with MyEconLab

- **Real-Time Data Analysis Exercises**—Using current macro data to help students understand the impact of changes in economic variables, Real-Time Data Analysis Exercises communicate directly with the Federal Reserve Bank of St. Louis's FRED® site and update as new data are available.

- **Current News Exercises**—Every week, current microeconomic and macroeconomic news articles or videos, with accompanying exercises, are posted to MyEconLab. Assignable and auto-graded, these multi-part exercises ask students to recognize and apply economic concepts to real-world events.

- **Experiments**—Flexible, easy-to-assign, auto-graded, and available in Single Player and Multiplayer versions, Experiments in MyEconLab make learning fun and engaging.

- **Reporting Dashboard**—View, analyze, and report learning outcomes clearly and easily. Available via the Gradebook and fully mobile-ready, the Reporting Dashboard presents student performance data at the class, section, and program levels in an accessible, visual manner.

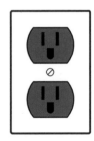

- **LMS Integration**—Link from any LMS platform to access assignments, rosters, and resources, and synchronize MyLab grades with your LMS gradebook. For students, new direct, single sign-on provides access to all the personalized learning MyLab resources that make studying more efficient and effective.

- **Mobile Ready**—Students and instructors can access multimedia resources and complete assessments right at their fingertips, on any mobile device.

MONEY, BANKING, AND THE FINANCIAL SYSTEM

THIRD EDITION

R. Glenn Hubbard

Columbia University

Anthony Patrick O'Brien

Lehigh University

 Pearson

New York, NY

Dedication

For Constance, Raph, and Will
—*R. Glenn Hubbard*

For Cindy, Matthew, Andrew, and Daniel
—*Anthony Patrick O'Brien*

Vice President, Business Publishing: Donna Battista
Director of Portfolio Management: Adrienne D'Ambrosio
Executive Portfolio Manager: David Alexander
Content Development Specialist: Lena Buonanno
Editorial Assistant: Michelle Zeng
Vice President, Product Marketing: Roxanne McCarley
Director of Strategic Marketing: Brad Parkins
Strategic Marketing Manager: Deborah Strickland
Product Marketer: Tricia Murphy
Field Marketing Manager: Ramona Elmer
Field Marketing Assistant: Kristen Compton
Product Marketing Assistant: Jessica Quazza
Vice President, Production and Digital Studio, Arts and Business: Etain O'Dea
Director of Production, Business: Jeff Holcomb
Managing Producer, Business: Alison Kalil
Content Producer: Christine Donovan

Operations Specialist: Carol Melville
Creative Director: Blair Brown
Manager, Learning Tools: Brian Surette
Managing Producer, Digital Studio, Arts and Business: Diane Lombardo
Digital Studio Producer: Melissa Honig
Digital Studio Producer: Alana Coles
Digital Content Team Lead: Noel Lotz
Digital Content Project Lead: Noel Lotz
Full-Service Project Management and Composition: Cenveo® Publisher Services
Interior Design: Cenveo® Publisher Services
Cover Design: Jonathan Boylan
Cover Photo Credit: top: Fotolia/Monkey Business; **bottom**: United States Federal Reserve
Printer/Binder: LSC Communications
Cover Printer: LSC Communications

Library of Congress Cataloging-in-Publication Data on file

3 17

ISBN 10:   0-13-452406-3
ISBN 13: 978-0-13-452406-1

Glenn Hubbard, Professor, Researcher, and Policymaker

R. Glenn Hubbard is the dean and Russell L. Carson Professor of Finance and Economics in the Graduate School of Business at Columbia University and professor of economics in Columbia's Faculty of Arts and Sciences. He is also a research associate of the National Bureau of Economic Research and a director of Automatic Data Processing, Black Rock Closed-End Funds, and MetLife. He received a Ph.D. in economics from Harvard University in 1983. From 2001 to 2003, he served as chair of the White House Council of Economic Advisers and chair of the OECD Economy Policy Committee, and from 1991 to 1993, he was deputy assistant secretary of the U.S. Treasury Department. He currently serves as co-chair of the nonpartisan Committee on Capital Markets Regulation. Hubbard's fields of specialization are public economics, financial markets and institutions, corporate finance, macroeconomics, industrial organization, and public policy. He is the author of more than 100 articles in leading journals, including *American Economic Review, Brookings Papers on Economic Activity, Journal of Finance, Journal of Financial Economics, Journal of Money, Credit, and Banking, Journal of Political Economy, Journal of Public Economics, Quarterly Journal of Economics, RAND Journal of Economics,* and *Review of Economics and Statistics.* His research has been supported by grants from the National Science Foundation, the National Bureau of Economic Research, and numerous private foundations.

Tony O'Brien, Award-Winning Professor and Researcher

Anthony Patrick O'Brien is a professor of economics at Lehigh University. He received a Ph.D. from the University of California, Berkeley, in 1987. He has taught money, banking, and financial markets courses for more than 25 years. He received the Lehigh University Award for Distinguished Teaching. He was formerly the director of the Diamond Center for Economic Education and was named a Dana Foundation Faculty Fellow and Lehigh Class of 1961 Professor of Economics. He has been a visiting professor at the University of California, Santa Barbara, and at Carnegie Mellon University. O'Brien's research has dealt with such issues as the evolution of the U.S. automobile industry, the sources of U.S. economic competitiveness, the development of U.S. trade policy, the causes of the Great Depression, and the causes of black–white income differences. His research has been published in leading journals, including *American Economic Review, Quarterly Journal of Economics, Journal of Money, Credit, and Banking, Industrial Relations, Journal of Economic History,* and the *Journal of Policy History.* His research has been supported by grants from government agencies and private foundations.

Brief Contents

Contents

Chapter 3   Interest Rates and Rates of Return   53

Chapter 4   Determining Interest Rates   92

Chapter 5   The Risk Structure and Term Structure of Interest Rates   139

Chapter 6   The Stock Market, Information, and Financial Market Efficiency

Chapter 7   Derivatives and Derivative Markets

Chapter 10   The Economics of Banking   306

Chapter 11   Beyond Commercial Banks:
Shadow Banks and Nonbank Financial Institutions   344

Chapter 12   Financial Crises and Financial Regulation   387

Chapter 15   Monetary Policy   494

Chapter 18   Monetary Theory II: The *IS–MP* Model   613

Preface

Do You Think This Might Be Important?

It's customary for authors to begin textbooks by trying to convince readers that their subject is important—even exciting. Following the events of recent years, with dramatic swings in stock prices, negative interest rates, unprecedented monetary policy actions, and a slow recovery from the devastating financial crisis of 2007–2009, we doubt anyone needs to be convinced that the study of money, banking, and financial markets is important. And it's exciting … sometimes maybe a little too exciting. The past 10 years has seen dramatic changes to virtually every aspect of how money is borrowed and lent, how banks and other financial firms operate, and how policymakers regulate the financial system. As a colleague of ours remarked: "I believe if I gave students the same exam I gave 10 years ago, I would require different answers to most of the questions!" Our goal in this textbook is to provide instructors and students with tools to understand these changes in the financial system and in the conduct of monetary policy.

New to This Edition

We were gratified by the enthusiastic response of students and instructors who used the previous two editions of this book. The response confirmed our view that a modern approach, paying close attention to recent developments in policy and theory, would find a receptive audience. In this third edition, we retain the key features of our previous editions while making several changes to address feedback from instructors and students and also to reflect our own classroom experiences. Here is a summary of our key changes, which are discussed in detail in the pages that follow:

- Added new coverage of how interest rates are determined using the money market model in Section 4.4, "Interest Rates and the Money Market Model." The section on the loanable funds model, which appeared in the body of the text in the previous edition, has been moved to a new appendix.

- Expanded the discussion of stock market indexes in Section 6.1, "Stocks and the Stock Market."

- Changed the organization of topics in Chapter 8, "The Market for Foreign Exchange," by moving the section on hedging exchange rate risk to the last section of the chapter where it can be easily omitted by instructors who do not cover this material.

- Added new coverage of why economists believe economic performance depends on the financial system in Section 9.1, "The Financial System and Economic Performance."

- Added new coverage of the effect of the Wall Street Reform and Consumer Protection Act (Dodd-Frank) on the Federal Reserve's ability to act as a lender of last resort in Section 12.4, "Financial Crises and Financial Regulations."

- Added new coverage of how the huge increase in bank reserves has affected the determination of the federal funds rate in Section 15.2, "Monetary Policy Tools and the Federal Funds Rate."

- Added new coverage of how the Fed manages the federal funds rate now that reserves are no longer scarce in Section 15.3, "The Fed's Monetary Policy Tools and Its New Approach to Managing the Federal Funds Rate."

- Revised coverage of China's interventions in the exchange rate market in Section 16.4, "Exchange Rate Regimes and the International Financial System," and added coverage of the policy trilemma.

- Added new coverage of the shadow bank lending channel in Section 18.4, "Are Interest Rates All That Matter for Monetary Policy?"

- Replaced 11 chapter-opening cases and updated retained cases.

- Added 18 new *Making the Connection* features, including several that are relevant to students' personal lives and decisions.

- Added 2 new *Solved Problem* features and updated retained *Solved Problems*. Some *Solved Problems* also involve subjects that are relevant to students' personal lives and financial decisions.

- Added 23 new figures and 5 new tables and updated the remaining graphs and tables with the latest available data.

- Replaced or updated approximately one-half of the *Review Questions* and the *Problems and Applications*, which students can complete on MyEconLab.

- Retained 46 real-time data exercises that students can complete on MyEconLab, where students and instructors can view the very *latest data* from FRED, the online macroeconomic data bank of the Federal Reserve Bank of St. Louis.

New Key Coverage

- Chapter 4, "Determining Interest Rates," includes new coverage of the determination of the short-run nominal interest rate using the money market model (also called the liquidity preference model) in Section 4.4, "Interest Rates and the Money Market Model." Including this new section in an early chapter allows professors to cover the relationship between changes in the money supply and short-term interest rates as part of the initial discussion of how interest rates are determined. We moved the section "The Loanable Funds Model and the International Capital Market," which appeared in the body of Chapter 4 in previous editions, to an appendix. This change is based on market feedback indicating that some instructors want the option to delay or skip covering the open-economy framework.

- Chapter 6, "The Stock Market, Information, and Financial Market Efficiency," has expanded coverage of stock market indexes to carefully illustrate why economists, policymakers, and investors use averages of stock prices, rather than the prices of any one company, to evaluate the state of the stock market.

- Changed the organization of topics in Chapter 8, "The Market for Foreign Exchange." The material in Section 8.2, "Foreign-Exchange Markets," of the previous edition that covered the use of derivatives in foreign-exchange markets has been moved to the end of the chapter, Section 8.3, "A Demand and Supply Model of Short-Run Movements in Exchange Rates," where it can be easily omitted by instructors who do not wish to cover this material. The remainder of the material from the previous edition's Section 8.2 has been integrated into Section 8.1. The relationship between the demand and supply approach to analyzing exchange rates and the interest-rate parity approach in the final section has been rewritten and clarified.

- Chapter 9, "Transactions Costs, Asymmetric Information, and the Structure of the Financial System," now covers why economists believe economic performance depends on the financial system in a new Section 9.1, "The Financial System and Economic Performance." This topic remains central in the aftermath of the 2007–2009 financial crisis, and the discussion helps reinforce the importance of many of the topics discussed in this and other chapters.

- Chapter 12, "Financial Crises and Financial Regulation," now includes a discussion of whether the Wall Street Reform and Consumer Protection Act (Dodd-Frank) has narrowed the Federal Reserve's ability to act as a lender of last resort in the event of another financial crisis (see the *Making the Connection* "Will Dodd-Frank Tie the Fed's Hands in the Next Financial Crisis?" in Section 12.4, "Financial Crises and Financial Regulations").

- The most important changes to this edition are in Chapter 15, "Monetary Policy." In previous editions, we followed the conventional approach of showing the equilibrium federal funds rate as being determined by the demand and supply for reserves. This approach assumes that reserves are scarce, which was an accurate assumption until the financial crisis of 2007–2009. But with banks currently holding $2 trillion in reserves, the traditional approach to explaining changes in the federal funds rate is no longer accurate. We explain the consequences of dropping the traditional assumption of scarce reserves in Section 15.2, "Monetary Policy Tools and the Federal Funds Rate." Then, in Section 15.3, "The Fed's Monetary Policy Tools and Its New Approach to Managing the Federal Funds Rate," we provide a new discussion of how the Federal Reserve currently manages the federal funds rate. This new discussion focuses on how the Fed uses the interest rate it pays on reserve balances (IOER) and the interest rate it pays on overnight reverse repurchase agreements (the ON RPP rate) to change its target for the federal funds rate. The discussion is summarized in new Figure 15.8, "The Fed's New Procedures for Managing the Federal Funds Rate." We believe that our new approach is essential if students are to understand this crucial aspect of Fed policymaking.

- Chapter 16, "The International Financial System and Monetary Policy," includes updated and revised coverage of China's interventions in the exchange-rate market in Section 16.4, "Exchange Rate Regimes and the International Financial System." This coverage is not only more current but points to the heightened risks facing China's economy and financial system. Section 16.4 also includes new coverage and a figure on the policy trilemma, which is the hypothesis that it is impossible for a country to have exchange rate stability, monetary policy independence, and free capital flows at the same time.

- Chapter 18, "Monetary Theory II: The *IS–MP* Model," includes new coverage of the shadow bank lending channel in Section 18.4, "Are Interest Rates All That Matter for Monetary Policy?" The role of shadow banking in the 2007–2009 financial crisis—and in the current financial system—makes this topic important for analyzing monetary policy.

New Chapter-Opening Cases

Each chapter-opening case provides a real-world context for learning, sparks students' interest in money and banking, and helps to unify the chapter. The third edition includes the following new chapter-opening cases:

- "You Get a Bright Idea … but Then What?" (Chapter 1, "Introducing Money and the Financial System")
- "The Federal Reserve: Good for Main Street or Wall Street—or Both?" (Chapter 2, "Money and the Payments System")
- "Why Are Interest Rates So Low?" (Chapter 4, "Determining Interest Rates")
- "The Long and the Short of Interest Rates" (Chapter 5, "The Risk Structure and Term Structure of Interest Rates")
- "You, Too, Can Buy and Sell Crude Oil … But Should You?" (Chapter 7, "Derivatives and Derivative Markets")
- "Who Is Mario Draghi, and Why Should Proctor & Gamble Care?" (Chapter 8, "The Market for Foreign Exchange")
- "Small Businesses Flock to the Bank of Bird-in-Hand" (Chapter 10, "The Economics of Banking")
- "Wells Fargo Owns Part of the Fed. Does It Matter?" (Chapter 13, "The Federal Reserve and Central Banking")

- "The End of 'Normal' Monetary Policy?" (Chapter 15, "Monetary Policy")
- "Why Did Employment Grow Slowly After the Great Recession?" (Chapter 17, "Monetary Theory I: The Aggregate Demand and Aggregate Supply Model")
- "Forecasting the Federal Funds Rate Is Difficult … Even for the Fed!" (Chapter 18, "Monetary Theory II: The *IS–MP* Model")

New *Making the Connection* Features and Supporting End-of-Chapter Exercises

Each chapter includes two or more *Making the Connection* features that provide real-world reinforcement of key concepts. Several of these *Making the Connections* cover topics that apply directly to the personal lives and decisions that students make and include the subtitle *In Your Interest*. The following are the new *Making the Connections*:

- "The Rise of Peer-to-Peer Lending and Fintech" (Chapter 1, "Introducing Money and the Financial System")
- "Will Sweden Become the First Cashless Society?" (Chapter 2, "Money and the Payments System")
- "*In Your Interest*: Does Your Portfolio Have Enough Risk?" (Chapter 4, "Determining Interest Rates")
- "*In Your Interest*: If Stock Prices Can't Be Predicted, Why Invest in the Market?" (Chapter 6, "The Stock Market, Information, and Financial Market Efficiency")
- "Brexit, Exchange Rates, and the Profitability of British Firms" (Chapter 8, "The Market for Foreign Exchange")
- "*In Your Interest*: FICO: Can One Number Forecast Your Financial Life—and Your Romantic Life?" (Chapter 10, "The Economics of Banking")
- "*In Your Interest*: Starting a Small Business? See Your Community Banker" (Chapter 10, "The Economics of Banking")
- "Will Dodd-Frank Tie the Fed's Hands in the Next Financial Crisis?" (Chapter 12, "Financial Crises and Financial Regulation")
- "Should Bankers Have a Role in Running the Fed?" (Chapter 13, "The Federal Reserve and Central Banking")
- "Are Negative Interest Rates an Effective Monetary Policy Tool?" (Chapter 15, "Monetary Policy")
- "The 'Exorbitant Privilege' of the U.S. Dollar?" (Chapter 16, "The International Financial System and Monetary Policy")
- "Free Fannie and Freddie?" (Chapter 18, "Monetary Theory II: The *IS–MP* Model")

46 Retained Real-Time Data Exercises That Students Can Complete on MyEconLab Using the Latest FRED Data

MyEconLab is a powerful assessment and tutorial system that works hand-in-hand with *Money, Banking, and the Financial System*. MyEconLab includes comprehensive homework, quiz, test, and tutorial options, allowing instructors to manage all assessment needs in one program. Key innovations in the MyEconLab course for *Money, Banking, and the Financial System*, third edition, include the following:

- Real-time *Data Analysis Exercises*, marked with 🌐, allow students and instructors to use the very latest data from FRED, the online macroeconomic data bank from the Federal Reserve Bank of St. Louis. By completing the exercises, students become familiar with a key data source, learn how to locate data, and develop skills to interpret data.

- In the Multimedia Library available in MyEconLab, select figures labeled MyEconLab Real-time data allow students to display a popup graph updated with real-time data from FRED.
- Current News Exercises provide a turn-key way to assign gradable news-based exercises in MyEconLab. Every week, Pearson locates a current news article, creates an exercise around the article, and adds it to MyEconLab.

Other Changes

- New *Solved Problems* have been added. Many students have difficulty handling problems in applied economics. We help students overcome this hurdle by including worked-out problems in each chapter. The following *Solved Problems* are new to this edition:
  - "Political Uncertainty and Bond Yields" (Chapter 5, "The Risk Structure and Term Structure of Interest Rates")
  - "The Bank of Japan Counters the Rising Yen" (Chapter 16, "The International Financial System and Monetary Policy")
- Approximately one-half of the *Review Questions* and *Problems and Applications* at the end of each chapter have been replaced or updated.
- Graphs and tables have been updated with the latest available data.

Our Approach

In this book, we provide extensive analysis of the financial events of recent years. We believe these events are sufficiently important to be incorporated into the body of the text rather than just added as boxed features. In particular, we stress a lesson policymakers learned the hard way: What happens in the shadow banking system is as important to the economy as what happens in the commercial banking system.

We realize, however, that the details of the financial crisis and recession will eventually pass into history. In this text, we don't want to just add to the laundry list of facts that students must memorize. Instead, we lead students through the economic analysis of why the financial system is organized as it is and how the financial system is connected to the broader economy. We are gratified by the success of our principles of economics textbook, and we have employed a similar approach in this textbook: We provide students with a framework that allows them to apply the theory that they learn in the classroom to the practice of the real world. By learning this framework, students will have the tools to understand developments in the financial system during the years to come. To achieve this goal, we have built four advantages into this text:

1. A framework for understanding, evaluating, and predicting
2. A modern approach
3. Integration of international topics
4. A focus on the Federal Reserve

Framework of the Text: Understand, Evaluate, Predict

The framework underlying all discussions in this text has three levels:

- First, students learn to *understand* economic analysis. "Understanding" refers to students developing the economic intuition they need to organize concepts and facts.
- Second, students learn to *evaluate* current developments and the financial news. Here, we challenge students to use financial data and economic analysis to think critically about how to interpret current events.

- Finally, students learn to use economic analysis to *predict* likely changes in the economy and the financial system.

Having just come through a period in which Federal Reserve officials, members of Congress, heads of Wall Street firms, and nearly everyone else failed to predict a huge financial crisis, the idea that we can prepare students to predict the future of the financial system may seem overly ambitious—to say the least. We admit, of course, that some important events are difficult to anticipate. But knowledge of the economic analysis we present in this book does make it possible to predict many aspects of how the financial system will evolve. For example, in Chapter 12, "Financial Crises and Financial Regulation," we discuss the ongoing cycle of financial crisis, regulatory response (such as the 2010 Wall Street Reform and Consumer Protection Act [Dodd-Frank]), financial innovation, and further regulatory response. We also cover the continuing debate over whether the Fed has retained sufficient authority as a lender of last resort to stabilize the financial system in the event of another crisis. With our approach, students learn not just the new regulations contained in Dodd-Frank but, more importantly, the key lesson that over time innovations by financial firms are likely to supersede many of the provisions of Dodd-Frank. In other words, students will learn that the financial system is not static but evolves in ways that can be understood using economic analysis.

A Modern Approach

Textbooks are funny things. Most contain a mixture of the current and the modern alongside the traditional. Material that is helpful to students is often presented along with material that is not so helpful or that is—frankly—counterproductive. We believe the ideal is to produce a textbook that is modern and incorporates the best of recent research on monetary policy and the financial system without chasing every fad in economics or finance. In writing this book, we have looked at the topics in the money and banking course with fresh eyes. We have pruned discussion of material that is less relevant to the modern financial system or no longer considered by most economists to be theoretically sound. We have also tried to be as direct as possible in informing students of what is and is not important in the financial system and policymaking as they exist today.

For example, rather than include the traditional long discussion of the role of reserve requirements as a monetary policy tool, we provide a brief overview and note that the Federal Reserve has not changed reserve requirements since 1992. Perhaps the most important distinction between our text and other texts is that we provide a complete discussion of how the Fed changes its target for the federal funds rate at a time when reserves are no longer scarce. The Fed's new procedures are at the center of monetary policy, and students need an accurate and up-to-date discussion.

Similarly, it has been several decades since the Fed paid serious attention to targets for M1 and M2. Therefore, in Chapter 18, "Monetary Theory II: The *IS–MP* Model," we replace the *IS–LM* model—which assumes that the central bank targets the money stock rather than an interest rate—with the *IS–MP* model, first suggested by David Romer more than 15 years ago. We believe that our modern approach helps students make the connection between the text material and the economic and financial world they read about. (For those instructors who wish to cover the *IS–LM* model, we provide an appendix on that model at the end of Chapter 18.)

By cutting out-of-date material, we have achieved two important goals: (1) We provide a much briefer and more readable text, and (2) we have made room for discussion of essential topics, such as the shadow banking system of investment banks, hedge funds, and mutual funds, as well as the origins and consequences of financial crises. See Chapter 11, "Beyond Commercial Banks: Shadow Banks and Nonbank Financial Institutions," and Chapter 12, "Financial Crises and Financial Regulation." Other texts either omit these topics or cover them only briefly.

We have taught money and banking to undergraduate and graduate students for many years. We believe that the modern, real-world approach in our text will engage students in ways that no other text can.

Integration of International Topics

When the crisis in subprime mortgages began, Federal Reserve Chairman Ben Bernanke famously observed that it was unlikely to cause much damage to the U.S. housing market, much less the wider economy. As it turned out, of course, the subprime crisis devastated not only the U.S. housing market but the U.S. financial system, the U.S. economy, and the economies of most of the developed world. That a problem in one part of one sector of one economy could cause a worldwide crisis is an indication that a textbook on money and banking must take seriously the linkages between the U.S. and other economies. We devote two full chapters to international topics: Chapter 8, "The Market for Foreign Exchange," and Chapter 16, "The International Financial System and Monetary Policy." In these chapters, we discuss such issues as the European sovereign debt crisis, the use of a negative interest rate policy by the European Central Bank, the Bank of Japan, and some other foreign central banks, and the increased coordination of monetary policy actions among central banks. We realize, however, that, particularly in this course, what is essential to one instructor is optional to another. So, we have written the text in a way that allows instructors to skip one or both of the international chapters.

A Focus on the Federal Reserve

We can hardly claim to be unusual in focusing on the Federal Reserve in a money and banking textbook ... but we do! Of course, all money and banking texts discuss the Fed, but generally not until near the end of the book—and the semester. After speaking to instructors in focus groups and based on our own years of teaching, we believe that approach is a serious mistake. In our experience, students often have trouble integrating the material in the money and banking course. To them, the course can seem a jumble of unrelated topics. The role of the Fed can serve as a unifying theme for the course. Accordingly, we provide an introduction and overview of the Fed in Chapter 1, "Introducing Money and the Financial System," and in each subsequent chapter, we expand on the Fed's role in the financial system. So, by the time students read Chapter 13, "The Federal Reserve and Central Banking," where we discuss the details of the Fed's operation, students already have a good idea of the Fed's importance and its role in the system.

Special Features

We can summarize our objective in writing this textbook as follows: to produce a streamlined, modern discussion of the economics of the financial system and of the links between the financial system and the economy. To implement this objective, we have developed a number of special features. Some are similar to the features that have proven popular and effective aids to learning in our principles of economics textbook, while others were developed specifically for this book.

Key Issue and Question Approach

KEY ISSUE AND QUESTION

Issue: Some economists and policymakers believe that bond rating agencies have a conflict of interest because they are paid by the firms whose bonds they are rating.

Question: Should the government more closely regulate the credit rating agencies?

Answered on page 167

139

We believe that having a key issue and related key question in each chapter provides us with an opportunity to explain how the financial system works in the context of topics students read about online and in newspapers and discuss among themselves and with their families. In Chapter 1, "Introducing Money and the Financial System," we cover the key components of the financial system, introduce the Federal Reserve, and preview the important issues facing the financial system. At the end of Chapter 1, we present 17 key issues and questions that provide students with a roadmap for the rest of the book and help them to understand that learning the principles of money, banking, and the financial system will allow them to analyze the most important issues about the financial system and monetary policy. The goal here is not to make students memorize a catalog of facts. Instead, we use these key issues and questions to demonstrate that an economic analysis of the financial system is essential to understanding recent events. See pages 19–21 in Chapter 1 for a complete list of the issues and questions.

We start each subsequent chapter with a key issue and key question and end each of those chapters by using the concepts introduced in the chapter to answer the question.

Contemporary Opening Cases

Each chapter-opening case provides a real-world context for learning, sparks students' interest in money and banking, and helps to unify the chapter. For example, Chapter 11, "Beyond Commercial Banks: Shadow Banks and Nonbank Financial Institutions," opens with a discussion of the rise of the shadow banking system in a case study entitled "When Is a Bank Not a Bank? When It's a Shadow Bank!" We revisit this topic throughout the chapter.

ANSWERING THE KEY QUESTION

Continued from page 139

At the beginning of this chapter, we asked:

"Should the government more closely regulate credit rating agencies?"

Like some other policy questions we will encounter in this book, this one has no definitive answer. We have seen in this chapter that investors often rely on the credit rating agencies for important information on the default risk on bonds. During the financial crisis of 2007–2009, many bonds—particularly mortgage-backed securities—turned out to have much higher levels of default risk than the credit rating agencies had indicated. Some economists and members of Congress argued that the rating agencies had given those bonds inflated ratings because the agencies have a conflict of interest in being paid by the firms whose bond issues they rate. Other economists, though, argued that the ratings may have been accurate when given, but the creditworthiness of the bonds declined rapidly following the unexpected severity of the housing bust and the resulting financial crisis. Despite increased regulation of the rating agencies following the financial crisis, the companies and governments that issue bonds continue to pay the agencies that rate them. It seems unlikely at this point that significant further changes in regulations will occur in the absence of another financial crisis.

CHAPTER 11

Beyond Commercial Banks: Shadow Banks and Nonbank Financial Institutions

Learning Objectives

After studying this chapter, you should be able to:

11.1 Explain how investment banks operate (pages 345–362)

11.2 Distinguish between mutual funds and hedge funds and describe their roles in the financial system (pages 362–369)

11.3 Explain the roles that pension funds and insurance companies play in the financial system (pages 369–374)

11.4 Explain the connection between the shadow banking system and systemic risk (pages 374–378)

When Is a Bank Not a Bank? When It's a Shadow Bank!

What is a hedge fund? What is the difference between a commercial bank and an investment bank? At the beginning of the financial crisis of 2007–2009, most Americans and even many members of Congress would have been unable to answer these questions. Most people were also unfamiliar with mortgage-backed securities (MBSs), collateralized debt obligations (CDOs), credit default swaps (CDSs), and other ingredients in the alphabet soup of new financial securities. During the financial crisis, these terms became all too familiar, as economists, policymakers, and the general public came to realize that commercial banks no longer

to borrowers. Instead, a variety of "nonbank" financial institutions, including mutual funds, hedge funds, and investment banks, were acquiring funds that had previously been deposited in banks. They were then using these funds to provide credit that banks had previously provided. These nonbanks were using newly developed financial securities that even long-time veterans of Wall Street often did not fully understand.

At a conference hosted by the Federal Reserve Bank of Kansas City in 2007, just as the financial crisis was beginning, Paul McCulley, a managing director of Pacific Investment Management Company (PIMCO),

---

Investment Banking **345**

new role of nonbank financial firms. A year later, the term became well known after Timothy Geithner used it in a speech to the Economic Club of New York. Geithner was then the president of the Federal Reserve Bank of New York and later became secretary of the Treasury in the Obama administration. He cited a Federal Reserve study indicating that by 2008, the shadow banking system had grown to be more than 50% larger than the commercial banking system.

As the financial crisis worsened, two large investment banks—Bear Stearns and Lehman Brothers—and an insurance company—American International Group (AIG)—were at the center of the storm. Although many commercial banks were also drawn into the crisis, 2007–2009 represented the first time in U.S. history that a major financial crisis had originated outside of the commercial banking system. Problems with nonbanks made dealing with the crisis more difficult because U.S. policymaking and regulatory structures were based on the assumption that commercial banks were the most important financial firms. In particular, the Federal Reserve System had been established in 1914 to regulate the commercial banking system and to

use discount loans to help banks suffering from short-run liquidity problems. Similarly, the Federal Deposit Insurance Corporation (FDIC) had been established in 1934 to insure deposits in commercial banks. As we will see in this chapter, the FDIC does not insure short-term borrowing by shadow banks, and shadow banks are normally not eligible to receive loans from the Fed when they suffer liquidity problems. As a result, the shadow banking system can be subject to some of the same sources of instability that afflicted the commercial banking system before the establishment of the Fed and the FDIC.

Partly as a result of the financial crisis, the size of the shadow banking system has declined relative to the size of the commercial banking system, although shadow banking remains larger. Following the financial crisis, in 2010 Congress passed the Wall Street Reform and Consumer Protection Act, or the Dodd-Frank Act, which to some extent increased federal regulation of the shadow banking system by creating the Federal Stability Oversight Council. But some policymakers and economists continue to believe that shadow banking remains a source of instability in the financial system.

Making the Connection Features

Each chapter includes two to four *Making the Connection* features that present real-world reinforcement of key concepts and help students learn how to interpret what they read online and in newspapers. Most *Making the Connection* features use relevant, stimulating, and provocative news stories, many focused on pressing policy issues. Several of these *Making the Connections* cover topics that apply directly to the personal lives and decisions that students make and include the subtitle *In Your Interest*.

MAKING THE CONNECTION | IN YOUR INTEREST

How Much Volatility Should You Expect in the Stock Market?

You may be reluctant to invest in the stock market because of the volatility of stock prices. After all, the larger the swings in an asset's price, the greater the risk to you as an investor. But is it possible to measure the degree of volatility that investors expect in the future? Such a measure might give you a way of comparing investing in stocks with investing in other financial assets.

One way to construct such a measure is by using the prices of options. In 1993, Robert E. Whaley, now of Vanderbilt University, noted that the prices of options on stock market indexes—such as the S&P 500—implicitly include a measure of investors' expectations of future market volatility. The measure of volatility is implicit, rather than explicit, because an option's price includes the option's intrinsic value plus other factors, including volatility, that affect the likelihood of an investor exercising the option. Whaley suggested a method to isolate the part of the option's price that represents investors' forecast of volatility.

Using the prices of put and call options on the S&P 500 index, the Chicago Board Options Exchange (CBOE) constructed the *Market Volatility Index*, called the VIX, to measure the expected volatility in the U.S. stock market over the following 30 days. Many people refer to the VIX as the "fear gauge" because when investors expect volatility in stock prices to increase, they increase their demand for options, thereby driving up their prices and increasing the value of the VIX. The following graph shows movements in the VIX from January 2004 to June 2016:

ranty. The VIX did not May 2010 and again in atility, this time tied to e might spill over into 6, as investors worried ncertainty in financial ote in the United King-

and in February 2006, against an increase in culator who wanted to peculator who wanted

volatility investors are

Sources: Robert E. Whaley, "Understanding the VIX," *Journal of Portfolio Management*," Vol. 35, No. 3, Spring 2009, pp. 98–105; Robert E. Whaley, "Derivatives on Market Volatility: Hedging Tools Long Overdue," *Journal of Derivatives*, Vol. 1, Fall 1993, pp. 71–84; Saumya Vaishampayan, "Fear Flashes in Options Market; VIX Nearly Doubles," *Wall Street Journal*, August 21, 2015; and Federal Reserve Bank of St. Louis.

See related problem 4.12 at the end of the chapter.

Here are examples:

- *"In Your Interest*: Interest Rates and Student Loans" (Chapter 3, page 65)
- *"In Your Interest*: Does Your Portfolio Have Enough Risk?" (Chapter 4, page 100)
- *"In Your Interest*: Should You Invest in Junk Bonds?" (Chapter 5, page 151)
- *"In Your Interest*: If Stock Prices Can't Be Predicted, Why Invest in the Market?" (Chapter 6, page 194)
- *"In Your Interest*: How Much Volatility Should You Expect in the Stock Market?" (Chapter 7, page 233)
- *"In Your Interest*: Corporations Are Issuing More Bonds; Should You Buy Them?" (Chapter 9, page 299)
- *"In Your Interest:* Starting a Small Business? See Your Community Banker" (Chapter 10, page 332)
- *"In Your Interest:* So, You Want to Be an Investment Banker?" (Chapter 11, page 360)
- *"In Your Interest:* If You Are Worried About Inflation, Shoud You Invest in Gold?" (Chapter 14, page 484)

Each *Making the Connection* has at least one supporting end-of-chapter problem to allow students to test their understanding of the topic discussed.

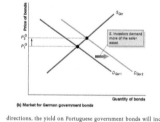

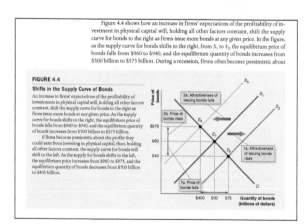

Solved Problem Features

Many students have difficulty handling problems in applied economics. We help students overcome this hurdle by including worked-out problems in each chapter. Our goals are to keep students focused on the main ideas of each chapter and to give them a model of how to solve an economic problem by breaking it down step by step. Several of these *Solved Problems* cover topics that apply directly to the personal lives and decisions that students make and include the subtitle *In Your Interest.*

Additional exercises in the end-of-chapter *Problems and Applications* section are tied to every *Solved Problem*. Students can also complete related *Solved Problems* on www.myeconlab.com. (See pages xxv-xxvi of this preface for more on MyEconLab.)

Graphs and Summary Tables

We use four devices to help students read and interpret graphs:

1. Detailed captions
2. Boxed notes
3. Color-coded curves
4. Summary tables with graphs

Review Questions and Problems and Applications—Grouped by Learning Objective to Improve Assessment

The end-of-chapter *Review Questions* and *Problems and Applications* are grouped under learning objectives. The goals of this organization are to make it easier for instructors to assign problems based on learning objectives, both in the book and in MyEconLab, and to help students efficiently review material that they find difficult. If students have difficulty with a particular learning objective, an instructor can easily identify which end-of-chapter questions and problems support that objective and assign them as homework or discuss them in class. Exercises in a chapter's *Problems and Applications* section are available in MyEconLab. Using MyEconLab, students can complete these and many other exercises online, get tutorial help, and receive instant feedback and assistance on exercises they answer incorrectly. Each major section of the chapter, paired with a learning objective, has at least two review questions and three problems.

We include one or more end-of-chapter problems that test students' understanding of the content presented in each *Solved Problem*, *Making the Connection*, and chapter opener. Instructors can cover a feature in class and assign the corresponding problem for homework. The *Test Item File* also includes test questions that pertain to these special features.

Data Exercises

Each chapter ends with at least two *Data Exercises* that help students become familiar with a key data source, learn how to locate data, and develop skills to interpret data.

Real-time *Data Analysis Exercises*, marked with 🌐, allow students and instructors to use the very latest data from FRED, the online macroeconomic data bank from the Federal Reserve Bank of St. Louis.

Supplements

The authors and Pearson Education have worked together to integrate the text, print, and media resources to make teaching and learning easier.

MyEconLab

MyEconLab is a powerful assessment and tutorial system that works hand-in-hand with *Money, Banking, and the Financial System*, third edition. MyEconLab includes comprehensive homework, quiz, test, and tutorial options, allowing instructors to manage all assessment needs in one program. Key innovations in the MyEconLab course for this edition include the following:

Key Terms and Problems

Key Terms

Bond rating, p. 141
Default risk (or credit risk), p. 141
Expectations theory, p. 155

Liquidity premium theory (or preferred habitat theory), p. 162
Municipal bonds, p. 149
Risk structure of interest rates, p. 140

Segmented markets theory, p. 161
Term premium, p. 162
Term structure of interest rates, p. 152

5.1 The Risk Structure of Interest Rates
Explain why bonds with the same maturity can have different interest rates.

Review Questions

1.1 Briefly explain why bonds that have the same maturities often do not have the same interest rates.

1.2 How is a bond's rating related to the bond issuer's creditworthiness?

1.3 How does the interest rate on an illiquid bond compare with the interest rate on a liquid bond? How does the interest rate on a bond with high information costs compare with the interest rate on a bond with low information costs?

1.4 What are the two types of income an investor can earn on a bond? How is each taxed?

1.5 Compare the tax treatment of the coupons on the following three bonds: a bond issued by the city

a. Do these ratings help explain the difference in the yields on the firms' bonds noted in the chapter opener? Briefly explain.

b. At the same time that AMD's bonds had yields above 10%, an article in the *Wall Street Journal* noted that AMD "is angling to lower the cost of virtual reality, targeting the field with a new line of graphics hardware priced at $199—half or less the cost of comparable products." If AMD is successful in earning large profits from selling its new virtual reality hardware, what is the effect likely to be on its bond yields? Illustrate your answer with a graph showing the market for AMD's bonds.

Source: Don Clark, "AMD Prices 3-D Tech to Spur Virtual Reality Market," *Wall Street Journal*, May 31, 2016.

5.2 The Term Structure of Interest Rates
Explain why bonds with different maturities can have different interest rates.

Review Questions

2.1 In his memoir, former Federal Reserve Chair Ben Bernanke remarked: "In setting longer-term rates, market participants take into account their expectations for the evolution of short-term rates." Explain what he meant.
Source: Ben S. Bernanke, *The Courage to Act: A Memoir of a Crisis and Its Aftermath*, New York: W.W. Norton, & Company, 2015, p. 75.

2.2 How does the Treasury yield curve illustrate the term structure of interest rates?

2.3 What are three key facts about the term structure?

2.4 Briefly describe the three theories of the term structure.

Problems and Applications

2.5 [Related to the Chapter Opener on page 139] The chapter opener noted that in mid-2016, you could earn an interest rate of 0.25% by buying

that bond matures into a one-year bond with an interest rate of 7%; or (c) buy a three-year bond with an interest rate of 8.5%. Assuming annual compounding, no coupon payments, and no cost of buying or selling bonds, which option should you choose?

2.7 Suppose that you have $1,000 to invest in the bond market on January 1, 2018. You could buy a one-year bond with an interest rate of 4%, a two-year bond with an interest rate of 5%, a three-year bond with an interest rate of 5.5%, or a four-year bond with an interest rate of 6%. You expect interest rates on one-year bonds in the future to be 6.5% on January 1, 2019, 7% on January 1, 2020, and 9% on January 1, 2021. You want to hold your investment until January 1, 2022. Which of the following investment alternatives gives you the highest return by 2022: (a) Buy a four-year bond on January 1, 2014; (b) buy a three-year bond January 1, 2014, and a one-year bond Janu-

---

Data Exercises

D5.1: [The yield curve and recessions] Go to the web site of the Federal Reserve Bank of St. Louis (FRED) (fred.stlouisfed.org) and for the period from January 1957 to the present download to the same graph the data series for the 3-month Treasury bill (TB3MS) and the 10-year Treasury note (GS10). Go to the web site of the National Bureau of Economic Research (nber.org) and find the dates for business cycle peaks and troughs (the period between a business cycle peak and trough is a recession). During which months was the yield curve inverted? How many of these periods were followed within a year by a recession?

D5.2: [Predicting with the yield curve] Go to www.treasury.gov and find the page "Daily Treasury Yield Curve Rates." Briefly describe the current shape of the

yield curve. Can you use the yield curve to draw any conclusion about what investors in the bond market expect will happen to the economy in the future?

D5.3: [The spread between high-grade bonds and junk bonds] Go to the web site of the Federal Reserve Bank of St. Louis (FRED) (fred.stlouisfed.org) and for the period from January 1997 to the present, download to the same graph the data series for the BofA Merrill Lynch US Corporate AAA Effective Yield (BAMLC0A1CAAAEY) and the BofA Merrill Lynch US High Yield CCC or Below Effective Yield (BAMLH0A3HYCEY). Describe how the difference between the yields on high-grade corporate bonds and on junk bonds have changed over this period.

- Real-time *Data Analysis Exercises*, marked with ⊕, allow students and instructors to use the very latest data from FRED, the online macroeconomic data bank from the Federal Reserve Bank of St. Louis. By completing the exercises, students become familiar with a key data source, learn how to locate data, and develop skills to interpret data.

- In the Multimedia Library available in MyEconLab, select figures labeled MyEconLab Real-time data allow students to display a popup graph updated with real-time data from FRED.

- Current News Exercises provide a turn-key way to assign gradable news-based exercises in MyEconLab. Each week, Pearson locates a current news article, creates an exercise around this article, and then automatically adds it to MyEconLab. Assigning and grading current news-based exercises that deal with the latest macro events and policy issues has never been more convenient.

  Other features of MyEconLab include:

- All end-of-chapter *Review Questions* and *Problems and Application*, including algorithmic, graphing, and numerical questions and problems, are available for student practice and instructor assignment. *Test Item File* multiple-choice questions are available for assignment as homework.

- The Custom Exercise Builder allows instructors the flexibility of creating their own problems or modifying existing problems for assignment.

- The powerful Gradebook records each student's performance and time spent on the Tests and Study Plan and generates reports by student or chapter.

A more detailed walk-through of the student benefits and features of MyEconLab can be found at the beginning of this book. Visit **www.myeconlab.com** for more information and an online demonstration of instructor and student features.

MyEconLab content has been created through the efforts of Melissa Honig, digital studio producer, and Noel Lotz and Courtney Kamauf, digital content project leads.

Access to MyEconLab can be bundled with your printed text or purchased directly with or without the full eText, at **www.myeconlab.com**.

Instructor's Resource Manual

Ed Scahill of the University of Scranton prepared the *Instructor's Resource Manual*, which includes chapter-by-chapter summaries, learning objectives, extended examples and class exercises, teaching outlines incorporating key terms and definitions, teaching tips, topics for class discussion, and additional applications. The *Instructor's Resource Manual* also contains solutions to the end-of-chapters problems revised by J. Robert Gillette of the University of Kentucky. *The Instructor's Resource Manual* is available for download from the Instructor's Resource Center (**www.pearsonhighered.com**).

Test Item File

Randy Methenitis of Richland College prepared the *Test Item File*, which includes more than 1,500 multiple-choice and short-answer questions. Test questions are annotated with the following information:

- **Difficulty:** 1 for straight recall, 2 for some analysis, and 3 for complex analysis
- **Type:** Multiple-choice, short-answer, and essay
- **Topic:** The term or concept that the question supports
- **Learning objective:** The major sections of the main text and its end-of-chapter questions and problems are organized by learning objective. The *Test Item File* questions

continue with this organization to make it easy for instructors to assign questions based on the objective they wish to emphasize.

- **Advanced Collegiate Schools of Business (AACSB) Assurance of Learning Standards:**

  Communication

  Ethical Reasoning

  Analytic Skills

  Use of Information Technology

  Multicultural and Diversity

  Reflective Thinking

- **Page number:** The page in the main text where the answer appears allows instructors to direct students to where supporting content appears.

- **Special features in the main book:** Chapter-opening story, *Key Issue and Question*, *Solved Problems*, and *Making the Connections*.

The *Test Item File* is available for download from the Instructor's Resource Center (**www.pearsonhighered.com**).

TestGen

TestGen is a computerized test generation program, available exclusively from Pearson, that allows instructors to easily create and administer tests on paper, electronically, or online. Instructors can select test items from the publisher-supplied test bank, which is organized by chapter and based on the associated textbook material, or create their own questions from scratch. With both quick-and-simple test creation and flexible and robust editing tools, TestGen is a complete test generator system for today's educators.

PowerPoint Lecture Presentation

Jim Lee of Texas A&M University–Corpus Christi prepared the PowerPoint slides, which instructors can use for classroom presentations and students can use for lecture preview or review. These slides include all the graphs, tables, and equations from the textbook. Student versions of the PowerPoint slides are available as PDF files. These files allow students to print the slides and bring them to class for note taking. Instructors can download these PowerPoint presentations from the Instructor's Resource Center (**www.pearsonhighered.com**).

This title is available as an eBook and can be purchased at most eBook retailers.

Third Edition Reviewers and Accuracy Checkers

The guidance and recommendations of the following instructors helped us revise the content and features of this text. While we could not incorporate every suggestion from every reviewer, we carefully considered each piece of advice we received. We are grateful for the hard work that went into their reviews and truly believe that the feedback was indispensable in revising this text. We appreciate their assistance in making this the best text it could be; they have helped teach a new generation of students about the exciting world of money and banking:

James C.W. Ahiakpor, California State University–East Bay
Thomas Bernardin, St. Olaf College
Oscar T. Brookins, Northeastern University
Georgia Bush, Banco de Mexico

Darian Chin, California State University–Los Angeles
Marc Fusaro, Emporia State University
Edgar Ghossoub, University of Texas–San Antonio

Mark J. Gibson, Washington State University
J. Robert Gillette, University of Kentucky
Anthony Gyapong, Pennsylvania State University–Abington
C. James Hueng, Western Michigan University

Kim Hyeongwoo, Auburn University
Syed H. Jafri, Tarleton State University
Kathy A. Kelly, University of Texas–Arlington
Stephen L. Kiser, University of Texas–Dallas

Paul Kubik, DePaul University
Carrie A. Meyer, George Mason University
John Neri, University of Maryland
Richard G. Stahl, Louisiana State University

Yongsheng Wang, Washington & Jefferson College
David A. Zalewski, Providence College

Special thanks to J. Robert Gillette of the University of Kentucky and Anthony Gyapong of Pennsylvania State University–Abington for their extraordinary work accuracy checking the chapters in page proof format and playing a critical role in improving the quality of the final product.

Second Edition Reviewers and Accuracy Checkers

The guidance and recommendations of the following instructors helped us to revise the content and features of the previous edition:

Mohammed Akacem, Metropolitan State College of Denver
Maharukh Bhiladwalla, New York University
Tina A. Carter, Tallahassee Community College
Darian Chin, California State University–Los Angeles
Dennis Farley, Trinity Washington University

Amanda S. Freeman, Kansas State University
J. Robert Gillette, University of Kentucky
Anthony Gyapong, Pennsylvania State University–Abington
Sungkyu Kwak, Washburn University
Raoul Minetti, Michigan State University

Hilde E. Patron-Boenheim, University of West Georgia
Andrew Prevost, Ohio University
Edward Scahill, University of Scranton
Heather L.R. Tierney, University of California, San Diego

First Edition Accuracy Checkers, Class Testers, and Reviewers

Special thanks to Ed Scahill of the University of Scranton for preparing the *An Inside Look* news feature in the first edition. Nathan Perry of Mesa State College and J. Robert Gillette of the University of Kentucky helped the authors prepare the end-of-chapter problems.

We are also grateful to J. Robert Gillette of the University of Kentucky, Duane Graddy of Middle Tennessee State University, Lee Stone of the State University of New York at Geneseo, and their students for class-testing manuscript versions and providing us with guidance on improving the chapters.

First Edition Accuracy Checkers

In the long and relatively complicated first edition manuscript, accuracy checking was of critical importance. Special thanks to Timothy Yeager of the University of Arkansas for both commenting on and checking the accuracy of all 18 chapters of the manuscript. Our thanks also go to this dedicated group, who provided thorough accuracy checking of both the manuscript and page proof chapters:

Clare Battista, California Polytechnic State University–San Luis Obispo
Howard Bodenhorn, Clemson University
Lee A. Craig, North Carolina State University

Anthony Gyapong, Pennsylvania State University–Abington
J. Robert Gillette, University of Kentucky
Woodrow W. Hughes, Jr., Converse College

Andrew Prevost, Ohio University
Ellis W. Tallman, Oberlin College
Timothy Yeager, University of Arkansas

First Edition Reviewers and Focus Group Participants

We appreciate the thoughtful comments of our first edition reviewers and focus group participants. They brought home to us once again that there are many ways to teach a money and banking class. We hope that we have written a text with sufficient flexibility to meet the needs of most instructors. We carefully read and considered every comment and suggestion we received and incorporated many of them into the text. We believe that our text has been greatly improved as a result of the reviewing process.

Mohammed Akacem, Metropolitan State College of Denver

Stefania Albanesi, Columbia University

Giuliana Andreopoulos-Campanelli, William Paterson University

Mohammad Ashraf, University of North Carolina–Pembroke

Cynthia Bansak, St. Lawrence University

Clare Battista, California Polytechnic State University–San Luis Obispo

Natalia Boliari, Manhattan College

Oscar Brookins, Northeastern University

Michael Carew, Baruch College

Tina A. Carter, Tallahassee Community College

Darian Chin, California State University– Los Angeles

Chi-Young Choi, University of Texas–Arlington

Julie Dahlquist, University of Texas–San Antonio

Peggy Dalton, Frostburg State University

H. Evren Damar, State University of New York– Brockport

Ranjit Dighe, State University of New York College–Oswego

Carter Doyle, Georgia State University

Mark Eschenfelder, Robert Morris University

Robert Eyler, Sonoma State University

Bill Ford, Middle Tennessee State University

Amanda S. Freeman, Kansas State University

Joseph Friedman, Temple University

Marc Fusaro, Arkansas Tech University

Soma Ghosh, Albright College

Mark J. Gibson, Washington State University

Anthony Gyapong, Pennsylvania State University–Abington

Denise Hazlett, Whitman College

Scott Hein, Texas Tech University

Tahereh Hojjat, DeSales University

Woodrow W. Hughes, Jr., Converse College

Aaron Jackson, Bentley University

Christian Jensen, University of South Carolina

Eungmin Kang, St. Cloud State University

Leonie Karkoviata, University of Houston

Hugo M. Kaufmann, Queens College, City University of New York

Randall Kesselring, Arkansas State University

Ann Marie Klingenhagen, DePaul University

Sungkyu Kwak, Washburn University

John Lapp, North Carolina State University

Robert J. Martel, University of Connecticut

Don Mathews, College of Coastal Georgia

James McCague, University of North Florida

Christopher McHugh, Tufts University

Doug McMillin, Louisiana State University

Carrie Meyer, George Mason University

Jason E. Murasko, University of Houston– Clear Lake

Theodore Muzio, St. John's University

Nick Noble, Miami University

Hilde E. Patron-Boenheim, University of West Georgia

Douglas Pearce, North Carolina State University

Robert Pennington, University of Central Florida

Dennis Placone, Clemson University

Stephen Pollard, California State University– Los Angeles

Andrew Prevost, Ohio University

Maria Hamideh Ramjerdi, William Paterson University

Luis E. Rivera, Dowling College

Joseph T. Salerno, Pace University

Eugene J. Sherman, Baruch College

Leonie Stone, State University of New York– Geneseo

Ellis W. Tallman, Oberlin College

Richard Trainer, State University of New York– Nassau

Raúl Velázquez, Manhattan College

John Wagner, Westfield State College

Christopher Westley, Jacksonville State University

Shu Wu, The University of Kansas

David Zalewski, Providence College

A Word of Thanks

We benefited greatly from the dedication and professionalism of the Pearson Economics team. Portfolio Manager David Alexander's energy and support were indispensable. David shares our view that the time has come for a new approach to the money and banking textbook. Just as importantly, he provided words of encouragement whenever our energy flagged. Development Editor Craig Leonard provided revision recommendations and helped coordinate the responses of reviewers. Content Development Specialist Lena Buonanno provided additional revision insights and edits. Lena's help with our texts over many years has been indispensable. Her hard work and cheerful outlook have lightened the burden of writing and revising our texts on tight schedules.

We thank Editorial Assistant Michelle Zeng for managing the review program and Content Producer Christine Donovan for managing production process for the book and the supplement package.

Fernando Quijano, formerly of Dickinson State University, created the graphs that appear in both the figures and the tables. As instructors, we recognize how important it is for students to view graphs that are clear and accessible. We are fortunate to have Fernando render all the figures in our texts and also our supplements. Market feedback on the figures continues to be very positive. We extend our thanks to Fernando not only for collaborating with us in creating the best figures possible but also for his patience with our demanding schedule.

We received excellent and speedy research assistance on the first edition from Andrey Zagorchev, now an assistant professor of finance at Rhodes College. We thank Pam Smith, Elena Zeller, and Jennifer Brailsford for their careful proofreading of two rounds of page proofs.

A good part of the burden of a project of this magnitude is borne by our families, and we appreciate their patience, support, and encouragement.

CHAPTER 1

Introducing Money and the Financial System

Learning Objectives

After studying this chapter, you should be able to:

1.1 Identify the key components of the financial system (pages 2–15)

1.2 Provide an overview of the financial crisis of 2007–2009 (pages 16–19)

1.3 Explain the key issues and questions concerning the financial system (pages 19–21)

You Get a Bright Idea ... but Then What?

Suppose it was impossible to borrow or lend money. Maybe life would be better. A character in Shakespeare's play *Hamlet* advises his son: "Neither a borrower nor a lender be." Some financial advisers suggest that new college graduates should buy things only with cash—no taking out a loan to buy a car and no putting the purchase of a new bed or refrigerator on a credit card. But could an economy operate successfully without borrowing or lending? We don't have to guess at the answer because we have examples of economies both in the modern world and in the past where there was little borrowing or lending. The results have been low incomes and very little economic progress.

To see the importance of borrowing and lending to an economy, suppose that you come up with an idea for a company: You design a smartphone application ("app") that will deliver a textbook chapter to a student's phone for a limited time for a low price. For example, if a student hasn't purchased her assigned calculus text but needs to use Chapter 10 to do her homework, the app will make that chapter available for six hours for $5.[1] You have a lot of work to do to

get your company off the ground—perfecting the software, designing the page in the app store where you will sell it, negotiating with textbook publishers to gain access to their books, and marketing your idea to students. You will have to spend a lot of money before you receive any revenue from sales of the app. Where will you get this money?

You face the same challenge as nearly every other entrepreneur around the world—both today and in the past. The role of the *financial system* is to channel funds from households and other savers to businesses. Businesses need access to funds in order to launch, survive, and grow. They depend on funds the way farms depend on water. For example, consider the large areas of southern Arizona and California's central valley that have rich soils but receive very little rain. Without an elaborate irrigation system of reservoirs and canals, water would not flow to these areas, and farmers could not raise their vast crops of lettuce, asparagus, cotton, and more. The financial system is like an irrigation system, although money, not water, flows through the financial system.

---

[1] If you start this company and it succeeds, please remember where you got the idea!

Continued on next page

During the economic crisis that began in 2007, the financial system was disrupted, and large sections of the U.S. economy were cut off from the flow of funds they needed to thrive. Just as cutting off the irrigation water in California's San Joaquin Valley would halt the production of crops, the financial crisis resulted in a devastating decline in production of goods and services throughout the economy. The result was the worst economic recession the world had experienced since the Great Depression of the 1930s.

Like engineers trying to repair a damaged irrigation canal to restore the flow of water, officials of the U.S. Treasury Department and the Federal Reserve (the Fed) took strong actions during the financial crisis to restore the flow of money through banks and financial markets to the firms and households that depend on it. Although some of these policies were controversial, most economists believe that some government intervention was necessary to pull the economy out of a deep recession.

Few households or firms escaped the fallout from the financial crisis and the recession it caused, giving them further evidence that the financial system affects everyone's lives.

In this chapter, we provide an overview of the important components of the financial system and introduce key issues and questions that we will explore throughout the book.

Key Components of the Financial System

LEARNING OBJECTIVE: Identify the key components of the financial system.

The purpose of this book is to provide you with the tools you need to understand the modern financial system. First, you should be familiar with the three major components of the financial system:

1. Financial assets
2. Financial institutions
3. The Federal Reserve and other financial regulators

We will briefly consider each of these components now and then return to them in later chapters.

Financial Assets

Asset Anything of value owned by a person or a firm.

Financial asset An asset that represents a claim on someone else for a payment.

Security A financial asset that can be bought and sold in a financial market.

Financial market A place or channel for buying or selling stocks, bonds, and other securities.

An **asset** is anything of value owned by a person or a firm. A **financial asset** is a financial claim, which means that if you own a financial asset, you have a claim on someone else to pay you money. For instance, a bank checking account is a financial asset because it represents a claim you have against a bank to pay you an amount of money equal to the dollar value of your account. Economists divide financial assets into those that are *securities* and those that aren't. A **security** is *tradable*, which means it can be bought and sold in a *financial market*. **Financial markets** are places or channels for buying and selling stocks, bonds, and other securities, such as the New York Stock Exchange. If you own a share of stock in Apple or Facebook, you own a security because you can sell that share in the stock market. If you have a checking account at Citibank or Wells Fargo, you can't sell it. So, your checking account is an asset but not a security.

In this book, we will discuss many financial assets. It is helpful to place them into the following five key categories:

1. Money
2. Stocks
3. Bonds
4. Foreign exchange
5. Securitized loans

Money Although we typically think of "money" as coins and paper currency, even the narrowest government definition of *money* includes funds in checking accounts. In fact, economists have a very general definition of **money**: Anything that people are willing to accept in payment for goods and services or to pay off debts. The **money supply** is the total quantity of money in the economy. As we will see in Chapter 2, money plays an important role in the economy, and there is some debate about the best way to measure it.

Money Anything that is generally accepted in payment for goods and services or to pay off debts.

Stocks **Stocks**, also called *equities*, are financial securities that represent partial ownership of a corporation. When you buy a share of Microsoft stock, you become a Microsoft *shareholder*, and you own part of the firm, although only a tiny part because Microsoft has issued millions of shares of stock. When a firm sells additional stock, it is doing the same thing that the owner of a small firm does when taking on a partner: increasing the funds available to the firm, its *financial capital*, in exchange for increasing the number of the firm's owners. As an owner of a share of stock in a corporation, you have a legal claim to a part of the corporation's assets and to a part of its profits, if there are any. Firms keep some of their profits as *retained earnings* and pay the remainder to shareholders in the form of **dividends**, which are payments corporations typically make every quarter.

Money supply The total quantity of money in the economy.

Stock Financial securities that represent partial ownership of a corporation; also called *equities*.

Dividend A payment that a corporation makes to its shareholders.

Bonds When you buy a **bond** issued by a corporation or a government, you are lending the corporation or the government a fixed amount of money. The **interest rate** is the cost of borrowing funds (or the payment for lending funds), usually expressed as a percentage of the amount borrowed. For instance, if you borrow $1,000 from a friend and pay him back $1,100 a year later, the interest rate on the loan was $100/$1,000 = 0.10, or 10%. Bonds typically pay interest in fixed dollar amounts called *coupons*. When a bond *matures*, the seller of the bond repays the principal. For example, if you buy a $1,000 bond issued by IBM that has a coupon of $40 per year and a maturity of 30 years, IBM will pay you $40 per year for the next 30 years, at the end of which IBM will pay you the $1,000 principal. A bond that matures in one year or less is a *short-term bond*. A bond that matures in more than one year is a *long-term bond*. Bonds can be bought and sold in financial markets, so bonds are securities just as stocks are.

Bond A financial security issued by a corporation or a government that represents a promise to repay a fixed amount of money.

Interest rate The cost of borrowing funds (or the payment for lending funds), usually expressed as a percentage of the amount borrowed.

Foreign Exchange Many goods and services purchased in a country are produced outside that country. Similarly, many investors buy financial assets issued by foreign governments and firms. To buy foreign goods and services or foreign assets, a domestic business or a domestic investor must first exchange domestic currency for foreign currency. For example, consumer electronics giant Best Buy exchanges U.S. dollars for

Foreign exchange Units of foreign currency.

Japanese yen when importing Sony televisions. **Foreign exchange** refers to units of foreign currency. The most important buyers and sellers of foreign exchange are large banks. Banks engage in foreign currency transactions on behalf of investors who want to buy foreign financial assets. Banks also engage in foreign currency transactions on behalf of firms that want to import or export goods and services or to invest in physical assets, such as factories, in foreign countries.

Securitized Loans If you don't have the cash to pay the full price of a car or a house, you can apply for a loan at a bank. Similarly, if a developer wants to build a new office building or shopping mall, the developer can also take out a loan with a bank. Until about 30 years ago, banks made loans with the intention of earning a profit by collecting interest payments on a loan until the borrower paid off the loan. It wasn't possible to sell most loans in financial markets, so loans were financial assets but not securities. Then, the federal government and some financial firms created markets for many types of loans, as we will discuss in Chapter 11. Loans that banks could sell on financial markets became securities, so the process of converting loans into securities is known as **securitization**.

Securitization The process of converting loans and other financial assets that are not tradable into securities.

For example, a bank might grant a *mortgage*, which is a loan a borrower uses to buy a home, and sell it to a government agency or a financial firm that will bundle the mortgage together with similar mortgages that other banks granted. This bundle of mortgages will form the basis of a new security called a *mortgage-backed security* that will function like a bond. Just as an investor can buy a bond from IBM, the investor can buy a mortgage-backed security from the government agency or financial firm. The bank that grants, or *originates*, the original mortgages will still collect the interest paid by the borrowers and send those interest payments to the government agency or financial firm to distribute to the investors who have bought the mortgage-backed security. The bank will receive fees for originating the loan and for collecting the loan payments from borrowers and sending them to the issuers of the mortgage-backed securities.

Financial liability A financial claim owed by a person or a firm.

Note that what a saver views as a financial asset a borrower views as a *financial liability*. A **financial liability** is a financial claim owed by a person or a firm. For example, if you take out a car loan from a bank, the loan is an asset from the viewpoint of the bank because it represents your promise to make a certain payment to the bank every month until the loan is paid off. But the loan is a liability to you, the borrower, because you owe the bank the payments specified in the loan.

Financial Institutions

Financial intermediary A financial firm, such as a bank, that borrows funds from savers and lends them to borrowers.

The financial system matches savers and borrowers through two channels: (1) banks and other *financial intermediaries* and (2) *financial markets*. These two channels are distinguished by how funds flow from savers, or lenders, to borrowers and by the financial institutions involved.[2] Funds flow from lenders to borrowers indirectly through **financial intermediaries**, such as banks, or directly through financial markets, such as the New York Stock Exchange.

---

[2] Note that for convenience, we sometimes refer to households, firms, and governments that have funds they are willing to lend or invest as *lenders*, and we refer to households, firms, and governments that wish to use those funds as *borrowers*. These labels are not strictly accurate because the flow of funds does not always take the form of loans. For instance, investors who buy stock are buying part ownership in a firm, not lending money to the firm.

If you get a loan from a bank to buy a car, economists refer to this flow of funds as *indirect finance*. The flow is indirect because the funds the bank lends to you come from people who have put money in checking or savings deposits in the bank; in that sense, the bank is not lending its own funds directly to you. On the other hand, if you buy stock that a firm has just issued, the flow of funds is *direct finance* because the funds are flowing directly from you to the firm.

Savers and borrowers can be households, firms, or governments, both domestic and foreign. Figure 1.1 shows that the financial system channels funds from savers to borrowers, and it channels *returns* back to savers, both directly and indirectly. Savers receive their returns in various forms, including dividend payments on stock, coupon payments on bonds, and interest payments on loans. Funds also flow between financial intermediaries and financial markets as, for example, when a commercial bank buys a bond in a financial market. Figure 1.1 is intended to give an overview of how funds flow

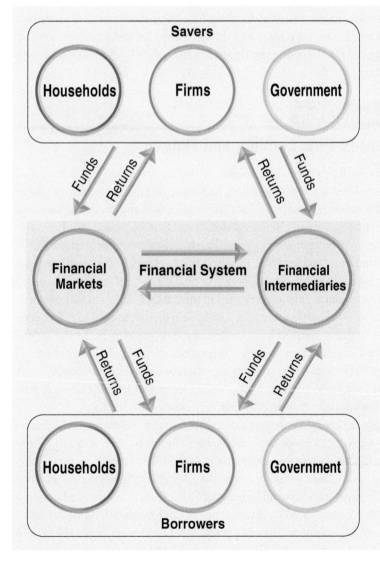

FIGURE 1.1

Moving Funds Through the Financial System

The financial system sends funds from savers to borrowers. Borrowers send returns back to savers through the financial system. Savers and borrowers include domestic and foreign households, businesses, and governments.

through the financial system. We will explain some of the key concepts below, but most of the discussion will be in later chapters.

Commercial bank A financial firm that serves as a financial intermediary by taking in deposits and using them to make loans.

Financial Intermediaries **Commercial banks** are the most important financial intermediaries. Commercial banks play a key role in the financial system by taking in deposits from households and firms and investing most of those deposits, either by making loans to households and firms or by buying securities, such as government bonds or securitized loans. Most households rely on borrowing money from banks when they purchase "big-ticket items," such as cars or homes. Similarly, many firms rely on bank loans to meet their short-term needs for *credit*, such as funds to pay for inventories (which are goods firms have produced or purchased but not yet sold) or to meet their payrolls. Many firms rely on bank loans to bridge the gap between the time they must pay for inventories or meet their payrolls and when they receive revenues from the sales of goods and services. Some firms also rely on bank loans to meet their long-term credit needs, such as funds they require to physically expand the firm.

In each chapter, the *Making the Connection* feature discusses a news story or another application related to the chapter material. Read the following *Making the Connection* for a discussion of how advances in technology and the difficulty that some households and firms had borrowing money following the financial crisis of 2007–2009 led to the rise of peer-to-peer lending.

MAKING THE CONNECTION

The Rise of Peer-to-Peer Lending and Fintech

Large businesses can raise funds in financial markets by selling stocks and bonds, but small businesses and households don't have this option. Because it's costly for investors to gather information on small businesses, these businesses cannot sell stocks and bonds and must rely instead on loans from banks. Similarly, when individuals and families (which economists refer to as *households*) borrow to buy homes, they typically rely on bank loans. When households borrow to buy cars, appliances, and furniture, they have three options: They can rely on bank loans, on loans provided by the sellers of those goods, or on their own personal credit cards.

At one time, government regulations resulted in most banks being small. Loan officers employed by these small banks often relied on their own judgment and experience in deciding whether to grant loans to local businesses and households. By the 2000s, changes in banking law meant that many small businesses and households were receiving loans from large banks that operated on a regional, or even national, basis. These large banks typically used fixed guidelines for granting loans that left little room for the personal judgment traditionally exercised by loan officers of small banks.

By the mid-2000s, many banks became convinced that it would be profitable to loosen their loan guidelines to make more borrowers eligible to receive credit. These banks believed that the larger number of borrowers who would *default* on their loans because of the looser guidelines would be more than offset by the payments received from the additional borrowers who would now qualify for loans. Unfortunately, during the financial crisis that began in 2007, the number of borrowers defaulting on loans turned out to be much higher than banks had predicted. Loan losses began rising, and by the end of 2009 they were four times greater than at the end of 2007.

In fact, the loan losses during 2007–2009 were by far the largest since the Great Depression of the 1930s. In response to these losses, federal government regulators began pushing banks to tighten their loan guidelines. Banks also became more cautious in making loans as they tried to avoid further loses. As a result of these factors, it became much more difficult for businesses and households to qualify for loans.

New firms, known as *peer-to-peer lenders*, or *marketplace lenders*, began to fill the demand for loans that banks were no longer meeting. Peer-to-peer lending sites, such as LendingClub, Prosper, and SoFi, allow small businesses and households to apply for loans online. The funds for those loans come from three key sources: individuals, other businesses, and—increasingly—financial firms, including insurance companies and pension funds. Banks have traditionally earned a profit on loans by paying a lower interest rate to depositors than they charge to borrowers. In contrast, peer-to-peer lenders make a profit by charging borrowers a one-time fee and charging the people providing funds a fee for collecting the payments from borrowers.

Like banks, peer-to-peer lenders are able to estimate the likelihood that borrowers will pay back loans by using data on a borrower's income, record of paying bills on time, and other aspects of her credit history. Because peer-to-peer lenders take advantage of software that rapidly evaluates information on borrowers, and because they rely heavily on smartphone technology in the loan application process, the lending sites are an example of *financial technology*, or *fintech*. Many borrowers find peer-to-peer lending attractive because the interest rates are lower than those on credit cards. Instead of paying 18% on a credit card balance, a borrower might pay only 10% on a peer-to-peer loan. Following the financial crisis, interest rates on bonds, bank savings accounts, and other financial assets had fallen to historically low levels. So, many investors were willing to make loans at the higher interest rates available on peer-to-peer lending sites even though they could lose money if borrowers defaulted on the loans.

By 2017, peer-to-peer lending was expanding rapidly, although it still remained much smaller than bank lending to small businesses and households. The industry had begun to experience some growing pains. LendingClub and some of the other marketplace lenders had begun securitizing the loans they were making and selling them to investors. In May 2016, LendingClub fired Renaud Laplanche, its chief executive officer (CEO), when the firm's board of directors discovered that LendingClub had not been disclosing all the required information to the investors it sold some loans to. The U.S. Treasury Department was also evaluating whether peer-to-peer lending might require further regulation to protect both borrowers and the investors providing the funds lent on these sites.

It remains to be seen how extensively peer-to-peer lending and the other examples of fintech that we will discuss in this book will affect the flow of funds from lenders to borrowers in the financial system.

Sources: U.S. Department of the Treasury, *Opportunities and Challenges in Online Marketplace Lending*, May 10, 2016; Peter Rudegeair and Anne Steele, "LendingClub CEO Fired over Faulty Loans," *Wall Street Journal*, May 19, 2016; "From the People, for the People," *Economist*, May 9, 2015; and Amy Cortese, "Loans That Avoid Banks? Maybe Not," *New York Times*, May 3, 2014.

See related problem 1.8 at the end of the chapter.

Nonbank Financial Intermediaries   Some financial intermediaries, such as *savings and loans*, *savings banks*, and *credit unions*, are legally different from banks, although these "nonbanks" operate in a very similar way by taking in deposits and making loans. Other financial intermediaries include investment banks, insurance companies, pension funds, mutual funds, and hedge funds. Although these institutions don't at first glance appear to be very similar to banks, they fulfill a similar function in the financial system by channeling funds from savers to borrowers.

Investment Banks   Investment banks, such as Goldman Sachs and Morgan Stanley, differ from commercial banks in that they do not take in deposits and until very recently rarely lent directly to households. (In late 2016, Goldman Sachs began engaging in fintech online lending, offering loans of up to $30,000 to households with high credit card balances but good credit histories.) Instead, they concentrate on providing advice to firms issuing stocks and bonds or considering mergers with other firms. They also engage in *underwriting*, in which they guarantee a price to a firm issuing stocks or bonds and then make a profit by selling the stocks or bonds at a higher price. In the late 1990s, investment banks increased their importance as financial intermediaries by becoming heavily involved in the securitization of loans, particularly mortgage loans. Investment banks also began to engage in *proprietary trading*, which involves earning profits by buying and selling securities.

Insurance Companies   Insurance companies specialize in writing contracts to protect their policyholders from the risk of financial losses associated with particular events, such as automobile accidents or fires. Insurance companies collect *premiums* from policyholders, which the companies then invest to obtain the funds necessary to pay claims to policyholders and to cover their other costs. So, for instance, when you buy an automobile insurance policy, the insurance company may lend the premiums you pay to a hotel chain that needs funds to expand.

Pension Funds   For many people, saving for retirement is the most important form of saving. Pension funds invest contributions from workers and firms in stocks, bonds, and mortgages to earn the money necessary to pay pension benefit payments during workers' retirements. With over $18 trillion in assets in 2016, private and state and local government pension funds are an important source of demand for financial securities.

Portfolio A collection of assets, such as stocks and bonds.

Mutual Funds   A mutual fund, such as Fidelity Investment's Magellan Fund, obtains money by selling shares to investors. The mutual fund then invests the money in a **portfolio** of financial assets, such as stocks and bonds, typically charging a small management fee for its services. By buying shares in a mutual fund, savers reduce the costs they would incur if they were to buy many individual stocks and bonds. Small savers who have only enough money to buy a few individual stocks and bonds can also lower their investment risk by buying shares in a mutual fund because most mutual funds hold a large number of stocks and bonds. If a firm issuing a stock or a bond declares bankruptcy, causing the stock or bond to lose all of its value, the effect on a mutual fund's portfolio is likely to be small. The effect might be devastating, though, on a small investor who had invested most of his or her savings in the stock or bond. Because most mutual funds are willing to buy back their shares at any time, they also provide savers with easy access to their money.

Hedge Funds Hedge funds, such as Bridgewater, run by Ray Dalio, are similar to mutual funds in that they accept money from investors and use the funds to buy a portfolio of assets. However, a hedge fund typically has no more than 99 investors, all of whom are wealthy individuals or institutions such as pension funds. Hedge funds usually make riskier investments than do mutual funds, and they charge investors much higher fees.

Financial Markets Financial markets are places or channels for buying and selling stocks, bonds, and other securities. Traditionally, financial markets have been physical places, such as the New York Stock Exchange, which is located on Wall Street in New York City, or the London Stock Exchange, which is located in Paternoster Square in London. On these exchanges, dealers would meet face-to-face to trade stocks and bonds. Today, most securities trading takes place electronically between dealers linked by computers and is called "over-the-counter" trading. *NASDAQ*, which originally stood for the *National Association of Securities Dealers Automated Quotation System*, is an over-the-counter market on which the stocks of many high-tech firms such as Apple and Intel are traded. Stocks and bonds sold in a particular market are "listed" on that market. For instance, General Electric is listed on the New York Stock Exchange, and Apple is listed on NASDAQ.

Economists make a distinction between *primary markets* and *secondary markets*. A **primary market** is a financial market in which stocks, bonds, and other securities are sold for the first time. An *initial public offering (IPO)* refers to a company selling its stock for the first time in the primary market. For example, Facebook's IPO took place in May 2012. A **secondary market** is a financial market in which investors buy and sell existing securities. For example, if you purchase Facebook stock today and sell it next year, that sale takes place in the secondary market. Primary and secondary markets can be in the same physical—or virtual—place, as when an IPO takes place for a stock listed on the New York Stock Exchange or on NASDAQ.

> **Primary market** A financial market in which stocks, bonds, and other securities are sold for the first time.
>
> **Secondary market** A financial market in which investors buy and sell existing securities.

MAKING THE CONNECTION

What Do People Do with Their Savings?

If you're like most college students, your primary financial asset is your checking account. After you begin your career, though, you'll accumulate a variety of different assets. The Federal Reserve System publishes data on household holdings of financial assets that shows how households divide up their total financial wealth. The following figure compares households' holdings of financial assets in 1978 and 2016. Some assets, such as stocks and bonds, are supplied by financial markets. Other assets, such as bank deposits and mutual fund shares, are supplied by financial intermediaries.

The figure shows that there have been significant changes over the decades in how households hold their financial wealth. The categories of wealth held in assets supplied by financial markets show that households increased their holdings of stocks issued by corporations from about 14% of their total wealth in 1978 to nearly 19% in 2016. But households now have only about half as much equity in *unincorporated businesses*, which include *partnerships* (businesses that are owned by two or more people

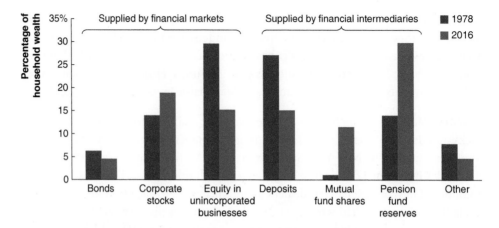

but are not corporations) and *sole proprietorships* (businesses that are owned by a single person). The equity in these businesses represents the difference between what the businesses could be sold for minus their debts. This equity is a less important part of household wealth partly because many relatively large firms that were organized as partnerships in 1978 had become corporations by 2016.

The categories of wealth held in assets supplied by financial intermediaries show that households now hold a much smaller percentage of their wealth in bank deposits, including checking accounts, savings accounts, and certificates of deposit. Households hold much larger percentages of their wealth in mutual fund shares and as pension fund reserves, which represent the value of household claims on pension plans at private companies, state and local government pension plans, and the value of individual retirement accounts (IRAs). The increase in the value of household pensions is a result of substantial increases in pensions that state and local governments have provided to their workers and an increase in the funds workers have deposited in IRAs and 401(k) plans offered by companies. The income workers deposit in IRAs and 401(k) accounts is not taxed until they withdraw the funds after they retire, which makes these accounts a very attractive way for most people to save.

Source: Board of Governors of the Federal Reserve, *Flow of Funds Accounts of the United States*, various issues.

See related problem 1.9 at the end of the chapter.

The Federal Reserve and Other Financial Regulators

During the financial crisis of 2007–2009, many people looked around at failing banks, the frozen markets for some financial assets, and plummeting stock prices and asked: "Who's in charge here? Who runs the financial system?" In a sense, these are unusual questions to ask because in a market system, no one individual or group is in charge. Consumers decide which goods and services they value the most, and firms compete to offer those goods and services at the lowest price. Few people think to ask: "Who's in charge of the frozen pizza market?" or "Who's in charge of the breakfast cereal market?" In most markets, the government plays a very limited role in deciding what gets produced, how it gets produced, what prices firms charge, or how firms operate.

But policymakers in the United States and most other countries view the financial system as different from the markets for most goods and services. It is different because, when left largely alone, the financial system has experienced periods of instability that have led to economic recessions.

The federal government of the United States has several agencies that are devoted to regulating the financial system, including these:

- The Securities and Exchange Commission (SEC), which regulates financial markets
- The Federal Deposit Insurance Corporation (FDIC), which insures deposits in banks
- The Office of the Comptroller of the Currency, which regulates federally chartered banks
- The Federal Reserve System, which is the central bank of the United States
- The Consumer Finance Protection Bureau (CFPB), which was created by Congress in response to the financial crisis of 2007–2009 to protect consumers from fraud or deceptive practices in financial markets

Although we will discuss all these federal agencies in this book, because of its importance, we will focus on the Federal Reserve System. Here we provide a brief overview of the Federal Reserve. We explore its operations in greater detail in later chapters.

What Is the Federal Reserve? The **Federal Reserve** (usually referred to as "the Fed") is the central bank of the United States. Congress established the Fed in 1913 to deal with problems in the banking system. As we have seen, the main business of banking is to take in deposits and to make loans. Banks can run into difficulties, though, because depositors have the right to withdraw their money at any time, while many of the loans banks grant to people buying cars or houses will not be repaid for years. As a result, if large numbers of depositors simultaneously demand their money back, banks may not have the funds necessary to satisfy the demand. One solution to this problem is for a country's central bank to act as a *lender of last resort* and make short-term loans that provide banks with funds to pay out to their depositors. Because Congress believed that the Fed had failed to carry out its duties as a lender of last resort during the Great Depression of the 1930s, it established the Federal Deposit Insurance Corporation (FDIC) in 1934. The FDIC insures deposits in banks up to a limit of $250,000 per depositor, per bank, which makes it less likely that depositors will withdraw their funds during a financial crisis.

Federal Reserve The central bank of the United States; usually referred to as "the Fed."

What Does the Federal Reserve Do? The modern Fed has moved far beyond its original role as a lender of last resort. In particular, the Fed is now responsible for *monetary policy*. **Monetary policy** refers to the actions the Federal Reserve takes to manage the money supply and interest rates to pursue macroeconomic policy objectives. These policy objectives include high levels of employment, low rates of inflation, high rates of growth, and stability in the financial system. The Fed is run by the Board of Governors, which consists of seven members who are appointed by the president of the United States and confirmed by the U.S. Senate. One member of the Board of Governors is designated as chair. In 2017, the chair was Janet Yellen, appointed by President Barack Obama in 2014. The Federal Reserve System

Monetary policy The actions the Federal Reserve takes to manage the money supply and interest rates to pursue macroeconomic policy objectives.

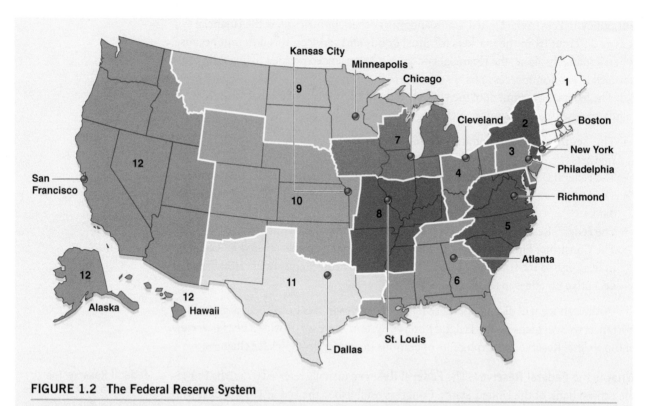

FIGURE 1.2 The Federal Reserve System

The Federal Reserve System is divided into 12 districts, each of which has a Federal Reserve Bank, identified by a purple dot in the figure. The federal government created the Federal Reserve System, but each regional Federal Reserve Bank is owned by the commercial banks within its district. Note that Hawaii and Alaska are included in the Twelfth Federal Reserve District.

Source: Board of Governors of the Federal Reserve System.

is divided into 12 districts, each of which has a Federal Reserve Bank, as shown in Figure 1.2. The Federal Open Market Committee (FOMC) is the main policymaking body of the Fed. The FOMC consists of:

- The seven members of the Board of Governors
- The president of the Federal Reserve Bank of New York
- Four presidents from the other 11 Federal Reserve District Banks

The FOMC meets in Washington, DC, eight times per year to discuss monetary policy. At these meetings, the FOMC decides on a target for a particularly important interest rate—the **federal funds rate**, which is the interest rate that banks charge each other on short-term loans.

Federal funds rate The interest rate that banks charge each other on short-term loans.

The Fed was heavily involved in the financial crisis of 2007–2009. Before providing a brief discussion of the financial crisis, we conclude our overview of the financial system by discussing the key services that the financial system provides.

What Does the Financial System Do?

In this book, we will do much more than just describe the financial system. We will also use the basic tools of economics to *analyze* how the system works. In your principles of economics class, you learned about these tools, including the model of demand and supply and marginal analysis. You also learned the basic economic idea that firms compete to supply the goods and services that consumers most want. In the financial system, banks, insurance companies, mutual funds, stockbrokers, and other *financial services firms* compete to provide financial services to households and businesses.

Economists believe there are three key services that the financial system provides to savers and borrowers: *risk sharing*, *liquidity*, and *information*. Financial services firms provide these services in different ways, which makes different financial assets and financial liabilities more or less attractive to individual savers and borrowers.

Risk Sharing *Risk* is the chance that the value of financial assets will change relative to what you expect. One advantage of using the financial system to match individual savers and borrowers is that it allows the sharing of risk. For example, if you buy a share of Apple stock for $100, that share may be worth $70 or $120 in one year's time, depending on how profitable Apple is. Most individual savers seek a steady return on their assets rather than erratic swings between high and low earnings. One way to improve the chances of a steady return is by holding a portfolio of assets. For example, you might hold some U.S. savings bonds, some shares of stock, and some shares in a mutual fund. Although during any particular period one asset or set of assets may perform well and another not so well, overall the returns tend to average out. This splitting of wealth into many assets to reduce risk is known as **diversification**. The financial system provides **risk sharing** by allowing savers to hold many assets.

Diversification Splitting wealth among many different assets to reduce risk.

The ability of the financial system to provide risk sharing makes savers more willing to buy stocks, bonds, and other financial assets. This willingness, in turn, increases the ability of borrowers to raise funds in the financial system.

Risk sharing A service the financial system provides that allows savers to spread and transfer risk.

Liquidity The second key service that the financial system offers savers and borrowers is **liquidity**, which is the ease with which an asset can be exchanged for money. Savers view the liquidity of financial assets as a benefit. They want to be able to sell their assets easily when they need to use the funds to buy goods or services or to make financial investments. More liquid assets can be quickly and easily exchanged for money, while less liquid—or *illiquid*—assets can be exchanged for money only after a delay or by incurring costs. For instance, if you want to buy groceries or clothes, you can easily use dollar bills or a debit card linked to your checking account. Selling your car, however, takes more time because personal property is illiquid. To sell your car, you may incur the costs of advertising or have to accept a relatively low price from a used car dealer. By holding financial claims on a factory—such as stocks or bonds issued by the firm that owns the factory—individual investors have more liquid savings than they would if they owned the machines in the factory. Investors could convert the stocks or bonds into money much more easily than they could convert a specialized machine into money.

Liquidity The ease with which an asset can be exchanged for money.

In general, we can say that assets created by the financial system, such as stocks, bonds, or checking accounts, are more liquid than are physical assets, such as cars, machinery, or real estate. Similarly, if you lend $100,000 directly to a small business, you probably can't resell the loan, so your investment would be illiquid. If, however, you deposit the $100,000 in a bank, which then makes the loan to the business, your deposit is a much more liquid asset than the loan.

Financial markets and intermediaries help make financial assets more liquid. Investors can easily sell their holdings of government securities and the stocks and bonds of large corporations, making those assets very liquid. As we noted earlier, during the past two decades, the financial system has increased the liquidity of many other assets besides stocks and bonds. The process of securitization has made it possible to buy and sell securities based on loans. As a result, mortgages and other loans have become more desirable assets for savers to hold. Savers are willing to accept lower interest rates on assets with greater liquidity, which reduces the costs of borrowing for many households and firms. One measure of the efficiency of the financial system is the extent to which it can transform illiquid assets into the liquid assets that savers want to buy.

Information A third service of the financial system is the collection and communication of **information**, or facts about borrowers and expectations of returns on financial assets. Your local bank is a warehouse of information. It collects information on borrowers to forecast their likelihood of repaying loans. Borrowers fill out detailed loan applications, and the bank's loan officers determine how well each borrower is doing financially. Because the bank specializes in collecting and processing information, its costs for information gathering are lower than yours would be if you tried to gather information about a pool of borrowers. The profit the bank earns on its loans are partly compensation for the resources and time bank employees spend to gather and store information.

> **Information** Facts about borrowers and expectations of returns on financial assets.

Financial markets convey information to both savers and borrowers by determining the prices of stocks, bonds, and other securities. When the price of your shares of Apple stock rises, you know that other investors must expect that Apple's profits will be higher. This information can help you decide whether to continue investing in Apple stock. Likewise, the managers of Apple can use the price of the firm's stock to determine how well investors think the firm is doing. For example, a major increase in Apple's stock price conveys investors' positive outlook for the firm. Apple may use this information in deciding whether to sell more stock or bonds to finance an expansion of the firm. The incorporation of available information into asset prices is an important feature of well-functioning financial markets.

In each chapter of this book, you will see the special feature *Solved Problem*. This feature will increase your understanding of the material by leading you through the steps of solving an applied problem in money, banking, and financial markets. After reading the problem, you can test your understanding by working the related problems that appear at the end of the chapter. You can also complete related Solved Problems on **www.myeconlab.com** and receive tutorial help.

SOLVED PROBLEM 1.1

The Services Securitized Loans Provide

We noted earlier that securitized loans are an important new financial asset that has increased in importance during the past 20 years. Briefly discuss whether securitized loans provide the key services of risk sharing, liquidity, and information. In your answer, be sure to define *securitized loans* and explain whether they are financial assets, financial securities, or both.

Solving the Problem

Step 1 **Review the chapter material.** This problem is about the services securitized loans provide, so you may want to review the sections "Financial Assets," which begins on page 2, and "What Does the Financial System Do?" which begins on page 13.

Step 2 **Define *securitized loans* and explain whether they are financial assets, financial securities, or both.** Ordinary (non-securitized) loans cannot be resold after they have been granted by a bank or another lender. Therefore, non-securitized loans are financial assets but not financial securities. Securitized loans are loans that have been bundled with other loans and resold to investors. Therefore, securitized loans are both financial assets and financial securities.

Step 3 **Explain whether securitized loans provide risk sharing, liquidity, and information.** Securitized loans provide all three of these key services. For example, before mortgage loans were securitized, the risk that the borrower would default, or stop making payments on the loan, was borne by the bank or other lender. When a mortgage is bundled together with similar mortgages in mortgage-backed securities, the buyers of the securities jointly share the risk of a default. Because any individual mortgage represents only a small part of the value of the security in which it is included, the buyers of the securities will suffer only a small loss if a borrower defaults on that individual mortgage.

A loan that is not securitized is illiquid because it cannot be resold. A securitized loan can be resold and so has a secondary market, which makes it liquid. One reason individual investors are reluctant to make loans directly to firms or households is that they lack good information on the financial condition of the borrowers. When loans are securitized, investors can, in effect, make loans to households and firms by buying a securitized loan without needing to have direct information on the financial condition of the borrowers. In buying the securitized loan, investors are relying on the bank or other *loan originator* to have gathered the necessary information.

So, securitized loans provide all three key financial services: risk sharing, liquidity, and information.

See related problem 1.12 at the end of the chapter.

1.2 The Financial Crisis of 2007–2009

LEARNING OBJECTIVE: Provide an overview of the financial crisis of 2007–2009.

In 2007, the United States entered what is likely to be the worst recession of your lifetime. Millions of people lost their jobs during the recession. Although the recession ended in June 2009, the recovery was weak, and it took more than five years for unemployment to return to normal levels.

The only comparable episode in the past 100 years was the Great Depression of the 1930s. In 1931, President Herbert Hoover famously announced, "We have now passed the worst . . . and we shall rapidly recover," even though nine more years of high unemployment lay ahead. During and after the recession of 2007–2009, some policymakers and economists made similarly incorrect predictions that prosperity would soon return.

Why was the recession of 2007–2009 so severe, and why did the recovery take much longer than expected? The simple answer is that unlike any other recession since the Great Depression of the 1930s, the recession of 2007–2009 was accompanied by a financial crisis. As we will see in the following chapters, the financial system changed in important ways as a result of the crisis. So, even though the financial crisis is now nearly a decade in the past, understanding it remains important for understanding the financial system.

Financial crisis
A significant disruption in the flow of funds from lenders to borrowers.

We can use the discussion of the financial system in this chapter to provide an overview of the financial crisis of 2007–2009. A **financial crisis** is a significant disruption in the flow of funds from lenders to borrowers. Because the financial crisis of 2007–2009 has had far-reaching and lasting effects on the financial system, we will discuss it in later chapters as well.

Origins of the Financial Crisis

Bubble An unsustainable increase in the price of a class of assets.

The financial crisis was primarily caused by the housing bubble of 2000–2005. A **bubble** is an unsustainable increase in the price of a class of assets, such as stocks issued by high-tech companies, oil and other commodities, or houses. Figure 1.3 shows the growth of the housing bubble and its eventual collapse. Panel (a) shows new home sales in the United States, and panel (b) shows the Case-Shiller index, which measures changes in the prices of single-family homes. Panel (a) shows that new home sales, after rising steadily through July 2005, fell by an astonishing 80% between July 2005 and July 2010. Panel (b) shows that home prices followed a similar pattern: They increased rapidly through the beginning of 2006, before declining more than 30% between the beginning of 2006 and the beginning of 2009. Starting in 2011, two years after the end of the financial crisis, home prices began a steady increase, while homes sales increased much more slowly.

Many economists believe that changes in the market for mortgages played a key role in the housing bubble. Mortgages were the first loans to be widely securitized. To promote homeownership, Congress wanted to create a secondary market in mortgages to make it easier for families to borrow money to buy houses. To reach this goal, in 1968 Congress began relying on *government-sponsored enterprises* (*GSEs*): the Federal National Mortgage Association ("Fannie Mae") and the Federal Home Loan Mortgage Corporation ("Freddie Mac"). Fannie Mae and Freddie Mac sell bonds to investors and use the funds to purchase mortgages from banks. By the 1990s, a large secondary market existed

MyEconLab Real-time data

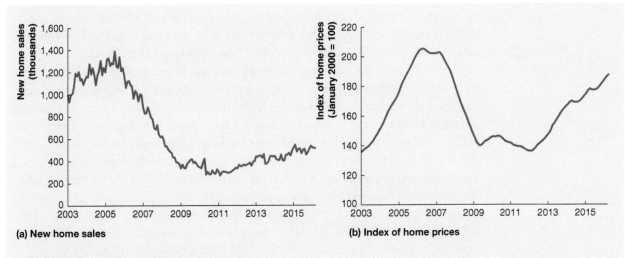

(a) New home sales

(b) Index of home prices

FIGURE 1.3 The Housing Bubble

Panel (a) shows that the housing bubble resulted in rapid increases in sales of new houses until 2005, followed by a sharp decrease in sales beginning in July 2005. A slow revival in house sales started in 2011.

Panel (b) shows that home prices followed a similar pattern to home sales, although after 2011, home prices increased more rapidly than did home sales.

Source: Federal Reserve Bank of St. Louis.

in mortgages, with funds flowing from investors through Fannie Mae and Freddie Mac to banks and, ultimately, to people borrowing money to buy houses.

By the 2000s, important changes had taken place in the mortgage market. First, investment banks became significant participants in the secondary market for mortgages. Investment banks began buying mortgages, bundling large numbers of them together as mortgage-backed securities, and reselling them to investors. Mortgage-backed securities proved very popular with investors because they often paid higher interest rates than other securities with comparable risk that the seller would default, or stop making payments on the security. Second, by the height of the housing bubble in 2005 and early 2006, lenders had greatly loosened the standards for obtaining a mortgage loan. Traditionally, only borrowers who had good credit histories and who were willing to make a down payment equal to at least 20% of the value of the house they were buying would be able to receive a mortgage. By 2005, however, many mortgages were being issued to *subprime borrowers* with flawed credit histories. In addition, *Alt-A borrowers*, who stated their incomes—but did not document them with income tax returns—and borrowers who made very small down payments found it easier to take out loans. Lenders also created new types of *adjustable-rate mortgages* that allowed borrowers to pay a very low interest rate for the first few years of the mortgage and then pay a higher rate in later years.

The chance that the borrowers using these nontraditional mortgages would stop making payments and default on their mortgages was higher than for borrowers using traditional mortgages. Why would borrowers take out mortgages on which they might have trouble making the payments, and why would lenders grant such mortgages? Both borrowers and lenders anticipated that housing prices would continue to rise, which would reduce the chance of borrowers defaulting on their mortgages and also make it easier for borrowers to convert to more traditional mortgages in the future.

Unfortunately, the decline in housing prices that began in 2006 resulted in many borrowers defaulting on their mortgages. As a result, the value of mortgage-backed securities declined sharply, and investors feared that they would lose money by purchasing them. Many commercial and investment banks owned mortgage-backed securities, and the decline in their value caused those banks to suffer heavy losses. By mid-2007, the decline in the value of mortgage-backed securities and the large losses suffered by commercial and investment banks began to cause turmoil in the financial system. Many investors refused to buy mortgage-backed securities, and some investors would buy only bonds issued by the U.S. Treasury. Banks began to restrict credit to all but the safest borrowers. The flow of funds from savers to borrowers, on which the economy depends, began to be greatly reduced.

Beginning in the spring of 2008, the Federal Reserve and the U.S. Department of the Treasury took unusual policy actions to deal with the results of the financial crisis and the recession that began in December 2007. Although the Fed had traditionally made loans only to commercial banks, in March 2008 it began making loans to some investment banks. Also in March, the Fed and the Treasury helped JPMorgan Chase acquire the investment bank Bear Stearns, which was in danger of failing. The Fed and Treasury were convinced that a failure by Bear Stearns had the potential of causing a financial panic, as many investors and financial firms would have stopped making short-term loans to other investment banks.

The Deepening Crisis and the Response of the Fed and Treasury

Some economists and policymakers criticized the decision by the Fed and the Treasury to help arrange the sale of Bear Stearns to JPMorgan Chase. The main concern was with the *moral hazard problem*, which is the possibility that managers of financial firms such as Bear Stearns might make riskier investments if they believe that the federal government will save them from bankruptcy. The Fed and the Treasury acted in March 2008 to save Bear Stearns because they believed that the failure of a large financial firm could have wider economic repercussions. In September 2008, when the investment bank Lehman Brothers was near bankruptcy, the Fed and the Treasury were again concerned that the failure of the firm would endanger the flow of funds through the financial system.

The Fed and the Treasury allowed Lehman Brothers to go bankrupt, which it did on September 15, 2008. The adverse reaction in financial markets was stronger than the Fed and Treasury had expected, which led them to decide two days later to have the Fed provide an $85 billion loan to American International Group (AIG)—the largest insurance company in the United States—in exchange for an 80% ownership stake, effectively giving the federal government control of the company. However, the fallout from the Lehman Brothers bankruptcy had widespread repercussions, including a sharp decline in most types of lending. Finally, in October 2008, Congress passed the *Troubled Asset Relief Program (TARP)*, under which the Treasury provided funds to commercial banks in exchange for stock in those banks. Taking partial ownership of private commercial banks was an unprecedented action for the federal government. Many policies of the Fed and Treasury during the recession of 2007–2009 were controversial because they involved partial government ownership of financial firms, implicit guarantees to large financial firms that they would not be allowed to go bankrupt, and unprecedented intervention in financial markets. These actions by the Fed and the Treasury were meant to restore the flow of funds from savers to borrowers. Without an increase in the flow of funds to more normal levels, households would lack the credit they needed to buy houses, cars, and other consumer durables, and firms would lack the credit they needed to finance new investment in plant and equipment, or, in many cases, even to finance their inventories and meet their payrolls.

Most economists and policymakers believed the severity of the crisis justified the Fed's use of innovative policies, but some worried that the Fed had overstepped the authority given to it by Congress. Others worried that the Fed's actions in working closely with the Treasury during the crisis might reduce the Fed's independence. As we will see in later chapters, the Fed's proper role in the financial system continues to be hotly debated.

1.3 Key Issues and Questions About Money, Banking, and the Financial System

LEARNING OBJECTIVE: Explain the key issues and questions concerning the financial system.

In this text, we will cover many different topics. Beginning in Chapter 2, we highlight one key issue and related question at the start of each chapter, and we end each chapter by using the analysis from the chapter to answer the question. Here are the issues and questions that provide a framework for the chapters that follow:

Chapter 2: Money and the Payments System

Issue: The Federal Reserve's actions during the financial crisis of 2007–2009 led to questions about whether it should continue to operate largely independently of oversight by the president and Congress.

Question: Should a central bank be independent of the rest of the government?

Chapter 3: Interest Rates and Rates of Return

Issue: Some investment analysts argue that very low interest rates on some long-term bonds make them risky investments.

Question: Why do interest rates and the prices of financial securities move in opposite directions?

Chapter 4: Determining Interest Rates

Issue: Following the financial crisis of 2007–2009, interest rates remained at historically low levels for an extended period.

Question: What factors are most important in determining interest rates?

Chapter 5: The Risk Structure and Term Structure of Interest Rates

Issue: Some economists and policymakers believe that bond rating agencies have a conflict of interest because they are paid by the firms whose bonds they are rating.

Question: Should the government more closely regulate bond rating agencies?

Chapter 6: The Stock Market, Information, and Financial Market Efficiency

Issue: Stock prices go through large swings up and down.

Question: Does the volatility of the stock market affect the broader economy?

Chapter 7: Derivatives and Derivative Markets

Issue: During and after the 2007–2009 financial crisis, some investors, economists, and policymakers argued that financial derivatives had contributed to the severity of the crisis.

Question: Are financial derivatives "financial weapons of financial mass destruction"?

Chapter 8: The Market for Foreign Exchange

Issue: The exchange rate between the dollar and other currencies has gone through wide fluctuations in recent years.

Question: Why hasn't the value of the dollar remained stable when measured against other currencies?

Chapter 9: Transactions Costs, Asymmetric Information, and the Structure of the Financial System

Issue: Acquiring funds to expand their operations is a significant challenge for many firms.

Question: Why do firms rely more on loans and bonds than on stocks as a source of external finance?

Chapter 10: The Economics of Banking

Issue: During the past 35 years, the U.S. financial system has experienced two periods during which there was a sharp increase in the number of bank failures.

Question: Is banking a particularly risky business? If so, what types of risks do banks face?

Chapter 11: Beyond Commercial Banks: Shadow Banks and Nonbank Financial Institutions

Issue: Today there is a substantial flow of funds from lenders to borrowers outside of the banking system.

Question: Does the shadow banking system pose a threat to the stability of the U.S. financial system?

Chapter 12: Financial Crises and Financial Regulation

Issue: The financial crisis of 2007–2009 was the most severe since the Great Depression of the 1930s.

Question: Was the severity of the 2007–2009 recession due to the financial crisis?

Chapter 13: The Federal Reserve and Central Banking

Issue: Following the financial crisis of 2007–2009, Congress debated whether to reduce the independence of the Federal Reserve.

Question: Should Congress and the president have greater authority over the Federal Reserve?

Chapter 14: The Federal Reserve's Balance Sheet and the Money Supply Process

Issue: Years after the end of the financial crisis of 2007–2009, banks continued to hold record levels of reserves.

Question: Why did bank reserves increase rapidly during and after the financial crisis of 2007–2009, and should policymakers be concerned about the increase?

Chapter 15: Monetary Policy

Issue: During the financial crisis of 2007–2009, the Federal Reserve implemented unusual monetary policy actions to stabilize the financial system and help bring the economy out of recession.

Question: Is the Fed likely ever to return to using normal monetary policy procedures?

Chapter 16: The International Financial System and Monetary Policy

Issue: The financial crisis of 2007–2009 and its aftermath led to controversy over the European Central Bank's monetary policy.

Question: Should European countries abandon using a common currency?

Chapter 17: Monetary Theory I: The Aggregate Demand and Aggregate Supply Model

Issue: During the recovery from the financial crisis of 2007–2009, the employment–population ratio remained low.

Question: What explains the relatively slow growth of employment during the economic expansion that began in 2009?

Chapter 18: Monetary Theory II: The *IS–MP* Model

Issue: By December 2008, the Federal Reserve had driven the target for the federal funds rate to near zero.

Question: In what circumstances is lowering the target for the federal funds rate unlikely to be effective in fighting a recession?

Key Terms and Problems

Key Terms

Asset, p. 2
Bond, p. 3
Bubble, p. 16
Commercial bank, p. 6
Diversification, p. 13
Dividend, p. 3
Federal funds rate, p. 12
Federal Reserve, p. 11
Financial asset, p. 2

Financial crisis, p. 16
Financial intermediary, p. 4
Financial liability, p. 4
Financial market, p. 2
Foreign exchange, p. 4
Information, p. 14
Interest rate, p. 3
Liquidity, p. 13
Monetary policy, p. 11

Money, p. 3
Money supply, p. 3
Portfolio, p. 8
Primary market, p. 9
Risk sharing, p. 13
Secondary market, p. 9
Securitization, p. 4
Security, p. 2
Stock, p. 3

1.1 Key Components of the Financial System

Identify the key components of the financial system.

Review Questions

1.1 Briefly define each of the five key financial assets. Is every financial asset also a financial security? Is it possible that what a saver would consider a financial asset a borrower would consider a financial liability?

1.2 What is the difference between direct finance and indirect finance? Which involves financial intermediaries, and which involves financial markets?

1.3 Briefly explain why the financial system is one of the most highly regulated sectors of the economy.

1.4 What is the Federal Reserve? Who appoints the members of the Federal Reserve's Board of Governors? How do the Fed's current responsibilities compare with its responsibilities when Congress created it?

1.5 Briefly describe the three key services that the financial system provides to savers.

Problems and Applications

1.6 A student remarks:

> When I pay my car insurance premiums, I never get that money back. My insurance premiums represent payments for a service I receive from the insurance company. When I deposit money in the bank, I can always withdraw the money later if I want to. So, my bank deposit represents a financial investment for me. Therefore, a bank is a financial intermediary, but an insurance company is not.

Briefly explain whether you agree with the student's argument.

1.7 [Related to the Chapter Opener on page 1]
In a talk at the White House after the end of the financial crisis, President Barack Obama argued: "Ultimately in this country we rise and fall together: banks and small businesses, consumers and large corporations." Why in this statement did the president single out banks? Aren't supermarkets, airlines, software companies, and many other businesses also important to the economy?
Source: Helene Cooper and Javier C. Hernandez, "Obama Tells Bankers That Lending Can Spur Economy," *New York Times*, December 14, 2009.

1.8 [Related to the Making the Connection on page 6]
An article in the *Economist* magazine notes the following about peer-to-peer lending sites: "Instead of a bank intermediating between savers and borrowers, the two parties deal with each other directly."

   a. What does the article mean when it describes banks as "intermediating" between savers and borrowers?

   b. What advantages might a peer-to-peer lending site have for savers and borrowers when compared with using a bank?

Source: "From the People, for the People," *Economist*, May 9, 2015.

1.9 [Related to the Making the Connection on page 9]
Households have a much larger fraction of their savings in pension funds than in bank deposits. If you are saving for retirement, why might you be better off putting your funds in an IRA or a 401(k) account than in a bank account? In your answer, be sure to explain what IRAs and 401(k) accounts are.

1.10 Typically, you will receive a very low interest rate on money you deposit in a bank. Interest rates on car loans and business loans are much higher. Why, then, do most people prefer putting their money in a bank to lending it directly to individuals or businesses?

1.11 Suppose financial intermediaries did not exist and only direct finance were possible. How would this affect the process of an individual buying a car or a house?

1.12 [Related to Solved Problem 1.1 on page 15]
During the 2007–2009 recession, many people who had taken out mortgages to buy homes had

trouble making the payments on their mortgages. Because housing prices were falling, the amount that people owed on their mortgages was greater than the price of their homes. Significant numbers of people defaulted on their mortgages. The following appeared in an article discussing this issue in the *Economist* magazine:

> Since foreclosures are costly for lenders as well as painful for borrowers, both sides could be better off by renegotiating a mortgage. The sticking-point, according to conventional wisdom, is securitization.

When mortgages are sliced into numerous pieces it is far harder to get lenders to agree on changing their terms.

Why might both lenders and borrowers be better off as a result of renegotiating a mortgage? How does securitization result in mortgages being "sliced into numerous pieces"? Why would securitization make renegotiating a loan more difficult? How would these difficulties affect the services that securitization provides to savers and borrowers?

Source: "Mortgage Mistakes," *Economist*, July 9, 2009.

1.2 ## The Financial Crisis of 2007–2009
Provide an overview of the financial crisis of 2007–2009.

Review Questions

2.1 What do economists mean by a "bubble"? Why do many economists believe that there was a housing bubble in the United States between 2000 and 2005?

2.2 By the 2000s, what significant changes had taken place in the mortgage market? What is a "subprime" borrower? What is an "Alt-A" borrower?

2.3 What problems did the decline in housing prices that began in 2006 cause for the financial system?

2.4 What actions did the Federal Reserve and Treasury take in dealing with the financial crisis? What is the moral hazard problem? How is it related to the Federal Reserve's and Treasury's actions?

Problems and Applications

2.5 Why is a bubble more likely to occur in the housing market than in the market for automobiles or the market for refrigerators?

2.6 Panel (b) of Figure 1.3 on page 17 shows a price index of houses. The late Karl Case of Wellesley College and Robert Shiller of Yale University developed this index. Many economists consider changes in the average price of houses in the United States to be difficult to measure. What challenges might exist in accurately measuring housing prices?

2.7 How does the creation of a secondary market in mortgages help to promote home ownership? Why might the federal government decide to intervene in the housing market to promote home ownership?

Data Exercises

D1.1: Go to the web site of the Bureau of Economic Analysis (www.bea.gov) and use the data there to calculate the percentage change in GDP for each year from 2000 through 2015. Graph your data.

Briefly compare the movements in GDP to the movements in the price index of houses shown in panel (b) of Figure 1.3 on page 17.

MyEconLab   Visit **www.myeconlab.com** to complete these exercises online and get instant feedback. Exercises that update with real-time data are marked with .

Money and the Payments System

Learning Objectives

After studying this chapter, you should be able to:

2.1 Analyze the inefficiencies of a barter system (pages 25–27)

2.2 List and describe the four key functions of money (pages 27–32)

2.3 Explain the role of the payments system in the economy (pages 32–37)

2.4 Explain how the U.S. money supply is measured (pages 37–39)

2.5 Use the quantity theory of money to analyze the relationship between money and prices in the long run (pages 40–47)

The Federal Reserve: Good for Main Street or Wall Street—or Both?

During the hotly contested 2016 presidential race, the candidates didn't agree on many of the issues. But most of them did agree that changes were needed in the operations of the Federal Reserve System (the "Fed"), which is the country's central bank. Democrats Hillary Clinton and Bernie Sanders proposed changes in the law to remove private banking executives from their roles in running the Fed. Republicans Donald Trump and Ted Cruz proposed that Congress's General Accountability Office audit the Fed's monetary policy decisions. Dissatisfaction with the Fed extended beyond presidential candidates to many members of Congress and to the general public—fewer than half of whom had a favorable view of the Fed.

Was dissatisfaction with the Fed the result of poor economic performance? As we will see in later chapters, Congress has given the Fed a "dual mandate" to achieve low inflation and low unemployment, and, in fact, both inflation and unemployment were low in 2016. The source of dissatisfaction with the Fed seemed to lie more with its actions during the financial crisis of 2007–2009, because some of those actions were far removed from its normal policies. Some economists and policymakers argued that the Fed had acted contrary to the basic idea embodied in the Federal Reserve Act of 1913. With that act, the Fed was granted substantial independence from Congress and the president, but

Continued on next page

KEY ISSUE AND QUESTION

Issue: The Federal Reserve's actions during and after the financial crisis of 2007-2009 led to questions about whether it should continue to operate largely independently of oversight by the president and Congress.

Question: Should a central bank be independent of the rest of the government?

Answered on page 47

in exchange, the Fed was only to engage in monetary policy, narrowly defined. Some critics argued that the Fed had used its independence to pursue policies that favored "Wall Street"—large financial firms—rather than "Main Street"—households and small businesses.

But why doesn't the Fed operate like other agencies of the federal government, such as the FBI or the Defense Department? In Chapter 13, we will discuss the reasons why Congress established the Fed with its current structure. At this point, we can note that a key reason many countries have granted their central banks considerable independence is because of the effect of changes in the money supply on the inflation rate. When a central bank is under direct control of the government, the money supply often increases rapidly, and so does the inflation rate.

In the African country of Zimbabwe, the government ordered the country's central bank to rapidly increase the money supply to help pay for the government's spending. The result was an inflation rate that reached an almost unimaginable 15 *billion* percent in 2008. The central bank began printing Zimbabwean dollar currency in denominations of $50 billion, then

$100 billion, and then $100 trillion. The extraordinary inflation rates in Zimbabwe contributed to disastrous declines in production and employment. Finally, in 2009, in an attempt to rein in inflation, the Zimbabwean government decided to abandon its own currency entirely in favor of the U.S. dollar. More recently, the government of Venezuela also financed much of its government spending by requiring the central bank to print money at a rapid rate. The result was an estimated inflation rate of more than 500% in 2016.

Very high inflation rates like these usually hit households and small businesses harder than they hit large financial firms, which are better able to protect themselves from the effects of rapid price increases. In that sense, Main Street has a large stake in good central bank policy.

But is the current structure of the Fed necessary to avoid economic disasters like those in Zimbabwe and Venezuela? We will continue to discuss central bank policy—and the political debate over the Fed—in later chapters. In this chapter, we will focus on the money supply and the connection between money and inflation.

Sources: Michael S. Derby, "Clinton Wants Bankers Off Regional Fed Boards," *Wall Street Journal*, May 12, 2016; Bernie Sanders, "To Rein in Wall Street, Fix the Fed," *New York Times*, December 23, 2015; "Spot the Difference," *Economist*, April 2, 2016; and Andrew Dugan, "Confidence in Obama's Economic Decisions Rises in U.S.," gallup.com, April 24, 2015.

Because very high rates of inflation in a country almost always lead to declines in production and employment, the links between money, inflation, and the policies of a country's central bank are very important. In this chapter, we begin to explore these links, starting with a brief discussion of what money is and how it is measured. At the end of the chapter, we discuss the quantity theory of money, which shows the links between changes in the money supply and the inflation rate in the long run.

 ## Do We Need Money?

LEARNING OBJECTIVE: Analyze the inefficiencies of a barter system.

Economists define **money** very broadly as *anything* that is generally accepted as payment for goods and services or in the settlement of debts. Do we need money? It may seem obvious that an economy needs money to operate, but think back to your introductory economics course. In the discussions of supply and demand, production, competition, and other microeconomic topics, money may not have been mentioned. Of course, there was an unstated understanding that money is involved in all the buying and selling. But the fact that you can tell the basic story of how a market system operates without mentioning money suggests that the services that money provides to households and firms are not always obvious.

Money Anything that is generally accepted as payment for goods and services or in the settlement of debts.

Barter

Barter A system of exchange in which individuals trade goods and services directly for other goods and services.

Economies *can* function without money. In the early stages of an economy's development, individuals often exchange goods and services by trading output directly with each other. This type of exchange is called **barter**. For example, on the frontier in colonial America, a farmer whose cow died might trade several pigs to a neighboring farmer in exchange for one of the neighbor's cows. In principle, people in a barter economy could satisfy all their needs by trading for goods and services, in which case they would not need money. In practice, though, barter economies are inefficient.

There are four main sources of inefficiency in a barter economy. First, a buyer or seller must spend time and effort searching for trading partners. The first neighbor the farmer approaches may not want to trade a cow for pigs. In a barter system, each party to a trade must want what the other party has available to trade. That is, there must be a *double coincidence of wants*. Because of the time and effort spent searching for trading partners in a barter economy, the **transactions costs**, or the costs in time or other resources of making a trade or exchange, will be high. A second source of inefficiency is that under barter, each good has many prices. The farmer might be able to exchange three pigs for a cow, 10 bushels of wheat for a plow, or a table for a wagon. So, what is the price of a cow, a plow, or a wagon? The answer is that each good will have many prices—one for every other good it might be exchanged for. A cow will have a price in terms of pigs, a price in terms of wheat, a price in terms of wagons, and so forth. A barter economy with only 100 goods would have 4,950 prices; one with 10,000 goods would have 49,995,000 prices![1] A third source of inefficiency arises from a lack of standardization: All pigs and cows are not the same, so the price of cows in terms of pigs would have to specify the size and other characteristics of the animals. Finally, imagine the difficulty of accumulating wealth. The only way to do so in a barter system would be by accumulating stockpiles of goods.

Transactions costs The costs in time or other resources that parties incur in the process of agreeing and carrying out an exchange of goods and services.

The Invention of Money

The inefficiencies of barter forced most people to be self-sufficient. On the frontier in colonial America, most people grew their own food, built their own homes, and made their own clothes and tools. Such economies have trouble growing because, in doing everything, an individual does some tasks well and does others poorly. To improve on barter, people had an incentive to identify a specific product that most other people would generally accept in an exchange. In other words, they had a strong incentive to invent money. For example, in colonial times, animal skins were very useful in making clothing. The first governor of Tennessee received a salary of 1,000 deerskins per year, and the state's secretary of the treasury received 450 otter skins per year. A good used as money that also has value independent of its use as money is called **commodity money**. Historically, once a good became widely accepted as money, people who did not have an immediate use for it were still willing to accept it. A colonial farmer—or the governor of Tennessee—might not want a deerskin, but as long as he knew he could use it to buy other goods and services, he would be willing to accept it in exchange for what he had to sell.

Commodity money A good used as money that has value independent of its use as money.

[1] These calculations are based on the formula for determining how many prices we need with N goods–that is, the number of prices when there are N items: Number of prices = $N(N-1)/2$.

MAKING THE CONNECTION

What's Money? Ask a Taxi Driver in Moscow!

In August 1989, one of the authors of this book was part of a group of American economists that traveled to Moscow and Leningrad (now St. Petersburg) in what was then the Soviet Union to discuss with Soviet economists some economic problems both countries faced. While there, he learned a great lesson about money from Russian taxi drivers.

Taking taxis in Moscow to and from meetings and dinners was an ordeal. The author's hosts had given the U.S. economists rubles (Soviet currency at the time), but Russian merchants and taxi drivers discouraged payments in rubles. Taxi drivers quoted a bewildering array of fares in terms of U.S. dollars, German marks, or Japanese yen. And the fares varied from cab to cab.

When the author relayed this frustration to his wife, she explained that she had no difficulties with taxis. She paid the fare with Marlboro cigarettes instead of currency! The author used Marlboros the next day (no other brand worked as well) and was able to pay taxi drivers with great success. He found that the taxi drivers could easily convert all major currencies to Marlboro equivalents.

At least during that period, Marlboro cigarettes had displaced the official currency (rubles) as the money most widely used by Moscow taxi drivers.

See related problems 1.6 and 1.7 at the end of the chapter.

Once a society invents money—as has happened many times and in many places around the world—transactions costs are greatly reduced, as are the other inefficiencies of barter. People can take advantage of **specialization**, producing the good or service for which they have relatively the best ability. Most people in modern economies are highly specialized. They do only one thing—work as an accountant, a teacher, or an engineer—and use the money they earn to buy everything else they need. Unlike in barter economies, few people today grow their own food, make their own clothing, or build their own houses. By specializing, people are far more productive than they would be if they tried to produce all the goods and services they consume themselves. The high income levels in modern economies are based on the specialization that money makes possible.

So, the answer to the question "Do we need money?" is "Yes, because money allows for specialization, higher productivity, and higher incomes."

Specialization A system in which individuals produce the goods or services for which they have relatively the best ability.

2.2 The Key Functions of Money

LEARNING OBJECTIVE: List and describe the four key functions of money.

Money serves four key functions in the economy:

1. It acts as a medium of exchange.
2. It is a unit of account.
3. It is a store of value.
4. It offers a standard of deferred payment.

Medium of Exchange

If you are a teacher or an accountant, you are paid money for your services. You then use that money to buy goods and services. You essentially exchange your teaching or accounting services for food, clothing, rent, and other goods and services. But unlike with barter, where goods and services are exchanged directly for other goods and services, the exchanges you participate in involve money. Money is providing the service of a **medium of exchange**. That is, money is the *medium* through which exchange takes place. Because, by definition, money is generally accepted as payment for goods and services or as payment for debts, you know that the money your employer pays you will be accepted at the stores where you purchase food, clothing, and other goods and services. In other words, you can specialize in producing teaching or accounting services without having to worry about directly producing the other goods and services you require to meet your needs, as you would in a barter economy.

Medium of exchange Something that is generally accepted as payment for goods and services; a function of money.

Unit of Account

Using a good as a medium of exchange provides another benefit: Instead of having to quote the price of a single good in terms of many other goods—as is the case with barter—each good has a single price quoted in terms of the medium of exchange. This function of money gives households and firms a **unit of account**, or a way of measuring value in the economy in terms of money. For instance, in the U.S. economy, each good or service has a price in terms of dollars.

Unit of account A way of measuring value in an economy in terms of money; a function of money.

Store of Value

Money allows value to be stored easily, thereby providing the service of a **store of value**. If you do not use all the dollars you currently have to buy goods and services today, you can hold the rest for future use. Note, though, that if prices in an economy rise rapidly over time, the amount of goods and services a given amount of money can purchase declines, and money's usefulness as a store of value is reduced.

Store of value The accumulation of wealth by holding dollars or other assets that can be used to buy goods and services in the future; a function of money.

Of course, money is only one of many *assets* that can be used to store value. In fact, any asset—shares of Apple stock, Treasury bonds, real estate, or Renoir paintings, for example—represents a store of value. Indeed, *financial assets*, such as stocks and bonds, offer an important benefit relative to holding money because they generally pay interest or may increase in value. Other assets also have advantages relative to money because they provide services. For instance, a house provides its owner with a place to sleep. Why, then, does anyone bother to hold money? The answer is *liquidity*, or the ease with which an asset can be exchanged for money. Money itself is, of course, perfectly liquid, while you incur transactions costs when you exchange other assets for money. When you sell bonds or shares of stock, for example, you pay a fee, or commission, either online or to your broker. If you have to sell your house on short notice because you take a job in a different state, you will have to pay a commission to a real estate agent and probably have to accept a lower price to sell the house quickly. To avoid such transactions costs, people are willing to hold money as well as other assets, even though other assets offer a greater return as a store of value.

Standard of Deferred Payment

Money is also useful because of its ability to serve as a **standard of deferred payment**. Money can facilitate exchange at a *given point in time* by providing a medium of exchange and unit of account. Money can also facilitate exchange *over time* by providing a store of value and standard of deferred payment. For example, a furniture store may order 25 dining room tables from a furniture manufacturer by promising to make full payment at an agreed price in 60 days.

Remember That Money, Income, and Wealth Measure Different Things

It's important to keep straight the differences among *money*, *income*, and *wealth*. We often say that people in *Forbes* magazine's list of richest Americans have a lot of money. We don't really mean that they have a lot of paper currency in their pockets (or hidden away in their mansions or yachts); instead, we mean that they own valuable assets, such as stocks, bonds, or houses. Money, like other assets, is a component of **wealth**, which is the difference between the value of a person's assets and the value of the person's liabilities. Only if an asset serves as a medium of exchange can we call it *money*. A person's *income* is equal to his or her earnings over a period of time. So, a person typically has considerably less money than income or wealth.

What Can Serve as Money?

We noted earlier that any asset can be used as money, provided that it is generally accepted as payment. In practical terms, an asset is suitable to use as a medium of exchange if it is:

- *Acceptable* to (that is, usable by) most people
- *Standardized in terms of quality*, so that any two units are identical
- *Durable*, so that it does not quickly become too worn out to be usable
- *Valuable* relative to its weight, so that amounts large enough to be useful in trade can be easily transported
- *Divisible*, because prices of goods and services vary

U.S. paper currency—Federal Reserve Notes—meet all these criteria.

The Mystery of Fiat Money

Notice that paper currency has no intrinsic value: You can use a $20 bill to buy goods and services, but beyond that, it has no value to you—except, perhaps, as a bookmark. The Federal Reserve issues the paper currency of the United States, but the Fed is under no obligation to redeem it for gold or any other commodity. Money, such as paper currency, that has no value apart from its use as money is called **fiat money**.

People accept paper currency in exchange for goods and services partly because the federal government has designated it to be **legal tender**, which means the government accepts paper currency in payment of taxes and requires that individuals and firms accept it in payment of debts. If Federal Reserve Notes are legal tender, doesn't that mean that everyone in the United States, including every business, has to accept paper money? It's a surprise to many people to learn that the answer to this question is "no." As the U.S. Treasury Department explains on its web site:

> There is … no Federal statute mandating that a private business, a person or an organization must accept currency or coins as payment for goods and/or services…. For example, a bus line may prohibit payment of fares in pennies or dollar bills. In addition, movie theaters, convenience stores and gas stations may refuse to accept large denomination currency (usually notes above $20) as a matter of policy.

In fact, it's *not* the government's designation of currency as legal tender that explains why paper currency circulates as a medium of exchange. Rather, paper currency circulates because of the confidence of consumers and firms that if they accept paper currency, they will be able to pass it along to someone else when they need to buy goods and services. Basically, it is a case of self-fulfilling expectations: You value something as money only if you believe that others will accept it from you as payment. Our society's willingness to use green pieces of paper issued by the Federal Reserve System as money makes them an acceptable medium of exchange.

As we will see in Section 2.5, if consumers and firms ever lose confidence that they will be able to pass along currency in buying goods and services, then the currency will cease to be a medium of exchange.

MAKING THE CONNECTION

Say Goodbye to the Benjamins?

In late 2016, there were about $1.4 trillion in Federal Reserve Notes *in circulation*—that is, held outside of banks, the U.S. Treasury, and the Federal Reserve. As the graph below shows, total currency in circulation has almost tripled since 2000. That's a lot of cash—more than $4,300 for every person in the United States. Although some businesses may have that much cash on hand, few individuals hold more than a few hundred dollars in currency at any given time.

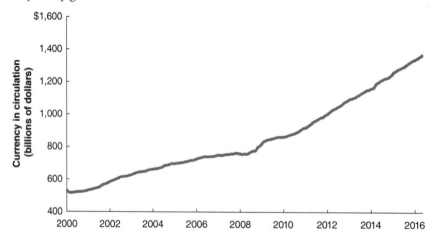

So, where is all that currency? The Federal Reserve estimates that as much as two-thirds of U.S. currency is held by individuals, firms, and governments outside the

United States—all of which is still counted as part of the U.S. money supply. In countries such as Venezuela, where—as we saw in the chapter opener—inflation rates have soared, many households and firms have switched to conducting transactions in U.S. dollars rather than in their domestic currencies. The purchasing power of the dollar is stable, while the purchasing power of their own currencies has rapidly declined. Some countries, including Panama, El Salvador, Ecuador, and Zimbabwe, use the U.S. dollar as their official currency, which they can do without the formal approval of the U.S. government.

There is another reason, though, that in many countries, including the United States, some people prefer to use cash rather than checks or credit cards in their transaction: They are engaging in illegal activities or are attempting to avoid paying taxes on legal activities. For these purposes, large-denomination bills are useful because they allow substantial transactions to be carried out in cash. The graph below shows the percentage of total currency made up of various bill denominations. (We ignore the value of bills from $500 to $10,000 that are still technically in circulation but have not been issued since 1969.) Most people use only smaller-denomination bills in their day-to-day lives. But bills with face values of $20 or less make up only about 15% of the value of all bills in circulation. More than three-quarters of the value of all U.S. currency consists of $100 bills. Because they have a portrait of Benjamin Franklin on them, criminals and terrorists in television shows and movies often refer to these bills as "Benjamins."

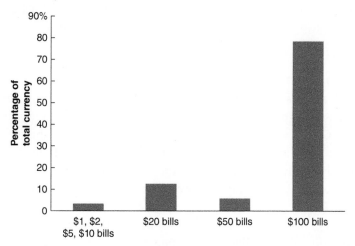

Many policymakers and economists believe that it's not just in the movies that $100 bills help criminals and terrorists; they argue that the ability to make cash transactions using large-denomination bills facilitates illegal activities by making the activities hard for governments to monitor. As a result, some policymakers have proposed eliminating the $100 bill, as well as the €500 note and similar high-denomination bills in other countries. One economist who has studied the issue argues: "High denomination notes are the payment instrument of choice for those evading taxes, committing crimes, financing terrorism or giving or receiving bribes." In 2016, the European Central Bank announced that it would stop issuing €500 notes because of "concerns that this banknote could facilitate illicit activities."

Will the fight against crime, tax avoidance, and terrorism cause the $100 bill to follow the €500 notes into the history books? Former Treasury Secretary Lawrence Summers and a number of other economists and policymakers argue that it should. As of this writing, though, the Federal Reserve has indicated that it has no immediate plans to stop issuing $100 bills. With more than 10 billion of these bills in circulation around the world, even if the Fed were to stop issuing new bills, it would be many years before they ceased to be widely available.

Sources: Mike Bird, "The Death of the € 500 Note Could Boost Its Black Market Price," *Wall Street Journal*, May 6, 2016; European Central Bank, "ECB Ends Production and Issuance of € 500 Note," press release, May 6, 2016; John Carney and Joshua Zumbrun, "The Plot to Kill the $100 Bill," *Wall Street Journal*, February 16, 2016; Peter Sands, "Making It Harder for the Bad Guys: The Case for Eliminating High Denomination Notes," Harvard Kennedy School, Working Paper Series, No. 52, February 2016; and Federal Reserve Board of Governors, "Currency in Circulation: Volume," February 5, 2016.

See related problems 2.8 and 2.9 at the end of the chapter.

2.3 The Payments System

LEARNING OBJECTIVE: Explain the role of the payments system in the economy.

Payments system The mechanism for conducting transactions in the economy.

Money facilitates transactions in the economy. The mechanism for conducting such transactions is called a **payments system**. The payments system has evolved over time from relying on payments made in gold and silver coins, to payments made with paper currency and checks written on deposits in banks, to payments made by electronic funds transfers.

The Transition from Commodity Money to Fiat Money

Historians disagree about precisely when people began using metallic coins. Evidence suggests that people in China were using metallic coins in the year 1000 B.C., and people in Greece were using them in 700 B.C. For centuries thereafter, buyers and sellers used coins minted from precious metals, such as gold, silver, and copper, as money. Gold and silver coins suffer from some drawbacks, however. For instance, from the days of the Roman Empire, governments seeking additional funds would sometimes *debase* the currency, melting down coins and re-minting them with a greater amount of less valuable metals mixed in with the gold and silver. An economy's reliance on gold and silver coins alone makes for a cumbersome payments system. People had difficulty transporting large numbers of gold coins to settle transactions and also ran the risk of being robbed. To get around this problem, beginning around the year A.D. 1500 in Europe, governments and private firms—early banks—began to store gold coins in safe places and issue paper certificates. Anyone receiving a paper certificate could claim the equivalent amount of gold. As long as people had confidence that the gold was available if they demanded it, the paper certificates would circulate as a medium of exchange. In effect, paper currency had been invented.

In modern economies, the central bank, such as the Federal Reserve in the United States, issues paper currency. The modern U.S. payments system is a fiat money system because the Federal Reserve does not exchange paper currency for gold or any other commodity money. The Federal Reserve issues paper currency and holds deposits from banks and the federal government. Banks can use these deposits to settle transactions with one another. Today, the Fed has a legal monopoly on the right to issue currency. Although in the nineteenth century private banks issued their own currency, they can no longer do so.

The Importance of Checks

Paper money has drawbacks. For instance, it can be expensive to transport paper money to settle large commercial or financial transactions. Imagine going to buy a car with a suitcase full of dollar bills! Another major innovation in the payments system came in the early twentieth century, with the increasing use of *checks*. **Checks** are promises to pay on demand money deposited with a bank or other financial institution. They can be written for any amount, and using them is a convenient way to settle transactions.

Check A promise to pay on demand money deposited with a bank or other financial institution.

Settling transactions with checks does, however, require more steps than settling transactions with currency. Suppose that your roommate owes you $50. If she gives you $50 in cash, the transaction is settled. Suppose, however, that she writes you a check for $50. You first must take the check to your bank. Your bank, in turn, must present the check for payment to your roommate's bank, which must then collect the money from her account. Processing the enormous flow of checks in the United States costs the economy several billion dollars each year. There are also information costs to using checks—the time and effort required for the seller to verify whether the check writer (the buyer) has a sufficient amount of money in her checking account to cover the amount of the check. Accepting checks requires more trust on the part of the seller than does accepting dollar bills.

New Technology and the Payments System

The Federal Reserve supervises the payments system but doesn't directly control it because many payments are processed by banks and other private firms. The Fed has listed what it believes to be the five most desirable outcomes for a payments system:[2]

1. **Speed.** Fast settlement of payments facilitates transactions by both households and businesses.
2. **Security.** Episodes in which criminals have hacked into retail credit card systems and other parts of the payments system have raised concerns about security. Better security increases consumers' and businesses' confidence that funds will not be stolen electronically.
3. **Efficiency.** Resources devoted to processing paper checks or other aspects of processing payments are diverted from producing other goods and services. Increasing the efficiency of the payments system allows it to function using fewer workers and computers, or other capital, which benefits the economy.

---

[2] This list is adapted from the one in Federal Reserve System, *Strategies for Improving the Payments System*, January 26, 2015, p. 2.

4. **Smooth international transactions.** The increasing amount of business that takes place across borders can be facilitated if payments can be made quickly and conveniently.
5. **Effective collaboration among participants in the system.** The payments system needs to efficiently involve governments, financial firms such as banks, and other businesses around the world. Such involvement ensures smooth transfers of funds in transactions.

Reaching these outcomes is made easier by breakthroughs in electronic telecommunication that have greatly reduced the time needed for clearing checks and for transferring funds. Settling and clearing transactions now occur over *electronic funds transfer systems,* which are computerized payment-clearing devices such as *debit cards, Automated Clearing House (ACH)* transactions, *automated teller machines (ATMs),* and *e-money.*

Debit cards can be used like checks: Cash registers in supermarkets and retail stores are linked to bank computers, so when you use a debit card to buy groceries or other products, your bank instantly credits the store's account with the amount and deducts it from your account. Such a system eliminates the problem of trust between the buyer and seller that is associated with checks because the bank computer authorizes the transaction. In recent years, many consumers have begun using apps on their smartphones or smartwatches that are linked to credit or debit cards. For example, Apple Pay and Android Pay allow consumers to buy goods at any store with a compatible register at the checkout counter by waving their phone or watch. Apple Pay and Android Pay are examples of *proximity mobile payments.* While the total volume of transactions using such payments is relatively small, it has been increasing rapidly.

ACH transactions include direct deposits of payroll checks into the checking accounts of workers and electronic payments on car loans and mortgages, where the payments are sent electronically from the borrower's account and deposited in the lender's account. ACH transactions reduce the transactions costs associated with processing checks, reduce the likelihood of missed payments, and reduce the costs lenders incur in notifying borrowers of missed payments.

Forty years ago, ATMs did not exist; to deposit or withdraw money from your checking account, you needed to fill out a deposit or withdrawal slip and wait in line at a bank teller's window. Adding to the inconvenience was the fact that many banks were open only between the hours of 10 A.M. and 3 P.M. (which were called *bankers' hours*). Today, ATMs allow you to carry out the same transactions at your bank whenever it is most convenient for you. Moreover, ATMs are connected to networks (such as Cirrus) so you can withdraw cash from the ATMs of banks other than your own.

E-Money, Bitcoin, and Blockchain

E-money Digital cash people use to buy goods and services over the Internet; short for electronic money.

The boundaries of electronic funds transfers have expanded to include **e-money**, or electronic money, which is digital cash people use to buy goods and services. The best-known form of e-money is the PayPal service. An individual or a firm can set up a PayPal account by linking to a checking account or credit card. As long as sellers are willing to accept funds transferred from a buyer's PayPal (or other e-money) account, e-money functions as if it were conventional, government-issued money. The central bank does not control e-money, though, so it is essentially a private payments system.

Recently, journalists, economists, and policymakers have been debating the merits of bitcoin, a new form of e-money. Unlike PayPal, bitcoin is not owned by a firm but is instead the product of a decentralized system of linked computers. Bitcoins are produced by people performing the complicated calculations necessary to ensure that online purchases made with bitcoins are legitimate—that is, that someone doesn't try to spend the same bitcoin multiple times. People who successfully complete these calculations are awarded a fixed number of bitcoins—typically 25. This process of bitcoin "mining" will continue until a maximum of 21 million bitcoins has been produced—a total expected to be reached in 2030.

Because people can buy and sell bitcoins in exchange for dollars and other currencies on web sites, some people refer to it as a "cryptocurrency." You can buy bitcoins and store them in a "digital wallet" on a smartphone. You can then buy something in a store that accepts bitcoins by scanning a bar code with your phone. A number of web sites, such as BitPay, which is based in Atlanta, allow merchants to process purchases made with bitcoins in a way similar to how they process credit card payments.

Why would buyers and sellers prefer to use bitcoins rather than cash or a credit card? The popularity of bitcoins with some buyers may be due to its being a new and trendy way to make purchases and because of the convenience of using a smartphone to make a purchase. In addition, when you buy something with a credit card, the credit card company has a permanent record of your transaction. Bitcoin transactions are more private because no such record of your transaction exists.

Some retailers prefer bitcoins to credit card purchases because the retailers pay only about 1% of the sale in processing costs, as opposed to about 3% for a credit card purchase. In addition, a bitcoin sale is final, just as if the purchase were made with cash, unlike credit card sales, where the buyer can dispute the purchase even months after it was made.

Despite these possible benefits to using bitcoin, it has not yet been widely adopted. The introduction of Apple Pay and Android Pay provided consumers with a way to use their smartphones linked to a credit card to make payments, which undercut one of bitcoin's advantages. Some firms also question whether the software underlying bitcoin is capable of dealing with a large number of transactions. The most popular online bitcoin exchange, Japan-based Mt. Gox, closed in 2015, further reducing confidence in the cryptocurrency.

Some policymakers are concerned that investors on exchanges might manipulate the prices of bitcoins and other virtual currencies. Between 2012 and 2016, the value of bitcoins in exchange for dollars has been as low as $5 per bitcoin and as high as $287 per bitcoin. Whether these swings in value represented underlying movements in demand and supply for bitcoins or the effects of investors manipulating their values was not clear.

Despite the problems with bitcoin, the underlying technology behind it, known as *blockchain*, has attracted interest from both firms and governments as they attempt to increase the speed, efficiency, and security of the payments system. Blockchain is technically a *distributed ledger*, or an online network that registers ownership of funds, securities, or any other good, including movies and songs. Blockchain allows individuals and businesses around the world to settle transactions instantly and securely on encrypted sites. The ability to direct transactions through blockchain could eliminate banks and other intermediaries, potentially greatly reducing costs. The greatest stumbling block to businesses adopting blockchain is the complexity of the technology and its resulting high cost. If the cost declines over time, blockchain may become a key part of the payments system.

Blockchain and other new payment technologies are exciting and lead some commentators to predict a "cashless society." A Federal Reserve study found that noncash payments continue to increase as a fraction of all payments, and electronic payments now make up more than two-thirds of all noncash payments. Not surprisingly, the number of checks written has been dropping by more than 2 billion per year. In reality, though, an entirely cashless (or checkless) society may be difficult to attain in the near future for two key reasons. First, as we noted with respect to blockchain, the infrastructure for an e-payments system is expensive to build. Second, many households and firms worry about protecting their privacy in an electronic system that is subject to computer hackers, although supporters of blockchain believe its encryption technology can overcome this problem. While the flow of paper in the payments system is likely to continue to shrink, it is unlikely to disappear.

MAKING THE CONNECTION

Will Sweden Become the First Cashless Society?

Can you imagine an economy in which no one uses cash? While no economy has yet arrived at this point, Sweden probably has come the closest. Swish, a mobile banking app, has become very popular in Sweden and other Scandinavian countries. The app makes it easy to transfer funds from one person's bank account to another, and because most stores and restaurants in Sweden are equipped to handle these payments, many people find that they rarely need to use cash.

Some stores and restaurants have stopped accepting cash and now require payment by credit card or using Swish or a similar app. These stores have eliminated their cash registers and rely entirely on people paying using mobile apps. Because many of their parishioners no longer carry cash, Swedish churches encourage them to make donations at church services using Swish.

Many branches of Sweden's banks no longer have cash available and do not accept cash deposits. Banks are removing many ATMs. Some bank managers note that the absence of cash has reduced the likelihood of bank robbery. Cash now accounts for only about 2% of transactions in Sweden, as compared with an average of about 10% in other European countries, while households in the United States still make 40% of their transactions using cash.

Young Swedes, in particular, are likely to rely on Swish or other apps rather than cash or even credit cards. One college student was quoted as saying: "No one uses cash. I think our generation can live without it." Some people in Sweden, though, still must rely on cash. For example, some older people do not know how to use smartphone apps; people with vision problems may have trouble using apps; and low-income people may not be able to afford smartphones or credit cards. Some privacy advocates are also concerned that apps and credit cards provide a public record of purchases that consumers may have legitimate reasons for keeping private. Finally, some people are afraid that using a credit card or an app leaves them exposed to hackers who may be able to steal money from their accounts.

To this point, Sweden is closer to becoming a cashless economy than are the United States and other countries. It remains to be seen whether more countries will follow Sweden's path or whether the drawbacks some people see to making all their transactions electronically will allow cash to remain important in their economies.

Sources: Mac William Bishop, "Sweden Sees Shift Away from Cash," nbcnews.com, February 6, 2016; Liz Alderman, "In Sweden, a Cash-Free Future Nears," *New York Times*, December 26, 2015; "Money for Everything," *Economist*, October 3, 2015; and Barbara Bennett, Douglas Conover, Shaun O'Brien, and Ross Advincula, "Cash Continues to Play a Key Role in Consumer Spending: Evidence from the Diary of Consumer Payment Choice," Federal Reserve Bank of San Francisco, *Fed Notes*, August 29, 2014.

See related problems 3.8 and 3.9 at the end of the chapter.

2.4 Measuring the Money Supply

LEARNING OBJECTIVE: Explain how the U.S. money supply is measured.

Economists and policymakers are interested in measuring money because, as we will see in later chapters, changes in the quantity of money are associated with changes in interest rates, prices, production, and employment. If the only function of money was to serve as a medium of exchange, we might want to include in the money supply only currency, checking account deposits, and traveler's checks because households and firms can easily use these assets to buy goods and services.

But including just these three assets would result in too narrow a measure of the money supply in the real world. Households and firms can use many other assets as mediums of exchange, even though they are not as liquid as cash or a checking account deposit. For example, you can easily convert your savings account at a bank into cash. Similarly, if you own shares in a money market mutual fund—which is a mutual fund that invests exclusively in short-term bonds, such as Treasury bills—you can write checks against the value of your shares. (See Chapter 1 for a definition of *mutual funds*.) So, we may want to consider assets such as savings accounts and money market mutual fund shares to be part of the medium of exchange.

Measuring Monetary Aggregates

As part of its responsibility to regulate the quantity of money in the United States, the Federal Reserve currently publishes data on two different definitions of the money supply. Figure 2.1 illustrates these definitions—referred to as **monetary aggregates**.

M1 Aggregate The narrow definition of the money supply is **M1**. As panel (a) in Figure 2.1 shows, M1 measures money as the traditional medium of exchange: currency, checking account deposits, and traveler's checks. Through the early 1980s, government regulations did not allow banks to pay interest on checking accounts, which made them

Monetary aggregate A measure of the quantity of money that is broader than currency; M1 and M2 are monetary aggregates.

M1 A narrow definition of the money supply: The sum of currency in circulation, checking account deposits, and holdings of traveler's checks.

MyEconLab Real-time data

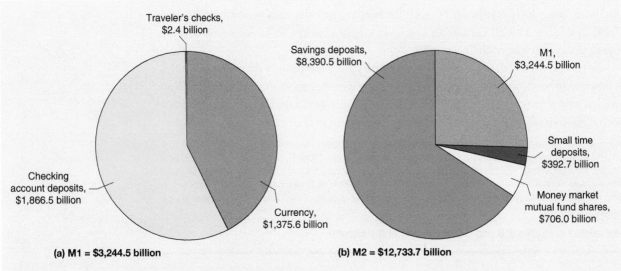

(a) M1 = $3,244.5 billion   (b) M2 = $12,733.7 billion

FIGURE 2.1 Measuring the Money Supply, May 2016

The Federal Reserve uses two different measures of the money supply: M1 and M2. M1 includes currency, checking account deposits, and traveler's checks. M2 includes all the assets in M1, as well as the additional assets shown in panel (b).

Note: In panel (b), savings deposits include money market deposit accounts.

Source: Board of Governors of the Federal Reserve System, *Federal Reserve Statistical Release, H6*, May 26, 2016.

close substitutes for currency. Financial innovation in the banking industry and government deregulation in the 1970s, 1980s, and 1990s have made other types of accounts close substitutes for traditional bank checking accounts. These accounts include checking accounts at savings institutions and credit unions, as well as interest-bearing checking accounts at commercial banks. Measures of M1 now include these other deposits against which checks may be written, along with non-interest-bearing checking account deposits called *demand deposits*, traveler's checks, and currency.

M2 A broader definition of the money supply: all the assets that are included in M1, as well as time deposits with a value of less than $100,000, savings accounts, money market deposit accounts, and non-institutional money market mutual fund shares.

M2 Aggregate M2 is a broader definition of the money supply than M1 and includes accounts that many households treat as short-term investments. These accounts can be converted into currency, although not as easily as the components of M1. As shown in panel (b) of Figure 2.1, in addition to the assets included in M1, M2 includes:

- Time deposits with a value of less than $100,000, primarily *certificates of deposits* in banks
- Savings accounts
- Money market deposit accounts at banks
- Noninstitutional money market mutual fund shares ("Noninstitutional" means that individual investors rather than institutional investors, such as pension funds, own the money market fund shares. Noninstitutional is also sometimes referred to as "retail.")

Does It Matter Which Definition of the Money Supply We Use?

Which is the better measure of money: M1 or M2? If M1 and M2 move together closely enough, the Fed could use either of them to try to influence the economy's output, prices, or interest rates. If M1 and M2 do not move together, they may tell different stories about what is happening to the money supply.

Panel (a) of Figure 2.2 shows the levels of M1 and M2 from January 1970 through April 2016. Note that M2 grew much more over these years than did M1. This result is not surprising because households and firms have increased their demand for certificates of deposit, money market mutual fund shares, and other assets that are included only in M2 much more than their demand for currency or checking accounts. Economists believe that *changes* in an economic variable are usually more important than are *levels* of the variable. For instance, as you consider borrowing to buy a house, you are more interested in the *inflation rate*—which measures the percentage change in the price level—than in the current price level. If we believe that changes in the money supply cause inflation, then a graph like panel (b), showing growth rates M1 and M2, measured as percentage changes at an annual rate, provides more information than does a graph like panel (a).

Panel (b) in Figure 2.2 shows that growth rates of M1 and M2 have been significantly different. Overall, the growth rate of M2 has been more stable than the growth rate of M1, which soared during the recessions of 1990–1991, 2001, and 2007–2009 and also had several periods of being negative. A negative growth rate means that the money supply measured by M1 actually became smaller during those periods. Given the difference in growth rates of M1 and M2, how do the Fed and private forecasters decide which measures to use to explain changes in other economic variables, such as the economy's total output, the price level, and interest rates? In fact, which measure of the money supply is best for forecasting remains an open question that Federal Reserve economists, academic economists, and private forecasters continue to research.

MyEconLab Real-time data

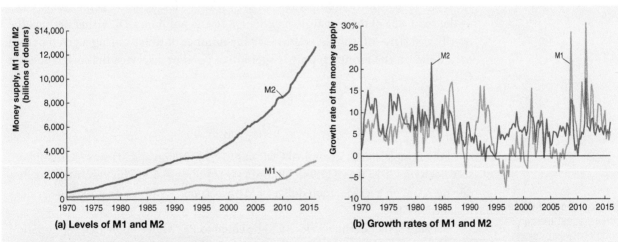

(a) Levels of M1 and M2

(b) Growth rates of M1 and M2

FIGURE 2.2 M1 and M2, 1970–2016

Panel (a) shows that since 1970, M2 has increased much more rapidly than has M1. Panel (b) uses quarterly data to show the annual growth rates of M1 and M2 since 1970. M1 has experienced much more instability than has M2.

Note: In panel (b), percentage changes are measured as the compound annual rate of change using quarterly data.

Source: Federal Reserve Bank of St. Louis.

2.5 The Quantity Theory of Money: A First Look at the Link Between Money and Prices

LEARNING OBJECTIVE: Use the quantity theory of money to analyze the relationship between money and prices in the long run.

The relationship between increases in the money supply and increases in prices has been discussed by writers dating back at least as far as the Greek philosopher Aristotle in the fourth century B.C. During the sixteenth century, the Spanish conquest of Mexico and Peru resulted in huge quantities of gold and silver being exported to Europe, where they were minted into coins, greatly increasing the European money supply. Many writers noted that this increase in the money supply was followed by an increase in the price level and a corresponding loss of *purchasing power*, which is the ability of consumers to use money to acquire goods and services. In this section, we explore how economists continue to study this link between changes in the money supply and changes in the price level.

Irving Fisher and the Equation of Exchange

In the early twentieth century, Irving Fisher, an economist at Yale University, developed the quantity theory of money to make more explicit the relationship between the money supply and inflation. Fisher began his analysis by using the *equation of exchange*:

$$M \times V = P \times Y.$$

The equation states that the quantity of money, M, multiplied by the velocity of money, V, equals the price level, P, multiplied by the level of real GDP, Y. Recall that the price level measures the average level of the prices of goods and services in the economy. There are several measures of the price level. The measure that is most relevant here is the *GDP deflator*, which incorporates the prices of all goods and services included in GDP. If we multiply real GDP by the GDP deflator, we get nominal GDP, so the right side of the equation of exchange equals nominal GDP. Fisher defined the *velocity of money*—or, simply, *velocity*—as the number of times during a given period each dollar in the money supply is spent on a good or a service that is included in GDP, or:

$$V = \frac{PY}{M}.$$

For example, in 2015, nominal GDP was \$17,947 billion and M1 was \$3,022 billion, so velocity in 2015 was \$17,947 billion/\$3,022 billion = 5.9. This result tells us that during 2015, on average, each dollar of M1 was spent 5.9 times on goods or services included in GDP.

Because Fisher defined velocity to be equal to PY/M, we know that the equation of exchange must always be true. The left side *must* be equal to the right side. A theory is a statement about the world that might possibly be false. Therefore, the equation of exchange is not a theory. Fisher turned the equation of exchange into the **quantity theory of money**, by arguing that the value of velocity was likely to be roughly constant in the short run. Fisher argued that the average number of times a

Quantity theory of money
A theory about the connection between money and prices that assumes that the velocity of money is determined mainly by institutional factors and so is roughly constant in the short run.

dollar is spent depends on institutional factors that change very slowly, such as how often people get paid, how often they go shopping, and how often businesses send out bills. The factors that affect velocity do not depend on the quantity of money or the value of real GDP. Therefore, Fisher argued, the value of velocity would not change as the quantity of money changes or as the value of real GDP changes. Because these assertions about velocity may be true or false, the quantity theory of money is, in fact, a theory.

The Quantity Theory Explanation of Inflation

To investigate the effects of changes in the money supply on inflation, we need to rewrite the equation of exchange from levels to percentage changes. We can do this by using a handy mathematical rule that states that an equation where variables are multiplied together is equal to an equation where the *percentage changes* of those variables are *added* together. So, we can rewrite the quantity equation as:

$$\% \text{ Change in } M \ + \ \% \text{ Change in } V \ = \ \% \text{ Change in } P \ + \ \% \text{ Change in } Y.$$

If Irving Fisher was correct that velocity is roughly constant in the short run and is unaffected by changes in the quantity of money or the value of real GDP, then the percentage change in velocity will be zero. Remember that the percentage change in the price level equals the inflation rate. Taking these two facts into account, we can rewrite the quantity equation one last time:

$$\text{Inflation rate } = \ \% \text{ Change in } M \ - \ \% \text{ Change in } Y.$$

This relationship gives us a useful way of thinking about the relationship between money and prices: Provided that velocity is constant, inflation will occur when the quantity of money increases faster than real GDP. The greater the percentage change in the quantity of money, the greater the inflation rate. In the United States, the long-run rate of growth of real GDP has been about 3% per year. So, the quantity theory indicates that if over the long run the Federal Reserve allows the money supply to increase at a rate faster than this, the result will be inflation.

SOLVED PROBLEM 2.5

Relationship Between Money and Income

A student makes the following assertion: "It isn't possible for the total value of production to increase unless the money supply also increases. After all, how can the value of the goods and services being bought and sold increase unless there is more money available?" Explain whether you agree with this assertion.

Solving the Problem

Step 1   **Review the chapter material.** This problem is about the relationship between money growth and changes in production or income, so you may want to review the section "Irving Fisher and the Equation of Exchange," which begins on page 40.

Step 2 **Explain whether output in an economy can grow without the money supply also growing.** Nominal GDP measures the value of total production, or, in symbols, *PY*. *PY* is the right side of the equation of exchange, so for it to increase, the left side—*MV*—must also increase. The student is asserting that nominal GDP cannot increase unless the money supply increases, but the equation of exchange shows us that nominal GDP could increase with the money supply remaining constant, provided that *V* increases. In other words, the total amount of spending in the economy as represented by nominal GDP could increase, even if the total number of dollars remains constant, provided that the average number of times those dollars are spent—*V*—increases.

EXTRA CREDIT: Remember the distinction between money and income. As you learned in your introductory economics course, at the level of the economy as a whole, total production is equal to total income, or GDP = National income. (Although, technically, we need to subtract depreciation from GDP to arrive at national income, this distinction does not matter for most macroeconomic issues.) But the value of GDP or national income is much greater than the value of the money supply. In the United States, the value of GDP is typically more than five times as large as the value of the M1 measure of the money supply.

See related problem 5.6 at the end of the chapter.

How Accurate Are Forecasts of Inflation Based on the Quantity Theory?

Note that the accuracy of the quantity theory depends on whether the key assumption that velocity is constant is correct. If velocity is not constant, then there may not be a tight link between increases in the money supply and increases in the price level. For example, an increase in the quantity of money might be offset by a decline in velocity, leaving the price level unaffected. As it turns out, velocity can move erratically in the short run, so we would not expect the quantity equation to provide good short-run forecasts of inflation. Over the long run, however, there is a strong link between changes in the money supply and inflation. Panel (a) of Figure 2.3 shows the relationship between the growth of the M2 measure of the money supply and the inflation rate by decade in the United States. (We use M2 here because data on M2 are available for a longer period of time than for M1.) Because of variations in the rate of growth of real GDP and in velocity, there is not an exact relationship between the growth rate of M2 and the inflation rate. But there is a clear pattern: Decades with higher growth rates in the money supply were also decades with higher inflation rates. In other words, most of the variation in inflation rates across decades can be explained by variation in the rates of growth of the money supply.

Panel (b) provides further evidence consistent with the quantity theory by looking at rates of growth of the money supply and rates of inflation across countries for the period from 2002 to 2015. Although there is not an exact relationship between rates of growth of the money supply and rates of inflation across countries, panel (b) shows that countries where the money supply grew rapidly tended to have high

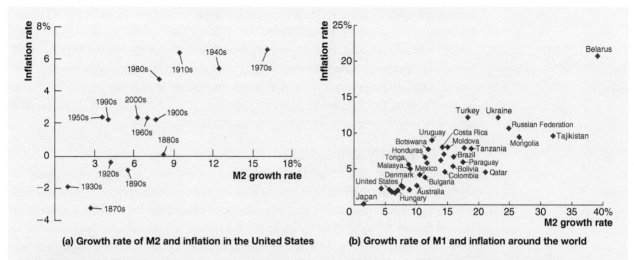

FIGURE 2.3 The Relationship Between Money Growth and Inflation over Time and Around the World

Panel (a) shows the relationship between the growth rate of M2 and the inflation rate for the United States from the 1870s to the 2000s. Panel (b) shows the relationship between the growth rate of M1 and inflation for 35 countries during the 2002–2015 period. In both panels, high money growth rates are associated with higher inflation rates.

Sources: Panel (a): for 1870s to 1960s, Milton Friedman and Anna J. Schwartz, *Monetary Trends in the United States and United Kingdom: Their Relation to Income, Prices, and Interest Rates, 1867–1975,* Chicago: University of Chicago Press, 1982, Table 4.8; for the 1970s to 2000s: Federal Reserve Board of Governors and U.S. Bureau of Economic Analysis; panel (b): International Monetary Fund, *International Financial Statistics.*

inflation rates, while countries where the money supply grew more slowly tended to have much lower inflation rates. Not included in panel (b) are data for the African country of Zimbabwe, which we mentioned at the beginning of the chapter. Between 1999 and 2008, the money supply in Zimbabwe grew by more than 7,500% per year. The result was an accelerating rate of inflation that eventually reached 15 *billion* percent during 2008. Zimbabwe was suffering from **hyperinflation**—that is, a rate of inflation that exceeds 50% per month. Venezuela is also not included in panel (b) because in recent years the government of Venezuela has stopped releasing accurate data. Economists estimate, though, that the money supply doubled in both 2015 and 2016, and prices increased at the hyperinflation rate of more than 500% in 2016. In the next section, we discuss the problems that hyperinflation can cause to a nation's economy.

Hyperinflation Extremely high rates of inflation, exceeding 50% per month.

The Hazards of Hyperinflation

Episodes of hyperinflation are rare. Some examples are the Confederate States of America during the last years of the Civil War, Germany during the early 1920s, Argentina during the 1990s, and Zimbabwe and Venezuela during more recent times. In these cases of extreme inflation, prices rise so rapidly that a given amount of money can purchase fewer and fewer goods and services each day. Eventually, if prices rise as rapidly as they did in Zimbabwe during 2008, anyone holding money for even a few hours finds that the money has lost most of its value before he or she can spend it. In those circumstances, households and firms may refuse to accept money at all, in which case money no longer functions as a medium of exchange. When economies don't use money, the specialization necessary to maintain high rates of productivity breaks down. For instance, during the German hyperinflation of the early 1920s, many workers abandoned their jobs because the money firms paid them lost its value before they had time to spend it. Not surprisingly, economic activity contracted sharply, and unemployment soared. The resulting economic hardships helped pave the way for the rise of Adolf Hitler and the Nazi Party. In recent years, hyperinflation in Zimbabwe and Venezuela has led to sharp declines in production and employment and to political turmoil.

What Causes Hyperinflation?

The quantity theory indicates that hyperinflation is caused by the money supply increasing far more rapidly than real output of goods and services. Once prices begin to rise rapidly enough that money loses a significant amount of its value, households and firms try to hold money for as brief a time as possible. In other words, velocity begins to rise as money changes hands at a faster and faster rate. In quantity theory terms, during a hyperinflation, both M and V on the left side of the equation increase rapidly. Because there are limits in the rate at which Y can grow, as a matter of arithmetic the inflation rate must soar.

Although the quantity theory can help us understand the arithmetic of *how* a hyperinflation occurs, it doesn't explain *why* it occurs. Central banks control the money supply and, so, have the means to avoid the economic disaster of a hyperinflation. Why, then, have some central banks at times allowed the money supply to increase at very rapid rates? The answer is that central banks are not always free to act independently of the rest of the government. The ultimate cause of hyperinflation is usually governments spending more than they collect in taxes, which results in government *budget deficits*. A budget deficit forces the government to borrow the difference between government spending and tax collections, usually by selling bonds. High-income countries, such as the United States, Germany, and Canada, can sell government bonds to private investors because those investors are confident that governments can make the interest payments. But private investors are often unwilling to buy bonds issued by developing countries, such as Zimbabwe or Venezuela, because they doubt that those governments will make the payments due on the bonds.

Governments that can't sell bonds to private investors will often sell them to their central banks. In paying for the bonds, the central bank increases the country's money supply. This process is called *monetizing the government's debt*, or, more casually, funding government spending by *printing money*.

MAKING THE CONNECTION

Deutsche Bank During the German Hyperinflation

Banks don't like inflation. Banks earn most of their revenue from making loans, and inflation results in borrowers paying back those loans in dollars that have less purchasing power. Particularly if the rate of inflation turns out to be higher than the bank expected it to be when making the loans, inflation will reduce bank profits. During a hyperinflation, the problems for banks are magnified because any loans will be repaid in money that will have lost most or all of its value.

One of the most famous hyperinflations occurred in Germany during the early 1920s. In 1918, when Germany lost World War I, the Allies—the United States, Great Britain, France, and Italy—imposed payments called *reparations* on the new German government. After a few years, the German government fell far behind in its reparations payment. In January 1923, the French government sent troops into the German industrial area known as the Ruhr to try to collect the payments directly. German workers in the Ruhr went on strike, and the German government decided to support them by paying their salaries. The government obtained the funds by selling bonds to the German central bank, the Reichsbank, thereby increasing the money supply.

The increase in the money supply was very large: The total number of marks—the German currency—in circulation rose from 115 million in January 1922 to 1.3 billion in January 1923 and then to 497 billion billion, or 497,000,000,000,000,000,000, in December 1923. Just as the quantity theory predicts, the result was a staggeringly high rate of inflation. The German price index that stood at 100 in 1914 and 1,440 in January 1922 rose to 126,160,000,000,000 in December 1923. The German mark became worthless. The German government ended the hyperinflation by (1) negotiating a new agreement with the Allies that reduced its reparations payments, (2) balancing the budget by reducing government expenditures and raising taxes, and (3) replacing the existing mark with a new mark. Each new mark was worth 1 trillion old marks. The Reichsbank was also limited to issuing a total of 3.2 billion new marks.

Deutsche Bank was the largest bank in Germany at the time of the hyperinflation, and it remains the largest today. The hyperinflation put enormous strain on the bank. Because German currency was losing value so quickly, households and firms wanted their transactions processed as rapidly as possible. To handle these transactions, the bank had to increase its employees by six times compared with pre–World War I levels. Households and firms were anxious to borrow money to meet their own soaring expenses, and they expected to be able to pay back loans using money that had lost most of its purchasing power. According to one economic historian, the demand for loans increased "geometrically from day to day." Because most of these loans would have been unprofitable to the bank, the bank's managers ordered its branches to sharply reduce the number of loans granted. Eventually, as German currency became nearly worthless, Deutsche Bank would make loans only to borrowers who would repay them in either foreign currencies or commodities, such as coal or wheat.

Despite the intense financial strains on the bank, Deutsche Bank emerged from the hyperinflation in a stronger competitive position in Germany. The bank's managers believed that with the value of currency and financial investments rapidly disappearing, they would be better off acquiring other banks because they would be acquiring land and buildings that would be likely to retain their value. This strategy turned out to be shrewd. When the hyperinflation ended in 1924 and the German economy resumed growing, Deutsche Bank was in an excellent position to profit from that growth.

Sources: Thomas Sargent, "The End of Four Big Hyperinflations," in *Rational Expectations and Inflation*, New York: Harper & Row, 1986; and David A. Moss, "The Deutsche Bank," in Thomas K. McCraw, *Creating Modern Capitalism*, Cambridge, MA: Harvard University Press, 1997.

See related problems 5.11 and 5.12 at the end of the chapter.

Should Central Banks Be Independent?

In the modern economy, hyperinflations occur primarily in developing countries when their central banks are forced to create so much money to fund government spending that the inflation rate soars. But central banks in high-income countries may also come under political pressure to buy government bonds to help fund government budget deficits. The more independent a central bank is of the rest of the government, the more it can resist political pressures to increase the money supply, and the lower the country's inflation rate is likely to be.

In a classic study, Alberto Alesina and Lawrence Summers of Harvard University tested the link between the degree of independence of a country's central bank and the country's inflation rate for 16 high-income countries during the years 1955–1988. Figure 2.4 shows the results. Countries with highly independent central banks, such as the United States, Switzerland, and Germany, had lower inflation rates than did countries whose central banks had little independence, such as New Zealand, Italy, and Spain. In recent years, New Zealand and Canada have granted their banks more independence, at least partly to better fight inflation.

It appears likely that the independence of the Federal Reserve helps to explain the relatively low inflation rates in the United States during the past 30 years. But the actions of the Fed during the 2007–2009 recession led many members of Congress to argue that the Fed's independence should be reduced. Some members had been long-time critics of the Fed and believed that in a democracy, monetary policy should be set by Congress and the president of the United States and implemented by officials who must directly answer to the president. Under existing law, the Federal Reserve operates independently because it is run by the seven-member Board of Governors who serve 14-year terms and are appointed by the president but cannot be replaced by the president or Congress

FIGURE 2.4

The Relationship Between Central Bank Independence and the Inflation Rate

For 16 high-income countries, the greater the degree of central bank independence, the lower the inflation rate. Central bank independence is measured by an index ranging from 1 (minimum independence) to 4 (maximum independence).

Source: Alberto Alesina and Lawrence H. Summers, "Central Bank Independence and Macroeconomic Performance: Some Comparative Evidence," *Journal of Money, Credit and Banking*, Vol. 25, No. 2, May 1993, pp. 151–162. Copyright 1993 by Ohio State University Press (Journals). Reproduced with permission of Ohio State University Press via Copyright Clearance Center.

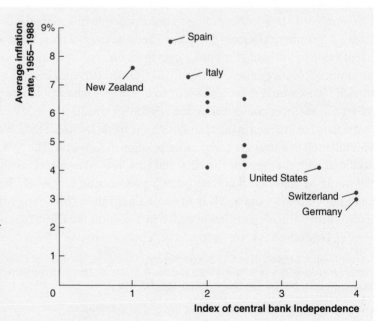

unless they resign or their terms expire. Because the members of the Board of Governors do not run for election, they are not accountable for their actions to the ultimate authorities in a democracy—the voters. Other members of Congress objected to the actions of the Fed during the recession because they believed the actions exceeded the authority granted to the Fed under federal law. Some members were particularly concerned that the Fed had brought about increases in the money supply and bank reserves that threatened higher inflation rates in the future.

Other members of Congress and many economists saw the Fed's actions as appropriate, given the severity of the crisis. As we will see in later chapters, the debate over the Fed may result in important changes in a key part of the financial system.

ANSWERING THE KEY QUESTION

Continued from page 24

At the beginning of this chapter, we asked:

"Should a central bank be independent of the rest of the government?"

We have seen that policymakers disagree on the answer to this question. The degree of independence that a country grants to its central bank is ultimately a political question. We have also seen, though, that most economists believe that an independent central bank helps to control inflation.

Key Terms and Problems

Key Terms

Barter, p. 26
Check, p. 33
Commodity money, p. 26
E-money, p. 34
Fiat money, p. 29
Hyperinflation, p. 43
Legal tender, p. 29

M1, p. 37
M2, p. 38
Medium of exchange, p. 28
Monetary aggregate, p. 37
Money, p. 25
Payments system, p. 32
Quantity theory of money, p. 40

Specialization, p. 27
Standard of deferred payment, p. 29
Store of value, p. 28
Transactions cost, p. 26
Unit of account, p. 28
Wealth, p. 29

2.1 **Do We Need Money?**
Analyze the inefficiencies of a barter system.

Review Questions

1.1 What are the costs of a barter system?

1.2 Give two examples of commodity money.

1.3 What role does specialization play in an economy's standard of living?

Problems and Applications

1.4 Why might an individual find a $20 Federal Reserve Note to be more desirable as a form of money than a $20 gold coin? Which would the government find more desirable to produce? Briefly explain.

MyEconLab   Visit **www.myeconlab.com** to complete these exercises online and get instant feedback. Exercises that update with real-time data are marked with .

1.5   What are the key differences between using a deer-skin as money and using a dollar bill as money?

1.6   [Related to the Making the Connection on page 27] Should the packs of Marlboro cigarettes used to pay taxi drivers in Russia in the late 1980s be considered money? Briefly explain.

1.7   [Related to the Making the Connection on page 27] Following the end of World War II in 1945, the Reichsmark, the German currency, lost so much value that a barter economy developed. During this period, many Germans used U.S. cigarettes as currency. Why might people have used cigarettes, rather than another commodity, as currency in these circumstances? Would only people who smoked cigarettes have been willing to use them as money? Briefly explain.

2.2 **The Key Functions of Money**
List and describe the four key functions of money.

Review Questions

2.1   What makes a dollar bill money? What makes a personal check money? Are there circumstances under which you would be reluctant to accept a dollar bill as money? A personal check?

2.2   Briefly describe each of the four main functions of money.

2.3   Is money the only store of value? If not, give some other examples of stores of value. Must money be a store of value to serve its function as a medium of exchange? Briefly explain.

2.4   What is the difference between commodity money and fiat money?

Problems and Applications

2.5   Suppose that you live in a simple farm economy where milk is accepted as the primary form of money. Discuss the difficulties with using milk as money in regard to:
a. A medium of exchange
b. A unit of account
c. A store of value
d. A standard of deferred payment

2.6   Discuss whether your money, wealth, or income increases in each of the following situations:
a. The value of your house increases.
b. Your boss gives you a 10% raise.
c. You take cash out of the bank and use it to buy an Apple iPad.

2.7   Suppose that Congress changes the law to require all firms to accept paper currency in exchange for whatever they are selling. Briefly discuss who would gain and who would lose from this legislation.

2.8   [Related to the Making the Connection on page 30] According to an article in the *Wall Street Journal*: "The highest U.S. dollar denomination, the $100 bill, trades at a significant premium in many emerging markets." Why might people in these countries wish to use U.S. currencies rather than the currencies issued by their governments? Why might their demand for $100 bills be greater than their demand for lower-denomination bills?
Source: Mike Bird, "The Death of the € 500 Note Could Boost Its Black Market Price," *Wall Street Journal*, May 6, 2016.

2.9   [Related to the Making the Connection on page 30] According to an article in the *Wall Street Journal*: "The $100 bill is America's most popular currency denomination. It also could be the most endangered."
a. Have you ever used a $100 bill to buy something? Why is the $100 bill the most popular U.S. currency denomination?
b. If the $100 bill is so popular, why is it endangered?
Source: John Carney and Joshua Zumbrun, "The Plot to Kill the $100 Bill," *Wall Street Journal*, February 16, 2016.

MyEconLab   Visit **www.myeconlab.com** to complete these exercises online and get instant feedback. Exercises that update with real-time data are marked with ⬤ .

2.3 The Payments System
Explain the role of the payments system in the economy.

Review Questions

3.1 Why does the Federal Reserve care about the payments system? What does the Fed consider to be the five desirable outcomes for the payments system?

3.2 Why did governments begin issuing paper currency?

3.3 What is the "blockchain" technology? Is it likely to lead to the United States becoming a "cashless society"? Briefly explain.

Problems and Applications

3.4 Suppose that an economy in 10,000 B.C. used a rare stone as its money. Suppose also that the number of stones declined over time as stones were accidentally destroyed or used as weapons. What would have happened to the value of the stones over time? What would the consequences likely have been if someone had discovered a large quantity of new stones?

3.5 One historian has given the following description of the economy of the Roman Empire in the third century under the emperor Diocletian:

> The coinage had become so debased as to be virtually worthless. Diocletian's attempt to re-issue good gold and silver coins failed because there simply was not enough gold and silver available to restore confidence in the currency…. Diocletian finally accepted the ruin of the money economy and revised the tax system so that it was based on payments in kind. The soldiers too came to be paid in kind.

a. What does it mean to describe coinage as having become debased?

b. Why would government officials need to restore confidence in the coins before people would use them as money?

c. What are "in-kind" payments? How might moving from a system of payments being made in gold and silver coins to a system of payments being made in kind affect the economy of the empire?

Source: Ralph W. Mathisen, "Diocletian," *An Online Encyclopedia of Roman Emperors*, www.roman-emperors.org/dioclet.htm. Reprinted with permission from Professor Ralph W. Mathisen.

3.6 An article in the *Wall Street Journal* on blockchain notes: "The technology could cut $20 billion in annual costs in global banking." What is blockchain technology, and how would it reduce the costs of banking?

Source: Kim S. Nash, "Blockchain: Catalyst for Massive Change Across Industries," *Wall Street Journal*, February 2, 2016.

3.7 In late 2009, Amazon introduced PayPhrase, an electronic payments system intended to compete with PayPal. Less than three years later, in early 2012, Amazon discontinued the program. PayPal is by far the largest electronic payments system. What problems might competitors encounter in trying to set up a competing system?

3.8 [Related to the Making the Connection on page 36] In Sweden, some banks have closed their ATMs, no longer allow depositors to make cash withdrawals in person at branches, and no longer accept cash deposits.

a. What are the benefits to a bank from taking these actions? What are the costs?

b. How might a bank measure the costs and benefits in making a decision about whether to go cashless?

3.9 [Related to the Making the Connection on page 36] According to an article on nbcnews.com, in Sweden, "Shoe stores, clothing shops and restaurants are increasingly reliant on card-only or mobile banking transactions, and some—like the brand Swedish Hasbeens—don't even have cash registers."

a. What are the benefits to a store or restaurant refusing to accept cash as payment from customers? What are the costs?

b. How might a store go about measuring the costs and benefits in making a decision about whether to go cashless?

Source: Mac William Bishop, "Sweden Sees Shift Away from Cash," nbcnews.com, February 6, 2016.

2.4 Measuring the Money Supply
Explain how the U.S. money supply is measured.

Review Questions

4.1 Are the assets included in M1 more or less liquid than the assets included in M2? Briefly explain.

4.2 Since 1970, which measure of the money supply has grown more rapidly, M1 or M2? Briefly explain why. Has the growth of M1 been more or less stable than the growth rate of M2?

Problems and Applications

4.3 Define *liquidity*. Rank the following assets in terms of liquidity, from most to least liquid: money market mutual fund, savings account, corporate stock, dollar bill, house, gold bar, checking account.

4.4 If you ask someone who hasn't taken a course in economics to define the money supply, he or she is likely to say something like: "The money supply equals the total amount of paper currency and coins in circulation." Why does the Fed include more than just currency in M1, its narrow definition of the money supply?

4.5 Explain whether each of the following is included in only M1, only M2, or both M1 and M2:

a. Traveler's checks

b. Savings deposits

c. Certificates of deposit

d. Checking account deposits

4.6 Until 1933, the United States was on the gold standard, and people could receive gold from the federal government in exchange for their paper currency. Although the federal government is no longer willing to exchange paper currency for gold, the Federal Reserve still stores more than 500,000 gold bars in the basement of the New York Federal Reserve building in Manhattan. Are these gold bars included in either the M1 or M2 definition of the money supply? Briefly explain why they are, or are not, included.

4.7 Suppose you withdraw $1,000 from your checking account and use the funds to buy a certificate of deposit at your bank. What is the immediate effect of these actions on M1 and M2?

4.8 Why aren't credit cards included in M1 or M2?

4.9 In Figure 2.2 on page 39, panel (b) shows that during a period in the early 1990s, the rate of M1 growth was increasing rapidly, while the rate of M2 growth was decreasing. Briefly explain how this outcome was possible.

2.5 The Quantity Theory of Money: A First Look at the Link Between Money and Prices

Use the quantity theory of money to analyze the relationship between money and prices in the long run.

Review Questions

5.1 Is the equation of exchange a theory? Briefly explain.

5.2 What does the quantity theory indicate is the cause of inflation?

5.3 Why do governments allow hyperinflation to occur?

5.4 Briefly discuss the pros and cons of a central bank being independent of the rest of the government.

Problems and Applications

5.5 If during 2018 the money supply increases by 4%, the inflation rate is 2%, and the growth of real GDP is 3%, what must have happened to the value of velocity during 2018?

5.6 [Related to Solved Problem 2.5 on page 41] A student makes the following statement: "If the money supply in a country increases, then the level of total production in that country must also increase." Briefly explain whether you agree with this statement.

5.7 During the late nineteenth century, the United States experienced a period of sustained *deflation*, or a falling price level. Explain in terms of the quantity theory of money how a deflation is possible. Is it necessary for the quantity of money to decline for deflation to occur?

5.8 How does a high rate of inflation affect the value of money? How does it affect the usefulness of money as a medium of exchange?

5.9 What does the statistical evidence show about the link between the growth rate of the money supply and the inflation rate in the long run? Is the link between the growth rate of the money supply and the inflation rate stronger in the short run or in the long run?

5.10 [Related to the Chapter Opener on page 24] According to an article in the *Economist*, "Zimbabwe abandoned its worthless currency not long after monthly inflation hit 80 billion per cent in November 2008. Zimbabweans now use American dollars." The article also notes that average incomes in Zimbabwe had fallen by two-thirds, but after the country abandoned its currency for the U.S. dollar, economic growth began to occur.

a. Why would Zimbabwe abandon its own currency to begin using U.S. dollars?

b. Why would using the U.S. dollar as its currency have enabled the economy of Zimbabwe to resume growing?

c. What potential problems could using U.S. dollars rather than its own currency pose for the Zimbabwean government?

Source: "Spot the Difference," *Economist*, April 2, 2016.

5.11 [Related to the Making the Connection on page 44] When the German government succeeded in ending the hyperinflation in 1924, was this better news for borrowers or for lenders? Briefly explain.

5.12 [Related to the Making the Connection on page 44] In 1919, the British economist John Maynard Keynes wrote the influential book *The Economic Consequences of the Peace*, in which he argued that the reparations for World War I that Germany was being forced to pay to the United States, France, Italy, and the United Kingdom would have devastating consequences: "But who can say how much is endurable, or in what direction men will seek at last to escape from their misfortunes?" What is the connection between the war reparations that Germany was forced to pay and the later hyperinflation? Why might hyperinflation lead to political unrest?

Source: John Maynard Keynes, *The Economic Consequences of the Peace*, New York: Harcourt, Brace and Howe, 1920, p. 251.

5.13 [Related to the Chapter Opener on page 24] An article in the *Wall Street Journal* notes: "The Federal

Reserve, though it has enormous power over the U.S. economy, is designed to be independent of Congress and the president." If the Fed has enormous power over the U.S. economy, why was it designed to be independent of Congress and the president rather than under their direct control?

Source: David Wessel, "Explaining 'Audit the Fed,'" *Wall Street Journal*, February 15, 2015.

5.14 One of the ways the Federal Reserve carries out its responsibilities for conducting monetary policy is by trying to affect the level of key interest rates. In early 2016, Federal Reserve Chair Janet Yellen met with President Barack Obama in the White House. According to an article in the *Wall Street Journal*, a spokesman for the president stated that "he 'would not anticipate' that Ms. Yellen would go into detail on the path of

interest rates at the meeting in order to preserve 'both the appearance of and the fact of the independence of the Federal Reserve and the chair.'"

a. What did the spokesman mean by "the appearance of and the fact of the independence of the Federal Reserve"?

b. Why might a president discussing the details of monetary policy with a Fed chair undermine the appearance that the Fed operates independently of the president? Why would the president worry about the possibility that the appearance of Fed independence might be undermined?

Source: David Harrison, "Barack Obama, Janet Yellen Discuss Economy, Regulation at White House," *Wall Street Journal*, April 11, 2016.

Data Exercises

D2.1: [The components of M1] Go to the web site of the Federal Reserve Bank of St. Louis (FRED) (fred.stlouisfed.org) and find the most recent values for the M1 Money Stock (M1), the Currency Component of M1 (CURRENCY), Total Checkable Deposits (TCD), and Travelers Checks Outstanding (WTCSL). Which of the components of M1 is the largest? Which is the smallest?

D2.2: [The relationship between M1 and M2] Go to the web site of the Federal Reserve Bank of St. Louis (FRED) (fred.stlouisfed.org) and find the most recent monthly values and values from the same month 5 years and 10 years earlier from FRED for the M1 Money Stock (M1SL) and the M2 Money Stock (M2SL).

a. Using these data, calculate M1 as a proportion of M2 for each of the years.

b. Explain whether this proportion has increased, decreased, or remained the same over time. Can you think of an explanation for any changes you observe?

D2.3: [The equation of exchange] Go to the web site of the Federal Reserve Bank of St. Louis (FRED) (fred.stlouisfed.org) and find the most recent values and values for the same quarter in 1985 for nominal Gross Domestic Product (GDP), the Velocity of M1 Money Stock (M1V), and the Velocity of M2 Money Stock (M2V).

a. Using the data found above, compute the M1 money supply and the M2 money supply for both periods.

b. Describe how M1 velocity and M2 velocity differ in the two quarters.

D2.4: [The relationship between changes in M2 and inflation] Go to the St. Louis Fed's data site (FRED) (fred.stlouisfed.org) and, for January 1990 to the most recent available month, download and graph both the compounded annual rates of change of M2 (M2SL) and the rate of change of the CPI (CPIAUCSL). What relationship do you see between the two variables?

CHAPTER

3

Interest Rates and Rates of Return

Learning Objectives

After studying this chapter, you should be able to:

3.1 Use the interest rate to calculate present values and future values (pages 54–62)

3.2 Distinguish among different debt instruments and understand how their prices are determined (pages 62–66)

3.3 Explain the relationship between the yield to maturity on a bond and its price (pages 66–71)

3.4 Understand the inverse relationship between bond prices and bond yields (pages 71–77)

3.5 Explain the difference between interest rates and rates of return (pages 78–80)

3.6 Explain the difference between nominal interest rates and real interest rates (pages 80–83)

Are Treasury Bonds a Risky Investment?

Want a safe investment? How about U.S. Treasury bonds? The Treasury sells bonds with a face value of $100 when it needs to borrow money to pay the federal government's bills. When you buy a bond, the Treasury will pay you interest every six months and pay you back the $100 face value of the bond when it matures. Unlike some local governments, corporations, or foreign governments that issue bonds, the U.S. government is almost certain to make the payments on these bonds. In other words, the *default risk* is effectively zero.

But in 2016, many financial advisers believed Treasury bonds were too risky and therefore warned investors

not to buy them. A contradiction? Not necessarily. At that time, 30-year Treasury bonds—bonds that would mature and pay the owner $100 in 30 years—had an interest rate of about 2.5%, which was much higher than the interest rate you would receive on a checking account or a savings account in a bank. But 2.5% was a historically low interest rate for 30-year Treasury bonds compared to the 15% they had paid in 1981 or even the 5.25% they had paid in mid-2007. Why had the interest rate on Treasury bonds declined? As we will discuss in more detail in Chapter 4, interest rates are determined by the interaction of the demand for funds by borrowers

Continued on next page

KEY ISSUE AND QUESTION

Issue: Some investment analysts argue that very low interest rates on some long-term bonds make them risky investments.

Question: Why do interest rates and the prices of financial securities move in opposite directions?

Answered on page 83

and the supply of funds by lenders or investors. One important factor that borrowers and investors take into account is the expected inflation rate. The higher the inflation rate, the lower the purchasing power of the dollars with which the borrower will repay the investor. When investors expect that future inflation rates will be high, they insist on being paid high interest rates on bonds.

One important reason 30-year Treasury bonds had such low interest rates in 2016 was that many investors expected that the inflation rate would remain 2% or less for years into the future. If this expectation proves to be accurate, low interest rates on long-term bonds might be the "new normal." But some economists and investment advisors weren't so sure. During the 2007–2009 financial crisis, the Federal Reserve had taken a number of unusual monetary policy actions, some of which were continuing in 2016. Federal Reserve Chair Janet Yellen argued that the Fed would be able to manage a transition back to more normal financial conditions. But if Yellen was wrong, particularly if inflation increased faster than expected, the Treasury would have to pay higher interest rates on newly issued bonds.

What happens if you buy a Treasury bond with an interest rate of 2.5%, when the Treasury begins selling new bonds with interest rates of 5%? If you hold your bond to maturity, you will continue receiving an interest rate of 2.5%. But what if you need the funds to buy a car or house and you decide to sell the bond *before* it matures? Your bond pays only 2.5% interest, while the Treasury is selling new bonds that pay 5%. To find a buyer for your bond, your broker will have to cut its price to compensate the buyer for receiving the lower interest rate. In other words, you will have to accept a loss on your bond.

So, while it is true that in buying a Treasury bond, you do not face *default risk*, you will face *interest-rate risk*, which is the risk that the price of your bond will fluctuate in response to changes in market interest rates. If predictions of higher future inflation rates turn out to be accurate, many investors who owned bonds in 2016 stood to lose a substantial amount as the prices of their bonds declined.

In this chapter, we will begin exploring bonds and similar securities. Bonds play an important role in the financial system because they facilitate funds moving from savers to borrowers. A solid understanding of interest rates will help you make sense of bonds and nearly every other aspect of the financial system.

3.1   The Interest Rate, Present Value, and Future Value

LEARNING OBJECTIVE: Use the interest rate to calculate present values and future values.

During the Middle Ages in Europe, governments often banned lenders from charging interest on loans, partly because some people interpreted the Bible as prohibiting the practice and partly because most people believed that anyone with funds to spare should be willing to lend them to poorer friends and neighbors to purchase basic necessities, without charging interest on the loan. In modern economies, households borrow money primarily to finance spending on such things as houses, furniture, college educations, and cars, and firms borrow money to finance spending on such things as factories, offices, and information technology. Perhaps because in modern economies very little borrowing is intended to finance spending on day-to-day necessities, charging interest on loans is no longer banned in most countries. Today, economists consider the interest rate to be the cost of credit.

Why Do Lenders Charge Interest on Loans?

If apple growers charged a zero price for apples, very few apples would be supplied. Similarly, if lenders, who are suppliers of credit, didn't charge interest on loans, there would be very little credit supplied. Recall from your introductory economics course the important concept of *opportunity cost*, which is the value of what you have to give up to engage in an activity. Just as the price of apples has to cover the grower's opportunity cost of supplying apples, the interest rate has to cover the lender's opportunity cost of supplying credit.

Consider the following situation: You loan $1,000 to a friend who promises to pay back the money in one year. There are three key facts you need to take into account when deciding how much interest to charge him:

1. By the time your friend pays you back, prices are likely to have risen, so you will be able to buy fewer goods and services than you could have if you had spent the money today rather than lending it.
2. Your friend might not pay you back; in other words, he might *default* on the loan.
3. During the period of the loan, your friend has use of your money, and you don't. If he uses the money to buy a laptop, he gets the use of the laptop for a year, while you wait for him to pay you back. In other words, by lending your money, you incur the opportunity cost of not being able to spend it on goods and services today.

So, we can think of the interest you charge on the loan as being the result of:

• Compensation for inflation
• Compensation for default risk—the chance that the borrower will not pay back the loan
• Compensation for the opportunity cost of waiting to spend your money

Notice two things about this list. First, even if lenders are convinced that there will be no inflation during the period of the loan and that there is no chance the borrower will default, lenders will still charge interest to compensate them for waiting for their money to be paid back. Second, these three factors vary from person to person and from loan to loan. For instance, during periods when lenders believe that the inflation rate will be high, they will charge more interest. Lenders will also charge more interest to borrowers who seem more likely to default.

Most Financial Transactions Involve Payments in the Future

We are all familiar with interest rates that are charged on car loans or college loans and interest rates paid on assets such as certificates of deposit in banks. But the interest rate is more important to the financial system than it might seem to be because of the following key fact: *Most financial transactions involve payments in the future.* When you take out a car loan, you promise to make payments every month until the loan is paid off. When you buy a bond issued by General Electric, General Electric promises to pay you interest every year until the bond matures. We could go on to list many other similar financial transactions that also involve future payments. The fact that financial transactions involve payments in the future poses a challenge: How is it possible to compare different transactions? For instance, suppose that you need to borrow $15,000 from your bank to buy a car. Consider two loans:

1. Loan A, which requires you to pay $366.19 per month for 48 months
2. Loan B, which requires you to pay $318.71 per month for 60 months

Which loan would you prefer? The interest rate helps answer questions like this because it provides a *link between the financial present and the financial future*. In this case, even though Loan A has a higher monthly payment, it has a lower interest rate: The interest rate on Loan A is 8%, and the interest rate on Loan B is 10%. While the interest rate is not the only factor to consider when evaluating a loan, it is an important factor.

Two key ideas—compounding and discounting—can help us further explore how the interest rate provides a link between the financial present and the financial future and can also help us understand how to calculate interest rates, like those on these two loans.

Compounding and Discounting

Future value The value at some future date of an investment made today.

Consider an example of compounding. Suppose that you deposit $1,000 in a one-year bank certificate of deposit (CD) that pays an interest rate of 5%. What will be the *future value* of this investment? **Future value** refers to the value at some future date of an investment made today. In one year, you will receive back your $1,000 *principal*—which is the amount invested (or borrowed)—and 5% interest on your $1,000, or:

$$\$1{,}000 + (\$1{,}000 \times 0.05) = \$1{,}050.$$

We can rewrite this compactly as:

$$\$1{,}000 \times (1 + 0.05) = \$1{,}050.$$

If:

$i =$ the interest rate

Principal = the amount of your investment (your original $1,000)

$FV_1 =$ the future value in one year,

then we can rewrite the expression as:

$$Principal \times (1 + i) = FV_1.$$

(Note that the subscript 1 in FV_1 indicates that we are looking at the future value after *one* year.) This relationship is important because it states that we can calculate a future value in one year by multiplying the principal invested by 1 plus the interest rate.

Compounding The process of earning interest on interest, as savings accumulate over time.

Compounding for More Than One Period Suppose that at the end of one year, you decide to reinvest in—or *roll over*—your CD for another year. If you reinvest your $1,050 for a second year, you will not only receive interest on your original investment of $1,000, you will also receive interest on the $50 in interest you earned the first year. The process of earning interest on interest as savings accumulate over time is called **compounding**. *Compound interest* is an important component of the total amount you earn on an investment.

We can calculate the future value after two years of your initial investment:

$$[\$1{,}000 \times (1 + 0.05)] \times (1 + 0.05) = \$1{,}102.50.$$

(Amount you earned after one year) $\times$ (Compounding during the second year)
$$= \text{Future value after two years.}$$

We can write this expression more compactly as:

$$\$1{,}000 \times (1 + 0.05)^2 = \$1{,}102.50,$$

or, in symbols, as:

$$Principal \times (1 + i)^2 = FV_2.$$

We could continue to compound your initial \$1,000 investment for as many years as you choose to roll over your CD. For instance, if you rolled it over for a third year at the same interest rate, at the end of the third year, you would have:

$$\$1{,}000 \times (1 + 0.05) \times (1 + 0.05) \times (1 + 0.05) = \$1{,}000 \times (1 + 0.05)^3 = \$1{,}157.63.$$

Note that the exponent on the compounding factor, $(1 + 0.05)$, equals the number of years over which the compounding takes place.

It's useful to generalize our result: If you invest \$1,000 for n years, where n can be any number of years, at an interest rate of 5%, then at the end of n years, you will have:

$$\$1{,}000 \times (1 + 0.05)^n,$$

or, in symbols:

$$Principal \times (1 + i)^n = FV_n.$$

SOLVED PROBLEM 3.1A   IN YOUR INTEREST

Using Compound Interest to Select a Bank CD

Suppose you are considering investing \$1,000 in one of the following bank CDs:

- The first CD will pay an interest rate of 4% per year for three years

- The second CD will pay an interest rate of 8% the first year, 1% the second year, and 1% the third year

Which CD should you choose?

Solving the Problem

Step 1 **Review the chapter material.** This problem is about compound interest, so you may want to review the section "Compounding for More Than One Period" on page 56.

Step 2 **Calculate the future value of your investment with the first CD.** Because the interest rate is the same each year for the first CD, the future value in three years will be equal to the present value of \$1,000, which is the amount of your principal, multiplied by 1 plus the interest rate raised to the third power, or:

$$\$1{,}000 \times (1 + 0.04)^3 = \$1{,}124.86.$$

Step 3 **Calculate the future value of your investment with the second CD.** For the second CD, the interest rate is not the same each year. So, you need to use a different compounding factor for each year:

$$\$1{,}000 \times (1 + 0.08) \times (1 + 0.01) \times (1 + 0.01) = \$1{,}101.71.$$

Step 4 **Decide which CD you should choose.** You should choose the investment with the highest future value, so you should choose the first CD.

EXTRA CREDIT: When asked to guess the answer to this problem without first doing the calculations, many students choose the second CD. They reason that the high 8% interest rate received in the first year means that even though the interest rates in the second and third years are low, the second CD will end up with the higher future value. As the following table shows, although the first CD starts out well behind after the first year, it finishes the third year with the higher value. This example illustrates the sometimes surprising results of compounding.

	First CD	Second CD
After 1 year	$1,040.00	$1,080.00
After 2 years	1,081.60	1,090.80
After 3 years	1,124.86	1,101.71

See related problem 1.6 at the end of the chapter.

An Example of Discounting We have just used the interest rate to link the financial future with the financial present by starting with a dollar amount in the present and seeing what the amount will grow to in the future as a result of compounding. We can reverse the process and use the interest rate to calculate the **present value**, or the value today, of funds to be received in the future. A key point is: *Funds in the future are worth less than funds in the present, so we have to reduce, or discount, funds in the future to find their present value.* The **time value of money** refers to the way that the value of a payment changes depending on when the payment is received. Why are funds in the future worth less than funds in the present? For the same three reasons that lenders charge interest on loans, as we noted earlier in this chapter:

Present value The value in today's dollars of funds to be paid or received in the future.

Time value of money The way that the value of a payment changes depending on when the payment is received.

1. Dollars in the future will usually buy less than dollars can today because the price level usually increases over time.
2. Dollars that are promised to be paid in the future may not actually be received because a borrower may default by failing to make promised payments.
3. There is an opportunity cost in waiting to receive a payment because you cannot get the benefits of the goods and services you could have bought if you had the money today.

Discounting The process of determining the present value of funds that will be paid or received in the future.

To carry out **discounting**, we reverse the compounding process we just discussed. In our example, you are willing to part with your $1,000 for one year (by buying a one-year CD), provided that you receive $1,050 after one year. In other words, $1,000 in present value is the equivalent of $1,050 in future value to be received in one year. We could reverse the story and ask: How much would you be willing to pay the bank today if it promised to pay you $1,050 in one year? The answer, of course, is $1,000. Looked at this way, for you, $1,050 to be received from the bank in one year has a present value of $1,000. From this perspective, compounding and discounting are equivalent processes. We can summarize this result (where PV = present value):

Compounding: $\$1{,}000 \times (1 + 0.05) = \$1{,}050$; or $PV \times (1 + i) = FV_1$.

Discounting: $\$1{,}000 = \dfrac{\$1{,}050}{(1 + 0.05)}$; or $PV = \dfrac{FV_1}{(1 + i)}$.

Note that while $(1 + i)$ is the compounding factor, which we use to calculate the future value of money we invest today, $1/(1 + i)$ is the discount factor, which we use to calculate the present value of money to be received in the future.

We can generalize this result for any number of periods:

Compounding: $PV \times (1 + i)^n = FV_n$.

Discounting: $PV = \dfrac{FV_n}{(1 + i)^n}$.

Some Important Points About Discounting We will use the idea of discounting future payments many times in this book, so it is important to understand the following four important points:

1. *Present value is sometimes called "present discounted value."* This terminology emphasizes that in converting dollars received in the future into their equivalent value in dollars today, we are discounting, or reducing, the value of the future dollars.
2. *The further in the future a payment is to be received, the smaller its present value.* We can see that this point is true by examining the discounting formula:

$$PV = \frac{FV_n}{(1 + i)^n}.$$

The larger the value of n, the larger the value of the denominator in the fraction and the smaller the present value.
3. *The higher the interest rate we use to discount future payments, the smaller the present value of the payments.* Once again, we can see that this point is true by examining the discounting formula:

$$PV = \frac{FV_n}{(1 + i)^n}.$$

Because the interest rate appears in the denominator of the fraction, the larger the interest rate, the smaller the present value. From an economic perspective, if you require a higher interest rate in order to be willing to lend your money, you are saying that a larger number of dollars in the future is worth as much to you as a dollar today. That is the equivalent of saying that each dollar in the future is worth less to you today than if the interest rate were lower.

TABLE 3.1 Time, the Interest Rate, and the Present Value of a Payment

	Present value of a $1,000 payment to be received in ...			
Interest rate	1 year	5 years	15 years	30 years
1%	$990.10	$951.47	$861.35	$741.92
2%	980.39	905.73	743.01	552.07
5%	952.38	783.53	481.02	231.38
10%	909.09	620.92	239.39	57.31
20%	833.33	401.88	64.91	4.21

We can illustrate the second and third points by using Table 3.1. The rows in the table show that for any given interest rate, the further in the future a payment is received, the smaller its present value. For example, at an interest rate of 5%, a $1,000 payment you receive in one year has a present value of $952.38, but the present value drops to only $231.38 if you receive the payment in 30 years. The columns show that for any given number of years in the future you will receive a payment, the higher the interest rate is, the smaller the payment's present value will be. For example, a $1,000 payment you receive in 15 years has a present value of $861.35 when discounted at an interest rate of 1% (column 4, first row), but the payment is worth only $64.91 when discounted at an interest rate of 20% (column 4, last row). Note that a $1,000 payment you will receive in 30 years has a present value of only $4.21 when discounted at an interest rate of 20% (column 5, last row).

4. *The present value of a series of future payments is simply the sum of the discounted value of each individual payment.* For example, what would someone's promise to pay you $1,000 in one year and another $1,000 in five years be worth to you? If we assume an interest rate of 10%, Table 3.1 shows that the present value of the payment you will receive in one year is $909.09, and the present value of the payment you will receive in five years is $620.92. So, the present value of the promise to make both these payments is equal to $909.09 + $620.92 = $1,530.01.

A Word of Caution About Notation This book will *always* enter interest rates in numerical calculations as decimals. For instance, 5% will be 0.05, *not* 5. Failing to follow this rule will, obviously, result in your calculations being inaccurate: It makes a big difference whether you multiply (or divide) by 0.05 or by 5! This caution is so important that we gave it its own little section.

SOLVED PROBLEM 3.1B   **IN YOUR INTEREST**

How Do You Value a College Education?

According to the Census Bureau's Current Population Survey, at age 22, the typical college graduate makes about $7,200 more per year than does the typical high school graduate who has not attended college. The earnings gap between high school graduates and college graduates grows until about age 42.

Consider the following data on the gap between earnings by college graduates and high school graduates (for the sake of simplicity, suppose that the additional income received by a college graduate is all received at the end of the year):

Age 22: $7,200
Age 23: $7,200
Age 24: $7,300
Age 25: $7,300

a. Considering just ages 22 to 25, what is the present value of the higher earnings from a college education? Assume an interest rate of 5%.

b. Suppose you are 18 years old and considering whether to enter the labor force by taking a job immediately after graduating from high school or to attend college and enter the labor force at age 22. Briefly explain how you might calculate the present value to you of a college education. (Hint: Are there costs and other factors beyond just the earnings gap between all high school graduates and all college graduates you should take into account?)

Source: Christopher Avery and Sarah Turner, "Student Loans: Do College Students Borrow Too Much, or Not Enough?" *Journal of Economic Perspectives*, Vol.26, No. 1, Winter 2012, pp. 165–192.

Solving the Problem

Step 1 **Review the chapter material.** This problem is about discounting future payments, so you may want to review the section "Some Important Points About Discounting," which begins on page 59.

Step 2 **Answer part (a) by using the data given to calculate the present value of a college education for these years.** Point 4 in the section "Some Important Points About Discounting" is: *The present value of a series of future payments is simply the sum of the discounted value of each individual payment.* You can consider the annual earnings gap between college graduates and high school graduates as being, in effect, a payment that a college graduate receives. Therefore, the calculation of the present value of a college education for these years is (remembering to enter the interest rate as a decimal):

$$PV = \frac{\$7,200}{1 + 0.05} + \frac{\$7,200}{(1 + 0.05)^2} + \frac{\$7,300}{(1 + 0.05)^3} + \frac{\$7,300}{(1 + 0.05)^4} = \$25,699.50.$$

Step 3 **Answer part (b) by considering how you might calculate the present value to you of a college education.** The first step would be to extend the present value calculation you did in part (a) through the normal retirement age of 67. (This is the age at which you would be eligible to receive full Social Security payments from the federal government.) But to better tailor the calculation to your circumstance, you would need to take into account the following points:

1. You incur explicit costs by attending college, including the costs of tuition and books. You should take these costs into account to calculate the net present value—that is, the present value after taking into account costs—of a college education. Because these costs will be incurred over the next few years, their present value will be significant.

2. By attending college, assuming that you can't also work full time, you will lose the wages you would have earned had you immediately entered the labor force after high school. These lost wages are an opportunity cost to you.

This cost will also have a high present value because it is incurred close to the present.

3. Finally, rather than use in your present value calculation the gap between the average income of college graduates and the average income of high school graduates, you should use the gap between the average income of the occupation you intend to enter and the income of the job you would accept if you entered the labor force immediately after graduating from high school.

See related problems 1.7 and 1.8 at the end of the chapter.

Discounting and the Prices of Financial Assets

Most financial assets, such as loans, stocks, and bonds, are basically promises by the borrower to make certain payments to the lender in the future. Discounting lets us compare financial assets by giving us a means of determining the present value of payments to be received at different times in the future. In particular, discounting gives us a way of determining the prices of financial assets. To see this point, think about why an investor would want to buy a financial asset, such as a stock or a bond. Presumably, investors buy financial assets to receive payments from the sellers of the assets. What are those payments worth to the buyer? The payments are worth their present value. By adding up the present values of all the payments, we have the dollar amount that a buyer will pay for the asset. In other words, we have determined the asset's price.

3.2 Debt Instruments and Their Prices

LEARNING OBJECTIVE: Distinguish among different debt instruments and understand how their prices are determined.

Our conclusion at the end of the last section is a key fact about the financial system: *The price of a financial asset is equal to the present value of the payments to be received from owning it.* In this section, we apply this key fact to an important class of financial assets called *debt instruments*. **Debt instruments** (also called **credit market instruments** or **fixed-income assets**) include loans granted by banks and bonds issued by corporations and governments. Stocks are not debt instruments but **equities** that represent part ownership of the firms that issue them. Debt instruments can vary in their terms, but they are all IOUs, or promises by the borrower both to pay interest and repay principal to the lender. Debt instruments take different forms because lenders and borrowers have different needs.

Debt instruments (also known as credit market instruments or fixed-income assets) Methods of financing debt, including simple loans, discount bonds, coupon bonds, and fixed payment loans.

Equity A claim to part ownership of a firm; stock issued by a corporation.

Loans, Bonds, and the Timing of Payments

There are four basic categories of debt instruments:

1. Simple loans
2. Discount bonds
3. Coupon bonds
4. Fixed-payment loans

We can use these four categories to identify the variations in the timing of payments that borrowers make to lenders. We know that these variations will affect the present values and, therefore, the prices of the debt instruments. In addition to describing each type of debt instrument, we represent the payments on a loan or bond on a *timeline* to make it easier to measure the inflows and outflows of funds.

Simple Loan With a **simple loan**, the borrower receives from the lender an amount of funds called the *principal* and agrees to repay the lender the principal plus interest on a specific date when the loan matures. The most common simple loan is a short-term business loan—called a *commercial and industrial loan*—from a bank. For example, suppose that the Bank of America makes a one-year simple loan of $10,000 at an interest rate of 10% to Nate's Nurseries. We can illustrate this transaction on a *timeline* to show the payment of interest and principal by the borrower to the lender.

After one year, Nate's would repay the principal plus interest: $10,000 + ($10,000 × 0.10) or $11,000. On a timeline, the lender views the transaction as follows:

Simple loan A debt instrument in which the borrower receives from the lender an amount called the principal and agrees to repay the lender the principal plus interest on a specific date when the loan matures.

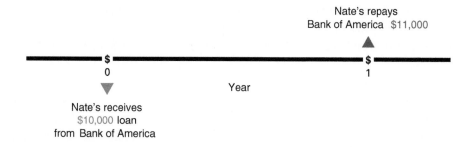

Discount Bond As with a simple loan, a borrower also repays a **discount bond** in a single payment. In this case, however, the borrower pays the lender an amount called the *face value* (or par value) at maturity but receives less than the face value initially. The interest paid on the loan is the difference between the amount repaid and the amount borrowed. Suppose that Nate's Nurseries issues a one-year discount bond and receives $9,091, repaying the $10,000 face value to the buyer of the bond after one year. So, the timeline for Nate's Nurseries discount bond is:

Discount bond A debt instrument in which the borrower repays the amount of the loan in a single payment at maturity but receives less than the face value of the bond initially.

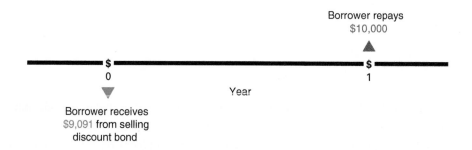

The lender receives interest of $10,000 − $9,091 = $909 for the year. Therefore, the interest rate is $909/$9,091 = 0.10, or 10%. The most common types of discount bonds are U.S. savings bonds, U.S. Treasury bills, and zero-coupon bonds.

Coupon Bonds Although they share the word "bond," *coupon bonds* are quite different from discount bonds. Borrowers issuing **coupon bonds** make interest payments in the

Coupon bond A debt instrument that requires multiple payments of interest on a regular basis, such as semiannually or annually, and a payment of the face value at maturity.

form of coupons at regular intervals, typically either once or twice per year, and repay the face value at maturity. The U.S. Treasury, state and local governments, and large corporations all issue coupon bonds. Because of the importance of coupon bonds in the financial system, you should be familiar with the following terminology related to them:

- *Face value*, or *par value*. The amount to be repaid by the bond issuer (the borrower) at maturity. The face value of the typical coupon bond is $1,000.
- *Coupon*. The annual fixed dollar amount of interest paid by the issuer of the bond to the buyer.
- *Coupon rate*. The value of the coupon expressed as a percentage of the par value of the bond. For example, if a bond has an annual coupon of $50 and a face value of $1,000, its coupon rate is $50/$1,000 = 0.05, or 5%.
- *Current yield*. As we will see in Section 3.4, after a coupon bond has been issued, it will often be resold many times in financial markets. As a result of this buying and selling, the bond's price may on a particular day be higher or lower than its $1,000 face value. The current yield is the value of the coupon expressed as a percentage of the current price of the bond. For example, if a bond has a coupon of $50, a par value of $1,000, and a current price of $900, its current yield is $50/$900 = 0.056, or 5.6%.
- *Maturity*. The length of time before the bond expires and the issuer makes the face value payment to the buyer. Many government and corporate bonds have maturities of 30 years, which means the issuer will make coupon payments each year for 30 years before making one last payment of the face value at the end of the thirtieth year. For example, if IBM issued a bond with a face value of $1,000 that has a maturity of 30 years and a coupon rate of 10%, it would pay $100 per year for 30 years and a final payment of $1,000 at the end of 30 years. The timeline on the IBM coupon bond is:

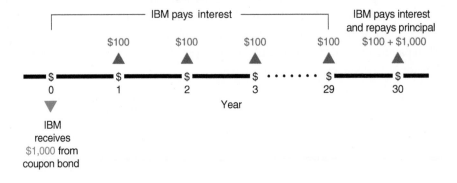

Fixed-payment loan A debt instrument that requires the borrower to make regular periodic payments of principal and interest to the lender.

Fixed-Payment Loan   With a **fixed-payment loan**, the borrower makes periodic payments (monthly, quarterly, or annually) to the lender. The payments include *both* interest and principal. Therefore, at maturity, the borrower has completely repaid the loan, and there is no lump-sum payment of principal. Loans with payments that include both interest and principal are called *amortized loans*. Common fixed-payment loans are home mortgages, student loans, and car loans. For example, if you are repaying a $10,000 10-year student loan with a 9% interest rate, your monthly payment is approximately $127. The timeline of payments is:

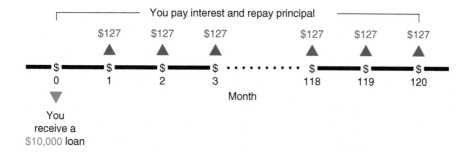

Fixed-payment loans are popular with households because as long as the household makes all the payments, the loan is completely paid off, and there is no large final payment to worry about, as with a simple loan. Fixed-payment loans also have the benefit to lenders that borrowers repay some principal with each loan payment, which reduces the chances of a borrower defaulting on the entire amount of the principal.

Although most debt instruments fall into these four categories, the changing needs of savers and borrowers have spurred the creation of new instruments having characteristics of more than one category.

MAKING THE CONNECTION | **IN YOUR INTEREST**

Interest Rates and Student Loans

With rising tuition costs, more students are taking out student loans, and the loans are for larger amounts. In 2016, the total amount of student loans in the United States was about $1.2 trillion—more than the total value of credit card debt. Student loan payments are often the largest item in the budgets of recent college graduates. Even future presidents are not immune. According to former First Lady Michelle Obama: "In fact, when [Barack and I] were first married … our combined monthly student loan bills were actually higher than our mortgage." After graduation, many students struggle to make the payments on their student loans. In 2016, about 43% of people with federal student loans were in default on them.

There are three main types of student loans:

1. Subsidized student loans
2. Unsubsidized student loans
3. Private loans

In 2016, federal student loans had a fixed interest rate of 4.29%. Under the standard repayment plan, federal student loans are paid back over 10 years. In late 2015, all borrowers under the federal student loan program became eligible for the Revised Pay As You Earn (or REPAYE) plan, under which payments are capped at 10% of the borrower's income and the loan balance is forgiven if it's not repaid after 20 years (or 25 years, if the loan was taken out for graduate study). Private student loans, obtained from banks, have a variety of interest rates and repayment times.

We can use the concepts of compounding and discounting to analyze some of the loan options students face:

1. *What are the consequences of not making interest payments while you are in college?* With an unsubsidized student loan, although you are responsible for paying the interest on your loan while you are in college, you usually have the option of postponing paying the interest until you graduate. However, the unpaid interest accumulates and is added to the principal of your loan. To take a simplified example, if you have a $20,000 student loan at a 4.29% interest rate, you would have been charged a total of $3,722 in interest during your four years in college. If you make no interest payments until you graduate, at that time your loan principal would be $23,722, which means the monthly payment during your 10-year payback period would rise from $205 to $243, and you would end up paying $1,152 more in total interest payments. Students' financial circumstances vary tremendously, of course, so postponing making interest payments may be appealing to one student but not to another.

2. *What are the consequences of extending your payback period from 10 years to 25 years?* Although the standard payback period for a federal student loan is 10 years for students not using the REPAYE plan, many students are able to extend the period to as long as 25 years. Suppose, once again, that you have a $20,000 student loan with a 4.29% interest rate. With a 10-year payback period, your monthly payment is $205. With a 25-year payback period, the payment drops to $109—a more manageable payment for many students who have other bills to cover with their first paychecks. But remember that fixed-payment loans are *amortized*, which means that each payment you make is a mixture of interest and principal. By extending the payback period for 15 years, you are paying down the $20,000 principal more slowly, so you are paying more in total interest over the life of your loan. With a 10-year payback period, your total interest payments are $4,642, while with a 25-year payback period, your total interest payments are nearly $12,639, or almost three times as high.

Being familiar with the interest rate concepts we are discussing in this chapter can help students and their parents as they decide how to finance a college education. Helpful loan calculators are available on the studentaid.ed.gov and bankrate.com sites.

Sources: Josh Mitchell, "More Than 40% of Student Borrowers Aren't Making Payments," *Wall Street Journal*, April 7, 2016; Jillian Berman, "America's Growing Student-Loan-Debt Crisis," marketwatch.com, January 19, 2016; and Charlie Spiering, "At Princeton, Michelle Obama Complains About Her Student Loans," *Washington Examiner*, September 24, 2012; and studentaid.ed.gov.

See related problems 2.6 and 2.7 at the end of the chapter.

 3.3 **Bond Prices and Yield to Maturity**

LEARNING OBJECTIVE: Explain the relationship between the yield to maturity on a bond and its price.

We have seen that the price of a bond—or any other financial security—should equal the present value of the payments the owner receives from the bond. We can apply this concept to determine the price of a coupon bond.

Bond Prices

Consider a five-year coupon bond with a coupon rate of 6% and a face value of $1,000. The coupon rate of 6% tells us that the seller of the bond will pay the buyer of the bond $60 per year for five years, as well as make a final payment of $1,000 at the end of the fifth year. (Note that, in practice, coupons are typically paid twice per year, so a 6% bond will pay $30 after six months and another $30 at the end of the year. For simplicity, we will assume throughout this book that any payments made on a security are received at the end of a year.) Therefore, the expression for the price, P, of the bond is the sum of the present values of the six payments (five coupon payments and the final payment of principal) the investor will receive:

$$P = \frac{\$60}{(1 + i)} + \frac{\$60}{(1 + i)^2} + \frac{\$60}{(1 + i)^3} + \frac{\$60}{(1 + i)^4} + \frac{\$60}{(1 + i)^5} + \frac{\$1,000}{(1 + i)^5}.$$

We can use this reasoning to arrive at the following general expression for a bond that makes coupon payments, C, has a face value, FV, and matures in n years:

$$P = \frac{C}{(1 + i)} + \frac{C}{(1 + i)^2} + \frac{C}{(1 + i)^3} + \; \dots \; + \frac{C}{(1 + i)^n} + \frac{FV}{(1 + i)^n}.$$

The dots (ellipsis) indicate that we have omitted the terms representing the years between the third year and the nth year—the final year in which the bond matures, which could be the tenth, twentieth, thirtieth, or other, year.

Yield to Maturity

To use the expression for a coupon bond to find the price of the bond, we need to know the future payments to be received and the interest rate. Suppose, though, we are in a situation where we know the price of a bond and the future payments, but we don't know the interest rate. For instance, what if you face a decision to choose between two potential investments:

1. A three-year, $1,000 face value coupon bond with a price of $1,050 and a coupon rate of 8%
2. A two-year, $1,000 face value coupon bond with a price of $980 and a coupon rate of 6%

One important factor in making a choice between these two investments is determining the interest rate you will receive on each. Because we know the prices and the payments for the two bonds, we can use the present value calculation to find the interest rate on each investment:

$$\text{Bond 1}: \$1,050 = \frac{\$80}{(1 + i)} + \frac{\$80}{(1 + i)^2} + \frac{\$80}{(1 + i)^3} + \frac{\$1,000}{(1 + i)^3}.$$

Using a financial calculator, an online calculator, or a spreadsheet program, we can solve this equation for i.[1] The solution for Bond 1 is $i = 0.061$, or 6.1%.

---

[1] See MyEconLab for instructions on using a spreadsheet or calculator to compute the interest rate in these types of equations.

$$\text{Bond 2}: \$980 = \frac{\$60}{(1 + i)} + \frac{\$60}{(1 + i)^2} + \frac{\$1,000}{(1 + i)^2}.$$

The solution for Bond 2 is $i = 0.071$, or 7.1%.

These calculations show us that even though Bond 1 may appear to be a better investment because it has a higher coupon rate than Bond 2, Bond 1's higher price means that it has a significantly lower interest rate than Bond 2. So, if you wanted to earn the highest interest rate on your investment, you would choose Bond 2.

Yield to maturity The interest rate that makes the present value of the payments from an asset equal to the asset's price today.

The interest rate we have just calculated is called the **yield to maturity**, which equates the present value of the payments from an asset with the asset's price today. The yield to maturity is based on the concept of present value and is the interest rate measure that economists, firms, and investors use most often. In fact, it is important to note that unless they indicate otherwise, *whenever economists or investors refer to the interest rate on a financial asset, the interest rate they mean is the yield to maturity.* Calculating yields to maturity for alternative investments allows investors to compare different types of debt instruments.

Keep in mind the close relationship between discounting and compounding. We just calculated the yield to maturity by using a discounting formula. We can also think of the yield to maturity in terms of compounding by asking: "If I pay a price, P, today for a bond with a particular set of future payments, what is the interest rate at which I could invest P and get the same set of future payments?" For example, instead of calculating the present value of the payments to be received on a 30-year Treasury bond, we can calculate the interest rate at which the money paid for the bond could be invested for 30 years to get the same present value.

Yields to Maturity on Other Debt Instruments

We saw in Section 3.2 that there are four categories of debt instruments. We have calculated the yield to maturity on a coupon bond. Now we can calculate the yield to maturity on each of the other three types of debt instruments.

Simple Loans Calculating the yield to maturity on a simple loan is straightforward. We need to find the interest rate that makes the lender indifferent between having the amount of the loan today or the final payment at maturity. Consider again the $10,000 loan to Nate's Nurseries. The loan requires payment of the $10,000 principal plus $1,000 in interest one year from now. We calculate the yield to maturity as follows:

$$\text{Value today} = \text{Present value of future payments}$$

$$\$10,000 = \frac{\$10,000 + \$1,000}{(1 + i)},$$

from which we can solve for i:

$$i = \frac{\$11,000 - \$10,000}{\$10,000} = 0.10, \text{ or } 10\%.$$

Note that the yield to maturity, 10%, is the same as the simple interest rate. From this example, we can conclude that, for a simple loan, the yield to maturity and the interest rate specified on the loan are the same.

Discount Bonds Calculating the yield to maturity on a discount bond is similar to calculating the yield to maturity on a simple loan. For example, suppose that Nate's Nurseries issues a $10,000 one-year discount bond. We can use the same equation to find the yield to maturity on the discount bond that we did in the case of a simple loan. If Nate's Nurseries receives $9,200 today from selling the bond, we can calculate the yield to maturity by setting the present value of the future payment equal to the value today, or $9,200 = $10,000/(1 + i)$. Solving for i gives us:

$$i = \frac{\$10,000 - \$9,200}{\$9,200} = 0.087, \text{ or } 8.7\%.$$

From this example, we can write a general equation for a *one-year* discount bond that sells for price, P, with face value, FV. The yield to maturity is:

$$i = \frac{FV - P}{P}.$$

Fixed-Payment Loans Calculating the yield to maturity on a fixed-payment loan is similar to calculating the yield to maturity on a coupon bond. Recall that fixed-payment loans require periodic payments that combine interest and principal, but there is no face value payment at maturity. Suppose that Nate's Nurseries borrows $100,000 to buy a new warehouse by taking out a mortgage loan from a bank. Nate's has to make annual payments of $12,731. After making the payments for 20 years, Nate's will have paid off the $100,000 principal of the loan. Because the loan's value today is $100,000, the yield to maturity can be calculated as the interest rate that solves the equation:

$$\text{Value today} = \text{Present value of payments}$$

$$\$100,000 = \frac{\$12,731}{(1 + i)} + \frac{\$12,731}{(1 + i)^2} + \ldots + \frac{\$12,731}{(1 + i)^{20}}.$$

Using a financial calculator, an online calculator, or a spreadsheet program, we can solve this equation to find that $i = 0.112$, or 11.2%. In general, for a fixed-payment loan with fixed payments, FP, and a maturity of n years, the equation is:

$$\text{Loan value} = \frac{FP}{(1 + i)} + \frac{FP}{(1 + i)^2} + \ldots + \frac{FP}{(1 + i)^n}.$$

To summarize, if i is the yield to maturity on a fixed-payment loan, the amount of the loan today equals the present value of the loan payments discounted at rate i.

Perpetuities Perpetuities are a special case of coupon bonds. A perpetuity pays a fixed coupon, but unlike a regular coupon bond, a perpetuity does not mature. The main example of a perpetuity is the *consol*, which the British government at one time issued, although it has not issued new perpetuities in decades. Existing consols with a coupon rate of 2.5% are still traded in financial markets. You may think that computing the yield to maturity on a perpetuity is difficult because the coupons are paid forever. However, the relationship between the price, coupon, and yield to maturity is simple. If your algebra skills are sharp, see if you can derive this equation from the equation for a coupon bond that pays an infinite number of coupons:[2]

$$P = \frac{C}{i}.$$

So, a perpetuity with a coupon of $25 and a price of $500 has a yield to maturity of $i = \$25/\$500 = 0.05$, or 5%.

SOLVED PROBLEM 3.3

Finding the Yield to Maturity for Different Types of Debt Instruments

For each of the following situations, write the equation that you would use to calculate the yield to maturity. You do *not* have to solve the equations for i. Instead, just write the appropriate equations.[3]

a. A simple business loan for $500,000 that requires a payment of $700,000 in four years.

b. A government discount bond with a price of $9,000, which has a face value of $10,000 and matures in one year.

c. A corporate bond with a face value of $1,000, a price of $975, a coupon rate of 10%, and a maturity of five years.

d. A student loan of $2,500, which requires payments of $315 per year for 25 years. The payments start in two years.

Solving the Problem

Step 1   **Review the chapter material.** This problem is about calculating yields to maturity for different debt instruments, so you may want to review the section "Bond Prices and Yield to Maturity," which begins on page 66.

Step 2   **Write an equation for the yield to maturity on the debt instrument in (a).** For a simple loan, the yield to maturity is the interest rate that results in the present value of the loan payment being equal to the amount of the loan. So, the correct equation is:

$$\$500{,}000 = \frac{\$700{,}000}{(1 + i)^4}.$$

---

[2] Here is the derivation: The price of a consol equals the present value of the infinite series of coupon payments the buyer will receive: $P = \frac{C}{1 + i} + \frac{C}{(1 + i)^2} + \frac{C}{(1 + i)^3} + \frac{C}{(1 + i)^4} + \ldots$ The rules of algebra tell us that an infinite series of the form $1 + x + x^2 + x^3 + x^4 + \ldots$ is equal to $\frac{1}{1 - x}$, provided that x is less than 1. In this case, $\frac{1}{1 + i}$ is less than 1, so we have the following expression for the price of a consol: $P = C \times \left[\dfrac{1}{1 - \left(\dfrac{1}{1 + i}\right)} - 1 \right]$. This expression simplifies to $P = \frac{C}{i}$ as given in the text.

[3] We provide instructions for solving these equations for i using a financial calculator and using a spreadsheet in MyEconLab.

Step 3   **Write an equation for the yield to maturity on the debt instrument in (b).**
For a discount bond, the yield to maturity is the interest rate that results in the present value of the bond's face value being equal to the bond's price. So, the correct equation is:

$$\$9{,}000 = \frac{\$10{,}000}{(1 + i)}, \text{or}, \; i = \frac{\$10{,}000 - \$9{,}000}{\$9{,}000}.$$

Step 4   **Write an equation for the yield to maturity on the debt instrument in (c).**
For a coupon bond, such as a long-term corporate bond, the yield to maturity is the interest rate that results in the present value of the payments the buyer receives being equal to the bond's price. Remember that a bond with a coupon rate of 10% pays an annual coupon of $100. So, the correct equation is:

$$\$975 = \frac{\$100}{(1 + i)} + \frac{\$100}{(1 + i)^2} + \frac{\$100}{(1 + i)^3} + \frac{\$100}{(1 + i)^4} + \frac{\$100}{(1 + i)^5} + \frac{\$1{,}000}{(1 + i)^5}.$$

Step 5   **Write an equation for the yield to maturity on the debt instrument in (d).**
For a fixed-payment loan, the yield to maturity is the interest rate that results in the present value of the loan payments being equal to the amount of the loan. Note that in this case, there is no payment due at the end of the first year, so the typical first term in the expression is omitted. Therefore, the correct equation is:

$$\$2{,}500 = \frac{\$315}{(1 + i)^2} + \frac{\$315}{(1 + i)^3} + \; \dots \; + \frac{\$315}{(1 + i)^{26}}.$$

See related problem 3.6 at the end of the chapter.

3.4 The Inverse Relationship Between Bond Prices and Bond Yields

LEARNING OBJECTIVE: Understand the inverse relationship between bond prices and bond yields.

Coupon bonds issued by governments and by large corporations typically have maturities of 30 years. During those 30 years, investors are likely to buy and sell a typical bond many times in the *secondary market*. Once a bond is sold the first time, the corporation or government issuing the bond is not directly involved in any of the later transactions. For instance, suppose that you pay $1,000 for a bond issued by the Ford Motor Company, and that the bond has a face value of $1,000 and a coupon rate of 5%. *Whenever the price of a bond is equal to its face value, the bond's yield to maturity will be equal to its coupon rate.* Presumably, you purchased the bond because you believed that 5% was a good interest rate to receive on your investment. If at some point you decide to sell your bond, the transaction is between you and the person buying your bond. Ford is not involved except for being informed that it should send future coupon payments to the new owner of the bond and not to you.

What Happens to Bond Prices When Interest Rates Change?

Suppose that one year after you purchased your bond, Ford issues more 30-year bonds, but these new bonds have coupon rates of 6% rather than 5%. Ford, like other corporations, varies the coupon rates on the bonds it sells based on conditions in the bond market. Ideally, corporations would like to borrow money at the lowest interest rate possible. But lenders—in this case, bond buyers—in some circumstances increase the interest rates they require to lend their funds. For instance, if bond buyers believe that future inflation will be higher than they had previously expected, they will require a higher interest rate before buying a bond. And if bond buyers believe that Ford is at a greater risk of defaulting on its bonds, they will also require a higher interest rate.

What effect will Ford's issuing new bonds with higher coupons have on your bond? First, note that once a firm issues a bond, its coupon rate does not change. So, even though Ford is paying buyers of its new bonds $60 per year, you are stuck receiving only $50 per year. If you decide to sell your bond, what price will you receive? Your bond clearly has a drawback to potential buyers: It pays a coupon of only $50, while newly issued Ford bonds pay coupons of $60. So, no investor would be willing to pay $1,000 for your 5% bond when he or she can pay $1,000 and receive a 6% bond from Ford. How much less than $1,000 will other investors be willing to pay you? We can answer this question by remembering the fundamental idea that the price of a financial security is equal to the present value of the payments to be received from owning the security. To calculate the price, we need to know what yield to maturity to use. When you purchased your bond, the yield to maturity was 5%. But conditions in the bond market have changed, and Ford has had to offer a 6% yield to maturity to attract buyers for its new bonds. If you want to sell your bond, it has to compete in the secondary market with the new 6% bonds, so 6% is the correct yield to maturity to use to calculate the new price of your bond.

In calculating the price of your bond (using a financial calculator, an online calculator, or a spreadsheet; see MyEconLab for instructions), keep in mind that the buyer of your bond will receive 29, rather than 30, coupon payments because one year has passed:

$$\$864.09 = \frac{\$50}{(1\ +\ 0.06)} + \frac{\$50}{(1\ +\ 0.06)^2} + \frac{\$50}{(1\ +\ 0.06)^3} + \ \cdots\ + \frac{\$50}{(1\ +\ 0.06)^{29}} + \frac{\$1,000}{(1\ +\ 0.06)^{29}}.$$

Capital gain An increase in the market price of an asset.

It may seem odd that your bond, which has a face value of $1,000 if held to maturity, would have a market price of only $864.09. Keep in mind, though, that you or a new owner of the bond will have to wait 29 years to receive the $1,000 face value. The present value of that $1,000 face value payment discounted at a 6% interest rate is only $184.56.

Capital loss A decrease in the market price of an asset.

If the market price of an asset increases, it is called a **capital gain**. If the market price of the asset declines, it is called a **capital loss**. In our example, you will have suffered a capital loss of $1,000 − $864.09 = $135.91.

MAKING THE CONNECTION

Banks Take a Bath on Mortgage-Backed Bonds

As we saw in Chapter 1, banks play a key role in the financial system. While large firms are able to sell stocks and bonds to investors, small and midsize firms rely on bank loans for the funds they need to operate and expand. Households also rely heavily on banks for the credit they need to make large purchases such as houses, cars, and furniture. Banks cut back on lending during the financial crisis, which deepened the recession of 2007–2009 by reducing the ability of firms and households to finance their spending.

Why did banks reduce lending during those years? The inverse relationship between interest rates and bond prices can help us answer this question. First, remember that the basis of commercial banking is to take in deposits from households and firms and invest the funds. Granting loans and buying bonds are the most important investments that banks make. During the housing boom of the early and mid-2000s, banks granted many residential mortgages to borrowers who had flawed credit histories and who in previous years would not have qualified for loans. Banks also granted many residential mortgages to borrowers who made small or no down payments. As we noted in Chapter 1, many of these mortgages were securitized, meaning they were pooled and turned into debt instruments known as *mortgage-backed securities*, and then sold to investors. Many mortgage-backed securities are similar to long-term bonds in that they pay regular interest based on the payments borrowers make on the underlying mortgages.

During the height of the housing boom, some banks invested heavily in mortgage-backed securities because their yields were higher than the yields on other investments with similar levels of default risk—or so the banks thought. When housing prices started to decline beginning in 2006, borrowers began to default on their mortgages. As borrowers stopped paying on their mortgages, owners of mortgage-backed securities received lower payments than they expected. In the secondary market for mortgage-backed securities, buyers—when they could be found at all—were willing to buy the securities only if the securities had much higher yields to compensate for the higher levels of default risk. Higher yields on these securities meant lower prices. By 2008, the prices of many mortgage-backed securities had declined by 50% or more.

By early 2009, U.S. commercial banks had suffered losses on their investments of about $1 *trillion*. Beginning in 2010, these losses were somewhat reduced as the housing market stabilized and the prices of some mortgage-backed securities rose. Nevertheless, these heavy losses forced some banks to close. Other banks were saved by injections of funds from the federal government under the Troubled Asset Relief Program (TARP). Surviving banks became much more cautious in making new loans. Banks had relearned the lesson that soaring interest rates can have a devastating effect on investors who hold existing debt instruments.

See related problem 4.10 at the end of the chapter.

If you own a long-term coupon bond, it is clearly not good news when interest rates rise. But what if interest rates fall? Suppose that one year after you bought a Ford bond with a coupon rate of 5%, the company begins to issue new bonds with coupon rates of 4%. Ford may be able to sell bonds with a lower coupon rate because investors expect that inflation in the future will be lower than they had previously expected or because they believe that Ford is less likely to default on the bonds. Your bond is now attractive to investors because it has a higher coupon rate than newly issued bonds. If you decide to sell your bond, it will be competing in the secondary market with the new 4% bonds, so 4% is the correct yield to maturity to use in calculating the new market price of your bond:

$$\$1,169.84 = \frac{\$50}{(1\ +\ 0.04)} + \frac{\$50}{(1\ +\ 0.04)^2} + \frac{\$50}{(1\ +\ 0.04)^3} + \ \cdots\ + \frac{\$50}{(1\ +\ 0.04)^{29}} + \frac{\$1,000}{(1\ +\ 0.04)^{29}}.$$

In this case, you will have a capital gain of $\$1,169.84\ -\ \$1,000 = \$169.84$.

Bond Prices and Yields to Maturity Move in Opposite Directions

The examples about Ford's bonds have demonstrated two very important points:

1. If interest rates on newly issued bonds rise, the prices of existing bonds will fall.
2. If interest rates on newly issued bonds fall, the prices of existing bonds will rise.

In other words, *yields to maturity and bond prices move in opposite directions*. This relationship must hold because in the bond price equation, the yield to maturity is in the denominator of each term. If the yield to maturity increases, the present values of the coupon payments and the face value payment must decline, causing the price of the bond to decline. The reverse is true when the yield to maturity decreases. The economic reasoning behind the inverse relationship between bond prices and yields to maturity is that if interest rates rise, existing bonds issued when interest rates were lower become less desirable to investors, and their prices fall. If interest rates fall, existing bonds become more desirable, and their prices rise.

Finally, notice that the inverse relationship between yields to maturity and bond prices should also hold for other debt instruments. The present value and, therefore, the price of any debt instrument should decline when market interest rates rise, and it should rise when market interest rates decline.

Secondary Markets, Arbitrage, and the Law of One Price

Let's consider the process by which bond prices and yields adjust to changes in market conditions. Buying and selling in the markets for financial assets such as bonds and stocks is similar to buying and selling in markets for goods and services, with two key differences. First, most trading of financial services is done electronically, with buyers and sellers linked together via computer systems, so very little trading occurs face-to-face. Second, most trading takes place very quickly, with millions of dollars of stocks and bonds being traded every second that the markets are open. Large volumes of bonds and stocks are traded over very brief periods because many participants in financial markets are *traders* rather than investors.

An investor in a financial market typically plans to earn a return by receiving payments on the securities he or she buys. For example, an investor in Apple buys the stock to receive dividend payments from Apple and to profit from an increase in the price of the stock over time. Traders, however, often buy and sell securities hoping to make profits by taking advantage of small differences in the prices of similar securities.

For example, recall what happens to prices of existing 5% coupon bonds when market interest rates fall to 4%: The price of an existing 5% bond increases from $1,000 to $1,169.84. Once this price increase occurs, the yields to maturity on those bonds and on newly issued 4% coupon bonds are the same—4%—so the bonds are equally desirable to investors. If market interest rates remain the same, no further price changes should occur. But, what about during the period *before* the prices of the 5% coupon bonds have risen all the way to $1,169.84? Clearly, a trader who buys the 5% bonds during that period can make a profit by, say, buying the bonds at $1,160 and reselling them when their prices have risen all the way to $1,169.84.

The process of buying and reselling securities to profit from price changes over a brief period of time is called **financial arbitrage**. The profits made from financial arbitrage are called *arbitrage profits*. In competing to buy securities where earning arbitrage profits is possible, traders force prices up to the level where they can no longer earn arbitrage profits. Prices of securities adjust very rapidly—sometimes in less than a second—to eliminate arbitrage profits because of the very large number of traders participating in financial markets and the speed of electronic trading. Economists conclude that *the prices of securities should adjust so that investors receive the same yields on comparable securities.* In our example, the prices of comparable coupon bonds adjust so that bonds with 5% coupon rates have the same yield as bonds with 4% coupon rates.

This description of how prices of financial securities adjust is an example of a general economic principle called the *law of one price*, which states that identical products should sell for the same price everywhere. The possibility of arbitrage profits explains the law of one price. For instance, if apples sell for $1.00 per pound in Minnesota and $1.50 per pound in Wisconsin, you could make an arbitrage profit by buying apples in Minnesota and reselling them in Wisconsin. As you and others took advantage of this opportunity, the price of apples in Minnesota would rise, and the price of apples in Wisconsin would fall. Leaving aside transportation costs, arbitrage should result in the price of apples being the same in the two states.

As you read this book, keep in mind that because of financial arbitrage, comparable securities should have the same yield, except during very brief periods of time.

Financial arbitrage The process of buying and selling securities to profit from price changes over a brief period of time.

MAKING THE CONNECTION   **IN YOUR INTEREST**

How to Follow the Bond Market: Reading the Bond Tables

Whether you want to invest in bonds or just want to follow developments in the bond market, where can you go to get information? You can find daily updates on the prices and yields for Treasury bills, notes, and bonds on the *Wall Street Journal* (wsj.com) web site or on Yahoo! Finance (finance.yahoo.com). The corporate bond listings given below are from the web site of the Financial Industry Regulatory Authority (FINRA). Data on corporate bonds can also be found on Yahoo! Finance.

Treasury Bonds and Notes

The table below contains data on five U.S. Treasury bonds and notes from among the many bonds and notes that were being traded on secondary markets on June 3, 2016. Treasury notes have maturities of 2 years to 10 years from their date of issue, while Treasury bonds typically have a maturity of 30 years from their date of issue.

The first two columns tell you the maturity date and the coupon rate. Bond A, for example, has a maturity date of May 15, 2019, and a coupon rate of 3.125%, so it pays $31.25 each year on its $1,000 face value.

	Maturity	Coupon	Bid	Asked	CHG	Asked YLD
Bond A—	May 15, 2019	3.125	106.3906	106.4063	0.2891	0.912
	February 15, 2020	8.500	127.0156	127.0313	0.4063	1.021
	May 15, 2020	3.500	109.1719	109.1875	0.4688	1.110
	February 15, 2025	7.625	148.8672	148.8828	1.1406	1.583
	August 15, 2029	6.125	149.7969	149.8954	1.5000	1.848

The next three columns refer to the bond's price. All prices are reported per $100 of face value. For Bond A, the first price listed, 106.3906, means a price of $1,063.906 for this $1,000 face value bond. The *bid* price is the price you will receive from a government securities dealer if you sell the bond. The *asked* price is the price you must pay the dealer if you buy the bond. The difference between the asked price and the bid price (known as the *bid–asked spread*) is the profit margin for dealers. Bid–asked spreads are low in the government securities markets, indicating low transactions costs and a liquid and competitive market. The "CHG" column tells you by how much the bid price increased or decreased from the preceding trading day. For Bond A, from the previous day, the bid price rose by $0.2891 per $100 of face value, or $2.891 for this $1,000 face value bond.

The final column contains the yield to maturity, calculated using the asked price by the method we discussed in Section 3.3 for coupon bonds. The *Wall Street Journal* reports the yield using the asked price because readers are interested in the yield from the perspective of an investor. So, you can construct three interest rates from the information contained in the table: the yield to maturity just described, the coupon rate, and the current yield (equal to the coupon divided by the price: ($31.25/$1,063.906) × 100, or 2.94% for Bond A). Note that the current yield of Bond A is well above the yield to maturity of 0.912%. This fact shows that the current yield is not a good substitute for the yield to maturity for bonds with a short time to maturity because the current yield does not include the effect of expected capital gains or losses.

Treasury Bills

The following table shows information about U.S. Treasury bill yields. Recall that Treasury bills are discount bonds, and unlike Treasury bonds and notes, they do not pay coupons. Accordingly, they are identified only by their maturity date (first column). In the Treasury bill market, following a very old tradition, yields are quoted as yields on a discount basis (or discount yields) rather than as yields to maturity.[4] The Bid and Asked columns of Treasury notes and bonds quote prices, while the Bid and Asked columns for Treasury bills quote yields. The bid yield is the discount yield for investors who want to sell the bill to dealers. The asked yield is the discount yield for investors who want to buy the bill from dealers. The dealers' profit margin is the difference between the asked yield and the bid yield. In comparing investments in Treasury bills with investments in other bonds, investors find it useful to know the yield to maturity. So, the last column shows the yield to maturity (based on the asked price). Because short-term interest rates were very low in 2016, the *asked yield* on the first bill listed is only 0.168%.

Maturity	Bid	Asked	CHG	Ask YLD
July 21, 2016	0.175	0.165	0.020	0.168
September 8, 2016	0.285	0.275	0.010	0.279
November 25, 2016	0.388	0.378	−0.063	0.383
February 2, 2017	0.460	0.450	−0.090	0.459

Note that in both the table for notes and bonds and the table for bills, the yield to maturity rises the further away the maturity date is.

New York Stock Exchange Corporation Bonds

The table below gives quotations for some of the corporate bonds that are most actively traded on the New York Stock Exchange. The first column tells you the name of the corporation issuing the bond—in the case of Bond B, the Goldman Sachs investment bank. The next column gives you the bond's symbol, GS.AEH. The third column gives you the coupon rate, 5.750%. The fourth column gives you the maturity, January 24, 2022. The next column gives you the bond's ratings from the three major bond rating agencies. The ratings provide investors with information on the likelihood that the firm will default on the bond, with AAA being the highest rating, given to bonds with very little chance of default. We will discuss bond ratings in more detail in Chapter 5. The next column presents the price of the bond the last time it was traded: $1,155.00. The last column gives the yield to maturity based on the last sale price: 2.757%.

	Issuer name	Symbol	Coupon	Maturity	Moody's/S&P/Fitch	Last sale price	Yield%
	Bank of America Corporation	BAC.ICB	7.625%	06/01/2019	Baa1/BBB+/A	116.188	2.007
Bond B	Goldman Sachs Group Inc.	GS.AEH	5.750%	01/24/2022	A3/BBB+/A	115.50	2.757
	Apple Inc.	AAPL4122390	3.450%	05/06/2024	Aa1/AA+/−−	106.789	2.499
	Walmart Stores Inc.	WMT.HV	5.250%	09/01/2035	Aa2/AA/AA	127.121	3.329

See related problem 4.11 at the end of the chapter.

---

[4] The yield on a discount basis for a bond with face value FV and a purchase price P is $[(FV - P)/FV] \times (360/\text{Number of days to maturity})$.

3.5 Interest Rates and Rates of Return

LEARNING OBJECTIVE: Explain the difference between interest rates and rates of return.

Return The total earnings from a security; for a bond during a holding period of one year, the coupon payment plus the change in the price of the bond.

When you make an investment, you are most concerned with what you earn during a given period of time, often called a *holding period*. If you buy a coupon bond and hold it for one year, the **return** on your investment in the bond for that year consists of (1) the coupon payment received and (2) the change in the price of the bond, which will result in a capital gain or loss. Usually, you are most interested in measuring your return as a percentage of your investment, which is your **rate of return, R**.

For example, consider again your purchase for $1,000 of a Ford bond with a face value of $1,000 and a coupon rate of 5%. If at the end of the year following your purchase, the price of the bond increases to $1,169.84, then during that year, you will have received a coupon payment of $50 and had a capital gain of $169.84. So, your rate of return for the year will have been:

Rate of return, R The return on a security as a percentage of the initial price; for a bond during a holding period of one year, the coupon payment plus the change in the price of a bond divided by the initial price.

$$R = \frac{\text{Coupon } + \text{ Capital gain}}{\text{Purchase price}} = \frac{\$50 + \$169.84}{\$1,000} = 0.220, \text{ or } 22.0\%.$$

If the price of your bond had declined to $864.09, then you would have received the $50 coupon payment but suffered a capital loss of $135.91. So, your rate of return for the year would have been negative:

$$R = \frac{\$50 - \$135.91}{\$1,000} = -0.086, \text{ or } -8.6\%.$$

A General Equation for the Rate of Return on a Bond

We can extend these examples to write a general equation for the rate of return on a coupon bond during a holding period of one year. First, recall that the *current yield* on a coupon bond is the coupon divided by the current price of the bond. The *rate of capital gain or loss* on a bond is the dollar amount of the capital gain or loss divided by the initial price. So, we have the following equation for the rate of return for a holding period of one year:

$$\text{Rate of return } = \text{ Current yield } + \text{ rate of capital gain.}$$
$$R = \frac{\text{Coupon}}{\text{Initial price}} + \frac{\text{Change in price}}{\text{Initial price}}.$$

Here are three important points about rates of return:

1. In calculating the rate of return, we use the price at the beginning of the year to calculate the current yield.
2. You incur a capital gain or loss on a bond even if you do not sell the bond at the end of the year. If you sell the bond, you have a *realized capital gain or loss*. If you do not sell the bond, your gain or loss is *unrealized*. In either case, the price of your bond has increased or decreased and needs to be included when calculating the rate of return on your investment.

3. If you buy a coupon bond, neither the current yield nor the yield to maturity may be a good indicator of the rate of return you will receive as a result of holding the bond during a particular time period because they do not take into account your potential capital gain or capital loss.

Interest-Rate Risk and Maturity

We have seen that holders of existing bonds suffer a capital loss when market interest rates rise. **Interest-rate risk** refers to the risk that the price of a financial asset will fluctuate in response to changes in market interest rates. But are all bonds equally subject to interest-rate risk? We might expect that bonds with fewer years to maturity will be less affected by a change in market interest rates than will bonds with more years to maturity. The economic reasoning is that the more years until a bond matures, the more years the buyer of the bond will potentially be receiving a below-market coupon rate, and, therefore, the lower the price a buyer would be willing to pay.

Table 3.2 shows that the arithmetic of bond prices bears out this reasoning. Assume that at the beginning of the year, you pay $1,000 for a $1,000 face value bond with a coupon rate of 5%. Assume that at the end of the year, the yield to maturity on similar bonds has risen to 7%. The table shows your rate of return, assuming that the bond you purchased has different maturities. For instance, the top row shows that if you purchased a one-year bond, your rate of return is equal to the current yield of 5%. You held the one-year bond for one year and received the $1,000 face value at maturity, so the change in market interest rates did not affect you. The second row (highlighted in red) shows that if your bond initially has a maturity of two years, you will take a capital loss, so your rate of return is less than the current yield. Your two-year bond now has only one year until maturity, so its price is:

$$\$981.31 = \frac{\$50}{(1 \ + \ 0.07)} + \frac{\$1,000}{(1 \ + \ 0.07)}.$$

The remaining rows show that the longer the maturity of your bond, the lower (more negative) your return. With a maturity of 50 years, your rate of return for the first year of owning your bond will be –22.5%.

Interest-rate risk The risk that the price of a financial asset will increase or decrease in response to changes in market interest rates.

TABLE 3.2   The Effect of Maturity on Interest-Rate Risk During the First Year of Owning a Bond When the Interest Rate Rises from 5% to 7%

Years to maturity	Current yield	Initial price	Price at the end of the year	Rate of capital gain or loss	Rate of return during the year
1	5%	$1,000	$1,000.00	0%	5.0%
2	5	1,000	981.31	−1.87	3.1
10	5	1,000	869.70	−13.0	−8.0
20	5	1,000	793.29	−20.7	−25.7
30	5	1,000	754.45	−24.6	−19.6
50	5	1,000	724.66	−27.5	−22.5

How Much Interest-Rate Risk Do Investors in Treasury Bonds Face?

We saw at the beginning of the chapter that in 2016, 30-year U.S. Treasury bonds had an interest rate of about 2.5%. Many people consider Treasury bonds to be a very safe investment. But are they? Although these bonds have no *default risk*, as long-term bonds, they have significant *interest-rate risk*. For example, suppose that at the beginning of 2017, you purchased for $1,000 a 30-year Treasury bond with a face value of $1,000 and a coupon rate of 2.5%. If at the end of the year, the yield to maturity on Treasury bonds had risen to a more normal rate of 5%, the price of your bond would decline to $621.47. You would suffer a capital loss of −37.9% and a rate of return of −35.4%. If the yield to maturity rose to 6%, your rate of return would be −45.1%. Some safe investment!

3.6 | Nominal Interest Rates Versus Real Interest Rates

LEARNING OBJECTIVE: Explain the difference between nominal interest rates and real interest rates.

Nominal interest rate An interest rate that is not adjusted for changes in purchasing power caused by changes in the price level.

To this point in the chapter, we have discussed only **nominal interest rates**—that is, interest rates that are not adjusted for changes in purchasing power caused by changes in the price level. In fact, inflation can reduce the purchasing power of returns on any investment. For example, suppose that you buy a $1,000 bond that pays you $50 in interest each year for 20 years. If the purchasing power of the dollars you receive declines over time, you are, in effect, losing part of your interest income to inflation. In addition, inflation causes the purchasing power of the principal to decline. For example, if inflation is 5% per year, the purchasing power of the $1,000 principal falls by $50 each year.

Real interest rate An interest rate that is adjusted for changes in purchasing power caused by changes in the price level.

Lenders and borrowers know that inflation reduces the purchasing power of interest income, so they base their investment decisions on interest rates adjusted for changes in purchasing power. Such adjusted interest rates are called **real interest rates**, and they represent the true return to lending and the true cost of borrowing. Because lenders and borrowers don't know what the *actual* real interest rate will be during the period of a loan, they must make saving or investing decisions on the basis of what they *expect* the real interest rate to be. So, to estimate the expected real interest rate, savers and borrowers must decide what they expect the inflation rate to be. The expected real interest rate, r, equals the nominal interest rate, i, minus the expected rate of inflation, π^e, or:[5]

$$r = i - \pi^e.$$

Note that this equation also means that the nominal interest rate equals the expected real interest rate plus the expected inflation rate: $i = r + \pi^e$.

For example, suppose you take out a car loan from your local bank. You are willing to pay, and the bank is willing to accept, a real interest rate of 3%. Both you and the bank

---

[5] To fully account for the effect of changes in purchasing power on the nominal interest rate, we should use the equation $\frac{1 + i}{1 + \pi^e} = 1 + r$. Rearranging terms gives us $1 + i = 1 + r + \pi^e + r\pi^e$. Or, $r = i - \pi^e - r\pi^e$. This equation is the same as the one in the text except for the term $r\pi^e$. The value of this term is usually quite small. For example, if the real interest rate is 2% and the expected inflation rate is 3%, then $r\pi^e = 0.02 \times 0.03 = 0.0006$. So, as long as the inflation rate is relatively low, the equation given in the text results in a value for the real interest rate that is close to the value that results from the exact equation.

expect that the inflation rate will be 2%. Therefore, you and the bank agree on a nominal interest rate of 5% on the loan. What happens if the inflation rate turns out to be 4%, which is higher than you and the bank had expected? In that case, the *real interest rate* that you end up paying (and the bank ends up receiving) equals 5% − 4% = 1%, which is less than the expected real interest rate of 3%. Because the inflation rate turns out to be higher than you and the bank expected, you gain by paying a lower real interest rate, and the bank loses by receiving a lower real interest rate.

We can generalize by noting that:

1. If the inflation rate is *greater* than the expected inflation rate, the real interest rate will be less than the expected real interest rate; in this case, borrowers will gain and lenders will lose.
2. If the inflation rate is *less* than the expected inflation rate, the real interest rate will be greater than the expected real interest rate; in this case, borrowers will lose and lenders will gain. Table 3.3 summarizes the important relationship among nominal interest rates, expected real interest rates, and real interest rates.

For the economy as a whole, economists often measure the nominal interest rate as the interest rate on U.S. Treasury bills that mature in three months. In Figure 3.1, we show the nominal interest rate, the real interest rate, and the expected real interest rate for the period from the first quarter of 1982 through the second quarter of 2016. To calculate the *expected* real interest rate, we used data from a survey of professional forecasters carried out by the Federal Reserve Bank of Philadelphia.

Figure 3.1 shows that the nominal and real interest rates tend to rise and fall together. Note that in some periods, particularly since the beginning of the financial crisis in 2007, the real interest rate has been negative. Why would investors buy Treasury bills if they expected to receive a negative real interest rate on their investments? The best explanation is that during and after the crisis, investors did not believe that the low interest rates on most other investments were sufficient compensation for the investments' higher default risk. So, investors were willing to receive a negative real interest rate on U.S. Treasury bills rather than risk losing money by investing in corporate bonds or other riskier securities. Finally, note that it is possible for the nominal interest rate to be lower than the real interest rate. For this outcome to occur, the inflation rate has to be negative, meaning that the price level is decreasing rather than

TABLE 3.3 The Relationship Among the Nominal Interest Rate, the Expected Real Interest Rate, and the Real Interest Rate

If the inflation rate is …	the real interest rate will be …	and borrowers will …	and lenders will …
greater than the expected inflation rate …	less than the expected real interest rate …	gain	lose.
less than the expected inflation rate …	greater than the expected real interest rate …	lose	gain.

MyEconLab Real-time data

FIGURE 3.1

Nominal and Real Interest Rates, 1982–2016

In this figure, the nominal interest rate is the interest rate on three-month U.S. Treasury bills. The real interest rate is the nominal interest rate minus the inflation rate, as measured by changes in the consumer price index. The expected real interest rate is the nominal interest rate minus the expected rate of inflation as measured by a survey of professional forecasters. When the U.S. economy experienced deflation during 2009 and 2015, the real interest rate was greater than the nominal interest rate.

Sources: Federal Reserve Bank of St. Louis, and Federal Reserve Bank of Philadelphia.

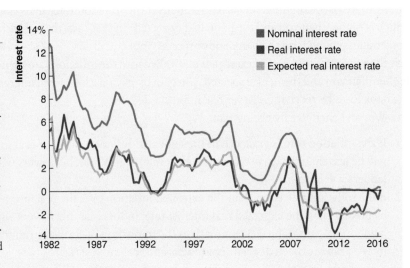

Deflation A sustained decline in the price level.

increasing. A sustained decline in the price level is called **deflation**. The United States experienced a period of deflation during the first 10 months of 2009 and again at the beginning of 2015.

In January 1997, the U.S. Treasury started issuing *indexed bonds* to address investors' concerns about the effects of inflation on real interest rates. With these bonds, called TIPS (Treasury Inflation-Protection Securities), the Treasury increases the principal as the price level, as measured by the consumer price index, increases. The stated interest rate on TIPS remains fixed once issued, but because it is applied to a principal amount that increases with inflation, the effective interest rate increases with inflation. For example, suppose that when issued, a 10-year TIPS has a principal of $1,000 and an interest rate of 3%. If the inflation rate during the year is 2%, then the principal increases to $1,020. The 3% interest rate is applied to this larger principal amount, so an investor would actually receive 0.03 × 1,020 = $30.60 in interest. Therefore, the actual interest rate the investor would have received on his or her original investment would be $30.60/$1,000 = 3.06%.[6] If the price level falls with deflation, the principal of a TIPS will decrease.

Figure 3.2 shows the value of TIPS as a percentage of the value of all U.S. Treasury securities. The share of TIPS in all Treasury securities increased steadily until 2008. During the following two years, as investors' expectations of inflation declined, TIPS became a smaller percentage of the value of all Treasury securities before increasing again as investors looked ahead to the possibility of rising inflation in the future.

---

[6] Note that this calculation is somewhat simplified because the Treasury actually adjusts the TIPS principal for inflation each month and pays interest on TIPS every six months.

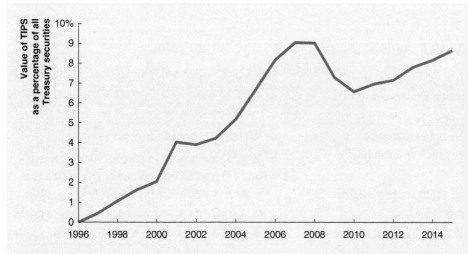

FIGURE 3.2

TIPS as a Percentage of All Treasury Securities

TIPS (Treasury Inflation-Protection Securities) were an increasing percentage of all U.S. Treasury securities until 2008. Demand for them fell during the following two years before rising again as investors looked to protect themselves against the possibility of future inflation.

Source: U.S. Treasury, *Treasury Bulletin*, various issues.

ANSWERING THE KEY QUESTION

Continued from page 53

At the beginning of this chapter, we asked:

"Why do interest rates and the prices of financial securities move in opposite directions?"

We have seen in this chapter that the price of a financial security equals the present value of the payments an investor will receive from owning the security. When interest rates rise, present values fall, and when interest rates fall, present values rise. Therefore, interest rates and the prices of financial securities should move in opposite directions.

Key Terms and Problems

Key Terms

Capital gain, p. 72
Capital loss, p. 72
Compounding, p. 56
Coupon bond, p. 63
Credit market instruments, p. 62
Debt instruments, p. 62
Deflation, p. 82
Discount bond, p. 63

Discounting, p. 58
Equity, p. 62
Financial arbitrage, p. 75
Fixed-income assets, p. 62
Fixed-payment loan, p. 64
Future value, p. 56
Interest-rate risk, p. 79
Nominal interest rate, p. 80

Present value, p. 58
Rate of return, R, p. 78
Real interest rate, p. 80
Return, p. 78
Simple loan, p. 63
Time value of money, p. 58
Yield to maturity, p. 68

3.1 The Interest Rate, Present Value, and Future Value
Use the interest rate to calculate present values and future values.

Review Questions

1.1 What are the main reasons that lenders charge interest on loans?

1.2 If you deposit $1,000 in a bank CD that pays interest of 2% per year, how much will you have after two years?

1.3 What is the present value of $1,200 to be received in one year if the interest rate is 5%?

1.4 How is the price of a financial asset related to the payments an investor receives from owning it?

Problems and Applications

1.5 Norman Jones, an economic historian at the University of Utah, has described the views of the ancient Greek philosopher Aristotle on interest:

> Aristotle defined money as a good that was consumed by use. Unlike houses and fields, which are not destroyed by use, money must be spent to be used. Therefore, as we cannot rent food, so we cannot rent money. Moreover, money does not reproduce. A house or a flock can produce new value by use, so it is not unreasonable to ask for a return on their use. Money, being barren, should not, therefore, be expected to produce excess value. Thus, interest is unnatural.

What did Aristotle mean in arguing that money is "barren"? Why would money being barren mean that lenders should not charge interest on loans? Do you agree with Aristotle's reasoning? Briefly explain.

Source: Norman Jones, "Usury," EH.Net Encyclopedia, edited by Robert Whaples, February 5, 2010, http://eh.net/encyclopedia/article/jones.usury.

1.6 [Related to Solved Problem 3.1A on page 57] Suppose that you are considering investing $1,000 in bank CDs.

a. First, you consider one of the following CDs:

• CD 1, which will pay an interest rate of 5% per year for three years

• CD 2, which will pay an interest rate of 8% the first year, 5% the second year, and 3% the third year

Which CD should you choose?

b. Would your answer to part (a) change if the second CD pays an interest rate of 1% the first two years and 10% in the third year? Briefly explain.

c. Now, suppose that in addition to the two CDs described in part (a), there is a third CD that pays an interest rate of 3% the first two years and an interest rate of 7% the third year. How does the future value of this investment compare to the other two? Which is the best investment?

1.7 [Related to Solved Problem 3.1B on page 60] Some companies offer their employees defined benefit pension plans. Under these plans, employees are promised a fixed monthly payment after they retire. The federal government regulates some aspects of these plans. A reporter for the *Wall Street Journal* wrote that under a former employer's pension plan, she was to receive $423 per month beginning in 14 years, when she turned 65 years old. She received a letter from her former employer offering a one-time payment of $32,088 in exchange for her agreeing *not* to receive the monthly pension payments.

a. Suppose that the reporter's former employer expects that the reporter will live to be 85 years old. That means she would receive the pension payments for 20 years. The total amount she would receive would be $423 per month × 12 months per year × 20 years = $101,520. Because the one-time payment her former employer offered her is less than one-third of this amount, is it obvious she should turn down the one-time payment? Briefly explain.

b. The reporter also noted: "Regulations that took effect in 2012 … allow companies to use corporate bond interest rates, rather than the lower ones of Treasury bonds, to calculate the discounted present value of an employee's future pension." If employers were still using the Treasury bond interest rate in offering employees one-time payments for giving up their right to a monthly pension, would her former employer's offer have been more or less than $32,088? Briefly explain.

Source: Anne Tergesen, "Should You Take a Lump-Sum Pension Offer?" *Wall Street Journal*, June 5, 2015.

1.8 **[Related to** Solved Problem 3.1B **on page 60]**
In 2015, the Washington Nationals baseball team signed pitcher Max Scherzer to a contract to play for the team for 7 years. He would be paid $15 million dollars per year for 14 years—an additional 7 years beyond the end of the time he would be committed to play for the Nationals. The contract was widely reported as being worth $210 million (or $15 million per year × 14 years). One baseball writer argued, though, that "this deal serves as a nice reminder that the payment terms of a deal can have an impact on the actual value of the contract."

a. What does the writer mean by the "actual value of the contract"? Isn't $210 million the actual value of the contract? Briefly explain.

b. The writer notes: "For a lot of reasons, money today is worth more than money in the future, and the further in the future you go, the less money is worth." What are the reasons that money today is worth more than money in the future? Briefly explain how we calculate the value today of money we will receive in the future.

c. Assume for simplicity that Scherzer receives his salary of $15 million per year for 2018, 2019, and 2020 at the end of each calendar year. At the beginning of 2018, what is the present value of the salaries he will receive for these three years? Use an interest rate of 7% in your calculation.

Source: Dave Cameron, "Max Scherzer and When $210 Million Isn't $210 Million," fangraphs.com, January 19, 2015.

3.2   **Debt Instruments and Their Prices**
Distinguish among different debt instruments and understand how their prices are determined.

Review Questions

2.1 What is the difference between a debt instrument and an equity?

2.2 What are the four basic categories of debt instruments? Which categories of debt instruments pay interest before the instrument matures? Which category of debt instrument pays back some of the principal before the instrument matures?

Problems and Applications

2.3 Explain in which category of debt instrument the following belong:

a. Car loan

b. U.S. Treasury bond

c. Three-month U.S. Treasury bill

d. Mortgage loan

2.4 Why do consumers usually prefer fixed-payment loans to simple loans when buying cars and houses?

2.5 Suppose that Ford issues a coupon bond at a price of $1,000. Draw a timeline for the bond, assuming that it has the following characteristics:

• Coupon rate of 5%
• Par value of $1,000
• Maturity of 20 years

2.6 **[Related to the** Making the Connection **on page 65]**
A student looking at the timeline for a student loan on page 65 of the text makes the following observation:

The text states that the interest rate on the loan is 9%, but this calculation is obviously wrong. Each monthly payment is $127, so the student will be paying back $127 × 12 = $1,524 per year. Therefore, because the principal of the loan is $10,000, the interest rate must be $1,524/$10,000 = 0.1524, or 15.24%.

Briefly explain whether you agree with the student's reasoning.

2.7 [Related to the Making the Connection on page 65] A certified financial planner notes that with an unsubsidized student loan, the borrower has the choice of whether to make interest payments on the loan while still in college. She advises that making the interest payments rather than postponing them until after graduation is "always to your financial benefit … because otherwise [the interest payments] will capitalize."

a. What does the financial planner mean when noting that the interest payments will "capitalize"?

b. Why does she believe that making the payments would be to your financial benefit? Are there good reasons some students decide to postpone making the interest payments until after they graduate? Briefly explain.

Source: Robert Powell, "How to Handle Your Student Loans While You're Still in School," marketwatch.com, January 29, 2016.

3.3 Bond Prices and Yield to Maturity
Explain the relationship between the yield to maturity on a bond and its price.

Review Questions

3.1 Why is yield to maturity a better measure of the interest rate on a bond than is the coupon rate?

3.2 In each of the following parts, write an expression that shows the relationship among the listed terms:

a. The price of a coupon bond, the coupon payments, the face value, and the yield to maturity

b. The amount borrowed on a simple loan, the required loan payment, and the yield to maturity

c. The price of a discount bond, the bond's face value, and the yield to maturity

d. The amount borrowed on a fixed-payment loan, the payments on the loan, and the yield to maturity

Problems and Applications

3.3 Assume that the interest rate is 10%. Briefly explain whether you would prefer to receive (a) $75 one year from now, (b) $85 two years from now, or (c) $90 three years from now. Would your answer change if the interest rate is 20%?

3.4 Suppose that you are considering subscribing to *Economist Analyst Today* magazine. The magazine is advertising a one-year subscription for $60 or a two-year subscription for $115. You plan to keep getting the magazine for at least two years. The advertisement notes that a two-year subscription saves you $5 compared to buying two successive one-year subscriptions. If the interest rate is 10%, should you subscribe for one year or for two years? (Assume that one year from now, a one-year subscription will still cost $60.)

3.5 Consider the case of a two-year discount bond—that is, a bond that pays no coupon and pays its face value after two years rather than one year. Suppose the face value of the bond is $1,000, and the price is $870. What is the bond's yield to maturity? (In this case, provide a numerical answer rather than just writing the appropriate equation.)

3.6 [Related to Solved Problem 3.3 on page 70] For each of the following situations, write the equation needed to calculate the yield to maturity. You do not have to solve the equations for i; just write the appropriate equations.

a. A simple loan for $350,000 that requires a payment of $475,000 in five years.

b. A discount bond with a price of $720 that has a face value of $1,000 and matures in five years.

c. A corporate bond with a face value of $1,000, a price of $950, a coupon rate of 8%, and a maturity of six years.

d. A student loan of $4,000 that requires payments of $275 per year for 20 years. The payments start in three years.

3.7 Consider a $1,000 face value bond that sells for an initial price of $450. It will pay no coupons for the first 10 years and will then pay a 6.25% coupon each year for the remaining 20 years. Write an equation that shows the relationship between the price of the bond, the coupon (in dollars), and the yield to maturity. You don't have to show every term in the expression, but be sure to show enough terms to demonstrate that you understand the relationship.

3.8 A few years ago, the British government was considering retiring, or buying back from investors, some outstanding consols that had annual coupons of £40.

a. What is a consol?

b. If the yield to maturity on other long-term British government bonds was 2.5%, what price was the British government likely to have offered investors? Briefly explain your answer.

Source: Tommy Stubbington and Ben Edwards, "U.K. to Repay First World War Bonds," *Wall Street Journal*, October 31, 2014.

3.9 Many retired people buy annuities. With an annuity, a saver pays an insurance company, such as Berkshire Hathaway Insurance Company or Northwestern Mutual Insurance Company, a lump-sum amount in return for the company's promise to pay a certain amount per year until the buyer dies. With an ordinary annuity, when the buyer dies, there is no final payment to his or her heirs. Suppose that at age 65, David Alexander pays $100,000 for an annuity that promises to pay him $10,000 per year for the remaining years of his life.

a. If David dies 20 years after buying the annuity, write an equation that would allow you to calculate the interest rate that David received on his annuity.

b. If David dies 40 years after buying the annuity, will the interest rate be higher or lower than if he dies after 20 years? Briefly explain.

3.4 | The Inverse Relationship Between Bond Prices and Bond Yields
Understand the inverse relationship between bond prices and bond yields.

Review Questions

4.1 What does it mean to describe a bond as being bought and sold in a "secondary market"?

4.2 If you own a bond and market interest rates increase, will you experience a capital gain or a capital loss? Briefly explain.

4.3 Briefly explain why yields to maturity and bond prices move in opposite directions.

4.4 What is the difference between an investor and a trader? What is financial arbitrage?

Problems and Applications

4.5 [Related to the Chapter Opener on page 53]
A student asks:

> If a coupon bond has a face value of $1,000, I don't understand why anyone who owns the bond would sell it for less than $1,000. After all, if the owner holds the bond to maturity, the owner knows he or she will receive $1,000, so why sell for less?

Answer the student's question.

4.6 Briefly explain whether you agree with the following statement:

> If interest rates rise, bonds become more attractive to investors, so bond prices will rise. Therefore, when interest rates rise, bond prices will also rise.

4.7 According to a *New York Times* article: "With yields on many municipal bonds extremely low … even a small increase in their price, which would cause the yield to go down, would cause a loss of principal."

a. What does the article mean by "loss of principal"?

b. Do you agree with the article's analysis? Briefly explain.

Source: Paul Sullivan, "Taxes Influence Investment Strategy, and Not Always for the Better," *New York Times*, May 3, 2013.

4.8 Consider the following information from September 15, 2016, for a coupon bond with a face value of $1,000 and a maturity date of September 15, 2018:

Coupon rate: 5.0%
Price: $955.11
Yield to maturity: 7.5%

a. What was the bond's current yield?

b. Why is the bond's yield to maturity greater than its coupon rate?

4.9 Ford Motor Company has issued bonds with a maturity date of November 1, 2046, that have a coupon rate of 7.40%, and it has issued coupon bonds with a maturity of February 15, 2047, that have a coupon rate of 9.80%. Why would Ford issue bonds with coupons of $74 and then a little more than a year later issue bonds with coupons of $98? Why didn't the company continue to issue bonds with the lower coupon?

4.10 [Related to the Making the Connection on page 73] A column in the *New York Times* noted that during the housing boom that ended in 2006: "Global banks had loaded up on these supposedly safe securities, and were at risk of becoming insolvent when their true value became known. Some banks blew up; others were bailed out."

a. Which securities is the columnist referring to?

b. What caused the value of these securities to decline?

c. Why did this result cause problems for banks?

Source: Neil Irwin, "What 'The Big Short' Gets Right, and Wrong, About the Housing Bubble," *New York Times*, December 22, 2015.

4.11 [Related to the Making the Connection on page 75] Consider the following information on two U.S. Treasury bonds:

	Maturity	Coupon	Bid	Asked	Chg	Asked Yield
Bond A	July 31, 2020	1.625	101.8984	101.9141	0.5000	1.151
Bond B	July 31, 2020	2.000	103.4141	103.4297	0.5000	1.151

Briefly explain how two securities that have the same yield to maturity can have different asked prices.

4.12 Consider the following analysis:

> The rise and fall of a bond's price has a direct inverse relationship to its yield to maturity, or interest rate. As prices go up, the yield declines and vice versa. For example, a $1,000 bond might carry a stated annual yield, known as the coupon of 8%, meaning that it pays $80 a year to the bondholder. If that bond was bought for $870, the actual yield to maturity would be 9.2% ($80 annual interest on $870 of principal).

Do you agree with this analysis? Briefly explain.

3.5	**Interest Rates and Rates of Return**

Explain the difference between interest rates and rates of return.

Review Questions

5.1 What is the difference between the yield to maturity on a coupon bond and the rate of return on the bond?

5.2 Why does a bond with a longer maturity have greater interest-rate risk than a bond with a shorter maturity?

Problems and Applications

5.3 Suppose that for a price of $950, you purchase a 10-year Treasury bond that has a face value of $1,000 and a coupon rate of 4%. If you sell the bond one year later for $1,150, what was your rate of return for that one-year holding period?

5.4 According to an article in the *Wall Street Journal*, "Companies and governments [in Europe] are increasingly borrowing at … terms of up to 100 years." The article notes: "That is good news for borrowers, but adds risks for investors." Why would any investor buy a bond with such a long maturity, given that the investor is unlikely to still be alive when the bond matures? Why might such bonds be considered particularly risky to investors?

Source: Christopher Whittall, "The Very Long Bet: 100-Year Bonds That Pay Peanuts," *Wall Street Journal*, May 11, 2016.

5.5 Suppose that on January 1, 2018, you purchased a coupon bond with the following characteristics:

- Face value: $1,000
- Coupon rate: 8 3/8
- Current yield: 7.5%
- Maturity date: 2020

If the bond is selling for $850 on January 1, 2019, then what was your rate of return on this bond during the holding period of calendar year 2018?

5.6 Suppose that you just bought a four-year $1,000 coupon bond with a coupon rate of 6% when the market interest rate is 6%. One year later, the market interest rate falls to 4%. What rate of return did you earn on the bond during the year?

5.7 Suppose that you are considering investing in a four-year bond that has a face value of $1,000 and a coupon rate of 6%.

a. What is the price of the bond if the market interest rate on similar bonds is 6%? What is the bond's current yield?

b. Suppose that you purchase the bond, and the next day the market interest rate on similar bonds falls to 5%. What will the price of your bond be now? What will its current yield be?

c. Now suppose that one year has gone by since you bought the bond, and you have received the first coupon payment. How much would another investor now be willing to pay for the bond? What was your total return on the bond? If another investor had bought the bond a year ago for the amount that you calculated in (b), what would that investor's total return have been?

d. Now suppose that two years have gone by since you bought the bond and that you have received the first two coupon payments. At this point, the market interest rate on similar bonds unexpectedly rises to 10%. How much would another investor be willing to pay for your bond? What will the bond's current yield be over the next year? Suppose that another investor had bought the bond at the price you calculated in (c). What would that investor's total return have been over the past year?

3.6 Nominal Interest Rates Versus Real Interest Rates
Explain the difference between nominal interest rates and real interest rates.

Review Questions

6.1 What is the difference between the nominal interest rate on a loan and the real interest rate?

6.2 What is the difference between the real interest rate and the expected real interest rate?

6.3 What are TIPS? Why would an investor buy TIPS rather than conventional Treasury bonds?

Problems and Applications

6.4 Suppose you are about to borrow $15,000 for four years to buy a new car. Briefly explain which of these situations you would prefer to be in:

    i. The interest rate on your loan is 10%, and you expect the annual inflation over the next four years to average 8%.

    ii. The interest rate on your loan is 6%, and you expect the annual inflation rate over the next four years to average 2%.

6.5 When will the real interest rate differ from the expected real interest rate? Would this possible difference be of more concern to you if you were considering making a loan to be paid back in 1 year or a loan to be paid back in 10 years? Briefly explain.

6.6 For several decades in the late nineteenth century, the price level in the United States declined. Was this likely to have helped or hurt U.S. farmers who borrowed money to buy land? Does your answer depend on whether the decline in the price level was expected or unexpected? Briefly explain.

6.7 Suppose that on January 1, 2018, the price of a one-year Treasury bill is $970.87. Investors expect that the inflation rate will be 2% during 2018, but at the end of the year, the inflation rate turns out to have been 1%. What are the nominal interest rate on the bill (measured as the yield to maturity), the expected real interest rate, and the real interest rate?

6.8 An article in the *Wall Street* Journal in 2016 noted: "Government-bond yields are heading higher around the world, a move typically linked to rising expectations of economic growth and inflation." Briefly explain why the yields on bonds will rise if investors expect inflation to be higher.

Source: Min Zeng and Christopher Whittall, "As Bond Yields Rise, Some Investors Fear Another False Dawn," *Wall Street Journal*, April 24, 2016.

Data Exercises

D3.1: [Compare interest rates on bonds of different maturities] Go to the web site of the Federal Reserve Bank of St. Louis (FRED) (fred.stlouisfed.org) and download and graph the data series for the 3-month Treasury bill (TB3MS), the 10-year Treasury note (GS10), and the 30-year Treasury bond (GS30) for the period from January 1990 to the most recent month. (Notice that there is a period when the Treasury stopped selling 30-year bonds, so no data are available for these months.) During which periods is the gap between the 10-year note and the 30-year bond the greatest? During which periods is the gap between the 10-year note and the 3-month bill the greatest?

D3.2: [Calculate the real interest rate using a 1-year Treasury bill and the consumer price index] Go to the web site of the Federal Reserve Bank of St. Louis (FRED) (fred.stlouisfed.org) and download the data for the 1-year Treasury bill (TB1YR) for the period from 1980 to the most recent month. Find the consumer price index for all urban consumers (CPIAUCSL) and then click on the link "Edit graph." In the pull-down menu for units, choose "Percentage change from year ago." Download the data. Subtract your measure of inflation from the values for the 1-year Treasury bill and graph both the resulting real interest rate and the values for the nominal Treasury bill interest rate. During which periods is the gap between the nominal interest rate and the real interest rate the greatest?

D3.3: [Compare interest rates on TIPS and regular Treasury bonds] Go to the web site of the Federal Reserve Bank of St. Louis (FRED) (fred.stlouisfed.org) and download and graph both the interest rate on the 10-year Treasury note (GS10) and the interest rate on the 10-year Treasury TIPS (FII10) for the period from January 2003 to the most recent month. What explains the difference between the two interest rates? When has the difference been the greatest?

D3.4: [Analyze real and nominal interest rates] Go to the web site of the Federal Reserve Bank of St. Louis (FRED) (fred.stlouisfed.org) and download the most recent values for the following five variables: (1) the 30-Year Conventional Mortgage Rate (MORTG); (2) BofA Merrill Lynch US Corporate AAA Effective Yield© (BAMLC0A1CAAAEY); (3) the 3-Month Treasury Bill: Secondary Market Rate (TB3MS); (4) the 10-Year Treasury Constant Maturity Rate (GS10); and

(5) the University of Michigan's measure of expected inflation over the next 12 months (MICH).

a. Using these data, take the most recent expected inflation rate and compute the expected real interest rate for each of the nominal interest rates: the 30-Year Conventional Mortgage Rate, BofA Merrill Lynch US Corporate AAA Effective Yield, the 3-Month Treasury Bill: Secondary Market Rate, and the 10-Year Treasury Constant Maturity Rate.

b. Suppose the actual inflation rate is greater than the expected inflation rate. Will borrowers or lenders be made worse off? Briefly explain.

D3.5: [Analyze bond prices and interest rates] Go to the web site of the Federal Reserve Bank of St. Louis (FRED) (fred.stlouisfed.org) and download the most recent values and values from the same month one year and two years earlier for the 1-Year Treasury Bill: Secondary Market Rate (TB1YR).

a. Suppose the 1-Year Treasury Bill has a face value of $1,000. Using the interest rates found above, calculate the price of a 1-Year Treasury Bill for each of the three months.

b. From the calculations you made in part (a), what can you conclude about the relationship between bond yields and bond prices?

Determining Interest Rates

Learning Objectives

After studying this chapter, you should be able to:

4.1 Discuss the most important factors in building an investment portfolio (pages 93–101)

4.2 Use a demand and supply model to determine market interest rates for bonds (pages 101–110)

4.3 Use the bond market model to explain changes in interest rates (pages 110–118)

4.4 Explain how interest rates are determined using the money market model (pages 118–122)

4.A Use the loanable funds model to determine interest rates in the international capital market (pages 128–136)

Why Are Interest Rates So Low?

Are you thinking about saving to buy a new car or a house a few years from now? Traditionally, many people saved for purchases like this by putting their money in certificates of deposit (CDs) at banks. As we will discuss in later chapters, even if your bank goes out of business, *federal deposit insurance* protects you against losses of up to $250,000 per deposit, per bank. So instead of risking funds on the stock or bond markets, many people choose the safer alternative of a CD.

Prior to the financial crisis that began in 2007, banks frequently offered CDs that paid annual interest rates of 5%. If you put $10,000 into a bank CD that has a 5% interest rate, at the end of five years, your savings will have grown to $12,763. By the end of seven years, your savings will have grown to $14,071.

During the financial crisis, however, interest rates, including those banks offered to depositors, declined sharply. By 2009, they had fallen below 1%, where they remained for more than seven years. In late 2016, Wells Fargo, one of the largest banks in the United States, was offering an interest rate of only 0.10% on a one-year CD. At that very low interest rate, if you deposit $10,000, in five years, your savings will have grown to only $10,050. After seven years, your savings will have grown to only $10,070. Your "reward" for letting the bank have use of your money for seven years will be only $70. If inflation during the seven years ends up being 2% per year, then the purchasing power of your savings will have declined by more 13%. In other words,

Continued on next page

Continued on next page

KEY ISSUE AND QUESTION

Issue: Following the financial crisis of 2007-2009, interest rates remained at historically low levels for an extended period.

Question: What factors are most important in determining interest rates?

Answered on page 122

seven years of saving will result in your being able to buy less than when you started.

In response to low bank deposit rates, some savers purchased Treasury bonds or corporate bonds. But the interest rates on these bonds were also low. For example, between 1980 and 2009, the average interest rate on a 10-year U.S. Treasury note was 7.2%. In late 2016, it was only 1.8%. Similarly, between 1980 and 2009, the average interest rate on long-term bonds issued by large, financially sound corporations was 8.4%. In late 2016, it was only 2.5%. As we saw in

Chapter 3, an increase in market interest rates causes prices of existing bonds to fall. So, if the interest rates on Treasury bonds or corporate bonds rose toward their historical averages, bond investors would suffer significant capital losses. Not surprisingly, many financial advisers warned investors that buying bonds could be risky.

In this chapter, we examine why interest rates have been at such historically low levels for such a long time and look more closely at how the bond market determines interest rates.

Sources: Paul H. Kupiec, "The High Cost of Ultralow Interest Rates," *Wall Street Journal*, May 22, 2016; wellsfargo.com; Federal Reserve Bank of St. Louis; and "Market Data Center," wjs.com.

In this chapter, we discuss how savers decide to allocate their wealth among alternative assets, such as stocks and bonds. We also further analyze the bond market and show that, as in other markets, the equilibrium price of bonds and the equilibrium interest rate are determined by the factors underlying demand and supply.

4.1 How to Build an Investment Portfolio

LEARNING OBJECTIVE: Discuss the most important factors in building an investment portfolio.

As you advance in your career and your income rises, you will begin to consider which financial assets you should invest in. You have many assets to choose from, ranging from basic checking and savings accounts in banks to stocks and bonds to complex financial securities. What principles should you follow as you build an investment *portfolio*? (Recall that a portfolio is a collection of assets owned by an investor.)

We begin by examining the objectives of the typical investor. You might expect that investors will attempt to earn the highest possible rate of return on their investments. But suppose you have the opportunity to invest $1,000 in an asset, such as a stock or bond, on which you expect a rate of return of 10%, but you also believe there is a significant chance of a return of -5%. Would you invest in that asset, or would you prefer to invest in an asset on which you expect a return of 5% but believe there is no chance of a negative return? Would it matter if you currently have only $1,000 in investments or if you currently have $1 million in investments? Would your answer be different if you were 60 years old rather than 20 years old?

The Determinants of Portfolio Choice

There are many ways to build an investment portfolio, depending on how an investor answers the questions we just asked. Even investors with the same income, wealth, and age will often have very different portfolios. Investors use the following *determinants of portfolio choice* (or *determinants of asset demand*) to evaluate different investment options:

1. The investor's *wealth,* or total amount of savings to be allocated among investments
2. The *expected rate of return* from an investment compared with the expected rates of return on other investments
3. The degree of *risk* in an investment compared with the degree of risk in other investments
4. The *liquidity* of an investment compared with the liquidity of other investments
5. The *cost of acquiring information* about an investment compared with the cost of acquiring information about other investments

We'll now consider each of these determinants.

Wealth Recall that income and wealth are different. *Income* is a person's earnings during a particular period, such as a year. Assets are anything of value, such as stocks and bonds, that a person owns. Liabilities are a person's loans or other debts. *Wealth* is the total value of assets a person *owns* minus the total value of any liabilities that a person *owes.* As a person's wealth increases, we would expect the size of the person's financial portfolio to increase but we would not expect the person to proportionally increase each individual asset in the portfolio. For instance, when you graduate from college, you may not have much wealth, and your only financial asset may be $500 in a checking account. Once you have a job and your wealth begins to increase, the amount in your checking account may not increase very much, but you may buy a bank certificate of deposit and some shares in a money market mutual fund. As your wealth continues to increase, you may purchase mutual funds that hold stocks and bonds. In general, when we view financial markets as a whole, we can assume that an increase in wealth will increase the quantity demanded for most financial assets.

Expected Rate of Return Given your wealth, how do you decide which assets to add to your portfolio? You probably want to invest in assets with high rates of return. As we saw in Chapter 3, though, the rate of return for a particular holding period includes the rate of capital gain, which an investor can calculate only at the end of the period. Suppose that you are considering investing in an IBM 8% coupon bond that has a current price of $950. You know that you will receive a coupon payment of $80 during the year, but you do not know what the price of the IBM bond will be at the end of the year, so you cannot calculate your rate of return ahead of time. You can, though, make informed estimates of the price of the bond one year from now, so you can calculate an *expected rate of return* (which we simplify to **expected return**).

Expected return The rate of return expected on an asset during a future period.

To keep the example simple, suppose you believe that at the end of the year, there are only two possible outcomes:

IBM bond	Bond price at the end of the year	Capital gain or loss	Rate of return for the year
Possibility 1	$1,016.50	7% gain	8% + 7% = 15%
Possibility 2	$ 921.50	−3% loss	8% − 3% = 5%

The *probability* of an event occurring is the chance that the event will occur, expressed as a percentage. In this case, let's assume that you believe that the probability of either of the prices occurring is 50%. In general, we calculate the expected return on an investment by using this formula:

$$\text{Expected return} = [(\text{Probability of event 1 occurring}) \times (\text{Value of event 1})] \\ + [(\text{Probability of event 2 occurring}) \times (\text{Value of event 2})].$$

This formula can be expanded to take into account as many events as the investor considers relevant. Applying the formula in this case, using decimals for the probabilities, gives us:

$$\text{Expected return} = (0.50 \times 15\%) + (0.50 \times 5\%) = 10\%.$$

One way to think of expected returns is as long-run averages. That is, if you invested in this bond over a period of years, and your probabilities of the two possible returns occurring are correct, then in half of the years, you would receive a return of 15%, and in the other half you would receive a return of 5%. So, on average, your return would be 10%. Of course, this example is simplified because we assumed that there are only two possible returns, when in reality there are likely to be many possible returns. We also assumed that it is possible to assign exact probabilities for each return, when in practice that would often be difficult to do. Nevertheless, this example captures the basic idea that in making choices among financial assets, investors need to consider possible returns and the probability of those returns occurring.

Risk Now suppose that you are choosing between investing in the IBM bond just described and investing in a Ford bond that you believe will have a return of 12% with a probability of 50% or a return of 8% with a probability of 50%. The expected return on the Ford bond is:

$$(0.50 \times 12\%) + (0.50 \times 8\%) = 10\%,$$

or the same as for the IBM bond. Although the expected returns are the same, most investors would prefer the Ford bond because, as we will see, the IBM bond has greater risk.

In Chapter 3, we mentioned default risk and interest-rate risk, but economists have a general definition of risk that includes these and other types of risk: **Risk** is the degree of uncertainty in the return on an asset. In particular, the greater the chance of receiving a return that is farther away from the asset's expected return, the greater the asset's risk. In the case of the two bonds, the IBM bond has greater risk because an investor could expect to receive returns that are either 5 percentage points higher or lower than the expected return, while an investor in the Ford bond could expect to receive returns that are only 2 percentage points higher or lower than the expected return. To provide a numerical measure of risk, economists measure the volatility of an asset's returns by calculating the standard deviation of an asset's actual returns over the years. If you have

Risk The degree of uncertainty in the return on an asset.

taken a course in statistics, recall that standard deviation is a measure of how dispersed a particular group of numbers is.[1]

Most investors are *risk averse*, which means that in choosing between two assets with the same expected returns, they would choose the asset with the lower risk. Investors are usually risk averse because many purchase financial assets as part of a savings plan to meet future expenses, such as buying a house, paying college tuition for their children, or having sufficient funds for retirement. They want to avoid having assets fall in value just when they need the funds. These investors will invest in an asset that has greater risk only if they are compensated by receiving a higher return. A consequence of most investors being risk averse is that in financial markets we observe a *trade-off between risk and return*. For example, assets such as bank CDs have low rates of return but also low risk, while assets such as shares of stock have high rates of return but also high risk.

Some investors are actually *risk loving*, which means they prefer to gamble by holding a risky asset with the possibility of maximizing returns. In our example, a risk-loving investor would be attracted to the IBM bond, with its 50% probability of a 15% return, even though the bond also has a 50% probability of a 5% return. Finally, some investors are *risk neutral*, which means they would make their investment decisions on the basis of expected returns, ignoring risk.

---

[1] We can use this example to show how to calculate the risk of investing in an asset as measured by the standard deviation of the returns on the asset. The first step in calculating the standard deviation is to find the deviation, or difference, between each return and the expected return on the bond. For example, for the IBM bond, the expected return equals 10% and the first return is 15%, so the difference from the expected return is 15% − 10% = 5%:

	Return 1	Deviation from the expected return	Return 2	Deviation from the expected return
IBM	15%	5%	5%	5%
Ford	12%	2%	8%	− 2%

Next, we need to square the deviations of the returns and add them together, weighted by the probability of the returns occurring. The result is the variance of the returns:

	Return 1	Deviation squared	Return 2	Deviation squared	Weighted deviations squared (variance of the returns)
IBM	15%	25%	5%	25%	(0.50 × 25%) + (0.50 × 25%) = 25%
Ford	12%	4%	8%	4%	(0.50 × 4%) + (0.50 × 4%) = 4%

Finally, taking the square root of the variance gives us the standard deviation of the returns. Using this measure of risk, we find that the IBM bond is riskier than the Ford bond:

	Variance	Standard deviation
IBM	25%	5%
Ford	4%	2%

Will a Black Swan Eat Your 401(k)?

If you go to work for a medium-size or large company, one of the benefits is likely to be a company-sponsored 401(k) retirement plan. Established under a law passed by Congress in 1978, these plans allow you to save for retirement by investing part of your salary in financial assets—typically mutual funds that buy stocks and bonds. You don't pay taxes on the funds you contribute to your 401(k) plan or on earnings on the funds if you don't withdraw them until after you reach retirement age.

In choosing among the options that most firms provide, you will want to take into account both the expected return and the level of risk. As we have just seen, in financial markets there is a trade-off between risk and return, with the riskiest assets typically having the highest expected returns. The following table provides data from 1926 to 2015 on four financial assets that are widely owned by investors. The "small" companies in the table are only small in the context of the U.S. stock market. In fact, they are fairly large, with the total value of their shares of stock being between $300 million and $2 billion. The "large" companies include General Motors, AT&T, McDonald's, Apple, and the other 500 firms included in the S&P 500, which is an average of the stock prices of firms valued at more than $5 billion. The average annual return is the simple average of the 89 yearly returns for each of the four assets during this period. Risk is measured as the volatility of the annual returns and is calculated as the standard deviation of each asset's annual returns during this period.

The data in the second and third columns of the table illustrate the trade-off between risk and return. Investors in stocks of small companies during these years experienced the highest average returns but also accepted the most risk. Investors in U.S. Treasury bills experienced the lowest average returns but also faced the least risk.

Financial asset	Average annual rate of return	Risk
Small company stocks	12.0%	23.0%
Large company stocks	10.0	17.4
Long-term Treasury bonds	5.6	12.2
U.S. Treasury bills	3.4	3.4

Source: Morningstar/Ibbotson.

The conventional measure of risk used in the table indicates the range within which returns typically fluctuate. Sometimes, though, returns occur that are far outside the usual range of returns. For instance, during 2008, at the height of the financial crisis, investors in large company stocks suffered a 37% loss. The probability of such a large loss was less than 5%. Stocks performed so poorly because the collapse of the housing market set off a financial crisis and the worst recession since the Great Depression of the 1930s. Nassim Nicholas Taleb, a professional investor and professor of economics at New York University, has popularized the term *black swan event* to refer to rare events that have a large effect on society or the economy. The name comes from the fact that Europeans believed that all swans were white—until 1697, when black swans were discovered in Australia. So, a black swan event is surprising and contrary to previous experience. Some economists see the financial crisis as a black swan event because before it occurred, few believed it was possible.

During 2008, the value of the average 401(k) account declined from $65,500 to $45,500, or by more than 30%. As a result, many risk-averse individual investors shifted the funds in their retirement accounts out of stock mutual funds and into bond mutual funds or even money market funds, which were paying interest rates of 1% or less. For people who had already retired or who were close to retirement, a decline of more than 30% in the value of their 401(k) accounts could be devastating if they were counting on those funds to finance their living expenses during retirement. But for younger investors, the problems caused by the decline were less severe. In fact, the value of large company stocks had regained their 2008 level by 2013.

So the black swan of the financial crisis may have done more damage to the average investor's portfolio by causing a shift to less risky—but lower return—assets than by the temporary decline in stock prices it caused.

Sources: Nassim Nicholas Taleb, *The Black Swan: The Impact of the Highly Improbable*, 2nd ed., New York: Random House, 2010; and Jack VanDerhei, Sarah Holden, Luis Alonso, and Steven Bass, Employee Benefit Research Institute, *Issue Brief*, No. 423, April 2016.

See related problem 1.6 at the end of the chapter.

Liquidity Recall from Chapter 2 that *liquidity* is the ease with which an asset can be exchanged for money. Assets with greater liquidity help savers to smooth spending over time or to access funds for emergencies. For example, if you have an unanticipated medical expense, you want to be able to sell assets quickly to meet the expense. The greater an asset's liquidity, the more desirable the asset is to investors. All else being equal, investors will accept a lower return on a more liquid asset than on a less liquid asset. Therefore, just as there is a trade-off between risk and return, there is a trade-off between liquidity and return. You are willing to accept a very low—possibly zero—interest rate on your checking account because you have immediate access to those funds.

The Cost of Acquiring Information Investors find assets more desirable if they don't have to spend much time or money acquiring information about them. For instance, the prices and yields on bonds issued by the U.S. Treasury are easy to obtain from the *Wall Street Journal* or from a web site such as Yahoo! Finance (finance.yahoo.com). And, guides to investment explain that the federal government is very unlikely to default on its bonds. If a new company issues bonds, however, investors must spend time and money collecting and analyzing information about the company before deciding whether to invest.

All else being equal, investors will accept a lower return on an asset that has lower costs of acquiring information. Therefore, just as there are trade-offs between risk and return and between liquidity and return, there is a trade-off between the cost of acquiring information and return. One reason interest rates on Treasury bonds are lower than interest rates on corporate bonds is that the cost of acquiring information on Treasury bonds is lower.

TABLE 4.1 Determinants of Portfolio Choice

An increase in ...	causes the quantity demanded of the asset in the portfolio to ...	because ...
wealth	rise	investors have a greater stock of savings to allocate.
expected return on an asset relative to expected returns on other assets	rise	investors gain more from holding the asset.
risk (that is, the variability of returns)	fall	most investors are risk averse.
liquidity (that is, the ease with which an asset can be converted to cash)	rise	investors can easily convert the asset into cash to finance consumption.
information costs	fall	investors must spend more time and money acquiring and analyzing information on the asset and its returns.

We can summarize our discussion of the determinants of portfolio choice as follows: *Desirable characteristics of a financial asset cause the quantity of the asset demanded by investors to increase, and undesirable characteristics of a financial asset cause the quantity of the asset demanded to decrease.* Table 4.1 lists the determinants of portfolio choice.

Diversification

Nearly all investors have multiple assets in their portfolios because the real world is full of uncertainty, and despite intensive analysis, an investor cannot be certain that an asset will perform as expected. To compensate for the inability to find one perfect asset, investors typically hold various types of assets, such as shares of stock issued by different firms. Dividing wealth among many different assets to reduce risk is called **diversification**.

Investors can take advantage of the fact that the returns on assets typically do not move together perfectly. For example, you may own shares of stock in Ford Motor Company and Apple. During a recession, the price of Ford's shares may fall as car sales decline, while the price of Apple's shares may rise if the firm introduces a popular new electronic product that consumers buy in large quantities, despite the recession. Similarly, the price of shares of the pharmaceutical firm Merck may fall if a new prescription drug unexpectedly fails to receive approval from the federal government, while the price of shares of Red Robin Gourmet Burgers may soar after the chain introduces a burger made of cauliflower and Brussels sprouts that becomes a sensation. So, the return on a diversified portfolio is more stable than are the returns on the individual assets that make up the portfolio.

Investors cannot eliminate risk entirely because assets share some common risk, called **market (or systematic) risk**. For example, economic recessions and economic expansions can decrease or increase returns on stocks as a whole. Few investments did well during the financial crisis of 2007–2009. Assets also carry their own unique risk

Diversification The division of wealth among many different assets to reduce risk.

Market (or systematic) risk Risk that is common to all assets of a certain type, such as the increases and decreases in stocks resulting from the business cycle.

Idiosyncratic (or unsystematic) risk Risk that pertains to a particular asset rather than to the market as a whole, as when the price of a particular firm's stock fluctuates because of the success or failure of a new product.

called **idiosyncratic** (or **unsystematic**) **risk**. For example, the price of an individual stock can be affected by unpredictable events such as scientific discoveries, worker strikes, and unfavorable lawsuits that affect the profitability of the firm. Diversification can eliminate idiosyncratic risk but not systematic risk.

MAKING THE CONNECTION | **IN YOUR INTEREST**

Does Your Portfolio Have Enough Risk?

Although all investments are risky, you can take steps to understand and manage risk when building your portfolio. Financial planners encourage their clients to evaluate their financial situation and their willingness to bear risk in determining whether an investment is appropriate.

Your *time horizon* is one important factor when choosing the degree of risk to accept. Funds you are saving in order to buy a home in the next few years should probably be invested in low-risk assets, such as bank certificates of deposit, even though those assets will have low returns. If you are saving for a retirement that won't begin for several decades, you can take advantage of the long-term gains from riskier investments, such as shares of stock, without much concern for short-term variability in returns. As you reach retirement, you can then switch to a more conservative strategy to avoid losing a substantial portion of your savings.

The following figure shows how households headed by people in two different age groups allocate their wealth. Younger households headed by someone 35 or younger have most of their wealth accounted for by the value of their homes and the value of the small businesses they own. They hold relatively little in stocks, retirement accounts, or other financial assets. Households headed by someone between 55 and 64 that are much closer to retirement still have the majority of wealth accounted for by their homes and small businesses. But these households have relatively more of their wealth in retirement accounts and in corporate stock owned outside of retirement accounts. Households headed by someone above the age of 75 (not shown in the figure) have a much larger fraction of their wealth in bank deposits and a much smaller fraction in stock than do households headed by someone aged 55 to 64.

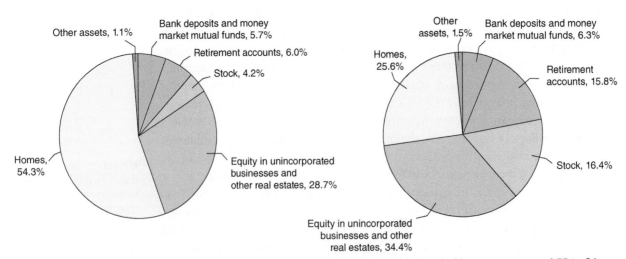

(a) Households headed by someone younger than age 35   **(b) Households headed by someone aged 55 to 64**

The following two typical financial plans of younger and older savers differ in their time horizons and saving goals:

	Financial plan for a younger saver	**Financial plan for an older saver**
Timeline for needing funds	Wants to build the value of a financial portfolio over more than 10 years.	Has a financial portfolio at or near the amount the investor needs to retire.
Financial goal	Accumulate funds by earning high long-term returns.	Conserve existing funds to earn a return slightly above the inflation rate.
Portfolio plan	Build a financial portfolio based on maximizing expected returns, with only limited concern for the variability of returns.	Reduce risk by selecting safe assets to earn an expected return *after inflation and taxes* of just above zero.

In assessing your saving plan, you need to consider the effects of inflation and taxes. Recall from Chapter 3 the important difference between real and nominal interest rates. A high nominal interest rate on an asset results in only a modest real return during a period of high inflation. In addition, the federal government taxes the returns from most investments, as do some state and local governments, and those taxes are usually imposed on nominal returns, not real returns. For example, if a bond pays you a 6% coupon (or $60) during a year when the inflation rate is 5%, the real interest rate you earned is only 1%—but you are taxed on your 6% nominal return. Depending on the investment, your *real, after-tax return* may be considerably different from your nominal pretax return. Many investors choose to invest in stocks because they understand that over the long run, investing in safe assets, such as U.S. Treasury bills, may leave them with a very small real, after-tax return. (In Chapter 5, we will look further at how differences in tax treatment can affect the returns on certain investments.)

Understanding how risk, inflation, and taxation affect your investments will help you make better-informed investment decisions.

Source: The figures are for 2013 and are based on data from Edward Wolff, "Household Wealth Trends in the United States, 1962–2013: What Happened over the Great Recession?" National Bureau of Economic Research Working Paper 20733, December 2014, Table 15. Note that "Bank deposits and money market mutual funds" also includes the cash surrender value of life insurance policies. "Stock" includes mutual funds and the value of personal trusts.

See related problem 1.7 at the end of the chapter.

Market Interest Rates and the Demand and Supply for Bonds

LEARNING OBJECTIVE: Use a demand and supply model to determine market interest rates for bonds.

We can use the determinants of portfolio choice just discussed to show how the interaction of the demand and supply for bonds determines market interest rates. Although demand and supply analysis should be familiar from your introductory economics course, applying this analysis to the bond market involves a complication. Typically, we draw demand and supply graphs with the price of the good or service on the vertical axis. Although we are interested in the prices of bonds, we are also interested in their interest rates. We know from Chapter 3 that the price of a bond, P, and its yield to maturity, i, are linked by the equation showing the price of a bond with coupon payments C that has a face value FV and that matures in n years:

$$P = \frac{C}{(1 + i)} + \frac{C}{(1 + i)^2} + \frac{C}{(1 + i)^3} + \ldots + \frac{C}{(1 + i)^n} + \frac{FV}{(1 + i)^n}.$$

Because the coupon payment and the face value do not change, once we have determined the equilibrium price in the bond market, we have also determined the equilibrium interest rate. With this approach to showing how market interest rates are determined, called the *bond market approach*, we are considering the bond as the "good" being traded in the market. The bond market approach is most useful when considering how the factors affecting the demand and supply for bonds affect the interest rate. In the appendix to the chapter, we will consider an alternative approach, called the *market for loanable funds approach*, that treats the funds being traded as the good. As in other areas of economics, which model we use depends on which aspects of a problem are most important in a particular situation.

A Demand and Supply Graph of the Bond Market

Figure 4.1 illustrates the market for bonds. For simplicity, let's assume that this is the market for a one-year discount bond that has a face value of $1,000 at maturity. The figure shows that the equilibrium price for this bond is $960, and the equilibrium quantity of bonds is $500 billion. Recall from Chapter 3 the formula for a one-year discount bond that sells for price P with face value FV:

$$i = \frac{FV - P}{P},$$

or, in this case:

$$i = \frac{\$1,000 - \$960}{\$960} = 0.042, \text{ or } 4.2\%.$$

As with markets for goods and services, we draw the demand and supply curves for bonds holding constant all factors that can affect demand and supply other than the price of bonds. The demand curve for bonds represents the relationship between the price of bonds and the quantity of bonds demanded by investors, holding all other factors constant. As the price of bonds increases, the interest rate on the bonds will fall, and the bonds will become less desirable to investors, so the quantity demanded will decline. Therefore, the demand curve for bonds is downward sloping, as shown in Figure 4.1.

Next, think about the supply curve for bonds. The supply curve represents the relationship between the price of bonds and the quantity of bonds supplied *by investors who own existing bonds and by firms that are considering issuing new bonds*. As the price of bonds increases, their interest rates will fall, and holders of existing bonds will be more willing to sell them. Some firms will also find it less expensive to finance projects by borrowing at

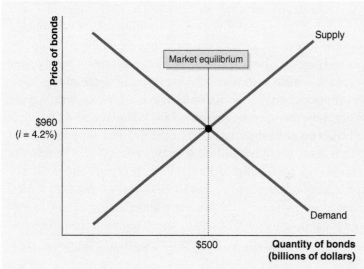

FIGURE 4.1

The Market for Bonds

The equilibrium price of bonds is determined in the bond market. By determining the price of bonds, the bond market also determines the interest rate on bonds. In this case, a one-year discount bond with a face value of $1,000 has an equilibrium price of $960, which means it has an interest rate (i) of 4.2%. The equilibrium quantity of bonds is $500 billion.

the lower interest rate and will issue new bonds. For both of these reasons, the quantity of bonds supplied will increase.

As with markets for goods and services, if the bond market is currently in equilibrium, it will stay there, and if it is not in equilibrium, it will move to equilibrium. For example, in Figure 4.2, suppose that the price of bonds is currently $980, which is above the equilibrium price of $960. At this higher price, the quantity demanded is $400 billion (point B), which is less than the equilibrium quantity demanded, while the quantity supplied is $600 billion (point C), which is greater than the equilibrium quantity

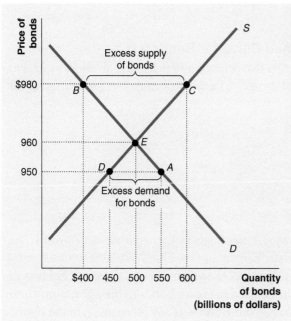

FIGURE 4.2

Equilibrium in Markets for Bonds

At the equilibrium price of bonds of $960, the quantity of bonds demanded by investors equals the quantity of bonds supplied by borrowers. At any price above $960, there is an excess supply of bonds, and the price of bonds will fall. At any price below $960, there is an excess demand for bonds, and the price of bonds will rise. The behavior of bond buyers and sellers pushes the price of bonds to the equilibrium price of $960.

supplied. The result is that there is an *excess supply of bonds* equal to $200 billion. Investors are buying all the bonds they want at the current price, but some sellers cannot find buyers. These sellers have an incentive to reduce the price they are willing to accept for bonds so that investors will buy their bonds. This downward pressure on bond prices will continue until the price has fallen to the equilibrium price of $960 (point *E*).

Now suppose that the price of bonds is $950, which is below the equilibrium price of $960. At this lower price, the quantity demanded is $550 billion (point *A*), which is greater than the equilibrium quantity demanded, while the quantity supplied is $450 billion (point *D*), which is less than the equilibrium quantity supplied. The result is that there is an *excess demand for bonds* equal to $100 billion. Investors and firms can sell all the bonds they want at the current price, but some buyers cannot find sellers. These buyers have an incentive to increase the price at which they are willing to buy bonds so that firms and other investors will be willing to sell bonds to them. This upward pressure on bond prices will continue until the price has risen to the equilibrium price of $960.

Explaining Changes in Equilibrium Interest Rates

In drawing the demand and supply curves for bonds in Figure 4.1, we held constant everything that could affect the willingness of investors to buy bonds—or firms and investors to sell bonds—except for the price of bonds. You may remember from your introductory economics course the distinction between a *change in the quantity demanded* (or *the quantity supplied*) and a *change in demand* (or *supply*). If the price of bonds changes, we move along the demand (or supply) curve, but the curve does not shift, so we have a change in quantity demanded (or supplied). If any other relevant variable—such as wealth or the expected rate of inflation—changes, then the demand (or supply) curve shifts, and we have a change in demand (or supply). In the next sections, we review the most important factors that cause the demand curve or the supply curve for bonds to shift.

Factors That Shift the Demand Curve for Bonds

In Section 4.1, we discussed the factors that determine which assets investors include in their portfolios. A change in any of these five factors will cause the demand curve for bonds to shift:

1. Wealth
2. Expected return on bonds
3. Risk
4. Liquidity
5. Information costs

Wealth When the economy is growing, households will accumulate more wealth. The wealthier savers are, the larger the stock of savings they have available to invest in financial assets, including bonds. As Figure 4.3 shows, an increase in wealth, holding all other factors constant, will shift the demand curve for bonds to the right, from D_1 to D_2, as savers are willing and able to buy more bonds at any given price. In the figure, as the demand curve for bonds shifts to the right, the equilibrium price of bonds rises

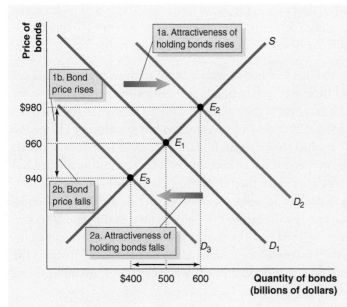

FIGURE 4.3

Shifts in the Demand Curve for Bonds

An increase in wealth, holding all other factors constant, will shift the demand curve for bonds to the right. As the demand curve for bonds shifts to the right, the equilibrium price of bonds rises from $960 to $980, and the equilibrium quantity of bonds increases from $500 billion to $600 billion.

A decrease in wealth, holding all other factors constant, will shift the demand curve for bonds to the left, reducing both the equilibrium price and equilibrium quantity. As the demand curve for bonds shifts to the left, the equilibrium price falls from $960 to $940, and the equilibrium quantity of bonds decreases from $500 billion to $400 billion.

from $960 to $980, and the equilibrium quantity of bonds increases from $500 billion to $600 billion. So, equilibrium in the bond market moves from point E_1 to point E_2. During a recession, as occurred during 2007–2009, households will experience declining wealth, and, holding all other factors constant, the demand curve for bonds will shift to the left, reducing both the equilibrium price and equilibrium quantity. In Figure 4.3, as the demand curve for bonds shifts to the left, from D_1 to D_3 the equilibrium price falls from $960 to $940, and the equilibrium quantity of bonds decreases from $500 billion to $400 billion. So, equilibrium in the bond market moves from point E_1 to point E_3.

Expected Return on Bonds If the expected return on bonds rises *relative to expected returns on other assets*, investors will increase their demand for bonds, and the demand curve for bonds will shift to the right. If the expected return on bonds falls relative to expected returns on other assets, the demand curve for bonds will shift to the left. Note that it is the expected return on bonds *relative* to the expected returns on other assets that causes the demand curve for bonds to shift. For instance, if the expected return on bonds remained unchanged, while investors decided that the return from investing in stocks would be higher than they had previously expected, the relative return on bonds would fall, and the demand curve for bonds would shift to the left.

The expected return on bonds is affected by the expected inflation rate. As we saw in Chapter 3, the expected real interest rate equals the nominal interest rate minus the expected inflation rate. Therefore, an increase in the expected inflation rate reduces the expected real interest rate. Similarly, the expected real return on bonds equals the nominal return minus the expected inflation rate. An increase in the expected inflation rate reduces the expected real return on bonds, which will reduce the willingness of investors to buy bonds at any given price and shift the demand curve for bonds to the left. A decrease in the expected inflation rate will increase the expected real return on bonds, increasing the willingness of investors to buy bonds at any given price and shift the demand curve for bonds to the right.

Risk An increase in the riskiness of bonds *relative to the riskiness of other assets* decreases the willingness of investors to buy bonds and causes the demand curve for bonds to shift to the left. A decrease in the riskiness of bonds relative to the riskiness of other assets increases the willingness of investors to buy bonds and causes the demand curve for bonds to shift to the right. It is the perceived riskiness of bonds *relative* to other assets that matters. If the riskiness of bonds remains unchanged but investors decide that stocks are riskier than they had previously believed, the relative riskiness of bonds will decline, investors will increase their demand for bonds, and the demand curve for bonds will shift to the right. In fact, during late 2008 and early 2009, many investors believed that the riskiness of investing in stocks had increased. As a result, investors increased their demand for bonds, which drove up the equilibrium price of bonds and, therefore, drove down the equilibrium interest rate on bonds.

Liquidity Investors value liquidity in an asset because an asset with greater liquidity can be sold more quickly and at a lower cost if the investor needs the funds to, say, buy a car or invest in another asset. If the liquidity of bonds increases, investors demand more bonds at any given price, and the demand curve for bonds shifts to the right. A decrease in the liquidity of bonds shifts the demand curve for bonds to the left. Once again, though, it is the relative liquidity of bonds that matters. For instance, online stock trading sites first appeared during the 1990s. These sites allowed investors to buy and sell stocks at a very low cost, so the liquidity of many stocks increased. The result was that the relative liquidity of bonds decreased, and the demand curve for bonds shifted to the left.

Information Costs The information costs investors must pay to evaluate assets affect their willingness to buy those assets. For instance, beginning in the 1990s, financial information began to be readily available on the Internet either for free or for a low price. Previously, an investor could find this information only by paying for a subscription to a newsletter or by spending hours in libraries, gathering data from annual reports and other records. Because stocks had been more widely discussed than bonds in newspapers such as the *Wall Street Journal* and magazines, the effect of the Internet on the information available on bonds was greater. As a result of the lower information costs, the demand curve for bonds shifted to the right. During the financial crisis, many investors believed that for certain types of bonds—particularly mortgage-backed securities—they lacked sufficient information to gauge the likelihood that the bonds might default. Gathering sufficient information appeared to be very costly, if it were possible at all. As a result of these higher information costs, the demand curve for bonds shifted to the left.

Table 4.2 summarizes the most important factors that shift the demand curve for bonds.

TABLE 4.2 Factors That Shift the Demand Curve for Bonds

All else being equal, an increase in ...	causes the demand for bonds to ...	because ...	Graph of effect on equilibrium in the bond market
wealth	increase	more funds are allocated to bonds.	
expected returns on bonds	increase	holding bonds is relatively more attractive.	
expected inflation	decrease	holding bonds is relatively less attractive.	
expected returns on other assets	decrease	holding bonds is relatively less attractive.	
riskiness of bonds relative to other assets	decrease	holding bonds is relatively less attractive.	
liquidity of bonds relative to other assets	increase	holding bonds is relatively more attractive.	
information costs of bonds relative to other assets	decrease	holding bonds is relatively less attractive.	

Factors That Shift the Supply Curve for Bonds

Shifts in the supply curve for bonds result from changes in factors other than the price of bonds that affect either the willingness of investors who own bonds to sell them or the willingness of firms and governments to issue additional bonds. Four factors are most important in explaining shifts in the supply curve for bonds:

1. Expected pretax profitability of physical capital investment
2. Business taxes
3. Expected inflation
4. Government borrowing

Expected Pretax Profitability of Physical Capital Investment Most firms borrow funds to finance the purchase of real physical capital assets, such as factories, machine tools, and information technology that they expect to use for several years to produce goods and services. The more profitable firms expect investment in physical assets to be, the more funds firms want to borrow by issuing bonds. During the late 1990s, many firms realized that investing in web sites that would allow them to make online sales to consumers would be very profitable. The result was a boom in investment in physical capital in the form of computers, servers, and other information technology, and an increase in bond sales.

Figure 4.4 shows how an increase in firms' expectations of the profitability of investment in physical capital will, holding all other factors constant, shift the supply curve for bonds to the right as firms issue more bonds at any given price. In the figure, as the supply curve for bonds shifts to the right, from S_1 to S_2, the equilibrium price of bonds falls from $960 to $940, and the equilibrium quantity of bonds increases from $500 billion to $575 billion. During a recession, firms often become pessimistic about

FIGURE 4.4

Shifts in the Supply Curve of Bonds

An increase in firms' expectations of the profitability of investments in physical capital will, holding all other factors constant, shift the supply curve for bonds to the right as firms issue more bonds at any given price. As the supply curve for bonds shifts to the right, the equilibrium price of bonds falls from $960 to $940, and the equilibrium quantity of bonds increases from $500 billion to $575 billion.

If firms become pessimistic about the profits they could earn from investing in physical capital, then, holding all other factors constant, the supply curve for bonds will shift to the left. As the supply for bonds shifts to the left, the equilibrium price increases from $960 to $975, and the equilibrium quantity of bonds decreases from $500 billion to $400 billion.

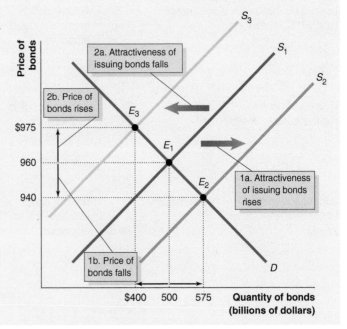

the profits they could earn from investing in physical capital, with the result that, holding all other factors constant, the supply curve for bonds will shift to the left, increasing the equilibrium price of bonds, while decreasing the equilibrium quantity. In Figure 4.4, as the supply curve for bonds shifts to the left, from S_1 to S_3, the equilibrium price increases from \$960 to \$975, and the equilibrium quantity of bonds decreases from \$500 billion to \$400 billion.

Business Taxes Taxes on businesses also affect firms' expectations about future profitability because firms focus on the profits that remain after paying taxes. When the government raises business taxes, the profits firms earn on new investment in physical capital decline, and firms issue fewer bonds. The result is that the supply curve for bonds will shift to the left. When the government cuts business taxes by, for example, enacting an investment tax credit, the lower taxes increase the profit firms earn on new investment projects, thereby leading firms to issue more bonds. So, the supply curve for bonds shifts to the right.

Expected Inflation We have seen that an increase in the expected rate of inflation reduces investors' demand for bonds by reducing the expected real interest rate that investors receive for any given *nominal* interest rate. From the point of view of a firm issuing a bond, a lower expected real interest rate is attractive because it means the firm pays less in real terms to borrow funds. So, an increase in the expected inflation rate results in the supply curve for bonds shifting to the right, as firms supply a greater quantity of bonds at every price. A decrease in the expected inflation rate results in the supply curve for bonds shifting to the left.

Government Borrowing So far, we have emphasized how the decisions of investors and firms affect bond prices and interest rates. Decisions by governments can also affect bond prices and interest rates. For example, many economists believe that a series of large U.S. federal government budget deficits during the 1980s and early 1990s caused interest rates to be somewhat higher than they otherwise would have been.

When we talk about the "government sector" in the United States, we include not just the federal government but also state and local governments. The government sector is typically both a lender—as when the federal government makes loans to college students and small businesses—and a borrower. In recent years, the federal government has borrowed an enormous amount from U.S. and foreign investors as tax receipts have fallen far short of spending. The result has been large *federal budget deficits*. Figure 4.5 shows the federal budget deficit and surplus in the years since 1965. (The shaded areas represent years when the economy was in a recession.) During most of these years, the federal budget has been in deficit, except for a few years in the late 1990s, when tax receipts exceeded government expenditures. The large deficits beginning in 2008 resulted, in part, from the severity of the 2007–2009 recession. When the economy enters a recession, tax receipts automatically decline as household incomes and business profits fall and the federal government automatically increases spending on unemployment insurance and other programs for the unemployed. The severity of the recession also led Congress and presidents George W. Bush and Barack Obama to increase spending dramatically and cut taxes. The economic recovery eventually reduced the size of the federal budget deficit, although the deficit remained large in 2016.

FIGURE 4.5

The Federal Budget, 1965–2015

With the exception of a few years in the late 1990s, the federal government has typically run a budget deficit. The recession of 2007–2009 led to record deficits that required the federal government to borrow heavily by selling bonds. The shaded areas represent years when the economy was in a recession.

Source: U.S. Bureau of Economic Analysis.

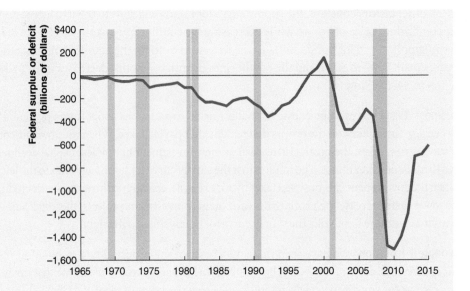

We can analyze the effect on the bond market of changes in the government's budget deficit or surplus. Suppose the federal government increases spending without increasing taxes. When the government finances the resulting deficit by issuing bonds, the supply curve for bonds will shift to the right. If we assume for now that households leave their saving unchanged in response to the government's increased borrowing, then the result of the government budget deficit, holding other factors constant, is to cause the equilibrium price of bonds to fall and the equilibrium quantity of bonds to rise. Because bond prices and interest rates move in opposite directions, the equilibrium interest rate will rise.

We can conclude that if nothing else changes, an increase in government borrowing shifts the bond supply curve to the right, decreasing the price of bonds and increasing the interest rate. A decrease in government borrowing shifts the bond supply curve to the left, increasing the price of bonds and decreasing the interest rate. Table 4.3 on the next page summarizes the factors that shift the supply curve for bonds.

Explaining Changes in Interest Rates

4.3

LEARNING OBJECTIVE: Use the bond market model to explain changes in interest rates.

Movements in interest rates occur because of shifts in either the demand for bonds, the supply of bonds, or both. In this section, we consider two examples of using the bond market model to explain changes in interest rates:

1. The movement of interest rates over the *business cycle*, which refers to the alternating periods of economic expansion and economic recession experienced by the United States and most other economies

2. The *Fisher effect*, which describes the movement of interest rates in response to changes in the rate of inflation

In practice, many shifts in bond demand and bond supply occur simultaneously, and economists sometimes have difficulty determining how much each curve may have shifted.

TABLE 4.3   Factors That Shift the Supply Curve for Bonds

All else being equal, an increase in ...	causes the supply of bonds to ...	because ...	Graph of effect on equilibrium in the bond market
expected profitability	increase	businesses borrow to finance profitable investments.	P, S₁, S₂, D, Q
business taxes	decrease	taxes reduce the profitability of investment.	P, S₂, S₁, D, Q
investment tax credits	increase	government tax credits lower the cost of investment, thereby increasing the profitability of investing.	P, S₁, S₂, D, Q
expected inflation	increase	at any given bond price, the real cost of borrowing falls.	P, S₁, S₂, D, Q
government borrowing	increase	more bonds are offered in the economy at any given interest rate.	P, S₁, S₂, D, Q

Why Do Interest Rates Fall During Recessions?

We can illustrate changes in interest rates over the business cycle by using the bond market graph. At the beginning of an economic recession, households and firms expect that for a period of time, levels of production and employment will be lower than usual. Households will experience declining wealth, and firms will become more pessimistic about the future profitability of investing in physical capital. As Figure 4.6 shows, declining household wealth causes the demand curve for bonds to shift to the left, from D_1 to D_2, and firms' declining expectations of the profitability of investments in physical capital cause them to issue fewer bonds, which shifts the supply curve for bonds to the left, from S_1 to S_2. The figure shows that the equilibrium price of bonds rises, from P_1 to P_2. We know that an increase in the equilibrium price of bonds results in a decline in the equilibrium interest rate.

Notice that if during a recession the demand curve for bonds shifted to the left by more than the supply curve for bonds, the equilibrium price of bonds might fall and, therefore, the equilibrium interest rate might rise. Evidence from U.S. data indicates that interest rates typically fall during recessions (and rise during economic expansions), which suggests that during the business cycle, the supply curve for bonds shifts more than does the demand curve.

How Do Changes in Expected Inflation Affect Interest Rates? The Fisher Effect

Equilibrium in the bond market determines the price of bonds and the *nominal* interest rate. But borrowers and lenders are more interested in the *real* interest rate because the real interest rate represents the value of the payments they make or receive *after* adjusting for the effects of inflation. After the fact, we can compute the real interest rate by subtracting

---

FIGURE 4.6

Interest Rate Changes in an Economic Downturn

1. From an initial equilibrium at E_1, an economic downturn reduces household wealth and decreases the demand for bonds at any bond price. The bond demand curve shifts to the left, from D_1 to D_2.

2. The fall in expected profitability reduces lenders' supply of bonds at any bond price. The bond supply curve shifts to the left, from S_1 to S_2.

3. In the new equilibrium, E_2, the bond price rises from P_1 to P_2.

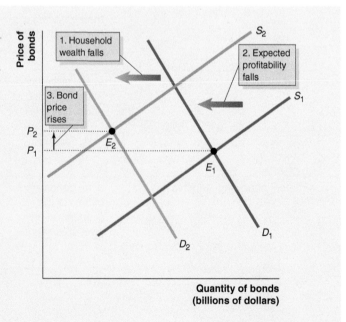

Explaining Changes in Interest Rates **113**

the inflation rate from the nominal interest rate. Because investors and firms don't know ahead of time what the inflation rate will be, they must form expectations of the inflation rate. Equilibrium in the bond market, then, should reflect the beliefs of borrowers and lenders about the *expected* real interest rate, which equals the nominal interest rate minus the *expected* inflation rate.

Irving Fisher, an economist at Yale University during the early twentieth century, argued that if equilibrium in the bond market indicated that lenders were willing to accept and borrowers were willing to pay a particular real interest rate, such as 3%, then any changes in expected inflation should cause changes in the nominal interest rate that would leave the real interest rate unchanged. For example, suppose that the current nominal interest rate is 5%, while the expected inflation rate is 2%. In that case, the expected real interest rate is 3%. Now suppose that investors and firms decide that the future inflation rate is likely to be 4%. Fisher argued that the result will be an increase in the nominal interest rate from 5% to 7%, which would leave the expected real interest rate unchanged, at 3%. More generally, the **Fisher effect** states that *the nominal interest rate rises or falls point-for-point with changes in the expected inflation rate.*

Is the Fisher effect consistent with our understanding of how demand and supply adjust in the bond market? Figure 4.7 shows that it is. Suppose that initially participants in the bond market expect the inflation rate to be 2% and that the market is currently in equilibrium at E_1, determined by the intersection of D_1 and S_1. Now suppose that participants in the bond market come to believe that the future inflation rate will be 4%. As we have seen in the previous section, an increase in the expected inflation rate will cause the demand curve for bonds to shift to the left, from D_1 to D_2, because the expected real interest rate investors receive from owning bonds will fall for any given bond price. At the same time, an increase in the expected inflation rate will cause the supply curve to shift to the right, from S_1 to S_2, as the expected real interest rate firms pay on bonds will fall for any given bond price.

Fisher effect The assertion by Irving Fisher that the nominal interest rate rises or falls point-for-point with changes in the expected inflation rate.

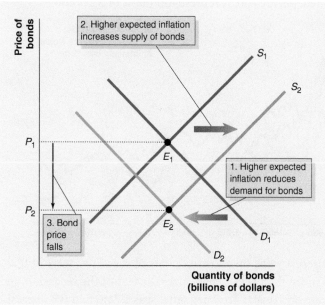

FIGURE 4.7

Expected Inflation and Interest Rates

1. From an initial equilibrium at E_1, an increase in expected inflation reduces investors' expected real return, reducing investors' willingness to buy bonds at any bond price. The demand curve for bonds shifts to the left, from D_1 to D_2.

2. The increase in expected inflation increases firms' willingness to issue bonds at any bond price. The supply curve for bonds shifts to the right, from S_1 to S_2.

3. In the new equilibrium, E_2, the bond price falls, from P_1 to P_2.

In response to the rise in expected inflation, both the demand curve and supply curve for bonds shift. In the new equilibrium, the price of bonds is lower, and, therefore, the nominal interest rate is higher. In Figure 4.7, the equilibrium quantity of bonds does not change because the nominal interest rate rises by an amount exactly equal to the change in expected inflation. In other words, the figure shows the Fisher effect working exactly. In practice, economists have found that various real-world frictions result in nominal interest rates not always increasing or decreasing by exactly the amount of a change in expected inflation. These real-world frictions include the payments brokers and dealers charge when buying and selling bonds for investors and the taxes investors must pay on some purchases and sales of bonds.

Even if it may not hold exactly, the Fisher effect alerts us to two important facts about the bond market:

1. Higher inflation rates result in higher nominal interest rates, and lower inflation rates result in lower nominal interest rates.
2. Changes in *expected* inflation can lead to changes in nominal interest rates before a change in *actual* inflation has occurred.

MAKING THE CONNECTION

Why Are Bond Interest Rates So Low?

In mid-2007, just before the financial crisis, the interest rate on 10-year Treasury notes was 5.0%, the interest rate on corporate bonds (issued by firms with good credit) was 6.7%, and the interest rate on three-month Treasury bills was 4.6%. We have seen that during a recession, we would expect that interest rates would decline. As the following graph shows, during the 2007–2009 recession, corporate bond rates temporarily rose because investors believed that default risk had increased, while Treasury note and Treasury bill rates declined. (Shaded areas represent months of recession.)

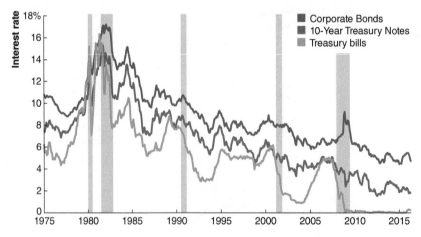

As the graph shows, interest rates on all three types of securities were still at historically very low levels more than seven years after the end of the recession. In October 2016, the interest rate on 10-year Treasury notes was 1.74%, and the interest rate on Treasury bills was 0.33%—the lowest those interest rates had been in more than 70 years. And it wasn't just in the United States that interest rates were at very low levels:

- Interest rates on 50-year bonds issued by the British government dropped below 2%, a result one financial columnist labeled "Bonkers. Totally Bonkers."

- Interest rates on Japanese government 30-year bonds dropped below 1%.

- Interest rates on German 10-year bonds fell to 0.05%. At that interest rate, if you invested €1,000 in buying a German government bond, after waiting 10 years you would receive back from the German government €1,005—a return of only €5 (or about $5.75) for lending your money for 10 years.

We can use the bond market model to analyze why bond interest rates remained so low for such a long time. First, as the analysis in Figure 4.7 indicates, because the actual and expected inflation rates remained very low, we would expect that the Fisher effect would result in low nominal bond interest rates. The following figure shows other developments in the bond market during this period. The increase in government budget deficits in the United States and many other high-income countries during and after the recession shifted the supply curve for bonds to the right, from S_{2007} to S_{2016}. By itself, this shift would have lowered the equilibrium price of bonds to P_1, raising the equilibrium interest rate. As the figure shows, however, the demand curve for bonds shifted from D_{2007} to D_{2016}, which was even greater than the shift in the supply curve. As a result, the equilibrium price of bonds increased from P_{2007} to P_{2016}, lowering the equilibrium interest rate.

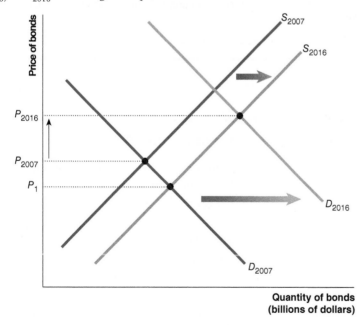

What caused the large increase in the demand for bonds? During the financial crisis, many investors engaged in a *flight to quality*, in which they sold stocks and other financial securities and bought government bonds. Even after the end of the financial crisis, growth was slow in most other high-income countries, leaving investors cautious about investing in riskier financial securities. In addition, high rates of saving in some countries, including China, Japan, and Korea, meant that investors in those countries added to the demand for U.S. Treasury securities.

Another key source of additional demand for government bonds came from central banks, which pursued a monetary policy of attempting to lower interest rates in order to increase production and employment. As we will see in later chapters, typically banks pursue expansionary monetary policy by buying short-term government securities, as the Fed does when it buys Treasury bills. But the sluggishness of the recovery led the Fed, the Bank of England, the European Central Bank, and the Bank of Japan all to pursue a policy of *quantitative easing*, which involves buying long-term securities to help stimulate the economy. For example, the Fed bought U.S. Treasury notes. The result of quantitative easing was a sharp increase in demand for government bonds, increasing their price and lowering their interest rate.

Bond interest rates seemed destined to remain low unless worldwide economic growth increased significantly. An increase in growth would likely increase inflation and reduce central bank purchases of government securities. The result would be falling bond prices and rising interest rates—which would result in capital losses to investors who owned bonds. But as one bond market participant put it, in 2016, among investors, "There is very little fear of economic strength. There is very little fear of inflation."

Sources: Justin Lahart, "The Yield Curve's Message for the Fed" *Wall Street Journal*, June 9, 2016; James Mackintosh, "A 2% Yield on a 50-Year Gilt? Bonkers. Totally Bonkers," *Wall Street Journal*, June 8, 2016; Min Zeng, "Foreign Demand for Treasurys Soars, the 'One-Eyed King,'" *Wall Street Journal*, June 9, 2016; and Ben Eisen, "The Yield Curve Is Flattening No Matter What the Fed Says," *Wall Street Journal*, June 9, 2016.

See related problem 3.5 at the end of the chapter.

SOLVED PROBLEM 4.3   **IN YOUR INTEREST**

What Happens to Your Investment in Bonds If the Inflation Rate Rises?

Following the unexpected election of President Donald Trump in November 2016, an article in the *Wall Street Journal* noted that: "Investors are geared for higher growth and inflation."

a. Why did interest rates on bonds remain at historically low levels years after the end of the financial crisis of 2007–2009?

b. When investors decided that the election of President Trump would lead to higher inflation, what was the effect on bond prices? Be sure to include in your answer a demand and supply graph of the bond market.

c. Suppose that you expect a greater increase in inflation than do other investors, but that you don't expect the increase to occur until three years in the future. Should you wait three years to sell your bonds? Briefly explain.

d. If expected inflation is increasing, would you have been better off investing in long-term bonds or in short-term bonds?

Source: Sam Goldfarb, "U.S. Government Bond Selloff Gains New Momentum," *Wall Street Journal*, November 30, 2016.

Solving the Problem

Step 1   **Review the chapter material.** This problem is about the persistence of very low interest rates on bonds and the effect of inflation on bond prices, so you may want to review the *Making the Connection* "Why Are Bond Interest Rates So Low?" which begins on page 114, and the section "How Do Changes in Expected Inflation Affect Interest Rates? The Fisher Effect," which begins on page 112.

Step 2   **Answer part (a) by explaining why interest rates on bonds remained at very low levels years after the end of the financial crisis of 2007–2009.** We saw in the *Making the Connection* that because the actual and expected inflation rates were very low during this period, the Fisher effect would lead us to expect that the nominal interest rate on bonds would also be low. In addition, we saw that the demand for bonds, particularly government bonds, has increased more than the supply of bonds, which has increased the price of bonds and lowered the nominal interest rate.

Step 3   **Answer part (b) by explaining the effect of an increase in expected inflation on bond prices and illustrate your response with a graph.** The article notes that the unexpected election of Donald Trump led investors to increase their expectations of the inflation rate. We have seen in this chapter that an increase in expected inflation will affect both the demand curve and the supply curve for bonds. Your graph should show the demand curve for bonds shifting to the left, the supply curve shifting to the right, and a new equilibrium with a lower price. You will suffer capital losses if you hold bonds during a period when their prices fall.

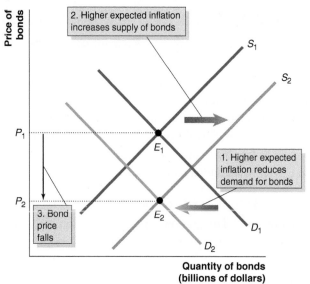

The equilibrium price falls from P_1 to P_2, while the quantity of bonds remains unchanged, as in Figure 4.7 on page 113. Note that even if the pure Fisher effect does not hold, we know that the price of bonds will still be lower in the new equilibrium because the demand for bonds shifts to the left, and the supply of bonds shifts to the right, even if the sizes of the shifts may not be the same.

Step 4 **Answer part (c) by discussing the difference in the effects of actual and expected inflation on changes in bond prices.** *Changes* in bond prices result from *changes* in the expected rate of inflation. Current expectations of inflation are already reflected in the nominal interest rate and, therefore, in the price of bonds. For example, if buyers and sellers of bonds are willing to accept an expected real interest rate of 2%, then if the expected inflation rate is 1%, the nominal interest rate will be 3%. If buyers and sellers change their expectations, the nominal interest rate will adjust. So, if you believe that future inflation is going to be higher than other investors think, you would be wise to sell your bonds right away. Waiting for inflation to increase would mean waiting until the nominal interest rate had risen and bond prices had fallen. By then, it would be too late for you to avoid the capital losses on your bonds.

Step 5 **Answer part (d) by explaining why long-term bonds are a particularly bad investment if expected inflation increases.** An increase in expected inflation will increase the nominal interest rate on both short-term and long-term bonds. But we know from Chapter 3 that the longer the maturity of a bond, the greater the change in price as a result of a change in market interest rates. So, if expected inflation and nominal interest rates rise, your capital losses on long-term bonds will be greater than your capital losses on short-term bonds.

See related problem 3.6 at the end of the chapter.

Interest Rates and the Money Market Model

LEARNING OBJECTIVE: Explain how interest rates are determined using the money market model.

The bond market analysis in the previous section focuses on the long-term nominal interest rate. As we will see in following chapters, monetary policy has traditionally focused on the short-term nominal interest rate. In particular, the Fed has targeted the *federal funds rate*—the rate that banks charge each other on overnight loans. In this section, we look at the determination of the short-run nominal interest rate using the money market model (which is also called the *liquidity preference model*).

The Demand and Supply for Money

Money market model A model that shows how the short-term nominal interest rate is determined by the demand and supply for money.

The **money market model** focuses on how the interaction of the demand and supply for money determines the short-term nominal interest rate.[2] Figure 4.8 shows the demand

---

[2] The money market model was first discussed by the British economist John Maynard Keynes in his book *The General Theory of Employment, Interest, and Money*, which was published in 1936. Keynes referred to the model as the "liquidity preference model," a term that some economists still use. Note one possible source of confusion: Economists sometimes also use the phrase "money market" to refer to the market for bonds, such as Treasury bills, that mature in one year or less.

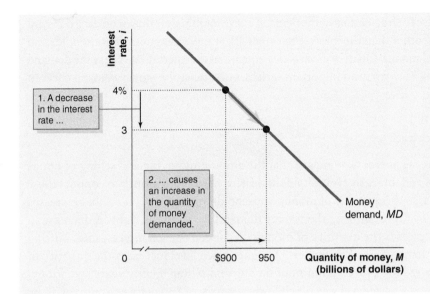

FIGURE 4.8

The Demand for Money

The money demand curve slopes downward because lower nominal interest rates cause households and firms to switch from financial assets such as U.S. Treasury bills to money. All other things being equal, a fall in the interest rate from 4% to 3% will increase the quantity of money demanded from $900 billion to $950 billion.

curve for money. The nominal interest rate is on the vertical axis, and the quantity of money is on the horizontal axis. Here we are using the M1 definition of money, which equals currency in circulation plus checking account deposits.

To understand why the demand curve for money in Figure 4.8 is downward sloping, consider that households and firms have a choice between holding money and holding other financial assets, such as U.S. Treasury bills. Money has one particularly desirable characteristic: It is perfectly liquid, so you can use it to buy goods, services, or financial assets. Money also has one undesirable characteristic: The currency in your wallet earns no interest, and the money in your checking account earns either no interest or very little interest. Alternatives to money, such as U.S. Treasury bills, pay interest, but you have to sell them if you want to use the funds to buy goods or services. When nominal interest rates rise on financial assets such as U.S. Treasury bills, the amount of interest that households and firms lose by holding money increases. When nominal interest rates fall, the amount of interest households and firms lose by holding money decreases. Remember that *opportunity cost* is what you have to forgo to engage in an activity. *The nominal interest rate is the opportunity cost of holding money.*

We now have an explanation for why the demand curve for money slopes downward: When nominal interest rates on Treasury bills and other financial assets are low, the opportunity cost of holding money is low, so the quantity of money demanded by households and firms will be high. When interest rates are high, the opportunity cost of holding money will be high, so the quantity of money demanded will be low. In Figure 4.8, a decrease in interest rates from 4% to 3% causes the quantity of money demanded by households and firms to rise from $900 billion to $950 billion.

Shifts in the Money Demand Curve

You know from your principles of economics course that the demand curve for a good is drawn holding constant all variables, other than the price, that affect the willingness of consumers to buy the good. Changes in variables other than the price cause the demand curve to shift. Similarly, the demand curve for money is drawn holding constant all variables, other than the interest rate, that affect the willingness of households and firms to hold money. Changes in variables other than the interest rate cause the demand curve to shift. The two most important variables that cause the money demand curve to shift are:

1. Real GDP
2. The price level

An increase in real GDP means that the amount of buying and selling of goods and services will increase. Households and firms need more money to conduct these transactions, so the quantity of money households and firms want to hold increases at each interest rate, shifting the money demand curve to the right. A decrease in real GDP decreases the quantity of money demanded at each interest rate, shifting the money demand curve to the left. A higher price level increases the quantity of money required for a given amount of buying and selling. Eighty years ago, for example, when the price level was much lower, a salary of $30 per week put you in the middle class, and you could purchase a new car for $500. As a result, the quantity of money demanded by households and firms was much lower than it is today, even adjusting for the effect of the lower real GDP and the smaller population of those years. An increase in the price level increases the quantity of money demanded at each interest rate, shifting the money demand curve to the right. A decrease in the price level decreases the quantity of money demanded at each interest rate, shifting the money demand curve to the left.

Figure 4.9 illustrates shifts in the money demand curve. An increase in real GDP or an increase in the price level will cause the money demand curve to shift to the right, from MD_1 to MD_2. A decrease in real GDP or a decrease in the price level will cause the money demand curve to shift to the left, from MD_1 to MD_3.

FIGURE 4.9

Shifts in the Money Demand Curve

Changes in real GDP or the price level cause the money demand curve to shift. An increase in real GDP or an increase in the price level will cause the money demand curve to shift to the right, from MD_1 to MD_2. A decrease in real GDP or a decrease in the price level will cause the money demand curve to shift to the left, from MD_1 to MD_3.

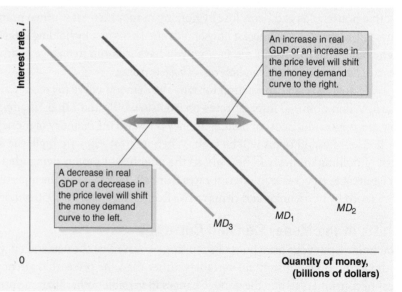

Equilibrium in the Money Market

As we will see in Chapter 14, central banks, including the U.S. Federal Reserve, do not have complete control of the supply of money. But at this point, we can focus on the effects of changes in the money supply on the short-term nominal interest rate by assuming that the Federal Reserve is able to set the supply of money at whatever level it chooses. Given this assumption, the money supply curve is a vertical line, and changes in the nominal interest rate have no effect on the quantity of money supplied. Figure 4.10 includes both the money demand and money supply curves to show how the equilibrium nominal interest rate is determined in the money market. Just as in other markets, equilibrium in the money market occurs where the money demand curve crosses the money supply curve. If the Fed increases the money supply, the money supply curve will shift to the right, and the equilibrium interest rate will fall. Figure 4.10 shows that when the Fed increases the money supply from \$900 billion to \$950 billion, the money supply curve shifts to the right, from MS_1 to MS_2, and the equilibrium interest rate falls from 4% to 3%.

In the money market, the adjustment from one equilibrium to another equilibrium is a little different from the adjustment in the market for a good. In Figure 4.10, the money market is initially in equilibrium, with an interest rate of 4% and a money supply of \$900 billion. When the Fed increases the money supply by \$50 billion, households and firms have more money than they want to hold at an interest rate of 4%. What do households and firms do with the extra \$50 billion? They are most likely to use the money to buy short-term financial assets, such as Treasury bills, which have maturities of one year or less. By buying short-term assets, households and firms drive up their prices and drive down their interest rates.

Table 4.4 summarizes the key factors that cause shifts in the demand and supply of money.

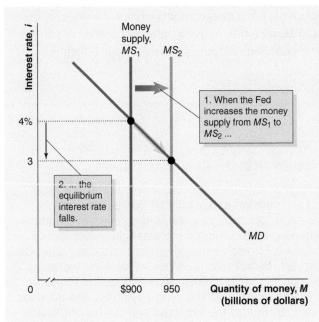

FIGURE 4.10

The Effect on the Interest Rate When the Fed Increases the Money Supply

When the Fed increases the money supply from \$900 billion to \$950 billion, the money supply curve shifts to the right, from MS_1 to MS_2, and the equilibrium nominal interest rate falls from 4% to 3%.

TABLE 4.4 Summary of the Money Market Model

An increase in ...	will shift the ...	causing ...	Graph of the effect on equilibrium in the money market
real GDP	money demand curve to the right	the nominal interest rate to increase.	
the price level	money demand curve to the right	the nominal interest rate to increase.	
money supply	money supply curve to the right	the nominal interest rate to decrease and the quantity of money to increase.	

The money market model shows us that, at least in the short run, the Fed can cause a decline in the short-term nominal interest rate by increasing the money supply. For the most part, though, long-run interest rates, such as those on Treasury bonds or corporate bonds, play a more important role in the financial system. In the following chapters, we will rely more on the bond market model when analyzing changes in interest rates. In Chapters 17 and 18, we return to using the money market model when discussing the effects of monetary policy on output, employment, and inflation.

ANSWERING THE KEY QUESTION

Continued from page 92

At the beginning of this chapter, we asked:

"What factors are most important in determining interest rates?"

We have seen in this chapter that long-term nominal interest rates are determined by the interaction of the demand and supply for bonds. Investors increase or decrease their demand for bonds as a result of changes in a number of factors. In particular, when expected inflation increases, investors reduce their demand for bonds because, for each nominal interest rate, the higher the inflation rate, the lower the real interest rate investors will receive. Increases in expected inflation lead to higher nominal interest rates and capital losses for investors who hold bonds in their portfolios. The supply of bonds also depends on the expected inflation rate, as well as the expected profitability of physical capital investments, the extent of government borrowing, and other factors.

Key Terms and Problems

Key Terms

Diversification, p. 99

Expected return, p. 94

Fisher effect, p. 113

Idiosyncratic (or unsystematic) risk, p. 100

Market (or systematic) risk, p. 99

Money market model, p. 118

Risk, p. 95

 4.1   How to Build an Investment Portfolio

Discuss the most important factors in building an investment portfolio.

Review Questions

1.1 What are the determinants of asset demand?

1.2 How do economists define expected return and risk? Are investors typically risk averse or risk loving? Briefly explain.

1.3 In what sense do investors face a trade-off between risk and return?

1.4 What is the difference between market risk and idiosyncratic risk? How does diversification reduce the risk of a financial portfolio?

Problems and Applications

1.5 A financial planner writing in the *New York Times* gave the following sarcastic investment advice: "On Jan. 1 of each year, just figure out which asset class will do really well and move all your money into that investment."

a. What does the financial planner mean by "asset class"?

b. Why isn't this advice something an investor should actually follow? What would an investor be better off doing instead?

Source: Carl Richards, "Diversification Is the Sane Alternative to Betting Big on One Investment," *New York Times*, March 16, 2015.

1.6 [Related to the Making the Connection on page 97]

The following is from a column on marketwatch.com: "There are lots of things we more or less know will happen…. But what are the potential black swans?"

a. What does the columnist mean by a "black swan"?

b. Is it likely that there is a good answer to the columnist's question? Briefly explain.

Source: Matthew Lynn, "5 Black Swans That Could Rock Markets in 2016," marketwatch.com, January 4, 2016.

1.7 [Related to the Making the Connection on page 100]

A report on 401(k) plans notes: "Younger participants tended to favor equity funds … while older participants were more likely to invest in fixed-income securities such as bond funds."

a. What are 401(k) plans?

b. What does the report mean by "equity funds"? Why might younger investors be more likely to invest in equity funds while older investors are more likely to invest in bond funds?

Source: Jack VanDerhei, Sarah Holden, Luis Alonso, and Steven Bass, Employee Benefit Research Institute, *Issue Brief*, No. 423, April 2016.

4.2 Market Interest Rates and the Demand and Supply for Bonds

Use a demand and supply model to determine market interest rates for bonds.

Review Questions

2.1 Why might the demand curve for bonds shift to the left? Why might the supply curve for bonds shift to the right?

2.2 Why does the supply curve for bonds slope up? Why does the demand curve for bonds slope down?

2.3 If the current price in the bond market is above the equilibrium price, explain how the bond market adjusts to equilibrium.

Problems and Applications

2.4 Briefly explain whether each of the following statements is true or false:

a. The higher the price of bonds, the greater the quantity of bonds demanded.

b. The lower the price of bonds, the smaller the quantity of bonds supplied.

c. As the wealth of investors increases, all else held constant, the interest rate on bonds should fall.

d. If investors start to believe that the U.S. government might default on its bonds, all else held constant, the interest rate on those bonds will fall.

2.5 For each of the following situations, explain whether the demand curve for bonds, the supply curve for bonds, or both would shift. Be sure to indicate whether the curve(s) would shift to the right or to the left.

a. The Federal Reserve publishes a forecast that the inflation rate will average 5% over the next five years. Previously, the Fed had been forecasting an inflation rate of 3%.

b. The economy experiences a period of rapid growth, with rising corporate profits.

c. The federal government runs a series of budget surpluses.

d. Investors believe that the level of risk in the stock market has declined.

e. The federal government imposes a tax of $10 per bond on bond sales and bond purchases.

2.6 Use a demand and supply graph for bonds to illustrate each of the following situations. Be sure that your graph shows any shifts in the demand or supply curves, the original equilibrium price and quantity, and the new equilibrium price and quantity. Also be sure to explain what is happening in your graphs.

a. The government runs a large deficit, holding everything else constant.

b. Households believe that future tax payments will be higher than current tax payments, so they increase their saving.

c. Both (a) and (b) occur.

2.7 Some economists argue that a boom in stock prices is a sign that profitable business opportunities are expected in the future. Use a demand and supply graph for bonds to show the effect of a boom in stock prices on the equilibrium interest rate.

4.3 Explaining Changes in Interest Rates

Use the bond market model to explain changes in interest rates.

Review Questions

3.1 Briefly explain what typically happens to interest rates during a recession. Use a demand and supply graph for bonds to illustrate your answer.

3.2 How will the bond market adjust to an increase in the expected inflation rate? Use a demand and supply graph for bonds to illustrate your answer.

Problems and Applications

3.3 Explain what will happen to the equilibrium price and equilibrium quantity of bonds in each of the following situations. (If it is uncertain in which direction either the equilibrium price or equilibrium quantity will change, explain why.)

a. Wealth in the economy increases at the same time that Congress raises the corporate income tax.

b. The economy experiences a business cycle expansion.

c. The expected rate of inflation decreases.

d. The federal government runs a budget deficit.

3.4 According to an article in the *Economist* about interest rates on European government bonds in 2016, investors were concerned that "European equities are almost 20% below their levels of a year ago; commodities have plunged in price; the default rates on corporate bonds are rising."

a. Would the factors listed in the article be expected to affect the demand or the supply for European government bonds? Briefly explain.

b. Holding other factors that affect the market for European bonds constant, would the result you identified in part (a) be likely to cause the interest rate on European government bonds to increase or to decrease? Use a demand and supply graph for the market for European government bonds to illustrate your answer.

Source: "Why Investors Buy Bonds with Negative Yields," *Economist*, February 9, 2016.

3.5 [Related to the Making the Connection on page 114] An article in the *Wall Street Journal* begins: "Yields on the 10-year government debt of Germany and the U.K. fell to all-time lows, a stark demonstration of the modern era of scant inflation, weak growth and outsize monetary policy." Discuss the effect on the equilibrium interest rate in the bond market of each of the three factors the article lists. Illustrate your answer with a graph of the bond market. Make

sure your graph shows any shifts in the demand curve or supply curve for bonds as a result of these factors and any change in the equilibrium price of bonds.

Source: Jon Sindreu, "Rock-Bottom Bond Yields in Europe Hit All-Time Lows," *Wall Street Journal*, June 8, 2016.

3.6 [Related to the Solved Problem 4.3 on page 116] According to an article in the *Wall Street Journal* in early 2016:

U.S. government bonds maturing in more than 25 years returned a negative 1.2% in the month through Thursday ... after chalking up a 8.7% gain between January and March.... The reversal reflects a shift in financial markets' preoccupation from the prospect of a recession to the risk of higher inflation.

a. Why would bond prices fall if investors believe that inflation will be higher than they had previously expected? Illustrate your answer with a graph showing demand and supply for bonds.

b. In this situation, would bonds that mature in 25 years be likely to have experienced larger or smaller price declines than bonds that mature in two years? Briefly explain.

Source: Min Zeng, "It Didn't Pay to Bet Against Inflation in April," *Wall Street Journal*, April 29, 2016.

3.7 [Related to the Chapter Opener on page 92] According to an article in the *Economist*, in Germany 80% of household wealth is in the form of bank deposits, as opposed to only 20% in the United States. The article notes: "If German ... savers are vulnerable to low rates, it is partly due to their own investment habits."

a. Would German savers be more vulnerable to low interest rates than U.S. savers? Briefly explain.

b. The article notes that "low rates ... are intended to encourage spending, not saving." Why would central bank policymakers focus more on encouraging spending than on encouraging saving?

Source: "Mario Battles the Wutsparer," *Economist*, April 30, 2016.

Interest Rates and the Money Market Model

4.4 Explain how interest rates are determined using the money market model.

Review Questions

4.1 Why is the demand for money curve downward sloping?

4.2 Draw a money demand and supply graph that shows how the Federal Reserve can decrease the short-run nominal interest rate.

Problems and Applications

4.3 Draw a graph of the money market. Show the effect on the money demand curve, the money supply curve, and the equilibrium short-term nominal interest rate of each of the following:

a. The Fed decreases the money supply.

b. A recession causes real GDP to fall.

c. The price level increases.

d. The Fed increases the money supply at the same time that the price level falls.

4.4 Suppose that the inflation rate increases, and the Federal Reserve responds by taking actions to raise the short-term nominal interest rate. Use a money market graph to show the result of the Fed's actions. Be sure to label any shifts in the money demand or money supply curve and any change in the equilibrium interest rate.

Data Exercises

D4.1: [The bond market and recessions] Go to the web site of the Federal Reserve Bank of St. Louis (FRED) (fred.stlouisfed.org) and download and graph the data series for the 10-year U.S. Treasury note (GS10) from January 1954 until the most recent month available. Go to the web site of the National Bureau of Economic Research (nber.org) and find the dates for business cycle peaks and troughs. (The period between a business cycle peak and trough is a recession.) Describe how the interest rate on the 10-year note moves just before, during, and just after a recession. Is the pattern the same across recessions?

D4.2: [Comparing movements in interest rates across countries] Go to the web site of the Federal Reserve Bank of St. Louis (FRED) (fred.stlouisfed.org) and download to the same graph the following data series from January 1957 until the most recent available month: (1) the interest rate on the

20-year U.S. Treasury note (GS20) and (2) the interest rate for 20-year UK government securities (INTGSBGBM193N). During which periods has the interest rate on long-term UK government bonds been higher than the interest rate on long-term U.S. government bonds? What has been the relationship between the two interest rates since 1995?

D4.3: [Find data on expected inflation from bond yields] Go to the web site of the Federal Reserve Bank of St. Louis (FRED) (fred.stlouisfed.org) and find the most recent values and values from the same month five years earlier for the 10-Year Treasury Constant Maturity Rate (GS10), and the 10-Year Treasury Inflation-Indexed Security, Constant Maturity (FII10). Using these data, explain what has happened to expected inflation between these two periods.

APPENDIX

The Loanable Funds Model and the International Capital Market

Learning Objective

4.A Use the loanable funds model to determine the interest rate in the international capital market.

In this chapter, we analyzed the bond market from the point of view of the demand and supply for bonds. An equivalent approach focuses on *loanable funds*. In this approach, the borrower is the buyer because the borrower purchases the use of the funds. The lender is the seller because the lender provides the funds being borrowed. Although the two approaches are equivalent, the loanable funds approach is more useful when looking at the flow of funds between the United States and foreign financial markets. Table 4A.1 summarizes the two views of the bond market.

The Demand and Supply for Loanable Funds

Figure 4A.1 shows that the demand curve for bonds is equivalent to the supply curve for loanable funds. In the figure, we consider again the case of a one-year discount bond with a face value of $1,000. In panel (a), we show the demand curve for bonds, which is the same as the one we showed in Figure 4.1 on page 103 (although we have

TABLE 4A.1 Two Approaches to Analyzing the Bond Market

	Demand and supply for bonds approach	Demand and supply for loanable funds approach
What is the good?	The bond	The use of funds
Who is the buyer?	The investor (lender) who buys a bond	The firm (borrower) raising funds
Who is the seller?	The firm (borrower) who issues a bond	The investor (lender) supplying funds
What is the price?	The bond price	The interest rate

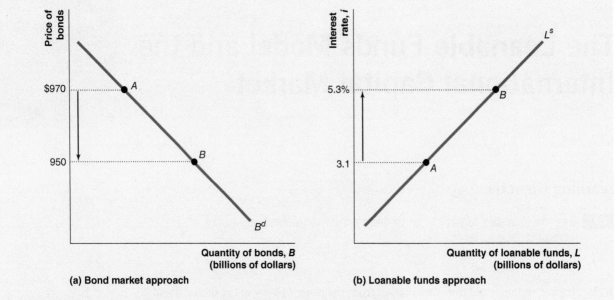

FIGURE 4A.1 The Demand for Bonds and the Supply of Loanable Funds

In panel (a), the bond demand curve, B^d, shows a negative relationship between the quantity of bonds demanded by lenders and the price of bonds, all else being equal.

In panel (b), the supply curve for loanable funds, L^S, shows a positive relationship between the quantity of loanable funds supplied by lenders and the interest rate, all else being equal.

labeled it B^d rather than Demand), with the price of bonds on the vertical axis and the quantity of bonds on the horizontal axis. In panel (b), we show the supply curve for loanable funds, with the interest rate on the vertical axis and the quantity of loanable funds on the horizontal axis. Suppose in panel (a) that the price of the bond is initially $970, which corresponds to point A on the demand curve for bonds. At that price, the bond will have an interest rate equal to ($1,000 − $970)/$970 = 0.031, or 3.1%, which we show as point A on the supply curve for loanable funds. Now suppose that the price of the bond declines to $950, which we show as point B on the demand curve for bonds. At this lower price, the bond will have a higher interest rate, equal to ($1,000 − $950)/$950 = 0.053, or 5.3%, which we show as point B on the supply curve for loanable funds. From the viewpoint of investors purchasing bonds—the bond market approach—the lower price increases the quantity of bonds demanded. Equivalently, from the viewpoint of investors providing loanable funds to borrowers—the loanable funds approach—the higher interest rate increases the quantity of loanable funds supplied.

Figure 4A.2 shows that the supply curve for bonds is equivalent to the demand curve for loanable funds. In panel (a), we show the supply curve for bonds. In panel (b),

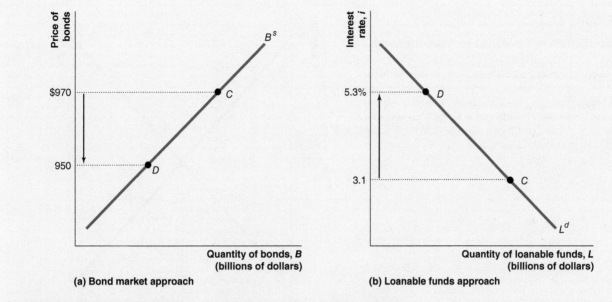

FIGURE 4A.2 The Supply of Bonds and the Demand for Loanable Funds

In panel (a), the bond supply curve, B^S, shows a positive relationship between the quantity of bonds supplied by borrowers and the price of bonds, all else being equal.

In panel (b), the demand curve for loanable funds, L^d, shows a negative relationship between the quantity of loanable funds demanded by borrowers and the interest rate, all else being equal.

we show the demand curve for loanable funds. Suppose in panel (a) that, once again, the price of the bond is initially $970, which corresponds to point C on the supply curve for bonds. At that price, we know that the bond will have an interest rate equal to 3.1%, which we show as point C on the demand curve for loanable funds. Now suppose that the price of the bond declines to $950, which we show as point D on the supply curve for bonds. At this lower price, the bond will have a higher interest rate, equal to 5.3%, which we show as point D on the demand curve for loanable funds. From the viewpoint of firms selling bonds—the bond market approach—the lower price decreases the quantity of bonds supplied. Equivalently, from the viewpoint of firms demanding loanable funds from borrowers—the loanable funds approach—the higher interest rate decreases the quantity of loanable funds demanded.

Equilibrium in the Bond Market from the Loanable Funds Perspective

Figure 4A.3 shows equilibrium in the bond market using the loanable funds approach. Equilibrium occurs when the quantity of loanable funds demanded is equal to the quantity of loanable funds supplied. In the figure, we assume that the funds

FIGURE 4A.3

Equilibrium in the Market for Loanable Funds

At the equilibrium interest rate, the quantity of loanable funds supplied by lenders equals the quantity of loanable funds demanded by borrowers. At any interest rate below the equilibrium, there is an excess demand for loanable funds. At any interest rate above equilibrium, there is an excess supply of loanable funds. The behavior of lenders and borrowers pushes the interest rate to 4.2%.

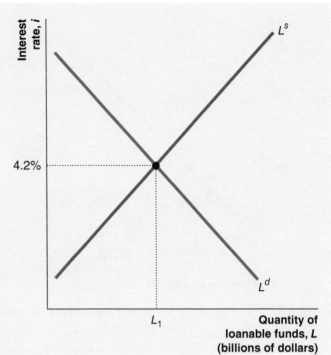

being traded are represented by a one-year discount bond with a face value of $1,000. The equilibrium interest rate is 4.2%, which is the interest rate on a one-year $1,000 bond with a price of $960. Notice that this analysis gives us the same interest rate as in Figure 4.1 on page 103, which reminds us that the demand and supply for bonds model and the demand and supply for loanable funds model are equivalent approaches.

Note that any of the factors that we listed on page 104 as causing the demand curve for bonds to shift will cause the supply curve for loanable funds to shift. Similarly, any of the factors that we listed on page 108 as causing the supply curve for bonds to shift will cause the demand curve for loanable funds to shift.

The International Capital Market and the Interest Rate

We have not directly taken into account how the foreign sector influences the domestic interest rate and the quantity of funds available in the domestic economy. In fact, foreign households, firms, and governments may want to lend funds to borrowers in the United States if the expected returns are higher than in other countries. Similarly, if opportunities are more profitable outside the United States, loanable funds will be drawn away from U.S. markets to investments abroad. The loanable funds approach provides a good framework for analyzing the interaction between U.S. and foreign bond markets. To keep matters simple, we assume that the interest rate is the expected real rate of interest—that is, the nominal interest rate minus the expected rate of inflation.

In a **closed economy**, households, firms, and governments do not borrow or lend internationally. In reality, nearly all economies are **open economies**, in which *financial capital* (or loanable funds) is internationally mobile. Borrowing and lending take place in the *international capital market*, which is the capital market in which households, firms, and governments borrow and lend across national borders. The *world real interest rate*, r_w, is the interest rate that is determined in the international capital market. The quantity of loanable funds that is supplied in an open economy can be used to fund projects in the domestic economy or abroad. Decisions about the supply of or demand for loanable funds in small open economies, such as the economies of the Netherlands and Belgium, do not have much effect on the world real interest rate. However, shifts in the behavior of lenders and borrowers in large open economies, such as the economies of Germany and the United States, do affect the world real interest rate. In the following sections, we consider interest rate determination in each case.

Small Open Economy

To this point, we have been implicitly assuming that we were analyzing a closed economy. In this type of economy, the equilibrium domestic interest rate is determined by the intersection of the demand curve and supply curve for loanable funds in the country, and we ignore the world interest rate. In an open economy, the world real interest rate is not determined by the intersection of the demand curve and supply curve of loanable funds in any one country; instead, it is determined in the international capital market. In the case of a **small open economy**, the quantity of loanable funds supplied or demanded is too small to affect the world real interest rate. So, a small open economy's domestic real interest rate equals the world real interest rate, as determined in the international capital market. For example, if the small country of Monaco, located on the Mediterranean coast to the south of France, had a large increase in domestic wealth, the resulting increase in loanable funds would have only a trivial effect on the total amount of loanable funds in the world and, therefore, a trivial effect on the world interest rate.

Why must the domestic interest rate in a small open economy equal the world interest rate? Suppose that the world real interest rate is 4%, but the domestic real interest rate in Monaco is 3%. A lender in Monaco would not accept an interest rate less than 4% because the lender could easily buy foreign bonds with a 4% interest rate. So, domestic borrowers would have to pay the world real interest rate of 4%, or they would be unable to borrow. Similarly, if the world real interest rate were 4%, but the domestic real interest

Closed economy An economy in which households, firms, and governments do not borrow or lend internationally.

Open economy An economy in which households, firms, and governments borrow and lend internationally.

Small open economy An economy in which the quantity of loanable funds supplied or demanded is too small to affect the world real interest rate.

rate in Monaco were 5%, borrowers in Monaco would borrow at the world rate of 4%. So, domestic lenders would have to lend at the world rate of 4%, or they would be unable to find anyone to lend to. This reasoning indicates why, for a small open economy, the domestic and world real interest rates must be the same.

Figure 4A.4 shows the supply and demand curves for loanable funds for a small open economy. If the world real interest rate, (r_w), is 3%, the quantity of loanable funds supplied and demanded domestically are equal (point E), and the country neither lends nor borrows funds in the international capital market. Suppose instead that the world real interest rate is 5%. In this case, the quantity of loanable funds supplied domestically (point C) is greater than the quantity of funds demanded domestically (point B). What happens to the excess supply of loanable funds? They are loaned on the international capital market at the world real interest rate of 5%. Because the country is small, the amount of funds it has to lend is small relative to the world market, so lenders in the country have no trouble finding borrowers in other countries.

Now suppose that the world real interest rate is 1%. As Figure 4A.4 shows, the quantity of loanable funds demanded domestically (point A) now exceeds the quantity of funds supplied domestically (point D). How is this excess demand for funds satisfied? By borrowing on the international capital market. Because the country is

FIGURE 4A.4

Determining the Real Interest Rate in a Small Open Economy

The domestic real interest rate in a small open economy is the world real interest rate, (r_w), which in this case is 3%.

If the world real interest rate is 5%, the quantity of loanable funds supplied domestically (point C) is greater than the quantity of loanable funds demanded domestically (point B). In this case, the country lends funds on the international capital market.

If the world real interest rate is 1%, the quantity of loanable funds supplied domestically (point D) is less than the quantity of loanable funds demanded domestically (point A). In this case, the country borrows funds on the international capital market.

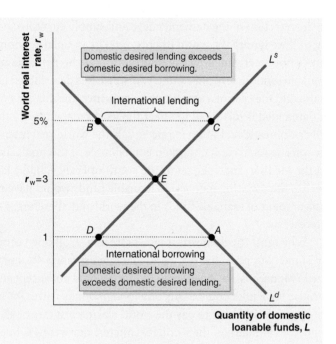

small, the amount of funds it wants to borrow is small relative to the world market, so borrowers in the country have no trouble finding lenders in other countries.

We can summarize as follows: The real interest rate in a small open economy is the same as the interest rate in the international capital market. If the quantity of loanable funds supplied domestically exceeds the quantity of funds demanded domestically at that interest rate, the country invests some of its loanable funds abroad. If the quantity of loanable funds demanded domestically exceeds the quantity of funds supplied domestically at that interest rate, the country finances some of its domestic borrowing needs with funds from abroad.

Large Open Economy

Changes in the demand and supply of loanable funds in many countries—such as the United States, Japan, and Germany—are sufficiently large that they *do* affect the world real interest rate—the interest rate in the international capital market. Such countries are considered **large open economies**, which are economies large enough to affect the world real interest rate.

Large open economy An economy in which changes in the demand and supply for loanable funds are large enough to affect the world real interest rate.

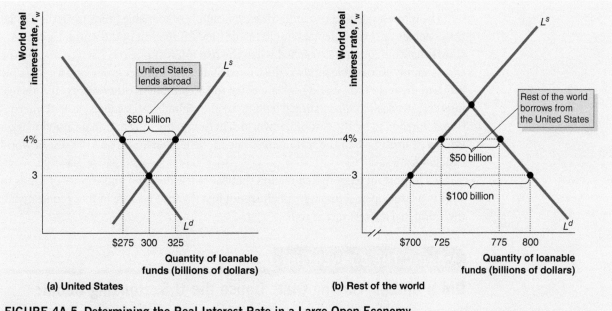

(a) United States

(b) Rest of the world

FIGURE 4A.5 Determining the Real Interest Rate in a Large Open Economy

Saving and investment shifts in a large open economy can affect the world real interest rate. The world real interest rate adjusts to equalize desired international borrowing and desired international lending. At a world real interest rate of 4%, desired international lending by the domestic economy in panel (a) equals desired international borrowing by the rest of the world in panel (b).

In the case of a large open economy, we cannot assume that the domestic real interest rate is equal to the world real interest rate. Recall that in a closed economy, the equilibrium interest rate equates the quantities of loanable funds supplied and demanded. Suppose we think of the world as two large open economies—the economy of the United States and the economy of the rest of the world. Then the real interest rate in the international capital market equates desired international lending (borrowing) by the United States with desired international borrowing (lending) by the rest of the world.

Figure 4A.5 illustrates how interest rates are determined in a large open economy. The figure presents a loanable funds graph for the United States in panel (a) and a loanable funds graph for the rest of the world in panel (b). In panel (a), if the world real interest rate is 3%, the quantity of loanable funds demanded and supplied in the United States are both equal to $300 billion. However, we can see in panel (b) that at an interest rate of 3%, the quantity of loanable funds demanded in the rest of the world is $800 billion, while the quantity of loanable funds supplied is only $700 billion. This gap tells us that foreign borrowers want to borrow $100 billion more from international capital markets than is available. Foreign borrowers therefore have an incentive to offer lenders in the United States and in the rest of the world an interest rate greater than 3%.

The interest rate will rise until the excess supply of loanable funds from the United States equals the excess demand for loanable funds in the rest of the world. Figure 4A.5 shows that this equality is reached when the real interest rate has risen to 4% and the excess supply of loanable funds in the United States and the excess demand for loanable funds in the rest of the world both are equal to $50 billion. In other words, at a 4% real interest rate, desired international lending by the United States equals desired international borrowing by the rest of the world. Therefore, the international capital market is in equilibrium when the real interest rate in the United States and the rest of world equals 4%.

It's important to note that factors that cause the demand and supply of funds to shift in a large open economy will affect not just the interest rate in that economy but the world real interest rate as well.

| **MAKING THE CONNECTION** |

Did a Global "Saving Glut" Cause the U.S. Housing Boom?

We saw in Chapter 1 that the financial crisis of 2007–2009 was brought on by the bursting of a "bubble" in housing prices. One cause of the bubble was the increase in mortgage loans to borrowers with poor credit histories who prior to the 2000s would not have qualified for mortgage loans. Some economists have argued that unusually low interest rates on mortgage loans also played a role in the rapid increase in housing prices

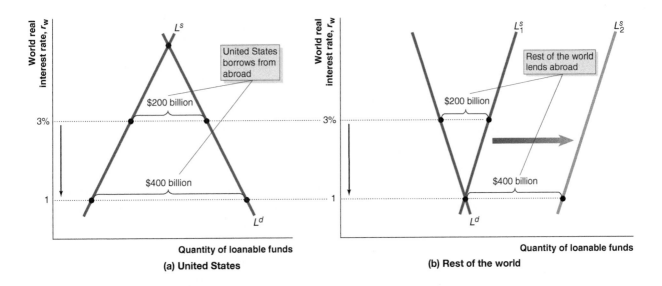

(a) United States

(b) Rest of the world

during the mid-2000s. Low interest rates increased the quantity of houses demanded, and, in particular, made it easier for investors who were speculating on future increases in house prices to buy multiple houses.

What explains the low interest rates during the 2000s? To help the U.S. economy recover from the 2001 recession, the Federal Reserve reduced interest rates and kept them at very low levels through mid-2004. Some economists have argued that the Fed persisted in a low-interest-rate policy for too long a period, thereby fueling the housing boom. Former Federal Reserve Chairman Ben Bernanke has disagreed, arguing that global factors, rather than Fed policy, were most responsible for low interest rates during the early 2000s. In 2005, near the height of the housing bubble, Bernanke, who was then serving on the Fed's Board of Governors, argued that "a significant increase in the global supply of saving—a global saving glut … helps to explain … the relatively low level of long-term interest rates in the world today." Bernanke argued that the saving glut was partly the result of high rates of saving in countries such as Japan, which had aging populations that increased their saving as they prepared for retirement. In addition, the level of global saving increased because beginning in the late 1990s, developing countries such as China and Korea increased their saving rates.

The following figure illustrates Bernanke's argument by using the loanable funds model for a large open economy. We start at equilibrium with the world real interest rate equal to 3%. In panel (a), at an interest rate of 3%, the United States is borrowing $200 billion from abroad. If the United States is borrowing $200 billion, then the rest of the world must be lending $200 billion, which is shown in panel (b). An increase in saving in the rest of the world—Bernanke's saving glut—shifts the supply curve of loanable funds to the right in panel (b). The real world interest rate begins to fall as the quantity of loanable funds that lenders in the rest of the world are willing to lend exceeds the quantity of loanable funds that borrowers in the United States are willing to borrow. The falling interest rate increases the quantity of funds demanded in the United States and decreases the quantity of funds supplied by the rest of the world. The real world interest rate declines to 1%, at which level the quantity of funds the United States borrows from abroad—$400 billion—once again equals the quantity of funds the rest of the world wishes to lend, and the international capital market is back in equilibrium.

Some economists, notably John Taylor of Stanford University, have been skeptical of the argument that there was a significant increase in global saving during the 2000s. Taylor argues that Federal Reserve policy, rather than a global saving glut, fueled the housing bubble in the United States.

Sources: Ben S. Bernanke, "The Global Saving Glut and the U.S. Current Account Deficit," Homer Jones Lecture, April 14, 2005 (available at www.federalreserve.gov/boarddocs/speeches/2005/20050414/default.htm); and John B. Taylor, *Getting Off Track*, Stanford, CA: Hoover Institution Press, 2009.

See related problem 4A.8 at the end of the appendix.

Key Terms and Problems

Key Terms

Closed economy, p. 131
Large open economy, p. 133

Open economy, p. 131
Small open economy, p. 132

4.A ### The Loanable Funds Model and the International Capital Market
Use the loanable funds model to determine the interest rate in the international capital market.

Review Questions

4A.1 Compare the bond market approach to the loanable funds approach by explaining the following for each approach:

a. What the good is

b. Who the buyer is

c. Who the seller is

d. What the price is

4A.2 In the loanable funds model, why is the demand curve downward sloping? Why is the supply curve upward sloping?

4A.3 When are economists most likely to use the bond market approach to analyze changes in interest rates? When are economists most likely to use the loanable funds approach?

Problems and Applications

4A.4 The federal government in the United States has been running large budget deficits.

  a. Use the loanable funds approach to show the effect of the U.S. budget deficit on the world real interest rate, holding everything else constant.

  b. Now suppose that households believe that deficits will be financed by higher taxes in the near future, and households increase their saving in anticipation of paying those higher taxes. Briefly explain how your analysis in part (a) will be affected.

4A.5 Suppose that in a large open economy, the quantity of loanable funds supplied domestically is initially equal to the quantity of funds demanded domestically. Then suppose that an increase in business taxes discourages investment. Show how this change affects the quantity of loanable funds and the world real interest rate. Does the economy now borrow or lend internationally?

4A.6 In a large open economy, how would each of the following events affect the equilibrium interest rate?

  a. A natural disaster causes extensive damage to homes, bridges, and highways, leading to increased investment spending to repair the damaged infrastructure.

  b. Households and firms expect that the government will increase taxes on businesses in the future.

  c. The World Cup soccer matches are being televised, and many people stay home to watch them rather than spending time shopping, thereby reducing consumption.

  d. The government proposes a new tax on saving, based on the value of people's investments as of December 31 each year.

4A.7 How would the following events affect the demand for loanable funds in the United States?

  a. Many U.S. cities increase business taxes to help close their budget deficits.

  b. Widespread use of tablet computers helps reduce business costs.

  c. The government eliminates the tax deduction for interest that homeowners pay on mortgage loans.

4A.8 [Related to the Making the Connection on page 135] We saw that former Federal Reserve Chairman Ben Bernanke argued that low interest rates in the United States during the mid-2000s were due to a global savings glut rather than to Federal Reserve policy. In an interview with Albert Hunt of Bloomberg Television, Alan Greenspan, who was Federal Reserve Chairman from August 1987 through January 2006, made the following similar argument:

> Behind the low level of long-term rates: a global savings glut as China, Russia and other emerging market economies earned more money on exports than they could easily invest.

  a. Use two loanable funds graphs to illustrate Greenspan's argument that a global savings glut caused low interest rates in the United States. One graph should illustrate the situation in the United States, and the other graph should illustrate the situation in the rest of the world.

  b. Why should Alan Greenspan care about a debate over the causes of low interest rates?

  Source: Rich Miller and Josh Zumbrun, "Greenspan Takes Issue with Yellen on Fed's Role in House Bubble," bloomberg.com, March 27, 2010.

Data Exercises

D4A.1: [Analyzing saving and investment] Go to the web site of the Federal Reserve Bank of St. Louis (FRED) (fred.stlouisfed.org) and find the most recent value and the value from the same quarter four years earlier for Gross Government Saving (GGSAVE).

   a. Total gross saving in the economy is composed of gross private saving and gross government saving. What does gross government saving represent?

   b. Using the values you found, explain whether the government budget was balanced, in a surplus, or in a deficit during these two quarters. From the first period to the most recent period, has government saving increased, decreased, or remained constant?

   c. Draw a graph to show the loanable funds market in equilibrium. Assuming gross private saving remains constant and given your answer in part (b), show the effect on the loanable funds market. Explain what will happen to the level of investment in the economy.

CHAPTER 5

The Risk Structure and Term Structure of Interest Rates

Learning Objectives

After studying this chapter, you should be able to:

5.1 Explain why bonds with the same maturity can have different interest rates (pages 140–152)

5.2 Explain why bonds with different maturities can have different interest rates (pages 152–167)

The Long and the Short of Interest Rates

In mid-2016, you could earn an interest rate of only 0.25% by buying a 3-month Treasury bill but a higher interest rate of 2.6% by buying a 30-year Treasury bond. It makes sense that the bond market rewards you with a higher interest rate for lending funds to the Treasury for 30 years rather than for just 3 months. But over the past 40 years, there have been many times when the gap between the interest rates on 3-month Treasury bills and on 30-year Treasury bonds has been much higher than it was in 2016. During a few other periods, the gap was actually negative: You could have earned a *higher* interest rate on a 3-month Treasury bill than on a 30-year Treasury bond. But why would an investor take that deal—receive less for lending money for 30 years than for lending it for 3 months?

In mid-2016, you could earn an interest rate of 2.5% on a corporate bond issued by the Aflac insurance company that matures in 2024. But you could earn an

interest rate of 10.2% on a corporate bond that matures the same year issued by AMD, the California semiconductor company. Why buy a bond with an interest rate of only 2.5% when you could earn an interest rate that is four times higher on another bond with the same maturity? As we will see in this chapter, one reason that some firms have to offer higher interest rates on their bonds is that the firms have a high risk of default—or failing to repay the interest and principal on the bond. Firms with a low risk of default can offer bonds with lower interest rates. Investors typically rely on private *bond rating agencies* when judging the default risk on bonds. But the firms that issue bonds pay the rating agencies for the ratings. Does this fact indicate that rating agencies have a conflict of interest and their ratings are unreliable?

Why are there so many different interest rates in the economy? The answer to this question is

Continued on next page

KEY ISSUE AND QUESTION

Issue: Some economists and policymakers believe that bond rating agencies have a conflict of interest because they are paid by the firms whose bonds they are rating.

Question: Should the government more closely regulate the bond rating agencies?

Answered on page 167

important to several groups. First, savers might be considering whether to buy a short-term Treasury bill, a long-term Treasury bond, or a corporate bond issued by a particular firm or to simply put their funds in a bank certificate of deposit (CD). Second, managers of firms track interest rates as they consider how much they will have to pay to borrow funds by selling bonds. Managers at firms like Aflac that can borrow at low interest rates can finance physical capital projects or research and development efforts that would be too costly for firms like AMD that have to borrow at much higher interest rates. Similarly, policymakers in federal, state, and local governments know that the interest rates they pay to borrow funds can have a substantial effect on their budgets. Finally, policymakers at the Federal Reserve have a very strong stake in determining which interest rates will be most affected by their actions and by how much those interest rates may increase or decrease.

Understanding the relationship among interest rates on bonds of different maturities—such as Treasury bills and Treasury bonds—and the relationship among interest rates on bonds issued by different corporations is one of the keys to understanding how the financial system works and how monetary policy affects the economy. We devote this chapter to exploring the relationships among the many different interest rates in the economy.

Sources: Data from Federal Reserve Bank of St. Louis and Financial Industry Regulatory Authority.

To this point, we have simplified our discussion of the bond market by assuming that there is a single type of bond and a single interest rate, and that the market for that bond determined the interest rate. That simplification was useful because it allowed us to analyze the factors that affect the demand and supply for all bonds. In this chapter, we look more closely at the bond market by analyzing why interest rates on bonds differ and what causes interest rates to change over time.

We look first at the *risk structure of interest rates*, which explains differences in yields across bonds with the same maturity. Then we turn to the *term structure of interest rates*, which explains why bond yields vary according to their time to maturity. Economists use both types of analyses to forecast future movements in the yields on individual bonds as well as broader movements in interest rates.

5.1 The Risk Structure of Interest Rates

LEARNING OBJECTIVE: Explain why bonds with the same maturity can have different interest rates.

Why might bonds that have the same maturities—for example, all the bonds that will mature in 30 years—have different interest rates, or yields to maturity?

The answer is that bonds that have the same maturity may differ with respect to other characteristics that investors believe are important, such as risk, liquidity, information costs, and taxation. Bonds with more favorable characteristics have lower interest rates because investors are willing to accept lower expected returns on those bonds. Similarly, bonds with less favorable characteristics have higher interest rates because investors require higher expected returns on those bonds. Economists use the term **risk structure of interest rates** to describe the relationship among the interest rates on bonds that have different characteristics but the same maturity.

Risk structure of interest rates The relationship among interest rates on bonds that have different characteristics but the same maturity.

Default Risk

Bonds differ with respect to **default risk** (sometimes called **credit risk**), which is the risk that a bond issuer will fail to make payments of interest or principal. To see the effect of default risk, let's use the example from the beginning of the chapter involving Aflac and AMD. If both companies issue bonds that have the same maturity, but investors believe that AMD has a higher default risk, the AMD bond will have a higher interest rate than the Aflac bond.

Measuring Default Risk U.S. Treasury bonds are considered to have *zero* default risk because the U.S. government guarantees that it will make all principal and interest payments. Investors therefore use U.S. Treasury bonds as a benchmark to determine the default risk on a bond. Of course, like all other bonds, U.S. Treasury bonds are subject to interest-rate risk.

The *default risk premium* on a bond is the difference between the interest rate on the bond and the interest rate on a Treasury bond that has the same maturity. We can think of the default risk premium as being the additional yield that an investor requires for holding a bond with some default risk. For example, if you were willing to buy a 30-year Treasury bond with an interest rate of 3%, but you would buy a 30-year bond issued by IBM only if it had an interest rate of 5% because the IBM bond carries some default risk, the default risk premium on the IBM bond is 5% − 3% = 2%.

The greater the probability that a bond's issuer will fail to make the payments on a bond, the higher the default risk premium investors will require. The cost of acquiring information on a bond issuer's *creditworthiness*, or ability to repay, can be high. As a result, many investors rely on *credit rating agencies*—such as Moody's Investors Service, Standard & Poor's Corporation, or Fitch Ratings—to provide them with information on the creditworthiness of corporations and governments that issue bonds. A **bond rating** is a single statistic that summarizes a rating agency's view of the issuer's likely ability to make the required payments on its bonds.

Table 5.1 shows the ratings of the three largest credit rating agencies. The higher the rating, the lower the default risk. (Although the capitalization practice differs among the agencies, they all rate bonds with the lowest default risk as "triple A.") Bonds receiving one of the top four ratings are considered to be "investment grade," which means they have low to moderate levels of default risk. Bonds receiving one of the lower ratings (such as B) are called "non-investment grade," "speculative," "high yield," or "junk bonds." These bonds have high levels of default risk. The rating agencies make their ratings publicly available and update them as the creditworthiness of issuers changes. For example, in 2016, Standard & Poor's (S&P) cut its rating on Exxon Mobil, the world's largest non-government oil company, because of falling oil prices.

Note that the rating agencies are offering *opinions*. Investors in financial markets may disagree with these opinions. A difference of opinion was evident in 2011, when S&P cut its rating on long-term U.S. government debt from AAA to AA+ because it believed that if the federal government continued to run large budget deficits, the government's ability to continue to make the interest and principal payments might be affected. However, most investors did not seem any more worried about default risk on U.S. Treasury bonds after S&P lowered its rating than they had been before.

Default risk (or **credit risk**) The risk that a bond issuer will fail to make payments of interest or principal.

Bond rating A single statistic that summarizes a rating agency's view of the issuer's likely ability to make the required payments on its bonds.

TABLE 5.1 Interpreting Bond Ratings

	Moody's Investors Service	Standard & Poor's (S&P)	Fitch Ratings	Meaning of the ratings
Investment-grade bonds	Aaa	AAA	AAA	Highest credit quality
	Aa	AA	AA	Very high credit quality
	A	A	A	High credit quality
	Baa	BBB	BBB	Good credit quality
Non-investment-grade bonds	Ba	BB	BB	Speculative
	B	B	B	Highly speculative
	Caa	CCC	CCC	Substantial default risk
	Ca	CC	CC	Very high levels of default risk
	C	C	C	Exceptionally high levels of default risk (for Moody's: "typically in default")
	—	D	D	Default

Note: The entries in the "Meaning of the ratings" column are slightly modified from those that Fitch uses. The other two rating agencies have similar descriptions. For each rating from Aa to Caa, Moody's adds a numerical modifier of 1, 2, or 3. The rating Aa1 is higher than the rating Aa2, and the rating Aa2 is higher than the rating Aa3. Similarly, Standard & Poor's and Fitch Ratings add a plus (+) or minus (−) sign. The rating AA + is higher than the rating AA, and the rating AA is higher than the rating AA − .

Sources: Moody's Investors Service, Rating Symbols and Definitions, May 2016; Fitch Ratings, Definitions of Ratings and Other Forms of Opinion, December 2014; and Standard & Poor's, Standard and Poor's Ratings Definitions, February 1, 2016.

Changes in Default Risk and in the Default Risk Premium How does a change in default risk affect the interest rate on a bond? If the rating agencies believe that a firm's ability to make payments on a bond has declined, they will give the bond a lower rating. If investors agree with the lower rating, they will demand a smaller quantity of the bond at any given price, so the demand curve for the bond will shift to the left. As we saw in Chapter 4, if the demand curve for a bond shifts to the left, the price of the bond will fall, and its yield will rise. For example, Bon-Ton Department Stores issued a bond that initially had an interest rate of 8%. But by June 2016, both Moody's and S&P had given the bond a non-investment-grade, or "junk," rating because they believed there was a significant probability that Bon-Ton would not make the remaining payments on the bond, which was scheduled to mature in 2021. As a result, the demand for the bond declined, and the price fell from $1,000 to $440. At such a low price, the bond's yield to maturity was 29%. Investors were requiring a great deal of extra return to compensate them for the high level of risk on the bond. In other words, the bond's default risk premium had soared.

Investors can decide that default risk has increased for a whole category of bonds. For instance, during recessions, the default risk on corporate bonds typically increases, which can cause a *flight to quality*. A flight to quality involves investors decreasing their demand for higher-risk bonds and increasing their demand for lower-risk bonds. Figure 5.1 illustrates this process. Panel (a) shows the market for Baa-rated corporate bonds. Typically during a recession, as corporate profits decline, investors become concerned that firms are less likely to make their bond payments. As a result, the demand curve for Baa-rated corporate bonds shifts to the left, causing the equilibrium price to fall from P_1^C to P_2^C. Panel (b) shows that investor concerns about increasing default risk causes the demand curve for U.S. Treasury bonds to shift to the right. The equilibrium price increases from P_1^T to P_2^T. Because the price of corporate bonds is falling, the yield to maturity on corporate bonds is rising. And because the price of Treasury bonds is increasing, the yield on Treasury bonds is falling. Therefore, the size of the default risk premium is increasing.

Figure 5.2 shows the spread between the average interest rate on Baa-rated corporate bonds and the interest rate on Treasury bonds from 1999 to 2016. The two shaded areas show the recessions of 2001 and 2007–2009. For the 2001 recession, the figure shows a fairly typical pattern, with the spread rising from about 2 percentage points before the recession to more than 3 percentage points during the recession. For the 2007–2009 recession, the figure shows that the increase in the default risk premium

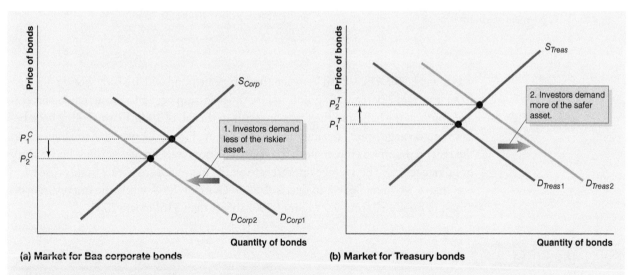

(a) Market for Baa corporate bonds

(b) Market for Treasury bonds

FIGURE 5.1 Determining Default Risk Premium in Yields

We can see the initial default risk premium by comparing yields associated with the prices P_1^T to P_1^C. Because the price of the safer U.S. Treasury bond is greater than that of the riskier corporate bond, we know that the yield on the corporate bond must be greater than the yield on the Treasury bond to compensate investors for bearing risk. As the default risk on corporate bonds increases, in panel (a), the demand for corporate bonds shifts to the left, from D_{Corp1} to D_{Corp2}. In panel (b), the demand for Treasury bonds shifts to the right, from D_{Treas1} to D_{Treas2}. The price of corporate bonds falls from P_1^C to P_2^C, and the price of Treasury bonds rises from P_1^T to P_2^T, so the yield on Treasury bonds falls relative to the yield on corporate bonds. Therefore, the default risk premium has increased.

MyEconLab Real-time data

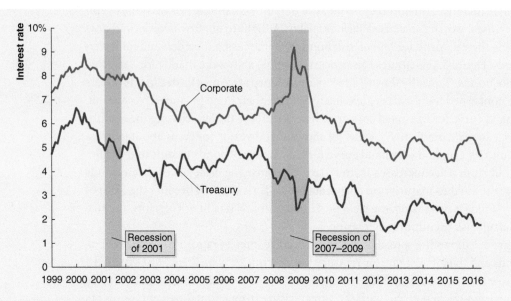

FIGURE 5.2 Rising Default Premiums During Recessions

The default premium typically rises during a recession. For the 2001 recession, the figure shows a fairly typical pattern, with the spread between the interest rate on corporate bonds and the interest rate on Treasury bonds rising from about 2 percentage points before the recession to more than 3 percentage points during the recession. For the 2007–2009 recession, the increase in the default risk premium was much larger. It rose from less than

2 percentage points before the recession began to more than 6 percentage points at the height of the financial crises in the fall of 2008.

Note: The corporate bond rate is for Baa-rated bonds. The Treasury bond rate is for 10-year Treasury notes.

Source: Federal Reserve Bank of St. Louis.

was much larger. The spread between the corporate bond and Treasury bond rates rose from less than 2 percentage points before the recession began to more than 6 percentage points at the height of the financial crisis in the fall of 2008, before falling back below 3 percentage points during the fall of 2009. As Figure 5.1 predicts, the increase in the risk premium was due to both the corporate bond rate increasing and the Treasury bond rate falling: The average interest rate on the Baa-rated corporate bonds rose from less than 6.5% in mid-2007 to nearly 9.5% in October 2008, while the interest rate on Treasury bonds fell from 5.0% in mid-2007 to less than 3.0% in late 2008.

SOLVED PROBLEM 5.1

Political Uncertainty and Bond Yields

In the summer of 2016, as Great Britain voted to leave the European Union (EU), some investors feared that economic instability might increase in the EU as a result of one of its key members leaving. An article in the *Wall Street Journal* noted that, in

particular, investors had become more concerned with the default risk on bonds issued by the governments of Portugal and Greece relative to the default risk on bonds issued by the governments of Germany, France, and the Netherlands. Suppose a student reads this article and argues: "Investors have become more worried that the governments of Portugal and Greece might default on their bonds. As a result, those bonds have become less desirable, so their yields have fallen, while the yields on bonds issued by Germany, France, and the Netherlands have risen."

Analyze the student's argument. Illustrate your answer using one graph showing the market for bonds issued by the German government and another graph showing the market for bonds issued by the Portuguese government.

Source: John Sindreu, "Global Safety Dash Highlights Eurozone Cracks," *Wall Street Journal*, June 15, 2016.

Solving the Problem

Step 1 **Review the chapter material.** This problem is about the effect of default risk in the bond market, so you may want to review the section "Default Risk," which begins on page 141.

Step 2 **Analyze whether the student's argument about movements in bond yields is correct.** The student's argument is incorrect. It's easy to make the student's mistake of reasoning that a more desirable bond—in this case, a German government bond—should have a higher interest rate than a less desirable bond—in this case, a Portuguese government bond. However, applying the analysis from this chapter and Chapter 4, we know that: (1) an increase in the demand for German government bonds will increase their price and lower their yield, and (2) a decrease in the demand for Portuguese government bonds will decrease their price and raise their yield. So, the student's analysis of the effects of a change in investors' perception of the default risk on these bonds is incorrect.

Step 3 **Illustrate your answer using graphs similar to those in Figure 5.1.** Panel (a) below shows the market for Portuguese government bonds. As investors decide that the probability of the Portuguese government defaulting on these bonds has increased, the demand curve will shift to the left, from D_{Port1} to D_{Port2}. The price of the bonds will fall from P_1^P to P_2^P. Because bond prices and bond yields move in opposite directions, the yield on Portuguese government

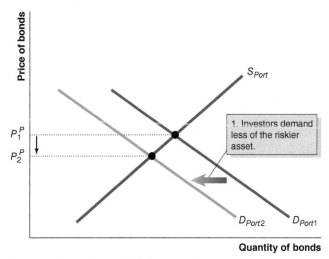

(a) Market for Portuguese government bonds

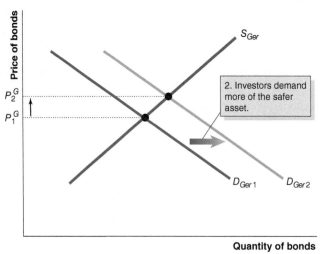

(b) Market for German government bonds

bonds will increase. Panel (b) shows the market for German government bonds. As investors engage in a *flight to quality* away from higher-risk bonds to lower-risk bonds, the demand curve will shift to the right, from D_{Ger1} to D_{Ger2}. The price of the bonds will increase from P_1^G to P_2^G. Because bond prices and bond yields move in opposite directions, the yield on German government bonds will decrease.

See related problem 1.10 at the end of the chapter.

MAKING THE CONNECTION

Do Credit Rating Agencies Have a Conflict of Interest?

The railroads in the nineteenth century were the first firms in the United States to issue large quantities of bonds. John Moody began the modern bond rating business by publishing *Moody's Analyses of Railroad Investments* in 1909. The firm that later became Standard & Poor's began publishing ratings in 1916. Fitch Ratings began publishing ratings in 1924. By the early twentieth century, firms in the steel, petroleum, chemical, and automobile industries, among others, were raising funds by issuing bonds, and the rating agencies expanded beyond rating just railroad bonds. By the 1920s, firms had difficulty selling bonds unless at least one of the rating agencies had rated them.

By the 1970s, the rating agencies were facing difficulties for two key reasons. First, the prosperity of the post–World War II period meant that defaults on bond issues were comparatively rare, so fewer investors were interested in the services the rating agencies offered. Second, the rating agencies could no longer earn a profit using their business model. The rating agencies were dependent primarily on selling their ratings to investors through subscriptions. The development of inexpensive photocopying in the 1970s undermined this model because one investor could purchase a subscription and then sell or give copies to nonsubscribers.

Beginning in the late 1970s, several developments turned around the fortunes of the rating agencies. First, periods of recession and high inflation increased the number of bond defaults, so more investors were willing to pay for information on the credit-worthiness of firms. Second, the rating agencies became involved in rating bonds issued by foreign firms and governments, both of which increased in volume beginning in the 1970s. Third, governments began to include bond ratings in their regulation of banks, mutual funds, and other financial firms. For instance, many mutual funds are required to hold only highly rated bonds. Finally, the rating agencies began to charge the firms and governments—rather than investors—for their services.

The last change raised the question of whether rating agencies face a conflict of interest. Because firms issuing bonds can choose which of the agencies to hire to rate their bonds, the agencies may have an incentive to give higher ratings than are justified in order to keep the firms' business. It became common for the agencies to provide bond issuers with "preview ratings" before the issuers agreed to hire the agencies. During the housing boom of the mid-2000s, investment banks issued many mortgage-backed bonds and other complex securities. When the housing market crashed beginning in 2006, many of these securities plunged in value, despite having high ratings from the rating agencies.

More than 90% of mortgage-backed securities issued during 2006 and 2007 with AAA ratings later defaulted or were eventually given junk ratings. Some economists and policymakers believed the rating agencies provided the high ratings primarily to ensure that the firms would continue to hire them. Many of the mortgage-backed securities had complicated structures. Some reports indicated that analysts at the rating agencies were reluctant to require issuers of these securities to provide sufficient information to rate the securities accurately because the analysts were afraid that doing so might offend the issuers. Some investors, including the managers of a number of state government pension plans, sued the rating agencies on the grounds that they had not carried out their responsibility to investors to provide accurate ratings. Eventually, the rating agencies paid fines and made other payments totaling $1.9 billion to resolve claims that they had improperly rated securities during the period leading up to the financial crisis. Some economists and policymakers were less critical of the agencies, though, arguing that they could not have anticipated how severe the housing crisis would be or the extent to which the crisis would affect the values of mortgage-backed securities.

In 2010, Congress passed the Wall Street Reform and Consumer Protection Act, or Dodd-Frank Act, which included provisions that affected the regulation of credit rating agencies. A new Office of Credit Ratings was created within the Securities and Exchange Commission (SEC) to oversee the agencies. The act put new restrictions on conflicts of interest at the rating agencies, authorized investors to bring lawsuits if an agency could be shown to have failed to gather sufficient information to properly rate a security, and gave the SEC the authority to deregister an agency that had provided inaccurate ratings over time. Critics of the regulations argued that they had not gone far enough in limiting the conflicts of interest at the rating agencies. The SEC official in charge of enforcing the regulations worried that changes at the rating agencies had not been sufficient and that the firms demonstrated "a failure to learn the lessons of the financial crisis."

But in evaluating the default risk on bonds, investors still rely heavily on the agencies, and in 2016 the agencies were earning record profits. Unless there is another financial crisis, it appears unlikely that there will be significant changes to how the agencies operate.

Sources: Timothy W. Martin, "What Crisis? Big Ratings Firms Stronger Than Ever," *Wall Street Journal*, March 11, 2016; Anusha Shrivastava, "Bond Sales? Don't Quote Us, Request Credit Firms," *Wall Street Journal*, July 21, 2010; David Segal, "Debt Raters Avoid Overhaul After Crisis," *New York Times*, December 8, 2009; and Richard Sylla, "An Historical Primer on the Business of Credit Rating," in Richard M. Levich et al., eds., *Ratings, Rating Agencies, and the Global Financial System*, Boston: Kluwer Academic Publishers, 2002.

See related problem 1.11 at the end of the chapter.

Liquidity and Information Costs

In addition to differences in default risk, differences in liquidity and information costs also lead to differences in interest rates. Because investors care about liquidity, they are willing to accept a lower interest rate on more liquid investments than on less liquid—or *illiquid*—investments, all other things being equal. So, investors expect to receive a higher return on an illiquid bond to compensate them for sacrificing liquidity.

Similarly, investors care about the costs of acquiring information on a bond. Spending time and money acquiring information on a bond reduces the bond's expected return. Not surprisingly, if two assets appear otherwise the same, an investor will prefer to hold the one with lower information costs. So, investors will accept a lower expected return on assets with lower costs for acquiring information than they will on a bond with higher costs for acquiring information.

An increase in a bond's liquidity or a decrease in the cost of acquiring information about the bond will increase the demand for the bond. In a bond market graph, the demand curve will shift to the right, increasing the bond's price and decreasing the bond's interest rate. Similarly, if a bond's liquidity declines or if the cost of acquiring information about the bond increases, the demand for the bond will decline. During the financial crisis of 2007–2009, many investors became reluctant to buy mortgage-backed bonds because homeowners were defaulting on many of the mortgages contained in the bonds. To make matters worse, investors came to realize that they did not fully understand these bonds and had difficulty finding information about the types of mortgages the bonds contained. We can illustrate this situation in a bond market graph by shifting the demand curve to the left, which will decrease the bond's price and increase the bond's interest rate.

Tax Treatment

Investors receive interest income in the form of coupon payments on bonds. Investors must include these coupons in their income when paying their taxes. The tax paid on the coupons differs, depending on who issued the bond. The tax also varies depending on where the investor lives. Investors care about the *after-tax return* on their investments—that is, the return the investors have left after paying their taxes. For example, consider two bonds each with $1,000 face values and 6% coupon rates, meaning they pay coupons of $60 per year. Suppose that on the first bond, issued by Ford, the investor has to pay a 40%

TABLE 5.2 How Taxes Affect the After-Tax Return on Two Bonds

Bond Issuer	Face value	Coupon rate	Tax investor owes	Coupon after paying tax	After-tax return
Ford	$1,000	6%	40%	$36	$36/$1,000 = 0.036, or 3. 6%
U.S. Treasury	$1,000	6%	25%	$45	$45/$1,000 = 0.045, or 4.5%

tax on the coupon received. On the second bond, issued by the U.S. Treasury, the investor pays only a 25% tax on the coupon received. So, after paying taxes, the investor will have only $36 left from the $60 coupon on the Ford bond but $45 left on the Treasury bond. If the investor paid $1,000 for each bond, then, ignoring any capital gains or losses during the year, the investor will have received an after-tax return of $45/$1,000 = 0.045, or 4.5%, on the Treasury bond, but only $36/$1,000 = 0.036, or 3.6%, on the Ford bond. If the investor considered the risk, liquidity, and information costs of the two bonds to be the same, the investor would clearly prefer the higher after-tax return on the Treasury bond. Table 5.2 summarizes this calculation.

How the Tax Treatment of Bonds Differs We can consider three categories of bonds: corporate bonds, U.S. Treasury bonds, and **municipal bonds**, which are bonds issued by state and local governments. The coupons on corporate bonds can be subject to federal, state, and local taxes. The coupons on Treasury bonds are subject to federal tax but not to state or local taxes. The coupons on municipal bonds are typically not subject to federal, state, or local taxes. The tax situation for corporate bonds is somewhat complex because eight states have no state income tax. Some local governments also have no income tax, or they tax wage and salary income but not income from investments. Table 5.3 summarizes the tax situation for the three types of bonds.

Municipal bonds Bonds issued by state and local governments.

Recall that bond investors can receive two types of income from owning bonds: (1) interest income from coupons and (2) capital gains (or losses) from price changes on the bonds. Interest income is taxed at the same rates as wage and salary income. In 2016, capital gains were taxed at a lower rate than interest income. Capital gains are also taxed only if they are *realized*—that is, if the investor sells the bond for a higher price than he or she paid for it. *Unrealized* capital gains are not taxed. For instance, if you buy a bond for

TABLE 5.3 Tax Treatment of Bond Coupon Payments

Type of bond	Taxed by state and local governments?	Taxed by the federal government?
Corporate bond	Taxed by most states and some cities	Yes
U.S. Treasury bond	No	Yes
Municipal bond	No	No

$800, and its price rises to $900, you have a taxable realized capital gain if you sell the bond; if you don't sell it, you have an unrealized gain, which is not taxed. Postponing the time when you pay capital gains tax has benefits because the further in the future you pay the tax, the lower the present value of the tax. Although interest income on municipal bonds is exempt from income tax, realized capital gains on these bonds are taxable.

The Effect of Tax Changes on Interest Rates We have seen that investors are interested in the after-tax return they receive on bonds and that tax rates on bonds differ according to the type of bond. So, a change in income tax rates will affect interest rates.

Figure 5.3 shows how a change in the federal income tax rate affects the interest rates on municipal bonds and Treasury bonds. We assume that initially the federal income tax rate is 35%. Panel (a) shows the market for municipal bonds, and panel (b) shows the market for Treasury bonds. The equilibrium price in panel (a), P_1^M, is higher than the equilibrium price in panel (b), P_1^T, which is the usual situation where the interest rate on municipal bonds is lower than the interest rate on Treasury bonds. Now suppose that the federal income tax rate rises to 45%. This higher tax rate will make the tax-exempt status of municipal bonds even more attractive to investors, and at the same time, it will reduce the after-tax return on Treasury bonds. In panel (a), the demand curve for municipal bonds shifts to the right, from D_{Muni1} to D_{Muni2}, increasing the price from P_1^M to P_2^M and lowering the interest rate. In panel (b), the demand curve for Treasury bonds shifts to the left, from D_{Treas1} to D_{Treas2}, lowering the price from P_1^T to P_2^T and raising the interest rate. If we assume that investors see the two bonds as having

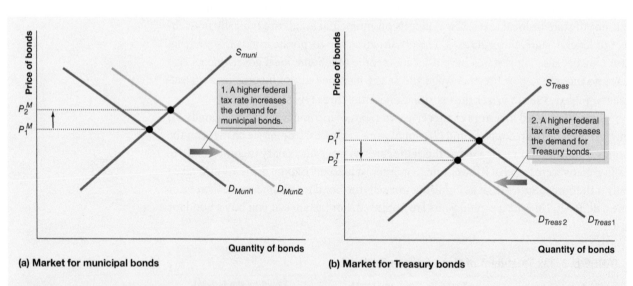

(a) Market for municipal bonds

(b) Market for Treasury bonds

FIGURE 5.3 The Effect of Changes in Taxes on Bond Prices

If the federal income tax rate increases, tax-exempt municipal bonds will be more attractive to investors, and Treasury bonds will be less attractive. In panel (a), the demand curve for municipal bonds shifts to the right, from D_{Muni1} to D_{Muni2}, increasing the price from P_1^M to P_2^M and lowering the interest rate. In panel (b), the demand curve for Treasury bonds shifts to the left, from D_{Treas1} to D_{Treas2}, lowering the price from P_1^T to P_2^T and raising the interest rate.

TABLE 5.4 The Risk Structure of Interest Rates

An increase in a bond's ...	causes its yield to ...	because ...
default risk	rise	investors must be compensated for bearing additional risk.
liquidity	fall	investors incur lower costs in selling the bond.
information costs	rise	investors must spend more resources to evaluate the bond.
tax liability	rise	investors care about after-tax returns and must be compensated for paying higher taxes.

the same characteristics, other than the tax treatment of their coupons, then after the increase in the tax rate, the interest rates on the bonds should adjust until investors receive the same after-tax yield on both bonds. From this analysis, we can conclude that an increase in income tax rates will tend to raise the interest rate on Treasury bonds and lower the interest rate on municipal bonds.

Table 5.4 summarizes the determinants of the risk structure of interest rates.

MAKING THE CONNECTION | IN YOUR INTEREST

Should You Invest in Junk Bonds?

As we saw in Chapter 4, interest rates in 2016 remained at historically low levels, with interest rates on bank CDs, Treasury bills, and other safe assets still well below 1%. As a result, many investors searched for ways to earn higher interest rates. Some individual investors moved into the risky junk bond market, attracted by the relatively high interest rates.

Junk bonds is the popular name for corporate bonds the rating agencies have given less than investment grade ratings to (for example, a rating of Ba or below from Moody's). At one time, corporations were able to sell only bonds that received an investment grade rating. As a result, all junk bonds were "fallen angels," a Wall Street term for a bond that was issued with an investment grade rating but was later downgraded, after the issuing corporation experienced financial problems. This situation changed in the late 1970s, after Michael Milken, a bond salesman at the investment bank Drexel Burnham Lambert, discovered academic research published by economist W. Bradock Hickman in his book *Corporate Bond Quality and Investor Experience*. Hickman used historical data to show that if an investor purchased a diversified portfolio of junk bonds, the investor would receive a return that was much higher than if the investor had invested in U.S. Treasury bonds. The difference in returns was more than enough to compensate for the additional risk from investing in junk bonds rather than in Treasuries. In other words, the interest rates on the junk bonds were high enough that even though some bonds in the investor's portfolio might default, causing losses on those bonds, the return on the whole portfolio would still be high.

Milken made Hickman's research the basis for presentations to institutional investors, such as pension funds and mutual funds, advocating that they invest in junk bonds. Milken was so successful in increasing demand for junk bonds that, for the first time, firms were able to issue new bonds with less than investment grade ratings. Although some institutional investors were prohibited from buying junk bonds either by their charters or by government regulators, other institutional investors began to make junk bonds a part of their investment portfolios.

In the years after the 2007–2009 financial crisis, some individual investors turned to investing in junk bonds, either by buying individual bonds or, more commonly, by buying mutual funds that invest in junk bonds. They did this because the average interest rate on junk bonds was much higher than the average interest rate on investment grade bonds or the interest rate on U.S. Treasury bonds. For instance, in October 2016, the average interest rate on junk bonds was 5.9%, while the average yield on investment grade bonds was 2.9%, and the yield on 10-year Treasury notes was 1.7%.

But should you consider junk bonds to be good investments? At the end of the financial crisis, the average interest rate on junk bonds was greater than 13%. But as the demand for junk bonds increased, their yields had declined. As a result, many financial advisers began to doubt that investors were receiving high enough yields to compensate them for the high risk of defaults on these bonds. As one article in the *Wall Street Journal* put it: "Investors with yield targets to hit may well be tempted by junk bonds. But they shouldn't assume there is easy money to be made here."

Only time will tell whether the enthusiasm that many individual investors developed for junk bonds will pay off for them. Many financial advisers doubted it would because they questioned whether individual investors fully understood the risks they were taking in making these investments.

Sources: Richard Barley, "Why Investors Should Handle High-Yield Bonds with Care," *Wall Street Journal*, April 18, 2016; W. Braddock Hickman, *Corporate Bond Quality and Investor Experience*, Princeton, NJ: Princeton University Press, 1958; and Federal Reserve Bank of St. Louis.

See related problem 1.15 at the end of the chapter.

5.2 | **The Term Structure of Interest Rates**

LEARNING OBJECTIVE: Explain why bonds with different maturities can have different interest rates.

Term structure of interest rates The relationship among the interest rates on bonds that are otherwise similar but that have different maturities.

We have seen why bonds with the same maturity may have different interest rates. We now consider the **term structure of interest rates**, which is the relationship among the interest rates on bonds that are otherwise similar but have different maturities. Theories of the term structure attempt to answer this question: Why should bonds that have the same default risk, liquidity, information cost, and taxation characteristics have different interest rates just because they have different maturities? It is easiest to hold constant these characteristics for Treasury bonds. So, a common way to analyze the term structure is by looking at the *Treasury yield curve*, which is the relationship on a particular day among the interest rates on Treasury bonds with different maturities. (Remember that Treasury bonds with a maturity of 1 year or less are *bills*, those with a maturity of 2 years to 10 years

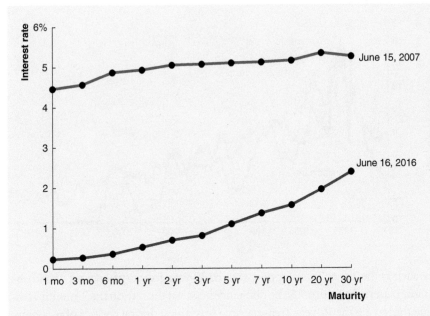

FIGURE 5.4

The Treasury Yield Curve

The yield curve for June 15, 2007, was nearly flat, while the yield curve for June 16, 2016, was upward sloping. The shape of the Treasury yield curve provides information on investors' expectations of future short-term interest rates.

Source: U.S. Department of the Treasury, *Daily Treasury Yield Curve Rates.*

are *notes*, and those with a maturity of more than 10 years are *bonds*. For simplicity, we often refer to all these securities as *bonds*.)

Figure 5.4 graphs the Treasury yield curves for two days: June 15, 2007, before the start of the financial crisis of 2007–2009, and June 16, 2016. We can note a couple of important points about these two yield curves. First, the interest rates, or yields, on all maturities were much lower in 2016 than in 2007. For example, on June 15, 2007, the yield on the three-month Treasury bill was 4.56%, while on June 16, 2016, the yield was only 0.27%, or 27-hundredths of 1%. The very low yields in 2016 were due primarily to the Federal Reserve's actions to keep interest rates low to aid economic recovery even years after the severe 2007–2009 recession. Second, on both days, the yields on long-term bonds were higher than the yields on short-term bonds, although the difference was much greater in 2016 than in 2007.

This pattern of long-term rates being higher than short-term rates is typical. Figure 5.5 illustrates this pattern by showing that in the years since 1976, interest rates on 3-month Treasury bills—the blue line—have generally been lower than interest rates on 10-year Treasury notes—the red line. When short-term rates are lower than long-term rates, there is an *upward-sloping yield curve*. Close inspection of Figure 5.5, though, shows that there have been periods when the interest rate on the 3-month Treasury bill has been higher than the interest rate on the 10-year Treasury note. These are periods of *downward-sloping yield curves*, with short-term interest rates that are higher than long-term interest rates. Because downward-sloping yield curves occur infrequently, they are also called *inverted yield curves.* Figure 5.5 also illustrates another important fact about the bond market: *Interest rates on bonds of different maturities tend to move together.* For instance, note that during the late 1970s, interest rates on both 3-month Treasury bills and 10-year Treasury notes increased, reaching peaks in the early 1980s, after which they both declined. If we graphed bonds of other

MyEconLab Real-time data

FIGURE 5.5

The Interest Rates on 3-Month Treasury Bills and 10-Year Treasury Notes, 1976–2016

The figure shows that most of the time since 1976, the interest rate on the 3-month Treasury bills (indicated by the blue line) have been lower than the interest rate on the 10-year Treasury notes (indicated by the red line). During a few periods, though, the interest rate on the 3-month Treasury bill has been higher than the interest rate on the 10-year Treasury note.

Source: Federal Reserve Bank of St. Louis.

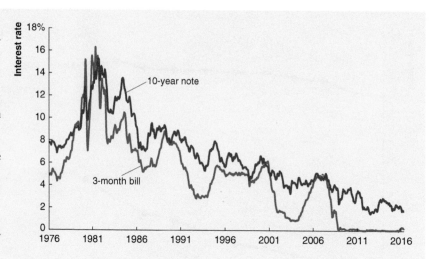

maturities, such as the 2-year Treasury note and the 30-year Treasury bond, we would observe the same pattern. In Figure 5.5, the difference between the rate on the 3-month Treasury bill and the rate on the 10-year Treasury note was largest during periods of recession, when the Federal Reserve drove short-term rates to low levels.

MAKING THE CONNECTION | **IN YOUR INTEREST**

Would You Ever Pay the Government to Keep Your Money?

Negative *real* interest rates happen frequently. For instance, during the third quarter of 2008, the nominal interest rate on the 3-month Treasury bill was 1.49%, while the inflation rate was 5.23%, so the real interest rate was 1.49% − 5.23% = −3.74%. But can the *nominal* interest rate ever be negative? You are probably thinking "no" because a negative nominal interest rate means that the *lender* is actually paying the *borrower* interest in return for borrowing the lender's money. What lender would ever do that?

During the Great Depression of the 1930s and again during the financial crisis of 2007–2009 and its aftermath, many investors were happy to *pay* interest to the U.S. Treasury for brief periods in return for the Treasury borrowing their money. In other words, these investors were willing to accept negative interest rates on the Treasury bills they purchased by paying prices that were higher than the bills' face values. In both cases, investors were looking for safe havens at a time when virtually all other investments seemed very risky. Holding their funds in cash would require paying for secure storage. Because interest rates on other short-term investments, such as bank certificates of deposit or money market mutual fund shares, were also very low, investors were giving up relatively little to temporarily park their funds in default-risk free Treasury bills.

Since 2012, both France and Germany have sold short-term government bonds with negative interest rates. In the spring of 2016, an extraordinary event occurred when the interest rate on both 10-year Japanese government bonds and 10-year German government bonds became negative. In other words, investors were willing to pay the

Japanese and German governments to keep their money for 10 years. This unlikely outcome resulted in part from action by the Bank of Japan and the European Central Bank (ECB). To help increase very slow economic growth, the central banks had switched from paying interest to commercial banks that had deposits with them to charging the banks interest. This change pushed banks to find other places to invest funds, including government bonds. There was also concern that the exit of Great Britain from the European Union might lead to economic problems, which caused a flight to safety as investors bought up AAA-rated German government bonds. We will discuss the central bank policies that helped lead to negative interest rates in Chapter 15.

For decades, negative interest rates on government debt had seemed like a historical curiosity from the Great Depression. Their reappearance indicates the difficulty the world financial system was still having recovering from the 2007–2009 crisis even more than seven years after it had ended.

Sources: Leslie Shaffer, "Why JGB Yields Won't Keep Falling Deeper into Negative Yield," cnbc. com, April 3, 2016; Mike Bird, "German 10-Year Government Bond Yields Dip Below Zero as Brexit Fears Hit Market," *Wall Street Journal*, June 14, 2016; Deborah Lynn Blumberg, "Some Treasury Bill Rates Negative Again Friday," *Wall Street Journal*, November 20, 2009; and Daniel Kruger and Cordell Eddings, "Treasury Bills Trade at Negative Rates as Haven Demand Surges," Bloomberg.com, December 9, 2008.

See related problem 2.9 at the end of the chapter.

Explaining the Term Structure

Our discussion of Figures 5.4 and 5.5 indicates that any explanation of the term structure should be able to account for three important facts:

1. Interest rates on long-term bonds are usually higher than interest rates on short-term bonds.
2. Interest rates on short-term bonds are occasionally higher than interest rates on long-term bonds.
3. Interest rates on bonds of all maturities tend to rise and fall together.

Economists have three theories to explain these facts: *the expectations theory, the segmented markets theory*, and *the liquidity premium theory* or *preferred habitat theory*. As we will see, although the expectations theory best captures the logic of how the bond market operates, the liquidity premium theory, which combines elements of the other two theories, is the one most economists accept. In evaluating the theories, two criteria prove useful. First is logical consistency: Does the theory offer a model of the bond market that is consistent with what we know of investor behavior? Second is predictive power: How well does the theory explain actual data on yield curves? We consider each of the theories in turn.

The Expectations Theory of the Term Structure

The *expectations theory* provides the basis for understanding the term structure. The **expectations theory** holds that the interest rate on a long-term bond is an average of the interest rates investors expect on short-term bonds over the lifetime of the long-term bond. The theory views investors in the bond market as sharing the primary objective

Expectations theory A theory of the term structure of interest rates which holds that the interest rate on a long-term bond is an average of the interest rates investors expect on short-term bonds over the lifetime of the long-term bond.

of receiving the highest expected return on their bond investments. For a given holding period, the theory assumes that investors do not care about the maturities of the bonds they invest in. That is, if an investor intends to invest in the bond market for, say, 10 years, the investor will look for the highest return and will not be concerned about whether he or she receives that return by, for example, buying a 10-year bond at the beginning of the period and holding the bond until it matures or by buying a 5-year bond, holding it until it matures in 5 years, and then buying a second 5-year bond.

So, the two key assumptions of the expectations theory are:

1. Investors have the same investment objectives.
2. For a given holding period, investors view bonds of different maturities as being perfect substitutes for one another. That is, holding a 10-year bond for 10 years is the same to investors as holding a 5-year bond for 5 years and another 5-year bond for a second 5 years.

Neither of these assumptions is entirely accurate, so while the expectations theory provides important insight into the term structure, it is not a complete explanation. It is essential, though, to understand the expectations theory before moving on to a more complete explanation of the term structure, so let's consider an example of how the expectations theory works.

The Expectations Theory Applied in a Simple Example Suppose that you intend to invest $1,000 for two years and are considering one of two strategies:

1. *The buy-and-hold strategy.* With this strategy, you buy a two-year bond and hold it until maturity. We will assume that you buy a two-year discount bond. This simplification allows us to avoid having to deal with coupon payments, although the result would not change if we added that complication. The interest rate on the two-year bond is i_{2t}, where the subscript 2 refers to the maturity of the bond and the subscript t refers to the time period, with time t being the present. After two years, the $1,000 investment will have grown to $\$1,000\,(1\ +\ i_{2t})\,(1\ +\ i_{2t})$, which is just an application of the basic compounding formula from Chapter 3.
2. *The rollover strategy.* With this strategy, you buy a one-year bond today and hold it until it matures in one year. At that time, you buy a second one-year bond and hold it until it matures at the end of the second year. Notice that with this strategy, you cannot be sure what interest rate you will receive on the one-year bond one year from now. Instead, you must rely on all the information you have about the bond market to form an *expectation* of what the interest rate on the one-year bond will be one year from now. The interest rate on the one-year bond today is i_{1t}, while the interest rate expected on the one-year bond one year from now (which is period $t\ +\ 1$) is $i^e_{1t\ +\ 1}$. So, if you follow this strategy, after two years, you will expect your $1,000 investment to have grown to $1,000(1\ +\ i_{1t})\,(1\ +\ i^e_{1t+1})$.

Under the assumptions of the expectations theory, the returns from the two strategies must be the same. To see why, remember from Chapter 3 that because of financial arbitrage, the prices of securities will adjust so that investors receive the same returns from holding comparable securities. According to the expectations theory, investors consider holding a two-year bond for two years or holding two one-year bonds for one year each as being comparable. Therefore, arbitrage should result in the returns from the two strategies being the same. So, your $1,000 should have grown to the same amount as a result of using either strategy, and we can write:

$$\$1,000\,(1 + i_{2t})\,(1 + i_{2t}) = \$1,000\,(1 + i_{1t})\,(1 + i^e_{1t+1}).$$

Multiplying out the expressions in the parentheses and then simplifying, we get:

$$2i_{2t} + i^2_{2t} = i_{1t} + i^e_{1t+1} + (i_{1t})\,(i^e_{1t+1}).$$

We can simplify further by noting that i^2_{2t} on the left side of the equation and $(i_{1t})\,(i^e_{1t+1})$ on the right side of the equation are likely to be small numbers because they are each the product of two interest rates. For instance, if the interest rate on the two-year bond is 3%, then $i^2_{2t} = 0.03 \times 0.03 = 0.0009$, which is a small enough number that we can ignore it without significantly affecting the result. If we ignore i^2_{2t} and $(i_{1t})\,(i^e_{1t+1})$ and divide both sides of the equation by 2, we are left with:

$$i_{2t} = \frac{i_{1t} + i^e_{1t+1}}{2}.$$

This equation tells us that the interest rate on the two-year bond is the average of the interest rate on the one-year bond today and the expected interest rate on the one-year bond one year from now. For example, if the interest rate on the one-year bond today is 2% and the interest rate expected on the one-year bond one year from now is 4%, then the interest rate on the two-year bond today should be 3% (= (2% + 4%)/2).

The equality between the buy-and-hold strategy and the rollover strategy should be true for any number of periods. For instance, the interest rate on a 10-year bond should equal the average of the interest rates on the 10 one-year bonds during that 10-year period. So, we can say generally that the interest rate on an n-year bond—where n can be any number of years—is equal to:

$$i_{nt} = \frac{i_{1t} + i^e_{1t+1} + i^e_{1t+2} + i^e_{1t+3} + \ \ldots \ + i^e_{1t+(n-1)}}{n}.$$

Interpreting the Term Structure Using the Expectations Theory If the expectations theory is correct, the term structure provides us with information on what bond investors must expect to happen to short-term rates in the future. For example, if the interest rate on the one-year bond is 2% and the interest rate on the two-year bond is 3%, investors must be expecting that the interest rate on the one-year bond one year from now will be 4%. Otherwise, the average of the interest rates on the two one-year bonds would not equal the interest rate on the two-year bond.

Figure 5.6 shows three possible yield curves. We can use the expectations theory to interpret their slopes. Panel (a) shows an upward-sloping yield curve with the interest rate on the one-year bond equal to 2%, the interest rate on the two-year bond equal to 3%, and the interest rate on the three-year bond equal to 4%. The two-year rate is an average of the current one-year rate and the expected one-year rate one year from now:

$$3\% = \frac{2\% + \text{Expected one-year rate one year from now}}{2}.$$

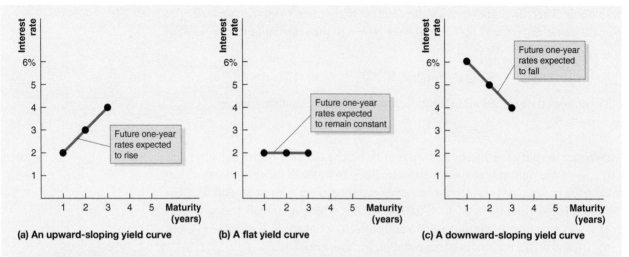

FIGURE 5.6 Using the Yield Curve to Predict Interest Rates: The Expectations Theory

Under the expectations theory, the slope of the yield curve shows that future short-term interest rates are expected to (a) rise, (b) remain the same, or (c) fall relative to current levels.

So, the expected one-year rate one year from now equals $(2 \times 3\%) - 2\% = 4\%$.

Similarly, we can calculate the expected one-year rate two years from now using the expected one-year rate one year from now that we just calculated:

$$4\% = \frac{2\% \; + \; 4\% \; + \; \text{Expected one-year rate two years from now}}{3}.$$

So, the expected one-year rate two years from now $= (3 \times 4\%) - (2\% + 4\%) = 6\%$.

We can conclude that the reason that the three-year bond has a higher interest rate than the two-year bond and the two-year bond has a higher interest rate than the one-year bond is because investors expect the interest rate on the one-year bond to increase from 2% to 4% to 6%. Or, more generally, *according to the expectations theory, an upward-sloping yield curve is the result of investors expecting future short-term rates to be higher than the current short-term rate.*

Panel (b) of Figure 5.6 shows a flat yield curve, with the two-year and three-year bonds having the same interest rates as the one-year bond. Under the expectations theory, we can infer that investors must be expecting that the interest rate on the one-year bond will remain unchanged, at 2%. Or, more generally, *according to the expectations theory, a flat yield curve is the result of investors expecting future short-term rates to be the same as the current short-term rate.*

Finally, panel (c) of Figure 5.6 shows a downward-sloping yield curve with the interest rate on the one-year bond being 6%, the interest rate on the two-year bond being 5%, and the interest rate on the three-year bond being 4%. We can apply the same arithmetic we did in the case of the upward-sloping yield curve to calculate the expected interest rates on the one-year bond one year from now and two years from now. Doing so shows that the expected interest rate on the one-year bond one year from now is 4%, and the expected interest rate on the one-year bond two years from now is 2%.

We can conclude that the three-year bond has a lower interest rate than the two-year bond and the two-year bond has a lower interest rate than the one-year bond because investors expect the interest rate on the one-year bond to decrease from 6% to 4% to 2%. Or, more generally, *according to the expectations theory, a downward-sloping yield curve is the result of investors expecting future short-term rates to be lower than the current short-term rate.*

Shortcomings of the Expectations Theory The expectations theory has an internally consistent explanation of the slope of the yield curve. It explains why we see upward-sloping, downward-sloping, and flat yield curves. The theory also explains why short-term and long-term rates tend to move up and down together, as shown in Figure 5.5 on page 154. Since the 1940s, movements in U.S. interest rates have been persistent: Increases or decreases in interest rates tend to continue for a considerable period of time. Therefore, if short-term interest rates increase today, investors will expect future short-term rates to also be high, which, according to the expectations theory, will also lead to an increase in long-term rates.

The expectations theory, though, does a poor job of explaining the first of the important facts about the term structure that we listed on page 155: Interest rates on long-term bonds are usually higher than interest rates on short-term bonds. In other words, the yield curve is typically upward sloping. The expectations theory explains an upward-sloping yield curve as being the result of investors expecting future short-term rates to be higher than the current short-term rate. But if the yield curve is typically upward sloping, investors must be expecting short-term rates to rise most of the time. This explanation seems unlikely because at any particular time, short-term rates are about as likely to fall as to rise. We can conclude that the expectations theory is overlooking something important about the behavior of investors in the bond market.

SOLVED PROBLEM 5.2A IN YOUR INTEREST

Can You Make Easy Money from the Term Structure?

The term *interest carry trade* refers to borrowing at a low short-term interest rate and using the borrowed funds to invest at a higher long-term interest rate.

a. Would you use an interest-carry-trade strategy for your personal investments? Identify the difficulties with this strategy for an individual investor. (Hint: Think about the ways you might be able to borrow money.)

b. If you were an investment adviser for an institutional investor, such as a pension fund or an insurance company, would you advise that investor to use an interest-carry-trade strategy? Identify the difficulties with this strategy for an institutional investor.

c. If the yield curve was inverted, or downward sloping, would an institutional investor still find an interest-carry-trade strategy to be possible? Briefly explain.

Solving the Problem

Step 1 **Review the chapter material.** This problem involves understanding the yield curve, so you may want to review the section "The Expectations Theory of the Term Structure," which begins on page 155.

Step 2 **Answer part (a) by explaining whether an individual investor can profitably engage in an interest carry trade.** The yield curve is typically upward sloping, so short-term interest rates are usually lower than long-term interest rates. Therefore, borrowing short term and investing the funds long term would seem to be a viable investment strategy. The average investor, though, would have difficulty using this strategy because the low short-term rates used in the yield curve—Treasury bill rates, for example—are well below the rates at which the typical investor can borrow. Most small investors would have to take out a personal loan from a bank, borrow from their broker using their security holdings as collateral, or borrow on their credit cards. The interest rates on these types of borrowings are far above the T-bill rate. So, if you are an average investor, the gap between the rate at which you can borrow and the rate at which you could invest in Treasury bonds or other long-term bonds is likely to be small or even negative.

Step 3 **Consider the situation of an institutional investor to answer part (b).** Unlike individual investors, institutional investors, such as pension funds and insurance companies, can borrow at a low short-term rate and invest at a higher long-term rate because the risk that these investors will default is low, and lenders can easily acquire information about them. In carrying out this strategy, though, institutional investors face the risk that as they roll over their short-term loans, the interest rates on them may have risen. For example, if a pension fund borrows $10 million for 6 months at a 1% interest rate to invest in 10-year Treasury notes at a 3% interest rate, it runs the risk that at the end of 6 months, short-term interest rates will have risen above 1%, thereby narrowing the pension fund's profit. In fact, if the expectations theory is correct, the average of the expected short-term interest rates over the life of the long-term investment should be roughly equal to the interest rate on the long-term investment, which would wipe out any potential profits from the interest carry trade. Moreover, if interest rates rise more rapidly than expected, the price of the long-term investment will decline, and the investor will suffer a capital loss.

Step 4 **Answer part (c) by explaining whether the interest carry trade would still be possible if the yield curve were inverted.** If the yield curve were inverted, with long-term rates lower than short-term rates, an institutional investor could borrow long term and invest the funds at the higher short-term rates. In this case, the investor would be subject to *reinvestment risk*, or the risk that after the short-term investment has matured, the interest rate on new short-term investments will have declined. For example, an insurance company that borrows $10 million by issuing long-term bonds at 5% and invests the funds in 6-month Treasury bills at 7% may find that when the Treasury bills mature, the interest rate on new Treasury bills has fallen to 4%. In fact, once again, the expectations theory predicts that the average of the expected short-term interest rates over the life of the long-term loan should be roughly equal to the interest on the long-term loan, which would wipe out any potential profits from the interest carry trade.

We can conclude that the expectations theory indicates that the interest-carry-trade strategy is not ordinarily a road to riches.

See related problems 2.10 and 2.11 at the end of the chapter.

The Segmented Markets Theory of the Term Structure

The **segmented markets theory** addresses the shortcomings of the expectations theory by making two related observations:

1. Investors in the bond market do not all have the same objectives.
2. Investors do not see bonds of different maturities as being perfect substitutes for each other.

These two observations imply that the markets for bonds of different maturities are separate, or *segmented*. Therefore, the interest rate on a bond of a particular maturity is determined only by the demand and supply for bonds of that maturity. The segmented markets theory recognizes that not all investors are the same. For instance, large firms often have significant amounts of cash on which they would like to earn interest but that they also want to have readily available. If you were managing this money for such a firm, you would probably put the funds in short-term Treasury bills rather than in longer-term Treasury notes or Treasury bonds so that the firm's money would be more readily accessible. Similarly, there are money market mutual funds that only buy Treasury bills, commercial paper issued by corporations, and other short-term assets and are not allowed by regulation to buy longer-term notes or bonds.

At the other end of the market, though, some investors who buy notes and bonds may buy few, if any, bills. For instance, insurance companies sell life insurance policies that require the companies to make payments when a policyholder dies. Actuaries who work for the companies can reliably estimate how much the company is likely to pay out during any particular year. The insurance companies use these estimates to buy bonds that will mature on a schedule that provides the funds needed to make payouts on the policies. If you were managing funds at an insurance company, you might be reluctant to invest in Treasury bills the funds that the company will need in 20 years to make expected payouts on its policies. Investing in bonds that mature in 20 years would be a better investment strategy than investing in Treasury bills.

In its pure form, the segmented markets theory indicates that investors who participate in the market for bonds of one maturity do not participate in markets for bonds of other maturities. Therefore, factors that affect the demand for Treasury bills or other short-term bonds have no effect on the demand for Treasury bonds or other long-term bonds.

In addition, the segmented markets theory indicates that investors do not view bonds of different maturities as being perfect substitutes for each other because long-term bonds have two shortcomings: (1) They are subject to greater interest-rate risk than short-term bonds, and (2) they are often less liquid than short-term bonds. As a result of these shortcomings, investors need to be compensated by receiving higher interest rates on long-term bonds than on short-term bonds. Economists who support the segmented markets

Segmented markets theory A theory of the term structure of interest rates which holds that the interest rate on a bond of a particular maturity is determined only by the demand and supply for bonds of that maturity.

theory also argue that investors who want to hold short-term bonds (for example, corporate money managers) outnumber investors who want to hold long-term bonds (for example, insurance companies). The result is that the prices of short-term bonds are driven up and their yields are driven down relative to those of long-term bonds.

The segmented markets theory, then, offers a plausible explanation of why the yield curve is typically upward sloping: There are more investors who are in the market for short-term bonds, causing their prices to be higher and their interest rates lower, and fewer investors who are in the market for long-term bonds, causing their prices to be lower and their interest rates higher. In addition, investors who buy long-term bonds require a higher interest rate to compensate them for the additional interest-rate risk and lower liquidity of long-term bonds. So, the segmented markets theory does a good job of accounting for the first of our important facts about the term structure.

The segmented markets theory, though, has a serious shortcoming: It does not provide a good explanation for the other two important facts about the term structure. The theory does not explain why short-term interest rates would ever be greater than long-term interest rates. In other words, the yield curve is occasionally downward sloping, though this theory does not tell us why. And if markets for bonds of different maturities truly are segmented (that is, completely independent of each other), it is difficult to understand the third important fact about the term structure: Interest rates of all maturities tend to rise and fall together.

The Liquidity Premium Theory

Neither the expectations theory nor the segmented markets theory provides a complete explanation of the term structure. Essentially, their shortcomings arise from the extreme position that each theory takes. Under the expectations theory, investors view bonds of different maturities as perfect substitutes for each other, while under the segmented markets theory, investors view bonds of different maturities as not being substitutes at all. The **liquidity premium theory** (or **preferred habitat theory**) of the term structure provides a more complete explanation by combining the insights of the other two theories while avoiding their extreme assumptions.

The liquidity premium theory holds that investors view bonds of different maturities as substitutes—but not perfect substitutes. Like the segmented markets theory, the liquidity premium theory assumes that investors prefer bonds with shorter maturities to bonds with longer maturities. Therefore, investors will not buy a long-term bond if it offers the same yield as a sequence of short-term bonds. Unlike in the segmented markets theory, however, investors will be willing to substitute a long-term bond for short-term bonds, provided that they receive a high enough interest rate on the long-term bond. The additional interest investors require in order to be willing to buy a long-term bond rather than a comparable sequence of short-term bonds is called a **term premium**. So, the liquidity premium theory holds that the interest rate on a long-term bond is an average of the interest rates investors expect on short-term bonds over the lifetime of the long-term bond plus a term premium that increases in value the longer the maturity of the bond.

For example, suppose that the one-year bond currently has an interest rate of 2%, and the interest rate expected on the one-year bond one year from now is 4%. Would investors be just as happy buying a two-year bond with an interest rate of 3%? The two-year bond offers the same interest rate as the average interest rate expected on the two

Liquidity premium theory (or preferred habitat theory) A theory of the term structure of interest rates which holds that the interest rate on a long-term bond is an average of the interest rates investors expect on short-term bonds over the lifetime of the long-term bond plus a term premium that increases in value the longer the maturity of the bond.

Term premium The additional interest investors require in order to be willing to buy a long-term bond rather than a comparable sequence of short-term bonds.

one-year bonds. But because investors *prefer* to buy one-year bonds, they must receive a higher interest rate—say 3.25%—as an incentive to buy the less desirable two-year bond. If investors were offered only 3% on the two-year bond, they would buy the two one-year bonds instead. The additional 0.25% that is needed to make investors see the two-year bond as being competitive with the two one-year bonds is the term premium.

The longer the maturity of a bond, the larger the term premium on the bond. So, a 5-year bond will have a larger term premium than will a 2-year bond, and a 20-year bond will have a larger term premium than will a 10-year bond. In effect, then, the liquidity premium theory adds a term premium to the expectations theory's equation, linking the interest rate on a long-term bond to the interest rate on short-term bonds. For example, if i_{2t}^{TP} is the term premium on a 2-year bond, then the interest rate on a 2-year bond is:

$$i_{2t} = \frac{i_{1t} + i_{1t+1}^e}{2} + i_{2t}^{TP}.$$

Or, more generally, the interest rate on an *n*-period bond is equal to:

$$i_{nt} = \frac{i_{1t} + i_{1t+1}^e + i_{1t+2}^e + i_{1t+3}^e + \ \dots \ + i_{1t+(n-1)}^e}{n} + i_{nt}^{TP}.$$

SOLVED PROBLEM 5.2B

Using the Liquidity Premium Theory to Calculate Expected Interest Rates

Use the data in the following table on Treasury securities of different maturities to solve this problem:

1 year	2 year	3 year
1.25%	2.00%	2.50%

Assume that the liquidity premium theory is correct. On this day, what did investors expect the interest rate to be on the one-year Treasury bill two years from that time if the term premium on a two-year Treasury note was 0.20% and the term premium on a three-year Treasury note was 0.40%? Assume that all three securities are discount bonds that do not pay coupons.

Solving the Problem

Step 1 Review the chapter material. This problem is about calculating expected interest rates using the liquidity premium theory, so you may want to review the section "The Liquidity Premium Theory," which begins on page 162.

Step 2 Use the liquidity premium equation, which links the interest rate on a long-term bond to the interest rates on short-term bonds, to calculate the interest rate that investors expected on the one-year Treasury bill in one year. According to the liquidity premium theory, the interest rate on a two-year bond should equal the average of the interest rate on the current one-year bond and the interest rate expected on the one-year bond in one year, plus the term premium. The problem tells us that the term premium on a two-year Treasury note is 0.20%, so we can calculate the interest rate expected on the one-year bond one year in the future:

$$i_{2t} = 2.00\% = \frac{1.25\% + i^e_{1t+1}}{2} + 0.20\%,$$

or,

$$i^e_{1t+1} = 2.35\%.$$

Step 3 **Answer the problem by using the result from step 2 to calculate the interest rate investors expected on the one-year Treasury bill in two years.**

$$i_{3t} = 2.50\% = \frac{1.25\% + 2.35\% + i^e_{1t+2}}{3} + 0.40\%,$$

or,

$$i^e_{1t+2} = 2.70\%.$$

See related problem 2.12 at the end of the chapter.

Table 5.5 summarizes key aspects of the three theories of the term structure of interest rates.

TABLE 5.5 Theories of the Term Structure of Interest Rates

Theory	Assumptions	Predictions	What the theory explains
Expectations	Investors have the same investment objectives, and, for a given holding period, investors view bonds of different maturities as perfect substitutes for each other.	The interest rate on a long-term bond equals the average of the interest rates expected on the one-year bonds during this holding period.	Explains the slope of the yield curve and why interest rates on short-term and long-term bonds move together. Drawback: Does not explain why the yield curve is usually upward sloping.
Segmented markets	Investors in the bond market do not all have the same objectives, and investors do not see bonds of different maturities as being substitutes for each other.	Interest rates on bonds of different maturities are determined in separate markets.	Explains why the yield curve is usually upward sloping. Drawback: Does not explain why the yield curve will ever be downward sloping or why interest rates on bonds of different maturities move together.
Liquidity premium	Investors view bonds of different maturities as substitutes for each other—but not as perfect substitutes.	The interest rate on an n-year bond equals the average of the interest rates expected on the n one-year bonds during these n years plus a term premium.	Explains all three important facts about the term structure.

Can the Term Structure Predict Recessions?

Investors, managers at firms, and policymakers can use information contained in the term structure of interest rates to forecast economic variables. Under the expectations and liquidity premium theories, the slope of the yield curve shows the short-term interest rates that bond market participants expect in the future. In addition, if fluctuations in expected real interest rates are small, the yield curve contains expectations of future inflation rates. To see why, suppose that you want to know the financial markets' prediction of the rate of inflation five years from now. If the real interest rate is expected to remain constant, you can interpret an upward-sloping yield curve to mean that inflation is expected to rise, leading investors to expect higher nominal interest rates in the future. To provide an accurate forecast of future inflation, you would also need to estimate the term premiums on long-term bonds. The Fed and many other financial market participants use the yield curve to forecast future inflation.

Economists and investors also consider the slope of the yield curve to predict the likelihood of a recession. Economists have focused on the *term spread*, which is the difference between the yield on the 10-year Treasury note and the yield on the 3-month Treasury bill. David C. Wheelock of the Federal Reserve Bank of St. Louis and Mark E. Wohar of the University of Nebraska, Omaha, have found that prior to every recession since 1953, the term spread has narrowed significantly. That is, the yield on the 10-year Treasury note has declined significantly relative to the yield on the 3-month Treasury bill. Wheelock and Wohar looked closely at what happened following periods when the yield curve was inverted, with short-term rates higher than long-term rates. With only one exception, every time the yield on the 3-month bill was higher than the yield on the 10-year note, a recession followed within a year. These results indicate that the slope of the yield curve is a useful tool in predicting recessions.[1]

We can see why the yield curve is useful in predicting recessions by examining several actual yield curves. Figure 5.7 shows three yield curves: one that slopes downward slightly, one that slopes upward slightly, and one that slopes upward steeply. If we apply the liquidity premium theory, these three yield curves—representing three particular days between 2007 and 2016—tell a story about financial markets' expectations about the economy.

[1] David C. Wheelock and Mark E. Wohar, "Can the Term Spread Predict Output Growth and Recessions? A Survey of the Literature," *Federal Reserve Bank of St. Louis Review*, Vol. 91, No. 5, September/October 2009, pp. 419–440.

MyEconLab Real-time data

FIGURE 5.7

Interpreting the Yield Curve

Models of the term structure, such as the liquidity premium theory, help analysts use data on the Treasury yield curve to forecast the future path of the economy. The yield curve from February 2007 is inverted as investors anticipated that a recession was likely to cause future short-term rates to be lower than current short-term rates. The yield curve from January 2008 is characteristic of a normal yield curve under the liquidity premium theory. The unusually low interest rates shown in the yield curve from June 2016 reflect the expectations of investors that slow growth in the U.S. and world economies would cause the Fed and foreign central banks to keep short-term interest rates low indefinitely and the effects of central banks purchases of long-term bonds under the policy of *quantitative easing*, which we discuss in Chapter 15.

Source: U.S. Department of the Treasury.

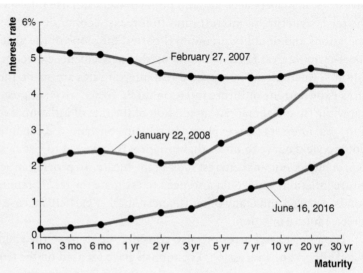

The yield curve from February 2007 is slightly inverted, with the short-term rates being higher than the long-term rates. During 2006 and 2007, the Fed wanted to keep short-term rates relatively high to deal with increasing rates of inflation resulting from rising oil prices and the lingering effects of the housing boom. Investors, though, may have anticipated the economic recession that was to begin in December 2007. As we saw in Chapter 4, during recessions, interest rates typically fall, and short-term rates tend to fall more than long-term rates, as the Fed takes actions to lower rates in hopes of stimulating the economy. In this situation, the liquidity premium theory of the term structure predicts that long-term rates should be lower than short-term rates, making the yield curve inverted.

The upward slope in the yield curve during January 2008 is characteristic of a normal yield curve under the liquidity premium theory. By that time, the economy was two months into the recession. However, investors expected that, as economic activity increased in the future, the demand for credit would increase, causing interest rates to increase. In other words, investors expected future short-term rates to rise above then-current levels. Therefore, the yield curve was upward sloping.

The bottom yield curve is from June 2016 (and is also shown in Figure 5.4). By that time, the Fed had taken policy actions to drive short-term rates to extremely low levels. Many investors were convinced that slow growth in the U.S. and world economies would cause the Fed and foreign central banks to keep short-term interest rates low indefinitely. In addition, central banks had made direct purchases of long-term bonds under a policy of *quantitative easing*, which we will discuss further in Chapter 15. These factors made the yield curve flatter than it typically is in normal economic times.

ANSWERING THE KEY QUESTION

Continued from page 139

At the beginning of this chapter, we asked:

"Should the government more closely regulate credit rating agencies?"

Like some other policy questions we will encounter in this book, this one has no definitive answer. We have seen in this chapter that investors often rely on the credit rating agencies for important information on the default risk on bonds. During the financial crisis of 2007–2009, many bonds—particularly mortgage-backed securities—turned out to have much higher levels of default risk than the credit rating agencies had indicated. Some economists and members of Congress argued that the rating agencies had given those bonds inflated ratings because the agencies have a conflict of interest in being paid by the firms whose bond issues they rate. Other economists, though, argued that the ratings may have been accurate when given, but the creditworthiness of the bonds declined rapidly following the unexpected severity of the housing bust and the resulting financial crisis. Despite increased regulation of the rating agencies following the financial crisis, the companies and governments that issue bonds continue to pay the agencies that rate them. It seems unlikely at this point that significant further changes in regulations will occur in the absence of another financial crisis.

Key Terms and Problems

Key Terms

Bond rating, p. 141

Default risk (or credit risk),
  p. 141

Expectations theory, p. 155

Liquidity premium theory (or
  preferred habitat theory), p. 162

Municipal bonds, p. 149

Risk structure of interest rates, p. 140

Segmented markets theory, p. 161

Term premium, p. 162

Term structure of interest rates,
  p. 152

5.1 The Risk Structure of Interest Rates
Explain why bonds with the same maturity can have different interest rates.

Review Questions

1.1 Briefly explain why bonds that have the same maturities often do not have the same interest rates.

1.2 How is a bond's rating related to the bond issuer's creditworthiness?

1.3 How does the interest rate on an illiquid bond compare with the interest rate on a liquid bond? How does the interest rate on a bond with high information costs compare with the interest rate on a bond with low information costs?

1.4 What are the two types of income an investor can earn on a bond? How is each taxed?

1.5 Compare the tax treatment of the coupons on the following three bonds: a bond issued by the city of Houston, a bond issued by Apple, and a bond issued by the U.S. Treasury.

Problems and Applications

1.6 Why might the bond rating agencies lower their ratings on a firm's bonds? Draw a demand and supply graph for bonds that shows the effect on a bond that has its rating lowered. Be sure to show the demand and supply curves and the equilibrium price of the bond before and after the rating is lowered.

1.7 According to Moody's, "Obligations rated Aaa are judged to be of the highest quality, subject to the lowest level of credit risk."

   a. What "obligations" is Moody's referring to?

   b. What does Moody's mean by "credit risk"?

Source: Moody's Investors Service, *Moody's Rating Symbols and Definitions*, May 2016, p. 5.

1.8 [Related to the Chapter Opener on page 139] The Aflac bond mentioned in the chapter opener was rated A− by Moody's, while the AMD bond was rated CCC.

   a. Do these ratings help explain the difference in the yields on the firms' bonds noted in the chapter opener? Briefly explain.

   b. At the same time that AMD's bonds had yields above 10%, an article in the *Wall Street Journal* noted that AMD "is angling to lower the cost of virtual reality, targeting the field with a new line of graphics hardware priced at $199—half or less the cost of comparable products." If AMD is successful in earning large profits from selling its new virtual reality hardware, what is the effect likely to be on its bond yields? Illustrate your answer with a graph showing the market for AMD's bonds.

Source: Don Clark, "AMD Prices 3-D Tech to Spur Virtual Reality Market," *Wall Street Journal*, May 31, 2016.

1.9 According to an article in the *Wall Street Journal*, bonds issued in 2016 by the toy store chain Toys "R" Us that matured in 2018 and had a 10% coupon were trading at "31 cents on the dollar." Why would an investor sell one of these bonds for 31 cents on the dollar rather than hold the bond for two years and receive 100 cents on the dollar when the bond matured? Which of the following ratings is this bond likely to have received: AAA, BBB, or CCC? Briefly explain.

Source: Matt Wirz and Matt Jarzemsky, "Toys 'R' Us Poses a Test for Junk-Bond Markets," *Wall Street Journal*, February 21, 2016.

1.10 [Related to Solved Problem 5.1 on page 144] In 2016, an article in the *Economist* about the bond market in China noted that the "spreads between yields on AAA-rated corporate bonds and government bonds fell to historic lows of less than 0.4 percentage points this January." What does this decline in spreads indicate about investors' expectations of the default risk on the corporate bonds? Illustrate what was happening in the bond market in China using one graph showing the market for corporate bonds and another graph showing the market for Chinese government bonds.

Source: "Risky Returns," *Economist*, May 7, 2016.

1.11 [Related to the Making the Connection on page 146]
According to an article in the *Wall Street Journal*, in May 2016, "Social Finance Inc., known as SoFi, for the first time received the highest possible credit rating from Moody's on a new bond deal."

a. What is Moody's highest possible credit rating? What information does this rating provide investors?

b. How does Moody's earn revenue from rating bonds like SoFi's? Should investors be concerned about how Moody's earns its revenue from rating bonds? Briefly explain.

Source: Telis Demos and Peter Rudegeair, "Online Lender SoFi's Bond Deal Receives Highest Moody's Rating," *Wall Street Journal*, May 21, 2016.

1.12 [Related to the Making the Connection on page 146]
According an article published in the *Wall Street Journal* in 2016, "Moody's Investors Service has agreed to pay $130 million to end a prominent lawsuit alleging crisis-era misconduct." The article also noted: "The industry's business model … remains in place."

a. What is the industry's business model?

b. Is there a relationship between the industry's business model and the misconduct the rating agencies were accused of during the financial crisis of 2007–2009? Briefly explain.

c. Why does the industry's business model remain in place?

Source: Timothy W. Martin, "Moody's to Pay Calpers $130 Million to Settle Lawsuit," *Wall Street Journal*, March 9, 2016.

1.13 Beginning in 2009, Congress authorized "Build America Bonds," which states and cities could issue to build roads, bridges, and schools. Unlike with regular municipal bonds, however, the coupons on Build America Bonds are taxable. Would

you expect the interest rates on these bonds to be higher or lower than the interest rates on comparable municipal bonds? Briefly explain.

1.14 An article appeared in the *New York Times* under the headline "Spanish Bond Yields Soar."

a. Can we tell from the headline whether the demand for Spanish government bonds was increasing or decreasing? Briefly explain.

b. Can we tell from the headline whether the prices of Spanish government bonds were increasing or decreasing? Briefly explain.

c. The article observes that Spain is "reaping the bitter harvest of a decade of ambitious and often unchecked spending on infrastructure and services." What does this observation have to do with the article's headline?

Source: Raphael Minder and Liz Alderman, "Spanish Bond Yields Soar," *New York Times*, July 23, 2012.

1.15 [Related to the Making the Connection on page 151]
According to an article on the junk bond market in Europe published in the *Economist* in 2016, "The spread (the interest premium over government borrowing rates) paid by junk-bond issuers has risen by nearly three-and-a-half percentage points since March last year."

a. How can you tell whether a newly issued bond is a junk bond?

b. Why would the spread between government bonds and junk bonds have been rising?

c. Does this increase in the spread make junk bonds a better or a worse investment compared with buying government-issued bonds? Briefly explain.

Source: "The Crazy World of Credit," *Economist*, January 30, 2016.

1.16 Suppose that, holding yield constant, investors are indifferent as to whether they hold bonds issued by the federal government or bonds issued by state and local governments (that is, they consider the bonds the same with respect to default risk, information costs, and liquidity). Suppose that state governments have issued perpetuities (or consols) with $75 coupons and that the federal government has also

issued perpetuities with $75 coupons. If the state and federal perpetuities both have after-tax yields of 8%, what are their pretax yields? (Assume that the relevant federal income tax rate is 39.6%.)

5.2 The Term Structure of Interest Rates

Explain why bonds with different maturities can have different interest rates.

Review Questions

2.1 In his memoir, former Federal Reserve Chair Ben Bernanke remarked: "In setting longer-term rates, market participants take into account their expectations for the evolution of short-term rates." Explain what he meant.

Source: Ben S. Bernanke, *The Courage to Act: A Memoir of a Crisis and Its Aftermath*, New York: W.W. Norton, & Company, 2015, p. 75.

2.2 How does the Treasury yield curve illustrate the term structure of interest rates?

2.3 What are three key facts about the term structure?

2.4 Briefly describe the three theories of the term structure.

Problems and Applications

2.5 [Related to the Chapter Opener on page 139] The chapter opener noted that in mid-2016, you could earn an interest rate of 0.25% by buying a 3-month Treasury bill or an interest rate of 2.6% by buying 30-year Treasury bond. Briefly explain how the Treasury is able to find buyers for 3-month Treasury bills when investors could earn an interest rate 10 times as high by buying 30-year Treasury bonds.

2.6 Suppose that you want to invest for three years to earn the highest possible return. You have three options: (a) Roll over three one-year bonds, which pay interest rates of 8% in the first year, 11% in the second year, and 7% in the third year; (b) buy a two-year bond with a 10% interest rate and then roll over the amount received when

that bond matures into a one-year bond with an interest rate of 7%; or (c) buy a three-year bond with an interest rate of 8.5%. Assuming annual compounding, no coupon payments, and no cost of buying or selling bonds, which option should you choose?

2.7 Suppose that you have $1,000 to invest in the bond market on January 1, 2018. You could buy a one-year bond with an interest rate of 4%, a two-year bond with an interest rate of 5%, a three-year bond with an interest rate of 5.5%, or a four-year bond with an interest rate of 6%. You expect interest rates on one-year bonds in the future to be 6.5% on January 1, 2019, 7% on January 1, 2020, and 9% on January 1, 2021. You want to hold your investment until January 1, 2022. Which of the following investment alternatives gives you the highest return by 2022: (a) Buy a four-year bond on January 1, 2018; (b) buy a three-year bond January 1, 2018, and a one-year bond January 1, 2021; (c) buy a two-year bond January 1, 2018, a one-year bond January 1, 2020, and another one-year bond January 1, 2021; or (d) buy a one-year bond January 1, 2018, and then additional one-year bonds on the first days of 2019, 2020, and 2021?

2.8 Suppose that the interest rate on a one-year Treasury bill is currently 1% and that investors expect that the interest rates on one-year Treasury bills over the next three years will be 2%, 3%, and 2%. Use the expectations theory to calculate the current interest rates on two-year, three-year, and four-year Treasury notes.

2.9 **[Related to the** Making the Connection **on page 154]** In the spring of 2016, an article on cnbc.com noted: "Yields on the benchmark 10-year JGB [Japanese government bond] have turned negative, which essentially means that bondholders are paying for the privilege of lending money to the Japanese government." Why would bondholders pay to lend money to the Japanese government? Shouldn't the Japanese government be paying the bondholders to borrow their money?

Source: Leslie Shaffer, "Why JGB Yields Won't Keep Falling Deeper into Negative Yield," cnbc.com, April 3, 2016.

2.10 **[Related to** Solved Problem 5.2A **on page 159]** An article in the *Wall Street Journal* quoted an anonymous billionaire investor as asking: "Has there ever been a carry trade that hasn't ended badly?" What is a carry trade? Why might it end badly?

Source: Robert Frank, "Where Billionaires Are Putting Their Money," *Wall Street Journal*, September 15, 2010.

2.11 **[Related to** Solved Problem 5.2A **on page 159]** Interest rates on U.S. Treasury bills are typically much lower than interest rates on U.S. Treasury notes and bonds. If the federal government wants to reduce the interest charges it pays when it borrows money, why doesn't the Treasury stop selling Treasury notes and bonds and sell only bills?

2.12 **[Related to** Solved Problem 5.2B **on page 163]** Use the data on Treasury securities in the table to answer the following question:

1 year	2 year	3 year
0.75%	1.25%	2.00%

Assuming that the liquidity premium theory is correct, what did investors on this day expect the interest rate to be on the one-year Treasury bill two years from now if the term premium on a two-year Treasury note was 0.10% and the term premium on a three-year Treasury note was 0.25%? Assume that all three securities are discount bonds that pay no coupons.

2.13 In 2016, when the interest rate on 10-year German government bonds became negative, an article in the *Wall Street Journal* noted that the interest rate on 10-year bonds depended in part on investors' expectations of future short-term interest rates. The article also noted that "investors don't seem to have changed their perception of ... [short-term] interest rates in the future." If the article is correct, can the expectations theory explain why the interest rate on 10-year German government bonds declined? Can the liquidity premium theory? Briefly explain.

Source: Jon Sindreu, "Are German Bonds Riding a Bubble?" *Wall Street Journal*, June 14, 2016.

2.14 The following quote from an article in the *Wall Street Journal* describes events in the market for Treasury securities that day: "Treasurys prices were mixed, with the shorter end of the curve rising and longer-dated Treasurys falling in price." On one graph, draw two Treasury yield curves: one curve showing the situation on that day (as described in the sentence) and one curve showing the situation on the day before. Label one curve "today" and the other curve "previous day." Be sure to label both axes of your yield curve graph.

Source: *Wall Street Journal*, February 22, 2008.

2.15 In 2016, an article in the *Wall Street Journal* argued that the "latest drop in the 10-year yield has caused a flattening of the yield curve ... that is disconcerting."

a. What does the article mean by a "flattening of the yield curve"?

b. Why might a flattening of the yield curve be disconcerting?

Source: Justin Lahart, "The Yield Curve's Message for the Fed," *Wall Street Journal*, June 9, 2016.

Data Exercises

D5.1: **[The yield curve and recessions]** Go to the web site of the Federal Reserve Bank of St. Louis (FRED) (fred.stlouisfed.org) and for the period from January 1957 to the present download to the same graph the data series for the 3-month Treasury bill (TB3MS) and the 10-year Treasury note (GS10). Go to the web site of the National Bureau of Economic Research (nber.org) and find the dates for business cycle peaks and troughs (the period between a business cycle peak and trough is a recession). During which months was the yield curve inverted? How many of these periods were followed within a year by a recession?

D5.2: **[Predicting with the yield curve]** Go to www.treasury.gov and find the page "Daily Treasury Yield Curve Rates." Briefly describe the current shape of the yield curve. Can you use the yield curve to draw any conclusion about what investors in the bond market expect will happen to the economy in the future?

D5.3: **[The spread between high-grade bonds and junk bonds]** Go to the web site of the Federal Reserve Bank of St. Louis (FRED) (fred.stlouisfed.org) and for the period from January 1997 to the present, download to the same graph the data series for the BofA Merrill Lynch US Corporate AAA Effective Yield (BAMLC0A1CAAAEY) and the BofA Merrill Lynch US High Yield CCC or Below Effective Yield (BAMLH0A3HYCEY). Describe how the difference between the yields on high-grade corporate bonds and on junk bonds have changed over this period.

The Stock Market, Information, and Financial Market Efficiency

Learning Objectives

After studying this chapter, you should be able to:

6.1 Describe the basic operations of the stock market (pages 174–181)

6.2 Explain how stock prices are determined (pages 182–188)

6.3 Explain the connection between the assumption of rational expectations and the efficient markets hypothesis (pages 188–197)

6.4 Discuss the actual efficiency of financial markets (pages 197–200)

6.5 Describe the basic concepts of behavioral finance (pages 201–203)

Are You Willing to Invest in the Stock Market?

Everybody seems to love Apple. From the iPod to the iPhone to the iPad to the Apple Watch, the firm has released one hit product after another. But how good an investment has Apple been? Suppose your grandparents had given you 1,000 shares of Apple's stock in 2000. If you had held on to the shares through June 2016, what would have happened to your investment? As the following table shows, the dollar value of your 1,000 shares would have been 23 times greater in 2016 than it was in 2000. But the table also shows that you would have been in for a wild ride, with the value of your investment bouncing up and down like a yo-yo. But Apple is just one stock. What if your stock market investment had been spread across a group of stocks?

Date	Price per share of Apple stock	Value of 1,000 shares of Apple stock
April 2000	$4.08	$4,080
December 2000	0.98	980
February 2005	5.90	5,900
November 2007	23.96	23,960
February 2009	11.74	11,740
May 2015	127.67	127,670
June 2016	95.33	95,330

Continued on next page

KEY ISSUE AND QUESTION

Issue: Stock prices go through large swings up and down.

Question: Does the volatility of the stock market affect the broader economy?

Answered on page 203

The Dow Jones Industrial Average (often called "the Dow") is the best-known measure of the performance of the U.S. stock market. The Dow is an average of the stock prices of 30 large corporations. If you had invested in the Dow in 2000, your investment would have declined by more than 25% by early 2003. But, good news! Between early 2003 and the fall of 2007, your investment would have increased by more than 75% ... before declining by more than 50% between the fall of 2007 and the spring of 2009 ... and then bouncing back almost 50% by the end of 2009. So, your investment in the Dow would have been as unstable as your investment in just Apple.

Clearly, buying stocks is not for cautious investors. But what explains the volatility of stock prices?

More importantly, what role does the stock market play in the financial system and the economy? Although the stock market has always been volatile, the movements in stock prices during the past 15 years have been particularly large. The plunge in stock prices during the 2007–2009 financial crisis unnerved many investors, some of whom took all their savings out of the stock market and vowed never to return.

Do swings in stock prices matter for production and employment in the economy? Or are they mainly of concern to investors? Should you avoid the stock market and keep your savings in less volatile investments? We explore these questions in this chapter.

The stock market is an important source of funds for large corporations. It is also where millions of individual investors save for large purchases and for retirement. Savers sometimes buy individual stocks, but more often their stock market investments are in mutual funds or pension funds. In this chapter, we discuss the stock market and look at the factors that determine stock prices.

6.1 Stocks and the Stock Market

LEARNING OBJECTIVE: Describe the basic operations of the stock market.

As we saw in Chapter 1, by buying stock in a company, an investor becomes a partial owner of the company. As an owner, a stockholder, sometimes called a *shareholder*, has a legal claim on the firm's profits and on its *equity*, which is the difference between the value of the firm's assets and the value of its liabilities. Because ownership of a firm's stock represents partial ownership of a firm, stocks are sometimes called *equities*. Bonds represent debt rather than equity. Most firms issue millions of shares of stock. For instance, by 2016, Apple had issued more than 5 *billion* shares of stock. So, most shareholders own only a very small fraction of the firms they invest in.

Corporation A legal form of business that provides owners with protection from losing more than their investment if the business fails.

People who are *sole proprietors*, which means they are the sole owners of a firm, and people who co-own a firm as a *partnership* typically have unlimited liability for the firm's debts. If these firms go bankrupt, anyone they owe money to can sue the owners for their personal assets. An investor who owns stock in a firm organized as a **corporation** is protected by *limited liability*. **Limited liability** is a legal provision that shields owners of a corporation from losing more than they have invested in the firm. If you had bought $10,000 worth of stock in Republic Airways, that was the most you could lose when the airline went bankrupt in 2016. In the eyes of the law, a corporation is a legal "person," separate from its owners. Without the protection of limited liability, many investors would be reluctant to invest in firms whose key decisions are made by the firm's managers rather than by its stockholders.

Limited liability A legal provision that shields owners of a corporation from losing more than they have invested in the firm.

Common Stock Versus Preferred Stock

There are two main categories of stock: common stock and preferred stock. Both represent partial ownership of a corporation, but they have some significant differences. A corporation is run by its *board of directors*, who appoint the firm's top management, such as the chief executive officer (CEO), chief operating officer (COO), and chief financial officer (CFO). *Common stockholders* elect the members of the board of directors, but *preferred stockholders* are not eligible to vote in these elections.

Corporations distribute some of their profits to their stockholders by making payments called **dividends**, which are typically paid quarterly. Preferred stockholders receive a fixed dividend that is set when the corporation issues the stock. Common stockholders receive a dividend that fluctuates as the profitability of the corporation varies over time. Corporations suffering losses may decide to suspend paying dividends, but if the corporation does pay dividends, it must first pay the dividend promised to preferred stockholders before making any dividend payments to the common stockholders. If the corporation declares bankruptcy, its debt holders—investors and financial institutions that have bought the corporation's bonds or made loans to the corporation—are paid off first, and then the preferred stockholders are paid off. If any money remains, the company pays the common stockholders.

The total market value of a firm's common and preferred stock is called the firm's *market capitalization*. For instance, in late 2016, the total value of Apple's outstanding stock—and, therefore, Apple's market capitalization—was about $628 billion, which was the largest among U.S. corporations.

Dividend A payment that a corporation makes to stockholders, typically on a quarterly basis.

How and Where Stocks Are Bought and Sold

Although there are more than 5 million corporations in the United States, only about 5,100 corporations are **publicly traded companies** that sell stock in the U.S. stock market. The remaining corporations, along with the millions of sole proprietorships and partnerships, are *private firms*, which means they do not issue stock that is bought and sold on the stock market.

Just as the "automobile market" refers to the many places where automobiles are bought and sold, the "stock market" refers to the many places where stocks are bought and sold. In the case of stocks, the "places" are both physical and virtual, as the electronic trading of stocks has become increasingly important. Still, when many people think of the U.S. stock market, they think of the New York Stock Exchange (NYSE) building, which is located on Wall Street in New York City. The NYSE is an example of a **stock exchange** where stocks are bought and sold face-to-face on a trading floor. Trading takes place every business day between the hours of 9:30 A.M. and 4:00 P.M. Many of the largest U.S. corporations, such as IBM, McDonald's, and Walmart, are listed on the NYSE's Big Board. In recent years, much of the trading on the NYSE has been done electronically, although some trading still takes place on the floor of the exchange. Trading on the NASDAQ stock market, which is named for the National Association of Securities Dealers, is entirely electronic. The NASDAQ is an example of an **over-the-counter market**, in which *dealers* linked by computer buy and sell stocks. Dealers in an over-the-counter market attempt to match up the orders they receive from investors to buy and sell the stocks. Dealers maintain an inventory of the stocks they trade to help balance buy and sell orders.

Publicly traded company A corporation that sells stock in the U.S. stock market; only 5,100 of the 5 million U.S. corporations are publicly traded companies.

Stock exchange A physical location where stocks are bought and sold face-to-face on a trading floor.

Over-the-counter market A market in which financial securities are bought and sold by dealers linked by computer.

Keep in mind the distinction between a primary market and a secondary market. In the stock market, just as in the bond market, most buying and selling is of existing stocks rather than stocks firms have newly issued. So, for both stocks and bonds, the secondary market is much larger than the primary market.

Traditionally, an individual investor purchased stocks by establishing an account with a stockbroker, such as Merrill Lynch (now part of Bank of America). Brokers buy and sell stocks for investors in return for a payment known as a *commission*. Today, many investors buying individual stocks use online brokerage firms, such as E*TRADE or TD Ameritrade. Online brokers typically charge lower commissions than do traditional brokers, but they often do not provide investment advice and other services that traditional brokers offer. Many investors prefer to buy stock mutual funds rather than individual stocks. Because stock mutual funds, such as Fidelity Investment's Magellan Fund, hold many stocks in their portfolios, they provide investors with the benefits of diversification.

The 5,100 publicly traded U.S. corporations represent only about 10% of the firms listed on stock exchanges worldwide. Figure 6.1 shows the 10 largest global stock markets, listed by the total value of the shares traded. Although the NYSE remains the world's largest, foreign stock markets have been rapidly increasing in size. The shares of the largest foreign firms, such as Sony, Toyota, and Nokia, trade indirectly on the NYSE in the form of *American Depository Receipts*, which are receipts for shares of stock held in a foreign country. Some mutual funds, such as Vanguard's Global Equity Fund, also invest in the stock of foreign firms. It is possible to buy individual stocks listed on foreign stock

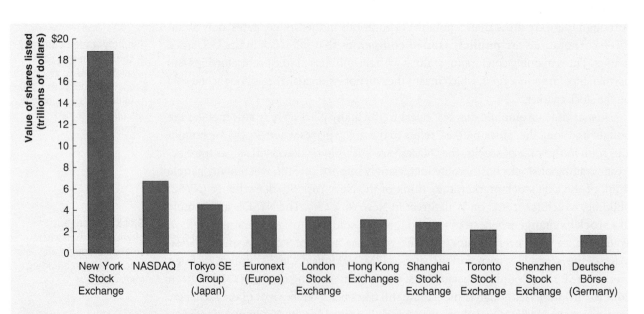

FIGURE 6.1 World Stock Exchanges, 2015

The New York Stock Exchange remains the largest stock exchange in the world, but other exchanges have been increasing in size. The exchanges are ranked on the basis of the total value of the shares traded on them.

Note: Although they operate independently, the New York Stock Exchange owns Euronext.

Source: www.world-exchanges.org.

exchanges by setting up an account with a local brokerage firm in the foreign country. Although at one time only the wealthy invested directly in foreign stock markets, today the Internet has made it much easier for the average investor to research foreign companies and establish foreign brokerage accounts.

Measuring the Performance of the Stock Market

If we want to measure inflation, we can't look at the price of just one good. Doing so could be misleading because, for instance, the price of gasoline might be falling at a time when many other prices are rising. Instead, when the government measures inflation, employees of the Bureau of Labor Statistics first calculate the consumer price index (CPI), which averages the prices of many goods and services. Similarly, when we are interested in measuring the performance of the stock market, we can't do so by following the price of any one company—even a company as large and important as Apple, Walmart, or General Motors.

Instead, we measure the overall performance of the stock market by using **stock market indexes**, which are averages of stock prices, just as the CPI is an average of the prices of goods and services. Keep in mind these two key points about index numbers like the CPI or the stock market indexes:

Stock market index An average of stock prices that investors use to measure the overall performance of the stock market.

1. The numbers are not measured in dollars or any other units. Indexes are set equal to 100 in a particular period, called the base period. Because indexes are designed to show movements in a variable over time, the year chosen as the base year is not important.
2. The values of index numbers aren't meaningful by themselves; *changes* in their values are important. For instance, the value of the CPI in June 2016 was 240. No one is particularly interested in that value by itself, but the fact that the CPI increased to 240 from 237 in June 2015 is interesting because it tells us that the inflation rate during that year was $\left(\dfrac{240-237}{237}\right) \times 100 = 1.3\%$. Similarly, the value of a stock market index on a particular day is less interesting than the change in the index's value from the previous day, or month, or year.

The most widely followed stock market indexes are the three that appear on the first page of the *Wall Street Journal*'s web site: the Dow Jones Industrial Average, the S&P 500, and the NASDAQ Composite index. Although the Dow is an average of the prices of the stocks of just 30 large firms, including Coca-Cola, Microsoft, and Walt Disney, it is the most familiar index to many individual investors. The S&P 500 index includes the 30 stocks that are in the Dow as well as stocks issued by 470 other large companies, each of which has a market capitalization of at least $5 billion. A committee of the Standard & Poor's Company chooses the firms to represent the different industries in the U.S. economy. Because these firms are so large, the total value of their stocks represents about 80% of the value of all publicly traded U.S. firms. The NASDAQ Composite index includes the 2,750 stocks that are traded in the NASDAQ over-the-counter market. Some firms in the NASDAQ Composite index, such as Microsoft and Intel, are also included in the Dow and in the S&P 500, but the NASDAQ includes stocks issued by many smaller technology firms that are not included in the other indexes.

Although these three stock indexes are averages of the stock prices of different companies, Figure 6.2 shows that the indexes move broadly together. All three indexes increased substantially in the late 1990s and reached peaks in early 2000. Much of the growth in stock prices during the late 1990s was fueled by the "dot-com boom," during which investors enthusiastically believed that many new online firms would become very profitable competing with traditional brick-and-mortar stores. Some dot-coms, such as Amazon.com, did succeed and became profitable, but others, such as Pets.com, eToys.com, and Webvan.com, did not. Because the NASDAQ Composite index contained many more dot-com stocks than did the other two indexes, it soared to a particularly high peak in early 2000. As investors became convinced that many dot-coms would not become profitable, all three indexes declined sharply, although the decline in the NASDAQ was the most severe. The recession of 2001 also contributed to a general fall in stock prices.

The Dow and the S&P 500 recovered from the dot-com crash, reaching new all-time highs in the fall of 2007. The financial crisis and the recession that began in December 2007 caused the three indexes to decline sharply until the spring of 2009, when all three began to recover. In Wall Street jargon, an increase in stock prices of more than 20% from a previous low is called a *bull market*, while a decline in stock prices of more than 20% from a previous high is called a *bear market*. So, during the period covered by the graphs, the U.S. stock market experienced three bull markets and two bear markets.

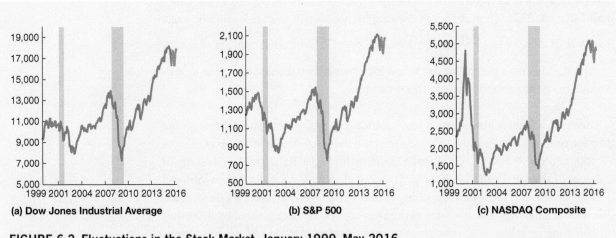

(a) Dow Jones Industrial Average   (b) S&P 500   (c) NASDAQ Composite

FIGURE 6.2 Fluctuations in the Stock Market, January 1999–May 2016

Investors can follow the performance of the U.S. stock market through stock market indexes, which are averages of stock prices. The most widely followed indexes are the Dow Jones Industrial Average, the S&P 500 index, and the NASDAQ Composite index.

The graphs show that all three indexes followed roughly similar patterns, although the NASDAQ reached a particularly high peak in early 2000 that it didn't attain again for more than 15 years. The shaded areas represent years when the economy was in a recession.

Does the Performance of the Stock Market Matter to the Economy?

Figure 6.2 shows that the stock market goes through substantial swings. These swings affect the personal finances of investors who own stocks, but do the swings affect the broader economy by causing fluctuations in employment and production? Increases and decreases in stock prices can affect the spending of households and firms, which in turn affects the economy. Rising stock prices can lead to increased spending, which can lead to increases in production and employment. Falling stock prices can lead to decreased spending, which can lead to decreases in production and employment. Most economic recessions are preceded by a decline in stock prices, which makes stock prices a *leading indicator* of recessions. However, not every recession is preceded by a decline in stock prices, and not every decline in stock prices is followed by a recession. So, declines in stock prices are not reliable predictors of recessions.

The effect of changes in stock prices on spending occurs primarily through three channels:

1. *Changes in the cost of equity funding for firms.* Large corporations use the stock market as an important source of funds for expansion. Financing spending through stock sales is called *equity funding*. Higher stock prices make it easier for firms to fund spending on real physical investments such as factories and machinery, or on research and development, by issuing new stock. Lower stock prices make it more difficult for firms to finance this type of spending.

2. *Changes in household wealth.* Stocks make up a significant portion of household wealth. When stock prices rise, so does household wealth, and when stock prices fall, so does household wealth. For example, the increase in stock prices between 1995 and 2000 increased wealth by $9 trillion, while the decline in stock prices between 2000 and 2002 wiped out $7 trillion in wealth. Similarly, the fall in stock prices between the fall of 2007 and the spring of 2009 wiped out $8.5 trillion in wealth. Households spend more when their wealth increases and less when their wealth decreases. So, fluctuations in stock prices can have a significant effect on the consumption spending of households.

3. *Changes in the expectations of households and firms.* The most important consequence of fluctuations in stock prices may be their effect on the expectations of consumers and firms. Significant declines in stock prices are typically followed by economic recessions. Consumers who are aware of this pattern may become more uncertain about their future incomes and jobs when they see a large fall in stock prices. Such uncertainty may lead them to postpone spending on houses and consumer durables, such as cars, furniture, and appliances. Firms have to be confident that demand for their products will be sustained for a period of years before they invest in physical capital, such as new factories, office buildings, or information technology, or in research and development of new products. A recession may cause this investment spending to become unprofitable. A significant decline in stock prices may lead firms to err on the side of safety and postpone spending until the uncertainty about the economy has diminished.

Did the Stock Market Crash of 1929 Cause the Great Depression?

The Great Depression of the 1930s was the worst economic downturn in U.S. history. Although production and employment began declining in August 1929, most people at the time dated the beginning of the Depression to the stock market crash in October. On Monday, October 28, prices on the New York Stock Exchange declined by more than 10%. The following day, called "Black Tuesday," has been described by one economist as "the most devastating day in the history of the New York stock market, and it may have been the most devastating day in the history of markets." Panel (a) in the following figure shows movements in the S&P 500 from 1920 to 1939. Panel (b) shows movements in real GDP for the same time period. (The shaded areas represent periods of recession during the Great Depression.)

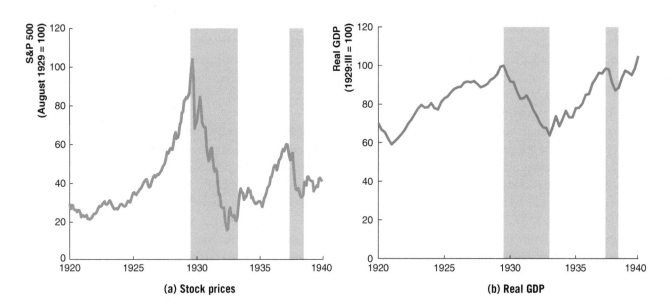

(a) Stock prices   **(b) Real GDP**

Does the decline in stock prices—particularly the crash in October 1929—explain the unprecedented decline in real GDP from 1929 to 1933? In a widely read book, *The Great Crash, 1929*, published in 1955, Harvard economist John Kenneth Galbraith argued that by destroying wealth and reducing income from capital gains, the stock market crash reduced consumption spending, particularly spending on consumer durables. The stock market crash also diminished the confidence of households and firms in future economic prosperity, further reducing spending. As a result, the crash increased the severity of the downturn that had begun in August, turning what would otherwise have been a normal recession into the Great Depression.

Later economists questioned Galbraith's analysis. The stock market has experienced sizable declines since 1929 without triggering another depression. For instance, on October 19, 1987, the S&P 500 declined by more than 20%—its largest one-day decline ever, and almost twice the size of the decline that occurred on October 29, 1929. Yet in the following months, the U.S. economy did not suffer even a recession, much less a depression. Nobel Laureate Milton Friedman of the University of Chicago and Anna Schwartz of the National Bureau of Economic Research made a very influential argument that it was the collapse of the U.S. banking system, beginning in the fall of 1930, rather than the stock market crash that explains the severity of the Great Depression. (We return to this argument in Chapter 12.)

Some economists, though, do believe that the stock market crash played an important role in the severity of the Depression. Christina Romer, an economist at the University of California, Berkeley, and former chair of the Council of Economic Advisers under President Barack Obama, argues that the crash of 1929 was more severe and prolonged than later crashes, such as the one in 1987. By December 1929, stock prices had already fallen by 32% from their peak. This decline increased uncertainty among consumers about their future incomes, which caused them to significantly reduce spending on consumer durables, such as cars, furniture, and appliances. In addition, consumers were more reluctant to borrow money to buy durable goods because consumer loan contracts were structured differently than they are today. As Martha Olney, of the University of California, Berkeley, has shown, if a consumer in the 1920s missed a payment, the lender could repossess the car or other durable without compensating the consumer for any equity. Even if you had paid off $500 of a $600 car loan, you would lose the full amount if you missed a payment. Car sales dropped by almost 25% between the crash and January 1930. Romer believes that this decline in consumer spending on durables is the key to understanding why real GDP declined so rapidly during the early months of the Depression.

The disagreements over how large an effect the stock market crash of 1929 had on the Great Depression reflect the wider differences of opinion among economists over the ways in which the financial system interacts with the real economy of production and employment. We will return to these issues in Chapter 12 when we discuss financial crises.

Sources: John Kenneth Galbraith, *The Great Crash, 1929*, Boston: Houghton-Mifflin, 1955; Milton Friedman and Anna J. Schwartz, *A Monetary History of the United States, 1867–1960*, Princeton: Princeton University Press, 1963; Christina D. Romer, "The Great Crash and the Onset of the Great Depression," *Quarterly Journal of Economics*, Vol. 105, No. 3, August 1990, pp. 597–624; and Martha Olney, *Buy Now, Pay Later: Advertising, Credit, and Consumer Durables in the 1920s*, Chapel Hill, NC: University of North Carolina Press, 1991. Data for the stock market graph are adapted from Robert J. Shiller, "Stock Market Data Used in 'Irrational Exuberance,' Princeton University Press, 2000, 2005, 2015, updated," and are adjusted to make the value for August 1929 equal to 100; data for the real GDP graph are adapted from Robert J. Gordon, ed., *The American Business Cycle, Continuity and Change*, Chicago: University of Chicago Press, 1986, Appendix B, as downloaded from nber.org, "Tables from 'The American Business Cycle,'" posted February 2008, and are adjusted from GNP to GDP and to make the value for the third quarter of 1929 equal to 100.

See related problem 1.8 at the end of the chapter.

| 6.2 | ## How Stock Prices Are Determined |

LEARNING OBJECTIVE: Explain how stock prices are determined.

We have seen that stock market indexes fluctuate, but what determines the prices of the individual stocks that make up those indexes? Recall a key fact about financial markets from Chapter 3: *The price of a financial asset is equal to the present value of the payments to be received from owning it.* We have applied this rule to the prices of bonds, but the rule holds equally for stocks, as we will see in the following sections.

Investing in Stock for One Year

Individual investors do not purchase stock in an attempt to control the firms whose stock they buy; they leave that to the firms' managers, supervised by their boards of directors. Instead, investors view purchases of stock as a financial investment on which they hope to receive a high rate of return. Suppose you intend to invest in Microsoft stock for one year. During the year, you expect to receive a dividend, and at the end of the year you could sell the stock for its market price at that time. Firms pay dividends quarterly, but for the sake of simplicity, we will assume that they make a single payment of dividends at the end of the year. Note that dividends on common stock are not fixed the way coupon payments on bonds are. A firm that suffers unexpected losses may decide to cut its dividend below what investors had expected it to pay. Suppose you expect that Microsoft will pay a dividend of $0.60 per share and that the price of Microsoft stock at the end of the year will be $32 per share. To the investor, the value of the stock equals the present value of these two dollar amounts, which are the *cash flows* from owning the stock.

We saw in Chapter 3 how investors in the bond market use an interest rate to discount future payments in calculating the present value of a bond. Similarly, you need to use a discount rate to calculate the present value of the cash flows from the stock. Rather than use the interest rate on, say, bank CDs to discount the cash flows, it makes sense to use a rate that represents your expected return on alternative investments of comparable risk to investing in shares of Microsoft. Taking the viewpoint of investors, economists refer to this rate as the **required return on equities, r_E.** From the viewpoint of firms, this is the rate of return they need to pay to attract investors, so it is called the *equity cost of capital.* The required return on equities and the equity cost of capital are the same rate—just looked at from the differing perspectives of investors and firms.

Required return on equities, r_E The expected return necessary to compensate for the risk of investing in stocks.

We can think of the required return on equities as the sum of a risk-free interest rate—usually measured as the return on Treasury bills—and a risk premium because investments in stocks are riskier than investments in Treasury bills. The risk premium included in the required return on equities is called the *equity premium* because it represents the additional return investors must receive in order to invest in stocks (equities) rather than Treasury bills. The equity premium for an individual stock, such as Microsoft, has two components. One component represents the *systematic risk* that results from general price fluctuations in the stock market that affect all stocks, such as the decline in stock prices during the financial crisis of 2007–2009. The other component is *unsystematic,* or *idiosyncratic,* risk that results from movements in the price of that particular stock that are not caused by general fluctuations in the stock market. An example of unsystematic risk would be the price of Microsoft's stock falling because a new version of Windows has poor sales.

Suppose that taking these factors into account, you require a 10% return in order to be willing to invest in Microsoft. In this case, to you, the present value of the two dollar amounts—the expected dividend and the expected price of the stock at the end of the year—is:

$$\frac{\$0.60}{1\ +\ 0.10}\ +\ \frac{\$32}{1\ +\ 0.10}\ =\ \$29.64.$$

If the price of a share of Microsoft is currently less than $29.64, you should buy the stock because it is selling for less than the present value of the funds you will receive from owning the stock. If the price is greater than $29.64, you should not buy the stock.

If we take the perspective of investors as a group, rather than that of a single investor, then we would expect the price of a stock today, P_t, to equal the sum of the present values of the dividend expected to be paid at the end of the year, D^e_{t+1}, and the expected price of the stock at the end of the year, P^e_{t+1}, discounted by the market's required return on equities, r_E, or

$$P_t\ =\ \frac{D^e_{t+1}}{(1\ +\ r_E)}\ +\ \frac{P^e_{t+1}}{(1\ +\ r_E)}.$$

Note that we use the superscript e to indicate that investors do not know with certainty either the dividend the firm will pay or the price of the firm's stock at the end of the year.

The Rate of Return on a One-Year Investment in a Stock

For a holding period of one year, the rate of return on an investment in a bond equals the current yield on the bond plus the rate of capital gain on the bond. We can calculate the rate of return on an investment in a stock in a similar way. Just as the coupon divided by the current price is the current yield on a bond, the expected annual dividend divided by the current price is the **dividend yield** on a stock. The rate of capital gain on a stock is equal to the change in the price of the stock during the year divided by the price at the beginning of the year. So, the expected rate of return from investing in a stock equals the dividend yield plus the expected rate of capital gain:

Dividend yield The expected annual dividend divided by the current price of a stock.

$$\text{Rate of return}\ =\ \frac{\text{Expected annual dividend}}{\text{Initial price}}\ +\ \frac{\text{Expected change in price}}{\text{Initial price}},$$

or,

$$R\ =\ \frac{D^e_{t+1}}{P_t}\ +\ \frac{(P^e_{t+1}\ -\ P_t)}{P_t}.$$

At the end of the year, you can calculate your actual rate of return by substituting the dividend actually received for the expected dividend and the actual price of the stock at the end of the year for the expected price. For example, suppose that you purchased a share of Microsoft for $30, Microsoft paid a dividend of $0.60, and the price of Microsoft at the end of the year was $33. Your rate of return for the year would be:

$$(\$0.60/\$30)\ +\ (\$33\ -\ \$30)/\$30\ =\ 0.02\ +\ 0.10\ =\ 0.12,\ \text{or } 12\%.$$

MAKING THE CONNECTION IN YOUR INTEREST

How Should the Government Tax Your Investment in Stocks?

If you invest in stocks, you will receive dividends and capital gains on your investments, which you must report as income on your tax return. Economists and policymakers debate the best way of taxing dividends and capital gains. Corporate profits are subject to the corporate income tax, which companies pay before they distribute some of the profits as dividends to their stockholders. Because stockholders must pay individual income taxes on the dividends they receive, the result is a *double taxation of dividends.*

This double taxation has three important effects: First, because dividends are taxed at both the firm level and the individual level, the return investors receive from buying stocks is reduced, which reduces the incentive people have to save in the form of stock investments and increases the costs to firms of raising funds. Second, because profits that firms distribute to stockholders are taxed a second time, firms have an incentive to retain profits rather than to distribute them. (Profits that firms keep rather than distribute as dividends are called *retained earnings.*) Retaining profits may be inefficient if firms are led to make investments that have lower returns than the investments stockholders would have made had they received dividends. Finally, because firms can deduct from their profits the interest payments they make on loans and bonds, the double taxation of dividends gives firms an incentive to take on what may be an excessive level of debt rather than issue stock.

Some economists have proposed eliminating the double taxation of dividends by integrating the corporate and individual income taxes. Under this plan, for tax purposes, firms would allocate all of their profits to their stockholders, even profits the firms don't distribute as dividends. Individuals would be responsible for paying all the taxes due on corporate profits. For example, in 2016 Apple was paying an annual dividend of $2.28, but that amount was only about 20% of Apple's profits. If you own 1,000 shares of Apple stock, you would pay tax not just on the $2,280 you receive in dividends but also on the $9,120 that represents your share of Apple's retained earnings. This plan would eliminate the corporate income tax and thereby end the problems caused by double taxation. But the plan would require an extensive revision of the current tax system and has not attracted much support from policymakers.

Capital gains are taxed only when an investor sells an asset and realizes the gain. Some economists argue that taxing capital gains results in a *lock-in effect* because investors may be reluctant to sell stocks that have substantial capital gains. This reluctance is increased by the fact that investors have to pay taxes on their nominal gains without an adjustment for inflation. For example, suppose you buy a share of Apple stock for $100, hold it for 10 years, and then sell it for $200. If inflation averaged 3% per year during that period, because of rising prices, $200 would buy about the same amount of goods and services as $150 could buy when you purchased the stock. Yet you would be taxed on your $100 nominal gain rather than on your $50 real gain. Having to pay taxes on nominal gains is another reason that investors sometimes avoid selling stock they have owned for years. If many investors are locked into their current portfolios, then the prices in those portfolios will be different than they would be in the absence of capital gains taxes, which may send misleading signals to investors and firms.

In 2003, Congress reduced from 35% to 15% both the tax on dividends and the tax on capital gains on stocks and other assets that investors held for at least one year. In 2013, Congress raised the tax rate on dividends and capital gains to 20% for high-income taxpayers. In addition, some taxpayers are required to pay an additional 3.8% on their capital gains and dividends, raising the top rate to 23.8%. Because these rates are still below the top individual tax rate of 39.6%, some of the inefficiencies resulting from the double taxation of dividends and the taxation of capital gains have been reduced. Some policymakers have criticized the lower tax rate on dividends, however, for adversely affecting the distribution of after-tax income. Households at the very top of the income distribution earn three-quarters of their income from dividends and capital gains. So, the low tax rate on dividends and capital gains can reduce the tax rate high-income households pay relative to the tax rate lower-income households pay because they depend more heavily on wage income that may be taxed at a higher rate.

In early 2017, President Donald Trump proposed cutting tax rates on both dividends and capital gains to improve financial market efficiency and increase economic growth. The trade-off between efficiency and equity is a recurring issue in economic policy. Policymakers must often balance the need to improve economic efficiency, which can increase incomes and growth, with the desire to distribute income more equally.

Sources: Donna Borak and Henry Williams, "Where Clinton and Trump Stand on Wall Street," *Wall Street Journal*, October 25, 2016; and Laura Saunders, "Taxes Under Trump," *Wall Street Journal*, December 2, 2016.

See related problem 2.10 at the end of the chapter.

The Fundamental Value of Stock

Now consider the case of an investor who intends to invest in a stock for two years. We apply the logic we used in the case of the one-year investment to the case of a two-year investment: The price of the stock should be equal to the sum of the present values of the dividend payments the investor expects to receive during the two years plus the present value of the expected price of the stock at the end of two years:

$$P_t = \frac{D_{t+1}^e}{(1\ +\ r_E)} + \frac{D_{t+2}^e}{(1\ +\ r_E)^2} + \frac{P_{t+2}^e}{(1\ +\ r_E)^2}.$$

We could continue to consider investments over more years, which would lead to similar equations, with the final expected price term being pushed further and further into the future. Ultimately, as we found when discussing bonds, the price of a share of stock should reflect the present value of all the payments to be received from owning the stock over however many periods. In fact, economists consider the *fundamental value* of a share of stock to be equal to the present value of all the dividends investors expect to receive into the indefinite future:

$$P_t = \frac{D_{t+1}^e}{(1 + r_E)} + \frac{D_{t+2}^e}{(1 + r_E)^2} + \frac{D_{t+3}^e}{(1 + r_E)^3} + \cdots \,,$$

where the ellipsis (...) indicates that the dividend payments continue forever. Because we are looking at an infinite stream of dividend payments, there is no longer a final price term, P^e, in the equation.

What about firms that pay no dividends, such as Facebook and Berkshire Hathaway, the company run by Warren Buffett, perhaps the best-known and most successful investor of recent decades? We can use this same equation to calculate the fundamental value of the firm, under the assumption that investors expect it to eventually start paying dividends. In that case, some of the initial expected dividend terms would be zero, and we would insert positive numbers starting in the year in which we expected the firm to begin paying dividends. Investors probably would not buy the stock of a firm that was never expected to pay dividends because in that case, investors would never expect to receive their proportionate share of the firm's profits.

The Gordon Growth Model

The equation given above for the fundamental value of a share of stock isn't very helpful to an investor who is trying to evaluate the price of a stock because it requires forecasting an infinite number of dividends. Fortunately, in 1959, Myron J. Gordon, then an economist at the Massachusetts Institute of Technology, developed a handy method of estimating the fundamental value of a stock. Gordon considered the case in which investors expect a firm's dividends to grow at a constant rate, g, which could be, say, 5%. In that case, each dividend term in the equation above would be 5% greater than the dividend received in the previous year. Using this assumption that dividends are expected to grow at a constant rate, Gordon developed an equation showing the relationship between the current price of the stock, the current dividend paid, the expected growth rate of dividends, and the required return on equities. This equation is called the **Gordon growth model** (or **dividend-discount model**):

Gordon growth model (or **dividend-discount model**)
A model that uses the current dividend paid, the expected growth rate of dividends, and the required return on equities to calculate the price of a stock.

$$P_t = D_t \times \frac{(1 + g)}{(r_E - g)}.$$

Suppose that Microsoft is currently paying an annual dividend of $0.60 per share. The dividend is expected to grow at a constant rate of 7% per year, and the return investors require to invest in Microsoft is 10%. Then, the current price of a share of Microsoft stock should be:

$$\$0.60 \times \frac{(1 + 0.07)}{(0.10 - 0.07)} = \$21.40.$$

There are several points to notice about the Gordon growth model:

1. The model assumes that the growth rate of dividends is constant. This assumption may be unrealistic because investors might believe that dividends will grow

in an uneven pattern. For instance, Microsoft's profits—and the dividends it pays—may grow more rapidly during the years following the introduction of a new version of Windows than during the following years. Nevertheless, the assumption of constant dividend growth is a useful approximation in analyzing stock prices.

2. To use the model, the required rate of return on the stock must be greater than the dividend growth rate. This is a reasonable condition because if a firm's dividends grow at a rate faster than the required return on equities, the firm will eventually become larger than the entire economy, which, of course, cannot happen.

3. Investors' expectations of the future profitability of firms and, therefore, their future dividends, are crucial in determining the prices of stocks.

SOLVED PROBLEM 6.2

Using the Gordon Growth Model to Evaluate GE Stock

The Gordon growth model is a useful tool for calculating the price of a stock. Apply the model to the following two problems:

a. If General Electric (GE) is currently paying an annual dividend of $0.40 per share, its dividend is expected to grow at a rate of 7% per year, and the return investors require to buy

GE's stock is 10%, calculate the price per share for GE's stock.

b. In June 2016, the price of IBM's stock was $155 per share. At the time, IBM was paying an annual dividend of $5.60 per share. If the return investors required to buy IBM's stock was 0.10, what growth rate in IBM's dividend must investors have been expecting?

Solving the Problem

Step 1 **Review the chapter material.** This problem is about using the Gordon growth model to calculate stock prices, so you may want to review the section "The Gordon Growth Model," which begins on page 186.

Step 2 **Calculate GE's stock price by applying the Gordon growth model equation to the numbers given in part (a).** The Gordon growth model equation is:

$$P_t = D_t \times \frac{(1 + g)}{(r_E - g)}.$$

Substituting the numbers given in the problem allows us to calculate the price of GE's stock:

$$\$0.40 \times \frac{(1 + 0.07)}{(0.10 - 0.07)} = \$14.27.$$

Step 3 **Calculate the expected growth rate of IBM's dividend by applying the Gordon growth model equation to the numbers given in part (b).** In this problem, we know the price of the stock but not the expected rate of dividend growth. To calculate the expected rate of dividend growth, we need to plug the numbers given into the Gordon growth equation and then solve for g:

$$\$155 = \$5.60 \times \frac{(1 + g)}{(0.10 - g)}$$

$$\$155 \times (0.10 - g) = \$5.60 \times (1 + g)$$

$$\$15.50 - \$155g = \$5.60 + \$5.60g$$

$$g = \frac{\$9.90}{\$160.60} = 0.062, \text{ or } 6.2\%.$$

Our calculation shows that investors must have been expecting IBM's dividend to grow at an annual rate of 6.2%.

See related problem 2.11 at the end of the chapter.

6.3 Rational Expectations and Efficient Markets

LEARNING OBJECTIVE: Explain the connection between the assumption of rational expectations and the efficient markets hypothesis.

The Gordon growth model shows that investors' expectations of the future profitability of firms play a crucial role in determining stock prices. In fact, expectations play an important role throughout the economy because many transactions require participants to forecast the future. For instance, if you are considering taking out a mortgage loan in which you agree to pay a fixed interest rate of 5% for 30 years, you will need to forecast such things as:

- Your future income: Will you be able to afford the mortgage payments?
- The future inflation rate: What will be the real interest rate on the loan?
- The future of the neighborhood the house is in: Will the city extend a bus or subway line to make it easier to travel downtown?

Adaptive Expectations Versus Rational Expectations

Adaptive expectations The assumption that people forecast future values of a variable using only past values of the variable.

Economists have spent considerable time studying how people form expectations. Early studies focused on the use of information from the past. For example, some economists assumed that investors' expectations of the price of a firm's stock depended only on past prices of the stock. This approach is called **adaptive expectations**. Some stock analysts employ a version of adaptive expectations known as *technical analysis*. These analysts believe that certain patterns in the history of a stock's price are likely to be repeated, and, therefore, can be used to forecast future prices.

Today, most economists are critical of the adaptive expectations approach because it assumes that people ignore information that would be useful in making forecasts. For example, in the late 1970s, the rate of inflation increased each year from 1976 through 1980. Anyone forecasting inflation by looking only at its past values would have expected inflation to be *lower* than it turned out to be. The rate of inflation declined each year from 1980 through 1983. During this period, anyone forecasting inflation by looking only at its past values would have expected inflation to be *higher* than it actually was. Taking into account additional information, such as Federal Reserve policy, movements in oil prices, or other factors that affect inflation rather than relying only on past values of inflation would have enabled someone to make a more accurate forecast.

In 1961, John Muth of Carnegie Mellon University proposed a new approach he labeled *rational expectations*. With **rational expectations**, people make forecasts using all available information. Muth argued that someone who did not use all available information would not be acting rationally. That is, the person would not be doing his or her best to achieve the goal of an accurate forecast. For example, in forecasting the price of a firm's stock, investors should use not just past prices of the stock but also any other information that is helpful in forecasting the future profitability of the firm, including the quality of the firm's management, new products the firm might be developing, and so on. If a sufficient number of investors and traders in the stock market have rational expectations, the market price of a stock should equal the best estimate of the present value of expected future dividends, which, as we saw earlier, is the stock's *fundamental value*. Therefore, if market participants have rational expectations, they can assume that the stock prices they observe represent the fundamental values of those stocks.

To economists, if people have rational expectations, their expectations equal the optimal forecast (the best estimate) of prices, using all information available to them. Although we are applying rational expectations to stocks, this concept applies to any financial security. If investors in the stock market have rational expectations, then the expectation of the future value of a stock should equal the optimal (best estimate) price forecast. Of course, saying that investors have rational expectations is not the same as saying that they can foretell the future. In other words, the optimal forecast is optimal, but it may be wrong.

To state this concept more exactly, suppose that at the end of trading today on the stock market, P^e_{t+1} is the optimal forecast of the price of Apple's stock at the end of trading tomorrow. If P_{t+1} is the *actual* price of Apple's stock at the end of trading tomorrow, then it is very unlikely that we will see $P^e_{t+1} = P_{t+1}$. Why? Because tomorrow, investors and traders are likely to obtain additional information about Apple—perhaps sales of the iPhones during the previous month are below what was forecast—that will change their view of the fundamental value of Apple's stock. So, there is likely to be a *forecast error*, which is the difference between the forecast price of Apple's stock and the actual price of Apple's stock. But no one can accurately forecast the size of that error ahead of time because the error is caused by *new* information that is not available when the forecast is made. If the information had been available, rational expectations tell us that it would have been incorporated into the forecast of the stock price. Therefore, the forecast error is unforecastable. To state the point more formally:

$$P_{t+1} - P^e_{t+1} = \text{Unforecastable error}_{t+1}.$$

So, when a forecast is made, we can be fairly sure that the forecast will turn out to be lower or higher than the actual value of the variable being forecast. But we have no way of telling how large the error will be or even whether it will be positive (that is, our forecast was too low) or negative (that is, our forecast was too high).

Rational expectations The assumption that people make forecasts of future values of a variable using all available information; formally, the assumption that expectations equal optimal forecasts, using all available information.

The Efficient Markets Hypothesis

Efficient markets hypothesis
The application of rational expectations to financial markets; the hypothesis that the equilibrium price of a security is equal to its fundamental value.

As originally developed by John Muth, the concept of rational expectations applies whenever people are making forecasts. The application of rational expectations to financial markets is known as the **efficient markets hypothesis**. With respect to the stock market, the efficient markets hypothesis states that when investors and traders use all available information in forming expectations of future dividend payments, the equilibrium price of a stock equals the market's optimal forecast—the best forecast given available information—of the stock's fundamental value. How can we be sure that markets will operate as the efficient markets hypothesis predicts and that equilibrium prices will equal fundamental values?

An Example of the Efficient Markets Hypothesis Consider an example. Suppose that it is 10:14 Monday morning, and the price of Microsoft stock is $32.10 per share, the company is currently paying an annual dividend of $0.90 per share, and its dividend is expected to grow at a rate of 7% per year. At 10:15, Microsoft releases new sales information indicating that sales of its latest version of Windows have been much higher than expected, and the firm expects higher sales to continue into the future. This news causes you and other investors to revise upward your forecast of the growth rate of Microsoft's annual dividend from 7% to 8%. At this higher growth rate and assuming an r_E of 10%, the present value of Microsoft's future dividends rises from $32.10 to $48.60. So, this new information causes you and other investors to buy shares of Microsoft. This increased demand will cause the price of Microsoft's shares to keep rising until they reach $48.60, which is the new fundamental value of the stock. Investors who have rational expectations can profit by buying or selling a stock when its market price is higher or lower than the optimal forecast of the stock's fundamental value. In this way, self-interested actions of informed traders cause available information to be incorporated into market prices.

Does the efficient markets hypothesis require that all investors and traders have rational expectations? Actually, it does not. As we saw in Chapter 3, the process of buying and reselling securities to profit from price changes over a brief period of time is called

Financial arbitrage The process of buying and selling securities to profit from price changes over a brief period of time.

financial arbitrage. The profits made from financial arbitrage are called *arbitrage profits*. In competing to buy securities where earning arbitrage profits is possible, traders will force prices to the level where investors can no longer earn arbitrage profits. As long as there are some traders with rational expectations, the arbitrage profits provided by new information will give these traders the incentive to push stock prices to their fundamental values. For instance, in the example just discussed, once the new information on Microsoft becomes available, traders can earn arbitrage profits equal to $16.50 per share, or the difference between the old fundamental value and the new fundamental value. Competition among even a few well-informed traders will be enough to quickly drive the price up to its new fundamental value.

Although the efficient markets hypothesis indicates that the price of a share of stock is based on all available information, our Microsoft example shows that the prices of stocks will change day-to-day, hour-to-hour, and minute-to-minute. Stock prices constantly change as news that affects fundamental values becomes available. Note that anything that affects the willingness of investors to hold a stock or another financial asset affects the stock's fundamental value. Therefore, we would expect that if new information leads investors to change their opinions about the risk, liquidity, information costs, or tax treatment of the returns from owning a stock, the price of the stock will change because the r_E will change.

What About "Inside Information"? The efficient markets hypothesis assumes that publicly available information is incorporated into the prices of stocks. But what about information that is not publicly available? Suppose, for example, that the managers of a pharmaceutical firm receive word that an important new cancer drug has unexpectedly received government approval, but this information has not yet been publicly released. Or suppose that economists at the U.S. Bureau of Labor Statistics have compiled data showing that unemployment was much higher than investors had expected, so demand for automobiles—and the profits of Ford and General Motors—will be lower than expected, but this information has also not yet been publicly released. Relevant information about a security that is not publicly available is called **inside information**. Some economists argue in favor of a version of the efficient markets hypothesis that holds that even inside information is quickly incorporated into stock prices. Many studies have shown, however, that it is possible to earn above-average returns by trading on the basis of inside information. For instance, the managers of the pharmaceutical firm could buy their company's stock and profit from the increase in the stock's price once the information on the drug's approval is released.

> **Inside information** Relevant information about a security that is not publicly available.

There is an important catch, though: Trading on inside information—known as *insider trading*—is illegal. Under U.S. securities laws, as enforced by the Securities and Exchange Commission (SEC), employees of a firm may not buy and sell the firm's stocks and bonds on the basis of information that is not publicly available. They also may not provide the information to others who would use it to buy and sell the firm's stocks and bonds. In 2012, a former Intel executive was among more than 20 people convicted of providing inside information about their firms to the manager of the Galleon hedge fund. The manager of the hedge fund was sentenced to 11 years in prison for having illegally earned $75 million trading stocks on the basis of inside information. Federal prosecutors called it the biggest insider trading case in history.

Are Stock Prices Predictable?

A key implication of the efficient markets hypothesis is that stock prices are not predictable. To see why, suppose that it is 4:00 P.M., stock trading has closed for the day, Apple stock has closed at a price of $95, and you are trying to forecast the price of Apple's stock at the close of trading tomorrow. What is your optimal forecast? The efficient markets hypothesis indicates that it is $95. In other words, the best forecast of the price of a stock tomorrow is its price today. Why? Because the price today reflects all relevant information that is currently available. While the price of Apple's stock is unlikely to actually be $95 at the close of trading tomorrow, you have no information today that will allow you to forecast whether it will be higher or lower.

Rather than being predictable, stock prices follow a **random walk**, which means that on any given day, they are as likely to rise as to fall. We can certainly observe stocks that rise for a number of days in a row, but this does not contradict the idea that stock

> **Random walk** The unpredictable movements in the price of a security.

prices follow a random walk. Even though when we flip a coin it is equally likely to come up heads or tails, we may still flip a number of heads or tails in a row.

Efficient Markets and Investment Strategies

Understanding the efficient markets hypothesis allows investors to formulate strategies for portfolio allocation as well as for trading and for assessing the value of financial analysis. We consider these strategies in the following sections.

Portfolio Allocation As long as all investors have the same information, the efficient markets hypothesis predicts that buying and selling in markets will eliminate opportunities for above-average profits. In other words, you may be convinced that Apple will make very high profits from selling iPhones, but if every other investor also has this information, it is unlikely that investing in Apple will provide you with a return higher than you would receive by investing in another stock because the high expected profits are already reflected in price of Apple's stock. Therefore, it is not a good strategy to risk your savings by buying only one stock. Instead, you should hold a diversified portfolio of assets. That way, news that may unfavorably affect the price of one stock can be off-set by news that will favorably affect the price of another stock. If sales of iPhones are disappointing, the price of Apple's stock will fall, while if sales of a new carrot burger at McDonald's are higher than expected, the price of McDonald's stock will rise. Because we can't know ahead of time what will happen, it makes sense to hold a diversified portfolio of stocks and other assets.

Trading If prices reflect all available information, regularly buying and selling individual stocks is not a profitable strategy. Investors should not move funds repeatedly from one stock to another, or *churn* a portfolio, particularly because they have to pay a commission to a broker on each sale or purchase. A better strategy is to *buy and hold* a diversified portfolio over a long period of time.

Financial Analysts and Hot Tips Financial analysts, like those employed by Wall Street firms such as Morgan Stanley and Goldman Sachs, fall into two broad categories: *technical analysts*, who rely on patterns of past stock prices to predict future stock prices, and *fundamental analysts*, who rely on forecasting future profits of firms in order to forecast future stock prices. We have already mentioned that technical analysis relies on adaptive expectations. Economists believe that technical analysis is unlikely to be a successful strategy for forecasting stock prices because it neglects all the available information except for past stock prices.

Fundamental analysis seems more consistent with the rational expectations approach because it uses all available information. But is fundamental analysis likely to be a successful strategy for forecasting stock prices? Many financial analysts appear to think so because they use fundamental analysis to advise their clients about which stocks to buy. They also use fundamental analysis when recommending stocks on cable news programs or in interviews with financial web sites. But the efficient markets hypothesis indicates that the stocks that financial analysts recommend are unlikely to outperform the market. Although analysts may be very good at identifying which firms have the best management, the most exciting new products, and the greatest capacity to earn profits in the future, investors and traders also know that information, and it is already incorporated into the prices of stocks.

Although it seems paradoxical, a firm that analysts and investors expect to be highly profitable in the future may be no better as an investment than a firm that they expect to be much less profitable. If investors require a 10% return to invest in the stock of either firm, the stock issued by the very profitable firm will have a much higher price than the stock issued by the less profitable firm. In fact, we know that the price of the more profitable firm's stock must be high enough and the price of the less profitable firm's stock must be low enough so that an investor would expect to earn 10% on either investment. The situation is the same as that in the bond market. If two bonds appear identical to investors in terms of risk, liquidity, information costs, and tax treatment, then competition among investors looking for the best investment will ensure that the two bonds have the same yield to maturity. If one bond has a coupon of $60 and the other bond has a coupon of $50, the bond with the higher coupon will also have a price high enough that it will have the same yield to maturity as the bond with the lower coupon.

Therefore, the efficient markets hypothesis indicates that the stock of a more profitable firm will not be a better investment than the stock of a less profitable firm.

Many people encountering the efficient markets hypothesis for the first time find it difficult to believe. They think: "Surely all the very smart, very hard-working men and women who are employed by Wall Street financial firms must be able to 'beat the market.' Otherwise, why are they paid such high salaries?" Many studies have shown, though, that mutual fund managers and other professional investors are unable to consistently earn better than the long-run average return on stocks. Most, in fact, do significantly worse. In other words, buying an index fund such as Vanguard's 500 Index Fund is likely to earn an investor a higher return than he or she could earn through any other investing strategy. *Index funds* buy a set portfolio of stocks—for instance, all the stocks in the S&P 500 stock index—and don't attempt to buy and sell the stocks of individual companies on the basis of news about those companies. *Actively managed funds* attempt to earn high returns by frequently buying and selling individual stocks. No manager of an actively managed fund has been able to consistently beat the returns on an index fund like the Vanguard 500 Index Fund.

In fact, one recent study found that over a five-year period, only 2 out of 2,862 actively managed stock funds were able to deliver consistently high returns to investors by being in the top 25% of funds, ranked by their returns. We would expect a larger number of funds to achieve such high returns even if the managers were choosing stocks by flipping coins rather than by carefully evaluating the likely future profitability of firms. In other words, during these five years, most fund managers would have done at least as well by randomly picking stocks. Burton Malkiel, an economist at Princeton University, has popularized the efficient markets hypothesis in his book *A Random Walk Down Wall Street*, which has sold more than 1 million copies. Malkiel made the following striking observation about the efficient markets hypothesis: "A blindfolded monkey throwing darts at a newspaper's financial pages could select a portfolio that would do just as well as one carefully selected by the experts."

Many investors have accepted the message of the efficient markets hypothesis that earning a return higher than the return earned by the stock market as a whole is very unlikely in the long run. As a result, many individual investors and even some institutional investors, such as pension funds, have been concentrating their investments in index mutual funds that track the S&P 500 or other market benchmarks rather than in actively managed mutual funds whose managers attempt to beat the market by picking individual stocks. Index funds are sometimes called passive funds, because their managers are just passively buying the stocks in the index, rather than actively choosing stocks. In the three years ending in August 31, 2016, about $1.3 trillion was invested in passive mutual funds while actively managed funds saw investors withdraw $250 billion. As an article in the *Wall Street Journal* put it: "Investors are giving up on stock picking." [1]

MAKING THE CONNECTION **IN YOUR INTEREST**

If Stock Prices Can't Be Predicted, Why Invest in the Market?

Many people have trouble accepting that there isn't some way to beat the market. As a result, they may follow an investment strategy such as buying high-yield (or junk) bonds thinking that bonds are less risky than stocks because coupons on bonds are fixed, unlike dividends on stock. But as we saw in Chapter 5, bond prices can fluctuate widely as interest rates on newly issued bonds rise and fall, and junk bonds are subject to substantial default risk.

Other people are lured to invest with money managers who "guarantee" above-average returns. Unfortunately, these managers either attempt to earn these high returns by making risky investments or they engage in outright fraud. One common type of fraud is a *Ponzi scheme*, under which the person running the fraud actually makes no investments with the money taken in. Instead, the fraudster uses the money from new investors to pay off old investors. In 2008, federal investigators determined that Bernard Madoff, who had been a respected Wall Street money manager, had been running a Ponzi scheme for decades, during which time he had defrauded investors out of billions of dollars.

The financial crisis of 2007–2009 caused many small investors to distrust the stock market. From its peak above 14,000 in October 2007, the Dow Jones Industrial Average dropped to about 6,500 in March 2009, a decline of nearly 54%. The S&P 500 index and the NASDAQ Composite index suffered similar declines. The value of the mutual funds held by households declined by almost $2 *trillion* during this period.

Economic research indicates that investors' willingness to participate in the stock market is affected by the returns they have experienced during their lives. For example, some investors who lived through the worst bear market in U.S. history, which occurred from 1929 to 1932, when the Dow declined by 89%, were reluctant to invest in the stock market even decades later. The impression that the market is not a level playing field may further reduce the participation of individual investors in the stock market. A poll taken right after the end of the 2007–2009 financial crisis showed that

[1] Anne Tergesen and Jason Zweig, "The Dying Business of Picking Stocks," *Wall Street Journal*, October 17, 2016.

while 24% of those polled had little or no faith in their local banks, 67% had little or no faith in Wall Street.

As a young investor, should you stay out of the stock market? The answer is that if you do, you may not meet your long-term investment goals. As we saw in Chapter 4, the long-run average annual return on investments in the stock market is far higher than the annual returns on investments in Treasury bills or bank certificates of deposit (CDs). Suppose that you start investing by saving $100 per month beginning at age 22. The table below shows how much you would accumulate at age 45 and at the normal retirement age of 67 if you save by buying bank CDs, U.S. Treasury bills, and stocks. The results in the first two rows of the table represent nominal returns, uncorrected for inflation. The final row shows how much you would accumulate in dollars that have the same purchasing power as they did when you were 22, assuming that inflation averages 2.5% per year.[2]

Results of Investing $100 per Month Beginning at Age 22

	CDs (at 1.5%)	Treasury bills (at 2.5%)	Stocks (at 10.0%)
At age 45	$33,076	$37,429	$107,543
At age 67	$77,253	$99,985	$1,057,086
At age 67, after inflation	$25,430	$32,913	$347,966

No one can forecast exactly what the returns to these investments may be in the decades ahead, but we have chosen reasonable estimates based on past returns. Bank CDs are a very safe investment that cautious investors trust, but the first row shows that at age 45, you will have accumulated significantly less than if you had taken on slightly more risk by investing in Treasury bills or considerably more risk by investing in stocks, perhaps by buying a diversified stock mutual fund such as the Vanguard Index 500 fund. The longer your time horizon, the greater the gap between the investments becomes. By retirement age of 67, investing in stocks will leave you with more than 13 times the amount you would have accumulated from bank CDs—$347,966 versus $25,430. The table shows again the trade-off between risk and return that we discussed in Chapter 4. As we noted there, most economists believe that younger savers who are decades away from retirement can afford to take on more risk than can savers who are approaching retirement age.[3]

---

[2] As a side note, investing regularly over time has advantages over occasionally investing large lump sums. Investing monthly, for instance, allows you to take advantage of *dollar cost averaging*. Dollar cost averaging results in your automatically buying more shares when prices are low and fewer shares when prices are high. This approach reduces the chance that you will have made most of your purchases when stock prices were high, making you more vulnerable to a later decline in prices.

[3] We should note that in 2016, some economists believed that stock prices were particularly high relative to firms' profitability. That is, the *P/E ratio*—the ratio of the price of a share stock to the firm's earnings, or profits, per share—was at a historically high level for many firms. When P/E ratios are particularly high, rates of return on stock investing tend to be lower in the following years. For instance, a study by the McKinsey consulting group forecast that the real average annual return to investing in the U.S. stock market over the next 20 years would be about 5.25% rather than the 7.5% we assumed in the last line of the table above. They concluded that, if their forecast is accurate: "Individuals would need to save more for retirement, retire later, or reduce consumption during retirement."

An important issue for the U.S. financial system in the future is whether young investors who experienced the high stock market volatility of recent years will be less willing than older investors to participate in the stock market. Economists debate the possible consequences for market efficiency if the share of stock market trading carried out by individual investors continues to shrink relative to the share carried out by institutional investors such as mutual funds, pension funds, and hedge funds.

Note: The calculations in the table assume an initial deposit of $100 and that the annual interest rates are compounded monthly.

Sources: McKinsey Global Institute, *Diminishing Returns: Why Investors May Need to Lower Their Expectations*, May 2016; Ulrike Malmendier and Stefan Nagel, "Depression Babies: Do Macroeconomic Experiences Affect Risk-Taking?" *Quarterly Journal of Economics*, Vol. 126, No. 1, February 2011, pp. 373–416; Luigi Guiso, Paola Sapienza, and Luigi Zingales, "Trusting the Stock Market," *Journal of Finance*, Vol. 63, No. 6, December 2008, pp. 2557–2600; and Zogby Interactive, "Voter Confidence in Big Banks, Corporations, and Wall Street Even Lower Than That of Government," zogby.com, February 18, 2010.

See related problem 3.9 at the end of the chapter.

SOLVED PROBLEM 6.3

Should You Follow the Advice of Investment Analysts?

Financial analysts typically advise investors to buy stocks whose prices they believe will increase rapidly and to sell stocks whose prices they believe will either fall or increase slowly. The following excerpt from an article by Bloomberg News describes how well stock market analysts succeeded in predicting prices during one year:

> Shares of JDS Uniphase, the company with the most "sell" recommendations among

analysts, has been a more profitable investment this year than Microsoft, the company with the most "buys."

The article notes: "Investors say JDS Uniphase is an example of Wall Street analysts basing recommendations on past events, rather than on earnings prospects and potential share gains." Briefly explain whether you agree with the analysis of these "investors" that the article is referring to.

Solving the Problem

Step 1 **Review the chapter material.** This problem is about whether we can expect financial analysts to successfully predict stock prices, so you may want to review the section "Are Stock Prices Predictable?" which begins on page 191.

Step 2 **Use your understanding of the efficient markets hypothesis to solve the problem.** From the point of view of the efficient markets hypothesis, it is not surprising that during that year, the price of JDS Uniphase's stock rose more than the price of Microsoft's stock. Although Microsoft may have had better managers and been more profitable than JDS Uniphase, Microsoft's stock price at the beginning of the year was correspondingly higher. At the beginning of the year, we know that as a result of financial arbitrage investors must have been expecting to get similar returns by investing in the stock of either firm.

Which firm would turn out to be the better investment depended on events during the year that investors could not have foreseen at the beginning of the year. As it turned out, these unforeseen events were more favorable toward JDS Uniphase, so with hindsight, we can say that it was the better investment.

The analysis of the "investors," as referred to in the article, is not correct from the efficient markets point of view. The key point is not that analysts were "basing recommendations on past events, rather than on earnings prospects and potential share gains." Even if analysts based their forecasts on the firms' earning prospects, they would have been no more successful because all the available information on the firms' earnings prospects was already incorporated into the firms' stock prices.

Source: Scott Lanman, "Analyst Ratings Based on Past Are Missing Mark," Bloomberg.com, September 23, 2003.

See related problem 3.11 at the end of the chapter.

 6.4
Actual Efficiency in Financial Markets

LEARNING OBJECTIVE: Discuss the actual efficiency of financial markets.

Many economists believe that movements in asset prices in most financial markets are consistent with the efficient markets hypothesis. Empirical work by Eugene Fama of the University of Chicago and many other economists has provided support for the conclusion that changes in stock prices are not predictable.

Other analysts—especially active traders and people giving investment advice—are more skeptical about whether the stock market, in particular, is an efficient market. They point to three differences between the theoretical behavior of financial markets and their actual behavior that raise doubts about the validity of the efficient markets hypothesis:

1. Some analysts believe that *pricing anomalies* in the market allow investors to earn consistently above-average returns. According to the efficient markets hypothesis, those opportunities for above-average returns should not exist—or at least should not exist very often or for very long.
2. These analysts also point to evidence that some price changes are predictable using available information. According to the efficient markets hypothesis, investors should not be able to predict future price changes using information that is publicly available.
3. These analysts also argue that changes in stock prices sometimes appear to be larger than changes in the fundamental values of the stocks. According to the efficient markets hypothesis, prices of securities should reflect their fundamental value.

Pricing Anomalies

The efficient markets hypothesis holds that an investor will not consistently be able to earn above-average returns by buying and selling individual stocks or groups of stocks. However, some analysts believe they have identified *stock trading strategies* that can result in above-average returns. From the perspective of the efficient markets hypothesis, these trading strategies are *anomalies,* or outcomes not consistent with the hypothesis. Two anomalies that analysts and economists often discuss are the *small firm effect* and the *January effect.*

The small firm effect refers to the fact that over the long run, investment in small firms has yielded a higher return than has investment in large firms. During the years 1926–2015, an investment in the stock of small firms would have received an average annual return of 12%, while an investment in the stock of large firms would have received an average annual return of only 10%. The January effect refers to the fact that during some years, rates of return on stocks have been abnormally high during January.

Do pricing anomalies indicate a flaw in the efficient markets hypothesis? Opinions among economists vary, but many are skeptical of the idea that these and other anomalies are actually inconsistent with the efficient markets hypothesis, for several reasons:

- *Data mining.* It is always possible to search through the data and construct trading strategies that would have earned above-average returns—if only we had thought of them ahead of time! This point is obvious when considering some frivolous trading strategies, such as the one incorporating the "NFC effect." In 1978, Leonard Koppett, a columnist for the *Sporting News,* noticed that during each of the previous 11 years the stock market had risen in years when a team from the National Football Conference (NFC) won the Super Bowl and had fallen in years when a team from the American Football Conference (AFC) won. Koppett's system correctly predicted whether the stock market would rise or fall for each of the following 11 years after he first published it. Of course, this effect represents a chance correlation between unrelated events. And as a predictor of the stock market's performance, the NFC effect has done a poor job in more recent years. For instance, in 2008, the NFC's New York Giants won the Super Bowl, but the Dow declined by more than 35%, while in 2009, the AFC's Pittsburgh Steelers won the Super Bowl, but the Dow rose 15%. More seriously, even if data mining could uncover a trading strategy that would earn above-average returns, once that strategy became widely known, it would be unlikely to continue to earn high returns. So, it's not surprising that once the January effect received substantial publicity in the 1980s, it largely disappeared.
- *Risk, liquidity, and information costs.* The efficient markets hypothesis does not predict that all stock investments should have the same expected rate of return. Instead, the hypothesis predicts that all stock investments should have the same return *after adjustment for differences in risk, liquidity, and information costs.* Investments in small firm stocks have had a higher average annual rate of return than investments in large firm stocks, but investing in small firm stocks has a significantly higher level of risk. In addition, markets for many small firm stocks are less liquid and have higher information costs than the markets for large firm stocks. So, some economists argue that the higher returns on investments in small firm stocks actually are just compensating investors for accepting higher risk, lower liquidity, and higher information costs.

- *Trading costs and taxes.* Some stock trading strategies popularized in books and online are quite complex and require buying and selling many individual stocks or groups of stocks during the year. When calculating the returns from these strategies, the writers promoting them rarely take into account the costs of all the required buying and selling. Each time an investor buys or sells a stock, the investor has to pay a commission, and this cost should be subtracted from the investor's return on the strategy. In addition, when an investor sells a stock for a higher price than the investor bought it for, the investor incurs a taxable capital gain. Taxes paid also need to be taken into account when calculating the return. Including trading costs and taxes eliminates the above-average returns supposedly earned using many trading strategies.

Mean Reversion and Momentum Investing

The efficient markets hypothesis holds that investors cannot predict changes in stock prices by using currently available information because only new information can change prices and returns. The efficient markets hypothesis therefore is inconsistent with what is known as *mean reversion*, which is the tendency for stocks that have recently been earning high returns to experience low returns in the future and for stocks that have recently been earning low returns to earn high returns in the future. If this pattern is sufficiently widespread, an investor could earn above-average returns on his or her portfolio by buying stocks whose returns have recently been low and selling stocks whose returns have recently been high.

However, some investors have claimed that they have earned above-average returns by following a strategy known as *momentum investing* that is almost the opposite of mean reversion. Momentum investing is based on the idea that there can be persistence in stock movements, so that a stock that is increasing in price is somewhat more likely to rise than to fall, and a stock that is decreasing in price is somewhat more likely to fall than to rise. So, if you follow the Wall Street saying "the trend is your friend," it may be advisable to buy when stock prices are rising and sell when they are falling.

Although opinions among economists about mean reversion and momentum investing differ, careful studies indicate that in practice, trading strategies based on either idea have difficulty earning above-average returns in the long run, particularly when trading costs and taxes are taken into account.

Excess Volatility

The efficient markets hypothesis tells us that the price of an asset equals the market's best estimate of its fundamental value. Fluctuations in actual market prices therefore should be no greater than fluctuations in fundamental value. Robert Shiller of Yale University has estimated the fundamental value of the stocks included in the S&P 500 over a period of decades. He has concluded that the actual fluctuations in the prices of these stocks have been much greater than the fluctuations in their fundamental value. Economists have debated the technical accuracy of Shiller's results because there are disagreements over estimates of stocks' fundamental value and other issues. Many economists believe, however, that Shiller's analysis does raise doubts as to whether the efficient markets hypothesis applies exactly to the stock market. In principle, Shiller's results could be used to earn above-average returns by, for instance, selling stocks when they are above their fundamental values and buying them when they are below their fundamental values. In practice, though, attempts to use this trading strategy have not been consistently able to produce above-average returns.

We can summarize by saying that evidence from empirical studies generally confirms that stock prices reflect available information, and no trading strategies have been discovered that can consistently earn higher than normal returns, taking into account risk, transactions costs, and taxes. However, examination of pricing anomalies, mean reversion, and excess volatility in stock prices has generated debate over whether fluctuations in stock prices reflect only changes in fundamental values.

MAKING THE CONNECTION

Does the Financial Crisis of 2007–2009 Disprove the Efficient Markets Hypothesis?

During the financial crisis of 2007–2009, the major stock indexes declined dramatically. Between October 2007 and March 2009, the Dow Jones Industrial Average declined by 54%, the S&P 500 declined by 57%, and the NASDAQ Composite index declined by 56%. The efficient markets hypothesis indicates that these price declines should represent declines in the fundamental values of these stocks. Is it plausible that the fundamental value of the firms included in these indexes had actually declined by more than 50%? After all, the firms had not been destroyed by the crisis. With a few exceptions, the firms still existed, and their factories, offices, research and development staffs, and other assets were largely intact.

The decline in stock prices, though, may have been consistent with substantial changes in the expectations of investors about both the future growth rate of dividends and the degree of risk involved in investing in stocks. When investors believe a category of investment has become riskier, they raise the expected return they require from that investment category. So, it seems likely that during the financial crisis, investors increased the required return on equities, r_E, and decreased the expected growth rate of dividends, g. The Gordon growth model indicates that an increase in r_E and a decrease in g will cause a decline in stock prices. So, a supporter of the efficient markets hypothesis would argue that the sharp decline in stock prices was caused by investors responding to new information on the increased riskiness of stocks and the lower future growth of dividends. Economists who are skeptical of the efficient markets hypothesis have argued, though, that the new information that became available to investors was not sufficient to account for the size of the decline in stock prices.

See related problem 4.6 at the end of the chapter.

Behavioral Finance

LEARNING OBJECTIVE: Describe the basic concepts of behavioral finance.

Over the past 25 years, some economists have argued that even if the efficient markets hypothesis is correct that trading strategies capable of delivering above-average returns are extremely rare, there is still a payoff to a better understanding of how investors make their decisions. *Behavioral economics* is the study of situations in which people make choices that do not appear to be economically rational. The field of **behavioral finance** applies concepts from behavioral economics to understand how people make choices in financial markets.

Behavioral finance The application of concepts from behavioral economics to understand how people make choices in financial markets.

When economists say that consumers, firms, or investors are behaving "rationally," they mean that they are taking actions that are appropriate to reach their goals, given the information available to them. There are many situations, though, in which people do not appear to be acting rationally in this sense. Why might people not act rationally? The most obvious reason is that they may not realize that their actions are inconsistent with their goals. For instance, there is evidence that people are often unrealistic about their future behavior. Although some people have the goal of being thin, they may decide to eat chocolate cake today because they intend to follow a healthier diet in the future. Unfortunately, if they persist each day in eating cake, they never attain their goal of being thin. Similarly, some people continue smoking because they intend to give it up sometime in the future. But that time never comes, and they end up suffering the long-term health effects of smoking. In both of these cases, people's current behavior is inconsistent with their long-term goals.

Some firms have noticed that fewer than the expected number of employees enroll in voluntary retirement savings plans known as 401(k) plans. Although these employees have a long-run goal of saving enough to enjoy a comfortable retirement, in the short run, they spend the money they should save to attain their goal. If, however, firms automatically enroll employees in these retirement plans, giving them the option to leave the plan if they choose to, most employees remain in the plans. To a fully rational employee, the decision about whether to save through a 401(k) plan should be independent of the minor amount of paperwork involved in either enrolling in a plan or leaving a plan in which the employer has enrolled the employee. In practice, though, automatically enrolling employees in a plan means that to leave the plan, the employees must confront the inconsistency between their short-run actions of spending too much and their long-run goal of a comfortable retirement. Rather than confront their inconsistency, most employees choose to remain in the plan.

Behavioral finance also helps to explain the popularity among some investors of technical analysis, which attempts to predict future stock prices on the basis of patterns in past prices. Studies indicate that when shown plots of stock prices generated by randomly choosing numbers, many people believe they see persistent patterns even though none actually exist. The results of these studies may explain why some investors believe they see useful patterns in plots of past stock prices even if the prices are actually following a random walk, as indicated by the efficient markets hypothesis. In addition, many investors exhibit *overconfidence* in their ability to predict stock prices. Contributing to this overconfidence is hindsight bias; when asked how successful their past investments have been, people often remember the stocks they bought that increased in price, while forgetting about some that fell in price. As a result, many individual investors have actually experienced lower returns than they believe they did. Some investors believe that their winning stock picks were the result of their superior insight, while their losing stock picks were the result of bad luck. As one researcher puts it: "Heads I win, tails it's chance."

Investors also show a reluctance to admit mistakes by selling their losing investments. Behavioral economists call this reluctance *loss aversion*. Once a stock whose price has declined is sold, there is no denying that investing in the stock was a mistake. As long as an investor holds on to a losing stock, the investor can hope that eventually the price will recover, and the loser will turn into a winner, even though the chances are equally good that the stock will continue to decline. Studies have shown that investors are more likely to sell stocks that have shown a price increase—thereby, "locking in" their gains—than they are to sell stocks that have experienced a price decline. For tax purposes, this approach is the opposite of an efficient strategy because capital gains are taxed only if the stock is sold. So, it makes sense to postpone the sale of these stocks to the future, while receiving the immediate tax benefit of selling the stocks whose prices have declined.

Noise Trading and Bubbles

Studies in behavioral finance have provided evidence that many investors exhibit overconfidence in their ability to carry out an investment strategy. One consequence of overconfidence can be *noise trading*, which involves investors overreacting to good or bad news. Noise trading can result from an investor's inflated view of his or her ability to understand the significance of a piece of news. For example, noise traders may aggressively sell shares of stock in a firm whose outlook is described unfavorably in the *Wall Street Journal* or *Fortune* magazine. Of course, information in a newspaper, a magazine, or online is readily available, and the efficient markets hypothesis holds that the price of the stock incorporates that information long before the noise trader has even read the article. Nonetheless, the selling pressure from noise traders can force the stock price down by more than the decrease in its fundamental value.

Can't better-informed traders profit at the expense of noise traders? Doing so may be difficult because the increased price fluctuations due to noise traders may increase the risk in the market. After noise traders have overreacted, an investor who believes in the efficient markets hypothesis cannot be sure how long it will take a price to return to its fundamental value.

Noise trading can also lead to *herd behavior*. With herd behavior, relatively uninformed investors imitate the behavior of other investors rather than attempt to trade on the basis of fundamental values. Investors imitating each other can help to fuel a speculative *bubble*. In a **bubble**, the price of an asset rises above its fundamental value. Once a bubble begins, investors may buy assets not to hold them but to resell them quickly at a profit, even if the investors know that the prices are greater than the assets' fundamental values. With a bubble, the *greater fool theory* comes into play: An investor is not a fool to buy an overvalued asset as long as there is a greater fool to buy it later for a still higher price. During the stock market dot-com boom in the late 1990s, some

Bubble A situation in which the price of an asset rises well above the asset's fundamental value.

investors knew that Pets.com and other Internet firms were unlikely to ever become profitable, but they bought these stocks anyway because they expected to be able to sell them for a higher price than they had paid. At some point, a bubble bursts as a significant number of investors finally become concerned that prices are too far above their fundamental values and begin to sell stocks. As panel (c) of Figure 6.2 on page 178 shows, once the dot-com bubble popped, the prices of stocks in the NASDAQ index dropped very rapidly.

How Great a Challenge Is Behavioral Finance to the Efficient Markets Hypothesis?

If many participants in financial markets are noise traders and exhibit herd behavior, and if bubbles in asset prices are common, is the efficient markets hypothesis the best approach to analyzing these markets? Particularly after the wide swings in stock prices during and after the financial crisis, more economists have become skeptical about the accuracy of the efficient markets hypothesis. Research in behavioral finance questioning the extent to which investors in financial markets exhibit rational expectations has added to this skepticism. As we noted earlier, during bubbles, it may be difficult for better-informed investors to force prices back to their fundamental levels. Some investors who bet against dot-com stocks a year or two before their peaks suffered heavy losses even though the stocks were already far above their fundamental values—which in many cases was zero.

Although fewer economists now believe that investors can rely on asset prices to continually reflect fundamental values, many economists still believe that it is unlikely that investors can hope to earn above-average profits in the long run by following trading strategies. Ongoing research in behavioral finance attempts to reconcile the actual behavior of investors with the rational behavior economists have traditionally assumed prevails in financial markets.

ANSWERING THE KEY QUESTION

Continued from page 173

At the beginning of this chapter, we asked:

"Does the volatility of the stock market affect the broader economy?"

The stock market plays an important role in the financial system by providing a source of funds to firms that issue stock and by providing investors a way to earn a higher return than on many other investments. But we've seen that stock prices can be volatile. This volatility can affect the economy in several ways: Increases in stock prices increase consumers' wealth and, therefore, their spending, while decreases in stock prices have the opposite effect. Increases in stock prices also increase the funds firms can raise, thereby increasing their spending on physical capital, while decreases in stock prices can have the opposite effect. Finally, increases and decreases in stock prices can affect the expectations of households and firms with respect to future economic growth, thereby affecting their spending. Most economists do not see these effects as typically being very large because historically there have been significant increases and decreases in stock prices that do not appear to have had much effect on real GDP or employment. Again, though, some economists believe the great stock market crash of 1929 contributed to the severity of the Great Depression.

Key Terms and Problems

Key Terms

Adaptive expectations, p. 188

Behavioral finance, p. 201

Bubble, p. 202

Corporation, p. 174

Dividend, p. 175

Dividend yield, p. 183

Efficient markets hypothesis, p. 190

Financial arbitrage, p. 190

Gordon growth model (or dividend-discount model), p. 186

Inside information, p. 191

Limited liability, p. 174

Over-the-counter market, p. 175

Publicly traded company, p. 175

Random walk, p. 191

Rational expectations, p. 189

Required return on equities, r_E, p. 182

Stock exchange, p. 175

Stock market index, p. 177

6.1 Stocks and the Stock Market
Describe the basic operations of the stock market.

Review Questions

1.1 Why are stocks called "equities"? Are bonds also equities?

1.2 In what ways are dividends similar to coupons on bonds? In what ways are dividends different from coupons on bonds?

1.3 What is the difference between a stock exchange and an over-the-counter market? What are the three most important stock market indexes?

1.4 How do fluctuations in stock prices affect the economy?

Problems and Applications

1.5 A student makes the following observation: "The Dow Jones Industrial Average currently has a value of 17,500, while the S&P 500 has a value of 2,000. Therefore, the prices of the stocks in the DJIA are more than eight times as high as the prices of the stocks in the S&P 500." Briefly explain whether you agree with the student's reasoning.

1.6 A student remarks: "135,000,000 shares of General Electric were sold yesterday on the New York Stock Exchange, at an average price of $25 per share. That means General Electric just received over $3.4 billion from investors." Briefly explain whether you agree with the student's analysis.

1.7 In a column in the *Wall Street Journal*, economist Burton Malkiel notes: "Preferred stock is a kind of hybrid security that sits between bonds and common stock."

a. In what sense is a share of preferred stock like a bond, and in what way is it like a share of common stock?

b. Many companies issue preferred stock with a provision that allows the company to buy it back at its original price after five years. When would companies be likely to buy back their preferred stock? Is it possible that these buy-backs cause losses to investors?

Source: Burton G. Malkiel, "The 'Preferred' Path to Higher Returns," *Wall Street Journal*, June 20, 2016.

1.8 [Related to the Making the Connection on page 180] Economist Peter Temin of MIT argues: "If the crash of 1929 was an important independent shock to the economy, then the crash of 1987 should have been equally disastrous."

a. What does Temin mean by "an important independent shock to the economy"?

b. Why does he argue that what happened to the economy following the crash of 1987 is evidence against the crash of 1929 being an important shock to the economy?

c. How would Christina Romer counter Temin's argument?

Source: Peter Temin, *Lessons from the Great Depression*, Cambridge, MA: MIT University Press, 1989, p. 44.

6.2 How Stock Prices Are Determined
Explain how stock prices are determined.

Review Questions

2.1 What is the relationship between the price of a financial asset and the payments investors expect to receive from owning that asset?

2.2 What is the relationship between the required return on equities and the equity cost of capital?

2.3 In words and symbols, write the two components of the rate of return on a stock investment for a holding period of one year.

2.4 What is the fundamental value of a share of stock?

2.5 Write the equation for the Gordon growth model. What key assumption does this model make?

Problems and Applications

2.6 Suppose that the price of Goldman Sachs stock is currently $142 per share. You expect that the firm will pay a dividend of $1.40 per share at the end of the year, at which time you expect that the stock will be selling for $160 per share. If you require a return of 8% to invest in this stock, should you buy it? Briefly explain.

2.7 At the beginning of the year, you buy a share of IBM stock for $120. If during the year you receive a dividend of $2.50, and IBM stock is selling for $130 at the end of year, what was your rate of return from investing in the stock?

2.8 A company is expected to pay a dividend per share of $20 per year forever. If investors require a 10% rate of return to invest in this stock, what is its price?

2.9 A friend has started a business selling software. The software is a great success, and the firm quickly grows large enough to sell stock. Your friend's firm promises to pay a dividend of $5 per share every year for the next 50 years, at which point your friend intends to shut down the business. The firm's stock is currently selling for $75

per share. If you believe that the company really will pay dividends as stated and if you require a 10% rate of return to make this investment, should you buy the stock? Briefly explain.

2.10 [Related to the Making the Connection on page 184]
A column in the *Wall Street Journal* asks the question: "Are capital gains so different from earned income that they should be taxed at a different rate?"

a. What is a capital gain?

b. In what ways are capital gains taxed differently than salary and wage income?

c. What is the economic argument for taxing capital gains differently than other income?

Source: Scott Sumner and Leonard E. Burman, "Is It Fair to Tax Capital Gains at Lower Rates Than Earned Income?" *Wall Street Journal*, March 1, 2015.

2.11 [Related to Solved Problem 6.2 on page 187]
Suppose that Coca-Cola is currently paying a dividend of $1.75 per share, the dividend is expected to grow at a rate of 5% per year, and the rate of return investors require to buy Coca-Cola's stock is 8%. Calculate the price per share for Coca-Cola's stock.

2.12 An article in the *Economist* in 2016 noted that since 2000, an investor in the United Kingdom would have earned a higher return from buying British government bonds than from buying stock issued by British firms. The article concluded: "There has been a negative equity risk premium this century."

a. Briefly explain how the author arrived at this conclusion. Be sure your answer includes an explanation of what the equity risk premium is.

b. Why might the equity risk premium in the United Kingdom have been negative during this period?

Source: Buttonwood, "Stocks for the Long Run?" *Economist*, January 13, 2016.

6.3

Rational Expectations and Efficient Markets

Explain the connection between the assumption of rational expectations and the efficient markets hypothesis.

Review Questions

3.1 What is the difference between adaptive expectations and rational expectations?

3.2 What is the relationship between rational expectations and the efficient markets hypothesis?

3.3 According to the efficient markets hypothesis, are stock prices predictable? What is a random walk?

Problems and Applications

3.4 An article in the *Economist* notes that according to the efficient markets hypothesis: "buying shares in Google because its latest profits were good, or because of a particular pattern in the price charts, was unlikely to deliver an excess return."

a. What does the article mean by "an excess return"?

b. Why would buying Google because its latest profits were good be unlikely to earn an investor an excess return?

c. Why would buying Google on the basis of a particular pattern in its past stock prices be unlikely to earn an investor an excess return?

Source: Buttonwood, "What's Wrong with Finance," *Economist*, May 1, 2015.

3.5 An article in the *Wall Street Journal* in 2016, observed that the price of Apple's stock had started to decline a year before "when fears of an iPhone slowdown surfaced." At the time the article was written, the author claims: "The iPhone slump is now more than priced in."

a. Why would the price of Apple's stock begin to fall just because investors anticipate that iPhone sales might slow down in the future?

Wouldn't we expect investors to wait until sales actually do slow down before selling the stock? Briefly explain.

b. What does the author mean when he describes the decline in iPhone sales as being "priced in"? If iPhone sales continue to decline as investors expect them to, will the decline lead to a further fall in the price of Apple's stock? Briefly explain.

Source: Dan Gallagher, "Apple Has Upside as Investors Worry," *Wall Street Journal*, April 24, 2016.

3.6 The following is from an article on cnbc.com:

Typically stock prices increase when the economy is expanding. But on a day when a measure of manufacturing production showed it had reached a three year high, stock prices declined. One stock market analyst was quoted as explaining why: "It's great news but not new news."

a. What does the analyst mean by "new news"?

b. Why would the effect of the announcement on stock prices depend on whether it was "new news"?

Source: Kate Gibson, "Stocks Decline with Oil; Traders Worry About ECB," cnbc.com, September 2, 2014.

3.7 An article in the *Wall Street Journal* contained the following: "Norfolk Southern Corp. on Thursday reported a surprise 25% profit jump in the first quarter." The article also noted that after the announcement, Norfolk Southern's stock rose 3.5%.

a. What is the relationship between a firm's profits and its stock price?

b. If the increase in Norfolk Southern's profits had not been a surprise, would the effect of the announcement on its stock price have been different? Briefly explain.

Source: Anne Steele, "Norfolk Southern Reports Surprise Jump in Profit," *Wall Street Journal*, April 21, 2016.

3.8 Suppose that Facebook's profits are expected to grow twice as fast as Amazon's. Which firm's stock should be the better investment for you? Briefly explain.

3.9 [Related to the Making the Connection on page 194] An article in the *Wall Street Journal* notes this about Burton Malkiel: "Even before index funds existed, the now-retired Princeton University professor argued that they could outperform actively managed funds."

a. What is the difference between an index fund and an actively managed fund?

b. Why might we expect investors to receive a higher return in the long run from buying index funds than from buying actively managed funds?

c. Does that fact that index funds provide higher returns in the long run than actively managed funds indicate that the people who run index funds know more about the stock market than do the people who run actively managed funds? Briefly explain.

Source: Silvia Ascarelli, "Burton Malkiel Is Still an Indexing Fan, but a 'Smart Beta' Skeptic," *Wall Street Journal*, May 8, 2016.

3.10 The business writer Michael Lewis has quoted Michael Burry, a fund manager, as saying:

I also immediately internalized the idea that no school could teach someone how to be a great investor. If that were true, it'd be the most popular school in the world, with an impossibly high tuition. So it must not be true.

Do you agree with Burry's reasoning? Briefly explain.

Source: Michael Lewis, *The Big Short: Inside the Doomsday Machine*, New York: W.W. Norton, 2010, p. 35.

3.11 [Related to Solved Problem 6.3 on page 196] An article in the *Wall Street Journal* described "a sea change in the fund business in which investors are increasingly opting for products that track the market rather than relying on managers to pick winners."

a. What does the article mean by "products that track the market"?

b. Shouldn't investors be able to earn a higher return by finding knowledgeable managers who can pick high-performing individual stocks than by investing in "products that track the market"? Briefly explain.

Source: Kirsten Grind, "Investors Pour into Vanguard, Eschewing Stock Pickers," *Wall Street Journal*, August 20, 2014.

3.12 [Related to the Chapter Opener on page 173] Many investors who bought stocks in 2000 and held them through 2010 found that they had received a negative real return on their investment over the 10-year period. Why would investors have invested in stocks during those years if they received a negative real return?

6.4 Actual Efficiency in Financial Markets
Discuss the actual efficiency of financial markets.

Review Questions

4.1 How might an investor use a pricing anomaly to earn above-average returns?

4.2 How might an investor use mean reversion or excess volatility to earn above-average returns?

4.3 Why are supporters of the efficient markets hypothesis unconvinced that differences between the theoretical and actual behavior of financial markets actually invalidate the hypothesis?

Problems and Applications

4.4 The policy committee of the Federal Reserve meets eight times per year in Washington, DC. After each meeting, the committee makes a public announcement about monetary policy. According to an article in the *Wall Street Journal*, going back to 1994, it was possible to earn an above average investment return using the following strategy: "On the day before a Fed policy announcement, buy the stocks in the S&P 500 index. Sell them a week later, and buy them again the following week." After this article was published, would you expect it would still be profitable to follow this strategy? Briefly explain.
Source: Justin Lahart, "Making Money with the Fed: Don't Get Mad, Get Even," *Wall Street Journal*, July 2, 2014.

4.5 An article in the *Wall Street Journal* describes one investment strategy that involves buying stocks on the London Stock Exchange at the beginning of November, selling them at the end of April, and then buying them again at the beginning of the following November. According to one investment analyst, this "Halloween effect" investment strategy will earn an above-average return. The article notes that the analyst's "results exclude transactions costs and taxes."
  a. What transactions costs is the article referring to?
  b. Does it matter that the results exclude transactions costs and taxes? Briefly explain.
Source: Corrie Driebusch and Aaron Kuriloff, "Sell Stocks in May? Tempting but Not Very Smart," *Wall Street Journal*, May 1, 2016.

4.6 [Related to the Making the Connection on page 200]
A columnist in the *Economist* argues that the efficient markets hypothesis has been "dealt a series of blows" because "in the late 1990s dot-com companies with no profits and barely any earnings were valued in billions of dollars; and in 2006 investors massively underestimated the risks in bundling together portfolios of American subprime mortgages."
  a. Explain how the incidents this columnist discusses may be inconsistent with the efficient markets hypothesis.
  b. Is it possible that these incidents might have occurred even though the efficient markets hypothesis is correct?
Source: Buttonwood, "The Grand Illusion," *Economist*, March 5, 2009.

4.7 Mutual funds that follow a "momentum trading" strategy are known on Wall Street as "momos." How might a mutual fund manager use a momentum trading strategy? Why might the fund manager expect to earn an above-average return?

4.8 Charles Dow was the original editor of the *Wall Street Journal*. He was the originator of "Dow Theory," which holds that the prices of transportation stocks, such as Heartland Express, can predict changes in the price of industrial stocks, such as ExxonMobil.
  a. An article in the *Wall Street Journal* refers to Dow Theory as the "granddaddy of technical analysis." Why would Dow Theory be considered technical analysis rather than fundamental analysis?
  b. Would an investor be able to earn an above-average return on her stock investments by selling industrial stocks whenever she saw declines in transportation stocks and buying industrial stocks whenever she saw increases in transportation stocks? Briefly explain.
Source: Spencer Jakab, "Keep on Trucking Despite Dow Theory," *Wall Street Journal*, July 16, 2012.

6.5 Behavioral Finance

Describe the basic concepts of behavioral finance.

Review Questions

5.1 How is behavioral finance related to behavioral economics?

5.2 What do economists mean when they describe investors as behaving rationally?

5.3 How can herd behavior lead to a bubble in a financial market?

Problems and Applications

5.4 According to an article in the *New York Times*, "millions of amateur investors continue to actively buy and sell securities regularly."

 a. Why might buying and selling securities regularly not be a good strategy for the average investor? What alternative strategy might an investor follow instead?

 b. What insights from behavioral finance might explain why some investors persist in trying to beat the market by picking individual stocks?

 Source: Gary Belsky, "Why We Think We're Better Investors Than We Are," *New York Times*, March 25, 2016.

5.5 Former Federal Reserve Chairman Alan Greenspan has argued that it is very difficult to identify bubbles until after they pop. What is a bubble, and why might bubbles be difficult to identify?

5.6 The British economist John Maynard Keynes once wrote that investors often do not rely on computing expected values when determining which investments to make:

 Most, probably, of our decisions to do something positive, the full consequences of which will be drawn out over many days to come, can only be taken as the result of animal spirits—a spontaneous urge to action rather than inaction—and not as the outcome of a weighted average of quantitative benefits multiplied by quantitative probabilities.

 If it is true that investors rely on "animal spirits" rather than expected values when making investments, is the efficient markets hypothesis accurate? Briefly explain.

 Source: John Maynard Keynes, *The General Theory of Employment, Interest, and Money*, London: Macmillan, 1936, p. 162.

5.7 An article in the *Economist* notes: "If other people are making a fortune by buying tech stocks, or by trading up in the housing market, then there is a huge temptation to take part, in case one gets left behind."

 a. What do economists call this type of behavior?

 b. What explains this type of behavior? Is it consistent with the assumption of the efficient markets hypothesis? Briefly explain.

 Source: Buttonwood, "What's Wrong with Finance," *Economist*, May 1, 2015.

5.8 An article in the *Economist* noted that while economic growth in China was slowing, Chinese "stocks have more than doubled in value." The article states that unlike in developed countries, where large institutional investors buy the overwhelming majority of the stock purchased, in China 90% of buying is done by individual investors. The article described the demand for stock by these investors as a "mania." What does the article mean when it describes stock buying by individual investors as a mania? Would individual investors be more likely than institutional investors to exhibit this behavior? Briefly explain.

 Source: "A Crazy Casino," *Economist*, May 26, 2015.

Data Exercises

D6.1: [The stock market and recessions] Go to the web site of macrotrends (macrotrends.net) and click the S&P 500 – 90 year historical chart. Describe how stock prices move just before, during, and just after a recession. Is the pattern the same across recessions? Briefly explain.

D6.2: [Exploring dividends] Go to wsj.com and find the dividend per share for each of the following firms:

a. Microsoft

b. Apple

c. Coca-Cola

d. Facebook

To find the dividend per share, enter the company's name in the search box on the home page. Which pays the highest dividend? Which has the highest dividend yield? Which does not pay a dividend? Why might a firm not pay a dividend? Why would investors buy the stock of a firm that does not pay a dividend?

CHAPTER 7

Derivatives and Derivative Markets

Learning Objectives

After studying this chapter, you should be able to:

7.1 Explain what derivatives are and distinguish between using them to hedge and using them to speculate (pages 213–214)

7.2 Define forward contracts and explain their role in the financial system (pages 214–215)

7.3 Explain how futures contracts can be used to hedge and to speculate (pages 215–224)

7.4 Distinguish between call options and put options and explain how they are used (pages 225–234)

7.5 Define swaps and explain how they can be used to reduce risk (pages 234–239)

You, Too, Can Buy and Sell Crude Oil … But Should You?

What's the best way to make money in the financial markets? As we saw in Chapter 6, most economists recommend investing by regularly buying shares in a mutual fund that tracks the stock market indexes, such as the S&P 500. Even professional financial managers have difficulty beating the market indexes by frequently buying and selling individual stocks. Nonetheless, some individuals use widely available software to "day trade," or buy and sell stocks after holding them only for brief periods—sometimes for just a few minutes. Typically, these investors are trying

to earn short-term profits. By comparison, savers who buy mutual funds typically seek to accumulate wealth slowly over the long term.

In recent years, oil prices have been particularly volatile, with the price of a barrel of oil peaking at $145 in 2008, falling to $34 in 2009, rising back above $100 in 2011, and falling below $30 in early 2016, only to rise again above $50. And there were many smaller price movements in between these dates. Some individual investors believe they have enough insight into what causes these price fluctuations to make a profit by

Continued on next page

KEY ISSUE AND QUESTION

Issue: During and after the 2007–2009 financial crisis, some investors, economists, and policymakers argued that financial derivatives had contributed to the severity of the crisis.

Question: Are financial derivatives "financial weapons of mass destruction"?

Answered on page 239

buying and selling oil. In effect, these investors have become oil day traders. Stock day traders often directly buy and sell firms' stock. Oil day traders aren't actually buying and selling barrels of oil; instead, they are placing bets on whether oil prices will rise or fall using *derivative securities*, or, simply, *derivatives*. Derivatives get their name from the fact that they are based on, or derived from, an underlying asset. These assets may be commodities, such as oil or wheat, or financial assets, such as stocks or bonds.

Economists use the term *speculators* to refer to investors who buy and sell derivatives with the hope of profiting from price changes in the underlying commodity or financial asset. Although some individual investors who day trade oil derivatives are able to make a profit, in the long run most suffer losses. Derivatives serve a more important purpose than allowing for speculation, though: They enable individuals and firms to *hedge*, or reduce the risk they face from price fluctuations. For example, both firms that use oil (or oil-based products), such as airlines, and firms that help produce oil, such as drilling companies, can use oil derivatives to hedge against fluctuations in the price of oil.

Although many U.S. businesses have used derivatives for decades, they were the subject of widespread debate during and after the financial crisis of 2007–2009. Warren Buffett, whose hometown is Omaha, Nebraska, may be the most successful financial investor in the world. In 2016, *Forbes* magazine estimated his wealth at $65 billion, making him the third-richest person in the world. Buffett's many shrewd investments have earned him the nickname the "Oracle of Omaha," so investors closely read his annual letters to Berkshire Hathaway's shareholders. In his letter for 2002, Buffett denounced financial derivatives as "time bombs, both for the parties that deal in them and for the economic system." He concluded that "derivatives are financial weapons of mass destruction, carrying dangers that, while now latent, are potentially lethal." Despite Buffett's warnings, the markets for financial derivatives exploded in size between 2002 and 2007. When the financial crisis began in 2007, just as Buffett had warned, financial derivatives played an important role.

As we will see, Buffett's criticisms were not aimed at the basic idea of using derivative securities, but rather at how some of the more exotic derivative securities were used in the years leading up to the financial crisis. In fact, derivatives play a useful role in the economy, and derivative markets offer investors and firms risk sharing, liquidity, and information services not otherwise available.

Sources: Ben Eisen, Nicole Friedman, and Saumya Vaishampayan, "The New Oil Traders: Moms and Millennials," *Wall Street Journal*, May 26, 2016; "The New Danger from Derivatives," bloomberg.com, March 7, 2016; Warren Buffet, "Chairman's Letter," in *Berkshire Hathaway, Inc. 2002 Annual Report*, February 21, 2003; and "The World's Billionaires," forbes.com.

Derivative securities (or derivatives) An asset, such as a futures contract or an option contract, that derives its economic value from an underlying asset, such as a stock or a bond.

Derivative securities (or **derivatives**) are financial securities whose economic value depends on the value of an underlying asset. In this chapter, we will concentrate on the most important derivatives: forward contracts, futures contracts, options contracts, and swaps. To understand why investors include derivatives in their portfolios and why firms use them to hedge risk, we describe the situations in which derivatives benefit the parties in a transaction, the obligations and benefits of each type of derivative, and the strategies investors and firms use in buying and selling derivatives. We discuss how derivatives are traded and how financial reforms following the 2007–2009 crisis have affected derivatives trading.

7.1 Derivatives, Hedging, and Speculating

LEARNING OBJECTIVE: Explain what derivatives are and distinguish between using them to hedge and using them to speculate.

Financial derivatives are financial securities whose economic value depends on an underlying financial asset, such as a stock, a bond, or a unit of foreign currency. The economic value of *commodity derivatives* depends on the underlying commodity, such as wheat, crude oil, or gold. Most derivatives are intended to allow investors and firms to profit from price movements in the underlying asset. An important use of derivatives is to **hedge**, or reduce risk. For example, consider the situation of the managers responsible for producing Tropicana orange juice. Suppose the managers are worried that orange prices may rise in the future, thereby reducing the profits from selling orange juice. It is possible for Tropicana to hedge this risk by using a derivative that will increase in value if the price of oranges rises. That way, if the price of oranges does rise, Tropicana's losses when it buys higher-priced oranges will be offset by the increase in the value of the derivative. If the price of oranges falls, Tropicana will gain from a reduced cost of buying oranges but will suffer a loss on the value of the derivative.

In this example, you may not see the net gain to Tropicana from using derivatives because in using them, the firm appears to gain sometimes, but at other times it appears to lose. Recall, though, from Chapter 4 that economists measure risk on a financial investment as the degree of uncertainty in an asset's return. Similarly, a key risk in producing orange juice is that orange prices will fluctuate, thereby causing fluctuations in the profits Tropicana can earn from selling orange juice. Because derivatives reduce the uncertainty in orange juice profits, Tropicana finds them valuable. In other words, even though using derivatives reduces how much Tropicana benefits from a decrease in the price of oranges, it also reduces the losses from an increase in the price of oranges, so Tropicana benefits from a net reduction in risk.

Similarly, suppose that you buy $20,000 worth of 10-year Treasury notes, intending to sell them next year to make a down payment on a house. You know that if interest rates rise, the market price of the notes will fall. You can hedge this risk by entering into a derivatives transaction that will earn a profit if interest rates rise. If interest rates fall rather than rise, you will benefit from the increase in the price of the notes. But you will suffer a loss on the derivatives transaction. Once again, though, you are willing to accept this trade-off because you gain a net reduction in risk.

In effect, derivatives can serve as a type of insurance against price changes in underlying assets. Insurance plays an important role in the economic system: If insurance is available on an economic activity, more of that activity will occur. For instance, if no fire insurance were available, many people would be afraid to own their own homes because of the heavy uninsured losses they would suffer in the event of a fire. The lower demand for housing would result in less residential construction. The availability of fire insurance increases the amount of residential construction. Similarly, if investors could not hedge the risk of financial investments, they would make fewer investments, which would reduce the flow of funds in the financial system. Firms and households would have reduced access to funds, which would slow economic growth.

Hedge To take action to reduce risk by, for example, purchasing a derivative contract that will increase in value when another asset in an investor's portfolio decreases in value.

Speculate To place financial bets, as in buying or selling futures or option contracts, in an attempt to profit from movements in asset prices.

Investors can also use derivatives to **speculate**, or place financial bets on movements in asset prices. For instance, suppose that your only connection with the orange business is to drink a glass of orange juice at breakfast every morning. However, your careful study of orange crop reports and long-range weather forecasts has convinced you that the price of oranges will rise in the future. A derivative that increases in value as orange prices rise gives you an opportunity to profit from your superior insight into the orange market. Of course, if your insight is wrong and orange prices fall, you will lose your bet.

Some investors and policymakers believe that speculation and speculators provide no benefit to financial markets. But, in fact, speculators help derivative markets operate by serving two useful purposes. First, hedgers are able to transfer risk to speculators. In derivatives markets, as in other markets, there must be two parties to a transaction. If a hedger sells a derivative security to a speculator, the speculator, by purchasing the security, has accepted the transfer of risk from the hedger. Second, studies of derivatives markets have shown that speculators provide essential liquidity. That is, without speculators, there would not be a sufficient number of buyers and sellers for the markets to operate efficiently. As with other securities, investors are reluctant to hold derivative securities unless there is a market in which to easily sell them.

In the following sections, we look at the most important types of derivatives and the roles they play in the functioning of financial markets.

7.2 Forward Contracts

LEARNING OBJECTIVE: Define forward contracts and explain their role in the financial system.

Firms, households, and investors often make plans that can be affected, for better or for worse, by changes in future prices. For instance, a farmer may plant wheat that will not be harvested for months. The farmer's profit or loss will depend on the price of wheat at the time the wheat is harvested. A bank may make a four-year automobile loan with an interest rate of 5% that is profitable as long as the interest rate the bank pays on deposits stays at 2% or less. If the interest rate on deposits rises to 4%, the bank will lose money on the loan because it will not be able to cover all of the costs related to making the loan.

Forward contract An agreement to buy or sell an asset at an agreed-upon price at a future time.

Forward contracts give firms and investors an opportunity to hedge the risk on transactions that depend on future prices. Forward contracts make possible *forward transactions*, which are transactions agreed to in the present but settled in the future. Generally, forward contracts involve an agreement in the present to exchange a given amount of a commodity, such as wheat, oil, or gold, or a financial asset, such as Treasury bills, at a particular date in the future for a set price. Forward contracts were first developed in agricultural markets. The supply of agricultural products depends on the weather and can therefore be subject to wide fluctuations. In addition, the demand for agricultural products is usually price inelastic. Recall from your principles of economics course that when demand is inelastic, fluctuations in supply cause large swings in equilibrium prices.

For example, suppose that you are a farmer who in May sows seeds with the expectation of a yield of 10,000 bushels of wheat. The price at which you can sell the wheat you have available immediately is called the **spot price**. Suppose the spot price in May is $5.00 per bushel. You are concerned that when you harvest the wheat in August, the spot price will have fallen below $5.00, so you will receive less than $50,000 for your wheat. When General Mills buys wheat to make Wheaties and other breakfast cereals, it has the opposite concern: A manager at General Mills is concerned that in August the price of wheat will have risen above $5.00, thereby raising the cost of producing cereal. You and the General Mills manager can hedge against an adverse movement in the price of wheat by entering into a forward contract under which you commit to sell 10,000 bushels of wheat to General Mills at a price of $5.00 per bushel at a date in the future known as the **settlement date**, which is the date on which the contracted delivery must take place. Both parties to the contract have locked in today the price they will receive or pay in the future, on the settlement date.

Although forward contracts provide risk sharing, they have important drawbacks. Because forward contracts usually contain terms specific to the particular buyer and seller involved in a transaction, selling the contract is difficult because a buyer would have to accept the same terms. Therefore, forward contracts tend to be illiquid. In addition, forward contracts are subject to default risk because the buyer or the seller may be unable or unwilling to fulfill the contract. For instance, in the previous example, General Mills might have declared bankruptcy shortly after signing the contract and may be unable to make the required payment to you. In this context, default risk is often called **counterparty risk**. The counterparty is the person or firm on the other side of the transaction. So, from the perspective of the seller, the buyer is the counterparty, and from the perspective of the buyer, the seller is the counterparty. Counterparty risk is the risk that the buyer will not fulfill his or her obligation to the seller or that the seller will not fulfill his or her obligation to the buyer. As a result of counterparty risk, buyers and sellers of forward contracts will incur information costs when analyzing the creditworthiness of potential trading partners.

Spot price The price at which a commodity or financial asset can be sold at the current date.

Settlement date The date on which the delivery of a commodity or financial asset specified in a forward contract must take place.

Counterparty risk The risk that the counterparty—the person or firm on the other side of the transaction—will default.

7.3 Futures Contracts

LEARNING OBJECTIVE: Explain how futures contracts can be used to hedge and to speculate.

Futures contracts first evolved in commodity markets to keep the risk-sharing benefits of forward contracts while increasing liquidity and lowering counterparty risk and information costs. Futures contracts differ from forward contracts in several ways:

1. Futures contracts are traded on exchanges, such as the Chicago Board of Trade (CBOT) and the New York Mercantile Exchange (NYMEX).
2. Futures contracts typically specify a quantity of the underlying asset to be delivered but do not fix the price on the settlement date when the asset is delivered. Instead, the price changes continually as contracts are bought and sold on the exchange.
3. Futures contracts are standardized in terms of the quantity of the underlying asset to be delivered and the settlement dates for the available contracts.

Futures contract A standardized contract to buy or sell a specified amount of a commodity or a financial asset on a specific future date.

Because futures contracts are standardized according to the rules of the exchanges they trade on, they lack some of the flexibility of forward contracts. For instance, although buyers and sellers of forward contracts in wheat may choose any settlement date they want, the CBOT offers wheat futures contracts with only five settlement dates per year. But many investors and firms like futures contracts because they have less counterparty risk and lower information costs, as well as greater liquidity. Counterparty risk is reduced because the exchange serves as a *clearinghouse* (or *clearing corporation*) that matches up buyers and sellers, and the exchange—rather than the buyers and sellers—stands as the counterparty on each trade. For instance, someone buying a futures contract on the CBOT has the CBOT as a counterparty, which greatly reduces default risk. Having the exchange as a counterparty also reduces information costs because buyers and sellers of futures contracts do not have to devote resources to determining the creditworthiness of trading partners. Finally, the reduced risk and information costs, along with the standardization of contract terms, increase the willingness of investors to buy and sell futures contracts. The markets for many futures contracts are highly liquid, with large numbers of buyers and sellers.

Hedging with Commodity Futures

Suppose that you want to hedge against falling wheat prices by using futures contracts. You plant wheat in May, when the spot price of wheat is $5.00 per bushel, which is the price you could sell the wheat for at that time. You are afraid that when you harvest the wheat in August, the price will have fallen. The CBOT doesn't offer a wheat futures contract with a settlement date in August, but it does offer one with a settlement date in September. Assume that the *futures price* in the contracts is $5.50. The futures price is $0.50 higher than the current spot price because buyers and sellers of futures contracts must be expecting that the spot price in September will be higher than the spot price in May. The buyers and sellers may base their expectation that the price of wheat will rise on information such as government crop reports and long-range weather forecasts.

Each wheat futures contract on the CBOT is standardized at 5,000 bushels, so to hedge against a price decline, you should sell two wheat futures contracts because you expect to harvest 10,000 bushels of wheat. To sell the contracts, you would need to use a registered futures broker who would be able to execute the trades for you on the CBOT. By selling wheat futures, you take a *short position* in the futures market. Someone has a **short position** if he or she has promised to sell or deliver the underlying asset. If a manager at General Mills who is worried about an increase in the future price of wheat buys the contract, he is taking the **long position** in the futures market, which means that he now has the right and obligation to buy or receive the underlying asset. *In general, the holder of a short position benefits from a fall in the price of the underlying asset, and the holder of a long position benefits from a rise in the price of the underlying asset.* Note that you are long in the spot market for wheat because you own wheat that you intend to sell after harvesting it, while the manager at General Mills is short in the spot market for wheat because he intends to buy wheat to make into breakfast cereal. We can generalize this important point:

> *Hedging involves taking a short position in the futures market to offset a long position in the spot market or taking a long position in the futures market to offset a short position in the spot market.*

Short position In a futures contract, the right and obligation of the seller to sell or deliver the underlying asset on the specified future date.

Long position In a futures contract, the right and obligation of the buyer to receive or buy the underlying asset on the specified future date.

The price in a wheat futures contract changes in the course of each day's trading, as new information becomes available that is relevant to forecasting the future spot price of wheat on the settlement day. As the time to deliver approaches, the futures price comes closer to the spot price, eventually equaling the spot price on the settlement date. Why must the spot price equal the futures price on the settlement date? Because if there were a difference between the two prices, arbitrage profits would be possible. For instance, if the spot price of wheat were $5.00 on the settlement date of the futures contract but the futures prices were $5.50, an investor could buy wheat on the spot market and simultaneously sell futures contracts. The buyers of the futures contract would have to accept delivery of wheat at $5.50, which would allow the investor to make a risk-free profit of $0.50 per bushel of wheat. In practice, investors selling additional futures contracts would drive down the futures price until it equaled the spot price. Only then would arbitrage profits be eliminated.

To continue with our example, suppose that when you harvest your wheat in August, the futures price has fallen to $5.25 per bushel, while the spot price is $4.75. The futures price is higher than the spot price because traders in the futures market expect that the spot price of wheat will increase between August and September, when the futures contract expires. For simplicity, assume that you harvest and sell your wheat on that same day. To fulfill your futures market obligation, you can engage in either *settlement by delivery* or *settlement by offset*. Because you want to sell your wheat as soon as it is harvested in August, you will use settlement by offset, so rather than actually delivering wheat, you will close your position at the CBOT by buying two futures contracts, thereby offsetting the two contracts you sold in May. You sold the contracts for $55,000 (= $5.50 per bushel × 10,000). By buying them back for $52,500 (= $5.25 × 10,000 bushels), you earn a profit of $2,500 in the futures market. In the spot market, you sell your wheat for $47,500, thereby receiving $2,500 less than you would have received at the May spot price. Because this $2,500 loss is offset by your $2,500 profit in the futures market, you have succeeded in hedging the risk of a price decline in the wheat market.

Notice that the manager at General Mills is in the reverse position. In settling his position in the futures market, he will sell two contracts at a futures price of $5.25 per bushel, thereby suffering a $2,500 loss—because the futures price when he bought the contracts in May was $5.50 per bushel. But he will buy wheat in the spot market for $2,500 less than he would have paid at the May spot price of $5.00 per bushel. If the spot price of wheat had risen rather than fallen, you would have lost money on your futures market position but earned a profit in the spot market, while the manager at General Mills would have earned a profit in the futures market but taken a loss in the spot market.

We can summarize the profits and losses of buyers and sellers of futures contracts:

Profit (or loss) to the buyer = Spot price at settlement − Futures price at purchase.

Profit (or loss) to seller = Futures price at purchase − Spot price at settlement.

Notice that the futures market is a *zero-sum game*, which means that if the seller makes a profit, the buyer must suffer a loss of exactly the same amount, and if the seller suffers a loss, the buyer will earn a profit of exactly the same amount. (To make sure you understand this point, review the example of the farmer and General Mills to check that whatever one gains the other loses.) Table 7.1 summarizes this example of using commodity futures contracts to hedge the risk of price fluctuations.

TABLE 7.1 Using Commodity Futures Contracts to Hedge

	Wheat farmer	Manager at General Mills
Concerned about ...	lower wheat prices	higher wheat prices
Hedges risk by ...	selling futures contracts	buying futures contracts
Position in futures market is ...	short	long
Position in spot market is ...	long	short
If wheat prices rise ...	loses in the futures market but gains in the spot market	gains in the futures market but loses in the spot market
If wheat prices fall ...	gains in the futures market but loses in the spot market	loses in the futures market but gains in the spot market

As we noted earlier, it may appear at first that hedging with futures contracts serves no useful purpose because buyers and sellers can expect to lose on their futures positions about as often as they can expect to gain. In fact, given that there are costs involved in buying and selling futures contracts, you and the General Mills manager in our example may seem to have made yourselves worse off. Remember, though, that using futures contracts reduces the variance of returns, which reduces risk. Investors and firms are willing to pay for a reduction in risk, which is why they hedge by using futures contracts.

Speculating with Commodity Futures

We have given an example of firms—farmers and General Mills—that are involved in the market for wheat and want to use futures to reduce the risk in their business operations. Investors who are not connected with the wheat market can use wheat futures to speculate on the price of wheat. For instance, suppose that it is May, and after carefully studying all the information relevant to forecasting the future demand and supply for wheat, you conclude that in September the price of wheat will be $6.25 per bushel. If September wheat futures have a futures price of $5.50 per bushel, you stand to make a profit by buying them. Although you do not actually want to take delivery of the wheat in September, you stand to make a profit by settling your position by selling wheat futures at some point between May and the September settlement date. If you were convinced that the spot price of wheat were going to be lower in September than the current futures price, you could sell wheat futures with the intention of buying them back at the lower price on or before the settlement date.

Notice, though, that because you lack an offsetting position in the spot market, an adverse movement in wheat prices will cause you to take losses. For instance, if you buy wheat futures, but the price of wheat falls rather than rises, you will have to settle your position for a loss. Similarly, if you sell wheat futures and wheat prices rise, you will also have to settle your position for a loss.

As we noted at the beginning of the chapter, speculators play an important role in futures markets by adding needed liquidity. Without speculators, most futures markets would not have enough buyers or sellers to operate, thereby reducing the risk sharing available to hedgers.

So You Think You Can Beat the Smart Money in the Oil Market?

Speculators tend to be attracted to securities or commodities that have volatile prices. After all, it's difficult to make money betting on price changes if prices don't change much! As noted in the chapter opener, in the past 15 years, oil prices have been quite volatile. The following figure shows the price of a barrel of West Texas Intermediate crude oil—oil that is produced in Texas and southern Oklahoma, and that serves as the benchmark for oil prices in the United States. The figure shows that the price of a barrel of oil has fluctuated dramatically over the past 11 years.

As with other prices, changes in the price of oil are determined by shifts in demand and supply. Many factors affect the demand for oil, including the rate of world economic growth, how many electric or hybrid cars consumers buy, and the prices of substitute goods such as natural gas or solar panels. Factors that affect supply include changes in the technology related to extracting oil, such as "fracking" of shale oil in the United States, and political instability that can disrupt production in countries such as Iraq, Nigeria, or Libya.

As we saw in Chapter 6, money managers and other Wall Street professionals who invest in the stock market carefully monitor news about firms. According to the efficient markets hypothesis, that news is instantly reflected in the prices of stocks. If Apple announces that sales of iPhones were unexpectedly strong, Apple's stock price will rise within a few seconds of the announcement. Wall Street professionals also closely follow developments in the markets for commodities so that they can move quickly to buy and sell derivatives as news causes their values to change. To make a profit buying and selling oil derivatives, you would therefore need to both follow news about the oil industry carefully and have a better understanding than Wall Street professionals of how that news is likely to affect oil prices. You couldn't realistically expect to react more quickly than Wall Street professionals to the news, so to make money speculating on oil prices, you would need to have superior insight into how the oil market works.

An increasing number of people apparently believe they can beat Wall Street professionals because in 2016, individual investors for the first time made up more than 10% of the volume of daily trading of oil futures on the Chicago Mercantile Exchange. Typically, only high-income investors are allowed to trade futures contracts directly, but many small investors can buy and sell financial securities that are linked to oil futures contracts.

For instance, one news story described a woman who cares for her two children full time and also speculates in the oil market by buying and selling such securities. According to the article, when she "read that wildfires were breaking out in an oil-producing region of Alberta [Canada], she sat down on the family room couch with a cup of hot chocolate and her laptop and bought shares of an investment linked to crude [oil]." When she sold the investment four days later, she had made about $400 on the transaction.

Many individual investors gain confidence from such anecdotes, but the question is: Are similar short-run investments likely to be profitable? It seems unlikely, given that few individual investors are able consistently to earn a profit either by buying and selling stocks or buying and selling derivatives. Although reliable statistics are scarce, a common estimate is that fewer than 5% of individuals who actively trade stocks or derivatives are able to just break even on their investments—much less earn a profit—taking into account the transactions costs of buying and selling and the taxes on any gains made.

The Chicago Mercantile Exchange provides the following advice to individuals thinking of trading futures contracts: "The funds you trade should be discretionary, separate from any savings you have set aside for college, retirement or emergencies. In other words, ask yourself if you can afford to lose whatever funds you expose to risk in your futures account." In other words: Proceed at your own risk!

Sources: Ben Eisen, Nicole Friedman, and Saumya Vaishampayan, "The New Oil Traders: Moms and Millennials," *Wall Street Journal*, May 26, 2016; Peter Hans, "The Long and Short of Crude Oil," forbes.com, May 12, 2016; and Chicago Mercantile Exchange, *A Trader's Guide to Futures*, September 19, 2011.

See related problem 3.10 at the end of the chapter.

Hedging and Speculating with Financial Futures

Futures contracts first appeared in commodity markets, such as the markets for wheat and oil, in the nineteenth century. Although trading in financial futures did not begin until 1972, today most futures traded are financial futures. Widely traded financial futures contracts include those for Treasury bills, notes, and bonds; stock indexes, such as the S&P 500 and the Dow Jones Industrial Average; and currencies, such as U.S. dollars, Japanese yen, euros, and British pounds. Financial futures contracts are regulated by exchange rules approved by the Commodity Futures Trading Commission (CFTC). The CFTC monitors potential price manipulation by traders on futures exchanges, as well as the conduct of the exchanges.

The process of hedging risk using financial futures is very similar to the process of hedging risk using commodity futures. Consider the following example of using financial futures to hedge interest-rate risk. Suppose you own Treasury notes but are concerned about being exposed to the risk of a decline in the price of the notes if market interest rates rise. Notice that you are in essentially the same situation as you were as a wheat farmer in our earlier example: (1) You would like to hedge against a price decline, and (2) you are long in the spot market—you own Treasury notes. So to hedge the risk of a price decline, you should go short in the futures market by selling Treasury note futures contracts. If, as you feared, market interest rates rise and the price of your notes falls, the futures price will also fall. You can settle your futures position by buying futures contracts to offset your earlier sale. Because you buy the contracts for a lower price than you sold them for, you make a profit that offsets the losses caused by the falling price of your Treasury notes.

Who would want to be on the other side of this transaction? That is, who might be willing to buy the futures contracts you want to sell? Consider, for example, the manager of a company's pension fund who expects to receive contributions to the fund in six months. The manager would like to invest the contributions in Treasury notes but may be afraid that the interest rate on the notes will have declined by then, reducing the return she would like to make on the investment. Worrying about a decline in the interest rate on Treasury notes is the same thing as worrying about an increase in their price, so the pension fund manager is like the manager at General Mills in our earlier example. The pension fund manager is short in the spot market for Treasury notes, so to hedge the risk of a price increase, she needs to go long in the futures market by buying Treasury futures contracts. If the interest rate on the Treasury notes falls and their price rises, the manager will be able to settle her Treasury futures position by selling futures contracts to offset her earlier purchase. Because she sells the contracts for a higher price than she bought them for, she makes a profit that offsets the lower returns she will receive when she buys the Treasury notes. Table 7.2 summarizes hedging with financial futures.

An investor who believes that he or she has superior insight into the likely path of future interest rates can use the futures market to speculate. For example, if you are convinced that in the future, interest rates on Treasury notes will be lower than indicated by the current price of Treasury futures, you could profit by buying Treasury futures. If you are correct, and future interest rates turn out to be lower than expected, the futures price will rise, and you can settle your position by selling Treasury futures contracts at a profit. If you wanted to speculate that future interest rates will be higher than expected, you could sell Treasury futures contracts.

TABLE 7.2 Using Financial Futures to Hedge Interest-Rate Risk

	Investor who owns Treasury notes	Pension fund manager who intends to buy Treasury notes in six months
Concerned about ...	lower Treasury note prices (higher interest rates)	higher Treasury note prices (lower interest rates)
Hedges risk by ...	selling futures contracts	buying futures contracts
Position in futures market ...	short	long
Position in spot market ...	long	short
If Treasury note prices rise (interest rates fall) ...	loses in the futures market but gains in the spot market	gains in the futures market but loses in the spot market
If Treasury note prices fall (interest rates rise) ...	gains in the futures market but loses in the spot market	loses in the futures market but gains in the spot market

MAKING THE CONNECTION | **IN YOUR INTEREST**

How to Follow the Futures Market: Reading the Financial Futures Listings

Following the futures market can help you understand developments in financial markets. Where can you go to get information? The *Wall Street Journal* reports online information on futures contracts each business day. You can also find data on the web site of the CME group (www.cmegroup.com), which was formed from a merger of the Chicago Board of Trade (CBOT) and the Chicago Mercantile Exchange (CME).

An example of a "quotation" on interest-rate futures on U.S. Treasury securities appears below. The quotation is from the end of trading on June 28, 2016, and is for a 10-year U.S. Treasury note futures traded on the CBOT. The quotation is for a standardized contract of $100,000 in face value of notes paying a 6% coupon. The first column states the contract month and year for delivery. The delivery date for the contract in the first row is September 2016. The next five columns present price information: the Last price, which is the price of the last trade that day; the change (Chg) in price from the previous day; the Open price, or the price at which the first trade of the day took place; the High price for the day; and the Low price for the day. Note that these prices are quoted per $100 of face value. For example, the Last price for the contract in the first row is $133.250 per $100 of face value. There are 1,000 $100s of face value in a $100,000 contract. Therefore, the price of this contract is $133.250 × 1,000 = $133,250. Because the price is above the face value of $100,000, we know that the yield to maturity on the contract must be less than the coupon rate of 6%.

10-year U.S. Treasury note futures

Month	Last	Chg	Open	High	Low	Volume	OpenInt
Sep 2016	133.250	0.266	133.031	133.922	132.984	1,306,807	2,753,697
Dec 2016	132.406	0.359	132.156	132.406	132.156	58	174

The Volume column tells you the number of contracts traded that day. In this case, 1,306,807 September 2016 contracts were traded. Open Interest (OpenInt) reports the volume of contracts outstanding—that is, not yet settled. For the September 2016 contract, open interest was 2,753,697 contracts.

You can get useful information from these quotes. The interest-rate futures contracts tell you market participants' expectations of future interest rates. Note that futures prices are slightly lower for December 2016 than for September 2016, which tells you that futures market investors expect long-term Treasury interest rates to *rise* slightly.

Although not shown here, you can also find interest-rate futures quotations for Treasury bonds and bills and foreign currencies. The financial futures listings also give you quotes on stock index futures, such as contracts on the S&P 500. Investors use stock index futures to anticipate broad stock market movements.

Sources of data: *Wall Street Journal*, July 2, 2016; and Chicago Board of Trade.

See related problem 3.13 at the end of the chapter.

SOLVED PROBLEM 7.3 IN YOUR INTEREST

How Can You Hedge an Investment in Treasury Notes When Interest Rates Are Low?

Following the financial crisis of 2007–2009, interest rates on Treasury bills, notes, and bonds and on many corporate and municipal bonds fell to very low levels. In 2016, many investors were still buying bonds despite their low yields, but forbes.com quoted one investment analyst as saying: "We are entering a period of a bond bear market."

a. What does a bear market in bonds mean?
b. What might cause a bear market in bonds?
c. How might you hedge the risk of investing in bonds?

Solving the Problem

Step 1 **Review the chapter material.** This problem is about hedging the risk of investing in bonds, so you may want to review the section "Hedging and Speculating with Financial Futures," which begins on page 220.

Step 2 **Answer part (a) by explaining what a bear market in bonds would be.** As we saw in discussing the stock market, a bear market refers to a price decline of at least 20% from a previous high.

Step 3 **Answer part (b) by explaining what might cause a bear market in bonds.** A bear market in bonds could result from investors believing that the inflation rate might rise in the future. The Fisher effect tells us that a higher expected inflation rate will result in higher nominal interest rates. Higher nominal interest rates mean lower bond prices.

Step 4 **Answer part (c) by explaining how you can hedge the risk of investing in bonds.** We have seen that investors can use the futures market to hedge the risk of investing in bonds. Because in this case you would be worried about rising interest rates and falling bond prices, the appropriate hedge would be for you to sell futures contracts, such as those available on the CBOT for Treasury notes. By owning bonds, you are long in the spot market for bonds, so the appropriate hedge would be for you to go short in the futures market for bonds by selling futures contracts. As an individual investor, you can sell the contracts by using a registered futures broker who would place the sell order on the CBOT. Many stockbrokers are also futures brokers. Some brokers are so-called full-service brokers who offer trading advice and provide research support, as well as executing trades. Other brokers are discount brokers, who charge a lower commission to execute trades but do not typically offer advice. Individual investors will sometimes hedge the risk of investing in bonds by buying shares in mutual funds that invest in derivative contracts rather than by buying or selling the contracts themselves.

Source: Kenneth Rapoza, "How to Avoid the Coming 25 Year Bond Bear Market," forbes.com, December 14, 2015.

See related problem 3.11 at the end of the chapter.

Trading in the Futures Market

As we have seen, buyers and sellers of futures contracts deal with an exchange rather than directly with each other, as would be the case with forward contracts. To reduce default risk, the exchange requires both the buyer and seller to place an initial deposit called a **margin requirement** into a *margin account*. For instance, on the CBOT, futures contracts for U.S. Treasury notes are standardized at a face value of $100,000 of notes, or the equivalent of 100 notes of $1,000 face value each. The CBOT requires that buyers and sellers of these contracts deposit a minimum of $1,100 for each contract into a margin account.

At the end of each trading day, the exchange carries out a daily settlement known as **marking to market**, in which, depending on the closing price of the contract, funds are transferred from the buyer's account to the seller's account or vice versa. For instance, suppose that you buy a Treasury note futures contract for a price of 100. From the *Making the Connection* on page 222, we know this price means that you paid $100,000 for the contract. Assume that you deposited just the minimum $1,100 required by the CBOT into your margin account, and the seller deposited the same amount into his or her account. The following day, at the end of trading in the market, the price of your contract has risen to 101, perhaps because new information has led traders to believe that interest rates will be lower in the future (and, therefore, Treasury note prices will be higher) than they had previously expected. Because the value of your contract has risen by $1,000, the exchange will transfer $1,000 from the seller's account to your account. The balance in the seller's account falls to $100. This amount is below the *maintenance margin*, which is sometimes less than the initial margin, but in the case of Treasury note futures contracts, is also $1,100. The seller will be subject to a *margin call*, which is an order from the exchange for the seller to add enough funds to his or her account to reach the $1,100 maintenance margin. Because of margin requirements and marking to market, traders rarely default on futures contracts, which limits the exchange's exposure to losses.

Table 7.3 summarizes the activities of buyers and sellers in the futures market.

Margin requirement In the futures market, the minimum deposit that an exchange requires from the buyer and seller of a financial asset; reduces default risk.

Marking to market In the futures market, a daily settlement in which the exchange transfers funds from a buyer's account to a seller's account or vice versa, depending on changes in the price of the contract.

TABLE 7.3 Buyers and Sellers in the Futures Market

Buyer of a futures contract	Seller of a futures contract
Has the obligation to buy the underlying asset on the settlement date.	Has the obligation to deliver the underlying asset on the settlement date.
Can use buying a futures contract to hedge if the buyer is someone who intends to buy the underlying asset and wants to insure against the price rising.	Can use selling a futures contract to hedge if the seller is the owner of the underlying asset and wants to insure against the price falling.
Can use buying a futures contract to speculate if the buyer believes that the price of the underlying asset will rise.	Can use selling a futures contract to speculate if the seller believes that the price of the underlying asset will fall.

7.4 Options

LEARNING OBJECTIVE: Distinguish between call options and put options and explain how they are used.

Options are another type of derivative contract. As with futures contracts, options contracts allow investors and firms to hedge risk or to speculate. The buyer of an option has the right to buy or sell the underlying asset at a set price during a set period of time. A **call option** gives the buyer the right to buy the underlying asset at the **strike price** (or **exercise price**), at any time up to the option's *expiration date*. For instance, if you buy a call option on Apple with a strike price of $110 and an expiration date of July, you have the right to buy one share of Apple stock for $110 at any time up to the expiration date in July (typically the third Friday of the month).

A **put option** gives the buyer the right to sell the underlying asset at the strike price at any time up to the option's expiration date. For instance, if you buy a put option on Apple with a strike price of $110 and an expiration date of July, you have the right to sell one share of Apple stock for $110 at any time up to the expiration date in July. Note that the options being described here are *American options*, which an investor may exercise at any time up to the expiration date. An investor may exercise *European options* only on the expiration date. The price of an option contract is also called *the option premium*.

With futures contracts, buyers and sellers have symmetric rights and obligations. That is, the seller must deliver the underlying asset, and the buyer must take delivery at the futures price on the delivery date (although, as we've seen, settlement typically occurs before delivery takes place). In contrast, with options contracts, the buyer has rights, and the seller, called the *option writer*, has obligations. For example, if you buy a call option and exercise your right to buy the underlying asset, the seller of the call option has no choice but to fulfill the obligation to sell the asset. However, as the buyer of the call option, you have no obligation to exercise it by buying the underlying asset and may choose, instead, to allow the option to expire, unexercised; the seller can't force you to exercise an option. Similarly, if you buy a put option and exercise your right to sell the underlying asset, the seller of the put option has no choice but to fulfill the obligation to buy the asset.

Options are traded both over the counter and on exchanges such as the Chicago Board Options Exchange (CBOE) and the New York Stock Exchange (NYSE). Options traded on exchanges are called *listed options*. Options contracts traded in the United States include stock options, which can be on individual stocks, stock indexes, or stock futures contracts; options on interest-rate futures (such as futures contracts on U.S. Treasury notes); and options on currencies and currency futures (such as futures contracts on the Japanese yen, euro, Canadian dollar, and British pound). One important distinction between futures and options contracts is that when you purchase a futures contract, funds change hands daily as the contract is marked to market. With an options contract, however, once you have purchased the option, funds change hands only when the option is exercised.

Option A type of derivative contract in which the buyer has the right to buy or sell the underlying asset at a set price during a set period of time.

Call option A type of derivative contract that gives the buyer the right to buy the underlying asset at a set price during a set period of time.

Strike price (or exercise price) The price at which the buyer of an option has the right to buy or sell the underlying asset.

Put option A type of derivative contract that gives the buyer the right to sell the underlying asset at a set price during a set period of time.

Why Would You Buy or Sell an Option?

Suppose that Apple stock has a current price of $100 per share, but you believe the price will rise to $120 at some point during the coming year. You could purchase shares of Apple and earn a profit if the price rises as you expect. There are two potential downsides to this strategy: Buying the shares outright will require a sizable investment, and if the price of Apple falls rather than rises, you will face a possibly substantial loss. As an alternative, you could buy call options that would allow you to buy Apple at a strike price of, say, $110. The price to buy the options will be much lower than the price to buy the underlying stock. In addition, if the price of Apple never rises above $110, you can allow the options to expire without exercising them, which limits your loss to the price of the options.

If Apple's stock is selling for $100 per share and you are convinced it will decline in price, you could engage in a *short sale*. With a short sale, you borrow the stock from your broker and sell it now, with the plan of buying it back—and repaying your broker—after the stock declines in price. But if the price of Apple rises rather than falls, you will lose money by having to buy back the stock—which is called "covering a short"—at a price that is higher than you sold it for. On the other hand, if you buy a put with a strike price of $90 per share, you will profit from a decline in the price of Apple's stock, while if the price rises, you can allow the option to expire and limit your loss to the price of the option.

Figure 7.1 illustrates the potential gains and losses from buying options on Apple stock. We assume that the buyer of the option pays a price for the option but does not incur any cost when buying or selling the underlying stock. We assume that the price a buyer pays to buy either the call option or the put option is $10 per share. Although the buyer of the option can exercise the option at any time, for simplicity we focus on how the payoff to owning the option varies with the price of the stock on the expiration date.[1] In panel (a), we illustrate the profit to buying a call option with a strike price of $110. When the price of Apple stock is between zero and $110 on the expiration date, the owner of the option will not exercise it and will suffer a loss equal to the $10 price of the option. As the price of Apple rises above $110 per share, the owner of the option will earn a positive amount from exercising it. For example, if the price is $115, the owner can exercise the option, buy a share of Apple from the seller of the option for the strike price of $110, sell the share in the market for $115, and make $5. Because the owner paid $10 for the option, he or she has a net loss of $5. If the price of Apple is $120, the owner will break even. For prices above $120, the owner earns a profit. For example, if the price of Apple is $150, the owner exercises the option, buys a share for $110, sells the share in the market for $150, and makes a profit of $30 [= ($150 − $110) − $10]. The higher the price of Apple stock rises, the greater the profit to the buyer of the call option.

In panel (b), we illustrate the profit to buying a put option with a strike price of $90. The owner of a put option earns a maximum profit when the price of Apple stock

---

[1] Alternatively, we can think of Figure 7.1 as illustrating the situation for the highest price—panel (a)—Apple stock reaches before the expiration date or the lowest price—panel (b).

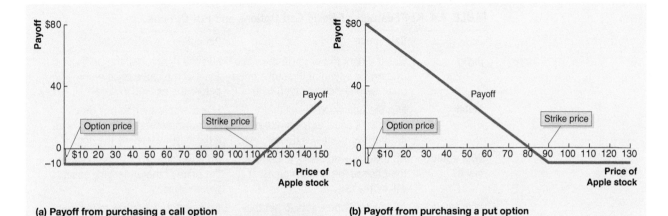

(a) Payoff from purchasing a call option   **(b) Payoff from purchasing a put option**

FIGURE 7.1 Payoffs to Owning Options on Apple Stock

In panel (a), we illustrate the profit from buying a call option with a strike price of $110. When the price of Apple stock is between zero and $110, the owner of the option will not exercise it and will suffer a loss equal to the $10 price of the option. As the price of Apple rises above $110 per share, the owner of the option will earn a positive amount from exercising it. For prices above $120, the owner earns a profit.

In panel (b), we illustrate the profit from buying a put option with a strike price of $90. The owner of a put option earns a maximum profit when the price of Apple is zero. As the price of Apple stock rises, the payoff from owning the put option falls. At a price of $80, the owner of the put would just break even. For prices above the $90 strike price, the owner of the put option would not exercise it and would suffer a loss equal to the option price of $10.

is zero.[2] The owner would buy a share of Apple for a price of zero, exercise the option, and sell the share to the seller of the put option for $90. Subtracting the $10 price of the option, the buyer of the option is left with a profit of $80. As the price of Apple stock rises, the payoff from owning the put option falls. At a price of $80, the owner of the put would just break even because the owner would make $10 from buying a share of Apple stock in the market for $80 and selling it to the option writer for $90, which would just offset the $10 price of the option. For prices above the $90 strike price, the owner of the put option would not exercise it and would lose an amount equal to the option price of $10.

Table 7.4 summarizes the key features of basic call options and put options.

Option Pricing and the Rise of the "Quants"

The price of an option is called an **option premium**. The seller of an option loses if the option is exercised. For instance, suppose that you sell a call option to buy Microsoft with a strike price of $50. If the buyer of the call option exercises it, we know that the market price of Microsoft must be higher than $50. In that case, you are obligated to sell Microsoft below its current price, so the buyer's gain is your loss.

Option premium The price of an option.

---

[2] In reality, of course, a stock has a price of zero only if the firm is bankrupt. In that case, trading in the stock would stop. A more realistic case would be a low price that would still be high enough that trading in the stock takes place.

TABLE 7.4 Key Features of Basic Call Options and Put Options

	Call option	Put option
Buyer	Has the right to purchase the underlying option at the strike price on or before the expiration date	Has the right to sell the underlying asset at the strike price on or before the expiration date
Seller	Has the obligation to sell the underlying asset at the strike price if the buyer exercises the option	Has the obligation to buy the underlying asset at the strike price if the buyer exercises the option
Who would buy it?	An investor who wants to bet that the price of the underlying asset will increase	An investor who wants to bet that the price of the underlying asset will decrease
Who would sell it?	An investor who wants to bet that the price of the underlying asset will not increase	An investor who wants to bet that the price of the underlying asset will not decrease

Not surprisingly, then, the size of the option premium reflects the probability that the option will be exercised, in the same way that a car insurance premium reflects the risk of an accident.

We can think of an option premium as having two parts: the option's intrinsic value and its time value. An option's *intrinsic value* equals the payoff to the buyer of the option from exercising it immediately. For example, if a call option on Microsoft stock has a strike price of $50 when the market price of Microsoft is $55, the option has an intrinsic value of $5 because the buyer could exercise it immediately, buy a share of Microsoft from the seller for $50, and resell the share in the market for $55. An option that has a positive intrinsic value is said to be *in the money*. A call option is in the money if the market price of the underlying asset is greater than the strike price, and a put option is in the money if the market price of the underlying asset is less than the strike price.

If the market price of the underlying asset:

- Is below the strike price, a call option is *out of the money*, or *underwater*.
- Is above the strike price, a put option is out of the money.
- Equals the strike price, a call option or a put option is *at the money*.

Notice that because a buyer does not have to exercise an option, an option's intrinsic value can never be less than zero.

In addition to its intrinsic value, an option premium has a *time value*, which is determined by how far away the expiration date is and by how volatile the stock price has been in the past. The further away the expiration date, the greater the chance that the intrinsic value of the option will increase. Suppose that the strike price on a call option on Microsoft is $50, and the current market price is $45. If the option expires tomorrow, the chance that the market price of Microsoft will rise above $50 is small. But if the option expires in six months, the chance is much greater. We can conclude that, all else being equal, *the further away in time an option's expiration date, the larger the option premium.*

Similarly, if the volatility in the price of the underlying asset is small, the chance that the intrinsic value of the option may increase substantially because of a large price swing is small. But if the volatility in the price of the underlying asset is large, the chance is much greater. Therefore, all else being equal, *the greater the volatility in the price of the underlying asset, the larger the option premium.*

Calculating the intrinsic value of an option is straightforward, but it is more difficult to determine exactly how the option premium should be affected by the time until the option expires or by the volatility in the price of the underlying asset. It is so difficult that for many years options were thinly traded—that is, investors seldom bought or sold them—because Wall Street firms and other professional investors were unsure how to price them. In 1973, a breakthrough occurred when Fischer Black and Myron Scholes, who were then economists at the University of Chicago, published an academic article in the *Journal of Political Economy* that used sophisticated mathematics to work out a formula for the optimal pricing of options. The Black-Scholes formula coincided with the establishment of the CBOE and led to an explosive growth in options trading.

The Black-Scholes formula had even wider significance because it demonstrated to Wall Street firms that sophisticated mathematical modeling could allow these firms to price complicated financial securities. The result was that Wall Street firms hired many people with advanced degrees in economics, finance, and mathematics to build mathematical models that the firms could use to price and evaluate new securities. These people became known as "rocket scientists," or "quants."

MAKING THE CONNECTION | **IN YOUR INTEREST**

How to Follow the Options Market: Reading the Options Listings

As with futures, investing in options is typically best left to sophisticated investors, but following the options listings can help you understand what changes in futures prices of commodities and financial assets investors expect. Newspaper and online listings of options contracts contain many of the same measures as futures listings. However, there are some differences in how options are listed depending on whether the underlying asset is a direct claim (for example, a bond or shares of stock) or a futures contract (for example, a stock index futures contract).

The quotations shown on the next page are for options contracts on shares of Apple stock and appeared on the google.com/finance site on July 1, 2016 (although the quotations are also widely available on other sites). The listing provides information on put options and call options with a strike price of $100.00. On the previous day, the closing price for a share of Apple was $95.60. In fact, there are many put and call options available on Apple stock, with different strike prices; here we list just four. The first column gives the expiration date for the options. The second column gives the strike price. The next three columns give information on call options, and the last three columns give information on put options.

Call and Put Options for Apple (AAPL)
Underlying stock price: 95.60

Expiration	Strike	Call			Put		
		Price	Volume	Open Interest	Price	Volume	Open Interest
(1)	(2)	(3)	(4)	(5)	(6)	(7)	(8)
Aug	100.00	1.26	2590	37734	5.72	743	9407
Oct	100.00	2.80	528	33996	7.15	97	12349
Jan	100.00	4.64	1122	150526	9.35	398	52623
Apr	100.00	6.20	37	641	11.00	19	148

Each of the two Price columns gives the last price the contract traded for on the previous day. For example, the August call option contract listed in the first row has a Last price of $1.26. Listed options contracts for stocks are for 100 shares of stock. So if you purchased the August call option contract, you would pay: $1.26 × 100 = $126. The Volume column provides information on how many contracts were traded that day, and the Open Interest column provides information on the number of contracts outstanding—that is, not yet exercised. Notice that the put options have higher prices than the call options with the same expiration date. These higher prices reflect the fact that because the strike price is above the underlying price, the put options are all *in the money*, while the call options are *out of the money*. Notice, also, that for both the call options and the put options, the further away the expiration date, the higher the price of the option.

Source of data: google.com/finance, July 1, 2016.

See related problem 4.8 at the end of the chapter.

SOLVED PROBLEM 7.4 **IN YOUR INTEREST**

Interpreting the Options Listings for Amazon.com

Use the following information on call and put options for Amazon.com to answer the questions. In your answers, ignore any costs connected with buying and selling options or the underlying stock apart from the prices of the options or the stock.

Amazon (AMZN) — Underlying stock price: 752.68

Expiration	Strike	Call			Put		
		Price	Volume	Open Interest	Price	Volume	Open Interest
Aug	700.00	52.65	101	2375	26.43	70	1341
Oct	700.00	64.03	12	519	37.97	10	409
Jan	700.00	81.67	26	2443	54.82	16	1200
Jun	700.00	100.95	0	41	77.40	2	92

a. Why are the call options selling for higher prices than the put options?

b. Why does the June call sell for a higher price than the October call?

c. Suppose you buy the June call. Briefly explain whether you would exercise that call immediately.

d. Suppose you buy the October call at the price listed and exercise it when the price of Amazon stock is $800. What will be your profit or loss?

(Remember that each options contract is for 100 shares of stock.)

e. Suppose you buy the June put at the price listed, and the price of Amazon stock remains $752.68. What will be your profit or loss?

Solving the Problem

Step 1 **Review the chapter material.** This problem is about interpreting the listings for options, so you may want to review the section "Option Pricing and the Rise of the 'Quants'," which begins on page 227, and the *Making the Connection* "How to Follow the Options Market: Reading the Options Listings," which begins on page 229.

Step 2 **Answer part (a) by explaining why the call options are selling for higher prices than the put options.** Notice that the strike price of $700.00 is less than the price of the underlying stock, which is $752.68. So, the call options are all in the money because if you exercised one, you would be able to buy 100 shares of Amazon for $700.00 each from the seller of the call option, and then sell the shares in the market for $752.68 each, thereby making a profit of $52.68 (= $752.68 − $700.00) per share. The puts are all out of the money because you would not want to exercise your right to sell a share of Amazon for $700.00 to the seller of the put when you could sell a share in the market for $752.68. Therefore, the puts have zero intrinsic value and their prices are all lower than the prices for the calls.

Step 3 **Answer part (b) by explaining why the June call sells for a higher price than the October call.** The price of an option equals the option's *intrinsic value* plus its *time value*, which represents all other factors that affect the likelihood of the option's being exercised. The further away the expiration date, the greater the chance that the intrinsic value of the option will increase, and the higher the price of the option. Therefore, because the two call options have the same strike price, the June call will have a higher price than the October call.

Step 4 **Answer part (c) by explaining whether you would exercise the June call immediately.** If you purchased the June call, you would be able to buy Amazon for $700.00 per share from the seller of the call and sell the shares in the market for $752.68 per share, earning $52.68 per share. But the price of the call is $100.95, so you would not buy the call to exercise it immediately. You would buy the call only if you expected that before the expiration date of the call, the price of Amazon would rise sufficiently that the intrinsic value of the call would be greater than $100.95.

Step 5 **Answer part (d) by calculating your profit or loss from buying the October call and exercising it when the price of Amazon stock is $800.** If you exercise the October call, which has a strike price of $700.00, when the price of Amazon stock is $800, you will earn $100.00 minus the option price of $64.03, for a profit of $35.97. There are 100 shares in the option contract, so your total profit equals $35.97 \times 100 = \$3,597.00$.

Step 6 **Answer part (e) by calculating your profit or loss from buying the June put if the price of Amazon remains at \$752.68.** If the price of Amazon remains at $752.68, the June put will remain out of the money. Therefore, you will not exercise it, instead taking a loss equal to the option's price of $77.40 per share. Your total loss will be $77.40 \times 100 = \$7,740.00$.

See related problem 4.8 at the end of the chapter.

Using Options to Manage Risk

Firms, banks, and individual investors can use options, as well as futures, to hedge the risk from fluctuations in commodity or stock prices, interest rates, and foreign currency exchange rates. Options have the disadvantage of being more expensive than futures. But options have the important advantage that an investor who buys them will not suffer a loss if prices move in the direction opposite to that being hedged against. For instance, we saw earlier that if you own Treasury notes and want to hedge against a decline in their price, you can sell Treasury note futures. But what if prices of Treasury notes increase? In this case, you have a gain on your holdings of Treasury notes, but you suffer a loss on your futures position. You have hedged your risk, but you cannot profit from an increase in prices of Treasury notes.

Instead of *selling* Treasury futures, you can hedge by *buying* Treasury put options. If prices of Treasury notes fall, you can exercise your puts and sell at the strike price, thereby minimizing your losses. If prices of Treasury notes rise, you can allow your puts to expire without exercising them, thereby keeping most of the gains from the price rise. Because options contracts guard against a negative outcome while still allowing profits from a positive outcome, they are more like insurance than are futures contracts. This insurance aspect of options is why options prices are called options premiums. (The payments a buyer of an insurance policy makes to an insurance company are called premiums.)

When choosing between hedging with options and hedging with futures, a firm or an investor has to trade off the generally higher cost of using options against the extra insurance benefit that options provide. As an options buyer, you assume less risk than with a futures contract because the maximum loss you can incur is the option premium. Note, though, that the options *seller* does not have a limit on his or her losses. For instance, if Treasury note prices fall to very low levels, the seller of a put option is still obligated to buy at the strike price, even if it is far above the current market price.

Many hedgers buy options not on the underlying financial asset but on a futures contract derived from that asset. For instance, in the previous example, rather than hedge against a decline in Treasury note prices by buying a put option on Treasury notes, you could buy a put option on Treasury note futures. Buying and selling *futures options* has several advantages over buying and selling options on the underlying assets. Futures contracts on Treasury notes and Treasury bonds are exchange-traded securities and, therefore, are more liquid than Treasury notes and bonds because the notes and bonds generally have to be traded through dealers. Similarly, the prices of futures contracts are readily available to investors on exchanges thoughout the trading day, while investors may have difficulty finding information on the prices of Treasury notes and bonds until the markets close for the day.

MAKING THE CONNECTION   IN YOUR INTEREST

How Much Volatility Should You Expect in the Stock Market?

You may be reluctant to invest in the stock market because of the volatility of stock prices. After all, the larger the swings in an asset's price, the greater the risk to you as an investor. But is it possible to measure the degree of volatility that investors expect in the future? Such a measure might give you a way of comparing investing in stocks with investing in other financial assets.

One way to construct such a measure is by using the prices of options. In 1993, Robert E. Whaley, now of Vanderbilt University, noted that the prices of options on stock market indexes—such as the S&P 500—implicitly include a measure of investors' expectations of future market volatility. The measure of volatility is implicit, rather than explicit, because an option's price includes the option's intrinsic value plus other factors, including volatility, that affect the likelihood of an investor exercising the option. Whaley suggested a method to isolate the part of the option's price that represents investors' forecast of volatility.

Using the prices of put and call options on the S&P 500 index, the Chicago Board Options Exchange (CBOE) constructed the *Market Volatility Index*, called the VIX, to measure the expected volatility in the U.S. stock market over the following 30 days. Many people refer to the VIX as the "fear gauge" because when investors expect volatility in stock prices to increase, they increase their demand for options, thereby driving up their prices and increasing the value of the VIX. The following graph shows movements in the VIX from January 2004 to June 2016:

MyEconLab Real-time data

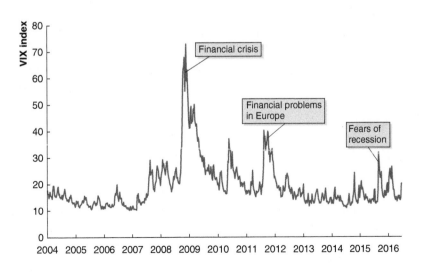

Through the middle of 2007, the VIX generally had a value between 10 and 20, meaning that investors were expecting that during the next 30 days, the S&P 500 would rise or fall by 10% to 20% at an annual rate. Then, as the financial crisis began in 2007, the VIX began to increase, reaching record levels of 80 in October and November 2008, following the bankruptcy of the Lehman Brothers investment bank. The rise in the VIX was driven by investors bidding up the prices of options as they attempted to hedge their stock market investments in the face of expected increases in volatility. The VIX did not fall back below 20 until December 2009. It rose sharply again in May 2010 and again in the fall of 2011, as the market experienced another period of volatility, this time tied to concerns about the possibility that financial problems in Europe might spill over into U.S. markets. The VIX also spiked several times in 2015 and 2016, as investors worried that slowing worldwide growth might lead to a recession and as uncertainty in financial markets increased following "Brexit," the June 2016 referendum vote in the United Kingdom to withdraw from the European Union.

In March 2004, the CBOE began trading futures on the VIX, and in February 2006, it began trading VIX options. An investor who wanted to hedge against an increase in volatility in the market would buy VIX futures. Similarly, a speculator who wanted to bet on an increase in market volatility would buy VIX futures. A speculator who wanted to bet on a decrease in market volatility would sell VIX futures.

The VIX index provides a handy tool for gauging how much volatility investors are anticipating in the market and for hedging against that volatility.

Sources: Robert E. Whaley, "Understanding the VIX," *Journal of Portfolio Management*," Vol. 35, No. 3, Spring 2009, pp. 98–105; Robert E. Whaley, "Derivatives on Market Volatility: Hedging Tools Long Overdue," *Journal of Derivatives*, Vol. 1, Fall 1993, pp. 71–84; Saumya Vaishampayan, "Fear Flashes in Options Market; VIX Nearly Doubles," *Wall Street Journal*, August 21, 2015; and Federal Reserve Bank of St. Louis.

See related problem 4.12 at the end of the chapter.

7.5 Swaps

LEARNING OBJECTIVE: Define swaps and explain how they can be used to reduce risk.

Swap An agreement between two or more counterparties to exchange sets of cash flows over some future period.

Although the standardization of futures and options contracts promotes liquidity, it also means that these contracts cannot be adjusted to meet the specific needs of investors and firms. This problem spurred the growth of *swap contracts*, or swaps. A **swap** is an agreement between two or more counterparties to exchange—or swap—sets of cash flows over some future period. In that sense, a swap resembles a futures contract, but as a private agreement between counterparties, its terms are flexible.

Interest-Rate Swaps

Interest-rate swap A contract under which counterparties agree to swap interest payments over a specified period on a fixed dollar amount, called the *notional principal*.

Consider a basic, or "plain vanilla," **interest-rate swap**, a contract under which the counterparties agree to swap interest payments over a specified period of time on a fixed dollar amount, called the *notional principal*. The notional principal is used as a base for calculations but is not an amount actually transferred between the counterparties. For example, suppose that Wells Fargo and IBM agree on a swap lasting five years and based on a notional principal of $10 million. IBM agrees to pay Wells Fargo an interest rate of 6% per year for five years on the $10 million. In return, Wells Fargo agrees to pay IBM a variable or floating interest rate. With interest-rate swaps, the floating interest rate is often based on the rate at which international banks lend to each other. This rate is known as *LIBOR*, which stands for London Interbank Offered Rate. Suppose that under the negotiated terms of the swap, the floating interest rate is set at a rate equal to the LIBOR plus 4%. Figure 7.2 summarizes the payments in the swap transaction.

If the first payment is based on a LIBOR of 3%, IBM owes Wells Fargo $600,000 (= $10,000,000 × 0.06), and Wells Fargo owes IBM $700,000 (= $10,000,000 × (0.03 + 0.04)). Netting the two payments, Wells Fargo pays $100,000 to IBM. Generally, parties exchange only the net payment.

There are five key reasons firms and financial institutions participate in interest-rate swaps. First, swaps allow the transfer of interest-rate risk to parties that are more willing to bear it. In our example, IBM is exposed to more interest-rate risk after the swap but is willing to bear the risk in anticipation of a return. On the first payment, IBM receives $100,000 more from Wells Fargo than it pays. Second, a bank that has many floating-rate assets, such as adjustable-rate mortgages, might want to engage in an interest-rate swap with a bank that has many fixed-rate mortgages. Banks and other firms often have good business reasons for acquiring floating-rate or fixed-rate assets. For example, a bank may find that home buyers prefer fixed-rate mortgages to adjustable-rate mortgages. Swaps allow them to retain those assets while changing the mix of fixed and floating payments that they receive. Third, as already noted, swaps are more flexible than futures or options because they can be custom-tailored to meet the needs of counterparties. Fourth, swaps also offer more privacy than exchange trading, and they are subject to relatively little government regulation. Finally, swaps can be written for long periods, even as long as 20 years. As a result, they offer longer-term hedging than is possible with financial futures and options, which typically settle or expire in a year or less.

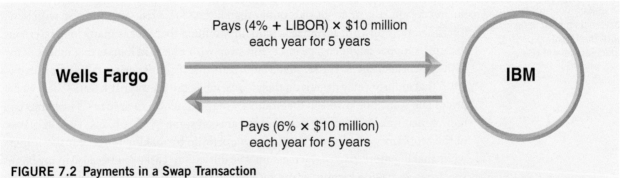

FIGURE 7.2 Payments in a Swap Transaction

Wells Fargo and IBM agree on a swap lasting five years and based on a notional principal of $10 million. IBM agrees to pay Wells Fargo an interest rate of 6% per year for five years on the $10 million. In return, Wells Fargo agrees to pay IBM a floating interest rate. In this example, IBM owes Wells Fargo $600,000 (= $10,000,000 × 0.06), and Wells Fargo owes IBM $700,000 (= $10,000,000 × (0.03 + 0.04)). Netting the two payments, Wells Fargo pays $100,000 to IBM. Generally, parties exchange only the net payment.

However, unlike with futures and exchange-traded options, with swaps, counterparties must be sure of the creditworthiness of their partners. This problem has led to the swaps market being dominated by large firms and financial institutions that have an easier time determining creditworthiness. In addition, swaps, like forward contracts, are not as liquid as futures and options. In fact, swaps are rarely resold.

The passage of the Dodd-Frank Act in 2010 increased regulation of swaps. Financial firms that engage in more than $8 billion in swaps contracts per year must now register with the Commodities Futures Trading Commission as "swap dealers." Swap dealers must trade swaps through a central clearinghouse. Data on these trades are publicly available, and dealers are required to deposit a fraction of the value of the swap contracts with the clearinghouse, as has long been the case when trading futures contracts.

Currency Swaps and Credit Swaps

In interest-rate swaps, counterparties exchange payments on fixed-rate and floating-rate debt. In a **currency swap**, counterparties agree to exchange principal amounts denominated in different currencies. For example, a French company might have euros and want to swap them for U.S. dollars. A U.S. company might have U.S. dollars and be willing to swap them for euros.

Currency swap A contract in which counterparties agree to exchange principal amounts denominated in different currencies.

A basic currency swap has three steps. First, the two parties exchange the principal amount in the two currencies. (Note the difference from the interest-rate swap, in which the counterparties deal in the same currency and typically exchange only the net interest amount, not the principal.) Second, the parties exchange periodic interest payments over the life of the agreement. Third, the parties exchange the principal amount again at the conclusion of the swap.

Why might firms and financial institutions participate in currency swaps? One reason is that firms may have a comparative advantage in borrowing in their domestic currency. They can then swap the proceeds with a foreign counterparty to obtain foreign currency for, say, investment projects. In this way, both parties may be able to borrow more cheaply than if they had borrowed directly in the currency they needed.

Credit swap A contract in which interest-rate payments are exchanged, with the intention of reducing default risk.

In a **credit swap**, interest-rate payments are exchanged, with the intention of reducing default risk, or credit risk, rather than interest-rate risk, as is the case with basic interest-rate swaps. For instance, a bank in Montana that makes many loans to firms that mine copper might engage in a credit swap with a bank in Kansas that makes many loans to wheat farmers. The Montana bank fears that if copper prices fall, some borrowers in that industry may default on their loans, while the Kansas bank fears that if wheat prices fall, some borrowers in that industry may default on their loans. The banks can reduce their risk by swapping payment streams on some of these loans. The alternative of the Montana bank diversifying its loan portfolio by making fewer loans to miners while making more loans to farmers may be difficult to carry out because many banks specialize in making loans to firms with which they have long-term relationships. The Kansas bank would face similar difficulties in diversifying its portfolio.

Credit Default Swaps

In the mid-1990s, Bankers Trust and the JPMorgan investment bank developed *credit default swaps*. The name is somewhat misleading because unlike the swaps we have discussed so far, **credit default swaps** are actually a type of insurance. During the financial crisis of 2007–2009, these swaps were most widely used in conjunction with mortgage-backed securities and collateralized debt obligations (CDOs), which are similar to mortgage-backed securities. The issuer of a credit default swap on a mortgage-backed security receives payments from the buyer in exchange for promising to make payments to the buyer if the security goes into default. For example, a buyer might purchase a credit default swap on a mortgage-backed security with a face value of $1,000 in exchange for paying the seller of the credit default swap $20 per year. If the issuer of the mortgage-backed security misses scheduled principal or interest payments and the bond defaults, its value will drop significantly. If the price of the bond drops to $300, the buyer of the credit default swap will receive $700 from the seller.

By 2005, some investors became convinced that many of the subprime mortgages included in the mortgage-backed securities and collateralized debt obligations were likely to default and decided to speculate by buying credit default swaps on these securities. These investors were speculating, rather than insuring, because most of them did not own the underlying mortgage-backed securities on which they were buying credit default swaps. American International Group (AIG), the largest insurance company in the United States, issued large amounts of credit default swaps on mortgage-backed securities. In hindsight, AIG charged the buyers relatively small amounts compared to the actual risk. The volume of credit default swaps AIG issued left the firm vulnerable to a decline in the U.S. housing market because that would lead to defaults on the mortgages underlying the mortgage-backed securities the firm was insuring. AIG underestimated the extent of the risk it was taking on, apparently because it relied on the high ratings that S&P and Moody's gave to many of these securities. Like the rating agencies, AIG used internal computer models for estimating risk that did not account for the effects of a nationwide decline in home prices.

By September 2008, the prices of the securities on which AIG had written credit default swaps appeared to have declined substantially in value. There was some disagreement on this point between AIG and the buyers of the credit default swaps because by that time the underlying securities were no longer being actively traded, so it was difficult to determine their true prices. The buyers insisted that AIG post collateral so that the buyers could offset the counterparty risk that AIG posed and be sure of collecting the payments they believed they were owed because of price declines in the underlying securities. Because AIG lacked sufficient collateral, it was pushed to the brink of bankruptcy. The Treasury and the Federal Reserve decided that if AIG went bankrupt and defaulted on its obligations, including its obligations to make payments to holders of credit default swaps, the financial system would be severely disrupted. So, in exchange for the federal government receiving 80% ownership of the company, the Federal Reserve loaned AIG $85 billion. AIG's losses increased, however, and ultimately it received $185 billion in funds from the federal government. Through sales of subsidiaries and a rebound in the prices of some of its financial holdings, AIG eventually repaid all of the funds it received from the federal government. By the end of 2012, the Treasury had sold its holdings of AIG stock for a profit of more than $22 billion.

The volume of credit default swaps from firms other than AIG also increased during the 2005–2006 period, even as the housing market began to decline. During the last

Credit default swap A derivative that requires the seller to make payments to the buyer if the price of the underlying security declines in value; in effect, a type of insurance.

months of the housing boom, the number of subprime mortgages being issued began to fall behind the demand for mortgage-backed securities and CDOs. Some commercial banks, investment banks, and other financial firms decided to place favorable bets on these securities by selling credit default swaps on them. Their reasoning was that the prices of the securities would remain high, so the firms would not have to pay anything to the buyers of the credit default swaps. The firms would earn a profit from the payments they would receive from the buyers. Unfortunately for these firms, the underlying securities plummeted in value, and the firms were liable for huge payments to the buyers of the credit default swaps.

A number of people in the financial community, as well as economists and policymakers, were concerned about the volume of credit default swaps outstanding. Because credit default swaps are traded over the counter rather than on exchanges, there are no reliable statistics on them. Credit default swaps were sold not just on securities but also on companies. It was very possible that multiple credit default swaps could have been sold on the same security or company. Therefore, a default on a security or a bankruptcy of a firm might lead to significant losses for the multiple firms that had sold credit default swaps on the security or firm. The heavy losses that AIG and other firms and investors suffered on credit default swaps deepened the financial crisis and led policymakers to consider imposing regulations on these derivatives.[3]

MAKING THE CONNECTION

Are Derivatives "Financial Weapons of Mass Destruction"?

We have seen that derivatives can play an important role in the financial system, particularly by facilitating risk sharing. As noted in the chapter opener, though, billionaire investor Warren Buffett considered them to be "financial weapons of mass destruction." Note that Buffett is not referring to futures contracts and exchange-traded options of the types we have focused on in this chapter. Instead, he is referring to derivatives that are not traded on exchanges. These derivatives include forward contracts, non-listed option contracts, and credit default swaps.

Buffett has identified three problems with these derivatives:

1. These derivatives are *thinly traded*—that is, they are not often bought and sold—which makes them difficult to value. Lack of a market value makes it difficult to evaluate the financial health of either the buyers or the sellers. In addition, dealers in some of these options mark them to market using prices predicted by computer models rather than actual market prices, which may not exist. This practice means that the dealers add money to the accounts of either the buyers or sellers—whichever

---

[3] An interesting and entertaining account of the development of credit default swaps during the financial crisis appears in Michael Lewis, *The Big Short: Inside the Doomsday Machine*, New York: W. W. Norton & Company, 2010. (Note that the book reproduces conversations with investors that involve substantial amounts of profanity.) An excellent source of information on collateralized debt obligations (CDOs) is an undergraduate senior thesis written at Harvard: Anna Katherine Barnett-Hart, "The Story of the CDO Market Meltdown," Harvard College, March 19, 2009.

benefits from the price change—and subtract money from the accounts of the other. The side gaining from the increasing value of its derivatives can count the gain as earnings in its financial statements. Buffett argues that because the models used to estimate the price changes may be inaccurate, the increased earnings are likely inaccurate as well.

2. Many of these derivatives are not subject to significant government regulation, so firms may not put aside reserves to offset potential losses. AIG suffered from this problem: When the firm had to provide collateral to the buyers of its credit default swaps, it lacked sufficient funds and needed to borrow from the Federal Reserve and the Treasury.

3. These derivatives are not traded on exchanges, so they involve substantial counterparty risk. Recall that with exchange-traded derivatives, the exchange provides clearinghouse services and stands as the counterparty to both the buyer and the seller. By acting as counterparty to both sides, the exchange greatly reduces default risk. During the financial crisis, worries about counterparty risk resulted in trading on some derivatives markets drying up, as potential buyers worried about default risk. This problem was particularly severe after Lehman Brothers declared bankruptcy in September 2008, defaulting on many of its contracts.

Many economists and policymakers share Buffett's concerns. During 2010, Congress passed the Wall Street Reform and Consumer Protection Act, also called the Dodd-Frank Act, in response to the financial crisis. Under the act, many derivatives now must be bought and sold on exchanges. Economists are debating whether the decline in counterparty risk and the increase in transparency will be worth the loss of flexibility from standardizing these derivative contracts.

Source: The best source for Warren Buffet's views on derivatives is the "Chairman's Letter," in Berkshire Hathaway's *Annual Report* for the years 2002–2010.

See related problems 5.8 and 5.9 at the end of the chapter.

ANSWERING THE KEY QUESTION

Continued from page 211

At the beginning of this chapter, we asked:

"Are financial derivatives 'financial weapons of mass destruction'?"

We have seen that futures and exchange-traded options play an important role in the financial system and provide the key service of risk sharing. Warren Buffett has argued that some derivatives that are not exchange traded contributed significantly to the financial crisis. While not all derivatives are financial weapons of mass destruction, policymakers have enacted new regulations that are intended to ensure that use of some derivatives does not destabilize the financial system.

Key Terms and Problems

Key Terms

Call option, p. 225

Counterparty risk, p. 215

Credit default swap, p. 237

Credit swap, p. 236

Currency swap, p. 236

Derivative securities (or
  derivatives), p. 212

Forward contract, p. 214

Futures contract, p. 215

Hedge, p. 213

Interest-rate swap, p. 234

Long position, p. 216

Margin requirement, p. 224

Marking to market, p. 224

Option, p. 225

Option premium, p. 227

Put option, p. 225

Settlement date, p. 215

Short position, p. 216

Speculate, p. 214

Spot price, p. 215

Strike price (or exercise price),
  p. 225

Swap, p. 234

Derivatives, Hedging, and Speculating

Explain what derivatives are and distinguish between using them to hedge and using them to speculate.

Review Questions

1.1 Why do investors buy and sell derivatives rather than the underlying assets?

1.2 What is the difference between hedging and speculating?

Problems and Applications

1.3 Would derivatives markets be better off if the only people buying and selling derivatives contracts were hedgers? Briefly explain.

1.4 In each of the following situations, what risk do you face from price fluctuations? What would have to be true of a derivative security if the security were to help you to hedge this risk?

a. You are a corn farmer.

b. You are a manufacturer of cornbread.

c. You are buying Treasury bonds to finance your child's future college tuition.

Forward Contracts

Define forward contracts and explain their role in the financial system.

Review Questions

2.1 What service do forward contracts provide in the financial system?

2.2 Why do forward contracts have counterparty risk?

Problems and Applications

2.3 Suppose that you are a wealthy investor. Although you have no connection with the oil industry, you are convinced from studying the determinants of demand and supply in the oil market that the price of oil will decline sharply in the future. How might you use forward contracts to profit from your forecast?

2.4 Suppose that oil prices decline by 50%. Which counterparty to a forward contract in oil has an incentive to default on the contract? Briefly explain.

7.3 Futures Contracts

Explain how futures contracts can be used to hedge and to speculate.

Review Questions

3.1 What are the key differences between forward contracts and futures contracts? What is the difference between a commodity future and a financial future? Give two examples of each.

3.2 Briefly explain why a firm might take a long position in the futures market for oil. Briefly explain why a firm might take a short position in the futures market for oil.

3.3 Give an example of speculating using commodity futures and speculating using financial futures.

Problems and Applications

3.4 Why did futures markets originate in agricultural markets? Would a farmer buy or sell futures contracts? What would a farmer hope to gain by doing so? Would General Mills buy or sell futures contracts in wheat? What would the company hope to gain by doing so?

3.5 According to an article in the *Wall Street Journal*, Canadian firms that import goods that are priced in U.S. dollars "buy futures contracts that guarantee that they can exchange Canadian dollars for U.S. [dollars] at fixed prices." Do you agree that a futures contract makes it possible to fix the price of the underlying asset?

Source: Phred Dvorak and Andy Georgiades, "Strong Loonie Sets Off a Retail Tiff," *Wall Street Journal*, May 19, 2010.

3.6 An article in the *Wall Street Journal* on the futures market for oil in the United Kingdom noted that on the day the article was published, "the number of long positions … fell by 6%."

a. What is a long position in the futures market?

b. The article also noted: "Speculative investors in oil cut their bullish bets on the price of crude." What does the article mean by a "bullish bet"? How would these investors have cut their bets?

Source: Georgi Kantchev, "Speculative Investors Cut Bullish Crude Oil Price Bets," *Wall Street Journal*, May 9, 2016.

3.7 An article in the *Wall Street Journal* noted: "U.S. oil producers … are using hedges to lock in prices."

a. Would oil producers be worried about prices rising or falling? Briefly explain.

b. How do oil producers use hedges to lock in prices?

Source: Timothy Puko and Erin Ailworth, "Oil Producers Lock In Once-Snubbed Prices," *Wall Street Journal*, April 24, 2016.

3.8 An article in the *Wall Street Journal* in 2016 noted: "After decades of spending billions of dollars to hedge against rising fuel costs, more airlines, including some of the world's largest, are backing off after getting burned by low oil prices."

a. How would airlines hedge against rising fuel costs?

b. Why would low oil prices cause airlines to be "burned"?

c. Does the fact that airlines were burned by their fuel hedges in 2016 mean that hedging their fuel costs was a bad idea? Briefly explain.

Source: Susan Carey, "Airlines Pull Back on Hedging Fuel Costs," *Wall Street Journal*, March 20, 2016.

3.9 Suppose that you are a wheat farmer. Answer the following questions.

a. It is September, and you intend to have 50,000 bushels of wheat harvested and ready to sell in November. The current spot market price of wheat is $2.50 per bushel, and the current December futures price of wheat is $2.75 per bushel. Should you buy or sell wheat futures? If each wheat futures contract is for 5,000 bushels, how many contracts will you buy or sell, and how much will you spend or receive in buying or selling futures contracts?

b. It is now November, and you sell 50,000 bushels of wheat at the spot price of $2.60 per bushel. If the futures price is $2.85 and you settle your position in the futures market, what was your gain or loss on your futures market position? Did you completely hedge your risk from price fluctuations in the wheat market? Give a numerical explanation.

3.10 [Related to the Making the Connection on page 219] An article in the *Wall Street Journal* quoted a young investor who works for the social network site LinkedIn as explaining that after losing money trading securities linked to crude oil futures prices, he was going to "stick to investing in what he knows, like tech."

a. Why might someone like this investor who has a full-time job have trouble earning a profit buying and selling oil futures (or other securities linked to the prices of oil futures)?

b. Is it likely that the investor would have more success buying and selling derivatives or other securities related to tech firms? Briefly explain.

Source: Ben Eisen, Nicole Friedman, and Saumya Vaishampayan, "The New Oil Traders: Moms and Millennials," *Wall Street Journal*, May 26, 2016.

3.11 [Related to Solved Problem 7.3 on page 223] Suppose that you are an investor who owns $10,000 in U.S. Treasury notes.

a. Will you be more worried about market interest rates rising or falling? Briefly explain.

b. How might you hedge against the risk you identified in part (a)?

3.12 According to an article in the *Economist* magazine:

> In 1958 American onion farmers, blaming speculators for the volatility of their crops' prices, lobbied a congressman

from Michigan named Gerald Ford to ban trading in onion futures. Supported by the president-to-be, they got their way. Onion futures have been prohibited ever since.

Is it likely that banning trading futures contracts in onions reduced the volatility in onion prices? Are onion farmers as a group better off because of the ban?

Source: "Over the Counter, Out of Sight," *Economist*, November 12, 2009.

3.13 [Related to the Making the Connection on page 222] Consider the hypothetical listing below for 10-year Treasury note futures on the Chicago Board of Trade. One futures contract for Treasury notes = $100,000 face value of 10-year 6% notes.

a. If today you bought two contracts expiring in December 2018, how much would you pay?

b. What does the "OpenInt" on a futures contract mean? What is the OpenInt on the contract expiring in March 2019?

c. If you were a speculator who expected interest rates to fall, would you buy or sell these futures contracts? Briefly explain.

d. Suppose you sell the December futures contract, and one day later, the Chicago Board of Trade informs you that it has credited funds to your margin account. What happened to interest rates during that day? Briefly explain.

Accompanies problem 3.13

Month	Last	Chg	Open	High	Low	Volume	OpenInt
Dec 2018	**130.500**	**0.301**	130.266	130.752	130.266	564,322	2,380,328
Mar 2019	**129.250**	**0.301**	129.000	129.500	128.950	4,325	118,728

Options

7.4 Distinguish between call options and put options and explain how they are used.

Review Questions

4.1 What is the difference between a call option and put option? What role does an option writer play?

4.2 How do the rights and obligations of options buyers and sellers differ from the rights and obligations of futures buyers and sellers?

4.3 What is an option premium? What is an option's intrinsic value? What other factors, besides intrinsic value, can affect the size of an option premium?

4.4 How can investors use options to manage risk?

Problems and Applications

4.5 A columnist on marketwatch.com offers the following advice: "If I were to hedge Apple, I'd use … 90-day puts as I've done at times in the past."

a. What does the columnist mean by "hedge Apple"?

b. Briefly explain how you would use put contracts to hedge Apple.

Source: Cody Willard, "What Happens When Apple Gets to $1,000 per Share?" marketwatch.com, February 24, 2015.

4.6 An article in the *New York Times* described how federal prosecutors accused a money manager of swindling his friends, family, and other investors out of $40 million. The article described the money manager as losing all the funds entrusted to him in "aggressive bearish options trades."

a. What is the difference between a bearish financial investment and a bullish financial investment?

b. To make these bearish trades, was the money manager buying put options or buying call options? Briefly explain.

Source: Matthew Goldstein and Alexandra Stevenson, "Andrew Caspersen, Charged in $40 Million Fraud, Had Gambling Addiction, Lawyer Says," *New York Times*, June 14, 2016.

4.7 An article in the *New York Times* with the headline "For Investors, 'Portfolio Insurance' Against Market Declines," observes: "You can, for example, buy 'put' options on a single stock or an entire index."

a. How does buying a put option provide insurance against a fall in stock prices?

b. Briefly compare the pros and cons of buying a put option versus selling stocks if you are worried that stock prices might decline.

Source: John F. Wasik, "For Investors, 'Portfolio Insurance' Against Market Declines," *New York Times*, November 11, 2015.

4.8 [Related to the Making the Connection on page 229 and Solved Problem 7.4 on page 230] Use the following information on call and put options for Facebook to answer the questions.

Facebook					Underlying stock price: 114.19		
		Call			Put		
Expiration	Strike	Price	Volume	Open Interest	Price	Volume	Open Interest
Aug	100.00	15.10	40	1632	1.00	247	3483
Dec	100.00	18.80	0	646	3.89	77	1841
Jan	100.00	19.19	2510	29807	4.58	184	20086
Jun	100.00	22.58	102	217	7.60	0	295
Aug	110.00	7.25	344	3260	3.14	586	6918
Dec	110.00	11.50	7	3393	7.09	7	4995
Jan	110.00	12.60	1351	2013	7.85	664	11074
Jun	110.00	16.37	23	329	11.30	4	682

a. What is the intrinsic value of the call option that expires in June and has a $100.00 strike price?

b. What is the intrinsic value of the put option that expires in January and has a $100.00 strike price?

c. Briefly explain why a call with a $110 strike price sells for less than a call with a $100 strike price (for all expiration dates), while a put with a $110 strike price sells for more than a put with a $100 strike price (for all expiration dates).

d. Suppose you buy the June call with a strike price of $110. If you exercise it when the price of Facebook is $125, what will be your profit or loss? (Remember that each options contract is for 100 shares of stock.)

e. Suppose you buy the June put with a strike price of $110 at the price listed, and the price of Facebook stock remains at $114.19. What will be your profit or loss?

4.9 An article in the *Wall Street Journal* observes: "When volatility is low, options are cheaper." Briefly explain the reasoning behind this observation.

Source: Ben Levisohn, "How to Rock at Lower Volume," *Wall Street Journal*, August 31, 2012.

4.10 According to an article in the *Wall Street Journal*, options traders were expecting a large move in the price of Facebook stock. They were buying both call options and put options with strike prices near the stock's current market price. The article described this strategy as a "bet on the size of the [price] move instead of its direction." Briefly explain how this investment strategy would work.

Source: Saumya Vaishampayan, "Options Traders Betting on Big Move for Facebook Shares," *Wall Street Journal*, April 27, 2016.

4.11 Suppose that the Dow Jones Industrial Average is above the 20,000 level. If the Dow were to fall to 17,000, who would gain the most: investors who had bought call options, investors who had sold call options, investors who had bought put options, or investors who had sold put options? Who would be hurt the most?

4.12 [Related to the Making the Connection on page 233] The CBOE web site quotes the CEO of an investment advisory firm as saying: "The VIX Index is an important and popular tool for measuring investor sentiment." Briefly explain in what sense the VIX is a measure of investor sentiment.

Source: www.cboe.com/micro/vix/introduction.aspx.

7.5 Swaps
Define swaps and explain how they can be used to reduce risk.

Review Questions

5.1 In what ways is a swap contract different from a futures contract?

5.2 In what ways is a credit swap different from an interest-rate swap?

5.3 How does a credit default swap differ from the other swap contracts discussed in this chapter? What difficulties did credit default swaps cause during the financial crisis of 2007–2009?

Problems and Applications

5.4 Suppose that you manage a bank that has made many loans at a fixed interest rate. You are worried that inflation might rise and the value of the loans will decline.

a. Why would an increase in inflation cause the value of your fixed-rate loans to decline?

b. How might you use swaps to reduce your risk?

5.5 A column in the *Wall Street Journal* observes: "Many regulators, politicians and academics consider credit default swaps to be insurance contracts." Briefly explain the reasoning behind this observation.

Source: Stuart M. Turnbull and Lee M. Wakeman, "Why Markets Need 'Naked' Credit Default Swaps," *Wall Street Journal*, September 11, 2012.

5.6 After the United Kingdom's electorate voted on June 23, 2016, to leave the European Union, an article in the *Wall Street Journal* noted: "Credit-default swaps on the debt of Bank of America and Citigroup Inc. are up 25% from a day earlier." What does an increase in the price of credit default swaps on bonds issued by Bank of America and Citigroup Inc. (which is also a bank) indicate about the bonds? What likely happened to the yields on those bonds?

Source: John Carney, "Bank Credit Default Swaps Surge on Brexit Fears," *Wall Street Journal*, June 24, 2016.

5.7 **[Related to the Chapter Opener on page 211]** In 2016, the Federal Reserve proposed a new rule that would limit how exposed a large bank could be to the risk of counterparty default by another large bank. At the same time, a report by a government agency indicated that by both buying and selling credit default swaps, banks may still be exposed to significant counterparty risk even though the use of credit default swaps had dropped by more than 75% since the financial crisis. An article in the *Wall Street Journal* on proposals to change the regulations governing the trading of financial derivatives contained the following:

> The SEC and the Commodity Futures Trading Commission are both seeking greater authority to police the over-the-counter market and hope new powers can help them reduce the risks that over-the-counter trading may pose to the broader system.

a. Why might a bank buy a credit default swap?

b. What counterparty risk exists for a buyer of a credit default swap?

Source: Katy Burne, "U.S. Watchdog Warns on Banks' Counterparty Exposures," *Wall Street Journal*, March 8, 2016.

5.8 **[Related to the Making the Connection on page 238]** In one of his annual letters to shareholders of Berkshire Hathaway, Warren Buffett wrote that trading derivatives has much more counterparty risk than does trading stocks or bonds because "a normal stock trade is completed in a few days with one party getting its cash, the other its securities. Counterparty risk therefore quickly disappears."

a. What is counterparty risk?

b. Why is counterparty risk greater for trading in derivatives than for trading in stocks and bonds?

Source: Warren Buffett, "Chairman's Letter," *Berkshire Hathaway Inc. 2008 Annual Report*, February 27, 2009.

5.9 **[Related to the Making the Connection on page 238]** In one of his annual letters to shareholders of Berkshire Hathaway, Warren Buffett wrote that: "Even experienced investors and analysts encounter major problems in analyzing the financial condition of firms that are heavily involved with derivatives contracts." Why might it be difficult for investors to analyze the financial condition of firms that are buying and selling large numbers of derivatives? Does it matter what type of derivatives the firms are buying and selling?

Source: Warren Buffett, "Chairman's Letter," *Berkshire Hathaway Inc. 2008 Annual Report*, February 27, 2009.

Data Exercises

D7.1: **[Comparing the volatility of one stock to the volatility of the whole market]** In addition to the VIX index based on S&P 500, there are VIX indexes available for some individual stocks. Go to the web site of the Federal Reserve Bank of St. Louis (FRED) (fred.stlouisfed.org) and for the period from June 2010 to the present, download and plot on the same graph the data series for the VIX index (VIXCLS) and the VIX index for Apple's stock (VXAPLCLS). Which of the two series is the more volatile? Would you expect the relationship between the two series to change during a recession? Briefly explain.

D7.2: **[Options and market expectations]** Go to finance.yahoo.com and in the search box type in *Facebook options*. Find the data on call and put options for Facebook. Find the calls and puts with a strike price within $5 of Facebook's closing stock price. Is the volume of trading and the open interest greater for the puts or for the calls? Interpret these data with respect to market expectations for Facebook's stock price to rise or fall.

The Market for Foreign Exchange

Learning Objectives

After studying this chapter, you should be able to:

8.1 Explain how markets for foreign exchange operate (pages 247–253)

8.2 Use the theory of purchasing power parity to explain how exchange rates are determined in the long run (pages 253–257)

8.3 Use a demand and supply model to explain how exchange rates are determined in the short run (pages 257–271)

Who Is Mario Draghi, and Why Should Proctor & Gamble Care?

To make a profit running a business, you need to worry about many things, including what price to charge, how to control your costs, how to manage your relationships with your employees and suppliers, how to market your product, and how to manage your social media presence. If you export your product overseas, import products for resale, or import some of your inputs, you have another important concern: the exchange rate, which measures how much one currency is worth in terms of another currency.

In today's global economy, many large firms manufacture products in several countries and sell them in other countries. Consider Procter & Gamble (P&G), a large consumer products company headquartered in Cincinnati, Ohio. Among many other products, the company sells Gillette razor blades. The blades it sells in Russia are

manufactured in Germany. During one recent period, the Russian ruble was declining in value in exchange for the euro, the currency used in Germany, which meant that more rubles were necessary to buy a euro. At the same time, the euro was declining in value in exchange for the U.S. dollar. So the cost to sell Gillette razor blades in Russia was rising in terms of rubles, leaving P&G to choose between making a smaller profit on its Russian sales or raising the ruble price of its blades, thereby losing sales to competitors. In addition, the euro profits made by its German manufacturing plants would translate into fewer dollars when P&G's headquarters in the United States reported on its financial statements the profits earned from its worldwide operations. It's no wonder that an article in the *Wall Street Journal* said the company was facing "foreign-exchange headwinds."

Continued on next page

KEY ISSUE AND QUESTION

Issue: The exchange rate between the dollar and other currencies has gone through wide fluctuations in recent years.

Question: Why hasn't the value of the dollar remained stable when measured against other currencies?

Answered on page 271

What explains the fluctuations in the exchange between the dollar and other currencies? One key factor is that during the past 25 years, financial investment across borders has increased, and investors have become more sensitive to differences in interest rates among countries. As a result, investors had a strong response in 2016 to the decision by the European Central Bank (ECB), led by its president Mario Draghi, to drive interest rates to very low levels in an attempt to stimulate spending by households and firms. These low interest rates, which on some government bonds were actually negative, led many investors to sell European financial assets to buy financial assets in other countries, particularly the United States. As a result of investors selling euros and buying other currencies, the value of the euro declined against these currencies, including the dollar. At the same time, investors were becoming concerned that investments in emerging countries, such as Russia, were at increased risk of default. As a result, these investors sold the currencies of those countries, driving down their values in exchange for both the euro and the dollar. So the policies of Mario Draghi and the ECB were affecting economies around the world.

As we will see in this chapter, other factors in addition to the actions of investors can help determine exchange rates, particularly in the long run. But in the modern international financial system, the European Central Bank, the Federal Reserve, and other central banks cannot ignore how their policies affect the economies of other countries and how financial and economic developments in other countries affect their economies.

Sources: Sharon Terlep, "P&G Posts Higher Profit, but Sales Volume Declines Across Most Businesses," *Wall Street Journal*, April 26, 2016; Paul Ziobro, Josh Mitchell, and Theo Francis, " Strong Dollar Squeezes U.S. Firms," *Wall Street Journal*, January 27, 2015; and Tom Fairless, "Mario Draghi to Face Tough Questions After ECB Meeting," *Wall Street Journal*, April 20, 2016.

In this chapter, we analyze how exchange rates are determined and why they change over time. Exchange rates experience short-run fluctuations around long-run trends. Understanding these changes will show why economic developments in the United States, including movements in U.S. interest rates, can affect international financial markets and the broader global economy.

8.1 Exchange Rates and the Foreign Exchange Market

LEARNING OBJECTIVE: Explain how markets for foreign exchange operate.

Today, markets for many products and financial assets are global, and both exports and imports of goods and services have grown tremendously. In 2016, foreign consumers, firms, and governments purchased about 13% of the goods and services produced in the United States, while almost 16% of goods and services consumed in the United States were produced abroad. These percentages were two to three times higher than they were in the 1960s. When individuals or firms in the United States import or export goods or make investments in other countries, they need to convert dollars into foreign currencies. The **nominal exchange rate**, which is usually referred to simply as the *exchange rate*, is the price of one country's currency in terms of another country's currency. For example, in October 2016, 1 U.S. dollar could buy 104 Japanese yen or 19 Mexican pesos.

Nominal exchange rate
The price of one currency in terms of another currency; also called the *exchange rate.*

Fluctuations in the exchange rate between the dollar and foreign currencies affect the prices that U.S. consumers pay for foreign imports. For instance, suppose that a Sony PlayStation 4 video game console has a price of ¥30,000 in Tokyo, and the exchange rate between the yen and the U.S. dollar is ¥100 = $1. Then, the dollar price of the PlayStation is $300 (= ¥30,000/(100¥/$)). If the exchange rate changes to

¥80 = $1, the dollar price of the PlayStation rises to $375 (= ¥30,000/(80¥/$)), even though the yen price of the PlayStation in Tokyo stays the same. In this case, the yen has gained in value against the dollar because it takes fewer yen to buy a dollar.

An increase in the value of one country's currency in exchange for another country's currency is called an **appreciation**. When the yen appreciates against the dollar, Japanese firms have more difficulty selling goods and services in the United States. In the same way, an appreciation of the yen against the dollar makes it easier for U.S. firms to sell goods and services in Japan. For instance, at an exchange rate of ¥100 = $1, a Hershey's candy bar that has a price of $1 in Philadelphia has a yen price of ¥100. But if the yen appreciates to ¥80 = $1, the candy bar has a yen price of only ¥80. When we say that the yen has experienced an *appreciation* against the dollar, this is equivalent to saying that the dollar has experienced a **depreciation**—or decrease in value—against the yen.

Appreciation An increase in the value of a currency in exchange for another currency.

Depreciation A decrease in the value of a currency in exchange for another currency.

MAKING THE CONNECTION

Brexit, Exchange Rates, and the Profitability of British Firms

Since 1973, the United Kingdom had been a member of the European Union (EU), an organization of 28 countries that have integrated their economies by eliminating most barriers to trade and by allowing mostly unrestricted movement of workers and firms between countries. In 2001, when most members of the EU began using the euro as their common currency, the United Kingdom decided to continue using the pound. In June 2016, the United Kingdom held a referendum in which a majority voted to leave the EU. The vote became known as *Brexit*, for "British exit."

Before the vote, many investors believed that the United Kingdom leaving the EU would have two key results: (1) The importance of London as a financial center would be reduced, and (2) the British economy would be hurt because British firms would most likely have to pay tariffs when exporting to EU countries. Most political analysts had predicted that a majority of people would vote to remain in the EU. So the actual outcome of the vote was a surprise to many investors and, as the figure below shows, when financial markets opened the morning after the vote, the value of the pound dropped by nearly 8% in exchange for the dollar: from an exchange rate of $1.48 = £1 to an exchange rate of $1.36 = £1.

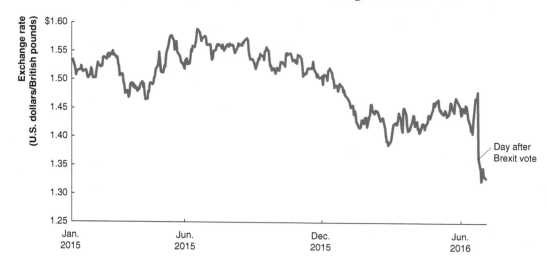

Leaving aside other consequences of the United Kingdom leaving the EU, was the decline in the value of the pound good news or bad news for British firms? The answer is that, by and large, the decline helped British firms that were exporters but hurt British firms that were competing against foreign imports or whose suppliers were located outside the United Kingdom. Among the winners was Brompton Bicycle, which makes a popular folding bike in a factory in London. The company exports 80% of its bicycles to other countries. Because of the decline in the exchange rate, each bike it sold in the United States for dollars resulted in higher earnings when the dollars were converted into pounds. Similarly, Rolls-Royce manufactures airplane engines in the United Kingdom and exports most of them. Its managers estimated that for every 1 cent decline in the dollar–pound exchange rate, its annual profits would increase by the equivalent of $2 million. The exchange rate declined by 16 cents in the days following the Brexit vote, so if this decline were sustained, Rolls-Royce's profits would increase by $32 million.

The Air and Grace shoe company, on the other hand, was hurt by the decline in the value of the pound. The company designs and sells its shoes in the United Kingdom but manufactures them in a factory in Portugal, which uses the euro as its currency. Because the value of the pound also declined against the euro, the cost of the shoes Air and Grace was importing had risen when translated into pounds. The firm's founder was quoted as saying: "There are two choices—let the business absorb the cost resulting in a reduced [profit] margin or pass it onto the consumer via increased retail prices." She indicated that her company was absorbing the higher costs but doubted it could continue to do so for long.

The fall in the value of the pound following the Brexit vote was another indication of the important role that exchange rates often play in determining the profitability of firms.

Sources: William Wilkes and Costas Paris, "Pound's Plunge Benefits Some Businesses, Punishes Others," *Wall Street Journal*, July 3, 2016; Suzanne Bearne and Helen Lock, "Opportunity or Disaster? Small Firms Describe the Impact of the Brexit Vote," guardian.com, July 3, 2016; and Mike Bird, "Pound Falls to Fresh Low as Brexit Fears Return," *Wall Street Journal*, July 5, 2016.

See related problem 1.7 at the end of the chapter.

Is It Dollars per Yen or Yen per Dollar?

There are two ways to express every exchange rate: (1) as units of foreign currency per unit of domestic currency or (2) as units of domestic currency per unit of foreign currency. For example, we can express the exchange rate between the U.S. dollar and the Japanese yen as ¥100 = $1 or as $0.01 = ¥1. The two expressions are mathematically equivalent, with one being the reciprocal of the other. Professional currency traders at banks and other financial institutions typically price, or "quote," exchange rates as units of domestic currency per unit of foreign currency, and these quotations are called *direct quotations*. *Indirect quotations* express exchange rates as units of foreign currency per unit of domestic currency.

In practice, there are certain conventions in reporting exchange rates in the financial news that are a mixture of direct and indirect quotations. For instance, the exchange rate between the U.S. dollar and the Japanese yen is almost always reported as yen per

	U.S. dollar	Euro	Pound	Swiss franc	Peso	Yen	Canadian dollar
Canada	1.30	1.44	1.69	1.33	0.07	0.01	.....
Japan	101.74	112.68	132.49	104.16	5.41	.....	78.37
Mexico	18.82	20.84	24.51	19.27	.....	0.19	14.50
Switzerland	0.98	1.08	1.27	.....	0.52	0.01	0.75
United Kingdom	0.77	0.85	.....	0.79	0.04	0.01	0.59
Eurozone	0.90	.....	1.18	0.92	0.05	0.01	0.70
United States	.....	1.11	1.30	1.02	0.05	0.01	0.77

FIGURE 8.1 Foreign-Exchange Cross Rates

Foreign-exchange rates can be expressed either as U.S. dollars per unit of foreign currency or as units of foreign currency per U.S. dollar. Reading across the rows, we see the direct quotations, while reading down the columns, we see the indirect quotations. For example, the third entry in the U.S. row shows that the exchange rate on this day was $1.30 per pound (£). The fifth entry in the U.S. dollar column shows that the exchange rate can also be expressed as £0.77 per dollar.

Source: "Key Cross Currency Rates," *Wall Street Journal*, July 6, 2016.

dollar, while the exchange rate between the euro and the dollar is reported as dollars per euro and the exchange rate between the British pound and the dollar is reported as dollars per pound. Many financial news outlets provide tables of currency "cross rates," such as the one shown in Figure 8.1, which provides both direct and indirect quotations for a day in July 2016. Reading across the rows, we see the direct quotations, while reading down the columns, we see the indirect quotations. For instance, the third entry in the U.S. row shows that the exchange rate on this day was $1.30 per pound (£). The next-to-last entry in the U.S. dollar column shows that the exchange rate can also be expressed as £0.77 per dollar.

Figure 8.2 shows fluctuations since 2004 in the exchange rates between the U.S. dollar and three other currencies: the yen, the Canadian dollar, and the euro. For consistency, in each case on the vertical axis we show the number of U.S. dollars necessary to buy one unit of the foreign currency. In showing the graphs this way, a larger value for the exchange rate represents a *depreciation* of the dollar and an *appreciation* of the other currency because more dollars are required to buy a unit of the foreign currency. These graphs show substantial fluctuations in the value of the dollar against these currencies. In Section 8.2, we investigate the factors that lead to fluctuations in exchange rates.

Nominal Exchange Rates Versus Real Exchange Rates

Nominal exchange rates tell you how many yen or euros or Canadian dollars you will receive in exchange for a U.S. dollar, but they do not tell you how much of another country's goods and services you can buy with a U.S. dollar. When we are interested in the relative purchasing power of two countries' currencies, we use the **real exchange rate**, which measures the rate at which goods and services in one country can be exchanged for goods and services in another country. For simplicity, let's consider the real exchange rate using one particular product: the McDonald's Big Mac. Suppose we want to know how many U.S. dollars and British pounds are needed to purchase a Big Mac, given the prices of Big

Real exchange rate The rate at which goods and services in one country can be exchanged for goods and services in another country.

(a) U.S. dollar–yen exchange rate   **(b) U.S. dollar–Canadian dollar exchange rate**   **(c) U.S. dollar–euro exchange rate**

FIGURE 8.2 Fluctuations in Exchange Rates, 2004–2016

The panels show fluctuations in the exchange rates between the U.S. dollar and the yen, the Canadian dollar, and the euro. Because we are measuring the exchange rate on the vertical axis as dollars per unit of foreign currency, an increase in the exchange rate represents a *depreciation* of the dollar and an *appreciation* of the other currency.

Source: Federal Reserve Bank of St. Louis.

Macs in the two countries. Let's assume that a Big Mac in New York has a price of $4.50, a Big Mac in London has a price of £5.00, and the nominal exchange rate between the dollar and the pound is $1.25 = £1. We can convert the pound price of the London Big Mac into a dollar price by multiplying by the nominal exchange rate: $5.00 × $1.25/£ = $6.25. So, a U.S. Big Mac can exchange for only $4.50/$6.25 = 0.72 Big Macs in London.

We can summarize the previous calculation as an expression for the real exchange rate between the dollar and the pound in terms of Big Macs:

Real Big Mac exchange rate =

$$\frac{\text{Dollar price of Big Macs in New York}}{\text{Pound price of Big Macs in London} \times \text{Dollars per pound}}$$
$$\text{(nominal exchange rate)}$$

Of course, we aren't much concerned about the real exchange rate in terms of a single product. But we can take the same approach to determine the real exchange rate between two currencies by substituting a consumer price index for each country in place of the price of a particular product. Recall that a consumer price index represents an average of the prices of all the goods and services purchased by a typical consumer and represents the *price level* in the country. Making this substitution gives us the following expression for the real exchange rate in terms of the nominal exchange rate and the price levels in each country:

Real exchange rate between the dollar and the pound =

$$\frac{\text{U.S. consumer price index}}{\text{British price index} \times \text{Dollars per pound exchange rate (nominal exchange rate)}}.$$

By rearranging terms and using symbols, we can write a more general equation showing the relationship between the nominal and real exchange rates:

$$e = E \times \left(\frac{P^{\text{Domestic}}}{P^{\text{Foreign}}} \right),$$

where:

E = nominal exchange rate, expressed as units of foreign currency per unit of domestic currency

e = real exchange rate

P^{Domestic} = domestic price level

P^{Foreign} = foreign price level

For example, if the real exchange rate between the British pound and the U.S. dollar were 2, this value would indicate that the average good or service produced in the United States can be exchanged for two of the average good or service in the United Kingdom. In other words, on average, goods and services in the United States would be expensive relative to goods and services in the United Kingdom. If the real exchange rate were less than 1, U.S. goods and services would be less expensive than British goods and services.

Foreign Exchange Markets

An individual consumer or investor can use exchange rates to convert one currency into another. If you travel to another country on business or for a vacation, you have to convert U.S. dollars into the local currency, which might be Canadian dollars, Japanese yen, euros, or British pounds. If the dollar rises in value relative to these currencies, you can buy more of other currencies during your travels, enabling you to enjoy a more expensive meal or bring back more souvenirs. Likewise, if you want to buy foreign stocks or bonds, you must convert U.S. dollars into the appropriate currency. Again, if the dollar appreciates, you can buy more Canadian, Japanese, or British stocks or bonds.

Foreign exchange market
An over-the-counter market where international currencies are traded and exchange rates are determined.

As with other prices, exchange rates are determined by the interaction of demand and supply. Currencies are traded in **foreign exchange markets** around the world. Traders in large commercial banks in North America, Europe, and Asia carry out the majority of the buying and selling of foreign exchange. Like the NASDAQ stock market, rather than being a physical place, the foreign exchange market is an over-the-counter market consisting of dealers linked together by computers. The large commercial banks are called *market makers* because they are willing to buy and sell the major currencies at any time. Rather than enter the foreign exchange market directly, most smaller banks and businesses pay a fee to a large commercial bank to carry out their foreign exchange transactions. Typically, traders are buying and selling bank deposits denominated in currencies—rather than the currencies themselves. For instance, a currency trader at Bank of America may exchange euros for yen by trading euros held in an account owned by Bank of America in a Paris bank for yen held in an account owned by Deutsche Bank in a bank in Tokyo. Most foreign exchange trading takes place among commercial banks located in London, New York, and Tokyo, with secondary centers in Hong Kong, Singapore, and Zurich.

Dollar deposits in banks outside the United States are called *Eurodollars*, and the market where they are bought and sold is called the *Eurodollar market*. Originally, Eurodollars referred only to dollar deposits in banks in Europe. However, today the term refers to deposits in any bank outside the United States. The Eurodollar market developed in the 1950s to serve two main purposes: First, in the late 1940s and early 1950s, most Western European countries had *capital controls*, or restrictions on the ability of investors or financial firms to freely trade one currency for another. One way of evading these capital controls was for European banks to offer their clients dollar deposits, which unlike European currencies, they could freely trade. Second, from the late 1940s on, the United States and the Soviet Union were engaged in the Cold War. Despite political hostility, the Soviet Union still needed access to dollars in order to pay for goods, including oil, that were priced in dollars. The Soviet government believed that keeping deposits in U.S. banks was risky because the U.S. government might seize the funds if the Cold War were to heat up. Instead, the Soviets were able to persuade European banks to allow them to hold dollar deposits. Today, U.S. banks have sometimes found that they can better serve the needs of multinational U.S. firms by holding dollar deposits in foreign banks. In fact, Eurodollars raised abroad have become an important source of funds for U.S. banks.

With daily trading in the trillions of dollars, the foreign exchange market is the largest financial market in the world. In addition to commercial banks, major participants in the foreign exchange market include investment portfolio managers and central banks, such as the Federal Reserve. Participants trade currencies such as the U.S. dollar, yen, pound, and euro around the clock. The busiest trading time is in the morning, U.S. east coast time, when the London and New York financial markets are both open for trading. But trading is always taking place somewhere. A currency trader in New York might receive a call in the middle of the night with news that leads him or her to buy or sell dollars or other currencies.

Exchange Rates in the Long Run

LEARNING OBJECTIVE: Use the theory of purchasing power parity to explain how exchange rates are determined in the long run.

We have seen that there can be substantial fluctuations in exchange rates. We turn now to explaining why exchange rates fluctuate. First we examine how exchange rates are determined in the long run.

The Law of One Price and the Theory of Purchasing Power Parity

Our analysis of what determines exchange rates in the long run, a period lasting at least several years, begins with a fundamental economic idea called the **law of one price**, which states that identical products should sell for the same price everywhere. To see why the law of one price should hold, consider the following example: Suppose that an iPhone is selling for $399 in stores in Houston and for $299 in stores in Boston. Anyone who lives in Boston could buy iPhones for $299 and resell them for $399 in Houston, using eBay or Craigslist or by shipping them to someone they know in Houston, who could sell them in local flea markets. As we saw in Chapter 3, when similar securities have different yields, the opportunity for *arbitrage profits* causes the prices of the securities to change until they have the same yields. Similarly, a gap in the prices of iPhones between Houston and Boston creates arbitrage profits that can be earned by buying cheap iPhones in Boston and reselling them in Houston. If there is no limit to the number of $299 iPhones available in Boston, the process of arbitrage will continue until the increased supply of iPhones being resold in Houston has driven the price there down to $299.

Law of one price The fundamental economic idea that identical products should sell for the same price everywhere.

Theory of purchasing power parity (PPP) The theory that exchange rates move to equalize the purchasing power of different currencies.

The law of one price holds not just for goods traded within one country but also for goods traded internationally. In the context of international trade, the law of one price is the basis for the **theory of purchasing power parity (PPP)**, which holds that exchange rates move to equalize the purchasing power of different currencies. In other words, in the long run, exchange rates should be at a level that makes it possible to buy the same amount of goods and services with the equivalent amount of any country's currency.

Consider a simple example: If you can buy a 2-liter bottle of Dr. Pepper for $1.50 in New York City or £1 in London, then the theory of purchasing power parity states that the exchange rate between the dollar and the pound should be $1.50 = £1. If exchange rates are not at the values indicated by PPP, then arbitrage profits are possible. Suppose that you can buy a bottle of Dr. Pepper for $1.50 in New York or £1 in London, but the exchange rate between the dollar and the pound is $1 = £1. You could exchange $10 million for £10 million, buy 10 million bottles of Dr. Pepper in London, and ship them to New York, where you could sell them for $15 million. The result would be an arbitrage profit of $5 million (minus any shipping costs). If the dollar–pound exchange rate does not reflect purchasing power parity for many products—not just bottles of Dr. Pepper— you could repeat this process for many goods and become extremely wealthy. In practice, though, as you and others attempted to earn these arbitrage profits by exchanging dollars for pounds, the demand for pounds would increase, causing the pound's value in terms of dollars to rise until it reached the PPP exchange rate of $1.50 = £1. Once the exchange rate reflected the purchasing power of the two currencies, the opportunity for arbitrage profits would be eliminated. At the PPP exchange rate, 1 bottle of Dr. Pepper in the United States exchanges for 1 bottle of Dr. Pepper in London, so the real exchange rate equals 1.

The reasoning we have just used suggests that, in the long run, nominal exchange rates adjust to equalize the purchasing power of different currencies. That is, in the long run, the real exchange rate should equal 1. (Recall from Section 8.1 that when the real exchange rate equals 1, goods and services in the United States can be exchanged for an equal amount of goods and services in the United Kingdom.) This theory should hold because, if it doesn't, opportunities for arbitrage profits exist. In the long run, by buying and selling currencies in the foreign exchange market, individuals pursuing profit opportunities should cause the nominal exchange rate to adjust so that the real exchange rate equals 1, and purchasing power parity holds. Although this logic may seem convincing, it is actually flawed, as we will discuss in the next section.

PPP leads to a prediction about movements in exchange rates in the long run: If one country has a higher inflation rate than another country, the currency of the high-inflation country will depreciate relative to the currency of the low-inflation country. To see why, look again at the expression for the real exchange rate:

$$e = E \times \left(\frac{P^{\text{Domestic}}}{P^{\text{Foreign}}} \right).$$

We can use a handy mathematical rule that states that an equation where variables are multiplied together is approximately equal to an equation where percentage changes in those variables are added together. Similarly, we can approximate the division of two variables by subtracting their percentage changes. Remember that the percentage change in the price level is the same thing as the inflation rate.

If we let π^{Domestic} stand for the domestic inflation rate and π^{Foreign} stand for the foreign inflation rate, then we have:

$$\% \text{ change in } e = \% \text{ change in } E + \pi^{\text{Domestic}} - \pi^{\text{Foreign}}.$$

If the theory of purchasing power parity is correct, then in the long run e, the real exchange rate, equals 1. If the real exchange rate is constant at 1, then its percentage change is zero, and we can rewrite the previous expression as:

$$\% \text{ change in } E = \pi^{\text{Foreign}} - \pi^{\text{Domestic}}.$$

This last equation tells us that the percentage change in the nominal exchange rate is equal to the difference between the foreign and domestic inflation rates. For example, if the inflation rate in the United Kingdom is higher than the inflation rate in the United States, we would expect over time fewer dollars would be needed to exchange for 1 pound; that is, the nominal exchange rate would appreciate. In fact, this prediction of PPP theory is correct. Over the past several decades, the value of the U.S. dollar has risen relative to the currencies of countries such as Mexico that have had higher inflation rates and fallen relative to the currencies of countries such as Japan that have had lower inflation rates.

Is PPP a Complete Theory of Exchange Rates?

Although the PPP theory generally makes correct predictions about movements in exchange rates in the long run, it has a much poorer track record in the short run. Three real-world complications keep purchasing power parity from being a complete theory of exchange rates:

1. **Not all products can be traded internationally.** When goods are traded internationally, arbitrage profits can be made whenever exchange rates do not reflect their PPP values. But more than half of the goods and services produced in most countries are not traded internationally. When goods are not traded internationally, arbitrage will not drive their prices to be the same. For example, suppose that the exchange rate is $1 = €1$, but the price of having your teeth cleaned is twice as high in Chicago as in Berlin. In this case, there is no way to buy up the lower-priced German service and resell it in the United States—and people in Chicago are not going to fly to Berlin just for that purpose. Because many goods and services are not traded internationally, exchange rates will not reflect exactly the relative purchasing power of currencies.

2. **Products are differentiated.** We expect the same product to sell for the same price around the world, but if two products are similar but not identical, their prices might be different. So, while oil, wheat, aluminum, and some other goods are essentially identical, automobiles, televisions, clothing, and many other goods are *differentiated*, so we would not expect them to have identical prices everywhere. In other words, for differentiated products, the law of one price doesn't hold.

3. **Governments impose barriers to trade.** The governments of most countries impose *tariffs* and *quotas* on imported goods. A **tariff** is a tax a government imposes on imports. A **quota** is a limit a government imposes on the quantity of a good that can be imported. The effect of both tariffs and quotas is to raise the domestic

Tariff A tax a government imposes on imports.

Quota A limit a government imposes on the quantity of a good that can be imported.

price of a good above the international price. For example, the U.S. government imposes a quota on imports of sugar. As a result, the U.S. price of sugar is typically two to three times the price of sugar in most other countries. Because of the quota, there is no legal way for someone to buy up low-priced foreign sugar and resell it in the United States. So, the law of one price doesn't hold for goods subject to tariffs and quotas.

SOLVED PROBLEM 8.2

Should Big Macs Have the Same Price Everywhere?

The *Economist* magazine tracks the prices of the McDonald's Big Mac hamburger in countries around the world. The following table shows the prices of Big Macs in the United States and in six other countries, along with the exchange rate between that country's currency and the U.S. dollar.

a. Explain whether the numbers in the table are consistent with the theory of purchasing power parity.

b. Explain whether your results in part (a) mean that arbitrage profits exist in the market for Big Macs.

Country	Big Mac price in domestic currency	Exchange rate (units of foreign currency per U.S. dollar)
United States	$4.93	—
Japan	370 yen	118.65
Mexico	49 pesos	17.44
United Kingdom	2.89 pounds	0.68
China	17.60 yuan	6.56
Russia	114 rubles	74.68
Norway	46.8 kroner	8.97

Source: "The *Economist* Big Mac Index," *Economist*, January 7, 2016.

Solving the Problem

Step 1 **Review the chapter material.** This problem is about the theory of purchasing power parity, so you may want to review the sections "The Law of One Price and the Theory of Purchasing Power Parity," which begins on page 253, and "Is PPP a Complete Theory of Exchange Rates?," which begins on page 255.

Step 2 **Answer part (a) by determining whether the theory of purchasing power parity applies to Big Macs.** If purchasing power parity holds for Big Macs, then their price should be the same—$4.93—in every country when we use the exchange rate to convert the domestic currency price into dollars. For example, the price of the Big Mac in Japan is ¥370, and we can convert this price into dollars by dividing by the number of yen per dollar: ¥370/(¥118.65/$) = $3.12. We can use this procedure to construct a table like this one:

Country	Domestic currency price	Dollar price
Japan	370 yen	$3.12
Mexico	49 pesos	$2.81
United Kingdom	2.89 pounds	$4.25
China	17.60 yuan	$2.68
Russia	114 rubles	$1.53
Norway	46.8 kroner	$5.22

The table shows that while the dollar prices of Big Macs in the United Kingdom and Norway are fairly close to the U.S. price, the dollar prices of Big Macs in the other four countries are significantly different from the U.S. price. So, we can conclude that the law of one price and, therefore, the theory of purchasing power parity, does not hold for Big Macs.

Step 3 **Answer part (b) by explaining whether arbitrage profits exist in the market for Big Macs.** We expect the law of one price to hold because if it doesn't, arbitrage profits are possible. However, it is not possible to make arbitrage profits by buying low-price Big Macs in Beijing and shipping them to Seattle or by buying low-price Big Macs in Moscow and shipping them to London. The Big Macs would be a cold, soggy mess by the time they arrived at their destination. As we discussed in this section, one reason that the theory of purchasing power parity does not provide a complete explanation of exchange rates is that many goods—such as Big Macs—cannot be traded internationally.

See related problem 2.7 at the end of the chapter.

 ## 8.3 A Demand and Supply Model of Short-Run Movements in Exchange Rates

LEARNING OBJECTIVE: Use a demand and supply model to explain how exchange rates are determined in the short run.

As we saw in Figure 8.2 on page 251, exchange rates fluctuate substantially. In fact, it is not unusual for exchange rates to fluctuate by several percentage points even during a single day. Because the purchasing power of currencies changes by only a tiny amount over the course of a few days, the size of short-run fluctuations in exchange rates is another indication that the theory of purchasing power parity cannot provide a complete explanation of exchange rates.

A Demand and Supply Model of Exchange Rates

Economists use the model of demand and supply to analyze how market prices are determined. Because the exchange rate is the price of foreign currency in terms of domestic currency, we can analyze the most important factors affecting exchange rates in the short run by using demand and supply. Here we are considering a short period of time, and we are analyzing currencies in high-income countries, such as the United States, Canada, Japan, and the countries of Western Europe, where annual inflation rates are low, so it is reasonable to assume that price levels are constant. We have already seen that the only factors that cause changes in the nominal exchange rate relative to the real exchange rate are the price levels in the two countries. Therefore, by assuming that price levels are constant, our model will determine *both* the equilibrium nominal exchange rate and the equilibrium real exchange rate.

The demand for U.S. dollars represents the demand by households and firms outside the United States for U.S. goods and U.S. financial assets. For example, a Japanese electronics store that wants to import Apple iPads has to exchange yen for dollars in

FIGURE 8.3

The Demand and Supply of Foreign Exchange

The lower the exchange rate, the cheaper it is to convert a foreign currency into dollars and the larger the quantity of dollars demanded. So, the demand curve for dollars in exchange for yen is downward sloping. The higher the exchange rate, the more yen households or firms will receive in exchange for dollars and the larger the quantity of dollars supplied. The supply curve of dollars in exchange for yen is upward sloping because the quantity of dollars supplied will increase as the exchange rate increases.

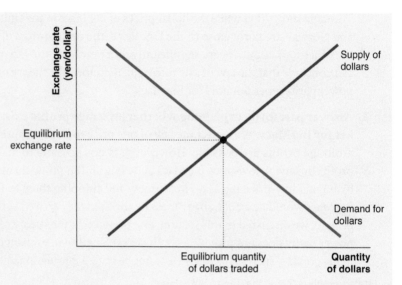

order to pay for them. It seems logical that the quantity of dollars demanded will depend on the exchange rate. The lower the exchange rate, the cheaper it is to convert a foreign currency into dollars and the larger the quantity of dollars demanded. For example, more dollars will be demanded at an exchange rate of ¥80 = $1 than at ¥100 = $1. In Figure 8.3, we plot the exchange rate on the vertical axis. In this case, the exchange rate is yen per dollar, but we could have used the exchange rate between any two currencies. On the horizontal axis, we measure the quantity of dollars being exchanged for yen. The demand curve for dollars in exchange for yen is downward sloping because the quantity of dollars demanded will increase as the exchange rate declines and the yen price of U.S. goods and financial assets becomes relatively less expensive.

The supply of dollars in exchange for yen is determined by the willingness of households and firms that own dollars to exchange them for yen. U.S. households and firms want yen in exchange for dollars in order to purchase Japanese goods and Japanese financial assets. It seems logical that the quantity of dollars supplied will depend on the exchange rate. The more yen a U.S. household or firm receives per dollar, the cheaper the dollar price of Japanese goods and Japanese financial assets will be. So, the higher the exchange rate, the more yen households or firms will receive in exchange for dollars, and the larger the quantity of dollars supplied. In Figure 8.3, the supply curve of dollars in exchange for yen is upward sloping because the quantity of dollars supplied will increase as the exchange rate increases.

Shifts in the Demand and Supply for Foreign Exchange

We assume that the demand and supply curves are drawn *holding constant all factors other than the exchange rate* that would affect the willingness of households and firms to demand or supply dollars. Changes in the exchange rate result in movements along the demand or supply curve—changes in the quantity of dollars demanded or supplied—but do not cause the demand or supply curve to shift. Changes in other factors cause either the demand or supply curve to shift.

Anything that increases the willingness of Japanese households and firms to buy U.S. goods or U.S. assets will cause the demand curve for dollars to shift to the right. For example, panel (a) of Figure 8.4 illustrates the effect of Japanese consumers increasing their demand for tablet computers sold by U.S. firms. As Japanese retail stores increase their orders for these tablets, they must increase their demand for dollars in exchange for yen. The figure shows that the demand curve for dollars shifts to the right, causing the equilibrium exchange rate to increase from ¥80 = $1 to ¥85 = $1 and the equilibrium quantity of dollars traded to increase from Dollars$_1$ to Dollars$_2$. Panel (b) illustrates the effect of U.S. consumers increasing their demand for Sony televisions. As U.S. retail stores increase their orders for these televisions, they must supply more dollars in exchange for yen. The figure shows that the supply curve for dollars in exchange for yen shifts to the right, causing the equilibrium exchange rate to decrease from ¥80 = $1 to ¥75 = $1 and the equilibrium quantity of dollars traded to increase from Dollars$_1$ to Dollars$_2$.

Up through the 1960s, short-run changes in exchange rates were primarily driven by the factors just discussed: shifts in the demand and supply for foreign currency to finance imports and exports. That is, trade in goods was more important, even in the short run, than was the flow of financial securities among countries. Comparatively few U.S. investors bought and sold European or Japanese stocks and bonds, and comparatively few investors in Europe or Japan bought and sold U.S. stocks and bonds. Today,

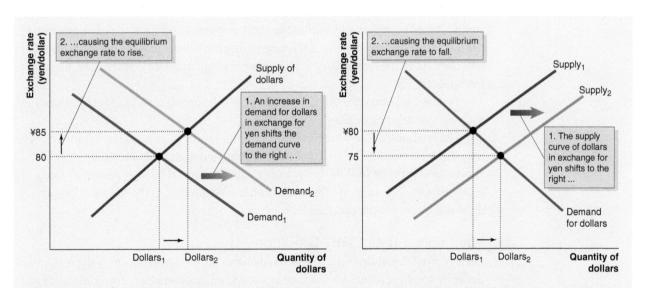

(a) The effect of an increase in the demand for dollars **(b) The effect of an increase in the supply of dollars**

FIGURE 8.4 The Effect of Changes in the Demand and Supply for Dollars

Panel (a) illustrates the effect of an increase in the demand for dollars in exchange for yen. The demand curve for dollars shifts to the right, causing the equilibrium exchange rate to increase from ¥80 = $1 to ¥85 = $1 and the equilibrium quantity of dollars traded to increase from Dollars$_1$ to Dollars$_2$.

Panel (b) illustrates the effect of an increase in the supply of dollars in exchange for yen. The supply curve for dollars in exchange for yen shifts to the right, causing the equilibrium exchange rate to decrease from ¥80 = $1 to ¥75 = $1 and the equilibrium quantity of dollars traded to increase from Dollars$_1$ to Dollars$_2$.

though, in the short run, the demand and supply of foreign currency originating from financial transactions is much more important than is the demand and supply of foreign currency originating from trade in goods. As a result, changes in interest rates are a key factor causing the demand curve and the supply curve for a currency to shift. For example, if interest rates in the United States rise relative to interest rates in Japan, the demand for U.S. dollars will increase as foreign investors exchange their currencies for dollars in order to purchase U.S. financial assets. The shift in the demand curve to the right results in a higher equilibrium exchange rate. If there is an increase in interest rates in Japan relative to interest rates in the United States, the supply curve for dollars will shift to the right, as U.S. investors exchange dollars for yen in order to purchase Japanese financial assets. The shift in the supply curve to the right results in a lower equilibrium exchange rate.

Similarly, if other characteristics of U.S. financial securities, apart from their interest rates, change relative to foreign securities, the demand for dollars will shift. For example, if investors believe that the probability of certain foreign governments defaulting on their bonds has increased, the demand curve for dollars will shift to the right as investors sell foreign bonds and buy U.S. bonds. Similarly, if investors believe that foreign bonds are becoming more liquid, the supply curve for dollars will shift to the right as investors exchange dollars for foreign currencies to buy foreign bonds.

Finally, some participants in financial markets analyze the effects of the factors that affect the demand and supply for a currency and use their analysis to *speculate* on future movements in exchange rates. For example, if investors decide that the value of the euro will increase in the future, they will supply dollars in exchange for euros. As a result, the supply curve for dollars will shift to the right, causing a decline in the exchange rate of the dollar for the euro. Similarly, if foreign investors believe that the value of the dollar will increase in the future, they will increase their demand for dollars in exchange for foreign currency.

Table 8.1 summarizes the factors that affect the demand and supply for dollars in exchange for other currencies.

The relationship between interest rates and exchange rates is important enough that many economists believe that in explaining movements in exchange rates in the short run, it is better to shift the focus entirely to financial investors and the effects of changes in interest rates in different countries. We do that in the next section, which discusses the *interest-rate parity condition*.

The Interest-Rate Parity Condition

On any given day, more than 95% of the demand for foreign exchange is the result of a desire by investors to buy foreign financial assets rather than a desire by households and firms to buy foreign goods and services. The tremendous demand for foreign exchange for purposes of financial investment reflects the importance of the increase in *international capital mobility* in recent decades. Policymakers in many countries have removed regulations that once hindered financial investments across national borders. The Internet allows investors in one country to easily access information about firms in other countries. The Internet also makes it easier for investors to contact financial firms, particularly

TABLE 8.1 Factors That Shift Demand and Supply for Dollars in Exchange for Foreign Currencies

All else being equal, an increase in ...	causes the ...	because ...	Graph of effect on equilibrium in the foreign exchange market
the foreign demand for U.S. goods	demand for dollars to increase	foreign firms need dollars to buy U.S. imports.	
U.S. interest rates relative to foreign interest rates	demand for dollars to increase	foreign investors need dollars to buy U.S. financial securities.	
desirable characteristics of U.S. financial securities	demand for dollars to increase	foreign investors need dollars to buy U.S. financial securities.	
the U.S. demand for foreign goods	supply of dollars to increase	U.S. firms need foreign currency to buy foreign exports.	
foreign interest rates relative to U.S interest rates	supply of dollars to increase	U.S. investors need foreign currency to buy foreign financial securities.	
desirable characteristics of foreign financial securities	supply of dollars to increase	U.S. investors need foreign currency to buy foreign financial securities.	

brokerage firms, to make investments in foreign firms for them. In this section, we explore the implications of international capital mobility for the determination of exchange rates.

Suppose that you intend to invest $10,000 in one-year government bonds. Also suppose that one-year U.S. Treasury bills currently have an interest rate of 1%, while one-year Japanese government bonds currently have an interest rate of 3%. To keep the example simple, assume that you consider the two bonds to be identical except for their interest rates. That is, you believe they have the same default risk, liquidity, information costs, and other characteristics. Which bonds should you purchase? The answer seems obvious: Because 3% is greater than 1%, you should purchase the Japanese government bonds. But bear in mind that to purchase the Japanese bonds, you have to exchange your dollars for yen, thereby assuming some **exchange-rate risk**, which is the risk that an investor or firm will suffer losses because of fluctuations in exchange rates. While your funds are invested in Japanese bonds, the value of the yen might decline relative to the dollar.

Exchange-rate risk The risk that an investor or firm will suffer losses because of fluctuations in exchange rates.

To continue with the example, if you buy U.S. government bonds, then after one year, you will have $10,100 (= $10,000 × 1.01). Assume that the exchange rate is ¥100 = $1. Then if you decide to purchase the Japanese government bonds, you must exchange $10,000 for ¥1,000,000 (= $10,000 × ¥100/$). At the end of one year, your investment in Japanese government bonds will give you ¥1,030,000 (= ¥1,000,000 × 1.03). If the exchange rate is still ¥100 = $1, you can convert your yen back into dollars and have $10,300 (= ¥1,030,000/(¥100/$)). So, the Japanese investment is clearly better. But what if during the year the value of the yen falls by 4%, to ¥104 = $1. (Note that this is the equivalent of the value of the dollar rising by 4%.) In this case, the ¥1,030,000 that you earn on your investment in the Japanese bond can be exchanged for only $9,903.85, which means you would have been better off investing in U.S. bonds.

As we first discussed in Chapter 3, economists assume that there are no arbitrage profits available in financial markets. Is this assumption consistent with a U.S. bond having a 1% interest rate, a Japanese bond having a 3% interest rate, and investors generally expecting a 4% depreciation in the yen (or, equivalently, a 4% appreciation of the dollar)? It is not consistent because investors would expect a much higher return on the U.S. investment than on the Japanese investment. This difference in returns would lead investors to buy U.S. government bonds, causing their prices to rise and their interest rates to fall, and it would lead investors to sell Japanese government bonds, causing their prices to fall and their interest rates to rise. By how much would the interest rate on the U.S. bond have to fall and the interest rate on the Japanese bond have to rise to eliminate the possibility of earning arbitrage profits? It would have to be enough so that *the difference between the two interest rates equals the expected change in the exchange rate between the yen and the dollar.*

For example, suppose that the interest rate on the Japanese bond rose to 5%, while the value of the yen was expected to decline by 4% relative to the dollar. Then you would receive either $10,100 from buying U.S. government bonds or ¥1,050,000/(¥104/$) = $10,096.15—nearly the same amount—from buying the Japanese government bond.

The **interest-rate parity condition** holds that differences in interest rates on similar bonds in different countries reflect expectations of future changes in exchange rates. We can state this condition generally as:[1]

Interest rate on domestic bond = Interest rate on foreign bond
— Expected appreciation of the domestic currency.

Interest-rate parity condition The proposition that differences in interest rates on similar bonds in different countries reflect expectations of future changes in exchange rates.

For instance, if the interest rate on a German government bond is 8% and the interest rate on an equivalent U.S. government bond is 6%, then the dollar must be expected to appreciate by 2% against the euro. The economic reasoning behind the interest-rate parity condition is the same as the economic reasoning behind the result that within a given country rates of return on similar securities will be the same: If this result does not hold, then investors can make arbitrage profits. The interest-rate parity condition extends this result to global investments: If the expected return from owning a foreign asset—including expected changes in the exchange rate—isn't the same as the return from owning a domestic asset, investors can make arbitrage profits because one asset or the other will be underpriced relative to its expected return.

Does the interest-rate parity condition always hold? That is, can we be sure that differences in interest rates on similar bonds in different countries always reflect expectations of future changes in exchange rates? In practice, we can't be sure, for several reasons:

1. **Differences in default risk and liquidity.** There are always some differences that matter to investors between bonds in different countries. For instance, U.S. investors may consider that the default risk on German or Japanese government bonds, while low, is higher than on U.S. government bonds. Similarly, from the point of view of a U.S. investor, U.S. government bonds will be more liquid than will foreign government bonds. So, some of the differences we see between interest rates on bonds in different countries is compensating investors for differences in the characteristics of the bonds. Particularly during times of turmoil in international financial markets, such as occurred during the financial crisis of 2007–2009 and following the Brexit vote in the United Kingdom, a *flight to quality* can occur when both U.S. and foreign investors prefer U.S. Treasury bonds to foreign bonds because of their very low default risk. This preference will drive down the interest rate on U.S. Treasury bonds relative to foreign bonds.

2. **Transactions costs.** Typically, the costs of purchasing foreign financial assets—the *transactions costs*—are higher than for domestic assets. For instance, foreign brokerage firms may charge higher commissions to buy a foreign firm's bonds than domestic brokerage firms or domestic online brokers would charge to buy a domestic firm's bonds.

---

[1] Note that this equation is an approximation, as can be seen by the fact that in the previous example, the amount earned on the investment in the Japanese bond isn't exactly equal to the $10,100 earned on the investment in the U.S. bond. In that example (and in general), the returns on the two investments will be equal only if the expected change in the exchange rate is slightly less than the difference between the two interest rates. So, the discussion in the text states a result that is only approximately correct. Stating the result exactly requires more algebra, thereby making the main point more difficult to understand. For our purposes, the result stated in the text is a sufficiently close approximation.

3. Exchange-rate risk. The interest-rate parity condition, as we have stated it, does not take into account the exchange-rate risk from investing in a foreign asset. If you could receive 4% on a one-year Treasury bill in the United States or expect to earn 4% on a one-year German government bond, the investment in the German government bond comes with more risk because the value of the dollar may appreciate more than expected against the euro. Economists sometimes account for the additional risk of investing in a foreign asset by including a *currency premium* in the interest-rate parity equation:

Interest rate on the domestic bond = Interest rate on the foreign bond
    − Expected appreciation of the domestic currency − Currency premium.

For example, suppose that the interest rate on the one-year U.S. Treasury bill is 1%, the interest rate on the one-year German government bond is 3%, the expected appreciation of the dollar versus the euro is expected to be 1%, and U.S. investors require a 1% higher expected rate of return on a one-year euro-denominated investment relative to a one-year U.S. dollar-denominated investment to make the two investments equally attractive. Then we would have interest-rate parity: 1% = 3% − 1% − 1%.

SOLVED PROBLEM 8.3 | **IN YOUR INTEREST**

Can You Make Money Investing in Mexican Bonds?

Suppose you read the following investment advice: "One strategy for earning an above-average return is to borrow money in the United States at 2% and invest it in Mexico in a comparable investment (with the same level of default risk, liquidity, and information costs) at 4%." Would you follow this strategy?

Solving the Problem

Step 1   **Review the chapter material.** This problem is about explaining differences in interest rates across countries, so you may want to review the section "The Interest-Rate Parity Condition," which begins on page 260.

Step 2   **Use the interest-rate parity condition to answer the question by explaining the relationship between expected changes in exchange rates and differences in interest rates across countries.** If the interest-rate parity condition holds, then a 2-percentage-point gap between the interest rate on a U.S. bond and the interest rate on a similar Mexican bond means that investors must be expecting that the value of the dollar will *appreciate* against the peso by 2% (= 4% − 2%). Therefore, the expected return on a U.S. investment and a Mexican investment should be the same. If, as a U.S. investor, you borrow money at 2% in the United States and invest it at 4% in the Mexican bond, you will not gain anything if the dollar appreciates by 2% because the true return on your Mexican investment will be 2% rather than 4%. In addition, you will be taking on exchange-rate risk because the dollar could appreciate by more than 2%.

See related problem 3.10 at the end of the chapter.

We saw in the previous section that we can use the demand and supply model for foreign exchange to analyze what happens to the exchange rate when a country's interest rate increases or decreases. Many economists prefer using the interest-rate parity approach because it focuses directly on the actions of financial investors. The two approaches, though, arrive at similar answers to the question of how changes in interest rates affect the exchange rate. For example, suppose that the interest rate on a one-year U.S. Treasury bill is currently 2%, the interest rate on a comparable French one-year government bond is 4%, and the dollar is expected to appreciate by 2% against the euro. If the Federal Reserve takes actions that lead to the Treasury bill rate increasing from 2% to 3%, we would expect that the demand for dollars will increase as investors in Europe attempt to exchange euros for dollars in order to invest in Treasury bills at the new higher interest rate. An increase in demand for dollars will cause the exchange rate to increase. In the new equilibrium, more euros will be required to buy a U.S. dollar.

This result of higher U.S. interest rates leading to a higher exchange rate is consistent with the interest-rate parity condition. If the exchange rate expected between the euro and the dollar one year from now remains the same, then an increase in the exchange rate now means that the rate of appreciation will be lower. In this example, an increase in the U.S. interest rate of 1%, with the French interest rate remaining unchanged, means that the expected rate of appreciation of the dollar will fall from 2% to 1%: 3% = 4% − 1%.

MAKING THE CONNECTION

What Explains Movements in the Dollar Exchange Rate?

Here are just some of the headlines that appeared in the *Wall Street Journal* in a span of three weeks in the summer of 2016:

> "Dollar Slips on Fed Minutes"
> "Sterling Selloff Sends Pound Plunging to 31 Year Low Against the Dollar"
> "Dollar Shoots Higher amid Brexit Woes"
> "Dollar Holds Gains as Yellen Comments on Economy"
> "Dollar Falls as Fed Softens Outlook for Interest Rate Increases"

These headlines indicate what most firms, consumers, and government policymakers know: The exchange rate between the dollar and other currencies can be volatile and is worth monitoring.

One way to measure the general value of one currency relative to other currencies is to calculate the *trade-weighted exchange rate*, which is an index number similar to the consumer price index. Just as the consumer price index weights individual prices by the share the product takes up in a household's budget, the trade-weighted exchange rate for the U.S. dollar weights each individual exchange rate by the share of that country's trade with the United States. The index is calculated so that the value for January 1997 is 100. The following figure shows movements in the trade-weighted dollar exchange rate from 1994 through 2016.

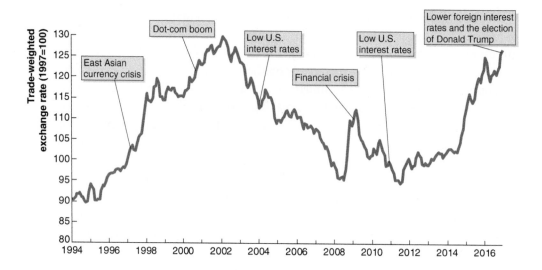

The increase in the value of the dollar during the late 1990s, as shown in the figure, was driven by strong demand from foreign investors for U.S. stocks and bonds, particularly U.S. Treasury securities. *Currency crises* in several East Asian countries, including South Korea, Thailand, Malaysia, and Indonesia, had resulted in sharp declines in the values of these currencies. As a result, many foreign investors engaged in a "flight to quality," in which they purchased assets denominated in U.S. dollars, particularly U.S. Treasury securities, because they appeared to be safe investments. In addition, some foreign investors wanted to participate in the boom in Internet ("dot-com") stocks. The increased demand from foreign investors increased the value of the dollar.

As the Fed began cutting its target for the federal funds rate during and after the recession of 2001, the value of the dollar declined. During the financial crisis of 2007–2009, many investors feared rising default risk on nearly all securities other than U.S. Treasury securities. The result was another flight to quality that increased the demand for dollars, raising the dollar exchange rate.

As the Fed aggressively cut interest rates in response to the financial crisis, the value of the dollar declined over the next several years except for a brief period in 2010, when investors feared that the governments of Greece and several other European countries might be at risk of defaulting on their bonds. By late 2012, investors began to anticipate the Fed would begin raising its target for the federal funds rate at the same time the European Central Bank began taking aggressive steps to lower interest rates. The result was a sharp appreciation in the value of the dollar that was extended by the election of Donald Trump in the November 2016 presidential election, which resulted in investors expecting higher economic growth and higher interest rates in the United States.

Going forward, it seems likely that headlines similar to the ones listed on the previous page will continue to appear as the exchange value of the dollar responds to shifts in demand and supply in international financial markets.

Sources: Chelsey Dulaney, "Dollar Slips on Fed Minutes," *Wall Street Journal*, July 6, 2016; Mike Bird, "Sterling Selloff Sends Pound Plunging to 31 Year Low Against the Dollar," *Wall Street Journal*, July 5, 2016; Ira Iosebashvili, "Dollar Holds Gains as Yellen Comments on Economy," *Wall Street Journal*, June 21, 2016; and Ira Iosebashvili, "Dollar Falls as Fed Soften Outlook for Interest Rate Increases," *Wall Street Journal*, June 15, 2016.

See related problem 3.11 at the end of the chapter.

Forward and Futures Contracts in Foreign Exchange

We saw in Chapter 7 that derivatives play an important role in the U.S. financial system. We can briefly examine their role in foreign exchange markets. In the foreign exchange market, a *spot market transaction* involves an exchange of currencies or bank deposits immediately (subject to a two-day settlement period) at the current exchange rate. In a *forward transaction*, traders agree today to a *forward contract* to exchange currencies or bank deposits at a specific future date at an exchange rate known as the *forward rate.*

Futures contracts differ from forward contracts in several ways. While forward contracts are private agreements among traders to exchange any amount of currency on any future date, futures contracts are traded on exchanges, such as the Chicago Mercantile Exchange (CME), and the quantity of currency being exchanged and the *settlement date* on which the exchange will take place are standardized. With forward contracts, the forward exchange rate is fixed at the time the contract is agreed to, while with futures contracts, the futures exchange rate changes continually as contracts are bought and sold on the exchange.

Counterparty risk refers to the risk that one party to the contract will default and fail to buy or sell the underlying asset. Counterparty risk is lower with futures contracts than with forward contracts because the exchange—rather than the buyers and sellers—stands as the counterparty on each trade. For instance, someone buying a futures contract on the Chicago Board of Trade (CBOT) has the CBOT as a counterparty, which reduces default risk. For many financial assets, the reduction in counterparty risk means more trading takes place in futures contracts than in forward contracts. This outcome does not hold for foreign exchange, however, because the bulk of the trading takes place among large banks whose traders ordinarily are confident that their trading partners will not default on forward contracts. Because banks like the flexibility of forward contracts, the amount of trading in forward contracts in foreign exchange is at least 10 times greater than the amount of trading in futures contracts. Table 8.2 summarizes the key differences between forward and futures contracts in foreign exchange.

Call and put options are available on foreign exchange. As we saw in Chapter 7, a call option gives the buyer the right to purchase the underlying asset at a set price, called the *strike price*, at any time until the option's expiration date. A put option gives the buyer the right to sell the underlying asset at the strike price.

TABLE 8.2 Key Differences Between Forward Contracts and Futures Contracts in Foreign Exchange

	Forward contracts	Futures contracts
How contracts are traded	Over the counter; often between banks	On futures exchanges, such as the Chicago Mercantile Exchange
Forward exchange rate	Fixed when contract is agreed to	Changes continually as contract is traded
Terms of contract	Flexible; settled by negotiation between buyer and seller	Fixed by the exchange
Settlement date	Flexible; settled by negotiation between buyer and seller	Fixed by the exchange
Counterparty risk	Potentially significant, although reduced because transactions are typically between large financial institutions	None; assumed by the exchange

Exchange-Rate Risk, Hedging, and Speculation

A U.S. firm is subject to exchange-rate risk when it sells goods and services in a foreign country. Assume that you work for Smucker's, a maker of jams, jellies, and other food products, headquartered in Orville, Ohio. Suppose Smucker's sells $300,000 worth of jams and jellies to a supermarket chain in England at a time when the exchange rate is $1.50 = £1. Smucker's agrees to ship the jams and jellies today, but—as is often the case—the English firm has 90 days to pay Smucker's the funds. Smucker's agrees that the English firm can pay in pounds, so Smucker's will receive a payment of £200,000 (= $300,000/$1.50/£) in 90 days. Smucker's is exposed to exchange-rate risk because if the pound falls in value relative to the dollar before the English supermarket chain makes its payment, Smucker's will receive less than $300,000. For instance, if in 90 days the exchange rate is $1.25 = £1, then Smucker's will be able to exchange the £200,000 it receives for only $250,000 (= £200,000 × $1.25/£).

As part of your job at Smucker's, you are responsible for reducing the firm's exposure to exchange-rate risk. You can *hedge*, or reduce, the exchange-rate risk by entering into a forward contract—or, more likely, having the firm's bank carry out the forward transaction for a fee. With a forward contract, Smucker's would agree today to *sell* the £200,000 it will receive in 90 days for dollars at the current forward rate. If the current forward rate is the same as the spot rate of $1.50 = £1 then Smucker's will have completely hedged its risk, at the cost of the fee its bank charges. The forward rate will reflect what traders in the forward market expect the spot exchange rate between the dollar and pound to be in 90 days, so the forward rate may not equal the current spot rate. Typically, though, the current spot rate and the 90-day forward rate are close together, allowing Smucker's to hedge most of the exchange-rate risk it faces.

Smucker's is hedging against the risk that the value of the pound will fall against the dollar. Now suppose you work for Burberry, a British clothing manufacturer. As part of your job, you need to hedge the exchange-rate risk on the following transaction:

Burberry sells £2 million of men's coats to Macy's, the U.S. department store chain. The current exchange rate is $1.50 = £1$, and Burberry agrees to accept payment of $3.5 million ($= £2$million $\times$ $1.50/£$) in 90 days. Burberry is exposed to the risk that over the next 90 days, the value of the pound will rise relative to the dollar, which would decrease the number of pounds it would receive in exchange for the $3.5 million payment it will receive from Macy's in 90 days. To hedge against this risk, you can arrange to *buy* pounds today at the current forward rate. Note that this is the opposite of the strategy Smucker's used: To hedge against a *fall* in the value of the pound, Smucker's *sells* pounds in the forward market; to hedge against a *rise* in the value of the pound, Burberry *buys* pounds in the forward market.

A hedger uses derivatives markets to reduce risk, while a *speculator* uses derivatives markets to place a bet on the future value of a currency. For example, if an investor becomes convinced that the future value of the euro will be lower than other people in the foreign exchange market currently believe it will be, the investor can sell euros in the forward market. If the value of euros does fall, then the spot price of the euro in the future will be lower, which will allow the investor to fulfill the forward contract at a profit. Similarly, if an investor believes that the future value of the euro will be higher than other people in the foreign exchange market currently believe it will be, the investor can make a profit by buying euros in the forward market. Of course, in either case, if the value of the euro moves in the opposite direction to the one the investor expects, the investor will suffer losses on his or her forward position.

Firms and investors can also use options contracts to hedge or to speculate. For example, a firm concerned that the value of a currency will fall more than expected—such as Smucker's, in our previous example—could hedge against this risk by buying put options on the currency. That way, if the value of the currency were to fall below the strike price, the firm could exercise the option and sell at the (above-market) strike price. Similarly, a firm concerned that the value of a currency will rise more than expected—such as Burberry, in our previous example—could hedge against this risk by buying call options on the currency. If the value of the currency were to rise above the strike price, the firm could exercise the option and buy at the (below-market) strike price.

Options contracts have the advantage to hedgers that if the price moves in the opposite direction from the one being hedged against, the hedger can decline to exercise the option and instead can gain from the favorable price movement. For instance, suppose that Smucker's decides to purchase put options on the pound rather than sell pounds in the forward market. Smucker's would still be protected against a fall in the value of the pound because it could exercise its put options, thereby selling pounds at an above-market price. But if the pound rises in value, Smucker's can allow the put options to expire without exercising them and profit from the additional dollars it receives when it exchanges the £200,000 from the English supermarket chain in 90 days. Although options appear to have an advantage over forward contracts in this respect, options prices (premiums) are higher than the fees incurred with forward contracts.

A speculator who believed that the value of a currency was likely to rise more than expected would buy calls, while a speculator who believed that the value of a currency was likely to fall more than expected would buy puts. If the value of the currency moves in the opposite direction to the one the speculator hopes, the speculator with an options contract doesn't have to exercise the option. So, the advantage of an options contract is that a speculator's losses are limited to whatever he or she paid for the option. But once again, the disadvantage of speculating with options contracts is that their prices are higher than those of forward contracts.

MAKING THE CONNECTION

Can Speculators Drive Down the Value of a Currency?

Participants in the market for foreign exchange can be divided into two groups: (1) hedgers, who—like Smucker's and Burberry in our examples—are motivated by the desire to reduce exchange-rate risk, and (2) speculators, who hope to profit from exchange rate movements. Currency speculators, like traders in stocks, bonds, and other financial assets, typically buy and sell a country's currency, hoping to make a profit over a short period of time. As we have seen, speculators serve a useful role by providing liquidity in financial markets. In order to hedge exchange-rate risk, firms need enough counterparties willing to be on the other side of the hedgers' buying or selling. Without speculators, many financial markets, including the foreign exchange market, would be significantly less liquid.

However, some policymakers believe speculators will sometimes drive down exchange rates to artificially low levels, thereby causing instability in foreign exchange markets. For example, in 2010, a controversy erupted over whether the managers of hedge funds were conspiring to earn billions of dollars by driving down the price of the euro. Hedge funds are similar to mutual funds in that they accept money from investors and invest the funds in a portfolio of assets. Unlike mutual funds, hedge funds typically make relatively risky investments, and they have fewer than 100 investors, all of whom are either institutions, such as pension funds, or wealthy individuals. According to an article in the *Wall Street Journal*, the managers of four hedge funds met in New York City to discuss whether it would be profitable to use derivatives to bet that the value of the euro would fall. Present at the meeting were representatives of a fund run by George Soros, who had famously earned $1 billion in the early 1990s by placing bets against the value of the British pound.

At the time of the meeting, the exchange rate between the euro and the dollar was $1.35 = €1, having already fallen from $1.51 = €1 the previous December. Some hedge fund managers were convinced that during the next year, the value of the euro was likely to fall all the way to parity with the dollar, or $1 = €1. The hedge funds could profit from this fall by selling euros in the forward market, selling euros futures contracts, or buying put contracts on the euro. The hedge funds could make these investments by putting up only about 5% of the value of the investments in cash and borrowing the other 95%. This high degree of *leverage*—or use of borrowed money in the investment—would magnify the size of any return as a fraction of their actual cash investment. Because the payoff to such a large decline in the value of the euro was potentially enormous, some observers called it a "career trade," meaning that this one investment alone—should it actually pay off!—would make the hedge fund managers both very wealthy and very famous.

Although some government officials in the United States and Europe criticized the hedge funds, many economists were skeptical that the managers' actions could have much effect on the value of the euro. The total value of euros being bought and sold in global foreign exchange markets is greater than $1.2 trillion *per day*. The four hedge fund managers present at the New York meeting were making long-term bets against the euro that amounted to only a few billion dollars. In any event, over the following two years, the euro–dollar exchange rate never dropped below $1.19 = €1, so anyone speculating on the value of the euro falling to parity had made a losing bet.

The exchange rates among major currencies such as the euro and the dollar are determined by factors that a few speculators probably can't affect, however large their resources.

Sources: Benoit Faucon and Katie Martin, "Pressures Drive Iran's Currency to New Low," *Wall Street Journal*, October 1, 2012; Susan Pulliam, Kate Kelly, and Carrick Mollenkamp, "Hedge Funds Try 'Career Trade' Against Euro," *Wall Street Journal*, February 26, 2010; and Michael Casey, "Justice Regulators Fall for Conspiracy Theories," *Wall Street Journal*, March 3, 2010.

See related problem 3.14 at the end of the chapter.

ANSWERING THE KEY QUESTION

Continued from page 246

At the beginning of this chapter, we asked:

"Why hasn't the value of the dollar remained stable when measured against other currencies?"

We have seen that the exchange rate between the dollar and other currencies is dependent in the short run on the level of interest rates in the United States relative to foreign interest rates and on the "safe haven" aspects of U.S. Treasury securities. Over the years, central banks have taken actions to raise and lower interest rates. In addition, turbulence has occurred in international financial markets as a result of the East Asian currency crisis, the 2007–2009 financial crisis, debt crises in Europe, and Brexit, which has caused investors to sell other securities to buy U.S. Treasury bonds. These developments have caused fluctuations in the demand for and supply of dollars and, therefore, in the exchange rate between the dollar and other currencies.

Key Terms and Problems

Key Terms

Appreciation, p. 248

Depreciation, p. 248

Exchange-rate risk, p. 262

Foreign exchange market, p. 252

Interest-rate parity condition, p. 263

Law of one price, p. 253

Nominal exchange rate, p. 247

Quota, p. 255

Real exchange rate, p. 250

Tariff, p. 255

Theory of purchasing power parity (PPP), p. 254

8.1 Exchange Rates and the Foreign Exchange Market
Explain how markets for foreign exchange operate.

Review Questions

1.1 What is the difference between the nominal exchange rate and the real exchange rate? When a newspaper article uses the phrase "the exchange rate," is the article typically referring to the nominal exchange rate or the real exchange rate?

1.2 What is the difference between a direct quotation of an exchange rate and an indirect quotation? If the exchange rate between the yen and the dollar changes from ¥80 = $1 to ¥90 = $1, has the yen appreciated or depreciated against the dollar? Has the dollar appreciated or depreciated against the yen?

1.3 Suppose that the euro falls in value relative to the dollar. What is the likely effect on European exports to the United States? What is the likely effect on U.S. exports to Europe?

1.4 What does it mean to describe the foreign exchange market as an "over-the-counter market"?

Problems and Applications

1.5 A student makes the following observation:

It currently takes 100 yen to buy 1 U.S. dollar, which shows that the United States must be a much wealthier country than Japan. But it takes more than 1 U.S. dollar to buy 1 British pound, which shows that the United Kingdom must be a wealthier country than the United States.

Briefly explain whether you agree with the student's reasoning.

1.6 A student makes the following observation:

This month the euro depreciated sharply against the U.S. dollar. That was good news for attendance at Disneyland Paris and bad news for attendance at Walt Disney World in Orlando, Florida.

Briefly explain whether you agree with the student.

1.7 [Related to the Making the Connection on page 248] If the exchange rate between the pound and the dollar changes from £1.45 = $1 to £1.30 = $1, is this good news for British firms such as Brompton Bicycle? Is it good news for U.S. consumers? Is it good news for U.S. firms that export to the United Kingdom? Is it good news for British consumers?

1.8 Suppose that an Apple iPhone costs $400 in the United States, £130 in the United Kingdom, and ¥70,000 in Japan. If the exchange rates are $1.50 = £1 and ¥100 = $1, what are the real exchange rates between the dollar and the yen and the dollar and the pound?

1.9 An article on the web site of the *Financial Times* describes Eurodollars as "dollars which somehow escaped the US system." Briefly explain what the author means.

Source: Izabella Kaminska, "All About the Eurodollars," ft.com, September 5, 2014.

8.2 Exchange Rates in the Long Run
Use the theory of purchasing power parity to explain how exchange rates are determined in the long run.

Review Questions

2.1 How is the law of one price related to the theory of purchasing power parity (PPP)?

2.2 Is PPP a theory of exchange rate determination in the long run or in the short run? Briefly explain.

2.3 According to the theory of purchasing power parity, if the inflation rate in Japan is lower than the inflation rate in Canada, what should happen to the exchange rate between the Japanese yen and the Canadian dollar in the long run?

MyEconLab   Visit **www.myeconlab.com** to complete these exercises online and get instant feedback. Exercises that update with real-time data are marked with ⓦ .

Problems and Applications

2.4 According to a survey of professional foreign exchange traders, the theory of purchasing power parity is considered to be "academic jargon." Why might foreign exchange traders not find PPP to be useful as they trade currencies day-to-day?

Source: Cheung, Yin-Wong, and Menzie David Chinn, "Currency Traders and Exchange Rate Dynamics: A Survey of the U.S. Market," *Journal of International Money and Finance*, Vol. 20, No. 4, August 2001, pp. 439–471.

2.5 Writing in the *Wall Street Journal*, economist William Easterly of New York University notes: "Around 2010, … the domestic currency in Brazil was so overvalued that tourists from Rio visiting Manhattan rented shipping containers to bring home their cheap purchases." What does Easterly mean when he writes that Brazil's currency was overvalued? How is he able to tell?

Source: William Easterly, "Making Sense of Meltdowns," *Wall Street Journal*, July 6, 2016.

2.6 A column in the *New York Times* discussed estimates by the International Monetary Fund (IMF) of growth in total world output, or GDP. The column noted that after adding up the value of each country's output in terms of that country's currency, the IMF could have converted each total into dollars using the current exchange rate between that country's currency and the U.S. dollar. The column further noted, though, that there was a significant problem with that approach: "The International Monetary Fund's solution to this problem is to use a formula involving purchasing power parity or P.P.P., which adjusts for the relative value of currencies and their purchasing power." What is the problem with calculating world GDP by converting each country's output to dollars using current exchange rates? Why would using exchange rates adjusted for the purchasing power of each country's currency be a better approach?

Source: Danny Hakim, "The World's Economy Soared Last Year (or Plunged)," *New York Times*, February 8, 2016.

2.7 [Related to Solved Problem 8.2 on page 256] The *Economist* magazine tracks the prices of the McDonald's Big Mac hamburger in countries around the world. The following table shows the prices of Big Macs in the United States and in five other countries, along with the exchange rate between each country's currency and the U.S. dollar.

Country	Big Mac price in domestic currency	Exchange rate (units of foreign currency per U.S. dollar)
United States	$4.93	—
Brazil	13.5 reals	4.02
Israel	16.9 shekels	3.94
South Korea	4,300 won	1,198
Switzerland	6.5 Swiss francs	1.01
Venezuela	132 Bolivars	198.7

a. Explain whether the statistics in the table are consistent with the theory of purchasing power parity.

b. If the purchasing power parity theory allowed us to exactly determine exchange rates in the short run, what would be the exchange rate between the Brazilian real and the Israeli shekel?

Source: "The *Economist* Big Mac Index," *Economist*, January 7, 2016.

2.8 According to the theory of purchasing power parity, what should happen to the value of the U.S. dollar relative to the Mexican peso if each of the following occurs?

a. Over the next 10 years, the United States experiences an average annual inflation rate of 3%, while Mexico experiences an average annual inflation rate of 8%.

b. The United States puts quotas and tariffs on many imported goods.

c. The United States enters a period of deflation, while Mexico experiences inflation.

8.3 A Demand and Supply Model of Short-Run Movements in Exchange Rates
Use a demand and supply model to explain how exchange rates are determined in the short run.

Review Questions

3.1 Look again at Figure 8.3 on page 258 and answer the following questions.

  a. Why is the demand curve for foreign exchange downward sloping?

  b. Why is the supply curve for foreign exchange upward sloping?

  c. Name three groups that would want to exchange dollars for yen.

  d. Name three groups that would want to exchange yen for dollars.

3.2 How does the interest-rate parity condition account for differences in interest rates on similar bonds in different countries? What are the main reasons that interest-rate parity may not hold exactly?

3.3 What is the difference between a spot transaction and a forward transaction in the foreign exchange market? What are the key differences between forward contracts in foreign exchange and futures contracts in foreign exchange? Why are forward contracts more widely used in the foreign exchange market than are futures contracts?

3.4 How can exchange-rate risk be hedged using forward, futures, and options contracts? How might an investor use forward, futures, and options contracts to speculate on the future value of a currency?

Problems and Applications

3.5 Draw a graph of the demand and supply of U.S. dollars in exchange for Japanese yen to illustrate each of the following situations:

  a. Sales of Apple iPhones and iPads soar in Japan.

  b. The interest rate on one-year Japanese government bonds rises relative to the interest rate on one-year U.S. Treasury bills.

  c. The Japanese government runs huge budget deficits, and investors believe that the government may default on its bonds.

3.6 An article in the Wall Street Journal contained the following observation: "Falling interest rates tend to boost bond prices ... but weigh on currencies."

  a. Why do falling interest rates increase bond prices?

  b. Why would falling interest rates "weigh on currencies"?

  Source: James Glynn and James Ramage, "Aussie Dollar Parity Talk Resumes," Wall Street Journal, July 1, 2014.

3.7 Suppose that the current exchange rate between the yen and the dollar is ¥100 = $1 and that the interest rate is 4% on a one-year bond in Japan and 3% on a comparable bond in the United States. According to the interest-rate parity condition, what do investors expect the exchange rate between the yen and the dollar to be in one year?

3.8 [Related to the Chapter Opener on page 246] An article in the New York Times observes that the high value of the yen "is dealing crippling blows to [Japan's] once all-important export machine." The article also observes, though, that "a high yen benefits Japan's rapidly expanding elderly population."

  a. Does a "high yen" mean that it takes more or fewer yen to exchange for one U.S. dollar?

  b. How does a high yen hurt Japanese exports?

  c. How might a high yen help the elderly population in Japan?

  Source: Martin Fackler, "Strong Yen Is Dividing Generations in Japan," New York Times, July 31, 2012.

3.9 Suppose that the current exchange rate is €1.50 = £1 but it is expected to be €1.35 = £1 in one year. If the current interest rate on a one-year government bond in Germany is 4%, what does the interest-rate parity condition indicate the interest rate will be on a one-year government bond in the United Kingdom? Assume that there are no differences in risk, liquidity, taxation, or information costs between the bonds.

3.10 [Related to Solved Problem 8.3 on page 264] Borrowing at a low interest rate in one currency to lend at a higher interest rate in another currency is sometimes called a "carry trade." An article in the *New York Times* observes: "China has been at the forefront of this so-called carry trade, in which corporations and countries tap dollar-based lenders and then invest the proceeds in higher-yielding assets denominated in local currencies."

a. What does the article mean by "higher-yielding assets denominated in local currencies"?

b. Would investors be certain to make a profit by following this strategy? Briefly explain.

c. Would investors engaging in this carry trade likely cause an increase or a decrease in the value of the Chinese yuan in exchange for U.S. dollars? Briefly explain.

Source: Landon Thomas, Jr., "A Big Bet That China's Currency Will Devalue Further," *New York Times*, September 23, 2015.

3.11 [Related to the Making the Connection on page 265] An article in the *New York Times* discusses the consequences in financial markets of Brexit, the vote in a 2016 referendum in the United Kingdom to leave the European Union: "Investors have dumped much that seems risky—the pound, the euro and shares on stock exchanges around the world. They have entrusted the proceeds to that rare sure thing, United States Treasury bills." The article described this process as a "flight to safety."

a. What is a "flight to safety"?

b. How would the flight to safety affect the exchange rate between the pound and the U.S. dollar? Illustrate your answer with a demand and supply graph showing the market for U.S. dollars in exchange for British pounds.

Source: Peter S. Goodman, "Taking Refuge in Dollar Could Expose World Economy to New Perils," *New York Times*, July 1, 2016.

3.12 Suppose that the U.S. firm Alcoa sells $2 million worth of aluminum to a British firm. Answer the following questions, assuming that the exchange rate is currently $1.50 = £1 and the British firm will pay Alcoa £1,333,333.33 in 90 days.

a. What exchange-rate risk does Alcoa face in this transaction?

b. In what alternative ways can Alcoa hedge this exchange-rate risk? In your answer, provide a specific example.

3.13 Suppose that the U.S. firm Halliburton buys construction equipment from the Japanese firm Komatsu at a price of ¥250 million. The equipment is to be delivered to the United States and paid for in one year. The current exchange rate is ¥100 = $1. The current interest rate on one-year U.S. Treasury bills is 6%, and the interest rate on one-year Japanese government bonds is 4%.

a. If Halliburton exchanges dollars for yen today and invests the yen in Japan for one year, how many dollars does it need to exchange today in order to have ¥250 million in one year?

b. If Halliburton enters a forward contract, agreeing to buy 250 million in one year at an exchange rate of ¥98 = $1 how many dollars does it need today if it plans to invest the dollars at the U.S. interest rate of 6%?

c. If Halliburton invests today at the U.S. interest rate of 6%, without entering into any other type of contract, does the firm know how many dollars it needs today to fulfill its equipment contract in one year? Briefly explain.

d. Which method(s) described in (a) through (c) provide(s) a hedge against exchange-rate risk? Which method do(es) not? Which method is Halliburton likely to prefer?

e. What does the forward contract exchange rate have to be in (b) in order for the results in (a) and (b) to be equivalent?

3.14 [Related to the Making the Connection on page 270] Suppose you are convinced that the value of the Canadian dollar will rise relative to the U.S. dollar. What steps could you take to make a profit based on this conviction?

Data Exercises

D8.1: [Exchange rate movements] Go to the web site of the Federal Reserve Bank of St. Louis (FRED) (fred.stlouisfed.org) and download the most recent value and the value from the same month one year earlier from FRED for the U.S. dollar–euro exchange rate (EXUSEU).

a. Using these values, compute the percentage change in the euro's value.

b. Explain whether the dollar appreciated or depreciated against the euro.

D8.2: [Exchange rate movements] Go to the web site of the Federal Reserve Bank of St. Louis (FRED) (fred.stlouisfed.org) and download and plot the U.S. dollar–euro exchange rate (EXUSEU), the U.S. dollar–yen exchange rate (EXJPUS), and the U.S. dollar–Canadian dollar exchange rate (EXCAUS) for the period from 2001 to the present. Answer the following questions on the basis of your graphs.

a. In what year did the euro reach its highest value?

b. During the financial crisis of 2007–2009, did the yen appreciate or depreciate against the dollar? Briefly explain.

c. Against which currency did the U.S. dollar depreciate the most during this period?

D8.3: [Exchange rate movements] Go to the web site of the Federal Reserve Bank of St. Louis Federal Reserve (FRED) (fred.stlouisfed.org) and download monthly data on the trade-weighted exchange rate for the U.S. dollar against major currencies (TWEXMMTH) from 1973 to the present.

a. What has been the long-term trend in the exchange value of the dollar? Leaving aside other factors, briefly explain the effect that changes in the exchange rate during this period have had on U.S. net exports.

b. What has been the trend in the exchange value of the dollar over the past year? Leaving aside other factors, briefly explain the effect that changes in the exchange rate during the past year have had on U.S. net exports.

D8.4: [Testing the theory of purchasing power parity] Go to the web site of the Federal Reserve Bank of St. Louis Federal Reserve (FRED) (fred.stlouisfed.org) and download the most recent values from FRED for the Japan/U.S. Foreign Exchange Rate (DEXJPUS), China/U.S. Foreign Exchange Rate (DEXCHUS), and the Mexico/U.S. Foreign Exchange Rate (DEXMXUS).

a. Explain whether the exchange rates are quoted as U.S. dollars per unit of foreign currency or units of foreign currency per U.S. dollar.

b. Use the data to report the exchange rate between the Japanese yen and the U.S. dollar.

c. Suppose a Big Mac sells for 300 yen in Japan, 14 yuan in China, and 34 pesos in Mexico. What is the price of a Big Mac in each country in terms of U.S. dollars?

d. Assuming no transportation costs, explain in which county you would want to purchase a Big Mac and in which country you would want to sell the same Big Mac in order to make the highest profit possible.

D8.5: [Interest rates and exchange rates] Go to the web site of the Federal Reserve Bank of St. Louis (FRED) (fred.stlouisfed.org) and download and plot the difference between the interest rate on the U.S. 3-month Treasury bill (TB3MS) and the interest rate on Japanese government securities (INTGSBJPM193N) from 1990 to the present. Next, download the data for the yen–dollar exchange rate (EXJPUS). Describe the relationship between the two series.

CHAPTER 9

Transactions Costs, Asymmetric Information, and the Structure of the Financial System

Learning Objectives

After studying this chapter, you should be able to:

9.1 Evaluate the reasons economists believe economic performance depends on the financial system (pages 279–281)

9.2 Analyze the problems that transactions costs, adverse selection, and moral hazard pose for the financial system (pages 281–296)

9.3 Use economic analysis to explain the structure of the U.S. financial system (pages 296–301)

Can Fintech or Crowdsourcing Fund Your Startup?

Great ideas for new businesses are fairly common: A few examples are opening a coffee shop in an underserved area, developing new applications for smartphones or tablets, and creating an innovative web site to provide tutorial help to students in money and banking courses. Locating the funding to actually start a new business is much more difficult. If you are like many entrepreneurs starting small businesses, you may have to rely for funds on your own savings or on loans from family members and friends. You will probably have difficulty borrowing from a bank unless you have good *collateral*, such as a home, that the bank can seize if you default on your loan.

Recently, though, some entrepreneurs have turned to *fintech* firms to find funding to start a business. Fintech,

which is short for *financial technology*, refers to firms using technology to provide financial services in innovative ways. To obtain funds to start your business, you might turn to fintech firms such as Kabbage, Lending-Club, or Social Finance (SoFi). These firms specialize in making loans to individuals and small businesses that have difficulty borrowing from banks. Unlike banks, these fintech firms finance their loans from funds provided by individual investors and other financial firms.

Typically, in deciding whether to grant a loan, banks have relied on certain standard data, such as how long you have worked at your current job, how long you have lived in your current apartment or house, and your FICO credit score, which is

Continued on next page

KEY ISSUE AND QUESTION

Issue: Acquiring funds to expand their operations is a significant challenge for many firms.

Question: Why do firms rely more on loans and bonds than on stocks as a source of external finance?

Answered on page 301

determined by such factors as how much money you owe, how many credit cards you have, and whether you make your payments on time. In contrast, fintech firms often use sophisticated software to analyze much different data in assessing your creditworthiness. For instance, ZestFinance looks at data such as how you fill out forms. ZestFinance's analysis indicates that people who fill out forms using all capital letters are more likely to miss a loan payment. SoFi believes a borrower's education should be given a greater weight in measuring creditworthiness; this company's data analysis shows that although many young college graduates don't have a long credit history, they are still very likely to make their loan payments on time.

You may also be able to obtain financing through *crowdfunding* sites, where you can raise small amounts of money from large numbers of people. In 2012, Congress passed the Jumpstart Our Business Startups Act (JOBS Act) to help make it easier for small businesses to obtain funding. Until 2016, under federal regulations, only wealthy investors could make equity investments in firms that had not gone through a formal initial public offering (IPO). In May 2016, when revised regulations went into effect, investors with incomes or net worth of less than $100,000 can buy up to $2,000 in equity in startups through online crowdfunding sites, and investors with incomes or net worth greater than $100,000 can invest more. One complication of funding your business this way is that each investor becomes part owner of your firm and is entitled to detailed information about it.

On balance, fintech and crowdsourcing are good news if you are an entrepreneur. But are they necessarily good news if you are a small investor? Traditionally, small investors have preferred to put their savings in banks or mutual funds to avoid the problem of *asymmetric information* in financial markets. Asymmetric information refers to a situation in which one party to an economic transaction has more information than the other party. In the case of crowdfunding, the startups raising funds will know much more about how likely they are to be successful than will small investors. Investors frequently face very high transactions costs in gathering enough information to distinguish firms that are likely to be successful from those that aren't. As a result, small investors have traditionally preferred depositing their savings in banks or buying mutual fund shares to making investments directly in firms. As one government regulator cautioned investors about crowdfunding: "These are companies that are new or close to brand new and are speculative. You don't want to invest more in any one company than you can afford to lose."

If you are a small investor, you might be searching for ways to earn higher returns than those available on bank CDs or money market mutual funds. Crowdfunding sites may provide a way for you to earn high returns—or a way to suffer significant losses.

Sources: Margaret Collins and Charles Stein, "The Vanguard Cyborg Takeover," bloomberg.com, March 24, 2016; Telis Demos and Deepa Seetharaman, "Facebook Isn't So Good at Judging Your Credit After All," *Wall Street Journal*, February 24, 2016; and Ruth Simon, "New Rules Give Startups Access to Main Street Investors, *Wall Street Journal*, May 11, 2016.

In earlier chapters, we have examined financial markets, including the markets for bonds, stocks, derivatives, and foreign exchange. We now begin to analyze the other part of the financial system: financial intermediaries. In this chapter, we step back from looking at the specifics of financial markets and financial intermediaries to consider the broader question of what determines the structure of the financial system. We look at the economic factors that have led households, nonfinancial firms, and financial firms to make the choices that have resulted in the current financial structure.

9.1 The Financial System and Economic Performance

LEARNING OBJECTIVE: Evaluate the reasons economists believe economic performance depends on the financial system.

As you learned in your principles of economics course, there are many factors that determine whether a country's economy can provide a high standard of living for its residents and whether that standard of living can increase over time. These factors include (1) the ability of the country's businesses to accumulate machinery, computers, and other physical capital; (2) the ability of businesses to adopt the latest technology; and (3) the ability of the country's government to provide a legal framework that protects property rights and enforces contracts.

In addition to these factors, many economists believe that developing a strong financial system can be essential to providing a foundation for a country to experience the robust economic growth required for a rising standard of living. The United States provides a good example. Richard Sylla, an economist at New York University, has argued that a series of decisions Treasury Secretary Alexander Hamilton made in the early years of George Washington's administration in the 1790s helped the United States develop a modern financial system. During the American Revolution, both the Continental Congress and the state governments had issued bonds they eventually stopped making payments on. The new federal government took responsibility for paying off these bonds—some of which were held by Europeans—thereby establishing the credit of the United States. As a result, investors in both the United States and Europe were reassured that in the future they could buy bonds with a reduced risk of default. As the bond market expanded, it became easier for the state and federal governments and for private businesses to raise funds by selling bonds.

Congress also chartered a central bank by establishing the Bank of the United States in 1791 (although we will see in Chapter 13 that the bank eventually ran into political difficulties). The bank was set up as a private corporation with stock sold to the general public. The bank had branches in several states, which made loans more widely available to businesses and motivated state governments to allow other private banks to be established.

Stock and bond markets were established in New York, Boston, and Philadelphia. Initially, the securities traded in these financial markets were primarily stock issued by the Bank of the United States and government bonds. But once these financial markets were organized, they provided other corporations with a way to raise funds and investors with a way to participate in the growth of the economy by buying part ownership of corporations.

Sylla argues that the early development of a modern financial system helps explain the rapid growth of the U.S. economy during the 1800s because the financial system provided a way for funds to flow from savers to entrepreneurs establishing and expanding businesses. During the 1800s, the United States experienced significantly higher growth rates than did other countries that, like the United States, had also experienced substantial European immigration, such as Australia, New Zealand, Canada, and the countries of Latin America.[1]

The connection between how developed a country's financial system is and the performance of the country's economy remains strong today. The World Bank is an international organization with the mission of promoting economic development. One measure this organization uses to evaluate a country's financial development is the total amount of credit banks and financial markets extend to households and firms as a percentage of GDP. Real GDP per capita is the best measure economists have of how successful a country is in providing a high standard of living to its residents. Figure 9.1 measures financial development on the horizontal axis and real GDP per capita on the vertical axis. The figure shows that although the relationship between financial development and economic performance is not exact, for the most part, the countries with limited financial development, such as Iraq, also have low levels of real GDP per capita, while countries with high levels of financial development, such as the United States and Japan, have high levels of real GDP per capita. Countries such as China and Vietnam that have lower levels of real

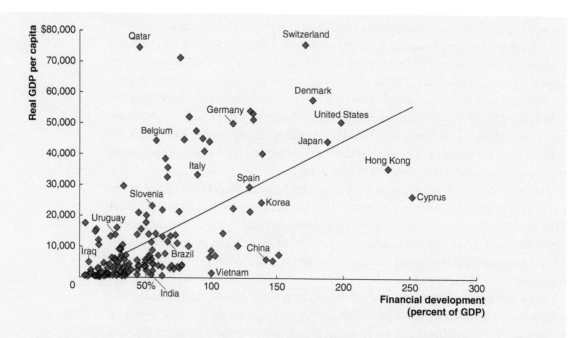

FIGURE 9.1 The Relationship Between Financial Development and Real GDP per Capita

The World Bank measures financial development by the total amount of credit banks and financial markets extend to households and firms as a percentage of GDP. Although the relationship is not exact, countries with higher levels of financial development tend to have higher levels of real GDP per capita, which indicates

they are better able to provide a higher standard of living for their residents.

Note: Data are for 2014.

Source: The World Bank, *World Development Indicators*.

---

[1] Richard Sylla, "Financial Foundations: Public Credit, the National Bank, and Securities Markets," in Douglas A. Irwin and Richard Sylla, eds., *Founding Choices: American Economic Policy in the 1790s*, Chicago: University of Chicago Press, 2011.

GDP per capita than might be expected from their levels of financial development have only recently begun to modernize their economies. High levels of financial development help firms in these countries acquire the funds they need to expand, so the countries' levels of real GDP per capita are likely to rise.

Having a developed financial system is not the only reason some countries are more successful economically than others, but many economists believe that the lack of a developed financial system makes it difficult for a country to have a high standard of living. In this chapter, we look further at how the financial system can enable prosperity and consider the role of asymmetric information and transactions costs on the structure of the financial system. At the end of the chapter, we highlight certain key facts about the U.S. financial system.

9.2 Transactions Costs, Adverse Selection, and Moral Hazard

LEARNING OBJECTIVE: Analyze the problems that transactions costs, adverse selection, and moral hazard pose for the financial system.

Some people have funds to lend, and some people would like to borrow funds. Bringing them together is a key role of the financial system. Bringing together savers and borrowers to make a deal—lending money—that can benefit both parties seems like a simple task. But as we have already seen in previous chapters, the financial system can be complex. Why the complexity? We can begin to answer this question by considering obstacles that make it difficult for savers to find borrowers they are willing to lend to and for borrowers to find savers who are willing to make loans.

The Problems Facing Small Investors

Suppose that you have saved $500, and you want to invest it. Should you invest in stocks? A stockbroker will tell you that the commissions you must pay will be large relative to the size of your purchases because you are investing a small amount of money. This cost will be particularly high if you are attempting to diversify by buying a few shares each of different stocks. Should you turn instead to the bond market to buy, say, a bond issued by Microsoft? Unfortunately, with the bond having a face value of $1,000, you lack the money to buy even one bond.

Having had no luck with financial markets, you look for another way to invest your money. Conveniently, your roommate's cousin needs $500 to develop a new application (app) for the Apple iPhone. He offers to pay you a 10% interest rate if you loan him your $500 for one year. But you don't know whether he is actually any good at writing apps. If his app fails, you suspect that he won't pay you back. Maybe you should seek out other borrowers and see what they would use your money for. Then you discover another problem: Your friend who is in law school tells you that to draw up a contract spelling out the terms of the loan—and what rights you would have if the borrower doesn't pay you back—would probably cost $300, which is more than half the money you have to invest. After hearing this news, you decide to forget about investing your $500. This outcome is not just bad news for you but also for the app developer, who will likely face the same difficulty in trying to raise funds from other individual investors.

Transactions costs
The cost of a trade or a financial transaction; for example, the brokerage commission charged for buying or selling a financial asset.

Your difficulty investing $500 illustrates the concept of **transactions costs**, which are the costs of making a direct financial transaction, such as buying a stock or bond, or making a loan. In this example, the transactions costs would include the legal fees you would have to pay to draw up a contract with the borrower of your money and the time you spent trying to identify a profitable investment. This example also illustrates the concept of **information costs**, which are the costs that savers incur to determine the creditworthiness of borrowers and to monitor how they use the acquired funds. Because of transactions costs and information costs, savers receive a lower return on their investments and borrowers must pay more for the funds they borrow. As we have just seen, these costs can sometimes mean that funds are never lent or borrowed at all. Although transactions costs and information costs reduce the efficiency of the financial system, they also create a profit opportunity for individuals and firms that can discover ways to reduce those costs.

Information costs
The costs that savers incur to determine the creditworthiness of borrowers and to monitor how they use the funds acquired.

How Financial Intermediaries Reduce Transactions Costs

High transactions costs make individual savers unlikely to lend directly to borrowers. For the same reason, small to medium-sized firms that need to borrow money—or sell part ownership of the firm to raise funds—are unlikely to find individuals willing to invest in them. As a result, both small investors and small to medium-sized firms turn to financial intermediaries, such as commercial banks and mutual funds, to meet their financial needs. For example, many small investors buy shares in mutual funds such as the Schwab Total Stock Market Index Fund, which invests in a portfolio of stocks issued by more than 2,000 U.S. firms. While an investor with just $500 to invest would find it difficult to buy a diversified portfolio without incurring substantial transactions costs, mutual funds provide diversification with low transactions costs. Similarly, an investor could purchase a certificate of deposit from a commercial bank. The commercial bank could then use the funds to make loans to household and business borrowers.

How are banks, mutual funds, and other financial intermediaries able to reduce transactions costs sufficiently to meet the needs of savers and borrowers while still making a profit? Financial intermediaries take advantage of **economies of scale**, which refers to the reduction in average cost that results from an increase in the volume of a good or service produced. For example, the fees dealers in Treasury bonds charge investors to purchase $1 million worth of bonds are not much higher than the fees they charge to purchase $10,000 worth of bonds. By buying $500 worth of shares in a bond mutual fund that purchases millions of dollars' worth of bonds, an individual investor can take advantage of economies of scale.

Economies of scale
The reduction in average cost that results from an increase in the volume of a good or service produced.

Financial intermediaries can also take advantage of economies of scale in other ways. For example, because banks make many loans, they rely on standardized legal contracts, so the costs of writing the contracts are spread over many loans. Similarly, bank loan officers devote their time to evaluating and processing loans, and through this specialization, they are able to process loans efficiently, reducing the time required—and, therefore, the cost per loan. Financial intermediaries also take advantage of technology to provide financial services, such as those that automated teller machine networks provide. Financial intermediaries also increasingly rely on sophisticated software to evaluate the creditworthiness of loan applicants.

To understand how financial intermediaries can help reduce information costs, we need to consider the nature of information costs more closely. We do so in the next section.

The Problems of Adverse Selection and Moral Hazard

A key consideration for savers is the financial health of borrowers. Savers don't lend to borrowers who are unlikely to pay them back. Unfortunately for savers, borrowers in poor financial health have an incentive to disguise this fact. For example, a company selling bonds to investors may know that its sales are declining rapidly, and it is near bankruptcy, but the buyers of the bonds may lack this information. **Asymmetric information** describes the situation in which one party to an economic transaction has better information than does the other party. In financial transactions, typically the borrower has more information than does the lender.

Economists distinguish between two problems arising from asymmetric information:

1. **Adverse selection** is the problem investors experience in distinguishing low-risk borrowers from high-risk borrowers before making an investment.
2. **Moral hazard** is the problem investors experience in verifying that borrowers are using their funds as intended.

Sometimes an investor will consider the costs arising from asymmetric information to be so great that the investor will lend only to borrowers who are transparently low risk, such as the federal government. However, more generally, there are practical solutions to the problems of asymmetric information, in which financial markets or financial intermediaries lower the cost of information needed to make investment decisions.

Adverse Selection

George Akerlof, of the University of California, Berkeley, was the first economist to analyze the problem of adverse selection. He did so in the context of the used car market. He was awarded the Nobel Prize in Economics in 2001 for his research into the economics of information. Akerlof noted that the seller of a used car will always have more information on the true condition of a car than will a potential buyer. A buyer might not realize that a car he is considering buying is a "lemon"—a car that has been poorly maintained by, for instance, not having its oil changed regularly. The prices that potential buyers are willing to pay for used cars will reflect the buyers' lack of complete information on the true condition of the cars.

Consider a simple example: Suppose that the used car market consists only of individual buyers and sellers; that is, there are no used car dealers. Suppose that you are in the market for a used 2014 Subaru WRX and that while you and other buyers would be willing to pay $20,000 for a good, well-maintained car, you will pay only $12,000 for a lemon. Unfortunately, you cannot tell the lemons from the good cars, but you have read an online report that indicates that about 75% of used 2014 Subarus are well maintained, while the other 25% are lemons. Recall from Chapter 4 that the *expected return* on an investment is calculated by adding up the probability of each event occurring

Asymmetric information
The situation in which one party to an economic transaction has better information than does the other party.

Adverse selection
The problem investors experience in distinguishing low-risk borrowers from high-risk borrowers before making an investment.

Moral hazard The risk that people will take actions after they have entered into a transaction that will make the other party worse off.

multiplied by the value of each event. In this case, we can calculate the *expected value* to you of a 2014 Subaru that you choose randomly from among those available for sale:

$$\text{Expected value} = (\text{Probability car is good}) \times (\text{Value if good})$$
$$+ (\text{Probability car is a lemon}) \times (\text{Value if a lemon}).$$

Or,

$$\text{Expected value} = (0.75 \times \$20,000) + (0.25 \times \$12,000) = \$18,000.$$

It seems reasonable for you to be willing to pay a price for a 2014 Subaru equal to the expected value of $18,000. Unfortunately, you are likely to run into a major problem: From your perspective, given that you don't know whether any particular car offered for sale is a good car or a lemon, an offer of $18,000 seems reasonable. But the sellers *do* know whether they are selling good cars or lemons. To a seller of a good car, an offer of $18,000 is $2,000 below the true value of the car, and the seller will be reluctant to sell. But to a seller of a lemon, an offer of $18,000 is $6,000 *above* the value of the car, and the seller will be happy to sell. Because sellers of lemons take advantage of knowing more about the cars they are selling than buyers do, the used car market is subject to adverse selection: Most used cars offered for sale will be lemons. In other words, because of asymmetric information, the used car market has adversely selected the cars that will be offered for sale. Notice as well that the problem of adverse selection reduces the total quantity of used cars bought and sold in the market because few good cars are offered for sale. From Akerlof's analysis of adverse selection in the used car market, we can conclude that information problems reduce economic efficiency in a market.

There are aspects of the actual used car market that reduce—but don't eliminate—the degree of adverse selection when compared with a market composed only of individual buyers and sellers. To reduce the costs of adverse selection, car dealers act as intermediaries between buyers and sellers. To maintain their reputations with buyers, dealers are less willing to take advantage of private information about the quality of the used cars they sell than are individual sellers, who will probably sell at most a handful of used cars during their lifetimes. As a result, dealers sell both lemons and good cars at close to their true values. In addition, government regulations require that car dealers disclose information about the cars to consumers.

"Lemons Problems" in Financial Markets   How do adverse selection problems affect the ability of stock and bond markets to channel funds from savers to investors? First, consider the stock market. Take a simple example, similar to the one we just used for the automobile market. Suppose that there are good, profitable firms and bad, currently unprofitable, or lemon, firms. The firms are aware of whether they are good or lemons, but on the basis of available information, potential investors cannot tell the difference. As we saw in Chapter 6, the fundamental value of a share of stock should be equal to the present value of all the dividends an investor expects to receive into the indefinite future. Suppose that given your expectations of future dividends to be paid, you believe the value of the stock issued by a good firm is $50 per share but the value of stock issued by a lemon firm is only $5 per share (based on the expectation that the firm will eventually become profitable). You are convinced from your reading of the *Wall Street Journal* and other financial web sites that 90% of firms offering stock for sale are good firms and 10% are lemon firms, but you lack the information to determine whether any particular firm is a good firm or a lemon firm.

You can use these assumptions to calculate the expected value to you of a share of stock issued by a randomly chosen firm among all the firms offering to sell stock:

$$\text{Expected value} = (0.90 \times \$50) + (0.10 \times \$5) = \$45.50.$$

So, you would be willing to pay \$45.50 for a share of stock, but to a good firm, this price is below the fundamental value of the stock. To sell shares at that low a price would be to sell part ownership of the firm—which is what shares of stock represent—for less than its true value. Therefore, good firms will be reluctant to sell stock at this price. Lemon firms, though, will be very willing to sell stock at this price because it is well above the true value of their shares. As lemon firms take advantage of knowing more about the true value of their firms than investors do, the stock market, like the used car market, is subject to adverse selection.

One of the consequences of adverse selection in the stock market is that many small to medium-sized firms will be unable or unwilling to issue stock. These firms will be unable to find investors willing to buy their shares—because the investors will be afraid of buying stock in what may turn out to be a lemon firm—or the firms will be unwilling to sell shares for far below their fundamental value. As a result, in the United States, only about 5,100 firms are *publicly traded*, which means that they are able to sell stock on stock markets. These firms are large enough that investors can easily find information about their financial health from sources such as reports by Wall Street analysts and articles by financial journalists. This information helps investors overcome the adverse selection problem.

Adverse selection is present in the bond market as well. Just as investors are reluctant to buy the stock of firms when the investors are unsure whether the firms are good firms or lemons, they are also reluctant to lend money to firms by buying their bonds. Because the risk in lending to lemon firms is greater than the risk in lending to good firms, if investors had complete information on the financial health of every firm, they would be willing to lend money to good firms at a low interest rate and lend money to lemon firms at a high interest rate. Because of asymmetric information, though, investors are often reluctant to make any loans at high interest rates. Investors often reason that as interest rates on bonds rise, a larger fraction of the firms willing to pay the high interest rates are lemon firms. After all, the managers of a firm facing bankruptcy may be willing to pay very high interest rates to borrow funds that can be used to finance risky investments. If the investments do not succeed, the managers are no worse off than they were before: The firm will still be facing bankruptcy. Investors who bought the bonds, however, will be considerably worse off than if they had put their funds in a less risky investment. In other words, as interest rates rise, the creditworthiness of potential borrowers is likely to deteriorate, making the adverse selection problem worse. Because investors realize this problem, they are likely to reduce the number of loans they are willing to make rather than to raise interest rates to the level at which the quantity of funds demanded and supplied are equal. This restriction of lending is known as

Credit rationing The restriction of credit by lenders such that borrowers cannot obtain the funds they desire at the given interest rate.

credit rationing. When lenders ration credit, firms—whether they are good firms or lemons—may have difficulty borrowing funds.

To summarize, in the market for used cars, adverse selection causes bad cars to push good cars from the market. In the stock market, adverse selection makes it difficult for any but the largest firms to sell stocks. And in the bond market, adverse selection leads to credit rationing.

Adverse selection is costly for the economy. When investors have difficulty obtaining information on good firms, the cost to those firms of raising funds increases. This situation forces many firms to grow primarily by investing *internal funds*, which are profits the firms have earned or funds raised from the owners of the firm. Since 1945, U.S. firms have raised more than two-thirds of the funds they need internally. Adverse selection problems are most likely to restrict opportunities for growth in younger firms in dynamic, emerging sectors of the economy, such as software and biotechnology, because with these firms investors have particular difficulty in distinguishing the good firms from the lemons.

Attempts to Reduce Adverse Selection   Financial market participants and the government have taken steps to try to reduce problems of adverse selection in financial markets. Following the great stock market crash of October 1929, it became clear that many firms selling stock on the New York Stock Exchange had not disclosed to investors crucial information on the firms' financial health or had actively misled investors about the firms' true condition. In response, in 1934, Congress established the Securities and Exchange Commission (SEC) to regulate the stock and bond markets. The SEC requires that publicly traded firms report their performance in financial statements, such as balance sheets, which show the value of a firm's assets, liabilities, and stockholders' equity (the difference between the value of the firm's assets and the value of its liabilities), and income statements, which show a firm's revenue, costs, and profit. Firms must prepare these statements using standard accounting methods. In addition, firms must disclose *material information*, which is information that, if known, would likely affect the price of a firm's stock.

The disclosure of information required by the SEC reduces the information costs of adverse selection, but it doesn't eliminate them for four key reasons:

1. Some good firms may be too young to have much information for potential investors to evaluate.
2. Lemon firms will try to present the information in the best possible light so that investors will overvalue their securities.
3. There can be legitimate differences of opinion about how to report some items on income statements and balance sheets. For example, during the financial crisis of 2007–2009, many banks and other financial firms had on their balance sheets assets, such as loans and mortgage-backed securities, that had become illiquid. The markets for these assets "seized up," meaning that little or no buying and selling was occurring. In that situation, investors had difficulty discovering the true prices of the assets by reading these firms' balance sheets.
4. The interpretation of whether information is material can be tricky. For example, some investors criticized Apple for not fully disclosing the extent of CEO Steve

Jobs's health problems in the years before he died. Although representatives of Apple argued that Jobs's health problems were a private matter, some investors believe that the company should have fully disclosed the problems because they could have affected the future profitability of the firm and, therefore, its stock price.

Private firms have tried to reduce the costs of adverse selection by collecting information on firms and selling that information to investors. As long as the firms gathering information do a good job, savers purchasing it will be better able to judge the quality of borrowers, improving the efficiency of lending. Although investors pay for the information, they can still benefit if it enables them to earn higher returns. Firms such as Moody's Investors Service, Standard & Poor's, Value Line, and Dun & Bradstreet specialize in collecting information from a variety of sources, including firms' income statements, balance sheets, interviews with firms' managers, and inspection of firms' offices or factories. These firms then sell this information to subscribers, including individual investors, libraries, and financial intermediaries. Some of these publications are available online.

Private information-gathering firms can help minimize the cost of adverse selection, but they can't eliminate it. Although only subscribers pay for the information collected, others can benefit without paying for it. Individuals who gain access to the information without paying for it are *free riders*. That is, they obtain the same benefits as those paying for the information, without incurring the costs. It's easy to photocopy and distribute the reports that private information-gathering firms prepare—or to scan them and post them on the Internet—so there may be many free riders for every paid subscriber. Because, in effect, private information-gathering firms end up providing their services to many investors for free, they are unable to collect as much information as they would if they didn't have to face the free-rider problem. As we saw in Chapter 5, in rating bonds, free rider problems forced Moody's and Standard & Poor's to shift from a business model that involved charging investors for information on the creditworthiness of firms issuing bonds to charging the issuing firms.

How Collateral and Net Worth Reduce Adverse Selection Problems The disclosure of information, either directly as a result of government regulation or indirectly as a result of the efforts of private information-gathering firms, diminishes but does not eliminate adverse selection. As a result, lenders often rely on financial contracts that are designed to help reduce adverse selection problems. If the owners of a firm have invested little of their own money in their firm, they don't have much to lose if they default on bonds or fail to pay back loans. To make it more costly for firms to take advantage of their asymmetric information, lenders often require borrowers to pledge some of their assets as **collateral**, which the lender claims if the borrower defaults. For example, a firm that owns a warehouse may have to pledge the warehouse as collateral when issuing a bond. If the firm fails to make the coupon payments on the bond, investors can seize the warehouse and sell it to cover their losses on the bond. Only very large, well-known firms, such as Microsoft and General Electric, are able to sell *debentures*, which are bonds issued without specific collateral.

Net worth, which is the difference between the value of a firm's assets and the value of its liabilities, provides the same assurance to lenders as does collateral. When

Collateral Assets that a borrower pledges to a lender that the lender may seize if the borrower defaults on the loan.

Net worth The difference between the value of a firm's assets and the value of its liabilities.

a firm's net worth is high, the firm's managers have more to lose by using borrowed money for high-risk investments. The managers of a firm with low net worth, on the other hand, have less to lose. Therefore, investors often reduce the chance of adverse selection by restricting their lending to high-net-worth firms.

In the end, though, the costs of adverse selection make it difficult for many firms to raise funds on financial markets. These costs are another reason, in addition to high transactions costs, why many firms turn to banks and other financial intermediaries when they need external finance.

How Financial Intermediaries Reduce Adverse Selection Problems Financial intermediaries, particularly banks, specialize in gathering information about the default risk of borrowers. Banks know from long experience which characteristics of borrowers— both households and firms—are likely to be good predictors of default risk. Some of the information that banks rely on is widely available to any financial institution. This information includes credit reports and the FICO credit score, compiled by the firm now called FICO and formerly called Fair Isaac. But individual banks also have access to information on particular borrowers that is not generally available. The ability of banks to assess credit risks on the basis of private information about borrowers is called **relationship banking**. For example, a local bank may have been making loans to a local car dealership over a period of years, so the bank will have gathered information on the creditworthiness of the dealership that other potential lenders would have difficulty acquiring.

Relationship banking The ability of banks to assess credit risks on the basis of private information about borrowers.

Banks raise funds from depositors, and, using their superior information on borrowers' creditworthiness, they lend the deposits to borrowers who represent good risks. Because banks are better able than individual savers to distinguish good borrowers from lemon borrowers, banks can earn a profit by charging a higher interest rate on loans than they pay to depositors. Depositors are willing to accept a lower interest rate because they know that transactions costs and information problems make it difficult for them to lend their funds directly to borrowers.

Banks can profit from their private information about borrowers because under relationship banking, they hold many of the loans they make. So, investors have a difficult time making a profit by making similar loans. Banks can profit from gathering information on local businesses and households because it is difficult for other investors to compete with them for this loan business. The information advantage banks gain from relationship banking allows them to reduce the costs of adverse selection and helps explain the key role banks play in providing external financing to firms.

MAKING THE CONNECTION

Has Securitization Increased Adverse Selection Problems?

The financial crisis of 2007–2009 emphasized the important role that securitization had come to play in the economy. *Securitization* involves bundling loans, such as mortgages, into securities that can be sold on financial markets. Some economists believe that the increase in securitization over the past 20 years may have led to an increase in adverse selection. As we have seen, with relationship banking, banks have an incentive to acquire information about potential borrowers and to use that information to make loans to households and firms. With relationship banking, banks earn a profit based on the difference between the interest rates they pay depositors and the interest rates they earn on loans, most of which they hold until maturity.

Securitization changes the focus of banks from relationship banking to the *originate-to-distribute* business model. With this model, banks still grant loans, but rather than hold them to maturity, banks either securitize the loans or sell them to other financial firms or to government agencies to be securitized. In either case, the banks hold the loans for a brief period rather than holding them to maturity. With the originate-to-distribute model, banks earn a profit from fees they receive from originating the loans and from fees they charge to process the loan payments that they receive from borrowers and pass on to the holders of the securities.

Some economists and policymakers argue that the originate-to-distribute model has reduced banks' incentive to distinguish between good borrowers and lemon borrowers. In other words, the model has reduced banks' incentive to reduce adverse selection. Once a loan has been securitized, if the borrower defaults, the owner of the security, rather than the bank that originated the loan, suffers most of the loss. In addition, some economists have argued that banks may use their information advantage to sell off the riskier loans while retaining the less risky loans for their own portfolios. It can be difficult for an investor purchasing securitized loans to evaluate the riskiness of loans included in the securities. Rating agencies, such as Moody's and Standard & Poor's, provide ratings for the securities, but the agencies also have less information about the riskiness of the loans contained in the securities than do the banks that originated the loans. Securitization provides certain advantages to the financial system: It allows increased risk sharing, it increases liquidity in loan markets, it reduces the interest rates borrowers pay on loans, and it allows investors to diversify their investment portfolios. The disadvantage of securitization is that it may inadvertently increase adverse selection problems.

Antje Berndt, of Carnegie Mellon University, and Anurag Gupta, of Case Western Reserve University, have studied the effects of the originate-to-distribute model on adverse selection. They examined loans banks made to corporations during the period from the beginning of 2000 through the end of 2004. They found that corporations whose bank loans ended up being securitized were significantly less profitable over the three-year period following the sale of their loans than were corporations whose bank loans were not sold or corporations that did not borrow funds from banks. Berndt and Gupta's results indicate that either banks were less careful in making loans that they intended to securitize or that they were more likely to sell loans that they had granted to less profitable firms.

In the Wall Street Reform and Consumer Protection Act, or Dodd-Frank Act, passed in 2010, Congress addressed the possibility that securitization has increased adverse selection in the financial system. The bill originally contained a *risk retention regulation* that required banks and other financial firms that sold mortgage-backed securities containing riskier mortgages to retain at least 5% of the total securities issued. However, in the end, federal regulators decided that this regulation was likely to substantially reduce mortgage lending, and the requirement was dropped. In December 2016, regulators did begin requiring sellers of collateralized loan obligations (CLOs), which are instruments that securitize riskier business loans, to retain at least 5% of the securities. Economists and policymakers continue to debate whether risk retention regulations are an effective means of dealing with adverse selection problems in securitized lending.

Sources: Antje Berndt and Anurag Gupta, "Moral Hazard and Adverse Selection in the Originate-to-Distribute Model of Bank Credit," *Journal of Monetary Economics*, July 2009, Vol. 56, No. 5, pp. 725–743; Floyd Norris, "Banks Again Avoid Having Any Skin in the Game," *New York Times*, October 23, 2014; and Carol J. Clouse, "Managers Untangle New Risk Retention Regulations for CLOs," institutionalinvestor.com, July 9, 2015.

See related problem 2.12 at the end of the chapter.

SOLVED PROBLEM 9.2

Why Do Banks Ration Credit to Households and Small Businesses?

In 2016, a business economist predicted that government regulations intended to increase the stability of the banking system would also raise the cost to banks of making loans. The rising cost of making loans would result in some "households and companies [being] effectively rationed out of credit markets."

a. If banks experience higher costs of making loans, why wouldn't they just charge a higher interest rate to compensate for the higher costs?

b. Why don't firms that are having trouble getting bank loans raise funds by selling bonds instead?

Source: Richard Barwell, "The Big Question in Banking Regulation," *Wall Street Journal*, March 15, 2016.

Solving the Problem

Step 1 **Review the chapter material.** This problem is about adverse selection and credit rationing, so you may want to review the section "Adverse Selection," which begins on page 283.

Step 2 **Answer part (a) by explaining how raising interest rates on loans can increase adverse selection problems for banks.** We've seen that lenders can be reluctant to increase the interest rates they charge borrowers because high interest rates may attract less creditworthy borrowers. That is, higher interest rates may increase adverse selection. Although banks specialize in gathering information on borrowers, they still know less about the true financial state of borrowers than do the borrowers. A small business that is close to declaring bankruptcy may see a bank loan as a financial lifeline and be less concerned about having to pay a high interest rate than would a borrower in better financial health. So, if banks experience higher costs in making loans, they may decide to engage in credit rationing by refusing to make loans to some borrowers rather than raising interest rates. This is the outcome the business economist quoted at the start of this Solved Problem predicted.

Step 3 **Answer part (b) by discussing why firms that are unable to get bank loans don't raise funds by selling bonds instead.** As we've seen in this section, adverse selection problems make it difficult for all but very large firms to raise funds by selling bonds.

See related problem 2.13 at the end of the chapter.

Moral Hazard

Even after a lender has gathered information on whether a borrower is a good borrower or a lemon borrower, the lender's information problems haven't ended. There is still a possibility that after a lender makes a loan to what appears to be a good borrower, the borrower will not use the funds as intended. This situation, known as *moral hazard*, is more likely to occur when the borrower has an incentive to conceal information or to act in a way that does not coincide with the lender's interests. Moral hazard arises because of asymmetric information: The borrower knows more than the lender does about how the borrowed funds will actually be used.

Moral Hazard in the Stock Market If you buy a firm's stock, you hope that the firm's management maximizes profit so that the value of your investment will increase. Unfortunately, monitoring whether the firm's management is actually maximizing profit is extremely difficult for an individual investor, which causes a significant moral hazard problem. When you buy stock Microsoft has newly issued, you can't tell whether the firm will spend your money wisely on research and development of a new version of Windows or fritter it away on gold faucets in the new executive restroom. The investment in research and development is likely to increase Microsoft's profit and your returns, while the gold faucets are not.

The organization of large, publicly traded corporations results in a *separation of ownership from control*. That is, legally, shareholders own the firm, but the firm is actually run by its top management, including the chief executive officer (CEO), the chief operating officer (COO), and the chief financial officer (CFO). In most large corporations, the top managers own only a small fraction of the firm's stock, typically less than 5%. Although the shareholders want the managers to run the firm so as to maximize the value of the shareholders' investment, the managers may have other objectives. Some top managers are accused of being "empire builders" who are interested in making the firm as large as possible through growth and the acquisition of other firms, even if the firm would be more profitable if it were smaller. Other top managers seem more concerned with using corporate jets and holding meetings in expensive vacation spots than with the firm's profit. Economists refer to the possibility that managers will pursue objectives different from those of shareholders as a **principal–agent problem**. The shareholders, as owners of the firm, are the *principals*, while the top managers, who are hired to carry out the owner's wishes, are the *agents*.

Managers even have an incentive to underreport their firms' profits so that they can reduce the dividends they owe to shareholders and retain the use of the funds. Problems of underreporting are reduced to some extent because the SEC requires

Principal–agent problem
The moral hazard problem of managers (the agents) pursuing their own interests rather than those of shareholders (the principals).

managers to issue financial statements prepared according to generally accepted accounting principles. Federal laws have made misreporting or stealing profit belonging to shareholders a federal offense, punishable by large fines or prison terms, or both. Continuing examples of the SEC bringing court cases against top managers who misstate the true financial state of firms show that fines and prison terms have not been complete deterrents.

Investors elect boards of directors to represent them in controlling corporations. Unfortunately, boards of directors are not a full solution to the problem of moral hazard in stock investing. First, boards of directors typically meet infrequently—often only four times per year—and generally rely on information provided to them by top management. Even highly motivated and skeptical boards of directors cannot hope to know as much about the firm as do the top managers. Therefore, it is often difficult for members of a board of directors to decide whether managers are acting in the best interests of shareholders. Boards of directors cannot use profitability as the sole measure of the performance of top managers because factors other than the efforts of the managers determine a firm's profitability. For instance, a recession may cause a firm to suffer losses that managers could do nothing to avoid. Second, boards of directors are not always independent of top managers. In fact, in some corporations, the firm's CEO also serves as chair of the board of directors. In addition, even though shareholders elect the members, many shareholders pay little attention to these elections, and CEOs can sometimes succeed in placing candidates favorable to them on the ballots. Some boards of directors include CEOs of other firms who are suppliers to the corporation. These board members may be reluctant to disagree with the CEO, for fear that he or she will retaliate by canceling their contracts. In recent years, the increased role of institutional investors, such as pension funds, in the election of boards of directors has helped to reduce moral hazard problems. For example, the California Public Employees' Retirement System (CalPERS) has a director of corporate governance who works to ensure that the pension fund invests in corporations that respect the interests of shareholders. Nevertheless, most economists believe that corporate boards of directors can reduce but not eliminate the moral hazard problem.

Some boards of directors have attempted to reduce moral hazard by using *incentive contracts* to better align the goals of top managers with the goals of shareholders. With some incentive contracts, part of a manager's compensation is tied to the performance of the firm. For example, a CEO may receive his or her full compensation only if the firm meets certain profit targets. Other incentive contracts provide top managers with options contracts. The options allow the managers to buy the firm's stock at a price above the market price on the day when the options were granted. The options give managers an incentive to make the firm more profitable, which will raise the price of the firm's stock and make the options more valuable. Although incentive contracts can reduce moral hazard, they can at times also increase it by leading managers to make decisions that are not in the best interests of shareholders. For instance, if top managers have their compensation tied to the firm's profit, they may undertake risky investments that will increase the firm's short-term profit but jeopardize the firm's long-term prospects.

Some economists have argued that top managers at some financial firms made riskier investments than they otherwise would have during the years leading up to the financial crisis because some of their compensation depended on the short-run profit of their firms. Similar problems exist when boards of directors provide top managers with stock options. During the 2000s, top managers at several firms were caught backdating their stock options contracts. Rather than having the contracts reflect the price of the firm's stock on the day the options were granted, the managers manipulated the contracts to appear to have been granted on an earlier date, when the firm's stock price had been much lower. As a result, the managers were able to earn substantial sums from the options even if the firm's stock price had not increased from the date the options were actually granted. The SEC considers backdating fraud, so several executives who engaged in this practice were convicted and sent to prison.

Moral Hazard in the Bond Market There is less moral hazard in the bond market than in the stock market. When you buy a share of stock, you are relying on the firm's top management to maximize profit. Whether they do is difficult for both you and the board of directors to verify. However, when you buy a bond, you only need the firm's top management to make the coupon payments and a final principal payment when the bond matures. Whether the managers are maximizing profit doesn't concern you. In other words, the cost of monitoring the firm's management is much lower for an investor who is a bondholder than for an investor who is a stockholder.

Even though investors are subject to less moral hazard when buying bonds than when buying stocks, buying bonds isn't entirely free from this problem. Because a bond allows a firm to keep any profit that exceeds the fixed payments due on the bond, the firm's managers have an incentive to assume more risk to earn this profit than is in the best interest of the bond investor. For example, suppose that you and other investors buy bonds issued by a software firm that has been successful in writing apps for the Apple iPhone. You expect that the firms will use the funds to develop new apps. Instead, the firm's management decides to use the funds on a much riskier venture—to develop a new smartphone to compete with the iPhone. In the likely event that the new phone fails to successfully compete with the iPhone, the firm will be forced into bankruptcy and won't be able to make the payments it promised you.

A key way investors try to reduce moral hazard in bond markets is by writing *restrictive covenants* into bond contracts. **Restrictive covenants** either place limits on the uses of the funds the borrower receives or require that the borrower pay off the bond if the borrower's net worth drops below a certain level. As an example of the first type of restrictive covenant, a firm might be restricted to using the funds from a bond issue to buy a warehouse or factory building. The purpose of restrictive covenants of the second type is to keep a firm's managers from taking on too much risk. The managers know that if they suffer losses on risky investments, the firm's net worth might drop below the level that would trigger the covenant. Having to pay off a bond issue possibly years before it would mature may be difficult for the firm and might cause the board of directors to question the competence of the managers.

> **Restrictive covenant** A clause in a bond contract that places limits on the uses of funds that a borrower receives.

Although restrictive covenants can reduce risk, they have the drawback of making bonds more complicated and possibly reducing the ease with which investors can sell them on secondary markets. The cost of monitoring whether firms actually are complying with restrictive covenants further hampers a bond's marketability and liquidity. And restrictive covenants can't be detailed enough to protect lenders against every possible risky activity in which the borrower might engage.

How Financial Intermediaries Reduce Moral Hazard Problems Just as financial intermediaries play an important role in reducing the extent of adverse selection in the financial system, they also play an important role in reducing moral hazard. Commercial banks specialize in monitoring borrowers and have developed effective techniques for ensuring that the funds they loan are actually used for their intended purpose. For instance, when you take out a loan to buy a car, a bank will often provide the funds by giving you a check made out to the car dealer rather than to you. Similarly, if the owner of a pizza parlor takes out a loan to enlarge her building, the bank is likely to release the funds in stages, requiring the owner to provide proof that each phase of the construction has been completed. Bank loans often contain restrictive covenants. For example, if you take out a loan to buy a new car, the bank will require you to carry a minimum amount of insurance against theft or collision damage, and the insurance policy will usually be written so that both the bank's name and your name will appear on the check you receive from the insurance company following an accident. If you take out a mortgage loan to buy a house, you will have to carry insurance on the house, and you can't sell the house without first repaying your mortgage loan.

In some countries, banks have an additional tool for overcoming moral hazard when providing funds to firms. For instance, in Germany, a bank such as Deutsche Bank can buy stock in a firm and place its employees on the firm's board of directors. This step gives a bank greater access to information and makes monitoring the behavior of managers easier. In the United States, however, federal regulations bar banks from buying stock—that is, making *equity investments*—in nonfinancial firms.

Other financial intermediaries have evolved to fill the gap in the financial system left by the legal ban on banks making equity investments in nonfinancial firms. **Venture capital firms**, such as Kleiner Perkins Caufield & Byers or Andreessen Horowitz, raise funds from investors and invest in small startup firms, often in high-technology industries. In recent years, venture capital firms have raised large amounts from institutional investors, such as pension funds and university endowments. A venture capital firm frequently takes a large ownership stake in a startup firm, often placing its own employees on the board of directors or even having them serve as managers. These steps can reduce principal–agent problems because the venture capital firm has a greater ability to closely monitor the managers of the firm it's investing in. The firm's managers are likely to be attentive to the wishes of a large investor because having a large investor sell its stake in the firm may make it difficult to raise funds from new investors. In addition, a venture capital firm avoids the free-rider problem when investing in a firm that is not publicly traded because other investors cannot copy the venture capital firm's investment strategy.

Venture capital firms target young firms. **Private equity firms** (or **corporate restructuring firms**), such as Blackstone, Carlyle, or Kohlberg Kravis Roberts & Co. (KKR), in contrast, usually invest in mature firms. Typically, they target firms where the managers appear not to be maximizing profit. By taking positions on the board of directors, they can monitor top managers and attempt to get them to

Venture capital firm A firm that raises equity capital from investors to invest in startup firms.

Private equity firm (or corporate restructuring firm) A firm that raises equity capital to acquire shares in other firms to reduce free-rider and moral hazard problems.

follow new policies. In some cases, they will acquire a controlling interest in the firm and replace the top management. Research by Steven Davis of the University of Chicago and colleagues indicates that when a private equity firm takes control of a company, it is usually able to increase that firm's productivity significantly, often by closing the firm's less productive establishments—factories or stores—reallocating employees to the firm's more productive establishments, and opening new establishments.[2] Often after improving the performance of an acquired firm, a private equity firm will then sell the firm, making a profit from the increased value of the acquired firm's stock. Private equity firms have helped to establish a *market for corporate control*, which can reduce moral hazard problems in the financial system by providing a means to remove top management that is failing to carry out the wishes of shareholders.

MAKING THE CONNECTION | **IN YOUR INTEREST**

Is It Safe to Invest Through Crowdfunding Sites?

As we saw in the chapter opener, in 2016, new regulations implementing provisions of the federal JOBS Act made it easier for startup firms to use crowdfunding. If your income or your net worth is less than $100,000 per year, you can use crowdfunding sites, such as Indiegogo or NextSeed, to invest up to $2,000 (but not more than 5% of your income or net worth) per year in equity shares in a startup firm. If your income or net worth is greater than $100,000, you can invest up to 10% of your income or net worth per year. But should you? Does crowdfunding overcome the problems of transactions costs and asymmetric information that have traditionally kept many small investors from directly investing in firms?

As we saw earlier, prior to crowdfunding, if you wanted to invest $10,000 in a startup, you would likely incur substantial transactions costs locating a suitable firm and making sure that your investment was legally protected. By acting as financial intermediaries, these sites reduce transactions costs for investors by identifying firms and by ensuring that the investors' funds are invested in accordance with federal securities laws.

It's less clear, however, whether crowdfunding sites can overcome information asymmetries. These sites typically screen firms that request permission to solicit investors on their site. The track record of firms raising money on crowdfunding sites has been mixed, however. In addition, unlike venture capital firms, these sites usually do not themselves invest in the startups that raise funds on their sites. So, the crowdfunding sites do not reduce the principal–agent problem through close monitoring of the startup's managers the way a venture capital firm does. One proposal to reduce this moral hazard problem is to have these sites hire independent analysts who can provide investors with additional information on the firms that are applying for funding on the

---

[2] Steven J. Davis, et al., "Private Equity, Jobs, and Productivity," *American Economic Review*, Vol. 104, No. 12, December 2014, pp. 3956–3990.

sites. However, the owners of a firm applying for funding would still have more information about the firm's prospects than would the analyst evaluating the firm.

One way in which crowdfunding sites can reassure investors is by insuring the investors' funds against the possibility of the funded firm going bankrupt. In 2016, American International Group, the largest insurance company in the United States, began offering such insurance to crowdfunding sites.

Some economists and policymakers worry that because the equity stakes investors are buying do not trade like the stocks of public corporations, the investments are illiquid. An investor who needs to quickly sell his or her equity investment is likely to have difficulty doing so. To address this problem, some economists and policymakers have urged the SEC to allow a secondary market in shares purchased through crowdfunding sites. As of 2016, the SEC had declined to do so, but the SEC commissioner has been quoted as acknowledging the difficulty: "The lack of a fair, liquid, and transparent secondary market for these securities is a long-standing problem that needs an effective solution."

If these problems can be overcome, crowdfunding may become an important source of funds to startup firms and a way for small investors to participate in the growth of these firms.

Sources: Leslie Scism, "AIG to Sell Crowdfunding Insurance, Looking to Make Money Off Investors' Worries," *Wall Street Journal*, May 24, 2016; Louise Lee, "The Missing Piece That Could Hold Back Equity Crowdfunding," *Wall Street Journal*, May 1, 2016. "Many Scrappy Returns," *Economist*, November 19, 2011; and Jenna Wortham, "Success of Crowdfunding Puts Pressure on Entrepreneurs," *New York Times*, September 17, 2012.

See related problem 2.15 at the end of the chapter.

9.3 Conclusions About the Structure of the U.S. Financial System

LEARNING OBJECTIVE: Use economic analysis to explain the structure of the U.S. financial system.

We have seen that transactions costs and information costs pose significant obstacles to the flow of funds from savers to borrowers. We have also seen how the financial system has adapted to reduce the effects of transactions costs and information costs. But what would the financial system look like if transactions costs and asymmetric information problems didn't exist? To understand how different it would be, we will review some key facts about the U.S. financial structure.

Figure 9.2 shows the most important sources of external funds for small to medium-sized firms during the years 2010–2015. These firms rely on loans of various types and on *trade credit*. Trade credit refers to the common situation where a firm ships goods ordered by another firm while agreeing to accept payment at a later date—typically after 30 to 90 days. For example, a home improvement store may receive a shipment of lawnmowers but have 60 days to pay the manufacturer for them. Figure 9.2 shows that mortgage loans are by far the most important source of external funds to these firms, with nonmortgage loans from banks being the next most important.

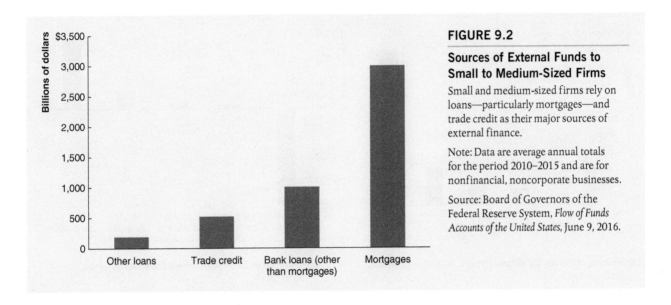

FIGURE 9.2

Sources of External Funds to Small to Medium-Sized Firms

Small and medium-sized firms rely on loans—particularly mortgages—and trade credit as their major sources of external finance.

Note: Data are average annual totals for the period 2010–2015 and are for nonfinancial, noncorporate businesses.

Source: Board of Governors of the Federal Reserve System, *Flow of Funds Accounts of the United States*, June 9, 2016.

Figure 9.3 shows the external sources of funds to corporations. In the United States, corporations account for more than 80% of sales by all businesses, so their sources of funding are particularly important. Panel (a) displays sources of funds to corporations by the average values outstanding at the end of the year during the period 2010–2015. Panel (a) displays *stock values*—that is, the total values of these variables at a point in time. Because they are stock values, they reflect how corporations are meeting their current financing needs and also how they have met those needs in the past. For instance, the total value of bonds that corporations have outstanding includes some bonds that may have been issued decades in the past. Panel (b) shows *net* changes in these categories of funds. For instance, net new bond issues equals the difference between the value of new bonds corporations have issued during the year minus the value of bonds that have matured during the year and been paid off. Net new stock issues equals the difference between the value of new shares issued minus the value of shares that firms have repurchased from investors. The values in panel (b) are also annual averages for the period 2010–2015. Panel (a) in Figure 9.3 shows that the value of the stocks corporations have issued is much greater than the value of bonds or the value of loans, while panel (b) shows that bonds and loans were much more important sources of external financing for corporations during these years than were stocks. In fact, in recent years, corporations have actually bought back from investors much more stock than they have issued.

We can use our discussion of transactions costs and information costs in Section 9.2 and the statistics in Figures 9.2 and 9.3 to discuss three key features of the financial system:

1. **Loans from financial intermediaries are the most important external source of funds for small to medium-sized firms.** As we have already noted, smaller businesses typically have to meet most of their funding needs *internally*, from the owners' personal funds or from the profits the firms earn. Figure 9.2 shows that

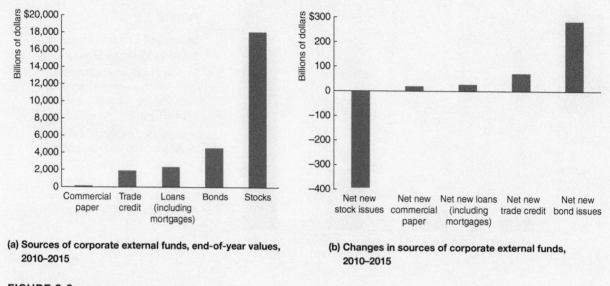

(a) Sources of corporate external funds, end-of-year values, 2010–2015

(b) Changes in sources of corporate external funds, 2010–2015

FIGURE 9.3

External Sources of Funds to Corporations

Panel (a) shows sources of funds to corporations, represented by the average values outstanding at the end of the year during the period 2010–2015. Panel (b) shows *net* changes in these categories. Panel (a) shows that the value of the stocks corporations have issued is much greater than the value of bonds or the value of loans, while panel (b) shows that bonds and loans were much more important sources of external financing for corporations during these years than were stocks.

Note: Data are for nonfarm, nonfinancial corporate businesses.

Source: Board of Governors of the Federal Reserve System, *Flow of Funds Accounts of the United States*, June 9, 2016.

loans are by far the most important *external* source of funds to smaller firms. Smaller firms cannot borrow directly from savers because savers encounter transactions costs that are too high when they attempt to make loans directly to businesses. Smaller firms cannot sell bonds or stocks because of the adverse selection and moral hazard problems that arise from asymmetric information. Because financial intermediaries—particularly commercial banks—can reduce both transactions costs and information costs, they are able to provide a channel by which funds can flow from savers to smaller firms.

2. **The stock market is a less important source of external funds to corporations than is the bond market.** What happens in the stock market each day is often the lead story in the financial news. The web site of the *Wall Street Journal* prominently displays a box showing what is happening minute-by-minute to each of the major stock market indexes. Yet most of the trading on the stock market involves buying and selling existing shares of stock, not sales of new stock issues. Sales of new shares of stock are very small when compared with sales of existing shares of stock. As noted earlier, panel (b) of Figure 9.3 illustrates the striking fact that in recent years corporations have actually bought back from investors more stock than they have issued. Panel (b) also shows that loans and bonds are the most

important categories of external credit to corporations. Why are corporations so much more likely to raise funds externally by selling bonds and by taking out loans—debt contracts—than by selling stock—equity? As we discussed earlier, moral hazard is less of a problem with debt contracts than with equity contracts. Investors who may doubt that the top managers of firms will actually maximize profit may still have confidence that the managers will be able to make the fixed payments due on bonds or loans.

3. **Debt contracts usually require collateral or restrictive covenants.** Households have difficulty borrowing money from banks unless they can provide collateral. Most of the large loans that households take out from banks use the good being purchased as collateral. For example, residential mortgage loans use the house being purchased as collateral, and automobile loans use the automobile as collateral. As discussed earlier, businesses are often in a similar situation. Figure 9.2 on page 297 shows that small to medium-sized businesses raise much more money from mortgage loans than they do from other business loans. Many corporate bonds also specify collateral that the bondholders can take possession of should the firm fail to make the required payments on its bonds. Both loans and bonds also typically contain restrictive covenants that specify how the firm can use the borrowed funds. Although debt contracts are subject to less moral hazard than are equity contracts, they still have some potential exposure. The purpose of collateral and restrictive covenants is to reduce the amount of moral hazard involved with debt contracts.

Savers would like to receive the highest interest rate on their investments, and borrowers would like to pay the lowest interest rate. Transactions costs and information costs drive a wedge between savers and borrowers, lowering the interest rate savers receive and raising the interest rate borrowers must pay. By reducing transactions and information costs, financial intermediaries can offer savers higher interest rates, offer borrowers lower interest rates, and still earn a profit.

MAKING THE CONNECTION | **IN YOUR INTEREST**

Corporations Are Issuing More Bonds, but Should You Buy Them?

Because the economy recovered very slowly from the recession of 2007–2009, the Federal Reserve took actions that resulted in interest rates on U.S. Treasury bonds falling to record low levels. As a result, investors searching for higher yields increased their demand for corporate bonds, which drove interest rates on these bonds also to record low levels. The following figure is an index prepared by Bank of America Merrill Lynch of interest rates on investment-grade corporate bonds. The figure shows the sharp decline in interest rates following the end of the recession of 2007–2009.

MyEconLab Real-time data

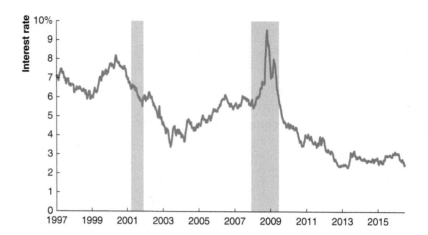

Corporations issued a record amount of investment-grade corporate bonds in 2016. In the previous few years, some corporations that hadn't recently issued long-term bonds, such as GE and Apple, decided to do so to take advantage of the low interest rates. One analyst with Moody's Investors Service was quoted as saying: "No treasurer or CFO [chief financial officer] wants to be the one treasurer or CFO who didn't get cheap long-term money when it was available."

Clearly, corporations are happy to sell bonds at such low interest rates, but as an investor, should you buy them? In October 2016, the average interest rate on investment-grade corporate bonds was just 2.8%, which was only about 1 percentage point above the expected inflation rate. While this interest rate was above the 1.8% interest rate on 10-year Treasury notes, the difference amounted to only a small default risk premium. The newly issued corporate bonds were primarily debentures, which means that the issuing corporations did not back them with any specific collateral. In the event of the issuing corporation defaulting, bondholders would likely absorb significant losses. Although at the time the bonds were issued, ratings agencies gave them investment-grade ratings, there was ample time before the bonds matured for the financial health of the issuing firms to decline.

In addition, long-term bonds have significant interest-rate risk. If interest rates on corporate bonds were to return to historically normal levels of 5% to 6%, investors who had purchased bonds in 2016 would suffer substantial losses. So, while 2016 was a great year for corporations to raise funds inexpensively by issuing long-term bonds, you would have been wise to proceed cautiously before investing in them.

Sources: Min Zeng, "After Record Week, How Much Lower Can Bond Yields Go?" *Wall Street Journal*, June 12, 2016; Ben Eisen and Sam Goldfarb, "Bond Trading Hits Record Level," *Wall Street Journal*, April 1, 2016; Vipal Monga, "Companies Feast on Cheap Money," *Wall Street Journal*, October 8, 2012; and Federal Reserve Bank of St. Louis.

See related problem 3.7 at the end of the chapter.

Banks and other financial firms are continually searching for ways to earn a profit by expediting the flow of funds from savers to borrowers. As we saw in the chapter opener, in recent years, some fintech firms have used sophisticated software to start web sites where small savers can be matched with small businesses. The savers receive a higher interest rate than they would receive from bank deposits, and the businesses pay a lower interest rate than they would pay on bank loans. Whether these new fintech web sites have the potential to displace a significant amount of the flow of funds through banks remains to be seen. As we saw in the previous section, one key issue is whether savers will consider using these web sites to be a safe way to invest their funds.

ANSWERING THE KEY QUESTION

Continued from page 277

At the beginning of this chapter, we asked:

"Why do firms rely more on loans and bonds than on stocks as a source of external finance?"

We have seen that both the bond market and the stock market are subject to problems of moral hazard. In both cases, investors have to be concerned that once firms have received investment funds, they will not use them for their intended purpose. The problem of moral hazard is considerably less serious when an investor buys a firm's bonds than when the investor buys a firm's stock. As a result, investors are more willing to buy bonds than stock, which explains why bonds are a more important source of external finance for firms. Small to medium-sized firms are unable to issue either bonds or stock and must rely on bank loans as their main source of external finance.

Key Terms and Problems

Key Terms

Adverse selection, p. 283
Asymmetric information, p. 283
Collateral, p. 287
Credit rationing, p. 286
Economies of scale, p. 282
Information costs, p. 282

Moral hazard, p. 283
Net worth, p. 287
Principal–agent problem, p. 291
Private equity firm (or corporate restructuring firm), p. 294
Relationship banking, p. 288

Restrictive covenant, p. 293
Transactions costs, p. 282
Venture capital firm, p. 294

9.1 | ### The Financial System and Economic Performance
Evaluate the reasons economists believe economic performance depends on the financial system.

Review Questions

1.1 Briefly explain why a country without a strong financial system might struggle to achieve high rates of economic growth.

1.2 What do the World Bank's data tell us about the relationship between the level of a country's financial development and the level of its real GDP per capita?

Problems and Applications

1.3 A 2016 article in the *Wall Street Journal* notes that banks in China have been experiencing problems with business borrowers defaulting on loans and have had difficulty attracting enough deposits to fund new loans. Are these problems likely to matter for the future growth of the Chinese economy? Briefly explain.

 Visit **www.myeconlab.com** to complete these exercises online and get instant feedback. Exercises that update with real-time data are marked with 🌐 .

Source: Anjani Trivedi, "Why China's Big Banks Aren't Looking So Large," *Wall Street Journal*, May 3, 2016.

1.4 Economist Richard Sylla of New York University has argued that in the 1790s, Treasury Secretary Alexander Hamilton "established the financial foundations that would make the United States the most successful emerging market in the nineteenth century, and the economic colossus of the next that some would call the 'American century.'"

a. What does Sylla mean by "the financial foundations'?

b. Why were these financial foundations important in making possible the rapid growth of the U.S. economy during the nineteenth and twentieth centuries?

Source: Richard Sylla, "Financial Foundations: Public Credit, the National Bank, and Securities Markets," in Douglas A. Irwin and Richard Sylla, eds., *Founding Choices: American Economic Policy in the 1790s*, Chicago: University of Chicago Press, 2011, p. 86.

1.5 Countries that are above the line in Figure 9.1 on page 280 have relatively high levels of real GDP per capita for their levels of financial development, and countries that are below the line have relatively low levels of real GDP per capita for their levels of financial development. Holding constant all other factors that might affect a country's rate of economic growth, would you expect future growth rates to be higher for countries above the line or for countries below the line? Briefly explain.

9.2 **Transactions Costs, Adverse Selection, and Moral Hazard**
Analyze the problems that transactions costs, adverse selection, and moral hazard pose for the financial system.

Review Questions

2.1 Why do savers with small amounts to invest rarely make loans directly to individuals or firms?

2.2 Why are financial intermediaries important to the financial system?

2.3 What is the difference between moral hazard and adverse selection? Explain the "lemons problem." How does the lemons problem lead many firms to borrow from banks rather than from individual investors?

2.4 Why was the Securities and Exchange Commission (SEC) founded? What effect has the SEC had on the level of asymmetric information in the U.S. financial system?

2.5 How is the principal–agent problem related to the concept of moral hazard?

2.6 What is the difference between venture capital firms and private equity firms? What roles do they play in the financial system? In what ways do the activities of these firms differ from crowdfunding?

Problems and Applications

2.7 How do financial intermediaries reduce the transactions costs involved in making loans? If we lived in a world in which everyone were perfectly honest, would the difference in the transactions costs faced by financial intermediaries when they make loans and those faced by small savers when they make loans disappear? Briefly explain.

2.8 Decades ago, many bank records were written by hand in ledgers. Were there significant economies of scale in keeping bank records under that system? How has the shift to keeping all records on computers affected economies of scale in banking?

2.9 The author of an article in the *New York Times* providing advice to renters observes that "landlords will always know more than you do."

a. Do you agree with this statement? If so, what do landlords know that potential renters might not know?

b. If the statement is correct, what are the implications for the market for rental apartments?

c. In what ways is the market for rental apartments like the market for used cars? In what ways is it different?

Source: Marc Santora, "How to Be a Brainy Renter," *New York Times*, June 4, 2010.

2.10 An article in the *Economist* observes: "Insurance companies often suspect the only people who buy insurance are the ones most likely to collect."

a. What do economists call the problem that is described in the article?

b. If insurance companies are correct in their suspicion, what are the consequences for the market for insurance?

Source: "The Money Talks," *Economist*, December 5, 2008.

2.11 [Related to the Chapter Opener on page 277] A 2016 article in the *Wall Street Journal* observes: "Equity crowdfunding promises to be a major new source of funding for small businesses."

a. What is equity crowdfunding, and what happened in 2016 that might make it a major source of funding to small businesses?

b. Why is crowdfunding likely to be a more important source of funding for small businesses than for large businesses?

Source: Louise Lee, "The Missing Piece That Could Hold Back Equity Crowdfunding," *Wall Street Journal*, May 1, 2016.

2.12 [Related to the Making the Connection on page 288] Commercial real estate loans are mortgages that use apartment buildings, office buildings, or other commercial real estate as collateral. An article in the *New York Times* discussing the securitization of commercial real estate loans makes the following observation:

The boom in commercial mortgage-backed securities in the middle of the last decade provided a lot of money for underwriters, enabled banks to earn fees from making and servicing bad loans and allowed property owners to withdraw large amounts of cash. The losers were the investors.

a. What is securitization?

b. Why would banks make bad commercial real estate loans? Don't banks lose money if these loans default?

c. Why would investors buy securities that contain bad commercial real estate loans? Is it likely that the interest rates on these securities were high enough to compensate investors for the additional risk involved with these securities? Briefly explain.

Source: Floyd Norris, "Commercial Mortgages Show How Bad It Got," *New York Times*, July 5, 2012.

2.13 [Related to Solved Problem 9.2 on page 290] A reader wrote to an advice column in the *New York Times*, complaining that his insurance company had canceled his homeowner's policy after he had filed two claims. The advice columnist observed: "A lot of people have shared a version of [this man's] experience … a couple of small claims … then nonrenewal." What problem are these insurance companies attempting to avoid by canceling these people's policies? Why don't the insurance companies raise the annual premiums they charge these people for their policies rather than cancel the policies?

Source: David Segal, "Spurned by an Insurer After Filing Small Claims," *New York Times*, April 25, 2015.

2.14 Aaron Levie, one of the founders of the Internet file-sharing site Box, Inc. explained the difficulty the firm had in raising funds from investors: "Investors had a hard time investing in a company where the founders acted 40, were 19 and looked 12. They thought we'd run off to Disneyland with the funding money." What do economists call the problem Levie encountered? Is the problem likely to be greater for small startup firms or for larger established firms? Briefly explain.

Source: Monica Langley, "Rich, but Not Silicon Valley Rich for Founders of Box," *Wall Street Journal*, April 23, 2015.

2.15 [Related to the Making the Connection on page 295] LendingClub, one of the largest fintech firms, attempts to match lenders and borrowers. Unlike some other fintech firms, LendingClub securitizes some of the loans it makes and sells them to investors. According to an article in the *Wall Street Journal*, it began to do that to "expand the pool of investors" in its loans. In 2016, its CEO was fired after LendingClub's board of directors learned that the dates on loans in some securities had been falsified.

a. What moral hazard problem do you face when investing funds on a site like LendingClub?

b. Is this problem increased or decreased if the site securitizes some of the loans it makes? Briefly explain.

Source: Peter Rudegeair and Annamaria Andriotis, "Inside the Final Days of LendingClub CEO Renaud Laplanche," *Wall Street Journal*, May 16, 2016.

 9.3

Conclusions About the Structure of the U.S. Financial System
Use economic analysis to explain the structure of the U.S. financial system.

Review Questions

3.1 What is the most important source of funds for small to medium-sized firms? What is the most important source of *external* funds for small to medium-sized firms?

3.2 What is the most important method of debt financing for corporations?

3.3 List the three key features of the financial system and provide a brief explanation for each.

Problems and Applications

3.4 Consider the possibility of income insurance. With income insurance, if a person loses his job or doesn't get as big a raise as anticipated, he would be compensated under his insurance coverage. Why don't insurance companies offer income insurance of this type?

3.5 An article in the *Economist* notes that: "From an insurance perspective, the co-payments that patients must sometimes make when receiving treatment are a waste; it would be better for people to be able to insure fully." Are restrictive covenants in loan agreements also a waste in this sense? If so, why do insurance companies use co-payments and why do lenders use restrictive covenants?

Source: "Oliver Hart and Bengt Holmstrom Win the Nobel Prize for Economic Sciences," *Economist*, October 10, 2016.

3.6 Describe some of the information problems in the financial system that lead firms to rely more heavily on internal funds than external funds to finance their growth. Do these information problems imply that firms are able to spend less on expansion than is economically optimal? Briefly explain.

3.7 [Related to the Making the Connection on page 299] An article in the *Wall Street Journal* in 2016 refers to the preceding 35 years as "the biggest bond bull market in history."

a. What does the article mean by a "bond bull market"? Does the graph in the *Making the Connection* indicate that there was a bond bull market during the time period shown? Briefly explain.

b. The article also notes: "Bonds are meant to be safe, dull investments." Is investing in bonds safe? What risks do bond investors face?

Source: James MacKintosh, "35-Year-Old Bond Bull Is on Its Last Legs," *Wall Street Journal*, July 13, 2016.

3.8 *Wall Street Journal* columnist Brett Arends offered the opinion that "as a rule of thumb, the more complex a [financial] product is, the worse the deal." Do you agree? Why would a more complex financial product be likely to be a worse deal for an investor than a simpler product?

Source: Brett Arends, "Four Lessons from the Goldman Case," *Wall Street Journal*, May 2, 2010.

Data Exercises

D9.1: [Comparing transaction fees] Online brokerages generally charge transaction fees per trade. This means that a $5,000 stock purchase is charged the same fee as a $100 stock purchase. Go to the following online brokerages and compare their transaction fees: TD Ameritrade, E-TRADE, and ScottTrade. Which has the highest transaction fee? If you had $200 to invest, and if the expected return in the stock market is 5% over one year, does the transactions cost affect your decision to buy stock? (Remember that you get charged the transactions fee for both the buy transactions and sell transactions.)

D9.2: [Recessions and the net worth of households] Go to the web site of the Federal Reserve Bank of St. Louis (FRED) (fred.stlouisfed.org) and download and graph the data series for the net worth of households (TNWBSHNO) from the first quarter of 1952 until the most recent quarter available. Go to the web site of the National Bureau of Economic Research (nber.org) and find the dates for business cycle peaks and troughs (the period between a business cycle peak and trough is a recession).

a. What is household net worth?

b. Describe how household net worth changes just before, during, and just after a typical recession.

c. Why did household net worth decline by so much during the recession of 2007–2009? How might the decline in household net worth have affected the severity of the 2007–2009 recession?

D9.3: [Recessions and the net worth of corporations] Go to the web site of the Federal Reserve Bank of St. Louis (FRED) (fred.stlouisfed.org) and download and graph the data series for the net worth of nonfinancial corporations (TNWMVBSNNCB) from the first quarter of 1952 until the most recent quarter available. Go to the web site of the National Bureau of Economic Research (nber. org) and find the dates for business cycle peaks and troughs (the period between a business cycle peak and trough is a recession).

a. What is a nonfinancial corporation? Give two examples. What is corporate net worth?

b. Describe how corporate net worth changes just before, during, and just after a typical recession.

c. Why did corporate net worth decline by so much during the recession of 2007–2009? How might the decline in corporate net worth have affected the severity of the 2007–2009 recession?

CHAPTER 10

The Economics of Banking

Learning Objectives

After studying this chapter, you should be able to:

10.1 Evaluate a bank's balance sheet (pages 307–317)

10.2 Describe the basic operations of a commercial bank (pages 317–320)

10.3 Explain how banks manage risk (pages 320–328)

10.4 Explain the trends in the U.S. commercial banking industry (pages 328–337)

Small Businesses Flock to the Bank of Bird-in-Hand

The Bank of Bird-in-Hand is a small bank in Pennsylvania's Amish country. The Amish are a religious denomination whose members avoid using modern technology such as cars and smartphones. Many of the bank's customers arrive at the drive-through window in a horse and buggy, make relatively small deposits, and ask for relatively small loans. Despite the small size of the transactions it makes, the Bank of Bird-in-Hand was prospering in 2016 while many larger banks were struggling. The struggles of larger banks were rooted in problems involving the basic business of banking, which is to take in deposits and use the funds to make loans to households and firms. The greater the gap between the interest rate at which banks lend and the interest rate they pay on deposits—known as the *spread*—the more profitable banks are. When the

Federal Reserve takes steps to lower interest rates, the result is usually a boost to bank profits. Fed policies have their greatest effect on short-run interest rates, so the rates that banks pay on deposits typically fall by more than the interest rates banks charge on loans to households and firms, which increases banks' spreads and their profits. As we have seen in previous chapters, though, the situation in 2016 was different because long-term interest rates on bonds and loans had also fallen to historically low levels, and as a result, bank profits were being squeezed. As one investment analyst put it: "It's just really tough for banks overall right now. I don't care how well-managed you are."

How was the Bank of Bird-in-Hand prospering while its larger rivals were hurting? If you were the owner of a small business in the town of Bird-in-Hand,

Continued on next page

KEY ISSUE AND QUESTION

Issue: During the past 35 years, the U.S. financial system has experienced two periods during which there was a sharp increase in the number of bank failures.

Question: Is banking a particularly risky business? If so, what types of risks do banks face?

Answered on page 338

you might well know the answer. Like other *community banks*, the Bank of Bird-in-Hand concentrates on making loans to small businesses. Community banks practice *relationship banking*, which as we saw in Chapter 9, involves banks gathering private information on borrowers to assess credit risks. Many large banks believe that the transactions costs involved in assessing risk on small business loans have made such loans unprofitable. As Rebel Cole, a finance professor at DePaul University, put it, large banks "have essentially abandoned the small business market." The chief loan officer of the Bank of Bird-in-Hand notes that larger banks in his area are usually not interested in loans for less than $1 million. As a result, small businesses have flocked to his bank.

The Bank of Bird-in-Hand has some advantages in lending to the Amish owners of farms and other small businesses in the area. One advantage is that for religious reasons, the owners are unlikely to turn to the new fintech web sites we discussed in previous chapters or to rely on credit cards or other sources of short-term credit. As we will discuss in Section 10.4, the presence of significant economies of scale in some aspects of banking have led to a rapid consolidation in the industry, with the 10 largest banks now having more than half of all deposits. But in some areas of banking services, such as loans to small businesses, economies of scale appear to be much more limited, allowing banks like the Bank of Bird-in-Hand to thrive.

Sources: Ryan Tracy, "A Local Bank in Amish Country Flourishes Amid Dearth of Small Lenders," *Wall Street Journal*, March 29, 2015; "Nice Gig: Lessons from One of America's Youngest Lenders," *Economist*, August 22, 2015; Ruth Simon, "Big Banks Cut Back on Loans to Small Business," *Wall Street Journal*, November 26, 2015; and Emily Glazer and Peter Rudegeair, "Wells Fargo's Quarterly Earnings Slip," *Wall Street Journal*, July 15, 2016.

We saw in Chapter 9 that banks are important to the efficient functioning of the financial system. In this chapter, we look more closely at how banks do business and how they earn a profit. We then consider the problems banks face in managing risks. In recent years, banks have faced competition from other financial institutions and from fintech firms that can offer savers and borrowers similar services at a potentially lower cost. We conclude this chapter by describing some of the steps banks have taken in response to increased competition.

10.1 The Basics of Commercial Banking: The Bank Balance Sheet

LEARNING OBJECTIVE: Evaluate a bank's balance sheet.

Commercial banking is a business. Banks fill a market need by providing a service, and they earn a profit by charging customers for that service. The key commercial banking activities are taking in deposits from savers and making loans to households and firms. To earn a profit, a bank needs to pay less for the funds it receives from depositors than it earns on the loans it makes. We begin our discussion of the business of banking by looking at a bank's *sources of funds*—primarily deposits—and *uses of funds*—primarily loans. A bank's sources and uses of funds are summarized on its **balance sheet**, which is a statement that lists an individual's or a firm's assets and liabilities to indicate the individual's or firm's financial position on a particular day. An **asset** is something of value that an individual or a firm owns. A **Liability** is something that an individual or a firm owes, particularly a financial claim on an individual or a firm. Table 10.1 combines data from all the banks in the country into a consolidated balance sheet for the whole U.S. commercial banking system for July 2016. Normally, balance sheets show dollar values for each entry.

Balance sheet A statement that lists an individual's or a firm's assets and liabilities to indicate the individual's or firm's financial position on a particular day.

Asset Something of value that an individual or a firm owns; in particular, a financial claim.

Liability Something that an individual or a firm owes; a claim on an individual or a firm.

TABLE 10.1 Consolidated Balance Sheet of U.S. Commercial Banks, July 2016

Assets (uses of funds)		Liabilities + Bank capital (sources of funds)	
	(Percentage of total assets)		(Percentage of total liabilities plus capital)
Reserves and other cash assets	10.6%	Deposits	74.8%
Securities	22.0	Checkable deposits	12.1
U.S. government	4.4	Nontransaction deposits	62.7
Mortgage-backed securities (MBS)	12.5	Small-denomination time deposits (CDs less than $100,000) plus savings deposits	56.2
State and local government and other securities	5.1		
Loans	58.8		
Commercial and industrial	12.3	Large-denomination time deposits (CDs greater than $100,000)	6.5
Real estate (including mortgages)	29.1		
Consumer	9.7	Borrowings	8.2
Interbank	1.2	From banks in the U.S.	0.5
Other loans	6.5	Other borrowings	7.7
Trading assets	1.1	Other liabilities	4.3
Other assets	7.5	Bank capital (or shareholders' equity)	12.7

Note: The data are for all domestically chartered commercial banks in the United States as of July 13, 2016.

Source: Federal Reserve Statistical Release H.8, July 22, 2016.

For ease of interpretation, we have converted the dollar values to percentages. Table 10.1 shows the typical layout of a balance sheet, which is based on the following accounting equation:

$$\text{Assets} = \text{Liabilities} + \text{Shareholders' equity.}$$

Shareholders' equity is the difference between the value of a firm's assets and the value of its liabilities. Shareholders' equity represents the dollar amount the owners of the firm would be left with if the firm were to be closed, its assets sold, and its liabilities paid off. For a public firm, the owners are the shareholders. Shareholders' equity is also called the firm's *net worth*. In banking, shareholders' equity is usually called **bank capital**. Bank capital is the funds contributed by the shareholders through their purchases of the bank's stock plus the bank's accumulated retained profits. The accounting equation above tells us that the left side of a firm's balance sheet must always have the same value as the right side. We can think of a bank's liabilities and its capital as the sources of its funds, and we can think of a bank's assets as the uses of its funds.

Bank capital The difference between the value of a bank's assets and the value of its liabilities; also called shareholders' equity.

Bank Liabilities

The most important bank liabilities are the funds a bank acquires from savers. The bank uses the funds to make investments, for instance, by buying bonds, or to make loans to households and firms. Bank deposits offer households and firms certain advantages over other ways in which they might hold their funds. For example, compared with holding cash, deposits offer greater safety against theft and may also pay interest. Compared with financial assets such as Treasury bills, deposits are more liquid. Deposits against which checks can be written offer a convenient way to make payments. Banks offer a variety of deposit accounts because savers have different needs. We next review the main types of deposit accounts.

Checkable Deposits Banks offer savers **checkable deposits**, which are accounts against which depositors can write checks. Checkable deposits are also called *transaction deposits*. Checkable deposits come in different varieties, which are determined partly by banking regulations and partly by the desire of bank managers to tailor the checking accounts they offer to meet the needs of households and firms. Demand deposits and NOW (negotiable order of withdrawal) accounts are the most important categories of checkable deposits. *Demand deposits* are checkable deposits on which banks do not pay interest. NOW accounts are checking accounts that pay interest. Businesses often hold substantial balances in demand deposits, partly because U.S. banking regulations do not allow them to hold NOW accounts but also because demand deposits represent a liquid asset that can be accessed with very low transactions costs.

Banks must pay all checkable deposits on demand. In other words, a bank must exchange a depositor's check for cash immediately, provided that the depositor has at least the amount of the check on deposit. Finally, note that checkable deposits are *liabilities to banks* because banks have the obligation to pay the funds to depositors on demand. But checkable deposits are *assets to households and firms* because even though banks have physical possession of the funds, households and firms still own the funds. An accounting note: It is important to grasp the idea that the same checking account can simultaneously be an asset to a household or firm and a liability to a bank. Understanding this point will make it easier for you to follow some of the discussion later in this chapter.

Nontransaction Deposits Savers use only some of their deposits for day-to-day transactions. Banks offer *nontransaction deposits* for savers who are willing to sacrifice immediate access to their funds in exchange for higher interest payments. The most important types of nontransaction deposits are savings accounts, money market deposit accounts (MMDAs), and *time deposits*, or certificates of deposit (CDs). With savings accounts—which at one time were generally called *passbook accounts*—depositors must give the bank 30 days' notice for a withdrawal. In practice, though, banks usually waive this requirement, so most depositors expect to receive immediate access to the funds in their savings accounts. MMDAs are a hybrid of savings accounts and checking accounts in that they pay interest, but depositors can write only three checks per month against them.

Checkable deposits
Accounts against which depositors can write checks.

Unlike savings deposits, CDs have specified maturities that typically range from a few months to several years. Banks penalize savers who withdraw funds prior to maturity by requiring the savers to forfeit part of the accrued interest. CDs are less liquid than savings accounts but pay depositors a higher rate of interest. There is an important difference between CDs of less than $100,000, which are called *small-denomination time deposits*, and CDs of $100,000 or more, which are called *large-denomination time deposits*. CDs worth $100,000 or more are *negotiable*, which means that investors can buy and sell them in secondary markets prior to maturity.

Federal deposit insurance
A government guarantee of deposit account balances up to $250,000.

Households with limited funds to save often prefer checkable deposits and small-denomination time deposits because these deposits are covered by **federal deposit insurance** up to a limit of $250,000 per depositor, per insured bank. Because of this insurance, even if your bank fails, you will not lose any of your funds, and typically you will have continuous access to them through ATMs or direct withdrawals. Deposit insurance gives banks an edge over other financial intermediaries in acquiring funds from small savers because, for instance, money market mutual fund shares lack this government insurance.

Borrowings Banks often have more opportunities to make loans than they can finance with funds they attract from depositors. To take advantage of these opportunities, banks raise funds by borrowing. A bank can earn a profit from this borrowing if the interest rate it pays to borrow funds is lower than the interest it earns by lending the funds to households and firms. Borrowings include short-term loans in the *federal funds market*, loans from a bank's foreign branches or other subsidiaries or affiliates, repurchase agreements, and *discount loans* from the Federal Reserve System. The federal funds market is the market in which banks make short-term loans—often just overnight—to other banks. Although the name indicates that government money is involved, in fact, the loans in the federal funds market involve the banks' own funds. The interest rate on these interbank loans is called the *federal funds rate*.

With *repurchase agreements*—otherwise known as "repos," or RPs—banks sell securities, such as Treasury bills, and agree to repurchase them, typically the next day. Banks use repos to borrow funds from business firms or other banks, using the underlying securities as collateral. A firm or another bank that buys the securities earns interest without any significant loss of liquidity. Repos are typically between large banks or corporations, so the degree of *counterparty risk*, or the risk that the other party to the transaction will default on its obligation, was at one time considered to be small. But during the financial crisis of 2007–2009, it became clear that even a large corporation might be quickly forced into bankruptcy, leaving the counterparties to its repos to suffer significant losses or a delay in accessing their funds, or both. For example, concern among the counterparties to the repos of the Lehman Brothers investment bank helped to force the firm into bankruptcy, worsening the financial crisis.

The Rise and Fall and (Partial) Rise of the Checking Account

In 1960, plain-vanilla demand deposits, which pay no interest, made up more than half of commercial bank liabilities. The following graph shows checkable deposits as a fraction of all bank liabilities for the period from January 1973 to June 2016. Although there were some fluctuations over the years, by and large, until the beginning of the financial crisis, checkable deposits made up a declining fraction of bank liabilities. By 2008, they reached a low point of a little more than 6% of all bank liabilities. Then the financial crisis hit, and households and firms began putting more funds into checkable deposits, so that by 2016, they had risen to more than 13% of bank liabilities.

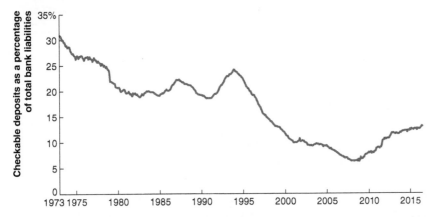

Sources: Federal Reserve Bank of St. Louis; and Board of Governors of the Federal Reserve System.

The long-run decline in the popularity of checking accounts until the financial crisis may seem puzzling because, in some ways, these accounts became more attractive over time. In the 1960s and 1970s, the only checkable deposits available were demand deposits, which paid no interest. Interest-paying NOW accounts were authorized by changes in bank regulations that took effect in 1980. In addition, because there were no ATMs in those days, to withdraw money from your checking account, you needed to go to your bank, stand in line, and fill out a withdrawal slip. Banks were typically open only during "banker's hours" of 10 A.M. to 3 P.M. from Monday to Friday. If stores or restaurants declined to accept checks—as many did—consumers could not spend the funds in their accounts. Today, debit cards make it possible for consumers to access the funds in their checking accounts even when buying from a store that doesn't accept checks.

Until the financial crisis, to many households and firms, the improved services that checking accounts provided were more than offset by alternative assets that offer higher interest rates. The following graph shows households' and firms' holdings of various short-term financial assets in July 2016. Even though checkable deposits have increased in popularity in recent years, the value of savings accounts and small time deposits (CDs of less than $100,000) was nearly five times greater than the value of checkable deposits.

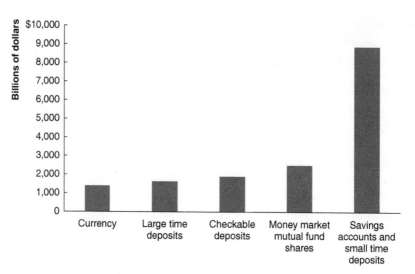

Sources: Federal Reserve Bank of St. Louis; and Board of Governors of the Federal Reserve System.

Households hold less in checking accounts relative to other financial assets than they once did, partly because households have become wealthier over time. With greater wealth, households have been better able to afford to hold assets, such as CDs, where their money is tied up for a while but on which they earn a higher rate of interest. Money market mutual funds, such as Vanguard's Prime Money Market Fund, which were first introduced in 1971, have also been popular. Like other mutual funds, money market mutual funds sell shares to investors and use the funds to buy financial assets. These funds buy only money market—or short-term—assets, such as Treasury bills and commercial paper issued by corporations. Money market mutual funds pay higher interest than bank deposit accounts, and they also allow for limited check writing, so they have been formidable competition for bank checking accounts.

The 2007–2009 financial crisis showed that checking accounts are still useful to households and firms, however. Checking accounts provide a safe haven for households and small businesses because their funds are protected up to the $250,000 federal deposit insurance ceiling. In addition, very low interest rates persisted for years after the end of the recession of 2007–2009. The interest rate on three-month CDs, which had been about 5% at the end of 2007, was only 0.15% in 2016. Similarly, yields on money market mutual funds, which had been about 5% in 2007, were only about 0.20% in 2016. As a result, many households moved their funds from CDs and money market mutual funds to checking accounts to take advantage of their greater liquidity without giving up much interest.

See related problem 1.5 at the end of the chapter.

Bank Assets

Banks acquire *bank assets* with the funds they receive from depositors, the funds they borrow, the funds they acquire from their shareholders purchasing the banks' new stock issues, and the profits they retain from their operations. A bank's managers build a portfolio of assets that reflect both the demand for loans by the bank's customers and the bank's need to balance returns against risk, liquidity, and information costs. The following are the most important bank assets.

Reserves and Other Cash Assets The most liquid asset that banks hold is **reserves**, which consist of **vault cash**—cash on hand in the bank (including in ATMs) or in deposits at other banks—and deposits banks have with the Federal Reserve System. As authorized by Congress, the Fed mandates that banks hold a percentage of their demand deposits and NOW accounts (but not MMDAs) as **required reserves**. Reserves that banks hold over and above those that are required are called **excess reserves**. Banks had long complained that the Fed's failure to pay interest on the banks' reserve deposits amounted to a tax because banks earned no interest on the required reserves they could otherwise have used to make loans or purchase securities. In October 2008, during the financial crisis, Congress authorized the Fed to begin paying interest on banks' required and excess reserve deposits. The interest rate is low—0.75% as of December 2016—and, of course, banks earn no interest on vault cash. Before the financial crisis of 2007–2009, excess reserves had fallen to very low levels, but because these reserves can provide an important source of liquidity to banks, during the financial crisis bank holdings of excess reserves soared. Years after the end of the financial crisis, banks have continued to hold substantial excess reserves because, in addition to receiving interest from the Fed on their reserve balances, many banks remain cautious about making loans, believing that the low interest rates they receive on most consumer and business loans are not sufficient compensation for the default risk on the loans except when the banks are lending to the most creditworthy borrowers.

Another important cash asset is claims banks have on other banks for uncollected funds, which is called *cash items in the process of collection*. Suppose your Aunt Tilly, who lives in Seattle, sends you a $100 check for your birthday. Aunt Tilly's check is written against her checking account in her bank in Seattle. If you deposit the check in your bank in Nashville, the check becomes a cash item in the process of collection. Eventually, your bank will collect the funds from the Seattle bank, and the cash item in the process of collection will be converted to reserves on your bank's balance sheet.

Small banks often maintain deposits at other banks to obtain foreign-exchange transactions, check collection, or other services. This activity, called *correspondent banking*, has diminished in importance over the past 50 years, as the financial system has provided small banks with other ways to obtain these services.

Securities *Marketable securities* are liquid assets that banks trade in financial markets. Banks are allowed to hold securities issued by the U.S. Treasury and other government agencies, corporate bonds that received investment-grade ratings when they were first issued, and some limited amounts of municipal bonds, which are bonds issued by state and local governments. Because of their liquidity, bank holdings of U.S. Treasury securities are sometimes called *secondary reserves*. In the United States, commercial banks cannot invest checkable deposits in corporate bonds (although they may purchase them

Reserves A bank asset consisting of vault cash plus bank deposits with the Federal Reserve.

Vault cash Cash on hand in a bank; includes currency in ATMs and deposits with other banks.

Required reserves Reserves the Fed requires banks to hold against demand deposit and NOW account balances.

Excess reserves Any reserves banks hold above those necessary to meet reserve requirements.

using other funds) or common stock in nonfinancial corporations. During the past 15 years, banks have increased their holdings of mortgage-backed securities. In 2016, mortgage-backed securities made up about 57% of the securities that banks held. During the financial crisis of 2007–2009, the value of many mortgage-backed securities declined sharply, which caused many banks to suffer heavy losses and some banks to fail.

Loans By far the largest category of bank assets is loans. Loans are illiquid relative to marketable securities and entail greater default risk and higher information costs. As a result, the interest rates banks receive on loans are higher than those they receive on marketable securities. Table 10.1 on page 308 shows that most bank loans fall into three categories:

1. Loans to businesses—called commercial and industrial, or C&I, loans
2. Consumer loans, made to households primarily to buy automobiles, furniture, and other goods
3. Real estate loans, which include mortgage loans and any other loans backed with real estate as collateral. Mortgage loans made to purchase homes are called *residential mortgages*, while mortgages made to purchase stores, offices, factories, and other commercial buildings are called *commercial mortgages*.

Figure 10.1 shows that the types of loans granted by banks have changed significantly since the early 1970s. Real estate loans have increased tremendously, growing from less than one-third of bank loans in 1973 to 57% of bank loans in 2016. C&I loans, which were the largest category of loans in 1973, have fallen from more than 40% of bank loans to 24%. Continuing slow growth in demand for housing since the financial

MyEconLab Real-time data

FIGURE 10.1

The Changing Mix of Bank Loans, 1973–2016

The types of loans granted by banks have changed significantly since the early 1970s. Real estate loans grew from less than one-third of bank loans in 1973 to 57% of bank loans in 2016. Commercial and industrial (C&I) loans fell from more than 40% of bank loans to 24%. Consumer loans fell from more than 27% of all loans to about 19%.

Note: The values are the shares of the total of C&I, consumer, and real estate loans at domestically chartered U.S. banks. Total loans do not include interbank loans or other loans.

Source: Federal Reserve Statistical Release H.8, July 29, 2016.

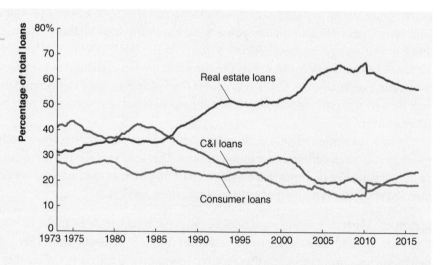

crisis has caused C&I loans to increase somewhat relative to real estate loans, although not by enough to reverse the long-run trends.

Firms take out C&I loans either to finance long-term investments, such as purchases of machinery and equipment, or to meet short-term needs, such as financing inventories. Beginning in the late 1970s, some firms that had previously used C&I loans began to meet their long-term funding needs by instead issuing junk bonds, which are bonds that receive below-investment-grade ratings from the bond-rating agencies. Once a market for newly issued junk bonds developed in the late 1970s, many firms found the interest rates on these bonds to be lower than what they would have paid on C&I loans from banks. When the market for commercial paper developed in the 1980s, some firms that had been using short-term C&I loans from banks began issuing commercial paper instead.

The decline in the importance of C&I loans has fundamentally changed the nature of commercial banking. Traditionally, it would not have been too much of an exaggeration to say that commercial banking consisted of taking in funds as checkable deposits and lending them to businesses. C&I loans were typically low-risk loans that banks could count on as the basis of their profits. Banks made C&I loans primarily to businesses on which they had gathered private information through long-term relationships. In addition, the loans were often well collateralized. Both of these factors reduced the chances that businesses would default on the loans. Banks usually did not face much competition in making the loans, which kept the interest rates on them relatively high. As the demand for C&I loans has declined, banks have been forced to turn to riskier uses of their funds, especially residential and commercial real estate lending. The bursting of the real estate bubble beginning in 2006 showed that replacing C&I loans with real estate loans had increased the degree of risk in a typical bank's loan portfolio.

Other Assets Other assets include banks' physical assets, such as computer equipment and buildings. This category also includes collateral received from borrowers who have defaulted on loans. Following the bursting of the real estate bubble, many banks ended up owning significant numbers of houses and residential lots, as borrowers and developers defaulted on their mortgages.

Bank Capital

Bank capital, also called shareholders' equity, or *bank net worth*, is the difference between the value of a bank's assets and the value of its liabilities. In 2016, bank capital for the U.S. banking system as a whole was about 14.5% of bank assets. A bank's capital equals the funds contributed by the bank's shareholders through their purchases of the bank's stock plus accumulated retained profits. As the value of a bank's assets or liabilities changes, so does the value of the bank's capital. For instance, during the financial crisis of 2007–2009, many banks saw declines in the values of loans and securities they owned. These declines in the value of bank assets resulted in declines in the value of their capital.

SOLVED PROBLEM 10.1

Constructing a Bank Balance Sheet

The following entries are from the actual balance sheet of a U.S. bank:

Cash, including cash items in the process of collection	$121
Non-interest-bearing deposits	275
Deposits with the Federal Reserve	190
Commercial loans	253
Long-term bonds (issued by the bank)	439
Real estate loans	460
Commercial paper and other short-term borrowing	70
Consumer loans	187
Securities	311
Interest-bearing deposits	717
Buildings and equipment	16
Other assets	685
Other liabilities	491

Note: Values are in billions of dollars.

a. Use the entries to construct a balance sheet similar to the one in Table 10.1, with assets on the left side of the balance sheet and liabilities and bank capital on the right side.

b. The bank's capital is what percentage of its assets?

Solving the Problem

Step 1 Review the chapter material. This problem is about bank balance sheets, so you may want to review the section "The Basics of Commercial Banking: The Bank Balance Sheet," which begins on page 307.

Step 2 Answer part (a) by using the entries to construct the bank's balance sheet, remembering that bank capital is equal to the value of assets minus the value of liabilities.

Assets		Liabilities and bank capital	
Cash, including cash items in the process of collection	$121	Non-interest-bearing deposits	$275
Deposits with the Federal Reserve	190	Interest-bearing deposits	717
Commercial loans	253	Commercial paper and other short-term borrowing	70
Real estate loans	460	Long-term bonds	439
Consumer loans	187	Other liabilities	491
Securities	311	Total liabilities	1,992
Buildings and equipment	16	Bank capital	231
Other assets	685		
Total assets	**$2,223**	**Total liabilities + bank capital**	**$2,223**

Step 3 **Answer part (b) by calculating the bank's capital as a percentage of its assets.**

Total assets $= \$2{,}223$ billion

Bank capital $= \$231$ billion

$$\text{Bank capital as a percentage of assets} = \frac{\$231 \text{ billion}}{\$2{,}223 \text{ billion}} = 0.104, \text{ or } 10.4\%$$

See related problem 1.7 at the end of the chapter.

10.2 The Basic Operations of a Commercial Bank

LEARNING OBJECTIVE: Describe the basic operations of a commercial bank.

In this section, we look at how banks earn a profit by matching savers and borrowers. When a depositor puts money in a checking account and the bank uses the money to finance a loan, the bank has transformed a financial asset (a deposit) for a saver into a liability (a loan) for a borrower. Like other businesses, a bank takes inputs, adds value to them, and delivers outputs.

To analyze further the basics of bank operations, we will work with an accounting tool known as a **T-account**, which shows *changes* in balance sheet items that result from a particular transaction. To take a simple example, suppose you use $100 in cash to open a checking account at Wells Fargo. As a result, Wells Fargo acquires $100 in vault cash, which it lists as an asset and, according to banking regulations, counts as part of its reserves. Because you can go to a Wells Fargo branch or an ATM at any time and withdraw your deposit, Wells Fargo lists your $100 as a liability in the form of checkable deposits. We can use a T-account to illustrate the changes in Wells Fargo's balance sheet that result:

T-account An accounting tool used to show changes in balance sheet items.

WELLS FARGO

Assets		Liabilities	
Vault cash	+$100	Checkable deposits	+$100

Note that Wells Fargo's balance sheet will have much larger amounts of vault cash and checkable deposits than the $100 shown here. The T-account shows only the changes in these items, not their levels.

What happens to the $100 that you deposited in Wells Fargo? By answering this question, we can see how a bank earns a profit. Suppose that Wells Fargo held no excess reserves before receiving your $100 deposit and that banking regulations require banks to hold 10% of their checkable deposits as reserves. Therefore, $10 of the $100 is required reserves, and the other $90 is excess reserves. To show the difference between required reserves and excess reserves, we rewrite the amount that Wells Fargo holds as reserves as follows:

WELLS FARGO

Assets		Liabilities	
Required reserves	+$10	Checkable deposits	+$100
Excess reserves	+$90		

Reserves that a bank keeps as cash pay no interest, and those the bank keeps in deposits at the Fed pay a low rate of interest. In addition, checkable deposits generate expenses for the bank: The bank must pay interest to depositors and pay the costs of maintaining checking accounts, including record keeping, operating a web site, and servicing ATMs. Therefore, the bank will typically want to use its excess reserves to make loans or buy securities to generate income. Suppose that Wells Fargo uses its excess reserves to buy Treasury bills worth $30 and make a loan worth $60. For simplicity, the units in this example are very small. (Thinking in thousands of dollars would be more realistic.) We can illustrate these transactions with the following T-account:

WELLS FARGO

Assets		Liabilities	
Reserves	+$10	Checkable deposits	+$100
Securities	+$30		
Loans	+$60		

Wells Fargo has used your $100 deposit to provide funds to the U.S. Treasury and to the person or business it granted the loan to. By using your deposit, the bank acquired interest-earning assets. If the interest Wells Fargo earns on these assets is greater than the interest the bank pays you on your deposit plus the other costs of servicing your deposit, then Wells Fargo will earn a profit on these transactions. The difference between the average interest rate banks receive on their assets and the average interest rate they pay on their liabilities is called the banks' *spread*.

To be successful, a bank must make prudent loans and investments so that it earns a high enough interest rate to cover its costs and to make a profit. This plan may sound simple, but it hasn't been easy for banks to earn a profit in the past decade. As we have seen, many banks purchased mortgage-backed securities, whose value declined sharply following the bursting of the housing bubble. In addition, many banks, particularly community banks, provided substantial loans to commercial real estate developers. The severity of the 2007–2009 recession meant that a greater-than-typical number of borrowers defaulted on their loans, forcing banks to take losses on those investments.

And, as we noted in the chapter opener, interest rates on bonds and loans fell to historically low levels following the financial crisis and remained there for years. As a result, banks found their spread squeezed and had difficulty making a profit on loans. This fact helps to explain the willingness of banks to maintain substantial excess reserves on deposit with the Fed, even though those reserves were earning a low interest rate.

Bank Capital and Bank Profit

As with any other business, a bank's profit is the difference between its revenue and its costs. A bank's revenue is earned primarily from interest on its securities and loans and from fees it charges for credit and debit cards, servicing deposit accounts, providing financial advice and wealth management services, originating and collecting payments on securitized loans, and carrying out foreign exchange transactions. A bank's costs are the interest it pays to its depositors, the interest it pays on loans or other debt, and its costs of providing its services. A bank's **net interest margin** is the difference between the interest

Net interest margin The difference between the interest a bank receives on its securities and loans and the interest it pays on deposits and debt, divided by the total value of its earning assets.

it receives on its securities and loans and the interest it pays on deposits and debt, divided by the total value of its earning assets.[1]

If we subtract the bank's cost of providing its services from the fees it receives, divide the result by the bank's total assets, and then add the bank's net interest margin, we have an expression for the bank's total profit earned per dollar of assets, which is called its **return on assets (ROA)**. ROA is usually measured in terms of *after-tax profit*, or the profit that remains after the bank has paid its taxes:

$$\text{ROA} = \frac{\text{After-tax profit}}{\text{Bank assets}}.$$

Return on assets (ROA) The ratio of the value of a bank's after-tax profit to the value of its assets.

A bank's shareholders own the bank's capital, which represents the value of their investment—or equity—in the firm. Naturally, shareholders are more interested in the profit the bank's managers are able to earn on the shareholders' investment than in the return on the bank's total assets. So, shareholders often judge bank managers not on the basis of ROA but on the basis of **return on equity (ROE)**, which is after-tax profit per dollar of equity, or bank capital:

$$\text{ROE} = \frac{\text{After-tax profit}}{\text{Bank capital}}.$$

Return on equity (ROE) The ratio of the value of a bank's after-tax profit to the value of its capital.

ROA and ROE are related by the ratio of a bank's assets to its capital:

$$\text{ROE} = \text{ROA} \times \frac{\text{Bank assets}}{\text{Bank capital}}.$$

In July 2016, total assets of U.S. commercial banks were $13.7 trillion, and bank capital was $1.7 trillion, meaning that the ratio of assets to capital for the banking system as a whole was 8.1. If a bank earned 2% ROA and had a ratio of assets to capital of 8.1, then its ROE would be 16.2% ($= 2\% \times 8.1$). However, if the bank's ratio of assets to capital was 15, then its ROE would be 30%. In the mid-2000s, some financial firms had ratios of assets to capital as high as 35. For those firms, a modest 2% ROA would translate to a whopping 70% ROE! We can draw the following important conclusion: *Managers of banks and other financial firms may have an incentive to hold a high ratio of assets to capital.*

The ratio of assets to capital is one measure of *bank leverage*, the inverse of which (the ratio of capital to assets) is called a bank's *leverage ratio*. **Leverage** is a measure of how much debt an investor assumes in making an investment. The ratio of assets to capital is a measure of **bank leverage** because banks take on debt by, for instance, accepting deposits to gain the funds to accumulate assets. A high ratio of assets to capital—high leverage—is a double-edged sword: Leverage can magnify relatively small ROAs into large ROEs, but it can do the same for losses. For example, suppose a bank suffers a 3% *loss* as a percentage of assets. With a ratio of assets to capital of 8.1, the result is a manageable −24.3% ROE. But if the bank's ratio of assets to capital were 35, the result would

Leverage A measure of how much debt an investor assumes in making an investment.

Bank leverage The ratio of the value of a bank's assets to the value of its capital, the inverse of which (capital to assets) is called a bank's leverage ratio.

---

[1] Earning assets do not include assets, such as vault cash, on which a bank does not earn a return.

be a −105% ROE. In other words, a relatively small loss on the bank's assets would wipe out *all* of the bank's capital. We can conclude that high leverage increases the degree of risk financial firms are exposed to by magnifying swings in profits as measured by ROE.

Moral hazard can contribute to high bank leverage in two ways. First, bank managers are typically compensated at least partly on the basis of their ability to provide shareholders with a high ROE. As we have seen, riskier investments normally have higher expected returns. So, to increase ROE, bank managers may make riskier investments by, for example, providing loans to risky commercial real estate developments or, as happened during the years just before the financial crisis of 2007–2009, by buying risky securities. Particularly if managers do not themselves own significant amounts of stock in the bank, they may have an incentive to take on more risk than shareholders would prefer. Second, federal deposit insurance has increased moral hazard by reducing the incentive depositors have to monitor the behavior of bank managers. Depositors with accounts below the deposit insurance limit do not suffer losses if their bank fails as a result of the bank's managers having taken on excessive risk. So, bank managers do not have to fear that becoming more highly leveraged will cause many depositors to withdraw their funds.

To deal with the risk of banks becoming too highly leveraged, government regulations called *capital requirements* have placed limits on the value of the assets commercial banks can acquire relative to their capital. Expanded capital requirements, both in the United States and globally, were an important regulatory response by governments to the 2007–2009 financial crisis. We will discuss the new requirements in Chapter 12.

10.3 Managing Bank Risk

LEARNING OBJECTIVE: Explain how banks manage risk.

In addition to risks that banks may face from inadequate capital relative to their assets, banks face several other types of risk. In this section, we examine how banks deal with the following three types of risks: liquidity risk, credit risk, and interest-rate risk.

Managing Liquidity Risk

Liquidity risk The possibility that a bank may not be able to meet its cash needs by selling assets or raising funds at a reasonable cost.

Liquidity risk is the possibility that a bank may not be able to meet its cash needs by selling assets or raising funds at a reasonable cost. For example, large deposit withdrawals might force a bank to sell relatively illiquid securities and possibly suffer losses on the sales. The challenge to banks in managing liquidity risk is to reduce their exposure to risk without sacrificing too much profitability. For example, a bank can minimize liquidity risk by holding fewer loans and securities and more reserves. Such a strategy reduces the bank's profitability, however, because the bank earns no interest on vault cash and only a low interest rate on its reserve deposits with the Fed. So, although the low interest rate environment during the years following the financial crisis caused many banks to hold large amounts of excess reserves, more typically banks reduce liquidity risk through strategies of *asset management* and *liquidity management*.

Banks can practice asset management by lending funds in the federal funds market, usually overnight. Normally, banks can earn a higher interest rate by lending to other banks in the federal funds market than they can by keeping the funds on deposit with the Fed, although this typical situation was not true during the years following the financial crisis. A second option is to use *reverse repurchase agreements*, which involve a bank buying Treasury securities owned by a business or another bank while agreeing to sell the securities back at a later date, often the next morning. (With a repurchase agreement, the bank would sell the Treasury securities and agree to buy them back at a later date.) The reverse repurchase agreement acts, in effect, as a short-term loan from the bank to a business or another bank, with the Treasury securities acting as collateral. Most banks use a combination of loans in the federal funds market and reverse repurchase agreements. Because these transactions have very short terms, the funds are available to meet deposit withdrawals.

Banks can also meet a surge in deposit withdrawals by increasing their liabilities—borrowings—rather than by increasing their reserves. Liability management involves determining the best mix of borrowings needed to obtain the funds necessary to satisfy deposit withdrawals. Banks can borrow from other banks in the federal funds market, borrow from businesses or other banks using repurchase agreements, or borrow from the Fed by taking out *discount loans*.

Managing Credit Risk

Credit risk is the risk that borrowers might default on their loans. One source of credit risk is asymmetric information, which often results in the problems of *adverse selection* and *moral hazard* that we discussed in Chapter 9. Because borrowers know more about their financial health and their true plans for using borrowed money than do banks, banks may find themselves inadvertently lending to poor credit risks or to borrowers who intend to use borrowed funds for something other than their intended purpose. We next briefly consider the different methods banks can use to manage credit risk.

Credit risk The risk that borrowers might default on their loans.

Diversification Investors—whether individuals or financial firms—can reduce their exposure to risk by diversifying their holdings, a concept we discussed in Chapter 5. If banks lend too much to one borrower, to borrowers in one region, or to borrowers in one industry, they are exposed to greater risks from those loans. For example, a bank that had granted most of its loans to oil exploration and drilling firms in Texas would have likely suffered serious losses on those loans following the decline in oil prices that began in June 2014 and lasted through January 2016. By diversifying across borrowers, regions, and industries, banks can reduce their credit risk.

Credit-Risk Analysis In performing **credit-risk analysis**, bank loan officers screen loan applicants to eliminate potentially bad risks and to obtain a pool of creditworthy borrowers. Individual borrowers usually must give loan officers information about their employment, income, and net worth. Business borrowers supply information about their current and projected profits and net worth. Banks often use *credit-scoring systems* to predict statistically whether a borrower is likely to default. For example, people who change jobs

Credit-risk analysis The process that bank loan officers use to screen loan applicants.

frequently are more likely to default than are people with more stable job histories. Loan officers collect information before granting a loan and also monitor the borrower during the term of the loan. Following the financial crisis of 2007–2009, many banks tightened their lending procedures to reduce credit risk on loans, particularly mortgage loans. Although this tightening may have helped banks reduce the risks they faced, it made it significantly harder for some households and small businesses to obtain loans.

MAKING THE CONNECTION | **IN YOUR INTEREST**

FICO: Can One Number Forecast Your Financial Life–*and* Your Romantic Life?

The interest rate you pay on a loan to buy a car or a house, or whether you receive the loan at all, can depend almost entirely on one three-digit number—your FICO score. (FICO is pronounced with a long i: Fīcō.) FICO is an abbreviation of the Fair Isaac Corporation, founded in 1956 by engineer William Fair and mathematician Earl Isaac. At the time the company started, there were no nationwide banks, and credit cards were not widely available. As a result, most households and small businesses depended on bank loans for credit. Bank loan officers typically relied to a significant extent on subjective judgments when granting loans. Because of asymmetric information problems, poor credit risks sometimes received loans and good credit risks were sometimes denied loans.

Fair and Isaac realized that advances in computer technology made it possible to use information on borrowers' credit histories to more accurately forecast whether borrowers would make their payments on time. Today, the company produces several credit scores, but the most widely used FICO score is a three-digit number ranging from 300 to 850, with a higher score indicating a better credit history. Your FICO score is based on information Fair and Isaac gather from the three major *credit reporting agencies*: Equifax, Experian, and TransUnion. Each agency compiles a credit report on anyone who uses a credit card, applies for a loan, or opens a bank account. Nearly every adult has a credit report, although some college students may not. Your credit report includes how much you owe on loans, how many credit cards you have and what their balances are, how reliably you pay your bills on time, where you live, and who you work for. (You can get a free copy of your credit report by going to the web site of the U.S. Federal Trade Commission: consumer.ftc.gov/articles/0155-free-credit-reports.)

For many years, consumers typically did not know their FICO scores because they were not included in the versions of credit reports made available to the public. Beginning in 2002, you could find out your FICO score by obtaining a copy of your credit report. Since 2015, many lenders will provide you with your FICO score for free. While Fair and Isaac do not make public the exact calculations they use in computing scores, they do explain how they weight broad categories of information they obtain from credit reports. The following graph shows these weights. The most important factor in determining your FICO score, with a weight of 35%, is whether you have a history of paying your bills on time. The next most important factor is how much you currently owe on your loans and credit cards.

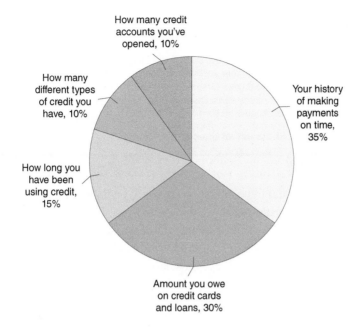

How many credit accounts you've opened, 10%

How many different types of credit you have, 10%

How long you have been using credit, 15%

Your history of making payments on time, 35%

Amount you owe on credit cards and loans, 30%

Most people have FICO scores between 600 and 750. Typically, you will need a score above 740 to qualify for the best interest rate on a car loan or mortgage loan from a bank. With a score below 620, you may have trouble getting a mortgage loan from a bank, in part because the government-sponsored enterprises Fannie Mae and Freddie Mac usually do not buy mortgages that banks have made to borrowers with lower scores. Since the financial crisis of 2007–2009, Fannie Mae and Freddie Mac have bought nearly all the mortgages that are securitized, making their requirements the ones that most banks follow.

Use of credit scores has spread beyond banks and credit card companies. Insurance companies use scores when they are deciding whether they are willing to offer policies to some applicants and in setting premiums. Some employers use credit scores to decide whether to make job offers, and some landlords use credit scores to determine who they will rent apartments to. Researchers at the Federal Reserve have even discovered that couples who have similar credit scores at the beginning of their relationship are more likely to stay together than are couples with very different scores. They conclude that apparently "credit scores reveal an individual's relationship skill and level of commitment." Time will tell whether this research leads to a new topic of conversation on first dates!

Some of the new fintech firms, such as Social Finance (SoFi), that have developed web sites for matching borrowers and lenders online are more skeptical of the usefulness of credit scores. These companies argue that credit scores are too backward looking— focusing on what people have done in the past rather than what they are likely to do in the future. In making lending decisions, SoFi, for instance, focuses on how much of their income borrowers have left after paying their bills, their employment history, and their level of education.

Despite these attempts to develop alternative measures of creditworthiness, to this point FICO scores continue to be used in evaluating 90% of credit applications.

So, for better or for worse, your score is likely to be important as you plan to buy a car or house.

Sources: Peter Rudegeair, "Silicon Valley: We Don't Trust FICO Scores," *Wall Street Journal*, January 11, 2016; Annamaria Andriotis, "Your FICO Credit Score: Actually, There Are Many," *Wall Street Journal*, June 26, 2015; and Jane Dokko, Geng Li, and Jessica Hayes, "Credit Scores and Committed Relationships," Finance and Economics Discussion Series 2015-081. Washington: Board of Governors of the Federal Reserve System, August 2015.

See related problem 3.7 at the end of the chapter.

Prime rate Formerly, the interest rate banks charged on six-month loans to high-quality borrowers; currently, an interest rate banks charge primarily to smaller borrowers.

Historically, loan rates to businesses were based on the **prime rate**, which was the interest rate banks charged on six-month loans to borrowers with the lowest expected default risk—so-called *high-quality borrowers*. Other loans carried interest rates greater than the prime rate, according to their credit risk. Higher-risk loans had higher interest rates. Today, however, banks charge most large to medium-sized businesses interest rates that reflect changing market interest rates instead of the stated prime rate, which is typically charged only to smaller borrowers.

Collateral To reduce problems of adverse selection, banks generally require that a borrower put up collateral, or assets pledged to the bank in the event that the borrower defaults. For example, if you are an entrepreneur who needs a bank loan to start a business, the bank will likely ask you to pledge some of your assets, such as your house, as collateral. In addition, the bank might require you to maintain a *compensating balance*, a required minimum amount that the business taking out the loan must maintain in a checking account with the lending bank.

Credit rationing The restriction of credit by lenders with the result that borrowers cannot obtain all the funds they desire at the given interest rate.

Credit Rationing In some circumstances, banks minimize the costs of adverse selection and moral hazard through *credit rationing*. In **credit rationing**, a bank either grants a borrower's loan application but limits the size of the loan or simply declines to lend any amount to the borrower at the current interest rate. The first type of credit rationing occurs in response to possible moral hazard. Limiting the size of bank loans reduces costs of moral hazard by increasing the chance that the borrower will repay the loan to maintain a sound credit rating. Banks place credit limits on the MasterCard and Visa cards they issue for the same reason. With a credit limit of $2,500 on your credit card, you are likely to repay the bank so that you can borrow again in the future. If the bank were willing to give you a $2.5 million credit limit, you might be tempted to spend more money than you could repay. So, limiting the size of borrowers' loans to amounts less than borrowers demand at the current interest rate is both rational and profit maximizing for banks.

The second type of credit rationing occurs in response to the adverse selection problem that arises when borrowers have little or no collateral to offer banks. What if a bank tries to raise the interest rate it charges to compensate itself for the higher default risk such borrowers represent? If the bank can't reliably distinguish the low-risk borrowers in this group from the high-risk borrowers, it runs the risk of having the low-risk borrowers drop out of the loan pool because of the high interest rate, leaving only the high-risk borrowers. So, keeping the interest rate at the lower level and denying loans altogether to some borrowers can be in the bank's best interest.

Monitoring and Restrictive Covenants To reduce the costs of moral hazard, banks monitor borrowers to make sure they don't use the funds borrowed to pursue unauthorized, risky activities. Banks keep track of whether borrowers are obeying *restrictive covenants*, or explicit provisions in the loan agreement that prohibit the borrower from engaging in certain activities. A business borrowing money to pay for new equipment might be explicitly barred from using the money to meet its payroll obligations or to finance inventories.

Long-Term Business Relationships As we noted in the chapter opener, the ability of banks to assess credit risks on the basis of private information on borrowers is called *relationship banking.* One of the best ways for a bank to gather information about a borrower's prospects or to monitor a borrower's activities is through a long-term business relationship. By observing the borrower over time—through the borrower's checking account activity and loan repayments—the bank can significantly reduce problems of asymmetric information by reducing its information gathering and monitoring costs. Borrowers also gain from long-term relationships with banks. The customer can obtain credit at a lower interest rate or with fewer restrictions because the bank avoids costly information-gathering tasks.

Managing Interest-Rate Risk

Banks experience **interest-rate risk** if changes in market interest rates cause a bank's profit or its capital to fluctuate. The effect of a change in market interest rates on the value of a bank's assets and liabilities is similar to the effect of a change in interest rates on bond prices. That is, a rise in the market interest rate will lower the present value of a bank's assets and liabilities, and a fall in the market interest rate will raise the present value of a bank's assets and liabilities. The effect of a change in interest rates on a bank's profit depends in part on the extent to which the bank's assets and liabilities are *variable rate* or *fixed rate*. The interest rate on a variable-rate asset or liability changes at least once per year, while the interest rate on a fixed-rate asset or liability changes less often than once per year.

> **Interest-rate risk** The effect of a change in market interest rates on a bank's profit or capital.

Table 10.2 shows the hypothetical balance sheet for Polktown National Bank. The table illustrates examples of fixed-rate and variable-rate assets and liabilities. If interest rates go up, Polktown will pay more interest on its $210 million in variable-rate liabilities, such as short-term CDs, while receiving more interest on only $150 million in variable-rate assets, such as adjustable-rate mortgage loans. As a result, its profit will decline, which means Polktown faces interest-rate risk.

The significant increase in the volatility of market interest rates during the 1980s caused heavy losses for banks and savings and loans that had made fixed-rate loans using funds from short-term, variable-rate deposits. For reasons we will explain in the next section, an increase in market interest rates also reduced the value of banks' assets relative to their liabilities, thereby reducing their capital and contributing to the increase in the failures of banks and savings and loans during the late 1980s.

TABLE 10.2 Hypothetical Balance Sheet for Polktown National Bank

Polktown National Bank			
Assets		**Liabilities plus bank capital**	
Fixed-rate assets	$350 million	Fixed-rate liabilities	$250 million
Reserves		Checkable deposits	
Long-term marketable securities		Savings deposits	
Long-term loans		Long-term CDs	
Variable-rate assets	$150 million	Variable-rate liabilities	$210 million
Adjustable-rate loans		Short-term CDs	
Short-term securities		Federal funds	
		Bank capital	$ 40 million
Total assets	**$500 million**	**Total liabilities plus bank capital**	**$500 million**

Gap analysis An analysis of the difference, or *gap*, between the dollar value of a bank's variable-rate assets and the dollar value of its variable-rate liabilities.

Measuring Interest-Rate Risk: Gap Analysis and Duration Analysis Bank managers use *gap analysis* and *duration analysis* to measure how vulnerable their banks are to interest-rate risk. **Gap analysis** looks at the difference, or *gap*, between the dollar value of a bank's variable-rate assets and the dollar value of its variable-rate liabilities. Most banks have negative gaps because their liabilities—mainly deposits—are more likely to have variable rates than are their assets—mainly loans and securities. For example, from Table 10.2, we can see that Polktown National Bank has a gap equal to $150 million − $210 million = −$60 million. To simplify the analysis, suppose that the interest rates on all of Polktown's variable-rate assets and variable-rate liabilities increase by 2 percentage points over a one-year period. Then Polktown will earn 0.02 × $150 million = $3 million more on its assets but pay 0.02 × $210 million = $4.2 million more on its liabilities, so its profit will fall by $1.2 million. We can also calculate the fall in Polktown's profit directly by multiplying the change in the market interest rate by Polktown's gap: 0.02 × −$60 million = 0.02 × −$60 million = −$1.2 million. This simple gap analysis conveys the basics of how to calculate the vulnerability of a bank's profits to changes in market interest rates. In practice, a bank manager will conduct a more sophisticated analysis that takes into account the fact that different assets and liabilities are likely to experience different changes in interest rates.

In addition to affecting a bank's profit, changes in interest rates can affect a bank's capital by changing the value of the bank's assets and liabilities. We know that the longer the maturity of a financial asset, the larger the change in the asset's price as a result of a given change in interest rates. During the 1930s, Frederick Macaulay, an economist at the National Bureau of Economic Research, developed the concept of *duration* as a more precise measure than maturity of the sensitivity of a financial asset's price to changes in the interest rate.[2] The longer the duration of a particular bank asset or bank liability, the more the value of the asset or liability will change as a result of a change in market interest rates. **Duration analysis** measures how sensitive a bank's capital is to changes in market interest rates. A bank's *duration gap* is the difference between the average duration of the bank's assets and the average duration of the bank's liabilities. If a bank has a positive duration gap, the duration of the bank's assets is greater than the duration of the bank's liabilities. In this case, an increase in market interest rates will reduce the value of the bank's assets more than the value of the bank's liabilities, which will decrease the bank's capital. Banks typically have positive duration gaps because their assets—mainly loans and securities—have longer durations than their liabilities—mainly deposits.

Duration analysis An analysis of how sensitive a bank's capital is to changes in market interest rates.

Table 10.3 summarizes gap and duration analysis and shows that *falling* market interest rates are typically good news for banks because they will *increase* bank profits and the value of bank capital, while *rising* market interest rates are bad news for banks because they will *decrease* bank profits and the value of bank capital. The difficulty many banks experienced following the financial crisis of 2007–2009 was that while falling interest rates initially helped banks' profits by reducing the interest rates they paid on deposits, persistently low interest rates eventually reduced the amount banks received on loans. The result was a decline in the interest rate spread between banks' deposits and their loans, which reduced their profits.

TABLE 10.3 Gap and Duration Analysis

Most banks have ...	so an increase in market interest rates will ...	and a decrease in market interest rates will ...
1. a negative gap,	*decrease* bank profits,	*increase* bank profits and
2. a positive duration gap,	*decrease* bank capital,	*increase* bank capital.

Reducing Interest-Rate Risk Bank managers can use a variety of strategies to reduce their exposure to interest-rate risk. Banks with negative gaps can make more adjustable-rate or *floating-rate* loans. That way, if market interest rates rise and banks must pay higher interest rates on deposits, they will also receive higher interest rates on their loans. Unfortunately for banks, many loan customers are reluctant to take out adjustable-rate loans because while the loans reduce the interest-rate risk banks face, they increase the interest-rate risk borrowers face. For example, if you buy a house using an adjustable-rate mortgage (ARM), your monthly payments will decline if market interest rates fall but rise if market interest rates rise. Many borrowers do not want to assume

---

[2] For the mathematically minded, here is a more precise definition of duration: Duration is the weighted sum of the maturities of the payments from a financial asset, where the weights are equal to the present value of the payment divided by the present value of the asset. If we denote the present value of a payment at time t by PV_t, then the market value, MV, of an asset that matures in T periods is:

$$MV = \sum_{t=1}^{T} PV_t, \text{ and the duration of the asset is } d = \sum_{t=1}^{T} t\left(\frac{PV_t}{MV}\right).$$

this interest-rate risk, so the great majority of residential mortgage loans are granted with fixed rates. Similarly, adjustable-rate car loans are rare. Fortunately for banks, they are able to sell many of their long-term loans as part of the securitization process that we have already discussed. In addition, many bank loans granted to businesses are short-term, variable-rate loans where the interest-rate risk is not very large.

As we saw in Chapter 7, banks can use *interest-rate swaps* in which they agree to exchange, or swap, the payments from a fixed-rate loan for the payments on an adjustable-rate loan owned by a corporation or another financial firm. Swaps allow banks to satisfy the demands of their loan customers for fixed-rate loans while still reducing exposure to interest-rate risk. Banks can also use futures contracts and options contracts to help hedge interest-rate risk. Suppose that Polktown National Bank uses funds from variable-rate certificates of deposit (CDs) to make a long-term fixed-rate loan to a local auto parts factory. If interest rates rise, Polktown will have to pay higher interest rates on the CDs or lose the funds to another bank but will not receive an increase in interest payments on the fixed-rate loan. To reduce, or *hedge*, this interest-rate risk, Polktown could sell Treasury bill futures contracts. If market interest rates rise, the value of Treasury bill futures contracts will fall, which will allow Polktown to earn a profit when it buys back the futures contracts to settle its position. This profit will offset the additional interest it will have to pay on the CDs. Polktown can undertake a similar hedge by using put options contracts on Treasury bills. (For a more complete discussion of futures and options contracts, see Chapter 7.)

10.4 Trends in the U.S. Commercial Banking Industry

LEARNING OBJECTIVE: Explain the trends in the U.S. commercial banking industry.

The U.S. commercial banking industry has gone through tremendous changes over the years. In this section, we present a brief overview of the history of banking and look at important developments during the past 20 years, including the effects of the financial crisis of 2007–2009.

The Early History of U.S. Banking

For most of U.S. history, the great majority of banks have been small and have typically operated in limited geographic areas. In the early years of the country, Congress established the Bank of the United States at the urging of the country's first Treasury secretary, Alexander Hamilton. This bank performed some of the same activities that modern central banks do, and it had nationwide branches. When the bank's initial 20-year charter expired in 1811, political opposition kept the charter from being renewed, and the bank went out of existence. The bank's opponents believed that the bank's actions had the effect of reducing loans to farmers and owners of small businesses and that Congress had exceeded its constitutional authority in establishing the bank. Financial problems during the War of 1812 led Congress to charter the Second Bank of the United States in 1816. But, again, political opposition, this time led by President Andrew Jackson, resulted in the bank's charter not being renewed in 1836.

After the failure of these two early attempts to establish a central bank with nation-wide branches, for several decades *state banks* were the only type of banks. Entrepreneurs wishing to start a bank had to obtain a charter—a legal document that allows a bank to operate—from their state government. The National Banking Act of 1863 made it possible for entrepreneurs to obtain a federal bank charter from the Office of the Comptroller of the Currency, which is part of the U.S. Treasury Department. Federally chartered banks are known as **national banks**. The United States currently has a **dual banking system** in which banks can be chartered either by state governments or by the federal government. The National Banking Acts of 1863 and 1864 also prohibited banks from using deposits to buy ownership of nonfinancial firms. This prohibition, which continues to the present, does not exist in some other countries, notably Germany and Japan.

National bank A federally chartered bank.

Dual banking system The system in the United States in which banks are chartered by either a state government or the federal government.

Bank Panics, the Federal Reserve, and the Federal Deposit Insurance Corporation

We have seen that banks can suffer from liquidity risk because of the possibility that depositors may collectively decide to withdraw more funds than the bank has immediately on hand. In the current banking system, this risk is relatively low because bank deposits, including those owned by businesses, are insured up to a limit of $250,000 per deposit, per bank, which reduces the concern that depositors might otherwise have of losing their money in the event that their banks fail. In addition, the Federal Reserve plays the role of a *lender of last resort* by making discount loans to banks suffering from temporary liquidity problems. For most of the nineteenth and early twentieth centuries, however, neither federal deposit insurance nor the Federal Reserve existed. As a result, banks were subject to periodic *bank runs*, in which large numbers of depositors would decide that a bank might be in danger of failure and would simultaneously demand their deposits back. If a few banks were hit with runs, they might be able to satisfy depositors' demand for funds by borrowing from other banks. But if many banks simultaneously experienced runs, the result would be a *bank panic*, which often resulted in banks being unable to return depositors' money and having to temporarily close their doors. With households and firms cut off from their deposits and from access to credit, bank panics typically resulted in recessions. A particularly severe panic in 1907 finally convinced Congress that the country needed a central bank capable of serving as a lender of last resort. Congress passed the Federal Reserve Act in December 1913, and the Federal Reserve System began operation in 1914.

Although the establishment of the Federal Reserve System put a temporary end to bank panics, they recurred in the early 1930s, during the Great Depression. Congress responded by setting up a system of federal deposit insurance run by the Federal Deposit Insurance Corporation (FDIC), which was established in 1934. All national banks were required to join the system, and state banks were given the option of joining. Today, about 99% of all depositors are fully insured, so most depositors have little incentive to withdraw their money and cause their bank to fail if there are questions about the bank's financial health. The FDIC generally handles bank failures in one of two ways: It closes the bank and pays off depositors, or it purchases and assumes control of the bank while finding another bank that is willing to purchase the failed bank. If the FDIC closes a bank, it pays off the insured depositors immediately, using the bank's assets. If those funds are insufficient, the FDIC makes up the difference from its insurance reserves, which come from payments insured banks make to the FDIC. After the FDIC has compensated insured depositors, any remaining funds are paid to uninsured depositors.

The FDIC prefers to keep failed banks open rather than close them. To keep a bank open, the FDIC will quickly find another bank that is willing to take over the failing bank—usually before the FDIC takes control of the failing bank. Another bank may be willing to take over the failing bank in order to enter a new geographic area or to gain access to the failed bank's deposit and loan customers. If the FDIC has to purchase and assume control of a failed bank, the FDIC typically incurs costs in the transition. Generally, it tries to find an acquiring bank to take on *all* of the failed bank's deposits. In that case, the FDIC subsidizes the acquisition by providing loans at low interest rates or by buying problem loans in the failed bank's portfolio. As Figure 10.2 shows, during the 2007–2009 financial crisis, there was a temporary sharp increase in the number of bank failures, although failures did not reach the high levels seen during the savings and loan crisis of the late 1980s. (We discuss the savings and loan crisis in Chapter 12.) A number of failures following the financial crisis were of large institutions, which required substantial expenditures by the FDIC.

Legal Changes, Economies of Scale, and the Rise of Nationwide Banking

Historically, a series of federal laws limited the ability of banks to operate in more than one state. The most recent of these was the McFadden Act, which Congress passed in 1927. In addition, most states were *unit banking states*, which means they had regulations prohibiting banks from having more than one branch. Research by David Wheelock of the Federal Reserve Bank of St. Louis has shown that in 1900, of the 12,427 commercial banks in the United States, only 87 had any branches. By contrast, for many years, most other countries have had relatively few banks, each operating branches nationwide.

The U.S. system of many small, geographically limited banks was the result of political views that the power of banks should be limited by keeping them small and that the deposits banks receive should be used only to fund loans in the local area. But most economists believe the U.S. system was inefficient because it failed to take full

MyEconLab Real-time data

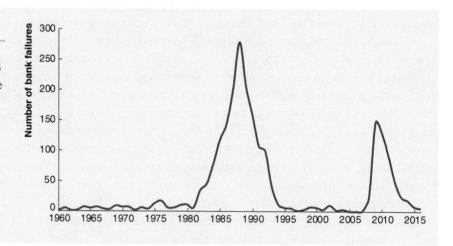

FIGURE 10.2

Commercial Bank Failures in the United States, 1960–2016

Bank failures in the United States were at low levels from 1960 until the savings and loan crisis of the mid-1980s. By the mid-1990s, bank failures had returned to low levels, where they remained until the beginning of the financial crisis in 2007. The financial crisis led to a sharp, but temporary, increase in bank failures.

Source: Federal Reserve Bank of St. Louis.

advantage of economies of scale in banking. *Economies of scale* refers to the reduction in average cost that results from an increase in the quantity of a good or service provided. Larger banks are able to spread their fixed costs, such as the salaries of loan officers, the cost of computer systems and software, and the cost of operating bank buildings, over a larger quantity of transactions. Keeping banks limited to a small geographic area was also inefficient because it exposed banks to greater credit risk by concentrating their loans in one area. If a bank is located in a town in downstate Illinois where most local businesses depend on agriculture, a drought could lead to a wave of loan defaults, causing the bank to suffer heavy losses and possibly fail.

Over time, restrictions on the size and geographic scope of banking were gradually removed. After the mid-1970s, most states eliminated restrictions on branching within the state. In 1994, Congress passed the Riegle–Neal Interstate Banking and Branching Efficiency Act, which allowed for the phased removal of restrictions on interstate banking. The 1998 merger of NationsBank, based in North Carolina, and Bank of America, based in California, produced the first bank with branches on both coasts.

Rapid consolidation in the U.S. banking industry has resulted from these regulatory changes. While in 1984, there were about 14,200 commercial banks in the United States, in 2016, there were only about 5,000. This consolidation is what we would expect in an industry with substantial economies of scale when firms are free to compete with each other, as has been the case since the removal of restrictions on banks branching and operating in more than one state. As you saw in your principles of economics course, when an industry has economies of scale, firms that expand have a lower average cost of producing goods or services. This lower cost allows the expanding firms to sell their goods or services at a lower price than smaller rivals, driving them out of business or forcing them to merge with other firms. Because large banks have lower costs than smaller banks, they can offer depositors higher interest rates, give borrowers lower interest rates, and provide investment advice and other financial services at a lower price.

Even though over the past 25 years there has been tremendous consolidation in the U.S. banking industry, 5,000 banks is still many more banks than in most other countries. So, it seems likely that further consolidation will take place, and the number of banks will continue to dwindle. The decline in the number of banks understates the degree of consolidation in the U.S. banking industry. As Table 10.4 shows, the largest 10 banks have more than half of all deposits, with the top 3 banks having more than one-third.

During 2010, as Congress enacted changes in financial regulation, some members of the House and Senate suggested placing limits on the size of banks. They argued that when banks become too large, they acquire market power that enables them to pay lower interest rates to depositors and charge higher interest rates on loans. In addition, some economists and policymakers worried that large banks were "too big to fail," meaning that their failure would cause such financial disruption that the Federal Reserve, the FDIC, and the U.S. Treasury would be forced to take measures to keep them from bankruptcy however poorly they may have been managed. As we will discuss in Chapter 12, the Dodd-Frank Act of 2010 did not specifically limit bank size, although it did put some limits on the methods the FDIC and other federal regulators can use to save large banks that are at risk of failing. The debate over whether there should be regulatory limits on the size of banks continues.

TABLE 10.4 The 10 Largest U.S. Banks, 2015

Bank	Share of total deposits
Bank of America	12.1%
JPMorgan Chase	11.5
Wells Fargo Bank	11.3
Citigroup	4.8
U.S. Bancorp	2.9
Capital One	2.6
PNC	2.4
TD Bank	2.1
Bank of New York Mellon	1.8
SunTrust	1.5
Total for top 10 banks	**53.0%**

Source: Federal Deposit Insurance Corporation; data are as of June 30, 2015.

MAKING THE CONNECTION   **IN YOUR INTEREST**

Starting a Small Business? See Your Community Banker

In the chapter opener, we saw that the small Bank of Bird-in-Hand was prospering at a time when many larger banks were struggling. Small banks are often called *community banks* because they receive most of their deposits and make most of their loans to households and firms in a particular geographic area, or community. At one time, most banks in the United States were community banks because states restricted the number of branches a bank could have, and federal law prohibited banks from operating in more than one state.

As we have just discussed, banks have substantial fixed costs that result in significant economies of scale. As a result, large regional or national banks can offer many banking services at a lower cost than can community banks. Not surprisingly, many community banks have disappeared, and they are often replaced by branches of regional or national banks. Larger banks, however, may fail to provide the same services that community banks do. For example, many large banks have cut back on small business loans, preferring to concentrate on loans of at least $1 million, which cost the bank about the same to process as do smaller loans of $100,000 or less. From the peak before the financial crisis, lending to small businesses by the largest banks has declined by about 40%.

One of the reasons that large banks have reduced their lending to small businesses is that small business loans are more difficult to securitize than are mortgage loans or balances on credit cards. Accordingly, some large banks have pushed their small business borrowers to rely on bank-issued credit cards, which carry higher interest rates, rather than on traditional bank loans. Some small businesses have turned to online lenders such as Kabbage Inc., but typically the interest rates these lenders charge are also much higher than the interest rates on bank loans.

Community banks attract small business borrowers by being more flexible in the standards they apply in granting loans. The standardized loan approval software used by most large banks often requires small businesses applying for loans to supply 10 years' worth of financial data—an impossibility for a small startup. Although community banks may charge higher interest rates on business loans than do large banks, the interest rates are still lower than on credit cards or on most online loans. In addition, community banks are often more flexible in allowing a borrower to miss a loan payment or overdraw a credit line without severe penalties.

Community banks do have problems, though. Since Congress passed the Dodd-Frank Act in 2010, all banks have faced greater regulation, which has raised their costs. The quarterly Call Reports that banks have to file with the FDIC, showing detailed accounts of their activities, are a particular burden on smaller banks because they require an extensive commitment of time from the bank's staff. In effect, these regulations are another large fixed cost that has to be spread over the smaller quantity of services a community bank supplies. Many community banks also cite the extensive regulatory burden of participating in the federal Small Business Administration's program that insures some loans to small businesses. These regulatory costs make it more difficult for entrepreneurs to start new community banks. For example, when the Bank of Bird-in-Hand opened in 2013, it was the first new bank to open in the United States since 2010. Prior to the financial crisis and the passage of the Dodd-Frank Act, an average of 100 new banks opened per year. In early 2017, President Donald Trump and members of Congress were considering loosening some of Dodd-Frank's regulatory requirements for small banks.

Currently, community banks offer clear advantages over larger banks for entrepreneurs seeking small business loans. But their small scale leaves them vulnerable in the future both to larger banks developing lower-cost ways of offering business loans of $100,000 or less and to fintech web sites, should these sites begin offering lower interest rate loans.

Sources: Michael Rapoport, "Small Banks Are in Good Shape, So Why Aren't They Doing Better?" *Wall Street Journal*, May 31, 2016; Ruth Simon, "Big Banks Cut Back on Loans to Small Business," *Wall Street Journal*, November 26, 2016; Robert G. Wilmers, "Shrinking Support for Small Businesses," *Wall Street Journal*, June 28, 2016; and Llewellyn Hinkes-Jones, "Community Banks Continue to Stabilize in 2015," bloomberg.com, March 7, 2016.

See related problem 4.9 at the end of the chapter.

Expanding the Boundaries of Banking

The activities of banks have changed dramatically during the past five decades. Between 1960 and 2017, banks: (1) increased the amount of funds they raise from time deposits and negotiable CDs; (2) increased their borrowings from repurchase agreements; (3) reduced their reliance on commercial and industrial (C&I) loans and on consumer loans; (4) increased their reliance on real estate loans; and (5) expanded into nontraditional lending activities and into activities where their revenue is generated from fees rather than from interest.

Off-Balance-Sheet Activities Banks have increasingly turned to generating *fee income* from *off-balance-sheet activities*. Traditional banking activity, such as taking in deposits and making loans, affects a bank's balance sheet because deposits appear on the balance sheet as liabilities, and loans appear as assets. **Off-balance-sheet activities** do not affect the bank's balance sheet because they do not increase either the bank's assets or its liabilities. For instance, when a bank buys and sells foreign exchange for customers, the bank charges the customers a fee for the service, but the foreign exchange does not appear on the bank's balance sheet. Banks also charge fees for *private banking* services to high-income households—those with a net worth of $1 million or more. Banks have come to rely particularly on the following four off-balance-sheet activities to earn fee income:

Off-balance-sheet activities Activities that do not affect a bank's balance sheet because they do not increase either the bank's assets or its liabilities.

1. **Standby letters of credit.** We have seen that during the 1970s and 1980s, banks lost some of their commercial lending business to the commercial paper market. As the commercial paper market developed, most buyers insisted that sellers provide a *standby letter of credit*. With a **standby letter of credit**, a bank promises to lend funds to the borrower—the seller of the commercial paper—to pay off its maturing commercial paper, if necessary. Banks generally charge a fee equal to 0.5% of the value of the commercial paper. Today, not only corporations but also state and local governments typically need standby letters of credit in order to sell commercial paper. Using standby letters of credit essentially splits the granting of credit into two parts: (1) credit-risk analysis through information gathering and (2) actual lending. Banks can provide credit-risk analysis efficiently, while financial markets can provide the actual lending more inexpensively. Unlike conventional loans, standby letters of credit do not appear on bank balance sheets.

Standby letter of credit A promise by a bank to lend funds, if necessary, to a seller of commercial paper at the time that the commercial paper matures.

2. **Loan commitments.** In a **loan commitment**, a bank agrees to provide a borrower with a stated amount of funds during a specified period of time. The borrower then has the option of deciding whether and when to take the loan. A bank earns a fee for a loan commitment. The fee is usually split into two parts: an *upfront fee* when the commitment is written and a *nonusage fee* on the unused portion of the loan. For loans that are actually made, the interest rate charged is a markup over a benchmark lending rate. Loan commitments fix the markup over the benchmark rate in advance but not the interest rate to be charged if the loan is made because the interest rate will vary with the benchmark rate. In addition, the bank's commitment to lend ceases if the borrower's financial condition deteriorates below a specified level.

Loan commitment An agreement by a bank to provide a borrower with a stated amount of funds during a specified period of time.

3. **Loan sales.** We have already seen that *loan securitization* has been an important development in the U.S. financial system. With securitization, rather than holding the loans in their own portfolios, banks convert bundles of loans into securities that are sold directly to investors through financial markets. As part of the trend toward securitization since the 1980s, the market for bank loan sales in the United States

grew from almost nothing to a substantial size. A **loan sale** is a financial contract in which a bank agrees to sell the expected future returns from an underlying bank loan to a third party. Loan sales are also called *secondary loan participations*. Formally, the loan contract is sold *without recourse*, which means the bank provides no guarantee of the value of the loan sold and no insurance. Large banks sell loans primarily to domestic and foreign banks and to other financial institutions. Originally, banks sold only short-term, high-quality loans with low information-gathering and monitoring costs. Increasingly, however, banks are selling lesser-quality and longer-term loans. By selling loans, banks put their reputations rather than their capital on the line. A bank whose loans perform poorly is unlikely to remain a successful player in that market.

4. **Trading activities.** Banks earn fees from trading in the multibillion-dollar markets for futures, options, and interest-rate swaps. Bank trading in these markets is primarily related to hedging the banks' own loan and securities portfolios or to hedging services provided for bank customers. But banks sometimes speculate in these markets by buying or selling, with the expectation that they can make a profit on changes in prices. Speculation, of course, carries the risk of losing money. The bank employees responsible for trading are often compensated on the basis of the profits they earn. So, a principal–agent problem can occur, with these employees taking on more risk—in the hope of earning higher profits and higher compensation—than the bank's top managers or its shareholders would prefer. During the financial crisis of 2007–2009, members of Congress became concerned that losses from trading in securities had worsened the financial situation at some banks. When Congress passed the Dodd-Frank Act in 2010, it included a provision based on a proposal developed by former Federal Reserve Chairman Paul Volcker, who was serving as head of President Obama's Economic Recovery Advisory Board. Under the "Volcker Rule," banks have to give up trading with their own funds, or *proprietary trading*. Both banks and regulators faced uncertainty as they attempted to distinguish what trading banks were doing on behalf of their customers—which was still allowed under the law—from proprietary trading—which was no longer allowed.

Banks generate fee income from off-balance-sheet activities, but they also take on additional risk. To assess their exposure to risk in off-balance-sheet activities, banks have developed sophisticated computer models. One popular model, known as the *value-at-risk (VAR) approach*, uses statistical models to estimate the maximum losses a portfolio's value is likely to sustain over a particular time period—hence the name "value at risk." These models have been helpful to banks in assessing risk, but they proved to be far less than foolproof in shielding banks from heavy losses during the financial crisis of 2007–2009, mainly because they did not fully account for credit risk in trading assets.

Electronic Banking and Mobile Banking The development of inexpensive computer processing and the rise of the Internet have revolutionized how many banking transactions are handled. The first important development in electronic banking was the spread of ATMs, which for the first time allowed depositors regular access to their funds outside normal banking hours. Rather than having to arrive at a bank between

> **Loan sale** A financial contract in which a bank agrees to sell the expected future returns from an underlying bank loan to a third party.

10 A.M. and 3 P.M., depositors could now withdraw money at 2 A.M. if they wanted to. ATMs were attractive to banks because once installed, the costs of running and maintaining them were far less than the costs of paying bank tellers. In addition, in states that restricted branch banking, ATMs were particularly appealing because they were not legally considered branches, so they allowed banks to extend their operations into areas where they could not have opened branches.

By the mid-1990s, *virtual banks* began to appear. These banks have no brick-and-mortar bank buildings but instead carry out all their banking activities online. Customers can open accounts, pay bills electronically, and have their paychecks directly deposited—all without paper. ING Direct, an online bank that is owned by Capital One, has more than 7.5 million depositors in the United States. By the mid-2000s, most traditional banks had also begun providing mobile banking services that allow depositors to easily pay some or all of their bills using their smartphones rather than by paper check, typically without being charged a fee. Borrowers can also use bank mobile apps to apply for loans, with the bulk of the approval process handled electronically. Banks have begun to clear the vast majority of checks electronically. Until a few years ago, if you deposited a check written against an account at another bank, your bank (or the Federal Reserve, which provided check-clearing services for banks) would have to physically send the check to the other bank in order to receive payment. Today, your bank is likely to clear the check by sending an electronic image of it to the other bank.

Electronic banking has played an increasing role in the banking industry, but brick-and-mortar bank branches continue to be built, and a majority of payments made using checking accounts still involve paper checks. The trend towards electronic provision of banking services seems clear, though.

The Financial Crisis, TARP, and Partial Government Ownership of Banks

Many of the high-risk mortgage loans that banks granted during the financial crisis of 2007–2009 had been securitized and resold to investors. Banks held some of these securities as investments, and, as Figure 10.1 on page 314 shows, banks had also become dependent on making real estate loans. As the financial crisis unfolded, first residential real estate mortgages and then commercial real estate mortgages suffered increased default rates, causing securities based on both types of mortgages to decline in value. By mid-2008, housing prices in the 20 largest metropolitan areas had declined by more than 15%, and more than 6% of all mortgages—and 25% of subprime mortgages—were at least 30 days past due. The market for mortgage-backed securities froze, meaning that buying and selling of these securities largely stopped, making it very difficult to determine their market prices. These securities began to be called "toxic assets."

Evaluating the balance sheets of banks became difficult because neither investors nor banks themselves were sure of the true market value of these toxic assets. So, the true value of bank capital—or even whether a bank still had positive net worth—was difficult to determine. Beginning in August 2007, banks responded to their worsening balance sheets by tightening credit standards for consumer and commercial loans. The resulting *credit crunch* helped cause the recession that started in December 2007, as households and firms had increased difficulty funding their spending.

In October 2008, to deal with the problems banks were facing, Congress passed the **Troubled Asset Relief Program (TARP)**. TARP provided the Treasury and the Fed with $700 billion in funding to help restore the market for mortgage-backed securities and other toxic assets in order to provide relief to financial firms that had trillions of dollars' worth of these assets on their balance sheets. Unfortunately, no good way of restoring a market for these assets was developed, so some of the funds were used instead for "capital injections" into banks. Under this program, called the Capital Purchase Program (CPP), the Treasury purchased stock in hundreds of banks, thereby increasing the banks' capital, just as any issuance of new stock would have done. Participating banks were required to pay the Treasury a yearly dividend equal to 5% of the value of the stock and to issue warrants that would allow the Treasury to purchase additional shares equal to 15% of the value of the Treasury's original investment. Although the Treasury stock purchases amounted to partial government ownership of hundreds of banks, the Treasury did not attempt to become involved in the management decisions of any of the banks. Table 10.5 shows the 10 largest Treasury investments under CPP.

Some economists and policymakers criticized the TARP/CPP program as a "bailout" of banks or of Wall Street. Some economists argued that by providing funds to banks that had made bad loans and invested in risky assets, the Treasury was encouraging bad business decisions, thereby increasing the extent of moral hazard in the financial system. Fears were also raised that the managers of banks that had received Treasury investments might feel pressure to make lending and investment decisions on the basis of political, rather than business, factors. However, Treasury and Fed officials feared that a surge in bank failures might plunge the U.S. economy into another Great Depression and argued that the program was justified, given the severity of the financial downturn. Criticism of the program lessened as the economy and banking system began to revive and many banks bought back the Treasury's stock investment. During the period from October 1, 2008, through September 30, 2009, the Treasury had invested $245 billion in the CPP. By mid-2016, $275 billion had been paid back or received as interest or dividends, leaving the program with a profit of $30 billion.

Troubled Asset Relief Program (TARP) A government program Congress passed in 2008 under which the U.S. Treasury purchased stock in hundreds of banks to increase the banks' capital.

TABLE 10.5 The 10 Banks Receiving the Largest Treasury Investments Under the TARP/CPP Program

Bank	Amount of Treasury investment
JPMorgan Chase	$25 billion
Citigroup Inc.	25 billion
Wells Fargo & Company	25 billion
Bank of America Corporation	10 billion
Goldman Sachs	10 billion
Morgan Stanley	10 billion
PNC Financial Services Group, Inc.	8 billion
U.S. Bancorp	7 billion
SunTrust Banks, Inc.	5 billion
Capital One Financial Corporation	4 billion

Source: U.S. Department of the Treasury.

Continued from page 306

ANSWERING THE KEY QUESTION

At the beginning of this chapter, we asked:

"Is banking a particularly risky business? If so, what types of risks do banks face?"

In a market system, businesses of all types face risks, and many businesses fail. Economists and policy-makers are particularly concerned about the risk and potential for failure that banks face because they play a vital role in the financial system. In this chapter, we have seen that the basic business of commercial banking—borrowing money short term from depositors and lending it long term to households and firms—entails several types of risks: liquidity risk, credit risk, and interest-rate risk.

Key Terms and Problems

Key Terms

Asset, p. 307
Balance sheet, p. 307
Bank capital, p. 308
Bank leverage, p. 319
Checkable deposits, p. 309
Credit rationing, p. 324
Credit risk, p. 321
Credit-risk analysis, p. 321
Dual banking system, p. 329
Duration analysis, p. 327
Excess reserves, p. 313

Federal deposit insurance, p. 310
Gap analysis, p. 326
Interest-rate risk, p. 325
Leverage, p. 319
Liability, p. 307
Liquidity risk, p. 320
Loan commitment, p. 334
Loan sale, p. 335
National bank, p. 329
Net interest margin, p. 318
Off-balance-sheet activities, p. 334

Prime rate, p. 324
Required reserves, p. 313
Reserves, p. 313
Return on assets (ROA), p. 319
Return on equity (ROE), p. 319
Standby letter of credit, p. 334
T-account, p. 317
Troubled Asset Relief Program
    (TARP), p. 337
Vault cash, p. 313

10.1 The Basics of Commercial Banking: The Bank Balance Sheet
Evaluate a bank's balance sheet.

Review Questions

1.1 Write the key accounting equation on which balance sheets are based. What are the most important bank assets? What are the most important bank liabilities?

1.2 According to this chapter: "We can think of a bank's liabilities as the sources of its funds, and we can think of a bank's assets as the uses of its funds." Briefly explain what this statement means.

1.3 How have the types of loans banks make changed over time?

Problems and Applications

1.4 If commercial banks were allowed to purchase significant amounts of stock in the companies to which they make loans, would this change increase or decrease the extent of moral hazard in the financial system? Briefly explain.

1.5 [Related to the Making the Connection on page 311] In 1960, federal regulations prohibited banks from paying interest on checking accounts. Banks are now legally allowed to pay interest on checking accounts, yet the value of checking accounts has shrunk from more than 50% of commercial bank liabilities in 1960 to about 13% today. Because checking accounts now pay interest, shouldn't they have become more popular with households rather than less popular? Briefly explain.

1.6 An article in the *Wall Street Journal* in 2016 discusses proposals by the Federal Reserve for new regulations that would affect banks' "long-term lending such as aircraft, shipping and project finance."

a. Does this long-term lending represent an asset or a liability to the banks doing the lending? Does it represent an asset or a liability to the firms borrowing the funds? Briefly explain.

b. The same article refers to a requirement implemented in 2014 that large banks hold more "highly liquid assets." Give an example of a highly liquid asset found on a bank's balance sheet.

Source: Donna Borak, "Regulators to Call for Banks to Have Year's Worth of Liquidity," *Wall Street Journal*, April 25, 2016.

1.7 **[Related to Solved Problem 10.1 on page 316]** The following entries (in millions of dollars) are from the balance sheet of Rivendell National Bank (RNB):

U.S. Treasury bills	$20
Demand deposits	40
Mortgage-backed securities	30
Loans from other banks	5
C&I loans	50
Discount loans	5
NOW accounts	40
Savings accounts	10
Reserve deposits with Federal Reserve	8
Cash items in the process of collection	5
Municipal bonds	5
Bank building	4

a. Use the entries to construct a balance sheet similar to the one in Table 10.1 on page 308, with assets on the left side of the balance sheet and liabilities and bank capital on the right side.

b. RNB's capital is what percentage of its assets?

1.8 At one time, Congress was considering having the federal government set up a "lending fund" for small banks. The U.S. Treasury would lend the funds to banks. The more of the funds the banks loaned to small businesses, the lower the interest rate the Treasury would charge the banks on the loans. A member of Congress was asked to comment on whether the bill would be helpful to small businesses. Here is part of the member's response:

> The bank that's struggling to write down their commercial real estate assets is having to take a hit to capital, and this provides replacement capital on very, very favorable terms. So it deals with the left side of the balance sheet.

a. Would a loan from the Treasury be counted as part of a bank's capital?

b. Does a bank's capital appear on the left side of the bank's balance sheet?

Source: Robb Mandelbaum, "Can Government Help Small Businesses?" *New York Times*, July 29, 2010.

10.2 The Basic Operations of a Commercial Bank
Describe the basic operations of a commercial bank.

Review Questions

2.1 Use a T-account to show the effect on Bank of America's balance sheet of your depositing $50 in currency in your checking account.

2.2 What is the difference between a bank's return on assets (ROA) and its return on equity (ROE)? How are they related?

 MyEconLab Visit **www.myeconlab.com** to complete these exercises online and get instant feedback. Exercises that update with real-time data are marked with 🌐 .

2.3 What does it mean to describe a bank as "highly leveraged"? Why might the managers of a bank want the bank to be highly leveraged? Why might the bank's shareholders want the bank to be less highly leveraged?

Problems and Applications

2.4 Suppose that Bank of America sells $10 million in Treasury bills to PNC Bank. Use T-accounts to show the effect of this transaction on the balance sheet of each bank.

2.5 Suppose that Lena, who has an account at Sun-Trust Bank, writes a check for $100 to José, who has an account at National City Bank. Use T-accounts to show how the balance sheets of each bank will be affected after the check clears.

2.6 Suppose that National Bank of Guerneville (NBG) has $34 million in checkable deposits, Commonwealth Bank has $47 million in checkable deposits, and the required reserve ratio for checkable deposits is 10%. If NBG has $4 million in reserves, and Commonwealth has $5 million in reserves, how much in excess reserves does each bank have? Now suppose that a customer of NBG writes a check for $1 million to a real estate broker who deposits the check at Commonwealth. After the check clears, how much does each bank have in excess reserves?

2.7 Suppose that the value of a bank's assets is $40 billion and the value of its liabilities is $36 billion. If the bank has a 2% ROA, then what is its ROE?

2.8 Suppose that First National Bank has $200 million in assets and $20 million in equity capital.

a. If First National has a 2% ROA, what is its ROE?

b. Suppose that First National's equity capital declines to $10 million, while its assets and ROA are unchanged. What is First National's ROE now?

2.9 An article in the *Wall Street Journal* in 2016 notes that in explaining the low stock price of the Citigroup bank: "Investors … have only to look to the bank's return on equity. That was just 7% in the second quarter."

a. Why would a bank's stock price be related to its return on equity?

b. Large banks like Citigroup hold more capital relative to their assets than they did prior to the 2007–2009 financial crisis. Briefly explain the effect this change has had on banks' return on equity, holding other factors that might affect banks' return on equity constant.

Source: John Carney, "From BofA to Wells Fargo, Here's a Breakdown of Bank Stress Test Results," *Wall Street Journal*, June 23, 2016.

2.10 According to an article in the *Wall Street Journal*, in 2016, JPMorgan Chase's leverage ratio was 6.2%. The bank's return on equity (ROE) was 9%. Calculate the bank's ROA.

Source: Stephen Grocer, "Citigroup, Wells Fargo Report Earnings—Recap," *Wall Street Journal*, July 15, 2016.

2.11 Suppose that you are considering investing in a bank that is earning a higher ROE than most other banks. You learn that the bank has $300 million in capital and $5 billion in assets. Would you become an investor in this bank? Briefly explain.

10.3 Managing Bank Risk
Explain how banks manage risk.

Review Questions

3.1 Discuss the steps banks take to manage liquidity risk, credit risk, and interest-rate risk.

3.2 What is a credit report? What is a credit score?

3.3 What is the difference between gap analysis and duration analysis? What is the purpose of gap analysis, and what is the purpose of duration analysis?

Problems and Applications

3.4 Before 1933, there was no federal deposit insurance. Was the liquidity risk faced by banks during those years likely to have been larger or smaller than it is today? Briefly explain.

3.5 Does the existence of reserve requirements make it easier for banks to deal with bank runs? Briefly explain.

3.6 Briefly explain whether you agree with each of the following statements:

a. "A bank that expects interest rates to increase in the future will want to hold more rate-sensitive assets and fewer rate-sensitive liabilities."

b. "A bank that expects interest rates to decrease in the future will want the duration of its assets to be greater than the duration of its liabilities—a positive duration gap."

c. "If a bank manager expects interest rates to fall in the future, the manager should increase the duration of the bank's liabilities."

3.7 [Related to the Making the Connection on page 322] According to an opinion column in the *Wall Street Journal*: "Former Google staffers founded the online lender Upstart, which [makes loans] based on [a borrower's] grade-point average, SAT score, college attended and even major." How does this approach to credit scoring differ from the approach Fair Isaac uses? Is it likely that Upstart is targeting a particular type of borrower? Briefly explain.
Source: Andy Kessler, "My Tour of FICO Scores, Fido Loans, Whatever," *Wall Street Journal*, November 15, 2015.

3.8 A Congresswoman introduces a bill to outlaw credit rationing by banks. The bill would require that every applicant be granted a loan, no matter how high the risk that the applicant will not pay back the loan. She defends the bill by arguing:

> There is nothing in this bill that precludes banks from charging whatever interest rate they would like on their loans; they simply have to give a loan to everyone who applies. If the banks are smart, they will set their interest rates so that the expected return on each loan—after taking into account the probability that the applicant will default on the loan—is the same.

Evaluate the Congresswoman's argument and describe the likely effects of the bill on the banking system.

3.9 The following entries (in millions of dollars) are from the balance sheet of Rivendell National Bank (RNB):

U.S. Treasury bills	$20
Demand deposits	40
Mortgage-backed securities	30
Loans from other banks	5
C&I loans	50
Discount loans	5
NOW accounts	40
Savings accounts	10
Reserve deposits with Federal Reserve	8
Cash items in the process of collection	5
Municipal bonds	5
Bank building	4

If RNB's assets have an average duration of five years and its liabilities have an average duration of three years, what is RNB's duration gap?

10.4 Trends in the U.S. Commercial Banking Industry

Explain the trends in the U.S. commercial banking industry.

Review Questions

4.1 Why is the United States said to have a dual banking system?

4.2 Why was the FDIC established?

4.3 Why did nationwide banking come relatively late to the United States compared with other countries?

4.4 List four off-balance-sheet activities and briefly explain what they are.

4.5 What are the key developments in electronic banking?

4.6 When and why was TARP created?

Problems and Applications

4.7 Evaluate the following statement:

> The United States has more than 5,000 banks, while Canada has only a few. Therefore, the U.S. banking industry must be more competitive than the Canadian banking industry.

4.8 A history of deposit insurance on the web site of the FDIC notes: "Some have argued at different points in time that there have been too few bank failures because of deposit insurance, that it undermines market discipline, … and that it amounts to a federal subsidy for banking companies."

a. What does it mean to describe deposit insurance as undermining "market discipline"? From this perspective, why might deposit insurance lead to too few bank failures?

b. In what sense might deposit insurance be considered a federal subsidy for banks?

c. If deposit insurance has these potential drawbacks, why do economists and members of Congress overwhelmingly support it?

Source: FDIC Bureau of Research and Statistics, "A Brief History of Deposit Insurance in the United States," fdic.gov/bank/historical/brief/brhist.pdf.

4.9 [Related to the Making the Connection on page 332] According to an article in the *Wall Street Journal*: "Jorge Rodriguez, owner of a Peruvian restaurant in Los Angeles, said Wells Fargo & Co.—his bank for several years—turned him down … when he sought financing to remodel and expand his business. 'They wouldn't even look at me as a viable client,' said Mr. Rodriguez." Why have large banks like Wells Fargo cut back on their lending to small businesses? In another article, the owner of a construction firm in New Hampshire stated: "We want a bank that will stick with us and ride out the tough times." Why might a small bank be more likely to provide credit to the construction firm's owner than would a large bank?

Sources: Ruth Simon, "Big Banks Cut Back on Loans to Small Business, *Wall Street Journal*, November 26, 2015; and Saabira Chaudhuri, "New Hampshire Businessman Files to Set Up Rare New Bank," *Wall Street Journal*, December 15, 2014.

4.10 The Capital Purchase Program carried out under TARP represented an attempt by the federal government to increase the capital of banks. Why would the federal government consider it important to increase bank capital? What might be some of the consequences of banks having insufficient capital?

4.11 A bank executive was quoted as arguing: "TARP successfully stabilized not only the banking industry but a number of other industries as well." Why might stabilizing the banking industry have stabilized other industries?

Source: Jeffrey Sparshott, "Bank CEO: History Will Be Kind to TARP," *Wall Street Journal*, August 15, 2012.

Data Exercises

D10.1: **[Movements in banks' net interest margins]** Go to the web site of the Federal Reserve Bank of St. Louis (FRED) (fred.stlouisfed.org) and download and graph the data series for the Net Interest Margin for All U.S. Banks (USNIM) from 1984 until the most recent quarter available. Go to the web site of the National Bureau of Economic Research (nber.org) and find the dates for business cycle peaks and troughs. (The period between a business cycle peak and trough is a recession.)

a. Describe how net interest margins move just before, during, and just after a recession.

b. Is there a long-term trend in net interest margins? What are the implications for bank profitability?

D10.2: **[Nonperforming loans and recessions]** Go to the web site of the Federal Reserve Bank of St. Louis (FRED) (fred.stlouisfed.org) and download and graph the data series for Nonperforming Total Loans (NPTLTL) from January 1988 until the most recent quarter available. Go to the web site of the National Bureau of Economic Research (nber.org) and find the dates for business cycle peaks and troughs. (The period between a business cycle peak and trough is a recession.)

a. Describe how nonperforming loans move just before, during, and just after a recession. Is the pattern the same across the three recessions in your data? Briefly explain.

b. Is there a long-term trend in nonperforming loans? What are the implications for bank profitability?

D10.3: **[Long-term trend in the number of banks]** Go to the web site of the Federal Reserve Bank of St. Louis (FRED) (fred.stlouisfed.org) and download and graph the data series for Banks (FREQ) from 1988 until the most recent quarter available. Go to the web site of the National Bureau of Economic Research (nber.org) and find the dates for business cycle peaks and troughs. (The period between a business cycle peak and trough is a recession.)

a. Describe the trend in the number of banks in the United States during these years. Briefly discuss the factors that account for this trend.

b. Do your data indicate a significant effect of recessions on the number of banks in the United States? Briefly explain.

 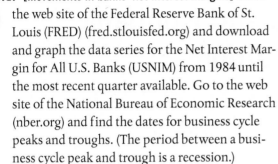

Beyond Commercial Banks: Shadow Banks and Nonbank Financial Institutions

Learning Objectives

After studying this chapter, you should be able to:

11.1 Explain how investment banks operate (pages 345–362)

11.2 Distinguish between mutual funds and hedge funds and describe their roles in the financial system (pages 362–369)

11.3 Explain the roles that pension funds and insurance companies play in the financial system (pages 369–374)

11.4 Explain the connection between the shadow banking system and systemic risk (pages 374–378)

When Is a Bank Not a Bank? When It's a Shadow Bank!

What is a hedge fund? What is the difference between a commercial bank and an investment bank? At the beginning of the financial crisis of 2007–2009, most Americans and even many members of Congress would have been unable to answer these questions. Most people were also unfamiliar with mortgage-backed securities (MBSs), collateralized debt obligations (CDOs), credit default swaps (CDSs), and other ingredients in the alphabet soup of new financial securities. During the financial crisis, these terms became all too familiar, as economists, policymakers, and the general public came to realize that commercial banks no longer played the dominant role in routing funds from savers

to borrowers. Instead, a variety of "nonbank" financial institutions, including mutual funds, hedge funds, and investment banks, were acquiring funds that had previously been deposited in banks. They were then using these funds to provide credit that banks had previously provided. These nonbanks were using newly developed financial securities that even long-time veterans of Wall Street often did not fully understand.

At a conference hosted by the Federal Reserve Bank of Kansas City in 2007, just as the financial crisis was beginning, Paul McCulley, a managing director of Pacific Investment Management Company (PIMCO), coined the term *shadow banking system* to describe the

Continued on next page

KEY ISSUE AND QUESTION

Issue: Today there is a substantial flow of funds from lenders to borrowers outside of the commercial banking system.

Question: Does the shadow banking system pose a threat to the stability of the U.S. financial system?

Answered on page 378

new role of nonbank financial firms. A year later, the term became well known after Timothy Geithner used it in a speech to the Economic Club of New York. Geithner was then the president of the Federal Reserve Bank of New York and later became secretary of the Treasury in the Obama administration. He cited a Federal Reserve study indicating that by 2008, the shadow banking system had grown to be more than 50% larger than the commercial banking system.

As the financial crisis worsened, two large investment banks—Bear Stearns and Lehman Brothers—and an insurance company—American International Group (AIG)—were at the center of the storm. Although many commercial banks were also drawn into the crisis, 2007–2009 represented the first time in U.S. history that a major financial crisis had originated outside of the commercial banking system. Problems with nonbanks made dealing with the crisis more difficult because U.S. policymaking and regulatory structures were based on the assumption that commercial banks were the most important financial firms. In particular, the Federal Reserve System had been established in 1914 to regulate the commercial banking system and to use discount loans to help banks suffering from short-run liquidity problems. Similarly, the Federal Deposit Insurance Corporation (FDIC) had been established in 1934 to insure deposits in commercial banks. As we will see in this chapter, the FDIC does not insure short-term borrowing by shadow banks, and shadow banks are normally not eligible to receive loans from the Fed when they suffer liquidity problems. As a result, the shadow banking system can be subject to some of the same sources of instability that afflicted the commercial banking system before the establishment of the Fed and the FDIC.

Partly as a result of the financial crisis, the size of the shadow banking system has declined relative to the size of the commercial banking system, although shadow banking remains larger. Following the financial crisis, in 2010 Congress passed the Wall Street Reform and Consumer Protection Act, or the Dodd-Frank Act, which to some extent increased federal regulation of the shadow banking system by creating the Federal Stability Oversight Council. But some policymakers and economists continue to believe that shadow banking remains a source of instability in the financial system.

Sources: Stanley Fischer, "The Importance of the Nonbank Financial Sector," Speech at the Debt and Financial Stability—Regulatory Challenges conference, the Bundesbank and the German Ministry of Finance, Frankfurt, Germany March 27, 2015; Zoltan Pozsar, et al., "The Shadow Banking System," Federal Reserve Bank of New York Staff Report No. 458, July 2010, Revised February 2012; Timothy F. Geithner, "Reducing Systemic Risk in a Dynamic Financial System," talk at The Economic Club of New York, June 9, 2008; and Paul McCulley, "Discussion," Federal Reserve Bank of Kansas City, *Housing, Housing Finance, and Monetary Policy*, 2007, p. 485.

In this chapter, we describe the different types of firms that make up the shadow banking system, explore why this system developed, and discuss whether it poses a threat to financial stability.

Investment Banking

LEARNING OBJECTIVE: Explain how investment banks operate.

When most people think of "Wall Street" or "Wall Street firms," they think of investment banks. Firms such as Goldman Sachs, Merrill Lynch, and JPMorgan have been familiar names from the business news. During the 2000s, the fabulous salaries and bonuses some of their employees earned inspired many undergraduates to pursue careers on Wall Street. In this section, we discuss the basics of investment banking and how it has changed over time.

What Is an Investment Bank?

The basis of commercial banking is taking in deposits and making loans. In contrast, **investment banking** is mainly concerned with the following activities:

Investment banking
Financial activities that involve underwriting new security issues and providing advice and financial services to clients, particularly with respect to mergers and acquisitions.

1. Providing advice on issuing new securities
2. Underwriting new securities
3. Providing advice and financing for mergers and acquisitions
4. Financial engineering, including risk management
5. Research
6. Proprietary trading and market making

The first three activities are central to investment banking. The remaining three activities have emerged more recently. We now briefly consider each of these activities.

Providing Advice on New Security Issues Microsoft is good at producing software, Campbell's is good at producing soup, and Coca-Cola is good at producing soft drinks. None of these firms, though, is good at knowing the ins and outs of financial markets. Firms usually turn to investment banks for advice on how to raise funds by issuing stock or bonds or by taking out loans. Investment banks have information about the current willingness of investors to buy different types of securities and on the prices investors are likely to require. This information would be difficult for firms to gather for themselves, but it is essential if they are to raise funds at a low cost.

Underwriting An activity in which an investment bank guarantees to the issuing corporation the price of a new security and then resells the security for a profit.

Underwriting New Security Issues One way for investment bankers to earn income is by *underwriting* firms' sales of new stocks or bonds to the public. In **underwriting**, investment banks typically guarantee a price to the issuing firm, sell the issue in financial markets or directly to investors at a higher price, and keep the difference, known as the *spread*. On average, investment banks earn 6% to 8% of the total dollar amount raised for an **initial public offering (IPO)**, which represents the first time a firm sells stock to the public. An investment bank typically earns 2% to 4% of the dollar amount raised in a *secondary offering* (or *seasoned offering*), which represents security sales by a firm that has sold securities previously. Fees for bond offerings are usually substantially lower: 0.375% for investment-grade bonds and 1% to 2% for non-investment-grade, or junk, bonds.

Initial public offering (IPO) The first time a firm sells stock to the public.

In return for the spread, the investment bank promises to use its "best effort" to resell the securities being underwritten. In a few cases, the investment bank will buy the securities outright, thereby taking on the *principal risk* that it may have misjudged the state of the market and may have to sell securities for a lower price than it had guaranteed to the issuing firm. The investment bank also agrees to make a secondary market in the securities. Doing so provides "support" for the IPO price. The support is only temporary, though. Once the investment bank stops buying shares in the IPO, the price of the shares may drop as investors buy and sell the shares in the secondary market. For instance, in mid-2016, average prices of the stock of companies that had gone public in 2015 were down 15% from their IPO prices.

Syndicate A group of investment banks that jointly underwrite a security issue.

While a single investment bank may underwrite a relatively small issue of stocks or bonds, groups of investment banks called **syndicates** underwrite large issues. Thirty-three banks participated in underwriting Facebook's IPO in 2012, which raised $18.4

billion for the firm. In a syndicated sale, the lead investment bank acts as a manager and keeps part of the spread, and the remainder of the spread is divided among the syndicate members and brokerage firms that sell the issue to the public. Once a firm has chosen the investment bank that will underwrite its securities, the bank carries out a *due diligence process*, during which it researches the firm's value. The investment bank then prepares a *prospectus*, which the Securities and Exchange Commission (SEC) requires of every firm before allowing it to sell securities to the public. The prospectus should contain all information about the firm that a potential investor would find relevant to making a decision to buy the firm's stocks or bonds, including the firm's profitability and net worth, as well as risks faced by the firm, such as pending lawsuits. The investment bank then conducts a "road show," with representatives visiting institutional investors, such as mutual funds, pension funds, and university endowment funds, that might be interested in buying the security issue. Finally, the investment bank sets a price for the stock that it estimates will equate the quantity of securities being sold with the quantity that investors will demand.

Underwriting can lower information costs between lenders and borrowers because investment banks put their reputations behind the firms they underwrite. Investors typically have confidence that because the underwriting investment bank has gathered sufficient information on the issuing firm during the due diligence process, the investors can purchase the firm's securities without incurring excessive risk. During the financial crisis of 2007–2009, this investor confidence was shaken when investment banks underwrote mortgage-backed securities that turned out to be very poor investments.

Providing Advice and Financing for Mergers and Acquisitions Large firms often expand by acquiring or merging with other firms. A small firm may decide that the fastest way to expand is to be acquired by another firm. For example, Swedish firm Mojang AB, developers of the hit video game Minecraft, agreed to be acquired by Microsoft for $2.5 billion. The company's founders believed the firm had grown too large for them to successfully manage. At the time of the acquisition, Markus Persson, the creator of Minecraft, told the game's fans: "Thank you for turning 'Minecraft' into what it has become, but there are too many of you, and I can't be responsible for something this big."[1]

Investment banks are very active in mergers and acquisitions (M&A). They advise both buyers—the "buy-side mandate"—and sellers—the "sell-side mandate." Typically, investment banks take the initiative in contacting firms about potential purchases, sales, or mergers. When advising a firm seeking to be acquired, investment banks attempt to find an acquiring firm willing to pay significantly more than the *market value* of the firm, which is the total value of its outstanding shares. In a typical acquisition, the acquiring firm will pay a premium of 25% to 30% above the market value for the acquired firm. Investment banks can estimate the value of firms, lead negotiations, and prepare acquisition bids. An investment bank provides a *fairness opinion* to an acquired firm's board of directors, indicating that a proposed offer is fair. An acquiring firm may

---

[1] Shira Ovide and Evelyn M. Rusli, "Microsoft Gets 'Minecraft'—Not the Founders," *Wall Street Journal*, September 15, 2014.

need to raise funds, through issuing stocks or bonds, or by taking out loans, in order to make the acquisition. As part of the advising process, an investment bank helps to arrange for this financing. Advising on M&A is particularly profitable for investment banks because, unlike with underwriting and most other investment banking activities, an investment bank does not have to invest its own capital. The only significant costs to advising on M&A are the salaries of the bankers involved in the deal and reserves to be used in the case of litigation.

In addition to giving advice on mergers and acquisitions, investment banks advise firms on their *capital structure*, which is the mix of stocks and bonds the firm uses to raise funds. With the very low interest rates on corporate bonds that persisted for years following the financial crisis, some investment banks advised client firms to issue bonds and use the funds to repurchase the firm's stock, particularly if the stock was selling for a low price. Investment banks can also provide advice on the size of the dividend a firm should pay on its stock.

Financial Engineering, Including Risk Management Investment banks have played a major role in designing new securities, a process called *financial engineering*. Financial engineering typically involves developing new financial securities or investment strategies, using sophisticated mathematical models developed by people with advanced degrees in economics, finance, and mathematics. These people have become known as "rocket scientists," or "quants." Many of the derivative securities we discussed in Chapter 7 are the result of financial engineering. As we have seen, firms can use derivatives to *hedge*, or reduce, risk. For example, an airline can use futures contracts in oil to reduce the risk that a sharp increase in oil prices will reduce the airline's profits. Just as most firms lack the specialized knowledge of financial markets to determine the best way to raise funds by selling stocks and bonds, most firms also need advice on how best to hedge risk using derivatives contracts. Investment banks supply this advice by constructing risk management strategies for firms in return for a fee.

During and after the financial crisis of 2007–2009, some policymakers and economists criticized investment banks because they believed the banks had financially engineered securities, particularly those based on mortgages, that were overly complex and had risk levels that were difficult to gauge. Most of these new securities were not well suited to hedging risk. It became clear that many senior managers at commercial and investment banks had not fully understood the newly created derivative products, including collateralized debt obligations (CDOs) and credit default swap (CDS) contracts, that they were buying, selling, and recommending to clients. These managers greatly underestimated the risk that the prices of these derivatives might fall if housing prices declined and homeowners began to default on their mortgages. The managers of investment banks often relied on the high ratings given to the securities by the rating agencies, such as Moody's, Standard & Poor's, and Fitch. As it turned out, the analysts at the rating agencies also didn't understand some of these securities and failed to accurately estimate their risk.

Research Investment banks conduct several types of research. Banks assign research analysts to large firms, such as Apple or General Electric, and to industries, such as the automobile or oil industries. These analysts gather publicly available information on firms and sometimes visit a firm's facilities and interview its managers. The investment bank uses some of the research material compiled to identify merger or acquisition targets for clients, and it makes some research material public through the financial media as "research notes." Research analysts often provide advice to investors to "buy," "sell," or "hold" particular stocks. In recent years, some analysts have used the terms *overweight* (in an investment portfolio) for a stock they recommend and *underweight* for a stock they do not recommend. The opinions of senior analysts at large investment banks can have a significant effect on the market. For example, a research note from a senior analyst that is unexpectedly negative about a particular firm can cause the price of the firm's stock to fall.

Some analysts specialize in offering opinions on the current state of the financial markets, sometimes minute by minute during the hours that the markets are open. These opinions can provide useful information for the investment bank's *trading desks*, where traders buy and sell securities. Analysts also engage in economic research, writing reports on economic trends and providing forecasts of macroeconomic variables, such as gross domestic product, the inflation rate, employment, and various interest rates. William Dudley, in 2017, the president of the Federal Reserve Bank of New York, holds a PhD in economics from the University of California, Berkeley, and was head of economic research at Goldman Sachs for many years.

Proprietary Trading and Market Making The three core investment banking activities are (1) providing advice on new security issues, (2) underwriting new securities, and (3) providing advice and financing for mergers and acquisitions. Traditionally, making investments in securities, commercial real estate, or other assets was a minor part of the operations of most investment banks. Beginning in the 1990s, however, *proprietary trading* (or *prop trading*), which involves buying and selling securities and other assets for a bank's own account rather than for clients, became a major part of the operations and an important source of profit for many investment banks. As discussed next, restrictions Congress placed on proprietary trading have reduced its importance to investment banks.

Proprietary trading exposed banks to *interest-rate risk, credit risk,* and *funding risk.* If investment banks held long-term securities, such as U.S. Treasury bonds or many mortgage-backed securities, the banks were exposed to the risk of an increase in market interest rates that would cause the prices of their long-term securities to decline. During the financial crisis it became clear that investment banks also faced substantial credit risk from proprietary trading. *Credit risk* is the risk that borrowers might default on their loans. The credit risk on mortgage-backed securities—particularly those that consisted of subprime or Alt-A mortgage loans—was much higher than the investment banks or the credit rating agencies had expected. During the mid-2000s, investment banks originated hundreds of billions of dollars of mortgage-backed securities. They retained some of these securities during the underwriting process and also because they believed that they would be good investments. Beginning in 2007, the market prices of many of these securities began to decline, and by 2008, the markets for these securities had *seized up,* or frozen, making them difficult to sell. As a result, some investment banks suffered significant losses.

The problems investment banks faced during the financial crisis were made worse because they had borrowed funds short term—sometimes just overnight—to finance their purchases of long-term securities. *Funding risk* is the risk that an investor who uses short-term borrowing to make long-term investments will be unable to renew the short-term borrowing. If lenders—typically other financial firms—making short-term loans to investment banks require that the loans be repaid rather than renewing them or allowing the loans to *roll over*, investment banks have to sell their long-term securities to repay the loans. During the financial crisis, many of the long-term securities investment banks had invested in declined in value, leaving them unable to pay off the short-term loans they had received from lenders. Using borrowed funds also increases leverage. We will further discuss both funding risk and leverage in the next section.

In an attempt to reduce the risks from proprietary trading, when Congress passed the Dodd-Frank Act in 2010, it included the Volcker Rule, which put strict limits on such trading. In response, most banks stopped proprietary trading, but continued to buy and sell securities in their role as market makers. A **market maker** is a firm that buys and sells securities, typically those that are not traded on exchanges, and maintains an inventory of the securities in order to serve as an intermediary between buyers and sellers. Investment banks earn a profit from market making from the spread between the price they pay for securities and the price for which they sell them. Although this spread is often small (and can occasionally be negative, in which case the bank will suffer a loss) it can also be substantial. For example, in October 2016, Goldman Sachs earned a profit of $100 million on a single junk bond when the price of the bond increased substantially between the time the bank purchased the bond and the time they sold it. Such gains raised the question of whether there is a significant difference between proprietary trading—which regulators no longer allow—and market making—which regulators continue to allow. Professor Hal Scott of the Harvard Law School was quoted as observing that: "No one has been able to distinguish between market making and prop trading." [2]

Market maker A firm that holds an inventory of a security and serves as an intermediary between buyers and sellers of the security.

"Repo Financing," Leverage, and Funding Risk in Investment Banking

We can consider further the funding risk investment banks face. Commercial banks finance their investments primarily from deposits. Using deposits to finance investments is called *retail funding*. Investment banks do not take in deposits, so they must finance their investments in other ways. One source of funds is the investment bank's capital, which consists of funds from shareholders plus profits the bank has retained over the years. Another source of funds is short-term borrowing, primarily from other financial firms. This type of financing is called *wholesale funding*. Prior to the 1990s, most investment banks were organized as partnerships, and they did relatively little proprietary trading or market making, concentrating instead on the traditional investment banking activities

[2] Justin Baer, "How One Goldman Sachs Trader Made More Than $100 Million," *Wall Street Journal*, October 19, 2016.

of underwriting and providing advice on mergers and acquisitions. The banks financed these activities largely from the partners' capital, or equity. During the 1990s and 2000s, however, most large investment banks converted from partnerships to publicly traded corporations, and proprietary trading became a more important source of profits.

Investment banks used wholesale funding to finance their investments in securities and their direct loans to firms, including mortgage loans to developers of commercial real estate. Financing investments by borrowing rather than by using capital, or equity, increases a bank's *leverage*. Using leverage in investing is a double-edged sword: Profits from the investment are increased, but so are losses. Recall that the ratio of a bank's assets to its capital is a measure of a bank's *leverage*. Because a bank's *return on equity* (ROE) equals its *return on assets* (ROA) multiplied by this measure of leverage, the greater the bank's leverage, the greater the ROE for a given ROA. But, the relationship holds whether the ROA is positive or negative, which means leverage can turn a small negative ROA into a large negative ROE.

SOLVED PROBLEM 11.1

The Perils of Leverage

Suppose that an investment bank is buying $10 million in long-term mortgage-backed securities. Consider three possible ways that the bank might finance its investment:

1. The bank finances the investment entirely out of its equity.
2. The bank finances the investment by borrowing $7.5 million and using $2.5 million of its equity.
3. The bank finances the investment by borrowing $9.5 million and using $0.5 million of its equity.

   a. Calculate the bank's leverage for each of these three ways of financing the investment.

b. For each of these methods of financing the investment, calculate the return on its equity investment that the bank receives, assuming that:

   i. The value of the mortgage-backed securities increases by 5% during the year after they are purchased.

   ii. The value of the mortgage-backed securities decreases by 5% during the year after they are purchased.

For simplicity, ignore the interest the bank receives from the securities, the interest it pays on funds it borrows to finance the purchase of the securities, and any taxes the bank must pay.

Solving the Problem

Step 1 **Review the chapter material.** This problem is about the interaction of leverage and risk, so you may want to review the section "'Repo Financing,' Leverage, and Funding Risk in Investment Banking," which begins on page 350.

Step 2 **Answer part (a) by calculating leverage for each method of financing the investment.** Leverage, as defined in this section, equals the value of assets divided by the value of capital (or equity). In this case, the value of the assets is a constant $10 million, but the bank is investing different amounts of its own funds—different amounts of capital or equity—with the three different ways of financing its investments. If the bank uses financing method 1, it uses

$10 million of its own funds; if it uses financing method 2, it uses $2.5 million of its own funds; and if it uses financing method 3, it uses $0.5 million of its own funds. Therefore, its leverage is as follows for each method:

1. $\dfrac{\$10,000,000}{\$10,000,000} = 1.$

2. $\dfrac{\$10,000,000}{\$2,500,000} = 4.$

3. $\dfrac{\$10,000,000}{\$500,000} = 20.$

Step 3 **Answer the first part of part (b) by calculating the bank's return on its equity investment for each of the three ways of financing the investment.** In each case, the bank experiences a gain of $500,000 from the increase in the prices of the mortgage-backed securities. Because the amount of equity the bank invests differs with the three methods of financing, the bank's returns also differ:

1. $\dfrac{\$500,000}{\$10,000,000} = 0.05,$ or 5%.

2. $\dfrac{\$500,000}{\$2,500,000} = 0.20,$ or 20%.

3. $\dfrac{\$500,000}{\$500,000} = 1.00,$ or 100%.

Step 4 **Answer the second part of part (b) by calculating the return for each of the three ways of financing the investment.** In this case, the investment bank suffers a loss of $500,000 from the fall in the prices of the mortgage-backed securities. Therefore, the bank's returns are:

1. $\dfrac{-\$500,000}{\$10,000,000} = -0.05,$ or −5%.

2. $\dfrac{-\$500,000}{\$2,500,000} = -0.20,$ or −20%.

3. $\dfrac{-\$500,000}{\$500,000} = -1.00,$ or −100%.

These results show that the more highly leveraged the bank's investment—that is, the more the bank relies on borrowing rather than on investing its own capital or equity—the greater the potential profit *and* the greater the potential loss. As we will see, even the highest leverage in this problem—20—is well below the leverage of the large investment banks in the years leading up to the financial crisis of 2007–2009!

See related problem 1.7 at the end of the chapter.

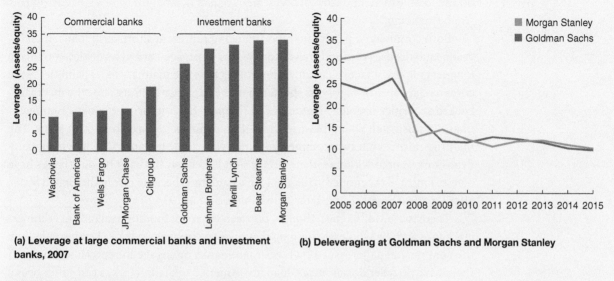

(a) Leverage at large commercial banks and investment banks, 2007

(b) Deleveraging at Goldman Sachs and Morgan Stanley

FIGURE 11.1 Leverage in Investment Banks

Panel (a) shows that at the start of the financial crisis in 2007, large investment banks were more highly leveraged than were large commercial banks.

Panel (b) shows that during and after the financial crisis, Goldman Sachs and Morgan Stanley reduced their leverage, or deleveraged.

Sources: Company annual reports and annual balance sheets.

As we saw in Chapter 10, federal banking regulations put limits on the size of a commercial bank's leverage. These regulations did not, however, apply to investment banks. As a result, during the 2000s, as investment banks increased their investments financed with borrowed funds, their leverage rose well above that of large commercial banks. Panel (a) of Figure 11.1 shows leverage for five large commercial banks and five large investment banks in 2007, as the financial crisis began. As a group, the investment banks were significantly more highly leveraged than the commercial banks. As we will discuss in the next section, by the end of 2008, Goldman Sachs and Morgan Stanley were the only large investment banks that remained independent. As panel (b) of Figure 11.1 shows, during and after the financial crisis, Goldman Sachs and Morgan Stanley reduced their leverage to levels more consistent with those of commercial banks. This process of reducing leverage is called *deleveraging*.

In addition to being highly leveraged, investment banks were vulnerable to funding risk because of how they financed their investments. Investment banks relied on wholesale funding, borrowed primarily by either issuing commercial paper or by using *repurchase agreements*. Repurchase agreements, or *repos*, are short-term loans backed by collateral. For example, an investment bank might borrow money by selling Treasury bills to another bank or a pension fund, and at the same time the investment bank would agree to buy the Treasury bills back at a slightly higher price either the next day or within a few days. The difference between the price of the Treasury bills when sold and when repurchased would represent the interest on the loan. By the mid-2000s, investment banks had begun to rely heavily on this "repo financing."[3]

Both commercial paper and repo financing represent short-term loans. If an investment bank uses the funds raised to invest in mortgage-backed securities or to make long-term loans, it faces a *maturity mismatch* because the maturity of its liabilities—the commercial paper or repos—is shorter than the maturity of its assets—the mortgage-backed securities or loans. As we saw in Chapter 10, commercial banks often face a maturity mismatch when they use short-term deposits to make long-term loans. The maturity mismatch leaves commercial banks vulnerable to bank runs, in which many depositors want to withdraw their money simultaneously but can't because banks have invested most of the money in illiquid loans. Bank runs became rare in the United States after Congress established federal deposit insurance in 1934.

There is a key difference, though, between the retail funding available to commercial banks and the wholesale funding that investment banks rely on. Lenders who buy the commercial paper issued by investment banks or engage in repo financing with them have no federal guarantees. If an investment bank fails, lenders can suffer heavy losses unless the loans are collateralized with assets that do not decline in value. This *counterparty risk,* or the risk that the party on the other side of a financial transaction will not fulfill its obligations, played an important role in the financial crisis of 2007–2009. As investment banks suffered losses on mortgage-backed securities, the funding risk they had undertaken became clear as lenders refused to buy the banks' commercial paper or enter into repo financing agreements with them. Several large investment banks, particularly Bear Stearns and Lehman Brothers, suffered severe financial difficulties because they had financed illiquid, long-term assets with short-term borrowing. As Jamie Dimon, the chairman and CEO of JPMorgan Chase, has put it: "There is one financial commandment that cannot be violated: Do not borrow short to invest long—particularly against illiquid, long-term assets."[4] Unfortunately, in the years leading up to the financial crisis, a number of investment banks violated this commandment.

MAKING THE CONNECTION

Did Moral Hazard Derail Investment Banks?

Until the early 1980s, all the large investment banks were partnerships. The funds the banks used to finance their operations came primarily from the partners' own equity in the firm. If a bank made a profit, the partners shared it, and if the bank suffered a loss, it was shared as well. The financial writer Roger Lowenstein has described the situation at the Salomon Brothers investment bank in the late 1970s, as the partners worried about an investment that had not been going well:

---

[3] The Lehman Brothers investment bank went bankrupt in 2008. A report released by a court-appointed bankruptcy examiner in 2010 indicated that the investment bank had accounted for some of its repos as sales rather than loans, as is typically done, in order to reduce both the assets and debt reported on its balance sheet, thereby reducing how leveraged the bank would appear to investors.

[4] Jamie Dimon, "Letter to Shareholders," March 10, 2008, in JPMorgan Chase's Annual Report, 2007, p. 12.

The firm's capital account used to be scribbled in a little book, left outside the office of a partner named Allan Fine, and each afternoon the partners would nervously tiptoe over to Fine's office to see how much they had lost.

In 1981, Salomon Brothers was the first of the large investment banks to "go public" by converting from a partnership to a corporation. By the time of the 2007–2009 financial crisis, all the large investment banks had become publicly traded corporations. As we saw in Chapter 9, corporations have a separation of ownership from control because although the shareholders own the firm, the top management actually controls it. The moral hazard involved can result in a principal–agent problem, as the top managers may take actions that are not in the best interest of the shareholders.

One way to reduce moral hazard is for shareholders to monitor the behavior of top managers. In the early 2000s, investment banks placed less emphasis on traditional activities such as underwriting and giving advice on mergers and acquisitions and began trading in complex financial securities, such as collateralized debt obligations (CDOs) and credit default swap (CDS) contracts. Shareholders and boards of directors often did not understand these activities or their risks and therefore could not effectively monitor the firms' managers. Some commentators and policymakers have argued that as a result, investment banks took on too much risk during the housing boom by increasing their leverage and buying what turned out to be risky mortgage-backed securities. They did so because top managers would not bear the consequences of heavy losses to the extent that they would have had the firms remained partnerships. Michael Lewis, who worked for several years as a bond salesman at Salomon Brothers and later became a financial author, has argued:

> No investment bank owned by its employees would have leveraged itself 35 to 1 or bought and held $50 billion in mezzanine CDOs. I doubt any partnership would have sought to game the rating agencies … or even allow mezzanine CDOs to be sold to its customers. The hope for short-term gain would not have justified the long-term hit.

Other commentators are skeptical of this argument. Many top managers of investment banks suffered significant losses during the financial crisis, which suggests that the moral hazard problem may not have been severe. At both Bear Stearns and Lehman Brothers, two of the most highly leveraged investment banks, most managers owned significant amounts of company stock. As the stock in these companies lost nearly all of its value during the financial crisis, the personal fortunes of many of the firms' managers dwindled. Richard Fuld, the chairman and CEO of Lehman Brothers at the time of its bankruptcy, suffered losses of about $930 million from the decline in the value of his Lehman Brothers stock.

The debate over why investment banks became more highly leveraged and took on more risk in the years before the financial crisis is likely to continue.

Sources: Michael Lewis, "The End," *Portfolio*, December 2008; Roger Lowenstein, *When Genius Failed: The Rise and Fall of Long-Term Capital Management*, New York: Random House, 2000, p. 4; and Aaron Lucchetti, "Lehman, Bear Executives Cashed Out Big," *Wall Street Journal*, November 22, 2009.

See related problem 1.8 at the end of the chapter.

The Investment Banking Industry

Prior to the Great Depression of the 1930s, the federal government allowed financial firms to engage in both commercial banking and investment banking. During the Depression, a financial panic occurred that involved a collapse in stock prices and the failure of more than 9,000 banks. As part of a series of laws intended to restructure the financial system, Congress passed the Glass-Steagall Act in 1933 to legally separate investment banking from commercial banking. Congress saw investment banking as inherently more risky than commercial banking. As a result, banks that had been engaging in both commercial and investment banking had to split into separate firms. Commercial banks were also not allowed to provide other financial services, such as life insurance, investment advice, or brokerage services. Why did Congress take this action? The great stock market crash of October 1929 had resulted in heavy losses from underwriting because investment banks were forced to sell securities for lower prices than they had guaranteed to the issuing firms. The Glass-Steagall Act also contained provisions for a system of federal deposit insurance (later made permanent with the establishment of the Federal Deposit Insurance Corporation). A majority in Congress believed that if the federal government was going to insure deposits, it should not allow banks to use the deposits to engage in what it saw as risky investment banking activities.

Following the passage of the Glass-Steagall Act, many larger banks saw their commercial banking activities as more profitable than their investment banking activities and so spun off their investment banking activities into separate firms. For example, JPMorgan, then a commercial bank, spun off Morgan Stanley, an investment bank, and First National Bank of Boston spun off First Boston Corporation, which became an independent investment bank.

As the decades passed and the disorderly conditions of the banking industry in the early 1930s faded from memory, economists and policymakers began to rethink the rationale for the Glass-Steagall Act. In principle, the act was designed to protect people with deposits in commercial banks from risky investment activities by banks. In practice, however, some economists argued that the act had protected the investment banking industry from competition because commercial banks could no longer offer investment banking services. These economists argued that the reduced competition enabled investment banks to earn larger profits than commercial banks. As a result, firms were forced to pay more for underwriting and other investment banking services than they would have if competition from commercial banks had been allowed.

By the 1990s, sentiment in Congress was gradually shifting toward repeal of the Glass-Steagall Act. Finally, in 1999, the Gramm-Leach-Bliley Act (formally called the Financial Services Modernization Act) repealed the Glass-Steagall Act. The Gramm-Leach-Bliley Act authorized new financial holding companies, which would permit securities and insurance firms to own commercial banks. The act also allowed commercial banks to participate in securities, insurance, and real estate activities. During the financial crisis of 2007–2009, some economists and policymakers argued that repeal of the Glass-Steagall Act had been a mistake. They argued that, just as during the 1930s, risky investment banking activity had damaged commercial banks and put government-insured deposits at risk.

Following the repeal of the Glass-Steagall Act in 1999, the investment banking industry underwent significant changes. The largest investment banks, known as "bulge bracket" firms, were of two types: Some, such as JPMorgan, Citigroup, and Credit Suisse, were part of larger financial firms with extensive commercial banking activity. Others, such as Goldman Sachs, Morgan Stanley, Lehman Brothers, Bear Stearns, and Merrill Lynch, were standalone investment banks that engaged in no significant commercial banking activity. Large commercial banks, such as Bank of America, UBS, Wachovia, and Deutsche Bank, also had investment banking affiliates. Finally, smaller or regional investment banks, known as "boutiques," such as the Blackstone Group, Piper Jaffray, Lazard, Raymond James, and Perella Weinberg, also played a significant role in the industry.

MAKING THE CONNECTION

Should Congress Bring Back Glass-Steagall?

As we just discussed, by the 1990s, most economists supported the repeal of the Glass-Steagall Act, arguing that the separation of commercial banking from investment banking reduced competition in the market for investment banking services and reduced opportunities for *economies of scope* in banking. Economies of scope exist when a firm can offer multiple goods or services at a lower cost than if they were produced separately. For example, some of a bank's costs for server time, software, and employees might be spread over both commercial banking services and investment banking services, allowing both types of services to be supplied at a lower price.

Although the Gramm-Leach-Bliley Act passed Congress with large majorities, following the financial crisis, some policymakers urged that the separation of commercial and investment banking be restored. During the 2016 presidential campaign, the platform of the Democratic Party urged passage of a "modernized version of Glass-Steagall," and the platform of the Republican Party stated: "We support reinstating the Glass-Steagall Act of 1933 which prohibits commercial banks from engaging in high-risk investment." Neither platform, however, gave details on which aspects of Glass-Steagall might be reinstated.

Senators Elizabeth Warren, John McCain, Maria Cantwell, and Angus King had put forward a more detailed proposal a few years earlier, when they introduced the "21st Century Glass-Steagall Act." That act, which did not become law, would have barred commercial banks from engaging in investment banking activities and offering other services, such as insurance, swaps, and most derivatives. The intent of the act was to confine commercial banks as closely as possible to the traditional banking activities of taking in deposits and making conventional loans to households and firms.

Policymakers have two main objectives in restoring Glass-Steagall: (1) to reduce risk in the financial system and (2) to reduce the size of banks. The first objective is similar to the goal of the supporters of the Glass-Steagall during the 1930s: to reduce risk in the financial system by keeping low-cost, government-insured deposits from being used to make risky financial investments. From this point of view, FDIC insurance of bank deposits creates a moral hazard problem. Depositors are unconcerned about the riskiness of investments made with the funds they provide because they will not suffer losses on the funds up to the $250,000 deposit insurance ceiling. Therefore, depositors don't require a return on the deposits high enough to compensate them for the riskiness of the investments being made with their funds. Because investment banking activity is being financed by low-cost government-insured deposits, banks receive an implicit subsidy from the federal government.

The second objective is motivated by a belief that very large banks are a threat to the stability of the financial system, use their market power to reduce competition in the financial system, and have substantial influence over government policy through campaign contributions to members of Congress and political lobbying. A reinstated Glass-Steagall Act would reduce the size of banks by confining different financial activities—such as commercial banking, security underwriting, insurance sales, and dealer or brokerage services—to separate firms.

Policymakers and economists who are skeptical of the need to reinstate Glass-Steagall believe that both of these objectives are better achieved by direct regulation of the types of investments banks are allowed to make or by taking steps—such as requiring banks to hold more capital—that reduce the effect on the financial system of losses from those investments. Since the financial crisis, regulations of these types have been enacted. The economists and policymakers who are skeptical of the need to reinstate Glass-Steagall also note that the firms whose problems are usually thought to have caused the most difficulty during the financial crisis either operated solely as investment banks—such as Bear Stearns and Lehman Brothers—or did not engage in any investment banking activity—such as Washington Mutual, a large mortgage lender. Large banks that combine commercial and investment banking activity were not at the center of the financial crisis. Moreover, during the crisis, the ability of JPMorgan Chase to purchase Bear Stearns and Bank of America to purchase Merrill Lynch may have helped stabilize the system. Neither purchase would have been allowable if Glass-Steagall restrictions had been in place.

One conclusion that nearly all policymakers and economists agree on is that the failure of a very large financial firm may lead to a financial crisis or worsen a crisis that is already under way. We will discuss this point further in Chapter 12. Knowing the problems that failure of a large financial firm may cause, regulators have an incentive to intervene to keep such firms from failing. The result of this *too-big-to-fail policy* is that moral hazard in the financial system is increased because managers of large firms may make very risky investments if they expect that the federal government will save them from failure. Separating commercial banking from investment banking is one way to make banks smaller, thereby potentially diminishing the too-big-to-fail problem. Following the financial crisis, federal regulators took a different approach to this problem. Rather than break up large banks, which might undercut the lower costs that large banks experience from economies of scale and scope, regulators instead were given the authority to take over a failing bank and gradually dispose of its assets in a way that would not disrupt the financial system. We will discuss this approach further in the Chapter 12.

The renewed debate over Glass-Steagall indicates that the effect of large banks on the efficiency and stability of the financial system remains an important issue for economists and policymakers.

Sources: Andrew Ross Sorkin, "One Thing Both Parties Want: To Break Up the Banks Again," *New York Times*, July 25, 2016; "Bernie Sanders's Obsession with Glass-Steagall Is Misplaced," *Economist*, February 18, 2016; 2016 Democratic Party Platform, July 21, 2016, demconvention.com/wp-content/uploads/2016/07/Democratic-Party-Platform-7.21.16-no-lines.pdf; and Republican Platform 2016, prod-static-ngop-pbl.s3.amazonaws.com/media/documents/DRAFT_12_FINAL[1]-ben_1468872234.pdf.

See related problems 1.9 and 1.10 at the end of the chapter.

Where Did All the Investment Banks Go?

The financial crisis of 2007–2009 had a profound effect on the investment banking industry. Firms that held significant amounts of mortgage-backed securities suffered heavy losses as the prices of those securities plummeted. The standalone investment banks had difficulty weathering the crisis, in part because they relied on short-term borrowing from institutional investors and from other financial firms to fund their long-term investments. As the crisis deepened, borrowing money short term became difficult, and these firms were forced to sell assets, often at low prices. In addition, because they were not commercial banks, they could not borrow by taking out discount loans from the Federal Reserve to meet temporary liquidity problems. In March 2008, Bear Stearns was on the edge of bankruptcy and sold itself at a very low price to JPMorgan Chase. In September 2008, Lehman Brothers filed for bankruptcy. Shortly thereafter, Merrill Lynch sold itself to Bank of America. In October, the only two remaining large standalone investment banks, Goldman Sachs and Morgan Stanley, petitioned the Federal Reserve to allow them to become *financial holding companies*, which are regulated by the Federal Reserve and eligible for discount loans through their bank subsidiaries. As financial holding companies, Goldman Sachs and Morgan Stanley could both borrow from the Fed; following Congress's passage of the Troubled Asset Relief Program (TARP) in October 2008, they were eligible for injections of capital from the U.S. Treasury purchasing their stock.

Some commentators labeled the effect of the financial crisis on investment banks as "the end of Wall Street" because large standalone investment banks had long been seen as the most important financial firms in the stock and bond markets. Table 11.1 shows the fates of 11 large investment banks. Although the structure of the industry has changed, the activities of investment banking—underwriting, providing advice on mergers and acquisitions, and so on—continue at subsidiaries of financial holding companies, at affiliates of commercial banks, and at boutique investment banks.

TABLE 11.1 The Fate of Large Investment Banks

Year	Investment bank	Fate of the bank
1988	First Boston	Bought by Credit Suisse
1997	Salomon Brothers	Bought by Travelers
2000	Donaldson, Lufkin, & Jenrette	Bought by Credit Suisse
	JPMorgan	Bought by Chase
	PaineWebber	Bought by UBS
2007	A.G. Edwards	Bought by Wachovia
2008	Bear Stearns	Bought by JPMorgan Chase
	Goldman Sachs	Became a financial holding company
	Lehman Brothers	Failed
	Merrill Lynch	Bought by Bank of America
	Morgan Stanley	Became a financial holding company

Notes: Credit Suisse is a bank headquartered in Zurich, Switzerland; Travelers is an insurance company headquartered in Hartford, Connecticut; UBS (originally the Union Bank of Switzerland) is a bank headquartered in Zurich, Switzerland; Chase is the Chase Manhattan Bank, headquartered in New York City, and is currently named JPMorgan Chase; and Wachovia is a bank headquartered in Charlotte, North Carolina, that subsequently merged with Wells Fargo Bank.

Source: Tabular adaptation of p. 80 ("The End of the Line") from Dave Kansas, *The Wall Street Guide to the End of the Wall Street as We Know It*, New York: Collins Business, 2009.

MAKING THE CONNECTION IN YOUR INTEREST

So, You Want to Be an Investment Banker?

Over the past 25 years, investment banking has been one of the most richly rewarded professions in the world. Top executives at investment banks such as Goldman Sachs, Morgan Stanley, and JPMorgan have earned tens of millions of dollars in salary and bonuses. This pay has been controversial. Some political commentators argue that the economic contribution from underwriting and providing advice on mergers and acquisitions is not worth the compensation these executives receive. Some critics lament that the high compensation is luring too many of the country's "best and brightest" to investment banking and away from what they see as more productive pursuits in industry, the sciences, and professions such as law, medicine, and teaching. Criticism of the top managers of investment banks increased during the financial crisis, and some policymakers and economists argued that investment banks had helped bring on the crisis by promoting risky mortgage-backed securities. As we have seen, following the financial crisis, none of the larger investment banks survived as standalone firms engaged only in investment banking.

But investment banking activity continues. The investment banking arms of commercial banks remain very active in underwriting and providing advice on mergers and acquisitions. Many boutique and regional investment banks continue to thrive, and Goldman Sachs and Morgan Stanley operate largely as they did before the crisis, although in 2016 Goldman Sachs made a limited move into traditional commercial banking online by both accepting small deposits and making personal loans. Goldman Sachs, which had made a profit of $17.6 billion in 2007, swung to a loss of $1.3 billion in 2008 during the worst of the crisis but was back to a profit of $19.8 billion in 2009 and remained profitable through 2016. Lloyd Blankfein, Goldman's CEO, earned $23 million in salary and bonus in 2015 (which was actually much lower than the $68.6 million he earned in 2007, before the financial crisis), and the average salary and bonus of the firm's 36,800 employees during 2015 was $344,511, although this compensation was down from $498,000 in 2009. Goldman's compensation was near the average for investment bank employees. Anyone climbing to the top managerial ranks at an investment bank (or other large financial firm) will have to deal with federal regulations on compensation arising from the financial crisis. For example, in 2016, federal regulators proposed that at least half of the bonuses banks pay top managers be deferred for four years and that bonuses would be subject to "claw backs" for seven years. (With *claw backs*, a top manager has to repay some of his or her compensation to his or her firm if it turns out that the manager had made decisions that ultimately harmed the firm.) Clearly, though, a career in investment banking offers compensation that is well above average.

Where do those interested in a career in investment banking get their start? New college graduates hired by investment banks will sometimes take so-called "back-office" jobs, in which they provide clerical or technical support for the firms' operations. Entry-level hires in investment banking proper are usually called *analysts*. These positions famously require workweeks of 80 hours or more. The day-to-day responsibilities of analysts include researching industries and firms, making presentations to the bank's clients, gathering and analyzing data, helping with the due diligence process for IPOs, drafting financial documents, and participating in "deal teams" for mergers and acquisitions. Investment banks typically have an "up or out" approach with analysts: After two to three years, the bank either promotes an analyst to the position of associate or asks him or her to leave the firm. New hires with MBAs, rather than only undergraduate degrees, are sometimes hired directly as associates. The higher rungs on the investment banking job ladder are typically titled vice president, director, and managing director.

New financial regulations enacted by Congress in the Dodd-Frank Act of 2010 have been changing the employment mix at investment banks. In particular, the Volcker rule, which limits the extent to which banks can trade securities using their own funds, has led to reduced employment on the banks' trading desks. Some investment banks, including Goldman Sachs, have responded by increasing their private equity activity, under which they raise funds to buy underperforming firms, improve the firms' management, and then sell the firms—for what the banks hope is a substantial profit. However investment banking evolves from here, it is likely to attract college graduates looking for careers in the financial world.

Sources: Donna Borak, Andrew Ackerman, and Christina Rexrode, "New Rules Curbing Wall Street Pay Proposed," *Wall Street Journal*, April 22, 2016; Justin Baer and Peter Rudegeair, "Goldman Shows the Big Problem for Banks: Revenue," *Wall Street Journal*, April 19, 2016; Liz Hoffman, "Goldman Sachs Raising Private-Equity Fund of $5 Billion to $8 Billion," *Wall Street Journal*, July 21, 2016; Liz Hoffman, "Goldman Sachs, Morgan Stanley Take a Tough Assignment: Reinventing Themselves," *Wall Street Journal*, August 28, 2016; and Goldman Sachs Group, *2015 Annual Report*.

See related problem 1.11 at the end of the chapter.

11.2 Investment Institutions: Mutual Funds, Hedge Funds, and Finance Companies

LEARNING OBJECTIVE: Distinguish between mutual funds and hedge funds and describe their roles in the financial system.

Investment institution A financial firm, such as a mutual fund or a hedge fund, that raises funds to invest in loans and securities.

Investment banks are not the only important nonbank financial firms. **Investment institutions** are financial firms that raise funds to invest in loans and securities. The most important investment institutions are mutual funds, hedge funds, and finance companies. Mutual funds and hedge funds, in particular, have come to play an increasingly important role in the financial system.

Mutual Funds

Mutual fund A financial intermediary that raises funds by selling shares to individual savers and invests the funds in a portfolio of stocks, bonds, mortgages, and money market securities.

Mutual funds are financial intermediaries that allow savers to purchase shares in a portfolio of financial assets, including stocks, bonds, mortgages, and money market securities. Mutual funds offer savers the advantage of reducing transactions costs. Rather than buy many stocks, bonds, or other financial assets individually—each with its own transactions cost—a saver can buy a proportional share of these assets by buying into the fund with one purchase. Mutual funds provide risk-sharing benefits by offering a diversified portfolio of assets and liquidity benefits because savers can easily sell the shares. Moreover, the company managing the fund—for example, Fidelity or Vanguard—specializes in gathering information about different investments.

The mutual fund industry in the United States dates back to the organization of the Massachusetts Investors Trust (managed by Massachusetts Financial Services, Inc.) in March 1924. The fund's marketing stressed the usefulness of mutual funds for achieving a diversified portfolio for retirement saving. Later in 1924, the State Street Investment Corporation was organized. In 1925, Putnam Management Company introduced the Incorporated Investment Fund. These three investment managers are still major players in the mutual fund industry.

Types of Mutual Funds Mutual funds operate as either closed-end or open-end funds. In *closed-end mutual funds*, the mutual fund company issues a fixed number of nonredeemable shares, which investors may then trade in over-the-counter markets, just as stocks are traded. The price of a share fluctuates with the market value of the assets—often called the net asset value (NAV)—in the fund. Due to differences in the quality of fund management or the liquidity of the shares, fund shares may sell at a discount or a premium relative to the market value of the underlying assets in the fund. More common are *open-end mutual funds*, which issue shares that investors can redeem each day after the markets close for a price tied to the NAV.

In the past 20 years, *exchange-traded funds (ETFs)* have become popular. ETFs hold portfolios of financial assets that investors can trade continually throughout the day, as they do stocks. In fact, ETFs first became popular in reaction to a sharp decline in stock prices on October 19, 1987—sometimes called Black Monday. Many investors were upset that they couldn't sell their open-end mutual funds until the stock market closed at 4 P.M. Although closed-end funds can be traded throughout the day, ETFs have an advantage over closed-end funds in that market prices of ETFs track the prices of the assets in the fund very closely. Unlike closed-end funds, ETFs are not actively managed, which means they hold a fixed portfolio of assets that managers do not change. (However, some actively managed ETFs are starting to appear.) Large institutional investors who purchase above a certain number of shares of an ETF—called a *creation unit aggregation*—have the right to redeem those shares for the assets in the fund. For instance, the Vanguard Large-Cap ETF contains 751 stocks. If the price of the underlying stocks were greater than the price of the ETF, institutional investors could make arbitrage profits by redeeming the ETF for the underlying stocks. Similarly, no institutional investor would buy an ETF if its price were greater than the prices of the underlying assets. Because arbitrage keeps the prices of ETFs very close to the prices of the underlying assets, small investors can use them as an inexpensive way of buying a diversified portfolio of assets.

Many mutual funds are called *no-load funds* because they do not charge buyers a commission, or "load." Mutual fund companies earn income on no-load funds by charging a management fee—typically about 0.5% of the value of the fund's assets—for running the fund. The alternative, called *load funds*, charge buyers a commission to both buy and sell shares.

Funds that invest in stocks or bonds are the largest category of mutual funds. Leading mutual fund companies, such as Fidelity, Vanguard, and T. Rowe Price, offer many stock and bond funds. Some funds hold a wide range of stocks or bonds, others specialize in securities issued by a particular industry or sector, and still others invest as an *index fund* in a fixed market basket of securities, such as the stocks in the S&P 500 index. Mutual fund companies also offer funds that specialize in the stocks and bonds of foreign firms, and these provide a convenient way for small investors to participate in foreign financial markets.

Money Market Mutual Funds   In recent years, **money market mutual funds**, which hold high-quality, short-term assets, such as Treasury bills, negotiable certificates of deposit, and commercial paper, have grown rapidly. Some funds, called *prime money market funds*, invest mainly in corporate commercial paper. Other funds invest primarily in government securities, such as Treasury bills. Most money market mutual funds allow savers to write checks above a specified amount, say $500, against their accounts. Money market mutual funds have become very popular with small savers as an alternative to commercial bank checking and savings accounts, which typically pay lower rates of interest.

Starting in the 1980s, prime money market mutual funds began successfully competing with commercial banks for the business of providing short-term credit to large firms. Rather than take out loans from banks, firms sold commercial paper to the funds. The interest rates the firms paid on the paper were lower than banks charged on

Money market mutual fund A mutual fund that invests exclusively in short-term assets, such as Treasury bills, negotiable certificates of deposit, and commercial paper.

loans but higher than the interest rate money market mutual funds would receive from investing in Treasury bills. The funds were taking on more credit risk by buying commercial paper rather than Treasury bills, but the risk was minimized because the maturities were short—generally less than 90 days—and the commercial paper received high ratings from the rating agencies. By the 2000s, many financial corporations, including investment banks, also began to rely on selling commercial paper to finance their need for short-term credit. As we have seen, some investment banks took on the risk of relying on commercial paper to finance long-term investments.

The financial crisis of 2007–2009 revealed that market participants had underestimated two sources of risk arising from the increased use of commercial paper. First, firms using commercial paper to fund their operations faced the funding risk that they might have difficulty selling new commercial paper when their existing commercial paper matured. Funding risk could leave firms scrambling to find alternative sources of credit. Second, money market mutual funds and other buyers of commercial paper faced the possibility that the modestly higher interest rates they were receiving compared with Treasury bills did not sufficiently compensate them for the credit risk they were taking on.

Because the underlying assets in a money market mutual fund are both short term and, presumably, of high quality, the funds keep their net asset values (NAVs) stable at $1 per share. Small day-to-day price declines that would otherwise drive the NAV of a fund's shares below $1 are absorbed by the fund because the fund's managers know that they will receive the face value of their investments in a brief period of time when the investments mature. So, unlike with other types of mutual funds, buyers do not have to worry about a loss of principal—or so most investors thought until the financial crisis.

To the shock of most investors, Reserve Management announced in September 2008 that its Reserve Primary Fund, a well-known money market mutual fund, had lost so much money when Lehman Brothers declared bankruptcy and defaulted on its commercial paper that Reserve would have to "break the buck." *Breaking the buck* meant that Reserve would allow the NAV of the fund to fall to $0.97, which would result in a 3% loss of principal for investors in the fund. In addition, Reserve announced that it would delay allowing investors to redeem their shares or write checks against them. The fact that investors in a well-known fund had suffered a loss of principal and had been unable to redeem their shares caused large withdrawals from other money market mutual funds. These withdrawals led the U.S. Treasury to announce that it would temporarily guarantee the holdings of money market mutual funds against losses, thereby ensuring that other funds would not be forced to break the buck.

Although the Treasury's guarantee slowed withdrawals from money market mutual funds, the funds cut back significantly on their purchases of commercial paper. Because the funds made up such a large fraction of the market for commercial paper and because many firms had become heavily dependent on sales of commercial paper to finance their operations, the adverse consequences for the financial system were severe. In October 2008, the Federal Reserve stepped in to stabilize the market by directly purchasing commercial paper for the first time since the Great Depression of the 1930s. The Fed's actions helped restore the flow of funds to firms that were dependent on commercial paper. We discuss recent regulatory changes affecting money market mutual funds in Section 11.4

Hedge Funds

Hedge funds are similar to mutual funds in that they use money collected from savers to make investments. There are several differences between mutual funds and hedge funds, however. Hedge funds are typically organized as partnerships of 99 investors or fewer, all of whom are either wealthy individuals or institutional investors, such as pension funds or university endowments. Because hedge funds consist of a relatively small number of wealthy and institutional investors, they are largely unregulated. Being unregulated allows hedge funds to make risky investments that mutual funds would be unable to make.

Hedge funds frequently *short* securities whose prices they think may decline, meaning that they borrow the securities from a dealer and sell them in the market, planning to buy them back after their prices decline. A typical strategy of early hedge funds was to pair a short position in a security with a long position by, for instance, buying a futures contract on the security, so that the fund would stand to gain from either an increase or a decrease in the price of the security. Because this type of strategy resembles the conventional hedging strategies we discussed in Chapter 7, these early funds acquired the name "hedge funds." Modern hedge funds, though, typically make investments that involve speculating, rather than hedging, so their name is no longer an accurate description of their strategies. Although reliable statistics on hedge funds are difficult to obtain, in 2016 there were as many as 10,000 of them operating in the United States, managing more than $3 trillion in assets.

Hedge funds have been controversial for the following four key reasons:

1. While mutual fund managers typically charge the fund a fee for managing it, hedge fund managers also receive a share of any profits the fund earns. A typical hedge fund charges investors a fee of 2% of the value of the fund's assets plus 20% of any profits the fund earns. (These fees are sometimes called "carried interest," on which managers pay taxes at the capital gains tax rate rather than the ordinary income tax rate, although in 2017, President Donald Trump was considering a proposal that carried interest be taxed as ordinary income.)
2. Investments in hedge funds are typically illiquid, with investors often not allowed to withdraw their funds for one to three years. And even then, typically investors are given only a narrow window of time during which they can redeem their investment.
3. In some cases, large hedge funds have experienced substantial losses that led to potential risk to the financial system. Most notably, in 1998 the hedge fund Long-Term Capital Management (LTCM), whose founders included Myron Scholes and Robert Merton, both winners of the Nobel Prize in Economics, made speculative investments that would return a profit if interest rates on high-risk debt fell relative to interest rates on low-risk debt. Unfortunately for LTCM, rather than narrowing, the spread between high-risk and low-risk debt widened, and LTCM was driven to the edge of bankruptcy. Although LTCM had used only $4 billion in equity to make its investments, through borrowing and using derivative contracts, the total value of its holdings was more than $1.1 trillion. The Federal Reserve feared that if LTCM declared bankruptcy and defaulted on its loans and derivative contracts, many of the hedge fund's counterparties would suffer losses, and these losses would

Hedge fund A financial firm organized as a partnership of wealthy investors that make relatively high-risk, speculative investments.

undermine the stability of the financial system. So in September 1998, the Federal Reserve Bank of New York organized a bailout in which 16 financial firms agreed to invest in LTCM to stabilize the firm so that its investments could be sold off—or "unwound"—in a way that would not destabilize financial markets. Some economists believe that the Fed's actions to support LTCM led other investment managers to take on more risk because they believed the Fed would also intervene to save their firms from failure. Other economists, though, are skeptical that the Fed's actions in the LTCM bailout had a significant effect on the actions of other financial firms.

4. Hedge funds have been criticized for their heavy use of short selling. Short selling can cause security prices to fall by increasing the volume of securities being sold. During the financial crisis, the leaders of the large investment banks claimed that short selling by hedge funds had driven the prices of their stocks to artificially low levels, thereby contributing to their financial problems. In 2010, the German government became concerned that speculation against bonds issued by some European governments and against the stocks of some German financial firms was destabilizing financial markets in Europe. In May, the German government banned "naked" short sales, which involve selling a security short without first borrowing the security.

Despite these criticisms, many economists believe that hedge funds play an important role in the financial system. Because hedge funds are able to mobilize large amounts of money and leverage the money when buying securities, they are able to quickly force price changes that can correct market inefficiencies.

MAKING THE CONNECTION **IN YOUR INTEREST**

Would You Invest in a Hedge Fund if You Could?

Many people are disappointed by what they see as the inadequate returns they are receiving on their investments in mutual funds. For these people, do hedge funds represent the promised land of investing? Potential hedge fund investors face two problems. To begin with, hedge funds are not available to the average investor. To buy into a hedge fund, you must be an "accredited investor," as defined by the Securities and Exchange Commission (SEC). In the fall of 2016, to be an accredited investor, you needed net worth of at least $1 million (not including the value of your house) or income of at least $200,000 in each of the two years prior to making the investment, as well as a reasonable expectation of having the same income in the year of the investment. Those requirements rule out most investors, but if you were an accredited investor, would buying into a hedge fund be likely to earn you a higher return than if you purchased shares in a mutual fund? The Vanguard 500 Index Fund, which invests in the stocks included in the S&P 500, for example, is within the reach of most investors because it has a minimum investment of only $3,000 and has no income requirement for investors.

Do hedge funds provide higher returns than the Vanguard 500 Index Fund and similar mutual funds? The answer to this question is not perfectly clear because, unlike mutual funds, most hedge funds do not have to provide detailed reports to the SEC on the returns their investors earn. While every year there are some funds that earn very high returns, which are widely publicized in the financial press, estimates of hedge fund returns indicate that in recent years they have on average underperformed. An analysis carried out for the *Wall Street Journal* indicated that from the second quarter of 2009—when the stock market began to recover from the financial crisis—through the second quarter of 2016, hedge funds had lower returns than a basic portfolio of stocks and bonds in 22 of 28 quarters. Even funds that have huge returns for a few years often suffer large losses in other years. For example, the hedge funds managed by John Paulson invested heavily in securities that would increase in value if housing prices declined. When housing prices did decline in 2007 and 2008, the funds earned a profit of $15 billion. Paulson's fees were more than $4 billion in 2007 alone—the largest return ever earned by an individual in a single year in U.S. financial markets. If you were an accredited investor, then of course you would jump at the chance to invest in Paulson's funds, right? In fact, in 2011, Paulson invested in securities that lost value when the U.S. recovery turned out to be slower than he had forecast. As a result, his largest fund suffered a 35% loss, and another of his funds lost more than 50%, leading a number of large investors to redeem their shares. One reason that hedge funds often incur large losses as well as large gains is that they tend to be much more heavily leveraged than are mutual funds.

In addition to earning erratic returns, hedge funds have several other drawbacks. As we have already noted, the fees hedge fund managers charge are much higher than the fees mutual fund managers charge. For example, Vanguard charges 0.16% of the value of the 500 Index Fund's assets as a management fee and returns all of the fund's profit to investors, while hedge fund managers such as John Paulson typically charge a fee of 2% of the value of the fund's assets plus 20% of any profit the fund earns—and some fund managers charge even more! With such high management fees, a hedge fund has to make very profitable investments for investors to receive an above-average return. Unlike an investment in a mutual fund, an investment in a hedge fund is typically illiquid because investors can withdraw their funds only at specific times. Hedge funds also often invest in assets that are more illiquid than the assets that mutual funds invest in. Because these illiquid assets may not frequently be bought and sold, it can be difficult for investors to determine their market prices and, therefore, the true value of the funds' investments.

The Dodd-Frank Act of 2010 required large hedge funds to register with the SEC for the first time, but hedge funds are not required to make detailed disclosures of their asset holdings, as mutual funds are. Hedge fund managers argue that full disclosure would allow other managers to copy their investment strategies. Lack of full disclosure makes it difficult for investors to evaluate hedge funds as easily as they can mutual funds. In extreme cases, the lack of disclosure can help conceal fraud. In 2008, the funds Bernard Madoff had been running for decades turned out to have been using money from new investors to pay off previous investors rather than using it to buy securities. Investors lost billions of dollars in the fraud, and Madoff was sentenced to more than 150 years in prison.

The table that follows summarizes the benefits and drawbacks of hedge funds relative to mutual funds.

Mutual funds		Hedge funds	
Benefits	**Drawbacks**	**Benefits**	**Drawbacks**
1. Low management fees	1. Not allowed to follow some investment strategies	1. Allowed to use sophisticated investment strategies	1. High management fees
2. Full disclosure of holdings	2. Possibly lower return	2. Possibly higher return	2. Limited disclosure of holdings
3. Shares are liquid			3. Investment in fund may be illiquid
4. Lower risk			4. Higher risk

The table shows that the key advantage of hedge funds is that they can use sophisticated investment strategies to earn high returns. An important idea in financial markets, though, is the trade-off between risk and return. Even if investors in hedge funds receive an above-average return on their investment—which is by no means clear—they take on substantially more risk than investors in diversified mutual funds. So, even if you were qualified to invest in a hedge fund, you would want to closely consider the fund's track record, its fees, and its investment strategy before doing so.

Sources: Rob Copeland and Timothy W. Martin, "Hedge Fund Star: We Are 'Under Assault,'" *Wall Street Journal*, May 12, 2016; Rob Copeland, "Wasted Opportunity: Hedge Funds Falter," *Wall Street Journal*, January 1, 2016; Julie Creswell and Azam Ahmed, "Large Hedge Funds Fared Well in 2011," *New York Times*, March 29, 2012; and Securities and Exchange Commission, *Investor Bulletin: Hedge Funds*.

See related problem 2.9 at the end of the chapter.

Finance Companies

Finance company
A nonbank financial intermediary that raises money through sales of commercial paper and other securities and uses the funds to make small loans to households and firms.

Finance companies are nonbank financial intermediaries that raise money through sales of commercial paper and other securities and use the funds to make small loans to households and firms. Some investment banks provide funds to finance companies through short-term loans or revolving lines of credit. Before making loans, finance companies gather information about borrowers' default risks. Because finance companies do not accept deposits as commercial banks do, however, federal and state governments generally have seen little need for regulation beyond information disclosure to potential borrowers and fraud prevention. The lower degree of regulation allows finance companies to provide loans tailored to match the needs of borrowers more closely than do the standard loans that other, more regulated institutions can provide.

The three main types of finance companies are consumer finance, business finance, and sales finance companies.

Consumer finance companies make loans to enable consumers to buy cars, furniture, and appliances; to finance home improvements; and to refinance household debts. Finance company customers have higher default risk than do good-quality bank customers and so are often charged higher interest rates.

Business finance companies engage in *factoring*—that is, purchasing at a discount the accounts receivable of small firms. Accounts receivable represent money that a firm is owed for goods or services sold on credit. For example, CIT, which is a business finance company headquartered in New York City, might buy $100,000 of short-term accounts receivable from Axle Tire Company for $90,000. CIT is effectively lending Axle $90,000 and earning a $10,000 return when CIT collects the accounts receivable. Axle Tire is willing to sell its receivables to CIT because it needs the cash to pay for inventory and labor costs, and it might have a cash flow problem if it waited for all its customers to pay their bills. Another activity of business finance companies is to purchase expensive equipment, such as airplanes or large bulldozers, and then lease the equipment to firms over a fixed length of time.

Sales finance companies are affiliated with department stores and companies that manufacture or sell big-ticket goods. For example, Macy's and JCPenney issue credit cards that consumers can use to finance purchases at those stores. This convenient access to credit is part of the store's marketing.

Many economists believe that finance companies fill an important niche in the financial system because they have an advantage over commercial banks in monitoring the value of collateral, making them logical players in lending for consumer durables, inventories, and business equipment. Other economists, though, note that finance companies take on more risk than do commercial banks and rely on short-term financing that may not be rolled over by lenders. These characteristics may make finance companies vulnerable to failure during a severe recession or financial crisis.

11.3 Contractual Savings Institutions: Pension Funds and Insurance Companies

LEARNING OBJECTIVE: Explain the roles that pension funds and insurance companies play in the financial system.

Pension funds and insurance companies may not seem much like commercial banks, but they are also financial intermediaries that accept payments from individuals and use the payments to make investments. Pension funds and insurance companies are called **contractual saving institutions** because the payments individuals make to them are the result of a contract, either an insurance policy or a pension fund agreement.

Pension Funds

For many people, saving for retirement is their most important form of saving. People can accumulate retirement savings in two ways: through **pension funds** sponsored by employers or through personal savings accounts. Because retirements are predictable, pension funds can invest the contributions of workers and firms in long-term assets, such as stocks, bonds, and mortgages, to provide for pension benefit payments during workers' retirements. Representing more than $12 trillion in assets in the United States in 2016, private, state, and local government pension funds are the largest institutional participants in capital markets. Figure 11.2 shows the investments of private and public pension funds during the first quarter of 2016. Total pension fund assets are equal to 17% of the assets of all U.S. households. Pension fund holdings of publicly traded stocks equal 39% of the holdings of all U.S. households.

Contractual saving institution A financial intermediary such as a pension fund or an insurance company that receives payments from individuals as a result of a contract and uses the funds to make investments.

Pension fund A financial intermediary that invests contributions of workers and firms in stocks, bonds, and mortgages to provide for pension benefit payments during workers' retirements.

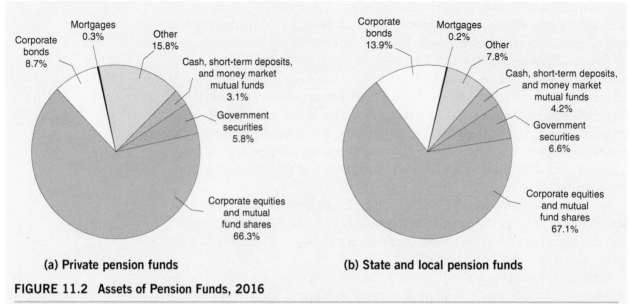

(a) Private pension funds

(b) State and local pension funds

FIGURE 11.2 Assets of Pension Funds, 2016

Both private and state and local pension funds concentrate their investments in stocks, bonds, and other capital market securities.

Source: Board of Governors of the Federal Reserve System, *Financial Accounts of the United States: Flow of Funds, Balance Sheets, and Integrated Macroeconomic Accounts, First Quarter 2016*, June 9, 2016.

When you work for a firm that has a pension fund, you receive pension benefits only if you are vested. *Vesting* is the number of years you must work in order to receive benefits after retirement. The vesting period required varies across pension plans. Employees may prefer to save through pension plans provided by employers rather than through savings accounts for three reasons. First, pension funds may be able to manage a financial portfolio more efficiently, with lower transactions costs, than employees can. Second, pension funds may be able to provide benefits such as life annuities, which are costly for individual savers to obtain on their own. Third, the special tax treatment of pensions can make pension benefits more valuable to employees than cash wages.[5]

A key distinction among pension plans is whether they have defined contributions or defined benefits. In a *defined benefit plan*, an employer promises employees a particular dollar benefit payment, based on each employee's earnings and years of service. The benefit payments may or may not be indexed to increase with inflation. If the funds in the pension plan exceed the amount promised, the excess remains with the employer running the plan. If the funds in the pension plan are insufficient to pay the promised benefit, the plan is *underfunded*, and the employer is liable for the difference.

---

[5] Your contribution to a pension fund can be excluded from your current income for tax purposes, and your employer's matching contribution is tax deductible for your employer. In addition, you aren't taxed on the investment earnings of a pension fund. Your taxation is deferred until you receive retirement benefits from your pension. You also have the option of transferring pension benefit payments into an individual retirement account (IRA) or another favorable distribution plan, which can reduce the tax you would otherwise owe on a lump-sum payment from your pension plan.

In a *defined contribution plan*, the employer places contributions from employees into investments, such as mutual funds, chosen by the employees. The employees own the value of the funds in the plan. If an employee's investments are profitable, the employee's income during retirement will be high; if the employee's investments are not profitable, the employee's income during retirement will be low. Although at one time defined benefit plans were more common, today most retirement plans are defined contribution plans. The notable exceptions are plans for public employees—such as teachers, firefighters, and police officers—and plans for private-sector workers in labor unions.

Most private employer defined contribution plans are 401(k) plans. Named after the section of the Internal Revenue Service Code in which they are described, 401(k) plans give many employees a chance to be their own pension managers. In a 401(k) plan, an employee can make tax-deductible contributions through regular payroll deductions, subject to an annual limit, and pay no tax on accumulated earnings until retirement. Some employers match employee contributions up to a certain amount. Many 401(k) participants invest through mutual funds, which enable them to hold a large collection of assets at a modest cost. By 2016, contributions to 401(k) plans equaled more than one-third of personal saving.

The shift from defined benefit plans to defined contribution plans has had pluses and minuses for employees. With a defined benefit plan, an employer's financial problems might result in the employee receiving a much smaller pension payment than was promised. In contrast, employees typically have clear ownership rights to the balances in their 401(k) plans, which should not be affected by an employer's bankruptcy. Employees also typically have an opportunity to choose from a range of mutual funds in which to invest their 401(k) contributions. But, with a defined benefit plan, the employer bears the risk that bad investments may require the firm to divert some current revenues to make promised pension payments. With a defined contribution plan, the employees bear the risk of poor investment returns.

In response to difficulties firms encountered in administering pension plans, Congress passed the Employee Retirement Income Security Act (ERISA) in 1974. This landmark legislation set national standards for pension fund vesting and funding, restricted plans' ownership of certain types of risky investments, and enacted standards for information reporting and disclosure. The act authorized creation of the Pension Benefit Guaranty Corporation (PBGC, or "Penny Benny") to insure pension benefits up to a dollar limit if a firm cannot meet its unfunded obligations under a defined benefit plan because of bankruptcy or other reasons. In 2016, the limit was $60,136 per year for a 65-year-old beneficiary. The PBGC charges firms a premium on pension liabilities and has an implicit line of credit from the U.S. Treasury. The current underfunding of defined benefit private pension funds greatly exceeds the reserves of the PBGC. This fact has led some economists to fear that a pension insurance crisis may be on the horizon.

Underfunding of state and local government pensions has become an even larger issue. In 2016, total underfunding of these pension plans was estimated at about $1 *trillion*. These pension payments are not insured by PBGC and are typically defined benefit plans. Detroit and some other cities that have undergone declines in population, resulting in falling incomes and tax collections, have had difficulty fulfilling pension promises made to employees in more prosperous times. In addition, low interest rates have reduced the investment earnings of many state and local pension plans. As a result, many city and state governments, as well as many school districts, have had to significantly raise taxes or cut back other spending in order to fulfill their pension obligations. Negotiations with public employee unions have in some cases resulted in reductions in future pension benefits or increases in employee contributions, but benefits for current retirees are sometimes protected by state constitutions and are rarely reduced unless a local government declares bankruptcy, as Detroit did in 2013. It seems likely that local governments will struggle with the problem of underfunded public pension plans for the indefinite future.

Insurance Companies

Insurance company A
financial intermediary
that specializes in writing
contracts to protect
policyholders from the risk
of financial loss associated
with particular events.

Insurance companies are financial intermediaries that specialize in writing contracts to protect their policyholders from the risk of financial loss associated with particular events—such as automobile accidents or house fires. Insurers obtain funds by charging *premiums* to policyholders and use these funds to make investments. For example, you might pay an annual premium of $1,000 to obtain a life insurance policy that would pay your beneficiary $1 million. The company might use your premium and those from other people purchasing policies to make a loan to a hotel chain that is remodeling or expanding. Policyholders pay the premiums in exchange for the insurance company assuming the risk that if the insured event occurs, the company will pay the policyholder. Insurance companies invest policyholders' premiums in stocks, bonds, mortgages, and direct loans to firms, known as *private placements*.

The insurance industry has two segments: *Life insurance companies* sell policies to protect households against a loss of earnings from the disability, retirement, or death of the insured person. *Property and casualty companies* sell policies to protect households and firms from the risks of illness, theft, fire, accidents, or natural disasters. Insurance companies typically do not make a profit on the insurance policies themselves because they pay out more in claims than they receive in premiums. Instead, their profit comes from investing the premiums. In the first quarter of 2016, life insurance companies held about $6.4 trillion in assets, while property and casualty insurance companies held about $1.6 trillion in assets. Figure 11.3 shows that the asset portfolios of property and casualty insurance companies differ from those of life insurance companies. The funds invested by life insurance companies are exempt from taxation, but property and casualty insurance companies do not receive this exemption. This tax difference is reflected in their asset portfolios: Property and casualty insurance companies invest more heavily in municipal bonds because the interest received is not taxable, while life insurance companies invest more heavily in corporate bonds, which pay higher interest rates.

The profitability of insurance companies depends in large part on their ability to reduce risks involved in providing insurance. The key risks to the profitability of insurers arise from adverse selection and moral hazard. Insurance companies have several ways of reducing the risks in providing insurance, which we discuss in the following sections.

Risk Pooling Insurance companies can reliably predict when and how much they will pay out to policyholders by using the *law of large numbers*. This statistical concept states

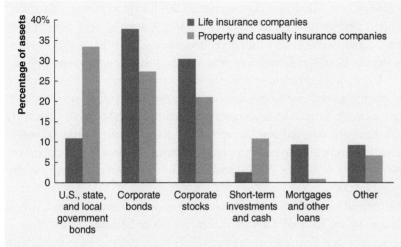

FIGURE 11.3

Financial Assets of U.S. Insurance Companies

Life insurance companies have larger asset portfolios than do property and casualty insurance companies. Property and casualty insurance companies hold more municipal bonds because the interest on them is tax exempt, while life insurance companies hold more corporate bonds because they pay higher interest rates.

Source: Board of Governors of the Federal Reserve System, *Financial Accounts of the United States: Flow of Funds, Balance Sheets, and Integrated Macroeconomic Accounts, First Quarter 2016*, June 9, 2016.

that although the death, illness, or injury risks of an individual are difficult to predict, the average occurrences of any such event for large numbers of people generally can be predicted. By issuing a sufficient number of policies, insurance companies take advantage of risk pooling and diversification to estimate the size of reserves, or funds they accumulate, needed to pay potential claims. Statisticians known as *actuaries* compile probability tables to help estimate the risk of an event occurring in the population. Insurance companies use these estimates to set policy premiums.

Reducing Adverse Selection Through Screening and Risk-Based Premiums Insurance companies suffer from adverse selections problems. The people most eager to purchase insurance are those with the highest probability of requiring an insurance payout. Severely ill people may want to buy large life insurance policies, and people in neighborhoods plagued by arson will want large fire insurance policies. To reduce adverse selection problems, insurance company managers gather information to screen out poor insurance risks. If you apply for automobile insurance, you have to supply information about your driving record, including speeding tickets and accidents.

Insurance companies also reduce adverse selection by charging *risk-based premiums*, which are premiums based on the probability that an individual will file a claim. For example, insurance companies charge higher premiums on automobile insurance policies for drivers who have had multiple accidents and speeding tickets than for drivers who have clean driving records. Similarly, premiums on life insurance policies are higher for older people than for younger people.

Reducing Moral Hazard with Deductibles, Coinsurance, and Restrictive Covenants Moral hazard is also a problem for insurance companies because policyholders may change their behavior once they have insurance. For example, after a firm has bought a fire insurance policy for a warehouse, the firm has less incentive to spend money fixing a broken sprinkler system in the warehouse. One way for insurance companies to reduce the likelihood that an insured event takes place is to make sure that some of the policyholder's money is at risk. Insurance companies do this by requiring a *deductible*, which is a specified amount of a claim that an insurance company does not pay. For example, a $500 deductible on your automobile insurance means that if you have an accident that results in $2,000 in damages to your car, the insurance company will pay you only $1,500. To give policyholders a further incentive to hold down costs, insurance companies may offer *coinsurance* as an option in exchange for charging a lower premium. This option requires policyholders to pay a certain percentage of the costs of a claim after the deductible has been satisfied. For example, if you have a health insurance policy with a $200 deductible and a 20% coinsurance requirement, then on a $1,000 claim, you would pay $360 (= $200 + (0.20 × $800)), and the insurance company would pay the other $640 on your behalf.

To cope with moral hazard, insurers also sometimes use *restrictive covenants*, which limit risky activities by the insured if a subsequent claim is to be paid. For example, a fire insurance company may refuse to pay a firm's claim if the firm failed to install and maintain smoke alarms, fire extinguishers, or a sprinkler system in accordance with its contract.

The tools that insurance companies use to reduce adverse selection and moral hazard problems are intended to align the interests of policyholders with the interests of the insurance companies. To the extent that the companies succeed, the cost of providing insurance is reduced. Competition among insurance companies results in these cost savings being passed along to policyholders, in the form of lower insurance premiums.

11.4 Risk, Regulation, and the Shadow Banking System

LEARNING OBJECTIVE: Explain the connection between the shadow banking system and systemic risk.

We have seen that in the years before the financial crisis of 2007–2009, nonbank financial institutions, such as investment banks, hedge funds, and money market mutual funds, had become an increasingly important means for channeling money from lenders to borrowers. These nonbank financial institutions have been labeled the *shadow banking system* because while they match savers and borrowers, they do so outside the commercial banking system. In principle, shadow banking firms have gained business from commercial banks by lowering costs to borrowers and raising returns to savers. On the eve of the financial crisis, the size of the shadow banking system was greater than the size of the commercial banking system.[6] What importance, if any, did this change in funding channels have for the financial system and the economy? Did the growth of the shadow banking system play a role in the financial crisis?

---

[6] Timothy Geithner, in the speech cited in the chapter opener, noted that in 2007, the value of the assets held by investment banks and hedge funds plus the value of asset-backed commercial paper plus repurchase agreements was greater than the value of loans, securities, and all other assets held by commercial banks.

Systemic Risk and the Shadow Banking System

In a market system, firms are generally free to operate as they please, subject to laws concerning fraud, racial and other discrimination, and so on. We saw in Chapter 10, though, that dating back to the early days of the country, fears of the financial power of banks had resulted in the government regulating banks in a number of ways, including restricting the number of bank branches and prohibiting interstate banking. Although some of these regulations had been removed by the 1990s, banks still remained more closely regulated than most other firms, including most financial firms.

During the 1930s, the sharp decline in stock prices and widespread bank failures led the federal government to enact new financial regulations. To help stabilize the banking system, Congress established the Federal Deposit Insurance Corporation (FDIC), which insures deposits in commercial banks. To help reduce information problems in financial markets, Congress established the Securities and Exchange Commission (SEC), which was given responsibility for regulating the stock and bond markets.

In the absence of deposit insurance, bank managers had an incentive to avoid risky investments that would alarm depositors and endanger the solvency of the bank. Depositors had an incentive to monitor how banks invested their deposits to avoid losses in the event that the bank failed. Although bank failures imposed losses on the owners of banks and on depositors, the possibility of losses always exists in a market system. Moreover, as Congress realized, the enactment of deposit insurance increased moral hazard by reducing the incentive bank managers had to avoid risky investments and by reducing the incentive depositors had to monitor the actions of bank managers. Why, then, did Congress establish the FDIC? The goal was not primarily to protect depositors from the risk of losing money if their banks failed. Instead, Congress was trying to stop bank panics. Congress intended to reduce the likelihood that the failure of an individual bank would lead depositors to withdraw their money from other banks, a process called *contagion*. Deposit insurance largely eliminated bank runs because depositors no longer had to fear the loss of funds in their checking and savings accounts in the event that their bank failed. Essentially, then, in enacting deposit insurance, Congress was less concerned with the risk to individual depositors than with **systemic risk** to the entire financial system.

Deposit insurance stabilized the banking system, maintaining the flow of funds from depositors through banks to borrowers, particularly businesses dependent on bank loans. But there is no equivalent to deposit insurance in the shadow banking system. In the shadow banking system, short-term loans take such forms as repurchase agreements, purchases of commercial paper, and purchases of money market mutual fund shares rather than the form of bank deposits. Or, using the terminology we introduced earlier, shadow banks rely on *wholesale funding* of their investments as opposed to the *retail funding* that commercial banks rely on. During the financial crisis, the Treasury temporarily guaranteed owners of money market mutual fund shares against losses of principal for shares they already owned, but that program ended in September 2009. With that exception, the government does not reimburse investors and firms who make loans to shadow banks in the event that they suffer losses. So, while commercial bank runs are largely a thing of the past, runs on shadow banks definitely are not. During the

Systemic risk Risk to the entire financial system rather than to individual firms or investors.

financial crisis, the shadow banking system was subject to the same type of systemic risk that the commercial banking system experienced during the years before Congress established the FDIC in 1934.

Regulation and the Shadow Banking System

Historically, the commercial banking system had been the primary source of credit to most firms and had been subject to periods of instability. So, the federal government has over the years regulated the types of assets commercial banks can hold and the extent of their leverage. Shadow banking firms, such as investment banks and hedge funds, had not been subject to these regulations. There have been two main rationales for exempting many nonbanks from restrictions on the assets they can hold and the degree of leverage they can have: First, policymakers did not consider these firms to be as important to the financial system as were commercial banks, and regulators did not believe that the failure of these firms would damage the financial system. Second, these firms deal primarily with other financial firms, institutional investors, or wealthy private investors rather than with unsophisticated private investors. Policymakers assumed that because investment banks and hedge funds were dealing with sophisticated investors, these investors could look after their own interests, without the need for federal regulations.

In 1934, Congress gave the SEC broad authority to regulate the stock and bond markets. With the growth of trading in futures contracts, Congress in 1974 established the Commodity Futures Trading Commission (CFTC) to regulate futures markets. Over time, though, financial innovation resulted in the development of complex financial securities that were not traded on exchanges and, therefore, not subject to regulation by the SEC and CFTC. By the time of the financial crisis, trillions of dollars' worth of securities such as credit default swaps were being traded in the shadow banking system, with little oversight from the SEC or CFTC. The financial crisis revealed that this trading involved substantial counterparty risk, particularly with respect to securities backed by mortgages. As we saw in Chapter 7, when derivatives are traded on exchanges, the exchange serves as the counterparty, which reduces the default risk to buyers and sellers. With the passage of the Dodd-Frank Act in 2010, Congress enacted regulatory changes that have pushed more trading in derivatives onto exchanges.

Counterparty risk in the shadow banking system also increased over time because some of these firms became highly leveraged. With high leverage, small losses would be magnified, increasing the probability of default.

The Fragility of the Shadow Banking System

We can summarize the vulnerability of the shadow banking system as follows: Many firms in the shadow banking system operate in a way similar to commercial banks in that they borrow short term—by issuing commercial paper or entering into repurchase agreements—and lend long term. However, for several reasons, they are more vulnerable than are commercial banks to incurring substantial losses and possible failure. First, unlike bank depositors, the investors providing investment banks and hedge funds with short-term loans have no federal insurance against loss of principal. This lack of federal insurance potentially makes investment banks and hedge funds as vulnerable to runs as commercial banks had been in the early 1930s. Second, because they are largely unregulated, shadow banks can invest in more risky assets and become more highly leveraged than commercial banks. Finally, shadow banks proved vulnerable in the financial crisis because during the early and mid-2000s, many had made investments that would rapidly lose value if housing prices in the United States were to decline. When housing prices began to decline, many shadow banks suffered heavy losses, and some were forced into bankruptcy. Given the increased importance of these firms in the financial system, the result was the worst financial crisis since the Great Depression.

Are Shadow Banks Still Vulnerable to Runs Today?

During and immediately following the financial crisis, some economists and policymakers called for extensive new regulations on shadow banks. In the end, the Dodd-Frank Act contained limited additional regulation of shadow banks. Some trading in derivatives was required to be carried out on exchanges, and large hedge funds were required for the first time to register with the SEC. In addition, federal regulators were given the authority to take over large financial firms—not just large commercial banks—that appeared likely to fail, and to require *systemically important financial firms (SIFIs)* to hold additional capital. Firms engaged in shadow banking that have become bank holding companies, such as the investment banks Goldman Sachs and Morgan Stanley, were also required to file resolution plans, or *living wills*, which, according to the Federal Reserve, "must describe the company's strategy for rapid and orderly resolution in the event of material financial distress or failure of the company." The intention is that living wills will better inform investors of the actions a firm's managers will take in the event of the firm failing and will help to limit the contagion from such a failure.

In addition, new SEC regulations require that beginning in 2016, prime money market funds sold to institutional investors must convert from the traditional price of $1 per share to a floating price determined by the actual market prices of the assets the funds hold. Basing share prices on the shares' net asset value (NAV) makes pricing of these money market funds consistent with the way investment firms have traditionally priced stock and bond mutual funds. These funds will also be able to impose fees on both retail and institutional investors redeeming funds and restrict withdrawals when the value of the funds' most liquid assets drops below certain levels. Some economists worried that these changes would lead institutional investors to switch out of prime funds, which invest primarily in short-term corporate debt such as commercial paper, and into money market funds that invest primarily in federal government debt such as Treasury bills and which are not subject to the new regulations. Such a switch might make it more difficult for some corporations to borrow by selling commercial paper.

Fundamentally, Dodd-Frank and other regulations left unchanged the basic problem the financial crisis revealed about shadow banks: Some shadow banks borrow short term to make (often leveraged) long-term investments. Because the lenders providing the short-term loans to shadow banks do not receive the same federal insurance as commercial bank deposits, shadow banks appear to be almost as vulnerable to runs now as they were at the time of the financial crisis. Some economists and policymakers advocate extending federal insurance to a wide range of short-term loans, thereby ending runs in the shadow banking system in the same way that the establishment of the FDIC ended runs in the commercial banking system. Other economists are skeptical of this proposal because they believe that insuring other types of short-term lending would greatly increase moral hazard problems, as lenders would have less incentive to monitor borrowers. In addition, the federal government would potentially be liable for enormous payments if during a financial crisis shadow banks defaulted on their short-term borrowing.

A more optimistic view held by some economists and policymakers is that there is an important distinction between runs on commercial banks and runs on shadow banks. Prior to the establishment of the FDIC, many people with commercial bank deposits had only limited ability to monitor the investments that bank managers were making with their deposits. Their deposits were also not secured by any specific collateral. In those circumstances, any bad news about a bank could set off a bank run and, through the mechanism of contagion, possibly a bank panic. The lenders to shadow banks, in contrast, are in many cases other financial firms, institutional investors, and wealthy investors. These lenders have much greater ability to monitor the quality of the investments managers of shadow banks are making and typically require specific collateral for their loans, as when repurchase agreements are secured by Treasury securities. In this view, the shadow bank runs during the financial crisis that led to the failure of Lehman Brothers and the near failure of Bear Stearns and AIG were the result of a historically unusual event—the widespread use of financial securities based on a single type of financial asset: residential mortgages. In this view, the likelihood is low that financial firms, institutional investors, and wealthy investors will again so greatly misjudge the riskiness of a financial asset. If this argument is correct, the original reason for exempting shadow banks from detailed regulation—that shadow banks deal primarily with sophisticated investors—still holds.

ANSWERING THE KEY QUESTION

Continued from page 344

At the beginning of this chapter, we asked:

"Does the shadow banking system pose a threat to the stability of the U.S. financial system?"

The shadow banking system clearly played a key role in the financial crisis of 2007–2009. Many shadow banks, particularly investment banks and hedge funds, were overly reliant on financing long-term investments with short-term borrowing, were highly leveraged, and held securities that would lose value if housing prices fell. When housing prices did fall beginning in 2006, these firms suffered heavy losses, and some were forced into bankruptcy. Given the importance of shadow banking to the financial system, the result was a financial crisis.

Do shadow banks still pose a threat to the stability of the financial system? Because shadow banks can fill a role in the financial system more efficiently than can commercial banks, shadow banks continue to operate much as they did before the financial crisis. In particular, shadow banks continue to borrow short-term funds that, unlike commercial bank deposits, are not federally insured, and they use those funds for long-term investments. Therefore, shadow banks remain vulnerable to runs similar to those that occurred during the financial crisis.

Key Terms and Problems

Key Terms

Contractual saving institution,
  p. 369
Finance company, p. 368
Hedge fund, p. 365
Initial public offering (IPO), p. 346

Insurance company, p. 372
Investment banking, p. 346
Investment institution, p. 362
Market maker, p. 350
Money market mutual fund, p. 363

Mutual fund, p. 362
Pension fund, p. 369
Syndicate, p. 346
Systemic risk, p. 375
Underwriting, p. 346

 Investment Banking
Explain how investment banks operate.

Review Questions

1.1 What are the key differences between investment banks and commercial banks?

1.2 What is the difference between retail funding and wholesale funding? Which type of funding do commercial banks mainly rely on? Which type of funding do investment banks mainly rely on?

1.3 What is leverage? Which were more highly leveraged prior to the financial crisis of 2007–2009: commercial banks or investment banks? Briefly explain why. What became of the large, stand-alone investment banks during the financial crisis?

Problems and Applications

1.4 A review of a biography of the British investment banker Siegmund Warburg states that Warburg believed:

> Investment banking should not be about gambling but about ... financial intermediation built on client relationships, not speculative trading.... Warburg was always queasy about profits made from [investing] the firm's own capital, preferring income from advisory and underwriting fees.

a. What is underwriting? In what sense is an investment bank that engages in underwriting acting as a financial intermediary?

b. Is an investment bank that buys securities with its own capital acting as a financial intermediary? Briefly explain.

Source: "Taking the Long View," *Economist*, June 24, 2010.

1.5 An article in the *Wall Street Journal* describes the following financial deal: "Private-equity firm KKR & Co. sold 15 million shares of Walgreens Boots Alliance Inc. to Citigroup Inc.... The bankers paid $80 a share and reoffered the shares to clients for $80.10, aiming to make as much as $1.5 million."

a. What is a private equity firm?

b. What investment banking activity was Citigroup performing in this deal?

c. Was Citigroup certain to make a profit on this deal? Briefly explain.

Source: Corrie Driebusch, "Big Banks Ladle On the Risk," *Wall Street Journal*, May 25, 2016.

1.6 In referring to the collapse of the Long-Term Capital Management hedge fund in 1998, an article in the *New York Times* noted:

> Starting with just $5 billion in capital, the fund was able to get $125 billion in

additional funds. Using that leverage, it took on trading positions with an estimated potential value of $1.25 trillion.

a. What is leverage? What information from this excerpt indicates that Long-Term Capital Management was highly leveraged?

b. What risks did Long-Term Capital Management's high leverage pose to the firm? What risks did it pose to the financial system?

Source: Anna Bernasek, "Hedge Funds' Heft Raises Increasing Concern About Their Risks," *New York Times*, July 5, 2005.

1.7 **[Related to** Solved Problem 11.1 **on page 351]** Suppose that you intend to buy a house for $200,000. Calculate your leverage for this investment in each of the following situations:

a. You pay the entire $200,000 price in cash.

b. You make a 20% down payment.

c. You make a 10% down payment.

d. You make a 5% down payment.

Now assume that at the end of the year, the price of the house has risen to $220,000. Calculate the return on your investment for each of the situations listed above. In your calculations, ignore interest you pay on the mortgage loan and the value of any housing services you receive from owning your home.

1.8 **[Related to the** Making the Connection **on page 354]** What incentives would the partners in an investment bank have to convert the firm into a public corporation? If becoming a public corporation increases the risk in investment banking, how do publicly traded investment banks succeed in selling stock to investors?

1.9 **[Related to the** Making the Connection **on page 357]** An article in the *New York Times* observes that "the Glass-Steagall Act … forced the separation of investment banking from commercial banking" and "Glass-Steagall aimed to protect the common folk who deposited money in their banks for safekeeping." In separating commercial banking from investment banking, was Congress's main goal the protection of the average person's bank deposits? Briefly explain.

Source: Andrew Ross Sorkin, "One Thing Both Parties Want: To Break Up the Banks Again," *New York Times*, July 25, 2016.

1.10 **[Related to the** Making the Connection **on page 357]** An editorial in the *Wall Street Journal* argues that: "there's no evidence that [repealing the Glass-Steagall Act in 1999] had anything to do with the [2007–2009 financial] crisis." Briefly discuss whether repealing the Glass-Steagall Act played a role in the financial crisis. Even if repealing Glass-Steagall played no role in the financial crisis, are there other reasons why its repeal may have been a bad idea? Briefly explain.

Source: "Glass-Steagall-Trump-Clinton Act," *Wall Street Journal*, July 28, 2016.

1.11 **[Related to the** Making the Connection **on page 360]** Many investment banks practice an "up or out" policy, with new hires being either fired or promoted within a few years. Many large law firms and accounting firms use a similar policy, as do colleges, with respect to their tenure-track faculty. Most firms, however, do not use this policy. In a typical firm, after a short probationary period, most employees continue to work for the firm indefinitely, with no set time before they are considered for promotion. What are the advantages and disadvantages to investment banks and other firms of using an "up or out" employment policy? Are there advantages to employees? If there are no advantages to employees, how are investment banks able to find people willing to work for them?

11.2 **Investment Institutions: Mutual Funds, Hedge Funds, and Finance Companies**
Distinguish between mutual funds and hedge funds and describe their roles in the financial system.

Review Questions

2.1 In what ways are investment institutions similar to commercial banks? In what ways are they different?

2.2 What are the key differences between mutual funds and hedge funds?

2.3 How are finance companies able to compete against commercial banks?

Problems and Applications

2.4 How are banks able to attract small savers if small savers can usually receive a higher interest rate from money market mutual funds than from bank savings accounts?

2.5 David Wessel of the Brookings Institution has described what happened with the Reserve Primary Fund, a money market mutual fund, on September 16, 2008:

> At 4:15 P.M., the fund issued a press release. The Lehman paper in its portfolio was worthless and the fund's shares were worth not $1, but only 97 cents: breaking the buck. The news triggered a run that spread through the $3.4 trillion [money market mutual fund] industry.

a. What is "Lehman paper"? Why was the Lehman paper in the fund's portfolio worthless?

b. What does "breaking the buck" mean? Why was it significant to the financial system?

c. What is a "run"? Why would one money market mutual fund having broken the buck cause a run on other money market mutual funds?

Source: David Wessel, *In Fed We Trust*, New York: Crown Business, 2009, p. 207.

2.6 In 2016, some industry analysts believed that automobile sales had reached a peak and might begin to decline. JPMorgan Chase CEO Jamie Dimon was quoted in an article in the *Wall Street Journal* as worrying about the possibility that auto finance companies might be facing "higher default rates from increased subprime lending [and] the growing use of longer repayment periods for borrowers." But the article also quoted the CEO of Ally Financial, one of the largest auto finance companies, as saying: "We know fully what we are originating … there are no skeletons in the closet."

a. What is an auto finance company?

b. What advantages might automobile dealers gain from using a finance company, rather than a bank, to finance their purchases of cars from the manufacturer and their customers' purchases of cars from the dealers? What advantages might customers gain?

c. What does the CEO of Ally Financial mean by saying that the company knows "fully what we are originating"? Why might Jamie Dimon have been worried about the types of loans auto finance companies were making, given the circumstances in the auto market in 2016?

Source: Emily Glazer and Annamaria Andriotis, "J.P. Morgan Chief James Dimon Sounds Alarm on Car Loans," *Wall Street Journal*, June 2, 2016.

2.7 An article in the *Wall Street Journal* notes: "Hedge funds typically charge higher fees than other money managers."

a. What is a hedge fund?

b. What fees do hedge funds typically charge? How do these fees compare with those that mutual funds typically charge?

c. What strategies do hedge funds use that mutual funds don't use that might allow the hedge funds to earn high returns in certain situations? Does evidence show that hedge funds consistently produce higher returns than do mutual funds that use more conventional strategies? Briefly explain.

Source: Timothy W. Martin and Rob Copeland, "Investors Pull Cash from Hedge Funds as Returns Lag Market," *Wall Street Journal*, March 30, 2016.

2.8 In describing the work of hedge funds, financial journalist Sebastian Mallaby has observed:

> [Research] showed that the unglamorous "value" stocks were underpriced relative to overhyped "growth" stocks. This mispricing meant that capital was being provided too expensively to solid, workhorse firms and too cheaply to their flashier rivals.... It was the function of hedge funds to correct inefficiencies like this.

a. Explain what the first two sentences in this excerpt mean: What is the connection between the relative prices of these two types of firms and their cost of raising capital? Who is "providing" capital to these firms?

b. How can hedge funds correct this inefficiency?

Source: Sebastian Mallaby, *More Money Than God: Hedge Funds and the Making of a New Elite*, New York: The Penguin Press, 2010, pp. 8–9.

2.9 [Related to the Making the Connection on page 366] A publication of the Securities and Exchange Commission (SEC) notes that to invest in a hedge fund, "you generally must be an accredited investor."

a. What is an accredited investor?

b. The publication also notes that hedge funds often use leverage and that "the use of leverage can turn an otherwise conservative investment into an extremely risky investment." Briefly explain what this observation means.

Source: Securities and Exchange Commission, *Investor Bulletin: Hedge Funds*.

11.3 | Contractual Savings Institutions: Pension Funds and Insurance Companies
Explain the roles that pension funds and insurance companies play in the financial system.

Review Questions

3.1 In what ways are contractual savings institutions similar to commercial banks? In what ways are they different?

3.2 What is the difference between a defined contribution pension plan and a defined benefit plan? What benefits do employees receive from saving for retirement using 401(k) plans?

3.3 In what ways are insurance companies financial intermediaries? What is the difference between a life insurance company and a property and casualty insurance company?

Problems and Applications

3.4 Suppose that as an employee of a large firm, you are given the choice between a defined benefit pension plan and a defined contribution pension plan. From your point of view, what are the advantages and disadvantages of each type of plan? From your employer's point of view, what are the advantages and disadvantages?

3.5 A 2016 column in the *New York Times* notes that: "about two decades ago ... employers began replacing traditional [pension] plans with 'defined contribution' plans like 401(k)'s."

a. What are "traditional pension plans," and how do they differ from 401(k) plans?

b. Briefly explain why 401(k) plans might be more desirable to employers and employees than traditional pension plans. Are there any reasons why 401(k) plans might be less desirable to either group?

Source: Steven Rattner, "Pension Holders Need a New Retirement Plan, Not Stock Tips," *New York Times*, June 21, 2016.

3.6 With 401(k) retirement plans, both the employer and the employee make contributions that are then invested, typically in mutual funds. A column in the *Wall Street Journal* describing these plans notes: "Vesting is the amount of time you must work for your company before gaining access to its payments to your 401(k). (Your payments, on the other hand, vest immediately.)" Why do 401(k) plans have vesting periods for the employer's contributions? Do vesting periods have any advantages to employees relative to a system without vesting periods? Briefly explain.

Source: "What Is a 401(k)?" *Wall Street Journal*.

3.7 In 2016, the long-run returns to the investments made by public pension funds fell to their lowest levels in many years and were expected to fall further as long-run interest rates remained low. One industry observer is quoted in the *Wall Street Journal* as observing: "Many states and local governments may be facing difficult choices if investment returns remain low." Briefly explain what these choices are.

Source: Timothy W. Martin, "Why Pensions' Last Defense Is Eroding," *Wall Street Journal*, July 25, 2016.

3.8 Suppose that insurance companies in Ohio are reluctant to offer fire insurance to firms in low-income neighborhoods because of the prevalence of arson fires in those neighborhoods. Suppose that the Ohio state legislature passes a law stating that insurance companies must offer fire insurance to every business in the state and may not take into account the prevalence of arson fires when setting insurance premiums. What will be the likely effect on the market for fire insurance in Ohio?

3.9 According to an article in the *Wall Street Journal*: "Life insurers earn much of their profit by investing customers' premiums in bonds until claims come due. They have typically favored high-quality, long-term corporate bonds." Insurance companies never know the exact amounts of their future payouts. So, why do they hold large amounts of long-term, relatively illiquid assets, such as corporate bonds, that may be difficult to sell quickly if they need to make payments to policyholders?

Source: Leslie Scism, "Low Rates Are Tormenting Insurers—and Their Customers," *Wall Street Journal*, March 20, 2016.

3.10 Private medical insurance companies sell policies that allow policyholders to make premium payments in exchange for the insurance company paying some or all of the policyholders' medical bills. An article in the *Economist* observes that: "health insurance is an unusual product in that it guarantees a basket of services which is always improving and getting more expensive."

a. What basket of services does a medical insurance policy guarantee?

b. Why might the fact that medical services are always improving and getting more expensive create difficulties for companies offering medical insurance policies?

Source: "You Didn't Pay for It," *Economist*, October 15, 2012.

11.4 Risk, Regulation, and the Shadow Banking System

Explain the connection between the shadow banking system and systemic risk.

Review Questions

4.1 In what ways does the shadow banking system differ from the commercial banking system?

4.2 Why have runs on commercial banks become rare, while several shadow banking firms experienced runs during the financial crisis?

4.3 What is *systemic risk*?

Problems and Applications

4.4 During the financial crisis of 2007–2009, the U.S. Treasury implemented the Guarantee Program for Money Market Funds, which insured investors against losses on their existing money market mutual fund shares. (The program ended in September 2009.) In explaining the program, a Treasury statement noted: "Maintaining confidence in the money market mutual fund industry was critical to protecting the integrity and stability of the global financial system." Why is the money market mutual fund industry so important? If money market mutual funds have problems, can't savers just deposit their money in banks?

Source: U.S. Department of the Treasury, "Treasury Announces Expiration of Guarantee Program for Money Market Funds," September 18, 2009.

4.5 As noted in the chapter, in 2016, new regulations meant that prime money market funds would have to price shares in a fund purchased by institutional investors at the fund's net asset value (NAV) rather than maintain the fund price at a constant $1. As a result, institutional investors might suffer losses on their holdings of these investments. In addition, during a financial crisis, the funds' managers could impose restrictions on redemption of fund shares. An article in the *Wall Street Journal* notes that just before the new regulations became effective, institutional investors pulled more than $400 billion out of

these funds, leaving the funds at their lowest level since 1999. The article concludes: "The test of the new rules [with respect to prime money market funds] will be whether the gains in safety will outweigh the economic impact of the decline in lending."

a. What type of risk did regulators hope to reduce with the new rules? How might the new rules reduce this type of risk?

b. Why does the article indicate that the new rules might result in a decline in lending? What type of lending is the article referring to?

Source: Ken Brown, "A $500 Billion Stampede in Money Markets Even Before New Rules Hit," *Wall Street Journal*, August 3, 2016.

4.6 In an account of the financial crisis, Roger Lowenstein described the problems affecting the Merrill Lynch investment bank: "too much leverage, too much relying on short-term [borrowing], and assets, especially real estate, of dubious value." Why might too much leverage be a problem for an investment bank? Why might relying too much on short-term borrowing be a problem?

Source: Roger Lowenstein, *The End of Wall Street*, New York: Penguin Press, 2010, p. 172.

4.7 An article by an economist at the International Monetary Fund about the shadow banking system notes:

> As long as investors understand what is going on and such activities do not pose undue risk to the financial system, there is nothing inherently shadowy about obtaining funds from various investors who might want their money back within a short period and investing those funds in assets with longer-term maturities.

a. What kind of funding is the author referring to that is obtained from "various investors who might want their money back within a short period"? What kind of investors are involved?

b. What type of problems did this funding cause during the financial crisis? Did investors "understand what is going on" during that period? Briefly explain.

Source: Laura E. Kodres, "What Is Shadow Banking?" *Finance and Development*, Vol. 50, No. 2, June 2013, p. 42.

4.8 In March 2008, the U.S. Treasury and the Federal Reserve arranged for the sale of the Bear Stearns investment bank to JPMorgan Chase in order to prevent Bear Stearns from having to declare bankruptcy. A columnist for the *New York Times* noted:

> It was an old-fashioned bank run that forced Bear Stearns to turn to the federal government for salvation…. The difference is that Bear Stearns is not a commercial bank, and is therefore not eligible for the protections those banks received 75 years ago when Franklin D. Roosevelt halted bank runs with government guarantees.

a. How can an investment bank be subject to a run?

b. What "government guarantees" did commercial banks receive 75 years ago?

c. How did these government guarantees halt commercial bank runs?

Source: Floyd Norris, "F.D.R.'s Safety Net Gets a Big Stretch," *New York Times*, March 15, 2008.

4.9 [Related to the Chapter Opener on page 344] Ben Bernanke served as chairman of the Federal Reserve during the financial crisis of 2007–2009. In his account of those years, he observed:

> Seen from the vantage point of early 2007, the economy's good performance, combined with the relatively small size of the subprime mortgage market and what appeared to be a healthy banking system led me and others to conclude that subprime problems … were unlikely to cause major damage…. [But] the panic in the short-term funding markets that began in August 2007 would ultimately transform a "correction" in the subprime mortgage market into a much greater crisis in the global financial system and global economy.

a. What does Bernanke mean by "the short-term funding markets"?

b. Why was there a panic in the short-term funding markets but not a panic among depositors at commercial banks?

c. Why might the financial crisis have been difficult to foresee, even by people working in high-level positions in the financial system? Were there changes in the financial system that—at least with hindsight—might have indicated that by 2007 a financial crisis had become more likely? Briefly explain.

Source: Ben S. Bernanke, *The Courage to Act: A Memoir of a Crisis and Its Aftermath*, New York: W. W. Norton, 2015, pp. 136, 139–140.

Data Exercises

D11.1: [Money market mutual funds] Go to the web site of the Federal Reserve Bank of St. Louis (FRED) (fred.stlouisfed.org) and download and graph the data series for Retail Money Funds (WRMFSL) and for Institutional Money Funds (WIMFNS) from the earliest week available until the most recent week available.

   a. Explain the difference between retail and institutional money market mutual funds.

   b. How have the trends in retail and institutional money market mutual funds differed?

D11.2: [Value of mutual fund shares and recessions] Go to the web site of the Federal Reserve Bank of St. Louis (FRED) (fred.stlouisfed.org) and download and graph the data series for the value of mutual fund shares owned by households (MF-SABSHNO) from the first quarter of 1952 until the most recent quarter available. Go to the web site of the National Bureau of Economic Research (nber.org) and find the dates for business cycle peaks and troughs (the period between a business cycle peak and trough is a recession).

   a. Describe how the value of mutual fund shares owned by households moves just before, during, and just after a recession. Is the pattern the same across recessions?

   b. What factors can cause the value of mutual fund shares owned by households to change?

chapter 12

Financial Crises and Financial Regulation

Learning Objectives

After studying this chapter, you should be able to:

12.1 Explain what financial crises are and what causes them (pages 389–397)

12.2 Describe the key elements of the financial crisis that occurred during the Great Depression (pages 397–403)

12.3 Describe what caused the financial crisis of 2007–2009 (pages 403–406)

12.4 Discuss the connection between financial crises and financial regulation (pages 406–421)

Bubbles, Bubbles, Everywhere! (Or Not)

The slow economic recovery after the 2007–2009 financial crisis led most central banks around the world to keep interest rates low for years. Before the financial crisis, the federal funds rate, which is the Federal Reserve's key target interest rate, had not been below 1%, except for very brief periods, since 1958. But in October 2008, the Fed cut its target for the federal funds rate to below 1%, and it remained there eight years later. In August 2016, the Bank of England cut its target interest rate to 0.25%—the lowest rate in the history of the bank, which dates to 1694.

As we will discuss further in Chapter 15, during times of recession and slow economic growth, central banks act to lower interest rates to spur borrowing by

households and firms. As households and firms borrow to buy new houses, appliances, computers, factories, office buildings, and machinery, aggregate demand, GDP, and employment should increase. Typically, though, once a recession is over, central banks keep interest rates low for only a limited time before allowing them to rise to more normal levels. In 2016, some economists and policymakers worried that keeping interest rates low for so long had caused distortions to the financial system.

In particular, these economists and policymakers worried that investors had taken advantage of being able to borrow at very low interest rates to purchase stocks, bonds, and other financial assets, as

Continued on next page

KEY ISSUE AND QUESTION

Issue: The financial crisis of 2007–2009 was the most severe since the Great Depression of the 1930s.

Question: Was the severity of the 2007–2009 recession due to the financial crisis?

Answered on page 421

well as real estate and commodities, driving up their prices to unsustainable levels. In other words, these markets were experiencing bubbles, which as we saw in Chapter 6, Section 6.5, occur when the price of an asset rises well above its fundamental value. At some point, a bubble bursts when a significant number of investors become convinced that price declines are likely and begin to sell the overvalued asset. The bursting of a bubble can cause major problems in the financial system, as happened when the bubble in housing prices burst in 2006.

But, were there really bubbles in the prices of financial and other assets during 2016? Bubbles are much easier to identify after the fact than before they have burst. Although we now know that housing prices in some markets had reached unsustainable levels by 2006, at the time, some industry observers argued that the high prices were justified by zoning restrictions and rising prices for construction supplies that had increased the cost of building new houses. Similarly, while in 2016, some economists and policymakers worried about bubbles in the stock market, the market for corporate bonds, or other markets, other economists argued that high prices in these markets were justified, particularly given the likelihood that interest rates would remain low for many years.

Policymakers in 2016 were also divided as to whether the U.S. and world economies were experiencing asset bubbles. Fed Chair Janet Yellen maintained: "I certainly wouldn't describe this as a bubble economy." But Esther George, president of the Federal Reserve Bank of Kansas City, was less optimistic, arguing that if the Fed failed to increase interest rates, the result could be to "distort the allocation of capital toward less fruitful—or perhaps excessively risky—endeavors…. When these types of imbalances tip, the entire economy can face the consequences of their fallout." Billionaire hedge fund manager George Soros argued: "When I look at the financial markets there is a serious challenge which reminds me of the crisis we had in 2008." The editors of the *Economist* were much less sure: "To the extent there [is] euphoria and rampant speculation (as there was in 2006–07), we are really talking about China rather than Europe or the US."

The point to note about these conflicting views is *not* that the financial system is impossible to understand but that financial crises are difficult to predict because they happen infrequently. Only people who had lived through the 1930s had experienced a financial crisis as severe as the one that began in 2007 following the collapse in the market for subprime mortgages. As we discuss financial crises in this chapter, keep in mind that when they occur, policymakers, managers of financial firms, investors, and households are forced to deal with highly unusual events.

Sources: Jason Douglas and Paul Hannon, "Bank of England Cuts Key Interest Rate to New Low," *Wall Street Journal*, August 4, 2016; Jonathan Spicer, "Yellen: 'I Certainly Wouldn't Describe This as a Bubble Economy,'" businessinsider.com, April 8, 2016; Esther L. George, "The Outlook and Monetary Policy," Speech to Economic Forum, York, Nebraska, April 7, 2016; Anusha Ondaatjie and Adam Haigh, "George Soros Sees Crisis in Global Markets That Echoes 2008," bloomberg.com, January 7, 2016; and "Is This Really 2008 All Over Again," *Economist*, January 7, 2016.

We have seen that the growth of the shadow banking system over the past 25 years has significantly changed the way funds flow from lenders to borrowers. In this chapter, we look at the origins and consequences of financial crises and then look specifically at how problems in the shadow banking system contributed to the financial crisis of 2007–2009.

12.1 The Origins of Financial Crises

LEARNING OBJECTIVE: Explain what financial crises are and what causes them.

The key function of the financial system is to facilitate the flow of funds from lenders to borrowers. A **financial crisis** is a significant disruption in this flow. Economic activity depends on the ability of households to borrow to finance purchases and the ability of firms to borrow to finance their day-to-day activities as well as their long-term investments in new factories, equipment, and research and development. So, a financial crisis typically leads to an economic recession as households and firms cut back their spending in the face of difficulty in borrowing money. From the early 1800s through the 1930s, most of the financial crises in the United States involved the commercial banking system. We begin our discussion of financial crises with bank panics.

The Underlying Fragility of Commercial Banking

The basic activities of commercial banks are to accept short-term deposits, such as checking account deposits, and use the funds to make loans—including car loans, mortgages, and business loans—and buy long-term securities, such as municipal bonds. In other words, banks borrow short term from depositors and lend, often long term, to households, firms, and governments. As a result, banks have a *maturity mismatch* because the maturity of their liabilities—primarily deposits—is much shorter than the maturity of their assets—primarily loans and securities. Banks are relatively *illiquid* because depositors can demand their money back at any time, while banks may have difficulty selling the loans in which they have invested depositors' money. Banks, therefore, face *liquidity risk* because they can have difficulty meeting their depositors' demands to withdraw their money. If more depositors ask to withdraw their money than a bank has money on hand, the bank has to borrow money, usually from other banks. If banks are unable to borrow to meet deposit withdrawals, then they have to sell assets to raise the funds. If a bank has made loans and bought securities that have declined in value, the bank may be **insolvent**, which means that the value of its assets is less than the value of its liabilities, so its net worth, or capital, is negative. An insolvent bank may be unable to meets its obligations to pay off its depositors.

Bank Runs, Contagion, and Bank Panics

Liquidity risk is a particular problem for banks if the government does not provide insurance for deposits and if there is no central bank. Between 1836 and 1914, the United States had no central bank. Prior to 1933, the federal government had no system of deposit insurance. In those years, if depositors suspected that a bank had made bad loans or other investments, depositors had a strong incentive to rush to the bank to withdraw their money. Depositors knew that the bank would only have enough cash and other liquid assets available to pay off a fraction of the bank's deposits. Once the bank's liquid assets were exhausted, the bank would have to shut its doors, at least temporarily, until it could raise additional funds. A bank that was forced to raise cash by selling illiquid assets at sharply discounted prices might become insolvent and permanently close its doors. Depositors of a failed bank were likely to receive only some of their money back, and then usually only after a long delay. The process by which simultaneous withdrawals by a bank's depositors results in the bank closing is called a **bank run**.

Financial crisis A situation in which serious problems in the financial system result in a significant disruption in the flow of funds from lenders to borrowers.

Insolvent The situation for a bank or other firm of having a negative net worth because the firm's assets have less value than its liabilities.

Bank run The process by which depositors who have lost confidence in a bank simultaneously withdraw enough funds to force the bank to close.

As a depositor in a bank during this period, if you had any reason to suspect that the bank was having problems, you had a strong incentive to be one of the first in line to withdraw your money. Even if you were convinced that your bank was well managed and its loans and investments were sound, if you believed the bank's other depositors thought the bank had a problem, you still had an incentive to withdraw your money before the other depositors arrived and forced the bank to close. In other words, in the absence of deposit insurance, *the stability of a bank depends on the confidence of its depositors*. In such a situation, if bad news—or even false rumors—shakes that confidence, a bank will experience a run.

Contagion The process by which a run on one bank spreads to other banks, resulting in a bank panic.

Moreover, without a system of government deposit insurance, bad news about one bank can snowball and affect other banks, in a process called **contagion**. Once one bank has experienced a run, depositors of other banks may become concerned that their banks might also have problems. These depositors have an incentive to withdraw their money from their banks to avoid losing it should their banks be forced to close. These other banks will be forced to sell loans and securities to raise money to pay off depositors. A key point is that if multiple banks have to sell the same assets—for example, mortgage-backed securities in the modern banking system—the prices of these assets are likely to decline. As asset prices fall, the net worth of banks is undermined, and some banks may even be pushed to insolvency. If multiple banks experience runs, the result is a **bank panic**, which may force many, perhaps all, banks in the system to close. A bank panic feeds on a self-fulfilling perception: If depositors *believe* that their banks are in trouble, the banks *are* in trouble.

Bank panic The situation in which many banks simultaneously experience runs.

The underlying problem in contagion and bank panics is that banks build their loan portfolios on the basis of private information about borrowers, information banks gather to determine which loans to make. Because this information is private, depositors can't review it to determine which banks are strong and which are weak. This situation is similar to adverse selection in financial markets, in which lenders cannot distinguish good from bad loan applicants. Because of the private information that banks obtain when accumulating assets, depositors have little basis for assessing the quality of their banks' portfolios and distinguishing solvent from insolvent banks. So, bad news about one bank can raise fears about the financial health of others, resulting in a bank panic.

Government Intervention to Stop Bank Panics

Policymakers want to maintain the health of the banking industry because banks reduce information costs and transactions costs in the financial system. The failure of financially healthy banks due to liquidity problems hurts the ability of households and small and medium-sized firms to obtain loans, thereby reducing the efficiency with which the financial system matches savers and borrowers.

Lender of last resort A central bank that acts as the ultimate source of credit to the banking system, making loans to solvent banks against their good, but illiquid, loans.

Governments have used two approaches to avoid bank panics: (1) A central bank can act as a lender of last resort, and (2) the government can insure deposits. Congress reacted to bank panics by establishing the Federal Reserve System in 1913. Policymakers and economists argued that the banking industry needed a "banker's bank," or *lender of last resort*. By acting as a **lender of last resort**, the Fed would be an ultimate source of credit to which banks could turn for loans during a panic. The Fed would make loans to solvent banks, using the banks' good, but illiquid, loans as collateral. Policymakers expected the Fed to make loans only to solvent banks, allowing insolvent banks to fail.

As we will see in this chapter, the Fed failed to stop the bank panics of the early 1930s, which led Congress to create the **Federal Deposit Insurance Corporation (FDIC)** in 1934. By reassuring depositors that they would receive their money back even if their bank failed, deposit insurance effectively ended the era of commercial bank panics in the United States.

> **Federal Deposit Insurance Corporation (FDIC)** A federal government agency established by Congress in 1934 to insure deposits in commercial banks.

SOLVED PROBLEM 12.1

Would Requiring Banks to Hold 100% Reserves Eliminate Bank Runs?

The Federal Reserve requires banks to hold reserves equal to 10% of their holdings of checkable deposits above a certain level. In the 1950s, Nobel Laureate Milton Friedman of the University of Chicago proposed that banks be required to hold 100% reserves. More recently, Laurence J. Kotlikoff of Boston University has advocated a similar plan. If required to hold 100% reserves, banks would make loans and buy securities with their capital rather than with deposits. Briefly discuss how this proposal would affect the likelihood of bank runs.

Source: Kotlikoff's account of 100% reserve banking is part of his general proposal for financial reform in Laurence J. Kotlikoff, *Jimmy Stewart Is Dead*, Hoboken, NJ: John Wiley & Sons, 2010.

Solving the Problem

Step 1 **Review the chapter material.** This problem is about what causes bank runs, so you may want to review the section "Bank Runs, Contagion, and Bank Panics," which begins on page 389.

Step 2 **Solve the problem by discussing what causes bank runs and whether requiring banks to hold 100% reserves would affect the likelihood of runs.** We have seen that bank runs are caused by depositors' knowledge that banks keep only a fraction of deposits on reserve and loan out or invest the remainder. In a system without a lender of last resort or government deposit insurance, banks can quickly exhaust their reserves in a run, so that only the first depositors in line will receive all their money back. If banks held 100% reserves rather than, say, 10%, depositors would no longer have to fear that their money would not be available should they choose to withdraw it. Depositors would also not be at risk of losing money if banks made poor investments because the value of a bank's loans and securities would no longer be connected to the bank's ability to refund depositors' money.

We can conclude that whatever the other merits or drawbacks of a system of 100% reserve banking, such a system would not be subject to runs.

See related problem 1.8 at the end of the chapter.

Bank Panics and Recessions

As Table 12.1 shows, the United States was plagued by bank panics from the mid nineteenth century until 1933, when federal deposit insurance was enacted. The National

TABLE 12.1 U.S. Bank Panics

Date of the bank panic	Did the bank panic occur during a recession?
August 1857	Yes
December 1861	No
April 1864	No
September 1873	Yes
June 1884	Yes
November 1890	Yes
May 1893	Yes
October 1896	Yes
October 1907	Yes
October 1930	Yes
April 1931	Yes
September–October 1931	Yes
January–February 1933	Yes

Note: Recessions are dated according to the National Bureau of Economic Research's (NBER's) business cycle reference dates, which begin in 1854. The bank panic of September 1873 occurred the month before a recession began.

Sources: Carmen M. Reinhart and Kenneth S. Rogoff, *This Time Is Different: Eight Centuries of Financial Folly*, Princeton, NJ: Princeton University Press, 2009, Table A.4.1; Michael Bordo, Barry Eichengreen, Daniela Klingebiel, and Maria Soledad Martinez-Peria, "Is the Crisis Problem Growing More Severe?" *Economic Policy*, Vol. 32, Spring 2001, pp. 52–82, web appendix; Michael Bordo and Joseph G. Haubrich, "Credit Crises, Money and Contractions: An Historical Review," *Journal of Monetary Economics*, Vol. 57, January 2010, pp. 1–18; and National Bureau of Economic Research.

Bureau of Economic Research (NBER) provides the generally accepted dates for recessions in the United States. From 1857 until 1933, every bank panic was associated with a recession, apart from the two panics that occurred in the 1860s, during the Civil War.

It isn't a coincidence that bank panics and recessions occurred together. A bank panic can lead to declines in production and employment, either causing a recession or making an existing recession worse. Bank failures can directly affect the ability of households and firms to spend by wiping out some of the wealth they hold as deposits. Shareholders of banks also suffer losses to their wealth when banks fail. In addition, households and firms that relied on failed banks for credit will no longer have access to the loans they need to fund some of their spending. Typically in a panic, even banks that remain solvent will reduce their lending as they attempt to accumulate reserves to meet deposit withdrawals. The result can be a *credit crunch*, as households and firms that previously qualified for bank loans no longer do. Finally, by destroying checking account deposits, bank failures can result in a decline in the money supply.

There can also be negative feedback between a bank panic and a recession. If a panic triggers a recession, the recession can make the panic worse. As the recession reduces

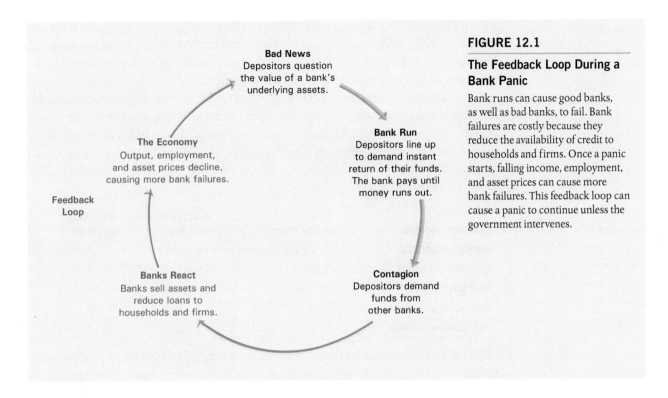

FIGURE 12.1

The Feedback Loop During a Bank Panic

Bank runs can cause good banks, as well as bad banks, to fail. Bank failures are costly because they reduce the availability of credit to households and firms. Once a panic starts, falling income, employment, and asset prices can cause more bank failures. This feedback loop can cause a panic to continue unless the government intervenes.

the profitability of firms and the incomes of households, more borrowers are likely to default on their loans, and the prices of securities held by banks are likely to fall, further undermining the confidence of depositors and leading to increased withdrawals. The threat of increased withdrawals and the decreasing number of creditworthy borrowers can lead banks to further curtail their loans, thereby reducing the ability of households and firms to spend, which deepens the recession. Figure 12.1 illustrates the negative feedback loop during a bank panic.

MAKING THE CONNECTION

Why Was the Severity of the 2007–2009 Recession So Difficult to Predict?

Policymakers, economists, and corporate CEOs were all surprised by the severity of the 2007–2009 recession in the United States. A key reason for the surprise was that the United States had not experienced a financial panic since the 1930s. Business cycle recessions can have a number of causes. The recession of 2001 was caused by a decline in investment spending after many firms had overspent on information technology during the "dot-com boom" of the late 1990s. Spikes in oil prices have also caused recessions. But recessions in the United States between 1933 and 2007, regardless of their cause, were not accompanied by bank panics. A series of bank panics occurred at the beginning of the Great Depression of the 1930s. The recession of 2007–2009 was also accompanied by a bank panic, but it was primarily in the "shadow banking system" rather than in the commercial banking system. Both the Great Depression and the recession of 2007–2009 were severe. Was their severity the result of the accompanying bank panics? More generally, do recessions accompanied by bank panics tend to be more severe than recessions that do not involve bank panics?

Carmen Reinhart and Kenneth Rogoff of Harvard University have gathered data on recessions and bank panics, or bank crises, in a number of countries in an attempt to answer this question. The table below shows the average change in key economic variables during the period following a bank crisis for the United States during the Great Depression and a variety of other countries in the post–World War II era, including Japan, Norway, Korea, and Sweden:

Economic variable	Average change	Average duration of change	Number of countries
Unemployment rate	+ 7 percentage points	4.8 years	14
Real GDP per capita	− 9.3%	1.9 years	14
Real stock prices	− 55.9%	3.4 years	22
Real house prices	− 35.5%	6 years	21
Real government debt	+ 86%	3 years	13

The table shows that for these countries, on average, the recessions following bank crises were quite severe. Unemployment rates increased by 7 percentage points—for example, from 5% to 12%—and continued increasing for nearly five years after a crisis had begun. Real GDP per capita also declined sharply. The average length of a recession following a bank crisis has been nearly two years. Adjusted for inflation, stock prices dropped by more than half, and housing prices dropped by more than one-third. Government debt soared by 86%. The increased public debt was partly the result of increased government spending, including spending to bail out failed financial institutions. But most of the increased debt was the result of government budget deficits resulting from sharp declines in tax revenues as incomes and profits fell as a result of the recession.

The table below shows some key indicators for the 2007–2009 U.S. recession compared with other U.S. recessions of the post–World War II period:

	Duration	Decline in real GDP	Peak unemployment rate
Average for postwar recessions	10.4 months	− 1.7%	7.6%
Recession of 2007–2009	18 months	− 4.1%	10.0%

Consistent with Reinhart and Rogoff's findings that recessions following bank panics tend to be unusually severe, the 2007–2009 recession was the worst in the United States since the Great Depression of the 1930s. The recession lasted nearly twice as long as the average of earlier postwar recessions, GDP declined by more than twice the average, and the peak unemployment rate was about one-third higher than the average.

Because most people did not see the financial crisis coming, they also failed to anticipate the severity of the 2007–2009 recession.

Note: In the second table, the duration of recessions is based on NBER business cycle dates, the decline in real GDP is measured as the simple percentage change from the quarter of the cyclical peak to the quarter of the cyclical trough, and the peak unemployment rate is the highest unemployment rate in any month following the cyclical peak.

Sources: The first table is adapted from data in Carmen M. Reinhart and Kenneth S. Rogoff, *This Time Is Different: Eight Centuries of Financial Folly*, Princeton, NJ: Princeton University Press, 2009, Figures 14.1–14.5; and the second table uses data from the U.S. Bureau of Labor Statistics, the U.S. Bureau of Economic Analysis, and the National Bureau of Economic Research.

See related problems 1.9 and 1.10 at the end of the chapter.

While the United States has experienced financial crises primarily as bank panics, other countries have experienced exchange-rate crises, sometimes called *currency crises*, and *sovereign debt crises*.

Exchange-Rate Crises

As we saw in Chapter 8, exchange rates between currencies—for instance, the exchange rate between the U.S. dollar and the euro or between the Japanese yen and the Australian dollar—are determined by the interaction of demand and supply, as are other prices. In some cases, though, countries have attempted to keep the value of their currency fixed by *pegging* it against another currency. For instance, during the 1990s, a number of developing countries pegged the value of their currencies against the U.S. dollar. Having a fixed exchange rate can provide important advantages for a country that has extensive trade with another country. When the exchange rate is fixed, business planning becomes much easier. For example, if the value of the South Korean won increases relative to the U.S. dollar, Korean television manufacturers may have to raise the dollar prices of televisions they export to the United States, which will reduce sales. If the exchange rate between the Korean won and the dollar is fixed, these manufacturers will have an easier job of planning.

In addition, if firms in a country want to borrow directly from foreign investors or indirectly from foreign banks, a fluctuating exchange rate will cause fluctuations in their debt payments. For example, a Thai firm might borrow U.S. dollars from a Japanese bank. If the Thai firm wants to build a new factory in Thailand with borrowed dollars, the firm has to exchange the dollars for an equivalent amount of Thai currency, the baht. When the factory opens and production begins, the Thai firm will be earning the additional baht it needs to exchange for dollars to make the interest payments on the loan. A problem arises if the value of the baht falls against the dollar because the Thai firm will now have to pay more baht to buy the dollars it needs. By pegging the value of the baht against the dollar, the Thai government reduces the risks to Thai firms from foreign-currency loans.

Pegging can lead to problems, particularly if the pegged exchange rate ends up substantially above the equilibrium rate that would prevail in the absence of the peg. Figure 12.2 illustrates the problem that several East Asian countries faced in the late 1990s, as they attempted to peg exchange rates against the dollar. In the absence of pegging, the equilibrium exchange rate between the Korean won and the dollar would be E_1, and the equilibrium quantity of won traded per day would be Won_1. Because the Korean government pegged the value at a level, E_2, that was above the equilibrium level, there was an excess supply of won equal to $Won_3 - Won_2$. With more people wanting to trade won for dollars at that exchange rate than want to trade dollars for won, the Korean central bank, which would be responsible for

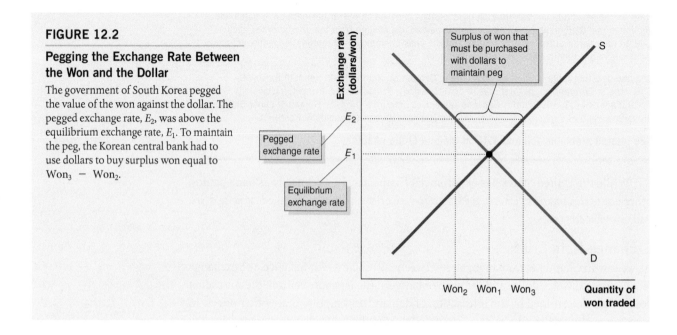

FIGURE 12.2

Pegging the Exchange Rate Between the Won and the Dollar

The government of South Korea pegged the value of the won against the dollar. The pegged exchange rate, E_2, was above the equilibrium exchange rate, E_1. To maintain the peg, the Korean central bank had to use dollars to buy surplus won equal to $Won_3 - Won_2$.

maintaining the peg, had to use its previously accumulated reserves of dollars to buy surplus won, or else the peg would be maintained.

Eventually, the central bank exhausted its holding of dollars. To maintain the peg as long as possible, Korea and other East Asian countries in similar situations took steps to raise domestic interest rates. Higher interest rates were intended to attract foreign investors to buy domestic bonds, thereby raising the demand for the domestic currency, and, potentially, preserving the peg. Unfortunately, higher domestic interest rates also discouraged domestic firms from engaging in real capital investment and domestic households from borrowing to finance spending on houses and consumer durables. In the end, the East Asian currency crises of the late 1990s resulted in recessions in these countries, and the countries decided to abandon their currency pegs.

Sovereign Debt Crises

Sovereign debt refers to bonds issued by a government. A sovereign debt crisis occurs when a country has difficulty making interest or principal payments on its bonds or when investors expect a country to have this difficulty in the future. If a sovereign debt crisis leads to actual default, a government may for a period of time be unable to issue bonds, which means it will have to rely exclusively on tax revenues to pay for government spending. Even if the government avoids default, it will probably have to pay much higher interest rates when it issues bonds. The resulting decreases in other government spending or increases in taxes can push the economy into recession.

Sovereign debt crises occur frequently and typically result from either of two circumstances:

1. Chronic government budget deficits that eventually result in the interest payments required on government bonds taking up an unsustainably large fraction of government spending

2. A severe recession that increases government spending and reduces tax revenues, resulting in soaring budget deficits

Following the 2007–2009 recession, several European governments, most notably that of Greece, were pushed to the edge of debt crises, as investors began to doubt their ability to pay the interest on their bonds. These countries imposed sharp spending cuts and higher taxes to reduce their government budget deficits.

12.2 The Financial Crisis of the Great Depression

LEARNING OBJECTIVE: Describe the key elements of the financial crisis that occurred during the Great Depression.

The two most significant financial crises in the past 100 years in the United States were the ones that accompanied the Great Depression of the 1930s and the recession of 2007–2009. In this section and the next section, we look more closely at these crises.

The Start of the Great Depression

Panel (a) of Figure 12.3 shows movements for the years from 1929 to 1939 in real GDP; real investment spending by firms on factories, office buildings, and other physical capital and by households on residential construction; and real consumption spending by households on goods and services. The data are expressed as index numbers relative to their values in 1929. Real GDP declined by 27% between 1929 and 1933, while real

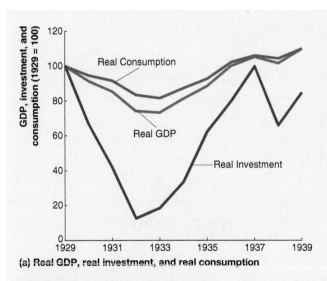

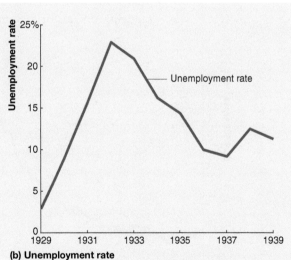

(a) Real GDP, real investment, and real consumption

(b) Unemployment rate

FIGURE 12.3 The Great Depression

In panel (a), the data are expressed as index numbers relative to their values in 1929. Real GDP declined by 27% between 1929 and 1933, while real consumption declined by 18%, and real investment fell by an astonishing 81%. These declines were by far the largest of the twentieth century. Panel (b) shows that the unemployment rate tripled from 1929 to 1930, was above 20% in 1932 and 1933, and was still above 10% in 1939, a decade after the Great Depression had begun.

Sources: Panel (a): U.S. Bureau of Economic Analysis; panel (b): Economic historians have compiled varying estimates of unemployment in the 1930s, years during which the federal government did not collect data on unemployment. The estimates used in the panel are from David R. Weir, "A Century of U.S. Unemployment, 1890–1990," in Roger L. Ransom, Richard Sutch, and Susan B. Carter (eds.), *Research in Economic History*, Vol. 14, Westport, CT: JAI Press, 1992, Table D3, pp. 341–343.

consumption declined by 18%, and real investment fell by an astonishing 81%. These declines were by far the largest of the twentieth century. Panel (b) shows the unemployment rate for the same years. The unemployment rate tripled from 1929 to 1930, was above 20% in 1932 and 1933, and was still above 10% in 1939, a decade after the Great Depression had begun.

Although many people think the Great Depression started with the famous stock market crash of October 1929, the NBER dates the Depression as having begun two months earlier, in August 1929. Figure 12.4 shows movements in the S&P 500 Composite Stock Price Index from 1920 through 1939. By 1928, the Federal Reserve had become concerned about the rapid increases in stock prices shown in the figure. As the Federal Reserve increased interest rates to reduce what it saw as a speculative bubble in stock prices, growth in the U.S. economy slowed during early 1929, and the economy eventually entered a recession.

Several factors increased the severity of the downturn during the period from the fall of 1929 to the fall of 1930. Between September 1929 and September 1930, stock prices plunged by more than 40%, reducing household wealth, making it more difficult for firms to raise funds by issuing stock, and increasing the uncertainty of households and firms about their future incomes. This increase in uncertainty may explain the sharp fall in household spending on consumer durables, such as automobiles, and firm spending on factories, office buildings, and other physical capital. (We discussed the stock market crash of 1929 at greater length in the *Making the Connection* that appears on page 180 of Chapter 6.) In addition, Congress passed the Smoot-Hawley Tariff Act in June 1930, which led foreign governments to increase tariffs in retaliation, thereby reducing U.S. exports. Some economists also believe that the downturn was made

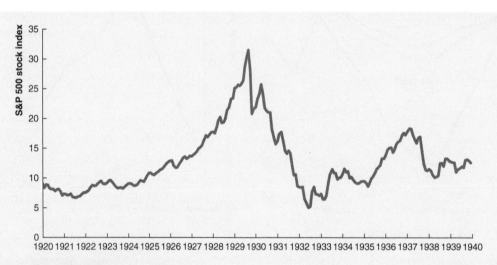

FIGURE 12.4 The S&P 500, 1920–1939

The Federal Reserve raised interest rates after it became concerned by the rapid increases in stock prices during 1928 and 1929. The decline in stock prices from 1929 to 1932 was the largest in U.S. history.

Source: Robert J. Shiller, *Irrational Exuberance*, Princeton, NJ: Princeton University Press, 2005, as updated at www.econ.yale.edu/~shiller/data.htm.

worse by a decline in spending on new houses. This decline resulted from a slowdown in population growth caused in part by legislation Congress passed in the early 1920s restricting immigration.

The Bank Panics of the Early 1930s

If the downturn that began in August 1929 had ended in the fall of 1930, it would still have been one of the most severe on record. Far from ending, though, the downturn continued until March 1933. A slow recovery then took place, until another recession began in May 1937 and lasted until June 1938. As a result, in 1939, a decade after the beginning of the Depression, many firms were still producing well below their capacity, and the unemployment rate remained high. The U.S. economy did not return to normal conditions until after the end of World War II in 1945.

Many economists believe that the series of bank panics that began in the fall of 1930 greatly contributed to the length and severity of the Depression. The bank panics came in several waves: the fall of 1930, the spring of 1931, the fall of 1931, and the spring of 1933. The large number of small, poorly diversified banks—particularly those that held agricultural loans as commodity prices fell—helped fuel the panics. A bank suspension occurs when a bank is closed to the public either temporarily or permanently. Figure 12.5 shows the number of bank suspensions for the years from 1920 to 1939. The bank panic of 1933 was the most severe, with several states declaring "bank holidays" in which all banks in the state were closed. Finally, shortly after taking office

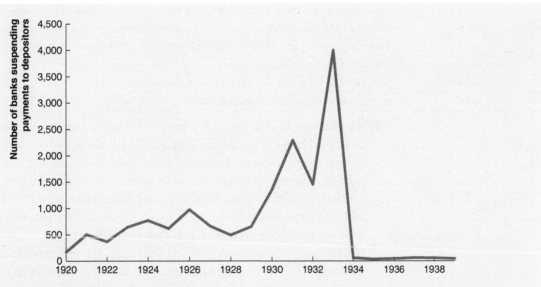

FIGURE 12.5 Bank Suspensions, 1920–1939

Bank suspensions, during which banks are closed to the public either temporarily or permanently, soared during the bank panics of the early 1930s before falling to low levels following the establishment of the FDIC in 1934.

Source: Board of Governors of the Federal Reserve System, *Banking and Monetary Statistics of the United States, 1914–1941*, Washington, DC: U.S. Government Printing Office, November 1943.

in March 1933, President Franklin Roosevelt declared a national bank holiday, and nearly every bank in the country closed. Of the 24,500 commercial banks operating in the United States in June 1929, only 15,400 were still operating in June 1934. Figure 12.5 shows that with the establishment of the FDIC in 1934, bank suspensions fell to low levels.

Debt-deflation process
The process first identified by Irving Fisher in which a cycle of falling asset prices and falling prices of goods and services can increase the severity of an economic downturn.

We have already discussed how bank panics can deepen a recession. In addition, during the Depression, the bank panics fueled a **debt-deflation process** first described at the time by Irving Fisher of Yale University. Fisher argued that as banks were forced to sell assets, the prices of those assets would decline, causing other banks and investors holding the assets to suffer declines in net worth, leading to additional bank failures and to investors going bankrupt. These failures and bankruptcies would lead to further asset sales and further declines in asset prices. In addition, as the economic downturn worsened, the price level would fall—as it did in the early 1930s—with two negative effects: Real interest rates would rise, and the real value of debts would increase. The consumer price index declined by about 25% between 1929 and 1933, which means that fixed payments on loans and bonds had to be made with dollars of greater purchasing power, increasing the burden on borrowers and raising the likelihood of defaults. The debt-deflation process—with falling asset prices, falling prices of goods and services, and increasing bankruptcies and defaults—can increase the severity of an economic downturn.

The Failure of Federal Reserve Policy During the Great Depression

Some bank failures during the early 1930s resulted from the severity of the Depression, as banks suffered losses on their loans and security investments, became insolvent, and failed. But some bank failures resulted from the instability of the system as banks that were illiquid, but not insolvent, suffered runs and were forced to close. Ironically, the Federal Reserve, which Congress established in 1913 to end bank panics, presided over the worst panics in U.S. history.

Why did the Fed not intervene to stabilize the banking system? Economists have discussed four possible explanations:

1. **No one was in charge.** Today, the person serving as Federal Reserve Chair is clearly in charge. That person is chair of both the Board of Governors and the Federal Open Market Committee, which determines the Fed's most important policies. Although any monetary policy action must be adopted by a formal vote, the chair is considered responsible for originating new policy initiatives and formulating responses to crises. The current structure of the Federal Reserve System was not put in place until 1935, however, and in the early 1930s, power within the Federal Reserve System was much more divided. The secretary of the Treasury and the comptroller of the currency, both of whom report directly to the president of the United States, served on the Federal Reserve Board, which was the predecessor to the Board of Governors. The secretary of the Treasury served as the board's chair. So, the Fed had less independence from the executive branch of the government than it does today. In addition, the heads of the 12 Federal Reserve District

Banks operated much more independently than they do today, with the head of the Federal Reserve Bank of New York having nearly as much influence within the system as the head of the Federal Reserve Board. At the time of the bank panics, George Harrison, the head of the Federal Reserve Bank of New York, served as chairman of the Open Market Policy Conference, the predecessor of the current Federal Open Market Committee. Harrison frequently acted independently of Roy Young and Eugene Meyer, who served as heads of the Federal Reserve Board during those years. Important decisions required forming a consensus among these different groups. During the early 1930s, consensus proved hard to come by, and taking decisive policy actions was difficult.

2. **The Fed was reluctant to rescue insolvent banks.** The Federal Reserve was established to serve as a lender of last resort to solvent banks that were experiencing temporary liquidity problems because of bank runs. Many of the banks that failed during the bank panics of the early 1930s were insolvent if their assets were valued at market prices. Some Fed officials believed that the Federal Reserve Act barred them from lending to insolvent banks. (As we will see in the *Making the Connection* on page 410, this issue was raised again during the debate over the Fed's failure to lend to Lehman Brothers as it slipped toward bankruptcy in 2008.) Leaving aside the legal issues, many Fed officials believed that taking actions to save insolvent banks was poor policy because it might encourage risky behavior by bank managers. In other words, the Fed was afraid of the problem that economists now call *moral hazard*.

3. **The Fed failed to understand the difference between nominal and real interest rates.** The Fed closely monitored nominal interest rates, particularly rates on short-term loans, which fell to very low levels during the early 1930s. Many Fed officials believed that these low interest rates indicated that demand for loans was low, so there had been no significant reduction in the supply of loans to borrowers. Economists, though, believe that the real interest rate is a better indicator than the nominal interest rate of conditions in the loan market. During the early 1930s, the U.S. economy experienced *deflation*, with the price level falling at an annual average rate of 6.6% between 1930 and 1933. So, measured in real terms, interest rates were much higher in the early 1930s than policymakers at the Fed believed them to be. Some economists argue that these high real interest rates indicate that the supply of loans had declined, which forced interest rates up as borrowers scrambled to find credit.

4. **The Fed wanted to "purge speculative excess."** Many members of the Fed believed that the Depression was the result of financial speculation during the late 1920s, particularly the bubble in stock prices that occurred in 1928 and 1929. They argued that only after the results of the excesses had been "purged" would a lasting recovery be possible. Some economists believe that the Fed followed the "liquidationist" policy said to be promoted by Secretary of the Treasury Andrew Mellon. According to this policy, allowing the price level to fall and weak banks and weak firms to fail was necessary before a recovery could begin.

MAKING THE CONNECTION

Did the Failure of the Bank of United States Cause the Great Depression?

In the early 1960s, Milton Friedman of the University of Chicago and Anna Schwartz of the National Bureau of Economic Research published an influential discussion of the importance of the bank panics of the 1930s in their book *A Monetary History of the United States, 1867–1960*. In that book and later writings, Friedman and Schwartz singled out the failure in December 1930 of the Bank of United States, a large private bank (despite its name) located in New York City, as being particularly important:

> [The bank's] failure on Dec. 11, 1930, marked a basic change in character of the contraction that had started in August 1929, from a severe recession, with no sign of any financial crisis, to a catastrophe that reached its climax in the banking holiday of March 1933, when all banks were closed for a week.

The Bank of United States ran into trouble in part because an unusually high percentage of its loans were in real estate, which by the fall of 1930 was suffering from declining prices and mortgage defaults. In addition, the bank's owners had been using its funds to buy the bank's stock in an attempt to keep the stock's price from falling. This practice is illegal and, two of the bank's owners later went to jail as a result. In the weeks leading up to the bank's closure, the Federal Reserve Bank of New York attempted to arrange for the bank to merge with two other New York City banks. When plans for the merger fell through, the bank was closed, becoming the largest bank to have failed in the United States up to that time.

The failure of the Bank of United States caused much discussion at the time, and economists continue to debate this episode today. The bank appears to have been insolvent at the time it closed, which may be why the plan to save it by merging it with other banks failed. There is some evidence, though, that George Harrison, who headed the Federal Reserve Bank of New York, did not support the merger plan, which may have played a role in its rejection by the other banks. Economists continue to disagree about whether the Federal Reserve should have moved more forcefully to keep the bank from closing.

Many economists are skeptical of Friedman and Schwartz's emphasis on the importance of the bank's failure. Immediately after the bank failed, other New York City banks did not suffer severe liquidity problems, and none failed. Several months passed before the next bank panic, and many of the banks involved in that panic were smaller banks outside New York City. In addition, whether that later panic had any connection to the failure of the Bank of United States is unclear. Following the failure of the Bank of United States, interest rates on low-rated corporate bonds began to rise relative to interest rates on high-rated corporate bonds, which might indicate that investors interpreted the bank's failure as bad news about the future state of the economy. But, once again, it is unclear whether this movement in interest rates was the result of the bank's failure.

The details of the failure of the Bank of United States are less important than the later effect of this episode on policymakers. Particularly after publication of

Friedman and Schwartz's book, many economists, both inside and outside the Fed, became convinced that allowing the bank to fail had been a significant policy mistake. Some economists even argue that this episode was important in leading the Fed to develop the "too-big-to-fail" doctrine, which holds that no large financial institution can be allowed to fail because its failure may destabilize the financial system. This doctrine was subject to intensive debate during the 2007–2009 financial crisis and its aftermath.

Although the Bank of United States failed more than 85 years ago, the consequences of its failure continue to influence current policy.

Sources: Milton Friedman and Anna Schwartz, *A Monetary History of the United States, 1867–1960*, Princeton, NJ: Princeton University Press, 1963, pp. 308–313; Friedman quote from Milton Friedman, "Anti-Semitism and the Great Depression," *Newsweek*, Vol. 84, November 16, 1974, p. 90; Allan H. Meltzer, *A History of the Federal Reserve: Volume 1: 1913–1951*, Chicago: University of Chicago Press, 2003, pp. 323–326; Elmus Wicker, *The Banking Panics of the Great Depression,* Cambridge, UK: Cambridge University Press, 1996; and Arthur J. Rolnick, "Interview with Ben S. Bernanke," Federal Reserve Bank of Minneapolis, *The Region*, June 2004.

See related problem 2.10 at the end of the chapter.

12.3 The Financial Crisis of 2007–2009

LEARNING OBJECTIVE: Describe what caused the financial crisis of 2007–2009.

Several factors contributed to the severity of the recession of 2007–2009, including an increase in oil prices from $34 per barrel in 2004 to $147 per barrel in 2008. The most important cause, though, was clearly the bursting of the housing market bubble.

The Housing Bubble Bursts

New home sales rose by 60% between January 2000 and July 2005, by which time many economists believed that a *bubble* had formed in the housing market. Recall that in a bubble, the price of an asset is greater than its fundamental value. We have seen that the fundamental value of a share of stock equals the present value of the dividends investors expect to receive from owning the stock. Similarly, the fundamental value of a house equals the present value of the housing services the homeowner expects to receive. We would anticipate, then, that housing prices and rents would increase at roughly the same rate.[1] Accordingly, if prices of single-family homes rise significantly relative to rental rates for single-family homes, it is more likely that the housing market is experiencing a bubble. As Figure 12.6 shows, housing prices and housing rents generally increase at about the same rate, but between January 2000 and May 2006, housing prices increased much more rapidly than rents. This divergence between housing prices and rents is evidence of a bubble.

As prices of new and existing homes began to decline during 2006, some homebuyers had trouble making the payments on their mortgage loans. When lenders foreclosed

---

[1] It is possible that housing prices might rise while current rents remain unchanged if homebuyers are anticipating an increase in *future* rents. But there was not much indication during 2000–2005 that homebuyers or economists were expecting sharp increases in rents in the future.

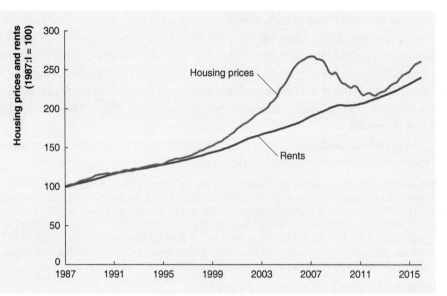

FIGURE 12.6

Housing Prices and Housing Rents, 1987–2016

Typically, housing prices increase at about the same rate as housing rents. But during the housing bubble, housing prices increased far more than did rents.

Sources: Federal Reserve Bank of St. Louis; and S&P/Case-Shiller, standardandpoors.com.

on defaulted mortgages, the lenders sold the homes, causing housing prices to decline further. Mortgage lenders that had concentrated on making subprime loans suffered heavy losses, and some went out of business. Most banks and other lenders tightened their requirements for borrowers. This *credit crunch* made it more difficult for potential homebuyers to obtain mortgages, which further depressed the housing market. The decline in the housing market not only resulted in lower spending on residential construction but also affected markets for furniture, appliances, and home improvements, as homeowners found it more difficult to borrow against the declining value of their homes.

Bank Runs at Bear Stearns and Lehman Brothers

By early 2007, it had become clear that investors, including banks and other financial firms, that owned mortgage-backed securities made up of subprime mortgages would suffer significant losses. Many economists and policymakers, though, still believed that rising defaults on subprime mortgages would not cause problems for the wider economy. For example, Fed Chairman Ben Bernanke argued: "We believe the effect of the troubles in the subprime sector on the broader housing market will likely be limited, and we do not expect significant spillovers from the subprime market to the rest of economy or to the financial system."[2] The first strong indication that a financial crisis might be approaching came in August 2007, when the French bank BNP Paribas announced that it would not allow investors in three of its investment funds to redeem their shares. The funds had held large amounts of mortgage-backed securities and because trading in these securities had dried up, it had become difficult to determine the securities' market prices and, therefore, the value of the funds' shares.

---

[2] Ben S. Bernanke, "The Subprime Mortgage Market," speech at the Federal Reserve Bank of Chicago's 43rd Annual Conference on Bank Structure and Competition, Chicago, May 17, 2007, www.federalreserve.gov/newsevents/speech/bernanke20070517a.htm.

In the fall of 2007 and the spring of 2008, credit conditions worsened. Many lenders became reluctant to lend to financial firms for more than very short terms and often insisted on government bonds as collateral. As we saw in Chapter 11, some investment banks had funded long-term investments with short-term borrowing from banks and other financial firms. These investment banks were in a situation similar to that of commercial banks before the establishment of federal deposit insurance. In particular, the investment banks were subject to runs if lenders declined to renew the banks' short-term loans, which is what happened to Bear Stearns in March 2008. Lenders became concerned that Bear's investments in mortgage-backed securities had declined in value so much that the investment bank was insolvent. With aid from the Federal Reserve, Bear was saved from bankruptcy only by being acquired by the bank JPMorgan Chase at a price of $10 per share; one year earlier, Bear's shares had sold for $170.

By August 2008, the crisis was deepening, as nearly 25% of subprime mortgages were at least 30 days past due. On September 15, the Lehman Brothers investment bank filed for bankruptcy protection after the Treasury and Federal Reserve declined to commit the funds necessary to attract another financial firm to purchase the bank. At the same time, the Merrill Lynch investment bank agreed to sell itself to Bank of America. The failure of Lehman Brothers marked a turning point in the crisis. As we saw in Chapter 11, on September 16, Reserve Primary Fund, a large money market mutual fund, announced that because it had suffered heavy losses on its holdings of Lehman Brothers commercial paper, it would "break the buck" by allowing the price of shares in the fund to fall from $1.00 to $0.97. This announcement led to a run on money market mutual funds, as investors cashed in their shares. Many parts of the financial system became frozen as trading in securitized loans largely stopped, and large firms as well as small ones had difficulty arranging for even short-term loans.

The Federal Government's Extraordinary Response to the Financial Crisis

Prior to the financial crisis, the federal government's policymaking and regulatory structure had been focused on the commercial banking system and the stock market. This focus left the government poorly equipped to deal with a crisis centered on the shadow banking system of investment banks, money market mutual funds, insurance companies, and hedge funds. In addition, as we have seen, most policymakers did not realize until well into 2007 that the subprime crisis might evolve into a full-blown financial crisis.

Nevertheless, the Federal Reserve, the Treasury, Congress, and President George W. Bush responded vigorously once the crisis had begun. On September 18, 2007, the Fed began aggressively driving down short-term interest rates by cutting its target for the federal funds rate, the interest rate that commercial banks charge each other for short-term loans. By December 2008, the federal funds rate was close to zero, its lowest rate in history. In September 2008, the federal government effectively nationalized Fannie Mae and Freddie Mac, the government-sponsored enterprises responsible for securitizing a majority of mortgage loans, by having the Treasury pledge to provide up to $100 billion to each firm in exchange for 80% ownership of the firms. The Treasury gave management control of the firms to the Federal Housing Finance Agency. That same month, the Treasury moved to stop the runs on money market mutual funds by announcing a $50 billion plan to insure shares in these funds. In October, the Fed announced that for the first time since the Great Depression, it would lend directly to corporations through the *Commercial Paper Funding Facility* by purchasing three-month commercial paper issued by nonfinancial corporations.

In September 2008, the Federal Reserve and the Treasury also unveiled a plan for Congress to authorize $700 billion to be used to purchase mortgages and mortgage-backed securities from financial firms and other investors. The objective of the *Troubled Asset Relief Program (TARP)*, which Congress passed in early October 2008, was to restore a market in these securities to provide relief to financial institutions that had trillions of dollars of these assets on their balance sheets. Ultimately, devising a program for purchasing mortgages and mortgage-backed securities proved difficult, and most of the TARP funds were used to make direct purchases of preferred stock in banks to increase their capital and to provide funds to automobile firms that were in danger of failing.

These policy initiatives represented one of the most extensive government interventions in the financial system in U.S. history. Whether these initiatives may have unintended negative consequences in the long run remains to be seen. But most economists and policymakers believe that they served the purpose of stabilizing the financial system during the fall of 2008 and the spring of 2009. Also helping to stabilize the system was a *stress test* administered by the Treasury to 19 large financial firms during early 2009. The test was intended to gauge how well these firms would fare if the recession deepened. Many investors were reassured when the tests indicated that the firms would need to raise only about $100 billion in new capital to have the resources to deal with a severe economic downturn.

After the crisis had passed, Congress turned to the task of examining whether regulations governing the financial system needed to be overhauled. In July 2010, Congress passed, and President Barack Obama signed, the Wall Street Reform and Consumer Protection Act, or Dodd-Frank Act, which we will discuss in the next section.

Financial Crises and Financial Regulation

LEARNING OBJECTIVE: Discuss the connection between financial crises and financial regulation.

The federal government's response to the 2007–2009 financial crisis highlights that new government financial regulations typically occur in response to a crisis. As we look at different types of regulations that the government has enacted over the years, we will see that there is a regular pattern:

1. A crisis in the financial system occurs.
2. The government responds to the crisis by adopting new regulations.
3. Financial firms respond to the new regulations.
4. Government regulators adapt policies as financial firms try to evade regulations.

The first stage in the regulatory pattern is a *crisis* in the financial system. For example, if savers lose confidence in banks, they will withdraw their funds, and a bank panic will result. In a panic, banks are unable to fulfill their role as financial intermediaries, and many households and firms lose access to loans.

The second stage occurs when the government steps in to end the crisis through *regulation*. The government generally intervenes when it perceives instability in financial institutions and when political pressures make intervention advisable. For example, government regulation in the United States and other countries has responded to bank panics by enacting deposit insurance.

The third stage is the *response by the financial system*. A major new regulation, such as deposit insurance, leads to changes and innovation in the activities of financial institutions. For example, banks may take on more risk once deposit insurance reduces the extent to which depositors monitor bank investments. As with manufacturing companies or other nonfinancial businesses, innovation (the development of new products or lines of business to serve consumers) gives one company an edge over its competitors. The motivation for financial innovation is the same as in other businesses: profit.

The fourth stage is the *regulatory response*. Regulators monitor the effect of regulation on how financial institutions do business. In particular, when financial innovations circumvent regulatory restrictions, regulators must adapt their policies or seek new authority as a regulatory response. For example, when Congress adopted a regulation to keep banks from paying interest on checking accounts, banks eventually circumvented the ban by developing accounts similar to checking accounts, called NOW accounts, that paid interest. Congress then had to adapt regulations to either ban NOW accounts or to allow them. In this case, Congress decided to allow the accounts.

Lender of Last Resort

We have already seen that Congress created the Federal Reserve System in 1913 as the lender of last resort to provide liquidity to banks during bank panics. We have also seen, though, that the Fed failed its first crucial test when it stood by while the banking system collapsed in the early 1930s. Congress responded to this failure by establishing the FDIC in 1934 and by reorganizing the Fed to make the Federal Open Market Committee (FOMC) the Fed's main policy body. The chairman of the Board of Governors, rather than the president of the Federal Reserve Bank of New York, was made the chairman of the FOMC. This last change helped to centralize decision making at the Fed by ensuring that the Board of Governors, based in Washington, DC, rather than the 12 Federal Reserve District Bank presidents, would be the dominant force in the system.

Success in the Postwar Years and the Development of the "Too-Big-to-Fail" Policy

Despite its shaky start as a lender of last resort during the Great Depression, the Fed has performed this role well during most of the post–World War II period. For example, when the Penn Central Railroad, once one of the largest corporations in the United States, filed for bankruptcy in 1970, it defaulted on $200 million of commercial paper. Investors started to doubt the quality of commercial paper issued by other large corporations and became cautious about investing in that market. The Fed helped to avoid a crisis by providing commercial banks with loans that allowed the banks to lend to firms that would ordinarily have borrowed in the commercial paper market.

In a similar episode in 1974, the Franklin National Bank began to experience a run by depositors who held negotiable certificates of deposit (CDs). Because these CDs were worth more than $40,000, they were beyond what was then the limit for federal deposit insurance, and investors worried that they would suffer heavy losses if the bank failed. Other banks feared that they would also be subject to runs by depositors holding negotiable CDs. Because negotiable CDs were a significant source of funds to banks, banks would have been forced to cut back on their own loans, reducing the credit available to households and firms. The Fed avoided this result by making short-term loans of more than $1.5 billion to Franklin National until the Fed was able to find another bank willing to merge with Franklin National. The Fed's prompt action avoided what could have been a significant blow to the financial system.

The stock market crash of October 19, 1987, raised fears of a repetition of the events that followed the 1929 crash. In particular, many securities firms had suffered heavy losses because of the fall in stock prices. These firms *make a market* in the securities traded on the floor of the New York Stock Exchange by being willing to buy, sell, and hold inventories of those securities. (Their role has been reduced in recent years, as most trading now takes place electronically rather than on the floor of the Exchange.) The failure of those firms would have disrupted trading on the New York Stock Exchange. Before the stock market opened for trading the following day, Federal Reserve Chairman Alan Greenspan announced to the news media the Fed's readiness to provide liquidity to support the economic and financial systems. At the same time, the Fed, acting as lender of last resort, encouraged banks to lend to securities firms and extended loans to banks. These actions reassured both banks and investors and preserved the smooth functioning of financial markets.

In these and other similar actions, the Fed had successfully used its role as lender of last resort to stabilize the financial system, thereby avoiding the errors of the 1930s, when the Fed's unwillingness to save banks that might be insolvent led it to stand by while the financial system collapsed. But was it possible that the Fed was starting to err in the opposite direction? In principle, central banks should provide short-term loans to banks that are illiquid but not insolvent. By lending to banks that are insolvent, the central bank confronts the danger that bank managers might take on too much risk, knowing that if their investments fail and they become insolvent, the central bank will save them. In other words, by taking steps to save insolvent banks, the Fed increases the level of moral hazard in the system. It became clear by the early 1980s that the Fed and the FDIC considered the largest banks "**too big to fail**." In 1984, the comptroller of the currency, who regulates national banks, provided Congress with a list of banks that were considered too big to fail. A failure by any of these banks was thought to pose *systemic risk* to the financial system, which, as we saw in Chapter 11, is risk to the entire financial system rather than to individual firms or investors.

Too-big-to-fail policy A policy under which the federal government does not allow large financial firms to fail, for fear of damaging the financial system.

Because the Fed and the FDIC would not allow these large banks to fail, depositors in them effectively had unlimited deposit insurance. Large depositors, including holders of negotiable CDs, would not lose any money if these banks failed, even though their deposits were above what was then the federal deposit limit of $100,000. So, these depositors had much less incentive to monitor the behavior of bank managers and to withdraw their deposits or demand higher interest rates if the managers made reckless investments.

Moreover, the too-big-to-fail policy was criticized for being unfair because it treated small and large banks differently. When the FDIC closed the African-American-owned Harlem's Freedom National Bank in 1990, its large depositors—including such charitable organizations as the United Negro College Fund and the Urban League—received only about 50 cents per dollar of uninsured deposits. Only a few months later, in January 1991, the much larger Bank of New England failed, as a result of a collapse of its real estate portfolio. Its large depositors were fully protected by the FDIC, costing taxpayers about $2.3 billion.

Concern with the unfairness and increased moral hazard resulting from the too-big-to-fail policy was one reason that Congress passed the Federal Deposit Insurance Corporation Improvement Act of 1991 (FDICIA). The act required the FDIC to deal with failed banks using the method that would be least costly to the taxpayer, which typically means closing the bank, reimbursing the bank's insured depositors, and using whatever funds can be raised from selling the bank's assets to reimburse uninsured depositors. Because the value of a failed bank's assets is almost always less than the value of its liabilities, uninsured depositors suffer losses. The act did contain an exception, however, for cases in which a bank's failure would cause "serious adverse effects on economic conditions or financial stability." To invoke this exception, two-thirds of the directors of the FDIC, two-thirds of the members of the Fed's Board of Governors, and the secretary of the Treasury would have to approve. During the financial crisis of 2007–2009, this exception proved to be important.

The Financial Crisis and a Broader Fed Role as Lender of Last Resort Because investment banks, rather than commercial banks, were most directly affected at the beginning of the financial crisis of 2007–2009, policymakers faced unexpected challenges. Unlike commercial banks, investment banks were not eligible to borrow directly from the Fed. While deposits in commercial banks are covered by insurance through the FDIC, loans to investment banks are not. We have already seen that the Fed dealt with these problems by lending to large investment banks and by buying commercial paper to ensure that corporations would be able to meet their short-term credit needs. In addition, the Treasury provided temporary insurance to investors owning money market mutual fund shares.

Perhaps the most controversial of the Fed's actions was the decision in March 2008 to participate with the Treasury to keep Bear Stearns from failing by arranging for the investment bank to be purchased by JPMorgan Chase. As part of the arrangement, the Fed agreed to cover up to $29 billion in losses that JPMorgan Chase might suffer on Bear's holdings of mortgage-backed securities. Some economists and policymakers criticized this action, saying that it increased moral hazard in the financial system. This criticism may have played a role in the Fed's decision not to attempt to save Lehman Brothers from bankruptcy in September 2008. A few days later, though, the Fed made a large loan to the American International Group (AIG) insurance company in exchange for 80% ownership of the firm. In fact, with the exception of Lehman Brothers, the Fed, FDIC, and Treasury combined to take actions that resulted in no large financial firms failing. The too-big-to-fail policy appeared to be back.

Could the Fed Have Saved Lehman Brothers?

Over the weekend of September 13 and 14, 2008, Federal Reserve and U.S. Treasury officials determined that they would not be able to save Lehman Brothers from bankruptcy, either by finding another financial firm to buy or merge with Lehman or by making loans that would allow the bank to deal with its inability to find short-term funding. Early Monday morning, September 15, Lehman Brothers filed for bankruptcy. The next day, the Fed and the Treasury saved the American International Group (AIG) from bankruptcy under the terms discussed earlier. The seemingly inconsistent decisions of allowing Lehman to fail while saving AIG surprised many observers at the time and have remained the subject of intense debate among economists and policymakers. As then Massachusetts Congressman Barney Frank observed: "The national commitment to the free market lasted one day. It was Monday."

The Fed's actions with respect to Lehman remain a source of controversy because most economists believe that Lehman's failure significantly worsened the financial crisis and recession. The effect of Lehman's failure can be seen in movements in an index of financial stress compiled by the Federal Reserve Bank of St. Louis. The index is an average of 18 financial variables, including spreads between interest rates on corporate bonds and Treasury securities, that tend to increase during periods when investors engage in a flight to safety and households and firms face difficulty securing credit. The following figure shows movements in the index from immediately before to immediately after the recession of 2007–2009. The average value of the index is zero, with periods of greater-than-normal financial stress having positive values and periods of lower-than-normal financial stress having negative values.

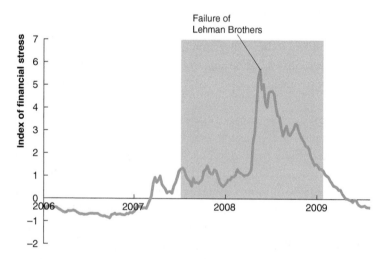

The figure shows that following the failure of Lehman, financial stress jumped dramatically. As households and firms had difficulty obtaining credit and as uncertainty about the economy markedly increased, spending declined sharply. The spending declines resulted in a contraction in production and employment. From the beginning of the recession in December 2007 to the failure of Lehman, total employment in the United States declined by about 1.2 million. From the failure of Lehman through the end of 2009, employment declined by an additional 7 million. This employment decline was by far the largest in such a brief period in U.S. history.

Policymakers and economists have offered two main explanations for why the Fed did not take steps that might have kept Lehman out of bankruptcy:

1. Criticism by members of Congress over the actions the Fed had taken to save Bear Stearns coupled with fear of increasing moral hazard in the financial system made the Fed decide to allow Lehman to declare bankruptcy.
2. Provisions of the Federal Reserve Act tied the Fed's hands and made it impossible for the Fed to legally save Lehman.

If correct, explanation 1 means that the Fed could have saved Lehman but chose not to, while explanation 2 means that, legally, the Fed could not have saved Lehman even if it had wanted to do so.

Ben Bernanke served as Fed chairman during the financial crisis. In his memoirs, published in 2015, Bernanke argued that because Lehman was insolvent, the Federal Reserve Act barred the Fed from saving it:

> It became evident that Lehman was deeply insolvent.... Lehman's insolvency made it impossible to save with Fed lending alone.... [W]e were required [by the Federal Reserve Act] to lend against adequate collateral. The Fed had no authority to inject capital or (what is more or less the same thing) make a loan that we were not reasonably sure could be fully repaid.

But was Lehman Brothers actually insolvent? After Lehman's bankruptcy, some of its creditors were paid back less than what the firm owed them, which seems to indicate that the value of the firm's assets was less than the value of its liabilities—the definition of insolvency. But in 2016, economist Laurence Ball of Johns Hopkins University released a working paper in which he disputed Bernanke's account. Ball argued that there is no evidence that Fed policymakers were concerned about Lehman's solvency at the time they were considering whether to make loans to the bank. Ball believes that Lehman did have sufficient collateral to secure a loan that would have met its short-run liquidity needs. He also notes that the Federal Reserve Act, as it was in 2008 (before it was subsequently amended by the Dodd-Frank Act in 2010), did not keep the Fed from making loans to insolvent firms, provided that the loan being made was secured by adequate collateral. In other words, the fact that Lehman proved to be insolvent once it declared bankruptcy did not necessarily preclude the Fed from making loans large enough to have kept the bank from failing.

Ball argues that explanation 1. above is the reason that the Fed allowed Lehman to fail. In particular, he believes that Treasury Secretary Henry Paulson was heavily involved in the decision and that he was sensitive to the political criticism he had received following the actions the Treasury and Fed had taken to save Bear Stearns the previous spring.

Providing some support for Ball's argument are interviews that financial journalists James Stewart and Peter Eavis conducted with economists at the Federal Reserve Bank of New York. The economists were members of two teams that were charged with evaluating Lehman's solvency. The weekend before Lehman's bankruptcy, the teams analyzed Lehman's balance sheet and concluded that the bank was, barely, solvent. Apparently, though, those reports did not reach Ben Bernanke, Henry Paulson, or New York Fed President Timothy Geithner before they made the decision to allow Lehman to declare bankruptcy. Some economists dispute Ball's conclusions because they believe that Ball (along with the New York Fed economists interviewed by Stewart and Eavis) underestimates Lehman's financial problems and that a loan from the Fed was unlikely to have saved the bank.

More than 85 years later, economists still debate the Fed's actions with respect to the failure of the Bank of United States in 1930. The debate over the failure of Lehman Brothers in 2008 may also continue for years to come.

Sources: Ben S. Bernanke, *The Courage to Act: The Financial Crisis and Its Aftermath*, New York: W.W. Norton, 2015, quoted passage is on p. 264; James Stewart, "Pointing a Finger at the Fed in the Lehman Disaster," *New York Times*, July 21, 2016; James B. Stewart and Peter Eavis, "Revisiting the Lehman Brothers Bailout That Never Was," *New York Times*, September 29, 2014; Laurence Ball, "The Fed and Lehman Brothers," working paper prepared for a meeting of the NBER Monetary Economics Program, July 14, 2016; and Federal Reserve Bank of St. Louis.

See related problem 4.8 at the end of the chapter.

The 2010 Financial Overhaul: The End of the Too-Big-to-Fail Policy? Although some economists and policymakers praised the actions of the Fed, FDIC, and Treasury in helping to restore stability to the financial system, many members of Congress and the general public criticized what was called the "Wall Street bailout" that they believed resulted from TARP and the actions taken to keep large financial firms from failing. Partially in response to these criticisms, Congress passed the Wall Street Reform and Consumer Protection Act, or Dodd-Frank Act, in July 2010, which included provisions intended to end the too-big-to-fail policy. The act allows the Fed, FDIC, and Treasury to seize and "wind down" large financial firms, which means that the firms' assets are to be sold off in a way that will not destabilize financial markets. Previously, only the FDIC had this power, and it could use it only in closing commercial banks. The intent of this provision of the Dodd-Frank Act was to give policymakers a third option besides allowing a large firm to go bankrupt or taking action to save it. Sheila Bair, who was then chair of the FDIC, predicted that the act would lead investors to shift funds toward smaller firms, where the information costs of determining the riskiness of investments would be lower. Larger firms would have to provide investors with higher expected returns to compensate them for the ending of the too-big-to-fail policy.

The Dodd-Frank Act also created the Financial Stability Oversight Council (FSOC), which is composed of the heads of the major federal financial regulatory agencies, including the Fed, the FDIC, and the Securities and Exchange Commission (SEC). The FSOC is chaired by the secretary of the Treasury and, among other responsibilities, is charged with identifying the financial firms that are *systemically important financial institutions* (SIFIs). A firm is considered a SIFI if its failure would potentially cause a financial crisis. These firms are subject to closer regulatory supervision, are required to hold additional capital, and are required to undergo annual *stress tests* to gauge their ability to withstand a severe recession or financial crisis. In addition, the firms must write

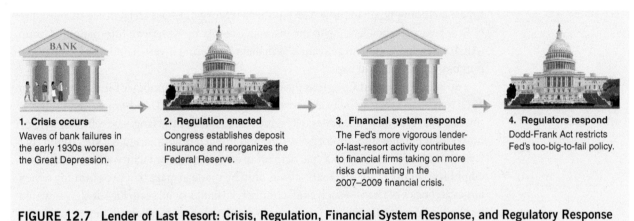

1. Crisis occurs

Waves of bank failures in the early 1930s worsen the Great Depression.

2. Regulation enacted

Congress establishes deposit insurance and reorganizes the Federal Reserve.

3. Financial system responds

The Fed's more vigorous lender-of-last-resort activity contributes to financial firms taking on more risks culminating in the 2007–2009 financial crisis.

4. Regulators respond

Dodd-Frank Act restricts Fed's too-big-to-fail policy.

FIGURE 12.7   Lender of Last Resort: Crisis, Regulation, Financial System Response, and Regulatory Response

living wills that show how they would be able to go through bankruptcy at no cost to the taxpayer. Finally, Dodd-Frank specified an *orderly liquidation authority*, under which the secretary of the Treasury, after receiving approval from the president of the United States and majorities of the Board of Governors of the Federal Reserve and the Board of Directors, could designate a failing financial firm to be taken over by the FDIC. The FDIC would operate the firm for as long as necessary to ensure that its ultimate failure did not jeopardize the financial system.

Whether these elaborate regulations will actually help reduce the downsides of the too-big-to-fail policy remains to be seen. As of 2017, the largest U.S. banks had maintained their importance in the financial system: The five largest bank holding companies owned more than one-half of all bank assets, compared with about one-quarter of all assets 15 years earlier. Some economists and policymakers questioned whether regulators could allow the failure of any of these banks—or even the failure of other somewhat smaller banks—without significant damage to the financial system, despite the greater capital these banks now hold and despite their having prepared living wills.

Figure 12.7 summarizes the Fed's role of lender of last resort in the context of financial crisis, regulation, financial system response, and regulatory response.

MAKING THE CONNECTION

Will Dodd-Frank Tie the Fed's Hands in the Next Financial Crisis?

As we have seen, Congress established the Federal Reserve in 1913 to make loans to commercial banks experiencing short-term liquidity problems. In 1932, Congress amended the Federal Reserve Act, adding Section 13(3), which gave the Fed broader powers during a financial crisis. That section authorized the Board of Governors under "unusual and exigent circumstances" to lend to "any individual, partnership, or corporation." In a further amendment to the Federal Reserve Act in 1991, Congress made explicit that in an emergency, the Fed could lend directly to nonbank firms.

After the 1930s, the Fed had not invoked this authority until the financial crisis of 2007–2009. Then, during the financial crisis, the Fed invoked the authority several times, including when lending $29 billion to JPMorgan Chase to facilitate its purchase of Bear Stearns, when lending to the insurance company American International Group (AIG), when lending to large securities dealers (including investment banks), and when purchasing commercial paper.

Some members of Congress disagreed with the Fed's policy of invoking Section 13(3) to lend to specific firms. As a result, as part of the 2010 Dodd-Frank Act, Congress rewrote that section of the Federal Reserve Act to remove the language referring to "any individual, partnership, or corporation" and replace it with language specifying that loans could only be made to a "participant in any program or facility with broad-based eligibility." In other words, loans could only be made as part of a program for which large categories of firms—such as all commercial banks or all securities dealers—would be eligible; loans to individual companies would no longer be allowed. In particular, the Fed was barred from making loans "for the purpose of assisting a single and specific company avoid bankruptcy." The loans that the Fed had made to JPMorgan Chase and AIG during the crisis were no longer permitted. In addition, any new programs beyond lending to commercial banks would require the approval of the secretary of the Treasury. During the financial crisis, the Fed needed the approval of only a majority of the Board of Governors to begin a new program.

Critics of these changes to the Fed's authority to act as a lender of last resort are concerned that in another financial crisis, the Fed may have difficulty stemming a panic if it is unable to make loans to individual firms. Although Dodd-Frank provides mechanisms for allowing large financial firms to fail without disrupting the financial system, these critics doubt that the mechanisms can be quickly implemented in a crisis. Large banks must prepare living wills, but in 2016 they were having difficulty doing so. Some economists and policymakers were skeptical that, in practice, large financial firms would be able to avoid runs during the period when they were preparing for bankruptcy. They also questioned whether the FDIC would be able to implement its orderly liquidation authority quickly enough in a crisis, given the multiple layers of approval required before the process could begin.

Some economists and policymakers were optimistic, though, that the Fed retained enough authority to effectively act as a lender of last resort. For instance, former Fed Chairman Ben Bernanke argued that the orderly liquidation authority was sufficient to remove the threat that failure of a single financial firm would start a panic, given that the Fed would retain its ability (with the approval of the secretary of the Treasury) to implement lending programs to groups of firms, such as investment banks or security dealers.

The debate is likely to continue over whether the Fed has retained sufficient authority as a lender of last resort to stabilize the financial system in the event of another crisis.

Sources: David Fettig, "The History of a Powerful Paragraph," Federal Reserve Bank of Minneapolis, *Region*, June 2008, pp. 33–34; Ryan Tracy, "Regulators Reject 'Living Wills' of Five Big U.S. Banks," *Wall Street Journal*, April 13, 2016; Glenn Hubbard and Hal Scott, "A Financial System Still Dangerously Vulnerable to a Panic," *Wall Street Journal*, March 1, 2015; Ryan Tracy and Erik Holm, "MetLife Wins Bid to Shed 'Systemically Important' Label," *Wall Street Journal*, March 20, 2016; and Ben S. Bernanke, *The Courage to Act: The Financial Crisis and Its Aftermath*, New York: W.W. Norton, 2015.

See related problems 4.9 and 4.10 at the end of the chapter.

Reducing Bank Instability

The banking crisis of the Great Depression led not only to a reorganization of the Federal Reserve and the establishment of the FDIC but also to Congress's enactment of new regulations aimed at directly increasing the stability of the commercial banking system. One way that Congress attempted to reach this goal was by reducing competition among banks. Congress's intention was to reduce both the likelihood of bank runs and the extent of moral hazard in banks' behavior. One argument for limiting competition is that it increases a bank's value, thereby reducing bankers' willingness to make excessively risky investments.

In the long run, however, anticompetitive regulations do not promote bank stability because they create incentives for unregulated financial institutions and markets to compete with banks by offering close substitutes for bank deposits and loans. A dramatic example of how anticompetitive regulation actually led to competition occurred in the fight over limits on the interest rates that banks could pay on deposits. The battle began with the Banking Act of 1933, which authorized *Regulation Q*. This regulation, which was administered by the Fed, placed ceilings on the interest rates bank could pay on time and savings deposits and prohibited banks from paying interest on demand deposits, which were then the only form of checkable deposits. Regulation Q was intended to maintain banks' profitability by limiting competition for funds among banks and by guaranteeing a reasonable spread between interest rates banks received on loans and interest rates they paid on deposits. In practice, the regulation forced banks to innovate in order to survive.

In setting a ceiling on interest rates that banks could pay depositors, Congress intended to give banks a competitive advantage in the market for loans. Because they paid relatively little for deposits, banks could charge lower interest rates on loans and were the leading lenders to households and firms. But whenever market interest rates rose above the Regulation Q interest rate ceilings, savers had an incentive to withdraw money from bank deposits, thereby starving banks of the funds they needed to make loans. For instance, in the late 1960s, as rising inflation rates drove interest rates above the Regulation Q ceilings, large corporations and wealthy households, in particular, substituted short-term investments in Treasury bills, commercial paper, and repurchase agreements for short-term deposits in banks. The introduction of money market mutual funds in 1971 gave savers an additional alternative to bank deposits.

As we have seen, the development of money market mutual funds also provided *borrowers* with a new source of funds. Large, well-established firms could raise short-term funds in the commercial paper market. Firms sold a substantial portion of their commercial paper to money market mutual funds. Banks suffered from losing their commercial loan business to the commercial paper market because, as our analysis of adverse selection predicts, only high-quality borrowers can successfully sell commercial paper, leaving banks with lower-quality borrowers. The exit of savers and borrowers from banks to financial markets is known as **disintermediation**, and it costs banks lost revenue because it means they do not have savers' funds to lend.

Disintermediation The exit of savers and borrowers from banks to financial markets.

To circumvent Regulation Q, banks developed four new financial instruments for savers:

1. Negotiable certificates of deposit (CDs)
2. Negotiable order of withdrawal (NOW) accounts
3. Automatic transfer system (ATS) accounts
4. Money market deposit accounts (MMDAs)

Citibank introduced *negotiable certificates of deposit* (or *negotiable CDs*) in 1961 as time deposits with a fixed maturity of, say, six months. These CDs had two important features: Because they had values of at least $100,000, they were not subject to Regulation Q interest rate ceilings. Because they could be bought and sold, negotiable CDs provided competition to commercial paper.

In addition, banks attempted to get around the prohibition of paying interest on demand deposits by developing *negotiable order of withdrawal (NOW) accounts* on which they paid interest. A depositor with a NOW account received "negotiable orders of withdrawal" that he or she could sign over when transferring funds to someone else. Although these negotiable orders of withdrawal were not called checks, they looked like checks and were treated like checks, so NOW accounts were effectively interest-paying checking accounts.

Banks also developed *automatic transfer system (ATS) accounts* as a means of helping large depositors avoid interest-rate ceilings. ATS accounts effectively pay interest on checking accounts by "sweeping" a customer's checking account balance at the end of the day into an interest-paying overnight repurchase agreement.

Finally, in response to the breakdown of interest-rate regulation in banking, Congress enacted two pieces of legislation: the Depository Institutions Deregulation and Monetary Control Act of 1980 (DIDMCA) and the Garn-St. Germain Act of 1982. With the passage of DIDMCA, Congress eased the anticompetitive burden on banks by phasing out Regulation Q—which disappeared entirely in 1986—and by formally allowing NOW and ATS accounts. In addition, the act eliminated interest-rate ceilings on mortgage loans and commercial loans. Congress passed the Garn-St. Germain Act to help reverse disintermediation by giving banks a more potent weapon against money market mutual funds. The act permitted banks to offer *money market deposit accounts (MMDAs)*, which would be covered by FDIC insurance, but against which banks were not required to hold reserves. Depositors were allowed to write only a limited number of checks per month. The costs of MMDAs to banks were low because the banks were not required to hold reserves against them or process many checks, so the banks could afford to pay higher interest rates on them than on NOW accounts. The combination of market interest rates and the safety and familiarity of banks made the new accounts instantly successful with depositors.

Figure 12.8 summarizes the process of financial crisis, regulation, financial system response, and regulatory response as it applies to interest-rate ceilings.

Capital Requirements

One way the federal government attempts to promote stability in the banking system is by sending examiners from the FDIC, the Fed, and the Office of the Comptroller of the Currency to banks to check whether they are following regulations. (The Office of the Comptroller of the Currency confines its examinations primarily to large national banks.) After an examination, a bank receives a grade in the form of a *CAMELS* rating, based on the following:

1. Crisis occurs
During the 1930–1933 crisis, public loses confidence in the banking system. Savers convert deposits to currency, and banks liquidate loans.

2. Regulation enacted
Banking instability produces a call for regulatory restrictions. To maintain bank profitability, Regulation Q imposes ceilings on deposit interest rates.

3. Financial system responds
Securities firms push growth of money market mutual funds and the commercial paper market. Banks innovate to bypass ceilings in raising funds and use information-cost advantages in lending.

4. Regulators respond
Competitive pressures force legislation (DIDMCA and Garn–St. Germain Act) to dismantle interest-rate ceilings, which allows banks to compete more effectively.

FIGURE 12.8 Interest-Rate Ceilings: Crisis, Regulation, Financial System Response, and Regulatory Response

Capital adequacy
Asset quality
Management
Earnings
Liquidity
Sensitivity to market risk

A poor CAMELS rating can lead to a cease-and-desist order being issued to a bank to change its behavior. Such a system mimics the way private markets approach moral hazard by inserting restrictive covenants in financial contracts.

Of the CAMELS categories, along with asset quality, capital adequacy has typically received the most attention. Regulating capital is an example of *macroprudential regulation* that attempts to reduce risk to the financial system by increasing the likelihood that the owners of financial firms absorb the cost of the firms' losses. Moral hazard occurs when banks make risky investments in an attempt to increase their return on equity. Regulating the minimum amount of capital that banks are required to hold reduces the potential for moral hazard and the cost to the FDIC of bank failures in two ways: (1) by increasing the ability of the bank to remain solvent after incurring losses and (2) by increasing the amount the bank's owners will lose in the event of the bank's failure, thereby giving the owners a greater incentive to avoid risky investments. Regulators increased their focus on capital requirements following the *savings-and-loan (S&L) crisis* of the 1980s. To promote mortgage lending, federal regulation created S&Ls in the 1930s. S&Ls held long-term, fixed-rate mortgages and financed them with short-term time deposits. Although this structure guaranteed that S&Ls would suffer from a severe maturity mismatch, as long as interest rates were stable and regulation limited the interest rates that S&Ls and banks could pay on deposits, little went wrong. Beginning in 1979, however, sharply rising market interest rates increased the cost of funds for S&Ls, decreased the present value of their existing mortgage assets, and caused their net worth to decline precipitously. S&Ls were also highly leveraged, with their capital often being as little as 3% of their assets, which magnified the effect of losses on their equity. A wave of S&L failures during the 1980s was ended only by a costly federal government bailout.

Many commercial banks also suffered losses during the 1980s, although the damage was limited by lower leverage and their lesser concentration in mortgage lending.

As a result of the fallout from the S&L crisis, policymakers resolved to address the problem of capital adequacy. The United States joined with other nations in a program begun by the Bank for International Settlements (BIS), located in Basel, Switzerland. The *Basel Committee on Banking Supervision* developed the **Basel accord** to regulate bank capital requirements. While the rulings of the Basel committee are only recommendations, they strongly influence the bank regulations of member countries.

Under the Basel accord, bank assets are grouped into four categories, based on their degree of risk. These categories are used to calculate a measure of a bank's *risk-adjusted assets* by multiplying the dollar value of each asset by a risk-adjustment factor. A bank's capital adequacy is then calculated using two measures of the bank's capital relative to its risk-adjusted assets. *Tier 1 capital* consists mostly of what we have been calling bank capital: shareholders' equity. *Tier 2 capital* equals the bank's loan loss reserves, its subordinated debt, and several other bank balance sheet items. Banks set aside part of their capital as a *loan loss reserve* to anticipate future loan losses. Using a loan loss reserve enables a bank to avoid large swings in its reported profits. When banks sell bonds, some of the bonds are *senior debt*, while others are *subordinated* debt, or *junior* debt. If the bank were to fail, the investors owning senior debt would be paid before the investors owning junior debt. Because the investors owning junior debt have a greater incentive to monitor the behavior of bank managers, junior debt was included in Tier 2 capital under the Basel accord.

Bank regulators determine a bank's capital adequacy by calculating two ratios: the bank's Tier 1 capital relative to its risk-adjusted assets and the bank's total capital (Tier 1 plus Tier 2) relative to its risk-adjusted assets. On the basis of these two *capital ratios*, banks are assigned to five risk categories, as shown in Table 12.2. Note that the higher a bank's capital ratio, the lower its leverage and the better able it is to weather short-term losses.

Banks in Category 1 have no restrictions on their activities beyond those specified in general banking regulations. Banks in Category 2 must abide by certain restrictions on their activities but are not required to take any actions. Banks in Categories 3, 4, and 5 must take steps to raise their capital ratios. Ordinarily, the FDIC enters a formal

Basel accord An international agreement about bank capital requirements.

TABLE 12.2 **Measuring Banks' Capital Adequacy**

Category	Description	Tier 1 capital ratio	Total capital ratio
1	Well capitalized	8% or greater	10% or greater
2	Adequately capitalized	6% or greater	8% or greater
3	Undercapitalized	Less than 6%	Less than 8%
4	Significantly undercapitalized	Less than 4%	Less than 6%
5	Critically undercapitalized	Less than 2%	—

Source: Federal Deposit Insurance Corporation.

agreement with a bank in Categories 3, 4, and 5, specifying the actions that must be taken and deadlines for completing the actions. A bank in Category 5 must convince the FDIC that it has a plan to immediately increase its capital, or it will be closed. Note that a bank in Category 5 might be solvent—its capital may be positive, so the value of its assets may be greater than the value of its liabilities—but it will still be closed by the FDIC if it cannot raise additional capital immediately.

Implementation of these capital requirements meant that banks with low capital ratios were forced to close or to raise additional capital, thereby increasing the stability of the commercial banking system. But the requirements also led to a response by large commercial banks involving financial innovations that allowed these banks to push some assets off their balance sheets. Because holding relatively risky assets, such as mortgage-backed securities, required banks to hold additional capital, some large banks, such as Citigroup, formed *special investment vehicles (SIVs)* to hold these assets. SIVs had separate management and separate capital from the banks that sponsored them. But in buying and selling securities, the SIVs benefited from their association with the sponsoring banks. By the time of the financial crisis, there were about 30 SIVs, holding about $320 billion in assets. As the assets held by the SIVs lost value, a sponsoring bank was faced with the hard choice of allowing the SIV to fail or bringing it back on the bank's balance sheet. In the end, most banks chose the second course, increasing the damage to their balance sheets during the financial crisis but preserving their relationships with customers who had invested in commercial paper and other debt issued by the SIVs.

Regulations under the Basel accord have continued to evolve, particularly with respect to the risk-adjustment factors used to gauge how much capital banks must hold against certain assets. In 2016, some banks in the United States and Europe argued that proposed changes in regulations would lead them to either have to hold additional capital or reduce some categories of lending. The banks argued that in either case, their ability to extend credit to households and firms might be reduced.

Figure 12.9 summarizes the process of financial crisis, regulation, financial system response, and regulatory response as it applies to capital requirements.

1. Crisis occurs
Inadequate capital contributes to losses at S&Ls and banks during the 1980s.

2. Regulation enacted
The United States joins other nations in the Basel accord, which strengthens capital requirements and penalizes the holding of risky assets.

3. Financial system responds
Banks increase off-balance-sheet activities with some banks setting up special investment vehicles (SIVs) to hold risky assets.

4. Regulators respond
The United States and other countries negotiate further increases in capital requirements under the Basel accord.

FIGURE 12.9 Capital Requirements: Crisis, Regulation, Financial System Response, and Regulatory Response

The 2007–2009 Financial Crisis and the Pattern of Crisis and Response

The events during and after the 2007–2009 financial crisis fit the pattern of crisis and response that we have seen several times in this chapter. Clearly, the housing collapse brought on a crisis greater than any the U.S. financial system had experienced since the Great Depression of the 1930s. The collapse of housing prices reduced the net worth of households, causing them to cut back on spending to pay down debt. Households that attempted to borrow, including borrowing to refinance mortgages, found it difficult to obtain credit because their net worth had declined and because lenders had tightened lending standards. Many smaller firms were in a similar position, as commercial real estate prices declined sharply, reducing the value of the buildings many firms rely on as collateral when borrowing.

Falling prices of mortgage-backed securities and other housing-related assets led to losses at banks and other intermediaries. The initial regulatory response by the Treasury and the Federal Reserve was to stabilize the financial system through bailouts of firms such as AIG, capital injections to commercial banks through TARP, and aggressive lending by the Federal Reserve.

Banks responded to the crisis and the regulatory pressure to rebuild their capital and reduce the nonperforming loans on their balance sheets by reducing lending and accumulating reserves in an attempt to *deleverage*. In addition, banks became more risk averse as they reassessed their lending rules. Many small businesses found themselves cut off from credit, even at banks with which they had had long-term relationships.

As the crisis passed, Congress attempted to overhaul regulation of the financial system with the passage in July 2010 of the Dodd-Frank Act. Here are some of the key provisions of the act:

- Created the Consumer Financial Protection Bureau, housed in the Federal Reserve, to write rules intended to protect consumers in their borrowing and investing activities.
- Established the Financial Stability Oversight Council, which includes representatives from all the major federal financial regulatory bodies, including the SEC, the FDIC, and the Fed. The council is intended to identify and act on systemic risks to the financial system.
- Attempted to end the too-big-to-fail policy for large financial firms, as discussed earlier in this chapter.
- Made several changes to the Fed's operations.
- Required certain derivatives to be traded on exchanges rather than over the counter.
- Implemented the *Volcker Rule*, which bans most proprietary trading at commercial banks.
- Required hedge funds and private equity firms to register with the SEC.

How the Dodd-Frank Act will affect the financial system remain to be seen, and in 2017, the incoming administration of President Donald Trump was considering changes to the act. In any event, if history is a guide, we can be certain that financial firms will respond with innovations intended to reduce the effect of the new rules on their activities.

Figure 12.10 summarizes the process of financial crisis, regulation, financial system response, and regulatory response as it applies to the financial crisis of 2007–2009.

1. Crisis occurs

The collapse of the housing bubble beginning in 2006 leads to falling net worth for households and disruption of financial intermediation.

2. Regulation enacted

The Treasury and Federal Reserve respond through bailouts of firms such as AIG, capital injections to commercial banks through TARP, and aggressive lending by the Federal Reserve.

3. Financial system responds

Banks and other financial firms increase their capital, deleverage, and become more risk averse in their loans and investments.

4. Regulators respond

Congress passes the Dodd-Frank Act to increase regulation of financial firms.

FIGURE 12.10 The Financial Crisis of 2007–2009: Crisis, Regulation, Financial System Response, and Regulatory Response

ANSWERING THE KEY QUESTION

Continued from page 387

At the beginning of this chapter, we asked:

"Was the severity of the 2007–2009 recession due to the financial crisis?"

We have seen that the recession of 2007–2009 was the most severe since the Great Depression of the 1930s. It was also the first recession since the 1930s to be accompanied by a financial crisis. In Section 12.1, we discussed research by Carmen Reinhart and Kenneth Rogoff that shows that recessions have typically been longer and deeper when they involve financial crises than when they don't. We noted that because financial crises disrupt the flow of funds from savers to households and firms, they cause substantial reductions in spending, which is the key reason they make recessions worse. So, it is likely that the severity of the 2007–2009 financial crisis explains the severity of the recession. Not all economists accept this conclusion. Some economists believe that policy errors by the Federal Reserve and policy uncertainty during and after the recession explain the severity of the recession and the weakness of the recovery.

Key Terms and Problems

Key Terms

Bank panic, p. 390

Bank run, p. 389

Basel accord, p. 418

Contagion, p. 390

Debt-deflation process, p. 400

Disintermediation, p. 415

Federal Deposit Insurance Corporation (FDIC), p. 391

Financial crisis, p. 389

Insolvent, p. 389

Lender of last resort, p. 390

Too-big-to-fail policy, p. 408

12.1 The Origins of Financial Crises
Explain what financial crises are and what causes them.

Review Questions

1.1 Why does a financial crisis typically result in a recession?

1.2 Does a bank have to be insolvent to experience a run?

1.3 What are the two methods that governments typically use to avoid bank panics?

1.4 How do currency crises occur? Why have some European countries been suffering from a sovereign debt crisis?

Problems and Applications

1.5 In describing the bank panic that occurred in the fall of 1930, Milton Friedman and Anna Schwartz wrote:

> A contagion of fear spread among depositors, starting from the agricultural areas, which had experienced the heaviest impact of bank failures in the twenties. But such contagion knows no geographical limits.

a. What do the authors mean by a "contagion of fear"?

b. What did bank depositors have to fear in the early 1930s? Do depositors today face similar fears? Briefly explain.

c. What do the authors mean when they write that "such contagion knows no geographical limits"?

Source: Milton Friedman and Anna Schwartz, *A Monetary History of the United States, 1867–1960*, Princeton, NJ: Princeton University Press, 1963, p. 308.

1.6 Former Federal Reserve Chairman Ben Bernanke has observed: "Even a bank that is solvent under normal conditions can rarely survive a sustained run."

a. What does Bernanke mean by "solvent under normal conditions"?

b. What does he mean by a "sustained run"? Why can't a bank survive a sustained run?

Source: Ben S. Bernanke, *The Courage to Act: The Financial Crisis and Its Aftermath*, New York: W.W. Norton, 2015, p. 45.

1.7 A classic account of bank panics was published in 1879 by Walter Bagehot, editor of the *Economist*, in his book *Lombard Street*: "In wild periods of alarm, one failure makes many, and the best way to prevent the derivative failures is to arrest the primary failure which causes them."

a. Why might one bank failure lead to many bank failures?

b. What are the two main ways in which the government can keep one bank failure from leading to a bank panic?

Source: Walter Bagehot, *Lombard Street: A Description of the Money Market*, New York: John Wiley, 1999 (first published 1873), p. 51.

1.8 [Related to Solved Problem 12.1 on page 391] Economist Laurence Kotlikoff of Boston University has proposed that the banking system be reformed so that all banks become "limited purpose banks." As he explains:

> [Banks] would simply function as middlemen. They would never own financial assets or borrow to invest in anything.... [Limited purpose banking] effectively provides for 100 percent reserve requirements on checking accounts. This eliminates any need for FDIC insurance and any possibility of traditional bank runs.

Why would 100% reserve requirements on checking accounts eliminate the need for FDIC insurance? Would depositors need to fear losing money if their bank failed?

Source: Laurence J. Kotlikoff, *Jimmy Stewart Is Dead*, Hoboken, NJ: John Wiley & Sons, 2010, pp. 123–124, 132.

1.9 [Related to the Making the Connection on page 393] In their book *This Time Is Different*, Carmen Reinhart and Kenneth Rogoff conclude: "An examination of the aftermath of severe postwar financial crises shows that they have had a deep and lasting effect on asset prices, output, and employment." Why should a recession accompanied by a financial crisis be more severe than a recession not accompanied by a financial crisis?

Source: Carmen M. Reinhart and Kenneth S. Rogoff, *This Time Is Different: Eight Centuries of Financial Folly*, Princeton, NJ: Princeton University Press, 2009, p. 248.

1.10 [Related to the Making the Connection on page 393] Carmen Reinhart and Kenneth Rogoff have argued that the 2007–2009 financial crisis explains not just the severity of the accompanying recession but also the slowness of the subsequent economic recovery. Michael Bordo of Rutgers University has argued that Reinhart and Rogoff's argument is incorrect. Instead, he argues that the slow recovery was due to "the unprecedented housing bust" and "uncertainty over changes in fiscal and regulatory policy." If you

were attempting to evaluate the relative merits of Reinhart and Rogoff's and Bordo's arguments, what type of evidence would you look at? Is it likely that you could definitively identify the causes of the slow recovery? Briefly explain.

Source: Michael Bordo, "Financial Recessions Don't Lead to Weak Recoveries," *Wall Street Journal*, September 27, 2012.

1.11 A column in the *Wall Street Journal* notes that "every heavily indebted country weighs the cost of repaying debt against the loss of confidence and creditworthiness that default entails." Whose confidence is an indebted country afraid of losing? What might be the consequences of losing that confidence?

Source: George Ip, "Sovereign Default: It's Not Personal, Just Business," *Wall Street Journal*, May 25, 2016.

12.2 The Financial Crisis of the Great Depression
Describe the key elements of the financial crisis that occurred during the Great Depression.

Review Questions

2.1 What role did the bank panics of the early 1930s play in explaining the severity of the Great Depression?

2.2 How did the debt-deflation process contribute to the severity of the Great Depression?

2.3 Briefly summarize the four explanations of why the Federal Reserve failed to intervene to stabilize the banking system in the early 1930s.

Problems and Applications

2.4 In June 1930, a delegation of businessmen appeared at the White House to urge President Herbert Hoover to propose an economic stimulus package. Hoover told them: "Gentlemen, you have come sixty days too late. The depression is over." When did the Great Depression begin? Why might Hoover have reasonably expected it to be over by June 1930? Why did the Depression continue much longer?

Source: Arthur M. Schlesinger, Jr., *The Crisis of the Old Order*, Boston: Houghton-Mifflin, 1957, p. 331.

2.5 In academic research published before he entered government, Fed Chairman Ben Bernanke wrote:

> [In] a system without deposit insurance, depositor runs and withdrawals deprive banks of funds for lending; to the extent that bank lending is specialized or information sensitive, these loans are not easily replaced by nonbank forms of credit.

a. What does it mean to say that bank lending is "information sensitive"?

b. What are "nonbank forms of credit"? Why would bank lending being "information sensitive" make it difficult to replace with nonbank forms of credit?

c. Does Bernanke's observation help explain the role bank panics played in the severity of the Great Depression?

Source: Ben S. Bernanke, *Essays on the Great Depression*, Princeton, NJ: Princeton University Press, 2000, p. 26.

2.6 In his memoirs, Herbert Hoover described the reaction of his Treasury secretary to the Great Depression:

> First was the "leave it alone liquidationists" headed by Secretary of the Treasury Mellon, who felt that government must keep its hands off and let the slump liquidate itself. Mr. Mellon had only one formula: "Liquidate labor, liquidate stocks, liquidate the farmers, liquidate real estate."

a. What does "liquidate" mean in this context?

b. Can these views help explain the Fed's actions during the early years of the Great Depression? Briefly explain.

Source: Herbert Hoover, *The Memoirs of Herbert Hoover: Volume 3: The Great Depression, 1929–1941*, New York: Macmillan, 1952, p. 30.

2.7 A columnist writing in the *Wall Street Journal* observed: "Franklin D. Roosevelt's March 1933 inaugural line 'that the only thing we have to fear is fear itself' was inspiring, but wrong. There was plenty to fear, not least the deflation that then gripped the nation."

a. Prices fall when a country experiences deflation, so isn't deflation good for consumers? Briefly explain.

b. Was deflation during the early 1930s good or bad for firms? Briefly explain.

Source: George Melloan, "Rising Global Debt and the Deflation Threat," *Wall Street Journal*, March 7, 2016.

2.8 In his history of the Federal Reserve, Allan Meltzer of Carnegie Mellon University describes the views of Federal Reserve officials in the fall of 1930:

> Most of the policymakers regarded the substantial decline in short-term market interest rates … as the main … indicators of the current position of the monetary system…. [Policy] was "easy" and had never been easier in the experience of the policymakers of the Federal Reserve System.

a. What does it mean to say that Fed policy is "easy"?

b. In the context of the early 1930s, were low nominal interest rates a good indicator that policy was easy? Why might Fed officials have believed that they were?

Source: Allan H. Meltzer, *A History of the Federal Reserve: Volume 1: 1913–1951*, Chicago: University of Chicago Press, 2003, p. 315.

2.9 In describing the performance of the Federal Reserve during the Great Depression, former Federal Reserve Chairman Ben Bernanke has written: "The Fed proved far too passive during the Depression. It was ineffective in its role of lender of last resort, failing to stop the runs that forced thousands of small banks to close."

a. What does Bernanke mean by the Fed's role as a lender of last resort?

b. How might the Fed have stopped the bank runs during the early 1930s?

c. Why didn't the Fed take the actions you describe in your answer to part (b)?

Source: Ben S. Bernanke, *The Courage to Act: The Financial Crisis and Its Aftermath*, New York: W.W. Norton, 2015, p. 47.

2.10 [Related to the Making the Connection on page 402] Arthur Rolnick of the Federal Reserve Bank of Minneapolis has argued that in their account of the failure of the Bank of United States:

> Friedman and Schwartz provide the rationale for the policy that today is known as "too big to fail"—that there are some institutions that are so big that we can't afford to let them fail because of the systemic impact on the rest of the economy…. They suggest that if the Fed had rescued this bank, the Great Depression might only have been a short, albeit severe, recession.

a. What was the Bank of United States? When did it fail? Why did it fail?

b. Why might the Fed's failure to save the Bank of United States provide a rationale for the too-big-to-fail policy?

c. Are there counterarguments to Rolnick's view?

Source: Arthur J. Rolnick, "Interview with Ben S. Bernanke," Federal Reserve Bank of Minneapolis, *The Region*, June 2004.

The Financial Crisis of 2007–2009

12.3 Describe what caused the financial crisis of 2007–2009.

Review Questions

3.1 What does it mean to say that there is a bubble in the housing market? Briefly describe the effect that the bursting of the housing bubble in 2006 had on the U.S. economy.

3.2 How can an investment bank experience a "run"? Briefly describe the effect the runs on Bear Stearns and Lehman Brothers had on the U.S. economy.

3.3 Briefly discuss the policy actions the Federal Reserve and the Treasury took during the financial crisis of 2007–2009.

Problems and Applications

3.4 An article in the *New York Times* quotes former Fed Chairman Alan Greenspan as arguing:

> The global house price bubble was a consequence of lower interest rates, but it was long-term interest rates that galvanized home asset prices, not the overnight rates of central banks, as has become the seemingly conventional wisdom.

a. What is a "house price bubble"?

b. Why would long-term interest rates have a closer connection than overnight interest rates to house prices?

c. Why would it matter to Greenspan whether low long-term interest rates were more responsible than low short-term interest rates for the housing bubble?

Source: Sewell Chan, "Greenspan Concedes That the Fed Failed to Gauge the Bubble," *New York Times*, March 18, 2010.

3.5 An article in the *New York Times* published just after the Fed helped save Bear Stearns from bankruptcy noted:

> If Bear Stearns failed, for example, it would result in a wholesale dumping of mortgage securities and other assets onto a market that is frozen and where buyers are in

hiding. This fire sale would force surviving institutions carrying the same types of securities on their books to mark down their positions.

a. Why did Bear Stearns almost fail?

b. How did the Federal Reserve rescue Bear Stearns?

c. What is the debt-deflation process? Does this process provide any insight into why the Federal Reserve rescued Bear Stearns?

Source: Gretchen Morgenson, "Rescue Me: A Fed Bailout Crosses a Line," *New York Times*, March 16, 2008.

3.6 In a blog post, former Federal Reserve Chairman Ben Bernanke described the four "basic elements" of a financial crisis: "broad-based loss of confidence in banks, runs by providers of short-term funding, fire sales of bank loans and other assets, [and] disruption of credit flows."

a. Why might each of these four elements occur during a financial crisis?

b. Briefly explain whether each of the four elements did occur during the 2007–2009 financial crisis.

Source: Ben S. Bernanke, "Ending Too Big to Fail: What's the Right Approach?" brookings.edu, May 13, 2016.

3.7 [Related to the Chapter Opener on page 387] Looking back at the financial crisis several years later, former Fed Chairman Alan Greenspan argued:

> At least partly responsible [for the severity of the financial collapse] may have been the failure of risk managers to fully understand the impact of the emergence of shadow banking that increased financial innovation, but as a consequence, also increased the level of risk. The added risk had not been compensated by higher capital.

a. How did the emergence of shadow banking increase the risk to the financial system?

b. What does Greenspan mean that "the added risk had not been compensated by higher capital"? By holding more capital, what problems could shadow banks have potentially avoided?

Source: Alan Greenspan, "The Crisis," *Brookings Papers on Economic Activity*, Spring 2010, p. 219.

3.8 In discussing the 2007–2009 financial crisis, Federal Reserve Vice Chairman Stanley Fischer observed: "The fact that losses in what was a relatively small part of the mortgage market quickly spread through the rest of the financial system illustrates how the complex interconnections among banks and nonbanks can amplify shocks in significant and unanticipated ways."

a. What "nonbanks" was Fischer referring to?

b. What interconnections among banks and nonbanks was he referring to?

c. What did he mean by writing that these interconnections can "amplify shocks"? What shocks were these interconnections amplifying?

Source: Stanley Fischer, "The Importance of the Nonbank Financial Sector," remarks at the conference "Debt and Financial Stability—Regulatory Challenges," sponsored by the Bundesbank and the German Ministry of Finance, March 27, 2015.

12.4 **Financial Crises and Financial Regulation**
Discuss the connection between financial crises and financial regulation.

Review Questions

4.1 How is being a lender of last resort connected to the too-big-to-fail policy?

4.2 What innovations did banks develop to get around ceilings on deposit interest rates?

4.3 Why might deposit insurance encourage banks to take on too much risk? Is deposit insurance, therefore, a bad idea? Briefly explain.

Problems and Applications

4.4 A column in the *Wall Street Journal* by the governor of the central bank of Sweden discussing the Basel accord makes the following observation: "One clear lesson from the [financial] crisis is that regulatory capital requirements for the banking system were too low. In other words, leverage was too high."

a. What are "regulatory capital requirements"?

b. Why would regulatory capital requirements being too low result in leverage being too high?

c. What does leverage being too high have to do with the financial crisis?

Source: Stefan Ingves, "Basel III Is Simpler and Stronger" *Wall Street Journal*, October 14, 2012.

4.5 The financial writer Sebastian Mallaby made the following observation about hedge funds:

Leverage also made hedge funds vulnerable to shocks: If their trades moved against them, they would burn through thin cushions of capital at lightning speed, obliging them to dump positions fast—*destabilizing* prices.

a. What does a hedge fund's trades "moving against it" mean?

b. Why would a fund's trades moving against it cause it to burn through its capital?

c. What is the connection between a fund's being highly leveraged and its having a "thin cushion of capital"?

d. What does a fund's "dumping its positions" mean?

e. Why might a fund's dumping its positions cause prices to be destabilized? Prices of what?

Source: Sebastian Mallaby, *More Money Than God*, New York: Penguin Press, 2010, p. 10.

4.6 An article in the *Wall Street Journal* notes: "Higher capital requirements effectively limit how much SIFIs can borrow, and can crimp profitability."

a. What is a SIFI? Why does the Dodd-Frank Act require SIFIs to hold more capital?

b. Why would holding more capital limit how much a financial firm can borrow and reduce the firm's profitability?

Source: Ryan Tracy, "What You Need to Know About SIFIs," *Wall Street Journal*, March 30, 2016.

4.7 [Related to the Chapter Opener on page 387] In a paper looking back at the financial crisis, former Fed Chairman Alan Greenspan wrote:

Some bubbles burst without severe economic consequences, the dotcom boom and the rapid run-up of stock prices in the spring of 1987, for example. Others burst with severe deflationary consequences. That class of bubbles … appears to be a function of the degree of debt leverage in the financial sector, particularly when the maturity of debt is less than the maturity of the assets it funds.

a. What does Greenspan mean by "debt leverage"?

b. Why would it matter if "the maturity of the debt is less than the maturity of the assets it funds"?

c. Does Greenspan's analysis provide insight into why the Fed during his tenure may have been reluctant to take action against asset bubbles?

Source: Alan Greenspan, "The Crisis," *Brookings Papers on Economic Activity*, Spring 2010, pp. 210–11.

4.8 [Related to the Making the Connection on page 410] Financial journalist James Stewart notes that in contrast to its actions with respect to Lehman Brothers: "the Fed did lend into continuing runs at both Bear Stearns and A.I.G., although officials argued then that those companies had adequate collateral to guarantee repayment."

a. What does Stewart mean by "lending into continuing runs"? Why would central banks lend into runs at financial firms?

b. Why is the issue of whether Bear Stearns and AIG held sufficient collateral important legally? Is it also important economically? Briefly explain.

c. How does your answer to part (b) relate to the Fed's decision not to lend to Lehman Brothers in the days before its bankruptcy?

Source: James Stewart, "Pointing a Finger at the Fed in the Lehman Disaster," *New York Times*, July 21, 2016.

4.9 [Related to the Making the Connection on page 413] An article in a Federal Reserve publication notes that during the financial crisis, the Federal Reserve lent $29 billion to help in JPMorgan Chase's purchase of Bear Stearns. The article asks: "by what legal authority did the Federal Reserve intervene in the business of a non-bank (in this case an investment firm)"?

a. Answer the article's question.

b. Would the Federal Reserve be legally able to take a similar action in a financial crisis today? Briefly explain.

Source: David Fettig, "The History of a Powerful Paragraph," Federal Reserve Bank of Minneapolis, *Region*, June 2008, pp. 33

4.10 [Related to the Making the Connection on page 413] In 2016, financial regulators ordered significant changes in the "living wills" prepared by five large banks. According to an article in the *Wall Street Journal*, the wills as submitted didn't "meet the legal standard laid out in the 2010 Dodd-Frank law, which requires that firms have credible plans to go through bankruptcy at no cost to taxpayers."

a. Why did Congress decide to require large financial firms to have living wills?

b. Was this requirement in the Dodd-Frank Act related to changes the act made in Section 13(3) of the Federal Reserve Act? Briefly explain.

Source: Ryan Tracy, "Regulators Reject 'Living Wills' of Five Big U.S. Banks," *Wall Street Journal*, April 13, 2016.

4.11 Shortly after the Federal Reserve arranged for JPMorgan Chase to purchase Bear Stearns in March 2008, the *Wall Street Journal* recounted the events that led to the extraordinarily low price that JPMorgan paid for Bear Stearns: "The bank was mulling a price of $4 or $5 a share. 'That sounds high to me,' Mr. Paulson said. 'I think this should be done at a low price.'"

a. Why did Treasury Secretary Paulson want Bear Stearns to sell for such a low price?

b. Why was the Fed's decision to orchestrate the purchase of Bear Stearns so controversial?

Source: Kate Kelly, "Bear Stearns Neared Collapse Twice in Frenzied Last Days," *Wall Street Journal*, May 29, 2008.

Data Exercises

D12.1: **[Unemployment and the recession of 2007–2009]**

 Go to the web site of the Federal Reserve Bank of St. Louis (FRED) (fred.stlouisfed.org) and download and graph the data series for the unemployment rate (UNRATE) from January 1948 until the most recent month available. Go to the web site of the National Bureau of Economic Research (nber.org) and find the dates for business cycle peaks and troughs. (The period between a business cycle peak and trough is a recession.) Describe how the unemployment rate moves just before, during, and just after a recession. How does the pattern for the 2007–2009 recession compare to the patterns for other recessions?

D12.2: **[Credit markets and the recession of 2007–2009]**

 Go to the web site of the Federal Reserve Bank of St. Louis (FRED) (fred.stlouisfed.org) and download and graph the data series for the interest rate on Baa-rated corporate bonds (DBAA) from January 1986 until the most recent data available. Go to the web site of the National Bureau of Economic Research (nber. org) and find the dates for business cycle peaks and troughs. (The period between a business cycle peak and trough is a recession.)

a. Describe how the interest rate on these bonds typically moves just before, during, and just after a recession.

b. How does the pattern for the 2007–2009 recession compare to the patterns for other recessions?

c. If you had to date the financial crisis just on the basis of movements in the interest rates on these bonds, in which month would you say the financial crisis began, and in which month would you say the financial crisis ended? Briefly explain your choices.

chapter 13

The Federal Reserve and Central Banking

Learning Objectives

After studying this chapter, you should be able to:

13.1 Explain why the Federal Reserve System is structured the way it is (pages 430–444)

13.2 Explain the Fed's relationship to the government and the arguments for and against its independence (pages 444–450)

13.3 Compare the extent of central bank independence in other countries (pages 451–454)

Wells Fargo Owns Part of the Fed. Does It Matter?

Who owns the FBI, the Department of Defense, or the Environmental Protection Agency? Because these agencies are part of the federal government, it's obvious that the agencies, the buildings they are housed in, and their computer systems are owned by the federal government. The question of who owns the 12 regional Federal Reserve Banks that make up the Federal Reserve System is much more complicated.

As we will see in this chapter, Congress struggled for more than 100 years before settling on a politically acceptable structure for the country's central bank. Under the compromise embodied in the Federal Reserve Act, passed in 1913, and later amended several times, the Board of Governors that controls the system is a federal government agency similar to the FBI or the

Department of Defense. But the 12 regional Federal Reserve Banks that conduct most of the business of the Federal Reserve System are legally the equivalent of private corporations, with the banks in their region that are part of the Federal Reserve System owning their stock. For example, there is a Federal Reserve Bank in San Francisco. Although Wells Fargo has branches across the country, it is headquartered in San Francisco, so it is part owner of the Federal Reserve Bank of San Francisco. But Wells Fargo and other member banks have few of the ownership rights that stockholders typically have in private corporations. The banks cannot sell or trade their stock, and the Federal Reserve Banks are not operated to maximize profit the way that commercial banks are, although member banks do receive

Continued on next page

KEY ISSUE AND QUESTION

Issue: Following the financial crisis of 2007–2009, Congress debated whether to reduce the independence of the Federal Reserve.

Question: Should Congress and the president have greater authority over the Federal Reserve?

Answered on page 454

an annual dividend payment. Banks also have some influence over how each Reserve Bank is run because they elect six of the nine members of the Reserve Banks' boards of directors. Those boards in turn appoint the Reserve Banks' presidents. Given that the Reserve Banks are responsible for supervising and regulating the member banks in their region, is it a conflict of interest for the member banks to have an important role in running the banks? Some policymakers have thought so, and in 2010, as part of the Dodd-Frank Act, Congress amended the Federal Reserve Act to exclude the bankers who serve on a Reserve Bank's board of directors from participating in the appointment of the Bank's president. During the 2016 presidential campaign, Democratic nominee Hillary Clinton went further and proposed that bankers be barred from serving on the Reserve Banks' boards of directors.

The debate over the role of banks in the Federal Reserve System was only one of several indications in recent years that many policymakers were in favor of changing the structure of the Fed. We have seen that the Federal Reserve Act intended to make the Fed financially independent from the rest of the federal government, and, to an extent, politically independent as well. But following the unusual policies the Fed pursued during the financial crisis of 2007–2009, some critics argue that the Fed has assumed far too important a role in the economy. In fact, many people consider the chair of the Federal Reserve second only to the president of the United States in his or her ability to affect the economy and the financial system.

Should the unelected head of the central bank have so much power? Or should Congress and the president have a more direct role in running the Federal Reserve System and setting policy, as they do in areas such as defense, the environment, taxes, and federal government spending? In this chapter, we discuss the current structure of the Fed to provide context for these debates.

Sources: Donna Borak and Henry Williams, "Where Clinton and Trump Stand on Wall Street," *Wall Street Journal*, June 20, 2016; and Board of Directors of the Federal Reserve System, "Federal Reserve Act: Section 4: Reserve Banks," August 2, 2013.

In this chapter, we discuss the Fed's organization and structure and its role as an economic policymaking body. We also describe the political arena in which the Fed operates and the debate over the independence of the central bank, which has become more intense in Congress in recent years. We then examine the organization and independence of central banks outside the United States, including the European Central Bank.

 ## The Structure of the Federal Reserve System

LEARNING OBJECTIVE: Explain why the Federal Reserve System is structured the way it is.

Few other central banks have as complex a structure as the Federal Reserve System. The Fed's organization was shaped by the same political struggle that gave the United States a fragmented banking system: advocates of strong financial institutions contending with those who feared such strong institutions would abuse their economic power. We hear echoes of those earlier political struggles in the fight over recent Congressional proposals for reducing the Fed's independence. To understand why the Fed is organized as it is, we need to look back in history at the nation's earlier attempts to create a central bank.

Creation of the Federal Reserve System

Not long after the United States won its independence, Treasury Secretary Alexander Hamilton organized the Bank of the United States, which was meant to function as a central bank but had both government and private shareholders. The Bank attempted to stabilize the financial system by taking steps to ensure that local banks did not extend too many loans relative to their capital. And the Bank rapidly accumulated enemies. Local banks resented the Bank's supervision of their operations. Many advocates of a limited federal government distrusted the Bank's power because the Constitution did not expressly provide Congress with the power to establish a central bank. Farmers and owners of small businesses, particularly in the West and South, resented the Bank's interfering with their ability to obtain loans from their local banks.

Congress granted the Bank a 20-year charter in 1791, making it the only federally chartered bank. All other banks at the time had their charters from state governments. In the face of political opposition, there was not enough congressional support to renew the charter, so the Bank ceased operations in 1811. Partly because of the federal government's problems in financing the War of 1812, political opinion in Congress shifted back toward the need for a central bank. In 1816, Congress established the Second Bank of the United States, also under a 20-year charter. The Second Bank encountered many of the same controversies as the First Bank. As the time approached for renewal of the Second Bank's charter, an epic political battle broke out between the populist President Andrew Jackson and Nicholas Biddle, the president of the Second Bank. Although in 1832, Congress passed a bill to recharter the Bank, Jackson vetoed the bill, and the Bank's charter expired in 1836. (The Bank survived for a time as a state-chartered bank in Pennsylvania.)

The disappearance of the Second Bank of the United States left the nation without a central bank and, therefore, without an official lender of last resort for banks. Private institutions, such as the New York Clearing House, attempted to fill the void, but severe nationwide financial panics in 1873, 1884, 1893, and 1907—and accompanying economic recessions—raised fears in Congress that the U.S. financial system was unstable. After a financial panic and economic recession in 1907, many policymakers worried that bankers such as New York financier J. P. Morgan, who in the past had helped organize loans to banks suffering temporary liquidity problems, would be unable to manage future crises. Congress appointed the National Monetary Commission in 1908 to study the possibility of establishing a central bank. Congress modified the commission's recommendations and, with the support of President Woodrow Wilson, the Federal Reserve Act became law in 1913.

The Federal Reserve Act established the **Federal Reserve System** as the central bank of the United States. Many in Congress believed that a unified central bank based in Washington, DC, would concentrate too much economic power in the hands of the officials running the bank. So, the act divided economic power within the Federal Reserve System in three ways: among bankers and business interests, among states and regions, and between government and the private sector. The act and subsequent legislation created four groups within the system, each empowered, in theory, to perform separate duties: the Federal Reserve Banks, private commercial member banks, the Board of Governors, and the Federal Open Market Committee (FOMC). All national banks— commercial banks with charters from the federal government—were required to join the

Federal Reserve System
The central bank of the United States.

system. State banks—commercial banks with charters from state governments—were given the option to join. The original intent of the Federal Reserve Act was to give the central bank control over the amount of currency outstanding and the volume of loans—known as *discount loans*—to member banks under the lender-of-last-resort function. In 1913, the president and Congress did not envision the Fed as a centralized authority with broad control over most aspects of money and the banking system. As we will see in the rest of this section, over time, the Fed has expanded its role in the financial system.

Federal Reserve Banks

Federal Reserve Bank
One of 12 district banks of the Federal Reserve System that, among other activities, conduct discount lending.

As part of its plan to divide authority within the Federal Reserve System, Congress decided not to establish a single central bank with branches, which had been the structure of both the First and Second Banks of the United States. Instead, the Federal Reserve Act divided the United States into 12 Federal Reserve districts, each of which has a **Federal Reserve Bank** in one city (and, in most cases, additional branches in other cities in the district). Congress intended that the primary function of the Reserve Banks would be to make discount loans to member banks in its region. These loans were to provide liquidity to banks, thereby fulfilling in a decentralized way the system's role as a lender of last resort and putting an end to bank panics—or so Congress hoped!

Figure 13.1 shows the Federal Reserve districts and locations of the Federal Reserve Banks. The map may appear strange at first glance because some states are split

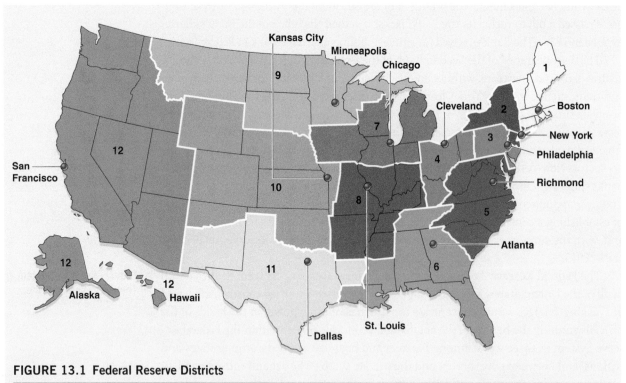

FIGURE 13.1 Federal Reserve Districts

Congress divided the United States into 12 Federal Reserve districts that each contains a mixture of urban and rural areas and manufacturing, agricultural, and service industries. Note that Hawaii and Alaska are included in the Twelfth Federal Reserve District.

Source: Federal Reserve Bulletin.

by district boundaries, and economically dissimilar states are grouped in the same district. The largest district geographically (San Francisco) is more than 10 times as large as the smallest (New York). Most Federal Reserve districts contain a mixture of urban and rural areas, as well as manufacturing, agriculture, and service business interests. This arrangement was intended to prevent any one interest group or any one state from obtaining preferential treatment from the district Federal Reserve Bank. The districts reflect the structure of the U.S. economy and the geographic distribution of industries and population as they were in 1914. But there have been substantial changes since that time. For example, the region served by the Federal Reserve Bank of San Francisco contained about 6% of the U.S. population in 1914 but has about 20% today. Proposals in Congress have suggested redrawing the district boundaries, but so far, none has been successful.

MAKING THE CONNECTION

St. Louis and Kansas City? What Explains the Locations of the District Banks?

The current Fed is not exactly what Congress had in mind when it passed the Federal Reserve Act. In particular, the Reserve Banks were intended to have much more independence than they have today. So, where the banks would be located was a significant issue during the Congressional debates over the act. The act allowed for 8 to 12 districts but did not specify their boundaries or indicate in which cities Federal Reserve Banks would be located. That decision was given to a Reserve Bank Organizing Committee, consisting of the secretary of the Treasury, the secretary of Agriculture, and the comptroller of the currency. The district boundaries and Federal Reserve Bank cities that the committee announced in April 1914 have remained unchanged to the present.

The committee's choices were controversial because the three committee members were all appointees of Democratic President Woodrow Wilson. Some critics argued that Democratic Party politics dictated which cities the committee chose. For instance, the only state with two banks is Missouri, with Kansas City serving as the Federal Reserve Bank for the tenth district and St. Louis serving as the bank for the eighth district. Critics pointed out that the Democratic speaker of the House was from Missouri. Similarly, Richmond, Virginia, the home of Democratic Senator Carter Glass, one of the sponsors of the Federal Reserve Act, was awarded a bank. Attempts were made to convince officials of the Federal Reserve System to overturn the committee's decisions, until finally in 1916, the U.S. attorney general ruled that the district boundaries and locations of the Federal Reserve Banks could be changed only if Congress amended the Federal Reserve Act.

Although the view that the locations of the Federal Reserve Banks represent early twentieth century politics is widespread among economists, recent research has questioned this idea. Michael McAvoy, of the State University of New York, Oneonta, reexamined the choices of the Reserve Bank Organizing Committee to see whether political or economic factors were more important. He found that there was agreement among most groups at the time on locating Federal Reserve Banks in six of the cities: Boston, Chicago, New York, Philadelphia, St. Louis, and San Francisco. McAvoy estimated a statistical model to see whether political variables—such as whether the city was represented by a Democrat in Congress—or economic variables—such as the city's population, the growth in bank capital, and the preferences of bankers surveyed by the committee—were able to predict the cities chosen. McAvoy's conclusion was that economic variables could correctly predict the cities chosen, while political factors could not.

David Wheelock, an economist at the Federal Reserve Bank of St. Louis, has studied why the Reserve Bank Organizing Committee chose to locate two Reserve Banks in Missouri. He noted that correspondent banking was particularly important in the early 1900s. Correspondent banks were typically located in larger cities and provided services such as check clearing and loans to smaller banks in the surrounding areas. Correspondent banks also helped facilitate the needs of the business customers of smaller banks. For example, a bank located in Kansas City might provide these services to smaller banks located in Kansas, Nebraska, or Colorado. Wheelock found that smaller banks surveyed by the Reserve Bank Organizing Committee were more likely to have correspondent relationships with banks in Kansas City and St. Louis than with banks in other cities, such as Denver or Omaha, that also wanted to be the location of a Reserve Bank. These smaller banks supported locating Reserve Banks in Kansas City and St. Louis over other cities.

So, while it may seem odd today for Missouri to have two Federal Reserve Banks, it appears to have made economic sense in 1914.

Sources: David C. Wheelock, "Economics and Politics in Selecting Federal Reserve Cities: Why Missouri Has Two Reserve Banks," Federal Reserve Bank of St. Louis *Review*, Vol. 97, No. 4, Fourth Quarter 2015, pp. 269–288; Michael R. McAvoy, "How Were the Federal Reserve Bank Locations Selected?" *Explorations in Economic History*, Vol. 43, No. 3, July 2006; and Allan H. Meltzer, *A History of the Federal Reserve, Volume I: 1913–1951*, Chicago: University of Chicago Press, 2003, pp. 73–75.

See related problem 1.8 at the end of the chapter.

In the chapter opener, we noted that the ownership structure of the Federal Reserve Banks remains controversial more than a century after they were first established. When banks join the Federal Reserve System, they are required to buy stock in their Federal Reserve Bank, which pays member banks a dividend on this stock. So, in principle, the private commercial banks in each district that are members of the Federal Reserve System own the District Bank. In fact, each Federal Reserve Bank is a private–government joint venture because the member banks enjoy few of the rights and privileges that shareholders ordinarily exercise. For example, member banks do not have a legal claim on the profits of the District Banks, as shareholders of private corporations do.

A guiding principle of the 1913 Federal Reserve Act was that one constituency (for example, finance, industry, commerce, or agriculture) would not be allowed to exploit the central bank's economic power at the expense of another constituency. Therefore, Congress restricted the composition of the boards of directors of the Federal Reserve Banks. The directors represent the interests of three groups: banks, businesses, and the general public. Member banks elect three bankers (Class A directors) and three leaders in industry, commerce, and agriculture (Class B directors). The Fed's Board of Governors appoints three public interest directors (Class C directors). For much of the Federal Reserve System's history, the nine directors of a Federal Reserve Bank have elected the president of that bank, subject to approval by the Board of Governors. Under the Dodd-Frank Act of 2010, the Class A directors no longer participate in the election of bank presidents. As we saw in the chapter opener, during the 2016 presidential campaign Democratic Party nominee Hillary Clinton proposed that banks no longer be allowed to elect the Class A and Class B directors and that bankers no longer serve as directors. We discuss this proposal later in this chapter.

The 12 Federal Reserve Banks carry out the following duties related to the Fed's roles in the payments system, control of the money supply, and financial regulation:

- Manage check clearing in the payments system
- Manage currency in circulation by issuing new Federal Reserve notes and withdrawing damaged notes from circulation
- Conduct discount lending by making and administering discount loans to banks within the district
- Perform supervisory and regulatory functions such as examining state member banks and evaluating merger applications
- Provide services to businesses and the general public by collecting and making available data on district business activities and by publishing articles on monetary and banking topics written by professional economists employed by the banks
- Serve on the Federal Open Market Committee, the Federal Reserve System's chief monetary policy body

The Federal Reserve Banks engage in monetary policy both directly (by making discount loans) and indirectly (through membership on Federal Reserve committees). In theory, Federal Reserve Banks establish the discount rate that banks pay on discount loans and determine the amounts that individual (member and nonmember) banks are allowed to borrow. In practice, however, since the 1920s, the discount rate has effectively been set by the Board of Governors in Washington, DC, and it is the same in all 12 districts. The Federal Reserve Banks also influence policy through their representatives on the Federal Open Market Committee and on the Federal Advisory Council, a consultative body composed of district bankers.

Member Banks

Although the Federal Reserve Act required all national banks to become member banks of the Federal Reserve System, state banks were given the option to join, and many chose not to. Currently, only about 20% of state banks are members. About 34% of all commercial banks in the United States now belong to the Federal Reserve System, although these member banks hold a substantial majority of all bank deposits.

Historically, state banks often chose not to join the Federal Reserve System because they saw membership as costly. In particular, state banks that did not join the system could avoid the Fed's reserve requirements. Because the Fed did not pay interest on required reserves, banks saw the reserve requirement as effectively being a tax because the banks were losing the interest they could have earned by lending the funds. In other words, being a member of the Fed imposed a significant opportunity cost on banks, in the form of lost interest earnings. As nominal interest rates rose during the 1960s and 1970s, the opportunity cost of Fed membership increased, and fewer state banks elected to become or remain members.

During the 1970s, the Fed argued that the so-called reserve tax on member banks placed these banks at a competitive disadvantage relative to nonmember banks. The Fed claimed that declining bank membership eroded its ability to control the money supply and urged Congress to compel all commercial banks to join the Federal Reserve System. Although Congress did not legislate such a requirement, the Depository Institutions Deregulation and Monetary Control Act (DIDMCA) of 1980 required that all banks maintain reserve deposits with the Fed on the same terms. This legislation gave member and nonmember banks equivalent access to discount loans and to payment system (check-clearing) services. DIDMCA effectively blurred the distinction between member and nonmember banks and halted the decline in Fed membership. In October 2008, the Fed began paying banks an interest rate of 0.25% on reserves, which lowered the opportunity cost to banks of holding reserves. In December 2016, the interest rate the Fed pays on reserves was 0.75%.

SOLVED PROBLEM 13.1

How Costly Are Reserve Requirements to Banks?

Suppose that Wells Fargo pays a 1% annual interest rate on checking account balances and has to meet a reserve requirement of 10%. Assume that the Fed pays Wells Fargo an interest rate of 0.50% on its holdings of reserves and that Wells Fargo can earn 5% on its loans and other investments.

a. How do reserve requirements affect the amount that Wells Fargo can earn on $1,000 in checking account deposits? Ignore any costs Wells Fargo incurs on the deposits other than the interest it pays to depositors.

b. Is the opportunity cost to banks of reserve requirements (the "reserve tax") likely to be higher during a recession or during an economic expansion? Briefly explain.

Solving the Problem

Step 1 **Review the chapter material.** This problem is about the effect of reserve requirements on banks, so you may want to review the section "Member Banks," which begins on page 435.

Step 2 **Answer part (a) by calculating the effective cost of funds to Wells Fargo.** With a 10% reserve requirement, Wells Fargo must hold $100 of a $1,000 checking account deposit as reserves with the Fed, on which it receives an interest rate of 0.50%. The bank can invest the remaining $900. So, it will earn:

$$(\$900 \times 0.05) + (\$100 \times 0.0050) = \$45.00 + \$0.50 = \$45.50.$$

If the bank did not need to hold reserves against the deposit, it would earn:

$$\$1,000 \times 0.05 = \$50.$$

So, the reserve requirement is reducing Well Fargo's return by $4.50, or:

$$(\$4.50/\$1,000) \times 100 = 0.45\%.$$

Step 3   **Answer part (b) by explaining how the reserve tax varies over the business cycle.** The higher the interest rate banks can earn on their loans and other investments, the higher the opportunity cost of having to hold reserves at the Fed that are earning a low interest rate. As we saw in Chapter 4, interest rates tend to fall during economic recessions and rise during economic expansions. So, the opportunity cost to banks of reserve requirements is likely to be higher during economic expansions than during economic recessions.

See related problem 1.9 at the end of the chapter.

Board of Governors

The **Board of Governors**, which is headquartered in Washington, DC, has ultimate authority over the Federal Reserve System. Its seven members are appointed by the president of the United States and confirmed by the U.S. Senate. To increase the Fed's independence, the terms of board members are set so that governors serve nonrenewable terms of 14 years, which are staggered so that one term expires every other January 31. As a result, it is unlikely that one U.S. president will be able to appoint a full Board of Governors. On average, presidents appoint a new member every other year. It is possible for one person to serve longer than 14 years: If the person begins by serving out the remainder of the unexpired term of a governor who has retired, he or she may be reappointed to a full term. By this method, Alan Greenspan served from 1987 to 2006. No Federal Reserve District can be represented by more than one member on the Board of Governors.

The president chooses one member of the Board of Governors to serve as chair. Chairs serve four-year terms and may be reappointed. For instance, Ben Bernanke was appointed chair in January 2006 by President George W. Bush and reappointed in January 2010 by President Barack Obama.

Currently, many board members are professional economists from business, government, and academia. Chairs of the Board of Governors since World War II have come from various backgrounds, including Wall Street (William McChesney Martin), academia (Arthur Burns, Ben Bernanke, and Janet Yellen), business (G. William Miller), public service (Paul Volcker), and economic forecasting (Alan Greenspan).

The Board of Governors administers monetary policy to influence the nation's money supply and interest rates through open market operations, reserve requirements, and discount lending. Since 1935, the board has had the authority to determine reserve requirements within limits set by Congress. The board also effectively sets the discount rate charged on loans to banks. It holds 7 of the 12 seats on the Federal Open Market Committee and therefore influences the setting of guidelines for open market operations. In addition to its formal responsibilities, the board informally influences national and international economic policy decisions. The chair of the Board of Governors advises the president and testifies before Congress on economic matters, such as economic growth, inflation, and unemployment.

Board of Governors The governing board of the Federal Reserve System, consisting of seven members appointed by the president of the United States.

The Board of Governors is responsible for some financial regulation. It sets margin requirements, or the proportion of the purchase price of securities that an investor must pay in cash rather than buy on credit. In addition, it determines permissible activities for bank holding companies and approves bank mergers. The chair of the Board of Governors also serves on the Financial Stability Oversight Council (FSOC), which the Dodd-Frank Act established in 2010 to regulate the financial system. Finally, the Board of Governors exercises administrative controls over individual Federal Reserve Banks, reviewing their budgets and setting the salaries of their presidents and officers.

The Federal Open Market Committee

The 12-member **Federal Open Market Committee (FOMC)** directs the Fed's open market operations. Members of the FOMC are the chair of the Board of Governors, the other Fed governors, and 5 of the 12 presidents of Federal Reserve Banks. The president of the Federal Reserve Bank of New York is always a member, with the other 11 Federal Reserve Bank presidents serving one-year terms on a rotating basis. All 12 Federal Reserve Bank presidents attend meetings and participate in discussions. The chair of the Board of Governors serves as chair of the FOMC. The committee meets in Washington, DC, eight times each year.

In recent decades, the FOMC has been at the center of Fed policymaking. As we will discuss in Chapter 15, until the financial crisis of 2007–2009, the Fed's most important policy tool was setting the target for the federal funds rate, which is the interest rate that banks charge each other on short-term loans. During the financial crisis, Fed Chairman Ben Bernanke needed to make decisions rapidly and to use new policy tools. As a result, the focus of monetary policy moved away from the FOMC. As more normal conditions have been returning to the economy and the financial system, the FOMC has regained its traditional importance.

Prior to each meeting, FOMC members access data from three books:

- The "Green Book," prepared by board staff, contains a national economic forecast for the next two years.
- The "Blue Book," also prepared by board staff, contains projections for monetary aggregates and other information useful in providing context for alternative monetary policies.
- The "Beige Book," prepared by the Federal Reserve Banks, contains summaries of economic conditions in each district.

At the end of each meeting, after all members of the Board of Governors and all Reserve Bank presidents have been heard from, the chair reviews the discussion. The FOMC then takes a formal vote that sets a target for the federal funds rate. The committee summarizes its views in a public statement of the balance of risks between higher inflation and a weaker economy. Typically, the board's staff has prepared three statements with slightly different language for the members to choose from. In times of uncertainty over the Fed's future policy, the precise wording of the statement can be very important.

The Fed doesn't administratively determine the federal funds rate but instead sets a target in a *domestic policy directive* that is sent to the Open Market Desk at the Federal

Reserve Bank of New York. There, the manager for domestic open market operations carries out the directive by buying and selling Treasury securities with *primary dealers,* which are private financial firms that have been authorized to buy and sell these securities with the Fed. As we will discuss in Chapter 15, in recent years the Open Market Desk has carried out the FOMC's policy directive primarily by executing reverse repurchase agreements with the primary dealers.

MAKING THE CONNECTION

On the Board of Governors, Four Can Be a Crowd

Because the Fed's most important monetary policy tool is setting the target for the federal funds rate, by the 1980s, the key monetary policy debates within the Fed took place during meetings of the FOMC. Economists and Wall Street analysts closely watched the outcome of each meeting for clues about the direction of Fed policy. During the financial crisis of 2007–2009, however, it became clear that the Fed could not confine its actions to changes in the target for the federal funds rate. As in other recessions, the FOMC moved quickly to cut the target beginning in September 2007. But by December 2008, although the target had effectively been cut to zero, the economy continued to contract, and the financial system was in crisis.

As we saw in Chapter 12, Fed Chairman Ben Bernanke responded by taking a series of policy actions, some of which were unprecedented. Because events were moving swiftly, waiting for the next FOMC meeting to discuss potential policy moves was not feasible. In addition, because FOMC meetings are attended by all the members of the Board of Governors and the 12 Reserve Bank presidents, their size was a barrier to quick decision making. The alternative of relying on the Board of Governors was also problematic. In 1976, Congress passed the Government in the Sunshine Act, which requires most federal government agencies to give public notice before a meeting. If four or more members of the Board of Governors meet to consider a policy action, it is considered an official meeting under the act and cannot be held without prior public notice. Given that Bernanke needed to make decisions rapidly as events unfolded hour by hour, the requirement of prior public notice made it infeasible for him to meet with more than two other members of the Board of Governors.

As a result, Bernanke relied on an informal group of advisers consisting of Board of Governors members Donald Kohn and Kevin Warsh and New York District Bank president Timothy Geithner. Geithner was a member of the FOMC but not of the Board of Governors, so his presence at meetings did not trigger the Sunshine Act requirement. The "four musketeers," as they came to be called, were the key policymaking body at the Fed for the duration of the crisis. The unintended consequence of the Sunshine Act requirements was to drastically limit the input of the other members of the FOMC into monetary policymaking.

Source: David Wessel, *In Fed We Trust: Ben Bernanke's War on the Great Panic*, New York: Crown Business, 2009.

See related problem 1.10 at the end of the chapter.

Power and Authority Within the Fed

Congress designed the Federal Reserve System to have checks and balances to ensure that no one group could control it. There was therefore little central (or national) control of the system during its first years. The Governors Conference, consisting of the heads of the 12 Federal Reserve Banks, competed with the Federal Reserve Board in Washington for control of the system.[1] After the severe banking crisis of the early 1930s, many analysts concluded that the decentralized Reserve Bank system could not adequately respond to national economic and financial disturbances. The Banking Acts of 1933 and 1935 gave the Board of Governors authority to set reserve requirements and the FOMC the authority to direct open market operations. The Banking Act of 1935 also centralized the Board of Governors' control of the system, giving it a majority (7 of 12) of votes on the FOMC. In addition, the secretary of the Treasury and the comptroller of the currency were removed from the Board of Governors, thereby increasing the Fed's independence.

Legislatively, Congress has given the Board of Governors and the FOMC *formal* authority over monetary policy. However, many Fed watchers believe that the *informal* authority of the chair often predominates. We can draw a contrast with the U.S. Supreme Court, for which the president of the United States nominates one member to be chief justice. Although the chief justice has certain administrative duties that allow him or her to influence the Court's actions, the chief justice has only 1 vote and has frequently been outvoted by other justices on important decisions. Federal Reserve chairs have only 1 vote of 7 on the Board of Governors and only 1 vote of 12 on the FOMC, yet chairs almost invariably are able to have the policies they favor adopted. Some board members and District Bank presidents on the FOMC may challenge the chair's agenda, but typically the chair's influence still prevails. The board's staff economists can also affect policymaking because they are responsible for presenting at each FOMC meeting summaries of economic conditions and potential policy options. Because the Federal Reserve Bank of New York always occupies a seat on the FOMC and is the home of the Open Market Desk through which open market operations are conducted, the president of that Bank can be quite influential. We can conclude that the informal power structure within the Fed is more concentrated than the formal power structure. Figure 13.2 shows the organizational and power-sharing arrangements within the Fed. Ultimately, the Fed chair wields the most power in the system.

Member banks, which are the nominal owners of Federal Reserve Banks, have little actual power within the system. The distinction between *ownership* and *control* within the Federal Reserve System is clear: Member banks own shares of stock in the Federal Reserve Banks, but this ownership confers few of the rights that are typically granted to shareholders of private corporations. For much of the Fed's history, member banks received a fixed 6% annual dividend. Whatever revenue the Fed has remaining after covering all of its expenses, including dividends it pays to member banks, it gives to the U.S.

---

[1] At the time, the heads of the Reserve Banks were called governors. The Governors Conference controlled open market operations in the early years of the Fed. Open market operations came under the control of the Open Market Investment Committee during the 1920s. The Open Market Investment Committee was replaced by the Federal Open Market Committee in 1933.

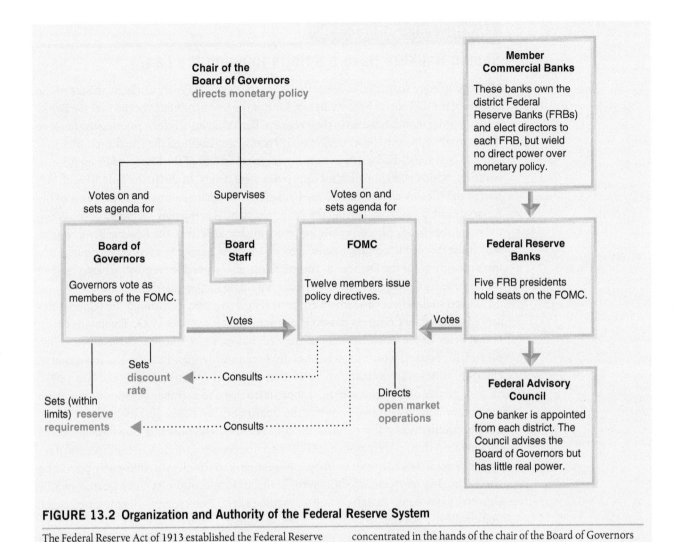

FIGURE 13.2 Organization and Authority of the Federal Reserve System

The Federal Reserve Act of 1913 established the Federal Reserve System and incorporated a series of checks and balances into the system. However, informal power within the Fed is more concentrated in the hands of the chair of the Board of Governors than the formal structure suggests.

Treasury to help fund the federal government's expenditures. In 2015, to raise funds to pay for repairs to the nation's highways, Congress changed the dividend the Fed pays to large member banks (those with assets greater than $10 billion) to equal the lesser of 6% or the interest rate on 10-year Treasury notes. In 2016, the interest rate on 10-year Treasury notes was below 3%, so large member banks received a significant cut in their dividend payments. Note that this change does not affect the basic fact that the dividend the Fed pays to member banks does not depend on the Fed's earnings, and member banks do not have the residual claim to a firm's profits that shareholders in a private corporation enjoy. Moreover, member banks have virtually no control over how their investment in the system is used because the Board of Governors in Washington, DC, formulates policy. Although member banks elect the six Class A and Class B directors, these are not contested elections. Officials at the Federal Reserve Bank or the Board of Governors typically suggest the one candidate for each position.

> **MAKING THE CONNECTION**

Should Bankers Have a Role in Running the Fed?

Many people are surprised to learn that bankers elect a majority of the members of the boards of the 12 Federal Reserve Banks. One of the responsibilities of the Reserve Banks is to supervise member banks in their regions. Banks having a role in running the Reserve Banks might appear to be a conflict of interest, comparable to the situation if pharmaceutical companies had a role in running regional offices of the Food and Drug Administration, which is responsible for approving new drugs. In 2010, the Dodd-Frank Act barred the Class A directors, who are bankers, from participating in the elections of the Reserve Bank presidents. During the 2016 presidential campaign, Democratic presidential nominee Hillary Clinton called for removing bankers from the Reserve Bank boards, which she labelled a "common sense reform." Senator Bernie Sanders of Vermont, Clinton's main rival for the Democratic nomination, also argued for removing bankers from the Reserve Bank boards, so that "the foxes would no longer guard the henhouse."

Given such objections, why were bankers given a role in running the regional Reserve Banks when Congress passed the Federal Reserve Act in 1913? The main reason is that prior to the establishment of the Fed, banks, particularly in large cities, relied on clearinghouses, which local banks could voluntarily join. Initially, the main role of clearinghouses was to clear checks written by member banks, but by the late 1800s, clearinghouses also were a source of short-term loans to member banks suffering from temporary liquidity problems. While the clearinghouses could deal with short-term liquidity problems of a few banks, they could be overwhelmed in a true bank panic, as became clear during the panic of 1907. When Congress responded to this problem, it set up the Federal Reserve System to operate similarly to the clearinghouses by providing check-clearing services and short-term loans. In fact, economist Gary Gorton of Yale University has noted that in certain ways, the Federal Reserve System amounted to the "nationalization of the private clearinghouse system."

Would there be a downside to removing bankers from any role in governing the Federal Reserve System? Federal Reserve Bank of Richmond President Jeffrey Lacker thinks so. He argues that if the law is changed so that banks no longer own the Federal Reserve Banks, the question arises as to who would own them: "If it is the Treasury, you are essentially nationalizing the Reserve Banks." He believes such a step would disturb the mix of public–private ownership that has prevailed since the founding of the system and might raise questions about whether the Fed would be able to undertake monetary policy free from political interference. Other economists and policymakers are unsure whether there actually is a problem with Fed oversight of member banks. As we saw in Chapter 12, the 2007–2009 financial crisis originated in the shadow banking system rather than the commercial banking system. Mutual funds, hedge funds, those investment banks that are not part of bank holding companies, and other shadow banking firms are *not* members of the Federal Reserve System and do not serve on the boards of the Reserve Banks. Fed Chair Janet Yellen summarized the thoughts of many Fed officials in testimony before Congress: "The structure of the Federal Reserve reflects choices that were hammered out 100 years ago, and I think the current structure works well, so I would not recommend changes."

Ultimately, it is up to Congress to decide the structure of the Federal Reserve System. The choices Congress makes can reflect economic issues but often are also influenced by political concerns.

Sources: Ylan Q. Mui, "Hillary Clinton to Support Federal Reserve Change Sought by Liberals," *Washington Post*, May 12, 2016; Bernie Sanders, "To Rein in Wall Street, Fix the Fed," *New York Times*, December 23. 2015; Gary Gorton, "Clearinghouses and the Origins of Central Banking in the United States," *Journal of Economic History*, Vol. 45, No. 2, June 1985, pp. 277–283; Craig Torres, Steve Matthews, and Elizabeth Dexheimer, "Reforming Fed Structure Could Harm Policy Independence: Lacker," bloomberg.com, May 24, 2016; and U.S. Senate Committee on Banking, Housing, and Urban Affairs, *Hearing on Fed's First Monetary Policy Report for 2015*, February 24, 2015.

See related problem 1.12 at the end of the chapter.

Changes to the Fed Under the Dodd-Frank Act

The severity of the financial crisis of 2007–2009 and some of the unprecedented policy actions the Fed took during that time led many economists and policymakers to reconsider the role of the Fed in the financial system. During the long debate over financial reform, members of Congress offered many proposals to alter the Fed's structure or its responsibilities. When the **Wall Street Reform and Consumer Protection Act**, also known as the **Dodd-Frank Act**, finally passed in July 2010, however, it contained none of the more extensive changes to the Fed that had been proposed. The following are the main provisions of the bill that affect the Fed:

Wall Street Reform and Consumer Protection Act (Dodd-Frank Act)
Legislation passed in 2010 that was intended to reform regulation of the financial system.

- **New regulatory responsibilities for the Fed.** The Fed was made a member of the new Financial Stability Oversight Council (FSOC), along with members of nine other regulatory agencies, including the SEC and the FDIC. Congress gave the FSOC authority to increase capital requirements at systemically important financial firms (SIFIs) and to require the firms to develop living wills that detail how the firms can be dissolved following a bankruptcy in a way that does not result in financial instability. The objective is to avoid situations, such as the failure of Lehman Brothers in 2008, in which the insolvency of one large financial firm threatens the stability of the system.
- **Restrictions on the Fed's role as a lender of last resort.** As we discussed in Chapter 11, Section 13(3) of the Federal Reserve Act was revised to remove the Fed's authority to lend to individual financial firms outside of broadly based lending programs. This change reflected dissatisfaction in Congress with the actions the Fed took during the financial crisis to keep Bear Stearns and AIG from being forced into bankruptcy.
- **New responsibilities for one member of the Board of Governors.** One member of the Board of Governors is now designated the vice chair for supervision, with particular responsibility for coordinating the Fed's regulatory actions.
- **GAO audit of emergency lending.** The Government Accountability Office (GAO) was ordered to perform an audit of the emergency lending programs the Fed had carried out during the financial crisis.
- **New process for electing Reserve Bank presidents.** As previously mentioned, the Class A directors of the Federal Reserve Banks will no longer participate in elections of the bank presidents.

- **Requirement for new disclosures of Fed borrowers and counterparties.** To increase the transparency of its operations, the Fed was ordered to disclose the names of financial institutions to which it makes loans and with which it buys and sells securities.
- **New regulatory bureau within the Fed.** The new Consumer Financial Protection Bureau was established at the Fed. Although the bureau is physically located in the Fed's Washington, DC building and its budget comes from Fed revenues, Fed officials have no managerial oversight of it. The bureau's director is appointed by the president, subject to confirmation by the Senate, and functions independently of other Fed officials. The purpose of the bureau is to write rules concerning consumer protection that will apply to all financial firms. Some of the responsibility that the Fed had for regulating consumer lending has been transferred to the bureau.

13.2 How the Fed Operates

LEARNING OBJECTIVE: Explain the Fed's relationship to the government and the arguments for and against its independence.

The government created the Fed to provide short-run liquidity to banks, to oversee aspects of the banking system, and to manage the money supply. The U.S. Constitution doesn't explicitly provide for the establishment of a central bank. As we saw in Section 13.1, twice in the nineteenth century Congress abolished the existing central bank. In this section, we describe how the political environment may affect how the Fed operates, and we discuss the debate over the Fed's independence.

Handling External Pressure

Congress intended the Federal Reserve System to operate largely independently of external pressures from the president, Congress, the banking industry, and business groups. Members of the Board of Governors are appointed for long, nonrenewable terms of office, reducing any one president's influence on the board's composition and reducing the temptation for governors to take actions merely to please the president and Congress.

The Fed's financial independence allows it to resist external pressure. Generally, federal agencies must ask Congress for the funds they need to operate. Congress scrutinizes these budgetary requests and can reduce the amounts requested by agencies that have fallen out of favor with key members of the House or Senate. Not only is the Fed exempt from this process, but it is also a profitable organization that actually contributes funds to the Treasury rather than receiving funds from it. Most of the Fed's earnings come from interest on the securities it holds, with smaller amounts coming from interest on discount loans and fees it receives from financial institutions for check-clearing and other services. In 2015, the Fed's profit was $103 *billion*, of which it contributed about $98 billion to the Treasury. The Fed's profit is substantial even when compared with the largest U.S. corporations. For instance, in 2015, Apple earned a profit of $78 billion, ExxonMobil earned $31 billion, Microsoft earned $27 billion, and Google (now using the corporate name Alphabet) earned $23 billion. But as noted, unlike with these corporations, the Fed turns over whatever it earns in excess of its expenses to the U.S. Treasury rather than retaining it.

Despite the attempt to give the Fed independence, it isn't completely insulated from external pressure. First, the president can exercise control over the membership of the Board of Governors. Often, governors do not serve their full 14-year terms because they can earn higher incomes in private business or because they wish to return to academic or other careers. Therefore, a president who serves two terms in office may be able to appoint several governors. In addition, the president may appoint a new chair every four years. A chair who is not reappointed may serve the remainder of his or her term as a governor but traditionally most have resigned, thereby giving the president another vacancy to fill.

Second, although the Fed's significant profit exempts it from requesting money from Congress, the Fed remains a creation of Congress. Congress can amend the Fed's charter and powers—or even abolish it entirely. Members of Congress are usually not shy about reminding the Fed of this fact. For example, with passage of the Humphrey-Hawkins Act (officially the Full Employment and Balanced Growth Act of 1978), Congress began requiring the Fed to explain how its procedures are consistent with the president's economic objectives. As we have seen, the Dodd-Frank Act changed some aspects of the Fed's organization and procedures. Recently, members of Congress have proposed that the GAO audit the Fed's monetary policy actions. Most Fed officials believe that this level of scrutiny of Fed policies would significantly reduce its independence, and to this point a majority of Congress appears to agree. So, in practice, Congress has reduced some aspects of the Fed's independence, but it has not yet limited the Fed's ability to conduct monetary policy independently.

Examples of Conflict Between the Fed and the Treasury

Congress and the president lack formal control of monetary policy, which has occasionally resulted in conflicts between the Fed and the president, who is often represented by the secretary of the Treasury. During World War II, the administration of President Franklin D. Roosevelt increased its control over the Fed. To help finance wartime budget deficits, the Fed agreed to hold interest rates on Treasury securities at low levels: 0.375% on Treasury bills and 2.5% on Treasury bonds. The Fed could keep interest rates at these low levels only by buying any bonds that were not purchased by private investors, thereby fixing, or *pegging*, the rates. When the war ended in 1945, the Treasury wanted to continue this policy, but the Fed didn't agree. The Fed's concern was inflation: Larger purchases of Treasury securities by the Fed could increase the growth rate of the money supply and the rate of inflation. As the war ended, the government lifted the price controls that had restrained inflation.

Fed Chairman Marriner Eccles strongly objected to the policy of fixing interest rates. His opposition led President Harry Truman not to reappoint him as chair in 1948, although Eccles continued to fight for Fed independence during the remainder of his time as a governor. On March 4, 1951, the federal government formally abandoned the wartime policy of fixing the interest rates on Treasury securities with the *Treasury–Federal Reserve Accord*. This agreement was important in reestablishing the Fed's ability to operate independently of the Treasury.

Conflicts between the Treasury and the Fed didn't end with that agreement, however. For example, President Ronald Reagan and Federal Reserve Chairman Paul Volcker argued over who was at fault for the severe economic recession of the early 1980s. Reagan blamed the Fed for soaring interest rates. Volcker held that the Fed could not take action to bring down interest rates until the budget deficit—which results from policy actions of the president and Congress—was reduced. Similar conflicts occurred during the administrations of George H. W. Bush and Bill Clinton, with the Treasury frequently pushing for lower short-term interest rates than the Fed considered advisable.

During the financial crisis of 2007–2009, the Fed worked closely with the Treasury. The relationship was so close, in fact, that some economists and policymakers worried that the Fed might be sacrificing some of its independence. The frequent consultations between Fed Chairman Ben Bernanke and Treasury Secretary Henry Paulson during the height of the crisis in the fall of 2008 were a break with the tradition of Fed chairs formulating policy independently of the administration. If such close collaboration were to become frequent, it would raise the question of whether the Fed would be able to pursue policies independently of those of the administration in power.

Factors That Motivate the Fed

We have shown that the Fed has legal authority for monetary policy. We now examine two views of what motivates the Fed in using its authority: the public interest view and the principal–agent view.

The Public Interest View The usual starting point for explaining the motivation of business managers is that they act in the interest of the constituency they serve: their shareholders. The **public interest view** of Fed motivation holds that the Fed, too, acts in the interest of its primary constituency—the general public—and that it seeks to achieve economic goals that are in the public interest. Examples of such goals are price stability, high employment, and economic growth.

Public interest view A theory of central bank decision making that holds that officials act in the best interest of the public.

Does the evidence support the public interest view of the Fed? Some economists argue that it doesn't with regard to price stability. The record of persistent inflation since World War II, particularly the high rates of inflation during the late 1970s and early 1980s, undercuts the claim that the Fed has emphasized price stability. Other economists argue that the Fed's record on price stability is relatively good and that the high inflation rates of the 1970s were primarily due to soaring oil prices that took the Fed by surprise. Since the early 1990s, the inflation rate has been closer to the Fed's target annual rate of 2%, although since the financial crisis, it has generally been below that rate. There are similar debates over whether the Fed's actions have been consistent with its goals of high employment and high rates of economic growth.

The Principal–Agent View Many economists view organizations as having conflicting goals. Although they are created to serve the public and perform a public service, government organizations also have internal goals that might not match their stated mission. In effect, public organizations face the principal–agent problem just as private corporations do.

Recall that when managers (agents) have little stake in their businesses, their incentives to maximize the value of shareholders' (principals') claims may be weak. In such situations, the agents don't always act in the interest of the principals. Gordon Tullock and Nobel Laureate James Buchanan of George Mason University formulated a **principal–agent view** of motivation in bureaucratic organizations such as the Fed. This view contends that the objective of bureaucrats is to maximize their personal well-being—power, influence, and prestige—rather than the well-being of the general public. So, the principal–agent view of Fed motivation predicts that the Fed acts to increase its power, influence, and prestige as an organization, subject to constraints placed on it by the principals: the president and Congress.

> **Principal–agent view**
> A theory of central bank decision making that holds that officials maximize their personal well-being rather than that of the general public.

If the principal–agent view accurately explains the Fed's motivation, we would expect the Fed to fight to maintain its autonomy—which it does. The Fed has frequently resisted Congressional attempts to control its budget. In fact, the Fed has been very successful at mobilizing constituents (such as bankers and business executives) in its own defense. Although early drafts of the Dodd-Frank Act included provisions that would have reduced the Fed's independence and its regulatory power, the Fed successfully lobbied Congress to strip most of these provisions from the final version of the act. Supporters of the public interest view, though, argue that the Fed guards its autonomy so as to better serve the public interest.

Proponents of the principal–agent view also predict that the Fed will avoid conflicts with groups that could limit its power, influence, and prestige. For example, the Fed can manage monetary policy to assist the reelection efforts of presidential incumbents who are unlikely to limit its power. The result would be a **political business cycle**, in which the Fed would try to lower interest rates to stimulate economic activity before an election to earn favor with the incumbent party running for reelection. After the election, the economy would face the consequences when the Fed contracted economic activity to reduce the inflationary pressure caused by its earlier expansion—but, by then, the president who was sympathetic to the Fed would have been reelected. The facts for the United States don't generally support the political business cycle theory, however. For example, an expansion of money supply growth preceded President Richard Nixon's reelection in 1972, but a contraction of money supply growth preceded President Jimmy Carter's and President George H. W. Bush's unsuccessful bids for reelection in 1980 and 1992, respectively.

> **Political business cycle** The theory that policymakers will urge the Fed to lower interest rates to stimulate the economy prior to an election.

Nevertheless, the president's desires may subtly influence Fed policy. One study of the influence of politics on changes in monetary policy from 1979 through 1984 measured the number of times members of the administration were quoted about desired changes in monetary policy in articles appearing in the *Wall Street Journal*. The author found a close correlation between changes in monetary policy and the number of these signals from the administration that they desired a policy change.[2]

One criticism of the principal–agent view addresses the need to separate the Fed's intentions from external pressure: The Fed itself might want to act in one way, whereas

[2] Thomas Havrilesky, "Monetary Policy Signaling from the Administration to the Federal Reserve," *Journal of Money, Credit, and Banking*, Vol. 20, No. 1, February 1988, pp. 83–101.

Congress and the president might try to get the Fed to pursue other goals. The principal–agent view also fails to explain why Congress allows the Fed to be relatively independent through self-financing. Some economists suggest that the Fed may provide Congress with long-run benefits through self-financing. If self-financing gives the Fed an incentive to conduct more open market purchases, thereby expanding the money supply, the Treasury will collect more revenue that Congress can spend. Certainly, the vast expansion in the Fed's holdings of securities during and after the 2007–2009 financial crisis resulted in the Fed increasing its interest income, most of which it then provided to the Treasury.

Fed Independence

Usually, the political issue of Fed independence arises not because of disagreement over monetary policy or even over the role of the Fed in managing monetary policy but because of the public's negative reaction to Fed policy. An example is the introduction of legislation in Congress that would have directed the GAO to audit the Fed's monetary policy actions. This legislation resulted in part from the public reaction to the Fed's inability to increase the speed of the economy's recovery from the 2007–2009 recession. We now analyze the arguments for and against Fed independence.

Arguments for Fed Independence The main argument for Fed independence is that monetary policy—which affects inflation, interest rates, exchange rates, and economic growth—is too important and technical to be determined by politicians. Because of the frequency of elections, politicians may be shortsighted, concerned with short-term benefits without regard for potential long-term costs. In particular, the short-term desire of politicians to be reelected may clash with the country's long-term goal of low inflation. Therefore, the Fed cannot assume that the objectives of politicians reflect public sentiment. The public may well prefer that the experts at the Fed, rather than politicians, make monetary policy decisions.

Another argument for Fed independence is that complete control of the Fed by elected officials increases the likelihood of political business cycle fluctuations in the money supply and interest rates. Elected officials might pressure the Fed to assist the Treasury's borrowing efforts by buying government bonds, which would increase the money supply, lower interest rates, and fuel inflation. Government officials pressuring central banks to buy bonds has been the primary cause of inflation in many other countries. For example, the inability of Venezuela's government to sell bonds to private investors led it to force the Central Bank of Venezuela to buy them. The result was a great expansion of the money supply and an annual inflation rate forecast to rise above 1,000% in 2017.

Arguments Against Fed Independence The importance of monetary policy for the economy is also the main argument against central bank independence. Supporters of this argument believe that in a democracy, elected officials should make public policy. Because the public can hold elected officials responsible for an ineffective monetary policy, some economists and policymakers advocate giving the president and Congress more control over monetary policy. The counterargument to the view that monetary policy is too technical for elected officials is that national security and foreign policy also require sophisticated analysis and a long time horizon, and these functions are entrusted to elected officials. In addition, critics of Fed independence argue that placing the central bank under the control of elected officials could confer benefits by coordinating and integrating monetary policy with government taxing and spending policies.

Those who argue for greater congressional control make the case that the Fed has not always used its independence well. For example, some critics note that the Fed failed to assist the banking system during the economic contraction of the early 1930s. Another example that many critics cite is that Fed policies were too inflationary in the 1960s and 1970s. Finally, some analysts believe that the Fed ignored the housing market bubble in the early 2000s and then moved too slowly to contain the effects on the financial system when the bubble finally burst in 2006.

Concluding Remarks Economists and policymakers don't universally agree on the merits of Fed independence. Under the present system, however, the Fed's independence is not absolute, and so it sometimes satisfies one group of critics or another. In practice, debates focus on proposals to limit Fed independence in some respects, not to eliminate its formal independence. The extended debate over the Dodd-Frank Act gave critics of Fed independence the opportunity to have a number of proposals considered. In the end, though, there was support among a majority of Congress for only relatively minor changes to the Federal Reserve Act.

MAKING THE CONNECTION

End the Fed?

There have been a number of recent proposals for relatively minor changes to the Fed's structure, including removing bankers from the boards of the regional Federal Reserve Banks, redrawing the Federal Reserve district boundaries, having the president of the United States appoint the Reserve Bank presidents, and having the Government Accountability Office (GAO) audit the Fed's monetary policy actions. A few economists and policymakers would go much further than these reforms and urge that the Fed be abolished.

Some critics of the Fed doubt its legality. The U.S. Constitution does not explicitly give the federal government the authority to establish a central bank. This fact was part of the debate over the First and Second Banks of the United States in the early 1800s. Some of the opponents of those banks saw them as a means of exerting federal power over the states in a way that was not authorized by the Constitution. Many slaveholders in the South opposed the Second Bank of the United States partly because they feared that if the federal government claimed to have the power to establish a central bank, it might also claim to have the power to abolish slavery.

During the debate over the Federal Reserve Act in 1913, the issue of whether a central bank was constitutional was raised again. The standard argument in favor of the constitutionality of the Federal Reserve is that Article 1, Section 8 of the U.S. Constitution states that Congress has the power "To coin money [and] regulate the value thereof." Congress delegated this power to the Federal Reserve in the Federal Reserve Act. The federal courts have upheld the constitutionality of the Federal Reserve Act, notably in the 1929 case *Raichle v. Federal Reserve Bank of New York*.

Modern arguments against the Fed have usually been based not on its supposed unconstitutionality but on the issue of whether having an independent central bank is the best means of carrying out monetary policy. During 2012, former Texas Congressman Ron Paul ran for the Republican nomination for president and argued forcefully that the Federal Reserve should be abolished. His book *End the Fed* was a bestseller. Among the benefits he saw from abolishing the Fed were "stopping the business cycle, ending inflation, building prosperity for all Americans, and putting an end to the corrupt collaboration between government and banks." In addition to abolishing the Fed, Congressman Paul advocated a return to the gold standard and a move to 100% reserve banking, which would eliminate the need for deposit insurance because banks could make loans and other investments only by using their capital.

In the debate in Congress over the Dodd-Frank Act, calls to abolish the Fed did not gain much support. But several proposals to significantly restructure the Fed or reduce its independence were included in early versions of the bill. For example, drafts of the bill contained provisions that would have stripped the Fed of most of its supervisory authority over banks and that would have set up a new agency, in which the Fed would have no role, to monitor the stability of the financial system. These provisions did not survive in the final version of the Dodd-Frank Act that became law in 2010.

Even after passage of the Dodd-Frank Act, some economists and members of Congress remained unhappy with both the unusual policy measures the Fed had adopted during and after the financial crisis and the possibility that Fed actions had contributed to the slow recovery from the recession. Following up on a proposal by his father, former Congressman Ron Paul, Kentucky Senator Rand Paul introduced a bill to have the GAO audit the Fed's monetary policy actions, but the bill was defeated in early 2016. The Fed's defenders argue that far from contributing to the slow recovery from the recession, the Fed's policy actions kept the economy from spiraling down into depression and aided what would otherwise have been an even slower recovery. The Fed's defenders also argue that in the long run, reducing the Fed's independence would reduce the effectiveness of monetary policy.

Given the Fed's power and the fact that its officials are unelected, its role is likely to remain a subject of debate among economists and policymakers.

Sources: David Harrison, "Senate Defeats 'Audit the Fed' Bill," *Wall Street Journal*, January 12, 2016; and Ron Paul, *End the Fed*, New York: Grand Central Publishing, 2009.

See related problems 2.10 and 2.11 at the end of the chapter.

13.3 Central Bank Independence Outside the United States

LEARNING OBJECTIVE: Compare the extent of central bank independence in other countries.

The degree of central bank independence varies greatly from country to country, but when we compare the structure of the Fed with that of central banks in Canada, Europe, and Japan, some patterns emerge. First, in countries in which central bank board members serve fixed terms of office, none is as long as the 14-year term for Federal Reserve governors, implying nominally greater central bank independence in the United States. Second, in those other countries, the head of the central bank has a longer term of office than the 4-year term of office of the chair of the Board of Governors in the United States, implying somewhat greater political control in the United States. So, whether the Fed's structure makes it more or less independent of political control than are other central banks is unclear.

An independent central bank is free to pursue its goals without direct interference from other government officials and legislators. Most economists believe that an independent central bank can more freely focus on keeping inflation low. The European Central Bank is, in principle, quite independent, whereas the Bank of Japan and the Bank of England traditionally have been less independent.

The Bank of England

The Bank of England, founded in 1694 and one of the world's oldest central banks, obtained the power to set interest rates independently of the government in 1997. The government can overrule the Bank of England in "extreme circumstances," but to date it has not done so. The chancellor of the Exchequer (a position similar to the secretary of the Treasury in the United States) does, however, set the Bank of England's inflation target. Interest rate determination falls to the Monetary Policy Committee, whose nine members are the Bank of England's governor (the equivalent of the Fed's chair), three deputy governors, the Bank's chief economist, and four external economic experts named by the chancellor of the Exchequer. A member of the Treasury Department attends the Monetary Policy Committee meetings but does not vote. Monetary policy focuses on the *bank rate*—the rate the Bank of England pays commercial banks on their reserves.

The Bank of Japan

The Bank of Japan's Policy Board members include the governor, two deputy governors, and six outside members named by the cabinet and confirmed by the Diet, which is Japan's national legislature. While the government may send representatives to meetings of the policy board, it lacks a vote. The Ministry of Finance does, however, retain control over parts of the Bank of Japan's budget that are unrelated to monetary policy. The Bank of Japan Law, in force since April 1998, gives the Policy Board more autonomy to pursue price stability. In 2016, the Bank of Japan announced that it would begin buying exchange-traded funds (ETFs), provided that the firms included in the funds were "proactively making investments in physical and human capital." This step was intended to prod firms into increasing their spending, as the Japanese economy remained stuck in an extended period of slow growth. Some economists and policymakers in Japan were concerned that this policy went well beyond typical monetary policy actions and into the sphere of fiscal policy, which is usually the domain of the Japanese prime minister and Diet. These observers were concerned that such actions might undermine the Bank of Japan's independence.

The Bank of Canada

The Bank of Canada has an inflation target as a goal for monetary policy, but that target is set jointly by the Bank of Canada and the government. While since 1967, the government has had the final responsibility for monetary policy, the Bank of Canada has generally controlled monetary policy. The finance minister can direct the bank's action, but such direction must be written and public, and none has been issued up to this time. In 2016, Bank of Canada Governor Stephen Poloz argued that while there was a need to coordinate the government's monetary and fiscal policies to help increase the growth rate of the Canadian economy, such coordination could be achieved without undermining the independence of the Bank of Canada.

The European Central Bank

As part of the move toward economic integration in Europe, the European Central Bank (ECB) is charged with conducting monetary policy for the 19 countries that participate in the European Monetary Union, or eurozone, and use the euro as their common currency. Representatives of many European nations signed an important agreement in Maastricht, the Netherlands, in December 1991. This agreement detailed a gradual approach to monetary union, which formally began on January 1, 1999.

The ECB's organization is in some respects similar to that of the U.S. Fed. The ECB's executive board, chaired in 2016 by Mario Draghi, who serves as president of the ECB, has six members. Board members (the president, a vice president, and four others) are appointed by the heads of state and government, based on the recommendation of the Council of Ministers of Economics and Finance, after consulting the European Parliament and the Governing Council of the ECB. Executive board members serve nonrenewable eight-year terms. Also participating in the governance of the ECB are the governors of each of the member national central banks; the governors of the national central banks serve terms of at least five years. The long terms of office are designed to increase the political independence of the ECB.

In principle, the ECB has a high degree of overall independence, with a clear mandate to emphasize price stability, and it is free from interference by the European Union or national governments in the conduct of policy. Moreover, the ECB's charter can be changed only by changing the Maastricht Treaty, which would require the agreement of all the countries that signed the original treaty. Whether legal independence is enough to guarantee actual independence is another matter, however. Based on the historical experience of the Federal Reserve, there may be cause for concern about the ECB. The decentralized central banking system envisioned in the original Federal Reserve Act of 1913 led to power struggles within the system and offered no mechanism to achieve consensus during the financial crisis of the early 1930s. National central banks have considerable power in the ECB. The governors of the European System of Central Banks

(ESCB) hold a majority of votes in the ECB's governing council. And national central banks collectively have a much larger staff than the ECB.

The European Central Bank has a complicated mission. Unlike the Fed, the Bank of England, or the Bank of Japan, which each conduct monetary policy for a single country, the ECB is responsible for the monetary policy of the 19 sovereign countries that use the euro as their currency. The 2007–2009 financial crisis and the recession that accompanied it affected these 19 countries to different extents. Even before euro coins and paper currency were introduced in 2002, some economists voiced doubts that a single currency controlled by one central bank could work, given the differences among the economies of the countries participating. Typically, during a recession, a country's central bank can pursue an expansionary policy that is as aggressive as might be needed. But during the 2007–2009 recession, the 19 countries that are part of the European Monetary Union had to rely on the ECB and were not able to pursue independent policies.

Europe experienced an extended period of slow growth following the 2007–2009 recession. In 2016, the ECB responded with aggressive monetary policy actions that led to negative interest rates on some government bonds. This result led to criticism from some policymakers in eurozone countries. For example, in Germany, both economic growth and employment were much higher than for the eurozone as a whole, and some German policymakers were critical of the ECB's policies. The German finance minister argued that the very low interest rates savers in Germany were receiving as a result of the ECB's policy had helped increase support for extremist parties. Some observers wondered whether the ECB's independence might ultimately be at stake if sharp differences in opinion persisted across eurozone policymakers.

The ECB also struggled with problems related to *sovereign debt*, or bonds issued by governments. The severe recession of 2007–2009 had hit some eurozone countries, including Portugal, Ireland, Greece, and Spain, much harder than others. These countries suffered from large government budget deficits as tax revenues declined and government spending increased. To finance the deficits, these governments had to issue bonds. By the spring of 2010, Greece had issued so many bonds that private investors began to doubt that Greece could afford to continue making the interest payments on this debt. Doubts also arose about debt issued by Ireland, Spain, and Portugal. The resulting *sovereign debt crisis* posed a dilemma for the ECB: It could intervene to buy some of the debt, but doing so might further increase the amount of liquidity in the European financial system, raising expectations of higher future inflation. In addition, buying debt might be seen as approving the poor budgetary policies of some of these governments, thereby increasing moral hazard.

Despite objections, then ECB President Jean-Claude Trichet began buying sovereign debt in May 2010. Trichet argued that the intervention was necessary to ensure that the affected governments would still be able to raise funds by selling bonds, and to protect the solvency of European banks that had purchased large amounts of these government bonds. The action resulted in considerable controversy, however. Nevertheless, Trichet's successor, Mario Draghi, expanded the buying program in an attempt to contain the sovereign debt crisis and ensure the stability of the European banking system. Although in 2016, the sovereign debt crisis appeared to be contained, whether the European experiment of a single currency and a single central bank would ultimately be successful remained in question.

Conclusions on Central Bank Independence

Although in most high-income countries, the central bank is insulated to some extent from the political process, in practice, the degree of independence in the conduct of monetary policy varies across countries. What conclusions should we draw from differences in central bank structure? Many analysts believe that an independent central bank improves the economy's performance by lowering inflation without raising output or employment fluctuations. As we saw in Chapter 2, a study by Alberto Alesina and Lawrence Summers found that the countries with the most independent central banks had the lowest average rates of inflation during the 1970s and 1980s. The countries with much less independent central banks had significantly higher rates of inflation.

What constitutes meaningful central bank independence? Economists emphasize that declarations by a government that the country's central bank is independent are insufficient. The central bank must be able to conduct policy without direct interference from the government. The central bank also must be able to set goals for which it can be held accountable. The leading example of such a goal is a target for inflation. Central banks in Canada, Finland, New Zealand, Sweden, and the United Kingdom have official inflation targets, as does the European Central Bank. After years of debate, the Fed followed these other central banks by adopting an inflation target of 2% in 2012.

ANSWERING THE KEY QUESTION

Continued from page 429

At the beginning of this chapter, we asked:

"Should Congress and the president have greater authority over the Federal Reserve?"

As we have seen in this chapter, almost since the founding of the Fed, economists and policymakers have debated how independent the Fed should be from the rest of the government. In 1913, the Federal Reserve Act placed the secretary of the Treasury and the comptroller of the currency—both presidential appointees—on the Federal Reserve Board, making the secretary of the Treasury the board's chair. In 1935, Congress removed these officials from the board to increase the Fed's independence. During the debate over financial reform in 2010, Congress seriously considered proposals that would have significantly reduced the Fed's independence, although these proposals were not included in the final version of the Dodd-Frank Act. During the 2016 presidential campaign, changes to the Fed's structure were again debated. Given its importance in the financial system, economists and policymakers will continue to debate the merits of the Fed's independence.

Key Terms and Problems

Key Terms

Board of Governors, p. 437

Federal Open Market Committee (FOMC), p. 438

Federal Reserve Bank, p. 432

Federal Reserve System, p. 431

Political business cycle, p. 447

Principal–agent view, p. 447

Public interest view, p. 446

Wall Street Reform and Consumer Protection Act (Dodd-Frank Act), p. 443

13.1 **The Structure of the Federal Reserve System**
Explain why the Federal Reserve System is structured the way it is.

Review Questions

1.1 Why did the United States have no central bank between 1836 and 1913? Why did Congress decide to establish the Federal Reserve System in 1913?

1.2 Why was the Federal Reserve System split into 12 districts?

1.3 Which body is more important within the Federal Reserve System: the Board of Governors or the Federal Open Market Committee? Briefly explain.

1.4 What changes did the Dodd-Frank Act make to the Fed?

Problems and Applications

1.5 Thomas Hoenig, former president of the Federal Reserve Bank of Kansas City, remarked about the Federal Reserve System: "It was designed as a public–private partnership, accountable to, and yet independent of, the government."

a. In what sense is the Federal Reserve System a "public–private partnership"?

b. In what sense is the Federal Reserve System both accountable to the government and independent of it?

Source: Thomas M. Hoenig, "Twelve Banks: The Strength of the Federal Reserve System," speech delivered at Copper Mountain, Colorado, September 15, 2006.

1.6 According to economist Allan Meltzer of Carnegie Mellon University, who has written about the history of the Federal Reserve:

Tension between the [Federal Reserve] Board and the reserve banks began before the System opened for business.... [Paul] Warburg described the problem. Dominance by the Board would allow political considerations to dominate decisions about interest rates. Dominance by the reserve banks "would ... reduce the Board to a position of impotence."

Paul Warburg was one of President Wilson's initial appointments when the Federal Reserve Board began operations in 1914.

a. Why did Congress set up a system that had this tension between the Federal Reserve Banks and the Federal Reserve Board?

b. Has the tension been resolved in the modern Fed? If so, how?

Source: Allan H. Meltzer, *A History of the Federal Reserve, Volume I: 1913–1951*, Chicago: University of Chicago Press, 2003, 75.

1.7 David Wheelock of the Federal Reserve Bank of St. Louis describes the following episode at the beginning of the Great Depression:

Following the stock market crash [of October 1929], the Federal Reserve Bank of New York used open market purchases [of Treasury securities] and liberal discount window lending [to commercial banks] to inject reserves into the banking system.... The Federal Reserve Board reluctantly approved the New York Fed's actions ex post, but many

---

 MyEconLab   Visit **www.myeconlab.com** to complete these exercises online and get instant feedback. Exercises that update with real-time data are marked with 🌐 .

members expressed displeasure that the New York Fed had acted independently.

a. What are the arguments for and against a Federal Reserve Bank operating independently?

b. In the modern Fed, would it be possible for a Federal Reserve Bank to act as the New York Fed did in 1929?

Source: David C. Wheelock, "Lessons Learned? Comparing the Federal Reserve's Responses to the Crises of 1929–1933 and 2007–2009," Federal Reserve Bank of St. Louis *Review*, Vol. 92, No. 2, March/April 2010, pp. 97–98.

1.8 **[Related to the** Making the Connection **on page 433]** Suppose Congress were to amend the Federal Reserve Act and set up a new commission to re-examine the Federal Reserve district boundaries. What considerations should the commission use in drawing the boundaries? Would the boundaries likely be much different than the original boundaries? Does it matter as much today as it did in 1914 where the district boundaries lie? Briefly explain.

1.9 **[Related to** Solved Problem 13.1 **on page 436]** Suppose that Bank of America pays a 2% annual interest rate on checking account balances while having to meet a reserve requirement of 10%. Assume that the Fed pays Bank of America an interest rate of 0.50% on its holdings of reserves and that Bank of America can earn 7% on its loans and other investments.

a. How do reserve requirements affect the amount that Bank of America can earn on $1,000 in checking account deposits? Ignore any costs Bank of America incurs on the deposits other than the interest it pays to depositors.

b. Is the opportunity cost to banks of reserve requirements likely to be higher during a period of high inflation or during a period of low inflation? Briefly explain.

1.10 **[Related to the** Making the Connection **on page 439]** What is the purpose of the Government in the Sunshine Act? In your opinion, was Fed Chairman Bernanke justified in evading the requirements of this act during the financial crisis of 2007–2009? Briefly explain.

1.11 **[Related to the** Chapter Opener **on page 429]** Defending the presence of bankers on the boards of directors of the Federal Reserve Banks, Jeffrey Lacker, president of the Federal Reserve Bank of Richmond argued: "This hybrid governance model has come to play an important role in the independence of monetary policy…. Political independence allows monetary policy to place greater weight on the long-term benefits of low and stable inflation."

a. What does Lacker mean by a "hybrid governance model"?

b. Why might a politically independent Fed give greater weight to low and stable inflation than Congress and the president would if they controlled monetary policy directly?

Source: Jeffrey M. Lacker, "The Fed-Bank Relationship Under Scrutiny," Federal Reserve Bank of Richmond *Econ Focus*, Fourth Quarter 2015, 1.

1.12 **[Related to the** Making the Connection **on page 442]** A Federal Reserve document states: "Due to concerns about potential conflicts of interest … Class A directors may not participate in most aspects of the appointment process of Reserve Bank presidents and first vice presidents."

a. Who are the Class A directors?

b. What potential conflicts of interest is this document referring to?

c. If there is a conflict of interest in the governance structure of the Federal Reserve Banks, why did Congress establish this structure when it passed the Federal Reserve Act in 1913?

Source: Board of Governors of the Federal Reserve System, "Directors—Appointment of Reserve Bank Presidents and Vice Presidents," federalreserve.gov/aboutthefed/directors/PDF/appointment-of-reserve-bank-presidents-first-vice-presidents.pdf.

13.2 **How the Fed Operates**
Explain the Fed's relationship to the government and the arguments for and against its independence.

Review Questions

2.1 In what ways is the Fed subject to external pressure?

2.2 What are the major differences between the public interest view of the Fed's motivation and the principal–agent view? How are these views connected to the theory of the political business cycle?

2.3 Briefly discuss the main arguments for and against the Fed's independence.

Problems and Applications

2.4 In the first volume of his history of the Federal Reserve System, Allan Meltzer titled one of his chapters "Under Treasury Control, 1942–1951." Why would Meltzer have considered the Fed to have been under Treasury control during those years?
Source: Allan H. Meltzer, *A History of the Federal Reserve, Volume I: 1913–1951*, Chicago: University of Chicago Press, 2003, Ch. 7.

2.5 At a hearing before a committee of the House of Representatives, former Fed Chairman Ben Bernanke was asked about legislation that would direct the GAO to audit the Fed's monetary policy actions. He replied:

> The term "audit the Fed" is deceptive. The public thinks that auditing means checking the books, looking at the financial statements, making sure that you're not doing special deals, and that kind of thing. All of those things are (already) completely open.… .
>
> The nightmare scenario I have is one in which some future Fed chairman would decide to raise the federal funds rate by 25 basis points, and somebody in this room would say, "I don't like that decision. I want the GAO to go in and get all the records, get all the transcripts, get all the

preparatory materials and give us an independent opinion on whether or not that was the right decision."

Why would the situation Bernanke is describing be a "nightmare scenario"? Wouldn't it be good to have the GAO give an independent opinion on whether a particular monetary policy action was the right decision?
Source: Board of Governors of the Federal Reserve System, "Testimony of Chairman Ben S. Bernanke before the House Financial Services Committee, July 18, 2012."

2.6 Evaluate the following statement: "Because the Fed does not have to ask Congress for money to fund its operations, the principal–agent view of the Fed's motivation cannot be correct."

2.7 Look again at the *Making the Connection* "St. Louis and Kansas City? What Explains the Locations of the District Banks?" on page 433 in Section 13.1. Are Michael McAvoy's and David Wheelock's explanations of how the Federal Reserve Bank cities were selected more consistent with a public interest view of how the decision was made or a principal–agent view? Briefly explain.

2.8 In his memoirs, former Fed Chairman Ben Bernanke discussed the reaction of the Federal Reserve Bank presidents to a congressional proposal that the Reserve Banks no longer be responsible for supervising state banks that were members of the Federal Reserve System:

> The Reserve Bank presidents were particularly alarmed at the prospect of losing bank supervision duties…. The [Reserve] banks had already endured rounds of staff layoffs over the previous decade as many of the Federal Reserve's financial services, such as check clearing, were consolidated into fewer locations…. [A] large proportion of their remaining employees examined and supervised banks and bank holding companies.

Are the positions of the Reserve Bank presidents during this episode better explained by the public interest view of Fed motivation or by the principal–agent view? Briefly explain.

Source: Ben S. Bernanke, *The Courage to Act: A Memoir of a Crisis and Its Aftermath*, New York: W.W. Norton, 2015, p. 458.

2.9 Fed Chair Janet Yellen was quoted in an article in the *Wall Street Journal* as asserting: "Academic studies establish beyond a shadow of a doubt that independent central banks perform better." What did Yellen likely mean by "perform better"? Why would a central bank that is independent be expected to perform better?

Source: David Harrison, "Senate Defeats 'Audit the Fed' Bill," *Wall Street Journal*, January 12, 2016.

2.10 [Related to the Making the Connection on page 449] When Kentucky Senator Rand Paul was running for the 2016 Republican presidential nomination,

an article in the *New York Times* noted: "Mr. Paul opposes the Federal Reserve's control of the money supply and interest rates, suggesting that such powers should be exercised by Congress." Why does Congress directly control fiscal policy—the federal government's decisions with respect to spending and taxes—but delegate the authority over monetary policy to the Federal Reserve?

Source: "Rand Paul on the Issues," *New York Times*, April 7, 2015.

2.11 [Related to the Making the Connection on page 449] Suppose that the U.S. Constitution were amended to include the following: "Congress shall establish a central bank that will be responsible for conducting the monetary policy of the United States." What effect would such an amendment be likely to have on the Fed?

13.3 Central Bank Independence Outside the United States
Compare the extent of central bank independence in other countries.

Review Questions

3.1 Compare the length of terms of office for central bank heads and members of central bank governing boards between the U.S. Federal Reserve and foreign central banks.

3.2 What is the main problem with having a central bank that is not independent of the rest of the government?

3.3 How is the European Central Bank organized? What special problems does it confront? What difficulties did it encounter during the financial crisis of 2007–2009 and the subsequent sovereign debt crisis?

Problems and Applications

3.4 Is it easier for a central bank to be independent in a high-income country or in a low-income country? What implications does your answer have for what the average inflation rate is likely

to be in high-income countries as opposed to low-income countries?

3.5 On its web site, the European Central Bank (ECB) states:

> The European Central Bank and the national central banks together constitute the Eurosystem, the central banking system of the euro area. The main objective of the Eurosystem is to maintain price stability: safeguarding the value of the euro.

The Federal Reserve, in contrast, has a dual mandate of both price stability and high employment. Why might a single objective of price stability be easier for the ECB to fulfill, given its circumstances?

Source: European Central Bank, "ECB Mission," ecb.europa.eu/ecb/orga/escb/ecb-mission/html/index.en.html.

3.6 In 2015, the Bank of Japan announced that it would begin buying exchange-traded funds

(ETFs), provided that the stocks included in the funds had been issued by firms that were "proactively making investments in physical and human capital." The Japanese government had been urging firms to increase their investment spending. An editorial in the *Wall Street Journal* observed: "Using the central bank's powers to promote the government's political goals also runs the risk of misallocating resources, which would harm growth. It sets a precedent that could undermine the bank's independence." Briefly explain whether you agree that these actions by the Bank of Japan might undermine its independence.

Source: "The Bank of Japan Lays an Egg," *Wall Street Journal*, December 20, 2015.

3.7 Adam Posen, then a member of the Bank of England's Monetary Policy Committee, was characterized as arguing in a speech that:

> Central banks' purchases of government debt … far from undermining their independence … should enhance their credibility…. Mr. Posen said, … "What matters for

our independence is our ability to say no and to mean it, and to be responsible about when we choose to say yes."

a. Why might purchasing government debt be seen as undermining a central bank's independence?

b. Why might a central bank sometimes want to say "no" to suggestions that it purchase government debt? Why might it sometimes want to say "yes"?

Source: Natasha Brereton, "BOE's Posen Defends ECB's Actions," *Wall Street Journal*, June 15, 2010.

3.8 A representative of the Treasury Department is present at every meeting of the Bank of England's Monetary Policy Committee. The representative can participate in the discussion but is not allowed to vote. In the United States, no member of the Treasury Department is present during meetings of the Federal Open Market Committee. What are the advantages and disadvantages of the British approach compared with the U.S. approach?

Data Exercises

D13.1: [The ECB and differences among European economies] Go to the web site of the Federal Reserve Bank of St. Louis (FRED) (fred. stlouisfed.org) and download and graph the growth rate for real GDP in Greece (GRCG-DPRQPSMEI) from the first quarter of 2000 to the most recent quarter available. On the same graph download the growth rate for real GDP in Germany (NAEXKP01DEQ1895) for the same period. Note that to add the data for Germany to the graph for Greece, you will first need to click on "Edit Graph," the click on "Add Data Series." When you

find the data series for real GDP for Germany, you will need to change the units to "Percentage Change from Year Ago." Briefly compare movements in the two series. What challenges do these movements in real GDP pose for the European Central Bank (ECB)?

D13.2: [The ECB and the sovereign debt crisis] Go to sdw. ecb.europa.eu and select "Government Debt (as a % of GDP)." What is the current eurozone debt/GDP ratio? What is the deficit/GDP ratio? What challenges do the deficit and debt data pose for the European Central Bank (ECB)?

CHAPTER 14

The Federal Reserve's Balance Sheet and the Money Supply Process

Learning Objectives

After studying this chapter, you should be able to:

14.1 Explain the relationship between the Fed's balance sheet and the monetary base (pages 462–470)

14.2 Derive the equation for the simple deposit multiplier and use T-accounts to illustrate multiple deposit expansion (pages 470–474)

14.3 Explain how the actions of banks and the nonbank public affect the money multiplier (pages 474–486)

14.A Appendix: Describe the money supply process for M2 (page 492–493)

Gold: The Perfect Hedge Against Economic Chaos?

In disaster movies and television shows, when civilization breaks down, the people who were smart enough to hide away a stash of gold coins or gold bars are usually the ones who survive.

After all, throughout history people have valued gold, and with the economy collapsing, who would sell anything for paper money? But what about a less cataclysmic event, such as the 2007–2009 financial crisis or Great Britain's vote in 2016 to leave the European Union ("Brexit"), which caused some people to be concerned about the international financial system? During uncertain financial times like these, many people see gold as a safe haven. But is it?

At one time, gold was the basis for the money supply in the United States and other high-income countries, but that is no longer the case. The United States left the gold standard in 1933 and stopped minting gold coins as currency. The U.S. Mint still produces gold coins that commemorate famous people and historical events, but collectors buy most of these coins. Some people are interested in gold coins as an investment, so the Mint also produces American Eagle Bullion coins. Beginning in 2008, as the financial crisis was at its worst, those coins were very hot. Sales of the 1-ounce American Eagle gold coin soared to more than 10 times the pre-crisis levels. BullionVault, a web-based

Continued on next page

KEY ISSUE AND QUESTION

Issue: Years after the end of the financial crisis of 2007–2009, banks continued to hold record levels of reserves.

Question: Why did bank reserves increase rapidly during and after the financial crisis of 2007–2009, and should policymakers be concerned about the increase?

Answered on page 486

company that sells investors title to gold bars stored in underground vaults in New York, London, and Zurich, reported very strong sales. There was a similar surge in gold buying in 2016, following Brexit. BullionVault experienced record sales, including many purchases from first-time investors. Although some investors like to have direct ownership of gold, other investors prefer to bet on gold indirectly by buying gold exchange-traded funds (ETFs). Gold ETFs can be bought and sold on financial markets and are designed to track the price of gold.

While some individual investors, known as "gold bugs," always want to hold gold, it wasn't just individual investors who were driving up the price of gold during these periods. Billionaire hedge fund managers George Soros and John Paulson invested in gold bullion and shares of stock in gold mining companies following the financial crisis. Soros is famous for having made more than $1 billion by betting against the value of the British pound in 1992. As you can imagine, his purchases of gold attracted the interest of many investors. Paulson, who had made billions during 2007 and 2008 by betting on a fall in housing prices, made an additional

$5 billion in profits in 2010 from an increase in gold prices. But while gold prices increased over most of the period from late 2008 through the end of 2012, they fell sharply during 2013, causing substantial losses for Paulson and other hedge fund managers who were betting on gold. However, gold prices began to rise again in 2016, and some hedge fund managers, including Soros, and many individual investors returned to buying gold.

Why the great interest in gold as an investment? The motives of investors differ, but many see it as a safe haven during times of economic uncertainty, particularly when they fear that inflation may rise. For instance, in many countries, including the United States, the money supply increased rapidly following the financial crisis, and banks were holding record amounts of reserves. Even though inflation remained low through 2016, some investors predicted soaring inflation in the years to come and saw holding gold as the best way to hedge that risk.

In this chapter, we explore why the money supply in the United States has risen so rapidly, how significant the risk of rising inflation is, and historically how well gold has served as a hedge against inflation.

Sources: Ese Erheriene and Jasmine Horsey, "Gold Continues to Climb on Brexit Safe-Haven Demand," *Wall Street Journal*, June 27, 2016; Stephanie Yang, "The Big Bet of 2016: Joining George Soros in Gold," *Wall Street Journal*, June 9, 2016; Gregory Zuckerman and Juliet Chung, "Paulson: All That Glitters Isn't Gold," *Wall Street Journal*, June 7, 2013; "Store of Value," *Economist*, July 8, 2010; and U.S. Mint, *American Eagle Bullion Sales Totals*, August 2016.

Economists, policymakers, and investors are interested in the money supply because it can affect interest rates, exchange rates, the inflation rate, and the economy's output of goods and services. One of the responsibilities of the central bank—whether it is the European Central Bank, the Fed in the United States, the Bank of Japan, or the Bank of England—is to manage the money supply. To understand how a central bank manages the money supply, we need to analyze the factors that determine the money supply and how a central bank can increase or decrease the quantity of money in circulation. In this chapter, we construct a model that explains the size of the money supply and explains why the money supply fluctuates. How a country's money supply is created is called the *money supply process*. We devote this chapter to understanding the money supply process in the United States. We will see why bank reserves in the United States soared during the 2007–2009 financial crisis and remained very high years later.

14.1 The Federal Reserve's Balance Sheet and the Monetary Base

LEARNING OBJECTIVE: Explain the relationship between the Fed's balance sheet and the monetary base.

We begin our analysis of the money supply process by first describing the monetary base and then determining how the monetary base is linked to the money supply. Our model of how the money supply is determined includes the behavior of three groups:

1. The *Federal Reserve*, which is responsible for controlling the money supply and regulating the banking system.
2. The *banking system*, which creates the checking accounts that are the most important component of the M1 measure of the money supply.
3. The *nonbank public*, which refers to all households and firms other than banks. The nonbank public decides the form in which they wish to hold money—for instance, as currency or as checking account balances.

Monetary base (or high-powered money) The sum of bank reserves and currency in circulation.

Figure 14.1 represents the money supply process and shows which groups in the economy influence each variable in the process. This figure is the backbone of our analysis in this chapter. The process starts with the **monetary base**, which is also called **high-powered money**. The monetary base equals the amount of currency in circulation plus the reserves of the banking system:[1]

$$\text{Monetary base} = \text{Currency in circulation} + \text{Reserves of banks.}$$

As we will see, the Fed has good control of the monetary base. The money multiplier links the monetary base to the money supply. As long as the value of the money multiplier is stable, the Fed can control the money supply by controlling the monetary base.

Our model of the money supply process applies to the monetary aggregate, M1, which is the Fed's narrow measure of money. The chapter appendix expands the model of the money supply process to the broader measure of the money supply, M2.

FIGURE 14.1

The Money Supply Process

Three groups determine the money supply: the central bank (the Fed), the banking system, and the nonbank public.

Monetary Base

Determined by
The Fed

×

Money Multiplier

Determined by
The Fed
The Banking System
The Nonbank Public

=

Money Supply

---

[1] Note that the "reserves" component of the monetary base is technically called "reserve balances" and includes deposits at the Fed by some nonbank depository institutions, such as savings and loans.

The Federal Reserve's Balance Sheet

There is a close connection between the monetary base and the Fed's balance sheet, which lists the Fed's assets and liabilities. In Table 14.1, we show both the full Fed balance sheet and a simplified version that includes only the four entries that are most relevant to the Fed's actions in increasing and decreasing the monetary base. In most years, the Fed's most important assets are its holdings of U.S. Treasury securities—Treasury bills, notes, and bonds—and the discount loans it has made to banks. The financial crisis of 2007–2009 and the slow economic recovery that followed led the Fed to greatly expand its purchases of Treasury securities as it tried to reduce interest rates and spur spending by households and firms. In addition, the Fed purchased mortgage-backed securities guaranteed by Fannie Mae and Freddie Mac in an attempt to help revive the very weak housing market. The Fed participated in actions to save the investment bank Bear Stearns and the insurance company AIG from bankruptcy, and securities related to those actions remained on the Fed's books in 2016, although to a much smaller extent than in earlier years. The Fed has participated in liquidity swaps with foreign central banks and has accumulated substantial assets related to those swaps.

TABLE 14.1 The Federal Reserve's Balance Sheet

(a) Federal Reserve balance sheet, August 2016

Assets		Liabilities and Capital	
Securities		Currency in circulation	$1,418,599
U.S. Treasury securities	$2,463,447	Reverse repurchase agreements	323,693
Federal agency debt securities	22,492	Reserve balances of banks (including term deposits)	2,394,467
Mortgage-backed and other securities	1,916,806	Treasury deposits, General Account	241,426
Discount loans to banks	212	Deposits of foreign governments and international organizations, and other deposits	40,748
Gold	11,037	Deferred availability cash items	552
Bear Stearns–related holdings	1,707	Other liabilities	6,852
Items in the process of collection	221	Total liabilities	$4,426,337
Buildings	2,211		
Coins	1,930	Capital	$40,139
Central bank liquidity swaps	105		
Foreign currency denominated assets	21,627		
Other assets	24,681		
Total assets	$4,466,476	Total liabilities and capital	$4,466,476

(b) Simplified Federal Reserve balance sheet

Assets	Liabilities
U.S. Government securities	Currency in circulation
Discount loans to banks	Reserves of banks

Note: Values for panel (a) are in millions of dollars. Components may not sum to totals because of rounding.

Source for panel (a): *Federal Reserve Statistical Release H.4.1, Factors Affecting Reserve Balances of Depository Institutions and Condition Statement of Federal Reserve Banks*, August 18, 2016.

When economists, policymakers, or journalists refer to the "size of the Fed's balance sheet," they are typically referring to the value of the Fed's assets. In this sense, in August 2016, the size of the Fed's balance sheet was $4.5 trillion—five times as large as it was in December 2007, at the beginning of the 2007–2009 recession and financial crisis.

Panel (a) of Table 14.1 also shows that the Fed's main liabilities are currency in circulation and reserve balances of banks—or, simply, *reserves*. In its role as the government's bank, the Fed also holds deposits for the U.S. Treasury and for foreign governments and international agencies. As part of its open market operations, the Fed incurs a liability in the form of reverse repurchase agreements. Finally, the asset "Items in the process of collection" and the liability "Deferred availability cash items" relate to the Fed's role in check clearing.

Panel (b) of Table 14.1 strips out the detail from the Fed's balance sheet to focus on the two assets and two liabilities that are most directly involved in the Fed's actions to increase or decrease the monetary base.

The Monetary Base

Notice that the sum of currency in circulation and bank reserves, the Fed's two liabilities shown in panel (b) of Table 14.1, equals the monetary base. We are treating currency in circulation as the amount of paper currency printed by the Fed, or *Federal Reserve Notes*, that is circulating in the economy.[2] **Currency in circulation** includes currency held by banks, which is called **vault cash**. Currency held by the nonbank public (households and firms) is called **currency in M1**. It equals currency in circulation minus vault cash:

Currency in circulation Paper money circulating outside the Fed.

Vault cash Currency held by banks.

$$\text{Currency in M1} = \text{Currency in circulation} - \text{Vault cash}.$$

Currency in M1 Currency held by the nonbank public.

Reserve balances of banks on the Fed's balance sheet equal deposits by commercial banks with the Fed. But by law, vault cash is also included in **bank reserves**. If we subtract vault cash from currency in circulation and add it to bank deposits with the Fed, we have a more exact definition of the monetary base:

Bank reserves Bank deposits with the Fed plus vault cash.

$$\text{Monetary base} = \text{Currency in M1} + \text{Total reserves of banks},$$

where the last term is the sum of vault cash and bank deposits with the Fed. Hereafter, for simplicity, we will refer to the monetary base as being equal to currency plus reserves.

Reserve deposits are assets for banks, but they are liabilities for the Fed because banks can request that the Fed repay the deposits on demand with Federal Reserve Notes. The situation is analogous to your checking account's being an asset to you but a liability to the bank where you have your account.

---

[2] Technically, the monetary base also includes U.S. Treasury currency outstanding, which is primarily coins. Because the value of coins in circulation is small compared to the Fed's currency outstanding or to bank reserves, we will ignore it. The reserve balances shown on the Fed's balance sheet include deposits at the Fed by all depository institutions, whether or not they are commercial banks. For convenience, we assume that all of these depository institutions are commercial banks.

Total reserves are made up of the amounts that the Fed requires banks to hold, called **required reserves**, and the extra amounts that banks elect to hold, called **excess reserves**:

$$\text{Reserves} = \text{Required reserves} + \text{Excess reserves}.$$

The Fed specifies a percentage of checkable deposits that banks must hold as reserves, which is called the **required reserve ratio**. For example, if the required reserve ratio is 10%, a bank must set aside 10% of its checkable deposits as reserve deposits with the Fed or as vault cash. In October 2008, the Fed for the first time began paying interest to banks on their reserve accounts, although the interest rate is quite modest (0.75% in early 2017). Historically, banks have not held much in excess reserves. Since the financial crisis of 2007–2009, however, banks have been holding much greater excess reserves. The key reason seems to be that although the interest rate the Fed pays on reserves is low, the investment is risk free, and the interest rate is competitive with the returns on other safe short-term investments the banks can make. In addition, given the historically high level of uncertainty in the financial system, many banks have wanted to increase their liquidity.

How the Fed Changes the Monetary Base

The Fed increases or decreases the monetary base by changing the levels of its assets—that is, the Fed changes the monetary base by buying and selling Treasury securities or by making discount loans to banks.

Open Market Operations The most direct method the Fed uses to change the monetary base is **open market operations**, which involve buying or selling securities, generally U.S. Treasury securities. Open market operations are carried out by the Fed's trading desk, located at the Federal Reserve Bank of New York. Fed employees on the trading desk buy and sell securities electronically with *primary dealers*. In 2016, there were 23 primary dealers, which are commercial banks, investment banks, and securities dealers. Dealers that are not commercial banks keep their accounts with commercial banks, so we can think of open market operations as being carried out between the Fed and the banking system. In an **open market purchase**, the Fed buys Treasury securities, which raises the monetary base. Suppose the Fed buys $1 million worth of Treasury bills from Wells Fargo. Wells Fargo electronically transfers ownership of the bills to the Fed, and the Fed pays for them by depositing $1 million in Wells Fargo's reserve account at the Fed.

We can illustrate the effect of the Fed's open market purchase by using a *T-account*, which is a stripped-down version of a balance sheet. We will use T-accounts to show only how a transaction *changes* a balance sheet. Although in our example, the Fed purchased securities from only one bank, in practice, the Fed typically buys securities from multiple banks at the same time. So, we use a T-account for the whole banking system to show the results of the Fed's open market purchase: The banking system's balance sheet shows a decrease in security holdings of $1 million and an increase in reserves of the same amount (note that the banking system's balance sheet

Required reserves
Reserves that the Fed requires banks to hold.

Excess reserves Reserves that banks hold over and above those the Fed requires them to hold.

Required reserve ratio The percentage of checkable deposits that the Fed specifies that banks must hold as reserves.

Open market operations The Federal Reserve's purchases and sales of securities, usually U.S. Treasury securities, in financial markets.

Open market purchase The Federal Reserve's purchase of securities, usually U.S. Treasury securities.

simply adds together the assets and liabilities of all the commercial banks in the United States):

BANKING SYSTEM

Assets		Liabilities
Securities	−$1 million	
Reserves	+$1 million	

We can use another T-account to show the changes in the Fed's balance sheet. The Fed's holdings of securities (an asset) increase by $1 million, and bank reserve deposits (a liability) also increase by $1 million:

FEDERAL RESERVE

Assets		Liabilities	
Securities	+$1 million	Reserves	+$1 million

The Fed's open market purchase from Wells Fargo increases reserves by $1 million and, therefore, the monetary base increases by $1 million. A key point is that *the monetary base increases by the dollar amount of an open market purchase.*

Open market sale The Fed's sale of securities, usually Treasury securities.

Similarly, the Fed can reduce the monetary base through an **open market sale** of Treasury securities. For example, suppose the Fed sells $1 million of Treasury securities to Barclays Bank. The Fed transfers the securities to Barclays, and Barclays pays with funds in its reserve account. As a result, the banking system's holdings of securities increase by $1 million, and its reserves fall by $1 milliion:

BANKING SYSTEM

Assets		Liabilities
Securities	+$1 million	
Reserves	−$1 million	

The Fed's holdings of securities decrease by $1 million, as do bank reserves:

FEDERAL RESERVE

Assets		Liabilities	
Securities	−$1 million	Reserves	−$1 million

Because reserves have fallen by $1 million, so has the U.S. monetary base. We can conclude that *the monetary base decreases by the dollar amount of an open market sale.*

As we will see, a key role the nonbank public plays in the money supply process is deciding how much currency it wishes to hold relative to checkable deposits. However, the public's preference for currency relative to checkable deposits does not affect the monetary base. To see why, consider what happens if households and firms decide to withdraw $1 million from their checking accounts. The following T-account shows the change in the balance sheet of the nonbank public (note that the nonbank public's balance sheet simply adds together the assets and liabilities of all of the households and firms in the United States):

NONBANK PUBLIC

Assets		Liabilities
Checkable deposits	−$1 million	
Currency	+$1 million	

As the banking system withdraws $1 million from its reserves at the Fed to provide the currency to households and firms, the banking system's balance sheet changes as follows:

BANKING SYSTEM

Assets		Liabilities	
Reserves	−$1 million	Checkable deposits	−$1 million

The Fed's balance sheet also changes as currency in circulation increases, while bank reserves fall:

FEDERAL RESERVE

Assets		Liabilities	
		Currency in circulation	+$1 million
		Reserves	−$1 million

Notice that although one component of the monetary base (reserves) has fallen by $1 million, the other component (currency in circulation) has risen by $1 million. So, the monetary base is unaffected. This result is important because it means that the Fed can increase and decrease the monetary base through open market operations without the changes being affected by how much currency the nonbank public wishes to hold relative to checkable deposits.

Discount Loans Although the Fed typically uses open market operations in managing the monetary base, it can also increase or decrease reserves by making **discount loans** to commercial banks. This change in bank reserves changes the monetary base.

Suppose that the Fed increases its discount loans to banks by $1 million. The Fed provides the funds to the banks by increasing their reserve accounts. For the Fed, assets rise by $1 million from the additional discount loans, and liabilities rise by $1 million from the additional bank reserves. So, the increase in discount loans affects both sides of the Fed's balance sheet:

Discount loan A loan made by the Federal Reserve, typically to a commercial bank.

FEDERAL RESERVE

Assets		Liabilities	
Discount loans	+$1 million	Reserves	+$1 million

Both sides of the banking system's balance sheet are also affected. Banks increase their assets by $1 million in the form of reserves and increase their liabilities by $1 million in the form of discount loans payable to the Fed:

BANKING SYSTEM

Assets		Liabilities	
Reserves	+$1 million	Discount loans	+$1 million

As a result of the Fed's making $1 million of discount loans, bank reserves and the monetary base increase by $1 million.

If banks repay $1 million in discount loans to the Fed, reducing the total amount of discount loans, the preceding transactions are reversed. Discount loans fall by $1 million, as do reserves and the monetary base:

FEDERAL RESERVE

Assets		Liabilities	
Discount loans	−$1 million	Reserves	−$1 million

BANKING SYSTEM

Assets		Liabilities	
Reserves	−$1 million	Discount loans	−$1 million

Comparing Open Market Operations and Discount Loans

Although open market operations and discount loans both change the monetary base, the Fed has greater control over open market operations than over discount loans. The Fed completely controls the volume of open market operations because it initiates purchases or sales of securities by having the trading desk at the New York Fed place orders with the primary dealers. The Fed is willing to buy and sell securities at whatever price is needed to carry out its open market operations successfully.

Discount rate The interest rate the Federal Reserve charges on discount loans.

The Fed's control over discount lending is much less complete than its control over open market operations because banks decide whether to borrow from the Fed. The Fed has some control over discount loans because it sets the **discount rate**, which is the interest rate the Fed charges on discount loans. In fact, the discount rate differs from most interest rates because it is set by the Fed, whereas most interest rates are determined by demand and supply in financial markets.

As a result of the difference between the Fed's control over open market operations and its control over discount loans, economists think of the monetary base as having two components: the nonborrowed monetary base, B_{non}, and borrowed reserves, BR, which is another name for discount loans. We can express the monetary base, B, as:

$$B = B_{non} + BR.$$

Although decisions by both the Fed and banks determine the volume of discount loans, the Fed by itself can control the nonborrowed monetary base.

MAKING THE CONNECTION

Explaining the Explosion in the Monetary Base

As the following graph shows, the monetary base increased sharply in the fall of 2008, doubling between September and the end of December. The base remained at high levels through the fall of 2016. The graph also shows that reserves, which had made up only about 5% of the monetary base before the financial crisis began, made up more than 50% by the spring of 2009. In fact, more than 80% of the increase in the monetary base occurred because of an increase in the bank reserves component rather than in the currency in circulation component.

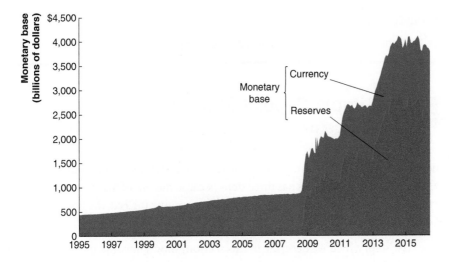

MyEconLab Real-time data

We have seen that the Fed has the ability through open market purchases of Treasury securities to increase bank reserves and, thereby, the monetary base. Typically, then, a large increase in the monetary base means that the Fed has made large purchases of Treasury bills and other Treasury securities. In this case, though, the Fed's holdings of Treasury securities actually *fell* while the base was exploding. The Fed held $779 billion in Treasury securities of all types in January 2007 but only $475 billion in January 2009. The Fed's holdings of Treasury bills plunged from $277 billion in January 2007 to only $18 billion in January 2009.

So the increase in the monetary base was not a result of typical open market purchases. Instead, the increase reflected the Fed's innovative policy measures. As the Fed began to purchase mortgage-backed securities, commercial paper, and assets connected with the investment bank Bear Stearns and the insurance company AIG, the asset side of its balance sheet expanded, and so did the monetary base. There is an important lesson from this episode for understanding the mechanics of increases in the monetary base: *Whenever the Fed purchases assets of any kind, the monetary base increases.* It doesn't matter if the assets are Treasury bills, mortgage-backed securities, or computer systems. For instance, if the Federal Reserve Bank of Dallas buys a computer system from a local information technology company for $10 million, it will pay for the computers with a check. When the company deposits the check into the company's bank, the bank will send the check to the Fed, which will increase the bank's reserves by $10 million. The result is an increase in the monetary base of $10 million. If the computer company decided to cash the check, the result would be the same: Currency in circulation would rise by $10 million, while the reserves of the computer company's bank would be unchanged, so the monetary base would still rise by $10 million.

When in the fall of 2008, the Fed began to purchase hundreds of billions of dollars' worth of mortgage-backed securities and other financial assets, it was inevitable that the monetary base would increase.

Sources: Federal Reserve Bank of St. Louis; and William T. Galvin, "More Money: Understanding Recent Changes in the Monetary Base," *Federal Reserve Bank of St. Louis Review*, Vol. 91, No. 2, March/April 2009, pp. 49–59.

See related problems 1.6 and 1.7 at the end of the chapter.

14.2 The Simple Deposit Multiplier

LEARNING OBJECTIVE: Derive the equation for the simple deposit multiplier and use T-accounts to illustrate multiple deposit expansion.

We now turn to the money multiplier to further understand the factors that determine the money supply. Our analysis has three steps because the size of the money multiplier is determined by the actions of three groups in the economy: the Fed, the nonbank public, and banks:

- The first step, which we describe in this section, shows how the money supply can be increased or decreased through a process called *multiple deposit expansion*. In this part of the analysis, we determine the *simple deposit multiplier*.
- The second step shows how the actions of the nonbank public affect the money multiplier.
- The third step incorporates the actions of banks.

We cover the second and third steps in Section 14.3.

Multiple Deposit Expansion

What happens to the money supply when the Fed increases bank reserves through an open market purchase? To answer this question, we first analyze the changes that occur at a single bank and then look at the changes for the whole banking system.

How a Single Bank Responds to an Increase in Reserves Suppose that the Fed purchases $100,000 in Treasury bills (or T-bills) from Wells Fargo, increasing Wells Fargo's reserves by $100,000. We can use a T-account to show how Wells Fargo's balance sheet changes to reflect these transactions:

WELLS FARGO

Assets		Liabilities
Securities	−$100,000	
Reserves	+$100,000	

The Fed's purchase of T-bills from Wells Fargo increases the bank's excess reserves but not its required reserves. Required reserves don't increase because they are determined as a percentage of the bank's checkable deposits, and because this transaction has no immediate effect on Wells Fargo's checkable deposits, it doesn't change the amount of reserves the bank is required to hold. Wells Fargo earns only a low interest rate from the

Fed on the additional reserves obtained from the T-bill sale and therefore has an incentive to loan out or invest these funds.

Suppose that Wells Fargo loans $100,000 to Rosie's Bakery to enable it to buy two new ovens. We will assume that Wells Fargo makes the loan by creating a checking account for Rosie's and depositing the $100,000 principal of the loan in it. Both the asset and liability sides of Wells Fargo's balance sheet increase by $100,000:

WELLS FARGO

Assets		Liabilities	
Securities	−$100,000	Checkable deposits	+$100,000
Reserves	+$100,000		
Loans	+$100,000		

Recall that the money supply—using the M1 definition—equals currency plus checkable deposits. By lending money to Rosie's, Wells Fargo creates checkable deposits and, therefore, increases the money supply. Suppose that Rosie's then spends the loan proceeds by writing a check for $100,000 to buy ovens from Bob's Bakery Equipment. Bob's deposits the check in its account with PNC Bank. Once the check has cleared and PNC Bank has collected the funds from Wells Fargo, Wells Fargo will have lost $100,000 of reserves and checkable deposits:

WELLS FARGO

Assets		Liabilities	
Securities	−$100,000	Checkable deposits	$0
Loans	+$100,000		
Reserves	$0		

Wells Fargo is now satisfied because it has exchanged some of its low-interest Treasury bill holdings for a higher-interest loan. But the effect of the open market purchase on the banking system is not finished.

How the Banking System Responds to an Increase in Reserves We can trace the further effect of the open market operation by considering the situation at PNC Bank after it has received the check for $100,000 from Bob's Bakery Equipment. After PNC has cleared the check and collected the funds from Wells Fargo, PNC's balance sheet changes as follows:

PNC BANK

Assets		Liabilities	
Reserves	+$100,000	Checkable deposits	+$100,000

PNC's deposits and reserves have both increased by $100,000. For simplicity, let's assume that when it received Bob's deposit, PNC had no excess reserves. If the required reserve ratio is 10%, PNC must hold $10,000 (= 0.10 × $100,000) against its increase of $100,000 in checkable deposits. The other $90,000 of the reserves it has gained are excess reserves. PNC knows that it should assume it will lose reserves equal to the amount of any loan it grants because the amount of the loan will be spent and the funds may be deposited in another bank. So, *PNC can only safely lend out an amount equal to its excess reserves.* Suppose that PNC makes a $90,000 loan to Santiago's Printing to purchase new office equipment. Initially, PNC's assets (loans) and liabilities (checkable deposits) rise by $90,000. But this is temporary because Santiago's will spend the loan proceeds by writing a $90,000 check to buy equipment from Computer Universe, which has an account at SunTrust Bank. When SunTrust clears the $90,000 check against PNC, PNC's balance sheet changes as follows:

PNC BANK

Assets		Liabilities	
Reserves	+$10,000	Checkable deposits	+$100,000
Loans	+$90,000		

These are the changes in SunTrust's balance sheet:

SUNTRUST BANK

Assets		Liabilities	
Reserves	+$90,000	Checkable deposits	+$90,000

To this point, checkable deposits in the banking system have risen by $190,000 as a result of the Fed's $100,000 open market purchase.

SunTrust faces the same decisions that Wells Fargo and PNC faced. SunTrust wants to use the increase in reserves to expand its loans, but it can safely lend only the increase in excess reserves. With a required reserve ratio of 10%, SunTrust must add $90,000 × 0.10 = $9,000 to its required reserves and can lend only $81,000. Suppose that SunTrust lends the $81,000 to Malik's Barber Shop to use for remodeling. Initially, SunTrust's assets (loans) and liabilities (checkable deposits) rise by $81,000. But when Malik's spends the loan proceeds and a check for $81,000 clears against it, the changes in SunTrust's balance sheet are as follows:

SUNTRUST BANK

Assets		Liabilities	
Reserves	+$9,000	Checkable deposits	+$90,000
Loans	+$81,000		

If the proceeds of the loan to Malik's Barber Shop are deposited in another bank, checkable deposits in the banking system will rise by another $81,000. To this point, the $100,000 increase in reserves supplied by the Fed has increased the level of checkable deposits by $100,000 + $90,000 + $81,000 = $271,000. This process is called **multiple deposit creation**. The money supply is growing with each loan. The initial increase in bank reserves and the monetary base results in the money supply growing by a multiple of the initial increase in reserves.

The process still isn't complete. The recipient of the $81,000 check from Malik's Barber Shop will deposit it, and checkable deposits at some other bank will expand. The process continues to ripple through the banking system and the economy. We illustrate the results in Table 14.2. Note from the table that new checkable deposits continue to be created each time checks are deposited and banks make new loans, but the size of the increase gets smaller each time because banks must hold part of the money at each step as required reserves.

Multiple deposit creation
Part of the money supply process in which an increase in bank reserves results in rounds of bank loans and creation of checkable deposits and an increase in the money supply that is a multiple of the initial increase in reserves.

TABLE 14.2 Multiple Deposit Creation, Assuming a Fed Open Market Purchase of $100,000 and a Required Reserve Ratio of 10%

Bank	Increase in deposits	Increase in loans	Increase in reserves
PNC Bank	$100,000	$90,000	$10,000
SunTrust Bank	90,000	81,000	9,000
Third Bank	81,000	72,900	8,100
Fourth Bank	72,900	65,610	7,290
Fifth Bank	65,610	59,049	6,561
.	.	.	.
.	.	.	.
.	.	.	.
Total increase	$1,000,000	$900,000	$100,000

Calculating the Simple Deposit Multiplier

Table 14.2 shows that the Fed's open market purchase of $100,000 increases the reserves of the banking system by $100,000 and, ultimately, increases checkable deposits by $1,000,000. The ratio of the amount of deposits created by banks to the amount of new reserves created is called the **simple deposit multiplier**. In this case, the simple deposit multiplier equals $1,000,000/$100,000 = 10. Why 10? How do we know that the initial increase in bank reserves of $100,000 ultimately leads to an increase in deposits of $1,000,000?

Simple deposit multiplier
The ratio of the amount of deposits created by banks to the amount of new reserves.

There are two ways to answer this question. First, each bank in this process is keeping reserves equal to 10% of its deposits because we are assuming that no bank holds excess reserves. For the banking system as a whole, the increase in reserves is $100,000—the amount of the Fed's open market purchase. Therefore, the system as a whole ends up with $1,000,000 in deposits because $100,000 is 10% of $1,000,000.

A second way to answer the question is by deriving an expression for the simple deposit multiplier. From Table 14.2, we can write an expression for the total increase in deposits:

$$\Delta D = \$100,000 + [0.9 \times \$100,000] + [(0.9 \times 0.9) \times \$100,000]$$
$$+ [(0.9 \times 0.9 \times 0.9) \times \$100,000] + \dots$$

Or, simplifying:

$$\Delta D = \$100,000 \times [1 + 0.9 + 0.9^2 + 0.9^3 + \dots].$$

The rules of algebra tell us that an infinite series like the one in the expression sums to:

$$\frac{1}{1 - 0.9} = \frac{1}{0.10} = 10.$$

So, $\Delta D = \$100,000 \times 10 = \$1,000,000$. Note that 10 is 1 divided by the required reserve ratio, rr_D, which in this case is 10%, or 0.10. This approach gives us another way of expressing the simple deposit multiplier:

$$\text{Simple deposit multiplier} = \frac{1}{rr_D}.$$

So, now we have an equation showing how a change in deposits, ΔD, is related to an initial change in reserves, ΔR:

$$\Delta D = \frac{\Delta R}{rr_D},$$

or, in our example,

$$\Delta D = \frac{\$100,000}{0.10} = \$1,000,000.$$

If a bank decides to invest all or some of its excess reserves in municipal bonds or other securities rather than make loans, the deposit expansion process will be the same as if the bank had made loans. Suppose that PNC decided to purchase $90,000 worth of municipal bonds from a bond dealer instead of extending the $90,000 loan to Santiago's. PNC would write the bond dealer a check in the amount of $90,000, which Goldman Sachs would deposit in its bank. The dealer's bank would then have excess reserves, which it could lend or invest, and so on. The effect on multiple deposit creation is the same whether banks use excess reserves to make loans or buy securities.

At first you might think that individual banks are creating money. However, an individual bank can lend only an amount equal to its excess reserves. New deposits are created when borrowers spend the funds they borrow from banks and the funds are then deposited back into the banking system. Multiple deposit creation refers to the actions of the banking system as a whole, not to the action of an individual bank.

Finally, note that just as the Fed can expand the volume of checkable deposits in the banking system by increasing reserves, it can also contract the volume of deposits by reducing reserves. The Fed reduces reserves by selling government securities in an *open market sale*. This action has a ripple effect that is similar to deposit expansion in the banking system but in the opposite direction. The result of the open market sale is *multiple deposit contraction*. Suppose that the Fed sells $100,000 in Treasury securities to Wells Fargo, thereby reducing that bank's reserves by $100,000. With a simple deposit multiplier of 10, we know that a decline in reserves of $100,000 will eventually lead to a decline in checkable deposits of $1,000,000.

14.3 Banks, the Nonbank Public, and the Money Multiplier

LEARNING OBJECTIVE: Explain how the actions of banks and the nonbank public affect the money multiplier.

Understanding the simple deposit multiplier is an important step in understanding the money supply process, but it is not the complete story. In deriving the simple deposit multiplier, we made two key assumptions:

1. Banks hold no excess reserves.
2. The nonbank public does not increase its holdings of currency.

In other words, we assumed in the previous section that whenever banks have excess reserves, they lend them all out. We also assumed that if households or firms receive a check, they deposit the whole amount in a checking account, keeping none of the funds as cash. Neither of these assumptions is correct: Banks hold excess reserves, and the nonbank public typically also increases its holdings of currency when its checking account balances rise. In this section, we find out what happens to our account of the money supply process if we relax these assumptions.

The Effect of Increases in Currency Holdings and Increases in Excess Reserves

In our account of the money supply process in Section 14.2, once Wells Fargo had acquired $100,000 in excess reserves as a result of selling Treasury bills to the Fed, the bank loaned the entire amount to Rosie's Bakery. Rosie's then spent the loan proceeds by writing a check for $100,000 to Bob's Bakery Equipment, and Bob's deposited the entire $100,000 check in its account with PNC Bank. Once the check cleared, PNC Bank gained $100,000 in reserves. But suppose that instead of depositing the whole $100,000, Bob's had deposited $90,000 and taken $10,000 in cash? In that case, PNC would have a gain in reserves of $90,000, not $100,000, thereby reducing the amount PNC had available to lend.

Throughout the process of banks making loans and creating new checkable deposits, households and firms will hold some of the increased funds as currency rather than as deposits. Funds deposited in banks are subject to the multiple deposit creation process, while funds held as currency are not. We can conclude that *the more currency the nonbank public holds relative to checkable deposits, the smaller the multiple deposit creation process will be.*

Now suppose that when Bob's Bakery deposits the $100,000 in its account at PNC Bank, the bank decides that instead of holding $10,000 as required reserves and loaning out the other $90,000, it will hold the entire $100,000 as excess reserves. If PNC takes this action, the process of multiple deposit creation comes to an immediate stop because no more loans are made, and no more deposits are created. Rather than resulting in a $1,000,000 increase in deposits, the Fed's $100,000 open market purchase will have resulted in only a $100,000 increase in deposits. The deposit multiplier will have declined from 10 to 1. We can conclude that *the more excess reserves banks hold relative to their checkable deposits, the smaller the multiple deposit creation process will be.*

Figure 14.1 on page 462 illustrates our ultimate goal in understanding the money supply process: to find a stable money multiplier that will link the monetary base to the money supply. We have seen that the Fed can control the size of the monetary base through open market operations. Provided that the money multiplier is stable, the Fed's control over the monetary base allows it to also control the money supply. The simple deposit multiplier is useful in understanding how reserve creation leads to increases in loans and deposits, which is the heart of the money supply process. But we need to elaborate on the simple deposit multiplier in three ways:

1. Rather than a link between reserves and deposits, we need a link between the monetary base and the money supply.

2. We need to include the effects on the money supply process of changes in the nonbank public's desire to hold currency relative to checkable deposits.

3. We need to include the effects of changes in banks' desire to hold excess reserves relative to deposits.

In the next section, we make these changes to the simple deposit multiplier story in order to build a complete account of the money supply process.

Deriving a Realistic Money Multiplier

We need to derive a money multiplier, m, that links the monetary base, B, to the money supply, M:

$$M = m \times B.$$

This equation tells us that the money multiplier is equal to the ratio of the money supply to the monetary base:

$$m = \frac{M}{B}.$$

Recall that the money supply is the sum of currency, C, and checkable deposits, D, while the monetary base is the sum of currency and bank reserves, R. Because we want to take into account banks' decisions about holding excess reserves, we can separate reserves into its components: required reserves, RR, and excess reserves, ER. So, we can expand the expression for the money multiplier to:

$$m = \frac{C + D}{C + RR + ER}.$$

Keep in mind that we are interested in the nonbank public's desire to hold currency relative to checkable deposits and banks' desire to hold excess reserves relative to checkable deposits. To capture this behavior in our expression for the money multiplier, we want to include the **currency-to-deposit ratio (C/D)**, which measures the nonbank public's holdings of currency relative to their holdings of checkable deposits, and the excess reserves-to-deposit ratio (**ER/D**), which measure banks' holdings of excess reserves relative to their checkable deposits. To include these ratios in the expression for the money multiplier, we can rely on the basic rule of arithmetic that multiplying the numerator and denominator of a fraction by the same variable preserves the value of the fraction. So, we can introduce the deposit ratios into our expression for the money multiplier this way:

Currency-to-deposit ratio (C/D) The nonbank public's holdings of currency, C, relative to their holdings of checkable deposits, D.

$$m = \left(\frac{C + D}{C + RR + ER}\right) \times \frac{(1/D)}{(1/D)} = \frac{(C/D) + 1}{(C/D) + (RR/D) + (ER/D)}.$$

Recall that the ratio of required reserves to checkable deposits is the required reserve ratio, r_D. We can use this fact to arrive at our final expression for the money multiplier:

$$m = \frac{(C/D) + 1}{(C/D) + r_D + (ER/D)}.$$

So, we can say that because:

$$\text{Money supply} = \text{Money multiplier} \times \text{Monetary base,}$$

then:

$$M = \left(\frac{(C/D) + 1}{(C/D) + m_D + (ER/D)} \right) \times B.$$

For example, suppose that we have the following values:

$$C = \$500 \text{ billion}$$
$$D = \$1,000 \text{ billion}$$
$$m_D = 0.1$$
$$ER = \$150 \text{ billion}$$

Then the currency-to-deposit ratio = $500 billion/$1,000 billion = 0.50, and the excess reserves-to-deposit ratio = $150 billion/$1,000 billion = 0.15. So, the value of the money multiplier is:

$$m = \frac{0.5 + 1}{0.5 + 0.1 + 0.15} = \frac{1.5}{0.75} = 2.$$

With a money multiplier of 2, every $1 billion increase in the monetary base will result in a $2 billion increase in the money supply.

There are several points to note about our expression linking the money supply to the monetary base:

1. The money supply will increase if either the monetary base or the money multiplier increases in value, and it will decrease if either the monetary base or the money multiplier decreases in value.
2. An increase in the currency-to-deposit ratio (C/D) causes the value of the money multiplier to decline and, if the monetary base is unchanged, it causes the value of the money supply to decline. For instance, in the previous example, if C/D increases from 0.5 to 0.6, then the value of the multiplier falls from $1.5/0.75 = 2$ to $1.6/0.85 = 1.88$. This result makes economic sense: If households and firms increase their holdings of currency relative to their holdings of checkable deposits, banks will have a relatively smaller amount of funds they can lend out, which reduces the multiple creation of deposits.
3. An increase in the required reserve ratio, m_D, causes the value of the money multiplier to decline and, if the monetary base is unchanged, it causes the value of the money supply to decline. The arithmetic of this result is straightforward: Because m_D is in the denominator of the money multiplier expression, as the value of m_D increases, the value of m declines. Economically, an increase in m_D means that for any increase in reserves banks receive, a larger fraction must be held as required reserves, which are therefore not available to be loaned out as part of the process of multiple deposit creation.
4. An increase in the excess reserves-to-deposit ratio (ER/D) causes the value of the money multiplier to decline and, if the monetary base is unchanged, it causes the

value of the money supply to decline. Once again, the arithmetic of this result is straightforward because ER/D is in the denominator of the money multiplier expression. Economically, an increase in ER/D means that banks are holding relatively more excess reserves, so they are not using these funds to make loans as part of the process of multiple deposit creation.

SOLVED PROBLEM 14.3

Using the Expression for the Money Multiplier

Consider the following information:

$$\text{Bank reserves} = \$500 \text{ billion}$$
$$\text{Currency} = \$400 \text{ billion}$$

a. If banks are holding $80 billion in required reserves, and the required reserve ratio $= 0.1$, what is the value of checkable deposits?

b. Given this information, what is the value of the money supply (M1)? What is the value of the monetary base? What is the value of the money multiplier?

Solving the Problem

Step 1 **Review the chapter material.** This problem is about the money multiplier, so you may want to review the section "Deriving a Realistic Money Multiplier," which begins on page 476.

Step 2 **Answer part (a) by calculating the value of checkable deposits.** The value of required reserves is equal to the value of checkable deposits multiplied by the required reserve ratio:

$$RR = D \times rr_D$$
$$\$80 \text{ billion} = D \times 0.1$$
$$D = (\$80 \text{ billion}/0.1) = \$800 \text{ billion}$$

Step 3 **Answer part (b) by calculating the values of the money supply, the monetary base, and the money multiplier.** The M1 measure of the money supply equals the value of currency plus the value of checkable deposits:

$$M = C + D$$
$$= \$400 \text{ billion} + \$800 \text{ billion}$$
$$= \$1,200 \text{ billion}.$$

The monetary base is equal to the value of currency plus the value of bank reserves:

$$B = C + R$$
$$= \$400 \text{ billion} + \$500 \text{ billion}$$
$$= \$900 \text{ billion}.$$

We can calculate the money multiplier two ways. First, note that the money multiplier is equal to the ratio of the money supply to the monetary base:

$$m = \frac{M}{B} = \frac{\$1{,}200 \text{ billion}}{\$900 \text{ billion}} = 1.33.$$

Or, we can calculate the value of the money multiplier using the expression derived on page 476:

$$m = \frac{(C/D) + 1}{(C/D) + rr_D + (ER/D)}.$$

To use this expression, we need to calculate the value of excess reserves. Because we know that total reserves equal $500 billion and required reserves equal $80 billion, the value of excess reserves must equal $420 billion. Inserting values into the expression for the money multiplier gives us:

$$m = \frac{(\$400 \text{ billion} / \$800 \text{ billion}) + 1}{(\$400 \text{ billion} / \$800 \text{ billion}) + 0.1 + (\$420 \text{ billion} / \$800 \text{ billion})}$$

$$= \frac{1.5}{1.125} = 1.33.$$

So, the two approaches to calculating the value of the money multiplier give us the same result.

See related problems 3.8 and 3.9 at the end of the chapter.

We saw in Section 14.1 that economists think of the monetary base as having two components—the nonborrowed monetary base, B_{non}, and borrowed reserves, BR, which is another name for discount loans: $B = B_{non} + BR$. Because the actions of both the Fed and banks determine the volume of discount loans, the Fed has greater control over the nonborrowed monetary base. We can recognize this fact by rewriting the relationship between the money supply and the monetary base:

$$M = \left(\frac{(C/D) + 1}{C/D + rr_D + (ER/D)} \right) \times (B_{non} + BR).$$

We now have a complete description of the money supply process:

1. The money supply equals the monetary base times the money multiplier.
2. The monetary base equals the nonborrowed base (which is determined primarily by the Fed through open market operations) and discount loans (which are determined jointly by banks and the Fed).
3. The money multiplier depends on the required reserve ratio (determined by the Fed), the ratio of excess reserves-to-deposits (determined by banks), and the currency-to-deposit ratio (determined by the nonbank public: households and firms).

TABLE 14.3 Variables in the Money Supply Process

An increase in the ...	based on the actions of ...	causes the money supply to ...	because ...
nonborrowed base, B_{non}	the Fed through open market operations	increase	the monetary base increases, and more reserves are available for deposit expansion.
required reserve ratio, rr_D	the Fed through changes in reserve requirements	decrease	fewer reserves can be lent out, and the value of the money multiplier falls.
currency-to-deposit ratio (C/D)	the nonbank public	decrease	the value of the money multiplier falls, reducing deposit expansion.
excess reserves-to-deposit ratio (ER/D)	banks	decrease	the value of the money multiplier falls, reducing deposit expansion.

Table 14.3 summarizes the variables that determine the money supply. Note that decreases in the variables listed in the first column would have the opposite effect on the money supply to that given in the third column.

We stated earlier that the Fed controls the money supply. We now know that this statement is not quite correct. The Fed can set the value of the nonborrowed base at whatever level it chooses. But the behavior of the nonbank public influences the money supply through the currency-to-deposit ratio, and the behavior of banks influences the money supply through the volume of discount loans and the excess reserves-to-deposit ratio. In the next section, we will use this analysis to understand changes in the monetary base and in the money supply since the beginning of the financial crisis of 2007–2009.

The Money Supply, the Money Multiplier, and the Monetary Base Since the Beginning of the 2007–2009 Financial Crisis

We have already seen that beginning in the fall of 2008, in response to the financial crisis, the Fed bought huge amounts of financial assets, including mortgage-backed securities. Panel (a) of Figure 14.2 shows that, as a result, the size of the monetary base soared. M1 also increased—but not by as much. As panel (b) shows, the value of the money multiplier declined sharply during the same period. The value of the money multiplier had been trending down, declining from a value of about 2.6 at the beginning of 1995 to about 1.7 at the beginning of 2007. The value then declined by more than 50% during the financial crisis, dropping below 1 by late 2008. In fact, with the value of the monetary base having risen above the value of the money supply, the money multiplier had turned into a money *divider*! The value of the money multiplier remained below 1 in 2016, more than seven years after the end of the financial crisis.

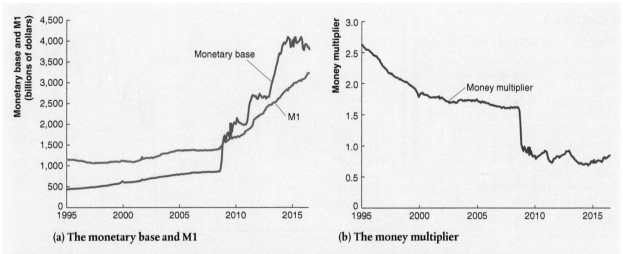

(a) The monetary base and M1 **(b) The money multiplier**

FIGURE 14.2 Movements in the Monetary Base, M1, and the Money Multiplier, 1995–2016

Panel (a) shows that beginning in the fall of 2008, the size of the monetary base soared. M1 also increased, but not nearly as much.

As panel (b) shows, the value of the money multiplier declined sharply during the same period.

Source: Federal Reserve Bank of St. Louis.

Why did the monetary base increase significantly more than M1? Figure 14.3 helps solve the mystery. The figure shows movements in the currency-to-deposit ratio (C/D) and the excess reserves-to-deposit ratio (ER/D). While the currency-to-deposit ratio had been gradually trending upward since 1995, it fell during the financial crisis because households and firms shifted funds into checkable deposits from money market mutual funds and other assets whose riskiness they believed had increased. With deposits increasing faster than currency, C/D fell. Recall from our discussion of the effect of changes in C/D on the money multiplier that a decrease in C/D, holding all else constant, will cause the value of the money multiplier to increase and the value of M1 to also increase for any given value of the monetary base. We know from panel (b) of Figure 14.2 that, in fact, the value of the money multiplier *decreased*. The reason is that the value of ER/D soared, increasing from almost zero in September 2008—because banks were holding very few excess reserves—to about 1.3 in the fall of 2009. In other words, banks began to hold more excess reserves than they had checkable deposits, causing ER/D to rise above 1.

Because the increase in ER/D was significantly larger than the decline in C/D, the value of the money multiplier declined, and the increase in the monetary base resulted in a much smaller increase in M1 than would have occurred if the value of the money multiplier had remained what it was at the beginning of the financial crisis.

Banks' holdings of excess reserves shot up during the fall of 2008 and remained high through the end of 2016 for several reasons. First, in October 2008, the Fed for the first time began paying banks interest on their excess reserves. Although the interest rate

MyEconLab Real-time data

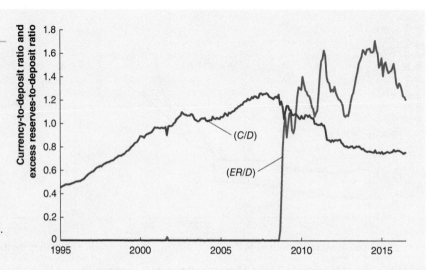

FIGURE 14.3

Movements in *C/D* and *ER/D*

The currency-to-deposit ratio (C/D) had been gradually trending upward since 1995, but it fell during the financial crisis of 2007–2009. At the same time, the excess reserves-to-deposit ratio (ER/D) soared, increasing from almost zero in September 2008—because banks were holding very few excess reserves—to about 1.3 in the fall of 2009. Banks began to hold more excess reserves than they had checkable deposits.

Source: Federal Reserve Bank of St. Louis.

was quite low—at that time, only 0.25%—other nominal interest rates had also declined sharply, and the return on deposits at the Fed was risk free. Second, during the financial crisis, banks had suffered heavy losses, particularly on their holdings of mortgage-backed securities and commercial real estate mortgages. These losses gave banks an incentive to remain liquid as they attempted to rebuild their capital. Finally, banks also tightened their lending standards in the face of increased uncertainty about the creditworthiness of borrowers and the implementation of stricter regulations. With fewer good alternatives, holding funds at the Fed became more attractive. The slow growth of the economy in the years following the end of the financial crisis resulted in historically low interest rates on loans and bonds, keeping very low the opportunity cost to banks of maintaining funds on deposit with the Fed. Continuing pressure from regulators to reduce the riskiness of their investments led to banks keeping lending standards tight. As a result of these factors, banks maintained high levels of excess reserves years after the end of the financial crisis.

MAKING THE CONNECTION

Did the Fed's Worry over Excess Reserves Cause the Recession of 1937–1938?

If the Fed is worried about the level of excess reserves in the banking system, one solution is to turn the *excess* reserves into *required* reserves by increasing the required reserve ratio. The Fed took this approach in the mid-1930s, during the Great Depression. As the following graph shows, after the bank panics ended in early 1933, excess reserves in the banking system rose sharply.

MyEconLab Real-time data

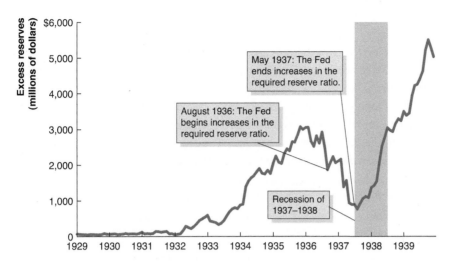

Source: Banking and Monetary Statistics of the United States.

Banks accumulated excess reserves during the mid-1930s for reasons similar to the reasons banks accumulated excess reserves after 2008. Although bank panics had ended following the establishment of the FDIC, many banks had suffered heavy losses and had a strong desire to remain liquid. Nominal interest rates had also fallen to very low levels, which reduced the opportunity cost of holding reserves at the Fed. Finally, given the severity of the Depression, the creditworthiness of most borrowers had deteriorated. By late 1935, the unemployment rate remained very high, at more than 14%, and the inflation rate remained low, at less than 2%. Nevertheless, some members of the Fed's Board of Governors were worried that stock prices were increasing rapidly. They felt that, despite the depressed economy, the increases might result in a speculative bubble similar to the one that had preceded the great stock market crash of October 1929. Some members were also afraid of an increase in the inflation rate. A memorandum by the Federal Reserve's staff referred to the "general fear which many people entertain that excess reserves of the present magnitude must sooner or later set in motion inflationary forces which, if not dealt with before they get strongly under way, may prove impossible to control."

The Board of Governors decided to reduce excess reserves in the banking system by raising the required reserve ratio on checkable deposits in four steps, from 10% to 20%, beginning in August 1936. The board also raised the required reserve ratio on time deposits from 3% to 6%. The graph above indicates that at first, the Fed's actions succeeded in reducing excess reserves. But the Fed's policy ignored the reasons banks during this period were holding excess reserves. Following the increases in the required reserve ratio, the only way banks could restore their previous holdings of excess reserves was to make fewer loans and, thereby, hold fewer demand deposits. As bank loans contracted, so did the money supply. Households and firms, unable to obtain credit, cut back on their spending, and the economy fell into a recession in 1937.

The unemployment rate, which was still far from the full employment levels of 1929, started increasing again.[3]

The Fed partly reversed course in April 1938 by cutting the required reserve ratio on checkable deposits from 20% to 17.5% and on time deposits from 6% to 5%. But the damage had been done. Many economists believe that the Fed's actions in raising the required reserve ratio contributed significantly to the recession of 1937–1938. The Fed had misjudged the desire of banks to hold excess reserves and, so, had failed to anticipate that banks would take action to restore their holdings of excess reserves despite the sharply higher reserve requirements. One Fed economist has observed: "The experience [of the 1930s] demonstrates that raising reserve requirements is surely *not* the best way to eliminate excess reserves."

Note: In the 1930s, the Fed set different reserve requirements for banks, depending on their size and location. The reserve requirements discussed here are for reserve city banks.

Sources: David Wheelock, "How *Not* to Reduce Excess Reserves," *Federal Reserve Bank of St. Louis Economic Synopses*, No. 38, 2009; Douglas A. Irwin, "Gold Sterilization and the Recession of 1937–1938," *Financial History Review*, Vol. 19, No. 3, December 2012, pp. 249–267; Board of Governors of the Federal Reserve System, *Banking and Monetary Statistics of the United States, 1914–1941*, Washington, DC, November 1943; the quote from the 1935 Fed memorandum is from Milton Friedman and Anna Schwartz, *A Monetary History of the United States, 1867–1960*, Princeton, NJ: Princeton University Press, 1963, p. 523.

See related problem 3.11 at the end of the chapter.

In 2016, banks' enormous holdings of excess reserves left some investors, policymakers, and economists concerned about the implications for future inflation. As we have seen, in normal economic times—and in the absence of the Fed paying interest on bank reserves—banks typically lend out nearly all of their excess reserves. If banks were to suddenly begin lending the $2 trillion in excess reserves they held in December 2016, the result would be an explosion in the money supply and, potentially, a rapid increase in inflation. Fear of inflation has traditionally led some investors to buy gold.

MAKING THE CONNECTION | IN YOUR INTEREST

If You Are Worried About Inflation, Should You Invest in Gold?

As we saw in the chapter opener, many people see gold as a safe haven investment—something to buy when financial markets seem chaotic. So, sales to individual investors of gold bars and coins and shares in ETFs that track the price of gold soared during the financial crisis of 2007–2009 and again in 2016, following the vote in Great Britain to

---

[3] Other factors also may have helped push the economy into recession in 1937. In 1936, Congress and President Franklin Roosevelt had enacted significant increases in both personal and corporate income tax rates. In addition, at the end of 1936, the U.S. Treasury decided to "sterilize" gold inflows. Although the United States was officially off the gold standard, the Treasury purchased most gold entering the United States at a fixed price of $35 per ounce. It purchased the gold using funds it had on deposit with the Fed. If the Treasury replaced those funds by depositing with the Fed gold certificates that represented claims on the physical gold, the gold inflow would lead to an increase in the monetary base. If it failed to do so, the gold inflow was sterilized, and the monetary base would be unchanged. Because the Treasury shared the Fed's fear that inflation might be increasing, it decided in December 1936 to begin sterilizing gold inflows. It continued to sterilize gold inflows for most of the period through February 1938. The Treasury's decision to sterilize gold inflows eliminated what had been an important source of increases in the monetary base and the money supply during previous years.

leave the European Union. Many investors who have been particularly worried about the possibility that increases in bank reserves and the money supply might lead to much higher rates of inflation in the future see gold as a hedge against inflation.

Historically, how good an investment has gold been? Gold clearly has some drawbacks as an investment: Unlike a bond, gold pays no interest; unlike a stock, gold pays no dividend. At a time when many investments—including most stocks and bonds—exist only in electronic form, gold is a real tangible asset that has to be stored and safeguarded. For instance, an individual investor who owns American Eagle coins issued by the U.S. Mint must find a place to store them—perhaps paying a fee to a bank for a safety deposit box—and may have to pay for insurance on them. An investor can avoid these costs by buying gold ETFs, although people who buy gold because they are afraid of a future collapse of the financial system prefer to hold physical gold.

Because gold pays no interest, it is difficult to determine its fundamental value as an investment. Ultimately, the minimum price of gold is set by its value as a metal that can be used in jewelry or for some industrial purposes, particularly in electronics, where its high conductivity and resistance to corrosion make it useful. Gold's value as an investment depends on how likely its price is to increase in the future because its rate of return is entirely in the form of capital gains. Many individual investors believe that gold is a good hedge against inflation because the price of gold can be relied on to rise if the general price level rises. But is this view correct? The blue line in the graph below shows the monthly price of gold from January 1976 through December 2016.

MyEconLab **Real-time data**

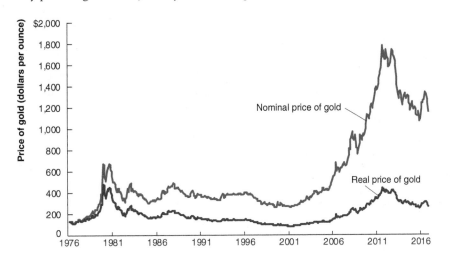

The graph shows that the price of gold soared during the high-inflation years of the late 1970s. Gold was selling for about $132 per ounce in January 1976 and increased to $670 in September 1980. Unfortunately for investors in gold, while the overall price level continued to rise during the years following 1980, the price of gold actually fell. In August 1999, gold was selling for only about $255 per ounce, or about 60% less than at its peak nearly 20 years earlier. Meanwhile, the price level, as measured by the consumer price index, had doubled. The red line on the graph shows the real price of gold, calculated by dividing the nominal price of gold by the consumer price index. The red line shows that even after the strong nominal price increases beginning in 2009, by the end of 2016, the real price of gold was more than 40% below its September 1980 level. In 1980, many newspaper stories and investment guides highlighted what a great investment gold had been during the late 1970s. Anyone who took this advice and bought gold bars or coins was in for a severe disappointment: After more than 35 years of paying to store and insure their bars and coins, all they would have to show for their investment was a −40% real return. If instead they had bought a mutual fund that invests in the S&P 500, they would have received a real return of more than 500%.

Contrary to its reputation among some investors, in the long run, gold has proven to be a *poor* hedge against inflation. Although investors who were buying gold in 2016 may have been making a shrewd investment, the record of the past 35 years was not encouraging.

Note: The nominal price of gold is the "gold fixing price" in the London Bullion Market. The real price of gold is calculated by dividing the nominal price by the consumer price index, using January 1976 = 100 as a base.

See related problem 3.13 at the end of the chapter.

ANSWERING THE KEY QUESTION

Continued from page 460

At the beginning of this chapter, we asked:

"Why did bank reserves increase rapidly during and after the financial crisis of 2007–2009, and should policymakers be concerned about the increase?"

As we have seen, the rapid increase in bank reserves that began in the fall of 2008 was a result of the Fed purchasing assets. Whenever the Fed purchases an asset, the monetary base increases. Both the currency and bank reserves components of the base increased in 2008, but the increase in reserves was particularly large. Banks were content to hold large balances of excess reserves because the Fed was paying interest on them and because of the increased risk in alternative uses of the funds. Inflation remained very low through 2016, but some policymakers were concerned that, ultimately, if banks began to lend out their holdings of excess reserves, the inflation rate could increase in the future.

Key Terms and Problems

Key Terms

Bank reserves, p. 464

Currency-to-deposit ratio (C/D), p. 476

Currency in circulation, p. 464

Currency in M1, p. 464

Discount loan, p. 467

Discount rate, p. 468

Excess reserves, p. 465

Monetary base (or high-powered money), p. 462

Multiple deposit creation, p. 472

Open market operations, p. 465

Open market purchase, p. 465

Open market sale, p. 466

Required reserve ratio, p. 465

Required reserves, p. 465

Simple deposit multiplier, p. 473

Vault cash, p. 464

14.1

The Federal Reserve's Balance Sheet and the Monetary Base
Explain the relationship between the Fed's balance sheet and the monetary base.

Review Questions

1.1 How does the monetary base differ from the money supply?

1.2 What are the two most important assets and the two most important liabilities on the Fed's balance sheet? Because currency is valuable, why is it a liability to the Fed rather than an asset?

1.3 Use a T-account for Wells Fargo and a T-account for the Fed to show the result of the Fed buying $1 million in Treasury bills from Wells Fargo.

Problems and Applications

1.4 An article in the *Economist* refers to the monetary base in China as "central bank-issued currency." Do you agree with this definition? Briefly explain.
Source: "How China's Cash Injections Add Up to Quantitative Squeezing," *Economist*, September 7, 2015.

1.5 Use T-accounts to show the initial effects of each of the following actions on the balance sheets of the Fed and the banking system:

   a. The Fed increases discount loans by $2 billion.

   b. The Fed carries out a $2 billion open market sale.

   c. The Fed spends $100 million on a new information technology system for the Federal Reserve Bank of Atlanta from DeShawn's Computer Services.

1.6 [Related to the Making the Connection on page 468] An article in the *Wall Street Journal* notes that by mid-2016, the Bank of Japan owned about one-third of all Japanese government bonds, "with its balance sheet ballooning to 85% of gross domestic product."

   a. Briefly explain whether the Bank of Japan's purchases of Japanese government bonds would appear on the asset side or the liability side of its balance sheet.

   b. Why have the balance sheets of most central banks increased substantially in recent years compared with the years before the financial crisis?
Source: Takashi Nakamichi and Megumi Fujikawa, "Bank of Japan Takes Modest Easing Action," *Wall Street Journal*, July 29, 2016.

1.7 [Related to the Making the Connection on page 468] An article in the *Wall Street Journal* in mid-2016 notes the persistence of slow economic growth and very low interest rates seven years after the end of the financial crisis. One consequence was "the persistence of the Fed's large balance sheet and financial institutions' desire to store large amounts of reserves at the central bank."

   a. How does a slow U.S. economic growth rate affect the size of the Fed's balance sheet?

   b. Why are banks storing large amounts of reserves with the Fed?

   c. Why are bank reserves a liability on the Fed's balance sheet? Are they also a liability on banks' balance sheets? Briefly explain.
Source: David Harrison, "Fed Discussed New Ways of Making Policy at July Meeting," *Wall Street Journal*, August 17, 2016.

 14.2

The Simple Deposit Multiplier
Derive the equation for the simple deposit multiplier and use T-accounts to illustrate multiple deposit expansion.

Review Questions

2.1 Suppose that PNC Bank sells $1 million in Treasury bills to the Fed and then makes a $1 million loan to David's Donut Emporium and Boat Repair. Use a T-account to show the results of these transactions on PNC's balance sheet.

2.2 Why does the Fed's purchase of Treasury bills lead to "multiple deposit expansion"?

2.3 If the required reserve ratio is 15%, what is the value of the simple deposit multiplier?

Problems and Applications

2.4 Suppose that Wells Fargo lends $100,000 to Jill's Jerseys. Using T-accounts, show how this transaction is recorded on the bank's balance sheet. If Jill's spends the money to buy materials from Zach's Zippers, which has its checking account at PNC Bank, show the effect on Wells Fargo's balance sheet. What is the total change in Wells Fargo's assets and liabilities?

2.5 Suppose that a bank with no excess reserves receives a deposit into a checking account of $10,000 in currency. If the required reserve ratio is 0.10, what is the maximum amount the bank can lend out?

2.6 Suppose that JPMorgan Chase sells $100 million in Treasury bills to the Fed.

a. Use T-accounts to show the initial effect of this sale on the balance sheets of JPMorgan Chase and the Fed.

b. Suppose that before selling the Treasury bills, JPMorgan Chase had no excess reserves. Suppose that the required reserve ratio is 20%. Suppose that JPMorgan Chase makes the maximum loan possible from the funds acquired by selling the Treasury bills. Use a T-account to show the initial effect of granting the loan on JPMorgan Chase's balance sheet. Also include on this T-account the transaction from part (a).

c. Now suppose that whoever took out the loan in part (b) writes a check for this amount and that the person receiving the check deposits it at Wells Fargo. Show the effects of these transactions on the balance sheets of JPMorgan Chase and Wells Fargo after the check has cleared. (On the T-account for JPMorgan Chase, include the transactions from parts (a) and (b).)

d. What is the maximum increase in the money supply that can result from the transaction in

part (a) (that is, the maximum increase after all actions resulting from the transaction in part (a) have occurred)?

2.7 In the following bank balance sheet, amounts are in millions of dollars. The required reserve ratio is 3% on the first $30 million of checkable deposits and 12% on any checkable deposits over $30 million.

Assets		Liabilities	
Reserves	$18.9	Checkable deposits	$180.0
Loans	150.0	Net worth	20.0
Securities	31.1		
	$200.0		$200.0

a. Calculate the bank's excess reserves.

b. Suppose that the bank sells $5 million in securities to an investor. Show the bank's balance sheet after this transaction. Now what are the bank's excess reserves?

c. Suppose that the bank loans its excess reserves in part (b) to a local business. Show the bank's balance sheet after the loan has been made but before the business has spent the proceeds of the loan. Now what are the bank's excess reserves?

d. Suppose that the business spends the amount of the loan by writing a check. Revise the bank's balance sheet and calculate its excess reserves after the check has cleared.

2.8 In medieval times, many goldsmiths would offer to store gold in return for a fee. They provided anyone depositing gold with a receipt, which represented a legal claim on the goldsmith to exchange the receipt for the amount of gold written on it.

a. How are the medieval goldsmiths like modern banks, and how are they unlike modern banks?

b. Is multiple deposit creation possible in this system? Does your answer depend on whether these receipts could be bought and sold and redeemed by someone other than the person who deposited the gold?

2.9 A Fed publication refers to the multiple expansion of deposits as "the heart of banking theory."

a. Why is the process of the multiple expansion of deposits important to understanding how the banking system operates?

b. The same publication contrasts "the banking system's ability to multiply loans and deposits with the individual bank's inability to do so." How is the banking system able to multiply loans and deposits if an individual bank is unable to do so?

Source: Thomas M. Humphrey, "The Theory of Multiple Expansion of Deposits: What It Is and Whence It Came," *Federal Reserve Bank of Richmond Economic Review*, March/April 1987.

14.3 **Banks, the Nonbank Public, and the Money Multiplier**
Explain how the actions of banks and the nonbank public affect the money multiplier.

Review Questions

3.1 What are the key differences between the simple deposit multiplier and the money multiplier?

3.2 Briefly explain whether under normal circumstances the money multiplier will increase or decrease following an increase in each of the following, holding other factors constant:

a. The currency-to-deposit ratio (C/D)

b. The excess reserves-to-deposit ratio (ER/D)

c. The required reserve ratio (rr_D)

3.3 Briefly explain what happened to the currency-to-deposit ratio (C/D) and the excess reserves-to-deposit ratio (ER/D) during the financial crisis of 2007–2009. What effect did these changes have on the size of the money multiplier?

Problems and Applications

3.4 A Federal Reserve publication notes that when economists analyze the money supply process, they typically assume that the money multiplier is "independent of the policy actions of the central bank."

a. Briefly explain what this assumption means.

b. Supposing that the assumption is *incorrect*, what would be the implications for the relationship between changes in the monetary base and changes in the money supply?

Source: Michelle R. Garfinkle and Daniel L. Thornton, "The Multiplier Approach to the Money Supply Process: A Precautionary Note," Federal Reserve Bank of St. Louis *Review*, Vol. 73, No. 4, July/August 1991, p. 47.

3.5 Explain whether you agree with the following observation: "If the required reserve ratio were zero, the process of multiple deposit expansion would go on forever."

3.6 What will be the value of the money multiplier if banks hold no excess reserves, the currency-to-deposit ratio is 1, and the required reserve ratio for checkable deposits is 100%?

3.7 An article in the *Economist* noted that the money supply in China "has grown considerably faster than" the monetary base. The article also noted that the Bank of China had reduced the required reserve ratio and that households and firms were relying less on currency to settle transactions. Use these last two developments to explain why the money supply in China was growing faster than the monetary base.

Source: "How China's Cash Injections Add Up to Quantitative Squeezing," *Economist*, September 7, 2015.

3.8 [Related to Solved Problem 14.3 on page 478] Consider the following data:

Currency	$ 100 billion
Bank reserves	200 billion
Checkable deposits	800 billion
Time deposits	1,200 billion
Excess reserves	40 billion

Calculate the values for the currency-to-deposit ratio, the ratio of total reserves to deposits, the monetary base, the money multiplier, and the M1 money supply.

3.9 [Related to Solved Problem 14.3 on page 478]
Consider the following data:

Currency	$850 billion
Checkable deposits	700 billion
Bank reserves	700 billion

a. Calculate the values for the currency-to-deposit ratio, the ratio of total reserves to deposits, the monetary base, the money multiplier, and the M1 money supply.

b. Suppose that the ratio of total reserves to deposits changes to 2.0 from the value you calculated in part (a). (Assume that the currency-to-deposit ratio remains the same.) Now what is the value of the money multiplier?

3.10 Consider the following data (where all values are in billions of dollars):

	June 1930	June 1931	June 1932
Currency	$3.681	$3.995	$4.959
Checkable deposits	21.612	19.888	15.490
Bank reserves	3.227	3.307	2.829

Calculate the values for each period for the currency-to-deposit ratio, the ratio of total reserves to deposits, the monetary base, the money multiplier, and the M1 money supply. Can you explain why the currency-to-deposit ratio and the ratio of total reserves to deposits moved as they did between 1930 and 1932?

3.11 [Related to the Making the Connection on page 482]
Allan Meltzer of Carnegie Mellon University wrote the following about how the Federal Reserve Board's staff analyzed the likely effects of the large excess reserves banks were holding in the mid-1930s:

> [The] Board's staff ... [assumed] that none of the excess reserves were held for reasons of safety based on experience. The result was a large overestimate of potential monetary and credit expansion and prospective inflation and an underestimate of the effect of higher reserve requirement ratios.

a. Why might banks in the mid-1930s have been holding reserves for "reasons of safety"?

b. What does Meltzer mean by "potential monetary and credit expansion"?

c. If banks were holding excess reserves for reasons of safety, why might the Fed's staff have been overestimating potential monetary and credit expansion?

d. What was the effect on banks of the Fed's decision to increase the required reserve ratio? What insight does Meltzer give into why the Fed's staff underestimated the effect of the increase?

Source: Allan H. Meltzer, *A History of the Federal Reserve, Volume I: 1913–1951*, Chicago: University of Chicago 2003, p. 496.

3.12 [Related to the Chapter Opener on page 460] The U.S. Mint describes the demand for the gold, silver, and platinum coins it produces as being dependent on the prices of these metals as commodities. In addition, the Mint notes: "These commodity prices are, in turn, dependent on variables such as ... perceived strength as a safe-haven asset ... and earnings potential from other commodities or investments." Briefly explain whether these two factors help account for the surge in demand for gold coins in 2016.

Source: U.S. Mint, *2015 Annual Report*, p. 12.

3.13 [Related to the Making the Connection on page 484]
A column in the *Wall Street Journal* in the summer of 2016 discussed gold as an investment. The columnist noted: "The future can always be different from the past. But if gold shoots far up from here, it won't be following the precedents of the past. It will be violating them."

a. Why were some investors in 2016 worried that there could be a dramatic increase in inflation in the coming years? Why did some of these investors see gold as a hedge against an expected increase in inflation?

b. What does the columnist mean by writing that "following the precedents of the past," gold might not be expected to increase rapidly in price?

Source: Jason Zweig, "Gold: It's Still a Pet Rock," *Wall Street Journal*, July 8, 2016.

Data Exercises

D14.1: [**Calculating the money multiplier**] Go to the web site of the Federal Reserve Bank of St. Louis (FRED) (fred.stlouisfed.org) and find the most recent values for the for the M1 Money Stock (M1SL) and the St. Louis Adjusted Monetary Base (AMBSL).

   a. Using these data, calculate the value of the money multiplier.

   b. Assuming that the multiplier is equal to the value computed in part (a), if the monetary base increases by $400 million, by how much will the money supply increase?

D14.2: [**Calculating the money multiplier**] Go to the web site of the Federal Reserve Bank of St. Louis (FRED) (fred.stlouisfed.org) and find the most recent values for the Currency Component of M1 (CURRNS), Total Checkable Deposits (TCDSL), and Excess Reserves of Depository Institutions (EXCSRESNS).

   a. Using these data, calculate the value of the currency-to-deposit ratio.

   b. Using these data, calculate the value of the excess reserves-to-deposit ratio.

   c. Using these data and assuming a required reserve ratio of 11%, calculate the value of the money multiplier.

D14.3: [**Analyzing changes in the money supply**] Go to the web site of the Federal Reserve Bank of St. Louis (FRED) (fred.stlouisfed.org) and find the most recent value and the value from the same month one year earlier for Excess Reserves of Depository Institutions (EXCSRESNS).

   a. Using these data, calculate the percentage change in excess reserve balances between the two periods.

   b. Based on your answer to part (a), briefly explain whether, holding all other factors that affect the money supply constant, the money supply should have increased, decreased, or remained the same during this period.

D14.4: [**The monetary base and recessions**] Go to the web site of the Federal Reserve Bank of St. Louis (FRED) (fred.stlouisfed.org) and download the data series for the St. Louis Adjusted Monetary Base (BASE) from July 1959 until the most recent month available. In addition to the levels of the monetary base also find the compound annual rates of changes (choose "Edit Graph" and then under "Units" choose Compound Annual Rate of Change). Graph both the levels and the rates of change of the monetary base. Go to the web site of the National Bureau of Economic Research (nber.org) and find the dates for business cycle peaks and troughs. (The period between a business cycle peak and trough is a recession.)

   a. What was the trend in the levels of the monetary base from 1959 through the most recent month available?

   b. Describe how the levels of the monetary base change just before, during, and just after a recession. Is the pattern the same across recessions?

   c. On the rate of change graph, which periods saw the most volatility in the monetary base?

The Money Supply Process for M2

Learning Objective

14.A Describe the money supply process for M2

In the aftermath of financial innovation during the 1980s and 1990s, such as Congress allowing banks to pay interest on checking accounts, many analysts and policymakers became concerned that M1 no longer adequately represented assets functioning as a medium of exchange. As a result, they focused more attention on M2. As we saw in Chapter 2, M2 is a broader monetary aggregate than M1, including not only currency, C, and checkable deposits, D, but also nontransaction accounts. We can divide these nontransaction accounts into two components:

1. N, which consists of savings accounts (including money market deposit accounts)
2. MM, which consists of retail money market mutual funds

So we can represent M2 as:

$$M2 = C + D + N + MM.$$

The M2 measure of the money supply is less sensitive than M1 to shifts by households and firms—the nonbank public—from holding funds in one type of account to holding them in another type of account. Suppose that, for instance, the nonbank public wants to switch funds from checkable deposits to savings accounts. In that case, D would fall, but N would rise by the same amount, leaving M2 unchanged. But M1, the sum of currency and checkable deposits, would fall.

We can express M2 as the product of an *M2 multiplier* and the monetary base:

$$M2 = (M2 \text{ multiplier}) \times \text{Monetary base}.$$

We can derive an expression for the M2 multiplier similar to the expression we derived for the M1 multiplier. The result is:

$$M2 \text{ multiplier} = \frac{1 + (C/D) + (N/D) + (MM/D)}{(C/D) + rr_D + (ER/D)}.$$

The M2 multiplier is significantly larger than the M1 multiplier because the terms N/D and MM/D are added to the numerator. With no reserve requirements for the accounts in N and MM, M2 money expansion from a change in the monetary base is greater than that for M1. The M2 multiplier has been more stable than the M1 multiplier since 1980.

Components of the M2 multiplier affect the size of the multiplier in a manner similar to that for M1. Increases in the required reserve ratio and the currency-to-deposit ratio reduce the extent of deposit expansion, thereby reducing the multiplier. However, an increase in the nonbank public's preference for nontransaction or money market–type accounts relative to checkable deposits increases the multiplier.

In recent years, many economists and policymakers have deemphasized the importance of changes in the money supply in forecasting future changes in other economic variables, such as real GDP. Nevertheless, some "Fed watchers" continue to study movements in the money supply. These Fed watchers predict the growth of M2 in much the same way as they do for M1. They forecast changes in the monetary base—particularly in the nonborrowed base—and changes in the components of the M2 multiplier.

Learning Objectives

After studying this chapter, you should be able to:

The End of "Normal" Monetary Policy?

In August 2016, as Federal Reserve policymakers gathered with economists and central bankers from other countries for an annual monetary policy conference in Jackson Hole, Wyoming, many observers were asking: Will monetary policy ever return to normal? During the financial crisis of 2007–2009, the Fed took extraordinary policy actions to keep the financial system from imploding. The crisis had deepened in the fall of 2008, following the bankruptcy of the Lehman Brothers investment bank. At that time, the Fed made huge asset purchases that greatly increased bank reserves, the monetary base, and the size of the Fed's balance sheet.

Fed policymakers expected that within two years of taking these actions, the economy would be in the middle of a strong recovery, and they could begin an "exit strategy." Although the Fed never described it in detail, the exit strategy was the process by which the Fed would shrink its balance sheet and return bank reserves and the monetary base to normal levels. In addition, the Fed had reduced its target for the federal funds rate—the interest rate banks charge each other on overnight loans—to a range of 0% to 0.25% in December 2008. As part of the exit strategy, Fed policymakers had expected to eventually raise the target to 4%. By the time of the 2016 Jackson Hole conference, however, more than seven years after the end of the 2007–2009 recession, the monetary base and the Fed's balance sheet remained very large, and the target

Continued on next page

KEY ISSUE AND QUESTION

Issue: During the financial crisis of 2007–2009, the Federal Reserve implemented unusual monetary policy actions to stabilize the financial system and help bring the economy out of recession.

Question: Is the Fed likely to return to using normal monetary policy procedures?

Answered on page 534

for the federal funds rate had risen only to a range of 0.25% to 0.50%. Normal monetary policy seemed very far off. As Fed Chair Janet Yellen remarked: "I certainly myself couldn't have imagined six, seven years ago that we would be employing the policies we are now."

Nor was the Fed alone in persisting in an unusual monetary policy. The Bank of Japan (BOJ), the Bank of England (BOE), and the European Central Bank (ECB) had pursued similar policies, with the BOJ and the ECB going so far as to push certain interest rates below zero. Although in 2016, the number of people employed in the United States had increased substantially since the end of the recession, the fraction of the population that was employed was far below pre-recession levels, and the growth rate of real GDP remained low. The recovery from the recession had been the weakest since at least the 1940s. The economies of the United Kingdom, the eurozone, and Japan were also experiencing slow growth.

To Chair Janet Yellen and some other Fed policymakers, the U.S. economy had yet to experience the strength that would allow them finally to start their exit strategy and return to normal monetary policy. Federal Reserve Bank of San Francisco President John Williams warned that even with the unconventional policies the Fed had been employing, the United States faced a "new normal [in which] recessions will tend to be longer and deeper [and] recoveries slower."

Some economists and policymakers were concerned, though, that the persistence of unconventional policies might have introduced distortions into the economy and the financial system that could lead to future economic instability. In particular, they were concerned that:

- A prolonged period of very low nominal interest rates had resulted in unsustainably high prices of stocks, corporate and government bonds, and other assets.
- Low interest rates had reduced the return to saving and had made it more difficult for risk-averse investors to adequately save for retirement using bank certificates of deposits (CDs) and other low-risk assets.
- The Fed's continuing to hold trillions of dollars in financial assets was distorting prices and yields in financial markets, particularly the housing market, by removing from the market securities usually held by private investors.

Would the Fed ever return to its pre-2007 policies? In remarks at the 2016 Jackson Hole conference, Yellen argued that the Fed should not go back to those policies because changes in the world economy and in the financial system meant the policies were no longer sufficient for the Fed to achieve its goals of high employment and price stability. As Yellen and other Fed policymakers left the conference, the debate over the future of monetary policy seemed likely to be prolonged and vigorous.

Source: Janet L. Yellen, "The Federal Reserve's Monetary Policy Toolkit: Past, Present, and Future," Remarks at "Designing Resilient Monetary Policy Frameworks for the Future," a symposium sponsored by the Federal Reserve Bank of Kansas City, Jackson Hole, Wyoming, August 26, 2016; Jon Hilsenrath, "Years of Fed Missteps Fueled Disillusion with the Economy and Washington," *Wall Street Journal*, August 25, 2016; Kevin Warsh, "The Federal Reserve Needs New Thinking," *Wall Street Journal*, August 24, 2016; and John C. Williams, "Monetary Policy in a Low R-Star World," *FRBSF Economic Letter*, 2016-23, August 15, 2016.

Although we can identify the goals of monetary policy, as the slow recovery from the 2007–2009 recession showed, it is not always easy for the Fed to achieve those goals. The Fed has a limited number of monetary policy tools to use in attaining its goals. It uses these policy tools primarily to change the money supply and short-term interest rates. During and after the financial crisis, though, the Fed had to move beyond a focus on the money supply and short-term interest rates. In this chapter, we describe how the Fed conducts monetary policy and identify the difficulties that it encounters in designing effective monetary policies.

15.1 The Goals of Monetary Policy

LEARNING OBJECTIVE: Describe the goals of monetary policy.

Most economists and policymakers agree that the ultimate aim of monetary policy is to advance the economic well-being of the population. Although there are many ways to assess economic well-being, it is typically determined by the quantity and quality of goods and services that individuals can enjoy. Economic well-being arises from efficient employment of labor and capital and steady growth in output. In addition, stable economic conditions—minimal fluctuations in production and employment, steady interest rates, and smoothly functioning financial markets—enhance economic well-being. The Fed has set six *monetary policy goals* that are intended to promote economic well-being:

1. Price stability
2. High employment
3. Economic growth
4. Stability of financial markets and institutions
5. Interest rate stability
6. Foreign exchange market stability

The Fed and other central banks use monetary policy to achieve these goals.

Price Stability

Inflation, or persistently rising prices, erodes the value of money as a medium of exchange and as a unit of account. Especially since the dramatic and unexpected rise in inflation during the 1970s, policymakers in the United States, Europe, Canada, and Japan have set price stability as a key policy goal. A market economy relies on prices to communicate information about costs and about demand for goods and services to households and firms. Inflation makes prices less useful as signals for resource allocation because households and firms have difficulty distinguishing changes in *relative prices*—which guide decision making—from changes in the general price level due to inflation. For example, if the relative price of corn rises by 5%, selling corn will be more profitable, and farmers will plant more corn. But if there is 5% inflation with no increase in the relative price of corn, selling corn is not more profitable because the price of corn and the price of inputs to corn growing will all have risen. In that case, farmers will not want to increase corn production but may do so if they have trouble recognizing that inflation rather than a relative increase in corn prices has occurred.

When inflation occurs, families have trouble deciding how much to save for their children's education or for retirement because they are uncertain how much they will be able to purchase in the future with a given amount of dollars saved. Firms facing uncertain future prices will hesitate to enter into long-term contracts with suppliers or customers. Fluctuations in inflation can also arbitrarily redistribute income, as when lenders suffer losses when inflation is higher than expected or when retired people on fixed dollar pensions suffer unexpected declines in purchasing power.

Severe inflation inflicts even greater economic costs. Rates of inflation in the hundreds or thousands of percent per year—known as *hyperinflation*—can severely damage an economy's productive capacity. In extreme cases, money loses value so quickly that it no longer functions as a store of value or medium of exchange. People need a wheelbarrow full of cash to buy groceries. During the hyperinflation of the 1920s in Germany, production plummeted and unemployment soared. The resulting economic instability paved the way for Hitler and the Nazi Party to come to power 10 years later. The range of problems caused by inflation—from uncertainty to economic devastation—makes price stability a key monetary policy goal.

High Employment

High employment, or a low rate of unemployment, is another key monetary policy goal. Unemployed workers and underused factories and machines lower an economy's output. Unemployment causes financial distress and decreases self-esteem for workers who lack jobs. Congress and the president share responsibility with the Fed for the goal of high employment. Congress enacted the Employment Act of 1946 and the Full Employment and Balanced Growth Act of 1978 (the Humphrey-Hawkins Act) to make explicit the federal government's commitment to achieving high employment and price stability.

Although the Fed is committed to high employment, it does not seek a zero percent rate of unemployment. Even under the best economic conditions, some workers move into or out of the job market or are between jobs. Workers sometimes leave one job to pursue another and might be unemployed in the meantime. Individuals also leave the labor force to obtain more education and training or to raise a family, and reentry may take time. This type of *frictional unemployment* enables workers to search for positions that maximize their well-being. *Structural unemployment* refers to unemployment that is caused by changes in the structure of the economy, such as shifts in manufacturing techniques toward automation, increased use of computer hardware and software in offices, and increases in the production of services instead of goods. The tools of monetary policy are ineffective in reducing the levels of frictional and structural unemployment because these types of unemployment depend on factors, such as long-run trends in technology, the age and gender composition of the workforce, changes in where industries are located, and the geographic mobility of workers, that do not depend on the changes in the money supply and interest rates that are the usual focus of monetary policy. Instead, the Fed attempts to reduce levels of *cyclical unemployment*, which is unemployment associated with business cycle recessions. Sometimes economists have difficulty distinguishing structural unemployment from cyclical unemployment. For example, in 2016, some economists and policymakers argued that the decline in the fraction of the U.S. population that was employed was due to the lingering effects of the 2007–2009 recession, while others believed that the decline had been caused by structural factors that could not be affected by monetary policy.

When all workers who want jobs have them (apart from the frictionally and structurally unemployed) and the demand and supply of labor are in equilibrium, economists say that unemployment is at its *natural rate* (sometimes called the *full-employment rate of unemployment*). Economists disagree on the exact value of the natural rate of unemployment, and there is good reason to believe that it varies over time in response to changes in the age and gender composition of the labor force and changes in government policies with respect to taxes, minimum wages, and unemployment insurance compensation. Currently, most economists estimate that the natural rate of unemployment is about 5%.

Economic Growth

Policymakers seek steady **economic growth**, or increases in the economy's output of goods and services over time. Economic growth provides the only source of sustained real increases in household incomes. Economic growth depends on high employment. With high employment, businesses are likely to grow by investing in new plant and equipment that raise profits, productivity, and workers' incomes. In contrast, when unemployment is high, businesses have unused productive capacity and are much less likely to invest in capital improvements. Policymakers attempt to encourage *stable* economic growth because a stable business environment allows firms and households to plan accurately and encourages the long-term investment that is needed to sustain growth.

Stability of Financial Markets and Institutions

When financial markets and institutions are not efficient in matching savers and borrowers, the economy loses resources. Some firms will be unable to obtain the financing they need to design, develop, and market goods and services. Savers waste resources looking for satisfactory investments. The stability of financial markets and institutions makes possible the efficient matching of savers and borrowers.

Congress and the president created the Fed in response to the financial panics of the late 1800s and early 1900s. However, as we saw in Chapter 12, the Fed failed to stop the bank panics of the early 1930s that increased the severity of the Great Depression. During the post–World War II period, the Fed experienced greater success in averting potential panics in the commercial paper, stock, and commodity markets. The Fed's attention to financial stability was shown by its interventions following the stock market crash of 1987 and the terrorist attacks of September 11, 2001 in the United States.

Although the Fed also responded vigorously to the financial crisis that began in 2007, it initially underestimated its severity and was unable to head off the deep recession of 2007–2009. The financial crisis led to renewed debate over whether the Fed should take action to forestall asset price bubbles such as those associated with the dot-com boom on the U.S. stock market in the late 1990s and the U.S. housing market in the mid-2000s. Fed policymakers and many economists have generally argued that asset bubbles are difficult to identify ahead of time and that actions to deflate them may be counterproductive. But the severity of the 2007–2009 recession led some economists and policymakers to reassess this position. Financial stability has clearly become a more important Fed policy goal.

MAKING THE CONNECTION

Should the Fed Deflate Asset Bubbles?

As we've seen in previous chapters, a bubble occurs when the price of an asset rises above the asset's fundamental value. We saw in Chapter 12 that during the early 2000s, the prices of houses in a number of U.S. cities soared far above what the rental value of the houses indicated. The bursting of the housing bubble was a key factor in causing the severity of the 2007–2009 financial crisis and recession. In the late 1990s, the prices of shares of stock in Internet companies such as Webvan and eToys rose to levels that were far above what could be explained by the likely future profitability of these firms. (In fact, these two firms and many other early Internet retailers eventually declared bankruptcy without earning any profits.) The bursting of the dot-com bubble contributed to the 2001 recession.

As part of its commitment to stabilizing the financial system, should the Fed monitor prices in asset markets and take steps to deflate bubbles before they can burst and potentially cause a recession? Some economists and policymakers believe that the lesson of the dot-com and housing bubbles is that the Fed needs to take steps to fight asset bubbles if it hopes to avoid the disruption to the financial system the bursting of these bubbles can cause. Some critics of Fed policy argued that in 2016, the Fed was actually feeding bubbles in financial assets by keeping interest rates at historically low levels, thereby making it easier for investors to borrow to make asset purchases. Other economists, and most Fed policymakers, were skeptical that the U.S. economy was experiencing asset bubbles and that the Fed had tools that would enable it to successfully fight bubbles.

To fight bubbles, the Fed would first need to identify them. Although in hindsight the prices of dot-com stocks in the late 1990s and the prices of houses in many markets in 2005 were clearly bubbles, such a conclusion was less clear at the time. As we saw in Chapter 6, the fundamental value of a share of stock depends on investor expectations of the future profitability of the company issuing the stock. We now know that Internet companies such as Webvan, eToys, and Pets.com would never earn the profits necessary to justify their stock prices. In the late 1990s, though, as Internet retailing was just beginning, each of these companies could make projections of their future profitability that were difficult to disprove. In addition to individual investors, who may have been swept along by enthusiasm rather than careful investigation of the companies' prospects, many professional money managers also invested heavily in these stocks. It's unclear how Fed policymakers could have identified a bubble when many market participants didn't believe one existed.

Similarly, as late as December 2004, economists at the Federal Reserve Bank of New York argued that there wasn't a housing price bubble. After analyzing the housing market, they concluded that: "Home prices have essentially moved in line with increases in family income and declines in nominal mortgage interest rates."[1] Although some insightful investors were able to earn large profits betting that housing prices would eventually decline significantly, other investors—including money managers at many large financial firms—persisted in buying mortgage-backed securities under the assumption that housing prices would continue to rise.

If the Fed did succeed in identifying a bubble in asset prices, there remains the question of what actions it could take to deflate the bubble without harming the financial system or the economy. As we will discuss in Section 15.2, the Fed's monetary policy actions are centered on changing the target for the federal funds rate, with the intention of affecting interest rates throughout the economy. Raising interest rates might help deflate an asset bubble by increasing the cost of borrowing the funds used to buy houses, stocks, or whatever other asset is experiencing a bubble.

Traditionally, Fed policymakers have been reluctant to use higher interest rates to head off potential asset bubbles, however. They argue that raising interest rates also

---

[1] Jonathan McCarthy and Richard W. Peach, "Are Home Prices the Next 'Bubble'?" *FRBNY Economic Policy Review*, Vol, 10, No. 3 , December 2004, pp. 1–17.

raises the costs to households and firms of financing all types of spending and may cause a slowdown in the economy or even a recession. Timothy Geithner served as president of the Federal Reserve Bank of New York from 2003 to 2009, a period that included the height of the bubble in housing prices. He argues that as the Fed considered the state of the housing and stock markets in early 2006, "the idea of slowing down the entire economy faster than we otherwise thought necessary just to try to push down home prices or stock prices seemed like amputating an arm to fix a wrist injury."

Former Fed Chairman Ben Bernanke has argued that regulation and supervision of financial firms can do a better job than can interest rate increases at restraining asset bubbles. Ensuring that financial firms hold increased capital against risky assets may restrain the growth of leverage that, as we saw in Chapter 12, helped contribute to the financial crisis. Current Fed Chair Janet Yellen argues that the steps that Congress, the Fed, and financial regulators have taken to reduce risk in the financial system have made the system more resilient, thereby reducing the threat that bubbles pose: "Because a resilient financial system can withstand unexpected developments, identification of bubbles is less critical."

Although currently most Fed policymakers do not consider fighting the growth of asset bubbles to be a key policy goal, the severity of the fallout from the bursting of the housing bubble means the issue is likely to continue to be debated.

Sources: David Harrison, "Fed's George Calls for Higher Interest Rates to Prevent Asset Bubbles," *Wall Street Journal*, April 7, 2016; Janet L. Yellen, "Speech at the 2014 Michel Camdessus Central Banking Lecture, International Monetary Fund, Washington, D.C.," July 2, 2014; Jonathan McCarthy and Richard W. Peach, "Are Home Prices the Next 'Bubble'?" *FRBNY Economic Policy Review*, Vol. 10, No. 3, December 2004, pp. 1–17; and Timothy F. Geithner, *Stress Test: Reflections on Financial Crises*, New York: Crown Publishers, 2014, p. 111.

See related problems 1.7 and 1.8 at the end of the chapter.

Interest Rate Stability

Like fluctuations in price levels, fluctuations in interest rates make planning and investment decisions difficult for households and firms. Substantial increases and decreases in interest rates make it hard for firms to plan investments in plant and equipment and make households more hesitant about long-term investments in houses. Because people often blame the Fed if they believe that interest rates are excessively high or excessively low, the Fed's goal of interest rate stability is motivated by political pressure as well as by a desire for a stable saving and investment environment. In addition, as we have seen, sharp interest rate fluctuations cause problems for banks and other financial firms. So, stabilizing interest rates can help stabilize the financial system.

Foreign Exchange Market Stability

In the global economy, foreign exchange market stability, or limited fluctuations in the foreign exchange value of the dollar, is an important monetary policy goal. A stable dollar simplifies planning for commercial and financial transactions. In addition, fluctuations in the dollar's value change the international competitiveness of U.S. industries: A rising dollar makes U.S. goods more expensive abroad and reduces exports, and a falling dollar makes foreign goods more expensive in the United States and reduces imports.

In practice, the U.S. Treasury often originates changes in foreign exchange policy, although the Fed implements these policy changes.

The Fed's Dual Mandate

How can the Fed pursue all six of these policy goals at once? As it turns out, these goals are really just two goals: price stability and high employment. If the Fed can attain these two goals, it will typically attain its other goals as well. Therefore, many economists and commentators refer to the Fed's *dual mandate* as price stability and high employment. An open question is whether the Fed's dual mandate is necessarily consistent with financial market stability, as we will discuss later in this chapter.

In the next section, we consider the monetary policy tools the Fed has available to reach its goals.

15.2 Monetary Policy Tools and the Federal Funds Rate

LEARNING OBJECTIVE: Understand how the Fed uses monetary policy tools to influence the federal funds rate.

Until the financial crisis of 2007–2009, the Fed primarily relied on three monetary policy tools. During the financial crisis, the Fed announced several new policy tools. We first consider the Fed's three traditional policy tools:

1. **Open market operations** are the Fed's purchases and sales of securities in financial markets. Traditionally, the Fed concentrated on purchases and sales of Treasury bills, with the aim of influencing the level of bank reserves and short-term interest rates. During the financial crisis, the Fed began purchasing a wider variety of securities to affect long-term interest rates and to support the flow of credit in the financial system.

2. **Discount policy** includes setting the discount rate and the terms of discount lending. When Congress passed the Federal Reserve Act in 1913, it expected that discount policy would be the Fed's primary monetary policy tool. The **discount window** is the means by which the Fed makes discount loans to banks, and it serves as the channel to meet banks' short-term liquidity needs.

3. **Reserve requirements** are the Fed's regulation requiring that banks hold a certain fraction of their checkable deposits as vault cash or deposits with the Fed.[2] In Chapter 14, we saw that the required reserve ratio is a determinant of the money multiplier in the money supply process.

During the financial crisis, the Fed introduced the following three new policy tools connected with bank reserve accounts. These new tools were still being used in 2017, and, in fact, the first two had become more important than the Fed's three traditional tools.

Open market operations The Federal Reserve's purchases and sales of securities, usually U.S. Treasury securities, in financial markets.

Discount policy The policy tool of setting the discount rate and the terms of discount lending.

Discount window The means by which the Fed makes discount loans to banks, serving as the channel for meeting the liquidity needs of banks.

Reserve requirement The regulation requiring banks to hold a fraction of checkable deposits as vault cash or deposits with the Fed.

---

[2] Required reserves vary with the level of checkable deposits. As of January 2017, banks do not have to hold reserves on their first $15.5 million of checkable deposits. They must hold reserves of 3% on the next $99.6 million in checkable deposits and reserves of 10% on checkable deposits above $115.1 million.

1. **Interest on reserve balances.** In October 2008, the Fed introduced a new tool when it began for the first time to pay interest on banks' required reserve and excess reserve deposits.[3] This interest rate is called the IOER, which stands for *interest rate on excess reserves*. Reserve requirements impose an implicit tax on banks because banks could otherwise receive interest on the funds by lending them out or by investing them. The Fed reduces the size of this tax by paying interest on reserve balances. The Fed also gains a greater ability to influence banks' reserve balances. By raising the interest rate it pays, the Fed can increase banks' holdings of reserves, potentially restraining banks' ability to extend loans and increase the money supply. By reducing the interest rate, the Fed can have the opposite effect. Finally, the interest rate the Fed pays on reserves can help put a floor on short-term interest rates because banks will typically not lend funds elsewhere at an interest rate lower than the rate they can earn on reserves deposited with the Fed.

2. **Overnight reverse repurchase agreement facility.** As we will discuss in the next section, the Fed's traditional means of raising short-term interest rates was to raise its target for the federal funds rate—the rate banks charge each other on overnight loans—by using open market sales to reduce the level of reserves in the banking system. But with banks still holding trillions of dollars of excess reserves years after the financial crisis, the Fed could not use open market sales to increase its target for the federal funds rate. Instead, in December 2015, when the Fed raised its target for the federal funds rate, it did so by increasing the interest rate it paid banks on reserves and the interest rate it offered on reverse repurchase agreements. We will discuss the details of this process in Section 15.3. For now, recall that a *repurchase agreement* (or *repo*) is a short-term loan backed by collateral. With a repurchase agreement, the Fed buys a security from a financial firm, which promises to buy it back from the Fed the following day. With a *reverse repurchase agreement* (sometimes called a *matched sale-purchase agreement* or *reverse repo*), the Fed does the opposite: It sells a security to a financial firm while at the same time promising to buy the security back the next day. In effect, the Fed is borrowing funds overnight from the firm that purchases the security. By raising the interest rate it is willing to pay on these loans, the Fed reduces the willingness of the firms it deals with in these transactions—its *counterparties*—to lend at a lower rate. The Fed refers to overnight reverse repurchase agreements as ON RRPs and the interest rate on these securities as the ON RRP rate. Although this procedure is more complex than the Fed's traditional means of raising the target for the federal funds rate, it is an effective way for the Fed to achieve that target at a time when banks are holding very large levels of excess reserves.

3. **Term deposit facility.** In April 2010, the Fed announced that it would offer banks the opportunity to purchase term deposits, which are similar to the certificates of deposit that banks offer to households and firms. The Fed offers term deposits to banks in periodic auctions. The interest rates are determined by the auctions and have been slightly above the interest rate the Fed offers on reserve balances. For example, in August 2016, the interest rate on the Fed's auction of $58 billion in

---

[3] Technically, the Fed can set separate interest rates on required reserve balances (IORR) and on excess reserve balances (IOER). In December 2016, the interest rate on both types of balances was the same: 0.75%.

7-day term deposits was 0.51%, which was higher than the interest rate of 0.50% the Fed was paying on reserve deposits. The term deposit facility gives the Fed another tool in managing bank reserve holdings. The more funds banks place in term deposits, the less they will have available to expand loans and the money supply. The term deposit facility is the least important of the Fed's three new monetary policy tools.

The Federal Funds Market and the Fed's Target Federal Funds Rate

For several decades, the focus of Fed policy has been setting a target for the **federal funds rate**, which is the interest rate that banks charge each other on very short-term loans. The target for the federal funds rate is set at meetings of the Federal Open Market Committee (FOMC), which take place eight times per year in Washington, DC. Although the Fed sets a target for the federal funds rate, the actual rate is determined by the interaction of demand and supply for bank reserves in the *federal funds market*.

To analyze the determinants of the federal funds rate, we need to examine the banking system's demand for and the Fed's supply of reserves. We will use graphs of the demand for and supply of reserves (like Figure 15.1 on page 504) to see how the Fed uses its policy tools to influence the federal funds rate and the money supply.

The Traditional Assumption of Scarce Reserves   The analysis that follows shows how the equilibrium federal funds rate is determined by the interaction of the demand and supply for reserves. A key assumption underlying the analysis is that reserves are scarce, by which we mean that on a typical day, there are many banks that meet their need for reserves by borrowing from other banks in the federal funds market. Prior to the financial crisis of 2007–2009, this assumption was accurate. For example, in June 2007, banks held only about $10 billion in reserves, while having $600 billion in checkable deposits. Since the financial crisis, however, this assumption has no longer been accurate because banks hold such large levels of reserves that they have little need to borrow from other banks. In December 2016, for instance, banks held $2.1 *trillion* in reserves, while having $1.9 trillion in checkable deposits. As we saw in Chapter 14, this increase in bank reserves was the result of the large increase in the size of the Fed's balance sheet during and after the financial crisis.

As we will see, the fact that reserves are no longer scarce has important implications for how the Fed conducts monetary policy. But to understand the Fed's current approach to policy, we still need to explore how the market for reserves functioned in the more normal times before the financial crisis. Doing so provides the background for understanding the Fed's current approach and also provides us with tools for understanding how the Fed might conduct monetary policy in the future if it shrinks its balance sheet enough that reserves once again become scarce.

Demand for Reserves   Banks demand reserves both to meet their legal obligation to hold required reserves and because they may wish to hold excess reserves to meet their short-term liquidity needs. The demand curve for reserves, *D*, shown in Figure 15.1, includes banks' demand for both required reserves, *RR*, and excess reserves, *ER*. The demand curve is drawn assuming that factors other than the federal funds rate—such as other market interest rates or the required reserve ratio—that would affect banks' demand for reserves are held constant. As with other types of loans, we would expect that the higher

Federal funds rate The interest rate that banks charge each other on very short-term loans; determined by the demand and supply for reserves in the federal funds market.

the interest rate, the lower the quantity of loans demanded. As the federal funds rate, i_{ff}, increases, the opportunity cost to banks of holding excess reserves increases because the return they could earn from lending out those reserves goes up. So, as the federal funds rate increases, the quantity of reserves demanded will decline. The result is that banks' demand curve for reserves will be downward sloping.

Notice that in Figure 15.1, the demand curve for reserves becomes horizontal (or perfectly elastic) at the interest rate i_{IOER}, which is the interest rate the Fed pays on banks' reserve balances. The interest rate that the Fed pays on reserves sets a floor for the federal funds rate. To see why, suppose that the Fed is paying banks 0.75% on their reserve balances, but the federal funds rate is only 0.30%. Banks could borrow funds in the federal funds market at 0.30%, deposit the money in their reserve balances at the Fed, and earn a risk-free 0.45%. Competition among banks to obtain the funds to carry out this risk-free arbitrage would force up the federal funds rate to 0.75%, which is the rate at which banks could no longer earn arbitrage profits. This analysis needs to be qualified, however, because it does not take into account that there are some nonbank financial institutions, such as Fannie Mae and Freddie Mac, that are eligible to participate in the federal funds market but are not eligible to receive interest on deposits with the Fed. We discuss this qualification later in this chapter, in the section "How the Fed Currently Manages the Federal Funds Rate."

Supply of Reserves Figure 15.1 also shows the supply curve for reserves, S. The Fed supplies borrowed reserves, in the form of discount loans, and nonborrowed reserves, through open market operations. During and after the financial crisis of 2007–2009, the Fed greatly increased the supply of reserves through its purchases of long-term Treasury securities and mortgage-backed securities during three rounds of quantitative easing. The vertical portion of the supply curve reflects the assumption that the Fed can set

FIGURE 15.1

Equilibrium in the Federal Funds Market

Equilibrium in the federal funds market occurs at the intersection of the demand curve for reserves, D, and the supply curve for reserves, S. The Fed determines the level of reserves, R, the discount rate, i_d, and the interest rate on banks' reserve balances at the Fed, i_{IOER}. Equilibrium reserves are R^*, and the equilibrium federal funds rate is i_{ff}^*.

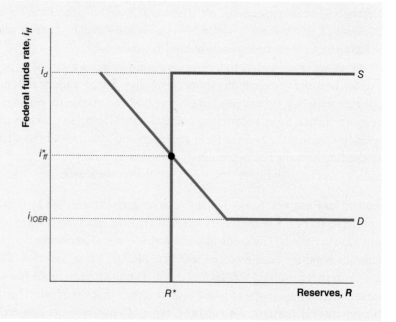

reserves, R, at whatever level it needs to meet its objectives. So, the quantity of reserves does not depend on the federal funds rate, making this portion of the supply curve vertical. Note, though, that the supply curve becomes horizontal (or perfectly elastic) at i_d, which is the discount rate that the Fed sets. At a federal funds rate below the discount rate, we assume that banks do not borrow from the Fed because they can borrow more cheaply from other banks. So, in this case, all bank reserves are nonborrowed reserves. The discount rate is a ceiling on the federal funds rate because banks would not pay a higher interest rate to borrow from other banks than the discount rate they can pay to borrow from the Fed. (For simplicity, we are assuming that banks face no restrictions on using the discount window.)

Equilibrium in the Federal Funds Market The equilibrium federal funds rate and level of reserves occur at the intersection of the demand and supply curves in Figure 15.1. Equilibrium reserves equal R^*, and the equilibrium federal funds rate equals i_{ff}^*.

Open Market Operations and the Fed's Target for the Federal Funds Rate

The centerpiece of Fed policymaking has been the meetings of the FOMC, at which the Fed announces a target for the federal funds rate. Although only banks and a few other financial institutions can borrow and lend at the federal funds rate, changes in this interest rate can have broad effects on the economy. For example, when the FOMC lowers the target for the federal funds rate, the lower cost of funds to banks typically leads to lower interest rates on bank loans to households and firms. Responding to the lower rates, firms increase their spending on machinery, equipment, and other investment goods, and households increase their spending on cars, furniture, and other consumer durables.

As Figure 15.2 shows, the federal funds rate, the mortgage interest rate, and the interest rates on corporate bonds generally move together. Note, though, that the federal funds rate often increases and decreases more than these long-term rates. For example, for several years after 2000, all interest rates fell, but the interest rates on mortgages and corporate bonds did not fall by as much or as rapidly as the federal funds rate. In this case, investors did not believe that these low short-term rates would continue for very long. In other words, investors expected that future short-term rates would increase. Generally, though, if the Fed increases or decreases its target for the federal funds rate, long-term nominal interest rates—for example, the interest rate on a 30-year mortgage—will also increase or decrease.

Traditionally, the Fed used open market operations to hit its target for the federal funds rate. For example, on October 29, 2008, to help ease the financial crisis and the recession, the FOMC lowered its target for the federal funds rate from 1.5% to 1%. To accomplish this goal, the Fed engaged in *open market purchases* of Treasury securities. At the same time that the Fed lowered its target for the federal funds rate, it cut the discount rate from 1.75% to 1.25%. Panel (a) of Figure 15.3 on page 507 illustrates the results of the Fed's actions. If nothing else changes in the federal funds market, an open market purchase shifts the reserve supply curve to the right, from S_1 to S_2, increasing bank reserves and decreasing the federal funds rate. Because the discount rate was lowered, the horizontal portion of the reserve supply curve also shifts down. The equilibrium level of bank reserves increases from R_1^* to R_2^*, and the equilibrium federal funds rate declines from 1.5% to 1%.

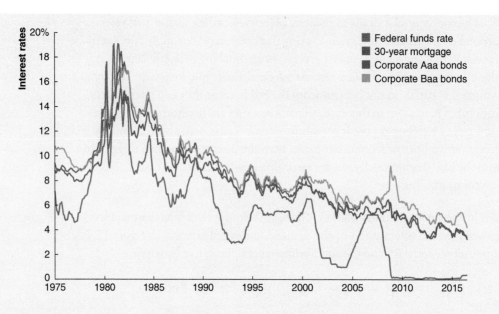

FIGURE 15.2 The Federal Funds Rate and the Interest Rates on Corporate Bonds and Mortgages

The Fed controls the federal funds rate. The long-term interest rates that households pay to purchase a house or that corporations pay to finance investment generally rise and fall with the federal funds rate.

Source: Board of Governors of the Federal Reserve System.

To increase its target for the federal funds rate, the Fed engaged in an *open market sale* of Treasury securities. For example, on June 29, 2006, the FOMC increased its target for the federal funds rate from 5% to 5.25%. At the same time, the Fed raised the discount rate from 6% to 6.25%. The Fed wanted to push up interest rates to slow the economy in the face of the housing bubble and a rising inflation rate. Panel (b) of Figure 15.3 illustrates the result of an open market sale. The supply curve for reserves shifts to the left, from S_1 to S_2, decreasing the equilibrium level of bank reserves from R_1^* to R_2^*, and increasing the equilibrium federal funds rate from 5% to 5.25%. Because the discount rate was increased, the horizontal portion of the reserve supply curve also shifts up. (Note that because these events took place before the Fed began paying interest on bank reserve deposits, we have omitted the horizontal segment of the demand curve for reserves.)

In summary, assuming that reserves are scarce, an open market purchase of securities by the Fed decreases the federal funds rate. An open market sale of securities increases the federal funds rate.

The Effect of Changes in the Discount Rate and in Reserve Requirements

The Fed adjusts the target for the federal funds rate almost exclusively through open market operations, but we can briefly consider the effect on the market for reserves of changes in the discount rate and changes in the required reserve ratio.

Changes in the Discount Rate Since 2003, the Fed has kept the discount rate higher than the target for the federal funds rate. This makes the discount rate a *penalty rate*, which means

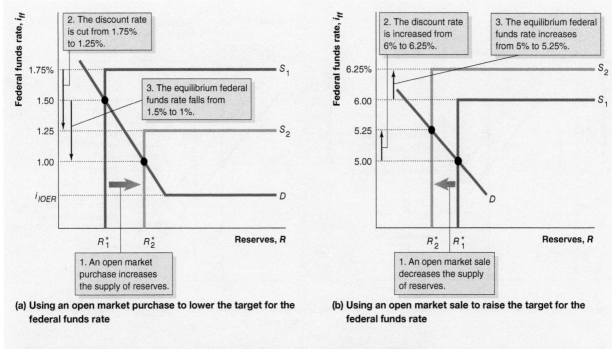

(a) Using an open market purchase to lower the target for the federal funds rate

(b) Using an open market sale to raise the target for the federal funds rate

FIGURE 15.3 Effects of Open Market Operations on the Federal Funds Market

In panel (a), an open market purchase of securities by the Fed increases reserves in the banking system, shifting the supply curve to the right, from S_1 to S_2. The equilibrium level of reserves increases from R_1^* to R_2^*, while the equilibrium federal funds rate falls from 1.5% to 1%. The discount rate also declines from 1.75% to 1.25%.

In panel (b), an open market sale of securities by the Fed reduces reserves, shifting the supply curve to the left, from S_1 to S_2. The equilibrium level of reserves decreases from R_1^* to R_2^*, while the equilibrium federal funds rate rises from 5% to 5.25%. The discount rate also increases from 6% to 6.25%.

that banks pay a penalty by borrowing from the Fed rather than from other banks in the federal funds market. Typically, the Fed has raised or lowered the discount rate at the same time that it raises or lowers the target for the federal funds rate.[4] As a result, changes in the discount rate have no independent effect on the federal funds rate. In the reserves market graph, the horizontal portion of the supply curve is always above the equilibrium federal funds rate.

Changes in the Required Reserve Ratio The Fed rarely changes the required reserve ratio. The last change took place in April 1992, when the required reserve ratio was reduced from 12% to 10%. It is possible, though, that the Fed might change the required reserve ratio in the future. Changing the required reserve ratio would cause a change in the equilibrium federal funds rate if the Fed did not also engage in an offsetting open market operations. We illustrate this result in panel (a) of Figure 15.4. If the other factors underlying the demand and supply curves for reserves are held constant, an increase in the required reserve ratio shifts the demand curve to the right, from D_1 to D_2, because banks have to hold more reserves. As a result, the equilibrium federal funds rate increases from i_{ff1}^* to i_{ff2}^*, while the equilibrium level of reserves remains unchanged, at R_1^*.

---

[4] An exception to this rule occurred in February 2010, when the Fed increased the discount rate from 0.50% to 0.75% while leaving the target for the federal funds rate unchanged.

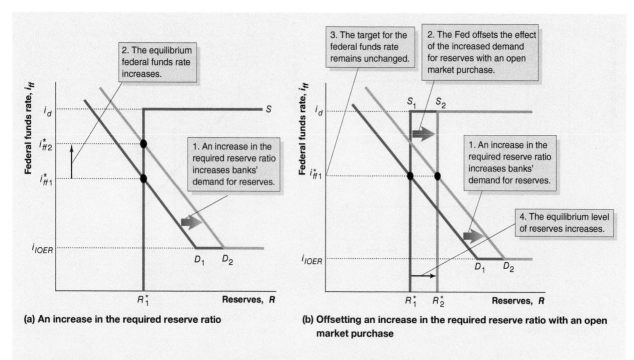

FIGURE 15.4 The Effect of a Change in the Required Reserve Ratio on the Federal Funds Market

In panel (a), the Fed increases the required reserve ratio, which shifts the demand curve for reserves from D_1 to D_2. The equilibrium federal funds rate rises from i^*_{ff1} to i^*_{ff2}. In panel (b), the Fed increases the required reserve ratio, which shifts the demand curve from D_1 to D_2. The Fed offsets the effects of the increase in the required reserve ratio with an open market purchase, shifting the supply curve from S_1 to S_2. The level of reserves increases from R^*_1 to R^*_2, while the target federal funds rate remains unchanged, at i^*_{ff1}.

It is unlikely that the Fed would begin using changes in the required reserve ratio as a means of changing its target for the federal funds rate. It is more likely that if the Fed changes the required reserve ratio, it will carry out offsetting open market operations to keep the target for the federal funds rate unchanged. Panel (b) shows the situation where the Fed combines an increase in the required reserve ratio with an open market purchase in order to keep unchanged its target for the federal funds rate. As in panel (a), the increase in the required reserve ratio shifts the demand curve to the right, from D_1 to D_2, but in this case the open market purchase shifts the supply curve to the right, from S_1 to S_2, keeping the target for the federal funds rate unchanged, at i^*_{ff1}. The equilibrium level of reserves increases from R^*_1 to R^*_2.

SOLVED PROBLEM 15.2

Analyzing the Federal Funds Market

Use demand and supply graphs for the federal funds market to analyze the following two situations. Be sure that your graphs clearly show changes in the equilibrium federal funds rate and equilibrium level of reserves, as well as any shifts in the demand and supply curves. In both parts of the problem, assume that reserves are scarce.

a. Suppose that banks decrease their demand for reserves. Show how the Fed can offset this change through open market operations in order to keep the equilibrium federal funds rate unchanged.

b. Suppose that in equilibrium the federal funds rate is equal to the interest rate the Fed is paying on reserves. If the Fed carries out an open market purchase, show the effect on the equilibrium federal funds rate.

Solving the Problem

Step 1 **Review the chapter material.** This problem is about the federal funds market, so you may want to review the following four sections: "Open Market Operations and the Fed's Target for the Federal Funds Rate," which begins on page 505, and the section "The Effect of Changes in the Discount Rate and in Reserve Requirements," which begins on page 506.

Step 2 **Answer part (a) by drawing the appropriate graph.** If banks decrease their demand for reserves, the demand curve will shift to the left. Given the assumption that reserves are scarce, unless the Fed offsets the effect of the shift, the equilibrium federal funds rate will decrease. To offset the decline in the demand for reserves, the Fed needs to carry out an open market sale, shifting the supply curve for reserves to the left. Your graph should show that after these two shifts, the equilibrium federal funds rate is unchanged.

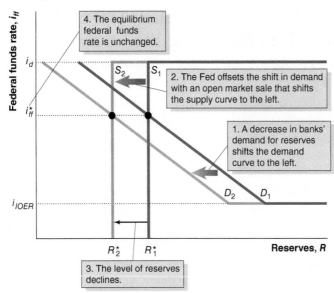

Step 3 **Answer part (b) by drawing the appropriate graph.** If the equilibrium federal funds rate is equal to the interest rate the Fed is paying banks on their reserve balances, the supply curve must be intersecting the demand curve on the horizontal segment of the demand curve. An open market purchase will shift the supply curve to the right, which increases the equilibrium level of reserves, but because the supply curve is already in the

horizontal segment of the demand curve, the equilibrium federal funds rate will not change.

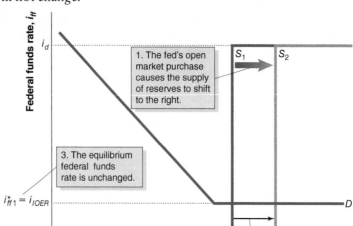

See related problems 2.7 and 2.8 at the end of the chapter.

15.3 The Fed's Monetary Policy Tools and Its New Approach to Managing the Federal Funds Rate

LEARNING OBJECTIVE: Trace how the Fed has changed its use of monetary policy tools over time.

Now that we have looked at how the Fed's monetary policy tools affect the federal funds rate, we can look more closely at each of the tools. We will also analyze how the Fed manages the federal funds rate in current circumstances when reserves are no longer scarce.

Open Market Operations

The original Federal Reserve Act of 1913 didn't specifically mention open market operations because, at that time, neither policymakers nor financial market participants understood them well. The Fed began to use open market purchases as a policy tool during the 1920s, when it acquired Liberty Bonds issued by the federal government during World War I from banks, enabling banks to finance more business loans. Before 1935, district Federal Reserve Banks conducted limited open market operations in securities markets, but these transactions lacked central coordination and were not always used to achieve a monetary policy goal. The lack of coordinated intervention by the Fed during the banking crisis of the early 1930s led Congress in 1935 to establish the FOMC to guide open market operations.

When the Fed carries out an open market purchase of Treasury securities, the prices of these securities increase, thereby decreasing their yield. Because the purchase will increase the monetary base, the money supply will expand. An open market sale decreases the price of Treasury securities, thereby increasing their yield. The sale decreases the monetary base and the money supply. Because open market purchases reduce interest rates, they are considered an *expansionary policy*. Open market sales increase interest rates and are considered a *contractionary policy*. (Note that an expansionary policy is also called a *loose policy*, and a contractionary policy is also called a *tight policy*.)

Implementing Open Market Operations How does the Fed carry out open market operations? At the end of each meeting, the FOMC issues a statement that includes its target for the federal funds rate and its assessment of the economy, particularly with respect to its policy goals of price stability and economic growth. In addition, the FOMC issues a *policy directive* to the Federal Reserve System's account manager, who is a vice president of the Federal Reserve Bank of New York and has the responsibility of implementing open market operations. Until the financial crisis of 2007–2009 and the vast expansion of bank reserves, the account manager at the New York Fed was responsible for hitting the FOMC's target for the federal funds rate. As we will see later in this section, open market operations by themselves are no longer capable of bringing about a change in the FOMC's target federal funds rate. Open market operations are conducted each morning on the Open Market Trading Desk at the Federal Reserve Bank of New York. The trading desk is linked electronically through a system called the Trading Room Automated Processing System (TRAPS) to *primary dealers*—who are private securities firms, such as Goldman Sachs and Cantor Fitzgerald, that the Fed has selected to participate in open market operations. (In December 2016, there were 23 primary dealers.) Each morning, the trading desk notifies the primary dealers of the size of the open market purchase or sale being conducted and asks them to submit offers to buy or sell Treasury securities. The dealers have just a few minutes to respond. Once the dealers' offers have been received, the Fed's account manager goes over the list, accepts the best offers, and then has the trading desk buy or sell the securities until the volume of reserves reaches the Fed's desired goal. These securities are either added to or subtracted from the portfolios of the various Federal Reserve banks, according to their shares of total assets in the system.

How does the account manager know what to do? The manager interprets the FOMC's most recent policy directive, holds daily conferences with two members of the FOMC, and personally analyzes financial market conditions. If the level of reserves needs to be increased over the current level, the account manager orders the trading desk to purchase securities. If the level of reserves needs to be decreased, the account manager orders the trading desk to sell securities.

In conducting the Fed's open market operations during normal times when reserves were scarce, the trading desk undertook both dynamic, or permanent, open market operations and defensive, or temporary, open market operations. *Dynamic open market operations* are intended to change monetary policy as directed by the FOMC. *Defensive open market operations* are intended to offset temporary fluctuations in the demand or supply for reserves, not to carry out changes in monetary policy. For example, when the U.S. Treasury purchases goods and services for the federal government, it does so by using funds in its account at the Fed. As the sellers of those goods and services deposit the funds in their banks, the supply of reserves in the banking system will increase. Similarly, if following a snowstorm transportation is delayed and there is a delay in check clearing, *Federal Reserve float* will increase. An increase in float temporarily increases the reserves of the banking system as banks that have had checks deposited see their reserves increase, while there is a delay in decreasing the reserves of banks against which checks have been written. Dynamic open market operations are likely to be conducted as outright purchases and sales of Treasury securities—that is, by buying from or selling to primary dealers. Defensive open market operations are much more common than dynamic operations. Defensive open market purchases are conducted through repurchase agreements. With these agreements, the Fed buys securities from a primary dealer, and the dealer agrees to buy them back at a given price at a specified future date, usually within one week. In effect, the government securities serve as collateral for a short-term loan. For defensive open market sales, the trading desk often engages in a reverse repurchase agreement (also called a *matched sale–purchase transactions* or a *reverse repo*), in which the Fed sells securities to primary dealers, and the dealers agree to sell them back to the Fed in the near future. Economic disturbances, such as natural disasters, also cause unexpected fluctuations in the demand for currency and bank reserves. The Fed's account manager must respond to these events and sell or buy securities to maintain the monetary policy indicated by the FOMC's guidelines.

Open Market Operations Versus Other Policy Tools Open market operations have several benefits that the Fed's other traditional policy tools—discount policy and reserve requirements—lack: control, flexibility, and speed of implementation. Because the Fed initiates open market purchases and sales, it completely controls their volume. Discount loans depend in part on the willingness of banks to request the loans and so are not as completely under the Fed's control.

Open market operations are flexible because the Fed can make both large and small open market operations. Often, dynamic operations require large purchases or sales, whereas defensive operations call for small purchases or sales. Other traditional policy tools lack such flexibility. Reversing open market operations is simple for the Fed. For example, if the Fed decides that its open market sales have made reserves grow too slowly, it can quickly authorize open market purchases. Discount loans and reserve requirement changes are more difficult to reverse quickly. This is a key reason the Fed has left reserve requirements unchanged since 1992.

The Fed can implement its open market operations rapidly, with no administrative delays. All that is required is for the trading desk to place buy or sell orders with the primary dealers. Changing the discount rate or reserve requirements requires lengthier deliberation.

"Quantitative Easing": Fed Bond Purchases During and After the Financial Crisis In recent decades, Fed open market operations have concentrated on buying and selling short-term Treasury securities, with the intention of affecting the market for bank reserves and the equilibrium federal funds rate. But by December 2008, the Fed had driven the target for the federal funds rate nearly to zero, while the financial crisis and the economic recession had deepened. These continuing problems led the Fed to take the unusual step of buying more than $1.7 trillion in mortgage-backed securities and longer-term Treasury securities during 2009 and early 2010. This policy of a central bank attempting to stimulate the economy by buying long-term securities is called **quantitative easing**. The Fed's objective was to reduce the interest rates on mortgages and on 10-year Treasury notes.

Quantitative easing A central bank policy that attempts to stimulate the economy by buying long-term securities.

The interest rate on 10-year Treasury notes plays an important role in the financial system because it is a benchmark default-free interest rate. A lower interest rate on 10-year Treasury notes can help to lower interest rates on corporate bonds, thereby increasing investment spending. In addition, many adjustable-rate mortgages have their interest rates determined by the interest rate on 10-year Treasury notes. When the interest rate on the 10-year Treasury note falls, the interest rates on these mortgages automatically fall. In November 2010, the Fed announced a second round of quantitative easing (dubbed QE2). With QE2, the Fed bought an additional $600 billion in long-term Treasury securities through June 2011.

In September 2011, with the economic recovery still proceeding more slowly than expected, the Fed announced that it would purchase $400 billion of long-term securities while also selling $400 billion of short-term securities. The financial press referred to this policy as *Operation Twist*. The policy's name reflects its goal of twisting the yield curve by increasing short-term interest rates and lowering long-term interest rates. Because Operation Twist attempted to directly reduce long-term interest rates through bond purchases, it was similar in its effects to quantitative easing. By selling $400 billion of short-term bonds at the same time that it bought $400 billion of long-term securities, the Fed did not increase the monetary base or the threat of future inflation.

In September 2012, the Fed announced a third round of quantitative easing (QE3), focused on purchases of mortgage-backed securities. The Fed ended QE3 in October 2014. Economists remain divided over whether the rounds of quantitative easing significantly expanded the growth of employment and output in the U.S. economy.

Figure 15.5 shows how the Fed's policies during the financial crisis of 2007–2009 and the following years affected the *Fed's balance sheet*. The turmoil following the collapse of Lehman Brothers on September 15, 2008, led to a dramatic change in Fed policy. The Fed's assets exploded from $927 billion before the Lehman Brothers bankruptcy to $2.2 trillion on November 12, 2008. The increase came primarily from new loans to financial institutions and attempts to increase the liquidity of key markets such as commercial paper under new *lending facilities*, as described in the next section. With the beginning of successive rounds of quantitative easing in early 2009, the Fed's holdings of mortgage-backed securities (including "agency securities" issued by Fannie Mae, Freddie Mac, and other government-sponsored enterprises [GSEs]) began to increase rapidly (shown by the dark brown area in the figure), as did its holdings of U.S. Treasury securities (shown by the green area in the figure). At the end of 2016, the Fed's holdings of these securities remained very large.

Discount Policy

Except for a brief period during 1966, before 1980, the Fed made discount loans only to banks that were members of the Federal Reserve System. Banks considered the ability to borrow from the Fed through the discount window as an advantage of membership that partially offset the cost of the Fed's reserve requirements. Since 1980, all depository institutions, including savings and loans and credit unions, have had access to the discount window. Each Federal Reserve Bank maintains its own discount window, although all Reserve Banks charge the same discount rate.

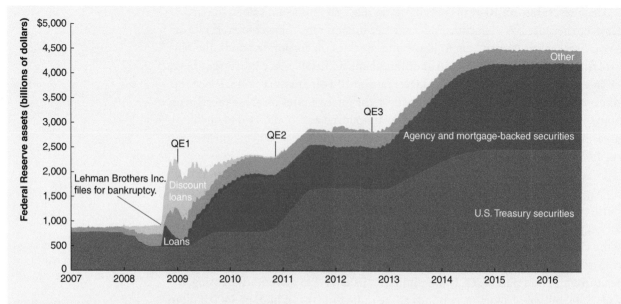

FIGURE 15.5 Federal Reserve Assets, 2007–2016

After the collapse of Lehman Brothers, the Fed dramatically increased the assets it owned from $927 billion to $2.2 trillion. Some of the increase came from loans to financial institutions, and the rest came from purchases of assets such as commercial paper and mortgage-backed securities. The Fed's three rounds of quantitative easing (QE) contributed to the increases in the Fed's assets.

Source: Board of Governors of the Federal Reserve System.

Categories of Discount Loans The Fed's discount loans to banks fall into three categories: (1) primary credit, (2) secondary credit, and (3) seasonal credit.

Primary credit is available to healthy banks that have adequate capital and supervisory ratings. Banks may use primary credit for any purpose and do not have to seek funds from other sources before requesting a discount window loan from the *primary credit facility*, or *standing lending facility*. The loans are usually very short term—often overnight—but they can be for as long as several weeks. The primary credit interest rate is set above the federal funds rate and so is only a backup source of funds because healthy banks will choose to borrow at a lower interest rate in the federal funds market or from other sources. The main purpose of primary credit is to make funds available to banks to deal with temporary liquidity problems. In that sense, primary credit represents the Fed's actions in its role as a lender of last resort. When economists and policymakers refer to the discount rate, they are referring to the interest rate on primary credit.

Secondary credit is intended for banks that are not eligible for primary credit because they have inadequate capital or low supervisory ratings. This type of credit is often used for banks that are suffering from severe liquidity problems, including those that may soon be closed. The Fed carefully monitors how banks are using the funds they obtain from these loans. The secondary credit interest rate is set above the primary credit rate, usually by 0.50 percentage point.

Primary credit Discount loans available to healthy banks experiencing temporary liquidity problems.

Secondary credit Discount loans available to banks that are not eligible for primary credit.

Seasonal credit consists of temporary, short-term loans to satisfy seasonal requirements of smaller banks in geographic areas where agriculture or tourism is important. For example, by using these loans, a bank in a ski resort area in Vermont won't have to maintain excess cash or sell loans and investments to meet the borrowing needs of local firms during the winter months. The seasonal credit interest rate is tied to the average of rates on certificates of deposit and the federal funds rate. Because of improvements in credit markets that allow even small banks access to market loans, many economists question whether a seasonal credit facility is still needed.

Seasonal credit Discount loans available to smaller banks in areas where agriculture or tourism is important.

Discount Lending During the Financial Crisis of 2007–2009 From its founding in 1914 until 1980, with a few brief exceptions, the Fed made loans only to members of the Federal Reserve System. In 1980, Congress authorized the Fed to make loans to all depository institutions. But, as we saw in Chapter 11, by the beginning of the financial crisis in 2007, a shadow banking system of investment banks, money market mutual funds, hedge funds, and other nonbank financial firms had grown to be as large as the commercial banking system. The initial stages of the financial crisis involved these shadow banks rather than commercial banks. When the crisis began, the Fed was handicapped in its role as a lender of last resort because it had no recent tradition of lending to any firms except depository institutions, such as commercial banks and savings and loans.

The Fed did, however, have the authority to lend more broadly. As it then was, Section 13(3) of the Federal Reserve Act authorized the Fed in "unusual and exigent circumstances" to lend to any "individual, partnership, or corporation" that could provide acceptable collateral and could demonstrate an inability to borrow from commercial banks. The Fed used this authority to set up several temporary *lending facilities*:

- **Primary Dealer Credit Facility.** Under this facility, primary dealers could borrow overnight using mortgage-backed securities as collateral. This facility was intended to allow the investment banks and large securities firms that are primary dealers to obtain emergency loans. The facility was established in March 2008 and closed in February 2010.
- **Term Securities Lending Facility.** Under this facility, the Fed would loan up to $200 billion of Treasury securities in exchange for mortgage-backed securities. By early 2008, selling mortgage-backed securities had become difficult. This facility was intended to allow financial firms to borrow against those illiquid assets. It was established in March 2008 and closed in February 2010.
- **Commercial Paper Funding Facility.** Under this facility, the Fed purchased three-month commercial paper issued by nonfinancial corporations. When Lehman Brothers defaulted on its commercial paper in October 2008, many money market mutual funds suffered significant losses. As investors began redeeming their shares in these funds, the funds stopped buying commercial paper. Many corporations had come to rely on selling commercial paper to meet their short-term financing needs, including funding their inventories and their payrolls. By buying commercial paper directly from these corporations, the Fed allowed them to continue normal operations. This facility was established in October 2008 and closed in February 2010.

- **Term Asset-Backed Securities Loan Facility (TALF).** Under this facility, the Federal Reserve Bank of New York extended three-year or five-year loans to help investors fund the purchase of asset-backed securities. These securities are securitized consumer and business loans, apart from mortgages. For instance, some asset-backed securities consist of consumer automobile loans that have been bundled together as a security to be resold to investors. Following the financial crisis, the market for asset-backed securities largely dried up. This facility was established in November 2007, and the last loans were made in June 2010.

By mid-2010, with the financial system having recovered from the worst of the crisis, the Fed had ended these innovative discount programs.

Figure 15.6 shows that there was an explosion in all types of lending by the Fed during the financial crisis. Borrowing from the Fed amounted to just $2.1 billion as late as December 5, 2007. However, as the financial crisis worsened during the first months of 2008, financial institutions borrowed more and more from the Fed. After the collapse of Bear Stearns on March 19, 2008, total borrowing from the Fed had increased to $108.9 billion. On September 17, 2008, just days after Lehman Brothers filed for bankruptcy, total borrowing had reached $271.3 billion, skyrocketing from there to $993.5 billion on December 10, 2008, during the worst part of the financial crisis. After that time, borrowing from the Fed decreased steadily, until it dropped to less than $1 billion by late 2011, where it remained in 2016.

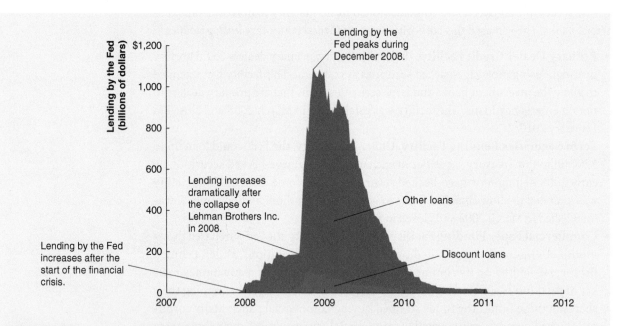

FIGURE 15.6 Lending by the Federal Reserve During the Financial Crisis of 2007–2009

During the financial crisis, lending by the Federal Reserve increased from just a few hundred million dollars before the financial crisis to $993.5 billion during December 2008. Since that time, lending by the Fed has steadily decreased.

Source: Board of Governors of the Federal Reserve System.

How the Fed Currently Manages the Federal Funds Rate

To help fight the adverse effects of the financial crisis and recession on household and business spending, in December 2008, the FOMC cut its target for the federal funds rate from 1% to a range of 0% to 0.25%. The target remained there until December 16, 2015, when the FOMC raised it to a range of 0.25% to 0.50%. By that time, the Fed believed that the U.S. economy was strong enough for the process of restoring more normal conditions in financial markets to begin. But unlike in the past, the FOMC knew that it could not increase the federal funds rate simply by directing the account manager at the New York Fed to engage in open market sales of Treasury securities. To raise the federal funds rate by this method would require draining as much as two trillion dollars in reserves from banks, which would have massively disrupted the financial system.

Instead, the Fed used two new monetary policy tools described earlier: It set the interest rate it pays on excess reserves (IOER) at 0.50% and the interest rate it pays on overnight reverse repurchase agreements (ON RRP) at 0.25%. The Fed needed both of these monetary policy tools because there are two distinct groups of financial institutions that borrow and lend in the federal funds market:

1. Depository institutions, such as commercial banks and savings and loans, that are eligible to borrow and lend in the federal funds market, and whose deposits with the Fed receive interest.
2. Financial institutions such as Fannie Mae, Freddie Mac, and the Federal Home Loan Banks (FHLBs) that are eligible to borrow and lend in the federal funds market, but whose deposits with the Fed *do not* receive interest. (Congress established the Federal Home Loan Bank System in 1932 to lend to savings and loans as the Federal Reserve does to commercial banks. The 12 district FHLBs sell debt in financial markets and use the funds to make loans, called *advances*, to member financial institutions. In recent years, the FHLBs have made substantial overnight loans in the federal funds market.)

As we explained on page 504 when discussing Figure 15.1, by raising the IOER to 0.50%, the Fed ensured that banks would rarely lend in the federal funds market at a lower interest rate.[5] But Fannie Mae, Freddie Mac, the FHLBs, and other financial institutions that are not eligible to receive interest on their deposits at the Fed would still be willing to lend in the federal funds market below the IOER. By setting the interest rate on its overnight reverse repurchase agreements at 0.25%, the Fed ensured that financial institutions that were eligible to be *counterparties*—that is, to enter into these agreements with the Fed—would be unlikely to lend elsewhere at a lower rate. This action ensured that the federal funds rate would be unlikely to drop below 0.25%, the lower end of the FOMC's target.

---

[5] There is a technical point we need to note: The actual federal funds rate may be below the IOER because banks incur costs for the funds they obtain and deposit at the Fed. Banks incur several costs when they acquire checkable deposits: (1) Banks may have to pay an insurance premium to the FDIC; (2) they may incur costs to service the accounts (such as the cost of clearing checks and preparing account statements); and (3) they may incur the cost of additional regulation by the Fed and other agencies as their balance sheets expand. These costs create a wedge between the IOER and the net return banks receive from depositing funds with the Fed.

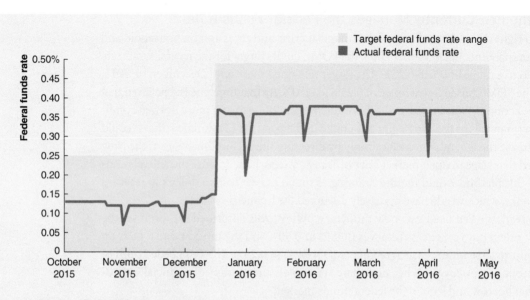

FIGURE 15.7 The Fed Raises Its Target for the Federal Funds Rate

On December 16, 2015, the FOMC announced that its target range for the federal funds rate would increase from 0%–0.25% to 0.25%–0.50%. The blue bands show the FOMC's target ranges for the months around the announcement. The red line shows the actual federal funds rate on each day. The actual federal funds rate increased by about the 0.25% that the Fed intended and on most days remained above the bottom (0.25%) of the FOMC's target range.

As of December 2016, in addition to the 23 primary dealers—which can also participate in reverse repurchase agreements with the Fed—61 other financial institutions were eligible to be counterparties on these agreements. These institutions included Fannie Mae, Freddie Mac, the FHLBs, and investment companies such as Fidelity, Vanguard, Charles Schwab, and Black Rock. Note that some of the investment companies, such as Vanguard and Fidelity, are not eligible to borrow and lend in the federal funds market. However, by accepting them as counterparties on overnight reverse repos, the Fed ensures that the interest rate it sets on these securities will have a wider effect on other short-term interest rates. For example, many of these investment companies operate money market mutual funds. Being able to earn a higher interest rate on overnight reverse repos with the Fed makes it possible for these companies to offer higher interest rates on their money market funds.

Figure 15.7 shows the effect of the FOMC's actions on December 16, 2015, to raise its target for the federal funds rate. The light blue band shows the FOMC's target for the federal funds rate, which had been 0% to 0.25% and was raised on that day to 0.25% to 0.50%. The red line shows the actual federal funds rate on each day. The figure shows that the actual federal funds rate increased by about the 0.25% that the Fed intended and on most days remained above the bottom (0.25%) of the FOMC's target range.

Figure 15.8 summarizes the Fed's new procedures for increasing its target for the federal funds rate. Panel (a) traces the steps by which the FOMC causes the actual federal funds rate to rise into its target range. Panel (b) uses the demand and supply for reserves

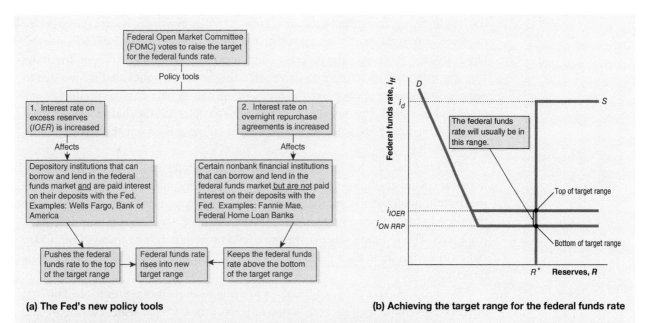

FIGURE 15.8 The Fed's New Procedures for Managing the Federal Funds Rate

Panel (a) summarizes how the Fed uses two new monetary policy tools—the interest rate it pays on excess reserves (IOER) and the interest rate it offers on overnight reverse repurchase agreements (ON RRP)—to manage the federal funds rate during a time when reserves are no longer scarce. Panel (b) shows the market for reserves in the circumstances where the supply curve for reserves intersects the demand curve in the demand curve's horizontal segment. The upper horizontal segment corresponds to the top of the Fed's target range for the federal funds rate and is determined by the interest rate the Fed pays on deposits from banks, i_{IOER}. The lower segment corresponds to the bottom of the Fed's target range for the federal funds rate and is determined by the interest rate the Fed offers on overnight reverse repurchase agreements, $i_{ON\ RRP}$.

graph to illustrate the Fed's new procedures. In panel (b), as a result of the Fed's massive purchases of Treasury securities and mortgage-backed securities, the supply curve of reserves has been shifted far to the right so that it intersects the demand curve in the demand curve's horizontal segment. Note that in this figure we have included two horizontal segments of the demand curve. The upper segment corresponds to the top of the Fed's target range for the federal funds rate and is determined by the interest rate the Fed pays on deposits from banks, i_{IOER}. The lower segment corresponds to the bottom of the Fed's target range for the federal funds rate and is determined by the interest rate the Fed offers on overnight reverse repurchase agreements, $i_{ON\ RRP}$. On a given day, the federal funds rate will ordinarily be somewhere in this range.

15.4 Monetary Targeting and Monetary Policy

LEARNING OBJECTIVE: Explain the role of monetary targeting in monetary policy.

Any central bank's objective in conducting monetary policy is to use its policy tools to achieve monetary policy goals. But the Fed often faces trade-offs in attempting to reach its goals, particularly the goals of high economic growth and employment on the one hand and low inflation on the other hand. To demonstrate the problem, suppose the Fed, intending to increase economic growth and employment, lowers the target for the federal funds rate with the expectation that other market interest rates will also fall. Lower interest rates typically increase consumer and business spending in the short run. But increased spending may drive prices higher. So, a policy that is intended to achieve one monetary policy goal (high employment) may have an adverse effect on another (low inflation). The Fed faced just this dilemma following the sharp increases in oil prices during the 1970s, when employment was falling at the same time that inflation was increasing.

The Fed faces another problem in reaching its monetary policy goals. Although it hopes to encourage high employment and price stability, it has no direct control over real output (which is the main determinant of employment in the short run) or the price level. Interactions among households and firms determine real output and the price level. The Fed can influence the price level or output only by using its monetary policy tools. But these tools don't permit the Fed to achieve its monetary policy goals directly.

The Fed also faces timing difficulties in using its monetary policy tools. The first obstacle preventing the Fed from acting quickly is the *information lag*. This lag occurs because it takes time for government agencies to gather data on changes in GDP, inflation, or other economic variables. If the Fed lacks timely information, it may implement a policy that doesn't match actual economic conditions, and its actions could actually worsen the problems it is trying to correct. For example, some economists argue that an information lag resulted in the Fed reducing the target for the federal funds rate too slowly during 2006 and 2007, following the collapse of the housing bubble. A second timing problem is the *impact lag*. This lag is the time that is required for monetary policy changes to affect output, employment, or inflation. Changes in interest rates and the money supply affect the economy over time, not immediately. Because of this lag, the Fed's actions may affect the economy at the wrong time, and the Fed might not be able to recognize its mistakes soon enough to correct them. In 2016, some economists and policymakers argued that the Fed was neglecting to take into account the impact lag in keeping the target of the federal funds rate near zero for such an extended period.

One possible solution to the problems caused by the information lag and impact lag is for the Fed to use targets to meet its goals. Targets partially solve the Fed's inability to directly control the variables that determine economic performance, and they reduce the timing lags in observing and reacting to economic fluctuations. Unfortunately, targets also have problems, and some traditional targeting approaches have fallen out of favor at the Fed during the past 25 years. In the remainder of this section, we describe targets, their benefits and drawbacks, and their use in setting monetary policy.

Using Targets to Meet Goals

Targets are variables that the Fed can influence directly and that help achieve monetary policy goals. Traditionally, the Fed has relied on two types of targets: *policy instruments*—sometimes called *operating targets*—and *intermediate targets*. Although using policy instruments and intermediate targets is no longer the favored approach at the Fed, reviewing how they work can provide some insight into the difficulties the Fed faces in executing monetary policy.

Intermediate Targets Intermediate targets are typically either monetary aggregates, such as M1 or M2, or interest rates. The Fed can use as an intermediate target either a short-term interest rate, such as the interest rate on Treasury bills, or a long-term interest rate, such as the interest rate on corporate bonds or residential mortgages. The Fed typically chose an intermediate target that it believed would directly help it to achieve its goals. The idea was that by using an intermediate target—say, a monetary aggregate such as M2—the Fed had a better chance of reaching a goal, such as price stability or full employment, that is not directly under its control, than it would if it had focused solely on the goal. Using an intermediate target could also provide feedback on whether the Fed's policy actions were consistent with achieving the goal. For instance, from statistical studies, the Fed might have estimated that increasing M2 at a steady rate of 3% per year was consistent with its goal of price stability. If M2 was actually growing by 6%, the Fed would know immediately that it was on a course to miss its long-run goal of price stability. It could then use its monetary policy tools (most likely open market operations) to slow M2 growth to the target rate of 3%. Hitting the M2 intermediate target would have had no value other than helping the Fed to achieve its stated goals.

Policy Instruments, or Operating Targets The Fed controls intermediate target variables, such as the mortgage interest rate or M2, only indirectly because the decisions of households, firms, and investors also influence these variables. The Fed would therefore need a target that was a better link between its policy tool and intermediate targets. Policy instruments, or operating targets, are closely related to intermediate targets; the Fed controlled these variables directly with its monetary policy tools. Examples of policy instruments include the federal funds rate and nonborrowed reserves. As we have seen, in recent decades, the federal funds rate has been the Fed's most commonly used policy instrument. Most central banks in high-income countries use interest rates as policy instruments.

Figure 15.9 shows the Fed's traditional approach of using policy instruments and intermediate targets to reach its goals. The figure also helps explain why we have used past tense in much of our discussion of targeting. Although the Fed selects goals, it ultimately controls only policy tools. For the targeting approach we have just outlined to be effective, the links between policy tools and policy instruments, between policy instruments and intermediate targets, and between intermediate targets and policy goals must be reliable. Over time, however, some of these links have broken down. For example, prior to 1980, there was a fairly consistent link between increases in the rate of growth of M1 and M2 and, after a lag of roughly two years, an increase in the inflation rate. This link made some economists argue that the Fed should concentrate on a monetary aggregate as its intermediate target. Unfortunately, the link between changes in the money supply and changes in inflation has been erratic since 1980. The growth of the money supply has varied widely, while the inflation rate has varied much less. In general, in recent years, many economists and policymakers no longer believe that a stable relationship exists between the alternative intermediate targets and the Fed's policy goals.

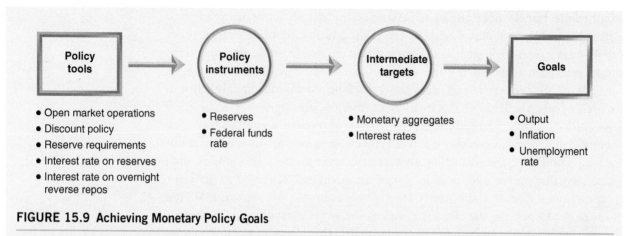

FIGURE 15.9 Achieving Monetary Policy Goals

The Federal Reserve establishes goals for economic variables such as the rate of inflation and the rate of unemployment. The Fed directly controls only its policy tools. It can use targets—intermediate targets and policy instruments—which are variables that the Fed can influence, to help achieve monetary policy goals. In recent years, the Fed has deemphasized the use of targeting procedures of this type.

Some discussion has continued, however, over whether the Fed should choose a reserve aggregate or the federal funds rate as its policy instrument. We analyze this discussion in the next section.

MAKING THE CONNECTION

What Happened to the Link Between Money and Prices?

In the United States, decades when the money supply has grown more rapidly have been decades when the inflation rate has been relatively high. But an economic relationship that holds over decades is not always useful for policymakers attempting to steer the economy in the short run. Prior to 1980, there was significant evidence that the link between money and prices held up in the short run of a year or two. In fact, many economists were convinced that the acceleration in inflation during the late 1960s and 1970s was due to the Fed's having allowed the growth rate of the money supply to sharply increase during those years.

The economists who argued this point most forcefully are known as *monetarists*. The most prominent monetarist was Nobel Laureate Milton Friedman of the University of Chicago. The monetarists appeared to have gained favor in July 1979, when President Jimmy Carter appointed Paul Volcker as chairman of the Board of Governors of the Federal Reserve System. Volcker was committed to reducing inflation and chose monetary aggregates as intermediate targets. Under Volcker, the Fed shifted its policy to emphasize nonborrowed reserves as a policy instrument, or operating target. This episode is sometimes referred to as "The Great Monetarist Experiment." At first, the Fed's policy seemed successful, as it reduced the rate of growth of the money supply and, with a lag, the inflation rate fell. A severe recession began in July 1981, however, and by the end of the year, the rate of the growth of the money supply was increasing. From the third quarter of 1981 to the third quarter of 1983, M1 grew at an annual rate of more than 9%. Friedman predicted that with a lag, the result of this high rate of money growth would be a much higher inflation rate.

To support his argument, in an article in the *American Economic Review*, Friedman presented some of the data in the table below. Focus first on the unshaded entries in the table. Friedman argued that there was a close connection between the rate of growth of M1 over a two-year period and the inflation rate two years later. The unshaded entries in the table show that this relationship holds for the period from 1973 through 1981. Note in particular that a decline in the growth of the money supply from 8.6% during 1977–1979 to 6.1% during 1979–1981—the result of Volcker's policies—was associated with a decline in the inflation rate from 9.4% to 4.8%. So, Friedman seemed justified in predicting that because the Fed had allowed the growth of the money supply to increase to 9.2% during the 1981–1983 period, the inflation rate was likely to increase significantly. In fact, though, the values in the shaded areas of the table show that despite the increase in the growth rate of the money supply, the inflation rate *decreased rather than increased*. Moreover, money growth remained high during the following two years, while the inflation rate decreased even further. In the years that followed, the link between the growth in M1 or M2 and the inflation rate was no stronger.

Period for money growth	Growth in M1	Inflation rate two years later	Period for inflation
Third quarter of 1973 to third quarter of 1975	5.2%	6.3%	Third quarter of 1975 to third quarter of 1977
Third quarter of 1975 to third quarter of 1977	6.4	8.3	Third quarter of 1977 to third quarter of 1979
Third quarter of 1977 to third quarter of 1979	8.6	9.4	Third quarter of 1979 to third quarter of 1981
Third quarter of 1979 to third quarter of 1981	6.1	4.8	Third quarter of 1981 to third quarter of 1983
Third quarter of 1981 to third quarter of 1983	9.2	3.3	Third quarter of 1983 to third quarter of 1985
Third quarter of 1983 to third quarter of 1985	8.1	2.8	Third quarter of 1985 to third quarter of 1987

Why did the short-run link between the growth of the money supply and inflation break down after 1980? Most economists believe that the breakdown occurred because the nature of M1 and M2 changed after 1980. Before 1980, banks were not allowed to pay interest on checkable deposits. In 1980, Congress authorized negotiable order of withdrawal (NOW) accounts, on which banks can pay interest, so M1 changed from representing a pure medium of exchange to also representing a store of value. In addition, financial innovations at banks increased the amount of checkable deposits households and firms were willing to hold without spending them. *Automatic transfer of saving* accounts move checkable deposit balances into higher-interest CDs each night and then back into checkable deposits in the morning. *Sweep accounts*, aimed at businesses, move their checkable deposits balances into money market deposit accounts at the end of each week and then move the funds back into checkable deposits at the beginning of the following week. (Recall that regulations bar firms from holding interest-earning checking [NOW] accounts.) As a result of these changes, a rapid increase in M1 need not translate directly into spending increases that would lead to higher inflation.

Because of the breakdown in the relationship between the growth of the money supply and inflation, since 1993, the Fed no longer announces targets for M1 and M2.

Although at one time investors closely followed the Fed's weekly publication of data on M1 and M2, looking for clues about future inflation rates, today publication of these data has little effect on financial markets.

Source: The table is adapted from Table 2 in Benjamin M. Friedman, "Lessons on Monetary Policy in the 1980s," *Journal of Economic Perspectives*, Vol. 2, No. 3, Summer 1988, p. 62. The original article by Milton Friedman is "Lessons from the 1979–1982 Monetary Policy Experiment," *American Economic Review*, Vol. 74, No. 2, May 1984, pp. 397–401.

See related problems 4.8 and 4.9 at the end of the chapter.

The Choice Between Targeting Reserves and Targeting the Federal Funds Rate

Traditionally, the Fed has used three criteria when evaluating variables that might be used as policy instruments. The Fed's main policy instruments have been *reserve aggregates*, such as total reserves or nonborrowed reserves, and the federal funds rate. We can briefly assess how well these instruments meet the Fed's three criteria:

1. **Measurable.** The variable must be measurable in a short time frame to overcome information lags. The Fed exercises significant control over both reserve aggregates and the federal funds rate and can accurately measure them hour by hour if it needs to.
2. **Controllable.** Although the Fed lacks complete control over the level of reserve aggregates and the federal funds rate because both depend on banks' demands for reserves, the Fed has the tools to keep both variables close to whatever target it selects. However, since December 2008, the Fed has chosen a range rather than a single number as its target for the federal funds rate.
3. **Predictable.** The Fed needs a policy instrument that has a predictable effect on its policy goals. The effect of a change in either reserves or the federal funds rate on goals such as economic growth or price stability is complex. This complexity is one reason the Fed at one time relied on intermediate targets. Because it is not clear whether reserves or the federal funds rate best meets this last criterion, economists continue to discuss which policy instrument is best, although this discussion has not been at the center of debates over monetary policy in recent years.

A key point to understand is that the Fed can choose a reserve aggregate for its policy instrument, or it can choose the federal funds rate, but it cannot choose both. To see why, look at Figure 15.10, which shows the demand and supply for reserves in the federal funds market. Note that once again, we are assuming that reserves are scarce and that, therefore, the demand curve for reserves intersects the supply curve for reserves on the downward-sloping segment of the demand curve. In panel (a), we assume that the Fed has decided to use the level of reserves as its policy instrument by keeping reserves constant at R^*. With demand for reserves at D_1, the equilibrium federal funds rate is i_{ff1}^*. If households and firms decide to hold more checkable deposits or if banks decide to hold more excess reserves, the demand for reserves will shift to the right, from D_1 to D_2. The result will be an increase in the equilibrium federal funds rate from i_{ff1}^* to i_{ff2}^*. Similarly, if households and firms decide to hold fewer checkable deposits or banks decide to hold fewer excess reserves, the demand for reserves will shift to the left, from D_1 to D_3.

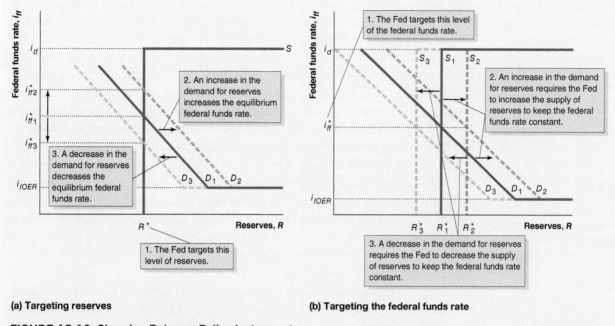

(a) Targeting reserves

(b) Targeting the federal funds rate

FIGURE 15.10 Choosing Between Policy Instruments

In panel (a), the Fed chooses the level of reserves as its policy instrument by keeping reserves constant, at R^*. With demand for reserves at D_1, the equilibrium federal funds rate is i^*_{ff1}. If the demand for reserves shifts to the right, from D_1 to D_2, the equilibrium federal funds rate increases from i^*_{ff1} to i^*_{ff2}. Similarly, if the demand for reserves shifts to the left, from D_1 to D_3, the equilibrium federal funds rate decreases from i^*_{ff1} to i^*_{ff3}.

In panel (b), the Fed chooses the federal funds rate as its policy instrument by keeping the rate constant, at i^*_{ff}. If the demand for reserves increases from D_1 to D_2, the Fed will have to increase the supply of reserves from S_1 to S_2 in order to maintain its target for the federal funds rate at i^*_{ff}. If the demand for reserves decreases from D_1 to D_3, the Fed will have to decrease the supply of reserves from S_1 to S_3 to maintain its target for the federal funds rate.

The result will be a decrease in the equilibrium federal funds rate from i^*_{ff1} to i^*_{ff3}. We can conclude that *using reserves as the Fed's policy instrument will cause the federal funds rate to fluctuate in response to changes in the demand for reserves.*

In panel (b) of Figure 15.10, we assume that the Fed has decided to use the federal funds rate as its policy instrument by keeping the rate constant, at i^*_{ff}. With demand for reserves at D_1, the equilibrium level of reserves is R^*_1. If the demand for reserves increases from D_1 to D_2, the Fed will have to increase the supply of reserves from S_1 to S_2 in order to maintain its target for the federal funds rate at i^*_{ff}. Shifting the supply curve from S_1 to S_2 causes the equilibrium level of reserves to increase from R^*_1 to R^*_2. Similarly, if the demand for reserves decreases from D_1 to D_3, the Fed will have to decrease the supply of reserves from S_1 to S_3 to maintain its target for the federal funds rate. The result will be a decrease in the equilibrium level of reserves from R^*_1 to R^*_3. We can conclude that *using the federal funds rate as the Fed's policy instrument will cause the level of reserves to fluctuate in response to changes in the demand for reserves.*

So, the Fed faces a trade-off: Choose reserves as its policy instrument and accept fluctuations in the federal funds rate or choose the federal funds rate as its policy instrument and accept fluctuations in the level of reserves. By the 1980s, the Fed had concluded that the link between the federal funds rate and its policy goals was closer than the link between the level of reserves and its policy goals. As a result, for the past 35 years, the Fed has used the federal funds rate as its policy instrument.

The Taylor Rule: A Summary Measure of Fed Policy

The decline in the Fed's use of traditional targeting largely coincided with Alan Greenspan's term as Fed Chairman. Greenspan was appointed in August 1987 and served until January 2006, when Ben Bernanke succeeded him. In speeches and testimony before Congress, Greenspan's explanations of his policies were famously difficult to understand. During a speech, he once joked: "I guess I should warn you if I turn out to be particularly clear, you've probably misunderstood what I said."[6] During this time, it was public knowledge that the Fed was using the federal funds rate as its policy instrument, or operating target. But how the FOMC settled on a particular target value for the federal funds rate wasn't clear.

Taylor rule A monetary policy guideline developed by economist John Taylor for determining the target for the federal funds rate.

Actual Fed deliberations are complex and incorporate many factors about the economy. John Taylor of Stanford University has summarized these factors in the **Taylor rule** for federal funds rate targeting.[7] The Taylor rule begins with an estimate of the value of the real federal funds rate, which is the federal funds rate—adjusted for inflation—that would be consistent with real GDP being equal to potential real GDP in the long run. With real GDP equal to potential real GDP, cyclical unemployment should be zero, and the Fed will have attained its policy goal of high employment. According to the Taylor rule, the Fed should set its current federal funds rate target equal to the sum of the current inflation rate, the equilibrium real federal funds rate, and two additional terms. The first of these terms is the *inflation gap*—the difference between current inflation and a target rate; the second term is the *output gap*—the percentage difference of real GDP from potential real GDP. The inflation gap and the output gap are each given "weights" that reflect their influence on the federal funds rate target. With weights of one-half for both gaps, we have the following Taylor rule:

$$\text{Federal funds rate target} = \text{Current inflation rate} + \text{Equilibrium real federal funds rate} + (1/2 \times \text{Inflation gap}) + (1/2 \times \text{Output gap}).$$

So when the inflation rate is above the Fed's target rate, the FOMC will raise the target for the federal funds rate. Similarly, when the output gap is negative—that is, when real GDP is less than potential GDP—the FOMC will lower the target for the federal funds rate. In calibrating this rule, Taylor assumed that the equilibrium real federal funds rate is 2% and the target rate of inflation is 2%. Figure 15.11 shows the level of the federal funds rate that would have occurred if the Fed had strictly followed the Taylor rule and the actual federal funds rate. The figure indicates that because the two lines are close together during most years, the Taylor rule does a reasonable job of explaining Federal Reserve policy. There are some periods when the lines diverge significantly. During the late 1960s and early to mid-1970s, the federal funds rate predicted from the Taylor rule is consistently above the target federal funds rate. This gap is consistent with the view of most economists that in the face of a worsening inflation rate during those years, the FOMC should have raised the target for the federal funds rate more than it did.

---

[6] Floyd Norris, "What if the Fed Chief Speaks Plainly?" *New York Times*, October 28, 2005.

[7] Taylor's original discussion of the rule appeared in John B. Taylor, "Discretion Versus Policy Rules in Practice," *Carnegie-Rochester Conference Series on Public Policy*, Vol. 39, 1993, pp. 195–214.

Figure 15.11 also indicates that the FOMC lowered the federal funds rate following the severe 1981–1982 recession more slowly than is consistent with the Taylor rule. The figure also indicates that the FOMC kept the federal funds rate at levels well below those indicated by the Taylor rule during the recovery from the 2001 recession. Some economists and policymakers have argued that by keeping the federal funds at a very low level for an extended period, the Fed helped provide fuel for the housing boom. The argument is that a low federal funds rate contributed to low mortgage interest rates, thereby increasing the demand for housing. At the time, Fed Chairman Alan Greenspan argued that low interest rates were needed to guard against the possibility that the economy might lapse into a period of deflation. Former Fed Chairman Ben Bernanke, who served on the Board of Governors during that period, has argued that a global saving glut, rather than Fed policy, was the main reason long-term interest rates were low in the United States during the early 2000s. Finally, notice that the Taylor rule indicates that the federal funds rate should have been *negative* throughout 2009, which is another indication of the severity of the 2007–2009 recession.

That the Taylor rule tracks the actual federal funds rate fairly closely confirms the view that targeting the federal funds rate has been central to Fed policymaking in recent decades.

MyEconLab Real-time data

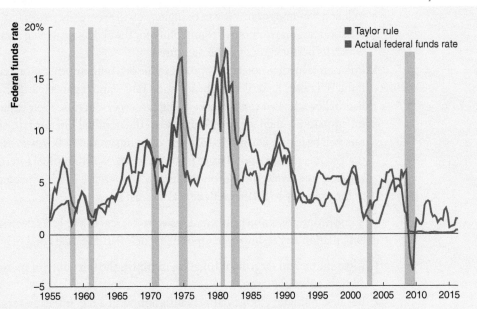

FIGURE 15.11 The Taylor Rule and the Actual Federal Funds Rate

The blue line shows the level of the federal funds rate that would have occurred if the Fed had strictly followed the Taylor rule, and the red line shows the actual federal funds rate. The figure shows that the Taylor rule does a good job of explaining Federal Reserve policy during some periods, but it also shows the periods in which the target federal funds rate diverges from the rate predicted by the Taylor rule. The shaded areas represent periods of recession.

Sources: Federal Reserve Bank of St. Louis; and Congressional Budget Office. We thank our late colleague Matthew Rafferty of Quinnipiac University for providing the data on the rate predicted by the Taylor rule.

Inflation Targeting: A New Monetary Policy Tool?

Particularly in the years just before the financial crisis of 2007–2009, many economists and central bankers expressed significant interest in using *inflation targeting* as a framework for conducting monetary policy. With inflation targeting, a central bank publically sets an explicit target for the inflation rate over a period of time, and the government and the public then judge the performance of the central bank on the basis of its success in hitting the target. After many years of not having an explicit inflation target, the Fed announced in 2012 that it would attempt to maintain an average inflation rate of 2% per year.

With inflation targeting, the Fed can still use its discretion to address special situations rather than follow an inflexible rule. Nevertheless, an inflation target allows monetary policy to focus on inflation and inflation forecasts, except during times of severe recession. Arguments in favor of the Fed using an explicit inflation target focus on four points:

1. Announcing explicit targets for inflation draws the public's attention to what the Fed can actually achieve in practice. Most economists believe that over the long run, monetary policy has a greater effect on inflation than on the growth of real output or employment.
2. Establishing transparent inflation targets for the United States provides an anchor for inflationary expectations. If households, firms, and participants in financial markets believe that the Fed will hit an annual inflation target of 2%, they will expect that if inflation was temporarily lower or higher, it will eventually return to the target rate.
3. Inflation targets promote accountability for the Fed by providing a yardstick against which its performance can be measured.
4. Inflation targeting potentially provides the Fed with another monetary policy tool. If the Fed raises its target for the inflation rate—and if participants in financial markets believe the Fed can hit its new, higher target and raise their expectations of the inflation rate—then for any given level of the nominal interest rate, the real interest rate will be lower. During 2016, some economists and policymakers suggested that the Fed raise its inflation target from 2% to 4%. With nominal interest rates at historically low levels, these economists saw an increase in the expected inflation rate as the only way to further reduce real interest rates.

Some economists and policymakers were critical of the Fed's decision to adopt an explicit inflation target, however. Opponents of inflation targets make five points:

1. Rigid numerical targets for inflation diminish the flexibility of monetary policy to address other policy goals.
2. Because monetary policy affects inflation with a lag, inflation targeting requires that the Fed depend on forecasts of future inflation, uncertainty about which can create problems for the conduct of policy.
3. Holding the Fed accountable only for a goal of low inflation may make it more difficult for elected officials to monitor the Fed's support for good economic policy overall.
4. Uncertainty about future levels of output and employment can impede economic decision making in the presence of an inflation target. That is, inflation targets may increase uncertainty over whether the Fed will take prompt action to return the economy to full employment following a recession.

5. Using the inflation target as another monetary policy tool could potentially be economically destabilizing. As the experience of the 1970s shows, once a higher inflation rate becomes embedded in the expectations of households and firms, it can be difficult to reduce the expectations again. In the context of 2016, forcing real interest rates lower ran the risk of increasing distortions in the financial system, possibly fueling speculative asset bubbles.

The jury is still out on the question of whether inflation targets improve economic policy. Many economists and central bankers have suggested that gains from transparency and accountability can be achieved without explicit inflation targets and that the credibility of monetary policy is better established through experience. Suggestions that the Fed use its inflation target as a monetary policy tool have been particularly controversial.

International Comparisons of Monetary Policy

Although there are institutional differences in how central banks conduct monetary policy, there are two important similarities in recent practices. First, most central banks in high-income countries have increasingly used short-term interest rates—similar to the federal funds rate in the United States—as the policy instrument, or operating target, through which goals are pursued. Second, many central banks took extraordinary policy measures—including using quantitative easing—in dealing with slow economic growth following the financial crisis of 2007–2009. In this section, we discuss these practices and the institutional settings for the conduct of monetary policy in Canada, Japan, the United Kingdom, and the European Union.

The Bank of Canada The Bank of Canada, like the U.S. Fed, became increasingly concerned about inflation during the 1970s. In 1975, the Bank of Canada announced a policy of gradually reducing the growth rate of M1. By late 1982, M1 targets were no longer used. In 1988, John Crow, then governor of the Bank of Canada, announced the bank's commitment to price stability by announcing a series of declining inflation targets. To meet the inflation targets, the Bank of Canada sets explicit operational target bands for the overnight rate (analogous to the federal funds rate). While Fed policy has been concerned primarily with the inflation gap and the output gap, the Bank of Canada has also made the exchange value of the Canadian dollar a focus of policy. This focus on exchange rates—particularly between the Canadian dollar and the U.S. dollar—reflects the large role that exports have traditionally played in the Canadian economy.

During 2007–2009, the Bank of Canada received praise for helping the Canadian financial system weather the financial crisis with much less instability than occurred in the United States. The Canadian banking system, in particular, avoided the heavy losses from investments in mortgage-backed securities and commercial real estate suffered by many banks in the United States. In 2010, the Bank of Canada was the first central bank in an industrial country to raise its target for the overnight bank lending rate. This was another indication of the relatively strong performance of the Canadian economy during the global downturn. However, falling oil prices, beginning in 2014, reduced economic growth in Canada and led the Bank of Canada in 2015 to cut its target for the overnight lending rate to 0.5%, where it remained in 2016.

The Bank of Japan In the aftermath of the first OPEC oil shock in 1973, Japan experienced an inflation rate in excess of 20%. This high inflation rate led the Bank of Japan (BOJ) to adopt explicit money growth targets. In particular, beginning in 1978, the BOJ announced targets for an aggregate corresponding to M2. Following the 1979 oil price shock, the central bank reduced money growth. The gradual decline in money growth over the period from 1978 through 1987 was associated with a faster decline in inflation than the United States experienced.

As also happened in the United States, Japanese banks and financial markets experienced a wave of deregulation and financial innovation during the 1980s. As a consequence, the BOJ began to rely less on the M2 aggregate in the conduct of monetary policy. From 1987 to 1989, the bank's concern over the foreign exchange value of the yen—which had risen significantly against the U.S. dollar—dominated monetary policy. The rapid rate of money growth during this period led to a boom in Japanese asset prices, particularly in land and stocks. In an attempt to reduce speculation in asset markets during the boom, the BOJ adopted a contractionary monetary policy, which led to a decline in asset prices and ultimately to a drop in Japanese economic growth.

Many financial market commentators viewed the continuing deflationary Japanese monetary policy in the late 1990s and 2000s as a significant factor in the weakness of Japanese economic performance during most of that period. A more expansionary monetary policy began to stimulate both economic growth and inflation in the mid-2000s. In 2006, the BOJ began to scale back its expansionary policy, but the financial crisis that began in 2007 led the BOJ to return to an expansionary policy. Since 2010, the BOJ has intervened several times to reverse the increasing value of the yen against the U.S. dollar. The high value of the yen hampered Japanese exports and impeded Japan's economic recovery. In the years following the financial crisis, the BOJ engaged in an ongoing struggle with the government of Japan, as the government attempted to pressure the BOJ to be more aggressive in bringing down the exchange value of the yen, while the BOJ fought to retain its independence in making monetary policy decisions.

When Shinzo Abe was elected prime minister in December 2012, he announced an economic program intended to reverse a period of nearly two decades of deflation and slow economic growth. The program, which became known as Abenomics, included the BOJ adopting an explicit inflation target of 2%, along with increased government spending, and structural reforms, such as improved corporate governance, making it easier for women to enter the workforce, and reducing impediments to international trade.

Although these measures had some success in ending deflation and increasing employment, the BOJ did not come close to hitting its inflation target, and economic growth was disappointingly slow. In response, the BOJ increased quantitative easing, including indirectly purchasing shares of stock in Japanese firms by buying exchange-traded funds (ETFs). (In contrast, the Fed's purchases under its quantitative easing programs had been confined to long-term Treasury bonds and mortgage-backed securities.) In addition, in February 2016, the BOJ took the unusual step of instituting a negative interest rate on the deposits it receives from Japanese banks. In effect, banks were required to pay the BOJ for keeping their deposits. This move was intended to push banks to lend out their reserves rather than leave them on deposit with the BOJ. In addition, lower interest rates could reduce the value of the yen in exchange for other currencies, giving a boost to

Japanese exports. In September 2016, the BOJ took the further step of announcing that it would begin targeting an interest rate of 0% on 10-year Japanese government bonds.

The Bank of England In the United Kingdom, the Bank of England (BOE) responded to rising inflation in the early 1970s by announcing that it would adopt targets for money supply growth. In response to accelerating inflation in the late 1970s, the government of Prime Minister Margaret Thatcher formally introduced in 1980 a strategy for gradual deceleration of money supply growth. Beginning in 1983, the BOE shifted its emphasis toward targeting growth in the monetary base (again with an eye toward a gradual reduction in the rate of growth of the money supply). In 1992, the United Kingdom adopted inflation targets, which are set by the chancellor of the Exchequer (a position similar to the secretary of the Treasury in the United States) rather than by the BOE.

The BOE obtained the power to set interest rates independently of the government in 1997. The government can overrule the BOE in "extreme circumstances," but to date it has not done so. Interest rate determination falls to the Monetary Policy Committee, whose nine members are the BOE's governor (the equivalent of the Fed's chair), three deputy governors, the BOE's chief economist, and four external economic experts named by the chancellor of the Exchequer. A representative of the Treasury attends the Monetary Policy Committee meetings but does not vote. Monetary policy focuses on the *Bank Rate*—the rate the BOE pays commercial banks on their reserves.

During the financial crisis of 2007–2009, the BOE took several dramatic policy actions. It lowered the Bank Rate in a series of steps from 5.75% in July 2007 to 0.5% in March 2009. In 2009, it also launched a program of quantitative easing that involved buying long-term British government bonds. The BOE ended quantitative easing in 2012, although it kept the bank rate at 0.5%. Following the vote to leave the European Union (called Brexit), the BOE, under Governor Mark Carney, took four steps to cushion the expected effects on the British economy: (1) It cut the Bank Rate to 0.25%; (2) it resumed buying long-term British government bonds; (3) it began buying bonds issued by British corporations; and (4) it started a program offering four-year loans to banks that would commit to using the funds to make loans to households and firms. These steps may have helped keep the British economy from sliding into a recession during the summer of 2016.

The European System of Central Banks The European System of Central Banks (ESCB), consisting of the European Central Bank (ECB) and the national central banks of all member states of the European Union, commenced operation in January 1999, following the signing of the Maastricht Treaty. Modeled on the law governing the German Bundesbank, the German central bank, the primary objective of the ESCB is to maintain price stability. As a secondary objective, the ESCB must also support the general economic policies of the European Union. The ECB has emphasized a goal of price stability, defined as an inflation range of 0% to 2%.

During the financial crisis of 2007–2009 and its aftermath, the ECB struggled to forge a monetary policy appropriate to the very different needs of the member countries. While some countries, notably Germany, had made a strong recovery from the recession, others, such as Greece, Ireland, Portugal, and Spain, struggled with high unemployment rates. In addition, the ECB felt obliged to intervene to buy Greek and Spanish government bonds when it appeared possible that those governments might default. This *sovereign debt crisis* put further strains on the ECB. In response to the debt crisis, eurozone governments for the first time gave the ECB additional authority to regulate the banking systems of member countries.

In June 2014, concern about slow growth and very low inflation throughout most of the eurozone led the ECB, under President Mario Draghi, to expand its quantitative easing program of purchasing government bonds and to introduce a new program of four-year low-interest rate loans to banks to encourage the banks to expand credit to households and firms. Most dramatically, the ECB cut the interest rate it paid banks on deposits to −0.10%. Three additional cuts in that rate to −0.40% meant that in late 2016, the eurozone had experienced more than two years with a key interest rate being negative.

MAKING THE CONNECTION

Are Negative Interest Rates an Effective Monetary Policy Tool?

The 2007–2009 financial crisis and recession were the most severe since the Great Depression of the 1930s. Central banks responded with a series of unprecedented monetary policy actions. As we have discussed in this and previous chapters, many of those actions were controversial. Possibly the most intense debate was over the action taken by several central banks, including the Bank of Japan, the European Central Bank, the Swiss National Bank, and Denmark's Nationalbank, to stimulate their economies using negative interest rates.

During and after the financial crisis, each of these central banks gradually lowered the interest rate it was paying on deposits received from banks. Starting in 2014, they began paying negative interest rates on these deposits, meaning that banks had to pay the central banks to keep funds on deposit. Other interest rates also were negative in these countries. Some commercial banks began charging their business customers fees on their checking account balances—effectively offering a negative interest rate on these accounts. Many short-term government bonds also began paying negative interest rates as investors, including banks, bid up their prices. In July 2016, the German government sold 10-year bonds with a yield of −0.05%. As one news article observed: "For investors, it means they are now paying for the privilege of lending money to Germany for 10 years." Because some bank loans, including mortgages, have interest rates that are adjusted according to changes in interest rates on government bonds, these loans began to have negative interest rates. Some homeowners discovered that banks were paying them interest on their mortgage loans!

The debate over the central bank policy of negative interest rates centered on two questions: (1) Was a policy of negative interest rates likely to result in short-run increases in output and employment? and (2) Was the policy likely to introduce distortions in the financial system? Economists have not yet had sufficient time to conduct thorough studies of the effect of negative interest rates. Initially, however, results appeared to be mixed. In some cases banks seemed to be raising the interest rates they were charging on loans—the opposite of the intended effect—to offset having to pay interest on their deposits at central banks. But BOJ Governor Haruhiko Kuroda argued that as a result of the BOJ's actions, interest rates on corporate bonds and mortgage loans had declined in Japan, thereby stimulating spending, production, and employment.

However, there was some evidence that negative interest rates were not having the desired effect of increasing consumer spending. In 2016, saving rates in Japan, Germany, Denmark, Sweden, and Switzerland were at their highest level since 1995. The increase in savings appeared to be the result of two factors: (1) Lower interest rates meant that households needed to save more to reach their goals of accumulating sufficient funds for large purchases or for retirement, and (2) some people saw negative interest rates as a signal from the central bank to expect future economic instability and increased their saving rate in response. Some economists and policymakers also worried that by reducing borrowing costs, low interest rates might be fueling bubbles in housing and other assets. In addition, many households searching for higher interest rates to help meet their savings goals were pushed out of bank certificates of deposit (CDs) and government bonds into riskier assets such as stocks or mutual funds or exchange-traded funds (ETFs) that invest in commodities, low-rated corporate bonds, or bonds issued by governments of developing countries. In a recession, the prices of these riskier assets might decline substantially. Many state and local pension funds have promised retirees fixed dollar benefits that have become increasingly difficult to fund as interest rates on the long-term bonds favored by pension funds have fallen to historically low levels.

Some economists and policymakers believed that the push to negative interest rates was an indication that macroeconomic policy had become unbalanced in most countries. Rather than rely on a mix of monetary and fiscal policies, governments were leaning almost exclusively on monetary policy. Fiscal policy, such as reductions in marginal tax rates on businesses and individuals; incentives to businesses to increase investment in factories, office buildings, and equipment; and increases in government spending on infrastructure, such as highways and bridges, had the potential to increase economic growth but had been not been included in the policy mix in recent years in most countries, except to a limited extent in Japan.

As of 2016, Fed policymakers were more concerned with the need to raise their target for the federal funds rate than with considering the possibility of negative interest rates. As Dennis Lockhart, president of the Federal Reserve Bank of Atlanta, put it, negative interest rates were "an experiment we have the luxury to watch from a distance."

Sources: Patricia Kowsmann and Jeannette Neumann, "A Battle Brews over Negative Rates on Mortgages," *Wall Street Journal*, May 16, 2016; Emese Bartha and Christopher Whittall, "Investors Now Pay Germany to Borrow for 10 Years," *Wall Street Journal*, July 13, 2016; John Wasik, "Trading Stocks for Bonds Poses Its Own Risks," *New York Times*, August 26, 2016; "Slow Suffocation," *Economist*, July 16, 2016; and Jon Hilsenrath and Harriet Torry, "Fed's Dislike of Negative Interest Rates Points to Limits of Stimulus Measures," *Wall Street Journal*, August 28, 2106.

See related problems 4.13 and 4.14 at the end of the chapter.

In this chapter we have discussed the mechanics of how monetary policy is carried out and the lively debates over the unusual monetary policies that central banks have been pursuing since the financial crisis of 2007–2009. In Chapters 17 and 18, we will explore in more detail how monetary policy affects output, employment, and inflation. First, though, in Chapter 16, we will look more closely at the international financial system and the role that central banks play in it.

ANSWERING THE KEY QUESTION

Continued from page 494

At the beginning of this chapter, we asked:

"Is the Fed likely to return to using normal monetary policy procedures?"

As we have seen in this chapter, prior to the financial crisis of 2007–2009, monetary policy was focused on using open market operations to raise and lower the federal funds rate. But that approach works only if reserves are scarce, which allows the Fed to affect the equilibrium federal funds rate by adjusting the level of reserves. In December 2015, when the Fed began raising its target for the federal funds rate for the first time since 2008, it did so by raising the interest rate it pays banks on their reserve deposits and the interest rate it offers on overnight reverse repurchase agreements. For the Fed to return to normal policy procedures, it would have to feel confident that its goals of high employment and price stability were being achieved. At that point, it could stop reinvesting the principal from Treasury bonds and mortgage-backed securities as those securities mature. Doing so would gradually shrink the Fed's balance sheet and once again make reserves sufficiently scarce that the Fed could return to using open market operations to hit its target for the federal funds rate.

Speaking at the Jackson Hole, Wyoming, conference mentioned in the chapter opener, Fed Chair Janet Yellen observed:

> At some point after the process of raising the federal funds rate is well under way, we will cease or phase out reinvesting repayments of principal from our securities holdings. Once we stop reinvestment, it should take several years for our asset holdings—and the bank reserves used to finance them—to passively decline to a more normal level.[8]

So, the answer to the key question is that while the Fed may eventually return to normal monetary policy procedures, it is unlikely to do so in the near future.

---

[8] Janet L. Yellen, "The Federal Reserve's Monetary Policy Toolkit: Past, Present, and Future," Remarks at "Designing Resilient Monetary Policy Frameworks for the Future" a symposium sponsored by the Federal Reserve Bank of Kansas City, Jackson Hole, Wyoming, August 26, 2016, p. 10.

Key Terms and Problems

Key Terms

Discount policy, p. 501

Discount window, p. 501

Economic growth, p. 498

Federal funds rate, p. 503

Open market operations, p. 501

Primary credit, p. 514

Quantitative easing, p. 512

Reserve requirement, p. 501

Seasonal credit, p. 515

Secondary credit, p. 514

Taylor rule, p. 526

15.1 **The Goals of Monetary Policy**
Describe the goals of monetary policy.

Review Questions

1.1 What is the purpose of monetary policy? What is meant by economic well-being? Why is the Fed said to have a "dual mandate"?

1.2 Which type of unemployment—frictional, structural, or cyclical—does the Federal Reserve seek to reduce? Why doesn't the Fed seek to reduce the unemployment rate to zero percent?

 MyEconLab Visit **www.myeconlab.com** to complete these exercises online and get instant feedback. Exercises that update with real-time data are marked with .

1.3 Why do fluctuations in interest rates make investment decisions by households and firms more difficult?

1.4 If you owned a firm that did business internationally, why would large fluctuations in the foreign exchange value of the dollar make planning for your business and financial transactions more difficult?

Problems and Applications

1.5 Given that *inflation* erodes the value of money, should the Federal Reserve pursue a goal of *deflation*? Would deflation create some of the same problems as inflation in terms of the information communicated by price changes and the arbitrary redistribution of income? Briefly explain.

1.6 A columnist in the *Wall Street Journal* has argued in favor of changing the Fed's dual mandate to a single mandate of price stability: "When an economy gets weak enough, extraordinary easing measures can be justified as the necessary battle against potentially highly damaging deflation rather than to reduce unemployment."

a. What does the columnist mean by "extraordinary easing measures"?

b. How would these measures end deflation? Why would deflation be "potentially highly damaging"?

c. Briefly explain whether you agree with the columnist's argument that the Fed's dual mandate should be replaced with a single mandate of price stability.

Source: Neal Lipschutz, "Should Fed Chairman Have a Single Term, Single Mandate?" *Wall Street Journal*, September 27, 2012.

1.7 [Related to the Making the Connection on page 498] A column in the *Wall Street Journal* mentions the famous billionaire investor "Warren Buffet, who in 1999 and early 2000 was widely derided as 'a dinosaur' and 'out of touch' for his refusal to buy technology stocks."

a. Why would anyone refer to an investor as out of touch if he wasn't investing in technology stocks in 1999 and early 2000?

b. What was the Fed's policy toward the increase in stock price during this period? Is your answer to part (a) relevant to evaluating the Fed's policy? Briefly explain.

Source: Jason Zweig, "When Does a Bubble Spell Trouble?" *Wall Street Journal*, January 10, 2014.

1.8 [Related to the Making the Connection on page 498] A columnist for bloomberg.com observes: "The Fed is easily able to tell when unemployment or inflation is high, but inflated asset prices are much, much harder to identify."

a. Briefly explain whether you agree with this columnist's statement.

b. What are the implications of your answer to part (a) for Fed policy?

Source: Noah Smith, "Fed Rates Are the Wrong Tools to Fight Bubbles,"bloomberg.com, July 6, 2016.

1.9 Achieving the goal of price stability with low and steady inflation allows the Fed to achieve other goals, such as stable interest rates and stable foreign exchange rates. If the Fed fails to achieve low and steady inflation, why will it be difficult to achieve stable interest rates?

15.2 **Monetary Policy Tools and the Federal Funds Rate**
Understand how the Fed uses monetary policy tools to influence the federal funds rate.

Review Questions

2.1 What are the Fed's three traditional monetary policy tools, and which is the most important?

2.2 Why does an increase in the federal funds rate decrease the quantity of reserves demanded? At what interest rate does the demand curve for reserves become perfectly elastic?

2.3 Briefly explain what determines the supply curve for reserves. Why does the supply curve have a horizontal segment?

2.4 What does it mean to say that bank reserves are scarce? In a period when bank reserves are *not* scarce, why have the interest rate the Fed pays on bank reserves and the interest rate the Fed offers on overnight reverse repurchase agreements increased in importance?

Problems and Applications

2.5 Use graphs of the federal funds market to illustrate the effect on the demand for reserves or the supply of reserves of each of the Fed policy actions listed below. Assume that reserves are scarce during the period the graphs represent. Be sure to explain what is happening in your graphs.

  a. A decrease in the required reserve ratio

  b. A decrease in the discount rate

  c. A decrease in the interest rate paid on reserves

  d. An open market sale of government securities

2.6 Suppose that the FOMC decides to lower its target for the federal funds rate. How can it use open market operations to accomplish this goal? How can the FOMC use open market operations to raise its target for the federal funds rate? Use a graph of the federal funds market to illustrate your answers. Does it matter for your answer whether reserves are scarce? Briefly explain.

2.7 [Related to Solved Problem 15.2 on page 508]
Use graphs of the federal funds market to analyze each of the following three situations. Be sure that your graphs clearly show changes in the equilibrium federal funds rate, changes in the equilibrium level of reserves, and any shifts in the demand and supply curves. Assume that you are analyzing a situation in which reserves are scarce.

  a. Suppose that the Fed decides to increase its target for the federal funds rate from 2% to 2.25% while also increasing the discount rate from 2.5% to 2.75%. Show how the Fed can use open market operations to bring about a higher equilibrium federal funds rate.

  b. Suppose that banks increase their demand for reserves. Show how the Fed can offset this change through open market operations in order to keep the equilibrium federal funds rate unchanged.

  c. Suppose that the Fed decides to decrease the required reserve ratio but does not want the

decrease to affect its target for the federal funds rate. Show how the Fed can use open market operations to accomplish this policy.

2.8 [Related to Solved Problem 15.2 on page 508]
Suppose that in equilibrium, the federal funds rate is equal to the interest rate the Fed is paying on reserves. Use a graph of the federal funds market to analyze the effect of an open market sale of Treasury securities on the equilibrium federal funds rate.

2.9 The December 13, 2005, press release of the Federal Open Market Committee (FOMC) stated that the FOMC "decided today to raise its target for the federal funds rate by 25 basis points to 4¼ percent." The press release also stated: "In a related action, the Board of Governors unanimously approved a 25-basis point increase in the discount rate to 5¼ percent." (Note: A *basis point* is one one-hundredth of a percentage point. So, there are 100 basis points in 1 percentage point.)

  a. Using a graph of the federal funds market, show the equilibrium federal funds rate and the discount rate before the policy action of December 13, 2005, when the federal funds rate was 4% and the discount rate 5%.

  b. Use your graph from part (a) to explain how the Fed would raise the federal funds rate by 25 basis points (¼%). Show in your graph the 25-basis-point increase in the discount rate. What policy action would the Fed use to bring about this increase in the target federal funds rate?

  c. Today, would the Fed use the same policy action you described in part (b) to raise the federal funds rate? Briefly explain.

Source: Board of Governors of the Federal Reserve System, "Press Release," December 13, 2005, www.federalreserve.gov/boarddocs/press/monetary/2005/20051213/.

2.10 The January 22, 2008 press release of the FOMC states that the FOMC "decided to lower its target for the federal funds rate by 75 basis points to 3½ percent." The press release goes on to say: "In a related action the Board of Governors approved a 75-basis point decrease in the discount rate to 4 percent."

  a. Use a graph of the federal funds market to show the equilibrium federal funds rate and the discount rate before the policy action of January 22, 2008, when the federal funds rate was 4¼% and the discount rate was 4¾%.

b. Use your graph to show how the Fed would lower the federal funds rate by 75 basis points (¾%). Show in your graph the 75-basis-point decrease in the discount rate. What policy

action would the Fed use to lower the federal funds rate by 75 basis points?

c. Today, would the Fed use the same policy action you described in part (b) to lower the federal funds rate? Briefly explain.

Source: Board of Governors of the Federal Reserve System, "Press Release," January 22, 2008, www.federalreserve.gov/newsevents/press/monetary/20080122b.htm.

15.3 **The Fed's Monetary Policy Tools and Its New Approach to Managing the Federal Funds Rate**
Trace how the Fed has changed its use of monetary policy tools over time.

Review Questions

3.1 How does an open market sale of Treasury securities by the Fed affect the price of Treasury securities, the interest rate on Treasury securities, the monetary base, and the money supply?

3.2 What is quantitative easing, and why did the Fed begin using it? What effect did quantitative easing have on bank reserves?

3.3 What are the three categories of discount loans? During the financial crisis of 2007–2009, how did the Fed's discount lending expand?

3.4 What two groups of financial institutions are eligible to borrow and lend in the federal funds market? Briefly describe the procedures the Fed now uses to increase the federal funds rate.

Problems and Applications

3.5 When it passed the Federal Reserve Act in 1913, Congress did not at first expect that the Fed would engage in open market operations. An article in a Federal Reserve publication notes that after the Fed first began buying Treasury securities: "Fed officials realized that by purchasing securities on the open market, Federal Reserve Banks could affect general credit conditions across the country."

a. What does the article mean by "general credit conditions in the country"?

b. How would the Fed's purchase of Treasury securities affect general credit conditions in the country?

Source: "Discovering Open Market Operations," Federal Reserve Bank of Minneapolis *Region*, August 1, 1988.

3.6 [Related to the Chapter Opener on page 494]
Following its meeting on July 27, 2016, the Federal Open Market Committee issued a statement that contains the following:

> The Committee is maintaining its existing policy of reinvesting principal payments from its holdings of agency debt and agency mortgage-backed securities in agency mortgage-backed securities and of rolling over maturing Treasury securities at auction, and it anticipates doing so until normalization of the level of the federal funds rate is well under way.

a. What are agency debt and agency mortgage-backed securities? Traditionally, the Fed's securities holdings have been composed primarily of short-term Treasury securities, such as T-bills. How did the Fed come to own agency debt and agency mortgage-backed securities?

b. What does it mean that the Fed intends to "roll over" maturing Treasury securities?

c. What are the implications of this statement for the level of reserves held by banks?

d. What does the statement mean by the "normalization of the level of the federal funds rate"? What was abnormal about the level of the federal funds rate in 2016?

Source: Federal Open Market Committee, "Federal Reserve Press Release," July 27, 2016.

 MyEconLab Visit **www.myeconlab.com** to complete these exercises online and get instant feedback. Exercises that update with real-time data are marked with .

3.7 [Related to the Chapter Opener on page 494] In a statement explaining how it intended at some point to normalize monetary policy, the FOMC wrote:

> The Committee intends that the Federal Reserve will, in the longer run, hold no more securities than necessary to implement monetary policy efficiently and effectively, and that it will hold primarily Treasury securities, thereby minimizing the effect of Federal Reserve holdings on the allocation of credit across sectors of the economy.

a. What does the Federal Reserve's holdings of securities have to do with implementing monetary policy?

b. What securities other than Treasury securities does the Fed currently hold? How does holding these securities affect "the allocation of credit across sectors of the economy"?

Source: Federal Open Market Committee, "Policy Normalization Principles and Plans," September 17, 2014.

3.8 [Related to the Chapter Opener on page 494] In a speech to the Fed conference in Jackson Hole, Wyoming, mentioned in the chapter opener, Fed Chair Janet Yellen observed that the financial crisis revealed the Fed's "inability to control the federal funds rate once reserves were no longer relatively scarce." She went on to state: "To address the challenges posed by the financial crisis … the Federal Reserve significantly expanded its monetary policy toolkit…. Our current toolkit proved effective last December. In an environment of superabundant reserves, the FOMC raised the effective federal funds rate."

a. What does Yellen mean by "reserves were no longer relatively scarce"?

b. Briefly explain why, with the monetary policy tools it had used prior to the financial crisis, the Fed could not control the federal funds rate.

c. How was the Fed able to use its new monetary policy tools to increase the federal funds rate in December 2015?

Source: Janet L. Yellen, "The Federal Reserve's Monetary Policy Toolkit: Past, Present, and Future," Remarks at "Designing Resilient Monetary Policy Frameworks for the Future" a symposium sponsored by the Federal Reserve Bank of Kansas City, Jackson Hole, Wyoming, August 26, 2016.

3.9 An article in the *Wall Street Journal* notes that the Fed sets "the lower bound, or a floor under short-term rates, with the interest rate it pays institutions like money-market funds on … reverse repurchase agreements."

a. What is a reverse repurchase agreement?

b. Why would the interest rate the Fed pays on reverse repurchase agreements set a floor under short-term interest rates?

Source: Michael S. Derby and Katy Burne, "Fed Bolsters Tool Kit for Lifting Interest Rates," *Wall Street Journal*, December 16, 2015.

3.10 According to an article in the *Wall Street Journal* in June 2016, Congressman Jeb Hensarling of Texas, chair of the House Financial Services Committee, criticized the Fed for paying banks an interest rate on their reserves that was higher than the federal funds rate. Briefly explain why the federal funds rate is typically lower than the interest rate the Fed pays banks on reserves. Is it likely that the Fed would be able to set the interest rate it pays banks on reserves equal to the actual federal funds rate? Briefly explain.

Source: Kate Davidson, "House Republicans Grill Janet Yellen on Fed Operations," *Wall Street Journal*, June 22, 2016.

3.11 In June 2016, the Fed had a target range for the federal funds rate of 0.25% to 0.50%. An article in the *Wall Street Journal* noted: "It has set the rate it pays on bank reserves at the top of that range and uses another rate it pays on reverse-repurchase agreements as the bottom."

a. Explain why these two interest rates serve to set the top and bottom of the Fed's target range for the federal funds rate.

b. Draw a graph of the market for reserves to illustrate your answer to part (a).

Source: Kate Davidson, "House Republicans Grill Janet Yellen on Fed Operations," *Wall Street Journal*, June 22, 2016.

MyEconLab Visit **www.myeconlab.com** to complete these exercises online and get instant feedback. Exercises that update with real-time data are marked with (⬤).

15.4	**Monetary Targeting and Monetary Policy**

Explain the role of monetary targeting in monetary policy.

Review Questions

4.1 What trade-offs does the Fed face, particularly in the short run, in attempting to reach its goals?

4.2 What two timing difficulties does the Fed face in using its monetary policy tools?

4.3 Place the following in sequence, from what the Fed has the most influence on to what the Fed has the least influence on: policy goals, policy tools, policy instruments, intermediate targets.

4.4 How can the Taylor rule be used as a guide to evaluating Federal Reserve monetary policy over time?

4.5 Which interest rates have some foreign central banks set at a negative level? Briefly explain why they have taken this action.

Problems and Applications

4.6 State whether each of the following variables is most likely to be a goal, an intermediate target, an operating target, or a monetary policy tool:

a. M2

b. Monetary base

c. Unemployment rate

d. Open market purchases

e. Federal funds rate

f. Nonborrowed reserves

g. M1

h. Real GDP

i. Discount rate

j. Inflation rate

4.7 If the Fed uses the federal funds rate as a policy instrument, will increases in the demand for reserves lead to an increase or a decrease in the level of reserves? If the Fed uses the level of reserves as a policy instrument, will increases in the demand for reserves lead to an increase or a decrease in the federal funds rate? Support your

answers with a graph of the demand and supply of reserves.

4.8 [Related to the Making the Connection on page 522] What legislative changes and financial innovations occurred after 1979 that affected M1? How did these changes affect the short-run link between money and inflation?

4.9 [Related to the Making the Connection on page 522] An article in the *Wall Street Journal* in June 2016 notes: "The Fed's preferred measure of consumer prices has fallen short of the central bank's 2% annual target for 48 consecutive months." Over the same period, the average annual growth rate of M1 was 9.5%, and over the four years prior to that, from June 2008 to June 2012, the average annual growth rate of M1 was 12.0%. Review the discussion of the quantity theory of money in Chapter 2, Section 2.5, which begins on page 40. Using the equation of exchange, explain how such high money supply growth rates can be consistent with an inflation rate of less than 2%. Prior to 1980, would we have expected to see an inflation rate less than 2%, given high growth rates of the money supply during the preceding few years? Briefly explain.

Sources: Ben Eisen, "Newest Inflation Expectations Likely to Trouble the Fed," *Wall Street Journal*, June 10, 2016.

4.10 In 2016, in a Federal Reserve publication, Federal Reserve Bank President of San Francisco President John Williams wrote that one way to prepare for a future of chronically low real interest rates would be for "central banks to pursue a somewhat higher inflation target. This would imply a higher average level of interest rates and thereby give monetary policy more room to maneuver."

a. Why would a higher inflation target result in a higher average level of interest rates?

b. What does Williams mean by writing that higher interest rates would give monetary policy "more room to maneuver"?

c. Are there any reasons that central banks raising their inflation targets might be a bad idea? Briefly explain.

Source: John C. Williams, "Monetary Policy in a Low R-Star World," *FRBSF Economic Letter*, 2016-23, August 15, 2016, p. 3.

4.11 Using the Taylor rule, calculate the target for the federal funds rate for June 2016, using the following information: equilibrium real federal funds rate of 2%, target inflation rate of 2%, current inflation rate of 1.0%, and an output gap of −1.9%. In your calculations, the inflation gap is negative if the current inflation rate is below the target inflation rate. How does the targeted federal funds rate calculated using the Taylor rule compare to the actual federal funds rate of 0.25% to 0.50%?

4.12 John Taylor has argued: "Considerable empirical work supports the view that interest rates were too low for too long in 2003–2005 and were a major factor in the housing boom and bust that resulted."

a. What evidence is there that interest rates were too low in 2003–2005?

b. How might interest rates that were too low in 2003–2005 have contributed to the housing boom and bust?

Source: John Taylor, *First Principles: Five Keys to Restoring America's Prosperity*, New York: W.W. Norton & Company, 2012, p. 133.

4.13 [Related to the Making the Connection on page 532] An article in the *Wall Street Journal* in 2016 begins: "Hans Peter Christensen got some unusual news when he opened his most recent mortgage statement. His quarterly interest payment was negative 249 Danish kroner." Briefly explain how and why this happened.

Source: Charles Duxbury and David Gauthier-Villars, "Negative Rates Around the World: How One Danish Couple Gets Paid Interest on Their Mortgage," *Wall Street Journal*, April 14, 2016.

4.14 [Related to the Making the Connection on page 532] An article in the *Wall Street Journal* in 2016 notes: "Over 30% of euro-denominated investment-grade corporate bonds trade at a negative yield … while 84% yield less than 1%." What caused so many European corporate bonds to have negative interest rates? Why would anyone buy a bond with a negative interest rate?

Source: Christopher Whittall, "Bond Investors Cash Out in Europe, Head to U.S.," *Wall Street Journal*, September 1, 2016.

Data Exercises

D15.1: [Following news of FOMC meetings] Go to www.federalreserve.gov, the web site for the Federal Reserve Board of Governors, and read the most recent Federal Open Market Committee (FOMC) press release. At the web site, select "Monetary Policy" at the top of the screen and then select "Federal Open Market Committee (FOMC) Calendar" on the far left of the screen. Scroll down and select the statement for the date of the most recent FOMC meeting. Answer the following questions on the basis of the FOMC press release:

a. Did the FOMC change the target for the federal funds rate? If so, what was the change?

b. On balance, in its statement does the FOMC appear to be more concerned about slow economic growth or high inflation?

c. Read the "Implementation Note" that accompanies the statement for the date of the most recent FOMC meeting. Did the Fed change the interest rate it pays on bank reserves and the interest rate it offers on reverse repurchase agreements?

d. Did the Fed announce any other monetary policy actions?

D15.2: [Movements in the federal funds rate relative to the target] Go to the web site of the Federal Reserve Bank of St. Louis (FRED)

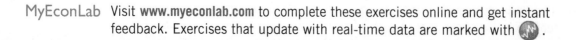

MyEconLab Visit **www.myeconlab.com** to complete these exercises online and get instant feedback. Exercises that update with real-time data are marked with .

(fred.stlouisfed.org) and download and graph the data series for the effective federal funds rate (DFF), the upper limit of the target range for the federal funds rate (DFEDTARU), and the lower limit for the target range (DFED-TARL). Plot values for all three data series from December 16, 2008, to the most recent day available on the same graph. Over this period, has the Fed been able to keep the effective federal funds rate within the target range? Briefly explain.

D15.3: [Central bank balance sheets] Go to the web site of the Bank of England, www.bankofengland.co.uk. The interactive database for the Bank of England has a section titled *Monetary financial institutions' balance sheets, income and expenditure*. That section has data on the Bank of England's balance sheet. What happened to the bank's balance sheet after 2007? How do these changes compare to the changes in the Fed's balance sheet during the same period?

D15.4: [Movements in discount loans] Go to the web site of the Federal Reserve Bank of St. Louis (FRED) (fred.stlouisfed.org) and download and graph the data series for discount loans (DISCBORR) from January 2000 until the most recent month available. Based only on these data, briefly explain when the financial crisis appears to have begun and when it ended.

chapter 16

The International Financial System and Monetary Policy

Learning Objectives

After studying this chapter, you should be able to:

16.1 Analyze how the Fed's interventions in foreign exchange markets affect the U.S. monetary base (pages 543–545)

16.2 Analyze how the Fed's interventions in foreign exchange markets affect the exchange rate (pages 545–549)

16.3 Describe how the balance of payments is calculated (pages 550–553)

16.4 Discuss the evolution of exchange-rate regimes (pages 553–573)

Can the Euro Survive?

From the start, the euro was a gamble. The decision by 12 sovereign countries to commit to using the same currency in 2002 was an unprecedented experiment. Although there have been examples of smaller countries abandoning their own currencies to use the currency of a larger country, never before had economies as large as those of Germany, France, and Italy agreed to use a common currency. Of the four largest economies in Europe, only the United Kingdom declined to join the "eurozone" and continued using its own currency. By 2016, 19 countries had adopted the euro. As we have seen, countries expect that their central banks will undertake monetary policy actions to achieve key policy goals, such as price stability and full employment. But to

undertake monetary policy, a country needs to control its money supply. With the French franc, German deutsche mark, Italian lira, and other currencies no longer in existence, these countries have surrendered control of monetary policy to the European Central Bank (ECB). The ECB, not the central banks of the individual member countries, determines such key monetary policy variables as the overnight bank lending rate and the size of the monetary base.

During its first five years, the euro gamble seemed to be paying off. Businesses and households were benefitting from the cost savings of buying and selling goods and investing across national borders without having to exchange currencies or worry about swings in the

Continued on next page

KEY ISSUE AND QUESTION

Issue: The financial crisis of 2007–2009 and its aftermath led to controversy over the European Central Bank's monetary policy.

Question: Should European countries abandon using a common currency?

Answered on page 573

values of the currencies. With steady growth in output and employment, few people in euro countries complained about the ECB's conduct of monetary policy. But then the financial crisis of 2007–2009 hit. Although the crisis caused all countries in the eurozone to experience declines in output and employment, Greece, Spain, Portugal, and Ireland were hit particularly hard. Before the euro, the central banks of those countries would have responded to the recession by allowing their currencies to depreciate, thereby boosting exports and reducing imports. Each country also could have expanded its monetary base. But these options for fighting recession were no longer available. Compounding the problem was the fact that falling government revenues and increasing government spending were leading to large government budget deficits that could be met only by selling bonds (which are known as *sovereign debt*).

Investors became concerned that so much debt was being sold that the governments of Greece, Spain, and Italy in particular might default on their interest or principal payments. In 2012, the ECB took the unusual step of buying the debt of Spain and Italy. In addition, the governments of eurozone countries agreed to give the ECB expanded powers to oversee banks in all member countries. As we discussed in Chapter 15, beginning in 2014, the ECB took the unusual step of making the interest rate on bank reserves negative. By 2016, the ECB had increased its purchases of government bonds, begun buying corporate bonds, and begun a program of four-year loans to banks to help them fund borrowing by households and firms. These actions helped stabilize the economies of the weakest eurozone members and increased the likelihood that the system would hold together, although some economists and policymakers continued to argue that the euro was not sustainable in the long run.

Whatever the outcome, the saga of the euro illustrates the lengths to which countries are willing to go to achieve stability in exchange rates and the difficulties those countries can encounter.

Source: Tom Fairless, "Draghi Stops Short of Pledging Fresh Stimulus," *Wall Street Journal*, July 21, 2016; "Unyielding," *Economist*, June 11, 2016; and Matt O'Brien, "The ECB's Big Bazooka Just Got Even Bigger," *Washington Post*, March 10, 2016.

In Chapter 8, we described how the foreign exchange market operates. In this chapter, we focus on how the Fed and other central banks intervene in foreign exchange markets. We also describe different exchange rate systems, such as the euro, and how these systems affect domestic monetary policy. We begin by looking at how the actions the Fed takes in foreign exchange markets can affect the monetary base in the United States.

16.1 Foreign Exchange Intervention and the Monetary Base

LEARNING OBJECTIVE: Analyze how the Fed's interventions in foreign exchange markets affect the U.S. monetary base.

In our analysis of the money supply process in Chapter 14, we described the actions of three participants: the central bank, the banking system, and the nonbank public. But because international financial markets are linked, foreign central banks, foreign banks, and foreign savers and borrowers can also affect the money supply in the United States. In particular, international financial transactions affect the money supply when central banks or governments try to influence the foreign exchange values of their currencies. As a result, such intervention may cause a conflict between the monetary policy goal of foreign exchange market stability and the policy goals of domestic price stability and economic growth.

The Federal Reserve and other central banks occasionally participate in international markets to affect the foreign exchange value of their nation's currency.

Foreign exchange market intervention A deliberate action by a central bank to influence the country's exchange rate.

International reserves (or foreign reserves) Central bank assets that are denominated in a foreign currency and used in international transactions.

A **foreign exchange market intervention** is a deliberate action by a central bank to influence the country's exchange rate. Foreign exchange market interventions alter a central bank's holdings of **international reserves** (or **foreign reserves**), which are assets that are denominated in a foreign currency and used in international transactions.

If the Fed wants the foreign exchange value of the dollar to rise, it can increase the demand for dollars by selling foreign assets and buying dollars in international currency markets. If the Fed wants the foreign exchange value of the dollar to fall, it can increase the supply of dollars by selling dollars and buying foreign assets. Such transactions affect not only the value of the dollar but also the domestic monetary base. We can show how the monetary base is affected by using T-accounts to trace the effect of a foreign exchange market intervention on the Fed's balance sheet.

Suppose that in an effort to reduce the foreign exchange value of the dollar, the Fed buys foreign assets—such as short-term securities issued by foreign governments—worth a dollar value of $1 billion. Typically, the Fed will buy from commercial banks the foreign exchange necessary to make the purchase of the foreign government bonds. This transaction increases the Fed's international reserves by $1 billion, so the entry for foreign assets on the Fed's balance sheet rises by $1 billion. The funds the Fed has paid to banks add $1 billion to banks' reserve deposits at the Fed, which are a Fed liability. We can summarize the effect of this transaction on the Fed's balance sheet as follows:

FEDERAL RESERVE

Assets		Liabilities	
Foreign assets (international reserves)	+$1 billion	Bank reserves at the Fed	+$1 billion

Alternatively, if the Fed paid for the foreign assets with $1 billion of U.S. currency, because currency in circulation also is a liability for the Fed, its liabilities still rise by $1 billion:

FEDERAL RESERVE

Assets		Liabilities	
Foreign assets (international reserves)	+$1 billion	Currency in circulation	+$1 billion

Because the monetary base equals the sum of currency and bank reserves, either transaction causes the monetary base to rise by the amount of the foreign assets (international reserves) purchased. *In other words, a purchase of foreign assets by a central bank has the same effect on the monetary base as an open market purchase of government bonds.* When a central bank buys foreign assets, its international reserves and the monetary base increase by the amount of foreign assets purchased.

Similarly, if the Fed, in an effort to increase the foreign exchange value of the dollar, sells foreign assets, the monetary base will decline, while the value of the dollar will rise. For instance, if the Fed sells $1 billion of short-term securities issued by foreign governments, the Fed's holdings of foreign assets will fall by $1 billion. At the same time, if the purchasers of the foreign assets sold by the Fed pay with checks drawn on U.S. banks, bank reserves at the Fed fall by $1 billion. The transaction affects the Fed's balance sheet as follows:

FEDERAL RESERVE

Assets		Liabilities	
Foreign assets (international reserves)	−$1 billion	Bank reserves at the Fed	−$1 billion

If the Fed instead purchased U.S. dollars with the proceeds of its sale of foreign assets, currency in circulation (another Fed liability) would fall by the value of the foreign assets sold. Because the monetary base is the sum of currency and reserves, it falls by the amount of foreign assets (international reserves) sold. Therefore, domestic bank reserves at the Fed or currency decline. *In other words, a sale of foreign assets by a central bank has the same effect on the monetary base as an open market sale of government bonds.* Purchases of domestic currency by a central bank financed by sales of foreign assets reduce international reserves and the monetary base by the amount of foreign assets sold.

When a central bank allows the monetary base to respond to the sale or purchase of domestic currency in the foreign exchange market, the transaction is called an **unsterilized foreign exchange intervention**. Alternatively, the central bank could use domestic open market operations to offset the change in the monetary base caused by a foreign exchange intervention. For example, consider a Fed sale of $1 billion of foreign assets. In the absence of any offsetting interventions, the monetary base falls by $1 billion. At the same time, however, the Fed could conduct an open market purchase of $1 billion of Treasury bills to eliminate the decrease in the monetary base arising from the foreign exchange intervention. The following T-account illustrates these transactions:

FEDERAL RESERVE

Assets		Liabilities	
Foreign assets (international reserves)	−$1 billion	Monetary base (currency plus reserves)	+$0 billion
Treasury bills	+$1 billion		

When a foreign exchange intervention is accompanied by offsetting domestic open market operations that leave the monetary base unchanged, it is called a **sterilized foreign exchange intervention**.

16.2 Foreign Exchange Interventions and the Exchange Rate

LEARNING OBJECTIVE: Analyze how the Fed's interventions in foreign exchange markets affect the exchange rate.

Foreign exchange interventions can affect the domestic money supply, with potentially unintended effects on the domestic economy. But central banks still occasionally intervene in foreign exchange markets because they seek to minimize fluctuations in exchange rates. A depreciating domestic currency raises the cost of foreign goods and may lead to inflation. As we saw in Section 16.1, central banks can attempt to limit depreciation

Unsterilized foreign exchange intervention
A foreign exchange market intervention in which the central bank does not offset the effect of the intervention on the monetary base.

Sterilized foreign exchange intervention
A foreign exchange market intervention in which the central bank offsets the effect of the intervention on the monetary base.

by buying assets denominated in the domestic currency and selling foreign currency denominated assets. An appreciating domestic currency can make a country's goods less competitive in world markets. Central banks attempt to limit appreciation by selling assets denominated in the domestic currency. In this section, we examine the effects of unsterilized and sterilized foreign exchange market interventions on the exchange rate.

Unsterilized Intervention

In Chapter 8, we saw that the exchange rate is determined by the demand and supply for dollars in the foreign exchange market. We can use demand and supply analysis to show the effects of central bank foreign exchange interventions on the exchange rate.

Assume that the Fed attempts to increase the exchange value of the dollar versus the Japanese yen through an unsterilized intervention. The Fed sells short-term Japanese government securities, which decreases the monetary base in the United States. The Fed has decreased the supply of dollars to the foreign exchange market, but as we saw in Chapter 15, a decrease in the monetary base may also raise U.S. interest rates (which is more likely if we are in a situation where bank reserves are scarce). As U.S. interest rates rise relative to Japanese interest rates, foreign investors will demand more U.S. dollars in order to buy U.S. financial assets, and U.S. investors will want to buy fewer Japanese financial assets, so their supply of U.S. dollars in exchange for Japanese yen will fall. Panel (a) of Figure 16.1 shows the results of the demand curve for dollars in exchange for yen shifting to the right, from D_1 to D_2, and the supply curve shifting to the left, from S_1 to S_2. The equilibrium exchange rate increases from E_1 to E_2, indicating that the Fed has successfully increased the exchange value of the dollar. So, if nothing else changes, an unsterilized intervention in which the central bank sells foreign assets in exchange for domestic currency leads to a decrease in international reserves and in the monetary base, and an appreciation of the domestic currency.

To lower the exchange rate with an unsterilized foreign exchange intervention, the Fed would buy short-term Japanese government securities, which increases the monetary base in the United States. If as the monetary base increases, U.S. interest rates fall, the demand curve for dollars in exchange for yen will shift to the left, and the supply curve of dollars will shift to the right. As panel (b) of Figure 16.1 shows, the result is a decrease in the equilibrium exchange rate. So, if nothing else changes, an unsterilized intervention in which the central bank buys foreign assets with domestic currency leads to an increase in international reserves and the monetary base, and depreciation of the domestic currency.

Sterilized Intervention

As we have seen, with a sterilized foreign exchange intervention, the central bank uses open market operations to offset the effects of the intervention on the monetary base. Because the monetary base is unaffected, domestic interest rates will not change. So, if the Fed sells short-term Japanese government securities but sterilizes the intervention by buying Treasury bills at the same time, U.S. interest rates will be unaffected. Therefore, the demand curve and supply curve for dollars in exchange for yen will also be unaffected, and the exchange rate will not change. We can conclude that a sterilized intervention does not affect the exchange rate. To be effective, central bank interventions that are intended to change the exchange rate need to be unsterilized.

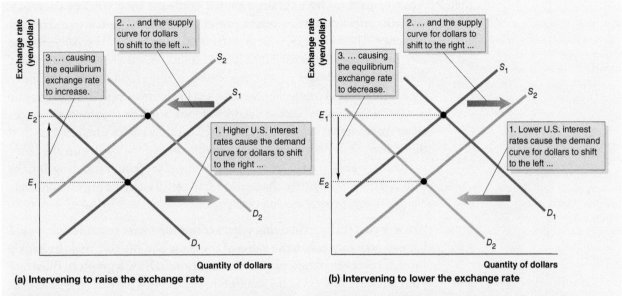

FIGURE 16.1 The Effect on the Exchange Rate of an Unsterilized Foreign Exchange Market Intervention

In panel (a), the Fed intervenes by selling short-term Japanese government securities. This action decreases the monetary base in the United States and raises U.S. interest rates. As a result, the demand for dollars in exchange for yen shifts to the right, from D_1 to D_2, and the supply of dollars shifts to the left, from S_1 to S_2. The equilibrium exchange rate increases from E_1 to E_2.

In panel (b), the Fed intervenes by buying short-term Japanese government securities. This action increases the monetary base in the United States and lowers U.S. interest rates. As a result, the demand for dollars in exchange for yen shifts to the left, from D_1 to D_2, and the supply of dollars shifts to the right, from S_1 to S_2. The equilibrium exchange rate decreases from E_1 to E_2. These two examples are both unsterilized interventions.

SOLVED PROBLEM 16.2

The Swiss Central Bank Counters the Rising Franc

In 2016, an article in the *Wall Street Journal* noted:

> Data Thursday from the Swiss central bank underscore the lengths to which officials have gone to keep their currencies from strengthening too much at a time most countries seem to prefer weaker, not stronger, exchange rates. Its foreign reserves rose to 95% of the size of the Swiss economy last month, exposing the central bank to huge losses if the franc keeps strengthening.

a. If the Swiss franc is stronger, will it take more francs or fewer francs to buy one euro? Why would most countries prefer a weaker currency to a stronger currency?

b. What actions would the Swiss central bank have to take to weaken the value of the franc against the euro? What are the Swiss central bank's "foreign reserves"? Why would its foreign reserves have risen? Use a graph of the market for Swiss francs in exchange for euros to illustrate the actions the Swiss central bank took to weaken the value of the franc.

Solving the Problem

Step 1   **Review the chapter material.** This problem is about how central banks intervene to affect the exchange rate, so you may want to review the section "Foreign Exchange Interventions and the Exchange Rate," which begins on page 545.

Step 2   **Answer part (a) by explaining what is meant by a weaker currency and why most countries might prefer a weaker currency to a stronger currency.** The Swiss franc is weaker if it takes more francs to exchange for one euro (or fewer euros to exchange for one franc). When the value of the franc falls relative to the euro, Swiss exporters, such as the food company Nestlé or the pharmaceutical companies Novartis and Roche, may experience an increase in sales within Europe because the price of their products in euros will have declined. For example, suppose that Nestlé sells a candy bar for 1 franc in Zurich. If the exchange rate between the franc and the euro is 1 franc = 1 euro, the candy bar has a price of 1 euro in Paris. But if the value of the franc weakens against the euro and the exchange rate changes to 1 franc = 0.9 euro, the price of the candy bar falls to 0.9 euro in Paris, increasing sales.

Step 3   **Answer part (b) by explaining what actions the Swiss central bank would have to take to weaken the value of the franc and the role that the bank's foreign reserves would play in these actions. Draw a graph to illustrate your answer.** To weaken the value of the franc versus the euro, the Swiss central bank has to sell francs in exchange for euros. As a result, the Swiss central bank's holdings or international reserves (or foreign reserves) will increase. The following graph shows that the Swiss central bank's sales have increased the supply of francs in exchange for euros from S_1 to S_2. As a result, the equilibrium exchange rate declines from E_1 to E_2. Notice that because you are drawing a graph from the perspective of the Swiss central bank, the vertical axis should be labeled "euros/franc."

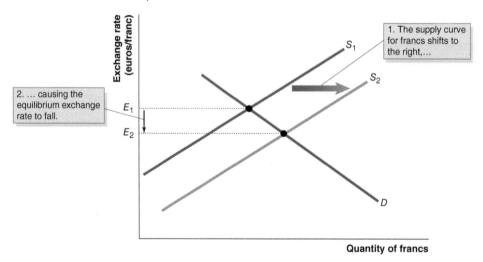

Source: Brian Blackstone, "Central Banks Still Intervene in Currency Markets Despite Weakened Effect," *Wall Street Journal*, July 7, 2016.

See related problem 2.6 at the end of the chapter.

Capital Controls

Mexico suffered a *currency crisis* during 1994–1995, and several East Asian countries suffered currency crises during 1997–1998. During these crises, the countries involved suffered sharp declines in the exchange value of their currencies, which disrupted their economies. These crises were fueled in part by sharp inflows and outflows of financial investments, or *capital inflows* and *capital outflows*, leading some economists and policymakers to advocate restrictions on capital mobility in emerging market countries. These restrictions, called **capital controls**, are government-imposed restrictions on foreign investors buying domestic assets or on domestic investors buying foreign assets. Governments intend capital controls to reduce the volatility of the exchange rate between their currency and foreign currencies.

Although capital outflows often play a role in currency crises—leading some political leaders to limit capital outflows, as Mahathir Mohamad, who was then prime minister of Malaysia, did in 1998—most economists are concerned about the effect of such controls on the domestic economy. Capital controls have significant problems. First, with capital controls, domestic firms and investors must receive permission from the government to exchange domestic currency for foreign currency. The government officials responsible for granting this permission may insist on receiving bribes before granting it. Most developing countries that have implemented capital controls have found that they result in a significant amount of government corruption. Second, multinational firms may be reluctant to invest in countries that have capital controls because the firms will have difficulty returning any profits they earn to their home countries if they can't exchange domestic currency for foreign currency. This problem is significant because to achieve high growth rates, many developing countries are dependent on the willingness of multinational firms to build factories and other facilities in their countries. Finally, in practice, many countries find that individuals and firms evade capital controls by using black markets where currency traders are willing to illegally exchange domestic currency for foreign currency.

Despite these drawbacks to using capital controls, the financial crisis of 2007–2009 and its aftermath revived interest in them among some economists and policymakers. In the years before the crisis, several European countries, including Spain, Greece, and Iceland, experienced large capital inflows, partly in response to the worldwide boom in real estate prices. Once the crisis began, these countries experienced sharp capital outflows, which helped deepen their recessions. The International Monetary Fund (an international agency that we discuss later in this chapter) was for many years opposed to capital controls. But more recently it has softened its opposition and has even recommended that governments and central banks consider using them in cases where they are experiencing particularly large capital inflows.

Restrictions on capital inflows receive more support from some economists than do restrictions on capital outflows, in part because such inflows often lead to domestic lending booms and increased risk taking by domestic banks. Other economists point out that the severity of this problem could be reduced by improving bank regulation and supervision in emerging-market countries. In this way, capital inflows could still serve as important financial mechanisms for channeling foreign investment to countries with promising investment opportunities.

Capital controls
Government-imposed restrictions on foreign investors buying domestic assets or on domestic investors buying foreign assets.

<table>
<tr><td>16.3</td><td></td></tr>
</table>

16.3 The Balance of Payments

LEARNING OBJECTIVE: Describe how the balance of payments is calculated.

In describing the Fed's foreign exchange market interventions, we simply noted the increase or decrease in international reserves on the Fed's balance sheet, without discussing why the Fed holds international reserves or what factors account for the size of its reserve holdings. Transactions in international reserves are one of several capital flows between the United States and other countries. To understand how the Fed accumulates international reserves and how much it has available for foreign exchange market interventions, we need to look at the broader flow of funds between the United States and foreign countries. We can use the balance-of-payments account to understand international capital flows. The **balance-of-payments account** measures all flows of private and government funds between a domestic economy (in this case, the United States) and all foreign countries.

Balance-of-payments account A measure of all flows of private and government funds between a domestic economy and all foreign countries.

The balance of payments for the United States is a bookkeeping procedure similar to ones that households or firms might use to record receipts and payments. In the balance of payments, inflows of funds to the United States from foreigners are receipts, which are recorded as positive numbers. Receipts include:

1. Purchases of U.S.-produced goods and services (exports)
2. Funds spent on purchases of U.S. assets by foreign households and businesses (capital inflows)
3. Gifts to U.S. citizens from foreigners (unilateral transfers)

Outflows of funds from the United States to foreigners are payments, which are recorded as negative numbers. Payments include:

1. Purchases of foreign goods and services (imports)
2. Money spent on purchases of foreign assets by U.S. households and businesses (capital outflows)
3. Gifts to foreigners, including foreign aid (unilateral transfers)

The principal components of the balance-of-payments account summarize transactions for purchases and sales of goods and services (the *current account balance*, which includes the *trade balance*) and flows of funds for international lending or borrowing (the *financial account balance*, which includes *official settlements*).

Each international transaction represents an exchange of goods, services, or assets among households, firms, or governments. Therefore, the two sides of the exchange must always balance. In other words, the payments and receipts of the balance-of-payments account must equal zero, or:

$$\text{Current account balance } + \text{ Financial account balance } = 0.$$

The Current Account

The current account summarizes transactions between a country and its foreign trading partners involving purchases and sales of currently produced goods and services. If the United States has a current account surplus (a positive number), U.S. residents are selling more goods and services to foreigners than they are buying imports from foreigners. Therefore, U.S. residents have funds to lend to foreigners. Typically, the U.S. current account has a negative balance, or is in deficit. In 2015, the United States had a current account deficit of $463 billion. When the United States has a current account deficit, it must borrow the difference to pay for goods and services purchased abroad. In general, a current account surplus or deficit must be balanced by international lending or borrowing or by changes in official reserve transactions. Some economists and policymakers have been concerned that the large U.S. current account deficits since the 1980s have caused the United States to rely heavily on savings from abroad—international borrowing—to finance domestic consumption, investment, and the federal budget deficit.

One reason for the U.S. current account deficits in the past 15 years may be a global "saving glut." The saving glut is partly the result of high rates of saving in countries such as Japan, which had aging populations that were preparing for retirement. In addition, the level of global saving has increased because developing countries such as China, Korea, and other Asian countries, as well as some countries in Eastern Europe, have increased their saving as their incomes have begun to rise. With high saving rates and relatively limited opportunities for investment, funds from these countries have flowed into the United States. In addition, slow growth and financial and political instability in Europe have led some investors to prefer U.S. securities as a safe haven. During some periods, these factors have led investors to bid up the value of the dollar. The high value of the dollar reduces U.S. exports and increases imports, contributing to the current account deficit.

The Financial Account

The financial account measures trade in existing financial or real assets among countries. When someone in a country sells an asset (a skyscraper, a bond, or shares of stock, for example) to a foreign investor, the transaction is recorded in the balance-of-payments accounts as a *capital inflow* because funds flow into the country to buy the asset. When someone in a country buys an asset abroad, the transaction is recorded in the balance-of-payments accounts as a *capital outflow* because funds flow from the country to buy the asset. For example, when a wealthy Chinese entrepreneur buys a penthouse apartment in a New York high rise, the transaction is recorded as a capital outflow for China and as a capital inflow for the United States.

The financial account balance is the amount of capital inflows minus capital outflows—plus the net value of debt forgiveness and transfers of financial assets by migrants when they enter the United States.[1] The financial account balance is in surplus if the residents of the country sell more assets to foreigners than they buy from foreigners.

[1] The capital account is a third, less important, part of the balance of payments. The capital account records relatively minor transactions, such as debt forgiveness, migrants' transfers—which consist of goods and financial assets people take with them when they leave or enter a country—and sales and purchases of nonproduced, nonfinancial assets. A nonproduced, nonfinancial asset is a copyright, patent, trademark, or right to natural resources. The definitions of the financial account and the capital account are often misunderstood because the capital account prior to 1999 recorded all the transactions included now in both the financial account and the capital account. In other words, capital account transactions went from being a very important part of the balance of payments to being a relatively unimportant part. Because the balance on what is now called the capital account is so small, for simplicity we merge it with the financial account here.

The financial account balance is in deficit if the residents of the country buy more assets from foreigners than they sell to foreigners. In 2015, the United States had capital inflows of $420.6 billion and capital outflows of $225.3 billion for a net financial account balance of $195.3 billion. This financial account balance represents an increase in U.S. assets held by foreigners.

Official Settlements

Not all capital flows among countries represent transactions by households and firms. Changes in asset holdings by governments and central banks supplement private capital flows. *Official reserve assets* are assets that central banks hold and that they use in making international payments to settle the balance of payments and to conduct international monetary policy. Historically, gold was the leading official reserve asset. Official reserves now are primarily government securities of the United States and other high-income countries, foreign bank deposits, and assets called Special Drawing Rights created by the International Monetary Fund. Official settlements equal the net increase (domestic holdings minus foreign holdings) in a country's official reserve assets.

The official settlements balance is sometimes called the *balance-of-payments surplus or deficit*. This terminology may be somewhat confusing. Earlier we saw that the balance of payments equals the sum of the current account and the financial account and is, therefore, always zero. An alternative way of thinking of the balance of payments is to exclude the official settlements balance from the financial account. This exclusion makes it possible for a country to have a balance of payments surplus or deficit. From this perspective, in 2015, the United States had a significant balance-of-payments deficit. When a country has a balance-of-payments surplus in this sense, it gains international reserves because its receipts exceed its payments. That is, foreign central banks provide the country's central bank with international reserves. When a country has a balance-of-payments deficit in this sense, it loses international reserves. Because U.S. dollars and dollar-denominated assets serve as the largest component of international reserves, a U.S. balance-of-payments deficit can be financed by a reduction in U.S. international reserves and an increase in dollar assets held by foreign central banks. Similarly, a combination of an increase in U.S. international reserves and a decrease in dollar assets held by foreign central banks can offset a U.S. balance-of-payments surplus.

The Relationship Among the Accounts

Recall that, in principle, the current account balance and financial account balance sum to zero. In reality, measurement problems keep this relationship from holding exactly. An adjustment for measurement errors, the *statistical discrepancy*, is reported in the financial account portion of the balance-of-payments accounts. The U.S. balance-of-payments account in 2015 had a statistical discrepancy of $267.8 billion (a capital inflow). Many analysts believe that similarly large statistical discrepancies in other countries' balance-of-payments accounts reflect hidden capital flows related to illegal activity, tax evasion, or capital flight because of political risk.

To summarize, international trade and financial transactions affect both the current account and the financial account in the balance of payments. To close out a country's international transactions from the balance of payments, its central bank and foreign central banks engage in official reserve transactions, which can affect the country's monetary base.

16.4 Exchange Rate Regimes and the International Financial System

LEARNING OBJECTIVE: Discuss the evolution of exchange rate regimes.

The Fed and other central banks engage in foreign exchange market interventions to maintain the foreign exchange value of their nations' currencies. Political agreements influence the size and timing of each central bank's purchases and sales of international reserves. Specifically, countries may agree to participate in a particular **exchange rate regime**, or system for adjusting exchange rates and flows of goods and capital among countries. At times, countries have agreed to fix exchange rates among their national currencies, and these agreements have committed their central banks to act to maintain these exchange rates. At other times, including the present, most countries have allowed exchange rates to fluctuate according to movements in demand and supply for different currencies, although central banks may still act to limit exchange-rate fluctuations.

> **Exchange rate regime**
> A system for adjusting exchange rates and flows of goods and capital among countries.

In this section, we analyze exchange rate regimes in terms of (1) how the agreement holds the system together, (2) how exchange rates adjust to maintain the agreement, and (3) how central banks act to maintain equilibrium in the international monetary and financial system. We also evaluate the successes and failures of each system and the *policy trilemma* that governments and central banks face.

Fixed Exchange Rates and the Gold Standard

In the past, most exchange rate regimes were **fixed exchange rate systems**, in which exchange rates were set at levels that were determined and maintained by governments. Under a **gold standard**, currencies of participating countries are convertible into an agreed-upon amount of gold. The exchange rates between any two countries' currencies are fixed by their relative gold weights. The classical gold standard that prevailed from the late nineteenth century to the outbreak of World War I in 1914 illustrates the successes and failures of a fixed exchange rate system. Figure 16.2 shows the spread of the gold standard between 1870 and 1913.

> **Fixed exchange rate system** A system in which exchange rates are set at levels determined and maintained by governments.

> **Gold standard** A fixed exchange rate system under which currencies of participating countries are convertible into an agreed-upon amount of gold.

Consider an example of how the gold standard operated: If $1 could be exchanged for 1/20 of an ounce of gold, while one French franc (FF1) could be exchanged for 1/80 of an ounce of gold, the exchange rate would be $1 = FF4, or $0.25 = FF1. Now let's consider an example of trade and capital flows between France and the United States to illustrate how this system of fixed exchange rates worked. Under a gold standard, a U.S. importer could buy goods from a French exporter by either (1) exchanging dollars for French francs in France and buying goods or (2) exchanging dollars for gold in the United States and shipping gold to France to buy francs and French goods.

Suppose that the demand for French goods rises relative to the demand for U.S. goods, leading to a rising demand for francs and a falling demand for dollars. The result is pressure for the exchange rate to move away from the official exchange rate—say, from $1 = FF4 to $1 = FF3. In this situation, U.S. importers could make a profit from

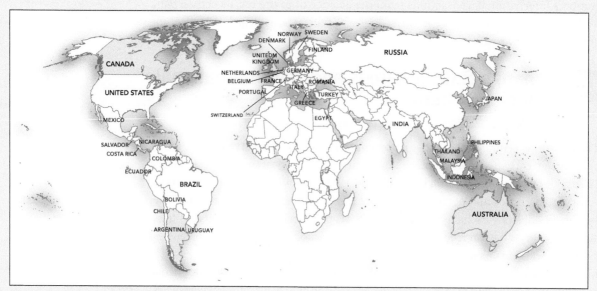

(a) Countries on the gold standard in 1870

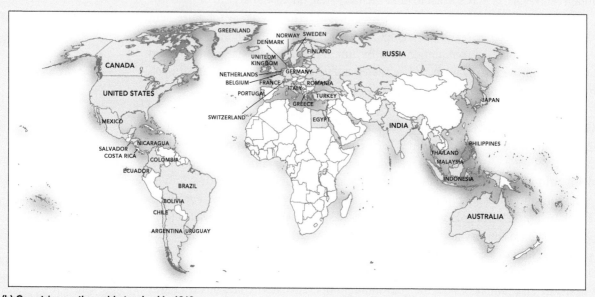

(b) Countries on the gold standard in 1913

FIGURE 16.2 The Spread of the Gold Standard

In 1870, the only countries on the gold standard were those shaded in yellow: Great Britain, Canada, Australia, Portugal, Argentina, and Uruguay. By 1913, most countries in Europe and the Western Hemisphere were on the gold standard. By the late 1930s, the gold standard had disappeared. Note that countries are shown with their current borders.

Source: Maps prepared by authors from information in Christopher M. Meissner, "A New World Order: Explaining the International Diffusion of the Classical Gold Standard, 1870–1913," *Journal of International Economics*, Vol. 66, No. 2, July 2005, Table 1, p. 391.

shipping gold to France to buy francs, as long as the governments of the United States and France continued to exchange currencies for gold at the agreed-upon rate.

Therefore, if Sally Sharp, a cloth importer in Philadelphia, wants to buy FF5,000 worth of cloth from Deluxe of Paris, she can use either of the two strategies described. First, if she tries to sell dollars for francs in the foreign exchange market, she will find that she must pay FF5,000 ÷ (3FF per $) = $1,666.67 for the cloth. Alternatively, she can exchange $1,250 for gold, ship the gold bars to France, and demand that the Bank of France exchange the gold for francs at the fixed exchange rate. At the official exchange rate of $1 = FF4, she will receive FF5,000 for her gold, which is enough to buy the cloth. The second strategy provides the cheaper solution for Sally. Her saving on this transaction, $416.67, makes it the better way to buy the cloth, as long as the cost of shipping the gold from Philadelphia to France does not exceed $416.67.

What happens in France as U.S. importers like Sally Sharp ship their gold to Paris? Gold flows into France, expanding that country's international reserves because gold is eventually exchanged for francs. The United States loses an equivalent amount of international reserves because dollars are given to the government in exchange for gold. An increase in a country's international reserves increases its monetary base, while a decrease in its international reserves lowers its monetary base. The monetary base rises in France and falls in the United States, putting upward pressure on the price level in France and downward pressure on the price level in the United States. French goods become more expensive relative to U.S. goods. Therefore, the relative demand for French goods falls, restoring the trade balance and causing the exchange rate to move toward the official rate of $1 = FF4.

Alternatively, if the relative demand for U.S. goods rises, gold flows from France to the United States, reducing the French monetary base and increasing the U.S. monetary base. In this case, the accompanying increase in the U.S. price level relative to the French price level makes French goods more attractive, restoring the trade balance. The exchange rate moves back toward the fixed rate of $1 = FF4. So, we can conclude that the gold standard had an automatic mechanism that would cause exchange rates to reflect the underlying gold content of countries' currencies. This automatic mechanism was called the *price-specie flow mechanism*.

One problem with the economic adjustment process under the gold standard was that countries with trade deficits and gold outflows experienced declines in price levels, or deflation. A period of unexpected and pronounced deflation could cause a recession or make a recession worse. During the 1870s, 1880s, and 1890s, several recessions occurred in the United States that were made more severe by deflation. A falling price level raised the real value of households' and firms' nominal debts, leading to financial distress for many sectors of the economy.

Another consequence of fixed exchange rates under the gold standard was that countries had little control over their domestic monetary policies. The reason was that gold flows caused changes in the monetary base. As a result, countries faced unexpected inflation or deflation from international trade. Moreover, gold discoveries and production strongly influenced changes in the world money supply, increasing instability. For example, in the 1870s and 1880s, few gold discoveries and rapid economic growth contributed to falling prices in many countries. This deflation caused substantial political unrest among farmers in the U.S. Midwest and Great Plains states, as they saw the real interest rates on their mortgages rise. In the 1890s, on the other hand, the gold discoveries in Alaska, the Yukon in Canada, and what is now South Africa increased price levels around the world.

In theory, the gold standard required that all countries maintain their promise to convert currencies freely into gold at fixed exchange rates. In practice, England made the exchange rate regime's promise credible. The strength of the British economy, its frequent trade surpluses, and its large gold reserves made England the anchor of the international monetary and financial system. During World War I, the disruption of the international trading system led countries to abandon their promises to convert currency into gold. The gold standard had a brief revival during the period between the two world wars but finally collapsed in the 1930s, during the Great Depression. President Franklin D. Roosevelt and Congress took the United States off the gold standard in 1933. Thereafter, the federal government would no longer redeem paper currency for gold, and U.S. citizens were barred from owning gold, except for some limited purposes, such as making jewelry, manufacturing, and coin collecting. The prohibition on U.S. citizens owning gold remained in effect until 1974.

MAKING THE CONNECTION

Did the Gold Standard Make the Great Depression Worse?

When the Great Depression began in 1929, governments came under pressure to abandon the gold standard in order to allow their central banks to more easily pursue expansionary monetary policies. In 1931, Britain became the first major country to abandon the gold standard. A number of other countries also went off the gold standard that year. The United States remained on the gold standard until 1933, and a few countries, including France, Italy, and Belgium, stayed on even longer. By the late 1930s, the gold standard no longer existed.

The earlier a country went off the gold standard, the easier time it had fighting the Depression with expansionary monetary policies. As the following figure shows, the countries that abandoned the gold standard before 1933 suffered an average decline in industrial production of only 3% between 1929 and 1934. The countries that stayed on the gold standard until 1933 or later suffered an average decline of more than 30%.

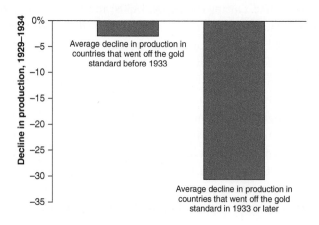

Why did countries that stayed on the gold standard suffer worse effects from the Great Depression? A key reason is that to remain on the gold standard, central banks often had to take actions that contracted production and employment rather than expanding them. For example, the United States experienced gold outflows during 1930 and 1931. Afraid that the gold outflows might force the country off the gold standard, the Fed attempted to stem them by raising the discount rate. Higher interest rates would make financial investments in the United States more attractive to foreign investors, leading them to increase their demand for dollars. But although higher interest rates were effective in stemming the gold outflow and keeping the United States on the gold standard, the economy actually needed *lower* interest rates to stimulate domestic spending. The United States did not begin to recover from the Depression until March 1933, the same month that it left the gold standard.

The devastating economic performance of the countries that stayed on the gold standard the longest during the 1930s is the key reason that policymakers did not attempt to bring back the classical gold standard in later years.

Sources: Ben Bernanke and Harold James, "The Gold Standard, Deflation, and Financial Crisis in the Great Depression: An International Comparison," in R. Glenn Hubbard, ed., *Financial Markets and Financial Crises*, Chicago: University of Chicago Press, 1991; Barry Eichengreen, *Golden Fetters: The Gold Standard and the Great Depression 1919–1939*, New York: Oxford University Press, 1992; dates for abandoning the gold standard used in the figure from Melchior Palyi, *The Twilight of Gold, 1914–1936*, Chicago: Henry Regnery, 1972, Table IV-I, pp. 116–117; the change in production in the figure is the change in industrial production from League of Nations, *World Production and Prices, 1925–1934*, Geneva: League of Nations, 1935, Appendix II, Table 1, p. 133.

See related problem 4.8 at the end of the chapter.

Adapting Fixed Exchange Rates: The Bretton Woods System

Despite the gold standard's demise, many countries remained interested in the concept of fixed exchange rates. As World War II drew to a close, representatives of the United States, the United Kingdom, France, and other Allied governments gathered at Bretton Woods, New Hampshire in 1944 to design a new international monetary and financial system. The resulting agreement, known as the **Bretton Woods system**, lasted from 1945 until 1971. Framers of the agreement, including the British economist John Maynard Keynes, intended to reinstate a system of fixed exchange rates but wanted to permit smoother short-term economic adjustments than were possible under the gold standard. The United States agreed to convert U.S. dollars into gold at a price of $35 per ounce— but only in dealing with foreign central banks. U.S. citizens continued to be prohibited from redeeming dollars for gold. The central banks of all other members of the system pledged to buy and sell their currencies at fixed rates against the dollar. By fixing their exchange rates against the dollar, these countries were fixing the exchange rates among their currencies as well. The United States was given a special role in the system because of its dominant position in the global economy at that time and because the country held much of the world's monetary gold. Because central banks used dollar assets and gold as international reserves, the dollar was known as the *international reserve currency*.

Under the Bretton Woods system, exchange rates were supposed to adjust only when a country experienced fundamental disequilibrium—that is, persistent deficits or

Bretton Woods system
An exchange rate system that lasted from 1945 to 1971, under which countries pledged to buy and sell their currencies at fixed rates against the dollar and the United States pledged to convert dollars into gold if foreign central banks requested it to.

International Monetary Fund (IMF) A multinational organization established in 1944 by the Bretton Woods agreement to administer a system of fixed exchange rates and to serve as a lender of last resort to countries undergoing balance-of-payments problems.

surpluses in its balance of payments at the fixed exchange rate. To help countries make a short-run economic adjustment to a balance-of-payments deficit or surplus while maintaining a fixed exchange rate, the Bretton Woods agreement created the **International Monetary Fund (IMF)**. Headquartered in Washington, DC, this multinational organization grew from 29 member countries in 1945 to 189 in 2016. In principle, the IMF was to administer the Bretton Woods system and to be a lender of last resort to ensure that short-term economic problems did not undermine the stability of the fixed exchange-rate system. In practice, the IMF—which survived the end of the Bretton Woods system—also encourages domestic economic policies that are consistent with exchange-rate stability and gathers and standardizes international economic and financial data to use in monitoring member countries.

Although the IMF no longer attempts to foster fixed exchange rates (its core Bretton Woods system function), its activities as an international lender of last resort have grown. During the developing world debt crises of the 1980s, the IMF provided credit to such countries to help them repay their loans. IMF lending during the Mexican financial crisis of 1994–1995 and the East Asian financial crisis of 1997–1998 inspired major controversy over its role in the international financial system.

Advocates of IMF intervention point to the need for a lender of last resort in emerging-market financial crises. Critics of the IMF raise two counterarguments. The first is that the IMF encourages moral hazard, in the form of excessive risk taking, by bailing out foreign lenders. According to this view, the IMF's bailout of foreign lenders in the Mexican crisis encouraged those lenders to make risky loans to East Asian countries, precipitating that crisis. The second argument is that, in contrast to the IMF's treatment of foreign lenders, the institution's *austerity programs* in developing countries focus on reducing government spending and raising interest rates, which are macroeconomic policies that can lead to unemployment and political upheaval.

Fixed Exchange Rates Under Bretton Woods Central bank interventions in the foreign exchange market to buy and sell dollar assets maintained the fixed exchange rates of the Bretton Woods system. Exchange rates could vary by 1% above or below the fixed rate before countries were required to intervene to stabilize them. If a foreign currency appreciated relative to the dollar, the central bank of that country would sell its own currency for dollars, thereby driving the exchange rate back to the fixed rate. If a foreign currency depreciated relative to the dollar, the central bank would sell dollar assets from its international reserves and buy its own currency to push the exchange rate back toward the fixed rate.

In general, a central bank can maintain a fixed exchange rate as long as it is willing and able to buy and sell the amounts of its own currency that are necessary for exchange rate stabilization. When a foreign central bank buys its own currency, it sells dollars (international reserves). When a foreign central bank sells its own currency, it buys dollars. The result is an important asymmetry in central banks' adjustments in response to market pressures on the exchange rate. A country with a balance-of-payments surplus has no constraint on its ability to sell its own currency to buy dollars to maintain the exchange rate. However, a country with a balance-of-payments deficit has its ability to buy its own currency (to raise its value relative to the dollar) limited by the country's stock of international reserves. As a result, reserve outflows caused by balance-of-payments deficits created problems for central banks that were bound by the Bretton Woods system. When a country's stock of international reserves was exhausted, the central bank and the government would have to implement restrictive economic policies, such as increasing interest rates, to reduce imports and the trade deficit or abandon the policy of stabilizing the exchange rate against the dollar.

Devaluations and Revaluations Under Bretton Woods Under the Bretton Woods system, a country could defend its fixed exchange rate by buying or selling reserves or changing domestic economic policies, or it could petition the IMF to be allowed to change its exchange rate. When its currency was overvalued relative to the dollar, with agreement from the IMF, the country could **devalue** its currency—that is, lower the official value of its currency relative to the dollar. A country whose currency was undervalued relative to the dollar could **revalue** its currency—that is, raise the official value of its currency relative to the dollar.[2]

In practice, countries didn't often pursue devaluations or revaluations. Under the Bretton Woods system, governments preferred to postpone devaluations rather than face political charges that their monetary policies were flawed. Revaluations were an even less popular choice. Domestic producers and their workers complained vigorously when the value of the currency was allowed to rise against the dollar because the prices of domestic goods rose in world markets, reducing profits and employment. The political pressures against devaluations and revaluations meant governments changed their exchange rates only in response to severe imbalances in the foreign exchange market.

Devaluation The lowering of the official value of a country's currency relative to other currencies.

Revaluation The raising of the official value of a country's currency relative to other currencies.

Speculative Attacks in the Bretton Woods System When investors came to believe that a government was unwilling or unable to maintain its exchange rate, they attempted to profit by selling a weak currency or buying a strong currency. These actions, known as *speculative attacks,* could force a devaluation or revaluation of the currency. Speculative attacks can produce international financial crises. Such an attack occurred in 1967, when the British pound was overvalued relative to the dollar. Figure 16.3 illustrates the speculative attack that took place against the pound. The intersection of the demand and supply for British pounds in exchange for dollars occurs at E_1, which was lower than the fixed exchange rate of £1 = $2.80. The result was a surplus of pounds in exchange for dollars. To defend the overvalued exchange rate, the Bank of England had to buy the surplus pounds equal to $Q_2 - Q_1$, using dollars from its international reserves.

As the Bank of England's international reserves shrank, currency traders knew that, at some point, the bank would run out of dollars and have to abandon its stabilization efforts. Speculators responded by selling pounds, including pounds borrowed from banks, to the Bank of England at the fixed exchange rate of $2.80/£1, expecting the pound to fall in value against the dollar. When the pound did eventually fall in value, the speculators used dollars to buy back the now cheaper pounds, earning a substantial profit. In terms of our graphical analysis, speculators were causing the supply of pounds to shift from S_1 to S_2, which caused the overvaluation of the pound to increase. This difference between the fixed and market exchange rates forced the Bank of England to buy

[2] Recall that in a flexible exchange rate system, a falling value of the exchange rate is known as *depreciation,* and a rising value of the exchange rate is known as *appreciation.*

FIGURE 16.3

The Speculative Attack on the British Pound, 1967

The intersection of the demand and supply curves for British pounds in exchange for dollars occurred at E_1, which was below the fixed exchange rate of £1 = $2.80. The result was a surplus of pounds in exchange for dollars. To defend the overvalued exchange rate, the Bank of England had to buy the surplus pounds equal to $Q_2 - Q_1$, using dollars from its international reserves. Speculators became convinced that England would devalue the pound, which caused the supply of pounds to shift from S_1 to S_2, increasing the overvaluation.

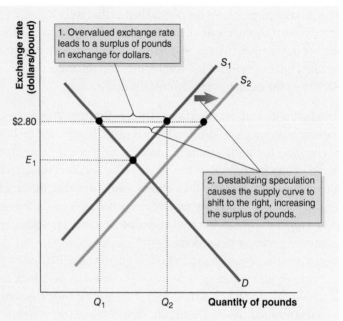

Callouts in figure:
1. Overvalued exchange rate leads to a surplus of pounds in exchange for dollars.
2. Destablizing speculation causes the supply curve to shift to the right, increasing the surplus of pounds.

even more pounds, until it ran out of dollars. On November 17, 1967, the Bank of England lost more than $1 billion of international reserves (on top of earlier losses of several billion dollars). On November 18, it devalued the pound by 14%.

Devaluations are forced by speculative attacks when a central bank is *unable* to defend the exchange rate, as in England's 1967 crisis. Revaluations, on the other hand, can be forced by speculative attacks when a central bank is *unwilling* to defend the exchange rate. A speculative attack on the undervalued deutsche mark in 1971 led to a revaluation of the mark against the dollar and hastened the demise of the Bretton Woods system.

The Speculative Attack on the Deutsche Mark and the Collapse of Bretton Woods

By 1970, the U.S. balance-of-payments deficit had grown significantly. By the first quarter of 1971, the large balance-of-payments surpluses outside the United States were causing fear in international financial markets because many currencies were undervalued relative to the dollar. Worries were greatest in West Germany, as the Bundesbank (the West German central bank) pursued policies to maintain a low inflation rate. The Bundesbank faced a dilemma. Because the German deutsche mark was undervalued against the dollar, if the Bundesbank defended the fixed exchange rate, it would have to sell marks and buy dollars in the foreign exchange market. By doing so, it would acquire international reserves, increasing the German monetary base and putting upward pressure on German prices. If Germany revalued the mark, it would avoid inflationary pressures but would break its promise under the Bretton Woods system and upset German firms that relied on exports to the United States.

The Bundesbank's dilemma set the stage for a speculative attack on the mark. In this case, speculators bought marks with dollars, expecting the mark to rise in value against the dollar. When the mark did rise, the speculators used the marks to buy back the now cheaper dollars, thereby earning a profit. By 1971, many investors were convinced that the Bundesbank would soon have to abandon the fixed exchange rate of $0.27 = DM1. On May 5, 1971, the Bundesbank purchased more than 1 billion U.S. dollars, expanding its monetary base by the same amount. Afraid that continued increases in the monetary base would spark inflation, the Bundesbank halted its intervention later that day. The mark began to *float* against the dollar, with its value being determined solely by the forces of demand and supply in the foreign exchange market.

The decision by the Bundesbank to abandon the fixed exchange rate against the dollar was a blow to the Bretton Woods system, but the system had even more fundamental problems. As U.S. inflation increased and U.S. balance-of-payments deficits mounted in the late 1960s, foreign central banks acquired large amounts of dollar-denominated assets. The Bretton Woods system was held together by the U.S. promise to exchange foreign central banks' dollars for gold at $35 per ounce. By 1971, however, the dollar assets that foreign central banks owned totaled more than three times the official U.S. gold holdings at the rate of $35 per ounce of gold. On August 15, 1971, the Nixon administration attempted to force revaluations of other currencies against the dollar. The United States suspended the convertibility of dollars into gold and imposed tariffs on imports that would be reduced only if a country revalued its exchange rate. This process of revaluations against the dollar was completed at the Smithsonian Conference in December 1971.

The exchange rate conditions that were agreed to at the Smithsonian Conference were not stable in the face of world events, however. In practice, many currencies began to float, although central banks intervened to prevent large fluctuations in exchange rates. At its January 1976 conference in Jamaica, the IMF formally agreed to allow currencies to float. At that conference, IMF members also agreed to eliminate gold's official role in the international monetary system. The conference represented the formal end of the Bretton Woods system, although in reality the system had stopped functioning five years earlier.

In 1970, even before countries formally abandoned the Bretton Woods system, the IMF had begun issuing a paper substitute for gold. The IMF created these international reserves, known as *Special Drawing Rights (SDRs)*, in its role as lender of last resort. The price of gold is now determined the same way that the prices of other commodities are determined—by the forces of demand and supply in the market.

To summarize, the Bretton Woods system was a fixed exchange rate system with a lender of last resort to smooth out short-term economic adjustments in response to balance-of-payments deficits. The system eventually collapsed because the United States was not committed to price stability and because other countries were reluctant to revalue their currencies against the dollar, which led to strong market pressures on the system's fixed exchange rates.

Central Bank Interventions After Bretton Woods

Since the demise of the Bretton Woods system, the United States has officially followed a **flexible exchange rate system**, in which the foreign exchange value of the dollar is determined in the foreign exchange market. Many other countries have followed the same course and allowed their exchange rates to float, or be determined by demand and supply. The Fed and foreign central banks have not, however, surrendered their right to intervene

Flexible exchange rate system A system in which the foreign exchange value of a currency is determined in the foreign exchange market.

in the foreign exchange market when they believe that their currency is significantly undervalued or overvalued. For example, in 2016, the Swiss central bank intervened to buy euros in exchange for Swiss francs in an attempt to lower the value of the franc against the euro. The present international financial system is a **managed float regime** (also called a *dirty float regime*), in which central banks occasionally intervene to affect exchange rates. As a result, international efforts to maintain exchange rates continue to affect domestic monetary policy.

Managed float regime
An exchange rate system in which central banks occasionally intervene to affect foreign exchange values; also called a dirty float regime.

MAKING THE CONNECTION

The "Exorbitant Privilege" of the U.S. Dollar?

During the height of the gold standard in the nineteenth and early twentieth centuries, the British pound was the key international currency. The majority of international borrowing was in pounds, and many products that were traded internationally—whether sold by British firms or not—were priced in pounds. To fight World War I between 1914 and 1918, the British government had to borrow large amounts, primarily from the United States. The United Kingdom's large foreign debts and the slow growth of the British economy relative to the U.S. economy during the twentieth century meant that by the time of the Bretton Woods conference in 1944, it was clear to the participants that the U.S. dollar would need to be the international reserve currency in the new international financial system.

By the 1960s, most economists and policymakers believed that the U.S. dollar had become overvalued relative to other key currencies, particularly the German mark and Japanese yen. The result was that the United States was running chronic current account deficits. Foreign central banks began accumulating increasing numbers of dollars. In effect, the dollar's role as international reserve currency meant that U.S. households and firms could consume more goods and services—including imports—than they produced. As a result, the standard of living in the United States was increased relative to other countries, which in total were consuming fewer goods and services than they produced. In a famous remark, French finance minister Valéry Giscard d'Estaing described the dollar in 1965 as enjoying an "exorbitant privilege" as a result of being the international reserve currency.

After the Bretton Woods system collapsed, the dollar retained its role as a reserve currency in the international monetary and financial system, with about 60% of international reserves being held in dollars as of 2016. Although euros, British pounds, Japanese yen, and Chinese yuan also serve as reserve currencies, a majority of international financial transactions are still carried out in dollars. In fact, most commodities—including oil—are priced in dollars, and, particularly in some developing countries, many foreign households and firms prefer using dollars to using their own currencies.

What if the dollar were to lose its place as the most important reserve currency? What advantages would the United States lose?

- First, U.S. households and firms might lose the advantage of being able to trade and borrow around the world in U.S. currency. This advantage translates into lower transactions costs and reduced exposure to exchange rate risk.

- Second, foreigners might be less willing to hold U.S. dollars. Currently, their willingness to do so confers a windfall on U.S. citizens because foreigners are essentially providing the United States with an interest-free loan.
- Third, there might be a decline in the ability of the U.S. government and U.S. firms to borrow at lower interest rates than can other governments or foreign firms. This ability is partly due to the dollar's role in the international financial system, and partly due to foreign investors often seeing U.S. securities as safe havens during periods of financial or political turmoil. As a result, typically U.S. investors earn more on their foreign investments than foreign investors earn on their investments in the United States.
- Finally, New York's leading international role as a financial center might be jeopardized.

Some economists and policymakers, though, are not convinced that the United States actually does gain an economic advantage from the dollar being a reserve currency. Because of its role as the key international reserve currency, the demand for the dollar is higher than it otherwise would be, which increases the exchange rate between the dollar and other currencies. As a consequence, U.S. firms have greater difficulty selling goods and services in foreign markets. If the dollar were to lose its reserve currency status, the value of the dollar versus other currencies might decline by as much as 30%, which would boost U.S. exports. Barry Eichengreen, an economist at the University of California, Berkeley, has noted that the result might be "a shift in the composition of what America exports from the treasury, agency, and derivative securities purchased by foreign central banks and private investors, toward John Deere earthmoving equipment, Boeing Dreamliners, and—who knows—maybe even motor vehicles and parts."

In the end, it seems likely that other currencies, such as the euro, yen, and yuan, will gradually increase their importance as reserve currencies relative to the dollar. This trend will have some effect on the U.S. economy, but in the long run, the ability of the U.S. economy to provide an increasing standard of living depends to a greater extent on factors such as the long-run growth rate of productivity and the pace of technological change than on the status of the dollar as a reserve currency.

Sources: Ben S. Bernanke, "Federal Reserve Policy in an International Context," Paper presented at the 16th Jacques Polak Annual Research Conference Hosted by the International Monetary Fund, Washington, DC, November 5–6, 2015; Barry Eichengreen, *Exorbitant Privilege: The Rise and Fall of the Dollar and the Future of the International Monetary System*, New York: Oxford University Press, 2011 (quotation is from p. 173); Robert J. Samuelson, "The 'Exorbitant Privilege' and Its Stubborn Costs," *Washington Post*, May 6, 2015; and Lewis E. Lehrman and John D. Mueller, "How the 'Reserve' Dollar Harms America." *Wall Street Journal*, November 20, 2014.

See related problem 4.11 at the end of the chapter.

Fixed Exchange Rates in Europe

One benefit of fixed exchange rates is that they reduce *exchange rate risk* in international commercial and financial transactions. Because of the large volume of commercial and financial trading among European countries, the governments of many of these countries have historically sought to reduce the costs of exchange rate fluctuations. Fixed exchange rates have also been used to constrain inflationary monetary policy. The theory of purchasing power parity indicates that a country's exchange rate will depreciate if it has a higher inflation rate than do its trading partners. So, when a government commits to a fixed exchange rate, it is also implicitly committing to restraining inflation. European countries that have suffered from high rates of inflation during some periods have favored fixed exchange rates for this reason.

The Exchange Rate Mechanism and European Monetary Union The countries that were members of the European Economic Community formed the *European Monetary System* in 1979. Eight European countries also agreed at that time to participate in an *exchange rate mechanism (ERM)* to limit fluctuations in the value of their currencies against each other. Specifically, the member countries promised to maintain the values of their currencies within a fixed range set in terms of a composite European currency unit (ECU). Member countries agreed to maintain exchange rates within these limits while allowing the rates to float jointly against the U.S. dollar and other currencies. The anchor currency of the ERM was the German mark. Both France and the United Kingdom reduced their inflation rates by tying their currencies to the German mark.

The United Kingdom withdrew from the ERM in 1992, as a result of one of the most celebrated speculative attacks in the history of foreign exchange markets. Although linking the pound to the German mark forced the British government to take actions to reduce the inflation rate, the rate still remained well above the rate in Germany. With such different inflation rates, it would be difficult on purchasing power parity grounds for the pound to maintain a fixed exchange rate with the mark. In addition, as West Germany unified with the former East Germany, the German government kept interest rates high to attract the foreign investment needed to finance reconstruction in East Germany. These high interest rates attracted foreign investors to German securities, bidding up the value of the mark relative to the pound.

Currency traders became convinced that the Bank of England would be unable to defend the exchange rate between the pound and the mark at the agreed-upon level. Although the British government raised interest rates and maintained that it would defend the value of the pound, currency traders persisted in selling pounds for marks until on Black Wednesday, September 16, 1992, the British government abandoned the ERM and allowed the value of the pound to float. A notable winner among currency traders was George Soros, the Hungarian-born hedge fund manager. The financial press estimated that Soros had made more than $1 billion by betting against the pound. Some commentators called him "The Man Who Broke the Bank of England." Soros has argued, though, that his actions had little to do with the decision by the British government to abandon the ERM: "Markets move currencies, so what happened with the British pound would have happened whether I was born or not, so therefore I take no responsibility."[3]

European Monetary Union
A plan drafted as part of the 1992 single European market initiative, in which exchange rates were fixed and eventually a common currency was adopted.

As part of the 1992 single European market initiative, European Community (EC) countries drafted plans for the **European Monetary Union**, in which exchange rates would be fixed by using a common currency, the **euro**. A single currency would eliminate transactions costs of currency conversion and reduce exchange rate risk. In addition, the removal of high transactions costs in cross-border trades would increase efficiency in production by offering the advantages of economies of scale.

euro The common currency of 19 European countries.

---

[3] Louise Story, "The Face of a Prophet," *New York Times*, April 11, 2008.

The European Monetary Union in Practice   In 1989, a report issued by the EC recommended establishing a common central bank, the **European Central Bank (ECB)**, to conduct monetary policy and, eventually, to control a single currency. The ECB, which formally commenced operation in January 1999, is structured along the lines of the Federal Reserve System in the United States, with an Executive Board (similar to the Board of Governors) appointed by the European Council and governors from the individual countries in the union (comparable to Federal Reserve Bank presidents). Like the Fed, the ECB is independent of member governments. Executive Board members are appointed for nonrenewable eight-year terms to increase their political independence. The ECB's charter states that the ECB's main objective is price stability.

Member countries met at Maastricht, the Netherlands in December 1991, and agreed to a gradual approach to monetary union. Their goals were to converge monetary policies by the mid-1990s and complete a monetary union in Europe by January 1, 1999. To have a single currency and monetary policy required more convergence of domestic inflation rates and budget deficits than existed in the mid-1990s. By the time monetary union began in 1999, 11 countries met the conditions for participation with respect to inflation rates, interest rates, and budget deficits. The United Kingdom declined to participate. Figure 16.4 shows the 19 countries that in 2016 were members of the *eurozone*, using the euro as their common currency.

European Central Bank (ECB) The central bank of the European countries that have adopted the euro.

FIGURE 16.4

Countries Using the Euro

The 19 member countries of the European Union that had adopted the euro as their common currency as of December 2016 are shaded with red hatch marks. The members of the EU that have not adopted the euro are colored tan. Countries in white are not members of the EU. Note that in June 2016, a majority of voters in a referendum in the United Kingdom favored taking the country out of the European Union. But as of December 2016, the United Kingdom had not yet formally left the European Union.

As noted in the chapter opener, in its early years, the euro seemed quite successful. From the time the euro was introduced in January 2002 through the beginning of the financial crisis in 2007, most of Europe experienced a period of relative economic stability. With low interest rates, low inflation rates, and expanding production and employment, the advantages of the euro seemed obvious. Some of the lower-income European countries appeared to particularly prosper under the euro. The Spanish economy grew at an annual rate of 3.9% between 1999 and 2007, and the country's unemployment rate dropped from nearly 20% in the mid-1990s to less than 8% in 2007. Ireland and Greece also experienced rapid growth during these years.

When the financial crisis of 2007–2009 hit and Europe entered a recession, the countries that were hardest hit could not pursue a more expansionary monetary policy than the ECB was willing to implement for the eurozone as a whole. These countries lacked the ability to revive their economies by depreciating their currencies and expanding their exports because they were committed to the euro, and most of their exports were to other eurozone countries. During the years of the gold standard, countries had similarly been unable to run expansionary monetary policies and were unable to have their exchange rates depreciate. As we have seen, these drawbacks led one country after another to abandon the gold standard in the 1930s until the system collapsed.

Will the same thing that happened to the gold standard happen to the euro? In 2016, some economists thought that it might, particularly those who had been doubtful that adopting the euro had been a good idea in the first place. Ideally, the economies of countries using the same currency should be harmonized, as the economies of the individual states are in the United States. Although the economies of the states differ and some were hit harder than others by the 2007–2009 recession, there is free movement of workers and firms across state borders; federal legislation results in many—but not all—rules with respect to labor, taxes, and environmental regulations being consistent across states; and the states share a common language and elect a common national government. The countries using the euro are much less harmonized in all these respects and are much more diverse economically, politically, and culturally than are the states of the United States. Some steps have been taken to aid the free flow of workers and firms across national borders, to coordinate some aspects of labor and tax legislation, and so on. In fact, one argument in favor of the euro was that it would aid the harmonization of Europe's economies. In 2016, though, the free flow of workers across countries had become a point of controversy, particularly after more than a million refugees fleeing unrest in the Middle East arrived in Europe. Political parties that were critical of the European Union and advocated withdrawal from it gained support in a number of countries.

But are the countries of Europe so diverse that using a common currency seriously hinders their economies in dealing with economic shocks like a significant recession? The answer may depend in part on whether the countries most affected by the recession can eventually return to higher growth and lower unemployment. Policymakers in Greece, Spain, Portugal, and Ireland—the countries that are perhaps most likely to abandon the euro—do not appear to see much gain from doing so. Abandoning the euro might allow these countries to increase their exports by depreciating their currencies and to spur recovery through expansionary monetary policies. But these actions would be at the expense of the long-term advantages these countries gain from the euro. So, while at the end of 2016 the euro was battered, it appeared likely to survive.

MAKING THE CONNECTION | IN YOUR INTEREST

If You Were Greek, Would You Prefer the Euro or the Drachma?

If you lived in Greece, would you prefer that the government continue using the euro or abandon it and resume using the drachma, its former currency? Like other countries in southern Europe, Greece had experienced an apparently strong economy during the early years of using the euro. From 2002, when the euro was introduced, through 2007, real GDP in Greece grew at average annual rate of 4.2%. The unemployment rate declined from 10.7% in 2001 to 7.7% in 2008.

Beginning in 2008, however, real GDP in Greece began to decline and unemployment began to rise. In 2016, real GDP in Greece was still more than 25% below its level in 2008. The unemployment rate rose from 7.4% in 2008 to depression levels of nearly 28% in 2013 and was still above 23% in 2016. In addition, the collapse in tax revenues led to a large government budget deficit and a national debt of 180% of GDP. Greece avoided defaulting on its debt only because of help from the "troika" made up of the European Commission, the European Central Bank (ECB), and the International Monetary Fund. The decision by the ECB to purchase Greek government bonds was controversial because some economists believed it would increase moral hazard by making it possible for European countries to issue more debt than private investors were willing to buy.

Because the unemployment rate in Greece for younger workers was about 50%, if you lived in Greece, it is likely that you would have difficulty finding a job as a new college graduate. But would your chances of finding a job and the chances of economic growth returning to Greece be higher if Greece continued using the euro or if it abandoned the euro for the drachma? As we have seen, countries using the euro cannot spur their exports by devaluing their currency. Not surprisingly, in 2008 Greece's current account deficit soared to nearly 15% of GDP.

Recall the expression for the real exchange rate from Chapter 8, page 252:

$$e = E \times \left(\frac{P^{\text{Domestic}}}{P^{\text{Foreign}}} \right),$$

where:

E = nominal exchange rate
e = real exchange rate
P^{Domestic} = domestic price level
P^{Foreign} = foreign price level

With a fixed nominal exchange rate, a country can still lower its real exchange rate, thereby increasing the competitiveness of its goods and services, if its price level falls relative to the price levels of other countries. Because the inflation rates in France, Germany, and other euro countries have been low, Greece would have to experience *deflation* to lower its relative price level. This *internal devaluation* is difficult to achieve because wages and prices tend to exhibit downward rigidity, which means that, in practice, cutting wages and prices is difficult. In fact, attempting to reduce wages and prices led to significant political unrest in Greece.

Abandoning the euro would allow Greece to increase the competitiveness of its exports, but there would also be significant drawbacks. For example, many people in Greece believed that if the government left the euro, it would exchange euro bank deposits for drachmas at a rate of one for one. If the drachma then depreciated—as was widely expected—as someone living in Greece, you would suffer heavy losses on your bank deposits. In addition, the Greek government would likely default on its bonds, forcing it to pay for government spending exclusively with tax revenues. The result would be dramatic cuts in government spending, potentially further depressing the Greek economy.

In addition, foreign lenders to Greek banks and firms would likely object to being paid in drachmas, which could result in legal disputes and undermine the ability of Greek companies to borrow outside Greece.

You and other people in Greece would probably be worse off in the short run if the country left the euro. In the long run, abandoning the euro might make it easier for Greek firms to compete with foreign firms, which could help the economy. Uncertainty about the short-run and long-term consequences of abandoning the euro was a key reason that people in Greece and the Greek government appeared unwilling at the end of 2016 to return to using the drachma.

Sources: Simon Nixon, "Real Greek Drama Is About Reforms, Not Debt Relief," *Wall Street Journal*, May 11, 2016; Stephen Fidler, "Euro Exit Would Bring Greece Trauma Before Growth," *Wall Street Journal*, June 25, 2016; and Organization for Economic Co-operation and Development, *Data*, September 2016.

See related problem 4.13 at the end of the chapter.

Currency Pegging

Pegging The decision by a country to keep the exchange rate fixed between its currency and another country's currency.

One way to maintain a fixed exchange rate is through pegging. With **pegging**, a country keeps its exchange rate fixed against another country's currency. It is not necessary for both countries in a currency peg to agree to it. For example, when in the 1990s, South Korea, Taiwan, Thailand, Indonesia, and other developing countries pegged their currencies to the U.S. dollar, the responsibility for maintaining the peg was entirely with the developing countries. Countries peg their currencies to gain the following advantages of a fixed exchange rate: reduced exchange-rate risk, a check against inflation, and protection for firms that have taken out loans in foreign currencies. This last advantage was important to many Asian countries during the 1990s because some of their firms had begun taking out dollar-denominated loans from U.S. and foreign banks. So, for instance, in the absence of a currency peg, if the value of the Korean won declined against the dollar, a Korean firm with loans in dollars would find its interest and principal payments rising in terms of the won.

A peg, though, can run into the problem faced by countries under the Bretton Woods system: A currency's equilibrium exchange rate, as determined by demand and supply, may be significantly different than the pegged exchange rate. As a result, the pegged currency may become overvalued or undervalued with respect to the dollar. In the 1990s, a number of Asian countries with overvalued currencies were subject to speculative attacks. During the resulting *East Asian currency crisis*, these countries attempted to defend their pegs by buying domestic currency with dollars, reducing their monetary bases, and raising their domestic interest rates. Higher interest rates plunged their economies into recession and, in the end, were ineffective in defending their pegs, which these countries all eventually abandoned.

Despite the drawbacks to pegging, many developing countries peg their currencies against either the dollar or the euro. Relatively few developing countries have adopted floating exchange rates.

Does China Manipulate Its Exchange Rate?

During the 2016 presidential election, both Democratic nominee Hillary Clinton and Republican nominee Donald Trump condemned the government of China for manipulating its exchange rate against the dollar. They argued that the Chinese government was intervening in exchange markets to keep the value of the yuan artificially low against the U.S. dollar in order to aid Chinese exports. How accurate was this argument?

As the Chinese government moved away from central planning toward a market system, an important part of Chinese economic policy was the decision in 1994 to peg the value of the yuan to the dollar at a fixed rate of 8.28 yuan to the dollar. Pegging against the dollar ensured that Chinese exporters would face stable dollar prices for the goods they sold in the United States. By the early 2000s, many economists argued that the yuan was undervalued against the dollar, possibly significantly so. To support the undervalued exchange rate, the People's Bank of China (PBOC), which is the central bank of China, had to buy large amounts of dollars with yuan. By 2005, the PBOC had accumulated $700 billion, a good portion of which it had used to buy U.S. Treasury bonds.

In July 2005, the Chinese government, under pressure from its trading partners, announced that it would switch from pegging the yuan against the dollar to linking the value of the yuan to the average value of a basket of currencies—the dollar, the Japanese yen, the euro, the Korean won, and several other currencies. Although the PBOC did not make public the details of how this linking of the yuan to other currencies would work, it declared that it had switched from a peg to a managed floating exchange rate. As Figure 16.5 shows, the value of the yuan gradually increased versus the dollar for most of the period from 2005 to the end of 2014. (Note that the figure shows the number of yuan per dollar, so an increase represents a *depreciation* of the yuan relative to the dollar, and a decrease represents an *appreciation* of yuan relative to the dollar.) The exception is the period from July 2008 to May 2010, when the exchange rate stabilized at about 6.83 yuan to the dollar, indicating that China had apparently returned to a "hard peg." This change in policy led to renewed criticism from policymakers in the United States. In mid-2010, President Barack Obama argued that "market-determined exchange rates are essential to global economic activity." In the face of this criticism, the PBOC allowed the yuan to resume its slow increase in value versus the dollar.

In 2015, the Chinese government was concerned that the growth rate of real GDP had slowed to about 7%, the lowest rate in more than 6 years. On August 11, the yuan was once again in the news, when the PBOC made a surprise announcement that it would buy dollars with yuan in order to reduce the yuan's value by about 3%—the largest one-day decline in the currency since 1994. Figure 16.5 shows that the value of the yuan continued to drift lower versus the dollar. The PBOC, though, insisted that the

MyEconLab Real-time data

FIGURE 16.5

The Yuan–Dollar Exchange Rate

China began explicitly pegging the value of the yuan to the dollar in 1994. Between July 2005 and July 2008, China allowed the value of the yuan to rise against the dollar before returning to a hard peg at about 6.83 yuan to the dollar until May 2010. In June 2010, the central bank of China announced that it would return to allowing the value of the yuan to rise against the dollar, which it did slowly through 2014. In 2015, the Chinese central bank took steps to reduce the value of the yuan versus the dollar, which led to criticism from U.S. politicians.

Source: Federal Reserve Bank of St. Louis.

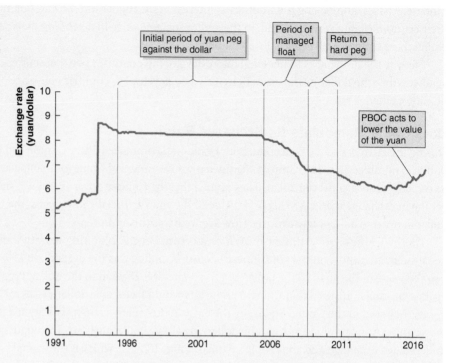

trend was the result of market forces and that it had not been taking action to push the value of the yuan lower. In fact, some economists believed that the PBOC had actually been buying yuan with dollars—keeping its value from falling more than it otherwise would have—as indicated by the fact that the PBOC's holdings of dollars had fallen by nearly $700 billion. Adding to the downward pressure on the yuan was the fact that many Chinese investors were taking advantage of new rules allowing them to invest abroad for the first time. To make these investments, the investors needed to exchange yuan for dollars or other foreign currency.

The continuing decline in the value of the yuan through the end of 2016 ensured that the Chinese government would face charges of currency manipulation from incoming President Donald Trump and other U.S. policymakers. Many economists were skeptical though that the value of the yuan was being kept artificially low.

The Policy Trilemma

Our analysis of monetary policy and exchange rates along with the actual experiences of many countries indicate that a country cannot achieve all three of the following goals:

1. Exchange rate stability
2. Monetary policy independence
3. Free capital flows

We discussed in Chapter 15 that exchange-rate stability is a monetary policy goal of the Fed and most other central banks because it simplifies planning for business and financial transactions and because it avoids sudden changes in the international competitiveness of domestic industries. For example, a sudden increase in the exchange value of the dollar could make it more difficult for Caterpillar, based in Peoria, Illinois, to export earth-moving equipment. *Monetary policy independence* means the ability of the central bank to use monetary policy to achieve its goals without regard to movements in exchange rates. The Fed is free to use monetary policy to achieve its goals of high employment and price stability because the United States has a floating exchange rate, so the Fed doesn't have to adjust interest rates to maintain the value of the dollar. In contrast, central banks in countries with fixed exchange rates must adjust interest rates to maintain their fixed exchange rate, which keeps them from simultaneously using interest rates to achieve their target levels of employment and inflation.

As we saw in Section 16.1, most economists see the free flow of capital across borders as desirable. One way for a country to finance investment in factories, machinery, and research and development is through capital flows from abroad. These flows can also finance government budget deficits so the deficits do not result in lower domestic investment. We've seen, though, that large capital inflows and outflows, particularly over a brief period, can be economically destabilizing. As a result, some countries have used *capital controls* to limit the free flow of capital across their borders. We've also seen that capital controls have an important drawback in that they may discourage foreign investment that may be indispensable to developing countries if they hope to increase their growth rates.

The hypothesis that it is impossible for a country to have exchange rate stability, monetary policy independence, and free capital flows at the same time is called the **policy trilemma**. This hypothesis is based on the work of Nobel Laureate Robert Mundell of Columbia University and Marcus Fleming of the International Monetary Fund. If the hypothesis is correct, it is possible to achieve at most two of the policy goals at the same time. Therefore, policymakers must choose which of the three goals they do not wish to pursue. Figure 16.6 illustrates the policy trilemma. Each side of the triangle indicates one of the three goals, and each point of the triangle indicates which goal is unattainable, given that the other two goals have been chosen.

Policy trilemma The hypothesis that it is impossible for a country to have exchange rate stability, monetary policy independence, and free capital flows at the same time.

The lower-left point of the triangle indicates that if policymakers choose to allow free capital flows and have an independent monetary policy, they must let the exchange rate float. The United States allows the free flow of capital, and the Fed is free to use monetary policy to pursue macroeconomic objectives such as low inflation and high employment. As a consequence of these choices, the United States must let the U.S. dollar float in foreign exchange markets. Why? Changes in the nominal exchange rate depend not only on domestic monetary policy but also on monetary policy in other countries. In 2016, as the Fed took steps to increase interest rates, while foreign central banks were lowering interest rates, the U.S. dollar appreciated, which was bad news for U.S. exporters. In general, the U.S. commitment to free capital flows and the Fed's focus on domestic policy objectives increases the exchange rate risk facing U.S. firms and households.

The lower-right point of the triangle indicates that if policymakers choose to allow free capital flows while also pursuing exchange rate stability, they must give up monetary policy independence. This dilemma is the one facing eurozone countries. For example, Greece is a member of the eurozone and allows free capital flows. In those circumstances,

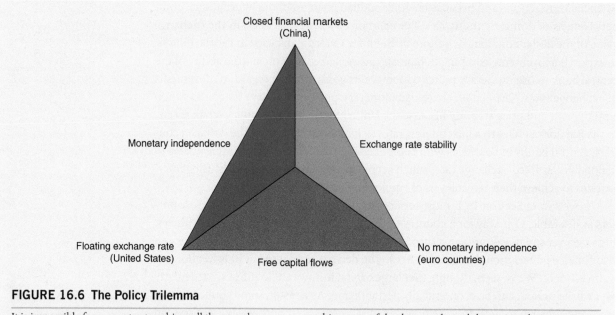

FIGURE 16.6 The Policy Trilemma

It is impossible for a country to achieve all three goals—exchange rate stability, monetary policy independence, and free capital flows—at the same time. At most, a country can achieve two of the three goals, and there is no clear consensus among economists on which of the two goals are best to pursue.

even if it had not ceded control over its monetary policy to the European Central Bank, it would not be able to pursue an independent monetary policy. Smaller European countries that do not use the euro, such as Switzerland, Denmark, and Sweden, are in a similar situation. Because most of their exports are to eurozone countries, their central banks feel obliged to stabilize the exchange rate between their country's currency and the euro. These countries also have free capital flows and, as a result, their monetary policies have to be focused more on stabilizing their exchange rate than on domestic policy goals. For example, in 2016 the Swiss National Bank pushed the interest rate it paid on bank reserves to −0.75% to keep the value of the Swiss franc from rising too much against the euro.

The top of the triangle indicates that, if policymakers choose monetary policy independence and a stable exchange rate, they must restrict the flow of capital. For years, China has maintained an independent monetary policy while essentially fixing the value of the yuan against a market basket of foreign currencies, so it had to restrict capital flows. Why? If China had allowed free capital flows, a large drop in the demand for Chinese assets would reduce the demand for its currency. This reduction in the demand for yuan would cause a large depreciation in the yuan. By restricting capital flows into and out of the country, China kept the value of the assets that foreigners own in China relatively stable, so the demand for yuan in foreign exchange markets was also relatively stable. In recent years, though, in an attempt to increase the integration of its economy into the international financial system, China has reduced regulations that were impeding capital flows. In 2016, as China was using an expansionary monetary policy to spur economic growth, many domestic investors began to sell Chinese securities to buy higher-yielding foreign securities, putting downward pressure on the exchange rate between the yuan and the dollar. It was unclear what steps the Chinese government might take to resolve the inconsistencies in its policy objectives. If it decided to maintain the free capital flows and an expansionary monetary policy, it would have to accept greater instability in its exchange rate—a move toward the position occupied by the United States at the lower-left point of the triangle.

ANSWERING THE KEY QUESTION

Continued from page 542

At the beginning of this chapter, we asked:

"Should European countries abandon using a common currency?"

As we have seen in this chapter, having a common currency in most of Europe has made it easier for households and firms to buy, sell, and invest across borders. From the introduction of the euro as a currency in 2002 until the beginning of the financial crisis in 2007, European economies experienced economic growth with low inflation. During the financial crisis, conflicts arose over the policies of the European Central Bank. The countries hit hardest by the crisis, such as Greece, Ireland, and Spain, were unable to allow their currencies to depreciate, as had happened in earlier recessions, to spur their exports. In 2016, the possibility that the euro system would collapse remained, and political opposition to it seemed to have been increasing. The system appeared likely to hold together, however, because of the conviction among many European economists and policymakers that the advantages of a common currency outweighed its disadvantages.

Key Terms and Problems

Key Terms

Balance-of-payments account, p. 550
Bretton Woods system, p. 557
Capital controls, p. 549
Devaluation, p. 559
euro, p. 564
European Central Bank (ECB), p. 565
European Monetary Union, p. 564
Exchange rate regime, p. 553
Fixed exchange rate system, p. 553

Flexible exchange rate system, p. 561
Foreign exchange market intervention, p. 544
Gold standard, p. 553
International Monetary Fund (IMF), p. 558
International reserves (or foreign reserves), p. 544
Managed float regime, p. 562

Pegging, p. 568
Policy trilemma, p. 571
Revaluation, p. 559
Sterilized foreign exchange intervention, p. 545
Unsterilized foreign exchange intervention, p. 545

16.1 Foreign Exchange Intervention and the Monetary Base

Analyze how the Fed's interventions in foreign exchange markets affect the U.S. monetary base.

Review Questions

1.1 If the Fed sells $2 billion of foreign assets, what happens to the Fed's holdings of international reserves and to the monetary base?

1.2 Does a purchase of foreign assets by the Fed have a greater effect, the same effect, or a smaller effect on the monetary base than an open market purchase of government bonds by the Fed? Briefly explain.

1.3 What is the difference between a sterilized foreign exchange intervention and an unsterilized foreign exchange intervention?

Problems and Applications

1.4 An article in the *Wall Street Journal* about the policies of the People's Bank of China observes: "Currency intervention … expands the central bank's balance sheet and adds to the money supply when left unsterilized, as it has been in the past."

a. What is a "currency intervention"? Why might a central bank undertake a currency intervention?

b. Why would a currency intervention expand the central bank's balance sheet?

c. Why does the effect of a currency intervention on a central bank's balance sheet depend on whether the intervention has been unsterilized? In your answer, be sure to explain the difference between a sterilized currency intervention and an unsterilized currency intervention.

Source: Aaron Back, "China's Central Bank Swoops to the Rescue," *Wall Street Journal*, April 28, 2015.

1.5 Allan Meltzer, an economist at Carnegie Mellon University, once argued:

I have yet to see a study that shows that sterilized intervention, the most common type of intervention used by the Fed in the foreign exchange markets, has any effect on the value of the dollar at all.

a. What is a "sterilized intervention"?

b. How would the Fed carry out a sterilized intervention in the foreign exchange market?

c. Why wouldn't a sterilized intervention have any effect on the value of the dollar?

Source: Joel Kurtzman, "Fed vs. Treasury on Dollar's Value," *New York Times*, March 28, 1990.

1.6 Use T-accounts to show the effect on the Fed's balance sheet of the Fed selling $5 billion in Japanese government bonds, denominated in yen. What happens to the Fed's international reserves and the monetary base? Briefly explain whether this is a sterilized foreign exchange intervention or an unsterilized foreign exchange intervention.

1.7 Use T-accounts to show the effect on the Fed's balance sheet of the Fed buying $2 billion in German government bonds, denominated in euros, and, at the same time, conducting an open market sale of $2 billion of U.S. Treasury securities. What happens to the monetary base? Briefly explain whether this is a sterilized foreign exchange intervention or an unsterilized foreign exchange intervention.

1.8 What effect does each of the following have on the U.S. monetary base?

a. The Fed purchases $10 billion of foreign assets.

b. The Fed sells $10 billion of foreign assets and purchases $10 billion of Treasury securities.

c. The Fed conducts a sterilized foreign exchange intervention.

d. The Fed sells $10 billion of foreign assets and sells $10 billion of Treasury securities.

16.2 Foreign Exchange Interventions and the Exchange Rate

Analyze how the Fed's interventions in foreign exchange markets affect the exchange rate.

Review Questions

2.1 To raise the exchange rate of its currency, would a central bank buy or sell foreign assets? What would be the effect on the monetary base? What would be the effect on domestic interest rates?

2.2 How does a sterilized central bank intervention affect the demand curve and the supply curve for a country's currency?

2.3 What are capital controls, and why might a country impose them? What are the disadvantages of imposing capital controls?

Problems and Applications

2.4 On the foreign exchange market, who demands dollars—U.S. investors or foreign investors? Why does an increase in U.S. interest rates relative to Japanese interest rates increase the demand for dollars? An investor who holds U.S. currency doesn't receive any interest, so why does the demand for dollars rise when U.S. interest rates rise?

2.5 Suppose the Bank of Japan sells $5 billion of U.S. Treasury securities. Use a graph of the demand and supply of yen in exchange for dollars to show the effect on the exchange rate between the yen and the dollar. Briefly explain what is happening in your graph. (Note that the exchange rate will be dollars per yen.)

2.6 [Related to Solved Problem 16.2 on page 547] An article in the *Wall Street Journal* in 2016 noted: "Denmark's central bank has sold Danish kroner to weaken its currency and keep the euro within a … target range."

a. What does it mean to "weaken" a currency? After weakening, would it take more or fewer Danish kroner to buy a euro?

b. How does the Danish central bank's selling kroner weaken that currency? Use a graph of the market for kroner in exchange for euros to illustrate your answer.

c. Why would it be important for the Danish central bank to keep the exchange rate between the kroner and the euro within a target range?

Source: Brian Blackstone, "Central Banks Still Intervene in Currency Markets Despite Weakened Effect," *Wall Street Journal*, July 7, 2016.

2.7 According to an article in the *Wall Street Journal* in 2016:

> Small changes in the yuan have touched off big swings in markets across the world, and the dollar has shot up against just about every currency. Amid the turmoil, financial- and economic-policy makers are advocating a tactic once anathema to all but the most mismanaged economies: capital controls.

a. What are capital controls?

b. Why might capital controls have been seen as a more desirable policy in 2016 than 10 years earlier?

c. Why does the article say that a government's using capital controls was once considered an indication that an economy was being mismanaged? Do the downsides to capital controls still exist? Briefly explain.

Source: Mike Bird, "The Hottest Idea in Finance: Capital Controls Are Good," *Wall Street Journal*, February 4, 2016.

16.3   The Balance of Payments
Describe how the balance of payments is calculated.

Review Questions

3.1 Distinguish between the types of transactions recorded in the current account and those recorded in the financial account. If a country runs a current account deficit, is the value of its exports of goods and services likely to be larger or smaller than the value of its imports of goods and services? Briefly explain.

3.2 Why must the current account balance plus the financial account balance equal zero? Briefly explain in what sense a country can run a balance-of-payments surplus or a balance-of-payments deficit.

3.3 How do central banks use official reserve assets?

Problems and Applications

3.4 If the U.S. current account deficit is $400 billion, and if the statistical discrepancy is zero, what is the financial account balance? Does this financial account balance represent a net capital outflow or a net capital inflow?

3.5 Suppose that a U.S. firm buys 10 Volkswagen cars for $20,000 each, and the German company uses the money to buy a $200,000 U.S. Treasury bond at a Treasury auction. How are these two transactions recorded in the balance-of-payments accounts for the United States?

3.6 Suppose that the U.S. government sells old warships worth $300 million to Japan, and Japan's government pays for them with its official holdings of dollar assets. How is this transaction recorded in the U.S. balance-of-payment accounts?

3.7 In 2016, Egypt was trying to keep the exchange rate between its currency (the Egyptian pound) and the U.S. dollar constant. An article in the *Wall Street Journal* observed that if the Egyptian government took steps to reduce the value of the pound, it "would boost foreign investors' confidence and increase the Egyptian market's competitiveness. It would also help reduce the strain in the balance of payments; Egypt's current-account deficit has widened to more than 5% of gross domestic product."

  a. Why would a reduction in value of the Egyptian pound help reduce Egypt's current account deficit?

  b. What does the article mean by "strain" on Egypt's balance of payments? Isn't any country's balance of payments always equal to zero? Why would reducing Egypt's current account deficit reduce strain on its balance of payments?

  Source: Dahlia Kholaif and Nikhil Lohade, "Bets on Egypt Currency Devaluation Rise," *Wall Street Journal*, July 25, 2016.

3.8 If a country imposes capital controls that result in its financial account balance being zero, would it be possible for the country to run a current account deficit? Briefly explain.

16.4   Exchange Rate Regimes and the International Financial System
Discuss the evolution of exchange rate regimes.

Review Questions

4.1 Briefly explain how the gold standard operated. What were the key differences between the gold standard and the Bretton Woods system?

4.2 Briefly answer each of the following questions about the gold standard:

  a. Was it a fixed exchange rate system or a flexible exchange rate system?

  b. Were countries able to pursue active monetary policies?

  c. Did countries that ran trade deficits experience gold inflows or gold outflows?

MyEconLab   Visit **www.myeconlab.com** to complete these exercises online and get instant feedback. Exercises that update with real-time data are marked with ⓦ.

d. How would a gold inflow affect a country's monetary base and its inflation rate?

e. During the Great Depression, how did the gold standard hinder economic recovery?

4.3 Under the Bretton Woods system, what were devaluations and revaluations? What is the difference between a devaluation and a depreciation? Why were countries hesitant to pursue a devaluation? Why were they even more hesitant to pursue a revaluation?

4.4 What is the eurozone? How do the countries of the eurozone benefit from using a single currency? What are the disadvantages to using a single currency?

4.5 What is pegging? What are the advantages of pegging? What are the disadvantages? Briefly discuss the controversy over China's management of the yuan-dollar exchange rate.

4.6 What is the policy trilemma? How do U.S. policymakers deal with the policy trilemma?

Problems and Applications

4.7 Under a gold standard, is inflation possible? Consider both the case for an individual country and the case for the world as a whole.

4.8 [Related to the Making the Connection on page 556] In discussing the situation of countries leaving the gold standard, or "unilaterally devaluing" during the 1930s, Barry Eichengreen of the University of California, Berkeley, and Jeffrey Sachs of Columbia University observe: "In all cases of unilateral devaluation, currency depreciation increases output and employment in the devaluing country." Explain how leaving the gold standard in the 1930s would lead to an increase in a country's output and employment.

Source: Barry Eichengreen and Jeffrey Sachs, "Exchange Rates and Economic Recovery in the 1930s," *Journal of Economic History*, Vol. 45, No. 4, December 1985, p. 934.

4.9 Evaluate the following argument:

The United States did not really leave the gold standard in 1933. Under the Bretton Woods system, the United States stood ready to redeem U.S. currency for gold at

a fixed price, and that is the basic requirement of the gold standard.

4.10 In discussing the Bretton Woods system, Michael Klein, an economist at Tufts University, observes: "Investors face a 'one-way bet' against central banks when they perceive an increased likelihood of a devaluation." In other words, investors will win if the country devalues, while not losing if it doesn't devalue.

a. How would speculators win if a country devalued under the Bretton Woods system?

b. Why wouldn't investors lose if the country didn't devalue under the Bretton Woods system?

c. Does your reasoning in parts (a) and (b) apply to any fixed exchange rate system? Briefly explain.

Source: Michael W. Klein, "European Monetary Union," *New England Economic Review*, March–April 1998, p. 5.

4.11 [Related to the Making the Connection on page 562] An opinion column in the *Washington Post* notes that the U.S. dollar is "the world's dominant international currency." The column also argues that, as a result, "we constantly run sizable trade deficits; and … U.S. manufacturers often are at a price disadvantage with foreign competitors."

a. In what sense is the dollar the world's dominant currency?

b. What is the connection between the dollar's dominance and the United States running trade deficits?

Source: Robert J. Samuelson, "The 'Exorbitant Privilege' and Its Stubborn Costs," *Washington Post*, May 6, 2015.

4.12 [Related to the Chapter Opener on page 542] An article in the *Economist* in 2016 notes that the "euro crisis" didn't keep four additional countries—Slovakia, Estonia, Latvia, and Lithuania—from joining the eurozone between 2009 and 2016: "Their experience suggests that the euro still has its benefits, but also some familiar risks."

a. What was the "euro crisis"?

b. What benefits does a country potentially gain from being a member of the eurozone? What are the familiar risks of being a member?

c. All four of these countries are small. Are there greater benefits to a smaller country being part of the eurozone than there are to a larger country? Briefly explain.

Source: "SELL Signals," *Economist*, May 14, 2016.

4.13 [Related to the Making the Connection on page 567] An article in the *Wall Street Journal* discussing the possibility that Greece might leave the eurozone observes: "Traditionally, devaluations are viewed as providing a short-run spur to growth."

a. Explain why the Greek economy might experience an increase in growth following a departure from the eurozone.

b. Why might Greece choose to remain in the eurozone despite your answer to part (a)?

Source: Stephen Fidler, "Euro Exit Would Bring Greece Trauma Before Growth," *Wall Street Journal*, June 25, 2015.

4.14 An article in the *New York Times* in 2016 notes that both Hillary Clinton and Donald Trump "want to label China as a currency manipulator."

a. What is a currency manipulator? Why would China want to manipulate its currency?

b. What are the arguments for and against China having actually manipulated its currency?

Source: Keith Bradsher, "In Trade Stances Toward China, Clinton and Trump Both Signal a Chill," *New York Times*, June 29, 2016.

4.15 Writing on his blog in 2016, former Fed Chairman Ben Bernanke noted: "Here is the trilemma in action: If China wants to use monetary policy to manage domestic demand and to simultaneously free up international capital flows, it may not be able to fix the exchange rate at current levels."

a. What does Bernanke mean by "the trilemma"?

b. Why might China be unable to fix its exchange rate if it is using an expansionary monetary policy and allowing free capital flows?

Source: Ben S. Bernanke, "China's Trilemma—And a Possible Solution," brookings.edu, March 9, 2016.

Data Exercises

D16.1: [Recent movements in the yuan–dollar exchange rate] Go to the web site of the Federal Reserve Bank of St. Louis (FRED) (fred.stlouisfed.org) and download and graph the data series for the yuan–dollar exchange rate (DEXCHUS) from July 2010 until the most recent day available. Since July 2010, how has the exchange rate between the yuan and the dollar changed?

D16.2: [The current account and the business cycle] Go to the web site of the Federal Reserve Bank of St. Louis (FRED) (fred.stlouisfed.org) and download and graph the data series for the U.S. current account balance (BOPBCA) from the first quarter of 1960 to the most recent quarter available. Go to the web site of the National Bureau of Economic Research (nber.org) and find the dates for business cycle peaks and troughs. (The period between a business cycle peak and trough is a recession.) Describe how the current account balance moves just before, during, and just after a recession. Is the pattern the same across recessions?

CHAPTER 17

Monetary Theory I: The Aggregate Demand and Aggregate Supply Model

Learning Objectives

After studying this chapter, you should be able to:

17.1 Explain how the aggregate demand curve is derived (pages 581–587)

17.2 Explain how the aggregate supply curve is derived (pages 587–595)

17.3 Demonstrate macroeconomic equilibrium using the aggregate demand and aggregate supply model (pages 595–599)

17.4 Use the aggregate demand and aggregate supply model to show the effects of monetary policy on the economy (pages 600–606)

Why Did Employment Grow Slowly After the Great Recession?

After a recession is over, real GDP and employment increase, and people find it easier to find jobs. According to the National Bureau of Economic Research, what economists call "The Great Recession" began in December 2007 and ended in June 2009. It was the longest and deepest recession since the Great Depression of the 1930s. The unemployment rate at the end of the recession was already a very high 9.5% in June 2009, and it rose to 10.0% by October 2009. Typically, the deeper the recession, the stronger the recovery. In the following months, unemployment did begin to decline but at a slow pace. It wasn't until late 2015—more than six years after the end of the recession—that the unemployment rate dropped to 5.0%, which is a level that most economists consider to be full employment.

But the unemployment rate does not always tell a complete story of the state of the labor market. To be counted as unemployed, someone has to be actively looking for work. What many economists and policymakers found disturbing in 2016 was that the fraction of the population working had not yet recovered to pre-recession levels. The following figure shows the employment–population ratio for three groups: the total population, the population between the ages of 25 and 54, and the male population between the ages of 25 and 54.

Continued on next page

KEY ISSUE AND QUESTION

Issue: During the recovery from the financial crisis of 2007–2009, the employment–population ratio remained low.

Question: What explains the relatively slow growth of employment during the economic expansion that began in 2009?

Answered on page 606

579

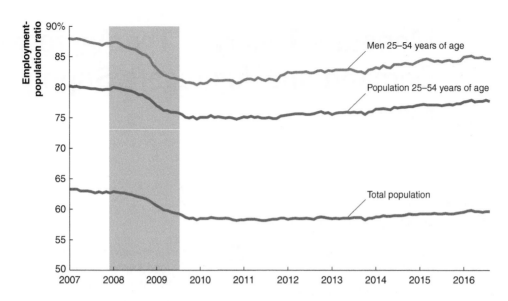

The declines in the employment–population ratio may seem small, but even a decline of a few percentage points means millions fewer people working. For instance, if the employment–population ratio for the total population (shown by the red line) had been as high in 2016 as it was in 2007, before the Great Recession had begun, 9 million more people would have been working. Some of the decline in the employment–population ratio was due to the effects of baby boomers—people who were born between 1946 and 1964—beginning to retire. But as the blue line shows, even focusing just on people in their prime-age years, ages 25 to 54, there was a significant decline representing more than 3 million fewer people working. The decline was particularly large for males in this age group, as shown by the green line.

In addition, the unemployed were staying unemployed for longer periods of time. In August 2016, 25.5% of the unemployed had been out of work for at least six months, compared with only 16.4% in June 2007, before the recession began. Low rates of inflation also indicated that there might be more slack in the labor market than the unemployment rate indicated. Ordinarily, as the unemployment rate declines and labor markets become tighter, competition among firms for workers causes wages to rise. Rising wages increase firms' costs and can lead to higher inflation. Yet in mid-2016, the inflation rate had been below the

Fed's target of 2% every month for more than four years.

Testifying before Congress in June 2016, Federal Reserve Chair Janet Yellen acknowledged the "continuing below-target inflation and the mixed readings on the labor market." As a result, she noted: "The [Federal Open Market] Committee expects that the federal funds rate is likely to remain, for some time, below the levels that are expected to prevail in the longer run."

The situation facing Fed policymakers raised the question of whether persistent slack in labor markets indicated that expansionary monetary policy should be continued. Some economists believed that the Fed policy would not be effective in increasing employment further because the remaining slack in labor markets was caused by factors beyond the Fed's control. The decline in the employment–population ratio, particularly for males, began decades ago. In the early 1950s, nearly 96% of males aged 25 to 54 were employed, while in 2016, fewer than 85% of males in this age group were employed. This long-run decline—which was greater than in most other high-income countries—suggests that structural factors unrelated to the overall state of the economy might be involved. These structural factors include: (1) an expansion of Social Security disability payments that has provided some men with an alternative source of income; (2) higher incarceration rates that have made some men less attractive to potential employers; and (3) the decline in demand for unskilled workers as a result of automation and the effects of globalization.

Monetary policy is intended to increase the total level of spending in the economy and is not suited to addressing the structural problems that may be partly responsible for low employment rates. But some economists believe that low employment rates are due in part to some workers having given up looking for jobs because the severity of the Great Recession meant that

these workers had spent many months unsuccessfully searching for jobs. Increasing the total level of spending in the economy might generate enough demand so that these workers would begin actively looking for jobs again. But after years of very low interest rates, was monetary policy the best way to expand the economy, or was it time for Congress and the president to consider fiscal policy measures—changes to spending and taxes?

In this chapter and Chapter 18, we provide a framework for better understanding these policy issues.

Sources: U.S. Bureau of Labor Statistics, *Employment Situation Summary, August 2016*, September 2, 2016; Federal Reserve Bank of St. Louis; President's Council of Economic Advisers, "The Long-Term Decline in Prime-Age Male Labor Force Participation," June 2016; and Janet L. Yellen, "Statement Before the Committee on Banking, Housing, and Urban Affairs, U.S. Senate," June 21, 2016.

The causes and consequences of business cycles like the 2007–2009 recession and the following expansion were not always a significant part of the study of economics. Modern macroeconomics began during the 1930s, as economists and policymakers struggled to understand why the Great Depression was so severe.

The U.S. economy has experienced business cycles dating back to at least the early nineteenth century. The business cycle is not uniform: Periods of expansion are not all the same length, nor are periods of recession. But every period of expansion in U.S. history has been followed by a period of recession, and every period of recession has been followed by a period of expansion. Economists have developed macroeconomic models to analyze the business cycle. The British economist John Maynard Keynes developed a particularly influential model in 1936, in response to the Great Depression.

In this chapter and the next, we explore *monetary theory*, which involves using macroeconomic models to explore the relationship between changes in the money supply and interest rates and changes in real GDP and the price level. We begin in this chapter with the *aggregate demand and aggregate supply (AD–AS) model*. This model captures some of the basic ideas first developed by Keynes in the 1930s.

17.1 The Aggregate Demand Curve

LEARNING OBJECTIVE: Explain how the aggregate demand curve is derived.

We start by looking at the relationship between the demand for goods and services and the price level. Economists analyze the demand for goods and services by households, firms, and the government in terms of aggregate expenditure. *Aggregate expenditure* on the economy's output of goods and services equals the sum of:

1. Spending by households on goods and services for consumption, C
2. Planned spending by firms on capital goods, such as factories, office buildings, and machine tools and by households on new homes, I
3. Local, state, and federal government purchases of goods and services (not including transfer payments—such as Social Security payments—to individuals), G

4. Net exports, which is spending by foreign firms and households on goods and services produced in the United States minus spending by U.S. firms and households on goods and services produced in other countries, *NX*

So, we can write that aggregate expenditure, *AE*, is:

$$AE = C + I + G + NX.$$

Aggregate demand (*AD*) curve A curve that shows the relationship between the price level and aggregate expenditure on goods and services.

We can use the concept of aggregate expenditure to develop the **aggregate demand (AD) curve**, which shows the relationship between the price level and aggregate expenditure on goods and services by households, firms, and the government. In Figure 17.1, we show the aggregate demand curve using a graph with the price level, *P*, on the vertical axis, and aggregate output, *Y*, on the horizontal axis. In the following section, we derive the aggregate demand curve by analyzing the effect of a change in the price level on the components of aggregate expenditure.

The Money Market and the Aggregate Demand Curve

The shape and position of the *AD* curve are important in determining the equilibrium values of real GDP and the price level.

The *AD* curve is downward sloping because, if nothing else changes, an increase in the price level reduces aggregate expenditure on goods and services. We can understand why an increase in the price level has this effect by reviewing and extending our discussion of the money market from Chapter 4.[1] The money market involves the interaction between the demand for M1—currency plus checkable deposits—by households and firms and the supply of M1, as determined by the Federal Reserve.

FIGURE 17.1

The Aggregate Demand Curve

The aggregate demand, *AD*, curve shows the relationship between the price level and the level of aggregate expenditure.

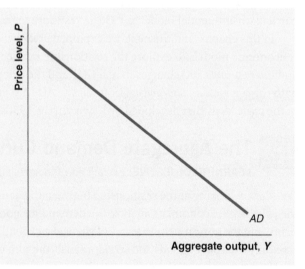

---

[1] Confusion alert: Recall our caution from Chapter 4: When economists refer to the "money market," they usually are referring to the market for bonds that mature in one year or less, such as Treasury bills. Here, though, we are using the phrase "money market" to refer to the analysis of money demand and money supply.

The analysis of the money market is sometimes called the *liquidity preference theory*, the term used by Keynes.

The quantity of M1 that households and firms demand depends on the price level. One hundred years ago, when the price level was much lower, households and firms needed fewer dollars to conduct their buying and selling. As the price level increases, households and firms require a larger quantity of dollars. In Chapter 4, we focused on the version of the money market model that involves the demand and supply for *nominal money balances*—that is, the quantity of money not corrected for changes in the price level. In this chapter, we take an alternative approach by assuming that households and firms demand, and the Federal Reserve supplies, **real money balances**, or M/P, where M is a monetary aggregate, such as M1, and P is a measure of the price level, such as the consumer price index or the GDP price deflator.

Panel (a) of Figure 17.2 illustrates the money market, using a graph with the short-term nominal interest rate, such as the interest rate on Treasury bills, on the vertical axis and the quantity of real money balances on the horizontal axis. The figure shows the demand for real money balances by households and firms as being downward sloping. We assume that the primary reason households and firms demand money is the *transactions motive*—which is the need to hold money as a medium of exchange to facilitate buying and selling. However, households and firms face a trade-off between the convenience of holding money and the low—or zero—interest rate they receive on money. The higher the interest rate on short-term assets such as Treasury bills, the more households and firms give up when they hold large money balances. So, the short-term nominal interest rate is the *opportunity cost of holding money*. The higher the interest rate, the smaller the quantity of real balances households and firms want to hold. The lower the interest rate, the larger the quantity of real balances households and firms want to hold. Therefore, the demand for real balances is downward sloping. We show the supply of real balances as a vertical line because we assume that the Fed can perfectly control the level of M1. The behavior of banks and the public also affect the level of M1, but our simplification here does not significantly affect the analysis.

In panel (b) of Figure 17.2, we show the effect of an increase in the price level on the money market, assuming that the nominal money supply—the dollar value of currency plus checkable deposits—is held constant. The increase in the price level reduces the supply of real balances, shifting the supply curve to the left, from $(M/P)^S_1$ to $(M/P)^S_2$. After the supply curve has shifted, at the original equilibrium interest rate, i_1, the quantity of real balances demanded will be greater than the quantity supplied. Households and firms will attempt to restore their desired holdings of real balances by selling short-term assets, such as Treasury bills. This increased supply of Treasury bills will drive down their prices and increase interest rates on those bills. A rising short-term interest rate will cause households and firms to reduce the quantity of real balances they demand until equilibrium is restored at interest rate i_2. We can conclude that an increase in the price level, holding all other things constant, will result in an increase in the interest rate.

An increase in the interest rate makes firms less willing to invest in plant and equipment and gives consumers an incentive to save rather than to spend. If we include this behavior in our expression for AE, then as P increases, C and I fall, and AE declines. There is also a change in net exports because of the effect of rising interest rates on the

Real money balances
The value of money held by households and firms, adjusted for changes in the price level; M/P.

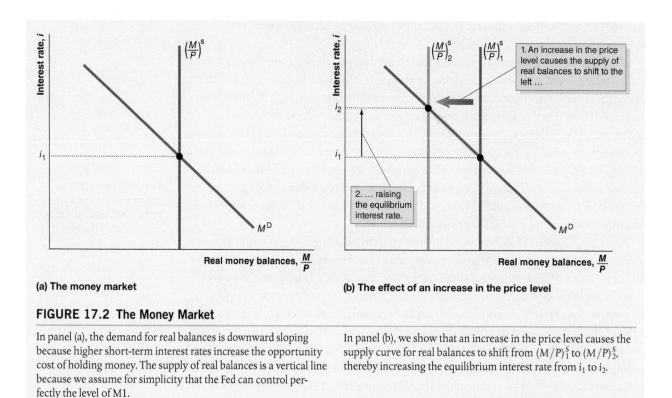

(a) The money market

(b) The effect of an increase in the price level

FIGURE 17.2 The Money Market

In panel (a), the demand for real balances is downward sloping because higher short-term interest rates increase the opportunity cost of holding money. The supply of real balances is a vertical line because we assume for simplicity that the Fed can control perfectly the level of M1.

In panel (b), we show that an increase in the price level causes the supply curve for real balances to shift from $(M/P)^S_1$ to $(M/P)^S_2$, thereby increasing the equilibrium interest rate from i_1 to i_2.

exchange rate. A higher domestic interest rate makes returns on domestic financial assets more attractive relative to those on foreign assets, which increases the demand for the domestic currency. The increased demand for the domestic currency raises the exchange rate, which increases imports and reduces exports, thereby reducing NX and AE.

Conversely, a decrease in the price level increases real money balances, leading to a drop in the interest rate in the money market. The lower interest rate reduces saving (thereby increasing consumption) and raises investment and net exports, so the level of aggregate expenditure rises.

We can see from Figure 17.1 that the AD curve slopes down and to the right, which gives it a slope like the demand curve for an individual good. But we know from our analysis that the reason for the AD curve's slope is quite different from that of a demand curve for an individual good. Points along the aggregate demand curve represent equilibrium combinations of the price level and total output. Which equilibrium point will actually prevail in the economy depends on the supply of output, as we will see in Section 17.3.

Shifts of the Aggregate Demand Curve

The placement of the AD curve on the graph is crucial to understanding the effects of policy measures. Shifts of the aggregate demand curve occur when aggregate expenditure on the economy's total output increases or decreases at a particular price level. A shift of the aggregate demand curve to the right is expansionary because each price level is associated with a higher level of aggregate expenditure. A shift of the aggregate demand curve to the left is contractionary because each price level is associated with a lower level of aggregate expenditure.

We now review the key factors that cause the aggregate demand curve to shift:

1. *Increases and decreases in the money supply.* If the Fed increases the nominal money supply and, at least initially, the price level does not increase as much, real money balances rise. The interest rate then falls in the money market, causing consumption, C, investment, I, and net exports, NX, all to increase. As a result, aggregate expenditure increases, shifting the aggregate demand curve to the right. Conversely, if the Fed reduces the nominal money supply, real money balances fall in the short run. As a result, the equilibrium interest rate rises, and consumption, investment, and net exports all decline. Aggregate expenditure falls, shifting the aggregate demand curve to the left.

2. *Changes in the household saving rate.* Aggregate demand will also shift to the right if consumers decrease their saving rate—the fraction of their income that they save. If households reduce their saving, consumption spending, C, will increase. As a result, the aggregate demand curve will shift to the right. An increase in the household saving rate will decrease consumption spending, shifting the aggregate demand curve to the left.

3. *Changes in households' expected future incomes.* Consumption spending will increase today if households expect their future income will increase, because many people base their consumption spending on their *permanent income*, rather than just on the income they are currently earning. A household's permanent income is the level of income that it expects to receive over time. So, if households expect their future incomes to increase, the aggregate demand curve will shift to the right. A decrease in permanent income as a result of households becoming pessimistic about the incomes they expect to receive in the future will reduce consumption spending today. As a result, the aggregate demand curve will shift to the left.

4. *The expected future profitability of capital.* Firms increase planned investment, I, if they expect the future profitability of capital to increase. Future profitability often depends on the state of the economy. So, firms will often increase planned investment if they anticipate that a recession will soon end and an economic recovery will begin. In that case, the aggregate demand curve will shift to the right. If firms believe that a recession is likely to begin in the near future, they are likely to decrease planned investment, which will shift the aggregate demand curve to the left.

5. *Changes in taxes on households and firms.* An increase in personal income taxes will reduce household's *disposable incomes*. The result is typically a decrease in consumption spending, which will shift the aggregate demand curve to the left. A decrease in personal income taxes will usually cause an increase in consumption spending, shifting the aggregate demand curve to the right. Similarly, an increase in business taxes, such as the corporate income tax, will reduce the profitability of new factories, office buildings, and equipment, and, therefore, cause a decline in planned investment spending. The aggregate demand curve will shift to the left. A decrease

in business taxes will increase planned investment spending, shifting the aggregate demand curve to the right.

6. *Changes in government purchases.* An increase in government purchases, G, directly adds to aggregate expenditure, and shifts the aggregate demand curve to the right. A decrease in government purchases decreases aggregate expenditure, and shifts the aggregate demand curve to the left.

7. *Changes in foreign demand for U.S.-produced goods and services.* An increase in foreign demand for U.S.-produced goods raises net exports, NX, and causes the aggregate demand curve to shift to the right. A decrease in foreign demand for U.S.-produced goods and services reduces net exports, and causes the aggregate demand curve to shift to the left. A key factor determining the demand for U.S.-produced goods and services is the exchange rate between the dollar and other currencies. When the value of the dollar increases, it takes more units of foreign currencies—such as the euro or the yen—to purchase a dollar, which increases the dollar price of U.S. goods in foreign currencies, thereby reducing exports. In addition, the dollar price of foreign goods declines, increasing imports of foreign goods. The result is a decline in net exports. A fall in the value of the dollar has the opposite effect.

Table 17.1 on page 587 summarizes the most important variables that shift the aggregate demand curve.

17.2 The Aggregate Supply Curve

LEARNING OBJECTIVE: Explain how the aggregate supply curve is derived.

Aggregate supply The total quantity of output, or GDP, that firms are willing to supply at a given price level.

The second component of the *AD–AS* model is **aggregate supply**, which is the total quantity of output, or real GDP, that firms are willing to supply at a given price level. Firms have different reactions to changes in the price level in the short run than in the long run. Therefore, we divide our analysis of aggregate supply according to the time horizon that firms face. Our initial goal is to construct a **short-run aggregate supply (SRAS) curve**, which shows the relationship between the price level and the quantity of aggregate output, or real GDP, that firms are willing to supply in the short run. We then discuss the long-run aggregate supply curve.

Short-run aggregate supply (*SRAS*) curve A curve that shows the relationship in the short run between the price level and the quantity of aggregate output, or real GDP, supplied by firms.

Economists are not in complete agreement about how firms respond in the short run to changes in the price level. Most economists believe that the aggregate quantity of output firms supply in the short run increases as the price level rises, so the short-run aggregate supply curve is upward sloping. And most economists also believe that, in the long run, changes in the price level have no effect on the aggregate quantity of output firms supply. But economists offer differing explanations of why the short-run aggregate supply curve is upward sloping.

Although the short-run aggregate supply curve may look like the supply curve facing an individual firm, it represents different behavior. The quantity of output that an individual firm is willing to supply depends on the price of its output *relative to the prices of other goods and services*. In contrast, the short-run aggregate supply curve relates the aggregate quantity of output supplied to the *price level*.

TABLE 17.1   Variables That Shift the Aggregate Demand Curve

An increase in ...	shifts the *AD* curve ...	because ...
the nominal money supply		real money balances rise, and the interest rate falls.
the household saving rate		consumption falls.
households' expected future incomes		consumption rises.
the expected future profitability of capital		investment rises.
income taxes and business taxes		consumption and planned investment decline.
government purchases		aggregate expenditure increases directly.
foreign demand for U.S.-produced goods and services		net exports increase.

The Short-Run Aggregate Supply (*SRAS*) Curve

One explanation of why the *SRAS* curve is upward sloping is called the *new classical view*, which was first proposed by Nobel Laureate Robert E. Lucas, Jr., of the University of Chicago. This approach is also sometimes called the *misperception theory* because it emphasizes the difficulty firms have in distinguishing relative increases in the prices of their products from general increases in the price level. For example, suppose that you are a toy manufacturer, and you see the price of toys increasing by 5%. If the price of toys has increased *relative* to other prices, you can conclude that the demand for toys has risen, and you should increase production. But if all prices in the economy are 5% higher, the relative price of toys is unchanged, and you are unlikely to increase your profit by producing more toys.

Of course, you are only one producer of many. Generalizing to include all producers in the economy, we can see why the misperception theory suggests a relationship between the quantity of aggregate output firms supply and the price level. Suppose that all prices in the economy rise by 5% but that relative prices don't change. If individual producers fail to recognize that relative prices haven't changed, aggregate output increases. This change in output occurs because producers think that some of the increase in prices represents increases in their products' relative prices, and they increase the quantity of their products supplied. According to the new classical view, firms that have perfect information about price changes would react by raising the quantity of toys supplied when prices of toys increased only if that increase differed from the expected increase in the general price level in the economy. If all producers expect the price level to increase by 5%, and as a toy manufacturer you see the price of toys increase by only 2%, you will *reduce* your toy production because you believe that the relative price of toys has declined. Across the economy, if the price level actually increases by only 2% when firms expected a 5% increase in the price level, many firms will cut output.

The new classical view suggests a positive relationship between the aggregate supply of goods and the difference between the actual and expected price levels. If P is the actual price level and P^e is the expected price level, the relationship between aggregate output and the price level, according to the new classical view, is:

$$Y = Y^P + a(P - P^e),$$

where:

Y = real aggregate output, or real GDP

Y^P = *potential* GDP, or the level of real output produced when the economy is at full employment (Y^P is also sometimes called *full-employment GDP*)

a = a positive coefficient that indicates by how much output responds when the actual price level is different from the expected price level.

The equation states that output supplied, Y, equals potential GDP, Y^P, when the actual price level and the expected price level are equal. When the actual price level is greater than the expected price level, firms increase output. When the actual price level is less than the expected price level, firms decrease output. As a result, output can be higher or lower than the full employment level in the short run—until firms can distinguish changes in relative prices from changes in the general price level. So, in the short run, for a particular expected price level, an increase in the actual price level raises the aggregate quantity of output supplied. Therefore, the *SRAS* curve is upward sloping.

An alternative explanation for why the *SRAS* curve is upward sloping comes from the argument of John Maynard Keynes and his followers that in the short run prices adjust slowly in response to changes in aggregate demand. That is, prices are *sticky* in the short run. In the most extreme view of price stickiness, we would observe a horizontal *SRAS* curve because prices would not adjust at all to increases or decreases in aggregate demand. Instead, firms would adjust their production levels to meet the new level of demand without changing their prices. Contemporary economists who follow Keynes's view of price stickiness have sought reasons for the failure of prices to adjust in the short run. Economists who embrace the *new Keynesian view* use characteristics of many real-world markets—in particular, the existence of long-term contracts and imperfect competition—to explain price behavior.

One form of rigidity arises from long-term nominal contracts for wages (between firms and workers) or prices for intermediate goods (between firms and their suppliers). Under a long-term nominal contract, a wage rate or price is set in advance in nominal terms for months or years. For example, an automobile manufacturer may have signed a long-term contract with a supplier of steel. If the automobile manufacturer and the steel company both expected that the inflation rate would be 3%, this fact would be reflected in the price of steel specified in the contract. If the inflation rate is actually 5%, the automobile manufacturer may be able to raise its prices more than it expected to, which will increase its profit, given that the cost of the steel it uses is fixed by the long-term contract. So, an unexpectedly large increase in the price level may result in an increase in output that would not have happened if all input prices were free to adjust. Similarly, if the inflation rate is actually 1%, when it had been expected to be 3%, firms may find their profits decline because some of their costs are not free to adjust. As a result, output will decline.

Many such long-term arrangements exist in the economy, and not all contracts come up for renewal during a particular period because they are overlapping or staggered. So, only some wages and prices can be adjusted in the current period. In the long run, firms and workers will renegotiate contracts in response to changes in demand, but they can't renegotiate all contracts immediately.

New Keynesians also attribute price stickiness to differences in market structure and the price-setting decisions that take place in different types of markets. In markets for wheat or Treasury bills, the product is standardized, many traders interact, and prices adjust freely and quickly to shifts in demand and supply. In such *perfectly competitive markets*, the purchases and sales of individual traders are small relative to the total market volume. For example, a few wheat farmers can't raise their prices above those of other wheat farmers because no one would buy their wheat.

However, many markets in the economy—such as the markets for high-fashion clothing, automobiles, and medical care—don't resemble the continuously adjusting price-taking markets for wheat or Treasury bills because the products in these markets are not standardized. Monopolistic competition results when products have individual characteristics. A seller who raises prices might see quantity demanded fall, but not to zero. In *monopolistically competitive markets*, sellers do not take prices as a given because they are *price setters* rather than *price takers*, as in perfectly competitive markets. New

Keynesian economists argue that prices will adjust only gradually in monopolistically competitive markets when there are costs to changing prices. The costs to a firm of changing prices—sometimes called *menu costs*—include informing current and potential customers of price changes and changing prices in online and print catalogs and on store shelves.

Why are menu costs potentially important in explaining movements in output and prices? Think again about a perfectly competitive market: When a seller of wheat charges a price that is slightly higher than other sellers charge, that seller will sell nothing at all. However, a monopolistically competitive firm (such as a clothing boutique) won't lose many of its customers if its prices are slightly higher than the market price. *If potential profits from making a price change are small relative to the cost of making the price change, the firm won't change its price.*

Rather than adjust prices continually in the short run, a monopolistically competitive firm is likely to meet fluctuations in demand by selling more or less at the posted price. This strategy is reasonable for a monopolistically competitive firm because the product price is higher than the marginal cost—that is, the cost of producing an extra unit. So, the firm is happy to sell extra output when demand increases. As a result of responding to the level of demand without adjusting prices, the firm's output will rise and fall, depending on aggregate demand.

When firms have sticky prices, an increase in the price level will tend to increase these firms' profit in the short run and so will lead them to increase output. The short-run aggregate supply curve that is implied by the new Keynesian view is upward sloping. The larger the proportion of firms in the economy with sticky prices, the flatter the *SRAS* curve will be. If all firms had sticky prices in the short run, the *SRAS* curve would be horizontal. Alternatively, if all firms had perfectly flexible prices in the short run, the *SRAS* curve would be vertical.

The Long-Run Aggregate Supply (*LRAS*) Curve

Long-run aggregate supply (*LRAS*) curve
A curve that shows the relationship in the long run between the price level and the quantity of aggregate output, or real GDP, supplied by firms.

The *SRAS* curve is upward sloping in both the new classical and new Keynesian explanations of aggregate supply, but the relationship between the price level and the quantity of aggregate output that firms are willing to supply won't be upward sloping in the long run. In the new classical view, firms eventually can distinguish changes in the relative prices of their products from changes in the price level. At that point, the actual and expected price levels are equal—that is, $P = P^e$. The new classical equation on page 588 indicates that when the actual price level equals the expected price level, current output, Y, equals potential GDP, Y^P. Therefore, the **long-run aggregate supply (*LRAS*) curve** is vertical at Y^P.

In the new Keynesian view, in the short run, many input costs are fixed, so firms can expand output without experiencing an increase in input cost that is proportional to the increase in the prices of their products. Over time, though, input costs increase in line with the price level, so in the long run, both firms with flexible prices and firms with sticky prices adjust their prices in response to a change in demand. As with the new classical view, the *LRAS* curve is vertical at potential GDP, or $Y = Y^P$.

Figure 17.3 displays the short-run and long-run aggregate supply curves on the same graph. Note that the curves intersect at a price level equal to P^e.

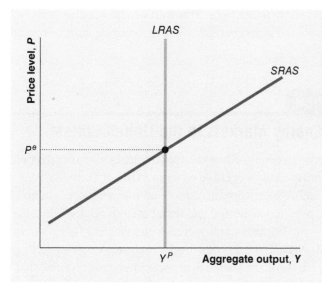

FIGURE 17.3

The Short-Run and Long-Run Aggregate Supply Curves

The *SRAS* curve is upward sloping because when the price level, *P*, exceeds the expected price level, P^e, the quantity of output supplied rises. In the long run, the actual and expected price levels are the same. Therefore, the *LRAS* curve is vertical at potential GDP, Y^P.

Shifts in the Short-Run Aggregate Supply Curve

Shifts in aggregate supply can explain changes in output in the short run. There are three main reasons the short-run aggregate supply curve shifts:

1. **Changes in labor costs.** Labor typically accounts for the majority of the costs of producing output. When output, *Y*, exceeds potential GDP, Y^P, the high level of output produced raises the demand for labor. The higher labor demand, in turn, bids up wages, increasing firms' labor costs. As a result, the short-run aggregate supply curve will eventually shift to the left because at any given price level, firms will supply less output when their costs are higher. In the case when output falls below potential GDP, firms begin to lay off workers, and workers' wages decline. The resulting drop in production costs eventually shifts the short-run aggregate supply curve to the right.

2. **Changes in other input costs.** Unexpected changes in the price or availability of raw materials, such as oil, or in the technology of producing goods and services affect production costs and the short-run aggregate supply curve. Such changes are called **supply shocks**. Positive supply shocks, such as the development of labor-saving technologies or lower food prices due to good growing seasons, shift the short-run aggregate supply curve to the right. Negative supply shocks, such as an increase in the price of oil, shift the short-run aggregate supply curve to the left.

3. **Changes in the expected price level.** When workers bargain for wages, they compare their wages to the costs of goods and services that they buy. When workers expect the price level to rise, they will demand higher nominal wages to preserve their real wages. Similarly, firms make decisions about how much output to supply by comparing the price of their output to the expected prices of other goods and services. When the expected price level rises, firms raise prices to cover higher labor and other costs. An increase in the expected price level shifts the short-run aggregate supply curve to the left. A decline in the expected price level shifts the

Supply shock An unexpected change in production costs or in technology that causes the short-run aggregate supply curve to shift.

short-run aggregate supply curve to the right. This shift occurs because firms reduce prices as nominal wages and other costs fall, thereby supplying more output at every given price level.

MAKING THE CONNECTION

Fracking Transforms Energy Markets in the United States

In the late 1850s, Edwin Drake, a career railroad conductor, invented a way to drill for oil and pumped the first significant quantities of crude oil from a field in Titusville, Pennsylvania. Until the 1960s, the United States produced more oil than any other country. During the late 1960s, as U.S. production slowed and then began to decline while the demand for oil continued to grow, imports of oil soared. The following figure shows that, particularly after the mid-1980s, U.S. oil production went into a long-run decline, and by the mid-1990s, for the first time the United States was importing more oil than it produced.

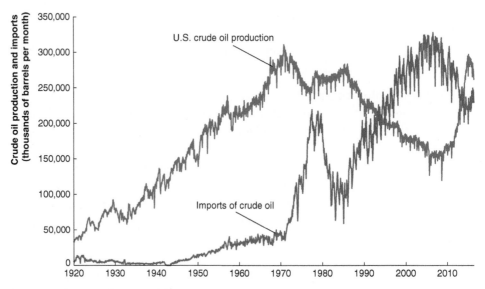

Source: U.S. Energy Information Administration.

Beginning in 2008, high crude oil prices led a number of U.S. energy companies to adopt a technology called hydraulic fracturing, or *fracking*. Fracking involves injecting a mixture of water, sand, and chemicals into a rock formation at high pressure to release oil and natural gas that could not have been recovered using traditional methods. The figure shows that as a result of fracking, U.S. oil production doubled between 2008 and 2015. Increased U.S. oil production helped cause a sharp decline in world oil prices from a high of $133 per barrel in 2008 to a low of only $30 per barrel in February 2016. Oil prices recovered to above $50 later in the year.

Oil wells typically also recover natural gas as a by-product of pumping oil. As a result, increased production of oil has also increased supplies of natural gas, and prices have fallen from a high of $13 per million British Thermal Units (BTUs, a measure of the heat content of fuel) in July 2008 to less than $3 in September 2016. Natural gas has long been a source of energy for manufacturing products such as chemicals and fertilizers. Falling natural gas prices led U.S. manufacturers of aluminum, glass, and other products to switch to natural gas from coal and other fuels. Many utilities also switched from coal to natural gas as it became cheaper. In addition to the benefits of a lower price, natural gas generates lower levels of the greenhouse gases that contribute to global warming. The percentage of U.S. electricity produced using natural gas increased from 20% in 2006 to 34% in 2016. As a result, many firms face lower electricity charges. But low-cost natural gas may prove to have its biggest effect on transportation markets. Firms in the long-haul trucking industry, which carries about three-quarters of the country's freight, have begun to switch from trucks powered by diesel fuel to trucks powered by much cheaper—and cleaner—natural gas.

As a result of these developments in energy markets, the *SRAS* curve for the United States has shifted to the right. Economist Philip Verlager has predicted that the United States will eventually have the lowest energy costs of any country in the industrialized world, and Citigroup economists have estimated that the increase in production of oil and gas in the United States could result in more than 3.5 million new jobs and substantially higher real GDP by 2020. Some business executives believe that lower prices for natural gas will continue for decades. "We convinced ourselves that this is not a temporary thing," says Peter Cella, chief executive of Chevron Phillips. "This is a real, durable phenomenon, a potential competitive advantage for the United States." Geologists estimate that the supply of natural gas in the United States is sufficient to maintain current production for over a century.

Despite the economic benefits of energy produced by hydraulic fracturing, the process has attracted critics. Fracking requires large amounts of energy and water, and people living close to production sites have complained of methane leaks. Some policymakers worry that the rush to take advantage of the new technology has overwhelmed the need to consider the risks to the environment. The International Energy Agency has estimated that many of the potential adverse effects from fracking can be contained through careful monitoring, but at an increase in average cost of about 7% for the typical gas well.

Lower oil and natural gas prices led some U.S. firms in 2016 to cut back on production, as shown in the figure on the previous page. But many economists and oil firm executives believe that over the long run, the effects of more abundant and cheaper supplies of oil and natural gas will have a large effect on the world economy. As a top manager at one oil firm put it in 2016: "There is now a massive amount of innovation—commercial innovation, changes in the business model, as well as technical innovation. There's an incredible window of opportunity at the moment."

Sources: Spencer Jakab, "Natural Gas: Don't Get Too Comfortable," *Wall Street Journal*, June 19, 2016; Sarah Kent, "Big Oil's New Focus on Natural Gas," *Wall Street Journal*, September 13, 2016; Ben Casselman and Russell Gold, "Cheap Natural Gas Gives Hope to the Rust Belt," *Wall Street Journal*, October 24, 2012; and "The Oil Conundrum," *Economist*, January 23, 2016.

See related problem 2.10 at the end of the chapter.

TABLE 17.2 Variables That Shift the Short-Run and Long-Run Aggregate Supply Curves

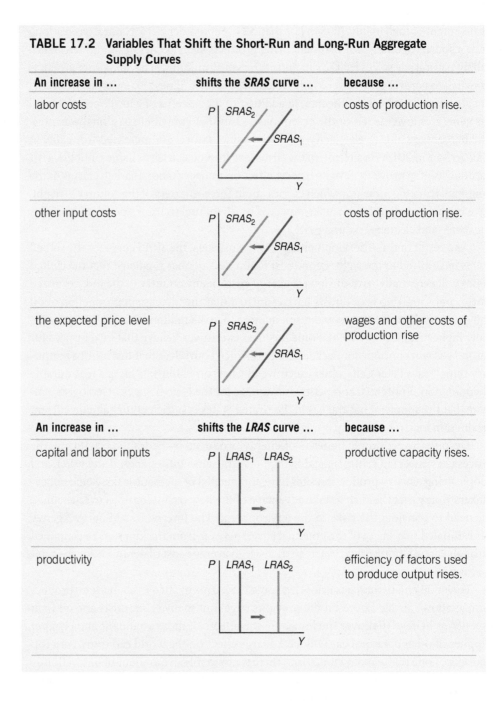

An increase in ...	shifts the *SRAS* curve ...	because ...
labor costs		costs of production rise.
other input costs		costs of production rise.
the expected price level		wages and other costs of production rise

An increase in ...	shifts the *LRAS* curve ...	because ...
capital and labor inputs		productive capacity rises.
productivity		efficiency of factors used to produce output rises.

Shifts in the Long-Run Aggregate Supply (*LRAS*) Curve

The long-run aggregate supply (*LRAS*) curve indicates the potential level of real output, or GDP, in the economy at a specific time. The *LRAS* curve shifts over time to reflect growth in potential GDP. Sources of this economic growth include (1) increases in capital and labor inputs and (2) technological change that increases the growth of productivity, or output produced per unit of input.

Growth in inputs raises the economy's productive capacity. When firms invest in new plant and equipment—beyond just replacing old plant and equipment—they increase the capital stock available for production. Labor inputs increase when the population grows or more people participate in the labor force. Studies of output growth in the United States and other countries show that over long periods of time, productivity growth significantly influences the pace of output growth. Productivity growth is driven primarily by technological change that allows firms to produce more output per unit of input. Economists have a broad definition of technological change that includes not just new or improved machinery and equipment, but also other ways of producing more output from a given amount of inputs, such as better methods of organizing production and improvements in worker training and education.

Table 17.2 on page 594 summarizes the most important variables that shift the short-run and long-run aggregate supply curves.

17.3 Equilibrium in the Aggregate Demand and Aggregate Supply Model

LEARNING OBJECTIVE: Demonstrate macroeconomic equilibrium using the aggregate demand and aggregate supply model.

Aggregate demand and short-run and long-run aggregate supply are the components of the *aggregate demand and aggregate supply (AD–AS) model*, which we can use to determine the equilibrium level of output and the equilibrium price level in the economy. Because there is a difference between the behavior of firms supplying output in the short run and in the long run, we have two equilibrium values for output and the price level—the short-run equilibrium and the long-run equilibrium.

Short-Run Equilibrium

To determine output and the price level in the short run, in Figure 17.4 we combine the aggregate demand (AD) curve and the short-run aggregate supply (SRAS) curve. The

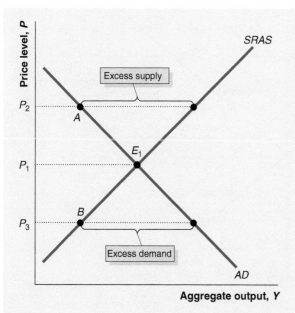

FIGURE 17.4

Short-Run Equilibrium

The economy's short-run equilibrium is represented by the intersection of the AD and SRAS curves at E_1. The equilibrium price level is P_1. Higher price levels are associated with an excess supply of output (at point A, for example), and lower price levels are associated with excess demand for output (at point B, for example).

economy's short-run equilibrium occurs at the intersection, E_1, of the AD and SRAS curves. No other point represents equilibrium. For example, point A lies on the AD curve, but at price level P_2, firms would supply more output than households and businesses would demand. The price level would fall to restore equilibrium at E_1. Point B lies on the SRAS curve. However, at price level P_3, households and businesses would demand more output than firms would be willing to produce. The price level would rise to P_1 to equate the quantity of output demanded and the quantity of output supplied.

Long-Run Equilibrium

Our analysis of the economy's equilibrium in the short run indicates that there are many possible combinations of output and the price level, depending on where the aggregate demand curve and the short-run aggregate supply curve intersect. In the long run, however, the price level adjusts to bring the economy into equilibrium at potential GDP, Y^P. So, the economy's long-run equilibrium occurs at the intersection of the AD, SRAS, and LRAS curves. In Figure 17.5, the aggregate demand curve AD_1 and the short-run aggregate supply curve $SRAS_1$ intersect at Y^P, with a price level of P_1.

Now suppose that aggregate demand increases unexpectedly, perhaps as a result of an increase in demand for housing. As a result, the aggregate demand curve will shift to the right, from AD_1 to AD_2, and output and the price level will both increase in the short run. The new short-run equilibrium, E_2, lies at the intersection of the AD_2 and $SRAS_1$ curves. But over time, as firms learn that the general price level has risen and as input costs rise, the SRAS curve will shift to the left, from $SRAS_1$ to $SRAS_2$, because at the new price level, firms are willing to supply less output. In the long run, the SRAS curve will have to shift far enough to intersect with AD_2 at Y^P. The new long-run equilibrium following the increase in aggregate demand is at point E_3, with a price level P_2 and output Y^P.

FIGURE 17.5

Adjustment to Long-Run Equilibrium

From an initial equilibrium at E_1, an increase in aggregate demand shifts the AD curve from AD_1 to AD_2, increasing output from Y^P to Y_2. Because Y_2 is greater than Y^P, prices rise, shifting the SRAS curve from $SRAS_1$ to $SRAS_2$. The economy's new equilibrium is at E_3. Output has returned to Y^P, but the price level has risen from P_1 to P_2. The LRAS curve is vertical at Y^P, potential GDP. Shifts in the AD curve affect the level of output only in the short run. This outcome holds in both the new classical and new Keynesian views, although price adjustment is more rapid in the new classical view.

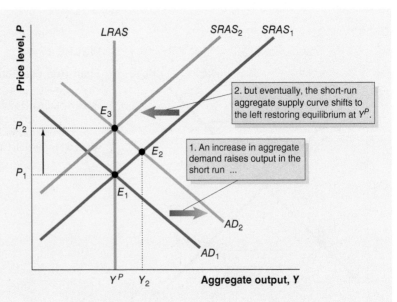

If aggregate demand contracts unexpectedly, so that the *AD* curve shifts to the left, the process will be reversed. Initially, output and the price level will decline. Over time, as firms learn that the price level has fallen and input costs fall, the *SRAS* curve will shift to the right. This process of adjustment is more gradual (due to sticky prices for many firms) in the new Keynesian view than in the new classical view. At the new long-run equilibrium, output equals Y^P, and the price level is lower than P_1.

Economists refer to the process of adjustment back to potential GDP just described as an *automatic mechanism* because it occurs without any actions by the government.

In the long run, the economy will produce Y^P, and the price level will adjust to shifts in aggregate demand to ensure that the economy is in equilibrium. Because the *LRAS* curve is vertical, economists generally agree that in the long run, changes in aggregate demand affect the price level but not the level of output. This long-run relationship between shifts in *AD* and the price level results in **monetary neutrality**. For example, if the Fed attempts to stimulate the economy by increasing the money supply, in the short run both output and the price level will increase, but in the long run only the price level increases because the level of output returns to Y^P. Conversely, a decline in the nominal money supply lowers the price level in the long run but has no effect on output. So, we can conclude that *changes in the money supply have no effect on output in the long run.*

Monetary neutrality The proposition that changes in the money supply have no effect on output in the long run because an increase (decrease) in the money supply raises (lowers) the price level in the long run but does not change the equilibrium level of output.

Economic Fluctuations in the United States

We can use the *AD–AS* model to explain past events and to predict future economic developments. Fluctuations in current output can be explained by shifts in the aggregate demand curve or the aggregate supply curve. In the following sections, we use *AD–AS* analysis to explain three episodes of economic fluctuations in the United States: (1) shocks to aggregate demand, 1964–1969; (2) supply shocks, negative during 1973–1975 and positive after 1995; and (3) a credit crunch shock to aggregate demand during and after the 2007–2009 recession. Then we use *AD–AS* analysis to predict the consequences for output and prices of pro-investment tax reform.

Shocks to Aggregate Demand, 1964–1969 By 1964, U.S. participation in the conflict in Vietnam had grown to a major war effort, and real government purchases—principally for military equipment and personnel—had expanded by 9% since 1960. Those expenditures would increase by another 21% between 1964 and 1969. The Fed was concerned that the rise in aggregate demand caused by these increases in government purchases would increase money demand and the interest rate. To avoid an increase in the interest rate, the Fed pursued an expansionary monetary policy: The annual growth rate of M1 rose from 3.7% in 1963 to 7.7% in 1964.

The combination of fiscal and monetary expansions led to a series of shifts of the aggregate demand curve to the right. Rising aggregate demand caused output to exceed potential GDP in the mid-1960s, putting upward pressure on production costs and the price level. As we demonstrated in the analysis of short-run and long-run equilibrium with the *AD–AS* model, when output rises above potential GDP, eventually the *SRAS* curve shifts to the left, restoring the economy's full employment equilibrium at a higher price level. Because fiscal and monetary expansion continued for several years, *AD–AS* analysis indicates that output growth and inflation (the rate of change in the price level) should have risen from 1964 through 1969, and, in fact, that is what happened.

Supply Shocks, 1973–1975 and After 1995 By the early 1970s, many economists and policymakers believed that inflation was mainly driven by increases in aggregate demand. In this view, inflation would only occur when output was also increasing. Then economists and policymakers in the United States and other industrialized countries were surprised by a period of rising inflation and *falling* output as a result of negative supply shocks in 1973 and 1974. In 1973, the Organization of the Petroleum Exporting Countries (OPEC) sharply reduced the supply of oil in the world oil market in an attempt to pressure the United States and other countries to stop supporting Israel in the 1973 Arab–Israeli war. Along with the quadrupling of world oil prices, poor crop harvests around the world caused food prices to rise significantly. In the United States, these two negative supply shocks were reinforced by the lifting of government wage and price controls that had been in effect since 1971. With the ending of these controls, firms raised prices, and workers pushed for higher wages to catch up with price increases and to recover the wage increases they had been unable to receive during the period of controls.

In *AD–AS* analysis, this set of negative supply shocks will shift the short-run aggregate supply curve to the left, raising the price level and reducing output. In fact, output fell in 1974 and 1975, while inflation rose. The combination of rising inflation with falling, or stagnating, output is called *stagflation*. Falling output and rising prices showed that aggregate supply shocks, as well as aggregate demand shocks, could change the economy's short-run equilibrium. A similar pattern occurred as a result of negative supply shocks caused by rising oil prices in the 1978–1980 period.

We can also examine favorable supply shocks, such as the acceleration in productivity growth experienced by the U.S. economy from 1996 to 2005. Many economists believe that investment in information technology, particularly technology connected with the "new economy" of the Internet, explains this increase in productivity growth. We can use *AD–AS* analysis to illustrate this positive supply shock. Both the *SRAS* and *LRAS* curves shifted to the right, raising output and causing the price level to rise by less than it otherwise would have. Beginning in 2006, productivity growth slowed, causing the *LRAS* curve to shift to the right at a slower rate. This slowdown in productivity growth contributed to the slow growth in real GDP in the years following the financial crisis of 2007–2009.

Credit Crunch and Aggregate Demand During and After the 2007–2009 Recession
As we have discussed in previous chapters, a *credit crunch*, or a reduction in the

ability or willingness of banks and other financial firms to lend, can cause a reduction in output. Many analysts believe that a credit crunch deepened the 2007–2009 recession and contributed to the slowness of the recovery from the recession. As we saw in Chapter 12, following the failure of the Lehman Brothers investment bank, a financial panic occurred. The process of securitization—apart from government-guaranteed residential mortgages—ground to a halt. As savers withdrew funds from money market mutual funds, corporations had difficulty selling commercial paper. As banks and other financial firms sold assets and cut back on lending to shore up their financial positions, the flow of funds from savers to borrowers was disrupted. Because households and small and medium-sized businesses weren't able to replace bank loans with funds from other sources, spending for consumer durable goods and business plant and equipment fell.

In *AD–AS* analysis, the decline in spending translates into a reduction in aggregate expenditure, shifting the *AD* curve to the left. Over time, the drop in aggregate demand puts downward pressure on prices, shifting the *SRAS* curve to the right. In fact, real GDP fell by 4.2% during the 2007–2009 recession, and the inflation rate as measured by the consumer price index (CPI) declined from 2.9% in 2007 to −0.3% in 2009. As we discussed in Chapter 12, other factors beyond the credit crunch contributed to the 2007–2009 recession, but most economists believe that the credit crunch was the factor mainly responsible for the severity of the recession.

Are Investment Incentives Inflationary? In the late 1990s, many economists and policymakers urged Congress to consider tax reforms that would stimulate business investment. And in 2002, President George W. Bush proposed and won Congressional approval for investment incentives. Such reforms included (1) the introduction of expensing—in which businesses write off the purchase of new plant and equipment all at once rather than gradually—and (2) cuts in dividend and capital gains taxes that reduced the cost of capital. Many economists argued that such reforms would significantly increase business investment demand and output of capital goods. Would these reforms also increase inflation?

In *AD–AS* analysis, the stimulus to investment translates into an increase in aggregate demand, shifting the *AD* curve to the right. However, as the new plant and equipment are installed, the economy's capacity to produce increases, and the *SRAS* and *LRAS* curves shift to the right, reducing the inflationary pressure from pro-investment tax reform. Recent evidence suggests that the supply response is substantial, and investment incentives are unlikely to be inflationary.

In 2010, the U.S. economy was struggling to recover from the 2007–2009 recession. In an attempt to stimulate aggregate demand, President Barack Obama proposed, and Congress enacted, the Small Business Jobs Act of 2010, which allowed businesses to expense their spending on investment goods through the end of 2011. This policy change increased the demand for investment goods, but did not have a signficant effect on the inflation rate.

17.4 **The Effects of Monetary Policy**

> **LEARNING OBJECTIVE:** Use the aggregate demand and aggregate supply model to show the effects of monetary policy on the economy.

Business cycle Alternating periods of economic expansion and economic recession.

The **business cycle** refers to alternating periods of economic expansion and economic recession. In a business cycle, output grows during an expansion until the business cycle peak. Then output declines as the economy moves into a contraction or recession until the business cycle trough, when output begins to expand again. This pattern varies from several months to several years, and expansions and recessions vary in intensity. In the period since the end of World War II in 1945, the recessions of 1981–1982 and 2007–2009 were particularly severe.

When the economy moves into a recession, output declines and unemployment increases, which results in hardships for some individuals and businesses. Most economists believe that increases in the money supply and decreases in interest rates can increase short-run output. It may be possible, then, for the Fed to use monetary policy to stabilize the economy by reducing the severity of recessions and smoothing short-run fluctuations in output. Such a **stabilization policy** attempts to shift the AD curve by changing the money supply and interest rates. It is also possible for Congress and the president to pursue *fiscal policy* actions, such as changing the level of government purchases or taxes to stabilize the economy. As with monetary policy, fiscal policy works primarily through shifts in the AD curve. But changes in tax policy that affect incentives to work, save, and invest may also increase aggregate supply in both the short and long runs.

Stabilization policy A monetary policy or fiscal policy intended to reduce the severity of the business cycle and stabilize the economy.

An Expansionary Monetary Policy

Suppose that the economy is hit by an *aggregate demand shock*, as happened in 2007, with the collapse of spending on new houses. Figure 17.6 illustrates the result. In panel (a), the economy starts at equilibrium at E_1, which is at the intersection of AD_1, $SRAS_1$, and $LRAS$. Output is at Y^P, and the price level is at P_1. As a result of the aggregate demand shock, the aggregate demand curve shifts from AD_1 to AD_2. The economy enters a recession at E_2, with output falling from Y^P to Y_2, and the price level falling from P_1 to P_2.

The Fed then has to decide whether to implement an expansionary monetary policy. If the Fed does nothing, we know from our earlier analysis that the economy will eventually correct itself. At E_2, with output less than full employment, over time input costs and prices will fall, shifting the short-run aggregate supply curve to the right, from $SRAS_1$ to $SRAS_2$, and bringing the economy back to potential GDP at E_3. The economy eventually returns to potential GDP at price level P_3, but the necessary adjustments to costs and prices may take years, during which time some workers suffer unemployment and some firms suffer losses.

Alternatively, as panel (b) of Figure 17.6 shows, the Fed could try to speed recovery by implementing an expansionary monetary policy. As we saw in Chapter 15, the Fed can implement an expansionary monetary policy by lowering the target for the federal funds rate. An expansionary policy will shift the aggregate demand curve back to the right, from AD_2 to AD_1. The economy moves from recession at E_2 back to its initial full

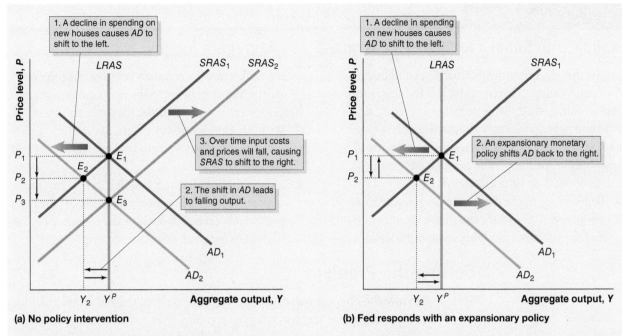

FIGURE 17.6 Effects of Monetary Policy

Panel (a) shows that from an initial full-employment equilibrium at E_1, an aggregate demand shock shifts the AD curve from AD_1 to AD_2, and output falls from Y^P to Y_2. At E_2, the economy is in a recession. Over time, the price level adjusts downward, restoring the economy's full employment equilibrium at E_3.

Panel (b) shows that from an initial full-employment equilibrium at E_1, an aggregate demand shock shifts the AD curve from AD_1 to AD_2. At E_2, the economy is in a recession. The Fed speeds recovery, using an expansionary monetary policy, which shifts the AD curve back from AD_2 to AD_1. Relative to the nonintervention case, the economy recovers more quickly back to full employment, but with a higher long-run price level.

employment equilibrium at E_1. The economy returns to potential GDP more quickly than it would have if the Fed had followed the alternative of refraining from active policy. Stabilization policy, however, has a side effect: It leads to a higher price level than would exist if no action were taken.

During the 1960s, many economists encouraged the use of monetary and fiscal policies to smooth fluctuations in the economy. However, other economists doubted that attempts to *fine-tune* the economy would be effective, given the potentially long lags in formulating and implementing stabilization policies. Most economists today believe that because of these lags, policymakers can't hope to successfully counterbalance every economic fluctuation. Therefore, economists generally advocate that policymakers focus on long-run objectives such as low inflation or steady economic growth. Many economists argue that policymakers should restrict the use of activist policy to fighting major downturns in the economy. A major downturn is, of course, exactly what the U.S. economy experienced beginning in 2007.

SOLVED PROBLEM 17.4

Dealing with Shocks to Aggregate Demand and Aggregate Supply

Assume that the economy is initially in equilibrium at full employment. Then suppose that the economy is hit simultaneously with negative aggregate demand and aggregate supply shocks: There is a large increase in oil prices, and there is a sharp decline in consumption spending as households become pessimistic about their future incomes.

a. Draw an aggregate demand and aggregate supply graph to illustrate the initial equilibrium and the short-run equilibrium after the shocks.

Do we know with certainty whether the price level will be higher or lower in the new equilibrium?

b. Suppose that the Fed decides not to intervene with an expansionary monetary policy. Show how the economy will adjust back to its long-run equilibrium.

c. Now suppose that the Fed decides to intervene with an expansionary monetary policy. If the Fed's policy is successful, show how the economy adjusts back to its long-run equilibrium.

Solving the Problem

Step 1 **Review the chapter material.** This problem is about the Fed's implementing an expansionary monetary policy, so you may want to review the section "An Expansionary Monetary Policy," which begins on page 600.

Step 2 **Answer part (a) by drawing the appropriate graph and explaining whether we know if the price level will rise or fall.** A negative supply shock will cause the aggregate supply curve to shift to the left, from $SRAS_1$ to $SRAS_2$, and a negative demand shock will cause the aggregate demand curve to shift to the left, from AD_1 to AD_2. Your graph should look like this:

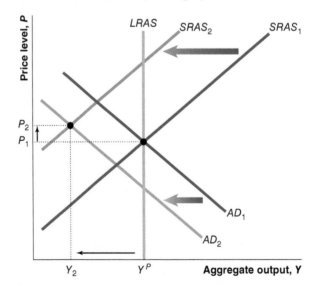

Note that as we have drawn the graph, the price level increases from P_1 to P_2, but it is possible that the AD curve will shift to the left by more than does the $SRAS$ curve. In that case, the price level will fall. So, we can't say with certainty whether the price level will rise or fall if the economy is hit by aggregate supply and aggregate demand shocks at the same time.

Step 3 **Answer part (b) by drawing the appropriate graph.** We start at the short-run equilibrium described in part (a), with output at Y_2 and the price level at P_2. With output at Y_2 being less than full employment, over time, prices and input costs will fall, shifting the short-run aggregate supply curve to the right, from $SRAS_2$ to $SRAS_3$, which will eventually bring the economy back to potential GDP, Y^P, at a lower price level, P_3.

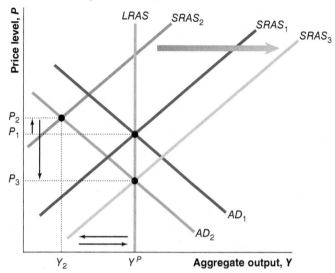

Step 4 **Answer part (c) by drawing the appropriate graph.** Starting again at the short-run equilibrium from part (a), an expansionary monetary policy will shift the aggregate demand curve from AD_2 to AD_3, restoring the economy to potential GDP, Y^P, at a higher price level, P_3.

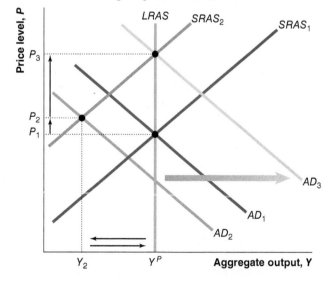

See related problem 4.7 at the end of the chapter.

Was Monetary Policy Ineffective During the 2007–2009 Recession?

As we saw in the chapter opener, the growth of employment and real GDP during the recovery from the 2007–2009 recession were slower than most economists and policymakers had expected. Do these facts indicate that monetary policy had failed? Not necessarily. Certainly, the Fed was unable to pull off a rapid and smooth return to full employment of the type illustrated in panel (b) of Figure 17.6 on page 601. But as we saw in Chapter 12, research has shown that both in the United States and in other countries, recessions accompanied by financial crises are almost always very severe. And the 2007–2009 recession was not caused simply by a temporary decline in aggregate demand. Instead, the declines in output in important industries, such as housing, may have resulted from structural changes in the economy and might be long-lived, perhaps even permanent. Therefore, expansionary monetary policy aimed at increasing aggregate demand would probably not succeed in re-employing workers who had lost their jobs in those industries.

In 2016, some economists inside and outside the Fed were also wondering whether prolonged levels of high unemployment had led to a reduction in the employment–population ratio that would be difficult to reverse. If so, the result would be a long-lived reduction in aggregate supply relative to what it would otherwise have been. Some economists believe that large negative shifts in aggregate demand actually reduce the full employment level of output, a situation known as *hysteresis*. With hysteresis, the process of the economy automatically returning to equilibrium, as illustrated in panel (a) of Figure 17.6, breaks down. This breakdown occurs because if high rates of unemployment persist, more workers lose their skills—or are viewed by employers as lacking current skills—and therefore have difficulty being rehired. Workers who are unemployed for long periods may also become discouraged and drop out of the labor force permanently. These obstacles to locating new jobs lead to chronic levels of lower employment and output.

Some economists have argued that persistently high rates of unemployment in many European countries during the 1980s and 1990s reflected hysteresis. Under this analysis, unemployment rose in those countries following the oil price shocks of the 1970s. When the unemployment rate remained persistently above the previous full employment level, hysteresis set in, and the unemployment rate remained stuck at high levels. Other economists are skeptical that hysteresis is a good explanation for persistent unemployment in Europe. These economists point to government policies, such as generous unemployment insurance benefits, high tax rates, and restrictions on firms hiring and firing workers, to explain why employment growth was sluggish in these countries.

So, in 2016, the Fed found itself in a dilemma: Using conventional expansionary monetary policy to increase the rate of output growth would be effective only if the main problem facing the economy was insufficient aggregate demand, which some economists and policymakers believed was indeed the case. If aggregate supply was the problem, however, conventional policy would be ineffective. Instead, Congress and the president might need to implement policies to deal with the reasons so many prime-age workers had dropped out of the labor force, even at a time when the unemployment rate had dropped to full-employment levels.

MAKING THE CONNECTION

The 1930s, Today, and the Limits to Monetary Policy

During and after the recession of 2007–2009, economists and policymakers studied whether events from the Great Depression of the 1930s might provide insight into what was happening. The Depression had also involved a financial crisis, and it had persisted over more than a decade. In 2016, low employment rates and sluggish growth of real GDP left policymakers concerned that the effects of the financial crisis of 2007–2009 might be similarly long-lived.

One of the striking facts about the Depression was the high unemployment rate in the late 1930s. This high unemployment rate was in part due to the recession of 1937–1938, which, as we saw in Chapter 14, the Fed had inadvertently helped cause through a series of increases in the required reserve ratio. Economist Robert Gordon of Northwestern University has analyzed the situation in the United States in 1939. Although estimates differ, Gordon believes that the unemployment rate that year was greater than 17% and that more than one-third of the unemployed had been without a job for more than a year. Despite the high unemployment rate, there was little indication of the falling wages and prices that would push the economy back to full employment by the process shown in panel (a) of Figure 17.6 on page 601. Some economists believe that the high unemployment of 1939 was due to problems with aggregate demand, while others believe it was due to problems with aggregate supply. Economists supporting the aggregate supply explanation point to these three key factors: (1) the substantial increases in tax rates Congress had enacted during the 1930s; (2) the sharp increase in unionization, strikes, and labor unrest; and (3) what these economists see as the undermining of private property rights under President Franklin Roosevelt's New Deal.

Gordon disagrees with the aggregate supply arguments, holding instead that the United States was suffering from hysteresis brought on by insufficient aggregate demand. He argues that once Congress began to substantially increase spending on military goods in 1940 to prepare for the entry of the United States into World War II, aggregate output rapidly expanded, and unemployment declined. In effect, the federal government engaged in a very large fiscal policy action by massively increasing spending on military goods. In Gordon's view, structural barriers to expanding output and employment disappeared once this large increase in aggregate demand had taken place.

Gordon's analysis of the events of the late 1930s and early 1940s has been challenged. Economist Robert Higgs of the Independent Institute has argued that the high unemployment of the 1930s was caused by "regime uncertainty" due to New Deal policies. He argues that because the 1940–1945 increases in output were largely in the war material and munitions industries, and the decline in unemployment was due to the draft and the growth in employment in war industries, true prosperity did not return until the end of the war in 1945. Higgs believes that the post-World War II prosperity was due to:

> the death of Roosevelt and the succession of Harry S Truman and his administration [which] completed the shift from a political regime investors perceived

as full of uncertainty to one in which they felt much more confident about the security of their private property rights... . [I]nvestors set in motion the postwar investment boom that powered the economy's return to sustained prosperity notwithstanding the drastic reduction of federal government spending from its extraordinarily elevated war-time levels.

Higgs's argument has been subject to criticism, though, by economists who see the shift in policies from the Roosevelt to Truman administrations as being less dramatic than he does.

In 2016, policy debates echoed those of the 1930s. Some economists argued in 2016 that sufficiently expansionary monetary policy could increase employment and the growth rate of real GDP, bringing the economy back to conditions similar to those that prevailed before the financial crisis of 2007–2009. Other economists believed that the Fed had taken expansionary monetary policy as far as it could go and that other approaches would be needed. For instance, some economists advocated the use of fiscal policy, particularly a program of spending on infrastructure, such as improvements to highways and bridges and tax reform that would increase incentives for investment in physical capital. The assurance of higher levels of aggregate demand might lead businesses to expand production and employment. In addition, new incentives could be enacted to spur businesses to increase hiring, leading workers who had dropped out of the labor market to return.

Other economists in 2016 echoed Higgs's arguments about the 1930s and 1940s, holding that greater policy certainty, particularly with respect to regulation and taxes, might lead businesses to increase spending on physical capital and to expand employment. Undoubtedly, economists will continue to explore the interesting parallels between the U.S. economy of the 1930s and the U.S. economy following the financial crisis of 2007–2009.

Sources: Robert J. Gordon, "Back to the Future: European Unemployment Today Viewed from America in 1939," *Brookings Papers on Economic Activity*, Vol. 19, No. 1, 1988, pp. 271–312; and Robert Higgs, *Depression, War, and Cold War: Challenging the Myths of Conflict and Prosperity*, Oakland, CA: Independent Institute, 2009.

See related problems 4.10, 4.11, and 4.12 at the end of the chapter.

ANSWERING THE KEY QUESTION

Continued from page 579

At the beginning of this chapter, we asked:

"What explains the relatively slow growth of employment during the economic expansion that began in 2009?"

We have seen in this chapter that in 2016 the employment–population ratio remained well below its pre-recession level. As a result, seven years after the end of the recession, millions of people were still without employment—a result that most economists and policymakers had not expected. Some economists believed that the slow growth in employment was the result of insufficient aggregate demand and suggested that production and employment could be increased through expansionary monetary policy.

Other economists, though, thought that structural problems might have resulted in the slow growth in employment and that those problems would have to be addressed by Congress and the president rather than by the Federal Reserve. Some economists believed that additional expansion of aggregate demand was needed, but favored fiscal policy actions involving infrastructure spending and changes to the tax code rather than additional monetary policy actions.

Key Terms and Problems

Key Terms

Aggregate demand (*AD*) curve, p. 582

Aggregate supply, p. 587

Business cycle, p. 600

Long-run aggregate supply (*LRAS*) curve, p. 590

Monetary neutrality, p. 597

Real money balances, p. 583

Short-run aggregate supply (*SRAS*) curve, p. 587

Stabilization policy, p. 600

Supply shock, p. 591

17.1 The Aggregate Demand Curve
Explain how the aggregate demand curve is derived.

Review Questions

1.1 Briefly describe each of the four components of aggregate expenditure.

1.2 Why is the *AD* curve downward sloping?

1.3 What is the primary reason that households and firms demand money? Why is the demand for real money balances downward sloping?

1.4 How does an increase in the interest rate affect each of the following categories of aggregate expenditure?

   a. Investment spending by firms on plant and equipment

   b. Consumption spending by households

   c. Net exports

Problems and Applications

1.5 Briefly explain whether each of the following events would shift the aggregate demand curve to the right or to the left.

   a. The Federal Reserve lowers the target for the federal funds rate.

   b. The federal government launches a massive program to rebuild the nation's highways.

   c. The federal government cuts the corporate profits tax.

   d. The foreign exchange value of the dollar rises.

   e. Firms become pessimistic about the future profitability of spending on factories and equipment.

1.6 Use a money market graph to explain the effect of a decrease in the price level on the equilibrium interest rate. How does the change in the interest rate affect planned investment spending, consumption spending, and net exports?

1.7 Stanley Fischer, vice-chair of the Federal Reserve, remarked that fluctuations in the exchange rate affects aggregate demand in the United States: "So that is the channel through which the exchange rate will affect our decisions."

   a. To which decisions would Fischer likely have been referring? Why would the Fed need to take into account the effect of movements in the exchange rate when making these decisions?

   b. Are there ways other than through their effects on aggregate demand that changes in exchange rates can affect the U.S. economy?

(You may want to review the discussion in Chapter 8, Section 8.1.)

Source: Ben Leubsdorf, "Fischer Says Fed Officials Will Watch Dollar for Impact on Aggregate Demand," *Wall Street Journal*, October 9, 2014.

1.8 In the early to mid-2000s, stock prices and housing prices rose substantially. What effect would these increases in household wealth have on the saving rate and on consumption spending? How would the increase in stock prices and housing prices have affected aggregate demand?

1.9 Shortly before leaving her position as chair of the President's Council of Economic Advisers in the Obama administration, Christina Romer observed: "The only surefire ways for policymakers to substantially increase aggregate demand in the short run are for the government to spend more and tax less." Which policymakers was Romer referring to? Briefly explain why the government's spending more and taxing less increases aggregate demand.

Source: Deborah Solomon, "Romer: 'Spend More, Tax Less' to Boost Economy," *Wall Street Journal*, September 1, 2010.

17.2 The Aggregate Supply Curve

Explain how the aggregate supply curve is derived.

Review Questions

2.1 How do the slopes of the short-run aggregate supply curve and the long-run aggregate supply curve differ?

2.2 In the new classical view, why can't firms distinguish between increases in the general price level and increases in the relative prices of their products?

2.3 What is meant by the term *price stickiness* in the new Keynesian view? What explains price stickiness?

2.4 What factors shift the short-run aggregate supply curve? What factors shift the long-run aggregate supply curve?

Problems and Applications

2.5 Use the equation $Y = Y^P + a(P - P^e)$ to explain why in the new classical view, the short-run aggregate supply curve is positively sloped and the long-run aggregate supply curve is vertical.

2.6 Draw graphs to show the effect of each of the following on the short-run aggregate supply curve:

a. A decrease in the expected price level

b. A decrease in oil prices

c. The development of laptop computers that are 10 times faster than existing laptops

d. An increase in wages, resulting from output exceeding the full-employment level of output

e. Severe winter storms that affect a large part of the United States

2.7 In an opinion column on bloomberg.com, economist Tyler Cowen of George Mason University notes: "Keynesian economics focuses on sticky nominal wages as one obstacle to increasing production." Briefly explain what he means.

Source: Tyler Cowen, "Maybe Supply-Side Economics Deserves a Second Look," bloomberg.com, September 7, 2016.

2.8 In 2015, the Chinese government announced that it would switch from relying on stimulating the economy through expansions in aggregate demand to relying on expansions in aggregate supply. According to a Chinese news site, the government had decided that "the best way to stimulate economic growth is to lower barriers to production, particularly through tax cuts." What kind of tax cuts did the government likely have in mind? How would these tax cuts serve to increase aggregate supply?

Source: "What Is China's Supply-Side Reform?" news. xinhuanet.com, December 22, 2015.

2.9 If the long-run aggregate supply curve shifts, does the short-run aggregate supply curve also have to shift? If the short-run aggregate supply curve shifts, does the long-run aggregate supply curve also have to shift? (Hint: Consider the factors that shift each curve and determine whether these factors also shift the other curve.)

2.10 [Related to the Making the Connection on page 592] Hydraulic fracturing has caused a dramatic reduction in the cost of producing natural gas and petroleum.

a. Briefly explain which industries are likely to be most directly affected by these cost reductions.

b. How will aggregate supply be affected by what happens in these industries as a result of the cost reductions from fracking? Is the effect likely to be greater in the short run or in the long run? Briefly explain.

17.3 Equilibrium in the Aggregate Demand and Aggregate Supply Model
Demonstrate macroeconomic equilibrium using the aggregate demand and aggregate supply model.

Review Questions

3.1 In a graph illustrating the *AD–AS* model, where does short-run equilibrium occur, and where does long-run equilibrium occur? At what level of output does long-run equilibrium occur?

3.2 When the economy is in a short-run equilibrium, with output greater than potential GDP, what will happen to the short-run aggregate supply curve? Briefly explain.

3.3 Suppose that the economy is initially in equilibrium at potential GDP. If there is a decrease in aggregate demand, use an *AD–AS* graph to show the effects on the price level and the output level in the short run and in the long run.

3.4 Does monetary neutrality mean that changes in the money supply can never affect real GDP? Briefly explain.

Problems and Applications

3.5 Can the economy be in a short-run macroeconomic equilibrium without being in a long-run macroeconomic equilibrium? Can the economy be in a long-run macroeconomic equilibrium without being in a short-run macroeconomic equilibrium? Support your answers with an *AD–AS* graph.

3.6 In an opinion column in the *Wall Street Journal* in 2016, Harvard economist Martin Feldstein referred to "a possible negative shock—such as

a sharp fall in exports or in construction—that could push the economy into a new recession." Briefly explain whether he was referring to a shock to aggregate demand or to aggregate supply. Illustrate your answer with an *AD–AS* graph.
Source: Martin Feldstein, "Federal Reserve Oblivious to Its Effect on Financial Markets," *Wall Street Journal*, January 13, 2016.

3.7 Suppose that in Year 1 the price level equals 110 and the output level equals $14 trillion and that in Year 2 the price level equals 104 and the output level equals $13 trillion. In the *AD–AS* model, what shift in the aggregate demand curve or the aggregate supply curve would explain the movement in the price level and the output level that occurred from Year 1 to Year 2?

3.8 Assume that the economy is initially in equilibrium at potential GDP. Use an *AD–AS* graph to show the effect of an increase in government purchases on the price level and the output level in the short run and in the long run. Explain what is happening in your graph.

3.9 Assume that the economy is initially in equilibrium at potential GDP. Suppose that there is a decrease in income in Europe that causes a decrease in demand for U.S.-produced goods. Use an *AD–AS* graph to show the effect of the decline in income in Europe on output and the price level in the United States in the short run and in the long run.

3.10 A Federal Reserve publication notes:

> During recessions, decreases in consumption [from an increase in saving] could inhibit economic recovery. However, in the long run, the accumulated money from individual savers is available for capital investment, a situation where businesses borrow to purchase capital (e.g., machinery and technology).

a. Briefly explain why decreases in consumption might inhibit economic recovery. Illustrate your answer with an *AD–AS* graph.

b. Use an *AD–AS* graph to illustrate the effect on the economy in the long run of the increase in saving described in the second sentence of the quotation.

Source: E. Katarina Vermann, "'Wait, Is Saving Good or Bad? The Paradox of Thrift,'" Federal Reserve Bank of St. Louis *Page One Economics*, May 2012.

17.4 | **The Effects of Monetary Policy**
Use the aggregate demand and aggregate supply model to show the effects of monetary policy on the economy.

Review Questions

4.1 Are all business cycles the same in terms of length and severity?

4.2 Why might attempts to fine-tune the economy be ineffective? Instead of fine-tuning, what do economists generally advocate that policymakers do?

4.3 What policies might the Federal Reserve use to counteract an aggregate demand shock?

4.4 What is hysteresis, and what problems might it pose for an economy?

Problems and Applications

4.5 The Federal Reserve can use expansionary or contractionary policy to shift the aggregate demand curve. Use an *AD–AS* graph to show how monetary policy should be used to return output to potential GDP when:

a. The aggregate demand curve intersects the short-run aggregate supply curve to the left of potential GDP.

b. The aggregate demand curve intersects the short-run aggregate supply curve to the right of potential GDP.

4.6 Given that the economy can correct itself and return to potential GDP, why would the Federal Reserve pursue expansionary monetary policy following a negative aggregate demand shock? How could the Fed pursuing an expansionary monetary policy be preferable to the economy correcting itself? Is it possible that an expansionary monetary policy could hurt the economy, given the lags in the impact of monetary policy actions? Briefly explain.

4.7 [Related to the Solved Problem 17.4 on page 602] Assume that the economy is initially in equilibrium at potential GDP. Then suppose that the economy is hit simultaneously with a *positive* aggregate demand shock and a *negative* aggregate supply shock: There is a large increase in U.S. exports to Europe and a large increase in oil prices.

a. Use an *AD–AS* graph to illustrate the initial equilibrium and the short-run equilibrium after the shocks. Do we know with certainty whether in the new equilibrium the output level will be higher or lower than potential GDP?

b. Suppose that the Fed decides not to intervene with monetary policy. Show how the economy will adjust back to long-run equilibrium.

c. Now suppose that the Fed decides to intervene with monetary policy. If the Fed's policy is successful, show how the economy adjusts back to long-run equilibrium.

4.8 Normally we think of the factors that cause the *AD* curve to shift as being different from the factors that cause the *LRAS* curve to shift. Is this still true in the case of hysteresis? Briefly explain.

4.9 [Related to the Chapter Opener on page 579] In a speech in June 2016, Jerome Powell, a member of the Federal Reserve's Board of Governors, noted that the fraction of the U.S. population aged 25 to 54 who were working or actively looking for work "is now below those of most other advanced economies, including the U.K., France and Germany, for example." He also stated: "I am inclined to believe that there are potential workers at the margins of the labor market who will return as the recovery continues."

a. Briefly explain how Governor Powell's two statements are related.

b. Why is it important for the Federal Reserve to accurately estimate how many people might still be brought back into the labor market as an economic recovery continues? Why might it be difficult for the Fed to make such estimates? What potential policy errors might the Fed make if its estimates are inaccurate?

Source: Jerome H. Powell, "Recent Economic Developments, Monetary Policy Considerations and Longer-Term Prospects," remarks at the Chicago Council on Global Affairs Chicago, Illinois, June 28, 2016.

4.10 [Related to the Making the Connection on page 605] Writing in the *New York Times*, economist Tyler Cowen of George Mason University argued:

In short, expansionary monetary policy and wartime orders from Europe, not the well-known policies of the New Deal, did the most to make the American economy climb out of the Depression.

Is Cowen's position more consistent with that of Robert Gordon or that of Robert Higgs? Briefly explain.

Source: Tyler Cowen, "The New Deal Didn't Always Work, Either," *New York Times*, November 21, 2008.

4.11 [Related to the Making the Connection on page 605] Economist Robert Gordon has written the following:

During 1939, more than any other year in the dismal Depression decade, the American economy exhibited every evidence of slipping into a low-employment trap. Prices were on a plateau, with no tendency to decline, despite high unemployment.

a. What does Gordon mean by a "low-employment trap"? (Hint: Think about Gordon's explanation for the high unemployment rate in 1939, as discussed in the *Making the Connection*.)

b. Why might the fact that prices were not declining despite high unemployment lead Gordon to conclude that the economy was in a low-employment trap?

Source: Robert J. Gordon, "Back to the Future: European Unemployment Today Viewed from America in 1939," *Brookings Papers on Economic Activity*, Vol. 19, No. 1, 1988, p. 272.

4.12 [Related to the Making the Connection on page 605] In 2016, a columnist for the *Wall Street Journal* wrote:

For years, the world has looked to central banks to deploy whatever tools they had to prop up economic growth. Now, just as those tools reach their limits, governments are quietly stepping up. Fiscal policy across the developed world is collectively turning more stimulative.

a. What tools were central banks using to "prop up growth"?

b. Why might some economists have believed that in 2016 those tools had reached their limits?

c. What is fiscal policy? What does it mean to say that fiscal policy was "turning more stimulative"?

Source: Greg Ip, "Fiscal Policy Makes a Quiet Turn Toward Stimulus," *Wall Street Journal*, September 14, 2016.

Data Exercises

D17.1: **[Showing movements in equilibrium real GDP and the price level]** Go to the web site of the Federal Reserve Bank of St. Louis (FRED) (fred.stlouisfed.org) and find data on real GDP (GDPCA) and the GDP price deflator (USAGDPDEFAISMEI) for 1960, 1973, 1975, and 2007.

    a. In an *AD–AS* graph, using the actual values for real GDP and the GDP price deflator, show equilibrium for 1960 and for 2007. Assume that the economy was at equilibrium at potential GDP in both years. From 1960 to 2007, what happened to long-run aggregate supply? Given the change in the GDP implicit price deflator, did aggregate demand grow more or less than long-run aggregate supply?

    b. In an *AD–AS* graph, using the actual values for real GDP and the GDP price deflator, show equilibrium for 1973 and for 1975. Assume that the economy was in equilibrium at potential GDP in 1973 but in only a short-run equilibrium in 1975. Given the changes in real GDP and the GDP implicit price deflator, briefly explain what happened to short-run aggregate supply from 1973 to 1975.

D17.2: **[The effects of a positive supply shock]** Using data from the St. Louis Federal Reserve (fred.stlouisfed.org) FRED database, examine the experience of the U.S. economy during the 1990s. The U.S. economy experienced a supply shock with the spread of information communication technology and the Internet after 1995.

    a. Download monthly data on the Personal Consumption Expenditure price index (PCEPI) from 1981 to the present. Calculate the inflation rate from 1982 to 2007 as the percentage change in the Personal Consumption Expenditure price index from the same month in the previous year.

    b. Calculate the average inflation rate from 1982 to 1995 and the average inflation rate from 1995 to 2007.

    c. Are your calculations consistent with a positive supply shock after 1995? Briefly explain.

D17.3: **[Comparing business cycles across countries]** During the 2007–2009 period, shocks affected the United Kingdom in ways similar to the United States. As in the United States, oil prices were high, and housing prices had sharply escalated after 2000. The financial crisis in the United States also affected investment in the United Kingdom, both by limiting credit and increasing risk premiums. Using data from the St. Louis Federal Reserve (fred.stlouisfed.org) FRED database, examine the behavior of the U.K. economy since 2007.

    a. Download quarterly data for real GDP (RGDPMPUKQ) and the GDP deflator (GBRGDPDEFQISMEI) from 2006 to the present. Calculate the growth rate of real GDP as the percentage change from the same quarter in the previous year and calculate the inflation rate as the percentage change in the GDP deflator from the same quarter in the previous year. Download data on the unemployment rate (GBRURHARMMDSMEI) for the same time period.

    b. Download the three data series from 2007 to the present in the same graph. After examining the data, briefly discuss how similar the experiences were of the United Kingdom and the United States during these years.

CHAPTER 18

Monetary Theory II: The *IS–MP* Model

Learning Objectives

After studying this chapter, you should be able to:

18.1 Explain what the *IS* curve is and how it is derived (pages 615–626)

18.2 Explain the significance of the *MP* curve and the Phillips curve (pages 626–633)

18.3 Use the *IS–MP* model to illustrate macroeconomic equilibrium (pages 633–643)

18.4 Discuss alternative channels of monetary policy (pages 643–646)

18.A Appendix: Use the *IS–LM* model to illustrate macroeconomic equilibrium (pages 654–657)

Forecasting the Federal Funds Rate Is Difficult … Even for the Fed!

At the end of 2016, many economists wondered why more than seven years after the end of the recession of 2007–2009, the Federal Open Market Committee (FOMC) had implemented only two small (0.25%) increases in its target for the federal funds rate. These two increases brought the target to a still historically low range of 0.50% to 0.75%. Some members of the FOMC worried about the consequences of keeping interest rates so low for so long. Federal Reserve Bank of Boston President Eric Rosengren cautioned that by not raising interest rates more quickly, the Fed was running the risk of allowing the U.S. economy to overheat: "It is important to note that an overheated economy—one that significantly exceeds sustainable out-put and employment—would pose risks to maintaining full employment over time." At about the same time, Federal Reserve Bank of San Francisco President John Williams made a similar point: "History teaches us that an economy that runs too hot for too long can generate imbalances, potentially leading to excessive inflation, asset market bubbles, and ultimately economic correction and recession."

In fact, as a group, the FOMC had expected that their target for the federal funds rate would be considerably higher in 2016 than it actually was. For instance, at the end of 2013, the participants in the discussion at the December FOMC meeting (all 12 Reserve Bank presidents and the 7 members of the Board of Governors

Continued on next page

KEY ISSUE AND QUESTION

Issue: By December 2008, the Federal Reserve had driven the target for the federal funds rate to near zero.

Question: In what circumstances is lowering the target for the federal funds rate unlikely to be effective in fighting a recession?

Answered on page 646

participate in FOMC discussions), expected that the target would be higher by the end of 2016 by an average of about 1.5 percentage points than it actually was. Typically, increases in the federal funds rate are reflected in other short-term interest rates. So, if the federal funds rate had been higher, interest rates on Treasury bills, bank CDs, and money market mutual funds would also have been higher, thereby increasing the return savers receive on these assets.

Long-term interest rates also typically rise as the federal funds rate rises, although the relationship is less certain. So, Treasury bond rates and rates on business loans and mortgages would likely have been higher as a result of a higher federal funds rate. In fact, a key reason that Boston Fed President Rosengren was concerned about the Fed's keeping interest rates so low for so long was that he feared low interest rates on commercial real estate mortgages may have been causing a bubble in prices in that market.

Why had FOMC members a few years earlier expected that their target for the federal funds rate in 2016 would be higher than it actually was? A key reason is that for most of the period since the end of the Great Recession, FOMC members had expected both the growth rate of real GDP and the inflation rate to be higher than they actually were. Slow growth rates of GDP and low inflation rates had convinced FOMC members to keep the target for the federal funds rate very low for longer than they had expected to.

In determining monetary policy, the Fed's forecasts of future economic growth and inflation are crucial. The Fed knows that changes in interest rates and the money supply affect the economy with a lag, so policies the Fed implements today will not have their full effect on the economy for a year or more. Therefore, having some idea of the likely state of the economy in the future helps to guide policy today. In preparing its forecasts, the Fed, foreign central banks, and private forecasters usually rely on macroeconomic models. In this chapter, we explore a model that helps us analyze how Fed policies affect key macroeconomic variables.

Sources: Eric S. Rosengren, "Exploring the Economy's Progress and Outlook," speech to the South Shore Chamber of Commerce Quincy, Massachusetts, September 9, 2016; John C. Williams, "Whiter Inflation Targeting," presentation to the Hayek Group, Reno, Nevada, September 6, 2016; Federal Reserve Open Market Committee, "Economic Projections of Federal Reserve Board Members and Federal Reserve Bank Presidents, December 2013," December 18, 2013; and David Harrison, "Fed's Eric Rosengren Sees 'Reasonable Case' for Gradual Rate Increases," *Wall Street Journal*, September 9, 2016.

In the previous chapter, we discussed the basic aggregate demand and aggregate supply (*AD–AS*) model. Although that model provides insights into how the price level and the level of real GDP are determined in the short run, it has some important shortcomings. First, the *AD–AS* model implicitly assumes that the full-employment level of real GDP remains constant when, in fact, it increases each year. Second, the model provides an explanation of the price level but not of *changes* in the price level—the inflation rate. Yet typically we are more interested in the inflation rate than we are in the price level. Finally, the model doesn't explicitly take into account how the Fed reacts to changing economic conditions. In this chapter, we develop a model that provides a more thorough explanation of changes in real GDP, the inflation rate, and the interest rate.

The *IS–MP model* is a more complete macroeconomic model than is the *AD–AS* model.[1] We can use the *IS–MP* model to provide a more detailed analysis of the effects of Federal Reserve policy. Note that to be useful, every model must simplify reality. The *IS–MP* model is more complete than the *AD–AS* model and can answer

---

[1] Economists love acronyms, even if they can sometimes be mysterious. In this case, *IS* stands for investment and saving, while *MP* stands for monetary policy. For a discussion of the historical origins of this model, see the *Making the Connection* on pages 634–635.

questions that the *AD–AS* model cannot. But the *IS–MP* model is less complete than many other macroeconomic models, including some that the Fed uses to prepare its forecasts. Whether a model is too simplified—or not simplified enough—depends on the context in which the model is being used. For our purposes, the *IS–MP* model is sufficiently complete to explain the key aspects of Federal Reserve policy.

The **IS–MP model** consists of three parts:

1. The **IS curve**, which represents equilibrium in the market for goods and services
2. The **MP curve**, which represents Federal Reserve monetary policy
3. The **Phillips curve**, which represents the short-run relationship between the output gap (which is the percentage difference between actual and potential real GDP) and the inflation rate

We begin by analyzing the *IS* curve.

 ## 18.1 The *IS* Curve

LEARNING OBJECTIVE: Explain what the *IS* curve is and how it is derived.

Equilibrium in the Goods Market

The *goods market* includes trade in all final goods and services that the economy produces at a particular point in time. Recall that gross domestic product (GDP)—for which we use the symbol Y—is the market value of all final goods and services produced in a country during a period of time, typically one year. Nominal GDP is calculated using the current year's prices, while real GDP is calculated using the prices in a base year. Because real GDP gives a good measure of a country's output, corrected for changes in the price level, it is the measure of aggregate output that we will use in this chapter.

Equilibrium occurs in the goods market when the value of goods and services demanded equals the value of goods and services produced—real GDP. Economists call total spending on goods and services *aggregate expenditure (AE)*. AE is equal to the sum of:

- Consumption demand by households, C
- Demand for investment in business plant and equipment, business inventories, and housing, I
- Government purchases of goods and services, G
- Net exports (or exports of goods and services minus imports of goods and services), NX

So, aggregate expenditure, *AE*, is:

$$AE = C + I + G + NX.$$

At equilibrium in the goods, *AE* equals real GDP, Y:

$$AE = Y.$$

The *IS* curve represents equilibrium in the goods market.

IS–MP model A macroeconomic model that consists of an *IS* curve, which represents equilibrium in the goods market; an *MP* curve, which represents monetary policy; and a Phillips curve, which represents the short-run relationship between the output gap (which is the percentage difference between actual and potential real GDP) and the inflation rate.

IS curve A curve in the *IS–MP* model that shows the combinations of the real interest rate and aggregate output that represent equilibrium in the market for goods and services.

MP curve A curve in the *IS–MP* model that represents Federal Reserve monetary policy.

Phillips curve A curve that shows the short-run relationship between the output gap (or the unemployment rate) and the inflation rate.

What if aggregate expenditure is less than real GDP? In that case, some goods that were produced are not sold, and inventories of unsold goods will increase. For example, if General Motors produces and ships to dealers 250,000 cars in a particular month but sells only 225,000, inventories of cars on the lots of GM's dealers will rise by 25,000 cars. (Notice that because inventories are counted as part of investment in the federal government's economic statistics, in this situation, *actual investment spending* will be greater than *planned investment spending*.) If the decline in demand is affecting not just automobiles but other goods as well, firms are likely to reduce production and lay off workers: Real GDP and employment will decline, and the economy will be in a recession.

If aggregate expenditure is greater than GDP, however, spending will be greater than production, and firms will sell more goods and services than they had expected to sell. If General Motors produces 250,000 cars but sells 300,000, then inventories of cars on dealers' lots will decline by 50,000 cars. (In this case, because firms are unexpectedly drawing down inventories, actual investment spending will be *less* than planned investment spending.) The dealers will be likely to increase their orders from GM's factories. If sales exceed production, not just for automobiles but for other goods as well, firms are likely to increase production and hire more workers: Real GDP and employment will increase, and the economy will be in an expansion.

Only when aggregate expenditure equals GDP will firms sell what they expected to sell. In that case, firms will experience no unexpected changes in their inventories, and they will not have an incentive to increase or decrease production. The goods market will be in equilibrium. Table 18.1 summarizes the relationship between aggregate expenditure and GDP.

Recall from your principles of economics course that using the *45°-line diagram* is one way to illustrate equilibrium in the goods market. The 45°-line diagram analysis is based on the simplifying assumption that of the four components of aggregate expenditure—C, I, G, and NX—changes in real GDP affect only C, consumption spending. To see why consumption depends on GDP, remember that when we measure the value of total production, we are at the same time measuring the value of total income. For example, when you buy a pizza at Domino's for $10, the whole $10—leaving aside the sales tax you pay—becomes someone's income. Some of the $10 becomes wages for the person cooking the pizza, some becomes profit for Domino's, and so on. If we add up the value of all the goods and services purchased, we have also added up all the current income produced during that period in the economy. (Sales taxes and some

TABLE 18.1 The Relationship Between Aggregate Expenditure and GDP

If aggregate expenditure is ...	then ...	and ...
equal to GDP	there are no unexpected changes in inventories	the goods market is in equilibrium.
less than GDP	inventories rise	GDP and employment decrease.
greater than GDP	inventories fall	GDP and employment increase.

other relatively minor items cause there to be a difference between the value for GDP and the value for *national income*, as shown in the federal government's statistics. But this difference is not important for our purposes.)

Studies have shown that households spend more when their current income is rising and spend less when their current income is falling.[2] The relationship between current consumption spending and current income, or GDP, is called the *consumption function*. Algebraically, we can write:

$$C = MPC \times Y,$$

where *MPC* stands for the marginal propensity to consume and is a number between zero and 1. If we look at the effect of changes in GDP on consumption, then $MPC = \Delta C/\Delta Y$, or the change in consumption divided by the change in GDP, or income. For instance, if the *MPC* is equal to 0.90, then households are spending $0.90 of every additional dollar they earn.

Because we are focusing on the effect of changes in GDP on aggregate expenditure, assuming that *I*, *G*, and *NX* don't depend on GDP is the same as assuming that their values are fixed. We can designate a variable with a bar over it as having a fixed value. So, we have the following expression for aggregate expenditure, substituting in the expression above for *C*:

$$AE = (MPC \times Y) + \bar{I} + \bar{G} + \overline{NX}.$$

Figure 18.1 shows equilibrium in the goods market using the 45°-line diagram. On the vertical axis, we measure total spending in the economy, or aggregate expenditure, *AE*. On the horizontal axis, we measure real GDP, or real total income, *Y*. The 45° line represents all points that are equal distances from the two axes, or in this case, all the points where *AE* = *Y*. Therefore, any point along the 45° line is potentially a point of equilibrium in the goods market. At any given time, though, there is just one equilibrium, which occurs at the point where the aggregate expenditure line crosses the 45° line. We draw the aggregate expenditure line as upward sloping because as GDP increases, consumption spending increases, while the other components of aggregate expenditure remain constant.

Panel (a) of Figure 18.1 shows that equilibrium in the goods market occurs at output level Y_1, where the *AE* line crosses the 45° line. Panel (b) shows why the goods market is not in equilibrium at other levels of output. For example, if the level of output is initially Y_2, aggregate expenditure is only AE_2. With spending less than production, there is an unexpected increase in inventories. Rising inventories cause firms to cut production, and output will fall until equilibrium is reached at Y_1. If the output level is initially Y_3, aggregate expenditure is AE_3. With spending greater than production, there is an unexpected decrease in inventories. Falling inventories cause firms to increase production, and output will increase until equilibrium is reached at Y_1.

---

[2] Many economists believe that consumption is better explained by a household's *permanent income* than by its current income. A household's permanent income is the level of income that it expects to receive over time. A household's current income might differ from its permanent income due to a temporary job loss, an illness, winning a lottery, having a year of particularly high or low investment income, and so forth. For our purposes, we can ignore this complication.

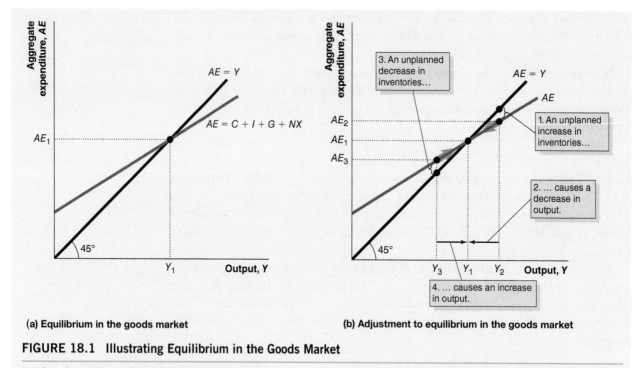

(a) Equilibrium in the goods market

(b) Adjustment to equilibrium in the goods market

FIGURE 18.1 Illustrating Equilibrium in the Goods Market

Panel (a) shows that equilibrium in the goods market occurs at output level Y_1, where the AE line crosses the 45° line. In panel (b), if the level of output is initially Y_2, aggregate expenditure is only AE_2. Rising inventories cause firms to cut production, and output will fall until equilibrium is reached at Y_1. If the output level is initially Y_3, aggregate expenditure is AE_3. Falling inventories cause firms to increase production, and output will increase until equilibrium is reached at Y_1.

Potential GDP and the Multiplier Effect

In Figure 18.1, Y_1 is the equilibrium level of GDP, but it is not necessarily the level policymakers want to achieve. The Fed's goal is to have equilibrium GDP close to **potential GDP**, which is the level of real GDP attained when all firms are producing at normal capacity. The normal capacity of a firm is *not* the maximum output the firm is capable of producing. Rather, it is the firm's production when operating on normal hours, using a workforce of normal size. At potential GDP, the economy achieves full employment, and cyclical unemployment is reduced to zero. So, potential GDP is sometimes called *full-employment GDP*. The level of potential GDP increases over time as the labor force grows, new factories and office buildings are built, new machinery and equipment are installed, and technological change takes place.

In Figure 18.2, we see what happens if the economy is initially in equilibrium at potential GDP, Y^P, and then aggregate expenditure falls. Assume that spending on residential construction declines, so the investment component, I, of aggregate expenditure falls. As a result, the aggregate expenditure line shifts down from AE_1 to AE_2. With spending now below production, there is an unintended increase in inventories. Firms respond to the inventory buildup by cutting production, and output declines until a new equilibrium is reached at Y_2. Note that the decline in output is greater than the decline in investment spending that caused it. In the context of this basic macroeconomic

Potential GDP The level of real GDP attained when all firms are producing at normal capacity.

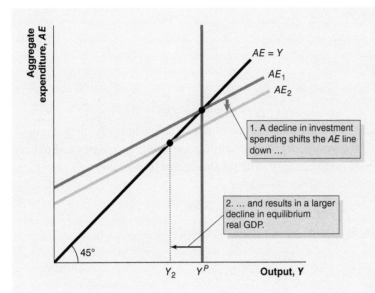

FIGURE 18.2

The Multiplier Effect

The economy is initially in equilibrium at potential GDP, Y^P, and then the investment component, I, of aggregate expenditure falls. As a result, the aggregate expenditure line shifts down from AE_1 to AE_2. Output declines until a new equilibrium is reached at Y_2. The decline in output is greater than the decline in investment spending that caused it.

model, *autonomous expenditure* is expenditure that does not depend on the level of GDP. So, investment spending, government purchases, and net exports are all autonomous, while consumption spending is not. A decline in autonomous expenditure results initially in an equivalent decline in income, which then leads to an *induced* decline in consumption. For example, as spending on residential construction declines, homebuilders cut production, lay off workers, and cut their demand for construction materials. Falling incomes in the construction industry lead individuals who work in that industry to reduce their spending on cars, furniture, appliances, and other goods and services. As production declines in those industries, so does income, leading to further declines in consumption, and so on.

The series of induced changes in consumption spending that result from an initial change in autonomous expenditure is called the **multiplier effect**. The **multiplier** is the change in equilibrium GDP divided by a change in autonomous expenditure. In symbols, the multiplier for a change in investment spending is:

$$\text{Multiplier} = \frac{\Delta Y}{\Delta I}.$$

How large is the multiplier? It is quite large in our simple model. To see this, recall that our expression for aggregate expenditure is:

$$AE = (MPC \times Y) + \bar{I} + \bar{G} + \overline{NX},$$

and that at equilibrium:

$$Y = AE.$$

Multiplier effect The process by which a change in autonomous expenditure leads to a larger change in equilibrium GDP.

Multiplier The change in equilibrium GDP divided by a change in autonomous expenditure.

Substituting, we have:

$$Y = (MPC \times Y) + \bar{I} + \bar{G} + \overline{NX},$$

or, rearranging terms:

$$Y = \frac{\bar{I} + \bar{G} + \overline{NX}}{(1 - MPC)}.$$

We can use this equation to analyze how much a change in investment changes equilibrium real GDP. If investment changes, while government purchases and net exports remain unchanged (so the change in their values equal 0), we have:

$$\Delta Y = \frac{\Delta I}{(1 - MPC)},$$

or, rearranging terms, we have an equation for the multiplier:

$$\frac{\Delta Y}{\Delta I} = \frac{1}{(1 - MPC)}.$$

If, as we assumed earlier, *MPC* is equal to 0.9, the value of the multiplier equals:

$$\frac{\Delta Y}{\Delta I} = \frac{1}{(1 - 0.9)} = \frac{1}{0.1} = 10.$$

In other words, a decline in investment spending of $1 billion would lead to a decline in equilibrium real GDP of $10 billion. When multiplier analysis was first developed in the 1930s by John Maynard Keynes and his colleagues, they believed that a large multiplier effect helped to explain the severity of the Great Depression: With a large multiplier, a relatively small decline in investment spending could have led to the large declines in GDP experienced in the United States and Europe.[3]

SOLVED PROBLEM 18.1

Calculating Equilibrium Real GDP

Use the following data to calculate the equilibrium level of real GDP and the value of the investment spending multiplier:

$$C = MPC \times Y = 0.8 \times Y$$
$$\bar{I} = \$1.6 \text{ trillion}$$
$$\bar{G} = \$1.3 \text{ trillion}$$
$$\overline{NX} = -\$0.4 \text{ trillion}$$

[3] Keynes thought that the value of the multiplier could be as large as 10. (John Maynard Keynes, *The General Theory of Employment, Interest, and Money*, London: Macmillan, 1936, p. 51.) Because macroeconomic statistics were not yet available in the 1930s, Keynes was unable to provide more than a rough estimate of the multiplier. He did note (p. 56) that Simon Kuznets's early estimates of investment and national income for the United States implied a multiplier of about 2.5. But Keynes thought the value of the *MPC* used in the calculation was "implausibly low," given the economic conditions in the United States during the 1930s.

Solving the Problem

Step 1 **Review the chapter material.** This problem is about calculating equilibrium real GDP and the value of the multiplier, so you may want to review the section "Equilibrium in the Goods Market," which begins on page 615, and the section "Potential GDP and the Multiplier Effect," which begins on page 618.

Step 2 **Use the data to calculate equilibrium real GDP.** We know that at equilibrium, aggregate expenditure equals real GDP. The expression for aggregate expenditure is:

$$AE = (MPC \times Y) + \bar{I} + \bar{G} + \overline{NX}.$$

So, at equilibrium:

$$Y = AE = (MPC \times Y) + \bar{I} + \bar{G} + \overline{NX}.$$

Substituting the values above gives us:

$$Y = 0.8Y + \$1.6 \text{ trillion} + \$1.3 \text{ trillion} + (-\$0.4 \text{ trillion})$$
$$Y = 0.8Y + \$2.5 \text{ trillion}$$
$$0.2Y = \$2.5 \text{ trillion}$$
$$Y = \frac{\$2.5 \text{ trillion}}{0.2} = \$12.5 \text{ trillion}$$

Step 3 **Calculate the value of the multiplier from the data given.** The equation for the investment spending multiplier is:

$$\frac{\Delta Y}{\Delta I} = \frac{1}{(1 - MPC)}.$$

With $MPC = 0.8$, the value of the multiplier is:

$$\frac{1}{(1 - 0.8)} = \frac{1}{0.2} = 5.$$

See related problem 1.6 at the end of the chapter.

Keynes and his followers believed in a large value for the multiplier, which led them to be optimistic about the effectiveness of fiscal policy. **Fiscal policy** refers to changes in federal government purchases and taxes intended to achieve macroeconomic policy objectives. Just as there is a multiplier for investment spending, there is a multiplier for government purchases:

$$\frac{\Delta Y}{\Delta G} = \frac{1}{(1 - MPC)}.$$

So, if the MPC is 0.9, the government purchases multiplier will also equal 10. In this case, if real GDP is $200 billion below its potential level, Congress and the president could bring real GDP back to potential GDP using fiscal policy by increasing government purchases by $20 billion (= $200 billion/10).

Fiscal policy Changes in federal government purchases and taxes intended to achieve macroeconomic policy objectives.

In fact, though, early estimates of the size of the multiplier turned out to be much too large. Our simple model—similar to those Keynes and his followers used in the 1930s—neglects several factors that cause the multiplier to be smaller than the value we have given here. These real-world complications include the effect that increases in GDP have on several variables: imports, the price level, interest rates, and individual income taxes.

In early 2009, the Obama administration proposed, and Congress passed, the American Recovery and Reinvestment Act, an $840 billion package of government spending increases and tax cuts that was by far the largest fiscal policy action in U.S. history. In proposing this policy action, White House economists estimated that the government purchases multiplier would have a value of 1.57, meaning that each $1 billion increase in government purchases would increase equilibrium real GDP by $1.57 billion. This estimate is much smaller than the simple multiplier of 10 that we computed earlier. But some economists argued that even an estimate of 1.57 is too high. A few economists argued that the government purchases multiplier has a value of less than 1. Estimating an exact number for the multiplier is difficult because after Congress and the president engage in a fiscal policy action, many other things can happen in the economy that affect real GDP. So, isolating the effect of a change in government purchases is not an easy task, and the debate over the size of the multiplier will likely continue.

Constructing the *IS* Curve

As we saw in Chapter 15, normally the focus of Fed policy is establishing a target for the federal funds rate, with the expectation that changes in the federal funds rate will cause changes in other market interest rates. Therefore, we need to incorporate the effect of changes in interest rates into the model of the goods market.

Movements in the interest rate affect three components of aggregate expenditure: consumption, C; investment, I; and net exports, NX. We are interested in the real interest rate, which is the interest rate most relevant to the decisions of households and firms in this context. Recall that the real interest rate equals the nominal interest rate minus the expected inflation rate. An increase in the real interest rate makes firms less willing to invest in plant and equipment and makes households less likely to purchase new houses, so I declines. Similarly, an increase in the real interest rate gives consumers an incentive to save rather than to spend, so C declines. And a higher domestic real interest rate increases returns on domestic financial assets relative to returns on foreign assets, increasing the demand for the domestic currency, thereby raising the exchange rate. The rise in the exchange rate increases imports and reduces exports, so NX declines. A decrease in the real interest rate will have the opposite effect—increasing I, C, and NX.

Panel (a) of Figure 18.3 uses the 45°-line diagram to show the effect of changes in the real interest rate on equilibrium in the goods market. With the real interest rate initially at r_1, the aggregate expenditure line is $AE(r_1)$, and the equilibrium level of output is Y_1 (point A). If the interest falls from r_1 to r_2, the aggregate expenditure line shifts up from $AE(r_1)$ to $AE(r_2)$, and the equilibrium level of output increases from Y_1 to Y_2 (point B). If the interest rate rises from r_1 to r_3, the aggregate expenditure line shifts down from $AE(r_1)$ to $AE(r_3)$, and the equilibrium level of output falls from Y_1 to Y_3 (point C).

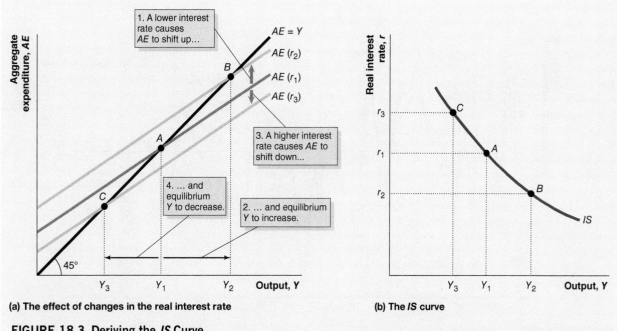

FIGURE 18.3 Deriving the *IS* Curve

Panel (a) uses the 45°-line diagram to show the effect of changes in the real interest rate on equilibrium in the goods market. With the real interest rate initially at r_1, the aggregate expenditure line is $AE(r_1)$, and the equilibrium level of output is Y_1 (point A). If the interest rate falls from r_1 to r_2, the aggregate expenditure line shifts up from $AE(r_1)$ to $AE(r_2)$, and the equilibrium level of output

increases from Y_1 to Y_2 (point B). If the interest rate rises from r_1 to r_3, the aggregate expenditure line shifts down from $AE(r_1)$ to $AE(r_3)$, and the equilibrium level of output falls from Y_1 to Y_3 (point C). In panel (b), we plot the points from panel (a) to form the *IS* curve. The points A, B, and C in panel (b) correspond to the points A, B, and C in panel (a).

In panel (b), we use the results from panel (a) to construct the *IS* curve, which shows the combinations of the real interest rate and total output where the goods market is in equilibrium. We know that at every equilibrium point in the 45°-line diagram in panel (a), aggregate expenditure equals total output, or GDP. In panel (b), we plot these points in a graph that has the real interest rate on the vertical axis and the level of total output on the horizontal axis. The points A, B, and C in panel (b) correspond to the points A, B, and C in panel (a). The *IS* curve is downward sloping because a higher interest rate causes a reduction in aggregate expenditure and a lower equilibrium level of output.

The Output Gap

In Chapter 15, we saw that the *Taylor rule* offers one explanation of the Fed's selection of a target for the federal funds rate. With the Taylor rule, the Fed has a target for the federal funds rate and adjusts that target on the basis of changes in two variables: the inflation gap and the output gap. The *inflation gap* is the difference between the current inflation rate and a target rate, and the **output gap** is the percentage difference between real GDP and potential GDP. Figure 18.4 shows movements in the output gap from 1952 through the second quarter of 2016.

Output gap The percentage difference between real GDP and potential GDP.

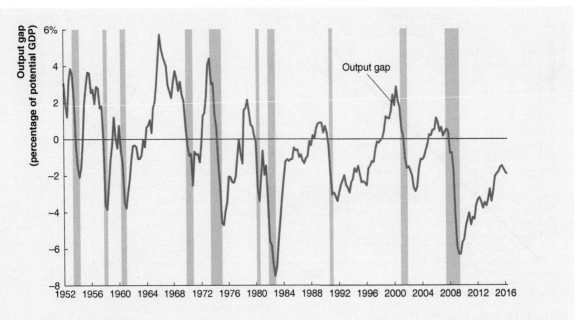

FIGURE 18.4 The Output Gap

The output gap is the percentage difference between real GDP and potential GDP. The output gap is negative during recessions because real GDP is below potential GDP.

Sources: Congressional Budget Office; and U.S. Bureau of Economic Analysis.

During recessions, the output gap is negative because real GDP is below potential GDP. During expansions, the output gap is positive once real GDP has risen above potential GDP. Figure 18.4 shows that the recessions of 1981–1982 and 2007–2009 were the most severe of the post–World War II era, as measured by the size of the output gap. Note that in 2016, seven years after the end of the 2007–2009 recession, the output gap remained negative, with real GDP still below potential GDP.

Because the Federal Reserve focuses on the output gap rather than on the level of real GDP, it would be useful to incorporate the output gap into our macroeconomic model. The graph of the *IS* curve shown in panel (b) of Figure 18.3 has the level of real GDP, rather than the output gap, on the horizontal axis. Can we replace the level of real GDP with the output gap in the *IS* curve graph? We can, with the following qualification: We should think of changes in the real interest rate as affecting the level of investment, consumption, and net exports *relative to potential GDP*. For instance, when the real interest rate falls and C, I, and NX increase, the increase in aggregate expenditure will cause real GDP, Y, to increase relative to potential GDP, Y^P. In that case, when we graph the *IS* curve with the real interest rate on the vertical axis and the output gap on the horizontal axis, the *IS* curve is still downward sloping.

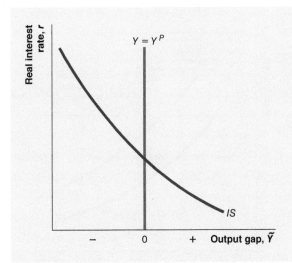

FIGURE 18.5

The *IS* Curve Using the Output Gap

This graph shows the *IS* curve with the output gap, rather than the level of real GDP, on the horizontal axis. Values to the left of zero on the horizontal axis represent negative values for the output gap—or periods of recession—and values to the right of zero on the horizontal axis represent positive values for the output gap—periods of expansion. The vertical line, $Y = Y^P$, is also the point where the output gap is zero.

Figure 18.5 shows the *IS* curve graph with the output gap on the horizontal axis. We use the symbol $\widetilde{Y}$ to distinguish the output gap from real GDP, Y. As a reference, we have included a vertical line where $Y = Y^P$, which is also the point where the output gap is zero. Normally, we draw graphs with the vertical axis beginning at a value of zero on the horizontal axis. In this case, though, our graphs are easier to understand if we move the vertical axis to the left, leaving zero in the middle of the horizontal axis. Note that values to the left of zero on the horizontal axis represent negative values for the output gap—or periods of recession—and values to the right of zero on the horizontal axis represent positive values for the output gap—periods of expansion.

Shifts of the *IS* Curve

We have derived the *IS* curve by looking at the effect of changes in the real interest rate on aggregate expenditure, holding constant all other factors that might affect the willingness of households, firms, and governments to spend. Therefore, an increase or a decrease in the real interest rate results in a *movement along the IS curve*. Changing other factors that affect aggregate expenditure will cause a *shift of the IS curve*. These other factors—apart from changes in the real interest rate—that lead to changes in aggregate expenditure are called **aggregate demand shocks**. For example, as we have seen, spending on residential construction declined rapidly in the United States beginning in 2006. This decline in a component of I was a *negative demand shock* that shifted the *IS* curve to the left. Beginning in mid-2014 and continuing through 2016, spending by state and local governments in the United States increased significantly. This increase in G was a *positive demand shock* that shifted the *IS* curve to the right. Figure 18.6 shows that for any given level of the real interest rate, positive demand shocks shift the *IS* curve to the right and negative demand shocks shift the *IS* curve to the left.

Aggregate demand shock
A change in one of the components of aggregate expenditure that causes the *IS* curve to shift.

FIGURE 18.6

Shifts in the *IS* Curve

For any given level of the real interest rate, positive demand shocks shift the *IS* curve to the right and negative demand shocks shift the *IS* curve to the left.

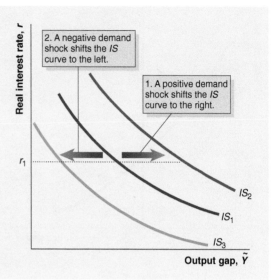

The *MP* Curve and the Phillips Curve

18.2

LEARNING OBJECTIVE: Explain the significance of the *MP* curve and the Phillips curve.

The second piece of the *IS–MP* model is the monetary policy, or *MP*, curve. The *MP* curve represents the Fed's monetary policy actions in setting a target for the federal funds rate following each meeting of the Federal Open Market Committee (FOMC). We assume that the Fed chooses a target for the federal funds rate according to the Taylor rule. Recall from Chapter 15, Section 15.4, the expression for the Taylor rule:

$$\text{Federal funds rate target} = \text{Current inflation rate} + \text{Equilibrium real} \\ \text{federal funds rate} + (1/2 \times \text{Inflation gap}) \\ + (1/2 \times \text{Output gap}).$$

The Taylor rule tells us that when the inflation rate rises above the Fed's target inflation rate of about 2%, as it did during late 2005 and early 2006, the FOMC will raise its target for the federal funds rate. And when the output gap is negative—that is, when real GDP is less than potential GDP, as it began to be in 2008—the FOMC will lower the target for the federal funds rate.

Although the FOMC can control the target for the federal funds rate, which is a short-term nominal interest rate, long-term real interest rates are more relevant in determining the level of aggregate expenditure. For instance, when people decide whether to buy a new house, they consider the real interest rate on 30-year mortgage loans, and when corporations borrow to finance new investment, they look at the real interest rate on long-term corporate bonds. However, short-term interest rates and long-term interest rates tend to rise and fall together. So, when the FOMC raises or lowers its target for the federal funds rate, long-term interest rates typically also rise or fall. Similarly, although the federal funds rate is a nominal interest rate, if expectations of future inflation remain stable, then by raising or lowering its target for the nominal federal funds rate, the FOMC is typically able to raise or lower the real interest rate.

The *MP* Curve

For the reasons described in the preceding section, we assume in the *IS–MP* model that the Fed is able to control the real interest rate by changing its target for the federal funds rate. Figure 18.7 shows the *MP* curve as a horizontal line at the real interest rate determined by the Fed because we assume that the Fed is able to keep the interest rate constant, despite increases or decreases in the output gap. When the Fed increases the real interest rate from r_1 to r_2, the *MP* curve shifts up from MP_1 to MP_2; consumption spending, investment spending, and net exports all decline, causing a movement up the *IS* curve; and the value of the output gap changes from $\widetilde{Y}_1$ to $\widetilde{Y}_2$ as real GDP falls relative to potential GDP. When the Fed decreases the real interest rate from r_1 to r_3, the *MP* curve shifts down from MP_1 to MP_3; consumption spending, investment spending, and net exports all increase, causing a movement down the *IS* curve; and the value of the output gap changes from $\widetilde{Y}_1$ to $\widetilde{Y}_3$ as real GDP increases relative to potential GDP.

The Phillips Curve

The Taylor rule indicates that the Fed typically increases the real interest rate when the inflation gap is positive—that is, when the current inflation rate is above the Fed's target inflation rate of 2%. Raising the real interest rate causes real GDP to decline relative to potential GDP. With real GDP below its potential level, firms operate below capacity, and the unemployment rate rises, which puts downward pressure on costs and prices, ultimately leading to a lower inflation rate. The Fed relies on *an inverse relationship between the inflation rate and the state of the economy*: When output and employment are increasing, the inflation rate tends to increase, and when output and employment are decreasing, the inflation rate tends to decrease.

The first economist to systematically analyze this inverse relationship was the New Zealand economist A.W. Phillips in 1958. Phillips plotted data on the inflation rate and the unemployment rate in the United Kingdom and drew a curve showing their average relationship. Since that time, a graph showing the short-run relationship between

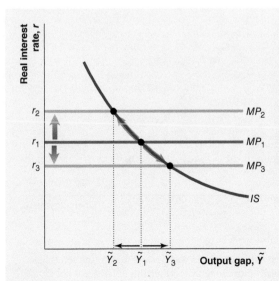

FIGURE 18.7

The *MP* Curve

The MP curve is a horizontal line at the real interest rate determined by the Fed. When the Fed increases the real interest rate from r_1 to r_2, the MP curve shifts up from MP_1 to MP_2, causing a movement up the *IS* curve, and the value of the output gap changes from $\widetilde{Y}_1$ to $\widetilde{Y}_2$. When the Fed decreases the real interest rate from r_1 to r_3, the MP curve shifts down from MP_1 to MP_3, causing a movement down the *IS* curve, and the value of the output gap changes from $\widetilde{Y}_1$ to $\widetilde{Y}_3$.

the unemployment rate and the inflation rate has been called a *Phillips curve*.[4] The graph in Figure 18.8 is similar to the one Phillips prepared. Each point on the Phillips curve represents a combination of the inflation rate and the unemployment rate that might be observed in a particular year. For example, point A represents the combination of a 4% unemployment rate and a 4% inflation rate in one year, and point B represents the combination of a 7% unemployment rate and a 1% inflation rate in another year.

Economists who have studied the Phillips curve relationship have concluded that rather than there being a single stable trade-off between inflation and unemployment, the position of the Phillips curve can shift over time in response to supply shocks and changes in expectations of the inflation rate. As we discussed in Chapter 17, Section 17.3, a negative supply shock, such as an unexpected increase in oil prices, can cause output to fall (and, therefore, unemployment to rise) at the same time that it causes upward pressure on the price level, which will increase the inflation rate. Unemployment and inflation both being higher means that the Phillips curve has shifted up. Changes in households' and firms' expectations about the inflation rate will also shift the position of the Phillips curve. For example, if workers and firms expect that the inflation rate will be 2% per year, but they experience an extended period of 4% inflation, they are likely to adjust their expectations of future inflation from 2% to 4%.

Expectations of inflation become embedded in the economy. For example, if workers believe that the future inflation rate will be 4%, rather than 2%, they know that unless their nominal wages increase by at least 4%, their real wages—their nominal wages divided by the price level—will decline. Similarly, the Fisher effect, which we discussed in Chapter 4, Section 4.3, indicates that an increase in the expected inflation rate will cause an increase in nominal interest rates. As workers, firms, and investors adjust from expecting an inflation rate of 2% to expecting an inflation rate of 4%, at any given unemployment rate, the inflation rate will be 2% higher. In other words, the Phillips curve will have shifted up by 2%.

FIGURE 18.8

The Phillips Curve

The Phillips curve illustrates the short-run relationship between the unemployment rate and the inflation rate. Point A represents the combination of a 4% unemployment rate and a 4% inflation rate in one year. Point B represents the combination of a 7% unemployment rate and a 1% inflation rate in another year.

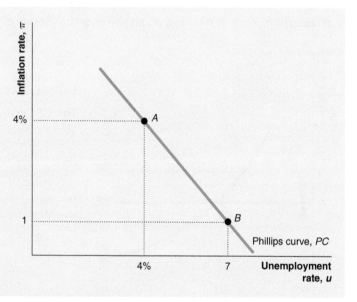

---

[4] Phillips actually measured inflation by the percentage change in wages rather than by the percentage change in prices. Because wages and prices usually move roughly together, this difference is not important to our discussion.

Finally, most economists believe that the best way to capture the effect of changes in the unemployment rate on the inflation rate is to look at the gap between the current unemployment rate and the unemployment rate when the economy is at full employment, which is called the *natural rate of unemployment*. The gap between the current rate of unemployment and the natural rate represents *cyclical unemployment* because it is unemployment caused by a business cycle recession raising the unemployment rate above its full employment level. When the current unemployment rate equals the natural rate, the inflation rate typically does not change, holding constant expectations of inflation and the effects of supply shocks. When the current unemployment rate is greater than the natural rate, there is slack in the labor market, and wage increases will be limited, as will firms' costs of production. So, the inflation rate will decrease. When the current unemployment rate is less than the natural rate of unemployment, labor market conditions will be tight, and wages are likely to increase, which pushes up firms' costs of production. So, the inflation rate will increase.

Taking all these factors into account gives us the following equation for the Phillips curve:

$$\pi = \pi^e - a(U - U^*) - s,$$

where:

π = the current inflation rate
π^e = the expected inflation rate
U = the current unemployment rate
U^* = the natural rate of unemployment
s = a variable representing the effects of a supply shock (*s* will have a negative value for a negative supply shock and a positive value for a positive supply shock)
a = a constant that represents how much the gap between the current rate of unemployment and the natural rate affects the inflation rate

The equation tells us that an increase in expected inflation or a negative aggregate supply shock will shift the Phillips curve up, while a decrease in expected inflation or a positive supply shock will shift the Phillips curve down.

What might cause the expected rate of inflation to change? Many economists believe that households and firms adjust their expectations of inflation if they experience persistent rates of actual inflation that are above the rates that they had expected. For example, inflation during the 1960s averaged about 2% per year but accelerated to 5% per year from 1970 to 1973 and 8.5% per year from 1974 to 1979. These persistently high rates of inflation led households and firms to revise upward their expectations of future inflation, and the Phillips curve shifted up. Notice that once the Phillips curve has shifted up, the short-run trade-off between inflation and unemployment becomes worse. That is, every unemployment rate becomes associated with a higher inflation rate. We saw in Chapter 15, Section 15.4, that Paul Volcker became Federal Reserve chairman in August 1979, with a mandate from President Jimmy Carter to bring down the inflation rate. When the economy experienced the severe recession of 1981–1982, the inflation rate declined sharply as the unemployment rate soared and firms experienced excess capacity. From 1983 to 1986, the inflation rate averaged 3.3% per year. Accordingly, households and firms lowered their expectations of future inflation, and the Phillips curve shifted down.

Figure 18.9 illustrates the Phillips curve shifting.

FIGURE 18.9

Shifts in the Phillips Curve

An increase in expected inflation or a negative aggregate supply shock will shift the Phillips curve up. A decrease in expected inflation or a positive aggregate supply shock will shift the Phillips curve down.

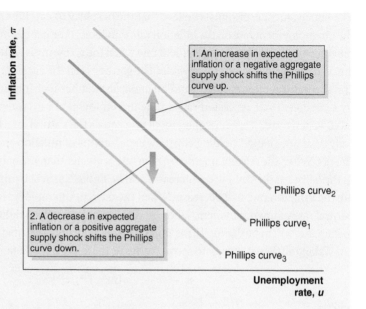

1. An increase in expected inflation or a negative aggregate supply shock shifts the Phillips curve up.

2. A decrease in expected inflation or a positive aggregate supply shock shifts the Phillips curve down.

Phillips curve₂

Phillips curve₁

Phillips curve₃

Okun's Law and an Output Gap Phillips Curve

The Phillips curve shows the short-run relationship between the inflation rate and the unemployment rate. We saw in Figure 18.7 on page 627 how we can use the *IS* curve and the *MP* curve to illustrate the Fed's use of monetary policy to affect the output gap. If we could show the relationship between the output gap and the inflation rate, we could integrate the Phillips curve into the *IS–MP* model. That would allow us to illustrate the effects of changes in the inflation rate on Fed policy and the effects of changes in Fed policy on the inflation rate. Fortunately, there is a straightforward way of modifying the Phillips curve to change it from a relationship between the inflation rate and the unemployment rate to a relationship between the inflation rate and the output gap.

Okun's law A statistical relationship discovered by Arthur Okun between the output gap and the cyclical rate of unemployment.

Okun's law, named after Arthur Okun, who served as chairman of the President's Council of Economic Advisers in the 1960s, conveniently summarizes the relationship between the output gap, $\widetilde{Y}$, and the gap between the current rate of unemployment (U) and the natural rate of unemployment (U^*):

$$\widetilde{Y} = -2 \times (U - U^*).$$

Remember that the difference between the current rate of unemployment and the natural rate of unemployment equals the cyclical rate of unemployment. Figure 18.10 shows the actual rate of cyclical unemployment and the rate of cyclical unemployment calculated using Okun's law for the years since 1950. Because the values track so closely in most years, we can be confident that substituting the output gap, $\widetilde{Y}$, for cyclical unemployment, $(U - U^*)$, in our Phillips curve equation will capture the effect of changes in the output gap on the inflation rate:

$$\pi = \pi^e + b\,\widetilde{Y} - s.$$

The coefficient b in the equation represents the effect of changes in the output gap on the inflation rate.

Figure 18.11 shows our revised Phillips curve, *PC*, with the output gap on the horizontal axis and the inflation rate on the vertical axis. Notice that with the output gap

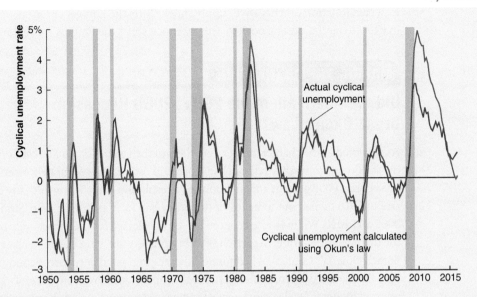

FIGURE 18.10 Using Okun's Law to Predict the Cyclical Unemployment Rate

Okun's law states that the output gap is equal to negative 2 times the gap between the current unemployment rate and the natural rate of unemployment. The graph shows that during most periods, Okun's law does a good job of accounting for the cyclical unemployment rate. Shaded areas represent months of recession.

Sources: Congressional Budget Office; and U.S. Bureau of Economic Analysis.

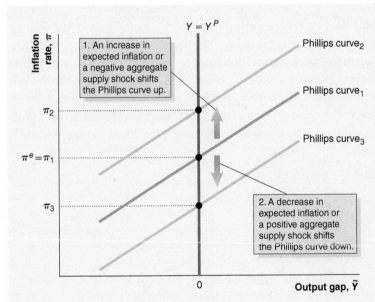

FIGURE 18.11

The Output Gap Version of the Phillips Curve

This Phillips curve differs from the one shown in Figure 18.8 on page 628 by having the output gap, rather than the unemployment rate, on the horizontal axis. As a result, the Phillips curve is upward sloping rather than downward sloping. When the output gap equals zero and there are no supply shocks, the actual inflation rate will equal the expected inflation rate. An increase in expected inflation or a negative supply shock shifts the Phillips curve up, and a decrease in expected inflation or a positive supply shock shifts the Phillips curve down.

version of the Phillips curve, the curve is upward sloping rather than downward sloping, as in Figure 18.8 on page 628. This change in slope occurs because inflation typically falls when the unemployment rate increases but rises when real GDP increases. When the output gap equals zero and there are no supply shocks, the actual inflation rate will equal the expected inflation rate. As with the original Phillips curve, an increase in expected inflation or a negative supply shock shifts the Phillips curve up, and a decrease in expected inflation or a positive supply shock shifts the Phillips curve down.

MAKING THE CONNECTION

Did the Aftermath of the 2007–2009 Recession Break Okun's Law?

As we noted in the chapter opener, members of the Federal Open Market Committee, and the staff economists they rely on, had trouble in recent years accurately forecasting future rates of real GDP growth and inflation. As a result, their actual target for the federal funds rate in 2016 turned out to be lower than they had forecast it would be. Similarly, during 2009 and 2010, White House economists were criticized for their inaccurate predictions of the unemployment rate. In early 2009, Christina Romer, who was then chair of President Barack Obama's Council of Economic Advisers, and Jared Bernstein, economic adviser to Vice President Joe Biden, predicted that if Congress passed President Obama's stimulus program of higher federal government spending and tax cuts, unemployment would peak at about 8% in the third quarter of 2009 and then decline in the following quarters. Although Congress passed the stimulus program, the unemployment rate was 9.6% in the third quarter of 2009. The unemployment rate rose to 9.9% in the fourth quarter of 2009 and didn't drop below 9% until the third quarter of 2011.

Romer and Bernstein were hardly alone in failing to forecast the severity of unemployment during 2009 and 2010. One reason for the faulty forecasts was that the decline in output was greater than expected, so, given Okun's law, the increase in the unemployment rate was also greater than expected. But the decline in real GDP can't account for all of the rise in unemployment. Figure 18.10 on page 631 shows that for the whole period since 1950, Okun's law does a good job of explaining movements in the unemployment rate. The following graph, which covers just the period from the first quarter of 2007 through the second quarter of 2016, shows that Okun's law did not do as well in explaining movements in the unemployment rate following the 2007–2009 recession.

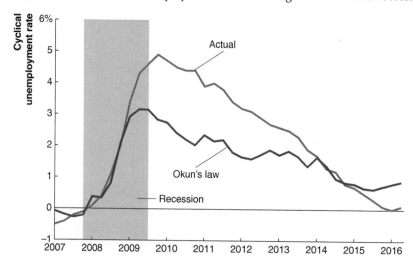

The graph shows that beginning in mid-2009 and continuing until mid-2013, Okun's law predicted a cyclical unemployment rate that was at least 1 percentage point and, during some periods, 2 percentage points lower than the actual unemployment rate. In other words, given the changes in GDP, economists relying on Okun's law would have expected the unemployment rate to be lower than it was. As then Fed Chair Ben Bernanke put it in testimony before Congress in 2012, the reduction in the unemployment rate was "frustratingly slow."

What explains the relatively poor performance of Okun's law during this period? Some economists have pointed to the behavior of labor productivity—the amount of output produced per worker—as one explanation. There was a temporary sharp increase in labor productivity in 2009 and 2010. When labor productivity increases, firms can produce either more output with a given number of workers or the same amount of output with fewer workers. Many firms appear to have taken the second option—maintaining their production levels with fewer workers—which led to a higher level of unemployment than many economists had forecast. But a difficulty with this explanation is that labor productivity declined to low levels in 2011 and remained there, while Okun's law continued to underpredict the unemployment rate for another two years. Another explanation offered by some economists is that because the 2007–2009 recession was so severe, many firms worried that they might be forced into bankruptcy. As a result, they took actions to cut their costs by laying off more workers than they ordinarily would have, given the extent of the decline in their sales.

Some economists argue that changes in the labor market may account for problems with Okun's law. For example, Robert Gordon of Northwestern University believes that a decline in unionization and a rise in temporary employment may have increased the willingness of firms to lay off workers when sales decline. If that is true, then the equation for Okun's law will have to be modified if it is to accurately predict changes in unemployment during future recessions.

It's unclear whether the strong relationship between changes in output and changes in unemployment Arthur Okun discovered 50 years ago will continue to hold.

Sources: Christina Romer and Jared Bernstein, "The Job Impact of the American Recovery and Reinvestment Plan," January 10, 2009; Mary Daly and Bart Hobijn, "Okun's Law and the Unemployment Surprise of 2009," Federal Reserve Bank of San Francisco *Economic Letter*, March 8, 2009; Robert J. Gordon, "Okun's Law and Productivity Innovations," *American Economic Review: Papers and Proceedings*, Vol. 100, No. 2, May 2010, pp. 11–15; Ben S. Bernanke, "Statement by Ben S. Bernanke Chairman Board of Governors of the Federal Reserve System before the Committee on Banking, Housing, and Urban Affairs U.S. Senate," July 17, 2012; and Jon Hilsenrath, "Piecing Together the Job-Picture Puzzle," *Wall Street Journal*, March 12, 2012.

See related problem 2.10 at the end of the chapter.

18.3 Equilibrium in the *IS–MP* Model

LEARNING OBJECTIVE: Use the *IS–MP* model to illustrate macroeconomic equilibrium.

We have now developed the three pieces of the *IS–MP* model: the *IS* curve, the *MP* curve, and the Phillips curve. Figure 18.12 shows a situation of long-run macroeconomic equilibrium using this model. In panel (a), the *IS* curve and the *MP* curve intersect where the

FIGURE 18.12

Equilibrium in the *IS–MP* Model

In panel (a), the *IS* curve and the *MP* curve intersect where the output gap is zero and the real interest rate is at the Fed's target level. In panel (b), the Phillips curve shows that because the output gap is zero, the actual and expected inflation rates are equal.

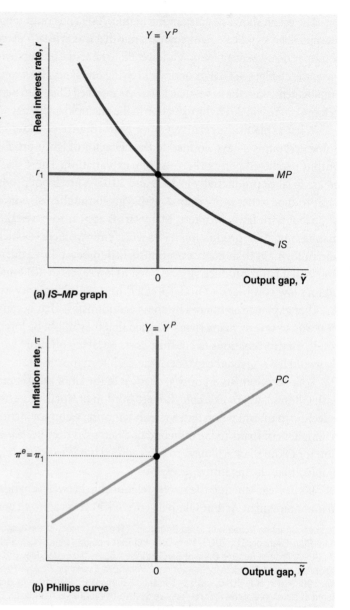

(a) *IS–MP* graph

(b) Phillips curve

output gap is zero and the real interest rate is at the Fed's target level. In panel (b), the Phillips curve shows that because the output gap is zero, the actual and expected inflation rates are equal.

> **MAKING THE CONNECTION**

Where Did the *IS–MP* Model Come From?

The macroeconomic model we have been discussing in this chapter has deep historical roots. British economist John Maynard Keynes developed the basic ideas behind the *IS* curve in his 1936 book *The General Theory of Employment, Interest, and Money*. Keynes was the first economist to discuss in detail the idea that total production would increase and decrease in response to fluctuations in aggregate expenditure. He believed that the collapse in aggregate expenditure beginning in 1929 caused the Great Depression.

Keynes did not explicitly draw the *IS* curve in *The General Theory*. The *IS* curve first appeared in an article written by John Hicks in 1937. Our discussion of the *IS* curve has left it something of a mystery as to why it is labeled *IS*. The mystery is solved by following Hicks's alternative approach to analyzing equilibrium in the goods market. If we look at a closed economy—one with no imports or exports—then aggregate expenditure equals $C + I + G$. And, in equilibrium, $Y = C + I + G$. We can rearrange this expression as $Y - C - G = I$. Because $Y - C - G$ represents output not consumed in the current period by households or the government, we can think of it as *national saving*, S. So, we can say that the goods market is in equilibrium when investment equals national saving, or $I = S$, which is why Hicks called the curve showing equilibrium in the goods market the *IS* curve. The two approaches to equilibrium in the goods market—(1) Total output = Aggregate expenditure, and (2) Investment = Saving—are exactly equivalent.

Hicks did not use the *MP* curve in his model. Instead, he used what became known as the *LM* curve, with *LM* standing for "liquidity" and "money." (In his original article, Hicks labeled the curve *LL*.) The *LM* curve shows combinations of the interest rate and output that would result in the money market being in equilibrium. (We discussed the money market in the previous chapter.) Hicks's approach is called the *IS–LM model*. (See the appendix on pages 654–657 for a further discussion of this model.) A shortcoming of the *IS–LM* model is that it assumes that monetary policy takes the form of the Federal Reserve's choosing a target for the money supply. We know, however, that since the early 1980s, the Fed has targeted the federal funds rate, not the money supply. In recent years, the Fed has paid very little attention to movements in the money supply when conducting short-term monetary policy. In 2000, David Romer of the University of California, Berkeley, suggested dropping the *LM* curve in favor of the *MP* curve approach that we have used in this chapter.

You can find out more about the original work of John Maynard Keynes, John R. Hicks, A.W. Phillips, and Arthur Okun by reading the references in the sources. Note that some of the discussion in these references is technical.

Sources: John Maynard Keynes, *The General Theory of Employment, Interest, and Money*, London: Macmillan, 1936; John R. Hicks, "Mr. Keynes and the 'Classics'; A Suggested Interpretation," *Econometrica*, Vol. 5, No. 2, April 1937, pp. 147–159; David Romer, "Keynesian Macroeconomics Without the *LM* Curve," *Journal of Economic Perspectives*, Vol. 14, No. 2, Spring 2000, pp. 149–169; A. W. Phillips, "The Relation Between Unemployment and the Rate of Change of Money Wage Rates in the United Kingdom, 1861–1957," *Economica*, Vol. 25, No. 100, November 1958, pp. 283–299; and Arthur M. Okun, "Potential GDP: Its Measurement and Significance," *Proceedings of the Business and Economic Statistics Section of the American Statistical Association*, 1962.

See related problems 3.5 and 3.6 at the end of the chapter.

Using Monetary Policy to Fight a Recession

Suppose that starting from the situation shown in Figure 18.12, the economy is hit by a demand shock, as happened, for example, in 2007 when spending on residential

FIGURE 18.13

Expansionary Monetary Policy

In panel (a), a demand shock causes the *IS* curve to shift to the left, from IS_1 to IS_2. Real GDP falls below potential GDP, so the economy has a negative output gap at $\widetilde{Y}_1$ and moves into a recession. Panel (b) shows that a negative output gap causes a movement down the Phillips curve, lowering the inflation rate from π_1 to π_2. The Fed lowers the real interest rate, shifting the monetary policy curve from MP_1 to MP_2 and causing a movement down the *IS* curve. Real GDP returns to its potential level, so the output gap is again zero. In panel (b), the inflation rate rises from π_2 back to π_1.

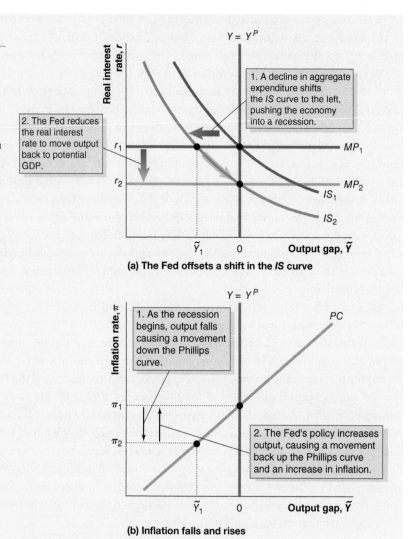

(a) The Fed offsets a shift in the *IS* curve

(b) Inflation falls and rises

construction declined following the collapse of the housing bubble. Panel (a) of Figure 18.13 shows that the demand shock causes the *IS* curve to shift to the left, from IS_1 to IS_2. Real GDP falls below potential GDP, so the economy has a negative output gap at $\widetilde{Y}_1$ and moves into a recession. Panel (b) shows that a negative output gap causes a movement down the Phillips curve, lowering the inflation rate from π_1 to π_2. The Fed typically fights recessions by lowering its target for the federal funds rate. This action lowers the real interest rate, shifting the monetary policy curve from MP_1 to MP_2. A lower real interest rate leads to increases in consumption spending, investment spending, and net exports, causing a movement down the *IS* curve. Real GDP returns to its potential level, so the output gap is again zero. In panel (b), the inflation rate rises from π_2 back to π_1.

Complications in Fighting the Recession of 2007–2009

As we saw in earlier discussions of Fed policy during the 2007–2009 recession, a smooth transition back to potential GDP, as shown in Figure 18.13, did not occur. One reason is that even though we have been assuming in the *IS–MP* model that the Fed controls the real interest rate, in fact, the Fed is able to target the federal funds rate but typically does not attempt to directly affect other market interest rates. Normally, the Fed can rely on the long-term real interest rate declining when the federal funds rate declines and rising when the federal funds rate rises. However, the recession of 2007–2009 did not represent normal times.

Recall from Chapter 5 that the default risk premium is the additional yield that an investor requires for holding a bond with some default risk. During the financial crisis, particularly after the failure of Lehman Brothers in September 2008, the default risk premium soared as investors feared that firms would have difficulty repaying their loans or making the coupon and principal payments on their bonds. Figure 18.14 shows two measures of how much investors increased the default risk premium they required to buy corporate bonds rated Baa by Moody's. The blue line shows the difference between the interest rate on Baa-rated corporate bonds and the interest rate on 10-year U.S. Treasury notes. The red line shows the difference between the interest rate on Baa-rated corporate bonds and the interest rate on Aaa-rated corporate bonds. Sales of Baa-rated bonds are an important source of funds to firms. Baa is Moody's lowest investment-grade rating, and the bonds of many more firms are able to qualify for that rating than for the Aaa rating. In fact, in 2016, only two nonfinancial corporations—Microsoft and Johnson & Johnson—qualified for Moody's Aaa rating. So, when the difference between Baa interest rate and the 10-year Treasury note interest rate soared from about 1.5% before the financial crisis to more than 6% at the height of the crisis, corporations had difficulty raising funds by issuing bonds. Note that Figure 18.14 shows that the increase in the risk premium during the 2007–2009 recession was much greater than the increase during the milder 2001 recession.

As we have seen, by the end of 2008, the Fed had caused the federal funds rate to fall nearly to zero, but the rise in the risk premium counteracted the effects of the Fed's expansionary policy. The Fed attempted to bring down long-term interest rates by taking

MyEconLab Real-time data

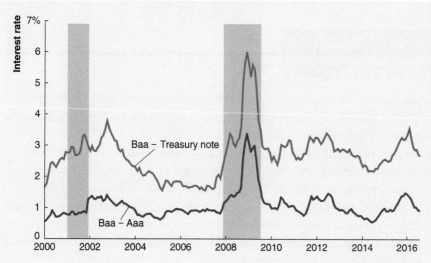

FIGURE 18.14

An Increasing Risk Premium During the 2007–2009 Recession

During the financial crisis of 2007–2009, the default risk premium soared, raising interest rates on Baa-rated bonds relative to those on Aaa-rated bonds (the red line in the figure) and 10-year U.S. Treasury notes (the blue line in the figure).

Source: Federal Reserve Bank of St. Louis.

FIGURE 18.15

Expansionary Monetary Policy in the Face of a Rising Risk Premium

During the recession of 2007–2009, the collapse in spending on residential construction shifted the *IS* curve from IS_1 to IS_2, and real GDP fell below potential GDP at $\widetilde{Y}_1$. The Fed responded by lowering the real interest rate from r_1 to r_2, but the increase in the risk premium caused the real interest rate actually to increase to r_3, pushing the economy into a deeper recession at $\widetilde{Y}_2$.

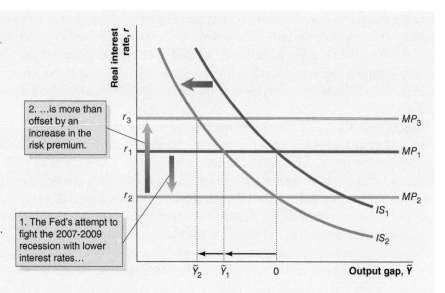

2. ...is more than offset by an increase in the risk premium.

1. The Fed's attempt to fight the 2007-2009 recession with lower interest rates...

the unusual step of directly buying both 10-year Treasury notes and mortgage-backed securities, but the Fed was not able to entirely offset the effects of the increase in the risk premium.

Figure 18.15 illustrates the problems the Fed had in implementing an expansionary monetary policy during 2008. The collapse in spending on residential construction shifted the *IS* curve from IS_1 to IS_2, and real GDP fell below potential GDP at $\widetilde{Y}_1$. The Fed responded by lowering the real interest rate from r_1 to r_2, which would in normal circumstances have been sufficient to bring the economy back to potential GDP. But the increase in the risk premium caused the real interest rate actually to increase to r_3, pushing the economy into a deeper recession at $\widetilde{Y}_2$. The economy started to recover in mid-2009 only after the risk premium began to decline to more normal levels. The Fed helped reduce the risk premium by undertaking unconventional policies such as buying mortgage-backed securities issued by Fannie Mae and Freddie Mac.

MAKING THE CONNECTION

Free Fannie and Freddie?

No aspect of the U.S. financial system was affected more by the 2007–2009 financial crisis than the market for residential mortgages. As we have seen, the financial crisis was brought on by a decline in housing prices that led to a fall in the prices of mortgage-backed securities (MBS). As financial firms suffered losses on their holdings of MBS, credit began to dry up, and the economy plunged into the most severe recession since the Great Depression of the 1930s. In September 2008, in response to the crisis, the federal government placed the Federal National Mortgage Association (Fannie Mae, or often just "Fannie") and the Federal Home Loan Mortgage Association (Freddie Mac, or often just "Freddie") under the conservatorship of a newly established federal agency, the Federal Housing Finance Agency (FHFA).

Fannie Mae and Freddie Mac had been *government-sponsored enterprises (GSEs)*, which Congress had established to create a secondary market in mortgages. Fannie and Freddie sell bonds to investors and use the funds to purchases mortgages from banks, which they then bundle into MBS. Legally, Fannie and Freddie were private corporations, whose stockholders expected them to make a profit. Although Congress had no responsibility to provide funds to Fannie and Freddie if they ran into financial problems, most investors were convinced that Congress would never allow them to fail because to do so would seriously disrupt the mortgage market, making it difficult for people to borrow funds to buy houses. As a result of this expectation, Fannie and Freddie were able to sell bonds with low interest rates because investors saw the bonds as having very low default risk.

The following figure shows the growing importance of the GSEs in the market for residential mortgages during the years leading up to the financial crisis. In the 1950s and 1960s, the traditional way of granting mortgages predominated, with banks and savings and loans granting most mortgages and keeping the mortgages on their books until they matured or were paid off by the borrowers. As a result, during those years banks, savings and loans, and insurance companies held 85% or more of all residential mortgages, shown by the blue line in the figure. By the early 1990s, Fannie Mae, Freddie Mac, and other federal agencies such as the Government National Mortgage Association (Ginnie Mae) and the Federal Housing Administration (FHA) were holding a majority of mortgages, shown by the red line in the figure. In addition, investment banks and some other financial firms began securitizing loans and issuing their own "private label" MBS, shown by the green line in the figure (which also includes private holders of mortgages, including individuals). Just prior to the financial crisis, the market share of private-label MBS was increasing at the expense of Fannie and Freddie's MBS (called *agency* MBS).

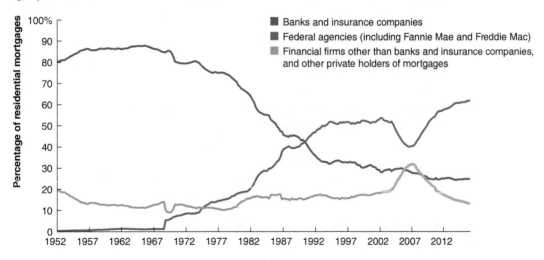

As housing prices declined, investors became concerned that Fannie and Freddie would be unable to honor their guarantees of the MBS they had issued. In addition, both held substantial amounts of their own MBS. Because Congress had allowed them to hold very little capital, it became evident that their losses were making the firms insolvent.

In September 2008, to avoid a meltdown in the mortgage market, Congress authorized the U.S. Treasury to inject $189 billion in new capital into Fannie and Freddie and put them under the conservatorship of the FHFA.

At the time the federal government took control of Fannie and Freddie the expectation among many economists and policymakers was that at some point, the firms would become private again. But as of the start of 2017, the firms were still under FHFA control, and no definite plans for privatizing them were in place. In addition, as part of its rounds of quantitative easing, the Fed held more than $1.75 trillion in MBS issued by Fannie and Freddie. This total amounted to about 17% of the value of all residential mortgages. Some economists and policymakers see the following significant problems with current conditions in the mortgage market:

- The federal government is effectively guaranteeing Fannie and Freddie's MBS. This guarantee makes private securitization of residential mortgages difficult because private securitizers, such as investment banks, would have to charge for insuring mortgages at rates far above those charged by Fannie and Freddie. In addition, by law, Fannie and Freddie are exempt from state and local corporate taxes, giving them a further advantage over potential private competitors. Not surprisingly, private securitization of mortgages has almost disappeared, as shown in the previous figure by the sharp decline in the green line following the financial crisis. In the absence of any private securitizers, the federal government is effectively in control of the mortgage market, a result that Congress did not expect to last indefinitely when it authorized the conservatorship of Fannie and Freddie in 2008.

- An agreement in 2010 between the FHFA and the Treasury resulted in nearly all of Fannie and Freddie's profits—more than $250 billion by 2016—being sent to the Treasury, leaving the firms with very little capital to cover any potential losses. If problems in the housing market were to cause a wave of mortgage defaults, Congress would have to provide substantial funds to sustain the firms.

- Because they are, in effect, government agencies, Fannie and Freddie may come under political pressure from Congress to weaken underwriting standards for the mortgages they buy. Although standards are higher than they were before the financial crisis, some economists are concerned about the increasing volume of mortgages granted with small down payments. When borrowers make only a small down payment, they are more likely to default on their mortgages if housing prices decline.

- The Fed's large purchases of MBS have increased their prices and lowered mortgage interest rates, which may have helped support the housing market but has meant that prices of these securities may not reflect their underlying risk.

Economists and policymakers have offered several proposals to restructure the mortgage market. In 2013, Senators Bob Corker of Tennessee and Mark Warner of Virginia introduced legislation to establish a new federal agency that for a fee would insure mortgages included in mortgage-backed securities in a way similar to how the FDIC ensures bank deposits. To reduce the moral hazard involved with the insurance, financial firms originating the mortgages would absorb any losses up to 10% of the value of the insured mortgages. The proposal was intended to induce other financial firms to enter the mortgage securitization market in competition with Fannie and Freddie. Eventually they would be phased out, leaving all mortgage securitization in private hands. Although the plan had bipartisan support, Congress declined to enact it.

Other proposals typically involve privatizing Fannie and Freddie by having the Treasury sell off its stock holdings in the firms. After privatization, financial regulators would treat them like other large financial firms by requiring them to hold substantial amounts of capital. Their legal exemption from state and local taxes would also be eliminated. Because investors are likely to continue to believe that Congress would save Fannie and Freddie from bankruptcy even if they are formally private firms again, some reform proposals would require the firms to pay fees to the federal government so that they would not have an advantage over other firms in raising funds from investors.

One stumbling block to enacting any reform is that mortgage interest rates are likely to increase as a result of privatizing the mortgage market because investors will insist on being fully compensated for risk that is no longer being absorbed by Fannie and Freddie. Rising interest rates are particularly likely if the Fed reduces its holdings of MBS over time as it normalizes monetary policy. Rising interest rates will deter some people from buying homes, and Congress may object, given that the fraction of the U.S. population that owns homes fell from 69.1% in 2005 to 63.5% in 2016.

As with some other Fed policies enacted in response to the financial crisis, it was unclear in 2016 what the exit strategy might be from the decision in September 2008 to nationalize Fannie and Freddie.

Sources: Joe Light, "Will Fannie and Freddie Need Another Bailout?" *Wall Street Journal*, May 24, 2016; James K. Glassman and Alex J. Pollock, "How to Fix Fannie and Freddie," aei.org, January 15, 2016; Office of the President, "A Better Bargain for the Middle Class: Housing," August 5, 2013; "Comradely Capitalism," *Economist*, August 20, 2016; U.S. Census Bureau, "Residential Vacancies and Homeownership in the Second Quarter 2016," July 28 2016; and Board of Governors of the Federal Reserve System.

See related problems 3.8 and 3.9 at the end of the chapter.

SOLVED PROBLEM 18.3

Using Monetary Policy to Fight Inflation

As we saw in Chapter 15, Section 15.4, Fed Chairman Paul Volcker took office in August 1979, with a mandate to bring down the inflation rate. Use the *IS–MP* model to analyze how the Fed can change expectations of inflation to permanently reduce the inflation rate. Be sure that your graphs include the *IS* curve, the *MP* curve, and the Phillips curve. Also be sure that your graphs show the initial effect of the Fed's policy on the output gap and the inflation rate. Finally, be sure to illustrate how the economy returns to long-run equilibrium at a lower inflation rate.

Solving the Problem

Step 1 **Review the chapter material.** This problem is about using the *IS–MP* model and the reasons for shifts in the Phillips curve, so you may want to review the section "The Phillips Curve," which beings on page 627, and the section "Equilibrium in the *IS–MP* Model," which begins on page 633.

Step 2 **Describe the policy the Fed would use to reduce the inflation rate and illustrate your answer with a graph.** To permanently reduce the inflation rate, the Fed needs to reduce the expected inflation rate. The expected inflation rate will decline if households and firms experience an inflation rate that is persistently lower than the inflation rate they had expected. The Phillips curve tells us that if real GDP falls below potential GDP, the inflation rate will decline. The Fed can cause a decline in real GDP by raising the real interest rate. Your graph should show the MP curve shifting up from MP_1 to MP_2, the new equilibrium output gap, $\widetilde{Y}_1$, and the reduction in the inflation rate from π_1 to π_2 along the Phillips curve.

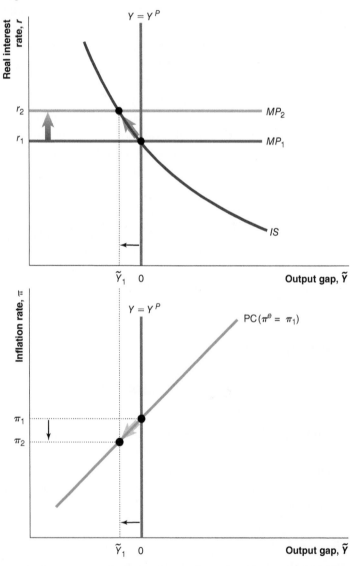

Step 3 **Show how after the Phillips curve shifts down, the Fed can return the economy to potential output at a lower inflation rate.** If the inflation rate persists at π_2, households will eventually lower their expectation of the inflation

rate from π_1 to π_2. Once that happens, the Phillips curve will shift down, and the Fed can lower the real interest rate from r_2 back to r_1, returning output to potential GDP.

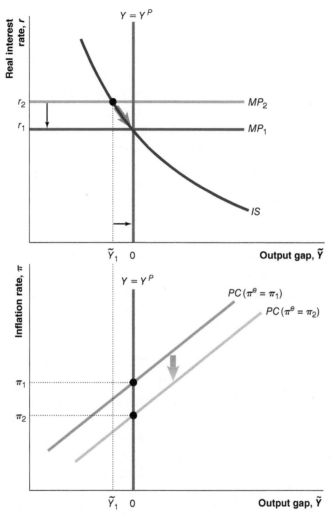

See related problem 3.10 at the end of the chapter.

18.4 Are Interest Rates All That Matter for Monetary Policy?

LEARNING OBJECTIVE: Discuss alternative channels of monetary policy.

Economists refer to the ways in which monetary policy can affect output and prices as the *channels of monetary policy*. In the *IS–MP* model, monetary policy works through interest rates: The Fed changes the real interest rate, which affects the components of aggregate expenditure, thereby changing the output gap and the inflation rate. Economists call this channel the *interest rate channel*. An underlying assumption in this approach is that borrowers are indifferent as to how or from whom they raise funds and regard alternative sources of funds as close substitutes. Bank loans play no special role in this channel.

The Bank Lending Channel and the Shadow Bank Lending Channel

Households and many firms depend on bank loans for credit because they have few or no alternative sources of funds. Some economists believe that the interest rate channel should be supplemented with consideration of the **bank lending channel**, which in its traditional form emphasizes the behavior of borrowers who depend on commercial bank loans. In this version of the bank lending channel, a change in banks' ability or willingness to lend affects the ability of bank-dependent borrowers to finance their spending plans. This channel's focus on bank loans also suggests a modified view of how monetary policy affects the economy. In this channel, a monetary expansion increases banks' ability to lend, and increases in loans to bank-dependent borrowers increase the spending of those borrowers. A monetary contraction decreases banks' ability to lend, and decreases in loans to bank-dependent borrowers lead to reductions in their spending.

In periods when reserves are scarce, the interest rate channel focuses on how the Fed, by increasing bank reserves through open market purchases, decreases the real interest rate and increases output in the short run. This increase in output occurs because the decline in the federal funds rate leads to declines in other interest rates that are important to the spending decisions of households and firms. The predictions of the bank lending channel are similar to those of the interest rate channel in one respect: In periods when reserves are scarce, when the Fed expands bank reserves through open market purchases, the increase in bank reserves leads to lower loan interest rates.

The bank lending channel holds further, however, that monetary policy affects the economy through the volume of bank lending to bank-dependent borrowers and by the spending of these borrowers. In the bank lending channel, an expansionary monetary policy causes aggregate expenditure to increase for two reasons: (1) the increase in households' and firms' spending from the drop in interest rates and (2) the increased availability of bank loans. In other words, if banks expand the availability of loans, the amount that bank-dependent borrowers can borrow and spend increases at any real interest rate. Therefore, *in the bank lending channel, an expansionary monetary policy is not dependent for its effectiveness on a reduction in interest rates.* Similarly, a contractionary monetary policy is not dependent for its effectiveness on an increase in interest rates.

Traditionally, discussion of the bank lending channel focuses on commercial banks, but as we discussed in Chapter 11, nonbank financial firms, or *shadow banks*, have increased their importance in the financial system over the past few decades. In particular, money market mutual funds have been an important source of credit to many businesses because the funds buy the commercial paper the firms sell. But because of the Federal Reserve's low interest rate policy, since 2008, the annual returns investors receive from owning money market mutual funds has been very low—often less than 0.25%. In response to such low returns, many investors have sold money market mutual funds and bought bond mutual funds, on which they can receive higher returns. As a result, the total value of the assets in money market mutual funds dropped by about $1 trillion between 2008 and 2015, and some money market funds closed.

Bank lending channel
A description of how monetary policy influences the spending decisions of borrowers who depend on commercial bank loans or on selling securities to shadow banks.

As investors sold money market funds, the funds cut back their purchases of commercial paper, forcing the firms issuing this paper to turn to other, possibly higher-cost, sources of financing. Total commercial paper outstanding declined from $2.2 trillion in 2007, just before the financial crisis, to less than $1 trillion in the fall of 2016.

We can conclude that the effect of the shadow bank lending channel is to make expansionary monetary policy somewhat less effective, at least when expansionary policy takes the form of very low interest rates. Because very low interest rates result in a contraction of commercial paper purchases by money market mutual funds, low interest rates may have a negative effect on firms that rely on issuing commercial paper to fund their short-term operations.

The Balance Sheet Channel: Monetary Policy and Net Worth

Monetary policy may also affect the economy through its effects on firms' balance sheet positions. Economists have modeled this channel through the effects of monetary policy on the value of firms' assets and liabilities and on the liquidity of balance sheet positions—that is, the quantity of liquid assets that households and firms hold relative to their liabilities. According to these economists, the liquidity of balance sheet positions is a determinant of spending on business investment, housing, and consumer durable goods. The **balance sheet channel** describes the ways in which, by changing interest rates, monetary policy affects borrowers' net worth and spending decisions. We know that when there are high information costs in lending, high levels of net worth and liquidity make it more likely that borrowers can obtain the funds they need to carry out their planned spending.

Balance sheet channel A description of how interest rate changes resulting from monetary policy affect borrowers' net worth and spending decisions.

How does monetary policy affect borrowers' balance sheets? Increases in interest rates in response to a contractionary monetary policy increase the amounts that borrowers with variable-rate loans pay on their debts and reduce the value of borrowers' net worth by reducing the present value of their assets. Recall that information problems increase the gap between the costs of external and internal funds as a borrower's net worth falls. That is, a decline in a borrower's net worth increases the cost of raising funds for capital investment because lenders require higher interest rates on loans to low net-worth borrowers and may also impose additional restrictions on their use of borrowed funds. This fall in net worth raises the cost of external financing by more than the increase that is implied by higher interest rates, and it reduces firms' ability to invest in plant and equipment. The balance sheet channel emphasizes this effect. *Even if monetary policy has no effect on banks' ability to lend, the decline in borrowers' net worth following a monetary contraction reduces aggregate demand and output.* Moreover, the balance sheet channel implies that spending by low-net-worth firms is particularly likely to fall following a monetary contraction.

The balance sheet channel, like the interest rate channel and the bank lending channel (with respect to commercial banks), holds that expansionary policy initially decreases interest rates, increasing output, while contractionary policy initially increases interest rates, reducing output. The balance sheet channel emphasizes the link between households' and businesses' net worth and liquidity and their spending. In the presence of information costs, changes in net worth and liquidity may significantly affect the volume of lending and economic activity.

Most economists believe that accepting the significance of the bank lending or balance sheet channel does not require rejecting the interest rate channel's implication that

TABLE 18.2 Channels of Monetary Policy

Channel	Focuses on ...	Monetary expansion ...	Monetary contraction ...
Interest rate channel	interest rates.	lowers interest rates, causing aggregate expenditure to increase.	raises interest rates, causing aggregate expenditure to decrease.
Bank lending channel (commercial banks)	bank loans.	increases banks' ability to lend to bank-dependent borrowers, causing aggregate expenditure to increase.	decreases banks' ability to lend to bank-dependent borrowers, causing aggregate expenditure to decrease.
Bank lending channel (shadow banks)	the ability of money market mutual funds to purchase commercial paper issued by firms.	lowers interest rates, which may lead investors to sell shares in money funds, thereby reducing the ability of the funds to purchase commercial paper.	raises interest rates, which may lead investors to purchase shares in money funds, thereby increasing the ability of the funds to purchase commercial paper.
Balance sheet channel	the link between the net worth and liquidity of households and firms and their spending.	increases net worth and liquidity, causing aggregate expenditure to increase.	decreases net worth and liquidity, causing aggregate expenditure to decrease.

monetary policy works through interest rates. Instead, the bank lending and balance sheet channels offer additional methods by which the financial system and monetary policy can affect the economy.

Table 18.2 summarizes the key points of these four channels of monetary policy.

ANSWERING THE KEY QUESTION

Continued from page 613

At the beginning of this chapter, we asked:

"In what circumstances is lowering the target for the federal funds rate unlikely to be effective in fighting a recession?"

As we have seen throughout this book, the recession of 2007–2009 was accompanied by a financial crisis that made the recession unusually severe. The Fed realized by the fall of 2008 that its normal policy of fighting recessions primarily by lowering its target for the federal funds rate was unlikely to be effective. The *IS–MP* model developed in this chapter provides one explanation of why normal monetary policy was ineffective. Although the Fed lowered the target for the federal funds rate nearly to zero, an increase in the risk premium demanded by investors caused a rise in the interest rates, such as the Baa bond rate, that many businesses pay, despite the Fed's actions.

Key Terms and Problems

Key Terms

Aggregate demand shock, p. 625
Balance sheet channel, p. 645
Bank lending channel, p. 644
Fiscal policy, p. 621
IS curve, p. 615

IS–MP model, p. 615
MP curve, p. 615
Multiplier, p. 619
Multiplier effect, p. 619
Okun's law, p. 630

Output gap, p. 623
Phillips curve, p. 615
Potential GDP, p. 618

18.1   **The *IS* Curve**
Explain what the *IS* curve is and how it is derived.

Review Questions

1.1   Describe each of the three parts of the *IS–MP* model.

1.2   Draw a 45°-line diagram showing an equilibrium in the goods market. Label the equilibrium level of real GDP, Y_1. Now show on your graph each of the following two situations:

1. Real GDP is equal to Y_2, where Y_2 is greater than Y_1

2. Real GDP is equal to Y_3, where Y_3 is less than Y_1

Be sure that your graph shows the level of aggregate expenditure and the level of unintended changes in inventories at Y_1, Y_2, and Y_3. Briefly explain how real GDP adjusts to equilibrium if it is initially equal to Y_2 or Y_3.

1.3   What is the relationship between the *MPC* and the multiplier?

1.4   Explain how the *IS* curve represents equilibrium in the goods market. Why is the *IS* curve downward sloping?

1.5   Give an example of a shock that could shift the *IS* curve to the left. Give an example of a shock that could shift the *IS* curve to the right.

Problems and Applications

1.6   [Related to Solved Problem 18.1 on page 620]
Use the following data to calculate the values of

equilibrium output and the investment spending multiplier:

$$C = MPC \times Y = 0.75 \times Y$$
$$\bar{I} = \$2.3 \text{ trillion}$$
$$\bar{G} = \$1.7 \text{ trillion}$$
$$\overline{NX} = -\$0.5 \text{ trillion}$$

1.7   Briefly explain whether you agree with the following argument:

Potential GDP is the level of real GDP attained when all firms are producing at capacity. Firms have the capacity to operate 24 hours per day if they have to, but they rarely do. Therefore, because firms can almost always produce much more output than they actually do, real GDP is almost always well below potential GDP.

1.8   John Maynard Keynes wrote that one requirement for a stable economy was that "the multiplier ... is greater than unity but not very large." Why might a large value for the multiplier make an economy less stable?

Source: John Maynard Keynes, *The General Theory of Employment, Interest, and Money*, London: Macmillan, 1936, p. 250.

1.9   In each of the following situations, briefly explain whether the *IS* curve will shift and, if it does shift, in which direction it will shift:

a. Consumers become more optimistic about their future incomes.

b. The federal government cuts the corporate profit tax.

c. The real interest rate rises.

d. Firms become pessimistic about the future profitability of spending on new information technology.

1.10 How would the size of the multiplier affect the slope of the *IS* curve? (Hint: In the 45°-line diagram, how does the multiplier affect the change in the equilibrium level of real GDP for a given change in the real interest rate?)

1.11 If consumption spending becomes more sensitive to changes in the real interest rate, how will the slope of the *IS* curve be affected?

1.12 An article in the *Wall Street Journal* in late 2015 noted: "One economic trend that hasn't done its bit for this 6½-year recovery: capital spending." Given that interest rates were at historically low levels during most of this period, what can we conclude about the shape of the *IS* curve during these years?

Source: Steven Russolillo, "Capital Spending: The Economy's Weak Spot," *Wall Street Journal*, December 22, 2015.

18.2 The *MP* Curve and the Phillips Curve

Explain the significance of the *MP* curve and the Phillips curve.

Review Questions

2.1 How can changes in the federal funds rate cause changes in long-term real interest rates?

2.2 Why is the *MP* curve a horizontal line? How is the Fed able to change the position of the *MP* curve?

2.3 When the Federal Reserve increases the real interest rate, is the result a movement up or down the *IS* curve? Does the value of the output gap increase or decrease?

2.4 What factors cause the Phillips curve to shift?

2.5 What is Okun's law, and how can it be used to derive an output gap Phillips curve?

Problems and Applications

2.6 An article in the *Wall Street Journal* in 2016 noted: "The 2016 rally in government bond prices has taken U.S. real yields … on the 10-year Treasury … below zero for the first time since 2012." Does this statement mean that if you had bought a 10-year Treasury note in 2016, in 10 years, when the note matures, the Treasury will pay you less than the price you paid for the bond? Briefly explain.

Source: Min Zeng, "By One Measure, U.S. Rates Are Already Negative," *Wall Street Journal*, April 8, 2016.

2.7 [Related to the Chapter Opener on page 613] An article in the *Economist* in 2016 argued: "If the Fed wants higher nominal rates in a world of low real rates, it must cultivate higher inflation." Briefly explain the author's reasoning.

Source: R.A., "Fed Officials Try to Understand Why They Cannot Keep Raising Rates," *Economist*, June 20, 2016.

2.8 In a lecture, Fed Chair Janet Yellen remarked: "The Phillips-curve approach to forecasting inflation has a long history in economics, and it has usefully informed monetary policy decision making around the globe." How might an economist use the Phillips curve to forecast inflation?

Source: Janet L. Yellen, "Inflation Dynamics and Monetary Policy," Philip Gamble Memorial Lecture, University of Massachusetts, Amherst, September 24, 2015, p. 16

2.9 In each of the following situations, briefly explain whether the short-run Phillips curve with the unemployment rate on the horizontal axis will shift, and if it does shift, in which direction it will shift:

a. The expected inflation rate decreases.

b. The actual inflation rate increases.

c. The price of oil substantially decreases.

d. Cyclical unemployment increases.

e. Favorable weather conditions result in bumper agricultural crops.

2.10 **[Related to the** Making the Connection **on page 632]** A Federal Reserve publication remarks: "For Okun's law to be useful as a rule of thumb, the relationship between real GDP growth and the unemployment rate needs to be stable across time."

a. What is the relationship between real GDP and unemployment, according to Okun's law?

b. Has Okun's law been stable across time? Briefly explain.

c. What does the authors mean by a "rule of thumb"? Is Okun's law a good rule of thumb?

Source: Brent Meyer and Murat Tasci, "An Unstable Okun's Law, Not the Best Rule of Thumb," Federal Reserve Bank of Cleveland *Economic Commentary*, June 12, 2012.

2.11 A columnist in the *Economist* asserts: "I would argue that the Fed has been targeting very low inflation, and falling inflation expectations imply much lower interest rates in future."

a. Will falling expectations of inflation lead to lower nominal interest rates, lower real interest rates, or both? Briefly explain.

b. If the Fed wanted to raise expectations of inflation, what actions might it take?

Source: R.A., "Fed Officials Try to Understand Why They Cannot Keep Raising Rates," *Economist*, June 20, 2016.

2.12 In a speech in 2016, Fed Chair Janet Yellen noted that there is some uncertainty in measuring the natural rate of unemployment: "it cannot be estimated precisely, and so it could be appreciably higher or lower—although given low readings on wages in recent years, I think the latter possibility is more likely than the former."

a. Why might a slow rate of wage growth make it likely that the natural rate of unemployment was lower than it had previously been estimated to be?

b. How would a lower natural rate of unemployment affect the short-run Phillips curve? Consider both the unemployment rate version of the Phillips curve and the output gap version of the Phillips curve.

Source: Janet L. Yellen, "The Outlook, Uncertainty, and Monetary Policy," Remarks at the Economic Club of New York, New York, New York, March 29, 2016, p. 11, fn. 8.

18.3 **Equilibrium in the *IS–MP* Model**
Use the *IS–MP* model to illustrate macroeconomic equilibrium.

Review Questions

3.1 Draw graphs showing long-run macroeconomic equilibrium in the *IS–MP* model. One of your graphs should show the output gap version of the Phillips curve. In long-run equilibrium, what does the output gap equal, and what is true about the actual and expected inflation rates?

3.2 When the Federal Reserve lowers the real interest rate, what happens to the output gap and to the inflation rate?

3.3 What is the default risk premium, and why did it dramatically increase during the 2007–2009 recession? How did this increase affect the *MP* curve and the output gap?

Problems and Applications

3.4 Use the *IS–MP* model (including the output gap Phillips curve) to analyze how the Federal Reserve would respond to a large positive demand shock. Assume that the economy was in long-run macroeconomic equilibrium before the demand shock. Use a graph to show both the effect of the positive demand shock and how the Fed might respond.

3.5 **[Related to the** Making the Connection **on page 634]** John Maynard Keynes developed a model, later elaborated by John Hicks, in which total output is determined solely by total spending with little consideration of the supply (production) side of the economy. Why would Keynes and Hicks, writing during the Great Depression, be likely to develop a model of the economy that focused on total spending?

3.6 **[Related to the** Making the Connection **on page 634]** John Hicks, in his original macroeconomic model, the *IS–LM* model, developed the *LM* curve to show the combinations of the real interest rate and output that result in equilibrium in the money market. The *LM* curve assumes that monetary policy takes the form of the Federal Reserve choosing a target for the money supply. Why would David Romer in 2000 suggest dropping the traditional *LM* curve and replacing it with the *MP* curve?

3.7 Economists debate whether the Federal Reserve, Congress, and the president should adopt an activist stabilization policy that attempts to "fine-tune" the economy—that is, smooth almost every fluctuation in GDP or inflation—or, instead, adopt a policy that focuses on long-run objectives, such as low inflation or steady economic growth, and restrict the use of activist policy to fighting major downturns in the economy. Does the reality that policymakers must rely on "real-time data" (data available at the time the Fed makes its decision) that is subject to revisions weaken or strengthen the argument against fine-tuning the economy with activist stabilization policy? Briefly explain.

3.8 **[Related to the** Making the Connection **on page 638]** An article on the U.S housing market in the *Economist* notes: "The status quo also means that, in the event of another crash, taxpayers would be landed with a big bill." Explain what aspect of the housing market makes it likely that if housing prices crashed again, as they did beginning in 2006, taxpayers would be landed with a big bill. Be sure to explain what taxpayers would be paying for with that big bill.

Source: "Comradely Capitalism," *Economist*, August 20, 2016.

3.9 **[Related to the** Making the Connection **on page 638]** In his memoirs, published in 2014, former Treasury Secretary Timothy Geithner observed:

"Eventually, Congress will have to make some tough choices about the mortgage market—not just how to reduce the government's dominant role, but how to balance the trade-off between safety and accessibility."

a. In what sense does the government have a dominant role in the mortgage market?

b. What steps would need to be taken to reduce the government's role in the mortgage market? As of 2016, the federal government had taken no steps to reduce its role in the mortgage market. Why has moving away from the current system proven to be difficult politically?

c. What is the trade-off between safety and accessibility with respect to home mortgages? How does the government's role in the mortgage market affect that trade-off?

Source: Timothy F. Geithner, *Stress Test: Reflection on Financial Crises*, New York: Crown, 2014, p. 435.

3.10 **[Related to** Solved Problem 18.3 **on page 641]** Suppose the Fed is concerned that deflation will harm the economy over the long run. Use the *IS–MP* model (including the Phillips curve) to analyze how the Federal Reserve would fight deflation.

a. Use an *IS–MP* model graph to show long-run macroeconomic equilibrium with a deflation rate of 2%.

b. If the Fed wants the economy to return to a long-run equilibrium with an inflation rate of 2%, how should it change its target for the federal funds rate? Show the effects of this change in the target for the federal funds rate on an *IS–MP* graph, including the Phillips curve. What happens to the output gap and to the inflation rate?

c. Use an *IS–MP* graph, including the Phillips curve, to illustrate how the economy returns to long-run equilibrium at the higher inflation rate.

3.11 **[Related to the** Solved Problem 18.3 **on page 641]** In testifying before Congress in mid-2012, then Fed Chairman Ben Bernanke noted that the economic recovery "could be endangered by the confluence of tax increases and [government] spending reductions that will take effect early next year if no legislative action is taken."

a. Use an *IS–MP* graph to show the effects of tax increases and government spending reductions on the output gap. Briefly explain what your graph shows.

b. In the same testimony, Bernanke referred to "the additional negative effects likely to result from public uncertainty about how these [taxing and

government spending] matters will be resolved." What components of aggregate expenditure might be affected by an increase in uncertainty? Use an *IS–MP* graph to show the effects of uncertainty on the output gap. Briefly explain what your graph is showing.

Source: Board of Governors of the Federal Reserve System, "Statement by Ben S. Bernanke Chairman Board of Governors of the Federal Reserve System before the Committee on Banking, Housing, and Urban Affairs, U.S. Senate," July 17, 2012.

18.4 Are Interest Rates All That Matter for Monetary Policy?
Discuss alternative channels of monetary policy.

Review Questions

4.1 What do economists mean by the "channels of monetary policy"?

4.2 If monetary policy does not cause a change in interest rates, can it still affect the output gap and the inflation rate? Briefly explain.

Problems and Applications

4.3 When the Federal Reserve changes the real interest rate to affect the output gap and inflation rate, do each of the following monetary policy channels reinforce or partially offset the effect of the change in the real interest rate: the bank lending channel (as it operates through commercial banks), the bank lending channel (as it operates through shadow banks), and the balance sheet channel? Briefly explain.

4.4 In the bank lending channel as it operates through commercial banks, an expansionary monetary policy is not dependent for its

effectiveness on a reduction in interest rates, and a contractionary monetary policy is not dependent for its effectiveness on an increase in interest rates. How can an expansionary monetary policy be effective without reducing interest rates to stimulate spending, and how can a contractionary monetary policy be effective without increasing interest rates to slow down spending?

4.5 Would you expect the bank lending channel (as it operates through commercial banks) to have a larger or a smaller effect in emerging economies, such as Brazil or India, than in the United States? Briefly explain.

4.6 For a brief period in 2008 and 2009, the U.S. Treasury guaranteed investors against losses on their holdings of money market mutual fund shares. If the program had become permanent, how would it have affected the bank lending channel as it operates through shadow banks?

Data Exercises

D18.1: [The Relationship between the federal funds rate and the long-term interest rate] Go to the web site of the Federal Reserve Bank of St. Louis (FRED) (fred.stlouisfed.org) and download to the same graph data from January 1984 to the most recent available month on the nominal federal

---

MyEconLab   Visit **www.myeconlab.com** to complete these exercises online and get instant feedback. Exercises that update with real-time data are marked with .

funds rate (FEDFUNDS) and the nominal 10-year constant maturity U.S. Treasury security (GS10).

a. Is the relationship between the federal funds rate and the long-term nominal interest rate as strong as the relationship between the federal funds rate and other short-term nominal interest rates? Briefly explain. Hint: Think of the term-structure of interest rates.

b. Now add the monthly interest rate of the 30-year fixed rate mortgage (MORTG) to your graph. Is the relationship between the federal funds rate and the mortgage rate stronger or weaker than the relationship between the federal funds rate and the interest rate on 10-year U.S. Treasury notes? Briefly explain. In particular, comment on the behavior of mortgage interest rates during the first part of the 2007–2009 recession. Hint: Think of the risk-structure of interest rates.

D18.2: [Analyzing the default risk premium] Go to the web site of the Federal Reserve Bank of St. Louis Federal Reserve (FRED) (fred.stlouisfed.org) and download data on the interest rate on AAA rated corporate bonds (AAA) and the interest rate on constant maturity 10-year U.S. Treasury notes (GS10) from January 1953 to the most recent available month.

a. Calculate the default risk premium and plot the resulting data series on a graph.

b. You can find the dates of U.S. recessions at the web site of the National Bureau of Economic Research (NBER) (www.nber.org/cycles/cyclesmain.html). What happens to the default risk premium during recessions? Holding everything else constant, what would you expect to happen to the *MP* curve during recessions?

c. What actions could the Fed take to offset the effect of the changes in the default risk premium on the *MP* curve?

D18.3: [Analyzing the real interest rate] Go to the web site of the Federal Reserve Bank of St. Louis Federal Reserve (FRED) (fred.stlouisfed.org) and download data from January 2003 to the most recent available month on the 10-year constant maturity U.S. Treasury notes (GS10) as a measure of the nominal interest rate and the 10-year U.S. Treasury inflation protected security (FII10) as a measure of the real interest rate.

a. The Fisher relationship tells us that the expected inflation rate is the nominal interest rate minus the real interest rate. Calculate the expected inflation rate over the next ten years using these data.

b. For January 2003 to the most recent available month, download data on Aaa corporate bonds (AAA). The Fisher relationship also tells us that the real interest rate equals the nominal interest rate minus the expected inflation rate. Calculate the real interest rate for Aaa corporate bonds using your results from part (a). Plot the resulting data series on a graph.

c. What happened to the real interest rate from the beginning of the recession in December 2007 to August 2008? Does this movement in the real interest rate suggest that shifts in the *IS* curve or *MP* curve were most likely to have been responsible for the start of the recession? Briefly explain.

d. What happens to the real interest rate during the period from September 2008 to November 2008? Does this movement in the real interest rate suggest that shifts in the *IS* curve or *MP* curve were responsible for the worsening of the recession during the fall of 2008? Briefly explain.

D18.4: **[Testing the Phillips curve]** Go to the web site

of the Federal Reserve Bank of St. Louis
(FRED) (fred.stlouisfed.org) and download
annual unemployment data (UNRATE) for
1962 to the present. (To convert the data
from a monthly frequency to an annual frequency, click on Edit Graph and Frequency.)
Next, download the annual inflation rate
measured using the consumer price index, or
CPI (CPIAUCSL). (Once you have converted
the data from a monthly frequency to an annual frequency, you can find the inflation rate
by clicking on Units and selecting Percentage Change from Year Ago.) Briefly explain
whether for each of the following periods,
the relationship between the annual unemployment rate and the annual inflation rate is
consistent with a movement along the short-
run Phillips curve or with a shift in the Phillips curve. If the data are consistent with the
Phillips curve having shifted, briefly explain
whether the shift resulted from a negative
shock or a positive shock.

a. 1966–1969

b. 1973–1975

c. 1992–1994

d. 2000–2002

The *IS–LM* Model

Learning Objective

18.A Use the *IS–LM* model to illustrate macroeconomic equilibrium.

IS–LM model A macroeconomic model of aggregate demand that assumes that the central bank targets the money supply.

LM curve A curve that shows the combinations of the interest rate and the output gap that result in equilibrium in the money market.

The *IS–MP* model that we developed in this chapter assumes that the Fed targets the federal funds rate. We used the *IS–MP* model to show the effects of monetary policy because the Fed and many other central banks today use as their monetary policy target a short-term bank lending rate, such as the federal funds rate.

At one time, though, some central banks targeted the money supply rather than a short-term interest rate. The **IS–LM model**, which we noted in the *Making the Connection* on pages 634–635 was first developed by British economist John Hicks in 1937, building on ideas developed by John Maynard Keynes, is similar to the *IS–MP* model. The difference is the *IS–LM* model assumes that the Fed is targeting the money supply rather than the federal funds rate. Both the *IS–MP* and *IS–LM* models use the *IS* curve to show the negative relationship between the real interest rate and expenditure in the market for goods and services. The *IS–LM* model differs from the *IS–MP* model because it substitutes an *LM* curve for the *MP* curve. The **LM curve** shows the combinations of the interest rate and the output gap that result in equilibrium in the money market.

Deriving the *LM* Curve

To derive the *LM* curve, we use the money market from Chapter 17. In that chapter, we assumed that equilibrium in the money market determined the short-term nominal interest rate. Because equilibrium in the goods market, as shown by the *IS* curve, depends on the real interest rate, we will make the simplifying assumption that the expected inflation rate is constant so that a change in the nominal interest rate is equivalent to a change in the real interest rate. In addition, we will assume that movements in short-term rates result in corresponding movements in the long-term interest rates that are important for consumption and investment decisions. If these assumptions hold, then the equilibrium long-term real interest rate is determined in the money market.

To derive the *LM* curve, we consider what happens to the demand for real balances when the output gap, or the percentage difference between real GDP and potential GDP, increases. (Note that we are measuring output as the output gap rather than as the level of output, to be consistent with the *IS–MP* model.) In panel (a) of Figure 18A.1, the economy begins in equilibrium at point A. A change in the output gap from $\widetilde{Y}_1$ to $\widetilde{Y}_2$ causes

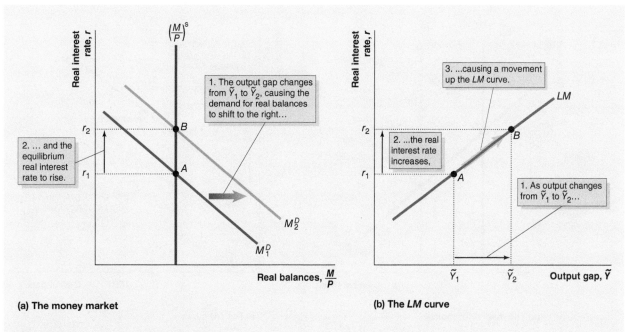

FIGURE 18A.1 Deriving the *LM* Curve

In panel (a), the economy begins in equilibrium at point A. A change in the output gap from $\tilde{Y}_1$ to $\tilde{Y}_2$ causes the demand for real balances to shift from M_1^D to M_2^D. The real interest rate must increase from r_1 to r_2 in order to maintain equilibrium in the money market at point B.

Panel (b) plots the combinations of the interest rate and the output gap from the equilibrium points A and B in panel (a). The *LM* curve shows all the combinations of the real interest rate and the output gap that result in equilibrium in the money market.

the demand for real balances to shift from M_1^D to M_2^D. The demand for real balances increases as output increases because households and firms need larger money balances to finance the increased transactions that result from higher levels of output. As the demand for real balances increases, the real interest rate must increase from r_1 to r_2 to maintain equilibrium in the money market at point B. This analysis tells us that, *holding the supply of real balances constant*, higher levels of output are associated with higher levels of the real interest rate in the money market. Panel (b) of Figure 18A.1 plots the combinations of the interest rate and the output gap from the equilibrium points A and B in panel (a). If we continued to vary the level of output in panel (a), we would trace out the combinations shown on the *LM* curve in panel (b). In other words, the *LM* curve shows all the combinations of the real interest rate and the output gap that result in equilibrium in the money market.

Shifting the *LM* Curve

If factors that affect the demand or supply for real balances, other than output, change, the *LM* curve will shift. For example, Figure 18A.2 shows the effect on the *LM* curve of an increase in the money supply. In panel (a), the money market begins in equilibrium at point A. The Fed then increases the supply of real balances from $(M/P)_1^S$ to $(M/P)_2^S$.

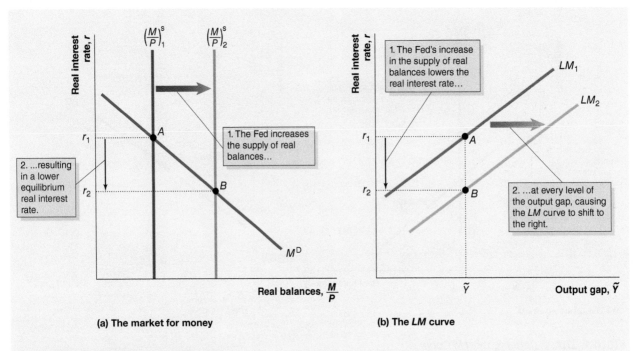

FIGURE 18A.2 Shifting the *LM* Curve

In panel (a), the money market begins in equilibrium at point *A*. The Fed then increases the supply of real balances from $(M/P)^S_1$ to $(M/P)^S_2$. The real interest rate falls from r_1 to r_2, and equilibrium in the money market is restored at point *B*. Panel (b) shows that the result of the increase in real money balances is to shift the *LM* curve to the right, from LM_1 to LM_2.

The real interest rate falls from r_1 to r_2, and equilibrium in the money market is restored at point *B*. In panel (b), we show that the result of the increase in real money balances is to shift the *LM* curve to the right, from LM_1 to LM_2. Compared with point *A*—which corresponds to point *A* in panel (a)—at point *B*, the output gap remains the same, and the real interest rate is lower.

Monetary Policy in the *IS–LM* Model

In Figure 18A.3, we bring together the *IS* curve and the *LM* curve. Where the two curves cross, we have equilibrium in both the goods market and the money market. We can use this graph to illustrate the effects of the Fed conducting an expansionary monetary policy that consists of increasing the supply of real balances rather than decreasing the target for the federal funds rate. At the initial equilibrium at point *A*, real GDP is below potential real GDP at $\widetilde{Y}_1$. As we saw in Figure 18A.2, increasing the supply of real balances shifts the *LM* curve to the right. If the Fed increases real money balances sufficiently to shift the

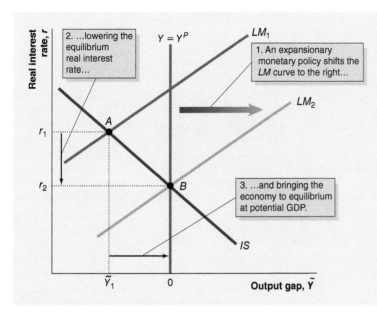

FIGURE 18A.3

Expansionary Monetary Policy

At the initial equilibrium at point *A*, real GDP is below potential real GDP. Increasing the supply of real balances shifts the *LM* curve to the right, from LM_1 to LM_2. Equilibrium will move to point *B* with real GDP at its potential level, and the real interest rate will fall from r_1 to r_2.

LM curve from LM_1 to LM_2, equilibrium will move to point *B* with real GDP at its potential level, and the real interest rate will fall from r_1 to r_2.

Key Terms

IS–LM model, p. 654
LM curve, p. 654

Adverse selection The problem investors experience in distinguishing low-risk borrowers from high-risk borrowers before making an investment. (p. 283)

Aggregate Demand (AD) curve A curve that shows the relationship between the price level and aggregate expenditure on goods and services. (p. 582)

Aggregate demand shock A change in one of the components of aggregate expenditure that causes the *IS* curve to shift. (p. 625)

Aggregate supply The total quantity of output, or GDP, that firms are willing to supply at a given price level. (p. 586)

Appreciation An increase in the value of a currency in exchange for another currency. (p. 248)

Asset Something of value that an individual or a firm owns; in particular, a financial claim. (pp. 2, 307)

Asymmetric information The situation in which one party to an economic transaction has better information than does the other party. (p. 283)

Balance-of-payments account A measure of all flows of private and government funds between a domestic economy and all foreign countries. (p. 550)

Balance sheet A statement that lists an individual's or a firm's assets and liabilities to indicate the individual's or firm's financial position on a particular day. (p. 307)

Bank capital The difference between the value of a bank's assets and the value of its liabilities; also called shareholders' equity. (p. 308)

Bank leverage The ratio of the value of a bank's assets to the value of its capital, the inverse of which (capital to assets) is called a bank's leverage ratio. (p. 319)

Bank panic The situation in which many banks simultaneously experience runs. (p. 390)

Bank reserves Bank deposits with the Fed plus vault cash. (p. 464)

Bank run The process by which depositors who have lost confidence in a bank simultaneously withdraw enough funds to force the bank to close. (p. 389)

Barter A system of exchange in which individuals trade goods and services directly for other goods and services. (p. 26)

Basel accord An international agreement about bank capital requirements. (p. 418)

Board of Governors The governing board of the Federal Reserve System, consisting of seven members appointed by the president of the United States. (p. 437)

Bond A financial security issued by a corporation or a government that represents a promise to repay a fixed amount of money. (p. 3)

Bond rating A single statistic that summarizes a rating agency's view of the issuer's likely ability to make the required payments on its bonds. (p. 141)

Bretton Woods system An exchange rate system that lasted from 1945 to 1971, under which countries pledged to buy and sell their currencies at fixed rates against the dollar and the United States pledged to convert dollars into gold if foreign central banks requested it to. (p. 557)

Bubble A situation in which the price of an asset rises well above the asset's fundamental value. (pp. 16, 202)

Business cycle Alternating periods of economic expansion and economic recession. (p. 600)

Call option A type of derivative contract that gives the buyer the right to buy the underlying asset at a set price during a set period of time. (p. 225)

Capital controls Government-imposed restrictions on foreign investors buying domestic assets or on domestic investors buying foreign assets. (p. 549)

Capital gain An increase in the market price of an asset. (p. 72)

Capital loss A decrease in the market price of an asset. (p. 72)

Check A promise to pay on demand money deposited with a bank or other financial institution. (p. 33)

Checkable deposits Accounts against which depositors can write checks. (p. 309)

Closed economy An economy in which households, firms, and governments do not borrow or lend internationally. (p. 131)

Collateral Assets that a borrower pledges to a lender that the lender may seize if the borrower defaults on the loan. (p. 287)

Commercial bank A financial firm that serves as a financial intermediary by taking in deposits and using them to make loans. (p. 6)

Commodity money A good used as money that has value independent of its use as money. (p. 26)

Compounding The process of earning interest on interest, as savings accumulate over time. (p. 56)

Contagion The process by which a run on one bank spreads to other banks, resulting in a bank panic. (p. 390)

Contractual saving institution A financial intermediary such as a pension fund or an insurance company that receives payments from individuals as a result of a contract and uses the funds to make investments. (p. 369)

Corporation A legal form of business that provides owners with protection from losing more than their investment if the business fails. (p. 174)

Counterparty risk The risk that the counterparty—the person or firm on the other side of the transaction—will default. (p. 215)

Coupon bond A debt instrument that requires multiple payments of interest on a regular basis, such as semiannually or annually, and a payment of the face value at maturity. (p. 63)

Credit default swap A derivative that requires the seller to make payments to the buyer if the price of the underlying security declines in value; in effect, a type of insurance. (p. 237)

Credit rationing The restriction of credit by lenders such that borrowers cannot obtain the funds they desire at the given interest rate. (pp. 286, 324)

Credit risk The risk that borrowers might default on their loans. (p. 321)

Credit-risk analysis The process that bank loan officers use to screen loan applicants. (p. 321)

Credit swap A contract in which interest-rate payments are exchanged, with the intention of reducing default risk. (p. 236)

Currency in circulation Paper money circulating outside the Fed. (p. 464)

Currency in M1 Currency held by the nonbank public. (p. 464)

Currency swap A contract in which counterparties agree to exchange principal amounts denominated in different currencies. (p. 236)

Currency-to-deposit ratio (C/D) The nonbank public's holdings of currency, C, relative to their holdings of checkable deposits, D. (p. 476)

Debt-deflation process The process first identified by Irving Fisher in which a cycle of falling asset prices and falling prices of goods and services can increase the severity of an economic downturn. (p. 400)

Debt instruments (also known as **credit market instruments** or **fixed-income assets**) Methods of financing debt, including simple loans, discount bonds, coupon bonds, and fixed payment loans. (p. 62)

Default risk (or **credit risk**) The risk that a bond issuer will fail to make payments of interest or principal. (p. 141)

Deflation A sustained decline in the price level. (p. 82)

Depreciation A decrease in the value of a currency in exchange for another currency. (p. 248)

Devaluation The lowering of the official value of a country's currency relative to other currencies. (p. 559)

Discount bond A debt instrument in which the borrower repays the amount of the loan in a single payment at maturity but receives less than the face value of the bond initially. (p. 63)

Discount policy The policy tool of setting the discount rate and the terms of discount lending. (p. 501)

Discount rate The interest rate the Federal Reserve charges on discount loans. (p. 468)

Discount window The means by which the Fed makes discount loans to banks, serving as the channel for meeting the liquidity needs of banks. (p. 501)

Discounting The process of determining the present value of funds that will be paid or received in the future. (p. 58)

Disintermediation The exit of savers and borrowers from banks to financial markets. (p. 415)

Diversification The division of wealth among many different assets to reduce risk. (pp. 13, 99)

Dividend A payment that a corporation makes to stockholders, typically on a quarterly basis. (pp. 3, 175)

Dividend yield The expected annual dividend divided by the current price of a stock. (p. 183)

Dual banking system The system in the United States in which banks are chartered by either a state government or the federal government. (p. 329)

Duration analysis An analysis of how sensitive a bank's capital is to changes in market interest rates. (p. 327)

Economic growth Increases in the economy's output of goods and services over time; a goal of monetary policy. (p. 498)

Economies of scale The reduction in average cost that results from an increase in the volume of a good or service produced. (p. 282)

Equity A claim to part ownership of a firm; stock issued by a corporation. (p. 62)

euro The common currency of 19 European countries. (p. 564)

European Central Bank (ECB) The central bank of the European countries that have adopted the euro. (p. 565)

European Monetary Union A plan drafted as part of the 1992 single European market initiative, in which exchange rates were fixed and eventually a common currency was adopted. (p. 564)

Excess reserves Any reserves banks hold above those necessary to meet reserve requirements. (pp. 313, 465)

Exchange rate regime A system for adjusting exchange rates and flows of goods and capital among countries. (p. 553)

Exchange-rate risk The risk that an investor or firm will suffer losses because of fluctuations in exchange rates. (p. 262)

Expectations theory A theory of the term structure of interest rates which holds that the interest rate on a long-term bond is an average of the interest rates investors expect on short-term bonds over the lifetime of the long-term bond. (p. 155)

Expected return The rate of return expected on an asset during a future period. (p. 94)

Federal deposit insurance A government guarantee of deposit account balances up to $250,000. (p. 310)

Federal Deposit Insurance Corporation (FDIC) A federal government agency established by Congress in 1934 to insure deposits in commercial banks. (p. 391)

Federal funds rate The interest rate that banks charge each other on very short-term loans; determined by the demand and supply for reserves in the federal funds market. (pp. 12, 503)

Federal Open Market Committee (FOMC) The 12-member Federal Reserve committee that directs open market operations. (p. 438)

Federal Reserve The central bank of the United States; usually referred to as "the Fed." (p. 11)

Federal Reserve Bank One of 12 district banks of the Federal Reserve System that, among other activities, conduct discount lending. (p. 432)

Federal Reserve System The central bank of the United States. (p. 431)

Fiat money Money, such as paper currency, that has no value apart from its use as money. (p. 29)

Finance company A nonbank financial intermediary that raises money through sales of commercial paper and other securities and uses the funds to make small loans to households and firms. (p. 368)

Financial arbitrage The process of buying and selling securities to profit from price changes over a brief period of time. (pp. 75, 190)

Financial asset An asset that represents a claim on someone else for a payment. (p. 2)

Financial crisis A significant disruption in the flow of funds from lenders to borrowers. (pp. 16, 389)

Financial intermediary A financial firm, such as a bank, that borrows funds from savers and lends them to borrowers. (p. 4)

Financial liability A financial claim owed by a person or a firm. (p. 4)

Financial market A place or channel for buying or selling stocks, bonds, and other securities. (p. 2)

Fiscal policy Changes in federal government purchases and taxes intended to achieve macroeconomic policy objectives. (p. 621)

Fisher effect The assertion by Irving Fisher that the nominal interest rate rises or falls point-for-point with changes in the expected inflation rate. (p. 113)

Fixed exchange rate system A system in which exchange rates are set at levels determined and maintained by governments. (p. 553)

Fixed-payment loan A debt instrument that requires the borrower to make regular periodic payments of principal and interest to the lender. (p. 64)

Flexible exchange rate system A system in which the foreign exchange value of a currency is determined in the foreign exchange market. (p. 561)

Foreign exchange Units of foreign currency. (p. 4)

Foreign exchange market An over-the-counter market where international currencies are traded and exchange rates are determined. (p. 252)

Foreign exchange market intervention A deliberate action by a central bank to influence the country's exchange rate. (p. 544)

Forward contract An agreement to buy or sell an asset at an agreed-upon price at a future time. (p. 214)

Future value The value at some future date of an investment made today. (p. 56)

Futures contract A standardized contract to buy or sell a specified amount of a commodity or a financial asset on a specific future date. (p. 215)

Gap analysis An analysis of the difference, or *gap*, between the dollar value of a bank's variable-rate assets and the dollar value of its variable-rate liabilities. (p. 326)

Gold standard A fixed exchange rate system under which currencies of participating countries are convertible into an agreed-upon amount of gold. (p. 553)

Gordon growth model (or **dividend-discount model**) A model that uses the current dividend paid, the expected growth rate of dividends, and the required return on equities to calculate the price of a stock. (p. 186)

Hedge To take action to reduce risk by, for example, purchasing a derivative contract that will increase in value when another asset in an investor's portfolio decreases in value. (p. 213)

Hedge fund A financial firm organized as a partnership of wealthy investors that make relatively high-risk, speculative investments. (p. 365)

Hyperinflation Extremely high rates of inflation, exceeding 50% per month. (p. 43)

Idiosyncratic (or **unsystematic**) **risk** Risk that pertains to a particular asset rather than to the market as a whole, as when the price of a particular firm's stock fluctuates because of the success or failure of a new product. (p. 100)

Information Facts about borrowers and expectations of returns on financial assets. (p. 14)

Information costs The costs that savers incur to determine the creditworthiness of borrowers and to monitor how they use the funds acquired. (p. 282)

Initial Public Offering (IPO) The first time a firm sells stock to the public. (p. 346)

Insolvent The situation for a bank or other firm of having a negative net worth because the firm's assets have less value than its liabilities. (p. 389)

Insurance company A financial intermediary that specializes in writing contracts to protect policyholders from the risk of financial loss associated with particular events. (p. 372)

Interest rate The cost of borrowing funds (or the payment for lending funds), usually expressed as a percentage of the amount borrowed. (p. 3)

Interest-rate parity condition The proposition that differences in interest rates on similar bonds in different countries reflect expectations of future changes in exchange rates. (p. 263)

Interest-rate risk The risk that the price of a financial asset will increase or decrease in response to changes in market interest rates. (pp. 79, 325)

Interest-rate swap A contract under which counterparties agree to swap interest payments over a specified period on a fixed dollar amount, called the *notional principal*. (p. 234)

International Monetary Fund (IMF) A multinational organization established in 1944 by the Bretton Woods agreement to administer a system of fixed exchange rates and to serve as a lender of last resort to countries undergoing balance-of-payments problems. (p. 558)

International reserves (or **foreign reserves**) Central bank assets that are denominated in a foreign currency and used in international transactions. (p. 544)

Investment banking Financial activities that involve underwriting new security issues and providing advice and financial services to clients, particularly with respect to mergers and acquisitions. (p. 346)

Investment institution A financial firm, such as a mutual fund or a hedge fund, that raises funds to invest in loans and securities. (p. 362)

IS curve A curve in the *IS–MP* model that shows the combinations of the real interest rate and aggregate output that represent equilibrium in the market for goods and services. (p. 615)

IS–MP model A macroeconomic model that consists of an *IS* curve, which represents equilibrium in the goods market; an *MP* curve, which represents monetary policy; and a Phillips curve, which represents the short-run relationship between the output gap (which is the percentage difference between actual and potential real GDP) and the inflation rate. (p. 615)

Law of one price The fundamental economic idea that identical products should sell for the same price everywhere. (p. 253)

Legal tender The government designation that currency is accepted as payment of taxes and must be accepted by individuals and firms in payment of debts. (p. 29)

Lender of last resort A central bank that acts as the ultimate source of credit to the banking system, making loans to solvent banks against their good, but illiquid, loans. (p. 390)

Leverage A measure of how much debt an investor assumes in making an investment. (p. 319)

Liability Something that an individual or a firm owes; a claim on an individual or a firm. (p. 307)

Limited liability A legal provision that shields owners of a corporation from losing more than they have invested in the firm. (p. 174)

Liquidity The ease with which an asset can be exchanged for money. (p. 13)

Liquidity premium theory (or **preferred habitat theory**) A theory of the term structure of interest rates which holds that the interest rate on a long-term bond is an average of the interest rates investors expect on short-term bonds over the lifetime of the long-term bond plus a term premium that increases in value the longer the maturity of the bond. (p. 162)

Liquidity risk The possibility that a bank may not be able to meet its cash needs by selling assets or raising funds at a reasonable cost. (p. 320)

Loan commitment An agreement by a bank to provide a borrower with a stated amount of funds during a specified period of time. (p. 334)

Loan sale A financial contract in which a bank agrees to sell the expected future returns from an underlying bank loan to a third party. (p. 335)

Long position In a futures contract, the right and obligation of the buyer to receive or buy the underlying asset on the specified future date. (p. 216)

Long-run aggregate supply (LRAS) curve A curve that shows the relationship in the long run between the price level and the quantity of aggregate output, or real GDP, supplied by firms. (p. 590)

M2 A broader definition of the money supply: all the assets that are included in M1, as well as time deposits with a value of less than $100,000, savings accounts, money market deposit accounts, and noninstitutional money market mutual fund shares. (p. 38)

Managed float regime An exchange rate system in which central banks occasionally intervene to affect foreign exchange values; also called a dirty float regime. (p. 562)

Margin requirement In the futures market, the minimum deposit that an exchange requires from the buyer and seller of a financial asset; reduces default risk. (p. 224)

Market (or **systematic**) **risk** Risk that is common to all assets of a certain type, such as the increases and decreases in stocks resulting from the business cycle. (p. 99)

Market maker A firm that holds an inventory of a security and serves as an intermediary between buyers and sellers of the security. (p. 350)

Marking to market In the futures market, a daily settlement in which the exchange transfers funds from a buyer's account to a seller's account or vice versa, depending on changes in the price of the contract. (p. 224)

Medium of exchange Something that is generally accepted as payment for goods and services; a function of money. (p. 28)

Monetary base (or **high-powered money**) The sum of bank reserves and currency in circulation. (p. 462)

Monetary neutrality The proposition that changes in the money supply have no effect on output in the long run because an increase (decrease) in the money supply raises (lowers) the price level in the long run but does not change the equilibrium level of output. (p. 597)

Monetary policy The actions the Federal Reserve takes to manage the money supply and interest rates to pursue macroeconomic policy objectives. (p. 11)

Money Anything that is generally accepted in payment for goods and services or to pay off debts. (pp. 3, 25)

Money market mutual fund A mutual fund that invests exclusively in short-term assets, such as Treasury bills, negotiable certificates of deposit, and commercial paper. (p. 363)

Money supply The total quantity of money in the economy. (p. 3)

Moral hazard The risk that people will take actions after they have entered into a transaction that will make the other party worse off. (p. 283)

MP curve A curve in the *IS–MP* model that represents Federal Reserve monetary policy. (p. 615)

Multiple deposit creation Part of the money supply process in which an increase in bank reserves results in rounds of bank loans and creation of checkable deposits and an increase in the money supply that is a multiple of the initial increase in reserves. (p. 472)

Multiplier The change in equilibrium GDP divided by a change in autonomous expenditure. (p. 619)

Multiplier effect The process by which a change in autonomous expenditure leads to a larger change in equilibrium GDP. (p. 619)

Municipal bonds Bonds issued by state and local governments. (p. 149)

Mutual fund A financial intermediary that raises funds by selling shares to individual savers and invests the funds in a portfolio of stocks, bonds, mortgages, and money market securities. (p. 362)

National bank A federally chartered bank. (p. 329)

Net interest margin The difference between the interest a bank receives on its securities and loans and the interest it pays on deposits and debt, divided by the total value of its earning assets. (p. 318)

Net worth The difference between the value of a firm's assets and the value of its liabilities. (p. 287)

Nominal exchange rate The price of one currency in terms of another currency; also called the *exchange rate*. (p. 247)

Nominal interest rate An interest rate that is not adjusted for changes in purchasing power caused by changes in the price level. (p. 80)

Off-balance-sheet activities Activities that do not affect a bank's balance sheet because they do not increase either the bank's assets or its liabilities. (p. 334)

Open economy An economy in which households, firms, and governments borrow and lend internationally. (p. 131)

Open market operations The Federal Reserve's purchases and sales of securities, usually U.S. Treasury securities, in financial markets. (p. 501)

Option A type of derivative contract in which the buyer has the right to buy or sell the underlying asset at a set price during a set period of time. (p. 225)

Option premium The price of an option. (p. 227)

Output gap The percentage difference between real GDP and potential GDP. (p. 623)

Over-the-counter market A market in which financial securities are bought and sold by dealers linked by computer. (p. 175)

Payments system The mechanism for conducting transactions in the economy. (p. 32)

Pegging The decision by a country to keep the exchange rate fixed between its currency and another country's currency. (p. 568)

Pension fund A financial intermediary that invests contributions of workers and firms in stocks, bonds, and mortgages to provide for pension benefit payments during workers' retirements. (p. 369)

Phillips curve A curve that shows the short-run relationship between the output gap (or the unemployment rate) and the inflation rate. (p. 615)

Policy trilemma The hypothesis that it is impossible for a country to have exchange rate stability, monetary policy independence, and free capital flows at the same time. (p. 571)

Political business cycle The theory that policymakers will urge the Fed to lower interest rates to stimulate the economy prior to an election. (p. 447)

Portfolio A collection of assets, such as stocks and bonds. (p. 8)

Potential GDP The level of real GDP attained when all firms are producing at normal capacity. (p. 618)

Present value The value in today's dollars of funds to be paid or received in the future. (p. 58)

Primary credit Discount loans available to healthy banks experiencing temporary liquidity problems. (p. 514)

Primary market A financial market in which stocks, bonds, and other securities are sold for the first time. (p. 9)

Prime rate Formerly, the interest rate banks charged on six-month loans to high-quality borrowers; currently, an interest rate banks charge primarily to smaller borrowers. (p. 324)

Principal–agent problem The moral hazard problem of managers (the agents) pursuing their own interests rather than those of shareholders (the principals). (p. 291)

Principal–agent view A theory of central bank decision making that holds that officials maximize their personal well-being rather than that of the general public. (p. 447)

Private equity firm (or **corporate restructuring firm**) A firm that raises equity capital to acquire shares in other firms to reduce free-rider and moral hazard problems. (p. 294)

Public interest view A theory of central bank decision making that holds that officials act in the best interest of the public. (p. 446)

Publicly traded company A corporation that sells stock in the U.S. stock market; only 5,100 of the 5 million U.S. corporations are publicly traded companies. (p. 175)

Put option A type of derivative contract that gives the buyer the right to sell the underlying asset at a set price during a set period of time. (p. 225)

Quantitative easing A central bank policy that attempts to stimulate the economy by buying long-term securities. (p. 512)

Quantity theory of money A theory about the connection between money and prices that assumes that the velocity of money is determined mainly by institutional factors and so is roughly constant in the short run. (p. 40)

Quota A limit a government imposes on the quantity of a good that can be imported. (p. 255)

Random walk The unpredictable movements in the price of a security. (p. 191)

Rate of return, R The return on a security as a percentage of the initial price; for a bond during a holding period of one year, the coupon payment plus the change in the price of a bond divided by the initial price. (p. 78)

Rational expectations The assumption that people make forecasts of future values of a variable using all available information; formally, the assumption that expectations equal optimal forecasts, using all available information. (p. 189)

Real exchange rate The rate at which goods and services in one country can be exchanged for goods and services in another country. (p. 250)

Real interest rate An interest rate that is adjusted for changes in purchasing power caused by changes in the price level. (p. 80)

Real money balances The value of money held by households and firms, adjusted for changes in the price level; M/P. (p. 583)

Relationship banking The ability of banks to assess credit risks on the basis of private information about borrowers. (p. 288)

Required reserve ratio The percentage of checkable deposits that the Fed specifies that banks must hold as reserves. (p. 465)

Required reserves Reserves the Fed requires banks to hold against demand deposit and NOW account balances. (pp. 313, 465)

Required return on equities, r_E The expected return necessary to compensate for the risk of investing in stocks. (p. 182)

Reserve requirement The regulation requiring banks to hold a fraction of checkable deposits as vault cash or deposits with the Fed. (p. 501)

Reserves A bank asset consisting of vault cash plus bank deposits with the Federal Reserve. (p. 313)

Restrictive covenant A clause in a bond contract that places limits on the uses of funds that a borrower receives. (p. 293)

Return The total earnings from a security; for a bond during a holding period of one year, the coupon payment plus the change in the price of the bond. (p. 78)

Return on assets (ROA) The ratio of the value of a bank's after-tax profit to the value of its assets. (p. 319)

Return on equity (ROE) The ratio of the value of a bank's after-tax profit to the value of its capital. (p. 319)

Revaluation The raising of the official value of a country's currency relative to other currencies. (p. 559)

Risk The degree of uncertainty in the return on an asset. (p. 95)

Risk sharing A service the financial system provides that allows savers to spread and transfer risk. (p. 13)

Risk structure of interest rates The relationship among interest rates on bonds that have different characteristics but the same maturity. (p. 140)

Seasonal credit Discount loans available to smaller banks in areas where agriculture or tourism is important. (p. 515)

Secondary credit Discount loans available to banks that are not eligible for primary credit. (p. 514)

Secondary market A financial market in which investors buy and sell existing securities. (p. 9)

Securitization The process of converting loans and other financial assets that are not tradable into securities. (p. 4)

Security A financial asset that can be bought and sold in a financial market. (p. 2)

Segmented markets theory A theory of the term structure of interest rates which holds that the interest rate on a bond of a particular maturity is determined only by the demand and supply for bonds of that maturity. (p. 161)

Settlement date The date on which the delivery of a commodity or financial asset specified in a forward contract must take place. (p. 215)

Short position In a futures contract, the right and obligation of the seller to sell or deliver the underlying asset on the specified future date. (p. 216)

Short-run aggregate supply (SRAS) curve A curve that shows the relationship in the short run between the price level and the quantity of aggregate output, or real GDP, supplied by firms. (p. 586)

Simple deposit multiplier The ratio of the amount of deposits created by banks to the amount of new reserves. (p. 473)

Simple loan A debt instrument in which the borrower receives from the lender an amount called the principal and agrees to repay the lender the principal plus interest on a specific date when the loan matures. (p. 63)

Specialization A system in which individuals produce the goods or services for which they have relatively the best ability. (p. 27)

Speculate To place financial bets, as in buying or selling futures or option contracts, in an attempt to profit from movements in asset prices. (p. 214)

Spot price The price at which a commodity or financial asset can be sold at the current date. (p. 215)

Stabilization policy A monetary policy or fiscal policy intended to reduce the severity of the business cycle and stabilize the economy. (p. 600)

Standard of deferred payment The characteristic of money by which it facilitates exchange over time; a function of money. (p. 29)

Standby letter of credit A promise by a bank to lend funds, if necessary, to a seller of commercial paper at the time that the commercial paper matures. (p. 334)

Sterilized foreign exchange intervention A foreign exchange market intervention in which the central bank offsets the effect of the intervention on the monetary base. (p. 545)

Stock Financial securities that represent partial ownership of a corporation; also called *equities*. (p. 3)

Stock exchange A physical location where stocks are bought and sold face-to-face on a trading floor. (p. 175)

Stock market index An average of stock prices that investors use to measure the overall performance of the stock market. (p. 177)

Store of value The accumulation of wealth by holding dollars or other assets that can be used to buy goods and services in the future; a function of money. (p. 28)

Strike price (or **exercise price**) The price at which the buyer of an option has the right to buy or sell the underlying asset. (p. 225)

Supply shock An unexpected change in production costs or in technology that causes the short-run aggregate supply curve to shift. (p. 591)

Swap An agreement between two or more counterparties to exchange sets of cash flows over some future period. (p. 234)

Syndicate A group of investment banks that jointly underwrite a security issue. (p. 346)

Systemic risk Risk to the entire financial system rather than to individual firms or investors. (p. 375)

T-account An accounting tool used to show changes in balance sheet items. (p. 317)

Tariff A tax a government imposes on imports. (p. 255)

Taylor rule A monetary policy guideline developed by economist John Taylor for determining the target for the federal funds rate. (p. 526)

Term premium The additional interest investors require in order to be willing to buy a long-term bond rather than a comparable sequence of short-term bonds. (p. 162)

Term structure of interest rates The relationship among the interest rates on bonds that are otherwise similar but that have different maturities. (p. 152)

Theory of Purchasing Power Parity (PPP) The theory that exchange rates move to equalize the purchasing power of different currencies. (p. 254)

Time value of money The way that the value of a payment changes depending on when the payment is received. (p. 58)

Too-big-to-fail policy A policy under which the federal government does not allow large financial firms to fail, for fear of damaging the financial system. (p. 408)

Transactions costs The cost of a trade or a financial transaction; for example, the brokerage commission charged for buying or selling a financial asset. (pp. 26, 282)

Troubled Asset Relief Program (TARP) A government program Congress passed in 2008 under which the U.S. Treasury purchased stock in hundreds of banks to increase the banks' capital. (p. 337)

Underwriting An activity in which an investment bank guarantees to the issuing corporation the price of a new security and then resells the security for a profit. (p. 346)

Unit of account A way of measuring value in an economy in terms of money; a function of money. (p. 28)

Unsterilized foreign exchange intervention A foreign exchange market intervention in which the central bank does not offset the effect of the intervention on the monetary base. (p. 545)

Vault cash Cash on hand in a bank; includes currency in ATMs and deposits with other banks. (p. 313, 464)

Venture capital firm A firm that raises equity capital from investors to invest in startup firms. (p. 294)

Wall Street Reform and Consumer Protection Act (Dodd-Frank Act) Legislation passed in 2010 that was intended to reform regulation of the financial system. (p. 443)

Wealth The sum of the value of a person's assets minus the value of the person's liabilities. (p. 29)

Yield to maturity The interest rate that makes the present value of the payments from an asset equal to the asset's price today. (p. 68)

Index

Key Symbols and Abbreviations

$*$: Equilibrium value of a variable

Δ: Change in a variable

ΔD: Change in deposits

ΔR: Change in reserves

π: Current inflation rate

π^e: Expected inflation rate

a: A constant that represents how much the gap between the current rate of unemployment and the natural rate affects the inflation rate

AD: Aggregate demand

AD–AS model: Aggregate demand and aggregate supply model

AE: Aggregate expenditure

AS: Aggregate supply

B: Monetary base

B_{non}: Nonborrowed monetary base

BR: Borrowed reserves

C: Consumption spending

C: Coupon (on a bond)

C: Currency in circulation

C/D: Currency-to-deposit ratio

D: Checkable deposits

e: Real exchange rate

E: Nominal exchange rate

ER: Excess reserves

ER/D: Excess reserves-to-deposit ratio

FP: Fixed payments

FV: Future value

g: Constant growth rate of dividends in the Gordon growth model

G: Local, state, and federal government purchases

i: Nominal interest rate

i_{1t}: Interest rate at time t on a one-year bond

i_{nt}: Interest rate at time t on an n-year bond

i_D: Discount rate; interest rate the Federal Reserve charges on discount loans to banks

i_{ff}: Federal funds rate

i_{IOER}: Interest rate paid by the Federal Reserve on banks' reserve deposits

I: Investment spending (on real physical capital)

IS curve: Equilibrium in the goods market

LRAS: Long-run aggregate supply

m: Money multiplier

M: Quantity of money

M1: Currency plus checkable deposits; narrow definition of the money supply

M2: Broad definition of the money supply

MP curve: Monetary policy

M/P: Real money balances

MPC: Marginal propensity to consume

n: Years

NX: Net exports

ON RPP: Overnight reverse repurchase agreements

P: Price level

P^e: Expected price level

PPP: Theory of purchasing power parity

r: Real interest rate

R: Rate of return

R: Total reserves equals required reserves (RR) plus excess reserves (ER)

r_E: Required return on equities

ROA: Return on assets

ROE: Return on equity

rr_D: Required reserve ratio

RR: Required reserves

s: A variable representing the effects of a supply shock

SRAS: Short-run aggregate supply

U: Current unemployment rate

U*: Natural rate of unemployment

V: Velocity of money

Y: Real aggregate output, or real GDP

Y^P: Potential GDP, sometimes referred to as *full-employment GDP*

Equations

Aggregate expenditure: $AE = C + I + G + NX$	Chapter 17, page 582
Assets $=$ Liabilities $+$ Shareholders' equity	Chapter 10, page 308
Bond price: $P = \dfrac{C}{(1 + i)} + \dfrac{C}{(1 + i)^2} + \dfrac{C}{(1 + i)^3} + \ldots + \dfrac{C}{(1 + i)^n} + \dfrac{FV}{(1 + i)^n}$	Chapter 3, page 67
Compounding: $PV \times (1 + i)^n = FV_n$	Chapter 3, page 59
Consumption function: $C = MPC \times Y$	Chapter 18, page 617
Currency in M1 $=$ Currency outstanding $-$ Vault cash	Chapter 14, page 464
Discounting: $PV = \dfrac{FV_n}{(1 + i)^n}$	Chapter 3, page 59
Equation of exchange: $M \times V = P \times Y$	Chapter 2, page 40